Practical Guide to Real Estate Taxation

2020 Edition

DAVID F. WINDISH

Wolters Kluwer

Editorial Staff

Editor . . . . Barbara L. Post, Esq.
Production . . . . Jennifer Schencker, Ranjith Rajaram, and Prabhu Meenakshisundaram

ISBN: 978-0-8080-5316-3

2700 Lake Cook Road
Riverwoods, IL 60015
800 344 3734
CCHCPELink.com

Printed in the United States of America

To those who fill my days and nights,

and give me troubles and delights.

To my family, wife, and children . . .
and must not forget the doodles and poodles.

Preface

The federal income tax impacts on real estate at every stage of its life cycle—acquisition, operation, and disposition. The essential structure of the major portion of *Practical Guide to Real Estate Taxation*, the first four parts, follows this life cycle and focuses on real estate used in business or held for the production of rental income. The remainder of the book is devoted to the tax consequences of the ownership of a personal residence and indirect ownership of real estate interests in the form of securities under federal law.

Part I looks at the acquisition of real property from a tax perspective, including the acquisition transaction itself, how the real estate is held, and how it is financed. Included in the first chapter is a very important discussion of allocating costs between real and personal property when a building is purchased. By allocating as much as possible to personal property, rather than real property, tax savings are maximized.

Parts II and III are concerned with the operational aspects of real estate. In the three chapters of Part II, the tax questions that arise from rental and leasing arrangements are explored. Tax deductions associated with real estate operation (including depreciation and maximizing that all-important deduction), the treatment of additions and improvements, and troubled real estate financings are the major topics in Part III. Also found in Part III is a chapter dealing with the tax questions and problems that arise in connection with the development, subdivision, and sale of real estate in the ordinary course of business—questions that are unique when compared to those involved in the one-time sale of business or investment property.

Part IV explores the last stage of the life cycle of real estate and examines the disposition of real estate through various taxable and nontaxable transactions. Included is a discussion of the all-important like-kind exchange rules for two-way, three-way, and even four-way exchanges. Also included is consideration of the involuntary disposition of real estate and the gratuitous transfer of real estate.

Ownership of a personal residence is favored by the tax law. The owner of a home is given advantages not available to the occupant of a rented residential apartment or home. Part V explores these advantages, including deductions available to all homeowners, use of part of a residence for business, cooperative and condominium ownership, and the avoidance of federal income tax on the sale of a residence.

The final three chapters, which make up Part VI, take a brief look at ownership interests in real estate that are indirect and mass-marketed. These three types of interests—real estate limited partnerships, real estate investment trusts, and real estate mortgage investment conduits—offer participation in real estate through interests that are securities under federal securities laws.

David F. Windish

August 2019

About the Author

David F. Windish, J.D., LL.M. in taxation, is a tax attorney and consultant. He has served as an instructor of tax-advantaged investments at the New York Institute of Finance; an Instructor of business law at the U.S. Merchant Marine Academy, Kings Point, N.Y.; and an adjunct professor at George Mason University, Fairfax, Va. He currently is the content consultant for Tax Talk Today, an online series of programs designed to educate all tax practitioners; and has served as executive editor for Tax Analysts; managing editor for *Business Strategies,* published by Wolters Kluwer; and senior editor for the Institute for Business Planning.

In addition to this book, Mr. Windish has authored *Tax Advantaged Investments* and *Investor's Guide to Limited Partnerships,* both published by the New York Institute of Finance. Through the Center for Video Education, he has authored continuing education courses dealing with real estate and closely held corporations. Those courses consisted of readings, case studies, and videotape segments.

Mr. Windish is a graduate of Rutgers University Law School and the New York University School of Law, Graduate Division. He has been heard as a guest speaker at professional meetings and seminars and on popular radio programs.

Contents

A more detailed Contents starts on page xi.

Chapter		Page
	PART I—ACQUIRING OWNERSHIP OF REAL PROPERTY	
1	The Acquisition Transaction	5
2	Form of Ownership	41
3	Financing Real Estate	97
	PART II—RENTAL AND LEASING ARRANGEMENTS	
4	Payments Between Landlord and Tenant	153
5	Lease Acquisition and Disposition	171
6	Leasehold Improvements and Additions	185
	PART III—REAL ESTATE OPERATION	
7	Operating Expenses and Taxes	207
8	Property Additions and Improvements	257
9	Depreciation	303
10	Development, Subdivision, and Sales in the Ordinary Course of Business	341
11	Passive Activity Loss Rules	363
12	Troubled Financings	407
	PART IV—DISPOSITION OF REAL ESTATE	
13	Sales and Exchanges	443
14	Seller-Financed Sales	505
15	Casualty, Condemnation, and Demolition	537
16	Contributions and Gifts	565
	PART V—PERSONAL RESIDENCES	
17	Deductions for Homeowners	589
18	Mixed-Use Residences	625
19	Cooperatives, Condominiums, and Associations	647
20	Sale of Residence	663
	PART VI—SECURITIZED REAL ESTATE INVESTMENTS	
21	Real Estate Limited Partnerships	685
22	Real Estate Investment Trusts	697
23	Real Estate Mortgage Investment Conduits	709
	Case Table	713
	Finding List	721
	Index	751

Contents in Detail

Paragraph

PART I—ACQUIRING OWNERSHIP OF REAL PROPERTY

Chapter 1—The Acquisition Transaction

OVERVIEW OF CHAPTER 100
IMPORTANCE OF BASIS 101
Calculation of Basis 101.01
Property Acquired by Purchase .... 101.01[A]
Property Constructed by or for the Owner .... 101.01[B]
Property Acquired in an Exchange .... 101.01[C]
Property Acquired on Exercise of an Option .... 101.01[D]
Property Acquired by Gift .... 101.01[E]
Property Acquired by Inheritance .... 101.01[F]
Property Acquired from a Spouse or Former Spouse .... 101.01[G]
Other Basis Rules .... 101.01[H]
Mortgage and Basis 101.02
Contingent or Speculative Obligations .... 101.02[A]
Borrowing Against Previously Owned Property .... 101.02[B]
Artificially Inflated Purchase Price .... 101.02[C]
PURCHASE OF REAL PROPERTY 102
Buying Expenses 102.01
Transaction Costs Under the Repair Regs .... 102.01[A]
Safe Harbor Expensing .... 102.01[B]
Allocation of Costs 102.02
Land and Buildings .... 102.02[A]
Land Improvements and Personal Property .... 102.02[B]
Buildings and Personal Property .... 102.02[C]
Real Estate as Part of a Going Business .... 102.02[D]
Reporting Requirements .... 102.02[E]
Apportionment of Real Property Taxes 102.03
Purchase from Foreign Person 102.04
CONSTRUCTION OF REAL PROPERTY 103
Capitalization of Construction Costs 103.01
Small Taxpayer Exception .... 103.01[A]
Expenses Other Than Interest .... 103.01[B]
Interest .... 103.01[C]
Interest and Taxes on Pre-1987 Construction 103.02
Capitalization of Carrying Charges 103.03
LOW-INCOME HOUSING TAX CREDIT 104
ENERGY EFFICIENT HOME TAX CREDIT 105

Paragraph

Chapter 2—Form of Ownership
OVERVIEW OF CHAPTER 200
OWNERSHIP FOR TAX PURPOSES 201
Use of Straw or Nominee Corporations 201.01
Agency Relationship Requirement 201.02
INDIVIDUAL AND JOINT OWNERSHIP 202
Sole Individual Ownership 202.01
Common and Joint Ownership 202.02
Joint Ownership by Spouses 202.03
Community Property 202.04
PARTNERSHIPS 203
Legal Characteristics 203.01
General Partnerships . . . . 203.01[A]
Limited Partnerships . . . . 203.01[B]
Joint Ventures . . . . 203.01[C]
Syndicates . . . . 203.01[D]
Taxation of Partnerships 203.02
Basis of Partnership Interest . . . . 203.02[A]
Contributions to Partnership . . . . 203.02[B]
Operation of Partnership . . . . 203.02[C]
Distributions . . . . 203.02[D]
Guaranteed Payments . . . . 203.02[E]
Elective Large Partnership Rules . . . . 203.02[F]
Post-2017 Partnership Audit Rules . . . . 203.02[G]
CORPORATIONS 204
Legal Characteristics 204.01
Taxation of Corporations 204.02
Organization of Corporation . . . . 204.02[A]
Operation of Corporation . . . . 204.02[B]
Property Distributions and Liquidations . . . . 204.02[C]
LIMITED LIABILITY COMPANIES 205
Entity Classification 205.01
Partnership Conversion to LLC 205.02
S CORPORATIONS 206
Qualification as an S Corporation 206.01
Income and Loss 206.02
Built-In Gain . . . . 206.02[A]
S Corporation Losses . . . . 206.02[B]
OWNERSHIP IN TRUST 207
Tax Treatment of Trusts 207.01
Depreciation 207.02
Grantor Trusts 207.03
CHOICE OF THE OWNING ENTITY 208
Corporation or Partnership 208.01

Paragraph

S Corporation or Partnership 208.02
Comparison Chart of Business Entities 208.03
QUALIFIED BUSINESS INCOME (PASSTHROUGH DEDUCTION) 209
Overview 209.01
Eligible Trades and Businesses 209.02
Specified Trades and Businesses .... 209.02[A]
Safe Harbor for Rental Real Estate .... 209.02[B]
Qualified Business Income 209.03
Calculating the Deduction 209.04
Agricultural or Horticultural Cooperatives 209.05

Chapter 3—Financing Real Estate

OVERVIEW OF CHAPTER 300
MORTGAGE FINANCING 301
Mortgage Costs 301.01
Borrower's Costs .... 301.01[A]
Lender's Costs .... 301.01[B]
Buy Downs and Similar Arrangements 301.02
Payoff of Mortgage 301.03
Prepayment Penalties .... 301.03[A]
Payment Discounts .... 301.03[B]
AT-RISK RULES 302
Taxpayers and Activities Subject to the Rules 302.01
Deduction Under the At-Risk Rules 302.02
Order of Deductions .... 302.02[A]
Recapture of Prior Deductions .... 302.02[B]
Determining Amount at Risk 302.03
Borrowed Amounts .... 302.03[A]
Avoidance of At-Risk Rules .... 302.03[B]
Computation of At-Risk Amount .... 302.03[C]
Qualified Nonrecourse Financing 302.04
Financing from Related Person .... 302.04[A]
Transfer of Property .... 302.04[B]
INTEREST 303
Interest Income 303.01
Interest Deduction 303.02
Prepaid Interest .... 303.02[A]
Investment Interest .... 303.02[B]
Tracing Debt Proceeds .... 303.02[C]
Business Interest .... 303.02[D]
Interest-Free and Below-Market Rate Loans 303.03
Gift Loans .... 303.03[A]
Compensation Loans .... 303.03[B]
Corporation-Shareholder Loans .... 303.03[C]

Paragraph

Reporting Requirements . . . . 303.03[D]
ORIGINAL ISSUE DISCOUNT AND IMPUTED INTEREST ON DEFERRED PAYMENT SALES 304
Imputed Interest 304.01
Unstated Interest . . . . 304.01[A]
Land Sales Between Family Members . . . . 304.01[B]
Original Issue Discount 304.02
Cash Method Accounting . . . . 304.02[A]
Assumptions and Modifications of Debt Instruments . . . . 304.02[B]
Interest Rates Under the Imputed Interest and OID Rules 304.03
Maximum Interest Rate . . . . 304.03[A]
Installment Obligations . . . . 304.03[B]
Variable Interest Rate Obligations . . . . 304.03[C]
Contingent Interest . . . . 304.03[D]
Excessive Interest . . . . 304.03[E]
SALE-LEASEBACKS AND OTHER LEASE FINANCING 305
Straight Sale-Leaseback 305.01
Tax Benefits . . . . 305.01[A]
Like-Kind Exchange and the Sale-Leaseback . . . . 305.01[B]
Recognition of a Sale-Leaseback for Tax Purposes 305.02
Supreme Court Guidelines . . . . 305.02[A]
IRS Guidelines . . . . 305.02[B]
Variations on the Sale-Leaseback 305.03
Split Financing . . . . 305.03[A]
Related Party Sale-Leasebacks . . . . 305.03[B]
Equity Participation . . . . 305.03[C]
Tax-Exempt Entity Leasing . . . . 305.03[D]
Lease with Option as Conditional Sales Contract 305.04

PART II—RENTAL AND LEASING ARRANGEMENTS

Chapter 4—Payments Between Landlord and Tenant

OVERVIEW OF CHAPTER 400
RENT 401
Percentage Rents 401.01
Payment of Lessor's Expenses 401.02
Property Transactions 401.03
Related Parties 401.04
Intra-Family Leases . . . . 401.04[A]
Controlled Corporations . . . . 401.04[B]
Matching Lessee's Deduction to Lessor's Income . . . . 401.04[C]
TENANT'S RENT DEDUCTION 402
Advance Rents 402.01
Graduated Rents 402.02
Decrease in Rents . . . . 402.02[A]

Paragraph

Increase in Rents ... 402.02[B]
LANDLORD'S RENT INCOME ... 403
Advance Rents ... 403.01
Assignments and Loans ... 403.02
DEFERRED OR STEPPED RENTAL AGREEMENTS ... 404
Section 467 Rental Agreements ... 404.01
Constant Rental Accrual in Tax Avoidance Transactions ... 404.02
Exemptions from Rental Agreement Rules ... 404.02[A]
Recapture in Leasebacks and Long-Term Agreements ... 404.02[B]
LEASES WITH PURCHASE OPTIONS ... 405
Lease as Sales Contract ... 405.01
Lease or Sale Distinguished ... 405.02
DEPOSITS ... 406
Lessee's Deduction ... 406.01
Lessor's Income ... 406.02

Chapter 5—Lease Acquisition and Disposition
OVERVIEW OF CHAPTER ... 500
LEASE ACQUISITION COSTS ... 501
Classification of Payments as Lease Acquisition Costs ... 501.01
Lessor's Costs ... 501.01[A]
Lessee's Costs ... 501.01[B]
Unsuccessful Lease Attempt ... 501.01[C]
Renewal Options ... 501.02
Existing Improvements Costs ... 501.03
LEASE CANCELLATION ... 502
Payments by Lessee ... 502.01
Lessee's Deduction ... 502.01[A]
Lessor's Income ... 502.01[B]
Payments by Lessor ... 502.02
Lessor's Deduction ... 502.02[A]
Lessee's Income ... 502.02[B]
Unamortized Costs on Cancellation of Lease ... 502.03
Modification of Lease ... 502.04
SALE OF LEASE ... 503

Chapter 6—Leasehold Improvements and Additions
OVERVIEW OF CHAPTER ... 600
IMPROVEMENTS AND ADDITIONS BY LESSOR ... 601
Restoration or Maintenance by Lessee ... 601.01
Improvements to Benefit a Particular Lessee ... 601.02
Purchase of Property with Lessee Improvements ... 601.03
IMPROVEMENTS AND ADDITIONS BY LESSEE ... 602
Improvements as Rent ... 602.01

	Paragraph
Improvements as Capital Investment	602.02
Pre-1987 Improvements	602.02[A]
Lease Termination	602.02[B]
INVESTMENT CREDIT	603
Qualified Rehabilitations by Lessee	603.01
Qualified Rehabilitations by Lessor	603.02
Election to Pass Credit to Lessee	603.02[A]
Credit Split on Short-Term Lease Property	603.02[B]

PART III—REAL ESTATE OPERATION

Chapter 7—Operating Expenses and Taxes

OVERVIEW OF CHAPTER	700
TAX ACCOUNTING FOR REAL ESTATE	701
Accounting Period	701.01
Required Tax Years for Partnerships, S Corporations, and Personal Service Corporations	701.01[A]
Election to Use Other Than a Required Year	701.01[B]
Accounting Method	701.02
Cash Method	701.02[A]
Accrual Method	701.02[B]
Long-Term Construction Contracts	701.02[C]
Controlling the Timing of Income and Expense	701.03
Deferring Income and Accelerating Deductions	701.03[A]
Accelerating Income and Deferring Deductions	701.03[B]
Related Party Transactions	701.04
Losses on Sales and Exchanges	701.04[A]
Deductions for Expenses and Interest	701.04[B]
Related Parties Defined	701.04[C]
START-UP EXPENSES	702
Write-off of Expenses	702.01
Investigatory Expenses	702.01[A]
Start-Up Expenses	702.01[B]
Pre-Opening Expenses	702.01[C]
Trade or Business Requirement	702.02
REAL ESTATE OPERATING EXPENSES	703
Repairs	703.01
Repair or Improvement	703.01[A]
De Minimis Safe Harbor	703.01[B]
Small Taxpayer Safe Harbor	703.01[C]
Routine Building Maintenance Safe Harbor	703.01[D]
Election to Capitalize Maintenance and Repairs	703.01[E]
Before the Repair Regulations	703.01[F]

Paragraph

Removal of Architectural Barriers 703.02
Materials and Supplies 703.03
Compensation 703.04
Real Estate Corporation Officers . . . . . . 703.04[A]
Family Members as Employees . . . . . . 703.04[B]
Independent Contractors and Employees . . . . . . 703.04[C]
Licensed Real Estate Agents . . . . . . 703.04[D]
Partners . . . . . . 703.04[E]
Commissions and Fees 703.05
Real Estate Commissions . . . . . . 703.05[A]
Kickbacks . . . . . . 703.05[B]
Insurance 703.06
Advertising 703.07
Legal Expenses 703.08
Interest 703.09
REAL ESTATE TAXES 704
Real Property Taxes 704.01
Deduction of Real Property Taxes . . . . . . 704.01[A]
Back Taxes Payments . . . . . . 704.01[B]
Payments in Lieu of Taxes . . . . . . 704.01[C]
Special Assessment and Local Benefit Taxes 704.02
Transfer Taxes 704.03
Impact Fees 704.04
EXCESS BUSINESS LOSSES 705
Excess Loss Defined 705.01
Partnerships and S corporations 705.02

Chapter 8—Property Additions and Improvements
OVERVIEW OF CHAPTER 800
IMPROVEMENTS TO REAL ESTATE AS CAPITAL EXPENDITURES 801
Unit of Property 801.01
Leased Buildings . . . . . . 801.01[A]
Condominiums and Cooperatives . . . . . . 801.01[B]
Other Property . . . . . . 801.01[C]
Improvements to Property . . . . . . 801.01[D]
Components as Separate Units . . . . . . 801.01[E]
Betterments to Property 801.02
Replacements . . . . . . 801.02[A]
Application to Buildings . . . . . . 801.02[B]
Building Refresh . . . . . . 801.02[C]
Building Remodel . . . . . . 801.02[D]
Amelioration of Pre-Existing Conditions . . . . . . 801.02[E]
Meeting Regulatory Requirements . . . . . . 801.02[F]
Increase in Efficiency, Capacity, Etc. . . . . . . 801.02[G]

	Paragraph
Restoration of Property	801.03
Restoration of Damage from Casualty	801.03[A]
Replacement of a Major Component or a Substantial Structural Part	801.03[B]
Previous Case Law	801.03[C]
Adaptation of Property	801.04
Abandonment of Improvement Plans	801.05
SPECIAL AMORTIZATION PROVISIONS	802
Pollution Control Facilities	802.01
Amortization Election Requirements	802.01[A]
Limitation for Longer-Lived Facilities	802.01[B]
Special Rule for Air Pollution Control Facilities	802.01[C]
Reforestation Expenses	802.02
Soil and Water Conservation Expenditures	802.03
ENERGY EFFICIENT COMMERCIAL BUILDINGS DEDUCTION	803
TAX CREDITS FOR BUILDING REHABILITATIONS	804
Rehabilitation of Older Commercial Buildings	804.01
Substantial Rehabilitation Test	804.01[A]
Expenditures Incurred by Predecessor	804.01[B]
The "Wall Test"	804.01[C]
Nonqualifying Expenditures	804.01[D]
Basis Reduction by Credit Amount	804.01[E]
Rehabilitations of Certified Historic Structures	804.02
Certification Requirements	804.02[A]
Nonqualified Buildings Credit Allowance	804.02[B]
Recapture of Rehabilitation Credits	804.03
LOW-INCOME HOUSING CREDIT	805
Overview of the Credit Process	805.01
Qualification for the Credit	805.02
Qualified Low-Income Building	805.02[A]
Qualified Low-Income Housing Project	805.02[B]
Calculation of the Low-Income Housing Credit	805.03
Applicable Credit Rates	805.03[A]
Qualified Basis for Determination of Credit	805.03[B]
Rehabilitation Expenditures	805.04
Compliance and Recapture Provisions	805.05
Increases in Tenant Income	805.05[A]
Large Partnerships	805.05[B]
Recapture Amount	805.05[C]
Casualty Losses	805.05[D]
RENEWAL COMMUNITIES AND NEW YORK LIBERTY ZONE	806
Commercial Revitalization Deduction	806.01
New York Liberty Zone	806.02

Paragraph

Chapter 9—Depreciation

OVERVIEW OF CHAPTER 900
MACRS DEPRECIATION SYSTEM 901
Computation of the Deduction 901.01
Recovery Periods .... 901.01[A]
Straight-Line Method .... 901.01[B]
Mid-Month Convention .... 901.01[C]
Use of Optional Tables .... 901.01[D]
Shorter Recovery Periods for Leasehold and Retail Improvements and Restaurant Property Before 2018 .... 901.01[E]
Improvement Property After 2017 .... 901.01[F]
Motorsports Entertainment Complexes .... 901.01[G]
Depreciation of Additions and Improvements 901.02
Land Improvements .... 901.02[A]
Property Under Construction .... 901.02[B]
Zoning and Variances .... 901.02[C]
Expensing and Bonus Depreciation 901.03
Expensing Election .... 901.03[A]
First-Year Bonus Depreciation .... 901.03[B]
ALTERNATIVE DEPRECIATION SYSTEM 902
Calculation of Alternative Depreciation 902.01
Election of Alternative Depreciation .... 902.01[A]
Use of Optional Tables .... 902.01[B]
Real Property Subject to Alternative Depreciation 902.02
Tax-Exempt Use Property .... 902.02[A]
Tax-Exempt Bond Financed Property .... 902.02[B]
Alternative Minimum Tax .... 902.02[C]
COST SEGREGATION 903
Recharacterizing Existing Property 903.01
ACRS DEPRECIATION FOR PRE-1987 PROPERTY 904
Computation of Deduction 904.01
Straight-Line Election .... 904.01[A]
ACRS Schedules .... 904.01[B]
Additions and Improvements 904.02
Substantial Improvements as Separate Property .... 904.02[A]
Qualification as Substantial Improvement .... 904.02[B]
DEPRECIATION OF PRE-1981 PROPERTY 905
Calculation of Deduction for Real Property 905.01
Depreciation Methods .... 905.01[A]
Change of Depreciation Methods .... 905.01[B]
Anti-Churning Rules 905.02
Real Property Rules .... 905.02[A]
Related Party Transfers .... 905.02[B]
Tax-Free Transfers .... 905.02[C]

Paragraph

Chapter 10—Development, Subdivision, and Sales in the Ordinary Course of Business

OVERVIEW OF CHAPTER 1000
DEVELOPMENT COSTS 1001
Equitable Apportionment Rule 1001.01
Manner of Apportionment of Basis . . . . 1001.01[A]
Methods of Apportionment of Basis . . . . 1001.01[B]
Inclusion of Development Costs in Basis 1001.02
Development Improvements as Separate Interest . . . . 1001.02[A]
Estimated Future Costs . . . . 1001.02[B]
Energy Efficient Home Credit 1001.03
DEALER STATUS 1002
Characterization of Dealer Property 1002.01
Tests Applied for Classification of Property . . . . 1002.01[A]
Subdivided Realty as Dealer Property . . . . 1002.01[B]
Tax Effects of Classification as a Dealer 1002.02
Dealer Installment Sales . . . . 1002.02[A]
Dealer Sales of Timeshares and Residential Lots . . . . 1002.02[B]
SUBDIVISION BY INVESTOR 1003
Qualification for Special Tax Treatment 1003.01
Holding Period Rules . . . . 1003.01[A]
Improvements to Land Tracts . . . . 1003.01[B]
Necessary Improvements to Property After Ten Years . . . . 1003.01[C]
Calculation of the Amount and Character of Gain 1003.02
Five-Percent Rule . . . . 1003.02[A]
Five-Year Rule . . . . 1003.02[B]

Chapter 11—Passive Activity Loss Rules

OVERVIEW OF CHAPTER 1100
GENERAL PROVISIONS 1101
Taxpayers Subject to the Rules 1101.01
Closely Held C Corporations . . . . 1101.01[A]
Personal Service Corporations . . . . 1101.01[B]
Activities Subject to the Rules 1101.02
Limited Partnership Interests . . . . 1101.02[A]
Oil and Gas Property Working Interests . . . . 1101.02[B]
Material Participation 1101.03
Material Participation by an Individual . . . . 1101.03[A]
Material Participation by a Corporation . . . . 1101.03[B]
IDENTIFICATION OF SEPARATE ACTIVITIES 1102
General Rule 1102.01
Limitations on Grouping 1102.02
Regrouping 1102.03

	Paragraph
Reporting Requirements for Grouping	1102.04
LIMITS ON RENTAL ACTIVITIES	1103
Rental Activity Defined	1103.01
Rentals Incidental to Nonrental Activities	1103.01[A]
Property Provided to a Partnership, Joint Venture, or S Corporation	1103.01[B]
Self-Rented Property	1103.02
Rental Incident to Development	1103.03
Rental of Nondepreciable Property	1103.04
Active Participation in Rental Real Estate	1103.05
$25,000 Limit	1103.05[A]
Filing Status	1103.05[B]
Phase-Out of Deduction	1103.05[C]
Real Property Business Exception	1103.06
Grouping Rental Real Estate Activities	1103.06[A]
Limited Partnership Interests	1103.06[B]
Coordination with Active Participation Exception	1103.06[C]
TAX TREATMENT OF PASSIVE LOSSES AND CREDITS	1104
Computation of Deductible Loss	1104.01
Passive Activity Gross Income	1104.01[A]
Passive Activity Deductions	1104.01[B]
Partners and S Corporation Shareholders	1104.01[C]
Closely Held Corporation's Passive Activity Loss	1104.02
Disallowed Losses	1104.03
Allocation of Disallowed Loss	1104.03[A]
Allocation Within Loss Activities	1104.03[B]
Carryover of Disallowed Deductions	1104.03[C]
Disposition of a Passive Activity	1104.03[D]
Passive Activity Credits	1104.04
Closely Held Corporation	1104.04[A]
Carryover of Suspended Credit	1104.04[B]
PUBLICLY TRADED PARTNERSHIPS	1105
Partnerships Subject to the Rule	1105.01
Partnerships Subject to Grandfather Rule	1105.02
Application of the Special Passive Activity Loss Rule	1105.03
Chapter 12—Troubled Financings	
OVERVIEW OF CHAPTER	1200
SETTLEMENT OF DEBT AT DISCOUNT	1201
Tax Treatment of Debtor	1201.01
Solvent Debtor	1201.01[A]
Insolvent or Bankrupt Debtor	1201.01[B]
Qualified Real Property Business Debt	1201.01[C]
Qualified Principal Residence Debt	1201.01[D]
Purchase-Money Mortgage Reduction	1201.01[E]

Paragraph

Tax Treatment of Creditor 1201.02
Loss on Discount .... 1201.02[A]
Bad Debt Deduction .... 1201.02[B]
Nonbusiness Bad Debts .... 1201.02[C]
FORECLOSURE 1202
Tax Treatment of the Debtor 1202.01
Calculation of Gain or Loss .... 1202.01[A]
Character of Gain or Loss .... 1202.01[B]
Tax Treatment of the Creditor 1202.02
Foreclosure Expenses .... 1202.02[A]
Purchase by Third Party .... 1202.02[B]
Purchase by Mortgagee .... 1202.02[C]
CONVEYANCE AND ABANDONMENT OF MORTGAGE 1203
Conveyance to Mortgagee 1203.01
Tax Treatment of Mortgagor .... 1203.01[A]
Tax Treatment of Mortgagee .... 1203.01[B]
Abandonment by Mortgagor 1203.02
REPOSSESSION OF SELLER-FINANCED PROPERTY 1204
Nonrecognition of Gain or Loss 1204.01
Prior Bad Debt Deductions .... 1204.01[A]
Holding Period of Reacquired Property .... 1204.01[B]
Basis of Reacquired Property .... 1204.01[C]
Recognition of Gain 1204.02
Reacquisition Following Installment Sale .... 1204.02[A]
Reacquisition Following Election Out of Installment Reporting .... 1204.02[B]
Third-Party Mortgages .... 1204.02[C]
Character of Gain .... 1204.02[D]

PART IV—DISPOSITION OF REAL ESTATE

Chapter 13—Sales and Exchanges

OVERVIEW OF CHAPTER 1300
SALE OF REAL ESTATE 1301
Computation of Gain or Loss 1301.01
Adjusted Basis .... 1301.01[A]
Amount Realized .... 1301.01[B]
Disallowed Losses .... 1301.01[C]
Sale Between Spouses and Former Spouses .... 1301.01[D]
Partial Dispositions .... 1301.01[E]
Character of Gain or Loss 1301.02
Capital Gains and Losses .... 1301.02[A]
Property Used in a Trade or Business: Section 1231 Assets .... 1301.02[B]
Holding Period .... 1301.02[C]

	Paragraph
Depreciation Recapture	1301.03
Section 1245 Property Recapture	1301.03[A]
Section 1250 Property Recapture	1301.03[B]
Alternative Minimum Tax	1301.04
Basic Computation	1301.04[A]
Small Business Exception	1301.04[B]
Adjustments to Taxable Income	1301.04[C]
Tax Preferences	1301.04[D]
Optional Ten-Year Writeoff	1301.04[E]
Alternative Minimum Tax Credit	1301.04[F]
TAX-FREE EXCHANGE OF PROPERTY	1302
Like-Kind Exchange Requirements	1302.01
Like-Kind Real Estate Defined	1302.01[A]
Basis Rule	1302.01[B]
Basis Allocation Among Multiple Properties	1302.01[C]
Exchange as Part of Business Acquisition	1302.01[D]
Partially Tax-Free Exchanges	1302.02
Other Property or Money	1302.02[A]
Mortgages and Other Liabilities	1302.02[B]
Basis in Partially Tax-Free Exchanges	1302.02[C]
Commissions and Other Expenses	1302.02[D]
Multi-Party Exchanges	1302.03
Three-Way Exchange	1302.03[A]
Four-Way Exchange	1302.02[B]
REPORTING REQUIREMENTS	1303
Transactions Subject to Reporting	1303.01
Reporting Person	1303.01[A]
Multiple Transferors	1303.01[B]
Information Return and Statement	1303.02
Form and Content of Return	1303.02[A]
Statement for Transferor	1303.02[B]
Penalties	1303.03
QUALIFIED OPPORTUNITY ZONES	1304
Opportunity Fund	1304.01
Opportunity Zone Property	1304.01[A]
90 Percent Test	1304.01[B]
Tax Deferral	1304.02
Eligible Gain	1304.02[A]
Gain Recognition	1304.02[B]
REDUCED TAXES ON DEPRESSED AREA PROPERTY	1305
Rollover of Empowerment Zone Investment	1305.01
Renewal Community Capital Gain	1305.02
D.C. Zone Capital Gain	1305.03

Paragraph

Chapter 14—Seller-Financed Sales

OVERVIEW OF CHAPTER 1400
INSTALLMENT SALES 1401
Sales that Qualify as Installment Sales 1401.01
Dealer Sales . . . . 1401.01[A]
Escrow Arrangements . . . . 1401.01[B]
Election Out of Installment Reporting . . . . 1401.01[C]
Reporting Installment Income 1401.02
General Rules . . . . 1401.02[A]
Payments . . . . 1401.02[B]
Sale of Multiple Assets . . . . 1401.02[C]
Like-Kind Exchanges . . . . 1401.02[D]
Contingent Sales . . . . 1401.02[E]
Unstated Interest . . . . 1401.02[F]
Sales to Related Party 1401.03
Sales of Depreciable Property . . . . 1401.03[A]
Resale by Related Purchaser . . . . 1401.03[B]
Interest on Deferred Tax 1401.04
DISPOSITION OR PLEDGE OF INSTALLMENT OBLIGATIONS . 1402
Sale or Satisfaction at Less than Face Value 1402.01
Exceptions to Rule for Recognition of Gain . . . . 1402.01[A]
Cancellation of Installment Obligations . . . . 1402.01[B]
Pledge of Installment Obligations 1402.02
Repossession of Property 1402.03

Chapter 15—Casualty, Condemnation, and Demolition

OVERVIEW OF CHAPTER 1500
BUSINESS CASUALTY 1501
Casualty Defined 1501.01
Casualty Gains and Losses 1501.02
Casualty Losses . . . . 1501.02[A]
Casualty Gains . . . . 1501.02[B]
Insurance and Other Reimbursements . . . . 1501.02[C]
Basis After Casualty . . . . 1501.02[D]
Disaster Area Losses 1501.03
Method of Taking Earlier Deduction . . . . 1501.03[A]
Revocation of Election . . . . 1501.03[B]
CONDEMNATIONS 1502
Condemnation Defined 1502.01
Gain or Loss from Condemnation 1502.02
Determination of the Condemnation Award 1502.03
Severance Damages . . . . 1502.03[A]
Special Assessments . . . . 1502.03[B]
TAX-FREE REPLACEMENT OF PROPERTY 1503

	Paragraph
Election to Postpone Gain	1503.01
Advantages and Disadvantages of the Election	1503.01[A]
Method of Election	1503.01[B]
Replacement Period	1503.01[C]
Replacement Property	1503.02
Similar Property	1503.02[A]
Required Replacement from Unrelated Person	1503.02[B]
Special Rule for Condemned Property	1503.02[C]
Federally Declared Disasters	1503.02[D]
Outdoor Advertising Displays	1503.02[E]
Acquisition of Corporate Control	1503.02[F]
Basis of Replacement Property	1503.03
Replacement with Corporate Stock	1503.03[A]
Direct Conversion to Replacement Property	1503.03[B]
DEMOLITION AND ABANDONMENT	1504
Demolition	1504.01
Abandonment	1504.02
Abandonment of Land	1504.02[A]
Abandonment of Improvements	1504.02[B]

Chapter 16—Contributions and Gifts

OVERVIEW OF CHAPTER	1600
CHARITABLE GIFTS	1601
Valuation of Real Estate Gifts	1601.01
Types of Appraisals	1601.01[A]
Required Appraisal	1601.01[B]
Gifts with Mixed Motives	1601.02
Gifts of Appreciated Property	1601.03
Ordinary Income Property	1601.03[A]
Capital Gain Property	1601.03[B]
Mixed Property	1601.03[C]
Gifts of Partial Interests	1601.04
Undivided Portion	1601.04[A]
Remainder Interest	1601.04[B]
Conservation Purposes	1601.04[C]
GIFTS AND CONTRIBUTIONS OF MORTGAGED PROPERTY	1602
Gifts to Family	1602.01
Charitable Gifts	1602.02
GIFTS OF LOSS PROPERTY	1603

PART V—PERSONAL RESIDENCES

Chapter 17—Deductions for Homeowners

OVERVIEW OF CHAPTER	1700
MORTGAGE INTEREST	1701

	Paragraph
Qualified Residence Interest	1701.01
Qualified Residence Defined	1701.01[A]
Acquisition Indebtedness	1701.01[B]
Home Equity Debt	1701.01[C]
Pre-1987 Indebtedness	1701.01[D]
Points	1701.02
Points Charged for Services	1701.02[A]
Refinancing	1701.02[B]
Special Mortgage Situations	1701.03
Redeemable Ground Rents	1701.03[A]
Shared Appreciation Mortgage (SAM)	1701.03[B]
Mortgage Interest Credit	1701.03[C]
Housing Allowances and Assistance Payments	1701.03[D]
Payment Penalties	1701.03[E]
REAL ESTATE TAXES	1702
CASUALTY LOSSES	1703
Limitations	1703.01
Deductible for Losses	1703.01[A]
Adjusted Gross Income Limitation	1703.01[B]
Calculation of the Casualty Deduction	1703.02
Real Estate	1703.02[A]
Personal Property	1703.02[B]
Loss to Real and Personal Property	1703.02[C]
Part Business and Part Personal-Use Property	1703.03
DISASTER RELIEF EXCLUSION	1704
MOVING EXPENSES	1705
Deduction Suspended for 2018 through 2025	1705.01
Qualification for the Deduction	1705.02
Distance	1705.02[A]
Length of Employment	1705.02[B]
Deductible Costs	1705.03
Reimbursements	1705.03[A]
Foreign Moves	1705.03[B]
DISTRICT OF COLUMBIA HOMEBUYER CREDIT	1706
FIRST-TIME HOMEBUYER CREDIT	1707
Recapture of Credit	1707.01
CREDITS FOR ENERGY SAVINGS	1708
Nonbusiness Energy Property Credit	1708.01
Energy Property Credit before 2011	1708.01[A]
Residential Energy Efficient Property	1708.02

Chapter 18—Mixed-Use Residences

OVERVIEW OF CHAPTER	1800
BUSINESS USE OF HOME	1801

	Paragraph
Safe Harbor Calculation	1801.01
Exclusive Use for Business Test	1801.02
Exceptions to Exclusive Use Test	1801.02[A]
Principal Place of Business	1801.02[B]
Place to Meet Patients, Clients, or Customers	1801.02[C]
Separate Structures	1801.02[D]
Allocation of Deductions	1801.03
Direct Expenses	1801.03[A]
Indirect Expenses	1801.03[B]
Limitation on Deductions	1801.04
Determination of Gross Income from Business Use of Home	1801.04[A]
Order of Deductions	1801.04[B]
Use of Home as Day-Care Facility	1801.05
Allocation Formula	1801.05[A]
Application of Formula	1801.05[B]
RENTAL OF PART OF HOME	1802
Rental Income	1802.01
Allocation of Expenses	1802.02
RENTAL OF VACATION OR OTHER RESIDENCE	1803
Dwelling Unit Classification	1803.01
Use as a Residence	1803.01[A]
Personal Use	1803.01[B]
Determination of Income and Deductions	1803.02
Rental for Less Than 15 Days	1803.02[A]
Rental for 15 Days or More	1803.02[B]
Other Limitations on Rental Losses	1803.03
RESIDENCE CONVERTED TO INVESTMENT	1804
Chapter 19—Cooperatives, Condominiums, and Associations	
OVERVIEW OF CHAPTER	1900
COOPERATIVE HOUSING CORPORATIONS	1901
Qualification as a Cooperative Housing Corporation	1901.01
One Class of Stock Requirement	1901.01[A]
Right of Occupancy	1901.01[B]
Distributions	1901.01[C]
Gross Income of Cooperative Housing Corporation	1901.01[D]
Deductions by Tenant-Stockholders	1901.02
Interest and Taxes	1901.02[A]
Depreciation	1901.02[B]
CONDOMINIUMS	1902
Tax Treatment of Unit Owner	1902.01
Tax Treatment of Condominium Association	1902.02
HOMEOWNERS ASSOCIATIONS	1903
Qualification for Tax-Exempt Status	1903.01

	Paragraph
Association Property	1903.01[A]
Use as Residences	1903.01[B]
Exempt Function Income	1903.01[C]
Expenditures	1903.01[D]
Inurement	1903.01[E]
Taxation of Homeowners Association	1903.02
Election of Exempt Status	1903.03
Nonexempt Associations	1903.04
Tax-Exempt Status	1903.04[A]
Cooperative Organization	1903.04[B]
Assessments	1903.04[C]

Chapter 20—Sale of Residence

OVERVIEW OF CHAPTER	2000
GAIN OR LOSS ON SALE OF RESIDENCE	2001
Business or Rental Use	2001.01
Residence Held for Gain	2001.02
TAX EXCLUSION FOR PRINCIPAL RESIDENCE	2002
Qualifications for Exclusion	2002.01
Joint Returns	2002.01[A]
Nonqualified Use	2002.01[B]
Special Situations	2002.01[C]
Employer Relocation Assistance	2002.01[D]
Exclusion for Mixed-Use Residence	2002.02
TAX-FREE ROLLOVER OF GAIN	2003
Postponement of Tax Requirements	2003.01
Replacement Period	2003.01[A]
Tax Treatment	2003.02
Gain on Old Residence	2003.02[A]
Gain on New Residence and Basis	2003.02[B]
Joint Ownership	2003.02[C]
Partial Business Use	2003.03
EXCLUSION OF GAIN FOR TAXPAYER OVER 55	2004
Exclusion Amount and Qualification Requirements	2004.01
Ownership and Use Requirements	2004.01[A]
Purchase of New Principal Residence	2004.01[B]
Election and Revocation of Election	2004.02
Election of the Exclusion	2004.02[A]
Revocation of the Election	2004.02[B]

PART VI—SECURITIZED REAL ESTATE INVESTMENTS

Chapter 21—Real Estate Limited Partnerships

OVERVIEW OF CHAPTER	2100
DEVELOPMENT OF LIMITED PARTNERSHIPS	2101

Paragraph

Limited Partnerships as Tax Shelters 2101.01
Real Estate Tax Shelters 2101.02
Real Estate Limited Partnerships 2101.03
TAX TREATMENT OF REAL ESTATE LIMITED PARTNERSHIPS 2102
Restrictions on Partnership-Generated Tax Losses 2102.01
At-Risk Rules .... 2102.01[A]
Passive Loss Rule .... 2102.01[B]
Limited Partnership Interests 2102.02
MASTER LIMITED PARTNERSHIPS 2103
Origins of Master Limited Partnerships 2103.01
Evolution and Growth of the MLP Concept 2103.02
Impact of Tax Legislation on MLPs 2103.03
Real Estate MLPs 2103.04

Chapter 22—Real Estate Investment Trusts

OVERVIEW OF CHAPTER 2200
TAX TREATMENT OF REITS 2201
Dividends-Paid Deduction 2201.01
Foreclosure Property .... 2201.01[A]
Designation of Qualified Dividends .... 2201.01[B]
Capital Gains .... 2201.01[C]
Built-in Gains Tax 2201.02
Other Taxes 2201.03
REIT Subsidiaries 2201.04
TAX TREATMENT OF REIT SHAREHOLDERS 2202
Capital Gain 2202.01
After-Tax Year Distributions 2202.02
QUALIFYING AS A REIT 2203
Ownership and Organization Requirements 2203.01
Income Requirements 2203.02
Asset Requirements 2203.03
Failure to Meet Asset Requirements .... 2203.03[A]
Ancillary Personal Property .... 2203.03[B]
Deficiency Dividends 2203.04

Chapter 23—Real Estate Mortgage Investment Conduits

OVERVIEW OF CHAPTER 2300
INVESTOR INTERESTS 2301
TAX TREATMENT OF REMICS 2302
Regular Interests 2302.01
Residual Interests 2302.02
Distributions .... 2302.02[A]
Income and Basis .... 2302.02[B]

Part I

ACQUIRING OWNERSHIP OF REAL PROPERTY

Introduction to Part I

Part I looks at the acquisition of real property from a tax perspective. Chapter 1 is concerned with the acquisition transaction itself. The acquisition puts into motion a host of tax provisions that will haunt the owner at every step of the property's life cycle. When a taxpayer acquires property, whether by purchase, construction, inheritance, or other means, the taxpayer must determine the tax basis for the property. It is this figure that determines many of the future tax consequences that will flow from the ownership of the property, including gain or loss on its eventual sale or disposition.

The vehicle that a taxpayer chooses to hold property also is a critical decision from a tax standpoint. If the real estate is business or investment property, individual or joint ownership, partnerships, limited liability companies, and corporations all have their advantages and disadvantages. The appropriate form of ownership and operation for real estate is explained in Chapter 2. Also, the very concept of ownership for federal tax purposes is explained so that taxpayers may assure themselves that the "right" person receives the tax benefits that flow from the ownership of real property.

Finally, a major concern in any real estate acquisition is how to finance the acquisition. Mortgage financing is common and raises tax questions for both the mortgagor and mortgagee. Is the interest paid by the mortgagor deductible for tax purposes? When is it deductible? When must the mortgagee include interest in income? Is there any hidden or unstated interest or original issue discount in the terms of the financing agreement? These questions, as well as many others, are explored in Chapter 3. Also explored in Chapter 3 are sale-leasebacks and other lease financing arrangements and the at-risk rules that limit deductions from property financed with nonrecourse financing.

Chapter 1
The Acquisition Transaction

¶ 100 Overview of Chapter
¶ 101 Importance of Basis
¶ 102 Purchase of Real Property
¶ 103 Construction of Real Property
¶ 104 Low-Income Housing Tax Credit
¶ 105 Energy Efficient Home Tax Credit

¶ 100 OVERVIEW OF CHAPTER

The acquisition of real estate itself, whether for investment, business, or personal use, has few immediate tax consequences. For the most part, the cost of real property is a capital expenditure that produces no immediate tax liability or benefit. The acquisition, however, does put into motion a host of tax provisions that will haunt the owner at every step of the property's life cycle.

The structure of the acquisition transaction, that is, the deal struck between the buyer and seller, affects the tax consequences that will ultimately flow from the ownership of the real property. There are also many expenses related to the actual acquisition. Some of these will be considered part of the cost of the property and, accordingly, will have no immediate tax consequences. Others, however, will not be part of the acquisition cost of the property and may produce current tax deductions. Moreover, it is sometimes difficult to distinguish between the expenses that are part of the cost of the property and those related to the acquisition of the property, which, for tax purposes, are not part of the cost of the property. This is especially true when real property assets are constructed rather than purchased in a completed state.

Although money spent for real property generally produces no immediate tax effect, there are a few cases in which the actual cost of purchasing or constructing real property can produce a tax savings. For example, the cost of low-income housing or the construction of energy efficient homes may, under certain circumstances produce an immediate tax credit.

These, then, are the topics of this first chapter: the cost of purchasing or constructing real property or otherwise determining the tax basis of property, the costs of acquiring the property which are not part of the tax basis of the property, and the tax credit for the purchase or construction of low-income housing.

¶ 101 IMPORTANCE OF BASIS

Knowing the basis of property is important for several reasons. It is the basis of property, adjusted for events that occur while the owner holds the property, that ultimately determines the amount of gain or loss on the disposition of the property.[1] This rule applies regardless of whether the real estate involved is used for business or personal purposes or is held for investment.

> ***Example 1:*** A building with a current market value of $250,000 has an adjusted basis of $100,000. If the building is sold for its market value, the owner reports a gain of $150,000, that is, the difference between the amount realized on the sale and the basis of the property at the time of the sale.

The adjusted basis of property (original basis adjusted for events occurring while the property is held) also serves as the outside limit on the amount of any deduction in the event of the loss or destruction of the property.[2]

> ***Example 2:*** A building with a current market value of $250,000 and an adjusted basis of $100,000 is destroyed by a hurricane. The maximum casualty loss that could be taken as a tax deduction is limited to $100,000. The amount of the actual deduction, of course, would depend on other factors, such as the amount of any insurance recovery and the type of property, that is, business or personal, involved.

In the case of real property that is used for business purposes or held for investment, basis is important for determining the amount of the annual depreciation deduction that may be permitted for the property.

.01 Calculation of Basis

The original basis of any property depends on how the owner acquires that property. The original basis is then increased or decreased by events occurring while the owner holds the property. The most common adjustments to original basis in the case of real property are increases for additions and improvements and decreases for depreciation and casualty losses. The various adjustments to original basis are discussed throughout this book in connection with the transactions giving rise to those adjustments.

How to determine original basis is discussed in the following paragraphs which relate to various ways in which real property may be acquired.

[A] Property Acquired by Purchase

When the owner acquires real property by purchase, the general basis rule of Code Sec. 1012 applies, that is, the original basis of the property is its cost. Cost, in addition to the cash paid by the buyer to the seller, includes the amount of any mortgage given to secure payment of the balance of the purchase price and expenses directly related to the acquisition of the property such as commissions, legal fees, and title insurance premiums.

---

[1] Code Sec. 1011.

[2] Code Sec. 165(b).

Cost does not include any amount for real property taxes that are treated as imposed on the purchaser under Code Sec. 164(d). Cost, however, does include real estate taxes that are treated as imposed on the seller but are assumed or paid by the buyer.

The acquisition of real property through purchase is considered in further detail at ¶ 102.

[B] Property Constructed by or for the Owner

As with real property acquired by purchase, the general basis rule of Code Sec. 1012 (that the original basis of property is its cost) applies to property constructed by or for the owner.

Cost, in the case of constructed property, includes the cost of materials and contractors' charges. In addition, the cost basis of real estate may include many items incurred during the construction period that would be currently deductible expenses in other settings. Under Code Sec. 263A, all direct costs and the property's proper share of any indirect costs, including taxes, that are allocable to the property during its construction must be capitalized as part of the original basis of the property. This capitalization rule applies to property that will be used in a trade or business or activity conducted for profit. It does not apply to a personal residence constructed by or for its owner.

The acquisition of real property by construction is considered in further detail at ¶ 103.

[C] Property Acquired in an Exchange

No gain or loss is recognized when property held for productive use in a trade or business or for investment is exchanged solely for property of like kind to be held either for productive use in a trade or business or for investment.[3] Under Code Sec. 1031(d), the basis of the old property given up in an exchange without recognition of gain or loss becomes the basis of the property received in the exchange. This like-kind exchange provision applies after 2017 only to real property held for productive use in a trade or business or for investment. Real property held primarily for sale remains ineligible for like-kind exchange treatment.

The new property acquired in a "tax-free" exchange is said to have a "substitute basis" in that the basis of the old property is substituted for the basis of the new property. This substitute basis preserves the gain or loss that went unrecognized at the time of the exchange for later taxation when the acquired property is disposed of in a taxable transaction.

If an exchange of property is an uneven exchange, that is, if cash or other nonlike-kind property is included in the exchange, the substituted basis must be adjusted to reflect the gain or loss that is recognized. Like-kind exchanges and the complications involved are considered at ¶ 1302.

[3] Code Sec. 1031.

[D] Property Acquired on Exercise of an Option

When real property is acquired through the exercise of an option on the property, the holder of the option adds the cost of the option to the price paid for the property at the time the holder exercises the option to determine the property's original basis. The holder of an option that allows it to lapse without exercising it is entitled to a loss deduction at that time.

[E] Property Acquired by Gift

The basis of property acquired by gift is determined under Code Sec. 1015. The rule has undergone several changes over the years, and slightly different versions apply, depending on the date of the gift. Earlier versions of the rule remain important in case it is necessary to trace basis back through a series of transfers.

Current Rule

The basis of property acquired by gift generally is the basis the donor had in the property prior to the gift, adjusted for any gift tax paid on the transfer. The adjustment for the gift tax is the amount of gift tax attributable to the appreciation in value the property experienced while held by the donor. The appreciation is measured by the difference between the donor's basis and the fair market value of the property at the time of the gift. The adjustment for gift taxes, however, cannot be used to increase the donee's basis over the fair market value of the property at the time of the gift.

> ***Example 3:*** The Donor has property with a basis of $100,000 and a fair market value of $250,000. On the transfer of this property to the donee, the Donor pays a gift tax in the amount of $50,000. The donee's basis for this property is $130,000, which reflects the Donor's basis of $100,000 increased by $30,000 of the gift tax, which is the amount of the gift tax attributable to the appreciation of the property while held by the Donor.
>
> The $30,000 adjustment is determined from the ratio of the appreciation (fair market value less basis) to the total value of the gift. In this case the appreciation is $150,000 ($250,000 - $100,000), and this is 60 percent of the value of the gift. Accordingly, the amount of the gift tax adjustment is 60 percent of the total gift tax paid on the transfer.

In the event that the donor's basis for the gift property exceeds the fair market value of the property at the time of the gift, a special rule limits the donee's basis to fair market value for purposes of determining any loss on the property on a later disposition by the donee.

> ***Example 4:*** The Donor makes a gift of property with a fair market value of $250,000 and a basis of $100,000. Assuming no gift tax is paid on the transfer, the donee's basis for the property is $100,000.
>
> If the figures were reversed and the property had a basis in the hands of the Donor of $250,000 but a value at the time of the gift of only $100,000, the donee's basis would be $250,000, unless use of that basis figure would produce a loss when the donee disposed of the property. For purposes of determining the amount of any loss realized by the donee on a disposition of the property, the basis would be $100,000, not $250,000.

Gifts Post-1958 and Pre-1977

The basis rule for gifts made after September 1, 1958, and before 1977, was the same as the current rule, except for the adjustment for gift taxes. The adjustment for gift taxes for gifts made during this period was the full amount of the tax, not just the portion attributable to appreciation.

> ***Example 5:*** The Donor had property with a basis of $100,000 and a fair market value of $250,000 when the Donor made a gift of the property before 1977. On the transfer of this property to the donee, the Donor paid a gift tax in the amount of $50,000. The donee's basis for this property is $150,000, which reflects the Donor's basis of $100,000 increased by the $50,000 gift tax paid on the transfer.

(Note that the basis adjustment as applied to gifts made after September 1, 1958, applied to gifts made before September 2, 1958, if the donee held the gift property on September 2, 1958.)

Gifts Post-1920 and Pre-1958

The basis rule for gifts made after 1920 and before September 2, 1958, was the same as the current rule, except that there was no adjustment for gift taxes paid. The donee's basis for a gift was simply the donor's basis before the gift or, for purposes of determining loss, the fair market value of the property on the date of the gift if lower than the donor's basis.

Gifts Pre-1921

The basis of property acquired by gift before 1921 was the fair market value of the property at the time of the gift.

[F] Property Acquired by Inheritance

Under Code Sec. 1014, the basis of property acquired from a decedent is generally the fair market value of the property on the date of the decedent's death. Under an election available to estates, the executor may elect to value estate property as of an alternate valuation date, which is generally six months after the decedent's death.[4] If this alternate valuation date is elected, the basis of property acquired from the decedent is its fair market value on the alternate valuation date.

There is also an election available to estates[5] which allows an executor to value certain real estate for estate tax purposes according to its use as farm property or in a trade or business, rather than at its fair market value. (Fair market value generally reflects the highest and best use of a particular parcel of real property.) If the executor elects this "special use" valuation, the basis of the property is its special use estate tax value rather than its fair market value.

Using the basis rules for gifts and for property acquired from a decedent, it might be possible to get an increased basis for appreciated property and avoid taxable gain by gifting the property to an elderly or terminally ill individual and then receiving back the property on the ultimate death of the donee. Making use of a

[4] Code Sec. 2032.

[5] Code Sec. 2032A.

deathbed-donee to get an increased basis for appreciated property, however, is blocked by Code Sec. 1014(e) if the donee dies within one year of the gift. In this case, the basis to the original donor who is receiving the property back from the donee-decedent is the adjusted basis of the property in the hands of the donee-decedent immediately before death. A similar rule applies if the estate of the donee-decedent sells the property and the original donor or spouse is entitled to the proceeds of the sale.

Effect of Delayed and Cancelled Estate Tax Repeal

The estate tax was scheduled to be repealed after 2009. This repeal was delayed and, ultimately, cancelled by the American Taxpayer Relief Act of 2012.[6] Had the estate tax been repealed, the rule that provides a fair market value basis for property acquired from a decedent would have been replaced with a modified carryover basis rule. Recipients of property on a decedent's death would have taken a basis equal to the lesser of the decedent's adjusted basis or the property's fair market value on the date of the decedent's death. In delaying the estate tax repeal, however, the Tax Relief Act of 2010[7] permitted the estates of decedents who died in 2010 to elect out of the estate tax and apply carryover basis to the decedent's property under Code Section 1022. The owner of property acquired from an estate that made this election, therefore, will have a carryover basis for the property. The IRS provided optional safe harbor guidance for this election in Rev. Proc. 2011-41.[8]

[G] Property Acquired from a Spouse or Former Spouse

Anytime property is transferred from one spouse to another, or from one spouse to a former spouse incident to a divorce, the transfer is treated as a gift, and the transferee spouse's basis for the property is the adjusted basis the property had in the hands of the transferor spouse.[9] This special basis rule applies regardless of the actual form of the transfer, whether a true gift, a sale for consideration, or otherwise. This rule complements the provision that makes all such transfers tax-free events.[10]

The transfer of property from a spouse to a former spouse is considered incident to the divorce if the transfer takes place within one year after the date on which the marriage ends or is related to the cessation of the marriage.

[H] Other Basis Rules

In addition to the basis rules discussed above, there are various basis rules throughout the Internal Revenue Code to cover special situations. These basis rules are covered at appropriate points throughout this volume. Notable among these special basis rules are those that determine basis following:

- Sale of a taxpayer's principal residence before May 7, 1997 (or later in specified situations) and its replacement with a new residence (see ¶ 2003).
- Foreclosure or repossession (see ¶ ¶ 1202 and 1204).

---

[6] P.L. 112-240.
[7] P.L. 111-312.
[8] 2011-35 IRB 188.
[9] Code Sec. 1041(b).
[10] Code Sec. 1041(a).

- Casualty, condemnation, or other involuntary conversion (see ¶ ¶ 1501 and 1502).
- Subdivision of a tract (see ¶ 1001.01).
- Contribution to a partnership or corporation (see ¶ ¶ 203.02[B]and 204.02[A]).

.02 Mortgage and Basis

The original cost basis of property includes the amount of any mortgage given to secure payment of any portion of the purchase price. It does not matter whether the money is borrowed from a financial institution, other third-party lender, or from the seller of the property in the form of a purchase-money mortgage. Cost basis also includes the amount of any existing mortgage on the property. This rule applies whether the buyer actually assumes the existing mortgage or purchases the property subject to the mortgage without personally assuming the mortgage.

(Note that basis does not include any principal amount that is recharacterized as interest under the imputed interest or original issue discount rules. Basis does include "interest" that is recharacterized as principal under these rules. The imputed interest and original issue discount rules are treated at ¶ ¶ 303 and 304.)

> ***Example 6:*** The Buyer purchases real estate from the Seller for $250,000. The Buyer pays for the property by giving the Seller $50,000 cash and a purchase-money mortgage in the amount of $75,000. The Buyer also assumes an existing mortgage on the property in the amount of $125,000. The Buyer's original cost basis for this real estate is $250,000.

The other side of the coin, of course, is that the seller includes in the amount realized from the sale of property the amount of any mortgage debt the seller is relieved of on the sale, as well as the amount of any purchase-money mortgage the seller grants to the buyer.

> ***Example 7:*** In the example above, the Buyer's basis is $250,000. By the same token, the amount the Seller has realized on the sale is $250,000—the $50,000 cash, the $125,000 mortgage obligation the Seller was relieved of when the Buyer assumed that mortgage in connection with the sale, and the $75,000 mortgage the Seller has taken back from the Buyer as part of the sale. The Seller's gain or loss is measured by the difference between the amount realized and the adjusted basis at the time of the sale.

This rule, which includes the amount of debt incurred to purchase property in the basis of the property for the buyer and the amount of debt discharged on the sale of property in the amount realized by the seller, can be traced back to the decision of the Supreme Court in *B.B. Crane.*[11]

Mrs. Crane inherited property from her husband. This property was valued for estate tax purposes at $262,000 and was subject to a $255,000 loan. At the time she inherited the property, there was $7,000 accrued interest due on the loan. In effect, the net value of Mrs. Crane's inheritance at the time of her husband's death was zero.

---

[11] S.Ct., 47-1 USTC ¶ 9217, 331 U.S. 1.

Mrs. Crane operated the property and claimed depreciation deductions for the property, but she never personally assumed the debt of $255,000. She ultimately sold the property and reported a taxable gain of $2,500, the net amount she received for the property. According to Mrs. Crane, all she inherited from her husband was her equity in the property, which was zero. All she sold when she sold the property was this equity. Therefore, her gain was only $2,500, the difference between the zero "basis" for her equity and the $2,500 "realized" from the sale of this equity.

According to the IRS, however, Mrs. Crane sold real estate and not just her equity in the real estate. Her adjusted basis at the time of the sale was the estate tax value of the property reduced by the $25,000 in depreciation deductions claimed while she held the property, or $237,000. The amount she realized on the sale of the property was the $2,500 cash received plus the $255,000 principal amount due on the loan against the property, or $257,500. Her gain, therefore, was not the $2,500 she received for her "equity," but the difference between her adjusted basis of $237,000 and her amount realized of $257,500, or a taxable gain of $20,500. The Supreme Court agreed with the IRS, and that has been the rule for basis and amount realized ever since.

In most cases, it is the face amount of a mortgage or other debt that controls in determining the amount to include in basis or amount realized. Old debts or debts carrying a below-current-market rate of interest are not discounted to reflect this. The imputed interest and original issue discount rules discussed at ¶¶ 304 and 304.01, however, may convert a portion of nominal principal to interest when an inadequate rate of interest is provided in a purchase-money mortgage. Also, in potentially abusive situations, the principal amount of debt incurred to purchase property may be equated to the fair market value of the property (see ¶ 101.02[C]).

Although original cost basis does include amounts borrowed to acquire property, there is no adjustment to basis as payments are made to reduce the debt. In other words, mortgage payments do not reduce or increase the basis of the mortgaged property.[12]

[A] Contingent or Speculative Obligations

While the rule is that basis includes the amount of any mortgage given to obtain the property, there must be a reasonable likelihood that an amount will actually have to be paid on the mortgage. If payments on a mortgage are contingent on the happening of some event or events that are uncertain and speculative, no real obligation is created by the mortgage until the future contingency occurs. If payments are actually made on a contingent and speculative obligation, the amount of the payments is added to basis at that time.

[12] Parker v. Delaney, CA-1, 51-1 USTC ¶ 9112, 186 F.2d 455.

See, for example, *S. Baron Est.*,[13] in which it was held that a recourse obligation was not treated as true debt because payment was too contingent.[14]

[B] Borrowing Against Previously Owned Property

A taxpayer that borrows against property already owned does not increase basis for the new obligation, unless the loan is used to improve or make additions to the property (see ¶ 803). In the latter case, it is the cost of the additions or improvements that is added to basis, regardless of how they are financed, just as original basis is the cost of the property, regardless of how it is financed.

While borrowing against previously owned property does not affect basis, neither does it produce taxable income to the borrower. In general, borrowing is not a taxable transaction. When a mortgage is placed against property that is already owned, the borrower receives money, but the borrower has a corresponding obligation to repay that results in no benefit, at least as far as the tax law is concerned.[15]

[C] Artificially Inflated Purchase Price

The use of debt to increase tax and financial benefits is a common and acceptable practice. In some cases, however, promoters have been known to artificially inflate basis (and claimed tax benefits) with liabilities incurred to purchase property at prices far in excess of the real value of the property. The IRS has waged a constant battle against this practice and has much case law on its side. When Congress passed the original issue discount rules in 1984, it made a direct attack on the use of debt to artificially inflate the basis of property in what are termed "potentially abusive situations."

In any potentially abusive situation, the principal amount of a debt instrument given to finance the purchase of property is considered to be the fair market value of the property reduced by the fair market value of any other consideration (such as a cash down payment) given for the property.[16] The effect of this rule when property is purchased with the use of debt in a potentially abusive situation is to limit the basis of the property to its fair market value regardless of the amount of the debt.

Potentially abusive situations include tax shelters, which are defined as partnerships, other entities, investment plans or arrangements, or any other plan or arrangement, if the principal purpose of the partnership, entity, plan, or arrangement is the avoidance or evasion of federal income tax. Other potentially abusive situations are those involving a recent sales transaction, nonrecourse financing, financing with a term in excess of the economic life of the property, or a debt instrument with clearly excessive interest.[17]

---

[13] CA-2, 86-2 USTC ¶ 9622, 798 F.2d 65.

[14] 1980-2 CB 229. *See also* Rev. Rul. 80-235, 1980-2 CB 229.

[15] *See* James v. U.S., S.Ct., 61-1 USTC ¶ 9449, 366 U.S. 213.

[16] Code Sec. 1274(b)(3).

[17] *See* Reg. § 1.1274-3.

Example 8: The Taxpayer purchases real estate with a $1,000,000 down payment and a nonrecourse mortgage with a stated principal amount of $7,000,000. The fair market value at the time of the purchase is $7,000,000.

Since the transaction is a potentially abusive situation, the principal amount of the debt for tax purposes is treated as being $6,000,000, the fair market value of the property ($7,000,000) reduced by the amount of the down payment ($1,000,000). This means that the basis of the property for tax purposes is $7,000,000 ($1,000,000 down payment plus the imputed principal amount of the debt of $6,000,000), not the $8,000,000 the basis would be if the basis included the down payment plus the stated amount of the mortgage debt.

The fair market value limitation in potentially abusive situations applies whether or not adequate stated interest is provided under the normal original issue discount rules. Moreover, the fair market value rule does not affect case law that has developed in connection with artificially inflated or overstated basis. In situations not covered by the statute, the IRS may still attack the basis of property that has been artificially inflated with excessive mortgage or debt financing.

The decision in *D.L. Narver, Jr.*[18] illustrates the case law that developed before passage of Code Sec. 1274 to limit the use of inflated or "soft" mortgages to increase basis. *Narver* involved the purchase of a building, property, and an adjacent parking lot by Jack R. Young and Associates from the Sutherland Foundation for $650,000. Young immediately resold only the building to two partnerships that it controlled for $1,800,000 in nonrecourse debt and $180,000 in prepaid interest.

After the sale, the partnerships leased the building to a wholly owned subsidiary of Young at a rental that exactly satisfied the partnerships' nonrecourse purchase obligation to Young. The partners, of course, took depreciation deductions based on the inflated $1,800,000 basis and interest deductions based on the nonrecourse $1,800,000 debt. (At the time, real estate was not subject to the at-risk rules.) The IRS challenged the partners' deductions and the Tax Court decided that in this situation, the partners actually had no equity in the building and were not building equity under the financing arrangement set up by Young. As a result, the partnerships had no basis in the building and there was nothing to depreciate.

In another case involving inflated mortgage financing, the Tax Court decided that there was no valid debt.[19] In this case, the promoter interposed a third party in the inflated mortgage sale. A limited partnership purchased properties from the Go Publishing Company for $1,000,000, which was 10 times the amount Go had paid to Cal-Am Corporation for the property. Cal-Am was controlled by the promoter and general partner of the limited partnership and had acquired the property for about $100,000 before its temporary sale to Go. When Go resold the property to the partnership, it accepted a minimum down payment and a nonrecourse mortgage for the balance.

---

[18] 75 TC 53, CCH Dec. 37,335, *aff'd per curiam*, CA-9, 82-1 USTC ¶ 9265, 670 F.2d 855.

[19] J.C. Beck, 74 TC 1534, CCH Dec. 37,305, *aff'd*, CA-9, 82-2 USTC ¶ 9427, 678 F.2d 818.

See also *C.T. Franklin Est.*,[20] in which it was held that a nonrecourse debt did not represent a valid debt or actual investment in property and was not includible in the basis of the property for purposes of computing depreciation because the debt unreasonably exceeded the value of the property. The same result also was reached in *Melvin W. Issacson Est.*[21]

¶ 102 PURCHASE OF REAL PROPERTY

While it is easy to state the rule that the basis of purchased property is its cost, it is not always as easy to determine the exact cost figure for a specific property. Most, if not all, purchases of real estate assets involve more than a few incidental expenses. For the most part, these incidental or extra expenses are part of the cost of the property.

Once the purchaser settles on a specific cost figure, that figure must be allocated among the several assets that generally compose the "real estate package." The most obvious allocation in the case of business or investment property is, of course, the allocation of purchase price between depreciable improvements and nondepreciable land. Further allocation between various classes of depreciable assets also may be required.

.01 Buying Expenses

The buyer of real estate has no choice in the treatment of expenditures made in connection with the purchase of real estate. Generally, any amounts paid out for new buildings or for permanent improvements or betterments made to increase the value of any property are not currently deductible expenses.[22] Rather, these expenses are capital expenditures that form part of the cost or basis of the property.

It does not matter whether these expenses are of the type normally born by the buyer in a real estate transaction or whether they are seller's expenses that are borne by the buyer under the terms of the purchase contract. It also does not matter that the type of expenditure involved would not be a capital expenditure but would be currently deductible in other circumstances. The buyer must treat all expenses related to the acquisition of the property as additions to cost. For instance, a buyer who agrees to pay for repairs already contracted for by the seller is required to add the cost of the repairs to the cost of the property.[23]

Some of the more typical expenses related to the acquisition of property that the buyer includes in the cost are:

- Appraisal fees
- Attorneys' fees
- Building line contest
- Clearing and grading
- Closing costs
- Commissions

[20] CA-9, 76-2 USTC ¶ 9773, 544 F.2d 1045.

[21] CA-2, 88-2 USTC ¶ 9572, 860 F.2d 55.

[22] Code Sec. 263; Reg. § 1.263(a)-1.

[23] Wilensky & Sons Co., 7 BTA 693, CCH Dec. 2624.

- Condemnation costs
- Credit investigations
- Deed of correction to perfect title
- Improvements to the property
- Mortgage title insurance
- Removing a cloud on title
- Survey costs
- Title abstract
- Title defense
- Title determination
- Title insurance
- Utility connection costs

Expenses for evaluating localities to determine the feasibility of selling residential property were capital expenditures and not currently deductible expenses for a taxpayer engaged in the business of acquiring residential properties for renovation and sale.[24] Similarly, the costs of exploration are part of the cost of property acquired or retained if property is acquired or retained based on the data obtained from geological and geophysical exploration.[25]

The proper treatment of points and other charges or expenses related to acquiring a mortgage on property, as distinguished from the acquisition of the property itself, is considered at ¶ 301.

[A] Transaction Costs Under the Repair Regs

The IRS has issued regulations to resolve several issues regarding capitalization.[26] The regulations, known as the "repair regs" because they primarily address whether an expenditure should be classified as a deductible repair or nondeductible capital improvement, also address the capitalization of transaction costs in connection with the acquisition or construction of real property. The regulations apply as of January 1, 2014. Taxpayers, however, may apply them as of 2012 if they chose. Alternatively, taxpayers may apply the temporary regulations (T.D. 9564) that were issued at the end of 2011 to tax years 2012 and 2013.[27] (The question of a repair versus an improvement is taken up beginning at ¶ 703.01.)

Under the repair regs, a taxpayer must capitalize amounts paid to facilitate the acquisition or production of real property.[28] An amount is paid to facilitate the acquisition of real or personal property if the amount is paid in the process of investigating or otherwise pursuing the acquisition. Except for inherently facilitative costs listed below, however, an amount paid in the process of investigating or pursuing the acquisition of real property does not facilitate the acquisition if it relates to activities performed in the process of determining whether to acquire real

[24] Rev. Rul. 74-104, 1974-1 CB 70.

[25] Rev. Rul. 77-188, 1977-1 CB 76; *see also* Rev. Rul. 83-105, 1983-2 CB 51.

[26] T.D. 9636.

[27] Reg. § 1.263(a)-1(h).

[28] Reg. § 1.263(a)-2.

property and which real property to acquire. These pre-decisional costs are deductible in the case of real property. Inherently facilitative acquisition costs allocable to real property are capitalized even if property is not eventually acquired.

According to the regs, the following are considered to be inherently facilitative:

1. Transporting the property (for example, shipping fees and moving costs);
2. Securing an appraisal or determining the value or price of property;
3. Negotiating the terms or structure of the acquisition and obtaining tax advice on the acquisition;
4. Computing application fees, bidding costs, or similar expenses;
5. Preparing and reviewing the documents that effectuate the acquisition of the property (for example, preparing the bid, offer, sales contract, or purchase agreement);
6. Examining and evaluating the title of property;
7. Obtaining regulatory approval of the acquisition or securing permits related to the acquisition, including application fees;
8. Conveying property between the parties, including sales and transfer taxes, and title registration costs;
9. Paying finders' fees or brokers' commissions, including amounts paid that are contingent on the successful closing of the acquisition;
10. Obtaining architectural, geological, engineering, environmental, or inspection services pertaining to particular properties; or
11. Securing services provided by a qualified intermediary or other facilitator of an exchange under Code Sec. 1031.[29]

The following example is based on Example 8 in Reg. § 1.263(a)-2(f)(4).

Example 9: A retail company owns several stores and decides to examine the feasibility of opening a new store in a distant city. The retailer hires and incurs costs for a development consulting firm to study the city and perform market surveys, evaluate zoning and environmental requirements, and make preliminary reports and recommendations as to possible locations. While continuing to consider whether to purchase property in the new city, the retailer pays an appraiser to appraise two different sites to determine reasonable offering prices for each site. The following year, the retailer decides to acquire one of these two sites for the location of its new store and not to acquire the other site.

The retailer is not required to capitalize payments to the development consultant because the payments relate to activities performed in the process of determining whether to acquire real property and which real property to acquire and the amounts are not inherently facilitative costs. The retailer, however, must capitalize amounts paid to the appraiser because the appraisal costs are inherently facilitative costs. The retailer must include the appraisal

[29] Reg. § 1.263(a)-2(f).

costs allocable to the property acquired in the basis of that property. The retailer may deduct the appraisal costs allocable to the property it did not acquire under Code Sec. 165.

Even after a buyer actually takes title to a property, until the buyer places that property in service, the buyer must capitalize the costs of work performed on that property, including repairs, installation costs, and testing costs.[30]

Example 10: A buyer purchases a building for use as a business office. Before placing the building in service, the buyer pays to repair cement steps, refinish wood floors, patch holes in walls, and paint the interiors and exteriors of the building. The following year, the buyer places the building in service and begins using the building as its business office. If the work the buyer did before placing the building in service is not considered an improvement to the building or its structural components, the buyer must capitalize the cost of the work as part of the cost of the office building.

[B] Safe Harbor Expensing

Under a safe harbor expensing provision,[31] a taxpayer may elect not to capitalize the cost of tangible property with a limited cost. However, the uniform capitalization rules may require a taxpayer to capitalize amounts that are deductible under the safe harbor as a direct or allocable indirect cost of property (see ¶ 103.01). Considering the limited amounts under this safe harbor, it certainly has wider application to the question of whether something is a repair or improvement, rather than the initial acquisition of real property. The question of whether an expenditure is a repair or improvement is considered in some detail in Chapter 7.

Under the election, provided the requirements are met, a taxpayer with an AFS may deduct up to $5,000 per item. For a taxpayer without an AFS, the deductible amount is limited to $500.

An AFS is whichever of the taxpayer's financial statements that is listed first on the following list:

1. A financial statement required to be filed with the Securities and Exchange Commission (SEC) (a 10-K or an Annual Statement to Shareholders);
2. A certified audited financial statement that is accompanied by the report of an independent certified public accountant (or in the case of a foreign entity, by the report of a similarly qualified independent professional) that is used for credit purposes; for reporting to shareholders, partners, or similar persons; or for any other substantial non-tax purpose; or
3. A financial statement (other than a tax return) required to be provided to the federal or a state government or any federal or state agency, other than the SEC or the IRS.[32]

[30] Reg. § 1.263(a)-2(d)(1).

[31] Reg. § 1.263(a)-1(f).

[32] Reg. § 1.263(a)-1(f)(4).

Requirements

A taxpayer with an AFS may elect the *de minimis* expensing safe harbor if:

1. It has written accounting procedures that treat amounts paid for property that cost less than a specified dollar amount or that has an economic useful life of 12 months or less as an expense for non-tax purposes; and
2. It treats those amounts as an expense on the AFS.

If a taxpayer does not have an AFS, its accounting procedures in effect at the beginning of the tax year do not need to be written. However, the taxpayer must expense the amount paid for the property on its books and records according to its accounting procedures.

.02 Allocation of Costs

When only one asset is purchased in a single transaction, such as a vacant lot, the purchase price plus related acquisition expenses is the tax basis for the asset as discussed above. Most real estate purchases, however, involve more than the purchase of a single asset, even though purchase price is stated as a single lump sum. When more than one asset is purchased for a single sum, cost must be apportioned among the several assets acquired in order to determine the basis of each.

[A] Land and Buildings

The most common example of the purchase of multiple assets for a single lump sum is the purchase of land and a building. The buyer and seller usually negotiate the purchase price as if a single asset were involved. For tax purposes, however, the cost must be allocated between the separate assets, the land and the building, in all cases except the purchase of a personal residence. The portion of the total cost allocated to the building is subject to depreciation (see ¶ 901), but the cost of the land is not. A personal residence, since it is not held for business or investment use, is not subject to depreciation so the cost allocation is not required.

In most cases, the cost allocation is based upon the relative fair market values of the separate assets. Reg. § 1.167(a)-5 provides that when buildings and land are acquired for a lump sum, the basis of the buildings for depreciation cannot exceed an amount which bears the same proportion to the lump sum as the value of the depreciable buildings at the time of acquisition bears to the value of the entire property at that time. Similarly, the IRS has ruled that legal expenses, such as title search, verification of mortgage balance, and similar expenses, must be allocated between the land and improvements according to the fair market values of each at the time of the purchase.[33]

> ***Example 11:*** The Buyer purchases a commercial office building and the underlying land for $500,000 and incurs $50,000 in expenses directly related to the acquisition. The Buyer's basis for the land and building is $550,000, and this must be allocated between the nondepreciable land and the depreciable building. If the value of the land represents 25 percent of the total value, then the basis for the land would be $137,500 ($550,000 × 25%). The basis for the building would be $412,500 ($550,000 × 75%).

[33] Rev. Rul. 68-528, 1968-2 CB 331.

Relative Values

Although the rule requiring allocation of cost based on relative fair market values is a conceptually simple rule, its application to specific situations may be anything but simple. The real problem is determining relative values.

As a starting point, buyer and seller may negotiate the relative values of land and buildings and provide for the allocation in the purchase agreement. The IRS is likely to respect the allocation made by the parties if the negotiations are truly arm's-length and the buyer and seller have some adverse interest as to how the allocation is finally made. However, an allocation made by the parties under the contract of sale may be rejected if the allocation does not reflect the economic reality of the transaction.[34]

In some cases, the valuations placed on land and buildings for local real property tax purposes have been used as a guide for determining relative fair market values. Even though valuations for real estate taxes often may be too low to be used to determine the correct value of a real estate parcel, the valuations used by the local property tax assessor often do point to the relative value of the land and buildings located on the land.[35]

Relative values also have been established through appraisal by experts. Mortgage appraisals may be another source of information as to the relative values of land and buildings.[36]

In *S.A. Meiers*,[37] the Tax Court allocated the total purchase price of two condominium properties based upon the buildings' replacement costs at the time rather than the local property tax assessor's relative valuation of the land and buildings. In this particular case, the court thought replacement cost was the more accurate gauge of relative values. Replacement cost was also used in *Pensacola Greyhound Racing, Inc.*[38]

The capitalization of rentals method was used to allocate cost when the buildings included two houses that were rented to tenants.[39] And in *D.N. Marks*,[40] the court also used the capitalization of earnings method because the purchasers were investors. An income or capitalization of earnings approach reflects that investors generally purchase property for the income it is expected to produce.

Building Demolition

Cost is not allocated between land and buildings when the buildings will be demolished. Rather, the entire cost for the property is the basis for the land. This same rule applies to all demolitions, even when the demolition is of a building that has been owned for some time by the taxpayer. The cost of demolition and any loss

[34] *See* D.N. Marks, 49 TCM 1222, CCH Dec. 42,022(M), T.C. Memo. 1985-179.

[35] 2554-58 Creston Corp., 40 TC 932, CCH Dec. 26,294; Offshore Operations Trust, 32 TCM 985, CCH Dec. 32,149(M), T.C. Memo. 1973-212.

[36] L.R. Akers, 40 TCM 574, CCH Dec. 37,044(M), T.C. Memo. 1980-238.

[37] 43 TCM 454, CCH Dec. 38,766(M), T.C. Memo. 1982-51.

[38] 32 TCM 1064, CCH Dec. 32,173(M), T.C. Memo. 1973-225.

[39] P. Hurd, 37 TCM 499, CCH Dec. 35,057(M), T.C. Memo. 1978-113.

[40] 49 TCM 1222, CCH Dec. 42,022(M), T.C. Memo. 1985-179.

sustained because of the demolition (usually, any remaining basis for the building) is added to the basis of the land on which the demolished structure was located.[41]

Prior to 1984, costs and other losses incurred in connection with the demolition of buildings generally could be claimed as a current deduction unless the building and the land on which the structure was located were purchased with an intent to demolish the building. Only if the purchaser intended to demolish the building at the time of purchase were costs and other losses added to the basis of the land. Needless to say, this rule led to many contests between taxpayers and the IRS over whether an intent to demolish a building existed when the building was purchased. Such controversies ended with the passage of Code Sec. 280B.

[B] Land Improvements and Personal Property

The division of real estate into land and buildings may be fairly obvious, but the purchase of real estate often involves more than the purchase of simply those two assets. The "bundle of assets" making up the real estate package may be further divided beyond land and buildings into land improvements and personal property. As with the allocation between land and buildings, these allocations should also be based on relative fair market values, with independent appraisals and costs analyses serving as the best means of establishing those relative values.

While the cost of land itself is not depreciable, various land improvements may be. Therefore, to take maximum advantage of available depreciation allowances, it is necessary to further allocate basis to those land improvements that qualify as depreciable. Generally, those land improvements that do not permanently improve the land but improve it only for use with a specific building are depreciable. As the IRS has put it, land improvement costs are depreciable if they are directly associated with buildings rather than inextricably associated with the land.[42]

In Rev. Rul. 65-265, the IRS ruled that the cost of general grading of land is part of the cost basis of the land and is nondepreciable. The cost of digging and removing soil necessary for the proper setting of the buildings and paving of the roadways, however, is part of their cost and is depreciable. This ruling was further clarified by Rev. Rul. 68-193,[43] which allowed depreciation for certain grading costs for roads constructed to provide for movement of heavy materials between buildings when the grading would be abandoned or replaced with the buildings with which it was directly associated.

Landscaping consisting of perennial shrubbery and ornamental trees adjacent to buildings was considered a depreciable land improvement when replacement of the buildings would require replacement of the landscaping. On the other hand, the cost of general landscaping of the grounds around the same buildings was considered a general land improvement cost and part of the basis of the nondepreciable land.[44]

---

[41] Code Sec. 280B.

[42] Rev. Rul. 65-265, 1965-2 CB 52.

[43] 1968-1 CB 79.

[44] Rev. Rul. 74-265, 1974-1 CB 56.

Rev. Proc. 87-56[45] contains the class lives and recovery periods for computing depreciation deductions for various assets. Under this Revenue Procedure, land improvements include depreciable improvements such as sidewalks, roads, canals, waterways, drainage facilities, docks, bridges, fences, landscaping and shrubbery.

(Depreciation and related concepts are considered further in Chapter 9.)

[C] Buildings and Personal Property

Just as land costs may be divided between land and land improvements to increase depreciation deductions, to the extent any portion of the cost of a building can be allocated to personal property, depreciation deductions may be increased. The cost of personal property may be recovered over much shorter periods than the cost of real property.[46] Making the allocation can be a troublesome undertaking. Nevertheless, the tax benefits that result usually make the effort worthwhile.

In order to allocate cost to those elements of the real estate package that may qualify as personal property it is necessary to identify those items. Historically, this was usually accomplished under the law as it developed for purposes of the investment credit. The investment credit, when it was in effect, generally was available for "tangible personal property," but not for "buildings or their structural components."

In a landmark decision,[47] the Tax Court ruled that, to the extent tangible personal property is included in an acquisition or in overall costs, it should be treated as such for depreciation purposes. The court also decided that the rules for determining whether property qualifies as tangible personal property for purposes of the investment tax credit (under pre-1981 tax law) are also applicable for determining depreciation under current law. The IRS acquiesced to the use of ITC rules for distinguishing personal (Code Sec. 1245) property from real (Code Sec. 1250) property.[48]

In determining whether or not a particular item of property is tangible personal property for tax purposes, local law is not controlling. This means that an item of property may be personal property for tax purposes even though it is real property for purposes of local law.[49] Tangible personal property includes all property contained in or attached to a building other than structural components.

Structural components that are considered part of a building include walls, partitions, floors, and ceilings, as well as any permanent coverings for them such as paneling or tiling, windows and doors, all components of a central air conditioning or heating system, plumbing and plumbing fixtures such as sinks and bathtubs, electric wiring and lighting fixtures, chimneys, stairs, sprinkler systems, fire escapes, and other components relating to the operation or maintenance of the building.[50]

---

[45] 1987-2 CB 674.

[46] *See* ¶ 901.

[47] Hospital Corporation of America, 109 TC 21 (1997).

[48] AOD CC-1999-008, 1999-2 CB. xvi.

[49] Reg. § 1.48-1(c).

[50] Reg. § 1.48-1(e)(2).

In an attempt to clarify existing law at the time, the Senate Finance Committee, in its report on the Revenue Act of 1978, included an extensive list of property associated with real estate that should be classified as personal property:

- Beverage bars
- Booths for seating
- Carpeting
- False balconies and other exterior ornamentation that have no more than an incidental relationship to the operation or maintenance of a building
- Floor coverings that are not an integral part of the floor itself, such as tile installed in a manner so that it is readily removed (not cemented, mudded or otherwise permanently affixed to the floor)
- Identity symbols that identify or relate to a particular retail establishment or restaurant and signs other than billboards
- Movable and removable partitions
- Ornamental fixtures, such as coats-of-arms, and depreciable artifacts
- Pictures of scenery, persons, etc., that are attached to walls or suspended from the ceiling
- Special lighting, including lighting to illuminate the exterior of a building or store, but not lighting to illuminate parking areas
- Wall panel inserts designed to contain condiments or serve as framing for pictures of products

Despite this "clarification" of existing law, the distinction between structural components and personal property remained a troublesome one and one that is often a matter of dispute between taxpayers and the IRS.

The IRS and the courts have, at times, applied a permanency test to determine whether assets attached to a structure are components of the building or are personal property. For instance, in *Minot Federal Savings & Loan Assn.*,[51] removable partitions that were not permanent and could be changed and moved without injury to the building were considered personal property.[52]

The classic pronouncement addressing inherent permanency was *Whiteco Industries, Inc.*[53] The Tax Court, based on an analysis of judicial precedent, developed six questions designed to determine whether a particular asset qualifies as tangible personal property. These questions, referred to as the Whiteco factors, are:

1. Can the property be moved and has it been moved?
2. Is the property designed or constructed to remain permanently in place?
3. Are there circumstances that show that the property may or will have to be moved?
4. Is the property readily movable?

[51] CA-8, 71-1 USTC ¶ 9131, 435 F.2d 1368.

[52] *See also* Rev. Rul. 75-178, 1975-1 CB 9; King Radio Corp. Inc., CA-10, 73-2 USTC ¶ 9766, 486 F.2d 1091; J.E. Fleming, 49 TCM 1134, CCH Dec. 42,005(M), T.C. Memo. 1985-165.

[53] 65 TC 664 (1975).

5. How much damage will the property sustain when it is removed?
6. How is the property affixed to land?

It should also be noted, however, that moveability is not the only determinative factor in measuring inherent permanency. In *L.L. Bean, Inc.*,[54] it was determined that, even though the structure could be moved, it was designed to remain permanently in place. Therefore, the court determined it to be an inherently permanent structure.

In its Cost Segregation Audit Technique Guide (October 2016), IRS tells its examiners to also consider the following points when addressing the Whiteco factors:

- The history of the item or similar items being moved;
- The manner in which an item is attached to a building or to the land;
- The weight and size of the item;
- The function and design of the item;
- The intent of the taxpayer in installing the item;
- The time, cost, manpower, and equipment required to move the components;
- The time, cost, manpower, and equipment required to reconfigure the existing space if the item is removed;
- The effect of the item's removal on the building; and
- The extent the item can be reused after removal.

The following checklists contain some additional authorities on just what is a building or structural component and what is personal property for many assets associated with real estate.

Building Components

- Canopies of concrete slab or steel frame over loading or storage docks which are integral parts of the walls[55]
- Cinderblock walls, doors, rest rooms, plumbing, office partitions and electrical wiring in an underground storage facility[56]
- Clean rooms within factory buildings[57]
- Docks at a factory for loading and unloading materials[58]
- Electrical distribution system servicing the overall electrical needs of the building[59]
- Enclosed modular office structures installed within a factory[60]
- Prefabricated, movable structure used as a restaurant[61]

[54] T.C. Memo. 1997-175, *aff'd*, CA-1, 145 F.3d 53 (1998).

[55] Rev. Rul. 74-2, 1974-1 CB 10.

[56] Rev. Rul. 70-103, 1970-1 CB 6.

[57] Rev. Rul. 68-530, 1968-2 CB 37.

[58] Rev. Rul. 74-392, 1974-2 CB 10.

[59] Rev. Rul. 70-160, 1970-1 CB 7.

[60] IRS Letter Ruling 8648005, April 21, 1986.

[61] H.L. Tennyson, DC Ida., 86-1 USTC ¶ 9147, 632 F. Supp. 2.

- Raised floor incorporated in original building design with no finished floor under raised floor[62]
- Remote control operator houses as part of a ski-lift facility[63]
- Structures housing machinery and equipment in breaker and fine-coal plants[64]
- Wall partitions that could not be stored, reused in their entirety, or removed without minor damage to the structure[65]

Personal Property

- Bank vault doors, night depository facilities and drive-up and walk-up teller's windows[66]
- Chandeliers and hanging lanterns that were accessories to a restaurant business rather than components relating to the operation or maintenance of the buildings in which they were located[67]
- Climate control system for processing cut roses in a greenhouse[68]
- Compressor station structures of natural gas transmission company[69]
- Electrical distribution system at large manufacturing complex except to the extent used to supply power for the overall operation and maintenance of buildings[70]
- Fire extinguishers,[71] but a fire protection system that is designed to remain in place permanently is a structural component[72]
- Individual room refrigeration units installed in a warehouse[73]
- Merchandising huts that could be removed from their locations[74]
- Raised floor built on existing floor to permit installation of wiring, ducts, and other services for computer equipment[75]
- Removable partitions that are not permanent and can be changed and moved without injury to the building[76]
- Wall-to-wall carpeting installed in the guest rooms, office space, bar areas and dining rooms of a motel[77]

---

[62] FSA 200110001.

[63] Rev. Rul. 69-169, 1969-1 CB 27.

[64] Rev. Rul. 68-50, 1968-1 CB 364.

[65] Mallinckrodt, Inc., CA-8, 85-2 USTC ¶ 9841, 778 F.2d 402, *aff'g per curiam* 48 TCM 1290, CCH Dec. 41,536(M), T.C. Memo. 1984-537; Dixie Manor Inc., CA-6, 81-1 USTC ¶ 9332.

[66] Rev. Rul. 65-79, 1965 1 CB 26.

[67] Shoney's South, Inc., 48 TCM 768, CCH Dec. 41,398(M), T.C. Memo. 1984-413; *but see also* L.A. Duaine, 49 TCM 588, CCH Dec. 41,845(M), T.C. Memo. 1985-39.

[68] Endres Floral Co., DC Ohio, 78-2 USTC ¶ 9614, 450 F. Supp. 16.

[69] Rev. Rul. 66-215, 1966-2 CB 11; *but see also* Rev. Rul. 86-15, 1986-1 CB 7.

[70] Scott Paper Co., 74 TC 137, CCH Dec. 36,920.

[71] Rev. Rul. 67-417, 1967-2 CB 49.

[72] Rev. Rul. 77-362, 1977-2 CB 8; *see also* Ponderosa Mouldings, Inc., 53 TC 92, CCH Dec. 29,802, holding that a sprinkler system that was movable and could be transferred to another location at the risk of some damage to the system was not personal property.

[73] Rev. Rul. 81-240, 1981-2 CB 11.

[74] Film N' Photos, Inc., 37 TCM 709, CCH Dec. 35,125(M), T.C. Memo. 1978-162.

[75] Rev. Rul. 74-391, 1974-2 CB 9; *see also* FSA 200033002.

[76] Rev. Rul. 75-178, 1975-1 CB 9.

[77] Rev. Rul. 67-349, 1967-2 CB 48.

For additional examples and authorities on what is a building or structural component and what is personal property, see the Appendix in Chapter 6 of the IRS's Cost Segregation Audit Techniques Guide.

[D] Real Estate as Part of a Going Business

When real estate is purchased as part of a going business, basis for the real estate will be limited to fair market value. Under Code Sec. 1060, the purchase price of assets that constitute a trade or business must be allocated for tax purposes using the residual method to determine the amount allocable to goodwill and going concern value. Under the residual method, the purchase price for the business is allocated first to tangible assets and specific intangible assets, including covenants not to compete, to the extent of their fair market values, and any excess is allocated to goodwill and going concern value.[78] The purpose of Code Sec. 1060 is to prevent amounts paid for goodwill or going concern value, which are amortizable over 15 years under Code Sec. 197, from being assigned to depreciable assets with shorter recovery periods, or for amounts paid for long-lived assets from being assigned to amortizable goodwill or going concern value. Reg. § 1.167(a)-5T provides that the basis of the depreciable property acquired cannot exceed the consideration allocated to that property under Code Sec. 1060.

A group of assets constitutes a trade or business under Code Sec. 1060 if their character is such that goodwill or going concern value could attach to the group under any circumstances. Even the sale of a business before it begins actual operations may be subject to Code Sec. 1060. The Court of Appeals for the Federal Circuit has held that the sale of a new wind farm business was subject to the residual method for the allocation of the purchase price. The business's power purchase agreements with its main customer also included a customer-based intangible element and, therefore, actual accrued goodwill was not required.[79]

Factors considered in determining whether a group of assets constitutes a trade or business include (1) whether any intangible assets are present (but the transfer of an intangible in the absence of other assets is not a trade or business for purposes of Code Sec. 1060), (2) whether total consideration exceeds the aggregate book value of tangible and intangible assets (other than goodwill and going concern value) as shown on the books of the purchaser, and (3) related transactions, including lease agreements, licenses, covenants not to compete, employment contracts, management contracts, or other similar agreements between the purchaser and seller in connection with the transfer.[80]

> ***Example 12:*** The Purchaser acquires a going business that includes real estate, other tangible assets and goodwill for total consideration of $100,000. The Purchaser and the Seller allocate $80,000 of the purchase price to real estate, $10,000 to other tangible assets, and $10,000 to goodwill. If the real estate's fair market value were only $60,000 and not $80,000, Code Sec. 1060 would require that only $60,000 of the purchase price be allocated to the real

[78] Reg. § 1.1060-1(c); Reg. § 1.338-6.

[79] Alta Wind I Owner Lessor C et al., CA-FC, 2018-2 USTC ¶ 50,357, 897 F.3d 1365.

[80] Reg. § 1.1060-1(b).

estate and, assuming the fair market value of the other tangible assets was $10,000, $30,000 to goodwill. Similarly, if the fair market value of the real estate actually were $90,000 and the value of the other tangible assets was $10,000, there would be nothing left to allocate to amortizable goodwill.

[E] Reporting Requirements

The purchaser and seller of a group of assets subject to Code Sec. 1060 must file asset acquisition statements on Form 8594 with their income tax returns for the taxable year that includes the purchase date.[81]

.03 Apportionment of Real Property Taxes

When real property is sold, the buyer and seller usually, but not always, apportion the property taxes for the year between them. In any event, regardless of whether the parties make such an apportionment, Code Sec. 164(d) governs each party's deduction of current real property taxes. This section allows a portion of the taxes for the real property tax year in which the property is sold to be deducted by the seller and a portion by the purchaser and limits the deductions to the portion of the taxes corresponding to the part of the real property tax year during which each owned the property.

When real property is sold, the portion of the real property tax allocable to that part of the real property tax year which ends on the day before the date of the sale is treated as a tax imposed on the seller, and the portion of the tax allocable to that part of the year which begins on the date of the sale is treated as imposed on the purchaser. This rule applies whether or not the seller and the purchaser apportion the tax.[82]

> ***Example 13:*** The Purchaser buys real property from the Seller on June 30, 2020. The real property tax year at the location of the property is April 1 to March 31, and the property tax for the year ending March 31, 2021, is $1,460. Under Code Sec. 164(d), $360 of the real property tax is treated as imposed on the Seller (90/365 × $1,460), and $1,100 is treated as imposed on the Purchaser (275/365 × $1,460).

If the real property tax becomes a personal liability or a lien before the beginning of the real property tax year to which it relates, and the property is sold after the tax becomes a personal liability or lien, but before the related tax year begins, the seller may not deduct any amount of the real property tax and the purchaser may deduct the taxes for the taxable year in which they are paid or accrued by the purchaser according to the purchaser's method of accounting. Similarly, if the real property tax becomes a personal liability or lien after the end of the real property tax year to which it relates, and the property is sold before the tax becomes a personal liability or lien, but after the end of the related real property tax year, the purchaser may not deduct any amount of the real property tax and the seller may deduct the taxes for the taxable year in which they are paid or accrued by the seller according to the seller's method of accounting.

---

[81] Reg. § 1.1060-1(e).

[82] Reg. § 1.164-6(b).

Example 14: The Seller sells real property to the Purchaser on November 15, 2020. The real property tax year at the location of the property is the calendar year and the tax becomes a lien on November 1 of the preceding calendar year. Under Code Sec. 164(d), the real property tax for the 2020 real property tax year, which became a lien on November 1, 2019, is apportioned between the Seller and the Purchaser. The entire real property tax for the 2021 real property tax year, which became a lien on November 1, 2020, may be deducted by the Purchaser when paid or accrued. No part of the 2021 real property tax may be deducted by the Seller even though the Seller owned the property when the 2021 tax became a lien.

A cash method seller may deduct the portion of taxes treated as imposed on the seller under Code Sec. 164(d) for the year of sale, whether or not they are actually paid in that year if the purchaser is liable for the real property tax or if the tax is not payable until after the date of sale. Alternatively, the seller may deduct the taxes for the year actually paid, if later than the year of sale.[83]

A cash method purchaser may deduct the portion of taxes treated as imposed on the purchaser under Code Sec. 164(d) for the year of sale, whether or not they are actually paid in that year if the seller is liable for the real property tax. Alternatively, the purchaser may deduct the taxes for the year actually paid, if later than the year of sale.[84]

Example 15: The Seller, a cash method taxpayer, sells real property to the Purchaser, also a cash method taxpayer, on May 30, 2020. The real property tax year where the property is located is the calendar year. The tax is a personal liability of the owner on June 30, but is not payable until February 28 of the following real property tax year. Under Code Sec. 164(d), 149/365 (January 1–May 29, 2020) of the real property tax payable on February 28, 2021, for the 2020 real property tax year is treated as imposed on the Seller and this portion may be deducted by the Seller for 2020 (the year of sale), whether or not actually paid that year or for the year the tax is actually paid. Also under Code Sec. 164(d), 216/365 (May 30–December 31, 2020) of the real property tax payable on February 28, 2021, for the 2020 real property tax year is treated as imposed on the Purchaser and may be deducted by the Purchaser for the taxable year in which the tax is actually paid.

If the real property tax is not a liability of any person, the person who holds the property at the time the tax becomes a lien on the property is considered liable for the tax.[85]

Example 16: The Seller, a cash method taxpayer, sells real property to the Purchaser, also a cash method taxpayer, on July 15, 2020. The real property tax year where the property is located is the calendar year and real property taxes are assessed and become a lien on June 30, but are not payable until September 1 of the current year. There is no personal liability for the real property taxes. Under Code Sec. 164(d)(1), 195/365 (January 1–July 14, 2020)

[83] *See* Reg. § 1.164-6(d)(1).

[84] *See* Reg. § 1.164-6(d)(2).

[85] *See* Reg. § 1.164-6(d)(3).

of the real property tax payable on September 1, 2020, for the 2020 real property tax year is treated as imposed on the Seller and this portion may be deducted by the Seller for the taxable year in which the sale occurs, whether or not actually paid or for the taxable year in which the tax is actually paid. Also under Code Sec. 164(d)(1), 170/365 (July 15–December 31, 2020) of the property tax is treated as imposed on the Purchaser and this portion may be deducted by the Purchaser for the taxable year in which the sale occurs, whether or not actually paid or for the taxable year in which the tax is actually paid.

For accrual method taxpayers who have not made the election to accrue property taxes under Code Sec. 461(c), the portion of any real property tax treated as imposed on the seller or purchaser under Code Sec. 164(d) which has not accrued as of the date of sale is treated as having accrued on the date of sale.[86]

Example 17: The Seller, an accrual method taxpayer who has not elected to accrue property taxes under Code Sec. 461(c), sells a parcel of real property to the Purchaser on June 30, 2020. The real property tax year where the property is located is the calendar year and the tax is assessed and becomes a lien on November 30 for the current year. There is no personal liability for the real property tax. Under Code Sec. 164(d), 180/365 of tax for the 2020 real property tax year is treated as imposed on the Seller and also is treated as accruing on June 30, 2020. The Purchaser, also an accrual method taxpayer who has not made the election under Code Sec. 461(c), accrues the share (185/365) of the real property tax on November 30, 2020.

Prior Deduction of Taxes

A taxpayer who, prior to the year of sale, has deducted an amount for real property taxes for the year of sale in excess of the portion of the tax treated as imposed on the taxpayer under Code Sec. 164(d) must include the excess in gross income for the taxable year of the sale.[87]

Reimbursements

If the seller pays real property taxes attributable to the year in which the sale occurs, the seller does not take into account in determining the amount realized from the sale any amount received as reimbursement for taxes which are treated under Code Sec. 164(d) as imposed on the purchaser. Similarly, in computing the cost basis under Code Sec. 1012, the purchaser does not take into account any amount paid to the seller as reimbursement for real property taxes which are treated as imposed on the purchaser under Code Sec. 164(d). These rules apply whether or not the contract of sale calls for the purchaser to reimburse the seller for the taxes paid by the seller.[88]

On the other hand, if the purchaser pays an amount representing property taxes that are treated as imposed on the seller, that amount is taken into account both in determining the amount realized from the sale by the seller and in

[86] Reg. § 1.164-6(d)(6).

[87] Reg. § 1.164-6(d)(5).

[88] Reg. § 1.1001-1(b)(1).

computing the purchaser's cost basis under Code Sec. 1012. It does not matter whether or not the contract of sale specifies that the sale price has been reduced by, or is in any way intended to reflect, the taxes allocable to the seller.[89]

> ***Example 18:*** The contract of sale on a parcel of real property specifies a contract price of $50,000. The property tax for the year of sale on the parcel is $1,000, which is paid entirely by the Purchaser. Under Code Sec. 164(d), $250 of the property tax is treated as imposed on the Seller and $750 is treated as imposed on the Purchaser. The Purchaser's cost basis for this parcel is $50,250, regardless of the taxable year in which the Purchaser makes actual payment of the taxes. Similarly, the Seller realizes $50,250 from the sale of the parcel.

.04 Purchase from Foreign Person

Code Sec. 1445 requires a purchaser or other transferee of a U.S. real property interest acquired from a foreign person to deduct and withhold a tax equal to 15 percent of the amount realized by the foreign person on the sale or other disposition. A purchaser or transferee who fails to withhold the required amount may be liable for the tax. There are several exemptions from the withholding requirement, the most important of which is the exemption for the purchase or acquisition, for $300,000 or less, of property for use as a personal residence by the transferee.

U.S. real property interests include any interest in real property located in the United States or the Virgin Islands and certain personal property, such as farm machinery, that is associated with the use of real property. Interests in mines, wells, or other natural deposits located in the United States are also considered U.S. real property interests.

An interest, other than as a creditor, in a domestic corporation may also be a U.S. real property interest. An interest in a corporation is not a real property interest if the corporation was not a U.S. real property holding corporation at any time during which the interest in the corporation was held, or during the five-year period ending on the date of disposition, if shorter. Also, if, on the date of disposition, the corporation did not hold any U.S. real property interests, and all U.S. real property interests held by the corporation at any time while the interest in the corporation was held, or during the five-year period ending on the date of disposition, if shorter, were disposed of in transactions in which the full amount of any gain was recognized, then an interest in the corporation is not a U.S. real property interest.

In addition to the exemption from withholding by the transferee for the purchase or acquisition of a personal residence for $300,000 or less, the other exemptions state that no withholding is required if:

1. The transferor furnishes to the transferee a certificate stating, under penalty of perjury, the transferor's U.S. taxpayer identification number and that the transferor is not a foreign person. (A foreign corporation that has

[89] Reg. § 1.1001-1(b)(2).

elected to be treated as a domestic corporation under Code Sec. 897(i) may file a non-foreign affidavit.)

2. In the case of a disposition of any interest in any domestic corporation, the corporation furnishes to the transferee a certification stating under penalty of perjury that the interest is not a U.S. real property interest. The corporation may issue the statement only if it was not a U.S. real property holding corporation as defined in Code Sec. 897 at any time during the previous five years (or period interest was held, if shorter), or if the interests in the corporation ceased to be U.S. real property interests under Code Sec. 897(c)(1)(B).
3. The transferee receives a withholding certificate from the IRS. (Such a certificate also can reduce the amount of the required withholding. Either the transferee or the transferor may request a withholding certificate based on the transferor's maximum tax liability or an agreement to pay the tax.)
4. The disposition is of a share of a class of stock that is regularly traded on an established securities market.

The regulations under Code Sec. 1445 provide a detailed explanation of the withholding requirements, and Rev. Proc. 2000-35[90] provides the procedures for obtaining a withholding certificate for exemption from the withholding requirement or for reduced withholding.

¶ 103 CONSTRUCTION OF REAL PROPERTY

The costs of constructing or improving buildings or other assets that have a useful life which extends beyond the end of the taxable year are not currently deductible.[91] Rather, these expenditures, referred to as capital expenditures, become part of the basis of the constructed or improved property. These capitalized costs are recovered through depreciation or amortization[92] if the property is used in a business or investment activity. The capitalized costs of property not used for business or held for investment are recovered at the time the property is sold or otherwise disposed of when unrecovered basis is offset against the amount realized in computing gain or loss.

Under the repair regulations, until property is actually placed in service, the cost of any work done on that property, including repairs, installation costs, and testing costs, must be capitalized as part of the cost of the property.[93]

.01 Capitalization of Construction Costs

It has long been clear that a taxpayer that constructs a building or other capital asset for its own use must capitalize all direct construction costs such as direct materials and labor. Also, depreciation on equipment used to construct the property may not be deducted currently but must be capitalized and added to the basis of the

[90] 2000-35 IRB 211.

[91] Code Sec. 263.

[92] *See* ¶ 901.

[93] Reg. § 1.263(a)-2(d)(1).

constructed property.[94] The tax treatment of many indirect expenses incurred in the construction of real property, however, was less certain.

In order to remove the uncertainty in this area, and to provide a single, comprehensive set of rules to govern the capitalization of costs, Congress enacted Code Sec. 263A. This section applies a single set of capitalization rules, the "uniform capitalization rules," to all costs incurred in manufacturing or constructing tangible property. These uniform capitalization rules require that amounts that are otherwise deductible under the safe harbor expensing rule (¶ 102.01[B]) be capitalized if they are direct or allocable indirect costs of property constructed by the taxpayer or property acquired for resale.[95]

The following discussion of these uniform capitalization rules is limited to their application to real estate. A comprehensive explanation of the uniform capitalization rules may be found in the regulations under Code Sec. 263A. Reg. 1.263A-0 contains an outline of those detailed regulations.

[A] Small Taxpayer Exception

The Tax Cuts and Jobs Act,[96] expanded the exception to the uniform capitalization rules for small taxpayers that purchase personal property for resale and extended the exception to real estate. For tax years beginning after December 31, 2017, a taxpayer is not required to apply the uniform capitalization rules for the tax year if its average annual gross receipts for the prior three-tax-year period do not exceed $25 million.[97] The average annual gross receipts amount of $25 million is adjusted for inflation for tax years beginning after December 31, 2018.

The steps for the gross receipts test are:

1. Determine gross receipts for each year in the three-tax-year period;
2. Compute the average annual gross receipts for the three-tax-year period; and
3. Determine if the average annual gross receipts for the three-tax-year period are $25 million or less.

A taxpayer that is not a corporation or partnership applies the gross receipts test as if each trade or business of the taxpayer were a corporation or a partnership. Tax shelters that are not allowed to use the cash method do not qualify as small businesses that can avoid the uniform capitalization rules. Before 2018, the exception to the uniform capitalization rules only applied to small taxpayers that purchased *personal* property for resale. The expanded exception applies to any *producer* or *reseller*, other than a tax shelter. Therefore, the exception now applies to real property acquired for resale.

[B] Expenses Other Than Interest

The uniform capitalization rules generally apply to real property built, constructed or improved by the taxpayer (or under contract for the taxpayer) for use in

[94] Idaho Power Co., S.Ct., 74-2 USTC ¶ 9521, 418 U.S. 1, 94 S.Ct. 2757.

[95] Reg. § 1.263(a)-1(f)(3).

[96] P.L. 115-97.

[97] Code Sec. 263A(i).

a trade or business or an activity conducted for profit. They also apply to real property acquired for resale which is not a capital asset and which is considered stock in trade or inventory property.[98] They do not apply to personal use property (such as a home constructed by a taxpayer for personal use). Also, the uniform capitalization rules do not apply to the development costs of oil and gas wells and other mineral property or to timber and ornamental trees and the real property underlying these trees.[99]

The costs that must be capitalized as part of the construction cost of real property are the direct costs of the property and the property's share of those indirect costs, including taxes, that are allocable to the property.[100] Interest expense is subject to some special allocation rules and is discussed separately below.

Direct Costs

Direct costs that must be capitalized in connection with the construction of real property include direct material costs and direct labor costs.[101]

Direct material costs include the cost of the materials that become an integral part of the real property and the cost of the materials that are consumed in the ordinary course of constructing the real property.

Direct labor costs include the cost of labor that can be identified or associated with the construction of the real property. The elements of direct labor costs include items such as basic compensation, overtime, vacation and holiday pay, sick pay, shift differentials, payroll taxes, and payments to a supplemental unemployment benefit plan paid for employees engaged in direct labor.

Indirect Costs

Indirect costs that must be capitalized in connection with the construction of real property include all costs that directly benefit the construction or are incurred because of the construction, subject to a few exceptions mentioned below.[102] In some cases, indirect costs may directly benefit, or be incurred because of, the construction even though the same costs also benefit other activities. In these cases, a reasonable allocation is required to determine the portion of the costs which is allocable to the construction of the real property.

Examples of indirect costs that must be capitalized in connection with the construction of real property include amounts incurred for:

1. Repair of equipment or facilities;
2. Maintenance of equipment or facilities;
3. Utilities (heat, light, power, etc.) relating to equipment or facilities;
4. Rent of equipment, facilities, or land;
5. Indirect labor and contract supervisory wages, including basic compensation, overtime, vacation, holiday and sick pay, shift differentials, payroll taxes and contributions to supplemental unemployment benefit plans;

---

[98] Code Sec. 263A(b).

[99] Code Sec. 263A(c).

[100] Code Sec. 263A(a)(2).

[101] Reg. § 1.263A-1(e)(2).

[102] Reg. § 1.263A-1(e)(3).

6. Indirect materials and supplies;
7. Tools and equipment (if their cost is not otherwise capitalized);
8. Quality control and inspection;
9. Taxes otherwise allowable as a deduction (except state, local and foreign income taxes) that relate to labor, materials, supplies, equipment, land or facilities, other than property taxes that are added to and considered part of the cost of equipment or facilities;
10. Depreciation, amortization and cost recovery allowances on equipment and facilities;
11. Administrative costs, whether or not performed on a construction site, but not any cost of selling or return on capital;
12. Direct and indirect costs incurred by any administrative, service or support function to the extent allocable to the construction (allocation rules are contained in Reg. § 1.263A-1(g));
13. Compensation paid to officers attributable to services performed in connection with the construction;
14. Insurance, including insurance on machinery and equipment or on the construction activity itself;
15. Deductible contributions to employee benefit plans;
16. Rework labor, scrap, and spoilage; and
17. Bidding, engineering, and design expenses.

Noncapitalized Costs

Costs that do not have to be capitalized in connection with the construction of real property include amounts incurred for:

1. Research and development;
2. Marketing, selling or advertising;
3. Casualty and theft losses and other losses under Code Sec. 165;
4. Income taxes;
5. Depreciation, amortization and cost recovery allowances on equipment and facilities that are temporarily idle (assets are not temporarily idle on nonworking days, but an asset used in construction is idle when it is not enroute to or located at a jobsite);
6. Deductible contributions to pension or annuity plans that represent past service costs; and
7. Cost attributable to strikes.

[C] Interest

Interest paid or incurred to finance the construction of certain real property must be capitalized under the uniform capitalization rules. The interest capitalization requirement generally applies to the same types of real property which are subject to the other capitalization requirements, except that interest on debt incurred or continued to finance the acquisition and holding of property for resale does not have to be capitalized.[103] Further, only interest costs paid or incurred during the construction period (see below) must be capitalized.[104]

The IRS Large Business and International Division has issued a Practice Unit that identifies taxpayers subject to Code Sec. 263A(f) and covers the steps involved in determining how much interest must be capitalized.[105] While Practice Units are not official pronouncements of law or directives, they do provide IRS staff with explanations of general tax concepts and information on specific types of transactions, and, in this regard, are useful to taxpayers and tax professionals.

The Practice Unit on Interest Capitalization for Self-Constructed Assets discusses the avoided cost method as the method used to determine the amount of interest to capitalize. The Practice Unit walks the user through steps to assist in determining the information needed to apply the avoided cost method. It assists the user in finding the pieces needed in order to make the computation. It includes a step for a Service-imposed change in accounting method and the calculation of a Code Sec. 481(a) adjustment. It also covers elections a taxpayer may adopt. The unit includes a comprehensive example walking the user through all the steps in computing capitalizable interest.

Allocation of Interest

The amount of interest on debt that is incurred or continued to finance the construction of property is determined using the avoided cost method. It is based on the amount of interest expense that would have been avoided if the construction had not taken place and all construction expenditures were used to repay any indebtedness.[106]

Debt that can be specifically traced to the construction must first be allocated to that construction activity. If construction expenditures exceed the amount of debt specifically traced to the construction, other debt (if any) of the taxpayer is allocated to the construction activity. The interest rate applied to any additional debt allocated to the construction activity is the weighted average of the interest rates on the taxpayer's debts outstanding during the construction period, other than debt specifically traced to the construction. In other words, not only must interest on debt that directly finances the construction be capitalized, but also any interest on debt that could have been paid off by construction expenditures that are not directly financed.

If the construction is being performed by a contractor and the customer makes progress payments or advance payments to the contractor, interest on debt incurred or continued during the construction period to finance the payments made and the costs incurred by the customer must be capitalized by the customer. The contractor must capitalize interest costs for the property under construction to the extent that the construction expenditures incurred by the contractor exceed the accumulated payments received from the customer.[107]

---

[103] Code Sec. 263A(f)(1)(B).

[104] Code Sec. 263A(f)(1)(A).

[105] Document Control Number INV/P/203_01_01-01.

[106] Reg. § 1.263A-9(a).

[107] *See* Reg. § 1.263A-11(c).

Interest on debt incurred or continued to finance assets, such as construction equipment, that is used to construct the property must be capitalized to the extent it is paid or incurred during the construction period of the property. If assets are used to construct property and for other purposes, only the portion of the interest allocable to the construction activity must be capitalized.[108]

Construction Period

The uniform capitalization requirements apply to interest only to the extent paid or incurred during the construction period of the property. The IRS has provided guidance in the regulations. According to the IRS, the production period of real property generally begins when physical activity is first performed on the property and ends when all production activities reasonably expected are completed and the property is placed in service.[109]

Physical production activities include, for example,

1. Clearing, grading, or excavating of raw land;
2. Demolishing a building or gutting a standing building;
3. Constructing infrastructure such as roads, sewers, sidewalks, cables, and wiring;
4. Structural, mechanical, or electrical work on a building or other structure; or
5. Landscaping.[110]

On the other hand, planning and design, such as soil testing, preparing architectural blueprints or models, and obtaining building permits, and incidental repairs are not physical production activities.[111]

The production period must be determined for each "unit" of real property. A unit of real property includes any components that are functionally interdependent and an allocable share of any common feature even though the common feature does not meet the functional interdependence test. When the production period begins for any functionally interdependent component or any common feature of the unit, the production period begins for the entire unit of real property. The portion of land included in a unit of real property includes land on which real property, including a common feature, included in the unit is situated, land subject to setback restriction for the property, and any other contiguous portion of the tract other than land held for a purpose unrelated to the unit being produced.[112]

> ***Example 19:*** Taxpayer is constructing a high-rise office building with two wings. At the end of the current year, Wing 1, but not Wing 2, is placed in service. Also at the end of the year, all production activities reasonably expected on Wing 1 are completed. Under Reg. § 1.263A-10(b)(1), Wing 1 and Wing 2 are separate units of property. The taxpayer may stop capitalizing interest on Wing 1 but not on Wing 2.

[108] *See* Reg. § 1.263A-11(d).

[109] Reg. § 1.263A-12(c)(2) and Reg. § 1.263A-12(d)(1).

[110] Reg. § 1.263A-12(e)(2).

[111] Reg. § 1.263A-12(f).

[112] *See* Reg. § 1.263A-10(b)(1).

Example 20: Taxpayer is in the home construction business. He generally paints and finishes the interior of a house, but not until after a potential buyer is found. Because the taxpayer reasonably expects to undertake production activity—the painting and finishing—the production period of each house does not end until those activities are completed.

.02 Interest and Taxes on Pre-1987 Construction

The uniform capitalization rules discussed at ¶ 103.01 generally did not apply to costs incurred before January 1, 1987. Also, they did not apply to costs incurred in connection with the construction of property if substantial construction occurred before March 1, 1986.

Prior to enactment of the uniform capitalization rules, former Code Sec. 189 required the capitalization of real property construction period interest and taxes.[113] Interest and taxes capitalized under former Code Sec. 189 were subject to 10-year amortization, that is, 10 percent of the capitalized amount could be deducted each year over a period of 10 years, beginning with the year the costs were incurred. If a building for which capitalized interest and taxes were incurred was not placed in service in the year the costs were incurred or the following year, the amortization deductions were suspended until the year the building was placed in service.

Real property construction period interest and taxes for former Code Sec. 189 were defined as interest paid or accrued on indebtedness incurred or continued to acquire, construct, or carry real property, and real property taxes, attributable to the construction period of the property and otherwise deductible for the taxable year in which paid or accrued.[114] The construction period for former Code Sec. 189 was essentially the same as the construction period for the interest capitalization requirement under the present uniform capitalization rules.

.03 Capitalization of Carrying Charges

Certain taxes and carrying charges otherwise expressly deductible under the Internal Revenue Code may be capitalized and added to the basis of property under the election provided by Code Sec. 266. For the most part, current deductions provide a greater tax benefit than capitalization and, for this reason, the election is seldom utilized. Also, since enactment of the uniform capitalization rules, many more expenses must be capitalized and less are available as current deductions.

Note that Reg. § 1.263A-8 through Reg. § 1.263A-15 on the requirement to capitalize interest (see ¶ 103.01[C]) apply before the application of the election to capitalize carrying charges under Code Sec. 266. After applying Reg. § 1.263A-8 through Reg. § 1.263A-15, a taxpayer may elect to capitalize interest under Code Sec. 266 for designated property within the meaning of Reg. § 1.263A-8(b), if a computation under any Internal Revenue Code provision is not materially distorted, including computations relating to the source of deductions.[115]

[113] Former Code Sec. 189 was repealed by the Tax Reform Act of 1986 for costs subject to the uniform capitalization rules.

[114] Former Code Sec. 189(e)(1).

[115] Reg. § 1.266-1(a)(2).

In any event, the election to capitalize otherwise deductible taxes and carrying charges relating to real property is available in the following cases.[116]

1. For unimproved and unproductive real property, annual taxes, interest on a mortgage, and other carrying charges. An election for these items relating to unimproved and unproductive real property is effective only for the year for which it is made.
2. For real property, whether improved or unimproved and whether productive or unproductive:
   a. Interest on a loan, but not theoretical interest of a taxpayer using his or her own funds,
   b. Taxes of the owner of the real property measured by compensation paid to the owner's employees,
   c. Taxes of the owner imposed on the purchase of materials, or on the storage, use, or other consumption of materials, and
   d. Other necessary expenditures.

   For these items to be subject to the election, they must be paid or incurred for the development of the real property or for the construction of an improvement or additional improvement to the real property, up to the time the development or construction work is completed. An election for these items is effective until the development or construction is completed.

   While taxes and carrying charges must be otherwise deductible to be subject to the election to capitalize costs under Code Sec. 266, not all deductible items are subject to the election. For instance, advertising expense on unproductive property and maintenance and upkeep costs attributable to improved and unimproved unproductive real property are not carrying charges subject to the election to capitalize.[117]

   Taxes or carrying charges that only partially relate to property for which taxes or carrying charges may be capitalized may be allocated between the two types of property to determine the amount subject to the election.[118]

   An election to capitalize otherwise deductible taxes and carrying charges is made by filing a statement listing the items that are being capitalized. This statement must be filed with the original tax return for the year for which the election is made.[119]

¶ 104 LOW-INCOME HOUSING TAX CREDIT

Over the years, Congress has provided various tax incentives to encourage the development and maintenance of low-income rental housing. These incentives have included special accelerated depreciation, five-year amortization of rehabilitation expenses, exemption from the capitalization requirement for construction period interest and taxes, and tax-exempt bond financing for multi-family rental properties.

---

[116] Reg. § 1.266-1(b).

[117] Rev. Rul. 71-475, 1971-2 CB 304.

[118] Reg. § 1.266-1(e).

[119] Reg. § 1.266-1(c)(3).

In the Tax Reform Act of 1986, Congress repealed many of the existing tax incentives for low-income housing and enacted a tax credit that may be claimed by owners of residential property used for low-income housing.[120] The credit is available for the cost of new construction, the cost of rehabilitation, or the cost of acquiring existing buildings by purchase and their rehabilitation. Generally, only the cost of buildings attributable to low-income units qualifies for the credit. Cost attributable to residential units other than low-income units and cost attributable to land are not eligible for the credit.

The low-income housing credit is taken annually, generally for a period of ten years. New construction and rehabilitation expenditures are eligible for a credit at a percentage that provides a total credit over the 10-year credit period equal to a present value of 70 percent of the qualified costs. The acquisition cost of existing projects and the cost of newly constructed projects receiving other federal subsidies are eligible for a credit at a percentage that provides a total credit over the 10-year credit period equal to a present value of 30 percent of the qualified costs.

The low-income housing credit is considered in further detail in ¶ 805.

¶ 105 ENERGY EFFICIENT HOME TAX CREDIT

A person who constructs an energy efficient home, or in the case of a manufactured home, produces an energy efficient home, may qualify for a tax credit. The credit is $1,000 for a home that meets the 30 percent standard and $2,000 for a home that meets the 50 percent standard.[121]

An energy-efficient home is a dwelling certified to have a projected level of annual heating and cooling energy consumption that provides either a 30 percent or 50 percent reduction in energy usage compared to a comparable dwelling constructed following the standards of chapter 4 of the 2006 International Energy Conservation Code and any applicable Federal minimum efficiency standards for equipment. Only manufactured homes may qualify for the credit using the 30 percent standard and one-third of the energy savings must come from the building envelope. For other homes that meet the 50 percent standard, one-fifth of the energy savings must come from the building envelope.[122]

In addition to providing the energy savings, the dwelling must be located in the United States, substantially completed after August 8, 2005, and purchased after 2005 and before 2018 (unless further extended by Congress as the credit has in the past).[123]

For more on the development and subdivision of property, see Chapter 10.

[120] Code Sec. 42.

[121] Code Sec. 45L.

[122] Code Sec. 45L(c).

[123] Code Sec. 45L(g).

Chapter 2
Form of Ownership

¶ 200 Overview of Chapter
¶ 201 Ownership for Tax Purposes
¶ 202 Individual and Joint Ownership
¶ 203 Partnerships
¶ 204 Corporations
¶ 205 Limited Liability Companies
¶ 206 S Corporations
¶ 207 Ownership in Trust
¶ 208 Choice of the Owning Entity
¶ 209 Qualified Business Income (Passthrough Deduction)

¶ 200 OVERVIEW OF CHAPTER

Most real estate acquisitions involve one buyer (or a husband and wife acting as one) using the buyer's own funds and a mortgage loan from a financial institution. If the real estate involved is a personal residence, the question of the optimum form of ownership does not arise, except, in the case of spouses, as to whether title should be in one spouse or they should own the property jointly. If the real estate is business or investment property, however, the choices available to the buyer increase. Should the real estate be owned and operated individually or through a corporation? If through a corporation, should it be a regular C corporation or an S corporation?

If, in connection with the acquisition of business or investment property, more than one individual buyer is involved, the number of choices for the owning entity increases again. Common or joint ownership is possible, as is the use of a C corporation or an S corporation. There is also the partnership form to consider and, if a partnership is chosen, whether a general partnership or limited partnership is appropriate. In most states, there is still another choice for the owning entity, a limited liability company, which may be treated as either a partnership or a corporation for federal tax purposes.

In some cases, the person who is to benefit from the property may not be a suitable owner, such as when the person is not capable of managing or dealing with the property for one reason or another. For example, a minor child might not be a suitable owner. In such cases, ownership in trust might be appropriate.

In any event, the form of ownership of real estate does have significant legal, financial, practical, and tax consequences. In this chapter, the appropriate form of ownership and operation for real estate is considered. Various forms of securitized real estate, that is, real estate ventures financed through a public offering, are considered at ¶ ¶ 2100 and 2200. Cooperatives and condominium ownership are considered at ¶ ¶ 1901 and 1902.

¶ 201 OWNERSHIP FOR TAX PURPOSES

It is generally the owner of real property who reports income from the property and who is entitled to the tax deductions, such as depreciation, generated by the property. But ownership for tax purposes, while it usually follows legal title, is not always the same as legal title. For example, an individual could deduct taxes paid on property even if the individual took title to the property in the names of a daughter and son-in-law for personal reasons and the record owners received no income and paid no expenses.[1] Similarly, it is the equitable owner, not the legal owner, who may deduct a loss on the foreclosure of property.[2]

The right to deduct depreciation does not depend on ownership of the legal title to property, but on the investment made in the property.[3] In *Gladdings Dry Goods Co.*, the test set is whether the taxpayer would suffer an economic loss as a result of a decrease in value of the property due to depreciation.[4]

In *Lazarus & Co.*,[5] the Supreme Court, citing *Gladdings Dry Goods Co.*, held that the test utilized to determine who is entitled to depreciation is who bears the burden of exhaustion of the capital investment. This test is usually applied by asking who has the "benefits and burdens of ownership." Factors the courts consider in answering this question include:

1. Whether legal title passes;
2. How the parties treat the transaction involved;
3. Whether an equity was acquired in the property;
4. Whether the contract creates a present obligation on the buyer of property to make payments;
5. Whether the right of possession is vested in the buyer;
6. Which party pays the property taxes;
7. Which party bears the risk of loss or damage to the property; and
8. Which party receives the profits from the operation and sale of the property.[6]

In the eyes of the IRS, it is apparently investment ***plus*** either possession or title that is controlling. Rev. Rul. 69-89[7] involved a company that entered into an executory contract for the purchase of land with a two-story building located in the state of Washington. Title to the property was retained by the seller until all payments called for by the contract were made by the purchaser. Under Washing-

[1] A.J. Gilbert, 11 TCM 457, CCH Dec. 18,958(M).

[2] S.J. Ritholz Est., 4 TCM 954, CCH Dec. 14,810(M).

[3] Gladding Dry Goods Co., 2 BTA 336, CCH Dec. 642.

[4] T.W. Blake, Jr., 20 TC 721, CCH Dec. 19,779, *acq.* 1954-2 CB 3.

[5] S.Ct., 39-2 USTC ¶ 9743, 308 U.S. 252.

[6] Grodt & McKay Realty, Inc., 77 TC 1221, CCH Dec. 38,472.

[7] 1969-1 CB 59.

ton law, the purchaser had no legal or equitable title or interest in the property under this contract, but the purchaser took possession of the property on the date of the contract and used the property for business purposes. The IRS ruled that the passing of title did not control who had the right to depreciation deductions for federal income tax purposes. According to the IRS, this situation is similar to the situation in which gain or loss on the sale of property arises at the time the deed passes or possession and the benefits and burdens of ownership are transferred to the buyer as a practical matter.

On the other hand, an investment without transfer of either title or possession may not be sufficient to produce ownership for tax purposes and allow the taxpayer making the investment to claim depreciation deductions.[8] In Rev. Rul. 68-431, the purchaser under a contract of sale made substantial improvements to some real estate before the seller was to surrender possession of the property and execute a land contract for the transfer of the property. The IRS ruled that the purchaser did not actually acquire the property and place it in service until the date possession of the property changed hands and the land contract was executed. The purchaser was not entitled to depreciation deductions until that time.

.01 Use of Straw or Nominee Corporations

For real estate, it is often desirable that ownership be in some unincorporated form in order to take maximum advantage of the tax benefits available from the ownership of real estate. When real estate is owned by a corporation, the deductions are locked in the corporation, and income is subject to a possible double tax. Also, a distribution of appreciated property by a corporation, either in the normal course of business or in liquidation of the corporation, generally produces a double tax on the appreciation—once at the corporate level and again at the shareholder level.

On the other hand, there may be good financial or practical reasons for using a corporation as the owning entity for real estate. In some cases, mortgage lenders may demand that title to real estate be held by a corporation to avoid state usury limits that apply to unincorporated entities and individuals. Corporations may also shield the underlying owners from liability, either on the mortgage or from other activities conducted on or in connection with the particular real estate involved. Corporations can also preserve the shareholders' anonymity.

When the use of a corporation has been necessitated by non-tax factors, yet the tax benefits of not using the corporation were high, individuals often attempted to get the best of both worlds by using what have come to be known as "straw," "nominee," or sometimes "dummy" corporations. The essential idea of the straw corporation is to have the corporation serve its non-tax functions while having the existence of the corporation ignored for tax purposes.

(It should be noted that since the rules relating to S corporations, a form of business organization more fully explored at ¶ 206, were liberalized to permit the holding of passive investment assets, the S corporation may fill the need for an

[8] Rev. Rul. 68-431, 1968-2 CB 99.

entity that provides the benefits of incorporation without the tax disadvantages and lessen the need for straw or nominee corporations in many situations. In any event, even when a nominee corporation is contemplated for holding real estate, it might be a good idea to elect S corporation status, if available, for the nominee in order to salvage some tax benefits in the event the corporation is treated as the taxpayer with respect to the real estate.)

As a general proposition, a corporation and its shareholders are treated as separate taxpayers. In an early case involving the question of the taxability of a straw corporation, the owner of real property transferred ownership to a corporation that the owner had organized at the request of, and for the protection of, the real property owner's creditors. On the eventual sale of the property, the taxpayer sought to have the corporation's existence ignored and the gain taxed to the shareholder in the shareholder's individual capacity. The Supreme Court,[9] however, ruled that the corporation's activities caused it to be taxable:

> The doctrine of corporate entity fills a useful purpose in business life. Whether the purpose be to gain an advantage under the law of the state of incorporation or to avoid or to comply with the demands of creditors or to serve the creator's personal or undisclosed convenience, so long as that purpose is the equivalent of business activity or is followed by the carrying on of business by the corporation, the corporation remains a separate taxable entity.

.02 Agency Relationship Requirement

Since it is very difficult to benefit from a straw corporation that carries on no business activity whatsoever, this decision proved to be very troublesome to anyone seeking to have the existence of a corporation ignored for tax purposes. But actually ignoring the corporate existence proved not to be necessary in order to benefit from a nominee corporation. Rather, it became a matter of shifting ownership for tax purposes away from the corporation and to the "beneficial owners" of the property. The corporation could be a valid taxable entity that held title to property and still not be taxable on the property if the corporation acted merely as the agent or nominal title holder on behalf of the true owner of the property.

This approach to the problem gained a boost from the Supreme Court decision in *National Carbide Corp.*[10] This case involved a corporation that organized several subsidiaries to act as agents for the parent in the sale of certain products. The subsidiaries maintained that they were mere collection agents for the parent and should not be taxed on profits that rightfully were taxable to the parent. While the Supreme Court did not agree in this case, it left the door open to the use of a corporate agent:

> What we have said does not foreclose a true corporate agent from handling the property and income of its owner-principal without being taxable therefor.

The Tax Court had occasion to examine the factors set out in *National Carbide Corp.* that would determine whether a true agency relationship existed in the context of a corporation formed to avoid state usury laws in *J.A. Roccaforte.*[11] The

[9] Moline Properties, Inc., S.Ct., 43-1 USTC ¶ 9464, 319 U.S. 436.

[10] S.Ct., 49-1 USTC ¶ 9223, 336 U.S. 422.

[11] 77 TC 263, CCH Dec. 38,122.

Tax Court, examining the following factors, found that a corporation formed by individual investors of a partnership engaged in the development of an apartment complex was a true corporate agent of its principals:

1. Whether the corporation operates in the name of and for the account of the principal;
2. Whether the principal is bound by the alleged corporate agent's acts;
3. Whether the alleged corporate agent transmits money it receives to the principal;
4. Whether the receipt of income is attributable to assets or employees of the principal;
5. Whether the alleged agent's relationship with the principal is based on its ownership and control by the principal; and
6. Whether the corporation's activities are consistent with the normal duties of an agent.

On appeal, however, the Fifth Circuit Court of Appeals reversed the Tax Court.[12] According to the Fifth Circuit, the Supreme Court decision in *National Carbide Corp.* holding that there is a possibility that an otherwise separate taxable corporate entity could, in some circumstances, qualify as a nontaxable agent of its principal set out two requirements that are mandatory: (1) the corporation's relations with its principal must not be dependent on the fact that it is owned by the principal, and (2) the corporation's business purpose must be the carrying on of the normal duties of an agent. Because the Tax Court found that the corporation's relations with the partners depended on their ownership and control of the corporation, the corporation was not a true nontaxable corporate agent.

While the Fourth Circuit adopted a similar position,[13] the Sixth Circuit refused to find such mandatory requirements and ruled that a valid agency is created when the attributes of an agency are present and the corporation conducts itself no differently than would an independent agent that had bargained with the principal at arm's length.[14] The split between the Circuits was resolved in favor of the Sixth Circuit position by the Supreme Court.[15]

In *Bollinger*, the Supreme Court ruled that a corporation that held record title to real property as agent for its shareholder was not the owner of the property for tax purposes. Rather, the shareholder, a partnership that developed and operated an apartment complex, was the true owner of the property. The corporation was formed to avoid Kentucky's usury law, and the corporation and the partnership entered into a written agreement that provided that the corporation would hold title to the apartment complex as the partnership's agent for the sole purpose of obtaining financing and would convey, assign, or encumber the property and disburse the proceeds only as directed by the partnership. The corporation had no obligation to maintain the property or assume any liability because of the execution

[12] J.A. Roccaforte, Jr., CA-5, 83-2 USTC ¶ 9452, 708 F.2d 986.

[13] F.R. Ourisman, CA-4, 85-1 USTC ¶ 9357, 760 F.2d 541.

[14] J.C. Bollinger, Jr., CA-6, 86-2 USTC ¶ 9821, 807 F.2d 65.

[15] J.C. Bollinger, Jr., S.Ct., 88-1 USTC ¶ 9233 485 U.S. 340, 108 S.Ct. 1173 (1988).

of promissory notes or otherwise, and the partnership agreed to indemnify and hold the corporation harmless from any liability it might sustain as its agent and nominee.

According to the Supreme Court, a true nontaxable corporate agent or nominee is created, and tax-avoiding manipulation adequately avoided, when:

1. There is a written agreement that states that the corporation is acting as agent for its shareholders with respect to the property at the time the property is acquired;
2. The corporation functions as an agent, and not as a principal, with respect to the property for all purposes; and
3. The corporation holds itself out as an agent, and not as a principal, in all dealings with third parties relating to the property.

The Supreme Court's *Bollinger* decision provides a clear safe harbor for the creation of a nominee corporation, without necessarily overturning the earlier tests based on *National Carbide Corp*. If the three criteria of *Bollinger* are followed though, a corporation dealing with real property is assured treatment as the true agent of its shareholders and the shareholders are assured treatment as the owners of the property for federal income tax purposes.

¶ 202 INDIVIDUAL AND JOINT OWNERSHIP

For tax purposes, the owner of real property can be only one of the following: an individual (proprietorship), a partnership, a corporation, or a trust or estate. This does not mean that if more than one person owns a particular parcel of real estate, the owners must form one of the available tax entities. As far as the tax law is concerned, two or more individuals together may own the same real estate and still be considered individual taxpayers with regard to that real estate. This section looks at the various ways individuals may own real estate without an intervening entity such as partnership, corporation or trust.

.01 Sole Individual Ownership

An individual may acquire real estate in his or her own name and all tax consequences of the acquisition, operation and disposition of that real estate will fall directly on the individual. Income generated by the real estate will be added to the individual's other income and taxed accordingly. Deductions generated by the real estate, subject to various loss limitations such as the at-risk rules (see ¶ 302) and the passive loss rules (see ¶ 1101.01), will reduce the individual's income subject to tax.

As a practical matter, individual ownership is the simplest and least costly form of ownership. On the other hand, individual ownership also opens the door to allow all potential liabilities arising out of the ownership and operation of the property to fall directly on the owner. In most cases, the individual owner will guard against the damage an unexpected liability could cause through careful management of the property and liability insurance sufficient to protect the individual's assets.

Individual ownership is not the only route available when one person acquires property. The individual may form a corporation to take title to the property and, in the case of business or investment property, to manage and operate the property. A corporate entity, however, may not be a practical alternative for ownership of property unless the property is of fairly large value or is part of a business that would justify the added expense and administrative burdens of creating a new legal and tax entity. (The formation, operation, advantages and disadvantages of corporations are discussed at ¶ 204—204.02.)

.02 Common and Joint Ownership

When two or more persons together own property, they may hold title as tenants in common or joint tenants. The distinction between the two forms of ownership is a legal one rather than a tax one. In either case, each owner owns an undivided interest in the entire property.

If the owners of property are tenants in common, each co-owner may deal with his or her interest as he or she pleases, that is, the co-owner may sell or encumber his or her interest and otherwise deal with it as his or her own property without the other co-owner's permission. The owner of an interest in real property as a tenant in common may bequeath the property to his or her heirs. As a practical matter, co-owners frequently limit their rights and arrange for the operation and management of the property in a separate contract or agreement.

The major difference between co-tenants and joint tenants is that, if the owners of property are joint tenants, each owner has a right of survivorship in the interest held by the other joint tenant. In other words, when one of two owners of property held as a joint tenancy dies, the surviving joint tenant automatically becomes the owner of the entire property. A joint tenant cannot bequeath his or her interest in the property and the joint tenant's interest does not pass to his or her heirs, unless they also happen to be surviving joint tenants. A joint tenant's interest in property on death remains out of the probate estate, while an interest as tenant in common is subject to probate.

While co-ownership may appear, at first glance, to be a form of partnership, it is not. Unlike partners, tenants in common or joint tenants cannot act on behalf of each other without authorization. Also, a co-owner is not liable for the contracts and debts of the other co-owner, even if the contracts or debts relate to the co-owned property. One partner, on the other hand, may bind all partners when that one partner is acting with respect to partnership business or property.

As long as co-owners do no more than hold the property and maintain, keep in repair, and rent or lease it, the status of the co-owners will not be challenged by the IRS. For example, if tenants in common of farm property lease it to a farmer for a cash rental or crop share, there is no partnership. Tenants in common, however, may be partners if they actively carry on a trade, business, financial operation, or venture and divide the profits from it. For example, a partnership exists if co-owners of an apartment building lease space and also provide services to the occupants either directly or through an agent.[16] The IRS has provided procedures for requesting a ruling that an undivided interest in rental real property (other than a mineral property) is not an interest in a partnership. The revenue procedure applies to co-ownership of rental real property in an arrangement classified under local law as a tenancy-in-common.[17]

From a practical standpoint, there may be little tax difference in the final result in many cases regardless of whether property is held as co-tenants or in partnership. Of course, if a co-tenancy rises to the level of a partnership, the partnership entity then must file returns and make those tax elections relating to the property which must be made at the partnership, rather than individual, level.

In the usual case, each co-tenant merely reports the share of income from the property and deducts the share of expenses on his or her own tax return, just as if the co-tenant were the sole owner of the property. Should a co-tenant actually pay more than his or her share of expenses, however, an amount over and above his or her proportionate share may not be deducted. Rather, the excess payments are treated for tax purposes as loans to the other co-tenants when the co-tenant paying expenses on behalf of another co-tenant is legally entitled to reimbursement.[18]

.03 Joint Ownership by Spouses

In most cases, the joint ownership of property by spouses, or ownership as tenants by the entirety, produces no special income tax consequences. As far as the joint ownership is concerned, the tax rules applied to spouses are the same as those applied to unrelated joint owners, except in the case of a sale or other transfer from one joint owner to the other.

If the spouses file a joint income tax return, then the joint ownership produces the same results as would individual ownership by one of the spouses, because each joint owner's share of the income and deductions from the property are combined on the joint return. On a sale of jointly owned property, each spouse reports his or her share of income or loss. On the death of a spouse, the surviving spouse receives a stepped-up basis for the interest acquired from the deceased spouse, but not for the interest already held by the surviving spouse. This can produce a tax disadvantage since the surviving spouse would receive a stepped-up basis for the entire property if the property were held solely by the deceased spouse and left to the surviving spouse by will.

On the sale or transfer of one spouse's interest to another, there is no gain or loss and the transfer is treated essentially as a gift. The transferee spouse takes the same basis for the interest received as the basis in the hands of the transferor spouse. This same rule applies on transfers incident to a divorce as well as on transfers between still married spouses.[19]

---

[16] Reg. §301.7701-1(a); *see also* L. Hahn, 22 TC 212, CCH Dec. 20,300; L.L. Powell, 26 TCM 161, CCH Dec. 28,348(M), T.C. Memo. 1967-32.

[17] Rev. Proc. 2002-22, 2002-14 IRB 733.

[18] *See* E.B. Boyd Est., 28 TC 564, CCH Dec. 22,410, involving tenants in common, and J. Conte, 42 TCM 1296, CCH Dec. 38,315(M), T.C. Memo. 1981-571, involving joint tenants.

[19] Code Sec. 1041.

.04 Community Property

Rights in and to real property are fixed by state law, but the federal tax treatment of income flowing from those rights is determined by federal law.[20] If the highest court of a state has made a determination as to ownership of a property interest, that decision controls in the federal courts for federal tax purposes. In the absence of a decision by the state's highest court, the federal courts must apply what they find the state law to be, after giving consideration to the decisions of lower state courts.[21]

There are nine community property states—Arizona, California, Idaho, Louisiana, Nevada, New Mexico, Texas, Washington, and Wisconsin. Also, Alaska allows both parties the option to make the property community property. If spouses in a community property state file a joint income tax return, the distinction between separate income and deductions and community income and deductions has little significance. The distinction becomes important when husband and wife file separate returns.

It is the date of acquisition that controls the status of property in community property states. In all community property states, real property acquired before marriage is treated as the separate property of the spouse who owned the property prior to the marriage. Income from separate property, however, may be community income, taxable one-half to each spouse in some states.

The states that follow the "Texas" or "Spanish" rule and treat income from separate property as community income are Idaho, Louisiana, Wisconsin, and Texas. The other five community property states (Arizona, California, Nevada, New Mexico, and Washington) follow the "California" or "American" rule and treat income from separate property as separate income.

Deductions relating to the separate property of one spouse are equally divided between the husband and wife if the income from the property is community income taxable one-half to each spouse. This rule applies on a sale of the property as well, even though the entire gain is taxable to the spouse who owned the separate property.[22]

¶ 203 PARTNERSHIPS

When an individual lacks the ability or resources (including seller or third-party financing) to acquire and operate real property, a partnership is often the answer. A partnership allows two or more persons to acquire and operate property without all of the formalities associated with corporate formation and operation.

.01 Legal Characteristics

A partnership is an association of two or more persons who join together as co-owners to carry on a business for profit. The partnership is a voluntary association and is formed by the agreement or contract among the partners who contribute

[20] Poe v. H.G. Seaborn, 2 USTC ¶ 611, S.Ct., 282 U.S. 101, 51 S.Ct. 58.

[21] H.J. Bosch Est., 67-2 USTC ¶ 12,472, S.Ct., 387 U.S. 456.

[22] L. Sanders, CA-10, 55-2 USTC ¶ 9636, 225 F.2d 629, *cert. denied*, 350 U.S. 967, 76 S.Ct. 435.

capital or services to the partnership. It is their agreement or contract that controls the relationship among the partners, and the partners are free to mutually agree to alter or vary their agreement as they see fit, provided their agreement is not contrary to state law.

The partnership form of business organization is recognized by state laws on the subject. In most states, the laws are similar because of the adoption of the Uniform Partnership Act, which governs all partnerships, and the Uniform Limited Partnership Act (or Revised Uniform Limited Partnership Act), which provides additional legal guidelines for limited partnerships.

[A] General Partnerships

The most important of the legal characteristics of a general partnership are those relating to the potential liability imposed on the partners and the ability of any one general partner to bind the others by his or her actions. The partnership is bound by the acts of any partner who is tending to partnership business. Outsiders to the partnership may rightfully assume that any one partner is acting for all when the partner conducts any partnership business.

This agency relationship among the partners means that any one partner can obligate all partners, and all partners are jointly and severally liable to third parties for the business acts of any partner. Also, partners are jointly and severally liable to third parties or outsiders for the acts of the employees and agents of the partnership. The joint and several liability imposed on general partners means that any one partner can be held responsible for the full amount of any third party claim against the partnership. While a partner who pays off a claim may have a right against other partners to seek contribution, the outsider is free to go after any one of the partners.

In addition to the agency relationship among the partners and the partners' potential for liability, other common characteristics that are associated with a general partnership include:

1. Management rights are vested in all general partners and all share equally in the right to conduct the business of the partnership.
2. Day-to-day operations of the partnership are controlled by a simple majority vote of the partners.
3. The partners are considered fiduciaries in their relationship with each other and are bound to look out for the interests of the partnership. A partner, either individually or through some other entity, cannot compete against the business of the partnership or interfere with the business of the partnership.
4. Partners must conserve and protect partnership capital. A partner may not transfer real estate, unless selling real estate is the partnership business and the transfer would be in the ordinary course of that business.

Keep in mind, of course, that the partnership is a creature of the agreement among the partners. Therefore, the partners may alter or change some of the usual characteristics of the general partnership if it suits their needs and is not contrary to state partnership law. For example, through agreement, partners may decide to give a larger voice in management to a partner who has contributed greater amounts of capital to the partnership, rather than allowing a simple majority vote of the partners to control.

[B] Limited Partnerships

A limited partnership is essentially a general partnership in which one or more partners have their liability limited in much the same fashion as shareholders in a corporation. These special partners with limited liability are limited partners. To obtain the limited liability protection for its limited partners, a limited partnership must file and record a certificate of limited partnership with the state authorities. The filing puts all on notice of the limited nature of some partners' liability.

In every limited partnership, there must be at least one general partner who is responsible for the management of the partnership and who is personally liable for the obligations of the partnership. The rights and liabilities of the general partner of a limited partnership are essentially the same as those of a partner in a general partnership. Limited partners, however, are exempt from liability for partnership debts, obligations, and losses in excess of their capital contributions, as long as they do not participate in the management of the partnership. The limited liability feature of limited partnerships makes them attractive as investment vehicles and popular vehicles for raising capital from outside investors. (Real estate limited partnerships, as securities and as vehicles for raising capital through public offerings or private placements, are given special consideration in Chapter 21.)

[C] Joint Ventures

A joint venture is a partnership-like organization that is formed to carry out one project or transaction or a series of related transactions over a short period of time. It is this feature that primarily distinguishes a joint venture from a partnership, which is usually involved in the management and operation of an ongoing enterprise. Also, a joint venture, unlike a partnership, can be organized for social or recreational purposes and need not be organized for a profit-making activity.

In real estate, a joint venture may be formed for the subdivision and sale of a specific parcel of real estate. Also, a joint venture may be formed to construct a specific building, housing project, or industrial park. If the "partners" involved in the project are corporations, the corporations are more likely to form a joint venture than a partnership to carry out their joint goals.

For tax purposes, a joint venture, in most cases, will be treated as a partnership. A married couple filing a joint return, however, may elect not to have a qualified joint venture treated as a partnership for federal tax purposes. The joint venture must involve the conduct of a trade or business. Further, the husband and wife must be the only members of the venture and both must materially participate in the business and elect to have the rule apply. If they elect, all items of income, gain, loss, deduction, and credit are divided between the spouses in accordance with their interests in the venture. Each spouse then takes into account his or her share of these items as a sole proprietor.[23]

[D] Syndicates

The term "syndicate" is a frequently used term in the real estate industry. When a real estate promoter uses the term, the promoter is most likely referring to the process of raising capital from investors, through either a public offering or private placement of participations or units.

In most cases, a syndicated real estate program will be organized as a partnership since this offers the most flexibility and freedom of operation for the promoter and tax advantages to the investors. There is no reason, however, why a real estate syndication may not refer to a venture organized as a corporation, or even some other arrangement, such as individual ownership of properties managed by the promoter or related party under an agency contract.

.02 Taxation of Partnerships

Federal law, specifically the Internal Revenue Code as interpreted by the federal courts and the Internal Revenue Service, determines whether or not an entity is a partnership for tax purposes. The Internal Revenue Code definition of a partnership is very broad and includes "a syndicate, group, pool, joint venture, or other unincorporated organization, through or by means of which any business, financial operation, or venture is carried on, and which is not, within the meaning of this title [the Internal Revenue Code], a trust or estate or a corporation."[24] For the most part, general partnerships and limited partnerships are treated alike for tax purposes. Also, joint ventures and similar arrangements are partnerships for tax purposes. (See the discussion of entity classification at ¶ 205.01.)

As a general rule, partnerships are not taxpayers, but rather serve as conduits through which business or investment results are passed to the partners. While a partnership does file a tax return, it pays no income taxes. Each individual partner must report his or her share of partnership results on the individual tax return and the final tax liability depends on the partner's other income and deductions as well as the share of partnership income and deductions. Note that partnership distributions are not required to trigger a tax liability on the part of the individual partners.

The following discussion is not meant to be a complete explanation of the partnership tax rules. Rather, the purpose is to merely highlight the critical areas that affect real estate that is owned and operated in partnership form.

[A] Basis of Partnership Interest

Every partner must know the tax basis for his or her interest in the partnership. It is the basis of a partnership interest that is used to determine the:

1. Amount of gain or loss realized by a partner on the sale of the interest;
2. Tax consequences at the time a partnership or partnership's interest is liquidated;

[23] Code Sec. 761(f).

[24] Code Sec. 7701(a)(2).

3. Primary limit on the amount of losses from the partnership that a partner can take as a tax deduction;
4. Amount of the distributions from the partnership that the partner can receive without taxes in addition to those that arise on the pass-through of partnership income.

The ownership of a partnership interest is separate from ownership of property by the partnership. When a partnership acquires real estate, the partnership's basis is determined under the rules discussed at ¶ 101.01. If the partnership acquires real estate as a result of a capital contribution by a partner, however, the partnership's basis is the same as the basis of the property in the hands of the contributing partner at the time of the contribution.[25] Each partner's basis for the interest in the partnership is determined according to how the partnership interest is acquired.[26]

The basis of a partnership interest acquired by a contribution of money or property to the partnership is the amount of money contributed plus the adjusted basis to the partner at the time of the contribution of any other property. If a partner realizes taxable income as a result of acquiring the interest in the partnership, that income is an addition to the partner's basis. If the partner contributes property, which is subject to a mortgage or liability, the partner's basis is reduced by the amount of the debt assumed by the other partners as a result of the contribution (the assumption of debt by a partnership is treated as a distribution of money to the partner whose debt is assumed and a contribution of money by the other partners, which in turn increases their bases).[27]

> ***Example 1:*** The New Partner acquires a 20 percent interest in a real estate partnership by contributing a parcel of real estate to the partnership. At the time of the contribution, the parcel had a fair market value of $100,000 and an adjusted basis to the New Partner of $40,000 and was subject to a mortgage in the amount of $20,000. The New Partner's basis for the 20 percent interest in the partnership is $24,000. This represents the New Partner's adjusted basis in the contributed property ($40,000) less the portion of the mortgage debt assumed by the other partners (80% × $20,000 = $16,000).

A partner who acquires an interest in a partnership other than by contributing money, property, or services to the partnership determines the basis under the rules applicable to the manner in which the interest is acquired (these are the basis rules discussed at ¶ 101.01). For instance, a partner who purchases an interest from another partner has a "cost basis" for the interest; an interest acquired by gift has the donor's basis, adjusted for gift taxes paid; an interest acquired from a decedent has a basis equal to its value on the date of the decedent's death; and so forth.[28]

The original tax basis of a partner's interest in a partnership must be adjusted for events that occur after the acquisition of the interest.[29] These adjustments are required to preserve the conduit nature of the partnership.

---

[25] Code Sec. 723.

[26] Code Sec. 705(a).

[27] Code Sec. 722 and Reg. § 1.722-1.

[28] Code Sec. 742 and Reg. § 1.742-1.

[29] Code Sec. 705.

The original basis of a partner's interest is increased by the partner's share of taxable income and tax-exempt income of the partnership. The original basis is decreased by the partner's share of partnership distributions, partnership losses, partnership expenditures that are not deductible in computing taxable income or loss and that are not capital expenditures, and the depletion deduction for oil and gas wells.

[B] Contributions to Partnership

The general rule of Code Sec. 721 is that no gain or loss is recognized by the partners or the partnership on the contribution of money or property to the partnership in exchange for a partnership interest. When real estate or services are contributed to a partnership, however, there are a number of exceptions to the general rule that can cause problems or an unexpected tax liability. Problems also may arise for existing partners when a new partner is admitted to an existing partnership if the admission of the new partner results in a decrease of the existing partners' shares of partnership liabilities and ordinary income items.

Mortgaged Property

A partner's basis for the partnership includes the adjusted basis in contributed property at the time of its contribution to the partnership reduced by any liabilities assumed by the other partners as a result of the contribution. As noted above, the reduction in the contributing partner's share of liabilities is treated as a distribution of money to the partner by the partnership.[30] As the example above illustrates, there is no problem as long as the liabilities assumed do not exceed the adjusted basis of the property. If liabilities assumed by the other partners exceed the adjusted basis, however, the contributing partner realizes income to the extent that the liabilities assumed by the other partners exceed the contributing partner's adjusted basis in the contributed property.

> ***Example 2:*** The New Partner acquires a 20 percent interest in a real estate partnership by contributing a parcel of real estate to the partnership. At the time of the contribution, the parcel had a fair market value of $100,000 and an adjusted basis to the New Partner of $40,000 and was subject to a mortgage in the amount of $60,000. The New Partner's basis for the 20 percent interest in the partnership is zero. This represents the New Partner's adjusted basis in the contributed property ($40,000) less the portion of the mortgage debt assumed by the other partners (80% × $60,000 = $48,000). The New Partner's basis is zero because a partner's tax basis for a partnership interest is never reduced below zero.
>
> The portion of the mortgage assumed by the other partners ($48,000) is treated as a distribution of money to the New Partner. Of this amount, $40,000 was used to reduce the New Partner's basis to zero. The remaining $8,000, the excess of the mortgage assumed by the other partners over the New Partner's adjusted basis for the contributed property, is treated as a taxable gain to the New Partner.

[30] Code Sec. 752(b).

Built-In Gain or Loss

At one time, a partner could contribute property to a partnership and shift a portion of the tax loss or gain that the partner would otherwise realize on the property to the other partners. Now, however, Code Sec. 704(c)(1) requires that gain and loss on property contributed to a partnership be shared among the partners in a way that takes into account any difference between the basis of the property to the partnership and its fair market value at the time of the contribution. This means that a contributing partner is taxed on any "built-in gain" on contributed property when that gain is realized by the partnership. Also, a "built-in tax loss" on contributed property cannot benefit partners other than the contributing partner.

> ***Example 3:*** Two equal partners form a partnership. Partner A contributes real estate worth $100,000, but that has a basis of $50,000. Partner B contributes $100,000 cash. The basis to the partnership for the real estate is $50,000.
>
> Under the usual partnership rules, if the partnership sold the real estate for its market value of $100,000, the partnership would have a $50,000 taxable gain that would be shared equally by A and B. A would have shifted $25,000 of taxable gain to B. Under Code Sec. 704(c)(1), however, A must report the entire $50,000 gain recognized by the partnership. If the partnership sells the real estate for more than $100,000, any gain in excess of the $50,000 "built-in gain" would be shared equally by the equal partners.

Also under Code Sec. 704(c)(1), gain or loss must be recognized by a partner who contributes property to a partnership if the partnership later distributes that property to the other partners within seven years of the contribution. No gain or loss is recognized, however, if the contributed property is redistributed to the contributing partner. The measure of the gain or loss recognized is the amount the contributing partner would have had to recognize had the property been sold by the partnership at its fair market value, that is, the difference between the partner's basis in the property and its fair market value at the time of the contribution (see the example above). An exception applies under Code Sec. 704(c)(2) if the distribution is related to a distribution of like-kind property to the contributing partner (like-kind property is determined under the Code Sec. 1031 rules, as discussed at ¶ 1302.01). Appropriate basis adjustments are made to reflect any gain or loss recognized.

Disguised Sales

The "disguised sale" rule of Code Sec. 707(a)(2) is intended to prevent partners and partnerships from characterizing a sale or exchange of property as a contribution to the partnership followed by a distribution from the partnership in order to avoid or defer tax. Generally, if a partner transfers money or other property to a partnership and there is a related transfer of money or other property by the partnership to that partner or to another partner, then the transactions are outside the partnership rules and are treated as a sale between the partner and the partnership or the two partners, depending on the actual transfers involved.

> ***Example 4:*** The New Partner contributes real estate worth $50,000 with a basis of $30,000 to a partnership in exchange for a 20 percent interest in the

partnership. As part of the deal, the partnership distributes $30,000 cash to the New Partner. In this case, the related transactions may be viewed as a sale of the real estate by the New Partner to the partnership rather than as a tax-free contribution of property to the partnership followed by a tax-free distribution of cash (an amount not in excess of the New Partner's basis in the partnership) to the New Partner.

If the related distribution of cash were made to existing partners rather than to the New Partner, the transaction could be viewed as a sale of a partnership interest by the existing partners to the New Partner.

Admission of New Partners

The admission of a new partner to a partnership may also trigger a tax to existing partners if the new partner assumes a share of partnership liability and is credited with a portion of any ordinary income items of the partnership that have not yet been realized.[31] The reduction of the existing partners' share of partnership liability is treated as a cash distribution to them. To the extent that the existing partners' share of "unrealized receivables" is also reduced, the deemed cash distribution triggers an immediate tax. The problem may be avoided when unrealized receivables are present, if the new partner does not assume a share of existing partnership liabilities. If there are no unrealized ordinary income items (receivables, depreciation recapture, substantially appreciated inventory, etc.), the problem usually does not arise, since the deemed cash distribution triggered by the new partner's assumption of liabilities merely serves to reduce the bases of the partnership interests of the existing partners.

Services

The contribution of services to a partnership in exchange for an interest in the partnership is outside the usual nonrecognition rule of Code Sec. 721. The partner contributing services realizes compensation income equal to the value of the partnership interest received for the services.[32] The value of the partnership interest received by the service partner generally is considered equal to the value of the services performed.[33]

[C] Operation of Partnership

A partnership, although generally not a taxable entity, must still compute its taxable income in a fashion similar to the way in which an individual computes his taxable income. The tax consequences of the income or loss are then passed on to the partners who must take into account every separate item of income, loss, deduction, or credit that enters into the computation of taxable income. Each partner, in effect, treats his or her share of each partnership item as if the partner had received the share directly from the source of the item to the partnership.

---

[31] Rev. Rul. 84-102, 1984-2 CB 119.

[32] S. Diamond, CA-7, 74-1 USTC ¶ 9306, 492 F.2d 286.

[33] Hensel Phelps Construction Co., CA-10, 83-1 USTC ¶ 9270, 703 F.2d 485.

Special Allocations

In some cases, a partnership agreement may give certain partners or classes of partners shares of certain items of income or loss that are greater or less than the shares they would receive under the general profit and loss sharing ratio of the partnership. This might occur as partners adjust their agreement to take into account their individual positions and strive to reach a bargain acceptable to all. In the heyday of tax shelters, special allocations of "tax losses" were common to attract investors.

The allocation of specific partnership items in a ratio that does not conform to the general profit and loss sharing ratio is called a special allocation. In order for a special allocation to be respected for tax purposes, the special allocation must have "substantial economic effect."[34] If a special allocation lacks substantial economic effect, the tax law ignores the allocation called for by the partnership agreement and makes an allocation that conforms to the normal profit and loss sharing ratio.

Regulations issued by the IRS in an attempt to define "substantial economic effect" run on for page after page.[35] In the simplest of terms, a special allocation has substantial economic effect if the allocation affects the capital accounts of the partners as well as the tax consequences to the partners. Since a partner's capital account reflects the partner's adjusted investment in the partnership, adjustment of capital accounts because of a special allocation means that the special allocation must ultimately affect the partner's share of the economic income or loss of the partnership and thus have substantial economic effect apart from the tax consequences.

Organization and Syndication Costs

In computing the taxable income of a partnership, organization and syndication costs are not currently deductible.[36] Rather, the actual costs of organizing a partnership must be charged to a capital account. A partnership may elect to deduct up to $5,000 of organizational expenditures in the tax year in which the trade or business begins. Each $5,000 amount is reduced, however, by the amount by which the cumulative cost of start-up or organizational expenditures exceeds $50,000. Expenditures that are not deductible under this provision must be amortized over 15 years. The costs of syndicating a partnership, however, are not deductible at all. Nondeductible syndication costs include all the expenses involved in selling partnership interests to investors and include:

1. Brokerage fees;
2. Registration fees;
3. Legal fees of the underwriter or placement agent and the issuer for securities advice and tax advice pertaining to the adequacy of tax disclosures in the prospectus or placement memorandum;

---

[34] Code Sec. 704(b).

[35] Reg. § 1.704-1.

[36] Code Sec. 709.

4. Accounting fees for the preparation of representations included in the offering materials; and
5. Printing costs of the prospectus, placement memorandum, and any other material for promoting and selling partnership interests.

Allocations for Services

In order to avoid the restrictions on deductions for organization and syndication costs, some partnerships would allocate partnership income to a general partner who would pay these costs. Instead of paying these costs directly, or providing a reimbursement for these costs to the paying partner out of invested funds, the partnership agreement would allocate a share of partnership income to the paying partner (a form of special allocation). The effect, as far as the other partners were concerned, was the equivalent of a deduction since their shares of partnership income would be reduced by the special allocation.

Code Sec. 707(a)(2) was a direct response to this type of tax trickery. The IRS now may treat allocations of partnership income made for property or services provided to the partnership as payments by the partnership for the property or services. This power goes beyond special allocations for organization and syndication costs and extends to all income allocations for property or services of any kind.

> ***Example 5:*** In an attempt to avoid the requirement that requires capitalization of construction costs, a partnership agreement may provide a special allocation of partnership income to a partner who provides architectural services to a partnership in connection with the construction of a commercial office building by the partnership. Under Code Sec. 707(a)(2), the IRS may treat the income allocation as payment for the architectural services by the partnership. If this is done, the amount of specially allocated income will become part of the capitalized cost of the building which may be recovered only through depreciation deductions.

[D] Distributions

The general rule is that gain is recognized by a partner from a partnership distribution only to the extent that there is a distribution of money in excess of the partner's basis in the partnership.[37] (But see the discussion of built-in gains and losses on contributions at ¶ 203.02[B].) A loss can be recognized only on a distribution that liquidates the partner's entire interest in the partnership.[38] If property is distributed, there is no immediate gain or loss, but the partner's basis for the property is the same as the partnership's basis before the distribution, but not more than the partner's basis in the partnership interest reduced by any cash distributed.[39]

It is the mechanism of the basis adjustment by which the conduit nature of the partnership is preserved. Income is taxed to partners as earned by the partnership and basis is increased. Money already taxed when earned is not subject to tax when

---

[37] Code Sec. 731(a).

[38] Code Sec. 731(b).

[39] Code Sec. 732.

distributed, but reduces basis. Taxing distributions only when they exceed a partner's adjusted basis for the partnership interest assures that a partner is not being taxed on the capital investment or on income for which the partner has already paid a tax.

[E] Guaranteed Payments

Sometimes, partners or a class of partners may be guaranteed a minimum return based on the amount of their capital contribution regardless of the income of the partnership. The same arrangement may be made for a partner who contributed services, that is, the "working partner" may be guaranteed a minimum amount for services regardless of the income of the partnership.

These guaranteed payments that are made without regard to partnership income are ordinary income to the recipient partners and, if otherwise deductible, are deductible in computing a partnership's taxable income.[40] In effect, guaranteed payments for the use of a partner's capital are in the nature of interest and are treated as such for tax purposes. Similarly, guaranteed payments in exchange for services are in the nature of wages or salary and are treated as such for federal income tax purposes.

[F] Elective Large Partnership Rules

The Taxpayer Relief Act of 1997 introduced several special provisions to simplify tax reporting for electing large partnerships and their partners. Electing large partnerships are partnerships with 100 or more partners in the preceding tax year that elect to have Code Secs. 771 through 777 apply. Service partnerships, however, such as accounting and law firms, and partnerships that primarily buy or sell commodities or related financial products, are not eligible to make the election. Special rules in Code Sec. 776 apply to oil and gas partnerships.

The large partnership rules are effective for tax years beginning after 1997 and before 2018. The general effect of the election is to reduce the items the partnership must report separately to its partners. For instance, income or loss from all passive activities of the partnership are combined into a single activity; all tax preferences are combined into a single line item; and capital gains and losses are netted at the partnership level and short-term capital gains in excess of short-term capital losses are added to ordinary income rather than reported separately.

Electing large partnerships also are subject to simplified audit rules contained in Code Secs. 6240–6255 for tax years beginning before 2018. For instance, an electing large partnership generally may report audit adjustments as additional distributive share items in the year the adjustment is imposed, rather than the year to which the adjusted item relates. Alternatively, the partnership may elect to pay the tax at the entity level, on behalf of the partners, rather than flowing the adjustment through to the partners.

Partners in an electing large partnership are not allowed to treat a partnership item differently on their returns than the way it was treated by the partnership. The partnership must provide Schedules K-1 to the partners no later than March 15 of the year after the close of the partnership tax year.

[40] Code Sec. 707(c).

[G] Post-2017 Partnership Audit Rules

The Bipartisan Budget Act of 2015, in addition to revoking the elective large partnership rules, provides a single set of rules for auditing partnerships and their partners at the partnership level that apply to tax years beginning after 2017.[41]

Under the revised audit rules, the IRS will examine partnership-related items that are relevant in determining income tax liability of any person including any imputed underpayment. Generally, any adjustment to a partnership-related item is determined at the partnership level.[42] The treatment of partnership-related items on a partner's return must be consistent with the treatment of the items on the partnership return in all respects, including the amount, timing, and characterization of the items. A partner does not meet this requirement if the treatment of the partnership-related item on the partner's return is consistent with how the item was treated on a schedule or other information furnished to the partner but inconsistent with the treatment of the item on the partnership return actually filed. A partner's return includes any return, statement, schedule, or list, and any amendment or supplement to them, filed by the partner for any tax imposed by the Internal Revenue Code.[43]

A partnership-related item is (1) any partnership item or amount relevant in determining the tax liability of any person; (2) any partner's distributive share of any such item or amount; and (3) any imputed underpayment. Examples of partnership-related items include:

- The character, timing, source, and amount of the partnership's income, gain, loss, deductions and credits;
- The character, timing, and source of the partnership's activities;
- The character, timing, source, value, and amount of any contributions to, and distributions from, the partnership;
- The partnership's basis in its assets, the character and type of the assets, and the value of the assets;
- The amount and character of partnership liabilities and any changes to those liabilities from the preceding tax year;
- The category, timing, and amount of the partnership's creditable expenditures;
- Any item or amount resulting from a partnership termination;
- Any item or amount of the partnership resulting from an election under Code Sec. 754;
- Partnership allocations and any special allocations; and
- The identity of a person as a partner in the partnership.[44]

The post-2017 partnership audit rules generally do not apply to self-employment taxes, the net investment income tax, withholding taxes for nonresident aliens or foreign corporations, or withholding taxes for foreign financial institutions and

[41] Code Secs. 6221 through 6241.

[42] Reg. § 301.6221-1(a).

[43] Reg. § 301.6222-1(a).

[44] Reg. § 301.6241-1(a)(6).

nonfinancial foreign entities under the Foreign Account Tax Compliance Act. However, any partnership adjustment for income taxes under the audit rules is taken into account in determining and assessing any of these other taxes to the extent relevant. For example, if a partnership adjustment results in a change in the amount of income an individual receives from the partnership, then the change is reflected in the calculation of the individual's net earnings from self-employment from the partnership.

Election Out

Partnerships with 100 or fewer partners for whom the partnership is required to furnish a Schedule K-1 may elect to opt out of the new partnership audit rules. In addition, each partner of the partnership must be:

- An individual;
- A C corporation, or foreign entity that would be treated as a C corporation if it were a domestic entity;
- An S corporation; or
- The estate of a deceased partner.

The election to opt out is not available to a partnership that has a partner classified as a partnership for federal tax purposes.

The election to opt out is made with a timely-filed tax return and must include the names and taxpayer identification numbers of all partners. The partnership also must notify each partner of the election. If any partner is an S corporation, the partnership also must disclose the name and TIN of each shareholder of the S corporation for the tax year of the corporation that ends with or within the partnership tax year. Each shareholder of the S corporation is counted as a partner for the purpose of qualifying to elect out.

Once a partnership makes the election, the partnership and partners will be audited under the general rules that apply to individual taxpayers.

¶ 204 CORPORATIONS

Corporations may hold real estate as investment property or engage in the active conduct of a trade or business involving real estate. Corporations also may own real estate assets, such as plants, warehouses, farmlands, etc., which are necessary for their primary business operations. For income and tax purposes, corporations are separate entities apart from their shareholders. Corporations are also "legal persons," that is, as a matter of law, corporations also are separate entities apart from their shareholders.

.01 Legal Characteristics

One reason why individuals may consider a corporation as the owning entity for real estate is that the corporation can insulate its shareholders from potential liabilities arising out of the ownership and operation of the real estate. As a general rule, a corporation's shareholders cannot be held personally liable for the debts, obligations, or any other liability that may attach to the corporation. Also, the assets within the corporation generally cannot be reached by creditors of the individual shareholders. A shareholder's interest in the corporation can be subject to claims against the shareholder, but those with such claims generally cannot touch the assets within the corporation.

The insulation from liability provided by a corporation, however, is not absolute. There are many instances in which the courts have "pierced the corporate veil" in order to reach shareholders. This is most likely to occur in the case of controlling shareholders in closely held corporations. It may also occur when shareholders themselves disregard the separate identity of the corporation and fail to follow corporate formalities.

Another reason individuals may consider the corporation as an owning entity for real estate is that the shares of stock representing ownership of the corporation are freely transferable and transfers of stock do not affect the corporate entity. All shareholders may sell their stock so that there is a complete change in corporate ownership, yet the "legal person" of the corporation remains undisturbed. Its business continues and its contracts and legal obligations are unaffected.

Corporate management is also removed from the shareholders, although shareholders do retain ultimate control over the corporation. It is the shareholders who elect the board of directors who are charged with the management of the day-to-day affairs of the business. In small corporations, those with few shareholders, the shareholders and the board may be the same persons. Nevertheless, it is those who own or control a majority of the corporation's stock who control the corporation and the board. In many cases, a minority interest in a corporation gives the minority shareholder virtually no say in corporate affairs. (Compare this to the partnership, in which each general partner, regardless of the partner's interest, has an equal say in management.)

Of course, all of the factors discussed above are general in nature. They are not all true for all corporations at all times. For instance, preferred stock and other classes of voting and nonvoting stock can alter the rights and obligations of shareholders. Also, shareholder agreements, stock restrictions, and various forms of indemnity and hold-harmless agreements may be used to affect the relative power of shareholders within a given corporation and to limit a shareholder's otherwise unrestricted right to sell or transfer shares of stock in the corporation.

.02 Taxation of Corporations

Corporations are taxpayers separate and apart from the shareholders who own the corporation. This is the critical tax difference between partnerships and corporations. There is, however, a type of corporation that has many of the tax features of partnership operation, the "S" corporation. The special tax features of S corporations are discussed at ¶ 206. The following discussion relates to regular or "C" corporations. (The letter designation is taken from the subchapter of the Internal Revenue Code that contains the tax rules relating to each of the two types of corporations.) The discussion is, by no means, an attempt to fully explain the tax rules applicable to corporations. The purpose is simply to call attention to those areas that may have special significance for a real estate corporation.

[A] Organization of Corporation

In most cases, a real estate corporation may be formed without a current tax. Code Sec. 351 provides that the transfer of money or property to a corporation is tax free if two conditions are met. First, the transfer must be made solely in exchange for stock of the corporation. Second, the transferors as a group must be in control of the corporation after the transfer. Control, in this case, means 80 percent of the total combined voting power of all classes of stock entitled to vote and at least 80 percent of each class of nonvoting stock.[45] Note that this tax-free transfer of money or property to a corporation may take place at any time, not just when the corporation is organized. The control group (or sole shareholder if there is only one shareholder) may transfer money or property to the corporation at any time and take advantage of Code Sec. 351.

Any potential tax that is avoided because of a Code Sec. 351 transfer, however, is not forgiven. The basis rules preserve any gain for future tax. The basis of the property transferred to the corporation has the same basis for the corporation as it had in the hands of the shareholders before the transfer.[46] Similarly, basis of stock received by the shareholders is the same as the basis of the property they transferred.[47]

While most incorporations can be accomplished on a tax-free basis, there are some potential problem areas that may create a tax liability when individuals set up a real estate corporation.

Transfer of Services

In some cases, individuals may contribute their services to the corporation in exchange for stock. The performance of services for stock is outside of the nonrecognition provision of Code Sec. 351. What's more, if individuals performing services in exchange for stock receive more than 20 percent of the corporation's stock, the entire incorporation becomes taxable because the 80 percent control requirement will not have been met by the other shareholders. In such a case, individuals transferring appreciated property to the corporation will be taxed on the appreciation.[48] The basis of the property to the corporation, as well as the shareholders' basis for the stock received, will be adjusted to reflect the taxable nature of the transaction by increasing basis for the amount of gain recognized.

Mortgaged Property

When mortgaged property is transferred to a corporation in a transaction subject to Code Sec. 351, the mortgage generally has no effect on the tax-free nature of the transaction. This rule, however, is subject to two important exceptions that apply to any liability transferred to or assumed by the corporation in the transaction.

---

[45] Code Sec. 368(c).

[46] Code Sec. 362.

[47] Code Sec. 358.

[48] *See*, for example, W.A. James, 53 TC 63, CCH Dec. 29,799.

1. If there is no business purpose for the assumption of the debt by the corporation but rather the only purpose of effecting the transaction is tax avoidance, the entire amount of the debt assumed is treated as a payment of money to the transferor.[49] This causes the transferor to recognize and be taxed on gain to the extent of this deemed payment of money. Basis is adjusted to reflect the amount of gain recognized.
2. If the liabilities transferred to the corporation exceed the basis of the property transferred, then gain is recognized by the transferor to the extent of the excess.[50] Again, basis on both sides of the transaction is adjusted to reflect the amount of gain recognized. There is an exception to exclude from this rule liabilities that are in the nature of trade accounts payable.

Taxable Incorporation

In some cases, incorporators may want the incorporation to be taxable in order to increase the basis of property in the hands of the corporation to its fair market value at the time of incorporation. This may allow for increased depreciation deductions by the corporation or lower amounts of income to be reported by the corporation at some later time. Of course, this is only desirable when it is thought that the future tax benefits to the corporation outweigh the current tax cost to the shareholders.

If a taxable incorporation is desired, however, it is sometimes very difficult to achieve. Code Sec. 351 nonrecognition is not elective. Anytime there is a transfer to a controlled corporation that meets the terms of the statute, Code Sec. 351 controls. Avoiding this section is usually a matter of having more than 20 percent of the corporation's stock issued to individuals who do not transfer money or property to the corporation.

Partnership Incorporation

Sometimes, it may be desirable to incorporate an existing partnership. When this is the case, the incorporation may be accomplished in any one of three ways:

1. The partnership transfers its assets to the new corporation in exchange for stock and then the partnership liquidates and distributes the stock to the partners;
2. The partnership liquidates and distributes assets to the partners who then transfer the assets to the corporation in exchange for stock; or
3. The partners transfer their partnership interest to the corporation in exchange for stock.

Regardless of how the incorporation of the partnership is accomplished, as long as the incorporation meets the requirements of Code Sec. 351, the incorporation is tax free. There are, however, other tax implications, depending on the method chosen. Rev. Rul. 84-111[51] discusses these tax implications for the corporation and its shareholders.

---

[49] Code Sec. 357(b).

[50] Code Sec. 357(c).

[51] 1984-2 CB 88.

Organization Costs

The costs associated with organizing a corporation are not currently deductible. Under Code Sec. 248, however, a corporation may elect to deduct up to $5,000 of organizational expenditures in the tax year in which it begins a trade or business. Each $5,000 amount is reduced, however, by the amount by which the cumulative cost of organizational expenditures exceeds $50,000. Expenditures that exceed the limit and are not deductible must be amortized over 15 years. Costs eligible for the deduction or amortization include expenses such as:

1. Accounting services necessary to get the corporation up and running;
2. Fees and other costs paid to the state in order to incorporate;
3. Legal services for drafting the corporate charter and by-laws, the minutes of the organizational meeting, and the terms of the stock certificate; and
4. Temporary directors and organizational meetings of directors and shareholders.

"Syndication" costs, that is, commissions, professional fees and printing costs, and other expenses associated with issuing stock or securities, are not considered organization costs eligible for deduction or amortization.

[B] Operation of Corporation

A C corporation reports income, takes deductions and credits, and pays taxes in much the same fashion as an individual taxpayer but under a different rate schedule.

For tax years beginning before 2018, corporate taxes were assessed at the following rates: 15 percent on the first $50,000 of taxable income; 25 percent on the next $25,000; and 34 percent on income in excess of $75,000. Corporations with taxable income in excess of $100,000 lost the benefit of all or some of the lower rate brackets. An additional five percent tax was imposed on corporate income in excess of $100,000 up to $335,000. This meant that corporations with $335,000 or more of taxable income were paying a flat tax of 34 percent on their income. A tax rate of 35 percent applied to corporations with taxable income of over $10,000,000. Corporations with taxable incomes of over $15,000,000 paid an additional three percent on the excess, up to a maximum additional tax of $100,000.

For tax years beginning after 2017, the graduated corporate tax rate structure is eliminated. Instead, a corporation's taxable income is taxed at a flat rate of 21 percent.[52]

After-tax corporate earnings paid out to shareholders can be subject to tax again, as dividends. This additional layer of taxation may increase the tax on income from an incorporated real estate venture. For instance, if a corporation has $100,000 of pre-tax earnings, it pays a tax of $21,000. If the corporation distributes the after-tax balance of $79,000 as a dividend to a shareholder in the 32 percent individual tax bracket but subject to a maximum 15 percent tax rate on qualified dividends, the shareholder ends up with $67,150 out of the original $100,000 in pre-

[52] Code Sec. 11.

tax earnings. The same pre-tax earnings realized directly by the individual or through a partnership would be reduced by $32,000, to $68,000, by taxes. Further, if the income were eligible for the passthrough deduction (see ¶ 209), the advantage to realizing the income directly would be even greater.

The double tax detriment of corporate operation, however, may not really exist for many corporations, especially in light of increased tax rates of up to 37 percent on higher-income individuals. Most closely held corporations pay out little or none of their earnings as dividends. There are other ways to take money out of a corporation. Salary payments, if reasonable in amount, are deductible as an expense by the corporation, and so are not subject to the double tax. Corporate-provided fringe benefits also eliminate the double tax and, in some cases, may be tax free to the recipients as well.

If earnings are to be retained for operations or additional investment by the corporation, the double tax problem also may be minimal. The corporate tax rate is substantially lower than top individual tax rates and this means that high tax-bracket individuals may be able to use a corporation as a tax shelter. At $200,000 of taxable income, a corporation is subject to a 21 percent tax, but a single individual moves into the 35 percent tax bracket (2018 rates). The lower tax rate means that more after-tax dollars may be left for reinvestment by the corporation than if an individual earned the income directly. Shareholders, however, must be aware of two penalty taxes that may be imposed when corporations retain income—the personal holding company tax and the accumulated earnings tax. These penalty taxes have no counterpart for individuals or partnerships.

Personal Holding Company Tax

A personal holding company is subject to a penalty tax on all ***undistributed*** personal holding company income at a rate of 20 percent. The tax[53] is intended to prevent taxpayers from using a corporation to hold passive investments so that the income from the investments is taxed at the lower corporate tax rates rather than the higher individual rates. A corporation is a personal holding company if five or fewer shareholders own more than 50 percent in value of the corporation's outstanding stock at any time during the last half of the taxable year (ownership is based on actual ownership and constructive ownership rules contained in the statute), and 60 percent of the corporation's adjusted ordinary gross income for the year is personal holding company income.

Personal holding company income includes such income items as dividends, interest, annuities, and royalties. In connection with real estate, rents are generally personal holding company income. However, an exception applies to what might be considered operating real estate corporations. Rents are not personal holding company income if rents are at least 50 percent of adjusted ordinary gross income and certain other requirements are met. Therefore, a corporation deriving most of its income from real estate generally will not be subject to this tax, but the tax may be a problem if the corporation holds other investment assets or temporarily invests funds in non-real estate assets.

[53] Code Secs. 541—547.

Accumulated Earnings Tax

The accumulated earnings tax[54] is a penalty tax assessed on the earnings accumulated during the year that are in excess of the reasonable needs of the business. The tax is intended to prevent corporations from accumulating earnings rather than paying out dividends that would be taxed to the shareholders. Most corporations are allowed to accumulate $250,000 without question. Above this amount, accumulations must be justified by reasonable business needs. The tax is applied to excess accumulations for the year at a rate of 20 percent.

As a practical matter, no corporation should be hit with this tax. The tax is usually imposed when shareholders ignore or are unaware of the tax and fail to make specific plans for the use of accumulated earnings. In this regard, shareholders may want to avoid falling into the potential trap of believing that the accumulated earnings tax can only apply when a corporation accumulates cash or liquid assets beyond the reasonable needs of the business. The IRS Chief Counsel has determined that a corporation was liable for the accumulated earnings tax even though it had no liquid capital from which to distribute earnings. The Chief Counsel rejected the argument that accumulated surplus must be represented by cash that is available for distribution.[55]

In the case considered by the IRS Chief Counsel, the corporation's shareholder transferred interests in several partnerships to the corporation. The partnerships made distributions to their partners sufficient to pay federal and state tax liability, but the remainder of the partners' shares of partnership income was retained in the partnerships. The corporation reported its share of partnership income, used distributions to pay its tax liability, and reported retained earnings representing its share of undistributed partnership income.

[C] Property Distributions and Liquidations

If a corporation sells appreciated property and distributes the proceeds to its shareholders, there is a double tax problem. This double tax is not avoided if the corporation distributes the appreciated property to shareholders or liquidates and distributes the property.

If a corporation distributes property to a shareholder and the fair market value of that property exceeds the adjusted basis of the property to the corporation, the corporation is taxed on the difference as if it had sold the property to the distributee at its fair market value.[56] If the property is subject to a liability, or the shareholder assumes a liability of the corporation in connection with the distribution, the amount of the liability is considered to be the minimum fair market value for the purpose of applying this rule. If the distribution represents a distribution of corporate earnings, that is, if it is considered a dividend for tax purposes, the shareholder is also taxed on the value of the property received.

---

[54] Code Secs. 531—537.

[55] CCA 201653017.

[56] Code Sec. 311(b).

A similar rule taxes a corporation that distributes appreciated property in liquidation.[57] Shareholders treat distributions in complete liquidation of the corporation as payment in exchange for their stock.[58]

Note how these rules differ significantly from the partnership rules which do not impose an immediate tax on property distributions to partners but use the basis mechanism to preserve the potential gain on property for tax at a later time. It is these rules that may be the greatest detriment to the use of a C corporation as the owning entity for real estate.

¶ 205 LIMITED LIABILITY COMPANIES

LLCs offer their members a flexible business entity that may be tailored and adopted to an endless number of business and investment situations. As a result of the advantages they offer, LLCs have become increasingly popular and often are the entity of choice when compared to partnerships. Many of the features that make LLCs attractive distinguish them from more traditional general and limited partnerships, although LLCs typically are structured to be classified as partnerships for federal income tax purposes.

Although local law varies as to the requirements for establishing an LLC, the common thread is that none of the members of an LLC are liable for the debts and obligations of the LLC beyond their contributions to the LLC, absent an express assumption of liability by a member if authorized under the applicable LLC statute. In addition, under local law LLCs frequently are managed by elected or designated "managers," who may be members of the LLC. When an LLC does not have managers, all members of the LLC ordinarily have rights, duties and obligations. If an LLC has elected or designated managers, who may or may not be members of the LLC, the managers ordinarily have many of the rights, duties and obligations that would otherwise be held by the members in an LLC without managers.

In short, LLCs offer the tax advantages of a partnership combined with the limited liability of a corporation.

.01 Entity Classification

The ability to obtain the benefits of partnership taxation for LLCs received a big boost when the IRS adopted new regulations under Code Sec. 7701 for classifying entities as partnerships or corporations (the "check-the-box" regulations). The previous regulations for classifying business organizations as associations taxable as corporations or as partnerships were based on the historical differences under local law between partnerships and corporations. The current regulations replaced those rules with a much simpler approach that generally is elective.

The first step in the classification process is to determine whether there is a separate entity for federal tax purposes.[59] The regulations explain that certain joint undertakings that are not entities under local law nonetheless may be separate

[57] Code Sec. 336.

[58] Code Sec. 331.

[59] Reg. § 1.301.7701-1.

entities for federal tax purposes, but not all entities formed under local law are recognized as separate entities for federal tax purposes. Whether an organization is treated as an entity for federal tax purposes is a matter of federal tax law, and does not affect the rights and obligations of its owners under local law. For instance, if a domestic limited liability company with a single individual owner is disregarded as an entity separate from its owner under Reg. § 301.7701-3, its individual owner is subject to federal income tax as if the company's business was operated as a sole proprietorship.

Business entities that are classified as corporations for federal tax purposes include corporations denominated as such under applicable law, as well as associations, joint-stock companies, insurance companies, organizations that conduct banking activities, organizations wholly owned by a State, and organizations that are taxable as corporations under a provision other than Code Sec. 7701(a)(3).[60]

Any business entity that is not required to be treated as a corporation for federal tax purposes (referred to in the regulation as an eligible entity) may choose its classification under the rules of Reg. § 301.7701-3. Those rules provide that an eligible entity with at least two members can be classified as either a partnership or an association, and that an eligible entity with a single member can be classified as an association or can be disregarded as an entity separate from its owner.

In order to provide most eligible entities with the classification they would choose without requiring them to file an election, the regulations provide default classification rules that aim to match taxpayers' expectations (and thus reduce the number of elections that will be needed). The regulations adopt a passthrough default for domestic entities, under which a newly formed eligible entity will be classified as a partnership if it has at least two members, or will be disregarded as an entity separate from its owner if it has a single owner.

An eligible entity may affirmatively elect its classification. The regulations require that the election be signed by each member of the entity or any officer, manager, or member of the entity who is authorized to make the election and who represents to having such authorization under penalties of perjury. An election will not be accepted unless it includes all of the required information, including the entity's taxpayer identifying number.

.02 Partnership Conversion to LLC

The IRS has applied the same rule to the conversion of an interest in a domestic partnership into an interest in a domestic limited liability company[61] as it has to the conversion of a general partnership into a limited partnership.[62] The conversion does not cause a termination of the partnership under Code Sec. 708, and does not cause the tax year of the partnership to close as to all or any of the partners under Code Sec. 706. The IRS also says that because the conversion does not cause a partnership termination, the resulting LLC does not have to obtain a

[60] Reg. § 1.301.7701-2.

[61] Rev. Rul. 95-37, 1995-17 IRB 10.

[62] Rev. Rul. 84-52, 1984-1 CB 157, and Rev. Rul. 86-101, 1986-2 CB 94.

new taxpayer identification number. The tax consequences are the same regardless of whether the resulting LLC is formed in the same state as the converting partnership or in a different state.

¶ 206 S CORPORATIONS

The S corporation is a creature of the federal tax law. For all purposes other than tax purposes, the S corporation is treated just as any other corporation. The corporation has a separate legal existence and its shareholders have the usual corporate shield against liability. For tax purposes, however, the treatment of S corporations is similar to the treatment of partnerships—*similar but not identical.* For state income tax purposes, many states recognize S corporation status and provide treatment under state law that is similar to the federal treatment.

S corporation status must be elected by all the shareholders of the corporation. If elected, each shareholder reports his or her share of corporate income, loss, deductions and credits on his or her own tax return, whether or not the corporation actually distributes income.[63] This pass-through of tax items to the shareholders is similar to the pass-through of partnership items to partners.

.01 Qualification as an S Corporation

For a corporation to become an S corporation, the shareholders of the corporation must unanimously consent to the election filed by the corporation.[64] The election must be filed with the IRS in the year before or by the 15th day of the third month of the year for which the election is to be effective.[65] To be eligible to elect S corporation status, the corporation must meet the following requirements contained in Code Sec. 1361:

1. The corporation must have no more than 100 shareholders.
2. All shareholders must be individuals or certain qualifying trusts, estates, or charitable organizations.
3. No shareholder can be a nonresident alien. (Effective as of January 1, 2018, a nonresident alien individual may be a potential current beneficiary of an electing small business trust, a trust that may qualify as an S corporation shareholder.[66] Nonresident aliens remain ineligible to be S corporation shareholders.)
4. The corporation must have only one class of stock.

The election terminates if the corporation fails to meet these requirements at any time.[67] Shareholders of an S corporation may terminate the election voluntarily by filing a notice of revocation with the IRS. This election to terminate requires the consent of shareholders who together own more than one-half of the shares of stock of the corporation.[68]

[63] Code Sec. 1366.

[64] Code Sec. 1362(a).

[65] Code Sec. 1362(b).

[66] Code Sec. 1361(c)(2)(B)(v).

[67] Code Sec. 1362(d)(2).

[68] Code Sec. 1362(d)(1).

S corporation status also may be terminated if the corporation has passive investment income and accumulated earnings.[69] If more than 25 percent of the S corporation's gross receipts for three years are from passive investment income and there are accumulated earnings, the S corporation election terminates. Prior to the termination, the passive investment income is taxed at the corporate level.[70] Passive investment income for this rule includes rents. Also included are the gross receipts from the sale of capital assets. For assets other than stocks and securities, only capital gain net income is included in measuring gross receipts from passive investment income. For stock or securities, gross receipts are taken into account only to the extent of gains.

.02 Income and Loss

The income of an S corporation is divided among shareholders according to their stock ownership.[71] This income is taxed to the shareholders whether or not there is an actual distribution to the shareholders. (Just as with a partnership, the basis mechanism assures that shareholders will pay but a single tax on S corporation income. A shareholder's basis is increased by the share of income passed through from the corporation. Distributions are tax free to the extent of a shareholder's basis and serve to reduce basis. Actual distributions are taxable only to the extent they exceed the shareholder's basis.)

The IRS Large Business and International Division has issued a Practice Unit that addresses whether a shareholder has sufficient basis to claim losses and deductions passed through from the S corporation.[72] The Unit provides IRS agents with a process to follow in determining or confirming an S corporation shareholder's basis. While Practice Units are not official pronouncements of law or directives, they do provide IRS staff with explanations of general tax concepts and information on specific types of transactions, and, in this regard, are useful to taxpayers and tax professionals.

If a shareholder was not a shareholder for the entire year, the income is apportioned based on stock ownership and the number of days during the year the shareholder held the stock. Note that this income-splitting rule is absolute—there is no possibility of any "special allocations" of income or loss, as is the case of a partnership when the special allocations have substantial economic effect.

> ***Example 6:*** An S corporation has three shareholders, A, B and C. A owns 25 percent, B owns 35 percent, and C owns 40 percent. Assuming these shareholders hold their stock for the entire tax year of the corporation and the corporation has $100,000 of income, A would report $25,000, B would report $35,000, and C would report $40,000.
>
> Suppose, however, that C sold the stock to new shareholder D on May 1 of the current year and the corporation is a calendar year corporation. In this case, the $40,000 of income must be apportioned between C and D. C would report $13,150 ($40,000 × 120/365), and D would report $26,850 ($40,000 × 245/365).

---

69 Code Sec. 1362(d)(3).

70 Code Sec. 1375.

71 Code Sec. 1366.

72 Document Control Number SCO/P/53_05_01_03-06 (2016).

[A] Built-In Gain

There is an exception to the pass-through of income to an S corporation's shareholders. This exception taxes the "built-in gain" on corporate assets at the corporate level if the gain is recognized by the corporation within five years of the S election.[73] "Built-in gain" is essentially the amount by which the value of an asset exceeded its basis at the time the corporation became an S corporation. This tax applies only if the corporation was a regular C corporation before electing S status. Any tax on built-in gains is passed on to S shareholders in pro rata fashion as a loss, as discussed below. In the case of an installment sale, if it occurs within the recognition period in effect at the time, all installments, even those falling outside the recognition period are subject to the built-in gains tax.[74]

Under Code Sec. 311(b), a corporation recognizes gain on a distribution of appreciated property to its shareholders. To the extent this appreciation represents built-in gain, the distribution of appreciated property by an S corporation to its shareholders may trigger the corporate level tax under Code Sec. 1374(d). Gain recognized by the corporation on a distribution of appreciated property to a shareholder, to the extent not taxed to the corporation, is passed through to the shareholders under the regular rule.

These rules can present a tax trap for unsuspecting S corporations that own appreciated real estate and for their shareholders. Individuals should become completely familiar with the S corporation provisions before choosing the S corporation as the owning entity for real estate or before converting a regular C corporation to S corporation status.

[B] S Corporation Losses

Losses of an S corporation, just as income, are passed through to the shareholders. A loss is apportioned among the shareholders based on stock ownership and the number of days during the tax year they held the stock. For instance, in the example above on the apportionment of income, if the corporation had a $100,000 loss instead of income, the apportionment of the loss would be calculated in the same fashion.

In the case of a partnership, the basis of a partner's interest in the partnership limits the partner's deduction for losses sustained by the partnership. A similar rule applies to shareholders of an S corporation. The amount of losses and deductions taken into account by an S corporation shareholder cannot exceed the shareholder's adjusted basis for the stock plus the adjusted basis for any debt owed the shareholder by the corporation.[75]

The IRS Large Business and International Division has issued a Practice Unit that addresses what qualifies as bona fide debt and whether that debt is owed directly to the shareholder creating debt basis.[76] The Unit lists factors that are often considered in determining whether a debt is bona fide and also lists cases in which

---

[73] Code Sec. 1374.

[74] Code Sec. 1374(d)(7).

[75] Code Sec. 1366(d).

[76] Document Control Number SCO/C/53_04_02_01-04 (2016).

the various Circuit Courts of Appeal have considered the question. While Practice Units are not official pronouncements of law or directives, they do provide IRS staff with explanations of general tax concepts and information on specific types of transactions, and, in this regard, are useful to taxpayers and tax professionals.

While the rule is similar to the partnership rule, there is one critical difference that must be noted. Unlike a partner's basis for the partnership interest, a shareholder's basis in an S corporation does not include debt owed to outsiders. An S corporation shareholder's basis is equal to the cost of the stock, or adjusted basis of property contributed to the corporation to acquire the stock, plus the shareholder's share of corporate income, less distributions received from the corporation and losses previously passed through from the corporation and deducted by the shareholder. Also, an S corporation shareholder can deduct corporate losses to the extent of any debt owed to the shareholder by the corporation, but there is no increase in a shareholder's basis for corporate debt to outsiders, as there is for partners, when a partnership incurs a liability.

The IRS Large Business and International Division has issued a Practice Unit that discusses the adjustments to shareholder's stock basis and basis in debt and the relationship of the two.[77] The Unit notes that shareholders must track stock basis and debt basis separately; they may not be combined. The taxability of distributions is determined by stock basis ONLY, therefore distributions reduce stock basis, but do not reduce debt basis. Conversely, the taxability of loan repayments are determined by debt basis ONLY. While Practice Units are not official pronouncements of law or directives, they do provide IRS staff with explanations of general tax concepts and information on specific types of transactions, and, in this regard, are useful to taxpayers and tax professionals.

The basis rule for S corporations may have two significant effects on an S corporation used as the owning entity for real estate. First, of course, is that shareholders may not be able to fully utilize loss deductions if mortgaged real estate produces tax deductions in excess of income. Second, if real estate is refinanced, the distribution of the proceeds of the new financing to the shareholders may trigger a tax.

In a partnership, if real estate is refinanced, the mortgage debt increases the bases of the partners in the partnership. A distribution of the refinancing proceeds is tax free to the partners to the extent of their bases in the partnership. In an S corporation, however, if real estate is refinanced, the mortgage debt to outsiders does not affect the bases of the shareholders in the S corporation. While the proceeds of the refinancing may be distributed tax free to the shareholders to the extent of their bases, their bases will not have been increased by the refinancing, and it is more likely that the distribution will be subject to tax.

[77] Document Control Number SCO/C/53_4_2_02-05 (2016).

¶ 207 OWNERSHIP IN TRUST

A trust is an entity that holds legal title to property for the benefit of another. The person who sets up or establishes a trust by transferring property to it is called the grantor of the trust. The property transferred by the grantor is managed by one or more trustees for the benefit of the beneficiaries of the trust. Legally, it is the trustees who hold the legal title to the trust property, while the beneficiaries hold what is termed beneficial title to the trust property.

As an owning entity for real estate operation or investment, the trust is likely to be used only when the beneficial owner is incapable of properly managing the property. It is a useful entity for making living or testamentary gifts to minors. Adults who do not have the time or experience to properly manage the trust property may also benefit from a trust, rather than being given the property outright. It is also a useful estate planning device when the grantor wants to preserve the property for more than one owner and more than one generation.

.01 Tax Treatment of Trusts

The trust has something of a split personality when it comes to federal income tax treatment, and the following discussion of trust taxation is but a brief summary of the rules found in Code Secs. 641-683.

Generally, a trust is a taxable entity just like an individual taxpayer or corporation. The tax on trust income is higher than the tax on the same amount of income realized by an individual, however, because the income required to reach the higher tax brackets is less.

The higher tax on trusts would be a major discouragement to the use of trusts if it were not for the other aspect of trust taxation. A trust can be a conduit in a fashion similar to a partnership or an S corporation. A trust computes taxable income in much the same way an individual does, but a trust also may deduct amounts that are required to be distributed or that are distributed to trust beneficiaries under the terms of the trust. This deduction is limited to trust income. The beneficiaries include in their income and pay taxes on amounts deducted by the trust.

.02 Depreciation

While the calculation of taxable income for a trust is similar to that made by an individual, there is a difference other than the distribution deduction that may be important for trusts owning real estate. The deduction for depreciation (and depletion as well) is allocated between the trust and its beneficiaries according to the terms of the trust or, if the trust is silent, according to the income of each. In other words, the trust instrument may spell out how depreciation is to be divided between the trust and its beneficiaries, but if no division is specified, then the division is made based on income. For instance, if the trust is silent on the apportionment of depreciation and 60 percent of trust income is distributed to beneficiaries, then 60 percent of any depreciation deduction is taken by the beneficiaries and the remaining 40 percent by the trust. (The tax deduction for depreciation is discussed at ¶ 901.01.)

.03 Grantor Trusts

An individual who sets up a trust to achieve tax savings may be disappointed if that individual retains too much control over the trust property or if the income from the trust can be used for his or her benefit. Under the grantor trust rules, the grantor rather than the trust or beneficiary is taxed on trust income when the grantor attaches too many strings to the transfer of the property to the trust. Generally, a grantor is taxed on trust income in the following situations:

1. It is reasonable to expect that the grantor will get the trust property back (there is an exception for reversion in the case of the death of a minor income beneficiary who is a lineal descendent of the grantor).
2. The grantor can direct who will enjoy the trust property or the income of the trust after the trust is set up (this is subject to several exceptions for certain very limited powers).
3. The grantor can buy or sell trust property for less than adequate consideration.
4. The grantor can borrow from the trust without adequate interest or security.
5. The grantor can revoke the trust and obtain the trust property.
6. The income of the trust can be used for the benefit of the grantor or the spouse of the grantor.

¶ 208 CHOICE OF THE OWNING ENTITY

Making the choice of the owning entity for real estate requires a careful evaluation of the principal's personal and financial situation, as well as the nature and type of real estate involved. In many cases, there may be little choice involved, or no real practical choice. When only one principal is involved in the acquisition and ownership of the property, the choice is between individual ownership and corporate ownership. Corporate ownership, however, entails additional expense and added complexity. The extra cost and trouble may not be justified by the type or value of the real estate to be acquired. For instance, there usually is no reason to set up a corporation to own a personal residence. When a corporation is not justified by the facts, then there is no practical alternative to individual ownership.

The choice of the owning entity usually becomes more of a consideration when there is more than one principal involved in the acquisition and ownership of the property. Ownership as tenants in common may be acceptable for merely holding real estate, but if development or operation is contemplated, the principals usually will desire the more formal arrangement of a partnership or corporation. If a corporation is the choice, the question remains as to whether the corporation should elect to be treated as an S corporation.

The following paragraphs make some general observations as to factors that might be considered in choosing the owning entity for real estate by comparing and contrasting the corporation with the partnership and then the S corporation with the partnership. Following this discussion is a chart that compares, in summary form, many of the features of partnerships, C corporations, and S corporations (see ¶ 208.03).

.01 Corporation or Partnership

The corporation boasts two possible advantages over a partnership that may make the corporation seem a likely choice as the owning entity for real estate. First, there is the liability protection afforded principals by the corporate veil. General partners are not protected by the partnership from liability arising out of the ownership or operation of real estate by the partnership. Second, shares of stock in a corporation are freely transferable, and transfers of stock do not affect the corporate entity. Partnership interests, on the other hand, generally are not readily transferable, and transfers of partnership interests may result in the termination of the partnership.

Unfortunately, these two possible advantages of corporate ownership over the use of a partnership may be more illusory than real. In a closely held corporation, true limited liability may be nonexistent from a practical standpoint. Banks and commercial lenders may require the personal guarantees of shareholders before lending to the corporation. Courts may "pierce the corporate veil" to provide relief to a party injured by the corporation. This is especially true if the corporation is undercapitalized or under-insured by the principals.

On the other hand, liability protection may be available in a partnership that equals or exceeds that available through a corporation. A limited partnership may protect limited partners from unlimited liability. (Although limited partnerships are discussed in greater detail in connection with securitized real estate in Part VI, limited partnerships may be set up by a small group of investors.) If the general partner in a limited partnership is a corporation, then the liability protection is essentially the same as with a corporation. Even in a general partnership, liability protection can be built in with insurance, nonrecourse financing and exculpatory provisions in mortgages.

The unlimited life and free transferability of stock in a closely held corporation also may be more theoretical than real. Shareholders often restrict stock transfers by shareholder agreement or restrictions incorporated in the stock. This is especially likely in an S corporation in order to prevent the transfer of stock to an ineligible shareholder. Partnership agreements may be drawn to allow continuation of the partnership following the death of a partner or other transfer of a partnership interest that would otherwise terminate the partnership.

What this all boils down to is that the choice between a corporation and a partnership may not really turn on the legal characteristics of the two entities. The extra expense of setting up and maintaining a corporation may be deciding in some cases. When expense is not a major factor, then the choice usually hinges on the tax treatment of the two entities.

Generally, organizing either a partnership or a corporation may be accomplished at no tax cost, so the initial tax burden will not be a deciding factor. Rather, it is in operation and liquidation that major tax differences occur which frequently tip the scale in favor of the partnership as the owning entity for real estate. Bear in mind, of course, that this is a general proposition that applies to "investment-type" real estate, that is, real estate that is owned to produce rents or held for appreciation rather than real estate that is owned to support a manufacturing or raw materials industry. In the latter case, it is the nature of the business that controls the choice of the form of business rather than the simple fact that the business owns real estate.

In any event, the separate existence of the corporation and its treatment as a separate taxpayer generally means that owning real estate through a corporation increases the tax costs and eliminates the tax benefits to the principals involved. If the real estate is producing taxable income, the income may be locked in the corporation and removed only at the cost of a double tax. This would not be the case, however, if the principals were employed by the corporation and could justify salary and fringe benefits to themselves that would eliminate the corporation's taxable income. But this is not always possible, especially when the income of the corporation is derived from passive sources such as rents.

A corporation is also subject to the accumulated earnings and personal holding company penalty taxes which simply may exacerbate the double tax problem, especially for a real estate corporation. Partnerships have no similar tax problems.

Should real estate produce tax losses, which is often the case when the real estate is highly leveraged, those losses would be locked in the corporation if it were chosen as the owning entity. The losses could only be used to offset corporate income and would provide no tax benefit to the principals. This may be less of a factor now that the use of passive losses by individuals to offset various other classes of income has been severely limited, but it is nevertheless a factor to consider.

Finally, the potential for tax on the transfer or distribution of property (whether or not in liquidation of the entity) is now a major factor tilting the scales in favor of partnerships for real estate ventures. Generally, a partnership may distribute appreciated property to its partners without an immediate tax to either the partnership or its partners. Any potential tax is preserved through the basis mechanism until such time as the partner receiving the property disposes of the property in a taxable sale or exchange. Should the partner hold the property until death, the appreciation escapes tax entirely. Even if a partnership sells appreciated property and distributes the proceeds, there is but a single tax at the partner level on the gain.

Distributions of appreciated property by a corporation, on the other hand, generally produce immediate tax consequences to both the corporation and its shareholders. The corporation is subject to tax as if it had sold the property and the shareholder is taxed on the value of the property to the extent it is considered a dividend for tax purposes. Even a liquidating distribution, which is not subject to dividend treatment, produces similar results because the corporation is taxed on the appreciation of the property and the shareholders are taxed to the extent the distribution exceeds their bases in the corporation's stock. A sale and distribution of the proceeds produces the same result as a distribution of appreciated property directly to the shareholders.

What the rules on distributions mean for the real estate entity is that it may be very costly to get real estate assets or their value out of a corporation and into the hands of shareholders if and when this becomes desirable. Use of a partnership, on the other hand, means a lower tax cost down the road when real estate assets are distributed to the principals or sold for their benefit.

.02 S Corporation or Partnership

The S corporation, with its special tax rules that are similar to a partnership, would seem to be a logical alternative to the partnership as the owning entity for real estate. The S corporation may offer the nontax advantages of a corporation combined with the tax advantages of a partnership. In some situations, this may, in fact, be the case. However, the dissimilarities between S corporation and partnership taxation are such that any hasty conclusion must be avoided.

Looking to the advantages of corporate operation found in the S corporation as compared to a partnership, the same general observations made in the comparison of regular C corporations to partnerships apply. Liability protection similar to that afforded by an S corporation can be built into a partnership with insurance, nonrecourse financing and exculpatory provisions. S corporation shareholders usually restrict stock transfers to protect the S election while partnership agreements can be drawn to allow continuation of the partnership following the death of a partner or other transfer of a partnership interest.

While the tax treatment of S corporations and partnerships is similar, it is not identical. Major differences in the two schemes of taxation do exist and, in many cases, will tip the choice of the owning entity for real estate to the partnership.

Leveraged real estate may produce tax losses that might be used to shelter other income of the owners, subject to the passive loss restrictions (passive loss rules are considered in some detail in Chapter 11). When leveraged real estate is owned by an S corporation, however, the loss ceiling imposed on shareholders may mean that they can derive no benefit from the losses produced by the leveraged property. S corporation shareholders do not get a basis step up for borrowings by the corporation to finance property, unlike partners who do get a basis step up to reflect borrowings by the partnership. With basis serving as the limiting factor on loss deductions in both partnerships and S corporations, the partnership has a clear tax advantage over the S corporation as a vehicle for owning and operating leveraged real estate.

Another potential drawback to the S corporation is the requirements that there be no more than 100 shareholders and only one class of stock. Partnerships are not limited to a certain number of partners and, perhaps more importantly in limited partnerships, various classes of partnership interests can be created. Also, the allocation of income, loss, deductions, and tax credits to shareholders in an S corporation must be made strictly according to stock ownership. The special allocations possible in a partnership, thereby permitting flexibility, are not available to an S corporation.

Finally, the S corporation, just as a regular corporation, presents some tax complications when appreciated property is distributed to shareholders. Unlike a partnership in which property distributions to partners generally produce no immediate tax, a property distribution to shareholders requires recognition of the gain on the property as if the corporation had sold the property. While this may not result in a tax at the corporate level because of the pass-through of the gain, the shareholders must report and pay taxes on their allocable shares of the recognized gain. Of course, if the gain recognized by the corporation is a built-in gain, the corporation as well as the shareholders will be subject to tax.

In sum, the S corporation, in some situations, may be a viable alternative to the partnership as the “entity of choice” for real estate investment and operation. The tax differences between the S corporation and partnership, however, are sufficiently broad as to require a very careful weighing of the factors involved. The potential tax disadvantages of an S corporation, although not as great as a C corporation, nevertheless may be enough to tip the scales in favor of partnership operation.

.03 Comparison Chart of Business Entities

The following chart provides a concise comparison of many of the attributes of partnerships, S corporations, and C corporations. An LLC, depending on the status its members elect for tax purposes, will have characteristics of a partnership or corporation.

COMPARISON OF THE ATTRIBUTES OF PARTNERSHIPS, S CORPORATIONS, AND C CORPORATIONS

Attribute	*Partnership*	*S Corporation*	*C Corporation*
Entity Status	No state filing or tax elections required (state filing required for limited partnership)	State filing for incorporation; status must be elected for tax purposes	State filing for incorporation; status must be elected for tax purposes
Number of Owners	No limitations	No more than 100 shareholders	No limitations
Eligible Owners	No limitations	Must be qualified shareholders, generally individuals and certain trusts and estates	No limitations
Classes of Ownership Interests	General and limited partners; different classes of limited partners	Only one class of stock; differences in voting rights permitted	Multiple classes of stock permitted, including common and preferred, voting and nonvoting, etc.
Transfer of Ownership Interests	No, subject to partnership agreement	Yes, subject to shareholder agreement or stock restrictions	Yes, subject to shareholder agreement or stock restrictions
Tax Year	Same as principal partners unless business purpose for a different year	Calendar year unless business purpose for a different year	May choose any permitted fiscal year or calendar year
Passive Investment Income Effect	None	May cause termination of status	None
Termination of Entity Status for Tax Purposes	Transfer of 50% or more of partnership interests within 12 months; cessation of operations	Election by stockholders owning at least 50% of stock; failure to meet S requirements; excess passive investment income	Cessation of operations

Attribute	*Partnership*	*S Corporation*	*C Corporation*
Basis of Interests or Stock	Money plus basis of contributed property and services, increased by share of partnership liabilities	Money plus basis of other property contributed; value of contributed services included in income	Money plus basis of other property contributed; value of contributed services included in income
Adjustments to Basis	Increased by partnership taxable income and increases in partnership liabilities; decreased by distributions, depletion, losses and decreases in partnership liabilities	Increased by corporate income; decreased by distributions and corporate losses; no adjustment for corporate liabilities	Increased only for additional capital contributions; decreased only by return of capital distributions
Limited Liability	No for general partners; Yes for limited partners	Yes	Yes
"Double Tax"	No	No, subject to some limited exceptions	Yes
Deduction of Entity Losses	Limited to adjusted basis of partnership interest	Limited to adjusted basis of stock and basis of debt owned to shareholder by corporation	No pass-through of entity losses to shareholders
Special Allocations	Permitted, provided substantial economic effect	No; allocation strictly on a per-share/per-day basis	No

Attribute	*Partnership*	*S Corporation*	*C Corporation*
Distributions of Property	Gain not recognized	Gain recognized to extent value of property exceeds basis of property to corporation; built-in gain subject to corporate level tax	Gain recognized by corporation to extent value of property exceeds basis of property to corporation; value taxed to shareholder as dividend to extent of corporation earnings and profits; if distribution is liquidating distribution, gain recognized by shareholder to extent value of property exceeds shareholder's basis in stock

¶ 209 QUALIFIED BUSINESS INCOME (PASSTHROUGH DEDUCTION)

Individuals compute their federal income tax liability for a tax year by multiplying their taxable income by the applicable tax rate, subtracting allowable credits, and adding other taxes, if warranted (*e.g.*, self-employment tax, household employment tax, etc.). There are four schedules of tax rates based on an individual's filing status: single, married filing jointly and surviving spouses, married filing separately, and head of household. The tax rates are graduated, so income is taxed at higher rates as the individual earns more. An unincorporated sole proprietorship is not treated as separate from its owner for federal income tax purposes, so the owner is taxed directly on the income from the business (see ¶ 202).

An individual who receives business income from a passthrough entity (such as a partnership or an S corporation) is taxed on that income at the regular individual income tax rates. A partner takes into account the partnership's items of income, gain, loss, deduction, and credit whether any income is distributed or not (see ¶ 203). Similarly, an S corporation shareholder takes into account the S corporation's items of income, gain, loss, deduction, and credit regardless of whether the income is distributed or not (see ¶ 206).

The Tax Cuts and Jobs Act[78] created a new deduction for business income that, essentially, is being taxed at the individual tax rates. The deduction applies to tax years beginning after December 31, 2017 and before January 1, 2026.[79]

[78] P.L. 115-97.

[79] Code Sec. 199A.

The Tax Cuts and Jobs Act slightly lowered the individual graduated tax rates (the graduated rates for 2018 range from ten percent to 37 percent) and, except for the first $50,000 of income, substantially lowered the corporate tax rate by providing a single flat rate of 21 percent for corporations. The passthrough deduction helps to equalize the tax burden imposed on business income regardless of the legal structure in which the business is conducted.

The discussion of the deduction in this paragraph is not intended as a complete exposition of the intricacies involved. On August 9, 2018, the IRS issued proposed regulations to provide taxpayers with computational, definitional, and anti-avoidance guidance regarding the application of Code Sec. 199A.[80] These proposed regulations contain six substantive sections, 1.199A-1 through 1.199A-6, each of which provides rules relevant to the calculation of the Code Sec. 199A deduction. Additionally, the proposed regulations would establish anti-abuse rules under Code Sec. 643(f) to prevent taxpayers from establishing multiple non-grantor trusts or contributing additional capital to multiple existing non-grantor trusts in order to avoid federal income tax, including abuse of Code Sec. 199A. These regulations also provide numerous examples of the passthrough deduction calculations.

The proposed regulations were largely adopted as final in January 2019.[81] However, the final regulations drop the rule that treated an incidental non-specified services trade or business (SSTB) as part of an SSTB if the businesses were commonly owned and shared expenses, and the non-SSTB's gross receipts were no more than five percent of the businesses' combined gross receipts. The final regulations also make several adjustments relating to trusts and estates. In conjunction with the final regulations, the IRS also issued additional proposed regulations that relate to previously disallowed losses of publicly traded partnerships, regulated investment companies that receive qualified REIT dividends, and rules for certain trusts.[82]

.01 Overview

An individual taxpayer in computing tax liability may deduct up to 20 percent of certain domestic qualified business income from a partnership, S corporation, or sole proprietorship.[83] The deduction is generally capped by the W-2 wages paid by the business and the unadjusted basis of property the business uses to produce business income.[84] This limit may be phased-in or eliminated if the taxpayer's taxable income meets certain threshold requirements (see ¶ 209.04). The deduction is generally not allowed for certain service trades or businesses, but this disallowance is phased-in for taxpayers whose taxable income meets certain threshold requirements (see ¶ 209.02[A]).

[80] NPRM REG-107892-18.
[81] T.D. 9847.
[82] NPRM REG-134652-18.
[83] Code Sec. 199A(a).
[84] Code Sec. 199A(b).

For individual taxpayers, the deduction is not allowed in determining adjusted gross income,[85] nor is it an itemized deduction.[86] It is available to individuals whether they itemize deductions or claim the standard deduction.[87]

A deduction is available for agricultural or horticultural cooperatives, but is computed in a fashion similar to the way in which the deduction for domestic production activities was computed under Code Sec. 199 prior to its repeal by the Tax Cuts and Jobs Act (see ¶ 209.05).

For partnerships and S corporations, the deduction is applied at the partner or shareholder level. Each partner takes into account his or her allocable share, and each shareholder must take into account his or her pro rata share, of each qualified item of income, gain, deduction, and loss. Further, each partner or shareholder is treated as having W-2 wages and unadjusted basis of property in an amount equal to his or her allocable or pro rata share of the partnership's or S corporation's W-2 wages and unadjusted basis of property. The share of W-2 wages is determined in the same manner as the partner's or shareholder's share of wage expenses. The share of the unadjusted basis of property is determined in the same manner as the partner's or shareholder's allocable share of depreciation.[88]

Trusts and estates are eligible for the deduction. Rules similar to those in effect on December 1, 2017 for the domestic production activities deduction apply for apportioning any W-2 wages and unadjusted basis of property between fiduciaries and beneficiaries.[89]

A taxpayer may be subject to a 20-percent accuracy-related penalty for a substantial understatement of income tax. In general, a substantial understatement exists when the tax understatement is more than the greater of ten percent of the tax required to be shown on the return, or $5,000. A taxpayer who claims the passthrough deduction may be subject to the 20-percent accuracy-related penalty for a substantial understatement of income tax if the understatement is more than the greater of five percent (not ten percent) of the tax required to be shown on the return for the tax year, or $5,000.[90]

.02 Eligible Trades and Businesses

A taxpayer can claim the passthrough deduction for income from many types of trades or businesses carried on by the taxpayer, but not for certain specified service trades or businesses (with exceptions). Also, performing services as an employee is not a qualified trade or business.[91]

[A] *Specified Trades and Businesses*

A specified service trade or business for which the passthrough deduction is *not* available is any trade or business:

---

[85] Code Sec. 62(a).
[86] Code Sec. 63(d).
[87] Code Sec. 63(b).
[88] Code Sec. 199A(f)(1)(A).
[89] Code Sec. 199A(f)(1)(B).
[90] Code Sec. 6662(d)(1)(C).
[91] Code Sec. 199A(d)(1).

- That involves the performance of services in the fields of accounting, actuarial science, athletics, brokerage services, consulting, financial services, health, law, or the performing arts; or
- That involves the performance of services consisting of investing and investment management, trading, or dealing in securities, partnership interests, or commodities; or
- Whose principal asset is the reputation or skill of one or more of its employees or owners.[92]

Architecture and engineering are *not* specified service trades or businesses, and so can be qualified trades or businesses if they otherwise qualify. The Conference Committee Report on the Tax Cuts and Jobs Act referred to the rules for determining whether a qualified personal service corporation may use the cash method of accounting for guidance on the types of activities that qualify as services in the fields of health, the performing arts, and consulting.[93]

A taxpayer carrying on a specified service trade or business can claim a modified qualified business deduction, however, if his or her taxable income for the tax year is less than

- $415,000 for taxpayers filing a joint return; or
- $207,500 for all other taxpayers.[94]

If this income requirement is met, the taxpayer takes into account only a percentage of his or her qualified items of income, gain, deduction, or loss, and W-2 wages and unadjusted basis of property, that are allocable to the specified service in computing qualified business income, W-2 wages, and unadjusted basis of property. The percentage is calculated by first determining the ratio of (1) the taxpayer's taxable income in excess of the $157,500 threshold amount ($315,000 for a joint return), over (2) $50,000 ($100,000 in the case of a joint return). This ratio is then subtracted from 100 percent.[95] (See ¶ 209.04 for how the actual passthrough deduction is calculated.)

[B] *Safe Harbor for Rental Real Estate*

The IRS has issued a revenue procedure that provides a safe harbor under which a rental real estate enterprise is treated as a trade or business for purposes of the qualified business income deduction.[96] A rental real estate enterprise is defined as an interest in real property held for the production of rents and may consist of an interest in multiple properties. An individual or relevant passthrough entity relying on the safe harbor must hold the interest directly or through an entity disregarded as an entity separate from its owner. Taxpayers must either treat each property held for the production of rents as a separate enterprise or treat all similar properties held for the production of rents as a single enterprise. Commercial and residential real estate may not be part of the same enterprise. Taxpayers may not vary this treatment from year to year. However, a taxpayer that chooses to treat its

[92] Code Sec. 199A(d)(2).

[93] *See* Reg. § 1.448-1T(e)(4).

[94] Code Sec. 199A(d)(3).

[95] Code Sec. 199A(d)(3)(B).

[96] Rev. Proc. 2019-38, 2019-42 IRB 942.

interest in each residential or commercial property as a separate rental real estate enterprise may choose to treat its interests in all similar commercial or all similar residential properties as a single rental real estate enterprise in a future year.

An interest in mixed-use property may be treated as a single rental real estate enterprise or may be bifurcated into separate residential and commercial interests. For this purpose, mixed-use property is defined as a single building that combines residential and commercial units. An interest in mixed-use property, if treated as a single rental real estate enterprise, may not be treated as part of the same enterprise as other residential, commercial, or mixed-use property.

To qualify for the safe harbor, a rental real estate enterprise must meet the following requirements:

1. Separate books and records are maintained to reflect income and expenses for each rental real estate enterprise;
2. For enterprises in existence for less than four years, 250 or more hours of rental services are performed per year for the rental enterprise. For enterprises in existence for four or more years, in any three of the five consecutive tax years that end with the tax year (or in each year if held for less than five years), 250 or more hours of rental services are performed per year for the rental real estate enterprise; and
3. The taxpayer maintains contemporaneous records, including time reports, logs, or similar documents, regarding:
   a. hours of all services performed;
   b. description of all services performed;
   c. dates on which such services were performed; and
   d. who performed the services.

   The records must be available for inspection at the request of the IRS.

Rental services for the safe harbor include, but are not limited to:

1. advertising to rent or lease the real estate;
2. negotiating and executing leases;
3. verifying information contained in prospective tenant applications;
4. collection of rent;
5. daily operation, maintenance, and repair of the property, including the purchase of materials and supplies;
6. management of the real estate; and
7. supervision of employees and independent contractors.

Rental services may be performed by owners or by employees, agents, and/or independent contractors of the owners. The term rental services does not include financial or investment management activities, such as arranging financing; procuring property; studying and reviewing financial statements or reports on operations; planning, managing, or constructing long-term capital improvements; or hours spent traveling to and from the real estate.

The following real estate is not eligible for the safe harbor:

1. Real estate used by the taxpayer (including an owner or beneficiary of a relevant passthrough entity relying on the safe harbor) as a residence for any part of the year;
2. Real estate rented or leased under a triple net lease;
3. Real estate rented to a trade or business conducted by a taxpayer or passthrough entity which is commonly controlled; and
4. The entire rental real estate interest if any portion of the interest is treated as a specified service trade or business under Reg. § 1.199A-5(c)(2), which provides special rules if property or services are provided to a specified service trade or business.

To claim the benefits of the safe harbor, the taxpayer (or passthrough entity) must include a statement attached to the return on which it claims the deduction (or passes through information for the deduction) that the requirements for the safe harbor have been satisfied. The statement also must include a description (including the address and rental category) of all rental real estate properties that are included in each rental real estate enterprise, and a description (including the address and rental category) of rental real estate properties acquired and disposed of during the tax year.

.03 Qualified Business Income

The qualified business income of a qualified trade or business carried on by a taxpayer is the net amount of the business's qualified items of income, gain, deduction, and loss. Items of income, gain, deduction, and loss are qualified to the extent they are effectively connected with the conduct of a trade or business within the United States, and are included or allowed in determining taxable income.[97]

> ***Example 7:*** ABC Company is a qualified business for purposes of the passthrough deduction. ABC has $100,000 of ordinary income from inventory sales, and makes a $25,000 expenditure that must be capitalized and amortized over five years. ABC's net business income is $95,000 ($100,000 minus the $5,000 current-year ordinary amortization deduction). ABC's qualified business income is not reduced by the entire amount of the capital expenditure, only by the amount deductible in determining taxable income for the year.

The source rules used to determine if items of income, deduction, etc., are "effectively connected" with a U.S. trade or business are the same as those used to determine whether the income of a nonresident alien or foreign corporation is effectively connected with a U.S. trade or business. Those source rules are applied for the purpose of determining the passthrough deduction by substituting "qualified trade or business (within the meaning of section 199A)" for "nonresident alien individual or a foreign corporation."[98]

[97] Code Sec. 199A(c)(3)(A).

[98] Code Sec. 199A(c)(3)(A)(i).

A taxpayer includes his or her qualified business income from sources within Puerto Rico if the income is taxable under Code Sec. 1.[99]

Qualified items of income, gain, deduction, or loss do not include:

1. Items of short-term capital gain or loss, or long-term capital gain or loss;
2. Dividends, income equivalent to a dividend, or payments in lieu of dividends;
3. Interest income which is not properly allocable to a trade or business;
4. The excess of gain over loss from commodities transactions, other than those entered into in the normal course of the trade or business or with respect to stock in trade or property held primarily for sale to customers in the ordinary course of the trade or business, property used in the trade or business, or supplies regularly used or consumed in the trade or business;
5. The excess of foreign currency gains over foreign currency losses from Code Sec. 988 transactions, other than transactions directly related to the business needs of the business activity;
6. Net income from notional principal contracts, other than clearly identified hedging transactions that are treated as ordinary (*i.e.,* not treated as capital assets);
7. Amounts from an annuity not received in connection with the trade or business; or
8. Items of deduction or loss properly allocable to an amount described in (1)—(7) above.[100]

Qualified business income does not include:

- Reasonable compensation paid to the taxpayer by the business for services rendered;
- Guaranteed payments to a partner for services rendered;
- Payments to a partner not in his capacity as a partner (Code Sec. 707(a) payments) for services rendered (to the extent provided in regulations);
- Qualified REIT dividends;
- Qualified cooperative dividends; or
- Qualified publicly traded partnership income.[101]

In determining alternative minimum taxable income, qualified business income is determined without regard to the minimum tax preferences and adjustments.[102]

If the net amount of qualified income, gain, deduction, and loss is less than zero, the loss is carried over to the next tax year. Any deduction allowed in the next tax year is reduced (but not below zero) by 20 percent of any carryover qualified business loss.[103]

---

[99] Code Sec. 199A(f)(1)(C)(i).
[100] Code Sec. 199A(c)(3)(B).
[101] Code Sec. 199A(c).
[102] Code Sec. 199A(f)(2).
[103] Code Sec. 199A(c)(2).

Example 8: Richard carries on two qualified businesses, Business A and Business B. In 2019, Richard has qualified business income of $20,000 from Business A and a qualified business loss of $50,000 from Business B. Richard cannot claim the passthrough deduction for 2019, but has a carryover qualified business loss of $30,000 to 2020. In 2020, Richard has qualified business income of $20,000 from Business A and $50,000 from Business B. To determine his passthrough deduction for 2020, Richard reduces the 20 percent deductible amount determined for the $70,000 qualified business income from Businesses A and B by 20 percent of the $30,000 carryover qualified business loss.

(See ¶ 209.04 for how the actual passthrough deduction is calculated and for additional examples of the calculation.)

.04 Calculating the Deduction

The basic calculation of the passthrough deduction is simply the lesser of two amounts. Those two amounts, however, are determined by still other calculations. Let's take it one step at a time.

Step 1: Basic Calculation. A noncorporate taxpayer can claim a passthrough deduction each year for the *lesser* of:

1. The taxpayer's "combined qualified business income amount" (see below); or
2. 20 percent of the excess of:
   a. The taxpayer's taxable income over,
   b. The taxpayer's net capital gain.

The deduction cannot be more than the taxpayer's taxable income (reduced by net capital gain) for the tax year. In determining the deduction amount, the taxpayer's taxable income is computed without regard to the passthrough deduction.[104]

Step 2: Combined Qualified Business Income Amount. A taxpayer's combined qualified business income amount equals:

1. The sum of the deductible amounts determined for each qualified trade or business carried on by the taxpayer; plus
2. 20 percent of the taxpayer's aggregate qualified REIT dividends and qualified publicly traded partnership income (each of these is defined below).[105]

A qualified trade or business's "deductible amount" is generally the *lesser* of:

1. 20 percent of the taxpayer's qualified business income from the trade or business; or
2. A "W-2 wages/qualified property limit," which is the *greater* of:
   a. 50 percent of the W-2 wages of the trade or business; or

[104] Code Sec. 199A(a).

[105] Code Sec. 199A(b)(1).

b. The sum of 25 percent of the W-2 wages of the trade or business, plus 2.5 percent of the unadjusted basis immediately after acquisition of all qualified property of the trade or business.[106]

The "W-2 wages/qualified property limit" does not apply or is modified for individuals with income below certain levels. See the discussion of the modifications to the W-2 wages/qualified property limit below. Rev. Proc. 2019-11[107] provides methods for calculating W-2 wages.

The qualified property component means that a taxpayer may be able to claim the deduction if the taxpayer carries on a qualified trade or business that has few or no employees but generates income using its depreciable tangible assets, for instance, a real estate business.

Example 9: Thomas operates a sole proprietorship that makes personalized protective covers for smartphones. The business buys a machine for $100,000 that can quickly produce the covers, and places the machine in service in 2020. In that year, the business has no employees. The W-2 wages/qualified property limit on the business's deductible amount for 2020 is $2,500, which is the greater of (1) 50 percent of W-2 wages ($0 × 50% = $0), or (2) the sum of 25 percent of W-2 wages ($0) plus 2.5 percent of the unadjusted basis of the machine immediately after its acquisition ($100,000 × 0.025 = $2,500).

Example 10: On January 5, 2013, Richard purchases real property for $1 million and places it in service for his trade or business. Richard's basis in the property under Code Sec. 1012 is $1 million. The real property is qualified property. As of December 31, 2019, Richard's basis in the property, as adjusted for depreciation deductions, is $821,550. Richard's unadjusted basis immediately after acquisition for the real property is its $1 million cost basis under Code Sec. 1012, regardless of any later depreciation deductions and resulting basis adjustments.

Now suppose that on January 15, 2020, Richard enters into a like-kind exchange under Code Sec. 1031 in which he exchanges his real property for a new parcel of property. The new property has a value of $1 million. No cash or other property is involved in the exchange. As of January 15, 2020, Richard's basis in the old property, as adjusted for depreciation deductions, is $820,482. Richard's unadjusted basis in the new property is $820,482 as determined under Code Sec. 1031(d) (his adjusted basis in the old property carried over to the new property). The new property is first placed in service by Richard on January 5, 2013, which is the date on which he first placed in service the old property given up in the exchange.

Guidance is expected from the IRS on how the combined qualified business income amount rules apply when the taxpayer has a short tax year, or acquires or disposes of the major portion of a trade or business or a separate unit of a trade or business.[108]

---

[106] Code Sec. 199A(b)(2).

[107] 2019-9 IRB 742.

[108] *See* Prop. Reg. § 1.199A-2(b)(2)(iv)(C).

A qualified REIT dividend is a dividend received from a real estate investment trust that is not a capital gain dividend or a qualified dividend income under Code Sec. 1(h)(11).[109]

Qualified publicly traded partnership income is the sum of:

1. The net amount of the taxpayer's allocable share of each qualified item of income, gain, deduction, and loss from a publicly traded partnership that is not treated as a corporation (without regard to reasonable compensation, guaranteed payments, or other payments to the taxpayer or partner for services rendered); plus
2. Any gain recognized by the taxpayer from disposing his or her partnership interest, to the extent the gain is treated as realized from the sale or exchange of property other than a capital asset.[110]

Step 3: Modifications to W-2 Wages/Qualified Property Limit. The W-2 wages/qualified property limit described above does not apply if the taxpayer's taxable income for the tax year is equal to or less than a $157,500 threshold amount ($315,000 for taxpayers filing a joint return).[111]

For other taxpayers, the W-2 wages/qualified property limit may be phased in. If the taxpayer's taxable income for the tax year is more than the $157,500 threshold amount ($315,000 for a joint return) but not more than $207,500 ($415,000 for a joint return), and if the W-2 wages/qualified property limit amount for the qualified trade or business is less than 20 percent of the taxpayer's qualified business income for that trade or business, then:

1. The W-2 wages/qualified property limit does not apply for the qualified trade or business; and
2. The amount that is 20 percent of the taxpayer's qualified business income from the qualified trade or business is reduced by a reduction amount.[112]

The reduction amount is calculated by:

1. Subtracting the qualified trade or business's W-2 wages/qualified property limit amount from the amount that is 20 percent of the taxpayer's qualified business income from the trade or business; then
2. Multiplying the difference determined in (1) above by a fraction: the numerator is the amount by which the taxpayer's taxable income for the tax year exceeds the $157,500 threshold amount ($315,000 for a joint return), and the denominator is $50,000 ($100,000 for a joint return).[113]

The threshold amounts are adjusted for inflation for tax years beginning after 2018.

> ***Example 11:*** Hans and Wendy are married. Wendy has a qualified business that is not a specified service business. For the 2019 tax year, they file a joint return reporting taxable income of $345,000. In that tax year, 20 percent

[109] Code Sec. 199A(e)(3).

[110] Code Sec. 199A(e)(5).

[111] Code Sec. 199A(b)(3)(A) and (e)(2)(A).

[112] Code Sec. 199A(b)(3)(B)(i) and (e)(2)(A).

[113] Code Sec. 199A(b)(3)(B)(ii) and (iii).

of the qualified business income from Wendy's business is $15,000. Wendy's share of wages paid by the business in the tax year is $20,000, so 50 percent of the W-2 wages from the business is $10,000. (For purposes of this example, assume that no qualified property factors into the calculation.) The $15,000 amount is reduced by 30 percent (($345,000 taxable income – $315,000 threshold amount) / $100,000) of $5,000 ($15,000 – $10,000), which equals $1,500 (0.3 × $5,000). Hans and Wendy take a passthrough deduction of $13,500 ($15,000 – $1,500).

Additional Examples. The following are additional examples of the calculation of the passthrough deduction. For further examples, see the regulations under Code Sec. 199A.[114]

Example 12: Harry, an unmarried individual, owns several parcels of land that he manages and that are leased to several suburban airports for parking lots. The business generated $1,000,000 of qualified business income in 2019. The business paid no wages and the property was not qualified property because it was not depreciable. After allowable deductions unrelated to the business, Harry's total taxable income for 2019 is $980,000. Because Harry's taxable income exceeds the applicable threshold amount, his Code Sec. 199A deduction is subject to the W-2 wage and unadjusted basis of qualified property limitations. Harry's deduction is limited to zero because the business paid no wages and held no qualified property.

Now suppose that Harry developed the land parcels in 2020, expending a total of $10,000,000 to build parking structures on each of the parcels, all of which are depreciable. During 2021, Harry leased the parking structures and the land to the suburban airports. He reports $4,000,000 of qualified business income for 2021. After allowable deductions unrelated to the business, Harry's total taxable income for 2021 is $3,980,000. Because his taxable income is above the threshold amount, the qualified business income component of his Code Sec. 199A deduction is subject to the W-2 wage and unadjusted basis of qualified property limitations. Because the business has no W-2 wages, the qualified business income component of Harry's deduction is limited to the lesser of 20 percent of the business's qualified business income or 2.5 percent of its unadjusted basis of qualified property. Twenty percent of the $4,000,000 of qualified business income is $800,000. Two and one-half percent of the $10,000,000 unadjusted basis of qualified property is $250,000. The qualified business income component of Harry's deduction, therefore, is limited to $250,000. Harry's deduction is equal to the lesser of (1) 20 percent of the qualified business income from the business as limited ($250,000) or (2) 20 percent of Harry's taxable income ($3,980,000 × 20% = $796,000). Therefore, Harry's Code Sec. 199A deduction for 2021 is $250,000.

Example 13: Theo has taxable income of $187,500, of which $134,000 is attributable to an accounting sole proprietorship (i.e., a specified service business, see ¶ 209.02[A]) after paying wages of $67,000 to employees. Be-

[114] T.D. 9847.

cause his taxable income is less than the $207,500 threshold for specified service businesses, Theo can claim the passthrough deduction, but only for an applicable percentage of his qualified items of income, gain, deduction, or loss, and the W-2 wages, from the accounting business. (For purposes of this example, assume that no qualified property factors into the calculation.) Theo has a 40 percent applicable percentage (1 – ($187,500 – $157,500)/$50,000 = 1 – 30,000/50,000 = 1 – 0.6 = 0.4). In determining includible qualified business income, Theo takes into account 40 percent of $134,000, or $53,600. In determining the includible W-2 wages, Theo takes into account 40 percent of $67,000, or $26,800. Theo calculates the deduction by taking the lesser of: 20 percent of $53,600 ($10,720), or 50 percent of $26,800 ($13,400). Theo can take a passthrough deduction for $10,720.

Example 14: Nick and Nora are married. They file a joint return on which they report taxable income of $345,000 (determined without regard to the passthrough deduction). Nick is a partner in the XYZ Partnership, a qualified trade or business that is not a specified service business. Nora operates Nora's Web Consulting, a sole proprietorship qualified trade or business that is a specified service business. They also received $10,000 in qualified REIT dividends during the tax year. Nick and Nora determine their passthrough deduction for the tax year as follows (for purposes of this example, assume that no qualified property factors into the calculation):

Nick's allocable share of qualified business income from the XYZ Partnership is $300,000, so 20 percent of the qualified business income from XYZ is $60,000 ($300,000 × 0.20). Nick's allocable share of wages paid by XYZ is $100,000, so 50 percent of the W-2 wages from the business is $50,000 ($100,000 × 0.5). Nick and Nora's taxable income is above the $315,000 threshold amount for a joint return, so the wage limit for XYZ is phased in. Accordingly, the $60,000 amount is reduced by 30 percent (($345,000 – $315,000)/$100,000) of the difference between $60,000 and $50,000, or $3,000 (($60,000 – $50,000) × 0.3). Nick's deductible amount for the XYZ Partnership is $57,000 ($60,000 – $3,000).

Nora's qualified business income and W-2 wages from Nora's Web Consulting are $325,000 and $150,000, respectively. Because their taxable income is less than the $415,000 joint-return threshold for specified service businesses, Nick and Nora can claim the passthrough deduction for Nora's consulting business, but only for an applicable percentage of the qualified items of income, gain, deduction, or loss, and the W-2 wages from that business. Further, because their taxable income is above the $315,000 threshold amount for a joint return, the exclusion of qualified business income and W-2 wages from Nora's consulting business are phased in.

Nora has an applicable percentage of 70 percent (1 – ($345,000 – $315,000)/$100,000 = 1 – $30,000/$100,000 = 1 – 0.3 = 0.7). In determining includible qualified business income, Nora takes into account $227,500 ($325,000 × 0.7). In determining includible W-2 wages, Nora takes into account $105,000 ($150,000 × 0.7). Nora calculates the deductible amount for her consulting business by taking the lesser of 20 percent of her $227,500 of includible qualified business income ($45,500) or 50 percent of her $105,000 of includible W-2 wages ($52,500). Although Nick and Nora's taxable income is above the threshold amount for a joint return, the wage limit is not binding because the 20 percent of includible qualified business income of the consulting business ($45,500) is less than 50 percent of its includible W-2 wages ($52,500). Nora's deductible amount for Nora's Web Consulting is $45,500.

Nick and Nora's combined qualified business income amount of $104,500, which consists of the $57,000 deductible amount for the XYZ Partnership, plus the $45,500 deductible amount for Nora's Web Consulting, plus 20 percent of the $10,000 qualified REIT dividends ($2,000). However, their passthrough deduction for the tax year is limited to $69,000, which is 20 percent of their $345,000 taxable income, because that amount is less than their qualified business income amount for the year.

Example 15: Herbert and Whitney are married. They file a joint return for the tax year, on which they report taxable income of $200,000 (determined without regard to the passthrough deduction). Herbert has a sole proprietorship qualified trade or business, and Whitney is a partner in the LMO Partnership, a qualified trade or business. Neither qualified business is a specified service business. They have a carryover qualified business loss of $50,000. Herbert and Whitney determine their passthrough deduction for the tax year as follows (for purposes of this example, assume that no qualified property factors into the calculation):

Herbert's qualified business income from his business is $150,000, so 20 percent of the qualified business income is $30,000. Herbert and Whitney's taxable income is below the $315,000 threshold amount for a joint return, so the wage limit does not apply to Herbert's business. Herbert's deductible amount for his business is $30,000.

Whitney's allocable share of qualified business loss from the LMO Partnership is $40,000, so 20 percent of the qualified business loss is $8,000. Because their taxable income is below the $315,000 threshold amount for a joint return, the wage limit does not apply to Whitney's partnership. Whitney's deductible amount for the LMO Partnership is an $8,000 reduction to the deduction amount.

Herbert and Whitney's combined qualified business income amount is $12,000, which consists of the $30,000 deductible amount for Herbert's business, the $8,000 reduction for the LMO Partnership, and a $10,000 reduction attributable to the carryover qualified business loss (20% × $50,000). Their deduction is limited to 20 percent of their $200,000 taxable income, or $40,000. Since their combined qualified business income amount is less than 20 percent of their taxable income, Herbert and Whitney's passthrough deduction amount for the tax year is $12,000.

.05 Agricultural or Horticultural Cooperatives

The deduction for specified agricultural or horticultural cooperatives is generally equal to nine percent of qualified production activity income, rather than 20 percent of qualified business income. The cooperatives deduction, generally, is calculated under the rules that applied to the calculation of the deduction for domestic production activities under Code Sec. 199 prior to its repeal by the Tax Cuts and Jobs Act. Further, in determining the combined qualified income of a patron of the cooperative, the deductible amount for the patron's qualified trade or business must be reduced by nine percent of the qualified business income that is allocable to qualified payments from the cooperative or, if less, by 50 percent of W-2 wages allocable to those payments. The coop may also pass through some or all of its own deduction to its patrons.[115]

A specified agricultural or horticultural cooperative is an organization that is subject to the cooperative income tax rules (Code Secs. 1381 through 1383) and engaged in:

1. Manufacturing, producing, growing, or extracting, in whole or significant part, an agricultural or horticultural product; or
2. Marketing agricultural or horticultural products. A specified cooperative that markets agricultural or horticultural products manufactured, produced, grown or extracted by its patrons is treated as having manufactured, produced, grown or extracted those products itself.[116]

Eligible taxpayers may deduct a portion of qualified payments they receive from a specified agricultural or horticultural cooperative. Eligible taxpayers are individuals, estates, trusts, and other specified agricultural or horticultural cooperatives. A qualified payment is any amount received from the coop that is a patronage dividend or per-unit retain allocation attributable to the portion of the coop's qualified production activity income for which the coop is allowed a deduction under Code Sec. 199A.[117]

The eligible taxpayer's deduction for qualified payments is equal to the portion of the coop's deduction for qualified production activities income that and identified by the coop in a written notice mailed to the patron by the 15th day of the ninth month following the end of its tax year.[118] The deduction is limited to the patron's taxable income, determined after taking into account the taxpayer's general qualified business income deduction, but without taking into account the taxpayer's passed-through deduction from the cooperative.[119]

The IRS has issued proposed regulations on the application of the qualified business income deduction to cooperatives and their patrons and to specified cooperatives and their patrons.[120] The proposed regulations are organized into six sections:

115 Code Sec. 199A(b) and (g).

116 Code Sec. 199A(g) (4).

117 Code Sec. 199(g) (1) and (g) (2) (E).

118 Code Sec. 199A(g) (2) (A).

119 Code Sec. 199A(g) (2) (B).

120 NPRM REG 118425-18.

- Prop. Reg. § 1.199A-7 describes rules for patrons of cooperatives to calculate their qualified business income deduction and rules for patrons of specified cooperatives to calculate the reduction to their deduction as required by Code Sec. 199A(b) (7).
- Prop. Reg. § 1.199A-8 sets out the criteria that specified cooperatives must satisfy to qualify for the Code Sec. 199A(g) deduction, and sets forth four steps necessary to calculate this deduction. These proposed regulations provide that the deduction available to specified cooperatives and their patrons is generally computed only on patronage gross receipts and related deductions.
- Prop. Reg. § 1.199A-9 provides additional rules for determining a Specified Cooperative's domestic production gross receipts (DPGR).
- Prop. Reg. § 1.199A-10 provides additional rules for calculating costs (including cost of goods sold (COGS) and other expenses, losses, and deductions) allocable to a Specified Cooperative's DPGR.
- Prop. Reg. § 1.199A-11 provides additional rules for determining the W-2 wage limitation in Code Sec. 199A(g) (1) (B).
- Prop. Reg. § 1.199A-12 details rules for applying Code Sec. 199A(g) in the context of an expanded affiliated group and other special rules that are not otherwise addressed in these proposed regulations.

The IRS has issued a proposed revenue procedure that provides computational guidance on methods and appropriate sources of data for calculating W-2 wages for purposes of Code Sec. 199A(g) and the proposed regulations.[121] The Notice provides three methods for calculating W-2 wages for the limitation on the deduction to 50 percent of the specified cooperative's W-2 wages for the tax year.

[121] Notice 2019-27, 2019-31 IRB 484.

Chapter 3
Financing Real Estate

¶ 300 Overview of Chapter
¶ 301 Mortgage Financing
¶ 302 At-Risk Rules
¶ 303 Interest
¶ 304 Original Issue Discount and Imputed Interest on Deferred Payment Sales
¶ 305 Sale-Leasebacks and Other Lease Financing

¶ 300 OVERVIEW OF CHAPTER

Financing the acquisition of real estate often involves third parties who are willing to lend money at interest based on the security afforded by the real estate. This financing is in addition to the equity financing in the form of money, property or services contributed to a partnership or corporation by its principals or the "down payment" made by an individual purchaser of real estate.

In most cases, the security for the real estate loan takes the form of a mortgage under which the borrower retains title to the property but gives the lender the right to take the property (foreclose) if the borrower fails to live up to the loan agreement. In some cases, however, financing real estate may involve the actual transfer of title to the "lender," who purchases the property but leases the property back to the "borrower" in a sale-leaseback transaction. Other leasing arrangements also may serve as financing devices.

Although seller financing is touched upon in this chapter, particularly in regard to the original issue discount and deferred payment sale rules of the tax code, installment sales and seller-financed transactions are explored further in Chapter 14. Also, interest on mortgages on taxpayers' personal residences is a topic covered in Chapter 17, along with other deductions for homeowners.

¶ 301 MORTGAGE FINANCING

As discussed at ¶ 101, the original cost basis of property includes the amount of any mortgage given to secure payment of any portion of the purchase price of the property. Similarly, the amount realized on the sale of property includes the amount of any mortgage that the seller is relieved of on the sale. If a mortgage is placed on previously owned property or an existing mortgage is refinanced, basis is not affected, nor does the owner realize taxable income from the proceeds of the loan. This rule applies even if the new mortgage exceeds the owner's adjusted basis in the property. Refinancing a previously owned property, therefore, is frequently a tax-free source of cash, but there is, of course, the obligation to repay the debt.

While mortgage financing is a popular way to finance real estate, it does entail certain costs for both the borrower and the lender, and these costs have tax consequences. Also, when a mortgage is satisfied at other than face amount, there may be tax consequences. These tax ramifications of mortgage financing are discussed in the following paragraphs. Gifts of mortgaged property are considered at ¶ 1602, and the sale of mortgaged property is discussed at ¶ 1301.01.

.01 Mortgage Costs

Both the borrower (mortgagor) and the lender (mortgagee) are likely to incur various costs in connection with a mortgage loan. These costs may include legal fees, finders' or placement fees, brokers' commissions, appraisal costs, and the costs of surveys and title investigation.

[A] Borrower's Costs

Fees, commissions, and other expenses paid by the borrower to obtain a mortgage or other loan on the property are not part of the cost of the property. Rather, they are more like capital expenditures that have a life that extends over the term of the loan. If business or income-producing property is involved, these costs may be amortized over the life of the loan and deducted accordingly.[1] Commissions paid to secure renewal of a loan also are subject to amortization.[2]

(For the treatment of the costs of obtaining a loan on a personal residence or other property that is held for personal rather than business or investment purposes, including the treatment of points, see ¶ ¶ 1701.01 and 1701.02.)

The term of the loan as specified in the loan agreement generally governs the period over which the borrower amortizes the costs, even if prepayment in full is allowed at any time. Amortization deductions for loan costs are taken on a straight-line basis. For instance, if a purchaser incurred $5,000 in costs in connection with a loan for the acquisition of business property and the term of the loan were 20 years, the purchaser would deduct $250 each year for 20 years. This would be the case regardless of whether the purchaser used the cash or accrual method of accounting.[3]

There are no rulings or case law actually on point governing the treatment of mortgage acquisition costs if the purchaser actually makes a partial prepayment on a loan for which the purchaser is amortizing costs. Presumably, if the prepayment merely shortens the term remaining on the loan, the purchaser may refigure the amortization deductions to spread any unamortized costs out over the shorter period remaining on the loan.

If prepayment of the unpaid balance of a loan is made in full at any time, any unamortized costs of obtaining the loan are deductible at that time.[4] The same rule

[1] Rev. Rul. 70-360, 1970-2 CB 103; Detroit Consolidated Theatres, Inc., CA-6, 43-1 USTC ¶ 9222, 133 F.2d 200.

[2] S. Spitzer, 23 BTA 776, CCH Dec. 7038.

[3] J.S. Lovejoy, 18 BTA 1179, CCH Dec. 5830.

[4] S&L Building Corp., 19 BTA 788, CCH Dec. 6019, *acq.* X-1 CB 60, *rev'd,* CA-2, 1932 CCH ¶ 9422, 60 F.2d 719, *rev'd,* S. Ct. 3 USTC ¶ 1064, 288 U.S. 406.

applies whenever the property is sold or disposed of before the costs are fully amortized. A taxpayer deducts the balance of unamortized loan costs when the liability for the loan and the property securing the loan are transferred.[5]

In the case of a corporation, any unamortized mortgage or loan costs are deductible in full in the year the corporation distributes assets to its shareholders in liquidation of the corporation.[6]

In the case of an individual, the balance of unamortized loan costs may be deducted on the income tax return for the year of the individual's death. Although the expenses incurred to obtain a loan are in the nature of capital expenditures that normally must be amortized over the term of the loan, the individual's death terminates the use of the loan proceeds, and the IRS has ruled that it is appropriate to deduct the balance of the unamortized loan costs on the deceased individual's final return.[7]

[B] Lender's Costs

Generally, a lender who regularly engages in the business of making loans is entitled to deduct most costs associated with the making of the loans as ordinary and necessary business expenses under Code Sec. 162. The costs falling into this ordinary and necessary category would include most overhead costs. The IRS has ruled, however, that finders' fees and buying commissions paid by banks, building and loan associations, other classes of banks and financial institutions to brokers, title companies, and others for their introduction of an acceptable applicant for a mortgage loan are part of the acquisition cost of the loan, which must be capitalized and amortized over the term of the mortgage loan.[8] Capitalization and amortization also seems to be the rule for the occasional lender, that is, the lender who is not regularly engaged in the business of lending money and who, therefore, has no expenses falling into the ordinary and necessary category.

.02 Buy Downs and Similar Arrangements

In order to move homes out of inventory in times of high interest rates, builders may make it easier for purchasers to meet monthly mortgage payments by buying down or otherwise subsidizing the mortgage payments. For instance, the builder may work out an arrangement with a financial institution under which the institution will charge a lower rate of interest to purchasers of the builder's homes in exchange for up-front payments by the builder. Such an arrangement reduces a purchaser's debt service and makes it easier for a purchaser to buy a home, thus increasing the builder's sales. These payments by the builder should be considered an ordinary and necessary expense in order to sell homes, and, therefore, should be deductible by the builder. Alternatively, the payments might be considered a reduction of the sales price, which would have the same practical effect as the deduction.

---

[5] *See* S&L Building Corp. above; *see also* O.C. Wacker, 40 TCM 1009, CCH Dec. 37,166(M), T.C. Memo. 1980-324.

[6] Longview Hilton Hotel Co., 9 TC 180, CCH Dec. 15,962, *acq*. 1947-2 CB 3; Anover Realty Corp., 33 TC 671, CCH Dec. 24, 2006.

[7] Rev. Rul. 86-67, 1986-1 CB 238.

[8] Rev. Rul. 57-400, 1957-2 CB 520.

In a Letter Ruling,[9] the IRS did rule that a builder who purchased loans from a financial institution which made below market-rate loans to purchasers of the builder's homes was entitled to deduct the excess of the purchase price paid for the loans over the fair market value of the loans. In this case, the builder was regularly engaged in the business of building and selling homes, and the premium paid by the builder for the loans was an expense incurred to permit the builder to sell his products. This ruling supports the idea that costs incurred by a builder to subsidize customers' mortgage payments, whatever the actual arrangement, are deductible ordinary and necessary business expenses.

.03 Payoff of Mortgage

Just as the receipt of the proceeds of a mortgage produces no tax consequences, the repayment of the amount borrowed also has no tax consequences. Sometimes, lenders charge a premium, a "prepayment penalty," for the privilege of retiring a mortgage debt before the end of the loan term. In other cases, the lender may discount the mortgage debt for early payment. In either case, tax consequences flow from the satisfaction of a mortgage debt at other than its face amount.

[A] Prepayment Penalties

A mortgagor who pays a penalty to the mortgagee for the privilege of prepaying a mortgage debt treats the prepayment penalty as additional interest.[10] When Rev. Rul. 57-198 was issued, of course, interest was deductible regardless of the nature of the underlying debt. Today, the interest deduction is subject to various limits based on the nature of the debt. Presumably, a prepayment penalty treated as interest is subject to the same limitations.

In *12701 Shaker Blvd. Co.,*[11] a taxpayer attempted to amortize, as a mortgage cost, a prepayment penalty paid to one lender over the life of a new mortgage obtained from a different lender. Since the penalty was paid to extinguish an existing debt in a transaction that was independent of the new financing and was not part of the cost of the new financing, it had to be deducted in the year in which it was paid.

On the other hand, the purchaser of an apartment building could not deduct currently a subordination fee paid to refinance existing loans on the property purchased. The fee in this case was distinguished from the prepayment penalty in *12701 Shaker Blvd.* because the fee was not paid to extinguish an already existing debt, but was paid to obtain refinancing of the existing first and second mortgages.[12]

The mortgagee who receives a prepayment penalty treats the penalty as additional interest income. The prepayment penalty is an additional charge which the borrower pays for the privilege of using the mortgage money for a shorter

[9] IRS Letter Ruling 8229120, April 23, 1982.

[10] Rev. Rul. 57-198, 1957-1 CB 94.

[11] 36 TC 255, CCH Dec. 24,825, *aff'd,* CA-6, 63-1 USTC ¶ 9194, 312 F.2d 749.

[12] IRS Letter Ruling 8614002, September 30, 1985.

period than originally agreed.[13] This is the rule regardless of whether the prepayment penalty is provided for in the loan agreement or is separately negotiated.[14]

[B] Payment Discounts

The reduction of a purchase-money mortgage for a solvent debtor is treated as a reduction or adjustment in the purchase price, rather than as the discharge of a debt.[15] Accordingly, the debtor realizes no income, and the debtor's basis for the property is reduced to reflect the reduced purchase price. For the seller-lender, the debt reduction also is an adjustment to the sale price. This rule applies only to adjustments to purchase-money debts between original purchasers and sellers. It does not apply to purchase-money debts held or transferred to third parties or to mortgages held by other than the seller of the property, nor does it apply if the purchaser of the property has transferred the property to someone else.

Congress enacted the rule of Code Sec. 108(e)(5) to resolve the problem of whether an adjustment to a purchase-money obligation was an adjustment to the purchase price or income from the discharge of indebtedness. Congress has also enacted special statutory rules governing insolvent and bankrupt debtors and the discharge of qualified real property business indebtedness, and these are considered beginning at ¶ 1201 in Chapter 12, in which issues relating to troubled financings are discussed. Unfortunately, the enactment of Code Sec. 108(e)(5) did not resolve whether a discount applied to a mortgage debt is income or an adjustment to purchase price in other situations. For this, we must rely on a hodgepodge of case law that attempts to distinguish between price reductions and income from the discharge of indebtedness.

Generally, a taxpayer realizes income on the nongratuitous discharge of indebtedness to the extent the debt is canceled or forgiven.[16] In Rev. Rul. 82-202,[17] the IRS ruled that an individual taxpayer realizes discharge of indebtedness income under Code Sec. 61(a)(12) on the discounted prepayment to a lender of all or a portion of mortgage debt. The amount of the discount is includible in income whether the mortgage note is recourse or nonrecourse. This would seem to be the rule whenever a mortgage debt is satisfied (other than in a gift situation) at less than face value and the fair market value of the property is more than the mortgage debt.[18] In Rev. Rul. 91-31,[19] the IRS amplified Rev. Rul. 82-202 so that it applies whether the fair market value of the property is greater or less than the principal balance of the mortgage.

There is, however, a line of cases that holds that when a buyer purchases property subject to a mortgage, or executes a mortgage as security for the unpaid portion of the purchase price or assumes an existing mortgage, and later satisfies the mortgage for less than the face amount of the mortgage but for more than the fair market value of the property at the time the mortgage is satisfied, the buyer

[13] General American Life Insurance Co., 25 TC 1265, CCH Dec. 21,631, *acq*. 1956-2 CB 5.

[14] S.R. Lewis, 65 TC 625, CCH Dec. 33,563.

[15] Code Sec. 108(e)(5).

[16] Code Sec. 61(a)(12).

[17] 1982-2 CB 35.

[18] *See* J.A. Michaels, 87 TC 1412, CCH Dec. 43,555; W. DiLaura, 53 TCM 1077, CCH Dec. 43,973(M), T.C. Memo. 1987-291; J.H. Sutphin, Cls. Ct., 88-1 USTC ¶ 9269, 14 Cls. Ct. 545.

[19] 1991-1 CB 19.

does not recognize income. Rather, in such a case, the reduction in the mortgage debt is treated as an adjustment to the cost basis of the property.[20]

In *Hirsch,* a taxpayer purchased real estate for $10,000 cash and a $19,000 mortgage, which was reduced to $15,000. When the mortgage matured, the property was worth only $8,000, and the mortgagee accepted $8,000 in discharge of the debt. This was held to be an adjustment of the purchase price, and the solvent mortgagor realized no income from the discharge of the mortgage at a discount. In *Fifth Ave.-14th Street Corp.,*[21] however, the court expressed the opinion that the rule applied in *Hirsch* and a series of cases that followed it would be "limited to a case of a purchase money obligation where the vendor-mortgagee, in negotiations directly relating to the purchase price, agrees to a reduction; it has not been applied where the reduction results from an arm's-length transaction relating solely to the debt itself, or from a purchase of the taxpayer's obligations at less than par in the market."

¶ 302 AT-RISK RULES

At one time, an investor could purchase an asset and take deductions for "tax losses" generated by the investment up to the full amount of the cost or other basis, even if the basis included borrowed amounts that the investor might never have to repay. With this as the rule, tax-shelter investments that were marketed primarily for their possible tax benefits proliferated. The main feature of many of these investments was the use of nonrecourse financing to provide investors with a high basis that could support large deductions, deductions that would exceed many times over any amount the investor might actually lose on the investment. (In a nonrecourse loan, the lender can look only to the asset financed by the loan for repayment, and the borrower is not personally liable for repayment of the borrowed amounts.)

Congress responded to the abuses in the use of nonrecourse financing by enacting "at-risk" rules in the Tax Reform Act of 1976. These original at-risk rules were limited in their application to four specific activities. A separate at-risk rule was enacted for partnerships, but real estate was not covered. Later, the rules were expanded to cover most activities, and the special partnership rule was dropped from the tax code; but again, real estate was exempted. In the Tax Reform Act of 1986, Congress finally extended the at-risk rules to real estate investments beginning in 1987, but limited the impact of the change by allowing nonrecourse financing from certain sources ("qualified nonrecourse financing") to be counted as amounts at risk.

Under the at-risk rules,[22] deductions from covered activities or investments are limited to the sum of the following amounts:

1. Money actually invested;
2. The adjusted basis of other property contributed to the activity;

[20] *See,* for example, K. Hirsch, CA-7, 40-2 USTC ¶ 9791, 115 F.2d 656.

[21] CA-2, 45-1 USTC ¶ 9115, 147 F.2d 453.

[22] Code Sec. 465.

3. Amounts borrowed for the activity for which the taxpayer is personally liable for repayment;
4. Amounts borrowed for the activity for which the taxpayer has pledged security property, other than property used in the activity, to the extent of the fair market value of the taxpayer's interest in the pledged property (but not if the pledged property has been financed with nonrecourse debt); and
5. Qualified nonrecourse financing for real estate.

Note that tax basis generally is not affected by the at-risk rules other than for the purpose of determining any available investment credit. Tax basis is still determined under the rules discussed in Chapter 1, but losses (deductions) from an activity cannot exceed the amount considered at risk in the activity. For instance, depreciation (see Chapter 9) is still calculated on tax basis, which may include nonrecourse debt, but the owner of the property cannot deduct losses generated by the depreciation deductions in excess of the amount at risk.

.01 Taxpayers and Activities Subject to the Rules

Taxpayers subject to the at-risk rules are:

1. Individuals;
2. Shareholders in S corporations; and
3. Corporations in which one-half of the stock (measured by value) is owned by five or fewer persons.[23]

There is a special exception for regular C corporations (but not S corporations) that are actively engaged in a trade or business other than a business involving master sound recordings, motion pictures, video tapes, or assets associated with literary, artistic, musical, or similar properties. This exception to the at-risk rules for regular corporations actively engaged in a trade or business, however, does not apply to personal holding companies and certain personal service corporations.[24] Also, regular corporations involved in equipment leasing are subject to the at-risk rules unless 50 percent or more of the corporation's gross receipts are from leasing or selling equipment.[25]

The at-risk rules generally apply to all activities including, since 1987, real estate. Each activity is treated separately under the rules, and a taxpayer cannot combine income from one activity and losses from another activity. There are, however, exceptions that permit the aggregation of income and losses from otherwise separate activities. Activities in connection with a trade or business are combined and treated together for purposes of applying the at-risk rules in the following situations:

1. If the person claiming the loss actively participates in the management of the business.[26]

---

[23] Code Sec. 465(a)(1).

[24] Code Sec. 465(c)(7).

[25] Code Sec. 465(c)(4).

[26] Code Sec. 465(c)(3)(B)(i).

2. If in a partnership or S corporation 65 percent or more of any losses go to partners or shareholders who actively participate in management.[27]

3. If a partnership or S corporation is engaged in equipment leasing, all leasing activities are treated together as a single activity.[28]

Generally, the aggregation rules in 1 and 3, above, apply to the activity of holding real property. Under these rules, if a taxpayer actively participates in the management of several partnerships, each engaged in a real estate business, the real estate activities of the various partnerships may be aggregated and treated as one activity as to that partner for purposes of the at-risk rules. Also, in the case of an affiliated group of corporations which is engaged principally in the real estate business, aggregation of the real estate activities is allowed if the component members of the group are actively engaged in the management of the real estate business (not including real estate financing other than between members of the affiliated group).[29]

.02 Deduction Under the At-Risk Rules

In any tax year, there are two ways in which deductions generated by an activity subject to the at-risk rules may be allowed.[30] First, deductions from an activity may be taken to the extent of income received or accrued from the activity in that taxable year. Income, in this case, includes gain on a sale of assets whether that gain is long-or short-term. Simply put, there are no at-risk limitations on deductions from an activity to the extent that activity is also producing income. In other words, deductions generated by an activity may always be used to offset income generated by that activity.

In addition to deductions equal to income, deductions may be taken in excess of income from the activity to the extent the taxpayer is at risk.

> ***Example 1:*** In 2019, the Taxpayer, who is on the calendar year, invested $50,000 in an activity subject to the at-risk rules by putting up $10,000 cash and obtaining nonrecourse financing for the balance. The Taxpayer's cost basis is $50,000, but the Taxpayer is at risk for only $10,000. At the end of 2019, the Taxpayer has a loss of $15,000 from the activity as a result of deductions generated by the activity.
>
> The $15,000 loss reduces the Taxpayer's basis so that at the end of 2019 the Taxpayer's adjusted basis is $35,000. Of the $15,000 loss, however, the Taxpayer may deduct only $10,000 for 2019, the amount at risk. This deduction reduces the Taxpayer's amount at risk in the activity to zero. The balance of the loss, $5,000, is disallowed, but it may be carried over to be used against future income or if the Taxpayer otherwise increases the amount at risk in the activity.[31]

---

[27] Code Sec. 465(c)(3)(B)(ii).

[28] Code Sec. 465(c)(2)(B)(i).

[29] *See* the Senate Finance Committee Report on the Tax Reform Act of 1986, P.L. 99-514.

[30] Prop. Reg. § 1.465-2(a).

[31] Prop. Reg. § 1.465-2(b).

Assume that at the beginning of 2020, the Taxpayer sells the activity for the amount of the nonrecourse debt, or $40,000. Since the Taxpayer's adjusted basis is $35,000, the sale produces a $5,000 gain. Since this gain is income from the activity, the disallowed loss from 2019 that is carried over to 2020 may be taken as a deduction for 2020 to the extent of this income. Accordingly, the Taxpayer reports the $5,000 as income for 2020, but the Taxpayer also can deduct the $5,000 loss that was previously disallowed.

For additional examples of permitted deductions under the at-risk rules, see Prop. Reg. § 1.465-11.

[A] Order of Deductions

When deductions from an activity exceed the amount at risk, the deductions are applied to the at-risk amounts and taken in the following order:[32]

1. Capital losses
2. All deductions that enter into the computation of Code Sec. 1231 gains and losses
3. Deductions that are not tax preferences under Code Sec. 57, to the extent not deducted under 1 or 2
4. All items of tax preference to the extent not deducted under 1 or 2

Deductions that are disallowed under the at-risk rules retain their identity according to this classification in succeeding years.

Example 2: The Taxpayer, who is on the calendar year, is engaged in an activity subject to the at-risk rules. At the end of 2019, the Taxpayer has $1,000 at risk in the activity. During 2020, the activity generates $3,000 of income and $7,500 in deductions. None of the deductions are capital losses or items subject to Code Sec. 1231, but $5,000 of the deductions are tax preferences. Assuming nothing else occurred in 2020 to affect the Taxpayer's amount at risk, the Taxpayer will be allowed $4,000 of deductions, and $3,500 will be disallowed by the at-risk rules. The $4,000 of allowed deductions will consist of the entire $2,500 of deductions that are not tax preferences and $1,500 of the $5,000 of tax preferences. The disallowed deductions in the amount of $3,500 will be carried over and will retain their classification as tax preferences for purposes of applying them against future income from the activity or increases in the Taxpayer's amount at risk in the activity.

[B] Recapture of Prior Deductions

Prior loss deductions that were allowed against amounts at risk in an activity must be recaptured and reported as income if an amount formerly at risk in the activity is converted to a nonrecourse liability or otherwise is no longer at risk.[33]

Example 3: The Taxpayer invested $100,000 in an activity in the form of $10,000 cash and $90,000 obtained through a recourse loan. The Taxpayer's original amount at risk in this activity, therefore, was $100,000. After taking

[32] Prop. Reg. § 1.465-38.

[33] Code Sec. 465(e).

$50,000 in loss deductions generated by this activity, the $90,000 recourse loan is converted to a nonrecourse loan. The Taxpayer now must report $40,000 of income, which represents a recapture of prior loss deductions to the extent the Taxpayer is no longer at risk.

.03 Determining Amount at Risk

Amounts at risk in an activity include the amount of money invested, the adjusted basis of any property contributed to the activity, and borrowed amounts for which the borrower is personally liable for repayment or has pledged property, other than property in the activity, to secure payment. Amounts at risk in the case of a real estate activity also include qualified nonrecourse financing, which is separately discussed below. Amounts at risk do not include any amount protected against loss by nonrecourse financing (other than qualified nonrecourse financing for real estate), guarantees, stop-loss arrangements, or any other similar arrangement.[34]

The amount at risk in an activity for subsequent years is reduced by any allowable loss for the current year.[35]

[A] Borrowed Amounts

Borrowed money is not included in the amount at risk if the money is borrowed from a person who has an interest in the activity other than as a creditor or who is related to a person who has an interest in the activity other than as a creditor.[36] Related persons include brothers and sisters, spouses, ancestors, and lineal descendants; shareholders and ten percent-owned corporations; partners and 10 percent-owned partnerships; beneficiaries and fiduciaries of a trust; and fiduciaries and grantors of a trust.

A special provision in Code Sec. 465(b)(2) prevents the use of circular arrangements to avoid the at-risk rules. For instance, if a taxpayer borrows money secured by livestock to buy real estate and borrows money secured by the real estate to pay for the livestock, none of the borrowed amounts would be considered at risk in either the livestock activity or the real estate activity.

Discounted Loans

In a case involving a recourse note that was not due for 10 years and for which the taxpayers were not liable for the stated interest on the note, the IRS asserted that the amount at risk should be discounted to reflect the time-value of money and that there was no personal liability for the interest. The Tax Court, however, ruled that the note did not have to be discounted to its value at the time of execution for purposes of determining the borrowed amount under the at-risk rules. The Court held that the tax code does not expressly or implicitly authorize a present value calculation in determining the borrowed amount.[37]

[34] Code Sec. 465(b)(4). *See also* Rev. Rul. 85-113, 1985-1 CB 184 (purported recourse note ruled nonrecourse because borrower could assign percentage of mine production in satisfaction of debt), and Rev. Rul. 80-72, 1980-1 CB 109 (option amounted to "other similar arrangement" to nonrecourse financing).

[35] Code Sec. 465(b)(5).

[36] Code Sec. 465(b)(3).

[37] D.B. Follender, 89 TC 943, CCH Dec. 44,305, *acq.* 1989-1 CB 1.

Guaranteed Loans

If a taxpayer guarantees repayment of an amount borrowed by another person (the primary obligor) for use in an activity, the guarantee does not increase the taxpayer's amount at risk.[38] If the taxpayer repays to the creditor the amount borrowed by the primary obligor, the taxpayer's amount at risk is increased when the taxpayer has no remaining legal rights against the primary obligor.

In *L.A. Bjerke*,[39] a limited partner was not entitled to deduct partnership losses based on debts that the partner guaranteed. The partnership debts that the partner guaranteed were not at risk because the partner could recover from the partnership as the primary obligor on the debt any guaranteed amounts that the partner might be compelled to pay.[40]

A limited partner was held to be at risk for the allocable share of the partnership's recourse indebtedness when the limited partner entered into legally enforceable contracts making the partner personally and ultimately liable for the share of the partnership's debt.[41] Since there was no primary obligor against whom the limited partner could recover amounts paid, the court concluded that the partner was not a mere guarantor of the share of the partnership's recourse debt but was ultimately liable for it.[42]

[B] Avoidance of At-Risk Rules

Knowing that taxpayers would attempt to get around the at-risk rules whenever possible, the IRS has put forth some proposed regulations that are designed to block such attempts. These regulations are directed against arrangements that are outside of normal commercial practices or that are designed to convert recourse debt to nonrecourse debt.

Beyond Normal Commercial Practice

The proposed at-risk regulations state that if a taxpayer engages in conduct that is not within "normal commercial practice" or has the effect of avoiding the at-risk rules, the amount at risk may be adjusted to reflect more accurately the amount that is actually at risk.[43] For instance, if an event increases the amount at risk near the close of the taxable year and has the effect of increasing the amount of losses that can be deducted, and a corresponding event decreases the amount at risk after year-end, these amounts will be disregarded unless there is a valid business reason for the arrangement and the arrangement is not a device to avoid the at-risk rules.

The circumstances the IRS considers in deciding whether to adjust the amount at risk include:

1. The length of time between an increase and decrease in the amount at risk;
2. The nature of the activity and deviations from normal business practice in the conduct of the activity;

[38] Prop. Reg. § 1.465-6(d).

[39] DC N.D., 87-2 USTC ¶ 9576, 677 F. Supp. 633.

[40] *See also* E.H. Allen, 55 TCM 641, CCH Dec. 44,718(M), T.C. Memo. 1988-166.

[41] T.S. Ockles, 54 TCM 785, CCH Dec. 44,245(M), T.C. Memo. 1987-507.

[42] IRS Letter Ruling 8749009, August 21, 1987.

[43] Prop. Reg. § 1.465-4(a).

3. The use of those amounts that increased the amount at risk toward the close of the tax year;
4. Contractual arrangements between parties to the activity; and
5. The occurrence of unanticipated events which make a decrease in the amount at risk necessary.

Recourse Liabilities Becoming Nonrecourse

If liabilities are recourse for a period of time and then later become nonrecourse, the amount of liabilities during the period they are recourse will be considered at risk only if the arrangement is primarily business motivated and consistent with the normal commercial practice of financing the activity for which the money is borrowed.[44]

In Rev. Rul. 82-225,[45] the IRS ruled that an investor was not at risk for a recourse note that could be converted into a nonrecourse note because the criteria for conversion did not require that the underlying property be of sufficient value to cover the amount of the note. Similarly, in *J. Porreca*,[46] a taxpayer that had a unilateral right to convert recourse notes to nonrecourse notes was not at risk because the right to convert was not tied to any substantial economic event.

A taxpayer was considered at risk, however, for a recourse note that was convertible to a nonrecourse note because substantial amounts were due and paid prior to the conversion of the note. The note could only be converted if payments were not in arrears. Also, the note provided no right to make up delinquencies, and payment was not contingent on the proceeds from the underlying activity. The at-risk amount, however, was limited to the extent of the payments made prior to conversion.[47]

[C] Computation of At-Risk Amount

To determine the amount at risk in an activity for a particular tax year, one begins with the at-risk amount at the end of the previous year and adjusts that amount for events occurring during the current year. The following summarizes the events that increase or decrease the amount at risk in an activity.

Increase Amount At Risk for:

- Money contributed
- Income from activity in excess of deductions
- Property contributed, measured by its adjusted basis (even if property is encumbered, but only to the extent that the taxpayer is personally liable)
- Loans for which the taxpayer is personally liable
- Loans secured by property not in the activity, limited to the fair market value of the property (but a later contribution of the property to the activity will reduce at-risk amount)
- Loans that are qualified nonrecourse financing for real estate

---

[44] Prop. Reg. § 1.465-5.

[45] 1982-2 CB 100.

[46] 86 TC 821, CCH Dec. 43,022.

[47] L. Lansburgh, 53 TCM 454, CCH Dec. 43,803(M), T.C. Memo. 1987-164; 54 TCM 691, CCH Dec. 44,227(M), T.C. Memo. 1987-491.

Decrease Amount At Risk for:

- Money withdrawn
- Loss allowed
- Property withdrawn or distributed from the activity, measured by adjusted basis of the property in the taxpayer's hands less liabilities to which the property is subject and for which the taxpayer is not personally liable

The following example illustrating the application of the at-risk rules and the provisions of the proposed at-risk regulations is drawn from Prop. Reg. § 1.465-41.

Example 4: On January 1, 2019, A and B form an equal partnership called the AB partnership. A and B each contribute $5,000 to the partnership on January 1. On August 1, 2019, AB borrows $6,000 from a bank and A and B assume personal liability. On December 31, 2019, the bank loan is reduced to $4,500. There is no income or loss for 2019. A's at-risk amount is calculated as follows:

At risk January 1, 2019	$0
Plus: Contributions	5,000
Share of loan for which A has personal liability	3,000
	$8,000
Less: Share of loan reduction	750
At risk December 31, 2019	$7,250

On February 1, 2020, AB borrows $20,000 on a nonrecourse basis with the loan secured by equipment. On May 1, 2020, the bank loan is reduced to $4,000. On August 1, 2020, the nonrecourse loan is reduced to $19,000. On October 1, 2020, AB distributes $2,000 to each of its partners. On December 1, 2020, the bank loan is reduced to $2,500. On December 31, 2020, A and B are each allocated their $3,000 share of AB income for 2020. A's at-risk amount for 2020 is calculated as follows:

At risk January 1, 2020	$7,250
Plus: Income from activity	3,000
	$10,250
Less: Share in bank loan reductions	1,000
	$9,250
Less: Distribution	2,000
At risk December 31, 2020	$7,250

Note that since the loans were repaid with money in the activity, the repayment to the bank reduced the amount at risk, and the repayment on the nonrecourse debt did not increase the amount at risk.

On March 1, 2021, A and B each contribute $1,000 to the partnership. On September 1, 2021, A and B each contribute $1,500. AB reduces the bank loan to zero by paying $2,500. AB pays $500 on the nonrecourse loan. On December 31, 2021, A and B have $10,500 allocated to each of them as their shares of AB losses. A's at-risk amount for 2021 is calculated as follows:

At risk January 1, 2021	$7,250
Plus: Contributions	2,500
	$9,750
Less: Share of bank loan reduction	1,250
At risk December 31, 2021	$8,500

Since A's loss allocation for 2021 is $10,500, but the at-risk amount is $8,500, A's loss deduction is limited. A deducts $8,500 of the loss for 2021, and this reduces the at-risk amount as of December 31, 2021 to zero. The $2,000 loss that is not allowed is treated as a loss in 2022.

During 2022, A and B each contribute $1,000 to the AB partnership. On December 31, 2022, A and B are each allocated $500 of income. A's at-risk amount for 2022 is calculated as follows:

At risk January 1, 2022	$8,500
Less: Loss allowed for 2021	8,500
	$0
Plus: Contribution	1,000
At risk December 31, 2022	$1,000

Of the $2,000 loss not allowed in 2021, $500 is deductible due to 2022 income and $1,000 is deductible because A is at risk for 2022 to this extent. The remaining $500 of the loss is not deductible in 2022 but it is carried over and treated as a loss for the following year. A begins 2023 with an at-risk amount of zero.

.04 Qualified Nonrecourse Financing

One reason real estate was exempted from the at-risk rules until 1987 was that it was generally thought that real estate investments were not subject to the abusive uses of nonrecourse financing to the same extent as other investments. Real estate has value that generally does not depreciate rapidly (in fact, it usually appreciates) and, therefore, investors have an incentive to protect their ownership of real estate even when financed on a nonrecourse basis. Abuse in real estate investments generally occurred when the nonrecourse financing was provided by the seller or promoter of the investment and the purchase price was set far above the actual fair market value of the property. With this in mind, when Congress extended the at-risk rules to real estate, it limited their application to truly abusive situations. Accordingly, qualified nonrecourse financing is treated as at risk under the rules.[48]

Qualified nonrecourse financing that is considered at risk must meet four requirements:

1. The borrowing must be for the activity of holding real property. Holding real property includes the holding of personal property and the provision of services that are incidental to the use of real property.
2. The borrowing must be from a qualified person or from any federal, state or local government or government instrumentality, or the loan must be guaranteed by federal, state or local government. Qualified persons include any person actively and regularly engaged in the business of lending money such as a bank, savings and loan, credit union, insurance company, or pension trust. Qualified persons do not include any person from which the taxpayer acquires the property or any person who receives a fee from the taxpayer's investment in the property or persons related to such persons. (Seller financing or promoter financing can never be qualified nonrecourse financing.)
3. No person may be personally liable for the financing, except as provided in regulations.
4. The borrowing may not be convertible debt.[49]

[A] Financing from Related Person

Qualified nonrecourse financing may be obtained from a related person, but, if it is, the terms of the borrowing must be commercially reasonable and on substantially the same terms as loans involving unrelated persons.

According to the Conference Committee Report on the Tax Reform Act of 1986, the terms of nonrecourse financing are commercially reasonable if the financing is a written unconditional promise to pay on demand or on a specified date or dates a sum or sums certain in money, and the interest rate is a reasonable market rate of interest, taking into account the maturity of the obligation.

Generally, an interest rate is not considered commercially reasonable if it is significantly below the market rate on comparable loans by qualified persons who are not related to the borrowers. Similarly, an interest rate that significantly exceeds the market rate on comparable loans by unrelated qualified persons is not considered commercially reasonable. Also, an interest rate that is contingent is not commercially reasonable, but floating rates keyed to a market index are permitted.

The terms of financing are not considered commercially reasonable if the term of the loan exceeds the useful life of the property. Also, if the right to foreclose or collect is limited, except to the extent provided under state law, the terms of the loan are not commercially reasonable. The intent of Congress, generally, is to limit qualified nonrecourse financing to financing that carries arm's-length terms.

[48] Code Sec. 465(b)(6).

[49] Prop. Reg. § 1.465-27.

[B] Transfer of Property

A taxpayer who acquires property subject to a nonrecourse debt that constituted qualified nonrecourse financing in the hands of the original borrower also may treat the debt as qualified nonrecourse financing, provided all the requirements are met. The same rule applies to subsequent transfers of the property taken subject to the debt, and to the admission of new partners to a partnership and the sale or exchange of a partnership interest, so long as the debt constitutes qualified nonrecourse financing as to each transferee or new partner.

¶ 303 INTEREST

Interest is compensation for the use or forbearance of money. It is the cost paid by the owner of real estate for the use of another's money to finance the acquisition. In the case of the supplier of the money, it is the "rent" received while another makes use of the money.

At one time, it may have been possible to say simply that interest paid is deductible and interest received is income when the acquisition of real estate is financed through a mortgage or other lending arrangement. Such is not the case today. Massive changes in the tax code in recent years have created traps and pitfalls that must be carefully negotiated when structuring a loan transaction. While most of the complications focus on interest as a deductible expense, certain provisions affect both the borrower and the lender, either as to the amount or timing of interest income and expense, or both. These provisions include the rules on interest-free and below-market rate loans and the original issue discount and imputed interest rules for deferred payment sales.

.01 Interest Income

Interest received by a mortgage lender is taxable income.[50] Interest income includes interest on a promissory note, a mortgage, and the interest portion of a condemnation award. Interest income also includes usurious interest, unless the usurious interest is automatically converted to principal payments under state law.[51] Prepayment penalties or premiums charged for the prepayment of a mortgage also are taxable as interest income to the recipient.[52]

Interest income, generally, is reported in the year it is received by a cash basis taxpayer and in the year it is earned by an accrual basis taxpayer.[53] An accrual basis taxpayer who receives an actual prepayment of interest, however, generally must report the interest income when received.[54] See, for example, *J.A. Mele*,[55] in which interest prepaid for five years on a promissory note was held accruable when received and could not be prorated over the five-year period; and *Bjornsen Investment Corp.*,[56] in which prepaid interest received by an accrual basis taxpayer in connection with a 20-year real estate contract was held taxable in full at time of receipt.

[50] Code Sec. 61.

[51] Reg. § 1.61-7.

[52] General American Life Insurance Co., 25 TC 1265, CCH Dec. 21,631, *acq.* 1956-2 CB 5.

[53] Code Sec. 451.

[54] Rev. Rul. 70-540, 1970-2 CB 101.

[55] 61 TC 358, CCH Dec. 32,260, *acq.* 1975-1 CB 2.

[56] DC Iowa, 81-1 USTC ¶ 9258.

Mortgage discount points charged to the seller by a mortgagee and deducted from the proceeds of the mortgage loan before they are paid to the seller, however, are not included in the mortgagee's income for the year the mortgage is originated.[57] The discount is included in income ratably as payments are received from the buyer.[58]

Keep in mind that the general rule regarding the amount and timing of interest income may be affected by the original issue discount and imputed interest rules for deferred payment sales which are discussed below.

.02 Interest Deduction

Code Sec. 163(a) states the general rule that a deduction is allowed for "all interest paid or accrued within the taxable year on indebtedness." Unfortunately, a plethora of other code provisions makes this general rule almost meaningless by limiting or denying completely deductions for interest relating to certain types of indebtedness. The provisions likely to apply to real estate financing include:

1. The deduction for interest on investment indebtedness is limited by Code Sec. 163(d) (see ¶ 303.02[B]).
2. Interest on personal debts is disallowed by Code Sec. 163(h), other than certain home mortgage debt (see ¶ 1701.01[C]).
3. Interest incurred during the construction of real estate generally must be capitalized under Code Sec. 263A (see ¶ 103.01).
4. Interest that qualifies as carrying charges on certain real estate may be capitalized under Code Sec. 266 (see ¶ 103.03).
5. An accrual basis taxpayer may deduct interest paid to a related cash basis taxpayer only when actually paid.[59]
6. Prepaid interest generally must be capitalized and deducted ratably over the term of the loan under Code Sec. 461(g) (see ¶ 303.02[A]).
7. Deductible interest may be limited under the at-risk rules of Code Sec. 465 (see ¶ 302).
8. Deductible interest may be limited under the passive loss limitations of Code Sec. 469 (see ¶ 1104.01[B]).
9. For tax years beginning after 2017, the deduction of interest on a debt incurred in a trade or business may be limited by Code Sec. 163(j) (see ¶ 303.02[D]).

To be deductible, generally, interest must be paid on the indebtedness of the taxpayer. In the case of interest paid by the legal or equitable owner on a mortgage on real property, the interest is deductible even if the owner is not directly liable on the bond or note secured by the mortgage.[60] Also, annual or periodic payments made under a redeemable ground rent are treated as interest payments under the tax code.[61] For instance, payments made under an agreement subject to the

[57] Rev. Rul. 65-95, 1965-1 CB 208.

[58] IRS Letter Ruling 7820003, January 20, 1978.

[59] Code Sec. 267.

[60] Reg. § 1.163-1(b).

[61] Code Sec. 163(c).

residential ground rent laws of Virginia are treated as interest.[62] Payments on nonredeemable ground rents, however, are not treated as interest, although the payments may be deductible if they qualify as a business or investment expense.

Subject to the special rules listed above, the general rule is that a cash basis taxpayer deducts interest when actually paid, and an accrual basis taxpayer deducts interest as it accrues ratably over the term or period of the debt.[63] For an accrual basis taxpayer, it is not material when actual payment occurs.[64] An accrual basis taxpayer, however, is placed on the cash method of accounting as to interest paid to a related cash basis person.[65] This rule prevents a related payor from taking advantage of an interest deduction before the interest is includible in the income of the recipient. The relationships covered by this rule are listed in Code Sec. 267(b) and include family members, controlled corporations, and various fiduciary relationships.

Cash basis taxpayers generally are allowed interest deductions only for interest actually paid in cash or its equivalent. Personal notes given to a creditor for interest due are not considered cash or its equivalent.[66] The IRS has announced that it will disallow any deduction claimed for interest paid on a loan if the payment is made with money obtained from the original creditor through a second loan, an advance, or any other arrangement that is similar to a loan.[67] A deduction is allowed, however, if the taxpayer borrows money from a third party and uses that money to pay interest which is owed to the original lender.

[A] Prepaid Interest

An accrual basis taxpayer can deduct prepaid interest only in the period in which the use of money occurs and only to the extent of the interest cost of using the borrowed funds during that period. It is not material when actual payment occurs, and the existence of a fixed liability to make a prepayment of interest is not sufficient to justify a deduction.[68] Code Sec. 461(g) makes cash basis taxpayers subject to essentially the same rule.

Under Code Sec. 461(g), a cash basis taxpayer who pays interest that is properly allocable to a later tax year must charge that interest to a capital account and treat it as paid in the periods in which the interest represents a charge for the use or forbearance of borrowed money during each year. Interest on a "wraparound mortgage" is subject to this prepaid interest rule, although the IRS may recharacterize part or all of a borrower's "interest" payment on a wraparound mortgage as, in substance, an additional down payment of principal or as a nondeductible deposit of interest with a third party.[69]

Once prepaid interest is allocated over the term of the loan, then it becomes subject to the various other provisions that restrict or limit the deduction for interest.

[62] Rev. Rul. 75-281, 1975-2 CB 65.

[63] Code Sec. 446; Reg. § 1.446-1(c).

[64] Rev. Rul. 68-643, 1968-2 CB 76.

[65] Code Sec. 267.

[66] Rev. Rul. 70-647, 1970-2 CB 38.

[67] IRS News Release 83-93, July 6, 1983; *see also* W.M. Roberts, 53 TCM 787, CCH Dec. 43,900(M), T.C. Memo. 1987-235.

[68] Rev. Rul. 68-643, 1968-2 CB 76.

[69] Rev. Rul. 75-99, 1975-1 CB 197.

Points are additional interest charges that are usually paid when a loan is closed and that generally are imposed by the lender in lieu of a higher interest rate. If points are paid as compensation for the use of borrowed money, and are therefore considered interest, rather than as payment for the lender's services, the points are prepaid interest and must be treated as paid over the term of the loan. Points paid in refinancing a mortgage are subject to this rule,[70] but an exception applies to points or prepaid interest to the extent the underlying debt is incurred for the purchase or improvement of the taxpayer's principal residence (see ¶ 1701.02).[71]

[B] Investment Interest

For noncorporate taxpayers, the deduction of "investment interest" is limited by Code Sec. 163(d). Generally, a noncorporate taxpayer may deduct investment interest only to the extent of net investment income. Any investment interest disallowed as a deduction under this provision may be carried over and deducted against investment income realized in future years.

Investment interest includes interest on debt attributable to property that produces interest income, dividends, annuities, or royalties not derived in the ordinary course of a trade or business. Investment interest also includes interest on debt allocable to oil and gas activities that are not passive activities and that constitute a trade or business. Also, interest expense allocable to portfolio income under the passive loss rules (see ¶ 1104.01[A]) and interest allocable to personal property used in a short sale is investment interest.

Investment interest does not include qualified residence interest (see ¶ 1701.01) or interest that is taken into account under the passive loss rules explained at ¶ 1101. Also, interest on debt allocable to rental real estate in which the taxpayer actively participates within the meaning of the passive loss rules (see ¶ 1103.06) is not considered investment interest.

Investment income is the income from property held for investment and includes capital gain derived from the sale of investment property. It includes interest income, annuities, and royalties not derived in the ordinary course of business, and income from activities that are trades or businesses in which the taxpayer does not materially participate but that are not passive activities under the passive loss rules. Investment income also generally includes dividends. However, a dividend that is otherwise eligible to be taxed at the same rate as capital gain is treated as investment income for purposes of determining the amount of deductible investment interest only if the individual elects to treat the dividend as not eligible for the reduced tax rate.

Investment income must be reduced by investment expenses to determine the ceiling amount for the deduction of investment interest. Investment expenses are any expenses other than interest that are deductible in connection with the production of investment income. Deductible expenses are those allowed after the application of the two percent of adjusted gross income floor for the deduction of

[70] Rev. Rul. 87-22, 1987-1 CB 146.

[71] Code Sec. 461(g)(2).

miscellaneous expenses by individual taxpayers. In computing the amount of investment expenses that exceed the two percent floor, non-investment expenses are disallowed before the disallowance of any investment expenses.

Investment income and expenses do not include any items taken into account under the passive loss rules.[72] (See Chapter 11 for a detailed discussion of the passive loss rules.)

Rental Real Estate

As noted above, interest on debt allocable to rental real estate in which the taxpayer actively participates within the meaning of the passive loss rules is not considered investment interest. Rental activities in which the taxpayer does not actively participate generally are considered passive activities under the passive loss rules. Therefore, income from such rental activities and interest on debt attributable to such activities would be covered by the passive loss rules and would not enter into the computation of the investment interest limitation.

Prior to 1987, interest on debt attributable to real property subject to a net lease was investment interest and income produced by net lease property was investment income. Now, of course, real property subject to a net lease produces income and loss subject to the passive loss rules, and not the investment interest limitation.

Vacant Land

Vacant land presents special problems in connection with the investment interest limitation. If land is acquired for investment, then interest on mortgages on that land would be investment interest deductible only to the extent of investment income.

Land, however, may be acquired for a number of reasons. A taxpayer may take the position that vacant land is acquired and held as part of a trade or business, that is, that the taxpayer is a dealer in property. In this case, interest attributable to debt on the land would not be subject to the investment interest limitation, but the sale of land would produce ordinary income, not capital gain.

Vacant land also may be acquired in order to construct rental real estate. If the rental real estate is a passive activity, then the interest on the land presumably would be governed by the passive loss rules rather than the investment interest limitation.

[C] Tracing Debt Proceeds

The number of limitations and restrictions on the deduction of interest requires that some way be found to classify interest under the various categories—investment interest subject to the Code Sec. 163(d) limitation, passive activity interest subject to the Code Sec. 469 passive loss rules, personal interest (other than qualified personal residence interest) disallowed under Code Sec. 163(h), and interest relating to a trade or business that may be limited by Code Sec. 163(j).

[72] Code Sec. 163(d)(4)(D).

In general, the IRS has prescribed regulations[73] that call for interest expense on a debt to be allocated in the same manner as the debt to which the interest relates is allocated. Debt is allocated by tracing disbursements of debt proceeds to specific expenditures.[74] In other words, debt proceeds and related interest expense are allocated based entirely on the use of the proceeds. The allocation is not affected by the type of property (other than in the case of qualified residence interest) that is used to secure the debt.[75]

> ***Example 5:*** The Taxpayer pledges corporate stock held for investment to secure a loan and uses the proceeds to purchase an automobile for personal use. Interest expense accruing on the debt is personal interest even though the debt is secured by investment property. If the automobile were used in the Taxpayer's trade or business, the interest would be business interest.

The amount of interest expense that accrues during any period is determined by taking into account relevant loan provisions and any applicable Internal Revenue Code provision that affects the accrual of interest expense, such as the original issue discount and imputed interest rules.[76]

Loan Proceeds Not Paid to Borrower

If a lender disburses debt proceeds to a person other than the borrower for the sale or use of property, for services, or for any other purposes, the debt is treated as if the borrower used the debt proceeds for the property, services, or other purpose.[77] The same tracing rule applies if a taxpayer incurs or assumes a debt for the sale or use of property, for services, or for any other purpose, or takes property subject to a debt, and no debt proceeds are disbursed to the taxpayer.

Loan Proceeds Received in Cash

Generally, any debt proceeds a taxpayer (other than a corporation) receives in cash (including withdrawal of cash from an account) are treated as used to make personal expenditures.[78] The taxpayer, however, may treat any cash expenditure made within 15 days after receiving the cash as made from the debt proceeds and may treat the expenditure as made on the date the cash was received.[79]

> ***Example 6:*** The Taxpayer incurs a $1,000 debt on August 4 and receives the proceeds in cash. The Taxpayer deposits $1,500 cash in an account on August 15 and on August 27 writes a check on the account for an investment expenditure. The Taxpayer also engages in many other cash transactions throughout the month of August, and numerous deposits of borrowed and unborrowed amounts and expenditures occur through the account. Despite these other transactions, the Taxpayer may treat $1,000 of the deposit on August 15 as an expenditure made from the debt proceeds received on August 4. Also, the Taxpayer may treat the investment expenditure on August 27 as made from the $1,000 debt proceeds treated as deposited in the account.

[73] Temp. Reg. § 1.163-8T.

[74] Temp. Reg. § 1.163-8T(a)(3).

[75] Temp. Reg. § 1.163-8T(c)(1).

[76] Temp. Reg. § 1.163-8T(c)(2)(C).

[77] Temp. Reg. § 1.163-8T(c)(3).

[78] Temp. Reg. § 1.163-8T(c)(5)(ii).

[79] Temp. Reg. § 1.163-8T(c)(5)(i).

Loan Proceeds Deposited in an Account

The deposit of debt proceeds in an account is an investment expenditure, and an amount held in an account (whether or not interest bearing) is considered property held for investment. The debt must be reallocated when the proceeds are withdrawn and used to make another expenditure.[80]

> ***Example 7:*** The Taxpayer borrows $100,000 on January 1 and immediately uses the proceeds to open a noninterest-bearing checking account. No other deposits are made to the account and none of the loan is repaid during the year. On April 1, the Taxpayer uses $20,000 from the account to make a passive activity expenditure. On September 1, the Taxpayer uses an additional $40,000 for personal expenditures.
>
> From January 1 through March 31, the entire $100,000 debt is allocated to an investment expenditure and the interest on the debt is investment interest. From April 1 through August 31, $20,000 of the debt is allocated to the passive activity, and $80,000 is allocated to the investment expenditure. Interest for this period is investment interest to the extent attributable to the $80,000 portion of the debt and interest subject to the passive loss rules to the extent attributable to the $20,000 portion of the debt. From September 1 through December 31, $40,000 of the debt is allocated to personal expenditures, $20,000 to the passive activity, and $40,000 to the investment expenditure. Interest on the debt is allocated accordingly.

When an account contains more than the proceeds of one loan and various deposits are made to the same account, an ordering rule is provided by Temp. Reg. § 1.163-8T(c)(4)(ii). Generally, debt proceeds deposited in an account are treated as expended before (1) any unborrowed amounts held in the account at the time the debt proceeds are deposited, and (2) any amounts (borrowed or unborrowed) that are deposited in the account after the debt proceeds are deposited.

> ***Example 8:*** The Taxpayer opens a checking account on January 10 and deposits $500 of proceeds of debt A and $1,000 of unborrowed funds. The following summarizes the transactions through the account during the year:
>
> January 10—$500 Debt A and $1,000 unborrowed funds deposited
>
> January 11—$500 proceeds of Debt B deposited
>
> February 17—$800 personal expenditure
>
> February 26—$700 passive activity expenditure
>
> June 21—$1,000 proceeds of Debt C deposited
>
> November 24—$800 investment expenditure
>
> December 20—$600 personal expenditure
>
> The $800 personal expenditure is treated as made from the $500 proceeds of Debt A and $300 of the proceeds of Debt B. The $700 passive activity expenditure is treated as made from the remaining $200 proceeds of Debt B

[80] Temp. Reg. § 1.163-8T(c)(4)(i).

and $500 of unborrowed funds. The $800 investment expenditure is treated as made entirely from the proceeds of Debt C. The $600 personal expenditure is treated as made from the remaining $200 proceeds of Debt C and $400 of unborrowed funds. Debt is allocated to an investment expenditure for periods during which debt proceeds are held in the account.

Despite the general ordering rules, a taxpayer may treat any expenditure made from an account within 15 days after debt proceeds are deposited as made from the debt proceeds.[81]

Example 9: The Taxpayer incurs a $1,000 debt on June 5 and immediately deposits the proceeds in an account (Account A). On June 17, the Taxpayer transfers $2,000 from Account A to another account (Account B). On June 30, the Taxpayer writes a $1,500 check on Account B for an investment expenditure. In addition, numerous deposits of borrowed and unborrowed amounts and expenditures occur through both accounts throughout the month of June.

The Taxpayer may treat $1,000 of the deposit to Account B on June 17 as an expenditure from the debt proceeds deposited in Account A on June 5. Also, the Taxpayer may treat $1,000 of the investment expenditure on June 30 as made from the debt proceeds treated as deposited in Account B on June 17.

If the proceeds of two or more debts are deposited in an account simultaneously, the proceeds are treated as deposited in the order in which the debts were incurred. If two or more debts are incurred simultaneously, the debts may be treated as incurred in any order the taxpayer selects.[82]

Debt Repayments

If debt is allocated to more than one expenditure when a portion of the debt is repaid, the debt is treated as repaid in the following order:

1. Amounts allocated to personal expenditures;
2. Amounts allocated to investment expenditures and passive activity expenditures other than rental real estate in which the taxpayer actively participates;
3. Amounts allocated to passive activity expenditures for rental real estate in which the taxpayer actively participates;
4. Amounts allocated to former passive activity expenditures; and
5. Amounts allocated to trade or business expenditures and to certain low-income housing projects.[83]

In the case of lines of credit or similar arrangements that permit borrowing periodically under a single loan agreement, all borrowings on which interest accrues at the same fixed or variable rate are treated as a single debt. Also, borrowings or portions of borrowings on which interest accrues at different fixed or

[81] Temp. Reg. § 1.163-8T(c)(4)(iii)(B).

[82] Temp. Reg. § 1.163-8T(c)(4)(v).

[83] Temp. Reg. § 1.163-8T(d)(1).

variable rates are treated as different debts, and the debts are treated as repaid in the order in which the borrowings are treated as repaid under the loan agreement.[84]

Debt Refinancing

To the extent the proceeds of any debt (the replacement debt) are used to repay any portion of a debt, the replacement debt is allocated to the expenditures to which the repaid debt was allocated. The amount of the replacement debt allocated is equal to the amount of debt allocated to the expenditures which was repaid with the proceeds of the replacement debt. If the replacement debt exceeds the repaid debt, the balance of the replacement debt is allocated to expenditures under the other tracing rules.[85]

Reallocation of Debt

Debt allocated to an expenditure relating to an asset is reallocated to another expenditure on the earlier of:

1. The date on which proceeds from a disposition of the asset are used for another expenditure, but not in excess of the proceeds from the disposition of the asset; or
2. The date on which the character of the first expenditure changes because of a change in the use of the asset, but not in excess of the fair market value of the asset on the date of change.[86]

If the proceeds from the disposition of an asset exceed the amount of debt reallocated because of the disposition, or two or more debts are reallocated because of the disposition of the asset, the proceeds of the disposition are treated as an account to which the rules discussed above for loan proceeds deposited to an account apply.[87]

> ***Example 10:*** On January 1, the Taxpayer sells an asset for $25,000. Just prior to the sale, the amount of debt allocated to the asset was $15,000. The proceeds of the disposition are treated as an account consisting of $15,000 of debt proceeds and $10,000 of unborrowed funds. If the Taxpayer immediately makes a $10,000 personal expenditure from the proceeds and within 15 days deposits the remaining proceeds in a bank account, the Taxpayer may treat the entire $15,000 deposited in the bank account as proceeds of a debt.

[D] Business Interest

For tax years beginning after 2017, the deduction of interest paid or accrued on a debt incurred in a trade or business is limited regardless of the form in which the business is organized.[88] An exception to the limitation is provided for a small business with average gross receipts of $25 million or less. Any interest not deductible generally may be carried forward indefinitely to succeeding tax years, subject to restrictions for partnerships and S corporations. There is also an election out for real property businesses.

---

[84] Temp. Reg. § 1.163-8T(d)(3).

[85] Temp. Reg. § 1.163-8T(e)(1).

[86] Temp. Reg. § 1.163-8T(j)(1).

[87] Temp. Reg. § 1.163-8T(j)(2).

[88] Code Sec. 163(j).

Under the limitation, deductible business interest for any taxpayer is limited in any tax year to the sum of:

1. Business interest income for the tax year;
2. 30 percent of the taxpayer's adjusted taxable income, including increases in adjusted taxable income as a result of a distributive share in a partnership or S corporation but not below zero; and
3. Floor plan financing interest (floor plan financing is used by car dealers to finance their inventory).[89]

The rule on business interest effectively limits the deduction of *net* interest expenses to 30 percent of the taxpayer's adjusted taxable income. The deduction for business interest and floor plan financing interest is permitted to the full extent of business interest income and floor plan financing interest.

Business interest is any interest paid or accrued on debt properly allocable to a trade or business. It does not include investment interest.[90] Business interest income is the amount of interest includible in gross income that is properly allocable to a trade or business. It does not include investment income.[91]

In Notice 2018-28,[92] the IRS announced that it intended to issue regulations clarifying that, for purposes of business interest limitation, all interest paid or accrued by a C corporation will be business interest and all interest includable in a C corporation's income will be business interest income. These regulations would not apply to a corporation that is an S corporation. Regulations also would address whether and to what extent interest paid, accrued, or includible in gross income by a non-corporate entity, such as a partnership in which a C corporation holds an interest, is properly characterized, to the C corporation, as business interest or business interest income.

Adjusted taxable income or purposes of the limitation is regular taxable income computed without regard to:

1. Any item of income, gain, deduction, or loss that is not properly allocable to a trade or business;
2. Any business interest or business interest income;
3. The amount of any net operating loss (NOL) deduction;
4. The 20-percent deduction for qualified business income of a passthrough entity (see ¶ 209); and
5. In tax years beginning before January 1, 2022, allowable deductions for depreciation, amortization, or depletion.[93]

The IRS may require other adjustments that it deems necessary.[94]

[89] Code Sec. 163(j)(1).

[90] Code Sec. 163(j)(5).

[91] Code Sec. 163(j)(6).

[92] 2018-16 IRB 492.

[93] Code Sec. 163(j)(8)(A).

[94] Code Sec. 163(j)(8)(B).

Proposed Regulations

The IRS issued proposed regulations on the business interest deduction limit on December 28, 2018.[95] Consistent with Code Sec. 163(j)(1), the proposed regulations limit a taxpayer's deduction for business interest expense and provide that any amount of business interest expense that cannot be deducted because of the limitation can be carried forward and treated as business interest expense in future years. The proposed regulations also provide special rules related to the business interest expense carried forward by passthrough entities, C corporations, and consolidated groups. The rather lengthy proposed regulations are organized into 11 sections:

- Prop. Reg. § 1.163(j)-1 contains common definitions used throughout the proposed regulations.
- Prop. Reg. § 1.163(j)-2 contains general rules on the computation of a taxpayer's business interest limitation.
- Prop. Reg. § 1.163(j)-3 contains ordering and other rules regarding the relationship of the limitation and other Code provisions affecting interest.
- Prop. Reg. § 1.163(j)-4 contains rules for C corporations (including REITs, RICs, and consolidated group members) and tax-exempt corporations.
- Prop. Reg. § 1.163(j)-5 contains rules governing the disallowed business interest expense carryforwards of C corporations.
- Prop. Reg. § 1.163(j)-6 contains special rules for applying the limitation to partnerships and S corporations.
- Prop. Reg. § 1.163(j)-7 contains rules on the application of the limitation to foreign corporations and their shareholders.
- Prop. Reg. § 1.163(j)-8 contains rules on the application of the limitation to foreign persons with effectively connected income.
- Prop. Reg. § 1.163(j)-9 contains rules on elections for excepted trades or businesses as well as a safe harbor for certain REITs (see below).
- Prop. Reg. § 1.163(j)-10 contains rules to allocate expense and income between non-excepted and excepted trades or businesses.
- Prop. Reg. § 1.163(j)-11 contains transition rules.

Election Procedure

An election to be treated as an excepted trade or business for real property or farming trades or businesses is made for a particular trade or business, not necessarily for a particular entity, and applies for the tax year that the election is made and all subsequent years.[96] An election is made by attaching a statement to a timely filed original income tax return, including extensions. The statement should include basic information of the taxpayer and the electing trade or business. If a taxpayer has multiple trades or businesses that may be eligible for the election, an election must be made for each trade or business, and the election statement must specify or describe the different electing trades or businesses.

[95] NPRM REG-106089-18.

[96] Prop. Reg. § 1.163(j)(9).

Because the election applies to the particular trade or business, the election generally terminates automatically if the taxpayer ceases to exist, or ceases the operation of the electing trade or business. However, if a taxpayer transfers all of the assets of an electing trade or business to a related party, the election does not terminate for that trade or business, and transfers to the related party.

An anti-abuse rule prevents a situation in which the taxpayer attempts to terminate the election through a transfer of the assets in the trade or business, but with the intent of resuming a trade or business of a similar nature. If a taxpayer re-acquires substantially all of the assets used in a trade or business, or substantially similar assets, and resumes conducting the prior trade or business within 60 months of ceasing the trade or business, the election is revived with the resumed trade or business.

Safe Harbor for Certain REITs

Prop. Reg. § 1.163(j)-9(g) provides a special safe harbor for REITs. For REITs that take advantage of this safe harbor, the rules applicable to REITs are substantially similar to the general rules provided for other taxpayers. However, certain modifications are applied to take into account the existing rules governing REIT taxation. If a REIT holds real property, interests in partnerships holding real property, or shares in other REITs holding real property, the safe harbor provides that the REIT is eligible to make an election to be an electing real property trade or business for all or part of its assets.

Election Out for Real Property Business

A taxpayer may elect to exclude from the limitation any real property trade or business as defined by the passive activity rules. A real property trade or business under the passive activity rules includes any real estate development, redevelopment, construction, reconstruction, acquisition, conversion, rental, operation, management, leasing, or brokerage trade or business. Interest expenses paid or accrued in an electing real property trade or business is not business interest subject to the limitation. The election is made at a time and manner as provided by the IRS. Once made, the election is irrevocable.[97]

The IRS has provided a safe harbor that allows taxpayers to treat certain infrastructure trades or businesses as electing real property trades or businesses. Eligible for this safe harbor are trades or businesses engaged in designing, building, managing, operating, or maintaining certain core infrastructure projects for purposes of private activity bond financing proposals.[98]

A business that elects to exclude a real property trade or business from the business interest limitation must use the alternative depreciation system (ADS) for any nonresidential real property, residential rental property, and qualified improvement property held by the electing real property trade or business.[99]

The IRS has issued an anti-abuse rule that affects electing real property trades or businesses. According to the IRS, it would be inappropriate to allow a business to

[97] Code Sec. 163(j)(7)(B).

[98] Rev. Proc. 2018-59, 2018-50 IRB 1018.

[99] Code Sec. 168(g)(1)(F).

be an excepted real property trade or business if the business leases substantially all of its real property to the owner of the business or to a related party. Allowing such an election, says the IRS, would encourage a taxpayer to enter into non-economic structures in which the real estate components of a non-real estate business are separated from the rest of the business in order to artificially reduce application of the business interest limitation.

Under the anti-abuse rule, if at least 80 percent of a business's real property, determined by fair market value, is leased to a trade or business under common control with a real property trade or business, the trade or business is not eligible for the election.[100] Common control in this case means that 50 percent of the direct and indirect ownership interests in both businesses are held by related parties within the meaning of Code Sec. 267(b) and Code Sec. 707(b). REITs that lease qualified lodging facilities and qualified healthcare properties are generally permitted to lease these properties to a taxable REIT subsidiary. The anti-abuse rule does not apply to these types of REITs.

Election Out for Farming Business

A taxpayer may elect to exclude from the limitation any farming business as defined under the uniform capitalization rules, as well as any trade or business of a specified agricultural or horticultural cooperative that makes the election. Interest expenses paid or accrued in an electing farming business is not business interest subject to the limitation. The election is made at a time and manner as provided by the IRS. Once made, the election is irrevocable.[101]

A business eligible to make the election is any trade or business involving the cultivation of land or the raising or harvesting of any agricultural or horticultural commodity. It also includes a trade or business of operating a nursery or sod farm, or the raising or harvesting of trees bearing fruit, nuts, or other crops, or ornamental trees (an evergreen tree that is more than six years old at the time it is severed from the roots is not an ornamental tree).

A business that elects to exclude a farming business from the business interest limitation must use the ADS for any property with a recovery period of ten years or more.[102]

Small Business Exception

The limitation on the deduction of business interest does not apply to any taxpayer that meets the $25 million gross receipts test for a corporation or partnership to use the cash method of accounting.[103] A taxpayer meets the small business test for the tax year if its average annual gross receipts for the three tax years ending with the prior tax year do not exceed $25 million, adjusted for inflation after 2018. In the case of a taxpayer that is not a corporation or partnership, the gross receipts test is applied in the same manner as if the taxpayer were a corporation or partner. The small business exception is not available to tax shelter.

---

[100] Prop. Reg. § 1.167(j)-9(h).

[101] Code Sec. 163(j)(7)(C).

[102] Code Sec. 168(g)(1)(F).

[103] Code Sec. 163(j)(3).

A real estate trade or business that can meet the small business exception has no need to elect to exclude the business from the application of the business interest limitation as discussed above. In such a case, the real estate trade or business presumably would not be required to use the ADS for its assets.

Carryforward of Disallowed Business Interest

Any business interest not allowed as a deduction for the tax year under the limitation may be carried forward and treated as business interest paid or accrued in the succeeding tax year. The interest may be carried forward indefinitely, subject to certain restrictions for partnerships and S corporations, as discussed below.[104]

Partnerships and S Corporations

In the case of a partnership or S corporation, the limitation on the deduction of business interest is applied at the entity level.[105] Any deduction for business interest is taken into account in determining the non-separately stated taxable income or loss of the partnership or S corporation. The adjusted taxable income of each partner or shareholder is determined without regard to the partner's or shareholder's distributive share of any item of income, gain, deduction, or loss of the partnership or S corporation. This prevents double counting of the same dollars used in the adjusted taxable income of the entity generating addition interest deductions passed through to the partners or shareholders.

If a partnership or S corporation has an excess taxable income for purposes of the deduction limit, then the excess is passed through to the partners or shareholders. Specifically, the adjusted taxable income of each partner or shareholder is increased by the partner's or shareholder's distributive share of the entity's excess taxable income. A partner's or shareholder's distributive share of partnership excess taxable income is determined in the same manner as the partner's or shareholder's distributive share of non-separately stated taxable income or loss of the entity.

The excess taxable income of a partnership or S corporation is a percentage of the entity's adjusted taxable income for the year. The percentage is:

- 30 percent of the entity's adjusted taxable income, over its net excess business interest (the excess of business interest of the entity, reduced by floor plan financing interest, over business interest income; over
- 30 percent of the entity's adjusted taxable income.

This addition to a partner's or shareholder's adjusted taxable income, allows them to deduct more interest than they may have paid or incurred during the year, to the extent the entity could have deducted more business interest.

Unlike other taxpayers, any disallowed interest of a partnership or S corporation is not carried forward to the succeeding tax year. Instead, the disallowed interest of the entity is treated as excess business interest that is allocated to each

[104] Code Sec. 163(j)(2).

[105] Code Sec. 163(j)(4).

partner or shareholder in the same manner as any non-separately state taxable income or loss.[106]

The allocated excess business interest for the current tax year is treated by the partner or shareholder as business interest paid or accrued by the partner or shareholder in the next succeeding year. In other words, the allocated excess business interest is carried forward to next succeeding tax year by the partner or shareholder but only to the extent the partner or shareholder is allocated excess taxable income from the entity in the succeeding year. Excess taxable income allocated to a partner or shareholder for any tax year must be used against excess business interest from the entity from all tax years before it may be used against any other business interest.

If the partner or shareholder does not have enough excess taxable income from the entity to offset the carried forward excess business interest, then the interest must continue to be carried forward to succeeding tax years. In all subsequent tax years, the excess business interest carried forward by the partner or shareholder is treated as paid or accrued in the next subsequent tax year that may only be used against excess taxable income allocated by the entity to the partner or shareholder for that tax year.

The adjusted basis of a partner's or shareholder's interest in the entity is reduced (but not below zero) by the amount of excess business interest allocated by the entity to the partner or shareholder. However, if the partner or shareholder sells or otherwise disposes of the interest in the partnership or S corporation, then their adjusted basis is increased immediately before the disposition by the excess (if any) of:

- The amount of the basis reduction due to the excess business interest allocated by the entity to the partner or shareholder, over
- Any portion of the excess business interest allocated to the partner or shareholder which has previously been treated as interest paid or accrued by the partner.

A disposition for purposes of an increase in the adjusted basis of a partnership or S corporation interest includes any transactions in which gain is not recognized in whole or part (including the death of the partner of shareholder). Also, no deduction is allowed to the transferor or transferee for any excess business interest that increases the adjusted basis in the entity.

.03 Interest-Free and Below-Market Rate Loans

In most contexts, an interest-free or below-market interest rate loan is really more than a simple borrow and lend transaction. Generally speaking, these loans are made in settings that are removed from traditional commercial lending and involve borrowers and lenders that have some relationship beyond mere debtor and creditor. In an effort to recognize the true nature of these transactions, Code Sec. 7872 takes certain interest-free and below-market rate loans and recharacterizes them as arm's-length transactions.

[106] Code Sec. 163(j)(4)(B).

In a loan transaction recharacterized under Code Sec. 7872, the lender is considered to have made a loan at a rate of interest fixed by statute and also made an additional payment to the borrower equal to the foregone interest. This additional payment may be considered a gift, dividend, contribution to capital, compensation, or some other payment, depending on the context of the loan. The borrower, in turn, is considered to have transferred back to the lender the amount of this foregone interest as an interest payment.

The amount of foregone interest is based on the "applicable federal rates" determined under the original issue discount rules.[107] These rates are announced by the IRS each month. For term loans, the federal short-term rate is used for loans of three years or less, the federal mid-term rate for loans of more than three years but not more than nine years, and the federal long-term rate for loans with terms of more than nine years. For demand loans, the short-term rate is used. A special blended rate may be used when an interest-free or below-market rate loan remains outstanding for the entire calendar year.[108] Numerous examples illustrating the computation of foregone interest may be found in Prop. Reg. § 1.7872-13.

The rules of Code Sec. 7872 apply to interest-free and below-market loans made in the following contexts.[109]

1. Gifts—These are loans in which the foregone interest is in the nature of a gift and generally involve family members, although it is possible for there to be a gift loan between other than family members.
2. Compensation—These are loans made in connection with the performance of services between an employer and employee, an independent contractor and the person hiring the contractor, or a partner and partnership if the loan is for services by the partner other than in the capacity as a partner.[110]
3. Corporation-Shareholder—These are loans from a corporation to a shareholder of the corporation or from a shareholder to a corporation. Loans to shareholders who are also employees are considered shareholder loans if certain minimal stock ownership requirements are met.[111]
4. Tax Avoidance—These are loans in which one of the principal purposes for the interest arrangement is avoidance of federal tax by the borrower or lender or both.[112]
5. Tax Effect Loans—These are loans that have a significant effect on the tax liability of the lender or borrower as defined by IRS regulations. The IRS has not yet issued regulations under this provision.

Gift loans, compensation loans, and shareholder-corporation loans are considered in more detail below. Keep in mind that the rules of Code Sec. 7872 for interest-free and below-market rate loans generally do not apply to any loan given in consideration for the sale or exchange of property and covered by the original issue discount rules or paid on account of the sale or exchange of property and covered

[107] Code Sec. 1274(d).
[108] Code Sec. 7872(f)(2).
[109] Code Sec. 7872(c).
[110] Prop. Reg. § 1.7872-4(c).
[111] Prop. Reg. § 1.7872-4(d).
[112] Prop. Reg. § 1.7872-4(e).

by the imputed interest rules.[113] (The original issue discount rules and imputed interest rules governing deferred payment sales of property are separately considered later in this chapter.)

[A] Gift Loans

An interest-free or below-market rate gift loan has both income and gift tax consequences. The same rules apply to the income tax treatment of both term loans and demand loans, but the gift tax treatment differs depending on whether a gift loan is a term loan or a demand loan.

Income Tax Treatment

In the case of a gift loan, the lender is treated as transferring to the borrower an amount equal to the interest foregone by the lender (the gift). The borrower, then, is treated as retransferring an equal amount back to the lender as interest. These transfers are considered to take place on the last day of the calendar year for loans outstanding for any period during the calendar year. Foregone interest is the difference between what would have been payable on the loan if interest accrued at the applicable federal rate and was paid on the last day of the calendar year and any interest actually payable on the loan allocable to the same period.

For the borrower, the amount of interest treated as transferred to the lender is subject to all the rules that govern the deductibility of interest. If the debt may be traced to a trade or business, the interest would be fully deductible. If the debt were traced to an investment, passive activity, or personal use, the interest deduction would be limited by the various provisions that apply to interest. For the lender, the interest received is, of course, gross income under Code Sec. 61.

The application of Code Sec. 7872 is limited in certain cases involving gift loans between individuals:

1. The rules do not apply to gift loans of $10,000 or less, as long as the loan is not used directly or indirectly to purchase or carry income producing assets.[114]
2. If gift loans between the parties do not exceed a total of $100,000 and one of the principal purposes of the loan arrangement is not the avoidance of federal income tax, then the interest treated as paid by the borrower is limited to the borrower's net investment income for the year (net investment income is the same as net investment income under the investment interest limitations discussed above). If the borrower's net investment income does not exceed $1,000, then it is treated as zero. In other words, if the borrower has under $1,000 net investment income, there is no deemed transfer of interest between the parties on a gift loan of $100,000 or less.[115]

Gift Tax Treatment

The gift tax treatment of a demand gift loan follows the income tax treatment. The amount of foregone interest that the lender treats as a gift to the borrower is

---

[113] Code Sec. 1274(c)(1); Code Sec. 483(c)(1); Prop. Reg. § 1.7872-2(a)(2)(ii).

[114] Code Sec. 7872(c)(2).

[115] Code Sec. 7872(d)(1).

the amount determined using the short-term federal rate on the last day of the calendar year. This means that, in the case of a demand loan that remains outstanding, a new gift is made each year equal to the foregone interest for the year.

If the gift loan is a term loan, however, the lender is treated as having made a gift of the interest on the date the loan is made. The amount of the gift is equal to the difference between the amount loaned and the present value of all payments that the borrower is required to make under the terms of the loan. Rather than a potential for a gift each year the loan remains outstanding, as is the case with a demand loan, a term loan generates but a single gift at the time of the loan.

The following example illustrates the difference between the income tax treatment and the gift tax treatment of term and demand loans under Code Sec. 7872 and is taken from the Conference Committee Report on the Tax Reform Act of 1984.

> ***Comprehensive Example 11:*** On January 1, the Father, a calendar year taxpayer, makes a $200,000 loan to the Son, also a calendar year taxpayer. The loan is repayable in two years, with five percent simple interest payable annually.
>
> Assuming that the applicable federal rate is 12 percent compounded semiannually, the amount of the gift made by the Father is $24,760. This is the difference between the $200,000 transferred to the Son and the present value at 12 percent of the $10,000 interest payment due at the end of year one and the $10,000 interest payment and $200,000 principal payment due at the end of year two.
>
> The amount treated as retransferred by the Son to the Father on the last day of each of the two calendar years is $14,720. This is the difference between interest computed at the applicable federal rate and the interest actually payable on the loan. This amount, in addition to the $10,000 interest called for by the loan agreement, is included in income by the Father and, subject to the rules that govern the interest deduction, is treated as interest paid by the Son.

[B] Compensation Loans

In the case of compensation-related interest-free or below-market rate loans, the treatment of the employer and employee or independent contractor depend on whether the loan is a demand loan or a term loan.

Demand Loans

When an employer makes an interest-free or below-market rate demand loan to an employee or independent contractor, the employer is considered to have paid compensation or wages equal to the amount of the foregone interest for any day that the loan is outstanding. The employee is considered to have received an equal amount of compensation income. The employee, in turn, is considered to retransfer an equal amount back to the employer as interest on the loan and the employer has interest income equal to the same amount.[116]

For the employer, an interest-free or below-market rate demand loan to an employee generally results in a wash as far as the tax consequences are concerned. The employer reports interest income from the loan, but is entitled to an equivalent deduction for the compensation deemed paid to the employee (provided the employee's compensation meets the usual "reasonable" requirement for deduction). For the employee, the interest foregone by the employer is compensation income, subject to FICA and FUTA taxes (but not income tax withholding). The equivalent amount deemed paid as interest back to the employer may or may not produce a tax deduction, depending on the use of the loan proceeds and the usual limits on the deduction of interest paid.

Term Loans

If a compensation-related loan is a term loan, the employee is treated as receiving compensation from the employer equal to the difference between the amount of the loan and the present value at the applicable federal rate of all payments that the employee is required to make under the terms of the loan. The employee must report this full amount of extra compensation as of the date the loan was received. The employee, however, is treated as making interest payments over the term of the loan.[117] In this case, even if the interest is deductible, the employee will not be able to fully offset the extra compensation received on the date of the term loan.

For the employer, the situation is reversed. The full amount of the foregone interest is deductible (assuming "reasonableness") when the loan is made, but additional interest income is reported over the term of the loan. Considering the harsh impact a term loan can have on the employee an employer is trying to benefit, the employer can structure a term loan to have it treated as a demand loan by making the benefits of the interest rate nontransferrable and conditioning them on the performance of substantial future services by the employee.[118]

De Minimis Exception

The rules of Code Sec. 7872 do not apply to compensation-related loans if the loans to an employee do not exceed $10,000 and do not have a principal purpose of tax avoidance.[119] In other words, an employee receiving an interest-free or below-market rate compensation loan of $10,000 or less reports no income and has no possible interest deduction as a result of the loan. Similarly, the employer is not considered to be paying additional compensation and reports no interest income (other than interest actually paid by the employee).

Employee Relocation Loans

Certain loans to employees are excepted from the interest-free and below-market rate loan rules of Code Sec. 7872 if they are to provide mortgage financing

[116] Code Sec. 7872(a).
[117] Code Sec. 7872(b).
[118] Prop. Reg. § 1.7872-10(a)(5).
[119] Code Sec. 7872(c)(3).

for an employee's new residence or bridge financing in connection with the transfer of the employee to a new principal place of work.[120]

[C] Corporation-Shareholder Loans

Interest-free and below-market rate loans between corporations and their shareholders are subject to essentially the same rules as compensation-related loans. The same distinction exists between term and demand loans, and the same $10,000 de minimis exception applies. The difference, of course, is the nature of the deemed payments equal to the foregone interest.

In the case of a loan from a corporation to a shareholder, the amount equal to the foregone interest transferred to the shareholder represents a dividend, not deductible by the corporation but taxable to the shareholder. The interest transferred back to the corporation from the shareholder is income to the corporation and is treated as interest paid by the shareholder, subject to the usual limits on the interest deduction. Since the corporation may not deduct dividends paid, and the corporation is taxed on the interest deemed received from the shareholder, an interest-free or below-market rate loan to a shareholder may be quite costly to the corporation.

In the case of an interest-free or below-market rate loan from a shareholder to the corporation, the amount of foregone interest deemed transferred to the corporation is treated as a contribution to capital, which is not income to the corporation and not deductible by the shareholder. The amount of the contribution to capital, however, does increase the shareholder's basis for the interest in the corporation. The interest payment transferred back to the shareholder from the corporation is deductible by the corporation and income to the shareholder.

[D] Reporting Requirements

A lender must attach a statement to the lender's income tax return for any taxable year in which the lender either has interest income or claims a deduction for an amount deemed transferred to a borrower under Code Sec. 7872. Similarly, a borrower must attach a statement to the borrower's return for any taxable year in which the borrower either has income from an imputed transfer or claims a deduction for interest under Code Sec. 7872.[121]

An individual who wants to take advantage of the provision that limits interest under Code Sec. 7872 to net investment income, in the case of gift loans totaling $100,000 or less, must notify the lender in a signed statement of the amount of the borrower's net investment income.[122]

¶ 304 ORIGINAL ISSUE DISCOUNT AND IMPUTED INTEREST ON DEFERRED PAYMENT SALES

In many cases, the sale of real estate does not involve outside third-party financing. Rather, the seller will provide financing and accept the buyer's debt in

[120] Temp. Reg. § 1.7872-5T(c).

[121] The exact contents of these statements are detailed in Prop. Reg. § 1.7872-11(g).

[122] Prop. Reg. § 1.7872-11(g)(3).

exchange for all or a part of the purchase price. Even when third-party financing is available, it may not be sufficient. In this case too, seller financing may be made available to the buyer to make up the difference. (Installment sales and seller-financed sales of real estate are considered in Chapter 14. Here we are concerned with the tax rules governing the financing of the transaction, rather than the sales transaction itself.)

On an installment or deferred payment sale of real estate, if the buyer and seller fail to provide adequate interest on the deferred payments, one of two Internal Revenue Code provisions may come into play to rewrite the parties' financing agreement for tax purposes. These provisions are the imputed interest rules of Code Sec. 483 and the original issue discount rules of Code Sec. 1274.

Before 1985, there was only one provision to deal with, the imputed interest rules of Code Sec. 483. In the Tax Reform Act of 1984, however, Congress expanded the original issue discount (OID) rules to cover many deferred payment sales of property. Previously, the OID rules were limited generally to publicly traded debt instruments and debt issued for publicly traded property.

The imputed interest rules were enacted in 1964 to close what was then perceived as a loophole in the tax law. At that time, an individual could convert what would be ordinary income into capital gain on the sale of a capital asset for installment or deferred payments. The strategy was simple. Instead of charging interest on the deferred payments, the seller would simply charge a higher price for the asset. The higher price, of course, was to compensate the seller for the interest the seller would otherwise receive. The buyer would pay no more than if the buyer paid a lower price plus interest, but the seller was able to report capital gain, which was subject to preferential tax treatment at that time, rather than ordinary interest income.

The imputed interest rules of Code Sec. 483 limited this strategy to convert ordinary income into capital gain by "imputing" interest in a contract for the sale of property unless a statutorily set minimum rate of interest was called for by the agreement. Since the fixed interest rate called for under the imputed interest rules did not always reflect current interest rates, Congress made the imputed interest rate under Code Sec. 483 conform to the OID rates when the OID rules were expanded in 1984 (how the rates are determined is discussed below for both the imputed interest rules and the OID rules).

While the imputed interest rules could block the conversion of ordinary income to capital gain as outlined above, Code Sec. 483 still left another loophole. If a cash basis seller sold an asset to an accrual basis buyer in an installment or deferred payment sale, a tax shelter of sorts could be constructed by manipulating the timing of the interest payments on the deferred amounts. The buyer could accrue and deduct the interest for the periods to which it related, even if the interest was not actually paid. The seller, however, would not have to report interest income until interest payments were actually received. In short, it was possible to generate an interest deduction for one taxpayer without a corresponding amount of interest income for another taxpayer. It is this second loophole, along with the conversion loophole, that the OID rules of Code Sec. 1274 are designed to close.

Unlike the imputed interest rules, the OID rules do more than merely convert "principal" into interest for tax purposes when insufficient interest is called for by the parties to a sale of property. The OID rules also require both the buyer and seller to account for any OID on an economic accrual basis by which OID is deemed to accrue at the applicable statutory rate with six-month compounding. Also, even if there is sufficient interest called for in a sale contract, the OID rules may require that the parties account for that interest for tax purposes under the OID accrual rule. (There is an exception that allows cash basis accounting in certain cases, and this is discussed in connection with the OID rules at ¶ 304.02[A].) In short, in addition to preventing the conversion of interest income into capital gain, the OID rules also match the buyer's interest deduction and the seller's interest income, regardless of their actual accounting methods and regardless of when interest payments are actually made.

Note: In 1986, the IRS issued proposed regulations that took up over 400 pages of typewritten copy and proposed additions or changes to the regulations under Code Secs. 163(e), 446, 482, 483, 1271, 1272, 1273, 1274, 1274A, and 1275. In 1992, the IRS withdrew most of those proposed regulations and issued new proposed regulations on the OID rules under Code Sec. 163(e) and Code Secs. 1271 through 1275, and proposed amendments to the Code Secs. 483, 1001, and 1012 regulations. The 1992 proposed regulations, with some changes, were adopted as final regulations on February 2, 1994.[123] Appropriate citations to the final regulations are made in the following discussion. The regulations also contain additional explanations and examples on how to determine imputed interest and original issue discount and how to accrue interest under the OID rules. The discussion here concentrates on the general concepts behind imputed interest and OID rather than any detailed mathematical computations. The reader who desires to delve into the mathematical intricacies is referred to the regulations.

.01 Imputed Interest

The imputed interest rules of Code Sec. 483 apply to an installment or deferred payment sale only if the OID rules of Code Sec. 1274 discussed below do not apply.[124] The real estate sales transactions that are not subject to the OID rules and, therefore, that are subject to the imputed interest rules are:

1. Sales of farms by individuals or small businesses (as defined by Code Sec. 1244(c)(3)), if the sales price of the farm is $1,000,000 or less.[125]
2. Sales by individuals of their principal residences.[126]
3. Sales of property if the aggregate amount of debt payments and other consideration for the sale does not exceed $250,000.[127]
4. Sales of land between certain family members if the sales price does not exceed $500,000.[128]

---

[123] T.D. 8517, 59 F.R. 4799-4831.

[124] Code Sec. 483(d)(1).

[125] Code Sec. 1274(c)(3)(A).

[126] Code Sec. 1274(c)(3)(B).

[127] Code Sec. 1274(c)(3)(C).

[128] Code Secs. 1274(c)(3)(F) and 483(e).

[A] Unstated Interest

Interest is imputed under Code Sec. 483 to a payment under a contract for the sale or exchange of property if the sales price is more than $3,000[129] and if the following conditions are met:

1. The payment is due more than six months after the date of the sale or exchange;
2. Some or all of the payments called for by the contract are due more than one year after the sale or exchange; and
3. There is "unstated interest."[130]

There is unstated interest in a contract of sale to the extent the sum of the payments due under the contract exceed the present values of the payments plus the present values of any interest payments due under the contract.[131] Present values are calculated using a discount rate that is equal to the applicable federal rate (see ¶ 304.03). In the case of a sale-leaseback transaction in which the seller or related party leases a portion of the property after the sale, however, 110 percent of the applicable federal rate is used (sale-leasebacks as financing tools are discussed at ¶ 305).

Under this rule, a contract that specifies interest equal to the applicable federal rate cannot have unstated interest and cannot be subject to the imputed interest rules. To the extent that there is unstated interest, however, the unstated interest is imputed to the contract and treated as interest for all tax purposes. This also reduces the amount of principal. Accordingly, the imputation of interest under Code Sec. 483 not only produces interest income for the seller and a possible interest deduction for the buyer, it also reduces the amount realized by the seller from the sale and reduces the buyer's cost basis in the property.

[B] Land Sales Between Family Members

In the case of a sale of land between family members for $500,000 or less, the discount rate used to determine if there is unstated interest is set at a maximum of six percent compounded semiannually.[132] Of course, this also means that the related parties may use this rate if it is lower than the applicable federal rate and avoid the imputed interest rules.

While the statute speaks to the sales price in applying the $500,000 limitation, the proposed regulations look to the amount of the debt instrument. Reg. § 1.483-3(b)(2) provides that the special imputed interest rate applies to a debt instrument issued in a sale or exchange of land by an individual to a member of the individual's family if:

1. The individuals are the only parties to the debt instrument;
2. The debt instrument is not given in consideration for any property other than land (the exception does not apply to the sale of depreciable structures or improvements); and

[129] Code Sec. 483(d)(2).

[130] Code Sec. 483(c).

[131] Code Sec. 483(b).

[132] Code Sec. 483(e).

3. The stated principal amount of the debt instrument, when added to the aggregate stated principal amount of any other debt instruments to which the exception applies and which were issued in prior qualified land sales between the individuals during the same calendar year, does not exceed $500,000.

If the property sold or exchanged does include property other than land, the maximum six percent rate applies only to the extent that the stated principal amount of the debt instrument issued in the sale or exchange is attributable to the land based on the relative fair market values of the land and the other property.[133]

Apparently, the regulations take the sensible position that sales for more than $500,000 can be fragmented so that the $500,000 limitation should be construed as applying to the debt. Presumably, the sales price may exceed $500,000, and even the amount of the sales price that is financed may exceed $500,000, but only $500,000 is eligible for the maximum six percent imputed interest rate.[134]

Family members eligible for the maximum six percent imputed interest rate on the sale of land are defined by Reg. § 1.483-3(b)(2)(i) to include only an individual's brother and sister (by the whole or half blood), spouse, parents, grandparents, children and grandchildren. Full effect is given to a legal adoption in determining these relationships.

.02 Original Issue Discount

Generally, the OID rules of Code Sec. 1274 may apply to any sale or exchange of property that is not one of the exceptions listed at ¶ 304.01 as covered by the imputed interest rules. If the sale of property is one that may be covered by the OID rules, the rules apply unless the contract of sale calls for interest at the applicable federal rate and the interest is payable currently at a constant rate over its term. If either inadequate interest is called for by the contract or adequate interest is not currently payable, the OID rules apply.[135]

If the interest rate called for by the contract is adequate but interest is not payable currently, the OID rules force the purchaser and seller to report the interest for tax purposes based on an economic accrual of interest with six-month compounding. If interest is less than the applicable federal rate, than an imputed principal amount is calculated by discounting all payments called for by the contract at the applicable federal rate. The difference between the stated principal amount and the imputed principal amount is original issue discount and is treated as interest for tax purposes. The parties account for the OID as if interest on the imputed principal amount were being compounded at six-month intervals.

Example 12: In a sale subject to the OID rules, the Buyer and the Seller agree to a purchase price of $1,500,000 for commercial property. The Seller agrees to accept $500,000 in cash and the Buyer's note and purchase-money mortgage for $1,000,000. The mortgage calls for five percent interest payable annually with the full amount of principal due at the end of five years, or

---

[133] Reg. § 1.483-3(b)(2)(iii).

[134] *See* the examples in Reg. § 1.483-4(b)(3).

[135] Code Sec. 1274(c).

payments by the Buyer to the Seller of $50,000 each year for four years and a final payment after five years of $1,050,000. At the time of the sale, the applicable federal rate that applies to this transaction is eight percent.

Since this deferred payment sale does not provide for adequate interest, an "imputed principal" amount and the original issue discount must be determined by discounting the payments required by the mortgage at eight percent compounded semiannually. Discounting the expected payments over the five-year term of the mortgage at eight percent gives a present value of $880,230, and this is the imputed principal amount. Subtracting the imputed principal from the stated principal ($1,000,000 - $880,230) yields original issue discount in the amount of $119,770.

The original issue discount of $119,770 must be treated as interest for tax purposes by both the Buyer and the Seller, so the Seller reports the appropriate portion of the OID as additional interest income each year, and the Buyer may deduct an equal amount as interest, subject to the usual limitations on the deduction of interest. Also, the imputed principal amount is treated as the principal amount of the debt for tax purposes. Accordingly, the Seller's gain or loss is determined based on his amount realized of $1,380,230 ($500,000 cash plus $880,230 mortgage debt), and the Buyer's cost basis for the property is also $1,380,230.[136]

[A] Cash Method Accounting

Generally, for purposes of the OID rules, any original issue discount must be treated by the parties to the transaction on an economic accrual basis regardless of their actual tax accounting methods and regardless of when interest is actually paid. There is, however, an exception to the OID accrual rule which permits the parties to elect cash method accounting for OID that would otherwise be subject to Code Sec. 1274, if certain requirements are met.[137] Cash method accounting is available if:

1. The stated principal amount of the debt does not exceed $2,000,000;
2. The seller/lender does not use an accrual method of accounting for tax purposes;
3. The seller/lender is not a dealer in the property sold or exchanged; and
4. The election[138] to use the cash method is made jointly by both the buyer and seller.

If a debt instrument subject to a cash method election is transferred by the lender or assumed by a successor to the borrower, the election applies to the new party or parties. If a seller/lender's transferee is an accrual basis taxpayer, however, the cash method election does not apply and the transferee must use accrual accounting under the rules of Code Sec. 1272 to report any OID.[139]

[136] For many additional examples relating to OID calculations, including the calculation of the amount of OID that is reported for any year over the term of the loan, *see* the regulations under Code Sec. 1274.

[137] Code Sec. 1274A(c).

[138] Reg. § 1.1274A-1(c)(1).

[139] Reg. § 1.1274A-1(c)(2).

[B] Assumptions and Modifications of Debt Instruments

Neither the OID rules of Code Sec. 1274 nor the imputed interest rules of Code Sec. 483 apply on the assumption of an existing debt instrument unless the terms and conditions of the debt instrument are modified or the nature of the transaction is changed in connection with the assumption.[140]

> ***Example 13:*** On the sale of property, the Seller provides a $3,000,000 purchase-money mortgage which calls for annual interest at 15 percent. Three years later, the property is resold and the new Buyer assumes the existing purchase-money mortgage, but the Seller agrees to lower the interest rate on the mortgage to nine percent. Because the mortgage debt has been modified on the assumption, the modified debt is treated as a new debt provided by the Seller in consideration for the old debt.

If the lender and borrower, or successors to either, modify a debt instrument materially either in kind or in extent, the modified debt instrument is treated as a new debt given in consideration for the old, unmodified debt. The new debt instrument is eligible for the cash method election (¶ 304.02[A]) if the other requirements are met. The new debt instrument is not eligible for the cash method election, however, if a principal purpose of the debt modification is to defer interest income or deductions through the election.[141]

.03 Interest Rates Under the Imputed Interest and OID Rules

The interest rates, called federal rates, on which imputed interest or OID is determined are keyed to the interest rate on United States government obligations and the terms of the deferred payment sale.[142] The rates are adjusted each month based on the average market yield on outstanding government obligations and announced by the IRS. The rate for a particular sale or exchange is the rate in effect on the date of the transaction.

The applicable federal rate as announced by the IRS is determined by the term of the deferred payment obligation. If the term is three years or less, the applicable federal rate is the announced federal short-term rate. If the term is more than three years but not more than nine years, the applicable federal rate is the federal mid-term rate; and for terms in excess of nine years, the federal long-term rate is used.

Note that in the case of a sale-leaseback transaction involving seller financing, the applicable federal rates are 110 percent of the announced federal rates.[143]

To prevent taxpayers' planning of the sale or purchase of property from being adversely affected by monthly changes in the federal rates, a special rule permits the use of the federal rates announced for one month in the following two months as well.[144] The test rate generally is the lowest of the applicable federal rates in effect during either the three-month period that ends with the first month in which there is a binding written contract that contains the terms of the sale or exchange, or the three-month period that ends with the month in which the sale or exchange

[140] Code Sec. 1274(c)(4).

[141] Reg. § 1.1274A-1(c)(3).

[142] Code Sec. 1274(d).

[143] Code Sec. 1274(e).

[144] Code Sec. 1274(d)(2).

occurs.[145] For instance, a real estate sale that closes in April may test for imputed interest or OID using the lowest federal rates announced for February, March, or April.

[A] Maximum Interest Rate

If seller financing or other debt subject to the imputed interest or OID rules does not exceed $2,800,000, the maximum rate under the imputed interest or OID rules is nine percent.[146] This rate is merely a maximum. If the applicable federal rate announced by the IRS for the month of sale (or preceding two months) is lower, the lower rate may be used in place of the nine percent rate. The maximum nine percent rate generally does not apply to new tangible personal property.[147]

[B] Installment Obligations

In the case of an installment obligation, the term of the instrument is the instrument's weighted average maturity as defined in Reg. § 1.1273-1(e)(3).[148]

[C] Variable Interest Rate Obligations

Generally, for purposes of determining whether there is adequate interest, a variable rate debt keyed to an objective index (such as prime, federal rate, LIBOR, or average yield on treasuries) is treated as if the debt called for a fixed rate equal to the variable rate at the time the debt is tested for adequate interest.[149]

The general rule for variable rate obligations does not apply if, as a result of interest rate restrictions, such as an interest rate cap, the expected yield of the obligation taking the restrictions into account is significantly less than the expected yield of the obligation without regard to the restrictions. In this case, the interest payments on the obligation, other than any fixed interest payments, are treated as contingent payments.[150] An obligation is not subject to this rule if it contains reasonably symmetric interest rate caps and floors, or reasonably symmetric governors, that are fixed throughout the term of the obligation.

> ***Example 14:*** A sells B property and as part of the consideration, B gives A a note for $1,000,000 payable in five years. Interest is payable monthly at a rate equal to one percentage point above the prime rate for the preceding month. If the applicable federal rate for this debt were 7.5 percent, and if, on the date this test rate is determined, the prime rate plus one percent equalled nine percent, the debt would have adequate interest.[151]

[D] Contingent Interest

If a debt instrument provides for one or more contingent payments, the issue price of the debt instrument is the lesser of the instrument's noncontingent principal payments and the sum of the present values of the noncontingent payments determined under Reg. § 1.1274-2(c). If the debt instrument is issued in a

---

145 Reg. § 1.1274-4(a)(1).
146 Code Sec. 1274A(a).
147 Code Sec. 1274A(b).
148 Reg. § 1.1274-4(c)(1).
149 Reg. § 1.1274-2(f)(1).
150 Reg. § 1.1274-2(f)(1)(ii).
151 For additional examples, *see* Reg. § 1.1274-2(h).

potentially abusive situation, however, the issue price is the fair market value of the noncontingent payments.[152]

When an obligation containing contingent payments is subject to Code Sec. 1274, any noncontingent payments are treated as a separate debt instrument. The issue price of the overall debt instrument is determined as above (Reg. § 1.1274-2(g)).[153]

A contingent payment is treated as a payment of principal to the extent of the present value of the payment, determined by discounting the payment at the test rate from the date of the payment is made to the issue date. Any amount in excess of part of the payment treated as principal is interest.[154] The test rate is the rate that would be the test rate for the overall debt instrument if the term of the overall debt instrument began on the issue date and ended when the contingent payment is made. In the case of a contingent payment that consists of a payment of stated principal accompanied by a payment of stated interest at a rate that exceeds this test rate, however, the test rate is the stated interest rate.[155]

> ***Example 15:*** On January 1, 1997, A sells a newly constructed office building to B for a $1,000,000 in cash and a debt instrument that matures on December 31, 2001. The debt instrument provides for a payment at maturity of $5,000,000 and a contingent payment of interest on December 31 of each year equal to a fixed percentage of the gross rents B receives from the building in that year. On January 1, 1997, the short-term applicable federal rate is 5 percent, compounded annually, and the mid-term rate is 6 percent, compounded annually.
>
> The issue price of the debt instrument, determined under the rules of Reg. § 1.1274-2(g) is $3,736,291—the present value of the $5,000,000 noncontingent payment due on December 31, 2001, based on a discount rate equal to the mid-term applicable federal rate of 6 percent. (B's basis in the building is $4,736,291, the $1,000,000 cash plus the present value of the noncontingent payment.) The noncontingent payment is treated as a separate debt instrument with an issue price of $3,736,291 and OID of $1,263,709.
>
> If the contingent payment that is fixed and payable on December 31, 1997, is $200,000, the present value of that amount discounted at the short-term federal rate of 5 percent from the date the payment is made to the issue date, or $190,476, is principal, and the remainder of $9,524 is interest. (The amount treated as principal increases B's basis in the building.) The remaining contingent payments are accounted for in a similar fashion—discounted at 5 percent for the payments due at the end of 1998 and 1999, and discounted at 6 percent for the contingent payments due at the end of 2000 and 2001.[156]

[152] Reg. § 1.1274-2(g).

[153] Reg. § 1.1275-4(c)(3).

[154] Reg. § 1.1275-4(c)(4)(ii).

[155] Reg. § 1.1275-4(c)(4)(ii)(B).

[156] For additional examples, *see* Reg. § 1.1275-4(c)(7).

[E] Excessive Interest

The imputed interest and OID rules generally set the minimum interest rate that can be charged for tax purposes in a contract for the sale of property. But what about a maximum rate of interest? May a buyer and seller lower the purchase price and charge a higher rate of interest to provide a tax advantage for one of the parties? Corporations that issue certain "high yield" discount obligations may lose a portion of their interest deductions, but what of other taxpayers?

As discussed at ¶ 101.02[C], the IRS does have the power under Code Sec. 1274(b)(3) to limit the imputed principal amount of a debt instrument to the fair market value of the property acquired with the debt, and this power would seem to apply equally to a reduced purchase price to gain a tax advantage from interest deductions as to an inflated purchase price to gain depreciation or other tax advantages. Reg. § 1.1274-2(b)(3) specifically provides that in the case of a debt instrument issued in a potentially abusive situation, the issue price of the debt instrument is the fair market value of the property received in exchange for the debt instrument, reduced by the fair market value of any consideration other than the debt. An abusive situation includes a debt instrument with clearly excessive interest.[157] According to the regulations, interest on a debt instrument is clearly excessive, if the interest, in light of the terms of the debt instrument and the creditworthiness of the borrower, is clearly greater than the arm's length amount of interest that would have been charged in a cash lending transaction between the same two persons.[158]

¶ 305 SALE-LEASEBACKS AND OTHER LEASE FINANCING

From a practical point of view, there may be very little difference between outright ownership of property and a long-term lease of the property, as far as the user of business property is concerned. In many cases, leasing transactions serve as a substitute for traditional financing. In a typical sale-leaseback, the owner of property sells the property to an investor and immediately leases the property back. A sale-leaseback can be arranged with any type of property, but it is real estate that is most often the subject of a sale and leaseback. The lease in a sale-leaseback is usually a net lease that assures the investor a return over and above the cost to him of financing the purchase of the property from the seller-lessee.

Apart from sale-leasebacks, a lease of property combined with an option to purchase by the lessee may be another way, in addition to a purchase-money mortgage, for the seller of property to provide financing for the prospective purchaser of property.

.01 Straight Sale-Leaseback

In a straight forward sale-leaseback, the owner of property sells the property to an investor. The property may be newly constructed property or property that has been owned by the seller for some time. (In some deals, the seller may be a builder or developer who has constructed the property to the specifications of the future

[157] Reg. § 1.1274-3(a)(2)(iv).

[158] Reg. § 1.1274-3(b)(3).

lessee. In these cases, the sale directly to the investor party eliminates the intermediate step of having the ultimate user of the property acquire title and then selling to the investor.) The investor may or may not obtain traditional mortgage financing from an outside third-party lender in order to finance the purchase. The investor then immediately leases the property back to the seller, usually on a long-term net lease. Under this arrangement, the seller-lessee is assured of the use of the property and is responsible for all property taxes, insurance, maintenance and upkeep expenses. The purchaser-lessor, through the net lease, is provided with a guaranteed return on his investment, and ownership of the property provides him with security for his investment.

In this form, the sale-leaseback is substituting for mortgage financing. Moreover, the amount of cash that is freed for the seller-lessee may be equal to the full value of the property, the equivalent of 100 percent financing.

> ***Example 16:*** A business owns a warehouse that is worth $500,000. The business would like to free up the cash that is tied up in the land and building for other uses, but wants to continue to use the warehouse in its business operations. One avenue open to this business is to borrow against the property by obtaining a mortgage loan for 80 percent of the property's value, or $400,000. Instead of a mortgage loan, however, the business may want to explore a sale-leaseback that could free the entire $500,000 value of the building.
>
> Assuming the mortgage loan could be obtained for a 25-year term at 10 percent, the business would be obligated to pay about $43,600 annually to amortize the loan over the 25 years. With a sale-leaseback, the business would sell the land and building to an investor for its full $500,000 value. Under the lease of the warehouse back from the investor, the lease might be for a 25-year term with annual payments of about $54,500, which is about the amount required to fully return the investor's $500,000 plus 10 percent interest over the 25-year term of the lease.

While the sale-leaseback as described above does free up the full value of the real estate assets, it does have significant drawbacks. First, at the end of the lease term, the investor and not the business owns the property, and the residual value, which may be significant, belongs to the purchaser-lessor. Second, the seller-lessee may want to continue using the property at the end of the lease term, but the property now belongs to the purchaser-lessor and the lease arrangement may have to be renegotiated. For these reasons, sale-leasebacks will contain various options for repurchase of the property or for the renewal of the lease on predetermined terms. These options, however, may complicate the tax treatment of the sale-leaseback.

[A] Tax Benefits

Provided that the sale-leaseback is recognized as a sale and a lease for tax purposes, the seller-lessee deducts the full amount of its rental payments. If there is a gain or a loss on the sale portion of the transaction, the gain or loss is taxable under the usual rules. The purchaser-lessor has income from the rents received from the seller-lessee, but this income may be sheltered by the operating expenses and depreciation deductions available to the owner of real estate.

(Lease payments are considered at ¶ 401, sales of real property at ¶ 1301, real estate operating expenses at ¶ 703, and depreciation at ¶ 901.)

For the seller-lessee, the sale-leaseback may provide a tax benefit because the deduction for rental payments may be greater than depreciation and interest deductions from traditional financing. This is more likely to be the case if the property has already been fully depreciated or if the property is leased back for less than its useful life. The sale-leaseback also may provide benefits for the seller-lessee when the seller-lessee cannot utilize the tax benefits associated with the ownership of depreciable property. The sale to an investor who can benefit from the tax advantages of ownership may permit the seller-lessee to lease at a favorable rate, in effect, splitting the tax benefits with the investor. Whether or not a sale-leaseback will actually provide a net benefit in a given situation may require extensive projections and computations. In many cases, the disadvantages of a sale-leaseback will outweigh the benefits.

Of course, to realize the tax benefits of a sale-leaseback, the transaction must be treated as a sale and leaseback for tax purposes, rather than as a mere financing device. The guidelines that have been applied are discussed at ¶ 305.02. If a sale-leaseback is not recognized as such for tax purposes, but is treated as a secured loan, the consequences are substantial. Since all calculations of the potential benefits of a sale-leaseback hinge on the tax treatment, it is essential that the parties to a proposed sale-leaseback be certain of the treatment of their transaction.

If a sale-leaseback is treated as a secured loan for tax purposes, the seller-lessee would be denied deductions for rent or lease payments. The seller-lessee's payments would be treated as payments on a loan—partly interest and partly the amortization of principal. Depreciation would be available to the seller-lessee who continues to be considered the owner of the property, but the rate and method of depreciation would be the same as before the purported sale of the property. The purchaser-lessor, instead of being in the position of the owner of property, would be in the position of a mortgagee. Depreciation deductions would not be available, nor would other deductions associated with the ownership of real property. To the extent payments received represent principal, however, the purchaser-lessor's income would be reduced.

When a utility engaged in a series of like-kind exchanges coupled with a sale and leaseback between an electricity distributor and tax-exempt public utilities, the Tax Court found that the sale-leaseback was actually a loan. Not only were the benefits of the sale-leaseback lost, but also the benefits of the like-kind exchanges. Because the sale-leasebacks were actually loans, the utility, in substance, exchanged its power plants for an interest in financial instruments. Because that exchange did not qualify as a like-kind exchange, the utility was required to include in income the gain on the sale of the power plants.[159]

---

[159] Exelon Corporation, CA-7, 2018-2 USTC ¶ 50,441, *aff'g* 147 TC 230, CCH Dec. 60,697.

[B] Like-Kind Exchange and the Sale-Leaseback

Real estate held as an investment or used in a trade or business may be exchanged for other investment or business real estate without recognition of gain or loss.[160] Reg. § 1.1031(a)-1(c) provides that no gain or loss is recognized if a taxpayer exchanges "a leasehold of a fee with 30 years or more to run for real estate." This raises the danger that if the lease in a sale-leaseback is for 30 years or more, the sale-leaseback may be treated as a like-kind exchange of property, although it is not entirely clear that this provision governs when only one property is involved, that is, when a fee interest is exchanged for a leasehold interest in the same property. There is a split of authority among the Circuit Courts of Appeals.

In *Century Electric Co.*,[161] the Eighth Circuit held that the sale of business property at a loss followed by a leaseback of the property for 95 years was a like-kind exchange which made the loss nondeductible. The court applied the regulation quoted above[162] and held it valid as applied to an exchange of a 30-year-or-longer leasehold for a fee interest, even though the rights exchanged are in the same property. On the other hand, the Second Circuit skirted the issue in *Jordan Marsh Co.*[163] In this case, a department store which sold the properties on which its store was operated for cash and simultaneously received a leaseback for 30 years and three days sustained a recognizable loss since, according to the court, there was in fact a sale for the full value of the properties conveyed, and not an exchange. The court found it unnecessary to pass on the validity of Reg. § 1.1031(a)-1(c) as applied to a leasehold of 30 years or more exchanged for a fee interest in the same property.[164] The key to sale-leaseback treatment rather than like-kind exchange treatment is that the sale must be for full fair market value and the rental must also be at fair rental value. Of course, if the term of the leaseback is less than 30 years, the problem cannot arise.

.02 Recognition of a Sale-Leaseback for Tax Purposes

Determining whether a particular sale-leaseback will be recognized as such for tax purposes, or whether it will be treated as a mortgage financing arrangement is not an easy task. The Supreme Court has established some guidelines, and further guidance may be distilled from IRS pronouncements.

[A] Supreme Court Guidelines

In *F. Lyon Co.*,[165] the Supreme Court held that the purchaser-lessor in a sale-leaseback was the owner of the building and that the arrangement was not merely a financing arrangement. The seller-lessee was a bank that could not itself finance the construction of a new building because of state and federal banking restrictions. The purchaser-lessor was a home furnishing company that agreed to take title to the building as it was being constructed and to lease it back to the bank with

[160] Code Sec. 1031; like-kind exchanges are considered fully at ¶ 1302.

[161] CA-8, 51-2 USTC ¶ 9482, 192 F.2d 155, *cert. denied*, 342 U.S. 954, 72 S.Ct. 625.

[162] Reg. § 1.1031(a)-1(c).

[163] CA-2, 59-2 USTC ¶ 9641, 269 F.2d 453.

[164] The IRS will not follow the decision in *Jordan Marsh*. *See* Rev. Rul. 60-43, 1960-1 CB 687. For additional cases holding that the like-kind provisions do not apply to a genuine sale-leaseback transaction, *see* Leslie Co., CA-3, 76-2 USTC ¶ 9553, 539 F.2d 943 and Crowley, Milner & Co., CA-6, 82-2 USTC ¶ 9612, 689 F.2d 635.

[165] 78-1 USTC ¶ 9370, 435 U.S. 561, 98 S.Ct. 1291.

options to repurchase at various times. The purchaser-lessor obtained both a construction loan and permanent mortgage financing, and made an initial investment of $500,000 in the building in order to diversify its operations.

The Court held that the sale-leaseback was genuine and pointed to the following factors:

1. A genuine multi-party transaction (financing was obtained from outside sources) with economic substance took place;
2. The sale-leaseback was compelled or encouraged by business or regulatory considerations and was not merely the result of tax avoidance considerations; and
3. The lessor retained significant and genuine attributes of the traditional lessor status.

Under these guidelines, if the purchaser-lessor supplied all of the funds for the purchase of the property, that is, did not obtain outside financing, and if the seller-lessee has a repurchase option that takes away any risk born by a lessor, the transaction would be treated as a financing arrangement, rather than as a sale and a leaseback.

[B] IRS Guidelines

In a series of pronouncements, the IRS has established some guidelines of its own for determining whether there is a true lease or merely a financing arrangement. Although most of these pronouncements are directed to leveraged leasing of equipment, they may offer guidance by way of analogy in the case of the sale-leaseback of real estate. As distilled from Rev. Rul. 55-540,[166] Rev. Proc. 75-21,[167] Rev. Proc. 75-28,[168] Rev. Proc. 76-30,[169] and Rev. Proc. 79-48,[170] the IRS may characterize a lease transaction as a financed sale transaction if one of the following factors is present:

1. The lessee acquires equity through the lease payments;
2. The lessee acquires title to the property after the required number of lease payments have been made;
3. The lessee's total lease payments are due in a relatively short time, and the payments substantially cover the amount required to purchase the asset;
4. The lease payments substantially exceed the fair rental value of the property indicating that the transaction is financed over less than the life of the asset;
5. The property will be acquired by the lessee at the end of the lease term for a nominal sum;

[166] 1955-2 CB 39.
[167] 1975-1 CB 715.
[168] 1975-1 CB 752.
[169] 1976-2 CB 647.
[170] 1979-2 CB 529.

6. The lessee participates with the lessor in the acquisition of the asset by guaranteeing a loan or through similar agreements; or
7. The lessor has little or no at-risk investment in the property (in a leveraged equipment lease, the IRS looks for a minimum at-risk investment of 20 percent of the asset's cost).

In a more recent pronouncement,[171] the IRS provided guidelines it will use for advance ruling purposes in determining whether certain transactions purporting to be leases of property are, in fact, leases for federal income tax purposes. Rev. Proc. 2001-28, like earlier pronouncements, is directed toward leveraged leases of equipment. The guidelines, says the IRS, clarify the circumstances in which an advance ruling recognizing the existence of a lease ordinarily will be issued solely to assist taxpayers in preparing ruling requests and the IRS in issuing advance ruling letters. The IRS cautions that the guidelines do not define, as a matter of law, whether a transaction is or is not a lease for federal income tax purposes and are not intended to be used for audit purposes.

.03 Variations on the Sale-Leaseback

The straightforward sale-leaseback transaction may be modified in several respects to provide advantages to the parties and to accommodate various situations. The following discusses some of the more common variations.

[A] Split Financing

Rather than a sale and leaseback of the entire real estate package, the real estate may be split into its components and only one component made the subject of the sale-leaseback. This is commonly done with a subordinated land lease. When a building is to be constructed, the land is sold to an investor and then leased back. Traditional mortgage financing is obtained by the seller-lessee of the land for the construction of the improvements. The lease is made subordinate to the mortgage. This arrangement provides financing for the land cost of a project which is not normally available through a traditional mortgage.

The tax treatment of these split financing sale-leasebacks hinges on the same factors as a regular sale-leaseback.

[B] Related Party Sale-Leasebacks

Related party sale-leasebacks present problems in several respects. First, under Code Sec. 267, a loss on the sale of property to a related party is disallowed. A related party is defined to include family members, controlled corporations, and trustees. This, of course, would only be a consideration if the subject of the sale-leaseback had a value less than its basis.

Even more important, a sale-leaseback involving related parties does not fall squarely within the Supreme Court guidelines for a valid sale-leaseback, which are discussed at ¶ 305.02[A]. There is also the danger that the sale and rental prices set by related parties will not be fair values.

Despite these problems, it is still possible to arrange a sale-leaseback between related parties, especially in light of Tax Court decisions upholding the validity of

[171] Rev. Proc. 2001-28, 2001-1 CB 1156.

gift-leaseback transactions. A gift-leaseback is essentially the same as a sale-leaseback, except that the lessee gives the property to the lessor prior to the leaseback. In many cases, these transactions are between a property owner and a trust set up for the benefit of the owner's children. The validity of a sale-leaseback between related parties is more likely to be upheld if the arrangement conforms to the guidelines that have been applied to gift-leasebacks. The Tax Court would also support the transaction if the sale is for less than full value, since this arrangement may be split into a part-sale, part-gift and leaseback.

According to the Tax Court, a gift-leaseback transaction is valid if the following conditions are met:

1. The donor must not retain substantially the same control over the property after the gift-leaseback transaction;
2. The lease must be in writing and call for a reasonable rent;
3. The leaseback must have a bona fide business purpose (although the Fourth and Fifth Circuit Courts seem to look for a business reason for the gift as well); and
4. The donor must not retain any equity in the property and must not have the right to regain the property.[172]

[C] Equity Participation

As noted above, one of the drawbacks in a sale-leaseback for the seller-lessee is that the property may have significant residual value at the end of the lease term. To overcome this, a sale-leaseback arrangement may give the seller-lessee an option to repurchase at the end of the lease term, although this may confuse the tax treatment of the transaction. Instead of an option to repurchase, the seller-lessee may be given a chance to share in any appreciation experienced by the property after the sale to the purchaser-lessee. This avoids the repurchase option, but may create other problems since, to the extent of the equity participation, the seller-lessee has not really parted with the property.

[D] Tax-Exempt Entity Leasing

Tax-exempt organizations and government units gain no advantage from depreciation on property that they own or use. This makes these entities prime candidates for the role of seller-lessee in a sale-leaseback. Through a sale of property to an investor followed by a leaseback, tax-exempt entities may obtain indirectly, through reduced rentals, the benefits of depreciation. For the purchaser-lessor, however, a sale-leaseback with a tax-exempt entity means reduced benefits from depreciation. For real estate leased to a tax-exempt entity, the depreciation period is generally 40 years. (Depreciation is considered in Chapter 9.)

.04 Lease with Option as Conditional Sales Contract

In any lease with an option to purchase, there is the danger that the IRS may view the transaction as a sales contract and the lease as a mere financing device in

[172] *See* C.J. Mathews, 61 TC 12, CCH Dec. 32,161, *rev'd*, CA-5, 75-2 USTC ¶ 9734, 520 F.2d 323, *cert. denied*, 424 U.S. 967, 96 S.Ct. 1463, and R.A. Serbousek, 36 TCM 479, CCH Dec. 34,353(M), T.C. Memo. 1977-105.

which the parties are attempting to gain the tax advantages of a lease while giving the lessee the right to take title to the property. In any lease arrangement with a purchase option, the parties must keep the option price high enough and the rental payments low enough so that the transaction will be treated as a lease and the rents will be deductible.

The Tax Court seems to apply an economic reality or intent to purchase test. If the option is exercisable within a period which is clearly less than the useful life of the property, and the rental payments cover a substantial part of what would be the purchase price, the Tax Court is likely to hold that a sale and purchase are intended. This was the result when a taxpayer paid $300,000 for two years' rent on a farm and then exercised an option to buy for an additional $100,000.[173]

In *M&W Gear Co.,*[174] the Court denied a deduction for rents. Through the purported rental payments, the taxpayer acquired a substantial equity in land. Factors the Court considered were:

1. Evidence of an initial intent to purchase by the lessee;
2. Unreasonably high rent;
3. No provision for cancellation of the lease without cause;
4. The lessee was obligated to exercise the purchase option as a matter of economics, since the lessee had made costly improvements that could not be removed and that could be retained only if the option to purchase were exercised.

On the other hand, a 10-year lease with an option to purchase real estate was a lease and not a sale, and payments under the lease were held deductible in *Calcasieu Paper Co., Inc.*[175] The value of the property was not in excess of the option price, only payments made in the last two years of the lease were applied to the purchase price, the amount paid on exercise of the option was 40 percent of the total payments under the lease, the option could be exercised only after a period of six years, and the parties intended to make a lease.

WBSR, Inc.[176] involved the lease of the physical properties of a radio station for one year at a rent of $4,000 and an option to buy for $44,000 less any rent paid. The lessee exercised the option to purchase but was entitled to a deduction for the rent paid under the agreement. The rent was not excessive in relation to the fair market value of the property. *See also Breece Veneer & Panel Co.,*[177] in which an agreement to pay rent of $100,000 in 60 monthly installments and an option to purchase for $50,000 was held a lease and the rent payments deductible because the lessee had no equity in the property until the option was exercised.

---

[173] M. Berry, 11 TCM 301, CCH Dec. 18,882(M).

[174] CA-7, 71-2 USTC ¶ 9555, 446 F.2d 841.

[175] 12 TCM 74, CCH Dec. 19,445(M).

[176] 30 TC 747, CCH Dec. 23,061, *acq.* 1958-2 CB 8.

[177] CA-7, 56-1 USTC ¶ 9485, 232 F.2d 319.

Part II

RENTAL AND LEASING ARRANGEMENTS

Introduction to Part II

Acquiring ownership of property is not a prerequisite to obtaining the use of property. Rental and leasing arrangements are common. The desire or necessity by some individuals and businesses to use property without the burdens of ownership, and the desire of others to profit from filling this need, fuels a multi-billion-dollar market in investment real estate.

The tax consequences flowing from the more common payments between tenants and landlords are discussed in Chapter 4. The most common payment, of course, is cash rent. But rent can take many forms and guises. For the business tenant, rent is a deductible expense. For the landlord, rent is taxable income. The amount and timing of a tenant's tax deduction and a landlord's income is explored in some detail, including the special timing and reporting rules for certain deferred or stepped rental agreements. The discussion reflects the IRS's adoption of final regulations that extend those special rules to decreasing, as well as increasing, rents.

While rent payments and deposits may be the most common payments that concern landlords and tenants, they are certainly not the only ones. Either party at both the inception and conclusion of a lease may incur substantial costs which are neither rents nor deposits. These costs, of course, have tax consequences. Careful advance planning, as discussed in Chapter 5, assures that all parties receive the most favorable tax treatment possible on the acquisition and the modification, cancellation, disposition, or other termination of a lease agreement.

Leasehold improvements and additions, the subject of Chapter 6, may be made by either the lessor or lessee, according to their agreement. How this responsibility is assigned determines the tax consequences, which can vary significantly depending on the exact arrangements made by the parties. This is one area in which the parties do have a great deal of power to shape the tax outcome by how they structure their lease agreement.

Chapter 4
Payments Between Landlord and Tenant

¶ 400 Overview of Chapter
¶ 401 Rent
¶ 402 Tenant's Rent Deduction
¶ 403 Landlord's Rent Income
¶ 404 Deferred or Stepped Rental Agreements
¶ 405 Leases with Purchase Options
¶ 406 Deposits

¶ 400 OVERVIEW OF CHAPTER

When a landlord and tenant enter into a lease agreement, the agreement may obligate the parties to make various payments. The most common of these payments, of course, are the periodic cash payments of rent. But rent can take many forms and guises. Other payments also may pass between landlord and tenant. For the landlord, the primary questions in any payment received from a tenant are whether the payment is income and, if so, when that income must be reported. For the tenant, the questions are whether a payment is deductible for tax purposes and, if so, when the deduction can be taken.

In this chapter, we examine the various forms of rent and their income tax consequences, beginning with an exploration of the concept of rent for tax purposes. The amount and timing of a tenant's tax deduction and a landlord's income are considered, as are the special timing and reporting rules for certain deferred or stepped rental agreements. In some cases, a purchase option written into a lease agreement may affect the characterization of payments between landlord and tenant, and this is also discussed in this chapter. The chapter concludes with a look at security deposits and similar payments.

While these topics cover most of the payments between landlord and tenant, there may be others that fall into the category of lease acquisition or disposition costs. These are considered in Chapter 5. Improvements and additions to leaseholds are the subjects of Chapter 6.

¶ 401 RENT

Rent is the payment by the user of property to the owner of property for its use and enjoyment. In general, gross income includes rentals received or accrued for the occupancy of real estate.[1] Rentals or other payments, required to be made as a condition to the continued use or possession, for purposes of the trade or business, of property to which the taxpayer has not taken title or in which the taxpayer has no equity, are deductible as ordinary and necessary business expenses.[2]

The usual form of rent is periodic cash payments, but rent may also be paid in property or services. When rent is paid in this manner, the amount of rent is measured by the value of the property or services. Other arrangements also may govern the payment of rent. Rent may be set as a percentage of the lessee's sales, profits, or some other figure, rather than as a fixed amount. Rent may be paid indirectly, for example, through the payment of the lessor's expenses or debts by the lessee. The key is that if a payment is made as a condition to the use or occupancy of property, other than as a payment toward the purchase of the property, the payment, regardless of its form, is rent.

.01 Percentage Rents

It is a common commercial practice to base rent or a portion of rent on a percentage of the lessee's sales, profits, or some other figure. Unless the parties to the lease are related (see ¶ 401.04), percentage lease agreements generally are respected for tax purposes and the percentage amounts are income to the lessor and deductible by the lessee. In upholding a lease which called for rent based on a percentage of gross sales, the Fifth Circuit Court of Appeals held that if a lease is fair and reasonable at the time it is executed, then deductions for rent paid during the term of the lease will be upheld regardless of the fact that the percentage of gross sales provision might produce low rental payments in poorer years and high rental payments in good years.[3]

.02 Payment of Lessor's Expenses

Generally, if a lessee pays any of the lessor's expenses, the payments are considered additional rent.[4] Payment of the lessor's expenses by the lessee is a common practice in commercial leases, and these leases are commonly referred to as "net leases." Expenses of the lessor that may be paid by the lessee as additional rent include maintenance and repair expenses, insurance, utilities, real estate taxes, and interest on mortgage or other debt of the lessor. Some leases have even required the lessee to pay principal amortization, as well as interest, on mortgage debt secured by the leased property.

When a lessee pays a lessor's expenses, the lessor reports rental income, even if the expense is a deductible item for the lessor. For example, Reg. § 1.162-11(a) provides that "taxes paid by a tenant to or for a landlord for business property are additional rent and constitute a deductible item to the tenant and taxable income to the landlord, the amount of the tax being deductible by the latter." In fact, any ordinary and necessary business expense[5] paid by the lessee attributable to the property leased would be deductible by the lessor as a business expense. The

[1] Code Sec. 61(a)(5); Reg. § 1.61-8(a).

[2] Code Sec. 162(a)(3).

[3] Brown Printing Co., CA-5, 58-2 USTC ¶ 9534, 255 F.2d 436.

[4] Reg. § 1.61-8(c).

[5] Code Sec. 162.

tenant, however, is paying rent and the amount is deductible by the lessee only if the property is being used for business purposes. For example, if the tenant in a residential apartment pays the landlord's property tax on the apartment, the tax is additional rent. The landlord has additional rental income, but a corresponding tax deduction. The tenant, however, is paying rent, and not a property tax, and would not be entitled to a tax deduction for the amount of the property tax paid on behalf of the landlord.

If a lease requires the lessee to pay, as additional rent, the income tax of the lessor attributable to the rental income, the income tax paid by the lessee is additional rent which increases the income tax due. The additional tax increases the rent that, in turn, once again increases the tax due, and so on. This pyramiding that occurs when the lessee is required to pay the lessor's income tax under a net lease is why most net leases do not provide for the payment of the lessor's income tax. There is also the problem of determining the lessor's income tax attributable to the rental income. Most lessors do not want to disclose to their lessees the financial information necessary to determine the amount.

Annual payments made by the lessee following the assumption by the lessee of the lessor's mortgage indebtedness are income to the lessor when made.[6] The same rule applies even if the lessor is not personally liable on the mortgage.[7]

.03 Property Transactions

In some situations, what appear to be transactions in, or sales or exchanges of, property may be treated as rental payments. In Rev. Rul. 73-276,[8] the IRS ruled that the payment of the rents collected by the purchaser after the sale, but which had accrued under a percentage rent agreement prior to the sale of a shopping center was rental income to the seller and not part of the purchase price.

A seller, who sold property for less than its fair value in exchange for the rent-free use of part of the property, received additional consideration for the property equal to the rental value of the property used. This rental value was then deductible by the seller as an advance rental.[9] (Treatment of advance rentals by lessors is considered at ¶ 403.01.) Another advance rental situation involved the lessor of land who received a share of the proceeds of a leasehold mortgage in return for subordinating his fee interest in the land to the leasehold mortgage. The share of the proceeds received by the land lessor was advance rent.[10]

The sale of property to a lessee who improves the property and then resells the property back to the lessor may be a rental situation rather than two sales transactions. In *W.J. Haag*,[11] the sale of property to the lessee who improved the property and then resold the property to the lessor resulted in a loss to the lessee. This loss was held to be rent paid by the lessee to the lessor, deductible by the lessee and includible in the lessor's income.

---

[6] L.P. Wentz v. Gentsch, DC Ohio, 40-2 USTC ¶ 9666.

[7] E.S. Amey, 22 TC 756, CCH Dec. 20,431.

[8] 1973-1 CB 210.

[9] Steinway & Sons, 46 TC 375, CCH Dec. 27,995, *acq.* 1967-2 CB 3.

[10] Rev. Rul. 75-226, 1975-1 CB 199.

[11] 40 TC 488, CCH Dec. 26,159, *acq.* 1964-2 CB 7, *aff'd*, CA-8, 64-2 USTC ¶ 9634, 334 F.2d 351.

.04 Related Parties

The lease of property between related persons offers the potential for tax avoidance, and for this reason the IRS is more sensitive to rental agreements between family members or corporations and their shareholders. As a general rule, as long as a lease agreement is reasonable when entered into and one that would be arrived at in an arm's-length dealing between strangers, the IRS will not challenge the lease and the lessee's rent deductions.[12]

[A] Intra-Family Leases

When business property is leased by a family member from another family member, there is the danger that the family may use the lease as a means of shifting income. If the lessee pays excessive rent, he will lose the deduction for rent above fair rental value (the amount of rent that would be charged in an arm's-length lease between strangers) since payment of the excess is not a "condition of the continued use or possession" of the property. In all likelihood, the excess rent will be treated as a gift to the lessor.

Determining the fair rental value of property leased to a family member, at times, may be difficult. If the property was previously leased to a stranger, the rent in that situation, most likely, would be considered the fair and reasonable rent that could be charged a family member. Rental figures for comparable properties, an appropriate capitalization rate applied to the value of the property, and professional appraisals also may be used to determine fair rental values.

[B] Controlled Corporations

Leases of property between a controlled corporation and its shareholders can run in either direction, that is, the corporation may be either the tenant or landlord. When the corporation is the tenant, the shareholder, through the rental agreement, is able to draw money out of the corporation in a tax-deductible manner. When the shareholder is the tenant, the shareholder may obtain use of the corporate property while, in effect, paying rent to oneself. In either case, there is the temptation to use the lease as a tax avoidance device, and the IRS is sensitive to such arrangements.

If a corporation pays excessive rent to a shareholder, the excess rent is treated as the payment of a nondeductible dividend.[13] Similarly, a bargain rental of corporate property to a shareholder may be construed as payment of a constructive dividend equal to the bargain element.[14] The shareholder, however, would be entitled to deduct the bargain rent paid in this situation, provided the leased property was used in a trade or business of the shareholder.

As in an intra-family lease, as long as the rent, including percentage rent, in a lease between a controlled corporation and shareholder is fair when agreed to and

[12] S. Imerman, 7 TC 1030, CCH Dec. 15,429, *acq.* 1947-1 CB 2; H.G. Bender, 6 TCM 421, CCH Dec. 15,762(M). *See also* Brown Printing Co. cited above.

[13] Limericks, Inc., 7 TC 1129, CCH Dec. 15,466, *aff'd,* CA-5, 48-1 USTC ¶ 9146, 165 F.2d 483.

[14] Rev. Rul. 58-1, 1958-1 CB 173.

would be accepted by parties dealing at arm's length, the IRS will accept the lease agreement.[15]

In some cases, it is possible for a shareholder to gain extra advantage by leasing unimproved property to a controlled corporation. If unimproved land, or property on which improvements can be made or added, is leased to the corporation, the corporation can make improvements. When the lease expires, the improvements become the property of the lessor-shareholder, and the shareholder may realize no taxable income because of the value added to the property by the corporation.[16] Although Code Sec. 109 does provide that the value of improvements made by the lessee is not gross income to the lessor on the termination of a lease, there is some danger that the IRS may find a constructive dividend if, following a lease to a controlled corporation, the property reverts to the shareholder-lessor long before the end of the improvement's useful life.[17]

Reallocation of Income

Lease agreements between shareholders and their controlled corporations also run the risk that the IRS may use its power to allocate income among commonly controlled trades, businesses or organizations in order to properly reflect income.[18] Leasing property to a controlled corporation may be a trade or business, and the Tax Court has supported reallocation of income among shareholders and their corporations by the IRS.[19]

Reallocation of Rental Income and Deductions

Code Sec. 482 also applies to leases between two corporations that are owned by the same shareholders. If the rent charged one corporation by the other is either too high or too low, rental income and deductions may be reallocated between the corporations and cause the shareholders to receive constructive dividends from one corporation which are deemed to be capital contributions to the other corporation.[20]

[C] Matching Lessee's Deduction to Lessor's Income

Were it not for Code Sec. 267, an accrual basis lessee could accrue and deduct rent owed to a related cash basis lessor before the lessor receives the rental income. Code Sec. 267(a)(2), however, requires the matching of deductions and income for expense and interest payments between certain related parties. Under this rule, a lessee is not allowed to deduct rent owed to a related taxpayer until the day that the corresponding income is includible in the lessor's income. In effect, an accrual basis lessee is placed on the cash basis as to rents owed to a related lessor.

The relationships that require the matching of deductions and income are the same as those for which losses on sales or exchanges are disallowed,[21] with one

[15] W.E. Davis & Sons, Inc., 41 TCM 1263, CCH Dec. 37,828(M), T.C. Memo. 1981-178; *see also* Brown Printing Co. cited above.

[16] Code Sec. 109.

[17] Safway Steel Scaffolds Co. of Georgia, CA-5, 79-1 USTC ¶ 9253, 590 F.2d 1360.

[18] Code Sec. 482.

[19] T.B. Fegan, 71 TC 791, CCH Dec. 35,880, *aff'd*, CA-10, 81-1 USTC ¶ 9436; R.D. Cooper, 64 TC 576, CCH Dec. 33,327; *see also* Rev. Rul. 88-38, 1988-1 CB 246.

[20] Equitable Publishing Co., CA-3, 66-1 USTC ¶ 9609, 356 F.2d 514, *cert. denied*, 385 U.S. 822, 87 S.Ct. 50.

[21] Code Sec. 267(b).

addition. Matching of expense deductions and income is required between a personal service corporation and any employee-owner of the corporation.[22] Matching is also required for any of the following relationships listed in Code Sec. 267(b):

1. Members of the same family, defined as including only brothers and sisters, spouse, ancestors, and lineal descendants;
2. A corporation and an individual who owns, directly or indirectly, more than 50 percent in value of the outstanding stock of the corporation;
3. Two corporations that are members of the same controlled group (50 percent parent-subsidiary or brother-sister corporations);[23]
4. The grantor and fiduciary of a trust;
5. Fiduciaries of two different trusts if the same person is the grantor of both trusts;
6. The fiduciary and beneficiary of a trust;
7. A fiduciary and beneficiary of different trusts if the same person is the grantor of both trusts;
8. A trust fiduciary and a corporation if more than 50 percent in value of the outstanding stock of the corporation is owned, directly or indirectly, by or for the trust or the grantor of the trust;
9. A tax-exempt educational or charitable organization and a person who controls, directly or indirectly, the organization, or a member of the control person's family;
10. A corporation and a partnership if the same persons own more than 50 percent in value of the outstanding stock of the corporation, and more than 50 percent of the capital or profit interest in the partnership;
11. An S corporation and another S corporation if the same persons own more than 50 percent of the value of the outstanding stock of each corporation; and
12. An S corporation and a regular corporation if the same persons own more than 50 percent in value of the outstanding stock of each corporation.

¶ 402 TENANT'S RENT DEDUCTION

Rent, if it is paid for the use of business property, is deductible.[24] Rent that is considered a personal, living or family expense, however, is not deductible.[25] Therefore, rent on a personal residence, apartment, or vacation property generally is not deductible (personal residences are considered generally in Part V; mixed-use residences, part business/part personal, are specifically considered in Chapter 18).

If rent is paid in property other than money, the amount deductible is the fair market value of the property. If a tenant pays for rent by providing services for the landlord, the amount deductible is the amount of cash rental that was agreed to

[22] Code Sec. 267(a)(2).

[23] Code Secs. 267(f) and 1563(a).

[24] Code Sec. 162(a)(3).

[25] Code Sec. 262.

(provided, of course, that the cash rental was a reasonable fair rental). The tenant who pays rent by providing services, however, must include the value of the services in income. Presumably, the value of the services and the fair rental value are the same. In other words, the tenant has income from providing services and an equal offsetting deduction for rent.

Not everything denominated rent by the parties is deductible. Rent paid under a lease with an option to purchase may, in some cases, be treated as part payment of the purchase price (see ¶ 405). There may be no deduction for excessive rent paid to a related party as discussed above.

A lessee using the accrual method of accounting deducts rent for the year in which the rent accrues, regardless of when it is paid.

> ***Example 1:*** The Taxpayer, who is an accrual-method, calendar-year taxpayer rents business property under a lease running from December 1, 2019, to November 30, 2020. Even if the Taxpayer makes no rent payments in 2019, the Taxpayer is still entitled to deduct the amount of rent attributable to December for the 2019 tax year. Similarly, if the Taxpayer pays three months' rent in December 2019, the deduction for 2019 is limited to one month's rent. The Taxpayer cannot deduct the other two months' rent in 2019, even though payment was made in 2019. The deduction for the two months' rent attributable to 2020 must be taken in 2020.

A lessee using the cash method of accounting cannot deduct rent until it is paid, regardless of the period to which it relates. Rent paid in advance, however, may not be currently deductible. Rather, the cash method lessee may have to take deductions for rent paid in advance over the periods to which the prepayment applies (see ¶ 402.01).

.01 Advance Rents

The rationale for denying a cash method taxpayer a full deduction for advance payments of rent is that the payment is creating an asset, the interest in the leasehold. Reg. § 1.263(a)-2(d) provides that a "taxpayer must capitalize amounts paid to acquire or produce a unit of real or personal property . . . , including leasehold improvement property, land and land improvements, buildings, machinery and equipment, and furniture and fixtures." Also, in providing rules for the timing of deductions, Reg. § 1.461-1(a) provides that "under the cash receipts and disbursements method of accounting . . . if an expenditure results in the creation of an asset having a useful life which extends substantially beyond the close of the taxable year, such an expenditure may not be deductible, or may be deductible only in part, for the taxable year in which made."

Accordingly, advance rentals are deductible on the cash basis only for the year to which they apply.[26] The same rule has been held to apply specifically to an accrual-method taxpayer.[27] See also Reg. § 1.162-11(a), which provides that "if a

[26] N.B. Smith, 51 TC 429, CCH Dec. 29,272; Baton Coal Co., CA-3, 2 USTC ¶ 788, 51 F.2d 469, *cert. denied,* 284 U.S. 674, 52 S.Ct. 129.

[27] G.W. Keeling, 30 TCM 954, CCH Dec. 30,968(M), T.C. Memo. 1971-224; H.L. Wood, 34 TCM 817, CCH Dec. 33,267(M), T.C. Memo. 1975-189.

leasehold is acquired for business purposes for a specified sum, the purchaser may take as a deduction in his return an aliquot part of such sum each year, based on the number of years the lease has to run." (Note that an advance payment that applies to the entire lease term may be considered a lease acquisition cost. Lease acquisition costs are discussed further at ¶ 501.)

Despite the general rule for advance rents, some court decisions have allowed deductions for rent paid in advance when the prepaid rent applied in part to the current year and in part to the following year.[28] In *M.J. Zaninovich*, the Ninth Circuit applied Reg. § 1.461-1(a) to a 20-year lease that required the first year's rent, for the period December-November, to be paid in advance. The court allowed the deduction for the full year's rent when paid because, in the opinion of the court, one year was not "substantially beyond the close of the taxable year." The court also noted that the prepayment of 12 months' rent was a common business practice in the type of lease involved and that the prepayment did not distort income or permit the evasion of tax.

While *M.J. Zaninovich* provides precedent for taking a deduction for up to a year's rent when at least part of the payment applies to the current year, it does not support a deduction for prepayment of a year's rent in the year of payment when the lease term does not begin until the following year. In such a case, the deduction, most likely, would have to be deferred until the year the lease begins. For instance, the "one-year rule" of *M.J. Zaninovich* was not followed in *G.S. Sorrell, Jr.*,[29] in which rent-up fees paid in 1977 by a partnership to the general partner were not deductible in 1977 since the lease terms began in 1978. The payment was considered a capital expenditure, amortizable over the life of the leases, beginning no earlier than the year the leases began.

.02 Graduated Rents

Rather than level rentals throughout the lease term, a lease may provide for graduated rentals that increase or decrease over time, beyond adjustments keyed to factors such as inflation or rises in taxes or other expenses. Graduated rent arrangements are generally designed to accommodate special situations of the lessor or lessee.

[A] Decrease in Rents

In the case of decreasing rents, there is the danger that the IRS may assert that the higher initial rents are advance rents that should be applied to later years of the lease. Advance rents do not have to be a single payment.

If advance rents are paid in installments over a period of years, the advance rents still must be deducted over the periods to which they relate. When a lease obligated the lessee to pay $10,000 annually during the first 25 years of a 99-year lease, with no payments required in the remaining years of the lease, only 1/99 of

[28] M.J. Zaninovich, CA-9, 80-1 USTC ¶ 9342, 616 F.2d 429; H.H. Hoopengarner, 80 TC 538, CCH Dec. 39,968, *aff'd*, CA-9, 745 F.2d 66.

[29] 53 TCM 1362, CCH Dec. 44,054(M), T.C. Memo. 1987-351, *rev'd on another issue* CA-11, 89-2 USTC ¶ 9521, 882 F.2d 484.

the aggregate rent was deductible in each year.[30] According to the court, "advance payments of rent, made in consideration of a lease for a longer period of time, have the character of capital investments whose benefits are spread throughout the life of the lease, and only an aliquot part of such expenditure is deductible in any tax year."

If there is some sound business reason for a lease with decreasing rents and the lease is a result of arm's-length bargaining, however, the lessee should take the higher deductions in the earlier years. See *Bellingham Cold Storage Co.*,[31] in which it was held that higher rents paid by the lessee on three leases in their earlier years were not advance rental payments allocable to the later years.

Renewal Options

Suppose that instead of decreasing rent over a fixed lease term, a lease fixes a level rent over the term of the lease, but also gives the lessee the option to renew at substantially reduced rental. Might the higher rents in the initial term be considered advance rentals applicable to the renewal term?

In Rev. Rul. 60-122,[32] the IRS ruled that a portion of the total payments in the first 36 months of a lease was advance rent applicable to a second 36-month renewal period that called for substantially reduced rents. While the lease involved equipment, the same rationale would seem applicable to real estate. Looking to whether the lessee would actually renew the lease, the IRS pointed to the nominal rent that had to be paid over the renewal period which made it "reasonable to assume . . . the lease will be renewed in accordance with the agreement." (See the discussion of the effect of renewal options on lease acquisition costs at ¶ 501.02.)

If factors other than low rent would influence the decision to renew beyond the initial term, it might be possible to show that it is not "reasonable to assume" that a lease will be renewed at a lower rent. In such a case, a lessee may be justified in taking the higher deductions during the initial term of the lease.[33]

Leases Involving More Than $250,000

Code Sec. 467(f) gives the IRS the power to prescribe regulations to make decreasing graduated rentals on leases involving more than $250,000 in rental payments subject to rules similar to those applicable to deferred or stepped rental agreements.

The IRS issued proposed regulations under Code Sec. 467 on June 3, 1996, that would apply to rental agreements that provide for decreasing, as well as increasing, rent, and to deferred or prepaid rent. The IRS adopted that rule as final in T.D. 8820 on April 30, 1999.

---

[30] Main & McKinney Bldg. Co. of Houston, Texas, CA-5, 40-2 USTC ¶ 9558, 113 F.2d 81, *cert. denied*, 311 U.S. 688, 61 S.Ct. 66.

[31] 64 TC 51, CCH Dec. 33,145.

[32] 1960-1 CB 56.

[33] Gem, Inc., DC Miss, 61-1 USTC ¶ 9361, 192 F. Supp. 841.

[B] Increase in Rents

If a lease calls for graduated rents that increase over time, there is no question of advance rents. Generally, the deduction for rent would follow the usual rules, that is, a deduction would be allowed for the increasing rents as they were paid or accrued, depending on the lessee's method of accounting. However, if the graduated rents are on a lease involving more than $250,000, the rent payments would be subject to the special rules of Code Sec. 467 that apply to deferred or stepped rents. These rules are discussed at ¶ 404.

¶ 403 LANDLORD'S RENT INCOME

Gross income includes rents received or accrued for the occupancy of real estate.[34] A cash method lessor includes rents in income for the year in which they are received. An accrual-method lessor includes rents in income for the year in which they accrue or are received, whichever is earlier (see the discussion of advance rents at ¶ 403.01).

When a lease calls for percentage rents based on a percentage of the lessee's sales, a lessor using accrual accounting includes the rents in income for the period during which the sales are made, even if actual payment is not due until the following year. In *Heer-Andres Investment Co.*,[35] the Tax Court ruled that additional rent measured by the lessee's net sales, which the lessor was entitled to for its fiscal year ending on January 31, accrued for the year ending on January 31, even though the additional rent was not payable until February. This ruling applies even if a portion of the additional rent might have to be returned to the lessee after the end of the taxable year.[36]

In some situations, improvements or additions made by a lessee to the lessor's property may be treated as rent income to the lessor (see ¶ 602).

.01 Advance Rents

The regulations are quite clear as to the treatment by the lessor of advance rents: "Except as provided in section 467 and the regulations thereunder, and except as otherwise provided by the Commissioner in published guidance, gross income includes advance rentals, which must be included in income for the year of receipt regardless of the period covered or the method of accounting employed by the taxpayer."[37] (See ¶ 404 for a discussion of the Code Sec. 467 rules.)

While the IRS has issued proposed regulations[38] to allow taxpayers a limited deferral beyond the tax year of receipt for certain advance payments, the regulations specifically exclude most rents. The limited deferral is available, however, for the lease or license of intellectual property and computer software. It is also available for the occupancy or use of property if the occupancy or use is ancillary to the provision of services. For example, the limited deferral is available for advance payments for the use of rooms or other quarters in a hotel, booth space at a trade

[34] Code Sec. 61(a)(5); Reg. § 1.61-8(a).

[35] 17 TC 786, CCH Dec. 18,623, *nonacq.* 1952-1 CB 5.

[36] Rod Realty Co., 26 TCM 243, CCH Dec. 28,374(M), T.C. Memo. 1967-49.

[37] Reg. § 1.61-8(b).

[38] NPRM REG-104554-18.

show, campsite space at a mobile home park, and recreational or banquet facilities, or other uses of property, so long as the use is ancillary to the provision of services to the property user.[39] See the discussion of deferral of advance payments at ¶ 701.02[B].)

If the Tax Code were symmetrical, of course, advance rents would be includible in income as earned rather than as received, just as payments of advance rents are deductible for the periods to which they relate rather than as paid. Unfortunately, the benefits of such symmetry are denied lessors. Despite the harshness of the rule and the possible bunching of income that it can create, the courts have been virtually unanimous in holding that rents received are income in the year of receipt, on a cash or accrual basis, even if no part of the advance payment is earned in the year of receipt.[40]

As long as the landlord has the unrestricted right to use advance rents, the rents must be included in income for the year received, even if the landlord may have to return some or all of the advance payment at some time in the future. For instance, the advance payment of the last year's rent under a 10-year lease was held to be income to an accrual basis lessor in the year received, even though the lessor was obligated to refund all or part of it if the premises were substantially destroyed prior to the expiration of the lease.[41]

.02 Assignments and Loans

Sometimes, the parties to a lease may attempt to cast their transaction in some other form in order to avoid the immediate taxation of advance rents. An amount paid by the "purchaser" for the assignment of a lease was treated as an advance rental payment, reportable by the "seller" as ordinary income in the year received, when the facts indicate the relationship between the parties to be that of lessor and lessee.[42] The value of a fee interest received on the execution of a lease, along with the right to annual rents, is an advance rental and taxable when received.[43]

W.B. Williams[44] involved an attempt to use a purported loan to avoid the inclusion of advance rents in the lessor's income when received. The lessee lent money to the lessor and the lessor was to repay the loan out of yearly payments received from the lessee for the use of land and timber. The court ruled that the "loan" was, in fact, prepaid rent. The lessor did not negotiate a loan separate from the lease, and the amount "loaned" was in direct relation to the annual rental payments. Of course, it should be possible for a lessor and lessee to work out a loan separate and apart from their lease agreement. The loan agreement should be embodied in a promissory note that contains a definite date for repayment. Also,

---

[39] Prop. Reg. § 1.1451-8(b)(i)(C)(4).

[40] *See*, for example, Hyde Park Realty, Inc., CA-2, 54-1 USTC ¶ 9305, 211 F.2d 462; B.D. Lyon, CA-9, 38-2 USTC ¶ 9356, 97 F.2d 70; Kohler-Campbell Corp., CA-4, 62-1 USTC ¶ 9237, 298 F.2d 911; J. & E. Enterprises, Inc., 26 TCM 944, CCH Dec. 28,622(M), T.C. Memo. 1967-191.

[41] New Capital Hotel, Inc., CA-6, 58-2 USTC ¶ 9912, 261 F.2d 437. *See also* Rev. Rul. 65-141, 1965-1 CB 210, in which the IRS ruled advance rents currently taxable even if paid to an escrow agent and even if the tenant may be entitled to a refund.

[42] Rev. Rul. 57-537, 1957-2 CB 52.

[43] Rev. Rul. 66-209, 1966-2 CB 299.

[44] CA-5, 68-1 USTC ¶ 9394, 395 F.2d 508.

the loan payments should not exactly match the rental payments called for in the lease agreement.

Not all payments received by a landlord, however, are immediately taxable. Advance payments that are in the nature of security deposits may escape current tax. See the discussion of deposits at ¶ 406.

¶ 404 DEFERRED OR STEPPED RENTAL AGREEMENTS

Deferred or stepped rental agreements offer the potential for tax savings when the lessor uses the cash method of accounting and the lessee uses the accrual method of accounting. Without some special statutory provision, the parties to a lease could agree to defer the payment of rent to the end of the lease. The amount of the payment, of course, would reflect the delay. In this fashion, the lessee could deduct rent as it accrued, but the landlord would not have to report income until the rent was actually paid. The Tax Reform Act of 1984 addressed this potential for tax avoidance with special rules for what are termed "Section 467 rental agreements."

Essentially, the rules of Code Sec. 467 are an extension of the original issue discount rules (discussed at ¶ 304) to leases that involve deferred or stepped rents. The essential thrust of the rules is to require the matching of rental income and deductions in Code Sec. 467 rental agreements and the inclusion of an interest factor on deferred rents in much the same fashion as the OID rules require the matching of income and deductions and the inclusion of an interest factor on deferred payment sales of property. Since April 30, 1999, similar rules apply to decreasing as well as increasing rentals.

.01 Section 467 Rental Agreements

A Section 467 rental agreement subject to Code Sec. 467 is any rental agreement for the use of tangible property under which:

1. There is at least one amount allocable to the use of property during a calendar year which is to be paid after the close of the following calendar year (a deferred rent), or
2. There are increases in the amount to be paid as rent under the agreement (stepped rents).

If the sum of the amounts to be paid under a rental agreement is $250,000 or less, Code Sec. 467 does not apply to the agreement, regardless of when the rent payments are made.[45]

In all Section 467 rental agreements that allocate rents (other than certain tax avoidance transactions discussed below), the lessor and lessee treat as rent for the current period the present value of rent to be paid after the close of the period that is allocable to the current period.[46] In addition, both the lessor and lessee take into account as interest an amount calculated by applying an interest rate equal to 110 percent of the applicable federal rate to the sum of rents taken into account in prior years but still unpaid as of the current year.[47] The applicable federal rates are the

[45] Code Sec. 467(d).

[46] Code Sec. 467(b)(1).

[47] Code Sec. 467(a)(2) and (e)(4).

same as those under the imputed interest and original issue discount rules discussed in Chapter 3.

When Code Sec. 467 applies to rental payments, the lessor and lessee are both placed on the accrual method of accounting as to deferred or stepped rents, and both must recognize an interest element on the deferred rent. The rule eliminates any mismatching of income and deductions that would otherwise occur when there is a cash-basis lessor and an accrual-basis lessee.

While the terms of Code Sec. 467 are directed to deferred or stepped rents, the IRS was directed to issue regulations with comparable rules for agreements involving decreasing rents.[48] The IRS issued proposed regulations under Code Sec. 467 on June 3, 1996, and final regulations on April 30, 1999, that apply to rental agreements that provide increasing or decreasing rents, or deferred or prepaid rent. The regulations do not address the application of Code Sec. 467 to transactions known as "lease strips" or "stripping transactions," which are described in Notice 95-53 (1995-44 IRB 21). Regulations were issued under Code Sec. 7701(l) recharacterizing stripping transactions. The regulations also do not provide for an adjustment to Code Sec. 467 rent and interest if a Code Sec. 467 rental agreement is modified. However, if a modification is "substantial," it is treated as a new Code Sec. 467 rental agreement.

As with the imputed interest and OID rules discussed in Chapter 3, the mathematics involved in the rent accrual and interest calculations for Code Sec. 467 rental agreements are best left to computers. The regulations do contain numerous examples.

.02 Constant Rental Accrual in Tax Avoidance Transactions

If a Section 467 rental agreement does not allocate rents, the rent that accrues in a taxable year is determined on a level present-value basis. The amount is the amount that, if paid at the close of each lease period, would result in an aggregate present value equal to the present value of the aggregate payments required under the lease.[49] Present value is determined using 110 percent of the applicable federal rate. The same rule applies to tax avoidance transactions as defined in Code Sec. 467(b)(4).

A tax avoidance transaction is any Section 467 rental agreement that has as a principal purpose the avoidance of income tax and that involves either a:

1. Leaseback to any person who had an interest in the property at any time within two years before the leaseback (or a person related to such person), or

2. Long-term agreement, which is a lease for a term in excess of 75 percent of the statutory recovery period for the property.

The statutory recovery period for residential rental property and nonresidential real property is 19 years, and the period for 15-year and 20-year property (for purposes

[48] Code Sec. 467(f).

[49] Code Sec. 467(b)(2) and (e)(1).

of computing depreciation under Code Sec. 168) is 15 years.[50] For most real property, therefore, a long-term lease agreement is one that is for a term of more than 14 years and three months.

Under regulations, the IRS, rather than the parties to the rental agreement, determine whether a rental agreement is a disqualified leaseback or long-term agreement.[51] The regulations also provide that if there is a significant difference in marginal tax rates of the lessor and the lessee, the rental agreement is closely scrutinized, and clear and convincing evidence is required to establish that tax avoidance is not as principal purpose for providing increasing or decreasing rent.[52]

[A] Exemptions from Rental Agreement Rules

Certain agreements may be exempt from the Section 467 rental agreement rules under regulations issued by the IRS.[53] The IRS has issued regulations that incorporate the circumstances the IRS was directed to consider in drawing the exceptions.[54] These safe harbors include:

1. Changes in amounts paid determined by reference to price indices,
2. Rents based on a fixed percentage of lessee receipts or similar amounts,
3. Reasonable rent holidays, or
4. Changes in amounts paid to unrelated third parties (this would allow increases in rent keyed to increases in the lessor's operating costs without subjecting the lease to the Code Sec. 467 rules).

The final regulations also contain several safe harbors for various types of contingent payments that either are intended to compensate the lessor for costs unrelated to the lessor's continuing investment in the leased property or are so contingent that they should not be taken into account for purposes of Code Sec. 467 until the liability for the payment becomes fixed. Safe harbors are provided for payments required to be made by the lessee: in the event of damage, destruction, or loss of the leased property; for the failure of the property to maintain a specified residual value; for the failure of the property to be returned to the lessor at the end of the lease term in the condition specified in the agreement; or for the failure of the lessor to obtain the income tax benefits contemplated by the agreement. In addition, a provision requiring late payment charges is not taken into account in determining whether tax avoidance is present in a leaseback or long-term agreement. Limitations on the scope of these safe harbors are provided in order to ensure that the provisions are included in the agreement for a valid business purpose and that the provisions are not used to achieve tax avoidance.

The final regulations also added a safe harbor for certain variable interest rate provisions. Under that safe harbor, a rent adjustment provision is disregarded if it is based solely on the dollar amount of changes in the lessor's interest costs, and only if the lessor and the lender are not related and the indebtedness is evidenced by a variable rate debt instrument.

[50] Code Sec. 467(e)(3).

[51] Reg. § 1.467-3(b).

[52] Reg. § 1.467-3(c).

[53] Code Sec. 467(b)(5).

[54] Reg. § 1.467-1(c)(2)(iii).

The regulations also contain a safe harbor that says that tax avoidance is not a principal purpose for providing increasing or decreasing rents, if the rents allocable to each calendar year of the lease do not vary from the average annual rents over the entire lease term by more than 10 percent (15 percent in the case of long-term leases of real estate).[55]

[B] Recapture in Leasebacks and Long-Term Agreements

If the lessor under a Section 467 rental agreement that involves a leaseback or a long-term agreement which is not subject to the constant rental accrual rule sells the property, the lessor must recapture as ordinary income a portion of the gain realized on the sale.[56] The recapture provision prevents the conversion of ordinary income into capital gain that would occur when the seller receives consideration for the property that includes, in part, consideration for the higher rentals to be paid to the purchaser after the sale. The recapture amount is generally the prior understated inclusions, defined as the excess, if any, of:

1. The amount the lessor would have taken into account prior to the disposition of the property had the lessor been required to reflect income under the constant rental amount of a tax avoidance transaction, over
2. The actual amount taken into account under Code Sec. 467 by the lessor prior to the disposition.[57]

Recapture, however, is generally limited to the amount of gain realized on the property and may not be more than the excess of the amount realized (or fair market value in case of a disposition other than by sale, exchange or involuntary conversion) over the adjusted basis of the property, reduced by the amount of gain treated as ordinary income under any other income tax provision.[58]

¶ 405 LEASES WITH PURCHASE OPTIONS

A lease with an option to buy is a common business arrangement. The lessee secures the use of the property without an immediate commitment to purchase the property. The lessor, who is probably looking to sell, receives immediate cash from rent to carry the property until it is sold. The question for tax purposes in lease-option situations is whether the lessee is actually leasing the property or, in fact, is buying the property. Since the tax treatment of a purchase transaction and a lease transaction is so different, it is important that the parties draft their agreement in order to obtain the desired results.

A deduction for rent under Code Sec. 162(a)(3) is available only if the taxpayer "has not taken or is not taking title" to the property or if the taxpayer "has no equity" in the property. If a purported lease is, in fact, a sale, the lessee may not deduct "rent" payments. Rather, these payments become part of the purchase price that must be capitalized and, in the case of business property, recovered through depreciation. Any payments received by the lessor that actually represent part of the purchase price for property might be treated as capital gain rather than ordinary income, and deductions for depreciation would be denied the lessor. As

[55] Reg. § 1.467-3(c)(3).

[56] Code Sec. 467(c)(1).

[57] Code Sec. 467(c)(3).

[58] Code Sec. 467(c)(2)(B).

long as the tax rates on capital gain and ordinary income were the same, there was little meaning to this distinction as far as the lessor was concerned. However, on a purchase, the purported lessor realizes income only to the extent of gain on the property, while rent is taxable in full.

.01 Lease as Sales Contract

In any lease with an option to purchase, there is the danger that the IRS may view the transaction as a sales contract and the lease as a mere financing device in which the parties are attempting to gain the tax advantages of a lease while giving the lessee an equity interest in the property. In any lease with a purchase option, the parties must keep the option price high enough and the rental payments low enough so that the transaction will be treated as a lease and the rents will be deductible. Rents that are unreasonably high when combined with an option price that is low indicate that the rent payments are, in fact, payments on the purchase price.

In *D.M. Haggard*,[59] a lease for land called for rent of $10,000 for 1948 and $12,000 for 1949. This was substantially higher than the rental value of the land. Along with the lease, the parties executed an option under which the lessor granted the lessee the right to purchase the land for $24,000 in 1950. The lessee paid the lessor $2,000 for this option. The lessor had previously negotiated for the sale of the land for $48,000. In this situation, the lessee was not allowed to deduct the "rent" payments because the lease and the option conferred an equity in the property to the lessee.[60]

In *W. Oesterreich*,[61] it was the nominal option price that tipped the scales in favor of a purchase rather than a lease transaction. The purported lease was for a term of 68 years, and, at the end of the lease, the lessee could acquire title to the property for a token consideration of $10. In this case, the payments under the "lease" were capital gains to the lessor and capital expenditures to the lessee because the "lease" was actually a contract of sale. Another factor in *W. Oesterreich* was that the lessee was required to make substantial improvements to the property and this investment could only be recovered by exercising the option to buy.[62]

.02 Lease or Sale Distinguished

For a further discussion of how to distinguish between a lease and a sale, see the discussion relating to sale-leaseback transactions at ¶ 305.02 and the discussion of the treatment of a lease with an option as a conditional sales contract at ¶ 305.04. The IRS guidelines for distinguishing between a lease and a sale of equipment contained in Rev. Rul. 55-540 and Rev. Proc. 2001-28, and discussed at ¶ 305.02[B], also may be helpful in distinguishing between a lease and a sale of real property.

---

[59] CA-9, 57-1 USTC ¶ 9230, 241 F.2d 288.

[60] *See also* E.H. Beus, 58-2 USTC ¶ 9945, CA-9, 261 F.2d 176.

[61] CA-9, 55-2 USTC ¶ 9733, 226 F.2d 798.

[62] *See also* Wilshire Holding Corp., CA-9, 59-1 USTC ¶ 9123, 262 F.2d 51.

¶ 406 DEPOSITS

The lessor of property may require the lessee to pay a deposit as security for faithful compliance with the terms of the lease. In a commercial transaction, the lessor may be free to use such deposits as the lessor sees fit and may not be required to pay the lessee interest on the deposit. In some states, however, the law requires that deposits be held in trust by lessors and that they be treated as the property of the lessee until such time as the lessor may apply the deposits to rent under the lease or until the lessee defaults on the lease.[63]

.01 Lessee's Deduction

The lessee may not deduct a security deposit when paid if the deposit is to be returned. If the lessor may apply the security deposit against rent owed by the lessee, the proper time for the lessee's deduction is when the deposit is actually applied against the rent. If the lessee forfeits a deposit because of a breach of the lease, the lessee deducts the amount in the year of the breach.

Note that the question of whether a deposit is actually the payment of advance rent does not really arise as to the proper timing of the lessee's deduction. Since advance rents are deductible by the lessee only for the period to which they relate, the timing of the deduction is the same regardless of whether a payment is advance rent or a security deposit that may be applied against future rent. Such is not the case with regard to the timing of the lessor's income.

.02 Lessor's Income

A lessor includes in income advance rents when they are received regardless of the method of accounting and regardless of the periods which the advance rents apply, subject to the rent accrual and interest rules that apply to Code Sec. 467 rental agreements discussed at ¶ 404. A security deposit that must be returned to the lessee on the termination of a lease in the absence of a default is clearly not taxable to the lessor on receipt, even if the lessor has the unrestricted right to use the funds for his or her own purposes. On the other hand, if a deposit is to be applied to the rent for the last period under the lease, it may be treated as advance rent, even if it also serves as security, unless the deposit must be held in trust or in escrow on behalf of the lessee, either under the terms of the lease or under state law.

If the intention of the parties is that an amount equal to the rent for one period paid on execution of a lease is to stand as security for the lessee's performance and the lessor must account to the lessee for the amount of the deposit plus interest, the lessor does not report income in the year of receipt, even if the amount is to be applied to the last year's rent.[64]

If the lessor is not required to account to the lessee for the principal amount of the payment and interest, a security deposit is includible in income.[65] In *J. & E.*

---

[63] *See*, for example, New York General Obligation Laws § 7-103.

[64] Clinton Hotel Realty Corp., CA-5, 42-2 USTC ¶ 9559, 128 F.2d 968; R.L. Harcum, DC Va, 58-2 USTC ¶ 9684, 164 F. Supp. 650; J. Mantell, 17 TC 1143, CCH Dec. 18,733, *acq.* 1952-1 CB 3.

[65] Astor Holding Co., CA-5, 43-1 USTC ¶ 9408, 135 F.2d 47.

Enterprises, Inc.,[66] security deposits that the lessor had the option to refund after five years or to apply to rental payments due during the sixth year of a 10-year lease were held to be advance rental payments includible in the lessor's income in the year of receipt. The lessor had unrestricted use of the money.

See also the discussion of the difference between advance payments and security deposits contained in Rev. Rul. 72-519.[67] The IRS ruled that a deposit received by a supplier of fuel from service stations to protect its title to, and interest in, the fuel before its sale was a security deposit, but a deposit paid by a new customer to a water company was an advance payment for water. By analogy, a deposit to secure the lessor's interest in the lease by securing the tenant's performance would not be currently taxable.

[66] 26 TCM 944, CCH Dec. 28,622(M), T.C. Memo. 1967-191.

[67] 1972-2 CB 32.

Chapter 5
Lease Acquisition and Disposition

¶ 500 Overview of Chapter
¶ 501 Lease Acquisition Costs
¶ 502 Lease Cancellation
¶ 503 Sale of Lease

¶ 500 OVERVIEW OF CHAPTER

While rent payments and deposits may be the most common payments that concern lessors and lessees in business and commercial leases, they are certainly not the only ones. There may be substantial payments at both the inception and conclusion of a lease that are not rents, advance or otherwise, or security deposits. Both the lessor and the lessee may incur substantial costs merely to obtain the lease. Also, the modification, cancellation, disposition or other termination of a lease may entail significant payments. These payments may be made by the lessor, the lessee, or some third party acquiring the lease from the existing lessee. All of these costs and payments have tax consequences. Careful advance planning will assure that all parties receive the most favorable tax treatment possible.

¶ 501 LEASE ACQUISITION COSTS

Lease acquisition costs may be incurred by the lessor or lessee, or both. The lessee must amortize costs incurred to acquire a lease over the term of the lease.[1] For the lessor, a similar rule applies. Costs incurred by a lessor to secure a lease are capital expenditures that must be spread ratably over the term of the lease, regardless of its length, and regardless of whether the lessor uses the cash or accrual method of accounting.[2] The same rule applies to a lessee who incurs costs to obtain a sublessee.[3]

> ***Example 1:*** A Corp. currently leases a building to B Corp. and the remaining term of the lease is five years. If C pays B Corp. $10,000 to assign the lease to C so that C can occupy the leased building, C would deduct $2,000 per year for each of the five years remaining on the lease to amortize the lease acquisition cost of $10,000.

---

[1] Reg. § 1.162-11(a).

[2] *See*, for example, M.C. Young, CA-9, 3 USTC ¶ 967 59 F.2d 691, *cert. denied*, 287 U.S. 652, 53 S.Ct. 116; E.A. Renwick, CA-7, 37-1 USTC ¶ 9010, 87 F.2d 123; P.W. Thielking, 53 TCM 746, CCH Dec. 43,891(M), T.C. Memo. 1987-227.

[3] Bonwit Teller & Co., CA-2, 2 USTC ¶ 797, 53 F.2d 381, *cert. denied*, 284 U.S. 690, 52 S.Ct. 266.

Similarly, if A Corp. paid B Corp. $10,000 in order to vacate the lease so that it could lease the property to C for five years, A Corp. would deduct $2,000 per year for each of the five years of the term of the new lease.

If B Corp. pays C $10,000 to sublease the building for the remaining five years on the lease, B Corp. would deduct $2,000 per year for each of the five years remaining on the lease.

As the example illustrates, the basic principle that lease acquisition costs must be amortized over the term of the lease is a simple one. Problems arise, however, in determining just what constitutes a lease acquisition cost and in fixing the exact term of the lease over which to amortize the costs when complicating factors such as renewal options are present.

.01 Classification of Payments as Lease Acquisition Costs

Generally, any payment made to acquire a lease and any other payments related to the acquisition of the lease are lease acquisition costs. The classification of a payment as a lease acquisition cost may work for or against a taxpayer. If an item that might otherwise qualify as an ordinary business expense or other currently deductible item is classified as a lease acquisition cost, the taxpayer loses the benefit of a current deduction. On the other hand, if an otherwise nondepreciable and nonamortizable capital expenditure can be classified as a lease acquisition cost, the taxpayer benefits from deductions over the term of the lease.

[A] Lessor's Costs

A lessor's normal expenses incurred to collect rents and manage property are ordinary and necessary business expenses that are currently deductible. The cost of acquiring a particular tenant, however, is a lease acquisition cost that must be amortized over the term of the lease. For instance, the entire amount of commission paid to a broker for obtaining a long-term lease is a lease acquisition cost.[4]

While some expenses, such as commissions for finding a tenant and attorney fees for services in connection with a particular lease, are readily seen as lease acquisition costs, other expenses may not be as obvious. Keep in mind that any payment that can be characterized as made to acquire a lease is amortizable over the life of the lease. In *G.S. Rush*,[5] a $2,500 expense for moving a house from one location on a lot to another, in order to lease the lot to an oil company, had to be amortized over the life of the lease. Similarly, the amount a lessor paid to a lessee in order to defray the cost of the lessee's move into the lessor's building had to be prorated over the lease term.[6]

Assume a lessor agrees to take over the leases between prospective tenants and other landlords in order to have the prospects move into the property. Is the rent paid by the lessor on the assigned leases a lease acquisition cost? It would seem to be similar to a lessor's payment of a lessee's expenses in order to induce the lessee to enter into a lease. In one case, however, the Second Circuit did not see

[4] Rev. Rul. 70-408, 1970-2 CB 68.

[5] DC Ala., 59-2 USTC ¶ 9752.

[6] C.F. Bachman, 21 BTA 36, CCH Dec. 6406.

it this way.[7] In this case, to obtain desirable tenants for its new office building, a taxpayer assumed the tenants' leases in other buildings and then attempted to rent these spaces for their remaining terms. The Tax Court denied a deduction to the taxpayer for the difference between what the taxpayer paid in rent and what was collected, characterizing this amount as a lease acquisition cost. On appeal, however, this decision was overturned. The Second Circuit Court characterized the payments on the old leases as part of the cost of operating the taxpayer's business, just as the income from subletting these spaces was part of the taxpayer's business income. The court pointed out that had the tenants remained in place and the owner of the old building granted a reduction in rent to keep them as tenants, the reduction would not be considered a capital investment to earn the reduced rent.

[B] Lessee's Costs

In the case of lease acquisition costs incurred by a lessee, the lessee is in the same position as the lessor in that these costs do not produce a current deduction, but must be amortized over the life of the lease. A lessee's acquisition costs may include items such as brokers' commissions, attorneys' fees, or even the cost of an outright purchase of an existing leasehold. Acquisition costs also may include some not so obvious items.

In order to expand a business, a taxpayer wanted to obtain adjoining property that was leased by a merchandising company under a lease that had eight years to run. In order to induce the merchandising company to assign the lease on the adjoining property, the taxpayer purchased the stock and fixtures of the company. Following the assignment of the lease, the taxpayer sold the stock and fixtures at a loss and deducted the loss. According to the IRS, however, the loss was a cost of acquiring the lease and, as such, had to be spread over the remaining eight-year life of the lease.[8]

Sometimes, a lease will be acquired as part of a larger transaction, such as the purchase of a business or corporation. Normally, the cost of a business (other than the cost of depreciable physical or other wasting assets) is not deductible or amortizable. The same is true for stock in a corporation. In these situations, the purchaser may be able to gain a deduction if the purchaser can show that some specific amount is being spent to acquire the lease. Advance planning and negotiation with the seller are required.

In *Washington Package Store, Inc.*,[9] the taxpayer purchased a liquor store that was operated from leased premises, but was denied an amortization deduction for any part of the purchase price because the taxpayer could not show that part of the consideration was paid to acquire the leasehold. Had the taxpayer separately negotiated to acquire the lease, in all likelihood, the cost would have been amortizable. In *N.W. Pugh Co., Inc.*,[10] the stock of a lessor corporation was acquired to obtain control of property leased to a corporation controlled by the taxpayer. The

[7] 379 Madison Ave., Inc., CA-2, 1932 CCH ¶ 9397, 60 F.2d 68.

[8] Rev. Rul. 68-260, 1968-1 CB 86.

[9] 23 TCM 1805, CCH Dec. 27,041(M), T.C. Memo. 1964-294.

[10] CA DC, 1934 CCH ¶ 9227, 70 F.2d 776, *cert. denied*, 293 U.S. 575, 55 S.Ct. 87.

court held that no part of the cost of the stock could be allocated to the lease. Again, advance planning may have allowed the taxpayer to negotiate separately for an amortizable leasehold interest and a reduced price for the stock of the corporation.

A lessee also may assume some obligations of the lessor on entering a lease. As discussed at ¶ 401.02, the assumption of a lessor's obligation may be treated as advance rent. It also may be treated as a lease acquisition cost (see ¶ 501.01). From a practical standpoint, the classification of the assumption by the lessee of a lessor's obligation as either advance rent or a lease acquisition cost is not that important. In either case, the lessee does not get a current deduction, but must amortize the payment over the lease term. Some items that have been treated as lease acquisition costs when assumed by the lessee include delinquent taxes due on the leased property and mortgages on the leased property. Payments made to creditors of a previous lessee also may be lease acquisition costs when made to free the lease from claims.

[C] Unsuccessful Lease Attempt

If the attempt to obtain a business lease is unsuccessful, the costs expended in the attempt generally are deductible when it is clear that the lease will not be acquired.[11] However, if the costs also are attributable to a later lease that is successful, the costs have to be amortized over the term of the successful lease. For example, attorney fees paid to negotiate a 20-year lease had to be deducted over the term of the lease.[12] The attorney had made several unsuccessful attempts to negotiate a lease with other prospects, but the attorney's work was not divisible. The successful negotiations were a continuation of the prior negotiations.

.02 Renewal Options

Once the amount of acquisition costs is determined, it is a simple matter to determine the annual amortization deduction when the lease has a fixed termination date. If the lease contains renewal options, however, the question arises as to whether acquisition costs should be amortized over the initial term of the lease only or over the initial term plus the periods of the renewal options.

Under Code Sec. 178, if a lease contains renewal options, lease acquisition costs are amortized over the initial term of the lease, ignoring any renewal periods, as long as at least 75 percent of the lease acquisition costs are attributable to the initial term. Lease acquisition costs must be amortized over the initial term plus any period for which the lease may be renewed or extended and any other period for which the parties reasonably expect the lease to be renewed, if more than 25 percent of the acquisition costs are attributable to the renewal periods.

> ***Example 2:*** The Lessee pays $10,000 to acquire a lease with an initial term of 20 years. The lease also contains two options to renew for periods of five years each. Of the $10,000 lease acquisition cost, $8,000 was paid for the initial 20-year term. Since at least 75 percent of the cost is attributable to the

[11] *See*, for example, Levenson & Klein, Inc., 67 TC 694, CCH Dec. 34,221.

[12] A.T. Galt, 19 TC 892, CCH Dec. 19,491, *aff'd and rev'd on other issues*, CA-7, 54-2 USTC ¶ 9457, 216 F.2d 41.

initial 20-year term, the $10,000 lease acquisition cost is deductible over the initial term at a rate of $500 per year.

Had only $7,000 of the costs been paid for the initial 20-year term, the proper amortization period for the lease acquisition cost would include the renewal periods. In this event, the $10,000 lease acquisition cost would be deductible over 30 years at a rate of $333.33 per year.

While this rule is all well and good when the lease acquisition costs can be apportioned easily between initial term and renewal periods, in most situations, the proper apportionment is not readily apparent. There may be some latitude for the parties to negotiate what portion of lease acquisition costs is attributable to initial term and renewal periods, but Reg. § 1.178-1(b)(5) provides that the portion of lease acquisition costs attributable to the term of the lease, ignoring renewal periods or options, must be determined "on the basis of the facts and circumstances of each case." This would indicate that any allocation arrived at by the parties may not be given validity, especially if the person receiving the payments has no interest in how the allocation is made.

The regulations do provide an annuity method for apportioning lease acquisition costs between initial term and renewal periods when other evidence is lacking.[13] The annuity method looks at the present value (at an appropriate rate of interest) of annual savings of $1 over the initial term compared to the present value of annual savings of $1 over the initial term plus renewal periods. While the regulations under Code Sec. 178 were adopted before Code Sec. 178 was amended in 1986, they presumably have continuing application to lease acquisition costs under revised Code Sec. 178.

Example 3: The Lessee acquires a lease from a previous tenant at a cost of $100,000. At the time of acquisition, there are 20 years remaining on the initial lease term and the lease contains two renewal options of ten years each. The lease calls for a uniform annual rental for the initial term and any renewal periods. If no other evidence of how much of the $100,000 of lease acquisition cost is attributable to the initial term, the Lessee may use the annuity method to apportion the cost. The annuity method calls for the use of a present value analysis based on a reasonable rate of interest. If the Lessee's cost of funds were 12 percent, this rate might be considered appropriate for the present value analysis.

The present value factor for the initial term of the lease, 20 years in this case, at 12 percent is 7.4694. The present value factor for 40 years, the initial term plus renewal periods, at 12 percent is 8.2438. The percentage of the $100,000 lease acquisition cost attributable to the initial term is: 7.4694/8.2438 = 90.6 percent. Since at least 75 percent of the acquisition cost is attributable to the initial term, the Lessee amortizes $100,000 over 20 years at a rate of $5,000 per year.

[13] Reg. § 1.178-1(b)(5)(i).

If the lease were such that the remaining initial term were ten years with two renewal periods of 15 years each, however, the acquisition cost would have to be amortized over 40 years. The present value factor for ten years at 12 percent is 5.6502, so the percentage of the lease acquisition cost attributable to the initial 10-year term would be calculated under the annuity method as follows: 5.6502/8.2438 = 68.5 percent. Since less than 75 percent of the lease acquisition cost is attributable to the initial term in this case, the Lessee would have to amortize $100,000 over the 40 years of the initial term plus renewal periods at a rate of $2,500 per year.

.03 Existing Improvements Costs

While lease acquisition costs must be amortized over the life of the lease, some costs incurred by a lessee to acquire a lease may not be lease acquisition costs. If a portion of the costs can be attributed to improvements on the leased property with a life shorter than the remaining lease term, those costs may be recovered through depreciation deductions over the remaining life of the improvements.[14]

This rule was reflected in Reg. § 1.167(a)-4, which applied to both improvements purchased and constructed by a lessee prior to amendment of Code Sec. 168(i)(8) by the Tax Reform Act of 1986. While the cost of improvements constructed by a lessee on leased property now must be recovered over the life of the improvements, even if longer than the lease term, Code Sec. 168(i)(8) does not seem to affect the depreciation of assets purchased with a lease when the life of the improvements is less than the term of the lease.

Reg. § 1.167(a)-4 provides:

> . . . If the useful life of such improvements in the hands of the taxpayer is equal to or shorter than the remaining period of the lease, the allowance shall take the form of depreciation . . . If, on the other hand, the estimated useful life of such property in the hands of the taxpayer, determined without regard to the terms of the lease, would be longer than the remaining period of such lease, the allowances shall take the form of annual deductions from gross income in an amount equal to the unrecovered cost of such capital expenditures divided by the number of years remaining of the term of the lease.

In Rev. Rul. 61-217, a lessee constructed a commercial building on leased land. The lessee then assigned its interest in the improved property and lease to another party. The IRS ruled, in effect, that the assignee's payment to the original lessee to acquire the lease with the improved property was payment for two distinct assets. The portion of the payment attributable to the building was recoverable through depreciation over the useful life of the building. The part of the capital investment by the assignee that represented consideration for increased rental value, the lease acquisition cost, was recoverable only through amortization over the remaining period of the lease.

The Sixth Circuit Court adopted a similar approach in a later case.[15] In that case, the taxpayer acquired two 99-year leases with 64 and 68 years still to run. The

[14] Rev. Rul. 61-217, 1961-2 CB 49.

[15] 1220 Realty Co., CA-6, 63-2 USTC ¶ 9703, 322 F.2d 495.

leases covered both land and buildings, and the court held that the portion of the cost allocable to the buildings was depreciable over their estimated useful lives.

Now, of course, the concept of useful life has been replaced by statutory recovery periods. These periods are used in place of useful life for determining depreciation deductions (see ¶ 901.01[A]). The key to tax savings on the acquisition of a lease is to allocate as much of the cost as is possible to improvements on the leased property that have a recovery period that is shorter than the remaining lease term.

> ***Example 4:*** The Lessee acquires a lease with 50 years remaining to run by paying the current tenant $100,000. If all of the $100,000 is treated as a lease acquisition cost amortizable over the remaining term of the lease, the Lessee's deduction for these costs would be $2,000 for each of the 50 years.
>
> Suppose, however, that the Lessee could show that $60,000 represented costs attributable to the acquisition of a commercial building located on the leased property. If this were the case, the Lessee would deduct $800 per year in each of 50 years as amortization of lease acquisition costs of $40,000. Also, the Lessee would deduct $1,538 in each of the first 39 years of the lease as depreciation of the cost attributable to acquiring the building.
>
> Deductions in the early years of the lease could be further increased if the Lessee could show that some of the costs were attributable to property acquired under the lease with shorter recovery periods than the 39-year period for commercial buildings. (See the discussion beginning at ¶ 102.02 on cost allocation. Recovery periods for various types of property are discussed at ¶ 901.01[A].)

¶ 502 LEASE CANCELLATION

For a wide variety of reasons, one party to a lease agreement may seek to cancel or terminate the agreement before the end of the lease term. Depending on the situation, the party seeking the cancellation may have to give some consideration to the other party in exchange for the cancellation.

If the lessee pays for the privilege of getting out of a business lease, the payment should be a deductible expense. For the lessor, of course, the payment from the lessee is income. On the other hand, if it is the lessor who pays the lessee for cancelling the lease agreement, the lessor is paying for the acquisition of property represented by the leasehold. A deduction for the payment may hinge on the reasons for the cancellation. For the lessee, the payment from the lessor is income. These concepts are explored more fully in the following paragraphs.

.01 Payments By Lessee

A lessee's payments to a lessor to cancel a lease have tax consequences for both parties. If the lessee simply pays the lessor to cancel the lease and walks away from the property, the tax treatment is relatively straightforward. Complications may arise, however, if the lessee enters into a new lease agreement or if the lessee acquires a fee interest in the property.

[A] Lessee's Deduction

An amount paid by a lessee to a lessor in consideration of the lessor's cancellation of a business lease is a deductible expense for years in which the payment is made or accrued depending on the lessee's accounting method. See Rev. Rul. 69-511,[16] in which the IRS ruled that a lump-sum payment by a lessee as damages for cancellation of a business lease that is equal to a certain amount for each month of the unexpired term is deductible.

The deduction for lease cancellation payments by an accrual basis lessee is taken when the lease is cancelled, even if the payments are spread out over a period of years. An accrual method lessee assumed the lessor's indebtedness of $45,100 in consideration of the cancellation of the lease. The lessee was required to deduct the amount in full in the year the lease was cancelled, even though the lessee would pay off the indebtedness assumed over an 11-year period.[17]

Not every payment by a lessee for the cancellation of a lease, however, gives rise to an immediate deduction. An amount paid by a lessee to obtain cancellation of a 20-year sublease on premises on which it owned a 99-year lease, in order to gain immediate possession, was amortizable over the remaining life of the 99-year lease.[18] Of course, in this situation, the payment made by the lessee is really in the nature of a payment made by a lessor to obtain possession of leased property (see ¶ 502.02).

What if the lessee pays to cancel a lease and then immediately enters into a new lease with the lessor? Are payments in this situation currently deductible? Generally, if a lease is cancelled on the acquisition of a new lease, any cost of the old lease, including the cost of its cancellation, becomes part of the cost of the new lease.[19] As a lease acquisition cost rather than a lease cancellation payment, the cost becomes deductible over the term of the new lease.

A lease agreement also may be cancelled by the lessee's acquisition of the fee interest in the leased property before the end of the lease term. The cost of acquiring the fee is a capital expenditure, not a currently deductible expense.[20] In *Millinery Building*, the taxpayer, as a lessee, constructed a building on leased property at a cost of $3 million. Title to the building was to vest in the lessor at the end of the lease, or the lessor could require the lessee to raze it. At the end of the 21-year initial term of the lease, the lessee exercised its option to renew and shortly after that bought the premises for $2,100,000. The lessee, now the owner of the property, contended that the land was worth $660,000, and that it should be allowed to deduct the remainder as the cost of cancelling a lease under which it was paying excessive rent. The Supreme Court disallowed the claimed deduction and held the purchase price was the cost of acquiring the complete fee to the land and building.

---

[16] 1969-2 CB 23.

[17] C.L. Baumann & Co., 2 TCM 188, CCH Dec. 13,239(M).

[18] Home Trust Co., CA-8, 3 USTC ¶ 1103, 65 F.2d 532.

[19] Phil Gluckstern's, Inc., 15 TCM 41, CCH Dec. 21,521(M), T.C. Memo. 1956-9; S. Peabody, BTA Memo., CCH Dec. 8260-A, October 26, 1933.

[20] Millinery Center Building Corp., S.Ct., 56-1 USTC ¶ 9391, 350 U.S. 456, 76 S.Ct. 493.

The purchase price had to be allocated to the land up to the land's value on the purchase date. Any amount paid over the value of the land had to be added to the lessee's remaining basis in the improvements.

[B] Lessor's Income

"An amount received by a lessor from a lessee for cancelling a lease constitutes gross income for the year in which it is received, since it is essentially a substitute for rental payments."[21] This essentially reflects the position of the Supreme Court announced in *W.M. Hort.*[22] According to the Supreme Court, consideration received for cancellation of a lease of realty is essentially a substitute for rental payments and not a return of capital. The consideration is taxable in full, even if there is a difference between the present value of the unmatured rental payments and the fair rental value of the property for the unexpired period of the lease. Any reduction in value of the property because of the lease cancellation becomes a deductible loss only when fixed by a closed transaction.

If a lessee relieves the lessor of the obligation to return a security deposit, two Circuit Courts have held that the proper measure of income to the lessor is the discounted value of the retained security deposit.[23] The IRS, however, does not follow these cases.[24] According to the IRS, the entire amount of the released security deposit is includible in the lessor's gross income in the year of release, whether or not the lessor had the use of the security deposit, with or without an obligation to pay interest to the lessee for the use. It would seem that the position of the IRS is the stronger one in this situation, and it is quite likely that the courts today would not follow the earlier decisions measuring current income in terms of the present value of the future obligation to return a deposit.

Payments by the lessee to the lessor on cancellation of a lease may be for something other than the cancellation of the lease. If a lessor can show that all or part of the payments are not for cancelling the lease but are consideration for something else, the lessor may escape current taxation. For example, damages received from the lessee for the loss or destruction of leased property are a return of capital. As a return of capital, the damages are applied to reduce the lessor's basis for the property rather than included in current income.[25] If the damages exceed the lessor's basis, the excess is a capital gain.[26]

In *Sirbo Holdings, Inc.*,[27] however, a distinction was drawn between a lessee's payment for damages to the lessor's property and payments to the lessor in exchange for the lessor's relieving the lessee of an obligation to remove additions to the leased property added by the lessee and to restore the property to the condition it was in at the time the lease was executed. In this latter case, the payment was held to be ordinary income to the landlord since there was no "sale or exchange" to support capital gain treatment.

---

[21] Reg. § 1.61-8(b).

[22] S.Ct., 41-1 USTC ¶ 9354, 313 U.S. 28, 61 S.Ct. 757.

[23] Warren Service Corp., CA-2, 40-1 USTC ¶ 9333, 110 F.2d 723; and Bradford Hotel Operating Co., CA-1, 57-2 USTC ¶ 9698, 244 F.2d 876.

[24] Rev. Rul. 68-19, 1968-1 CB 42.

[25] Hamilton & Main, Inc., 25 TC 878, CCH Dec. 21,542.

[26] Boston Fish Market, 57 TC 884, CCH Dec. 31,321.

[27] CA-2, 75-1 USTC ¶ 9178, 509 F.2d 1220.

.02 Payments by Lessor

Payments for the cancellation of a lease made by the lessor are treated as payments made for the acquisition of property rights. As such, the payments are capital expenditures under Code Sec. 263 and Reg. § 1.263(a)-2. For the lessee, the receipt of a lease cancellation payment from the lessor is income subject to the provisions of Code Sec. 1241.

[A] Lessor's Deduction

Since lease cancellation payments made by the lessor are capital expenditures, the lessor is not entitled to a current deduction for these costs. Nevertheless, if the cancellation payments are made in connection with business property, the lessor is entitled to recover his costs. The question, then, is one of the proper period over which lease cancellation payments may be deducted.

As a general rule, an amount paid by a lessor to the lessee for the cancellation of the lease is for a capital asset, and the lessor may deduct the amount through amortization deductions over the unexpired term of the cancelled lease.[28]

Suppose, however, that the reason the lessor pays to cancel an existing lease is to regain the property in order to lease it to a new tenant on more favorable terms. In this situation, the lease cancellation payment for the old lease also may be classified as a lease acquisition cost of the new lease. In fact, if the lessor makes the cancellation payment in order to enter a specific new lease, the lease cancellation payment is amortizable over the term of the new lease rather than the unexpired term of the old lease.[29]

In *Handlery Hotels, Inc.*, the court struggled with the question of when a lease cancellation payment should be treated as the cost of a new lease amortizable over the term of the new lease rather than over the unexpired term of the old lease. According to the court, the question is really one of clearly reflecting the lessor's income for the periods involved. In this case, the court decided that the payment involved was based on the value of the unexpired term of the old lease and, therefore, should be amortized over that period in order to clearly reflect the lessor's income over that period.

If a lessor pays an existing tenant to cancel an existing lease in order to execute a more favorable lease with a new tenant, the lessor may have a bunching of income problem if the lessor receives advance rent or bonus payments from the new tenant. The advance rent is reportable in full when received, as discussed at ¶ 403.01, but the lease cancellation payment is amortizable over either the term of the new lease or unexpired term of the old lease. In this case, the lessor may reduce taxes if a deal is struck to permit the new tenant to make a payment directly to the old tenant. As far as the old tenant is concerned, the tax treatment of the payment is the same whether it comes from the lessor or the new tenant. For the new tenant, advance rent paid to the lessor and a lease acquisition cost paid to the

[28] Rev. Rul. 71-283, 1971-2 CB 168; Peerless Weighing & Vending Machine Corp., 52 TC 850, CCH Dec. 29,713; Handlery Hotels, Inc., CA-9, 82-1 USTC ¶ 9106, 663 F.2d 892.

[29] Wells Fargo Bank & Union Trust Co., Trustee, CA-9, 47-1 USTC ¶ 9359, 163 F.2d 521; Montgomery Co., 54 TC 986, CCH Dec. 30,106, *acq.* 1970-2 CB xx; H. Latter, 20 TCM 336, CCH Dec. 24,710(M), T.C. Memo. 1961-67.

old tenant are both amortizable over the term of the lease, so the tax consequences for the new tenant are the same. The lessor, however, is better off, since advance rent is, in effect, immediately offset by what would otherwise be a lease cancellation payment.

If a lessor pays to cancel a lease in order to sell the property or in order to erect new buildings or improvements, the payments should be reflected in the basis of the property. In *Shirley Hill Coal Co.*,[30] it was held that an amount paid to a lessee for cancellation of a long-term lease of property which the lessor wished to sell enters into the computation of gain or loss on the sale. See also *American Spring & Wire Specialty Co.*,[31] in which it was held that a payment for accelerating the termination of a lease in order to obtain immediate possession of the property was part of the cost of the property and not deductible or amortizable over the remaining life of the lease.

When a taxpayer makes payments to acquire and cancel a lease and obtain early possession of the premises so that it can erect a new building for business use, the payments are part of the cost of the buildings and not of the land. The costs are recovered through depreciation over the useful life or recovery period of the new building and not over the shorter term of the cancelled lease.[32]

If a lessee makes lease cancellation payments to a sublessee, the lease cancellation payments are amortizable over the remaining term of the primary lease rather than the remaining term of the sublease.[33]

[B] Lessee's Income

Amounts received by a lessee for cancellation of the lease are treated as amounts received "in exchange for such lease."[34] Note that Code Sec. 1241 does not have any bearing on the characterization of the amount received by the lessee other than to provide the requisite "exchange" necessary to support capital gain or loss or Code Sec. 1231 gain or loss. The actual character of the income is determined by the nature of the leasehold asset (see the discussion of the sale of a lease at ¶ 503). Also, Code Sec. 1241 does not prevent a transaction that does not qualify under that section from being treated as a sale.[35]

The cancellation of a lease covered by Code Sec. 1241 is the termination of all the contractual rights of a lessee in a particular premises, other than by the expiration of the lease in accordance with its terms. A payment made in good faith for a partial cancellation of a lease is treated as a cancellation payment under Code Sec. 1241, if the cancellation relates to a severable economic unit, such as a portion of the premises covered by the lease or a reduction in the unexpired term of the

[30] 6 BTA 935, CCH Dec. 2374.

[31] 20 TCM 116, CCH Dec. 24,646(M), T.C. Memo. 1961-26.

[32] Third National Bank in Nashville, CA-6, 72-1 USTC ¶ 9223, 454 F.2d 689. *See also* J.W. Keiler, II, CA-6, 68-1 USTC ¶ 9360, 395 F.2d 991; Houston Chronicle Publishing Co., CA-5, 73-2 USTC ¶ 9537, 481 F.2d 1240, *cert. denied*, 414 U.S. 1129, 94 S.Ct. 867.

[33] Steele-Wedeles Co., 30 BTA 841, CCH Dec. 8585; Mid-State Products Co., 21 TC 696, CCH Dec. 20,157, *acq.* 1955-2 CB 7.

[34] Code Sec. 1241.

[35] Reg. § 1.1241-1(a).

lease.[36] Payments made for other modifications of leases, however, are not treated as amounts received for cancellation under Code Sec. 1241.

In a case decided under the law before enactment of Code Sec. 1241, a lessee was accorded sale or exchange treatment for payments received from the lessor in exchange for the lessee's relinquishment of a covenant that barred the lessor from leasing other parts of the building to competitors of the lessee.[37] In Rev. Rul. 56-531,[38] the IRS did rule that amounts received by a lessee from his lessor in consideration of the lessee's relinquishment of a lease covenant restricting the use of the real estate by the lessor are the proceeds of a sale. Arguably, even under Code Sec. 1241, such a covenant may be a "severable economic unit."

If a lessee receives payments in connection with the cancellation of a lease that are not actually for the cancellation, those amounts are not treated under Code Sec. 1241. For instance, the lessor may return a security deposit with interest. The amount of the deposit is, of course, a return of the lessee's own funds (provided the deposit was treated as such and not as advance rent), and the interest is taxable as interest income. Returned advance rents that were previously deducted by the lessee are ordinary income.[39]

.03 Unamortized Costs on Cancellation of Lease

As discussed at ¶ 501.01, lease acquisition costs are amortizable over the term of the lease. On the cancellation of a lease before its full term, either the lessor or lessee may have unamortized acquisition costs. Generally, a lessor's unamortized costs become fully deductible in the year of cancellation or termination.[40] A similar rule applies to the lessee, and a lessee may deduct unamortized lease acquisition costs in the year the lease is cancelled as a business expense.[41]

If the lessor cancels the lease in order to sell the property, however, unamortized costs are not deductible. Rather, they are added to the basis of the property and reduce the amount of gain or increase the amount of loss recognized.[42] Similarly, if the lessee purchases the property during the term of the lease, any unamortized lease acquisition cost becomes part of the basis of the property. The cost of the property then is the purchase price plus the remaining unamortized lease acquisition costs.[43]

Another situation in which the lessor does not enjoy an immediate deduction for remaining lease acquisition costs on the cancellation of a lease is when the lessor enters into a new lease for the same premises. In this case, the unamortized costs of acquiring the old lease are amortized over the term of the new lease.[44]

---

[36] Reg. § 1.1241-1(b).

[37] L.W. Ray, CA-5, 54-1 USTC ¶ 9235, 210 F.2d 390, *cert. denied*, 348 U.S. 829, 75 S.Ct. 53.

[38] 1956-2 CB 983.

[39] A.J. Gray, CA-9, 81-1 USTC ¶ 9371, 642 F.2d 320. *See also* Peerless Steel Equipment Co., 26 TCM 880, CCH Dec. 28,598(M), T.C. Memo. 1967-181.

[40] Oliver Iron Mining Co., 13 TC 416, CCH Dec. 17,202, *acq*. 1950-1 CB 4.

[41] Guelph Hotel Corp., 7 BTA 1043, CCH Dec. 2693, *acq*. VII-1 CB 13.

[42] R.H. Post, CA-2, 40-1 USTC ¶ 9187, 109 F.2d 135.

[43] H. Boos, 30 BTA 882, CCH Dec. 8593.

[44] Pig & Whistle Co., 9 BTA 668, CCH Dec. 3198; Phil Gluckstern's, Inc., 15 TCM 41, CCH Dec. 21,521(M), T.C. Memo. 1956-9.

Sometimes, a lease cancellation may be negotiated in one year, but the actual early termination of the lease will not take place until some time in the following year. In effect, the negotiation of early notice of cancellation shortens the remaining term of the lease. When this situation arises, any unrecovered lease acquisition costs, as of the time notice of cancellation is given, should be deducted ratably over the period from the beginning of the year in which notice is given until the termination of the lease.[45]

> ***Example 5:*** The Lessee, who is a calendar year, accrual basis taxpayer, received notice on April 1, 2019, that its lease is being terminated. Lessee is given until May 31, 2020, to vacate the leased premises. The original term of the lease was not to expire until 2025. As of 2019, Lessee has $17,000 of lease acquisition costs remaining unamortized.
>
> In this situation, Lessee's unamortized lease acquisition costs as of January 1, 2019, should be deducted ratably over the period from January 1, 2019, to May 31, 2020. This is a period of 17 months, so the Lessee should deduct 12/17 of the $17,000, or $12,000, for 2019, and 5/17 of the $17,000, or $5,000, for 2020.

Note that a rule similar to that for unamortized lease acquisition costs applies to unrecovered leasehold improvement costs when a lease is terminated. The unrecovered costs of improvements incurred by a lessee result in a loss in the year the lease is cancelled. See discussion at ¶ 602.02[B].

.04 Modification of Lease

A lessee who receives a payment for modifying an existing lease agreement realizes income. The question is whether that income may qualify as capital gain as an amount received in a sale or exchange, either because Code Sec. 1241 applies, as discussed at ¶ 502.02[B], or because there is a sale of a lease by the lessee, as discussed at ¶ 503.

On the other hand, when a lessee pays for the modification of an existing lease, the lessee wants to maximize current deductions. Rev. Rul. 73-176[46] illustrates the wrong way to do this. In the ruling, a lessee had entered into a 20-year lease for five floors of a building, but later found that it did not need that much space. The lessee negotiated a modification of the terms of the lease with a reduction in the amount of space leased. In addition to rent at the same rate per square foot as under the unmodified lease, the lessee agreed to pay a specific amount as "additional rent" over a period of 60 months. The IRS recharacterized this "rent" as a capital cost for the release from the future obligation to pay rent over the 20-year term of the lease. Accordingly, the deductions had to be spread out over the entire remaining term of the lease, rather than taken as paid over the five years.

Instead of a lease modification, the parties may have been able to increase the lessee's deductions by terminating the old lease and entering into an entirely new agreement. The lessor would not suffer because the lessor is taxed on receipt regardless of whether the extra amount is received as advance rent, a lease cancellation or modification payment, or as current rent.

---

[45] Guelph Hotel Corp., 7 BTA 1043, CCH Dec. 2693, *acq.* VII-1 CB 13.

[46] 1973-1 CB 146.

¶ 503 SALE OF LEASE

Leasehold interests generally qualify as capital assets. Accordingly, if a lessee transfers all of the interest in the property to a third party, there is a sale of a capital asset. If leased land or buildings are used in a trade or business, the lease is a Section 1231 asset if the leasehold has been held for the required holding period.[47] The transaction is a sale even if the original lessee remains contingently liable to the lessor for the performance of the assignee under the lease. An exception does apply, however, if the holder of the leasehold is a dealer in leases. Dealer treatment converts an otherwise capital or Section 1231 asset into an ordinary income asset.[48]

Sale or exchange treatment is available on the sale of a leasehold by a lessee regardless of the source of the payments or who is actually acquiring the lease. Of course, payments may come from the lessor, in which case the payments, most likely, would qualify as capital gains from a sale under Code Sec. 1241, provided the payment is for the lessee's entire interest or a severable economic unit. The assignment or transfer of a lease to a third party also qualifies as sale,[49] as does the transfer of a lease to a sublessee.[50] Amounts received by a lessee from a sublessee for the lessee's release of its rights to the lessor, with whom the sublessee desired to negotiate a direct lease, were capital gains from the sale of the leasehold.[51]

The distinction between the sale of a lease and a sublease is less critical when capital gain is subject to the same rate of tax as ordinary income. Nevertheless, the distinction remains important because of the limits on the deduction of capital losses that prevent their deduction against ordinary income. The transfer by a lessee of less than the entire interest in the leased property, other than a severable economic unit, generally is treated as a sublease giving rise to ordinary income, rather than as a sale giving rise to capital gain.

In Rev. Rul. 57-537,[52] the IRS ruled that the amount paid by the purchaser for the assignment of a lease was an advance rental, reportable by the seller-lessee as ordinary income in the year received, if the seller-lessee reserved the exclusive right and option to purchase the land that was the subject of the lease. Also, a sublease has been found when an agreement among the lessor, lessee, and a third party provided for the lessee's continuing liability to the lessor, gave the lessee a right of reentry for breach of the agreement, and provided for the monthly payment of the "selling price" that resembled the payment of rent.[53]

---

[47] Rev. Rul. 72-85, 1972-1 CB 234.

[48] *See* Chapter 13 for a general discussion of the sale or exchange of real estate, and Chapter 10 for a discussion of dealer sales.

[49] Metropolitan Building Co., TC 971, CCH Dec. 23,448, *acq.* 1959-2 CB 6.

[50] S.D. Miller, 48 TC 649, CCH Dec. 28,565, *acq.* 1968-1 CB 2.

[51] Metropolitan Building Co., CA-9, 60-2 USTC ¶ 9686, 282 F.2d 592, *rev'g and rem'g* 31 TC 971, CCH Dec. 23,448, *acq.* 1959-2 CB 6.

[52] 1957-2 CB 52.

[53] S. Voloudakis, CA-9, 60-1 USTC ¶ 9192, 274 F.2d 209; *see also* J.D. Price, 17 TCM 660, CCH Dec. 23,079(M), T.C. Memo. 1958-124.

Chapter 6
Leasehold Improvements and Additions

¶ 600 Overview of Chapter
¶ 601 Improvements and Additions by Lessor
¶ 602 Improvements and Additions by Lessee
¶ 603 Investment Credit

¶ 600 OVERVIEW OF CHAPTER

Improvements and additions to leased property may be made by either the lessor or lessee, according to their agreement. Lease provisions often dictate what improvements are to be made and who is to make them and bear their cost. In this regard, the lessor and lessee should engage in some advance planning. How the responsibility is assigned will determine which party is entitled to depreciation deductions for the cost of improvements. The agreement between the parties may also determine whether improvements made by the lessee are to be treated as additional rent, deductible costs for the lessee and income to the lessor, or as a capital expenditure, for which the lessee may take depreciation deductions and which passes tax-free to the lessor at the expiration of the lease.

Another consideration when making improvements to leased property is whether any possible investment credit is available and who is entitled to claim the credit. The investment credit for rehabilitating historic structures may be quite significant. In some cases, the lessee may earn this credit, and in others, the lessor. When the credit is earned by the lessor, the lessor may pass this credit on to the lessee, or share the credit with the lessee, in certain situations. How the parties decide to handle the credit, as well the overall cost of improvements and additions, will turn on their relative tax positions. Leasehold improvements and additions are one area in which the parties have a great deal of power to shape the tax outcome through how they structure their lease agreement.

¶ 601 IMPROVEMENTS AND ADDITIONS BY LESSOR

The lessor who erects buildings or makes other improvements or additions to the property he leases generally is entitled to depreciation deductions for the cost of those improvements. The lessee who rents improved property is not entitled to depreciation deductions for the improvements when it is the lessor who has made the capital expenditures necessary to support the deductions. The lessor's depreciation deductions are taken over the usual recovery period for the property involved, regardless of the period of the lease.[1] Similarly, a lessor has no depreciable interest in improvements made by his lessee, even though the improvements become the property of the lessor.[2] (The computation of depreciation deductions for real estate and related improvements is the subject of Chapter 9.)

When the cost of improvements is borne by both the lessor and the lessee, both are entitled to depreciation deductions. The lessor is allowed depreciation on the amount contributed.[3] The cost of improvements borne by the lessee but treated as rent is considered to be a lessor's cost.[4] (See the discussion of improvements as rent at ¶ 602.01.)

.01 Restoration or Maintenance by Lessee

Leases usually contain provisions that impose some burden on the lessee to maintain the property. If the maintenance provision in a lease requires the tenant to return the property in its original condition on the expiration of the lease, there is some danger that the lessor will be denied deductions for depreciation. If the tenant must return property in its original condition, the lessor arguably cannot suffer a loss due to depreciation. A maintenance provision that will not jeopardize the lessor's depreciation deductions for improvements is one that excepts the lessee from any obligation to make good ordinary wear and tear or obsolescence. It is ordinary wear and tear and obsolescence that the depreciation deduction is designed to compensate.

The lessor has not been entitled to depreciation on property on which the lessee was bound to make good all depreciation by replacement and additions so as to return to the lessor at the expiration of the lease the value which the property had when the lease was made.[5] Similarly, depreciation deductions have been denied for furniture and fixtures when the lessee was required to replace them if they could not otherwise be kept in first-class condition.[6]

On the other hand, a requirement that the lessee keep the property in good repair and replace all or any part of the property whenever necessary does not prevent the lessor from taking depreciation deductions.[7] A similar result obtains if the lessee agrees to yield up the leased premises and all buildings and improvements thereon in first-class condition and repair.[8]

The critical distinction between the cases that have allowed depreciation and those that have disallowed depreciation seems to be one of value. If the lessor is guaranteed to get back the equivalent value of the property leased, there is no depreciation. On the other hand, if the lessor will get back the property in good

[1] Reg. § 1.167(a)-4.

[2] C.H. Reisinger, CA-2, 44-2 USTC ¶ 9443, 144 F.2d 475.

[3] P. Wilson, 20 TCM 676, 20 TCM 676, CCH Dec. 24,833(M), T.C. Memo. 1961-135.

[4] Reg. § 1.263(a)-3(f)(2).

[5] Georgia Ry. & Electric Co., CA-5, 35-2 USTC ¶ 9417, 77 F.2d 897, *cert. denied*, 296 U.S. 601, 56 S.Ct. 117; Terre Haute Electric Co., Inc., CA-7, 38-1 USTC ¶ 9228, 96 F.2d 383, *cert. denied*, 292 U.S. 624, 54 S.Ct 629; Watson Land Co., CA-9, 86-2 USTC ¶ 9679, 799 F.2d 571.

[6] Royal St. Louis, Inc., CA-5, 78-2 USTC ¶ 9663, 578 F.2d 1017; *see also* Hibernia National Bank in New Orleans Tr. Div., CA-5, 84-2 USTC ¶ 9771, 740 F.2d 382, in which it was held that an amendment to the lease in *Royal St. Louis, Inc.* that incorporated a wear and tear exception did not entitle the lessor to depreciation because the lessor remained insulated from economic loss.

[7] Alaska Realty Co., CA-6, 44-1 USTC ¶ 9256, 141 F.2d 675; North Carolina Midland Ry. Co., Ct. Cls., 58-2 USTC ¶ 9701, 143 Ct. Cls. 30, 163 F. Supp. 610.

[8] Swoby Corp., 9 TC 887, CCH Dec. 16,123.

repair and condition, but there is no guarantee as to value, the lessor is entitled to depreciation deductions that reflect a possible loss due to obsolescence and ordinary wear and tear. This is supported by Rev. Rul. 62-8.[9]

In Rev. Rul. 62-8, the IRS ruled that a lessor may, upon proper showing, be entitled to some allowance for depreciation, including obsolescence, of leased depreciable property, even though the lessee has agreed to so preserve, replace, renew, and maintain the property and all additions, amendments, and improvements to it that the property will be in at least as good a condition on the termination of the lease as at its beginning. The ruling distinguished G.C.M. 11933, which held that a lessor should not be entitled to depreciation when the lease provides that the property be maintained by the lessee and the same property or its equivalent in value be returned to the lessor on the termination of the lease.

While many of the cases dealing with the depreciation of leasehold improvements and additions predate enactment of the Accelerated Cost Recovery System (ACRS) and the Modified Accelerated Cost Recovery System (MACRS) of depreciation spelled out in Code Sec. 168, the principles generally remain valid.[10]

The lessee, simply because required by the lease to keep buildings and improvements up to their present condition or to maintain and restore the property, is not entitled to depreciation deductions.[11] But the lessee is entitled to deductions for the cost of repairs and for the cost of restoration expenses on the termination of the lease.[12] The lessee also may deduct expenses during the term of the lease for replacements required under the lease to keep the property in good operating condition.[13]

.02 Improvements to Benefit a Particular Lessee

Suppose the owner of property erects a building or other structure on the property in order to lease the property to a particular tenant. Further suppose that the improvement is only usable by that particular tenant and that when the tenant leaves the improvement will have no further value. In this situation, it would seem that deductions by the lessor for the cost of the improvement should be taken over the term of the lease, rather than the normal recovery period for the property, if the term of the lease is less than the recovery period. True, Reg. § 1.167(a)-4 says that depreciation for improvements to leased property by the lessor must be computed over the recovery period of the property, regardless of the lease term, but this seems to be based on the idea that the improvements will remain a benefit to the property and to the lessor at the expiration of a lease. This is not the case when the improvements benefit only a particular tenant and cannot be used by anyone else.

In *L.S. Ames*,[14] the court held that the useful life of a facility specifically constructed as a state social service center was the physical life of the facility rather than the term of the state's shorter lease. In this case, the specialized facilities

[9] 1962-1 CB 31.

[10] Code Sec. 168(a).

[11] H.W. Weiss v. J. H. Wiener, 1 USTC ¶ 393, 279 U.S. 333, 49 S.Ct. 337; Ohio Cloverleaf Dairy Co., CA-6, 1929 CCH ¶ 9307, 34 F.2d 1022.

[12] G.C.M. 11933, XII-2 CB 52; O.D. 516, 2 CB 112.

[13] Journal-Tribune Publishing Co., CA-8, 54-2 USTC ¶ 9630, 216 F.2d 138.

[14] CA-9, 80-2 USTC ¶ 9641, 626 F.2d 693.

would not have been suited for any use except a social service center, and the lessor took depreciation based on the term of the lease. In denying the more rapid depreciation, the court pointed to the lessor's failure to prove that he could reasonably foresee that the state would not exercise its option to renew the lease. Presumably, had the lessor been able to make such a showing, the cost of the improvements could have been depreciated over the shorter term of the lease.[15]

Even with the limited authority that existed before the Tax Reform Act of 1986 for writing off the cost of improvements made to benefit a particular lessee over the term of the lease rather than the recovery period for the improvement, the 1986 Act has probably foreclosed any such possibility for the future. Code Sec. 168(i)(8) provides that in "the case of any building erected (or improvements made) on leased property, if such building or improvement is property to which this section applies, the depreciation deduction shall be determined under the provisions of this section."

Although the lessor generally cannot write off improvements made for a particular lessee over a lease term that is shorter than the recovery period for the property while the lessee occupies the property, the Small Business Job Protection Act of 1996 did amend Code Sec. 168 to allow a possible write off at the end of the lease. Generally, a lessor of leased property that disposes of a leasehold improvement made for the lessee of the property may take the adjusted basis of the improvement into account for determining gain or loss if the improvement is irrevocably disposed of or abandoned by the lessee at the termination of the lease.

This does not mean that some tax planning cannot improve the position of the lessor who makes improvements to benefit a particular lessee. In the normal course of events, the lessor who makes such improvements will charge a higher rent in order to compensate for the cost of the improvements. Increased rental payments made in order to reimburse a lessor for improvements made on leased property are income to the lessor.[16]

Suppose, however, that the lessor agrees to accept a lower rent if the lessee agrees to repay the lessor for the cost of the improvements? Could what otherwise would be taxable rental income be converted to a tax-free reimbursement in this case? The answer appears to be yes, provided that the improvements are specially suited only to the particular tenant and "enhance by little or nothing the value of [the lessor's] real estate."[17]

When the lessor makes an improvement "for the account of the lessee," as in the *Beecham* case, the payments by the lessee to reimburse the lessor would be the lessee's cost of the improvements. The lessee would have to treat the improvements as if they were made directly by the lessee. (See the discussion of lessee-made improvements at ¶ 602.)

---

[15] *See also* L.C. Fieland, 73 TC 743, CCH Dec. 36,749, in which there was no "practical certainty" that the improvements involved could not be used after the expiration of the lease.

[16] D.G. Satterfield, 34 TCM 872, CCH Dec. 33,287(M), T.C. Memo. 1975-203; *see also* Rev. Rul. 70-146, 1970-1 CB 18.

[17] Beecham, Inc., DC Tenn., 73-2 USTC ¶ 9719.

.03 Purchase of Property with Lessee Improvements

A lessor who makes no investment in improvements to the property leased is not entitled to depreciation based on the cost or value of the improvements. Rather, it is the lessee who has made the investment and who is entitled to depreciation (see below). Suppose, however, that a lessor who has permitted a lessee to make improvements to the leased property sells that property subject to the lease. The seller had no investment in the improvements, but can the same be said of the purchaser? A portion of the purchase price may reflect the increased value of the property that flows from the improvements constructed by the lessee. In this situation, may the purchaser take depreciation deductions even though the predecessor could not? The answer is less than clear.

In Rev. Rul. 55-89,[18] the IRS ruled that a person who inherits property on which a lessee has constructed a building without cost to the lessor is not entitled to depreciation deductions for the building when the lease extends beyond the useful life (recovery period) of the building. The person who inherits the property acquires no depreciable interest in the building since possession of the building cannot be obtained until after the expiration of the lease. The application of this same rationale to a purchaser is supported by a First Circuit decision.[19]

While the First Circuit did hold that the purchaser had no depreciable interest in a building built by a lessee on the land subject to the lease because the seller of the lease had no interest in the building, the court indicated that it might not apply the same rationale to a situation in which the lease term is less than the useful life (recovery period) of the building. More importantly, the court indicated that it might support the idea that the purchaser of property on which a lessee has made improvements is entitled to some deduction for amortization of lease acquisition costs related to the acquisition of the lease.

Prior to the decision in *DeMatteo,* the Eighth Circuit had adopted a more pragmatic approach to the question of whether the purchaser of property from a lessor would be entitled to depreciation for lessee-constructed improvements.[20] The Eight Circuit saw no problem in allowing, in effect, two taxpayers (the lessee and the purchaser) to take deductions for the same property. The critical matter was whether the purchaser, as well as the lessee, had made some investment in a depreciable or wasting asset. Accordingly, the purchaser of leased land on which the lessee has constructed a building is entitled to depreciate or amortize the part of the cost that represents either the value of the building or a premium for the rent to be received. See also *H.B. Pearson,*[21] in which it was held that it would be possible for the heir of a lessor to have a depreciable interest in a building erected by a lessee if the heir could show what part of the estate tax valuation was attributable to the building, as distinguished from the land.

---

[18] 1955-1 CB 284.

[19] M. DeMatteo Construction Co., CA-1, 70-2 USTC ¶ 9684, 433 F.2d 1263.

[20] World Publishing Co., CA-8, 62-1 USTC ¶ 9282, 299 F.2d 614.

[21] CA-5, 51-1 USTC ¶ 9236, 188 F.2d 72, 342 U.S. 861, 72 S.Ct. 88.

The most recent of the confusing line of cases dealing with depreciation or amortization by a lessor's successor for lessee-constructed improvements is *Geneva Drive-In Theatre, Inc.*[22] In this case, part of the purchase price paid for the property clearly could be allocated to the improvements on the leased property constructed by the lessee. In this case, the court conceded that the purchaser was entitled to depreciation for this portion of the cost, but that the depreciation deductions could not begin until after the termination of the lease. Under this approach, the purchaser's interest in the lessee-constructed improvements is a reversionary one, and the purchaser does not actually own the improvements until they revert to the purchaser on termination of the lease.

In trying to draw some meaningful planning strategies out of the cases cited above, one is left with the feeling that the purchaser of property subject to a lease on which the lessee has constructed improvements is on shaky ground in claiming depreciation deductions for improvements on which the seller could not take depreciation. In such situations, the purchaser may be on firmer ground if some part of the cost is attributable to the acquisition of the lease rather than to the fee interest on the underlying property. The purchaser could negotiate for the purchase of two assets—the property without the improvements and the lease between the seller and the lessee. The latter cost, as a lease acquisition cost, would be subject to amortization deductions as discussed at ¶ 501. In this way, the whole matter of depreciation for the improvements may be avoided.

¶ 602 IMPROVEMENTS AND ADDITIONS BY LESSEE

A lessee who rents improved property has not made any investment in the improvements and is not entitled to depreciation deductions for the improvements. Since it is the owner of the property, the lessor, who has made the capital investment in the improvements, it is the lessor who is entitled to depreciation deductions (see ¶ 601). Obviously, the lessor renting improved property charges more rent than if the property were unimproved, and the lessee has a larger deduction for rent paid.

Under Code Sec. 110, which was added to the Code by the Taxpayer Relief Act of 1997, a lessee of retail space for a term of 15 years or less does not have to include in income construction or improvement allowances from the lessor for property that is nonresidential real estate that reverts to the lessor at the termination of the lease. The lessor must treat the amount excluded by the lessee as nonresidential real property.

If the lessee rents unimproved property and proceeds to make improvements to the property other than with payments or allowances from the lessor, it is an entirely different matter. In this situation, it is the lessee who is making the capital expenditures that will support a depreciation deduction. The lessor is not entitled to depreciation for improvements when the cost is borne by the lessee. The cost of improvements, however, may be treated as rent by the parties. If this is the case, then it is the lessor who is treated as making the improvements. The cost is

[22] CA-9, 80-2 USTC ¶ 9544, 622 F.2d 995.

deductible as rent by the lessee and the lessor includes the cost in income as rental income. The lessor, then, is entitled to the depreciation deductions for the improvements.[23]

In any negotiation for the lease of property that will have to be improved, the parties should consider their tax and financial needs in deciding who should make the improvements and under what terms. Generally speaking, the process is one of trading off current and future income and deductions and current and future cash expenditures. When the lessee makes improvements, the lessor is accepting lower rents for the increase in value to the property that the lessor will realize at a later time. At the same time, the lessee will be paying less in rent, but will incur the up-front cost of the improvements. When the lessor makes improvements, the lessor charges more rent but incurs the up-front costs, while the lessee avoids the up-front improvement costs but pays more rent throughout the term of the lease.

.01 Improvements as Rent

Whether the cost of improvements made by a lessee is treated as rent for tax purposes depends on the intent of the parties.[24] This intent may be found in either the terms of the lease or the circumstances surrounding the lease and the making of the improvements. Reg. § 1.61-8(c) provides, in part: "Whether or not improvements made by a lessee result in rental income to the lessor in a particular case depends upon the intention of the parties, which may be indicated either by the terms of the lease or by the surrounding circumstances."

If the lease describes a payment by the lessee as a rental payment, that description will generally control, even if the payment compensates the lessor for the cost of improvements. In *F.T.B. Martin*,[25] amounts described in the lease as rentals, which the lessor claimed were repayments to it of advances for remodeling the premises, were held to be rental income. The terms of the lease governed the characterization of the payments. See also *D.G. Satterfield*,[26] in which increased rental payments made to a lessor as reimbursement for improvements made on leased property were rental income to the lessor. On the other hand, if the payments really do represent repayment for improvements, the payments are not rental income to the lessor.[27]

When the cost of improvements made by a lessee may be credited against the rental obligation of the lessee, the cost of the improvements is treated as rent.[28] Similarly, work performed by a tenant under an abatement agreement was additional rental income to the lessor since it was the intent of the parties to treat the improvements as a substitute for rent.[29] Also, when the lease permitted the tenant to make improvements and to reduce the amount of the stated rent by the cost of

[23] Reg. § 1.263(a)-3(f)(2).

[24] M.E. Blatt Co., S.Ct., 38-2 USTC ¶ 9599, 305 U.S. 267.

[25] 11 BTA 850, CCH Dec. 3893.

[26] 34 TCM 872, CCH Dec. 33,287(M), T.C. Memo. 1975-203.

[27] Beecham, Inc., DC Tenn., 73-2 USTC ¶ 9719; *but see* Rev. Rul. 70-146, 1970-1 CB 18, in which the entire amount, received by a lessor under a supplemental agreement by the lessee to pay an amount each month in addition to specified rent until the supplemental payments equaled one-half the cost of improvements made by the lessor, was ruled rental income.

[28] I. Brown, CA-7, 55-1 USTC ¶ 9258, 220 F.2d 12.

[29] B.E. McBride, 53 TCM 158, CCH Dec. 43,713(M), T.C. Memo. 1987-94.

the improvements, the cost of the improvements was treated as rent and the tenant was treated as having made no investment in the improvements. The entire cost of the improvements was deductible by the tenant as rent.[30]

Generally, the cost of the improvements is the amount of rental income realized by the lessor and the amount of rent deemed paid by the lessee when improvements are treated as rent. In a ruling that preceded enactment of the 1954 Code, the IRS had accepted the idea that the lessor could include in income the value of the improvements discounted to reflect the fact that the lessor would not obtain the improvements until the end of the lease term.[31] It is not clear that the IRS would be willing to accept the same position today.[32]

When the cost of improvements is a direct offset against the rent stated in the lease agreement, the lessor's income is measured by the cost. This amount also becomes the lessor's basis for the improvements on which depreciation is calculated.[33] The lessee's rent deduction is based on the same amount that the lessor includes as rental income. Bear in mind, however, that different rules apply to the timing of the rental deduction and the inclusion in income of rent.

If the cost of improvements treated as rent is substantial, there is the likelihood that the cost represents advance rentals. The deduction for advance rentals by the lessee must be spread over the periods to which they relate (see ¶ 402.01), while the lessor includes advance rentals in income in full (see ¶ 403.01). Also, if the cost of an improvement treated as rent plus other rental payments called for by the lease exceed $250,000, income and deductions may have to be spread out under regulations under Code Sec. 467, dealing with deferred and stepped rental agreements (see ¶ 404).

.02 Improvements as Capital Investment

A person who makes additions or improvements to his or her own business property may take depreciation deductions for the cost over the recovery period that applies to the particular addition or improvement involved. This same rule applies to a lessee who makes additions or improvements to business property that he or she leases, if the additions or improvements are not treated as rent.[34] It does not matter what the remaining term of the lease is at the time an improvement is made; depreciation is based on the full recovery period of the improvement. For improvements that were placed in service before 1987, their cost is recovered over the normal recovery period or amortized over the remaining term of the lease if shorter than the appropriate recovery period (see ¶ 602.02[A]). (See ¶ 901.01 for a discussion of how depreciation is calculated.)

As indicated at ¶ 602 and 602.01, whether lessee-made improvements are treated as a capital expenditure by the lessee or as additional rent depends on the intent of the parties.[35] The intent not to treat lessee-made improvements as addi-

[30] Your Health Club, Inc., 4 TC 385, CCH Dec. 14,250, *acq.* 1945 CB 7.

[31] *See* I.T. 4009, 1950-1 CB 13.

[32] *See*, for example, Rev. Rul. 67-123, 1967-1 CB 383.

[33] *See* I. Brown, 22 TC 147, CCH Dec. 20,293, *aff'd*, CA-7, 55-1 USTC ¶ 9258, 220 F.2d 12.

[34] Code Sec. 168(i)(8).

[35] M.E. Blatt Co., 38-2 USTC ¶ 9599, 305 U.S. 267; 59 S.Ct. 186; Reg. § 1.61-8(c).

tional rent may be found in the terms of the lease or in the circumstances of the situation. For example, if a lessee makes improvements that meet the special needs of the lessee and cannot be used by the lessor or other tenants, this would indicate that the improvements are not intended as rent.[36] In *G.H. Cunningham,* the principal stockholder of a corporation was held not to have received rental income from improvements made by the corporation to property it leased from the stockholder because neither party intended that the value of the improvements should be rent.

Another indication that improvements are not intended as rent is the actual rent charged for the property without the improvements. When controlled corporations erected buildings on land leased from the stockholder, it was held that the improvements were not in lieu of rent. The corporations were bona fide business corporations and if they had rented similar property on the open market from strangers, they could not have rented the property for any amount substantially less than the amount their actual occupancy cost them.[37]

[A] Pre-1987 Improvements

For improvements made by a lessee and placed in service before 1987 (or after 1986 if they are subject to the pre-1987 depreciation rules under various transition rules), the lessee may amortize the cost of the improvements over the remaining term of the lease if that is less than the recovery period for the improvements. There are, however, some exceptions to this rule.

If a pre-1987 improvement may be removed by the lessee and used elsewhere, amortization over the lease term is not permitted. A lessee was denied amortization deductions over a relatively short remaining lease term for the cost of fixtures, signs and wall cabinets. The lessee was unable to show that these assets could not be removed on termination of the lease and used elsewhere.[38] Also, a lessee who has a purchase option on the leased property may not amortize the cost of pre-1987 improvements over the lease term if it seems likely that the lessee will exercise the option, or if the lessee intends to exercise the option and it appears that the lessee will do so.[39]

Renewal Options

Generally, the lessee who made improvements to leased property and placed them in service before 1987 may amortize the cost over the remaining initial term of the lease and may ignore any renewal period or options, if the remaining initial term of the lease at the time the improvements were placed in service was at least 60 percent of the recovery period applicable to the improvements. If the remaining initial term was less than 60 percent of the recovery period, the renewal periods are counted as part of the lease term, unless the lessee can establish that it is more probable that the lease will not be renewed or extended than that the lease will be

[36] G.H. Cunningham, CA-9, 58-2 USTC ¶ 9771, 258 F.2d 231.

[37] O.L. Bardes, 37 TC 1134, CCH Dec. 25,416, *nonacq.* 1964-1 CB (Part 1) 6.

[38] Bell Electric Co., 45 TC 155, CCH Dec. 27,630, *acq.* 1966-2 CB 4.

[39] Dawson-Spatz Packing Co., CA-6, 61-1 USTC ¶ 9452, 289 F.2d 934; S.J. Moss, 38 TC 605, CCH Dec. 25,605.

renewed or extended. Also, the amortization period must include renewal periods if the lease has been renewed or extended or the facts show with reasonable certainty that the lease will be renewed or extended.[40]

Purchase of Fee

If a lessee constructed a building or other improvement on leased property and placed that building or improvement in service before 1987, the lessee is entitled to amortize the cost over the lease term, if the lease term is less than the recovery period of the improvement. But what if the lessee now purchases the complete fee in the property? Obviously, a portion of the purchase price reflects the value of the lessor's right to the improvement at the end of the lease term as well as the value of the property without the lessee's improvement.

The excess of the purchase price of the fee over the value of the property without the lessee's improvement is not a deductible expense, and the lessee cannot amortize the portion of the purchase price allocable to the improvement over the remaining period of the extinguished lease.[41] According to the IRS, a lessee who purchases the fee must depreciate improvements made by the lessee before the purchase over their remaining recovery period as of the date the lessee acquires the fee.[42] See also *Wilshire Medical Properties, Inc.*,[43] in which it was held that a lessee who constructed a medical building on leased land and then purchased the lessor's interest in the property was entitled to show that some allocation of the purchase price between the land and the building should be made for the purposes of depreciation.

In Rev. Rul. 60-180, the IRS ruled that the purchase price paid by a lessee who had made improvements to leased land must be allocated to the land and the improvements in proportion to (1) the fair market value of the land as of the date of purchase and (2) the fair market value on the same date of the right to acquire at the end of the lease term the improvements made by the lessee. The amount of the purchase price allocated to the improvements is depreciable over their remaining recovery period as of the date of the purchase.

Example 1: The Taxpayer entered into a 16-year lease for land in January 1986 and constructed a building on the land at a cost of $30,000. The building was completed in January 1987 and had a recovery period of 19 years. The Taxpayer is amortizing the cost of the building over the term of the lease at a rate of $2,000 per year ($30,000 cost divided by the 15 years remaining on the lease when the building was placed in service). On July 1, 1997, the Taxpayer purchases the premises from the lessor for $25,000. On that date, the fair market value of the land is $15,000 and the value of the lessor's right to acquire the building at the end of the lease term is $10,000. The Taxpayer's basis for depreciating the building over its remaining recovery period on July 1, 1997, is $19,000. This amount is the Taxpayer's unrecovered cost for the building of

[40] Former Code Sec. 178, as in effect before enactment of the Tax Reform Act of 1986, and the regulations under former Code Sec. 178.

[41] Millinery Center Building Corp., S.Ct., 56-1 USTC ¶ 9391, 350 U.S. 456, 76 S.Ct. 493.

[42] Rev. Rul. 60-180, 1960-1 CB 114.

[43] CA-9, 63-1 USTC ¶ 9334, 314 F.2d 333.

$9,000 ($30,000 less $21,000 in amortization for the period January 1987 through June 1997), plus $10,000 of the purchase price allocated to the building.

[B] Lease Termination

If a lessee has made improvements to leased property, those improvements become the property of the lessor on the termination of the lease. At that time, we must be concerned with two questions:

1. What are the tax consequences to the lessee, who has been taking depreciation for the cost of the improvements?
2. What are the tax consequences, if any, to the lessor, who now comes into possession of the improvements?

Lessee's Loss Deduction

According to the Senate Finance Committee Report on the Tax Reform Act of 1986, a lessee who does not retain improvements that the lessee made to the leased property realizes gain or loss on termination of the lease measured by the adjusted basis of the improvements at that time. In other words, the termination of the lease is treated as if the lessee is selling the improvements and unless the lessee realizes some amount for the lease, the lessee suffers a tax loss equal to any unrecovered cost for the improvements when the lessee surrenders possession of the leased property. If the improvements were capital assets, the loss would be a capital loss. If the improvements were Code Sec. 1231 business property, the loss would be a Code Sec. 1231 loss. (See the discussion of sales and exchanges in Chapter 13.)

Lessor's Tax-Free Receipt

On the termination of a lease, the lessor recognizes no income because of the receipt of improvements that were made by the lessee to the leased property.[44] This income exclusion does not apply if the improvements represent the liquidation in kind of lease rentals. The exclusion applies only to the income realized by the lessor upon the termination of the lease and has no application to the cost of improvements made by the lessee that is treated as rent during the period of the lease. The exclusion has no application to income which may be realized by the lessor on the termination of the lease and which is not attributable to the value of the improvements made by the lessee, and it does not apply to income derived by the lessor after the termination of the lease as a result of the ownership of the improvements.[45]

In *Boston Fish Market Corp.*,[46] it was held that a payment to a lessor in settlement of a tenant's obligation under the lease agreement to restore the leasehold improvements to their original pre-lease condition was not excludable from income under Code Sec. 109 and was taxable to the lessor. Reg. § 1.109-1(b) contains the following example.

[44] Code Sec. 109.

[45] Reg. § 1.109-1(a).

[46] 57 TC 884, CCH Dec. 31,321.

Example 2: The A Corporation leased in 1945, for a period of 50 years, unimproved real property to the B Corporation under a lease providing that the B Corporation erect on the leased premises an office building costing $500,000, in addition to paying the A Corporation a lease rental of $10,000 per annum beginning on the date of completion of the improvements, the sum of $100,000 being placed in escrow for the payment of the rental. The building was completed on January 1, 1950. The lease provided that all improvements made by the lessee on the leased property would become the absolute property of the A Corporation on the termination of the lease by forfeiture or otherwise and that the lessor would become entitled on such termination to the remainder of the sum, if any, remaining in the escrow fund. The B Corporation forfeited its lease on January 1, 1955, when the improvements had a value of $100,000. Under the provisions of section 109, the $100,000 is excluded from gross income. The amount of $50,000, representing the remainder in the escrow fund, is forfeited to the A Corporation and is included in the gross income of that taxpayer.

A corresponding basis provision[47] prevents a lessor from increasing the basis for the property by the value of lessee improvements that are excluded from income under Code Sec. 109. What this means, of course, is that the lessor will be taxed on the improvements when the lessor disposes of them in a taxable transaction. The overall effect of Code Secs. 109 and 1019 is to defer the tax on the lessor for lessee improvements that are not treated as rent to a time when the lessor is in a position to pay the tax.

Example 3: The Lessor purchased land at a cost of $20,000 and leased this land for a number of years. The lessee constructed improvements on the land for its use. The cost of the improvements was borne solely by the lessee and was not treated as rent by the parties. On the termination of the lease, when the improvements had a fair market value of $75,000, these improvements became the property of the Lessor. At this time, the fair market value of the land was $40,000.

On the termination of the lease, the Lessor's basis for the property, land, and buildings is $20,000, the Lessor's basis for the land. If the Lessor immediately sells the property for its total fair market value of $115,000, the Lessor realizes a gain of $95,000, which represents the $20,000 gain on the land plus the value of the improvements received tax-free from the lessee on the termination of the lease. Code Sec. 109 does not prevent the recognition of this gain on the sale or other taxable disposition of the property.

¶ 603 INVESTMENT CREDIT

Prior to the Tax Reform Act of 1986, an investment credit was available for most tangible personal business property. This credit was ten percent of the cost of qualifying property. For the most part, the credit was only of tangential interest to the owner of commercial or investment real estate since buildings and their structural components were not eligible for the credit. In addition to the regular ten percent investment credit, however, an investment credit for the cost of rehabilitat-

[47] Code Sec. 1019.

ing certain buildings was introduced in 1978. While the 1986 Act repealed the regular investment credit, it retained the credit for qualified rehabilitation expenditures, but in modified form.

The current tax credit for rehabilitation expenditures is available for the cost of rehabilitating existing commercial buildings before 2018 or residential and nonresidential historic structures. The tax credit is ten percent of the cost of the qualified rehabilitation of a commercial building before 2018, but the building must have been first placed in service before 1936. The cost of rehabilitating a certified historic structure, regardless of its age, is eligible for a 20 percent tax credit. For the rehabilitation of historic structures after 2017, the credit is taken over a period of five years. For qualified rehabilitations prior to 1987, commercial buildings 30 years old qualified for a 15 percent credit and buildings 40 years old qualified for a 20 percent credit. The pre-1987 credit for the rehabilitation of an historic structure was 25 percent of the cost of the rehabilitation.

The tax credit for rehabilitation expenditures is considered in detail at ¶ 804.

.01 Qualified Rehabilitations by Lessee

The lessee of a building who makes qualified expenditures to rehabilitate the building can qualify for the ten percent tax credit for older commercial buildings before 2018 or the 20 percent tax credit for historic structures. To be eligible to take the credit, however, the expenditures must be capitalized by the lessee and not treated as rent by the parties. Also, there must be at least 39 years remaining on the term of the lease at the time the rehabilitation is completed (27½ years in the case of residential rental property).[48] The remaining term of the lease is determined without regard to any renewal periods.

The rules governing how a lessor may pass an investment credit to a lessee were preserved when the investment credit provisions were restructured in the Revenue Reconciliation Act of 1990.[49] This would indicate that a lessor who makes qualified rehabilitation expenditures may elect to pass the credit to the lessee under former Code Sec. 48(d) as in effect prior to 1991 (see ¶ 603.02[A]). Presumably, the election to pass the credit through to the lessee would be available even if the remaining term of the lease is less than 39 years or other applicable recovery period for the property. A lessor who reimburses a lessee for the rehabilitation costs incurred by the lessee is treated as having made the qualified expenditures.

.02 Qualified Rehabilitations by Lessor

A lessor who rehabilitates a building that is leased is eligible for the rehabilitation tax credit if the expenditures otherwise qualify.

Since the parties to the lease may arrange who is to actually claim the credit, by fixing who is to make the rehabilitation expenditures or by use of the election to pass the credit to the lessee (see ¶ 603.02[A]), the lessor and lessee should carefully weigh who is in the best position to make full use of the credit. Various limits on the credit, which are discussed at ¶ 804.01[D], may limit the utility of the

[48] Code Sec. 47(c)(2)(B)(vi).

[49] Code Sec. 50(d)(5).

credit to certain taxpayers. By fixing who will claim the credit, and adjusting other lease terms accordingly, both lessor and lessee may gain from the credit.

[A] Election to Pass Credit to Lessee

Generally, the lessee of property is not entitled to an investment credit for leased property when it is the lessor who makes the investment that qualifies for the credit. Under an exception to this rule, however, a lessee may claim the investment credit if the lessor of new investment credit property elects to pass the credit to the lessee.[50] In some cases, the election results in a split of the credit between the lessor and the lessee (see ¶ 603.02[B]).

When the lessor elects to pass an investment credit to the lessee, the lessee calculates the credit on the basis of the fair market value of the property eligible for the credit.[51] If the lease is between component members of a controlled group of corporations, however, the credit is based on the lessor's basis in the property.[52] The election by a lessor to pass the credit to the lessee may be made on a property-by-property basis or under a general election. In either case, statements must be filed by the lessor with the lessee. Details on the procedure to pass the credit to the lessee may be found in Reg. § 1.48-4.

Lessee's Income

Generally, when a taxpayer makes qualified rehabilitation expenditures, the taxpayer must reduce the basis of the property for depreciation by the amount of the rehabilitation credit.[53] This basis reduction does not apply to the lessor, however, when the lessor elects to pass the credit through to the lessee.[54] Rather, when the lessor elects to pass the credit to the lessee, the lessee must include in gross income the amount of the credit ratably over the recovery period of the property.[55] The ratable income inclusion begins on the date the investment credit property is placed in service and continues on each one-year anniversary date thereafter until the end of the recovery period. The lessee must include the amount of its credit in income regardless of limitations on the amount of the credit based on the amount of the lessee's income tax.[56]

If the lessee of the property is a partnership (other than an electing large partnership) or an S corporation, the income inclusion that results from the credit is not an item of partnership income or an item of S corporation income. A partner or S corporation shareholder that is the ultimate credit claimant (the partner or S corporation shareholder that files Form 3468 to claim the investment credit) is treated as a lessee and includes an amount in income in proportion to the credit received by the partner or S corporation shareholder.[57]

---

[50] Former Code Sec. 48(d), as in effect prior to 1991; *see* Code Sec. 50(d)(5).

[51] Former Code Sec. 48(d)(1)(A), as in effect prior to 1991; *see* Code Sec. 50(d)(5).

[52] Former Code Sec. 48(d)(1)(B), as in effect prior to 1991; *see* Code Sec. 50(d)(5).

[53] Code Sec. 50(c).

[54] Former Code Sec. 48(d)(5)(A), as in effect prior to 1991; *see* Code Sec. 50(d)(5).

[55] Former Code Sec. 48(d)(5)(B), as in effect prior to 1991; *see* Code Sec. 50(d)(5) and Reg. § 1.50-1.

[56] Reg. § 1.50-1(b)(2).

[57] Reg. § 1.50-1(b)(3).

In the case of a credit recapture because of an early disposition (including a lease termination), the lessee or the ultimate credit claimant includes in gross income an amount equal to the excess, if any, of the amount of the credit that is not recaptured over the total increases in gross income previously taken. The amount is in addition to the amounts the lessee or the ultimate credit claimant previously included in gross income. The lessee's or the ultimate credit claimant's gross income is reduced by an amount equal to the excess, if any, of the total increases in gross income previously included, over the amount of the credit that is not recaptured.[58] Any adjustment required by credit recapture is taken into account in the tax year in which the property is disposed of or otherwise ceases to be investment credit property.[59]

If, after the credit recapture period but before the end of the recovery period, there is a lease termination, the lessee otherwise disposes of the lease, or a partner or S corporation shareholder that is an ultimate credit claimant disposes of its entire interest in the partnership or S corporation, the lessee or the ultimate credit claimant may irrevocably elect to take into account the remaining amount required to be included in gross income under this section in the tax year of the disposition or termination.[60]

Example 4: Jim and John, calendar year taxpayers, form a partnership that leases nonresidential real property. The property is placed in service on October 1, 2016, and the lessor elects to treat the partnership as having acquired the property. Jim's investment credit determined for 2016 is $3,900 and John's investment credit for 2016 is $7,800. The shortest recovery period that could be available to the property is 39 years. Because the lessor elected to treat the partnership as having acquired the property, the lessor does not reduce its basis in the building. Rather, Jim and John, the ultimate credit claimants, must include the amount of the credit ratably in gross income over 39 years. Jim's increase in gross income for each of the 39 years beginning with 2016 is $100 ($3,900/39-year recovery period). John's is $200 ($7,800/39-year recovery period). Because the gross income Jim and John are required to include is not an item of partnership income, Jim and John are not entitled to an increase in the outside basis of their partnership interests and are not entitled to an increase in their capital accounts.

Example 5: The facts are the same as in *Example 4* except that on January 1, 2019, the lease between the partnership and the lessor terminates (the lessor retains ownership of the property), and Jim's and John's income tax for 2019 is increased by $2,340 and $4,680 (60% of $3,900 and $7,800, assuming that the aggregate decrease in the credits was the full amount of the investment credits). Therefore, the amount of the unrecaptured credit as to Jim and John is $1,560 and $3,120 (40% of $3,900 and $7,800). The amounts that Jim and John previously included in gross income are $300 for Jim ($100 for each of 2016, 2017, and 2018) and $600 for John ($200 for each of 2016, 2017, and 2018). Jim and John are required to include in gross income an amount equal

[58] Reg. § 1.50-1(c).

[59] Reg. § 1.50-1(c)(3).

[60] Reg. § 1.50-1(d).

to the excess of the credit that is not recaptured ($1,560 for Jim and $3,120 for John) over the total increases in gross income previously made ($300 for Jim and $600 for John). Therefore, Jim and John must include in gross income $1,260 (Jim) and $2,520 (John) in the tax year of the lease termination (2019) in addition to the recapture amounts described above.

Example 6: The facts are the same as in *Example 5* except that on December 1, 2021, Jim sells his entire interest to Harry, and on January 1, 2022, the lease between partnership and lessor terminates. At the time of the lease termination, John is still a partner in the partnership. There is no recapture event because both the lease termination and the disposition of Jim's interest in the partnership occurred outside of the recapture period.

At the time that Jim sold his interest in the partnership to Harry, Jim had previously included $500 ($100 for each of 2016-2020) in gross income. Jim must continue to include the remaining $3,400 (including $100 in 2021) in gross income ratably over the remaining portion of the applicable recovery period of 39 years. Alternatively, Jim may irrevocably elect to include the remaining $3,400 in gross income in the tax year that Jim sold his entire interest in the partnership to Harry (2021). Jim cannot make this election in the tax year of the lease termination (2022).

At the time of the lease termination, John had previously included $1,200 ($200 for each of 2016-2021) in gross income. John must continue to include the remaining $6,600 required in gross income ratably over the remaining portion of the applicable recovery period of 39 years. Alternatively, John may irrevocably elect to include the remaining $6,600 in gross income in the tax year of the lease termination (2022).

Subleases

A lessee who subleases property on which the lessor elected to pass on an investment credit may, in turn, elect to pass the credit on to the sublessee. The lessee-sublessor, however, need not pass the credit on to the sublessee, but may retain it.[61]

When neither the lessor nor the lessee in a standard two-party lease can make immediate use of a rehabilitation investment tax credit, it may be possible to interpose a third party who can make use of the credit. This is essentially what happened in *Comdisco, Inc.*[62] A supplier corporation leased computer equipment directly to another corporation, but entered into a new lease for the property with a third party and assigned the former lease and elected to pass through the investment credit to the third party. The court ruled the transaction was a lease from the supplier to the third party and a sublease from the third party to the original lessee. The third party, as a lessee from the supplier, was entitled to the investment credit under the supplier's election to pass the credit to the lessee. It did not matter that the original lessee continued to make payments directly to the supplier because the third party was obligated to the primary lessor. While *Comdisco* involved the lease

[61] Rev. Rul. 71-243, 1971-1 CB 7.

[62] CA-7, 85-1 USTC ¶ 9245, 756 F.2d 569.

of equipment (which was eligible for the investment credit at the time), there would be no reason why the same principle could not apply to the lease of property that is being rehabilitated and is eligible for the investment credit for qualified rehabilitations.

[B] Credit Split on Short-Term Lease Property

A lessor who elects to pass the investment credit to a lessee can transfer only part of the credit in the case of property leased under "certain short term leases."[63] A lease is subject to this special rule if the lease is of property that:

1. Is new investment credit property (qualified rehabilitations are always treated as new property);
2. Has a class life of more than 14 years under the ADR system;[64]
3. Is leased for a period of less than 80 percent of its class life; and
4. Is not leased subject to a net lease under which the lessor is guaranteed a specific return or is guaranteed against loss of income.[65]

Since real estate is often leased under a net lease arrangement, there will be many occasions when an election to pass the credit to the lessee will result in a pass-through of the full credit, even if the lease term is relatively short. Unless the lessee remains in possession at least five years, however, all or part of the credit may be recaptured.[66] If the credit does have to be split between the lessor and the lessee when the lessor elects to pass the credit to the lessee, the credit is divided between the two parties in the same ratio that the lease term bears to the class life of the property.[67]

If the lessee of property subleases property that is subject to the short-term lease rules, the property is treated as being subject to a short-term lease in the hands of the sublessee. Property that is short-term lease property in the hands of the lessee is treated as such in the hand of the sublessee even if the property is leased to the sublessee under a net lease.[68] Of course, the credit must be split three ways if the sublessor elects to pass the credit to the sublessee after the primary lessor has elected to pass the credit to the sublessor.

---

[63] Former Code Sec. 48(d)(2), as in effect prior to 1991; *see* Code Sec. 50(d)(5).

[64] *See* Rev. Proc. 87-56, 1987-2 CB 674, for a listing of the class lives for various assets.

[65] *See* former Code Sec. 57(c)(1)(B) as in effect before the enactment of the Tax Reform Act of 1986 for the definition of net lease for this purpose.

[66] Code Sec. 50(a)(1).

[67] Reg. § 1.48-4(c)(3) and the examples in Reg. § 1.48-4(c)(4).

[68] Reg. § 1.48-4(e).

Part III

REAL ESTATE OPERATION

Introduction to Part III

Chapter 7 looks at many of the common deductions associated with real estate operation. Also, the general rules relating to tax accounting are considered in this chapter, with special regard to the rules that are likely to affect the ownership and operation of real estate and those entities that may hold real estate for business or investment purposes.

Chapter 8 deals with additions and improvements to real estate in general and the special amortization and tax credit provisions available for particular types of improvements. This includes the additional deductions to assist economically depressed areas and incentives for increasing energy efficiency. The more widely available deduction for depreciation is given special consideration in Chapter 9. Also included is a discussion on the use of cost segregation studies that may allow for faster depreciation writeoffs.

The development, subdivision, and sale of real estate in the ordinary course of business involves tax questions and problems that are unique when compared to those involved in the one-time sale of rental property or property used in a trade or business. These unique questions and problems are the subjects of Chapter 10. Also touched on is the incentive Congress has provided home builders for constructing more energy efficient homes.

While deductions generated by a specific property always can be used to reduce the taxable income from that property, there are limits on the use of deductions generated by real estate activities to reduce taxable income from other sources. Perhaps the most important limitations in this regard are the passive loss limitations discussed in Chapter 11. These limitations must be considered in any evaluation of the tax benefits that might be derived from the ownership and operation of real estate.

Finally, Part III concludes with an examination of one area of real estate operation that no one really wants to face—what happens when real estate just cannot support the debt incurred to finance its purchase, or support the debt incurred for other purposes and secured by the real estate. Troubled real estate financings, the topic of Chapter 12, may develop in the course of holding real estate for investment, for the production of rental income, or for use in a trade or business.

Chapter 7
Operating Expenses and Taxes

¶ 700 Overview of Chapter
¶ 701 Tax Accounting for Real Estate
¶ 702 Start-Up Expenses
¶ 703 Real Estate Operating Expenses
¶ 704 Real Estate Taxes
¶ 705 Excess Business Losses

¶ 700 OVERVIEW OF CHAPTER

The income tax rates are applied to "taxable income," that is, to income after permitted deductions. The ownership and operation of real estate give rise to a host of deductions that often reduce substantially the amount of income from the real estate that is subject to tax. In this Chapter, many of the most common deductions associated with real estate operation are examined. Depreciation, a "non-cash" expenditure that is often one of the largest deductions associated with real estate operation, however, is singled out and treated separately in Chapter 9. Also, the deduction for interest is considered in Chapter 3 in connection with real estate financing. Deductions related to leasehold acquisition and disposition are considered in Chapter 5, and those related to leasehold improvements and additions in Chapter 6.

While deductions generated by a specific property always can be used to reduce the taxable income from that property, there are limits on the use of deductions generated by real estate activities to reduce taxable income from other sources. One such limitation is the at-risk rules discussed in Chapter 3. Another is the passive loss limitations discussed in Chapter 11. These limitations must be considered in any evaluation of the tax benefits that might be derived from the ownership and operation of real estate.

Taxable income must be determined using a consistent method of accounting to fix the taxable amount in a specific accounting period. The two most widely used accounting methods are cash and accrual, and the two most widely used accounting periods are the calendar and fiscal years. The general rules relating to tax accounting also are considered in this chapter, with special regard to the rules that are likely to affect the ownership and operation of real estate and those entities that may hold real estate for business or investment purposes.

¶ 701 TAX ACCOUNTING FOR REAL ESTATE

Most individuals are cash method, calendar year taxpayers. Individual ownership or co-ownership of real estate generally does not present an opportunity to make accounting changes. When real estate is acquired for business or investment purposes by a new entity and a new taxpayer comes into existence, however, an opportunity exists to choose the accounting period and accounting method that will be most advantageous to the new entity and its owners. Of course, in many cases, the discretion to pick and choose among possible accounting periods and methods is not unfettered. The Internal Revenue Code contains a host of provisions designed to limit the tax advantages that might otherwise be gained through judicious tax accounting.

.01 Accounting Period

Taxable income is computed on the basis of an annual accounting period called the tax or taxable year. This period generally may be either a fiscal year or the calendar year. The calendar year is the 12 months ending on December 31. A fiscal year is a 12-month period ending on the last day of any calendar month. Also, a fiscal year may be adopted that varies from 52 to 53 weeks and that always ends on the same day of the week and that always ends either on whatever date that day of the week last occurs in a calendar month or on whatever date that day of the week falls which is nearest to the last day of a calendar month.[1]

Since a new taxpayer may adopt either a fiscal year or the calendar year on the first return,[2] the formation of a new entity in connection with the acquisition and ownership of real estate offers the opportunity to select the most advantageous tax year. The ability to select any fiscal year as the tax year, however, is limited by special rules that apply to partnerships, S corporations, and personal service corporations and which are discussed at ¶ 701.01[A]. When the choice of a tax year is not limited, the year may be selected to match income and deductions to limit tax liability, or to create a short initial year to minimize initial income taxes.

[A] Required Tax Years for Partnerships, S Corporations, and Personal Service Corporations

Various provisions of the Internal Revenue Code generally require that partnerships,[3] S corporations,[4] and personal service corporations[5] conform their tax years to the tax years of their owners unless a business purpose can be shown for the use of some other year. S corporations and personal service corporations generally must use the calendar year.

The IRS has issued Revenue Procedures that contain procedures for expeditious approval of requests by these entities to adopt, retain, or change their tax years. Rev. Proc. 2006-45[6] applies to corporations, and Rev. Proc. 2006-46[7] applies to partnerships, S corporations, personal service corporations, and trusts. The Reve-

[1] Reg. § 1.441-2.
[2] Reg. § 1.441-1(c).
[3] Code Sec. 706(b).
[4] Code Sec. 1378(b).
[5] Code Sec. 441(i).
[6] 2006-45 IRB 851.
[7] 2006-45 IRB 859.

nue Procedures also contain a test for determining a natural business year that, if met, automatically establishes a business purpose for a particular fiscal year. Rev. Rul. 87-57[8] contains examples of factors that are considered by the IRS in determining whether a business purpose exists for a specific tax year. Certain partnerships, S corporations, and personal service corporations may elect to use a tax year other than a required tax year,[9] as separately discussed at ¶ 701.01[B].

Partnerships

When a new partnership had the unrestricted right to choose a taxable year, partners often would take maximum advantage of this tax deferral opportunity. For example, if all partners were on the calendar year (which most likely would be the case when the partners were individuals), then choosing a fiscal year ending January 31 for the partnership would allow the partners to defer reporting partnership income for a period of 11 months. Partnership items from a partnership's tax year are reported by partners for their tax year that includes the last day of the partnership's tax year.

Now, however, Code Sec. 706(b) prevents this type of deferral by requiring a partnership to conform its tax year to that of the partners, unless the partnership can establish a business purpose for a different tax year. Under these tax year conformity rules, a partnership must use the same tax year as its majority partners, that is, the tax year used by the partners who have an aggregate interest in partnership profits and capital of more than 50 percent.[10] Since most individuals are calendar year taxpayers, this provision generally requires a partnership of individuals to use the calendar year.

If there is no combination of majority partners that have the same tax year, then the partnership's tax year must conform to the tax year of all the principal partners of the partnership, that is, all partners that have at least a five percent interest in partnership profits and capital.[11] If a partnership's tax year cannot be determined using majority partners or principal partners, then the tax year chosen must be the one that results in the least aggregate deferral of income to the partners.[12] Reg. § 1.706-1(b)(3)(iv) contains numerous examples of how to determine the tax year that results in the least aggregate deferral of income to the partners.

Once the partnership's tax year is fixed by the conformity rules (or by a business purpose), a partner cannot change tax years to achieve the deferral blocked by the conformity rules. A principal partner (five percent interest) cannot change to a tax year other than that of the partnership in which he or she is a principal partner unless a business purpose for the change is established.[13] The IRS, in effect, has extended this rule to all partners. Reg. § 1.706-1(b)(8)(ii) provides that no partner may change the taxable year without securing approval from the Commissioner of Internal Revenue.

---

[8] 1987-2 CB 117.

[9] Code Sec. 444.

[10] Code Sec. 706(b)(1)(B)(i).

[11] Code Sec. 706(b)(1)(B)(ii).

[12] Code Sec. 706(b)(1)(B)(iii); Reg. § 1.706-1(b)(3).

[13] Code Sec. 706(b)(2).

A partnership may elect a tax year other than a required tax year under Code Sec. 444 as discussed at ¶ 701.01[B].

S Corporations

S corporations must use a tax year that is a "permitted year."[14] A permitted year is defined as a year ending on December 31 or any other accounting period for which the corporation is able to establish a business purpose.[15] Deferral of income to shareholders is not a business purpose that would justify a tax year other than the calendar year.

An S corporation may elect a tax year other than a required tax year under Code Sec. 444 as discussed at ¶ 701.01[B].

Personal Service Corporations

A personal service corporation must use the calendar year as its taxable year unless the corporation establishes a business purpose for having a different period for its taxable year.[16] Deferral of income to shareholders is not a business purpose that would justify a tax year other than the calendar year.

A corporation is a personal service corporation if:

1. The corporation is a C corporation;
2. The principal activity of the corporation is the performance of personal services in the fields of health, law, engineering, architecture, accounting, actuarial science, performing arts, or consulting;
3. The personal services are substantially performed by employee-owners (a person is an employee-owner if he is an employee of the corporation and owns any outstanding stock of the corporation); and
4. Employee-owners own more than ten percent of the fair market value of the outstanding stock of the corporation.[17]

Reg. § 1.441-3 also contains an explanation of how to determine the "principal activity" of a corporation and how to determine whether personal services are "substantially performed" by employee-owners.

A personal service corporation may elect a tax year other than a required tax year under Code Sec. 444 as discussed at ¶ 701.01[B].

[B] Election to Use Other Than a Required Year

Partnerships, S corporations, and personal service corporations that have a required tax year under the rules discussed above may elect, on Form 8716, to use a tax year other than their required year.[18] The election to use a tax year other than a required year, however, carries a cost—a "required payment" in the case of a partnership or S corporation, and minimum distributions to owner-employees in the case of a personal service corporation. The election is available to an entity if it meets the following three conditions:

[14] Code Sec. 1378(a).
[15] Code Sec. 1378(b).
[16] Code Sec. 441(i)(1).
[17] Reg. § 1.441-3(c).
[18] Code Sec. 444.

1. The entity is not a member of a tiered structure (subject to a *de minimis* exception);
2. The entity did not previously have an election under Code Sec. 444 in effect; and
3. The elected tax year results in a deferral period of less than three months (or the deferral period of its current tax year if less than three months in the case of an entity that is changing its tax year).

For a partnership, S corporation, or personal service corporation that wants to adopt or change its taxable year by making the election under Code Sec. 444, the deferral period comprises the months that occur after the end of the taxable year desired under the election and before the close of the required tax year.[19] If an entity is using its required tax year as its tax year, the deferral period is deemed to be zero.[20] This latter precludes an entity that is already using its required tax year from changing to a different tax year, since an entity seeking to change its tax year cannot elect a tax year under Code Sec. 444 with a deferral period that is greater than the deferral period of its current tax year.

Example 1: The newly formed Partnership, in which all partners are calendar year individual taxpayers, desires to elect a tax year ending September 30. The Partnership's required tax year is the calendar year. The deferral period in this case is three months, the number of months between September 30 and December 31. The new Partnership would be permitted to elect a fiscal year ending September 30 under Code Sec. 444.

On the other hand, suppose the Partnership were an existing partnership that had historically used the calendar year, its required year, and that the Partnership desired to change its tax year to the fiscal year ending September 30. In this case, the deferral period of its current tax year is zero and the deferral period of its desired tax year would be three months. The Partnership would not be permitted to elect the fiscal year ending September 30 under Code Sec. 444 because the deferral period for the new year would be greater than the deferral period of its existing tax year.

Election by Partnerships and S Corporations

A partnership or S corporation that makes the election to have a tax year other than the required tax year must make the payments required by Code Sec. 7519 for any tax year for which the election is in effect. The "required payment" is intended to represent the value of the tax deferral that the owners of the partnership or S corporation receive as a result of the election to use other than a required tax year. The payment is due by May 15 of the calendar year following the calendar year in which the elected tax year begins.[21] Required payments under Code Sec. 7519 are assessed and collected as if they were employment taxes and are paid with Form 720 or by FTD deposit. A worksheet included with the instructions for Form 1065 and Form 1120S is used to compute the required payment and must be included

[19] Code Sec. 444(b)(4).

[20] Temp. Reg. § 1.444-1T(b)(4)(ii)(B).

[21] Temp. Reg. § 1.7519-2T(a)(4)(ii).

when the payment is made. A required payment is waived if it does not exceed $500. A partnership, S corporation, or its owners are not entitled to a deduction for any required payment under Code Sec. 7519.[22]

Election by Personal Service Corporations

A personal service corporation that elects a tax year other than the required tax year is subject to the deduction limits contained in Code Sec. 280H. These deduction limits are designed to eliminate the benefit that would otherwise result from the tax deferral. Code Sec. 280H limits the deductions that a personal service corporation using other than a required tax year may take for payments to employee-owners of the corporation unless certain minimum distributions are made to the employee-owners before the end of the calendar year. These minimum distributions must be made during the deferral period. See Temp. Reg. § 1.280H-1T for details on calculating the minimum distributions and any deduction limits imposed for failing to meet the minimum distribution requirements.

Termination of Election

The election to use a tax year other than the required tax year under Code Sec. 444 is terminated if:

1. The electing entity changes to its required tax year;
2. The electing entity liquidates;
3. A partnership or S corporation willfully fails to make the required payments or a personal service corporation willfully fails to comply with the minimum distribution requirements;
4. An entity becomes a member of a tiered structure (see discussion below);
5. An S corporation's S election is terminated (but a corporation that immediately becomes a personal service corporation following the termination of its status as an S corporation may continue the election); or
6. A personal service corporation ceases to be a personal service corporation (but a personal service corporation that ceases to be a personal service corporation but elects to be an S corporation may continue the election).

Once an election under Code Sec. 444 to use a tax year other than a required year is terminated under the above rules, the partnership, S corporation, or personal service corporation may not make another Code Sec. 444 election.[23]

Tiered Structures

An entity that is part of a tiered structure generally may not elect or continue a tax year other than a required year.[24] A partnership, S corporation, or personal service corporation is part of a tiered structure if the entity directly owns any portion of another partnership, S corporation, personal service corporation, or certain trusts. An entity is also a part of a tiered structure if any other partnership, S

---

[22] Temp. Reg. § 1.7519-2T(b).

[23] Code Sec. 444(d)(2)(B); Temp. Reg. § 1.444-1T(a)(5).

[24] Code Sec. 444(d)(3).

corporation, personal service corporation, or certain trusts directly own any portion of the entity.[25]

Certain ownership, however, may be disregarded under both "upstream" and "downstream" *de minimis* rules. Upstream, forbidden ownership in the entity seeking the Code Sec. 444 election is disregarded if it does not exceed five percent.[26] Downstream, forbidden ownership by the entity seeking the Code Sec. 444 election is disregarded if the forbidden ownership contributes five percent or less of the entity's taxable income or two percent or less of the entity's gross income.[27]

.02 Accounting Method

Taxpayers must compute taxable income using a method of accounting that clearly reflects income.[28] The two most commonly used methods of accounting are the cash receipts and disbursements method and the accrual method. Other methods may be allowed under other Internal Revenue Code sections, such as the installment method discussed at ¶ 1401, and hybrid methods may be authorized by regulations.[29] The general rules applicable to a specific accounting method may not always apply to specific items. Many income and expense items are subject to special rules that alter the timing or amount of reportable income or deduction from what would be the case under normal cash or accrual accounting rules. Examples of such items, include advance rents (see ¶ ¶ 402.02 and 403.01), prepaid and investment interest (see ¶ 303.02), original issue discount (see ¶ 304.02), and construction period expenses (see ¶ 103.01).

A taxpayer engaged in more than one trade or business may use a different method of accounting to compute taxable income for each trade or business.[30] This rule allows an individual to use the cash method for personal income and expenses and the accrual method for business income and expenses. It also allows an individual or other taxpayer to select a new method of accounting for a new business.[31]

[A] Cash Method

Under the cash method of accounting, income is reported for the year in which it is actually or constructively received in the form of cash or its equivalent or other property or services.[32] Under the doctrine of constructive receipt, income must be reported under the cash method when the income is credited to the taxpayer's account, set apart for the taxpayer, or otherwise made available so that the taxpayer may draw upon it at any time. Deductions under the cash method generally are taken for the year in which the amounts are actually paid. The cash method is the method of accounting used by most individuals.

---

[25] Temp. Reg. § 1.444-2T.

[26] Temp. Reg. § 1.444-2T(c)(3).

[27] Temp. Reg. § 1.444-2T(c)(2).

[28] Code Sec. 446.

[29] Code Sec. 446(c).

[30] Code Sec. 446(d).

[31] *See,* for example, R.C. Hoffman, 19 TCM 836, CCH Dec. 24,295(M), T.C. Memo. 1960-160, *aff'd,* CA-3, 62-1 USTC ¶ 9218, 298 F.2d 784; National Builders, Inc., 12 TC 852, CCH Dec. 16,985, *acq.* 1949-2 CB 3; Burgess Poultry Market, Inc., DC Tex, 64-2 USTC ¶ 9515.

[32] Reg. § 1.446-1(c).

A cash method taxpayer may control the timing of income, within the confines of the doctrine of constructive receipt, or deductions to the extent he has control over the timing of receipt of income or payment of expenses. Billing practices may hasten or defer collection of income, and accelerating or deferring payment of expenses may accelerate or defer tax deductions attributable to those expenses. There are, however, some limits on the taxpayers who are eligible to use the cash method of accounting, and these limitations are discussed below.

Limitations on Use of Cash Method

Under Code Sec. 448, certain taxpayers are not permitted to use the cash method of accounting, but must adopt and use the accrual method. These taxpayers are:

1. C corporations;
2. Partnerships that have at least one C corporation as a partner; and
3. Tax shelters.

Trusts that are subject to tax on unrelated trade or business income are treated as C corporations with respect to their unrelated business income.[33]

Tax shelters that are subject to the limitations on the use of the cash method of accounting are broadly defined to include:

1. Any enterprise, other than a C corporation, in which interests have been offered for sale in an offering that is subject to federal or state securities law registration;
2. A partnership or entity, other than a C corporation, if more than 35 percent of losses are allocable to limited partners or limited entrepreneurs; and
3. Any partnership or other entity, any investment plan or arrangement, or any other plan or arrangement, if the principal purpose is the avoidance of federal income tax.[34]

Exceptions to Limitations on Use of Cash Method

There are several exceptions to the limitations on the use of the cash method. Under these exceptions, small businesses, farmers and ranchers, and qualified personal service corporations may use the cash method of accounting, if otherwise qualified.

Except in the case of a tax shelter, a C corporation or partnership with a C corporation as a partner may use the cash method of accounting if its average annual gross receipts for the prior three-tax-year period (or shorter period if not in existence for three years) do not exceed $25 million ($5 million for tax years beginning before 2018). The average annual gross receipts amount of $25 million is adjusted for inflation after 2018.[35]

Also, except in the case of a tax shelter, Code Sec. 448 does not apply to a farming business.[36] It should be noted, however, that certain farm corporations are

[33] Code Sec. 448(d)(6).

[34] Temp. Reg. § 1.448-1T(b).

[35] Code Sec. 448(b)(3) and (c).

[36] Code Sec. 448(b)(1) and (d)(1).

required to use accrual accounting under the provisions of Code Sec. 447. Essentially, for tax years beginning after 2017, corporations engaged in farming are required to use accrual accounting unless the corporation is an S corporation or a corporation with less than $25 million in annual gross receipts.[37] For tax years beginning before 2018, the test was $1 million, except in the case of family farm corporations which were subject to a $25 million gross receipts test.

Again, except in the case of a tax shelter, a qualified personal service corporation may use the cash method of accounting. A qualified personal service corporation is a corporation in which substantially all of the activities involve the performance of services in the fields of health, law, engineering, architecture, accounting, actuarial science, performing arts, or consulting. Also, for a corporation to be a qualified personal service corporation, substantially all of the stock of the corporation must be owned by employees who perform services for the corporation or former employees or their estates or heirs.[38]

[B] Accrual Method

Under the accrual method of accounting, income is reported for the year in which it is earned, whether or not that income is actually or constructively received. Generally, it is the right to receive the income and not its actual receipt that controls.[39] Accrual of income may not be postponed because there is the possibility that some of the income may have to be returned or refunded.[40] Deductions or credits under the accrual method of accounting are taken in the year they are accrued or incurred, unless properly allowable in another year. As a general proposition, expenses incurred in and properly attributable to the process of earning income during an accounting period should be charged against that income, even if the expenses are not paid until a subsequent period.[41]

Economic Performance Requirement

In general, an accrual method taxpayer deducts expenses when (1) all events have occurred that determine the fact of the taxpayer's liability for the expense and (2) the taxpayer's liability can be determined with reasonable accuracy.[42] This "all events" test is not treated as satisfied with respect to a particular item unless and until economic performance with respect to that particular item has occurred.[43]

In the case of a liability that requires a payment for property or services provided to, or for the use of property by, an accrual method taxpayer, economic performance occurs when the property or services are provided or the property is used. In the case of a liability that requires a payment for property or services provided by an accrual method taxpayer, economic performance occurs and related expenses are deductible when the taxpayer actually provides the services or property.

---

[37] Code Sec. 447(c).

[38] Code Sec. 448(d)(2); Temp. Reg. § 1.448-1T(e).

[39] J.M. Enright Est., S.Ct., 41-1 USTC ¶ 9356, 312 U.S. 636, 61 S.Ct. 777.

[40] A.M. Brown, S.Ct., 4 USTC ¶ 1223, 291 U.S. 193, 54 S.Ct. 356.

[41] P.C. Anderson, S.Ct., 1 USTC ¶ 155, 269 U.S. 422, 46 S.Ct. 131.

[42] Code Sec. 461(h)(4); Reg. § 1.461-1(a)(2).

[43] Code Sec. 461(h).

Example 2: In November of 2018, an accrual-method Taxpayer, using the calendar year as the accounting period, contracted with a third party to have the third party clean and paint the walls within a warehouse that the Taxpayer owns at a cost of $15,000. The work is not performed until sometime in 2019. Although the Taxpayer was contractually bound to pay the $15,000 as of November 2018, economic performance does not occur until 2019, and the Taxpayer may not accrue the expense deduction until 2019.

In order to avoid disrupting normal business and accounting practices, an exception to the economic performance rules applies in the case of certain recurring expense items. An expense deduction is allowed for an item, even if economic performance has not occurred, if:

1. The all events test, other than economic performance, is met;
2. Economic performance occurs within a reasonable time, but not more than 8½ months after the close of the year;
3. The item is recurring in nature and similar items are treated as incurred in the year in which the all events test is met without regard to economic performance; and
4. The recurring item is not material or the deduction for the year in which the all events test is met, without regard to economic performance, results in a better matching of income and expense.[44]

The recurring item exception to the economic performance requirement is not available to taxpayers that are considered tax shelters.[45]

Inclusion Based on Financial Accounting Treatment

For an accrual-method taxpayer, the all-events test is met for any item of gross income if all the events have occurred which fix the right to receive such income and the amount of such income can be determined with reasonable accuracy. However, for tax years beginning after 2017 (2018 in the case of income from debt instruments with original issue discount), the all-events test for any item of gross income or portion of such item cannot be treated as met any later than when the item of gross income or portion of such item is taken into account in revenue in the taxpayer's applicable financial statement or other financial statement specified by the IRS.[46] Exceptions apply to taxpayers who do not have an applicable financial statement and to mortgage servicing contracts.

Deferral for Advance Payments

Generally, for tax years beginning after 2017 (2018 in the case of income from debt instruments with original issue discount), an accrual-method taxpayer who receives an advance payment during the tax year must either:

[44] Code Sec. 461(h)(3).

[45] Code Sec. 461(i).

[46] Code Sec. 451(b).

1. Include the advance payment in gross income for the tax year of receipt; or
2. Make an election to defer the inclusion of the advance payment in gross income with respect to the category of advance payments to which the advance payment belongs.[47]

Under the deferral election, any portion of the advance payment that is required to be included in gross income under the financial statement rule described above would be included in gross income in the tax year in which it is received and the remaining portion of the advance payment would be included in gross income in the tax year following the tax year in which it is received. An item of gross income is received by the taxpayer if it is actually or constructively received, or if it is due and payable to the taxpayer.

The rule for deferring advance payments from income essentially codified IRS guidance first issued in Rev. Proc. 2004-34[48] on deferral of advance payments. The IRS has issued proposed regulations on the treatment of advance payments to implement changes made to Code Sec. 451.[49]

An advance payment is any payment:

1. The full inclusion of which in the taxpayer's gross income for the tax year of receipt is a permissible method of accounting without regard to this advance payment rule;
2. Any portion of which is included in revenue by the taxpayer in a 10-K or Annual Statement to Shareholders that is required to be filed with the U.S. Securities and Exchange Commission (SEC) or an audited financial statement that is used for credit purposes, reporting to shareholders, partners, or other proprietors, or to beneficiaries, or any other substantial non-tax purpose, for a subsequent tax year; and
3. Which is for goods, services, or such items as may be identified by the IRS.

An advance payment does not include:

1. Rent;
2. Insurance premiums governed by subchapter L (insurance companies);
3. Payments with respect to financial instruments;
4. Payments with respect to warranty or guarantee contracts under which a third party is the primary obligor;
5. Payments subject to tax on certain amounts received from U.S. sources by a nonresident alien or foreign corporation or payments subject to the withholding rules for nonresident aliens or foreign corporations;
6. Payments for property transferred in connection with the performance of services; and
7. Any other payment identified by the IRS for this purpose.

[47] Code Sec. 451(c).

[48] 2004-22 IRB 991.

[49] NPRM REG 104554-18.

Accrual of Real Property Taxes

Accrual method taxpayers may elect to accrue real property taxes over the period of time to which the property taxes relate.[50] A separate election may be made for the real property taxes attributable to each separate trade or business of the taxpayer.[51] If this election is not made, state and local property taxes are deemed to accrue (1) on the date that fixes when the tax becomes a lien on the property, (2) when personal liability for the tax arises, or (3) on any other basis appropriate to the specific situation.

> ***Example 3:*** A calendar year Taxpayer using the accrual method owns real property for which the taxes become a lien on the property as of the first day of the property tax year, which runs from October 1 to September 30. Property taxes for the October 1, 2018, through September 30, 2019, period are $2,400. If the Taxpayer elects to ratably accrue the deduction for real property taxes, the Taxpayer deducts $600 of the $2,400 for the 2018 taxable year and $1,800 for the 2019 taxable year. In the absence of the election, the Taxpayer would accrue and deduct the entire $2,400 for the taxable year because the $2,400 becomes a lien against the property as of October 1, 2018.

[C] Long-Term Construction Contracts

In the case of long-term contracts, that is, contracts that cannot be completed within one year, taxpayers generally must use the percentage-of-completion method of accounting.[52] Under the percentage-of-completion method, the taxpayer includes in income for the tax year the portion of the gross contract price that corresponds to the percentage of the entire contract that has been completed during the tax year.[53] Under the percentage-of-completion—capitalized-cost method of long-term contract accounting, which was available before July 11, 1989, and which remains available for contracts resulting from the acceptance of a bid made before July 11, 1989, the taxpayer takes 90 percent of the items with respect to the long-term contract into account under the percentage-of-completion method and ten percent of the items under the completed-contract method or other normal method of accounting used by the taxpayer.[54]

These long-term contract rules of Code Sec. 460, which essentially require the use of the percentage-of-completion method of accounting for long-term contracts and block the use of the completed-contract method of accounting (under which income and expenses relating to a long-term contract are not taken into account until the contract is completed), do not apply to certain types of construction contracts.[55]

Small Construction Contracts

The long-term contract rules of Code Sec. 460 and the cost allocation rules for long-term contracts contained in Code Sec. 460(c) do not apply to "small construc-

[50] Code Sec. 461(c).

[51] Reg. § 1.461-1(c)(3).

[52] Code Sec. 460.

[53] Code Sec. 460(b).

[54] Former Code Sec. 460(a) as in effect prior to its amendment by Sec. 7621 of the Revenue Reconciliation Act of 1989, and Sec. 7621(d) of the 1989 Act.

[55] Code Sec. 460(e).

tion contracts." A small construction contract is one that is expected to be completed within the two-year period beginning on the commencement date of the contract and that is performed by a taxpayer whose average annual gross receipts do not exceed $25 million ($10 million for tax years before 2018). The exception for small construction contracts cannot be applied by a tax shelter that is not allowed to use the cash method of accounting.[56]

A taxpayer that is not a corporation or partnership applies the gross receipts test as if each trade or business of the taxpayer were a corporation or a partnership. For example, a sole proprietorship should apply the $25 million gross receipts test as if the sole proprietorship were a corporation or partnership.[57]

Home Construction Contracts

The long-term contract rules and cost allocation rules of Code Sec. 460 do not apply to "home construction contracts."[58] A home construction contract is a contract in which 80 percent or more of the estimated total contract costs are reasonably expected to be attributed to (1) the building, reconstruction or rehabilitation of dwelling units contained in buildings comprising four or fewer dwelling units, and (2) improvements to real property directly related to such dwelling units and located on the site of the dwelling units.[59]

The IRS Chief Counsel, in a Technical Advice Memorandum (TAM),[60] determined that long-term construction contracts requiring grading and soil compaction of the pad area necessary to construct home foundations qualified for the completed-contract method of accounting. According to the TAM, the grading and soil compaction of the pad area to construct the foundations were as essential to the support of the houses as the foundations themselves and were part of the dwelling units. Further, the taxpayer's work was regulated by state and local building codes and was the subject of home warranties. Therefore, the long-term construction contracts requiring grading and soil compaction of the pad area qualified for the completed-contract method of accounting.

The IRS Large Business and International Division has issued a Practice Unit that discusses the proper method of accounting for land developers and subcontractors.[61] The Practice Unit notes that land developers and the subcontractors they hire to construct common improvements (*e.g.*, water lines, utilities, roads, sewers, parks) may be taking the position that their contracts are home construction contracts eligible for the completed-contract method of accounting, even though they do not construct any homes. In general, the Practice Unit concludes the taxpayers are required to use the percentage-of-completion method for those contracts. While Practice Units are not official pronouncements of law or directives, they do provide IRS staff with explanations of general tax concepts and information on specific types of transactions, and, in this regard, are useful to taxpayers and tax professionals.

[56] Code Sec. 460(e)(1)(B).

[57] Code Sec. 460(e)(2).

[58] Code Sec. 460(e)(1)(A).

[59] Code Sec. 460(e)(5).

[60] TAM 201650014.

[61] Document Control Number MAT/C/213_01-02.

Residential Construction Contracts

"Residential construction contracts" are contracts other than home construction contracts for which 80 percent or more of the total estimated costs under the contract are reasonably expected to be attributed to the building, construction, reconstruction, or rehabilitation of, or improvements to, real estate directly related to and located on the site of dwelling units.[62] Under a special rule for residential construction contracts, the percentage-of-completion—capitalized-cost method of accounting is applied with 70 percent of the contract items taken into account under the percentage-of-completion method and the remaining 30 percent of the items under the completed-contract or other normal method of accounting used by the taxpayer.[63]

.03 Controlling the Timing of Income and Expense

The cash method taxpayer, because income is reported and deductions are taken as income is received or expenses paid, has a greater degree of control over the timing of income and expense than does the accrual method taxpayer. The accrual method taxpayer, because income and expense items must be reported in the year accrued or incurred, generally has less control over the timing of income and expense. Nevertheless, even the accrual method taxpayer has some strategies available to defer or accelerate income and expense items.

In the usual case, regardless of the method of accounting employed by the taxpayer, a taxpayer will want to defer income and accelerate deductions to reduce current taxes. Through income deferral and expense acceleration, taxes are shifted to future years and, in the meantime, the taxpayer has the use of funds that would otherwise go to pay taxes. In some situations, however, accelerating income and deferring deductions may produce better overall tax results, for instance, when current income will be subject to lower tax rates than income reportable in the following year, either through application of the regular tax rates or the alternative minimum tax. For example, if income reportable this year would be subject to the alternative minimum tax, but income next year would be subject to the highest regular tax rates, accelerating income and deferring deductions could produce a tax advantage.

[A] Deferring Income and Accelerating Deductions

As noted, the usual tax strategy is to seek to defer income and to accelerate deductions in order to shift tax liability to future years and gain the use of money that would otherwise go to the tax collector. The following is a checklist of some ideas for reducing current taxes through income deferral and expense acceleration.

1. A cash method taxpayer may delay billing and collection for property and services until after the end of the year.
2. An accrual method taxpayer may defer income by delaying the completion of services or the furnishing of property. For the accrual method taxpayer to achieve deferral, however, the taxpayer must actually hold back or delay

[62] Code Sec. 460(e)(5)(B).

[63] Code Sec. 460(e)(4).

completion of the work or delay shipment or transfer of the property. Merely delaying billing does not defer income once "all events" fixing the taxpayer's right to the income have occurred.

3. Profitable sales may be delayed, provided the delay is possible without undue risk of loss. Depending on the nature of the property, sales on consignment or approval may defer income realization while serving to fix price. In the case of real estate, simply setting a closing date after year end defers income from the sale.
4. When available, an installment sale may also defer income from the sale of property. An installment sale permits closing to take place in the current year while income is delayed until some future date. An installment sale also buys the taxpayer more time to assess the tax position. By electing out of installment reporting before a tax return is filed, the taxpayer can "reshift" income back into the year of sale.
5. Cash method taxpayers may prepay real estate or state income taxes and accelerate deductions for these items.
6. Expenses can be accelerated by advance purchases of supplies, repairs and other deductible items. Legal and accounting fees for work in progress at year end may be paid. Cash method taxpayers must actually pay these items to garner a deduction, and accrual method taxpayers must be certain the expenses are incurred and accrued and economic performance has occurred.
7. Cash method taxpayers may pay bonuses before year end to accelerate the deduction. Accrual method taxpayers need not actually pay bonuses before year end but must be certain the necessary actions have been taken to fix liability for the bonuses before year-end, and the bonuses must actually be paid within 2½ months after the close of the year. Special rules apply to bonuses paid to related cash method taxpayers as discussed at ¶ 701.04 in connection with related party transactions.
8. Lease cancellation payments can accelerate deductions for rent on leased property that is no longer desirable or being used.
9. Charitable contributions are easily controlled for maximum advantage. Gifts of easements and appreciated real estate should be considered to effect a charitable deduction with no out-of-pocket cash cost.
10. Sales of property at a loss can be accelerated into the current year in order to use the loss deduction to offset other income.
11. Purchase of depreciable personal property before year end generates a deduction for the current year.

[B] Accelerating Income and Deferring Deductions

When good tax planning calls for accelerating income into the current year and deferring deductions until the following year, the strategies available are essentially the opposite of those presented at ¶ 701.03[A]. The following checklist highlights some of the more common strategies:

1. Accelerate billing and speed up shipments and delivery of goods and services.
2. Conclude profitable sales expeditiously so that closing takes place before year end.
3. Installment obligations or receivables may be sold to accelerate the receipt of income.
4. Installment obligations may be pledged to accelerate the realization of income.
5. Cash method taxpayers may delay the payment of deductible business expenses.
6. Purchase of supplies and repairs may be delayed.
7. Acquisition of depreciable personal property may be delayed until after year end.
8. Sales of property at a loss can be delayed or closing dates can be set after year end.

.04 Related Party Transactions

Code Sec. 267 contains provisions that block the use of related parties to create tax losses through property sales and deductions for expenses and interest owed by an accrual method taxpayer to a related cash method taxpayer.

[A] Losses on Sales and Exchanges

Generally, a taxpayer may make a sale or exchange of property in order to establish a loss and reduce income from other sources. If the sale of property that results in a loss is between related parties, however, no deduction is allowed for that loss.[64] This loss disallowance rule applies to sales between those related parties that are listed in Code Sec. 267(b) and set out at ¶ 701.04[C].

Were it not for Code Sec. 267(a), taxpayers could use related party sales to reduce current taxes even though, as a practical matter, no actual loss is realized. For example, if the sole owner of a corporation sells property at a loss to the corporation, the shareholder retains ownership and control over the property through the ownership and control over the corporation. Code Sec. 267 blocks the shareholder from taking a loss deduction for the sale of property in this case because, in effect, the shareholder still owns the property or otherwise has dominion and control over the property.

Following the sale of property at a loss between related parties, the transferee's basis in the property is determined under the normal rules, that is, the basis is its cost. The transferor realizes no benefit from the disallowed loss. However, if the original transferee of the property later sells or disposes of the property at a gain, the amount of gain realized by the transferee is reduced by the amount of the loss previously disallowed under Code Sec. 267.[65] The reduction of gain on a subsequent

[64] Code Sec. 267(a)(1).

[65] Code Sec. 267(d).

sale applies only to the original transferee and only to the property received from the related party or property received in exchange for that property in a tax-free exchange.

[B] Deductions for Expenses and Interest

Code Sec. 267(a)(2) prevents the mismatching of expense and income that would otherwise occur when an accrual method taxpayer pays a deductible expense to a related cash method taxpayer. For example, an accrual method corporation could accrue salary owed to its sole shareholder. If the sole shareholder were a cash method taxpayer, the corporation could obtain a deduction even though the cash method shareholder would not be required to include the salary in income until such time as it is actually received. Under the current rule of Code Sec. 267(a)(2), however, an accrual method taxpayer may deduct expenses and interest owed to a related cash method taxpayer only when the related taxpayer is required to include the amount in his income. The rule applies to all deductible expenses and interest when the timing of the deduction depends on the taxpayer's method of accounting.

While the related persons covered by this matching of deductions and income rule are essentially the same as those covered by the loss disallowance rule, there are some additional related party rules for expenses and interest owed by partnerships and S corporations and their shareholders. Generally, the matching rules apply to amounts accrued by a partnership to its partners, by partners to their partnerships, by an S corporation to its shareholders, and by S corporation shareholders to their corporation.[66] Special constructive ownership rules apply to partnerships.[67]

[C] Related Parties Defined

Related parties that are subject to the loss disallowance rule and income and expense matching rule of Code Sec. 267 include:

1. Members of a family, which includes only brothers, sisters, spouse, ancestors and lineal descendants;
2. An individual and a corporation if the individual owns 50 percent or more in value of the outstanding stock of the corporation;
3. Two corporations that are members of the same controlled group;[68]
4. A grantor and a fiduciary of any trust;
5. A fiduciary of a trust and a fiduciary of another trust, if the same person is the grantor of both trusts;
6. A fiduciary of a trust and a beneficiary of the trust;
7. A fiduciary of a trust and a beneficiary of another trust, if the same person is the grantor of both trusts;

---

[66] Code Sec. 267(e)(1).

[67] Code Sec. 267(e)(1)(C) and (e)(3).

[68] Code Sec. 267(f).

8. A fiduciary of a trust and a corporation, if more than 50 percent in value of the corporation is owned by or for the trust or by or for the grantor of the trust;
9. A person and a tax-exempt charitable or educational organization if the organization is controlled by that person or members of that person's family;
10. A corporation and a partnership, if the same persons own more than 50 percent in value of the outstanding stock of the corporation and more than 50 percent of the capital or profit interest in the partnership;
11. An S corporation and another S corporation if the same persons own more than 50 percent in value of the outstanding stock of each corporation;
12. An S corporation and a C corporation if the same persons own more than 50 percent in value of the outstanding stock of each corporation; and
13. An executor of an estate and a beneficiary of the estate, except for a sale or exchange to satisfy a pecuniary bequest.[69]

Code Sec. 267(c) contains a series of constructive ownership rules for determining stock ownership for purposes of Code Sec. 267. Also, Code Sec. 267(e) contains special related party rules for partnerships and S corporations.

¶ 702 START-UP EXPENSES

In order for "business expenses" to be deductible, there must be a trade or business. But what about the numerous expenses that arise before a business actually comes into existence? Without some special provision, these expenses would not be deductible. What's more, since most businesses have indefinite lifetimes, there could be no amortization of the cost of creating an asset (the business) over the life of the business. In short, a taxpayer who created a business could recover start-up and related costs only when the business was sold or otherwise ceased operation.

Fortunately, Code Sec. 195 provides the authority for recovering the cost of business start-ups sooner than the end of the business. The taxpayer who starts a business after October 22, 2004, may elect to deduct up to $5,000 of start-up expenditures in the tax year in which the trade or business begins. Each $5,000 amount is reduced, however, by the amount by which the cumulative cost of start-up expenditures exceeds $50,000. Expenditures that are not deductible must be amortized over 15 years.[70] If the taxpayer disposes of the business before the end of the amortization period, the taxpayer may deduct any remaining start-up costs at that time, subject to the general provisions on deducting losses contained in Code Sec. 165.[71] For tax years beginning in 2010 only, the $5,000 and $50,000 amounts were increased to $6,000 and $60,000.[72]

The election to deduct business start-up costs must be made on the tax return for the year in which business begins by attaching a statement that sets out the

---

[69] Code Sec. 267(b).

[70] Code Sec. 195(b)(1).

[71] Code Sec. 195(b)(2).

[72] Code Sec. 195(b)(3).

amount and description of the expenditures, the dates incurred, the month business began, and the number of months over which the costs will be amortized. It is important to claim the deduction as early as possible should there be any doubt about when the business actually begins. The right to deduct the costs could be lost if the IRS determines that business actually began in the year before that for which the election is made.

.01 Write-off of Expenses

Generally, the expenditures eligible under Code Sec. 195 must be of the type that would be deductible if they were paid or incurred in connection with the expansion of an existing business in the same field.[73] In addition, the expenditures must fall within one of the three categories of expenses. The expenditures must be paid or incurred in connection with (1) investigating the creation or acquisition of an active trade or business, (2) creating an active trade or business, or (3) an activity engaged in for profit and for the production of income before active business begins and in anticipation of the activity becoming an active trade or business.[74]

Expenses eligible under Code Sec. 195 do not include interest deductible under Code Sec. 163(a), taxes deductible under Code Sec. 164, and research and experimental expenses under Code Sec. 174. Also, eligible expenditures do not include any amount for which a deduction would not be allowable to an existing trade or business. For example, securities registration expenses, underwriters' commissions, and other amounts paid in connection with the sale of stock, securities, or partnership interests are not deductible under Code Sec. 195.

The election also does not apply to amounts paid or incurred as part of the acquisition cost of a trade or business. Nor does it apply to amounts paid or incurred to acquire property for sale or for property that may be depreciated or amortized based on its useful life, including expenses relating to a lease and leasehold improvements. Corporate or partnership organization expenditures that may be deducted or amortized under Code Sec. 248 or Code Sec. 709 are covered by those provisions and are not subject to the election under Code Sec. 195.

[A] Investigatory Expenses

The first category of expenses eligible under Code Sec. 195 are those incurred in investigating the creation or acquisition of an active trade or business. These investigatory expenses are the costs incurred in reviewing a prospective business prior to reaching a final decision to acquire or enter that business. These costs include expenses incurred for the analysis or survey of potential markets, products, labor supply, transportation facilities, and similar expenses.

In the case of investigatory expenses incurred in connection with the acquisition of an existing business, the taxpayer must obtain an equity interest in, and actively participate in the management of, the trade or business. Amortization or deduction is not available for the costs incurred in investigating the acquisition of an investment interest represented by a bond or other debt instrument (even if

[73] Code Sec. 195(c)(1)(B).

[74] Code Sec. 195(c)(1)(A).

convertible), preferred stock, or limited partnership interest. A taxpayer acquiring common stock is ordinarily acquiring an investment interest rather than a qualifying trade or business, and investigatory expenses relating to the acquisition of corporate stock generally may not be deducted or amortized under Code Sec. 195. However, if a stock acquisition is in substance the acquisition of a trade or business, the investigatory expenses are eligible even though one of the steps of the transaction involves the acquisition of stock—for example, the acquisition of a corporation that is then liquidated. Also, a corporation is considered to acquire the trade or business assets of an acquired corporation, rather than to make a portfolio investment in stock, if the acquired corporation becomes a member of an affiliated group which includes the corporation incurring the investigatory expenses and a consolidated income tax return is filed for the group.

A sole proprietor always is treated as having an operator equity interest in the trade or business. In the case of the acquisition of a general partnership interest, the taxpayer is treated as acquiring an active interest if the taxpayer actively participates in the management of the trade or business of the partnership.

[B] Start-Up Expenses

The second category of expenses eligible under Code Sec. 195 are those incurred in actually creating an active trade or business. Start-up costs are those incurred after the decision is made to establish a particular business and before the time when the business begins. Start-up costs may be incurred by a taxpayer who is not engaged in any existing business, or by a taxpayer with an existing business who begins a new one that is unrelated, or only tangentially related, to the existing business.

Start-up costs include advertising, salaries and wages paid to employees who are being trained and their instructors, travel and other expenses incurred to line up prospective distributors, suppliers or customers, and salaries and fees paid for executives, consultants, and for similar professional services, including those for setting up books and records. In the case of an existing business, start-up expenses do not include ordinary and necessary business expenses paid or incurred in connection with an expansion of the business. These latter expenses are currently deductible and need not be amortized. Whether there is an expansion of an existing trade or business or a creation or acquisition of a new trade or business is, in the words of the Senate Finance Committee Report on P.L. 96-605, "based on the facts and circumstances of each case."

[C] Pre-Opening Expenses

The final category of expenses eligible under Code Sec. 195 are those incurred in any activity engaged in for profit and for the production of income in anticipation of the activity becoming an active trade or business but before the day on which the active trade or business begins. This category of expenses, which represents an expansion of the definition of expenditures eligible under Code Sec. 195, was added to the statute by the Tax Reform Act of 1984. The intent was to make pre-opening expenses, such as land rent during construction, eligible under Code Sec. 195.

.02 Trade or Business Requirement

To be eligible under Code Sec. 195, expenditures must relate to the investigation or creation of an active trade or business. Therefore, expenditures relating to an investment are not eligible. An activity for which related expenses are deductible only as itemized deductions for individuals under Code Sec. 212 is not treated as a trade or business. In addition, an activity is not treated as a trade or business activity solely because the property used in the activity may be eligible for capital gain or ordinary loss treatment under Code Sec. 1231.

In the case of rental activities, there must be significant furnishing of services incident to the rentals to constitute an active business rather than an investment. A rental activity is not considered an active business solely because deductions attributable to it are allowed in computing adjusted gross income. According to the Senate Finance Committee Report on P.L. 96-605, however, the operation of an apartment complex, an office building, or a shopping center would constitute an active trade or business.

¶ 703 REAL ESTATE OPERATING EXPENSES

Expenses of operating a real estate business or expenses associated with real estate used in a trade or business are deductible under Code Sec. 162, which allows a deduction for "all the ordinary and necessary expenses paid or incurred during the taxable year in carrying on any trade or business." Even if the holding of real estate does not rise to the level of a trade or business, an individual may deduct all the ordinary and necessary expenses paid "for the management, conservation, or maintenance of property held for the production of income."[75]

Under Code Sec. 212, it is not even necessary that the property be producing current income in order for a taxpayer to take deductions. Reg. § 1.212-1(b) provides that ordinary and necessary expenses of a building devoted to rental purposes are deductible "notwithstanding that there is actually no income therefrom in the taxable year, and regardless of the manner in which or the purpose for which the property in question was acquired." Further, if property is held for investment, expenses may be deductible under Code Sec. 212 even though the property is not currently productive and "there is no likelihood that the property will be sold at a profit or will otherwise be productive of income and even though the property is held merely to minimize a loss with respect thereto."

While the regulations seem to allow deductions for expenses related to the holding of raw land for investment, they apparently do not allow deductions when there is some use of the property beyond a mere passive holding of the property unless there is a profit motive. A taxpayer was denied deductions for maintenance expenses of a house owned with a brother as tenants in common when the brother had the exclusive right to live there rent free. The expectation that the property would appreciate and eventually be sold at a profit was not sufficient to establish that it was held for the production of income.[76]

---

[75] Code Sec. 212.

[76] J. Hirschel, 41 TCM 1298, CCH Dec. 37,842(M), T.C. Memo. 1981-189, *aff'd*, CA-2, February 25, 1982.

The proposition that rental property need not be producing current income in order for expenses to be deductible, however, has limits, although those limits may be hard to define. In *L. Hudson*,[77] a two-year vacancy in the other half of the taxpayer's duplex while the taxpayer was waiting for "desirable tenants" established that the property was no longer held for profit-making purposes. Longer periods of vacancy, however, may still not preclude deductions, given some special circumstances.[78]

In *Gorod*, the taxpayer constructed a duplex apartment building and occupied the upper unit of the building. The Court held that the taxpayer held the lower unit of the building for the production of income, even though the lower unit was never rented over a period of about ten years. The lack of rental income was explained by the building's location in a high crime, rundown area. The taxpayer continued to advertise the lower unit, spent money keeping it in habitable condition, and did not use it for personal purposes. However, the Tax Court was unwilling to stretch its generosity when the same taxpayer appeared before the court four years later. By this time, the apartment had been vacant for 13 years, rent had never been collected, and the residence had become uninhabitable and had been boarded up. The court held that the taxpayer did not have a profit motive in keeping the vacant space.[79]

Once it is established that real estate is part of a trade or business or held for the production of income, the deduction of the routine operating expenses usually does not present a tax problem. Sometimes, though, it becomes difficult to separate the ordinary and necessary business expenses from expenditures that produce an extended benefit and that must be capitalized and recovered through depreciation, amortization, or, in some cases, on the sale or disposition of the property.

The following discussion focuses on the more common expense items which may be associated with the ownership and operation of business or investment real estate and the questions that relate to the timing and amount of the deductions for these items. Keep in mind that, in addition to the tax accounting rules discussed at ¶ 701.02, deductions attributable to real estate may be limited by the at-risk rules discussed at ¶ 302, the passive loss rules discussed at ¶ 1101, and the excess business loss rule discussed at ¶ 705.

.01 Repairs

The cost of repairing and maintaining real property used in a trade or business or held for the production of income is deductible as an ordinary and necessary business expense under Code Sec. 162 or an ordinary and necessary expense under Code Sec. 212. Reg. § 1.162-4 provides:

> A taxpayer may deduct amounts paid for repairs and maintenance to tangible property if the amounts paid are not otherwise required to be capitalized.

[77] 41 TCM 1253, CCH Dec. 37,825(M), T.C. Memo. 1985-175.

[78] G.C. Gorod, 42 TCM 1569, CCH Dec. 38,388(M), T.C. Memo. 1981-632.

[79] G. Gorod, 49 TCM 526, CCH Dec. 41,827(M). T.C. Memo. 1985-33.

Optionally, § 1.263(a)-3(n) provides an election to capitalize amounts paid for repair and maintenance consistent with the taxpayer's books and records.

This regulation indicates the usual question that arises in taking a deduction for repairs, that is, whether the claimed deductible repair is actually a capital expenditure. An expenditure that goes beyond incidental repair for the purposes of keeping the property in ordinary efficient operating condition and materially adds to the value of the property or prolongs its life is not currently deductible. Rather, the cost of replacements, improvements or additions must be capitalized and recovered through depreciation or amortization. In the words of the Supreme Court in *Union Pacific R.R. Co.*:[80]

> Theoretically, the expenses chargeable to earnings include the general expenses of keeping up the organization of the company, and all expenses incurred in operating the works and keeping them in good condition and repair; whilst expenses chargeable to capital include those which are incurred in the original construction of the works, and in subsequent enlargement and improvement thereof.

As to what constitutes a deductible repair as opposed to a capital expenditure has been addressed by the IRS in what have been termed the "repair regulations."[81] The regulations apply as of January 1, 2014. Taxpayers, however, may apply them as of 2012 if they desire. Alternatively, taxpayers may apply the temporary regulations (T.D. 9564) that were issued at the end of 2011 to 2012 and 2013.[82]

[A] Repair or Improvement

A current deduction is not allowed for any amount paid out for new buildings or for permanent improvements or betterments made to increase the value of any property or estate, or for any amount expended in restoring property or in making good the exhaustion of property for which an allowance is or has been made.[83]

At one time or another, just about every expenditure imaginable made to repair or improve property has been subject to challenge by the IRS over whether it should be classified as a currently deductible repair expense or a capital improvement. Reg. § 1.263(a)-3, essentially, is an attempt by the IRS to bring together the rules and concepts developed over many years through court decisions and IRS pronouncements.

The focus of the repair regulations, not surprisingly, are the guidelines for determining a capital expenditure for which a current deduction is not available. Under the repair regulations, the cost of improving a "unit" of property must be capitalized. A unit of property is improved when the work performed on the property:

1. Results in a betterment to the unit of property;
2. Restores the unit of property; or
3. Adapts the unit of property to a new or different use.[84]

---

[80] S.Ct., 99 U.S. 402.

[81] T.D. 9636; Reg. § 1.162-4; Reg. § 1.263(a)-3.

[82] Reg. § 1.263(a)-1(h).

[83] Code Sec. 263(a); Reg. § 1.263(a)-1(a).

[84] Reg. § 1.263(a)-3(d).

The improvement of real property is taken up more fully in Chapter 8, especially the improvement of property as defined by the repair regulations beginning at ¶ 801. The repair regulations, however, do contain safe harbors for classifying certain amounts as deductible repairs. That is our focus here.

[B] De Minimis Safe Harbor

Under a safe harbor expensing provision,[85] a taxpayer may elect not to capitalize the cost of tangible property with a limited cost. However, the uniform capitalization rules of Code Sec. 263A may require a taxpayer to capitalize amounts that are deductible under the safe harbor as a direct or allocable indirect cost of property (see ¶ 103.01).

Under the election, provided the requirements are met, a taxpayer with an AFS (see below) may deduct up to $5,000 per item. For a taxpayer without an AFS, the deductible amount is limited to $500.

A taxpayer with an AFS (see below) may elect the *de minimis* expensing safe harbor if:

1. It has written accounting procedures that treat amounts paid for property that cost less than a specified dollar amount or that has an economic useful life of 12 months or less as an expense for non-tax purposes; and
2. It treats those amounts as an expense on the AFS.

If a taxpayer does not have an AFS, its accounting procedures in effect at the beginning of the tax year do not need to be written. However, the taxpayer must expense the amount paid for the property on its books and records according to its accounting procedures.

An AFS is whichever of the taxpayer's financial statements that is listed first on the following list:

1. A financial statement required to be filed with the Securities and Exchange Commission (SEC) (a 10-K or an Annual Statement to Shareholders);
2. A certified audited financial statement that is accompanied by the report of an independent certified public accountant (or in the case of a foreign entity, by the report of a similarly qualified independent professional) that is used for credit purposes; for reporting to shareholders, partners, or similar persons; or for any other substantial non-tax purpose; or
3. A financial statement (other than a tax return) required to be provided to the federal or a state government or any federal or state agency, other than the SEC or the IRS.[86]

[C] Small Taxpayer Safe Harbor

A taxpayer with average annual gross receipts for the three preceding tax years of $10 million or less may elect to deduct the total amount paid during the year for repairs, maintenance, improvements, and similar activities performed on an eligible building, provided the total paid does not exceed the lesser of:

---

[85] Reg. § 1.263(a)-1(f).

[86] Reg. § 1.263(a)-1(f)(4).

1. 2 percent of the unadjusted basis of the eligible building; or
2. $10,000.[87]

The property eligible under this small taxpayer safe harbor is a unit of property that is a building, including building systems and structural components, or a portion of a building that is a separate unit of property (see the discussion of what is a unit of property at ¶ 801.01), that has an unadjusted basis of $1 million or less.[88] If total amounts paid during the year for repairs, maintenance, improvements, and similar activities performed on the building property exceed the safe harbor limitations, the safe harbor election is not available for that property.[89]

The unadjusted basis is the basis as determined under Code Sec. 1012, generally cost, and not reduced by depreciation or other amounts treated as an expense, such as the Code Sec. 179 deduction. In the case of leased property, the lessee's unadjusted basis is the total amount of (undiscounted) rent paid or expected to be paid by the lessee for the entire term of the lease, including renewal periods if there is a reasonable expectation the lease will be renewed. Factors that are significant in determining whether there is a reasonable expectancy of renewal for this purposes are listed in Reg. § 1.263(a)-4(f)(5)(ii).[90]

Example 4: A consulting firm, a qualifying taxpayer, owns an office building in which the firm provides consulting services. The building has an unadjusted basis of $750,000. During the year, the firm pays $5,500 for repairs, maintenance, and improvements to the office building. Because the building has an unadjusted basis of $1,000,000 or less, the building is eligible building property under the small taxpayer safe harbor. The aggregate amount paid by the firm during the year for repairs, maintenance, improvements and similar activities does not exceed the lesser of two percent of the building's unadjusted basis ($15,000) or $10,000. Therefore, the firm may elect to not to capitalize the amount paid for repair, maintenance, improvements, or similar activities on the building and, provided the amount otherwise is an ordinary and necessary business expense, the firm may deduct the $5,500.

Coordination with Other Safe Harbors

Amounts for repairs, maintenance, improvements, and similar activities performed on eligible building property include amounts not capitalized under the de minimis safe harbor election (¶ 703.01[B]) and those amounts deemed not to improve property under the safe harbor for routine maintenance (¶ 703.01[D]).

[D] Routine Building Maintenance Safe Harbor

An amount paid for routine maintenance on a unit of property, including a building structure or a building system, is currently deductible.[91]

Routine maintenance for a building unit of property is the recurring activities that a taxpayer expects to perform to keep the building structure or each building

[87] Reg. § 1.263(a)-3(h).
[88] Reg.§ 1.263(a)-3(h)(4).
[89] Reg. § 1.263(a)-3(h)(8).
[90] Reg. § 1.263(a)-3(h)(5).
[91] Reg. § 1.263(a)-3(i).

system in its ordinarily efficient operating condition. Routine maintenance activities include, for example, the inspection, cleaning, and testing of the building structure or each building system, and the replacement of damaged or worn parts with comparable and commercially available replacement parts.

Routine maintenance may be performed any time during the useful life of the building structure or building systems. However, the activities are routine only if the taxpayer reasonably expects to perform the activities more than once during the ten-year period beginning when the building structure or the building system on which the maintenance is performed is placed in service.

A taxpayer's expectation is not unreasonable merely because the taxpayer does not actually perform the maintenance a second time during the ten-year period, if the taxpayer otherwise substantiates that its expectation was reasonable at the time the property was placed in service. Factors the IRS considers in determining whether maintenance is routine and whether a taxpayer's expectation is reasonable include the recurring nature of the activity, industry practice, manufacturers' recommendations, and the taxpayer's experience with similar or identical property. For a lessor of a building or a part of the building, the lessor's use of the building unit of property includes the lessee's use of its unit of property.

> ***Example 5:*** A development company purchases a retail mall with an escalator system including several escalators. The company expects to replace the escalator handrails every four years to keep the escalator system in an efficient operating condition. Four years later, the developer replaces the handrails. Because the developer reasonably expected to perform this activity more than once during the ten years after it placed the property in service, the amount paid by the developer for the handrail replacements are within the routine maintenance safe harbor and the cost does not have to be capitalized.
>
> Several years later, the developer must replace the steps of the escalators. The developer did not expect to have to replace the steps for 18 to 20 years. Because the replacement does not involve recurring activities that the developer expected to perform more than once during the ten years after it placed the property in service, the cost of the step replacement does not fall within the routine maintenance safe harbor and the cost must be capitalized if the replacement results in an improvement.

[E] Election to Capitalize Maintenance and Repairs

A taxpayer may elect to treat amounts paid for repair and maintenance as amounts paid to improve that property and as an asset subject to the allowance for depreciation if:

1. The taxpayer incurs these amounts in carrying on the taxpayer's trade or business, and
2. The taxpayer treats these amounts as capital expenditures on its books and records regularly used in computing income.[92]

[92] Reg. § 1.263(a)-3(n).

A taxpayer that makes this election for a tax year must capitalize all amounts paid for repair and maintenance to tangible property that it treats as capital expenditures on its books and records in that tax year.

Exception: The election does not apply to amounts paid for repairs or maintenance of rotable or temporary spare parts to which the taxpayer applies the optional method of accounting for rotable and temporary spare parts. See ¶ 703.03.

> ***Example 6:*** A company provides services to its customers from an office building that it owns. The building's HVAC system incorporates ten roof-mounted units that provide heating and air conditioning for different parts of the building. The company replaces two of the ten units to address climate control problems in various offices throughout the building. If the replacement of the two units is not an improvement to the HVAC system, the company may deduct the cost as a repair and maintenance cost.
>
> On its books and records, the company treats the cost of the two HVAC components as capital expenditures. If the company would prefer to account for the cost in the same way for federal income tax purposes, the company may elect to capitalize the cost, rather than take a current deduction. If the company does make the election to capitalize, it must capitalize all amounts paid for repair and maintenance to tangible property that it treats as capital expenditures on its books and records in that year.

[F] Before the Repair Regulations

While the repair regulations are extensive, it is interesting to note that they do not provide any bright-line tests as to which specific expenditures are deductible and which must be capitalized. Facts and circumstances will continue to play a major role in answering the question. In some situations, it may be useful to take a look at case law as it developed before the IRS promulgated the current repair regulations. After all, it is this law that is the source of much of what is contained in the regulations.

Initially, it is obvious that most repairs will add value to property when measured against the value of the property just prior to the repair. This simple addition to value need not be capitalized under the repair regulations, just as it need not have been capitalized under prior case law. The Tax Court explained the proper test for determining whether an expenditure should be treated as a capital expenditure, rather than a deductible repair, because of the value added to the property in *Oberman Mfg. Co.*[93] According to the Court, the proper test is whether "the expenditure materially enhances the value, use, life expectancy, strength, or capacity as compared with the status of the asset prior to the condition necessitating the expenditure."

Size of Expenditure

While large expenditures often fall into the capital expenditure category, it is not the size or amount of the expenditure that determines whether it is a deductible

[93] 47 TC 471, CCH Dec. 28,334.

repair expense or a capital expenditure. Rather, it is the purpose for which the expenditure is made that controls. An expenditure that returns property to the state it was in prior to the condition necessitating the expenditure and that does not make the property more valuable, useful or long-lived, is a deductible repair, regardless of the amount. See, for example, *Plainfield-Union Water Co.,*[94] in which it was held that a substantial expenditure for cleaning and cement-lining tar-coated cast-iron piping was deductible since the useful life, strength, value, and capacity of the pipes were not increased by the cleaning and the lining.

Even when there is some incidental expansion or enlargement, a large expenditure nevertheless may be classified as a deductible repair. How far the courts may be willing to go in this area is illustrated by the Fifth Circuit Court of Appeals decision in *S.C. Evans.*[95]

A farmer had a large earthen dam that began to allow water to seep through. The farmer made several efforts to patch the dam, but was unable to stop the leakage. Finally, the farmer hired a contractor who drained the reservoir, excavated soil from the dam's front, and replaced the soil with clay in order to seal the dam. The cost to the farmer for the work was $50,000, and the repaired reservoir was one-fourth to one-half acre larger than prior to the repair. The Tax Court had characterized the $50,000 repair cost as a capital expenditure, but the Fifth Circuit disagreed. According to the Appeals Court:

> [The] taxpayer's sole purpose in undertaking the expense was to prevent the dam from leaking and thus to keep it in an ordinary operating condition over its probable useful life and for the use for which it was acquired. The work did not create a replacement for the dam, but merely restored the capability of retaining water which it had, so far as the record reflects, at the time taxpayer acquired it. If the work is considered repair, it did not in our view materially add to the value or materially prolong its ordinary life. Nothing of record establishes that the alleged enlargement constituted a material increase in value.

Forced Expenditures

Sometimes, property owners must make repairs, alterations, improvements, or other changes to their property in order to comply with some law or ordinance, or the requirements of some regulatory agency. Simply because an expenditure is forced on a property owner does not affect how that expenditure is classified, whether as a deductible repair or capital expenditure. If the required expenditures do not result in value added to the property or a longer useful life, they are deductible. On the other hand, if the required expenditures result in long-lived additions or improvements, the expenditure must be capitalized and recovered through depreciation or amortization.[96]

Under an order of the city building commissioner, the owner of rental property shored up the walls with steel rods, inserted new beams to support the roof, repaired portions of the roof, and underpinned the foundation of the building with cinder blocks. The expenses were held to be capital in nature, even though the

[94] 39 TC 333, CCH Dec. 25,740, *nonacq.* 1964-2 CB 8.

[95] CA-5, 77-2 USTC ¶ 9596, 557 F.2d 1095.

[96] T.O. Campbell, 32 TCM 451, CCH Dec. 31,953(M), T.C. Memo. 1973-101; International Building Co., 21 BTA 617.

expenditures were forced on the building owner by government authority.[97] A similar result was reached when the expenditures were forced on the taxpayer by a pending lawsuit. In *Mt. Morris Drive-In Theatre Co.*,[98] the taxpayer constructed an outdoor theater on sloping land. Later, the taxpayer had to spend over $8,000 to construct a drainage system extending onto adjacent land in compromise of a pending lawsuit by the adjoining landowner, who complained of concentrated drainage onto the land. The cost of the drainage system was a capital expenditure and not a deductible expense.

Classification of Expenditures

At one time or another, just about every expenditure imaginable made to repair or improve real property has been subject to challenge by the IRS over whether it should be classified as a currently deductible repair expense or a capital expenditure. Needless to say, it would be virtually impossible to catalog all the cases, but it may help to look at some expenditures to see how they were treated.

The cost of painting, papering, whitewashing, decorating, etc., income-producing or business property is deductible.[99] But see the discussion below on general renovations and remodeling. The cost of painting must be capitalized when it is done as part of or incidental to a general reconditioning or remodeling of the property.[100]

Repairing rotting wood floors[101] and finishing a concrete floor in a storage room[102] are deductible repairs, but replacing a wood floor with a concrete floor is a capital expenditure.[103] Repairing a road without changing basic construction is a deductible repair expense,[104] but replacing a gravel driveway with a concrete driveway is a capital expenditure.[105] Sandblasting and pointing brick walls is a deductible repair,[106] but replacing a cracked old wall with a new wall is capital expenditure.[107] Replacing corrugated roofing that was blown away and replacing broken slate on slate roof are deductible repair expenses,[108] but replacing part of a foundry roof and supporting the roof are capital expenditures.[109]

---

[97] J.L. Boland, 19 TCM 1030, CCH Dec. 24,370(M), T.C. Memo. 1960-199.

[98] 25 TC 272, CCH Dec. 21,338, *aff'd per curiam* 56-2 USTC ¶ 9994, 238 F.2d 85.

[99] J.T. Rose v. Haverty Furniture Co., CA-5, 1927 CCH ¶ 7012, 15 F.2d 345; M. Markovitz, 11 TCM 823, CCH Dec. 19,138(M); R.O. Watts, 34 TCM 613, CCH Dec. 33,184(M), T.C. Memo. 1975-131.

[100] J.M. Jones, CA-5, 57-1 USTC ¶ 9517, 242 F.2d 616; Bank of Houston, 19 TCM 589, CCH Dec. 24,204(M), T.C. Memo. 1960-110.

[101] Farmers Creamery Corp. of Fredericksburg, Va., 14 TC 879, CCH Dec. 17,646, *acq.* 1954-1 CB 4 in part and *nonacq.* 1954-1 CB 8 in part.

[102] W.C. Hudlow, Jr., 30 TCM 894, CCH Dec. 30,959(M), T.C. Memo. 1971-218.

[103] L.J. Best, 13 TCM 948, CCH Dec. 20,601(M), T.C. Memo. 1954-170.

[104] Almac's, Inc., 20 TCM 56, CCH Dec. 24,620(M), T.C. Memo. 1961-13.

[105] A.R. Jones, 25 TC 1100, CCH Dec. 21,590, *acq.* 1958-2 CB 6, *rev'd and rem'd on another issue*, CA-5, 58-2 USTC ¶ 9832, 259 F.2d 300.

[106] City National Bank, 11 TCM 411, CCH Dec. 18,921(M), T.C. Memo. 1952.

[107] Stewart Supply Co., Inc., 22 TCM 246, CCH Dec. 25,986(M), T.C. Memo. 1963-62, *aff'd*, CA-2, 63-2 USTC ¶ 9824, 324 F.2d 233.

[108] Knoxville Iron Co., 18 TCM 251, CCH Dec. 23,504(M), T.C. Memo. 1959-54.

[109] Mountain State Steel Foundries, Inc., 18 TCM 306, CCH Dec. 23,522(M), T.C. Memo. 1959-59, *rev'd on another issue*, 60-2 USTC ¶ 9797, 284 F.2d 737.

Replacement, Renovation, and Reconditioning

Replacements that arrest deterioration and appreciably prolong the life of property are capital expenditures and are not currently deductible.[110] For example, the replacement of an old floor in a building with a new floor that permitted the use of heavy equipment made the building more valuable and was a capital expenditure and not a deductible repair.[111] Similarly, the replacement of a wooden factory door that had rotted because of termite damage with a new aluminum door and the construction of a new entrance had to be capitalized.[112] The cost of replacing a completely worn-out furnace and heating system is a capital expenditure when there is no repair of an existing system but a substantial replacement adding to the value of the property.[113]

Additions and improvements do not have to prolong useful life to be classified as capital expenditures, if the expenditures adapt the property to new or different uses, or make the property better suited to the business.[114] In *J.H. Rutter,*[115] expenditures made to add a lunch area, restrooms and loading and unloading ramps to clothing manufacturing plants were classed as capital expenditures. The purpose behind the expenditures was not merely to keep the property in efficient operating condition, but to add value to the plants and adapt them to different uses. Similarly, the cost of remodeling stores to adapt property to a different use is a capital expenditure.[116]

Courts generally hold that repairs that occur as part of an overall plan of renovation, modernization, alteration, or improvement must be capitalized. Items that would normally qualify as deductible repairs, such as painting, wallcovering, etc., are not deductible when they are incurred pursuant to an overall plan of capital improvements which substantially upgrade the condition of the property.[117] In *J.S. Moss,*[118] amounts spent on repairs as part of a renovation plan for a hotel were held not deductible by the Tax Court, but the decision was reversed by the Ninth Circuit Court of Appeals (see Improvements to Land and Buildings, below).

The propensity of courts to hold "repairs" made as part of overall renovations and reconditionings to be part of the capital expenditure, rather than separate deductible expenses, means that taxpayers should undertake to keep repairs separate from such general renovations. This usually requires that otherwise deductible repair procedures be undertaken at a different time from that at which the general renovations take place. If separating the time that repairs are done from the time of renovation is not possible, taxpayers should keep separate records for

[110] Reg. § 1.162-4.

[111] Phillips & Easton Supply Co., 20 TC 455, CCH Dec. 19,691.

[112] Alabama-Georgia Syrup Co., 36 TC 747, CCH Dec. 24,957, *rev'd and rem'd on another issue sub nom.*, L.B. Whitfield, Jr., 63-1 USTC ¶ 9124, 311 F.2d 640.

[113] C.A. Boddie, 20 TCM 350, CCH Dec. 24,717(M), T.C. Memo. 1961-72.

[114] Human Engineering Institute, 37 TCM 619, CCH Dec. 35,100(M), T.C. Memo. 1978-145, *aff'd*, CA-6, 80-2 USTC ¶ 9600, 629 F.2d 1160.

[115] 52 TCM 326, CCH Dec. 43,316(M), T.C. Memo. 1986-407, *aff'd*, CA-5, 88-2 USTC ¶ 9500, 853 F.2d 1267.

[116] Bee Holding Co., 17 TCM 963, CCH Dec. 23,253(M), T.C. Memo. 1958-195.

[117] First American National Bank of Nashville, CA-6, 72-2 USTC ¶ 9694, 467 F.2d 1098; Mountain Fuel Supply Co., CA-10, 71-2 USTC ¶ 9681; 449 F.2d 816, *cert. denied*, 405 U.S. 989, 92 S.Ct. 1251; Wolfsen Land & Cattle Co., 72 TC 1, CCH Dec. 35,975.

[118] 51 TCM 742, CCH Dec. 42,962(M), T.C. Memo. 1986-128, *rev'd*, 87-2 USTC ¶ 9590, 831 F.2d 833.

the cost of repairs, or even have the repairs done under separate contracts, in order to sustain the deduction for the repair costs.

In *B.W. Cohn,*[119] a taxpayer was allowed to deduct $50,000 as a repair expense out of $212,000 spent on improvements and repairs to a rundown farm purchased for $110,000. The district court held that the ordinary and necessary repairs to the farm buildings were deductible, even though they were made during an expansion and remodeling program.[120]

Improvements to Land and Buildings

Capital expenditures include not only the cost of original construction but also subsequent improvements[121] and the cost of converting property to commercial use.[122] It is not necessary that expenditures which are made to convert property to business use or to make property suitable for use in business increase the actual value or assessed value of the property in order to be classified as capital expenditures.[123]

Nondeductible capital expenditures include the cost of improvements to land, as well as improvements to buildings. For example, amounts paid by the developer of a mobile home park to a public utility for underground electric and gas distribution systems are capital expenditures that are included in the developer's cost basis for the land.[124] Similarly, the costs of revetments and a berm built in connection with a lake landfill program and the cost of filling in the area are costs of improving and acquiring land.[125] The costs of land preparation were held to be nondeductible capital expenditures when the costs were incurred to increase the value of the farms for eventual resale and the activity was more than necessary annual maintenance.[126]

Expenditures to rehabilitate and restore an old office that had been uninhabitable when the taxpayer moved into it were capital expenditures and were not made for incidental repairs.[127] Similarly, taxpayers who purchased and renovated two apartment buildings were required to capitalize their expenditures.[128] The expenditures were not just for cosmetic changes but were made as part of a plan of rehabilitation for capital improvement. Even expenditures incurred after the apartments were occupied had to be capitalized because the taxpayers could not show that the plan of renovation ended with occupancy and they had not segregated their various expenses.

[119] DC Tenn., 57-1 USTC ¶ 9457, *aff'd*, CA-6, 58-2 USTC ¶ 9840, 259 F.2d 371.

[120] *But see* A.L. Allen, 15 TCM 464, CCH Dec. 21,680(M), T.C. Memo. 1956-88, in which it was held that expenditures which might have been deductible expenses for repairs were not allowed as deductions, even though they could be segregated, because they were part of a general plan of rehabilitation and betterment. *See also* Wells, 115 TCM 1034, T.C. Memo. 2018-11, in which a farmer was not permitted to deduct as ordinary and necessary business expenses "repairs" she made to her farm, because the repairs were part of a general plan of rehabilitation, modernization and improvement.

[121] Simmons & Hammond Mfg. Co., 1 BTA 803, CCH Dec. 296.

[122] I.T. Burden, 1 TCM 610, CCH Dec. 12,991(M).

[123] E. Dumble Co., 9 BTA 591, CCH Dec. 3188.

[124] Rev. Rul. 80-93, 1980-1 CB 50.

[125] Rev. Rul. 77-270, 1977-2 CB 79.

[126] P.O. Huber, 49 TCM 57, CCH Dec. 41,606(M), T.C. Memo. 1984-593.

[127] K.A. Brown, 39 TCM 397, CCH Dec. 36,406(M), T.C. Memo. 1979-434.

[128] D.C. Ruttenberg, 52 TCM 370, CCH Dec. 43,323(M), T.C. Memo. 1986-414.

In *J.S. Moss*,[129] however, the Ninth Circuit allowed a current deduction for the costs of repairing a hotel and did not require capitalization of the costs merely because they were incurred as part of a plan to remodel the hotel with furniture and furnishings. The hotel remained in operation throughout the period of the remodeling and maintained its high rating throughout most of the period. The improvements merely served to maintain its status.

.02 Removal of Architectural Barriers

A special deduction, of up to $15,000 per year, is allowed at the election of the taxpayer for the cost of removing architectural barriers to elderly and handicapped persons from business facilities.[130] Without this special statutory election, the costs of removing architectural barriers from business facilities normally would be capital expenditures that would be added to basis and recovered through depreciation. Costs in excess of $15,000 in any one year are treated as capital expenditures. Elderly persons are those aged 65 or older, and handicapped refers to blindness and deafness, as well as to difficulty in walking or using one's hands.

To qualify for the expense deduction, the removal of the barrier must bring the property into conformity with standards established by the Treasury on the advice of the U.S. Architectural and Transportation Barriers Compliance Board. These standards are contained in Reg. § 1.190-2. The procedure for electing to take advantage of the special deduction and the recordkeeping requirements are contained in Reg. § 1.190-3.

.03 Materials and Supplies

As part of the repair regulations, the IRS also addressed the issue of deducting materials and supplies. Reg. § 1.162-3 contains these rules that are effective for tax years beginning on or after January 1, 2014, but may be applied to tax years beginning on or after January 1, 2012.

Reg. § 1.162-3(a) generally provides the same rule for most materials and supplies as under prior regulations, that is, that the cost of materials and supplies may be deducted as they are purchased unless the taxpayer maintains records of consumption or takes physical inventories, in which case the materials and supplies are deducted as consumed. Reg. § 1.162-3(a)(3), however, provides for the use or consumption of "rotable and temporary spare parts."

Rotable spare parts are materials and supplies that are acquired for installation on a unit of property, removable from that unit of property, generally repaired or improved, and either reinstalled on the same or other property or stored for later installation. Temporary spare parts are materials and supplies that are used temporarily until a new or repaired part can be installed and then are removed and stored for later (emergency or temporary) installation.[131]

Subject to exceptions, rotable and temporary spare parts are treated as used or consumed in the taxpayer's operations in the tax year in which the taxpayer

[129] CA-9, 87-2 USTC ¶ 9590, 831 F.2d 833.

[130] Code Sec. 190.

[131] Reg. § 1.162-3(c)(2).

disposes of the parts. This somewhat harsh rule is ameliorated by the option given to taxpayers to use an optional method to account for these parts. The optional method generally allows deductions as parts are installed but requires income inclusion and basis additions as parts are removed and stored or repaired.[132]

Under the regulations, materials and supplies are defined as tangible property that is used or consumed in the taxpayer's operations that is not inventory and that:

1. Is a component acquired to maintain, repair, or improve a unit of tangible property owned, leased, or serviced by the taxpayer and that is not acquired as part of any single unit of tangible property;
2. Consists of fuel, lubricants, water, and similar items, that are reasonably expected to be consumed in 12 months or less, beginning when used in taxpayer's operations;
3. Is a unit of property that has an economic useful life of 12 months or less, beginning when the property is used or consumed in the taxpayer's operations;
4. Is a unit of property that has an acquisition cost or production cost (as determined under section 263A) of $200 or less (or other amount as identified in published guidance); or
5. Is identified in published guidance as materials and supplies for which treatment is permitted under Reg. § 1.162-3.[133]

Published guidance includes IRS guidance issued before adoption of the repair regulations. For example, materials and supplies under the current regulations include inventoriable items of small businesses described in Rev. Proc. 2002-28[134] and restaurant smallwares described in Rev. Proc. 2002-12.[135]

A taxpayer generally may elect to treat as a capital expenditure and to treat as an asset subject to the allowance for depreciation the cost of any material or supply as defined above. The election to capitalize does not apply to rotable and temporary spare parts that the taxpayer elected to treat under the optional method. The election also does not apply to materials and supplies intended to be used as a component in the items listed in 3, 4, or 5, above, if the taxpayer has not elected to capitalize those items.[136]

.04 Compensation

Ordinary and necessary business expenses include a reasonable allowance for salaries or other compensation for personal services actually rendered.[137] This sets up the test for deducting compensation payments: the payments must be reasonable and the payments must be in fact payments purely for services.[138]

Reasonable compensation is the amount that would ordinarily be paid for like services by like enterprises under like circumstances as of the date when the

[132] Reg. § 1.162-3(e)(2).

[133] Reg. § 1.162-3(c)(1).

[134] 2002-1 CB 15.

[135] 2002-1 CB 334.

[136] Reg. § 1.162-3(d).

[137] Code Sec. 162(a)(1).

[138] Reg. § 1.162-7(a).

contract for services is made.[139] As a practical matter, the reasonable compensation question is likely to arise only in cases in which the business and the employee are related, such as when the employee is the sole or major stockholder of a corporate employer, or when the employee is a child, parent, or spouse of the employer. When an employee is not an owner or related to an owner, the arm's-length dealing involved means that the salary, almost by definition, is reasonable.

Any amount paid in the form of compensation, but not in fact as the purchase price of services, is not deductible.[140] For instance, if salaries paid to shareholder-employees of a corporation are in excess of those paid for similar services and the excessive payments correspond or bear a close relationship to the stockholdings of the employees, it is likely that the excess payments represent a distribution of earnings. Also, an ostensible salary may be in part a payment for property. For example, partners may sell out to a corporation and agree to continue to work for the corporation. In this case, part of the salaries paid to the former partners may actually be payment for the transfer of the business.

How compensation is determined does not control its deductibility.[141] Compensation may be contingent, although contingent compensation is more open to challenge as unreasonable. Nevertheless, according to the regulation, "if contingent compensation is paid pursuant to a free bargain between the employer and the individual made before the services are rendered, not influenced by any consideration on the part of the employer other than of securing on fair and advantageous terms the services of the individual, it should be allowed as a deduction even though in the actual working out of the contract it may prove to be greater than the amount which would ordinarily be paid."

Methods of compensating employees, including salary, fringe benefits, retirement plans, vacations, bonuses, etc. are almost as numerous as employers. It is impossible for this work on real estate taxation to go into these areas in any depth, and the author leaves this area to others. The following discussion relating to compensation focuses on some areas that are most critical for the closely held real estate corporation or family real estate business.

[A] Real Estate Corporation Officers

The Supreme Court has said that "extraordinary, unusual, and extravagant amounts paid by a corporation to its officers in the guise and form of compensation for their services, but having no substantial relation to the measure of services, and being utterly disproportioned to their value, are not in reality payment for services and cannot be regarded as 'ordinary and necessary expenses' . . . ".[142] Unfortunately, there is no set formula for determining the reasonableness of compensation, since reasonableness is a question of fact that is determined for each case. Many of the Tax Court's opinions on the reasonable compensation question begin with the following statement: "The question is one of fact. The finding [as to the amount which constitutes reasonable compensation] which has been made is dispositive of

[139] Reg. § 1.162-7(b)(3).

[140] Reg. § 1.162-7(b)(1).

[141] Reg. § 1.162-7(b)(2).

[142] Botany Worsted Mills, S.Ct., 1 USTC ¶ 348, 287 U.S. 282, 49 S.Ct. 129.

the sole issue. It would serve no purpose to review the evidence or attempt to rationalize the conclusion reached."

Even though what constitutes reasonable compensation depends on the facts of each individual situation, it may be helpful to see what has been held to be reasonable in various situations. There are a number of cases that have dealt with reasonable compensation in the context of a real estate corporation.[143]

[B] Family Members as Employees

The owner of a real estate business may achieve substantial tax savings by employing immediate family members in the business. The tax savings can be achieved without reducing the income to the total family unit.

Children

The owner of a real estate business may employ his or her children in the business. Each child can earn an amount equal to the standard deduction for the current year free of income tax, while the business deducts the amounts paid, provided they are reasonable compensation for the services actually rendered by the child. Even if the children earn more than the standard deduction, tax savings may be achieved since earned income is taxed in the child's tax bracket and not in the parent's tax bracket, as is the case with unearned income of a child under 14 years of age. The children, of course, are free to spend their earnings on personal items that would otherwise be purchased by the parents with their after-tax dollars. The personal exemptions for the children remain available to the parents, provided they continue to provide over half the support of the children, but the children are then not also entitled to the personal exemption.

It apparently does not matter how young a child is when the parent employs the child in the business, as long as the child can perform some useful service and effectively does perform the service. Even a seven-year-old child has been found able to perform valuable services for a parent's business so as to be entitled to reasonable compensation that is deductible by the business.[144] It does not matter that the child uses the pay received for part of his or her support.[145]

It is important that proper payroll records be keep for children who are employed by the business. Failure to keep the necessary records, and to withhold and pay any necessary payroll taxes, can result in the loss of the deduction.[146]

---

[143] Bev Anderson Chevrolet, Inc., 26 TCM 338, CCH Dec. 28,403(M), T.C. Memo. 1967-64; Langley Park Apartments, Sec. C., Inc., 44 TC 474, CCH Dec. 27,447, *aff'd per curiam*, CA-4, 66-1 USTC ¶ 9368, 359 F.2d 427; B. Perlmutter, 44 TC 382, CCH Dec. 27,434, *aff'd*, CA-10, 67-1 USTC ¶ 9246, 373 F.2d 45; Marlo Coil Co., Ct. Cls., 697 CCH ¶ 7915; S. & B. Realty Co., 54 TC 863, CCH Dec. 30,073, *acq.* 1970-2 CB XXI; Ettle Co., Inc., 30 TCM 351, CCH Dec. 30,751(M), T.C. Memo. 1971-86; R.J. Nicoll Co., 59 TC 37, CCH Dec. 31,566, *acq.* 1973-2 CB 3; Roth Properties Co., 33 TCM 104, CCH Dec. 32,438(M), T.C. Memo. 1974-33, *aff'd*, CA-6, 75-1 USTC ¶ 9337, 511 F.2d 526; P.E. Kummer Realty Co., 33 TCM 209 CCH Dec. 32,467(M), T.C. Memo. 1974-44, *aff'd*, CA-8, 75-1 USTC ¶ 9262, 511 F.2d 313; Chevy Chase Motor Co., Inc., 36 TCM 942, CCH Dec. 34,517(M), T.C. Memo. 1977-227; Keller Street Development Co., 37 TCM 1451, CCH Dec. 35,383(M), T.C. Memo. 1978-350; C.W. Clayton, Jr., 42 TCM 670, CCH Dec. 38,153(M), T.C. Memo. 1981-433.

[144] W.E. Eller, 77 TC 934, CCH Dec. 38,391, *acq.* 1984-2 CB 1.

[145] Rev. Rul. 73-393, 1973-2 CB 33.

[146] A.R. Furmanski, 33 TCM 225, CCH Dec. 32,472(M), T.C. Memo. 1974-47; C. Tschupp, 22 TCM 466, CCH Dec. 26,052(M), T.C. Memo. 1963-98.

Spouses

Generally, there is not the same advantage to putting a spouse on the payroll as there is with putting a child on the payroll. If a joint return is filed, the tax is the same regardless of which spouse earns the income. In the case of an incorporated business, however, there may be some indirect tax advantages to putting a spouse on the payroll. If the owner-spouse's compensation has reached the limits of reasonableness, putting the spouse on the payroll allows more money to be drawn out of the corporation without a double tax. A spouse on the corporate payroll may also benefit from qualified retirement plan coverage and various fringe benefits that may be offered by the corporation. Another consideration is the Individual Retirement Account deduction that may be available to a spouse who has earned income.

Payroll Taxes

One disadvantage of employing family members in an incorporated real estate business is the added social security taxes and possible unemployment taxes that have to be paid by the family member and the corporation. While the corporation's share of social security and other payroll taxes is deductible, social security taxes paid by the family member are not deductible. This added tax burden should be taken into consideration when assessing the tax savings from employing family members in the business.

The added social security taxes may not be as much of a burden if the family member employed in the business is a parent or older family member who has not had sufficient earnings to qualify for full social security benefits. Added taxes, in this case, may be offset by future benefits. The opposite consideration is also important when employing older family members who are past the retirement age. That is, earnings may reduce the social security benefits for which the family member is currently eligible, at least until the family member is old enough to earn unlimited amounts without a reduction in benefits.

The disadvantage of added payroll taxes when family members are employed by an incorporated business may not be present if the family members are employed by an unincorporated business. A child under 18 years of age who is employed in the business of a parent, or a spouse employed by a spouse, is exempt from social security and FUTA taxes. Income tax withholding generally is required, except in the case of a child who earns less than the standard deduction for the year.

A parent employed in a child's trade or business is subject to social security taxes, as well as income tax withholding. The parent is exempt from FUTA taxes. Just as in the case of an incorporated business, the added social security taxes paid by a parent employed in a child's business may be an advantage, if the added taxes purchase future benefits for the parent.

[C] Independent Contractors and Employees

An employee's income is subject to income tax withholding by the employer. Also, an employee requires employer-paid FUTA and unemployment taxes, employer and employee FICA (social security) contributions, and, in many cases, coverage under workers' compensation statutes. On the other hand, an independent contractor is responsible for making his own income tax and FICA payments and is not covered by unemployment insurance or workers' compensation. Obviously, if a business can use independent contractors rather than employees, its tax and administrative burden can be greatly reduced.

Whether a business can characterize someone it employs to perform services for it as an independent contractor depends on whether the business controls both what the person performing the services does and how the work is performed. If the business does both, the individual is an employee. An independent contractor has discretion in how the work is performed.

As an aid to determining whether an individual is an employee under the common law rules, the IRS has identified 20 factors that indicate whether sufficient control is present to establish an employer-employee relationship. The IRS developed the factors based on an examination of cases and rulings considering whether an individual is an employee. The 20 factors are set out in Rev. Rul. 87-41.[147]

[D] Licensed Real Estate Agents

Licensed real estate agents and direct salespersons may be exempt from income tax withholding, social security tax (FICA), and federal unemployment tax (FUTA). These individuals are treated as self-employed persons or independent contractors if the payments they receive are directly related to sales or other output and the services performed as a nonemployee are specified in a written contract. Direct sellers must be in the business of selling consumer products other than in a permanent retail place of business.

[E] Partners

A partner in a partnership may be compensated for services rendered to the partnership. If the services rendered are within the normal scope of partnership duties, any compensation is treated as part of the partner's distributive share of partnership income, rather than as a deductible expense of the partnership.[148] When the partner renders the services as an outsider and not in his or her capacity as a member of the partnership, however, then the partnership is entitled to a deduction for the compensation paid to the partner as an outsider. Also, when the partner performs services as an outsider, then the partnership is treated as an unrelated entity for all purposes.[149]

In Rev. Rul. 81-301,[150] an advisor general partner, a corporate investment advisor, rendered services to the partnership which were substantially the same as the services it rendered as an independent contractor or agent to other persons. The IRS ruled that the ten percent of daily gross income allocation paid to the advisor was not part of the advisor's distributive share of partnership income and was a payment that was subject to Code Sec. 707(a). As such, the payments were taxable to the advisor as compensation for services and were deductible by the partnership as a business expense.

[147] 1987-1 CB 296.

[148] E.T. Pratt, CA-5, 77-1 USTC ¶ 9347, 550 F.2d 1023.

[149] Code Sec. 707(a).

[150] 1981-2 CB 144.

Guaranteed Payments

Even when a partner is performing services in the capacity as a partner, payments to the partner for the services are deductible by the partnership if the payments can be classified as guaranteed payments under Code Sec. 707(c). Guaranteed payments are payments made by a partnership to a partner for services or capital, if the payments are determined without regard to the income of the partnership. Guaranteed payments are considered to be made to one who is not a partner, but only for the purpose of the partner's gross income under Code Sec. 61(a) and the partnership's expense deduction under Code Sec. 162(a).[151] Unlike payments under Code Sec. 707(a), which are treated as made to an outsider for all purposes, guaranteed payments under Code Sec. 707(c) are treated as made to an outsider only for the limited purpose of computing the partner's gross income and the partnership's deduction.

While guaranteed payments must be "determined without regard to the income of the partnership," the IRS has ruled that guaranteed payments may include payments for services determined by reference to an item of gross income of the partnership and need not be a fixed amount.[152] In the ruling, general partners of a real estate limited partnership each received a fee of five percent of the gross rentals received by the partnership in exchange for management services provided to the partnership. The fees were ruled to be guaranteed payments under Code Sec. 707(c) because they were reasonable in amount and the method used to determine the compensation would have been used for an unrelated party.

The classification of payments for services rendered by a partner as payments to an outsider under Code Sec. 707(a) or guaranteed payments under Code Sec. 707(c) can have a significant impact on the taxable incomes of the partners, as illustrated in Reg. § 1.707-1(c), Example 3.

> ***Example 7:*** Partner X in the XY partnership is to receive a payment of $10,000 for services, plus 30 percent of the taxable income or loss of the partnership. Partner Y receives 70 percent of the taxable income or loss. After deducting the payment of $10,000 made to Partner X as a guaranteed payment, the XY partnership has a loss of $9,000. Of this amount, $2,700 (30 percent of the loss) is Partner X's distributive share of the partnership loss. Partner X reports ordinary gross income in the amount of $10,000 and a loss from the partnership of $2,700. Partner Y's share of the loss is $6,300. If the $10,000 payment to Partner X did not qualify as a guaranteed payment or a deductible payment to an outsider under Code Sec. 707(a), the partnership would have taxable income of $1,000. Partner X would report only $300 of income, rather than $10,000 in gross income (which might be partially offset by Partner X's $2,700 share of the loss), and Partner Y's $6,300 loss would be converted into $700 of income.

[151] Reg. § 1.707-1(c).

[152] Rev. Rul. 81-300, 1981-2 CB 143.

Disguised Payments for Services

Sometimes, rather than seeking to classify payments to a partner as compensation, a partnership may want to disguise payments to a partner for services as a share of partnership income. This is likely to occur when the compensation would have to be capitalized and could not be taken as a deductible business expense. For example, payments to a partner that would be classified as organization or syndication fees, or payments relating to the construction of property (see ¶ 103.01), would have to be capitalized under the normal capitalization rules. If these otherwise nondeductible compensation payments could be characterized as distributions of partnership income, the partners who are not receiving the payments would have the equivalent of a deduction (through a reduction in their shares of partnership income) for the payments made to the partner rendering the services.

Attempts to disguise payments for services that must be capitalized as distributions of partnership income, however, are thwarted by Code Sec. 707(a)(2)(A). If a partner performs services for a partnership and, in connection therewith, receives a related partnership allocation and distribution, the transaction is treated as a transaction between the partnership and an outsider if the transaction is more properly characterized as a payment to the partner acting in a non-partner capacity. In such a case, the amount paid to the partner is treated as a payment for services provided to the partnership and, when appropriate, the partnership is required to capitalize these amounts or otherwise treat the amounts in a manner consistent with the recharacterization. The partnership must treat the purported allocation to the partner performing the services as a payment to a non-partner in determining the partner's shares of taxable income or loss.

.05 Commissions and Fees

Commissions and fees are deductible business expenses if they are incurred in connection with services for the business that produce only a short term benefit. For example, management fees that are paid to a real estate agent for collecting rents and managing rental property are deductible in the year paid or incurred.[153] If, however, the commissions or fees are paid for services that provide a long-lived benefit or a long-lived asset, the commissions or fees would have to be capitalized.[154] For example, a fee paid in connection with the negotiation of a long-term lease would have to be amortized over the term of the lease (see the discussion of lease acquisition costs at ¶ 501). Similarly, commitment fees or standby charges in connection with a bond sale agreement under which funds for construction are made available in stated amounts over a specified period must be amortized over the term of the loan.[155]

[A] Real Estate Commissions

Generally speaking, commissions and fees paid in connection with the acquisition of real estate represent part of the acquisition cost of the property and are

[153] Reg. § 1.162-1(a).

[154] Reg. § § 1.461-1(a) and 1.263(a)-2

[155] Rev. Rul. 81-160, 1981-1 CB 312.

capital expenditures rather than currently deductible business expenses.[156] This rule would seem to be the same regardless of whether the purchaser is a real estate dealer or not.

In the case of commissions paid on the sale of real estate, whether the sale is by a dealer or a non-dealer does make a difference in the treatment of the selling commissions. Real estate commissions paid by dealers in real estate for the sale of real estate are deductible as a business expense under Code Sec. 162 in the year in which paid or accrued.[157] Commissions on the sale of real estate by a non-dealer are not deductible as expenses, but they are an offset against the selling price and, accordingly, reduce the gain or increase the loss that is reportable on the sale.[158]

[B] Kickbacks

Kickbacks, in the nature of fees or commissions, are deductible, if they fall in the category of an ordinary and necessary expense and are not illegal or do not frustrate sharply defined national or state policies proscribing particular types of conduct.[159]

A subcontractor at a large shopping mall construction site was allowed deductions for the lawful kickback payments it made to the supervisor of the primary contractor.[160] The subcontractor understood that it would not be allowed to continue the subcontract work and would not be timely paid if the kickbacks were not forthcoming. The court found an obvious logical relationship between the subcontractor's construction business and the kickback payments that it made to retain its construction contracts. Accordingly, the kickbacks were an ordinary cost of doing business, as well as a necessary one. Because deductions are allowable for such costs as long as the payments are within the bounds of federal and state law, they were deductible as current expenses and were not capital in nature.

In a later case, however, the Sixth Circuit distinguished its decision in *Raymond Bertolini Trucking Co.* on the question of ordinary and necessary and refused to allow a paving subcontractor to deduct kickback payments. The subcontractor obtained contracts for the construction of a mall by paying for services and materials used to construct the personal residence of the general contractor's vice president in charge of awarding the contracts. According to the court, the kickbacks in this case were neither ordinary nor necessary, since the subcontractor had obtained nearly all of its contracts, including 20 with the same general contractor, without paying kickbacks.[161]

.06 Insurance

Taxpayers may deduct insurance premiums against fire, storm, theft, accident, or other similar losses in the case of a business.[162] Insurance premiums paid on

[156] R.V. Jacobson, 47 TCM 499, CCH Dec. 40,640(M), T.C. Memo. 1983-719.

[157] C. Whitman, CA-2, 1931 CCH ¶ 9393, 49 F.2d 1087.

[158] E.A. Giffin, 19 BTA 1243 CCH Dec. 6095; A. Pickard, 28 TCM 766, CCH Dec. 29,673(M), T.C. Memo. 1969-153; C.F. Frick, 47 TCM 564, CCH Dec. 40,656(M), T.C. Memo. 1983-733; I.T. 2340, VI-1 CB 43.

[159] S.B. Heininger, S.Ct., 44-1 USTC ¶ 9109, 320 U.S. 467, 64 S.Ct. 249.

[160] Raymond Bertolini Trucking Co., CA-6, 84-2 USTC ¶ 9591, 736 F.2d 1120.

[161] Car-Ron Asphalt Paving Co. Inc., CA-6, 85-1 USTC ¶ 9298, 758 F.2d 1132.

[162] Reg. § 1.162-1(a).

property under construction, however, must be capitalized as part of the cost of the property under the capitalization rules of Code Sec. 263A (see ¶ 103.01[B]). But even before enactment of the uniform capitalization rules, insurance premiums to protect property under construction were not currently deductible. The Tax Court ruled that insurance premiums for fire and extended coverage on buildings during construction were capital expenditures and thus not currently deductible[163] (similarly as to insurance premiums for public liability and workers' compensation insurance paid in connection with the construction of a new building when the taxpayer took on the responsibility of a general contractor).[164]

If insurance premiums on business property provide coverage extending beyond one year, a cash method taxpayer may have to spread the deduction out over the period to which the premiums relate. The IRS takes the position that the payment in advance of insurance premiums by a cash method taxpayer results in the creation of an asset, prepaid insurance, that is used up ratably over the period covered by the insurance contract. Only the pro rata portion of the insurance premium applicable to the taxable year is deductible.[165] But one-year premiums on fiscal year insurance are deductible in full in the calendar year in which paid by a taxpayer reporting on the calendar year.[166]

Life insurance premiums, even if business related, generally are not deductible if the payer is directly or indirectly a beneficiary under the policy. When a company that was selling homesites paid the premiums for llfe insurance on homesite purchasers, however, the IRS ruled that the life insurance premium payments were deductible as a business expense by the developer.[167]

The treatment of casualty losses is considered in Chapter 15.

.07 Advertising

Advertising and similar expenses are deductible business expenses.[168] Advertising expenses to develop goodwill or to influence the public through intermediary organizations are also deductible. To be deductible, however, the expenses must be reasonable in amount and have a reasonable relationship to the business activities in which the taxpayer is engaged. For instance, a builder was not allowed a business deduction for advertising and promotional expenses incurred as a result of polo playing because the builder could not show a relationship between these expenses and a business purpose.[169] Expenses incurred by an automobile agency in sponsoring cars in auto races, however, were properly deductible as advertising expenses.[170]

---

[163] H. Shainberg, 33 TC 241, CCH Dec. 23,838, *acq.* 1960-1 CB 5.

[164] Rev. Rul. 66-373, 1966-2 CB 103.

[165] Rev. Rul. 70-413, 1970-2 CB 103. *See also* Boylston Market Assn., CA-1, 42-2 USTC ¶ 9820, 131 F.2d 966; H.W. Guenther, 34 TCM 834, CCH Dec. 33,272(M), T.C. Memo. 1975-194; R.V. Jacobson, 47 TCM 499, CCH Dec. 40,640(M), T.C. Memo. 1983-719.

[166] Kauai Terminal, Ltd., 36 BTA 893, CCH Dec. 9810, *acq.* 1939-2 CB 18; I.L. Bell, 13 TC 344, CCH Dec. 17,192, *acq.* 1949-2 CB 1.

[167] Rev. Rul. 70-254, 1970-1 CB 31.

[168] Reg. § 1.162-1(a).

[169] R.J. Sieber, 38 TCM 48, CCH Dec. 35,816(M), T.C. Memo. 1979-15.

[170] Lang Chevrolet Co., 26 TCM 1054, CCH Dec. 28,648(M), T.C. Memo. 1967-212.

.08 Legal Expenses

Legal expenses paid or incurred as a result of a business transaction or paid to preserve an existing business are deductible under Code Sec. 162. On the other hand, expenditures incurred to defend or perfect title to property, or to recover property, or to develop or improve property are part of the cost of the property and are not deductible expenses.

Attorney fees paid to obtain a judicial determination of the title to land, or in successfully defending title to land, including suits to remove a cloud on the title, have been held to be additional costs of the land in numerous decisions.[171] Similarly, legal expenses in a suit to partition real property are nondeductible capital expenditures.[172] Expenses incurred in litigation to secure the right as a tenant to use and occupy a premises also have been held to be nondeductible costs of defending title to property.[173]

Legal expenses incurred in a condemnation proceeding are capital expenditures and are not deductible.[174] When the proceeding results in a condemnation and award, the expenses offset the award.[175]

Legal expenses incurred in connection with property held for the production of income or investment may not be deducted and must be capitalized, if they are incurred to defend or protect title, to acquire or dispose of the property, or to develop or improve the property.[176] Legal expenses incurred by a taxpayer in seeking a higher award in a state condemnation action against the taxpayer's property were not deductible as expenses paid or incurred for the production of income under Code Sec. 212, but were capital expenditures.[177] Similarly, amounts paid by an individual for attorneys' fees in connection with the condemnation of property held for investment and the rezoning of the remainder of the tract were capital expenditures and were not deductible.[178] While rezoning costs normally are considered nondeductible capital expenditures, a loss deduction may be available if a rezoning effort fails. In *Chevy Chase Land Co.*,[179] the Tax Court allowed a deduction for an abandonment loss when the costs of a zoning effort were completely lost and worthless when the zoning change was denied.

On the other hand, if the expenses result in the collection of taxable income, for instance rent, then the expenses are deductible under Code Sec. 212. In *B.V. Sickle*,[180] the reasonable attorney's fees paid in an action to recover rent were held

---

[171] *See*, for example, Louisiana Land & Exploration Co., CA-5, 47-1 USTC ¶ 9266, 161 F.2d 842; L.Q. Coupe, 52 TC 394, CCH Dec. 29,610, *acq.* 1970-2 CB xix; Anderson-Tully Co., 48 TCM 415, CCH Dec. 41,314(M), T.C. Memo. 1984-338.

[172] J.D. Cothran, 33 TCM 547, CCH Dec. 32,568(M), T.C. Memo. 1974-109.

[173] Bush Terminal Buildings Co., CA-2, 53-1 USTC ¶ 9392, 204 F.2d 575, *cert. denied*, 346 U.S. 856, 74 S.Ct. 72.

[174] Issac G. Johnson & Co., CA-2, 45-2 USTC ¶ 9338, 149 F.2d 851.

[175] Casalina Corp., CA-4, 75-1 USTC ¶ 9311, 511 F.2d 1162; J. Iske, 39 TCM 1161, CCH Dec. 36,807(M), T.C. Memo. 1980-61, *aff'd*, (unpublished opinion) November 18, 1980, *cert. denied*, 451 U.S. 909, 101 S.Ct. 1978; Rev. Rul. 71-476, 1971-2 CB 308.

[176] Reg. § 1.212-1(k).

[177] S.E. Stickles, DC NY, 70-1 USTC ¶ 9239; *see also* S. Marcus, 23 TCM 1240, CCH Dec. 26,908(M), T.C. Memo. 1964-206.

[178] W.M. Soelling, 70 TC 1052, CCH Dec. 35,429; *see also* J.D. Wallace, 48 TCM 157, CCH Dec. 41,263(M), T.C. Memo. 1984-277.

[179] 72 TC 481, CCH Dec. 36,127.

[180] 52 TCM 982, CCH Dec. 43,480(M), T.C. Memo. 1986-538.

fully deductible under Code Sec. 212. The taxpayer was able to prove that the entire amount paid to the attorney under a contingency fee arrangement was paid for the action to recover rent and that the fee was reasonable. The cost of ejecting a trespasser so that income could be realized from property has also been held to be a currently deductible expense.[181]

.09 Interest

The general rule is that a deduction is allowed for "all interest paid or accrued within the taxable year on indebtedness."[182] However, this rule is limited by many other provisions of the Internal Revenue Code. The interest deduction is considered in some detail at ¶ 303.

For a discussion of the requirement to capitalize construction period interest, see ¶ 103.01[C].

¶ 704 REAL ESTATE TAXES

Taxpayers may deduct state, local, and foreign real property taxes; state and local personal property taxes; and state, local, and foreign income taxes (or state and local sales taxes in lieu of income taxes), regardless of whether those taxes are incurred in connection with a trade or business, property held for the production of income or investment, or purely personal activities.[183] Individuals generally take these deductions as itemized deductions. These taxes are not deductible for purposes of the individual alternative minimum tax, however, unless they are business related and deductible in computing adjusted gross income.[184] An individual who will be subject to the alternative minimum tax in a particular tax year should attempt to accelerate or defer the payment of deductible taxes so as not to lose the benefit of the tax deduction.

State, local, and foreign taxes, other than property and income taxes, are deductible if they are incurred in carrying on a trade or business or an activity for the production of income. In the case of these other state and local taxes, Code Sec. 164(a) requires that the taxes be treated as part of the cost of the property, or a reduction in the amount realized, if these taxes are imposed on the acquisition or disposition of property. Examples of these other taxes include mortgage recording taxes and state transfer taxes.

Individual Deduction Limited

The itemized deduction by individuals for state, local, and foreign property taxes, and state and local income taxes and general sales taxes paid or accrued during the tax year is limited for tax years 2018 through 2025. An individual cannot deduct foreign real property taxes, but may still claim an itemized deduction of up to $10,000 ($5,000 for a married taxpayer filing a separate return) for state and local property taxes, income taxes, and general sales taxes. An individual may also still

---

[181] A. Bliss, CA-5, 3 USTC ¶ 928, 57 F.2d 984.

[182] Code Sec. 163(a).

[183] Code Sec. 164(a).

[184] Code Sec. 56(b)(1)(A)(ii).

claim a deduction for state and local real or personal property taxes paid or accrued in carrying on a trade or business or income-producing activity.[185]

Business taxpayers who make business-related payments to charities or government entities for which they receive state or local tax credits can generally deduct the payments as business expenses. The business expense deduction is available to any business taxpayer, regardless of whether it is doing business as a sole proprietor, partnership or corporation, as long as the payment qualifies as an ordinary and necessary business expense. Businesses generally still can deduct business-related payments in full as a business expense, regardless of the limitations on nonbusiness state and local taxes.[186]

Safe Harbors

The IRS has provided safe harbors for businesses that make payments to charitable organizations in exchange for state or local tax credits.[187]

If a C corporation makes a payment to a charitable organization and receives or expects to receive a tax credit that reduces a state or local tax imposed on the corporation in return, the corporation may treat the payment as an ordinary and necessary business expense to the extent of the credit.

If a specified passthrough entity makes a payment to a charitable organization and receives or expects to receive a tax credit that the entity applies to offset a state or local tax, other than a state or local income tax, the specified passthrough entity may treat the payment as an ordinary and necessary business expense to the extent of the credit. An entity qualifies for this safe harbor only if the following requirements are met:

1. The entity is a business entity other than a C corporation that is regarded as separate from its owners;
2. The entity operates a trade or business;
3. The entity is subject to a state or local tax incurred in carrying on its trade or business that is imposed directly on the entity; and
4. In return for a payment to a charitable organization, the entity receives or expects to receive a state or local tax credit that the entity applies or expects to apply to offset a state or local tax other than a state or local income tax.

.01 Real Property Taxes

Real property taxes deductible under Code Sec. 164(a) are taxes imposed on interests in real property that are levied for the general public welfare. Deductible real property taxes do not include taxes assessed against local benefits.[188] For example, a monthly charge based on usage made by a city for the use of its sewer system is not a tax and is not deductible as a tax.[189] Such a charge, however, may be deductible as a business expense or, if attributable to rental property, as an expense

[185] Code Sec. 164(b)(6).

[186] IR-2018-178.

[187] Rev. Proc. 2019-12, 2019-4 IRB 401.

[188] Reg. § 1.164-3(b).

[189] Rev. Rul. 75-346, 1975 CB-2 66.

incurred in the production of income.[190] On the other hand, real estate tax increases imposed on all property owners within a municipality to pay off general revenue bonds that were sold to build and maintain a sewage disposal system are deductible as real property taxes.[191]

Annual assessments of a homeowners' association paid by its members for the purposes of promoting the recreation, health, safety, and welfare of residents and maintaining common areas are not deductible as real property taxes.[192] Also, annual fees earmarked for sanitation services that are imposed on all property in a county, based on the assessed value of the property, but which are subject to a maximum limit with additional fees for commercial and special services, are not deductible as real property taxes.[193]

Cash method taxpayers generally deduct taxes when they are paid. In this case, "paid" means paid to the proper taxing authority. A cash method mortgagor who makes monthly payments to the mortgagee that equal one-twelfth of the estimated annual real property taxes may deduct the taxes only in the year in which payment of the taxes is made by the mortgagee to the proper taxing authorities.[194]

For a discussion on the accounting rule applicable to the accrual of real property taxes, see ¶ 701.02[B].

[A] Deduction of Real Property Taxes

Generally, it is the owner of the property against which real property taxes are assessed that is entitled to the deduction. The owner, in this case, is not necessarily the owner of the legal title, and the equitable owner of property may be entitled to the tax deduction if the equitable owner actually pays the tax.

When taxpayers acquired a residence, legal title to the property was held by others as nominees, and the record title was never held by the taxpayers. The taxpayer's wife, however, made all of the payments on the purchase price of the residence and the mortgage payments. She claimed deductions for real estate taxes that she paid, but the deductions were disallowed by the IRS since she was not the record owner of the property. The Tax Court, however, held that the wife was the equitable owner of the residence and was entitled to deduct the real estate taxes paid, even though legal title was in the names of others.[195] Similarly, a taxpayer who took title to rental property in the names of his daughter and son-in-law for personal reasons could deduct the taxes he paid on the property when the record owners received no income from the property and paid no expenses on the property.[196]

A husband and wife may deduct on separate returns only the amount of property tax actually paid by each on property held as tenants by the entirety or as

[190] M. Thornbrough, 11 TCM 227, CCH Dec. 18,832(M).

[191] Rev. Rul. 74-52, 1974-2 CB 50.

[192] Rev. Rul. 76-495, 1976-2 CB 43.

[193] Rev. Rul. 77-29, 1977-1 CB 44.

[194] Rev. Rul. 78-103, 1978-1 CB 58. *See also* F.L. Odom, Jr., 44 TCM 1132, CCH Dec. 39,344(M), T.C. Memo. 1982-531 (cash method taxpayer not credited with payment of taxes until paid out of escrow account to which taxpayer made deposits).

[195] G.B. Casey, 24 TCM 1558, CCH Dec. 27,604(M), T.C. Memo. 1965-282.

[196] A.J. Gilbert, 11 TCM 457, CCH Dec. 18,958(M).

joint tenants.[197] Taxes paid by a husband on a home owned by his wife, however, are not deductible by the husband.[198]

[B] Back Taxes Payments

Back taxes paid to redeem property to which the municipality had taken a tax collector's deed are deductible if, under local law, the taxpayer is personally liable for the arrearages until redemption or foreclosure of the right to redemption.[199] The same rule applies when the back tax payment is made directly to the person who acquired the property, subject to redemption, at a tax sale.[200]

For the apportionment of the real property tax deduction between buyer and seller on the purchase of real estate, see the discussion at ¶ 102.03.

[C] Payments in Lieu of Taxes

When state and local government and agencies undertake development of property, for example, to provide housing, the property may not be subject to regular property taxes because of the government ownership. Usually, local authorities then impose some equivalent payment requirement on the developers and eventually owners of the property. One example is the tax equivalency payments to the New York City Educational Construction Fund that were required to be paid by a cooperative housing corporation for the development of the air space over property owned by the public school system of New York. The payments were applied to debt service on obligations funding public school construction.

In Rev. Rul. 71-49,[201] the IRS ruled that the cooperative housing corporation may deduct the payments as real property taxes under Code Sec. 164 because (1) the payments are measured by and are equal to the amounts imposed by the regular taxing statutes, (2) the payments are imposed by a specific state statute, and (3) the proceeds are designated for a public purpose rather than for some privilege, service, or regulatory function, or for some other local benefit tending to increase the value of the property on which the payments are made. Each tenant-stockholder of the cooperative housing corporation then is entitled to deduct the payments in the amount of the stockholder's proportionate share.

A similar rule has been applied to PILOT payments (payments in lieu of taxes) made by private developers of government owned property under lease agreements. The PILOT obligations in the letter rulings satisfy the three-prong test of Rev. Rul. 71-49: (1) PILOT are imposed at the same general rate at which real property taxes are imposed; (2) PILOT are imposed by state statute although the law uses the vehicle of leasing agreements; and (3) PILOT may only be used by the government agency for public purposes, including debt service of bonds issued to construct municipal facilities and services, and payment of operating and administrative expenses.[202]

---

[197] W.R. Tracy, 25 BTA 1055, CCH Dec. 7510, *acq.* X1-2 CB 10, *rev'd on another issue,* CA-6, 4 USTC ¶ 1269, 70 F.2d 93; Rev. Rul. 71-268, 1971-1 CB 58.

[198] W.A. Colston, CA DC, 3 USTC ¶ 947, 59 F.2d 867, *cert. denied,* 287 U.S. 640, 53 S.Ct. 89; W. Buff, 58 TC 224, CCH Dec. 31,371.

[199] J.R. Hopkins, 15 TC 160, CCH Dec. 17,811, *acq.* 1951-1 CB 2.

[200] C.E. Baldwin, 14 TCM 794, CCH Dec. 21,141(M), T.C. Memo. 1955-200.

[201] Rev. Rul. 71-49, 1971-1 CB 103.

[202] *See* Ltr. Rul. 200730012 and Ltr. Rul. 200720016.

.02 Special Assessment and Local Benefit Taxes

Deductible real property taxes are those that are levied for the general public welfare by the proper taxing authorities at a like rate against all property in the territory over which the authorities have jurisdiction.[203] Taxes for local benefits or special assessments paid for local benefits such as streets, sidewalks, and other like improvements that are imposed because of and measured by some benefit that tends to increase the value of the property against which the assessment is levied are not deductible as taxes.[204] A tax is considered assessed against a local benefit when the property subject to the tax is limited to the property benefited. Special assessments are not deductible, even though an incidental benefit inures to the public welfare.[205] While the improvements envisioned by the statute are those that tend to increase the value of the property, there is no requirement that the improvements actually increase the value of the property assessed in every particular case.[206]

To the extent assessments against local benefits are made for maintenance or repair or to meet interest charges for the benefits, however, they are deductible.[207] It is up to the taxpayer to show the allocation of the assessments to the different purposes. If the allocation cannot be shown, none of the amount paid is deductible.[208] In Rev. Rul. 79-201,[209] the IRS ruled that the portion of a "front foot benefit charge" assessed against property benefited by the construction of a water system and added to the taxpayer's real property tax bill, which was properly allocated to interest and maintenance charges, was deductible as a tax under Code Sec. 164. However, the ruling went on to say that no part of a flat per unit charge or a two-part charge consisting of a metered charge and a uniform charge for maintenance and interest that a sewer or water authority imposed on all its customers was deductible.

The IRS has ruled that the following are taxes for local benefits and cannot be deducted under Code Sec. 164, except to the extent allocable to maintenance or interest charges:

1. Assessments paid by property owners to a city-created parking improvement district for the purpose of providing public parking facilities in or near the district.[210]
2. Assessments imposed by an irrigation district, a subdivision of a state, against farm property within the district for operation and maintenance, administration, water purchase costs, and repayment of the cost of a water distribution system.[211]
3. "Front foot benefit charges" assessed by the Washington Suburban Sanitary Commission against property in jurisdictions adjacent to the District of Columbia for water main and sewer improvements.[212]

---

[203] Reg. § 1.164-4(a).
[204] Code Sec. 164(c)(1).
[205] Reg. § 1.164-4(a).
[206] Caldwell Milling Co., 3 BTA 1232, CCH Dec. 1379.
[207] Code Sec. 164(c)(1).
[208] Reg. § 1.164-4(b)(1).
[209] 1979-1 CB 97.
[210] Rev. Rul. 60-327, 1960-2 CB 65.
[211] Rev. Rul. 67-337, 1967-2 CB 92.
[212] Rev. Rul. 75-455, 1975-2 CB 68.

4. Sewer, water, and solid waste disposal system taxes imposed on benefited lands only by municipal utility districts formed under state law to enhance the value and marketability of a certain tract of land.[213] But real estate tax increases imposed on all property owners within a municipality to pay off general revenue bonds sold to build a sewage disposal system and to provide for its maintenance are deductible as real estate taxes.[214]

.03 Transfer Taxes

Prior to the Tax Reform Act of 1986,[215] state and local real estate transfer taxes were deductible if incurred in connection with a trade, business, or income-producing property.[216] These transfer taxes were not deductible if incurred by an individual in connection with the purchase of a personal residence.[217]

The following was added to Code Sec. 164(a) by the Tax Reform Act of 1986: "... any tax [other than real property, personal property, income and certain other taxes] which is paid or accrued by the taxpayer in connection with an acquisition or disposition of property shall be treated as part of the cost of the acquired property or, in the case of a disposition, as a reduction in the amount realized on the disposition." Accordingly, a taxpayer purchasing property and paying a state or local real estate transfer tax adds the transfer tax to the tax basis for the property. A taxpayer selling property and paying a state or local transfer tax reduces the amount realized on the sale by the amount of the tax, and this, in turn, reduces the gain or increases the loss that must be reported as a result of the sale.

For the capitalization of taxes in connection with the construction of property, see the discussion at ¶ 103.01.

.04 Impact Fees

In some areas, developers must pay what are termed "impact fees" in order to develop land. These fees are designed to offset the increase in infrastructure cost that must be borne by the community caused by the influx of new residents in connection with the development. In Florida, these fees must be paid for the approval and recordation of plats. The question arises whether these impact fees are deductible business expenses or capital expenditures.

Oriole Homes Corp. is a large residential home builder that deducted impact fees as an ordinary and necessary business expense. The IRS, however, asserted that the impact fees were nondeductible capital expenditures. A district court in Florida decided that impact fees must be capitalized as a development cost and recovered through an increase in the cost of goods sold as each house in a

[213] Rev. Rul. 76-45, 1976-1 CB 51. *See also* G.A. Noble, 70 TC 916, CCH Dec. 35,400, *nonacq.* 1979-42 (taxpayer's one-time "tap fee" to hook up to city's sewer system is special assessment for improvement benefiting the taxpayer's business properties and is a nondeductible capital expenditure).

[214] Rev. Rul. 74-52, 1974-2 CB 50.

[215] P.L. 99-514.

[216] *See* Rev. Rul. 69-456, 1969-2 CB 30 (state and local transfer taxes paid by a corporation on the sale of a building used in the operation of its business); Rev. Rul. 71-590, 1971-2 CB 124 (Pennsylvania Realty Transfer Tax paid by a corporation on purchase of real estate).

[217] L.C. Black, 60 TC 108, CCH Dec. 31,942; J.M. Gibbons, 35 TCM 565, CCH Dec. 33,785(M), T.C. Memo. 1976-125.

development is sold.[218] Citing that court decision, the IRS has ruled that impact fees incurred in connection with the construction of new buildings are capitalized costs allocable to the new buildings under Code Secs. 263 and 263A.[219]

¶ 705 EXCESS BUSINESS LOSSES

Excess business losses of noncorporate taxpayers are not allowed for tax years beginning after December 31, 2017, and before January 1, 2026. An excess business loss that is disallowed is treated as a net operating loss (NOL) carryover to the following tax year. The passive activity loss rules (see Chapter 11) apply before the rules for excess business losses. The limit on excess farm losses of noncorporate taxpayers does not apply while the limit on excess business losses is in effect.[220]

.01 Excess Loss Defined

An excess business loss is the excess of:

1. The taxpayer's aggregate deductions for the tax year from trades or businesses, determined without regard to whether or not the deductions are disallowed under the excess business loss limitation; over
2. The sum of:
    a. The taxpayer's aggregate gross income or gain for the tax year from the trades or businesses, plus
    b. $250,000, adjusted annually for inflation after 2018 ($500,000 in the case of a joint return).[221]

Example 8: For 2018, the unmarried owner of a retail appliance business has $1,100,0000 in gross income and $1,490,000 in deductions from the appliance business that is his only business activity. The business is not a passive activity. The owner's excess business loss is $140,000 ($1,490,000 - ($1,100,000 + $250,000)). The owner treats his excess business loss of $140,000 as an NOL carryover to 2019.

.02 Partnerships and S Corporations

For partnerships and S corporations, the limit on excess business losses is applied at the partner or shareholder level.[222] A partner takes into account his or her distributive share of the partnership's items of income, gain, deduction, or loss in applying the excess business loss rules to his or her tax year within which the partnership's tax year ends. Similarly, a shareholder of an S corporation takes into account his or her pro rata share of the corporation's items of income, gain, deduction, or loss in applying the excess business loss rules to his or her tax year within which the corporation's tax year ends.

---

[218] Oriole Homes Corp. v. U.S., DC Fla., 89-2 USTC ¶ 9433.

[219] Rev. Rul. 2002-9, 2002-10 IRB 614.

[220] Code Sec. 461(l).

[221] Code Sec. 461(l)(3).

[222] Code Sec. 461(l)(4).

Chapter 8
Property Additions and Improvements

¶ 800 Overview of Chapter
¶ 801 Improvements to Real Estate as Capital Expenditures
¶ 802 Special Amortization Provisions
¶ 803 Energy Efficient Commercial Buildings Deduction
¶ 804 Tax Credits for Building Rehabilitations
¶ 805 Low-Income Housing Credit
¶ 806 Renewal Communities and New York Liberty Zone

¶ 800 OVERVIEW OF CHAPTER

When the owner of property makes additions or improvements to the property, generally the owner may not deduct the cost currently. Rather, the owner may add the cost to the tax basis of the property and recover the added cost through depreciation deductions, if available, or on the sale or other disposition of the property.

In some cases, however, the tax law provides for a faster recovery of the cost of certain additions or improvements to real property in order to encourage owners to take certain actions. An example of these special amortization provisions is the write-off for additions or improvements to industrial and other business property to control air and water pollution. Other incentives are provided for reforestation, soil and water conservation, and energy efficiency.

Another incentive that Congress often uses to promote socially desirable goals is a tax credit. Unlike a deduction, which reduces taxable income, a tax credit is a direct reduction in tax liability. Currently, there are two tax credits that may be used by owners of, and investors in, real estate. These tax credits are the investment credit for the rehabilitation of certain older commercial buildings before 2018 and historic structures and the credit for the acquisition or improvement of low-income housing.

This chapter discusses additions and improvements to real estate in general and the special amortization and tax credit provisions that are available for particular types of improvements. The more widely available deduction for depreciation and more limited expensing election are given special consideration in Chapter 9.

¶ 801 IMPROVEMENTS TO REAL ESTATE AS CAPITAL EXPENDITURES

The Internal Revenue Code denies a deduction for any amount paid out for new buildings or for permanent improvements or betterments made to increase the value of any property or estate.[1] It also denies a deduction for any amount expended in restoring property or in making good the exhaustion thereof for which an allowance is or has been made in the form of a deduction for depreciation, amortization, or depletion.[2]

As to what constitutes a capital expenditure as opposed to a currently deductible expense has been addressed by the IRS in what have been termed the "repair regulations." The regulations apply as of January 1, 2014. Taxpayers, however, may have applied them as of 2012 if they desired. Alternatively, taxpayers may have applied the temporary regulations that were issued at the end of 2011 to 2012 and 2013.[3]

Reg. § 1.263(a)-3 tells us that a taxpayer generally must capitalize the aggregate of related amounts paid to improve a "unit of property" owned by the taxpayer and that a unit of property is improved if the amounts paid for activities performed after the property is placed in service by the taxpayer:

1. Result in a betterment to the unit of property;
2. Restore the unit of property; or
3. Adapt the unit of property to a new or different use.[4]

.01 Unit of Property

Whether an item is a capital improvement and not a currently deductible expense under the repair regulations is affected by the size of the unit of property. The regulations provide a functional interdependence test in order to define a unit of property for most tangible property, other than buildings.[5]

In the case of a building, the regulations are quite specific as to what constitutes a unit of property. While an entire building is technically a unit of property, the regulations apply the improvement rules separately to the building structure and nine specific building systems. A building structure consists of the building (as defined in Reg. § 1.48-1(e)(1)), and its structural components (as defined in Reg. § 1.48-1(e)(2)), other than those designated as buildings systems. The following structural components are building systems that are separate from the building structure, and to which the improvement rules must be applied:

---

[1] Code Sec. 263(a)(1).

[2] Code Sec. 263(a)(2).

[3] Reg. § 1.263(a)-1(h). *See also* T.D. 9564.

[4] Reg. § 1.263(a)-3(d). *See also* the discussion of repair expenses and the safe harbors for deducting repairs under the repair regulations beginning at ¶ 703.01. For the special considerations involved when landlords and tenants make improvements or additions to leased property, *see* ¶ ¶ 601 and 602.

[5] Reg. § 1.263(a)-3(e).

1. Heating, ventilation, and air conditioning ("HVAC") systems (including motors, compressors, boilers, furnace, chillers, pipes, ducts, radiators);
2. Plumbing systems (including pipes, drains, valves, sinks, bathtubs, toilets, water and sanitary sewer collection equipment, and site utility equipment used to distribute water and waste to and from the property line and between buildings and other permanent structures);
3. Electrical systems (including wiring, outlets, junction boxes, lighting fixtures and associated connectors, and site utility equipment used to distribute electricity from property line to and between buildings and other permanent structures);
4. All escalators;
5. All elevators;
6. Fire-protection and alarm systems (including sensing devices, computer controls, sprinkler heads, sprinkler mains, associated piping or plumbing, pumps, visual and audible alarms, alarm control panels, heat and smoke detection devices, fire escapes, fire doors, emergency exit lighting and signage, and fire fighting equipment, such as extinguishers, hoses);
7. Security systems for the protection of the building and its occupants (including window and door locks, security cameras, recorders, monitors, motion detectors, security lighting, alarm systems, entry and access systems, related junction boxes, associated wiring and conduit);
8. Gas distribution system (including associated pipes and equipment used to distribute gas to and from property line and between buildings or permanent structures); and
9. Other structural components specifically designated as building systems that are excepted from the building structure in future published guidance.[6]

[A] Leased Buildings

A lessee who leases an entire building is treated in essentially the same fashion as the owner of a building. The lessee applies the improvement rules to the building structure and to each building system. For a lessee who leases only part of a building, the lessee applies the improvement rules to the entire portion of the building structure subject to the lease or the portion of any building system subject to the lease.[7]

[B] Condominiums and Cooperatives

The owner of an individual unit in a building with multiple units (such as a condominium), applies the improvement rules to the building structure that is part of the condominium or to the portion of any building system that is part of the condominium. In the case of the condominium management association, the association must apply the improvement rules to the building structure or to any building system.[8]

---

[6] Reg. § 1.263(a)-3(e)(2).

[7] Reg. § 1.263(a)-3(e)(2)(v).

[8] Reg. § 1.263(a)-3(e)(2)(iii).

A taxpayer that has an ownership interest in a cooperative housing corporation applies the improvement rules to the portion of the building structure in which the taxpayer has possessory rights or to the portion of any building system that is part of the portion of the building structure subject to the taxpayer's possessory rights. In the case of a cooperative housing corporation, the corporation must apply the improvement rules to the building structure or to any building system.[9]

[C] Other Property

In the case of real or personal property other than buildings, all the components that are functionally interdependent comprise a single unit of property. Components of property are functionally interdependent if the placing in service of one component is dependent on the placing in service of the other component.[10]

In the case of plant property, the unit of property is further divided into smaller units comprised of each component (or group of components) that performs a discrete and major function or operation within the functionally interdependent property. Plant property is functionally interdependent machinery or equipment, other than network assets, used to perform an industrial process, such as manufacturing, generation, warehousing, distribution, automated materials handling in service industries, or other similar activities.[11]

Network assets are railroad track, oil and gas pipelines, water and sewage pipelines, power transmission and distribution lines, and telephone and cable lines that are owned or leased by taxpayers in each of those industries. The term includes, for example, trunk and feeder lines, pole lines, and buried conduit. It does not include property that would be included as a building structure or building systems nor does it include separate property that is adjacent to, but not part of a network asset, such as bridges, culverts, or tunnels. In the case of network assets, the improvement rules are applied based on a taxpayer's particular facts and circumstances. The functional interdependence standard that generally applies to property other than buildings is not determinative.[12]

[D] Improvements to Property

An improvement to a unit of property generally is not a unit of property separate from the unit of property improved.[13] For example, a building addition is not a separate unit of property even though depreciation begins when the addition is placed in service as a separate asset. The unit of property is the entire building, including the addition, as long as the addition is depreciated in the same manner as the original building.[14] If the addition were depreciated using a different method or over a different period than the building, however, the addition would be a separate unit of property (see below).

---

[9] Reg. § 1.263(a)-3(e)(2)(iv).

[10] Reg. § 1.263(a)-3(e)(3)(i).

[11] Reg. § 1.263(a)-3(e)(3)(ii).

[12] Reg. § 1.263(a)-3(e)(3)(iii).

[13] Reg. § 1.263(a)-3(e)(4).

[14] *See* Example 15 in Reg. § 1.263(a)-3(e)(6).

[E] Components as Separate Units

A component (or group of components) of a unit of property must be treated as a separate unit of property if its depreciation method or period is different than the property of which it is a part when the property is placed in service.[15] For instance, tires on a truck would be considered a separate unit of property from the truck if the tires were depreciated over five years and the truck depreciated over three years.[16]

A similar rules applies if the IRS or taxpayer changes the depreciation period or method of a portion of a building or other unit of property after the unit of property is placed in service.[17] For example, if a cost segregation study is performed after a building is placed in service and as a result, components of the building are reclassified as personal property and depreciated over a shorter period than the building, the reclassified components are a separate unit of property.[18]

.02 Betterments to Property

A taxpayer must capitalize as an improvement an amount paid for a betterment to a unit of property. An amount is paid for a betterment to a unit of property only if it:

1. Ameliorates a material condition or defect that either existed prior to the taxpayer's acquisition of the unit of property or arose during the production of the unit of property, whether or not the taxpayer was aware of the condition or defect at the time of acquisition or production;
2. Is for a material addition, including a physical enlargement, expansion, extension, or addition of a major component to the unit of property or a material increase in the capacity, including additional cubic or linear space, of the unit of property; or
3. Is reasonably expected to materially increase the productivity, efficiency, strength, quality, or output of the unit of property.

The IRS says that it is appropriate to consider all the facts and circumstances including, but not limited to, the purpose of the expenditure, the physical nature of the work performed, and the effect of the expenditure on the unit of property.[19]

Generally, determining whether an expenditure is for a betterment of property involves comparing the condition of the property immediately after the expenditure with the condition of the property immediately before the circumstances necessitating the expenditure.[20]

If the expenditure is made to correct the effects of normal wear and tear that occurred during the taxpayer's use of property, the condition of the property immediately before the circumstances necessitating the expenditure is the condi-

[15] Reg. § 1.263(a)-3(e)(5)(i).

[16] *See* Example 16 in Reg. § 1.263(a)-3(e)(6).

[17] Reg. § 1.263(a)-3(e)(5)(ii).

[18] *See* Example 18 in Reg. § 1.263(a)-3(e)(6); *see also* Example 17 in which building improvements are reclassified as 15-year restaurant, leasehold, or retail improvement property in a year after being placed in service. For a discussion of cost segregation studies, *see* ¶ 903. Additional examples illustrating the application of the improvement rules to a unit of property may be found at Reg. § 1.263(a)-3(e)(6).

[19] Reg. § 1.263(a)-3(j).

[20] Reg. § 1.263(a)-3(j)(2)(iv).

tion of the property after the last time the taxpayer corrected the effects of normal wear and tear (whether through maintenance or improvements). If the taxpayer had not previously corrected the effects of normal wear and tear, the condition of the property when placed in service is used for comparison.[21]

If the expenditure is made to correct damage property that occurred during the taxpayer's use of the property, the condition of the property immediately before the circumstances necessitating the expenditure is the condition of the property immediately before the damage.[22]

[A] Replacements

If a taxpayer replaces a part of a unit of property that cannot reasonably be replaced with the same type of part (for example, because of technological advancements or product enhancements), the replacement of the part with an improved, but comparable, part does not, by itself, result in a betterment to the property.[23]

> ***Example 1:*** The owner of a building replaces cedar shakes with architectural asphalt shingles because the wood shingles are no longer available. The new shingles are somewhat stronger than the old shingles, but are otherwise comparable. The replacement is not a betterment. On the other hand, if the owner replaced the shingles with one made of a lightweight composite that is maintenance free, does not absorb moisture, has a Class A fire rating, and a 50-year warranty, the replacement would likely be considered a betterment.

[B] Application to Buildings

An amount is paid to improve a building if it is paid for a betterment to a building, condominium, cooperative, or a leased building or leased portion of building. For example, an amount is paid to improve a building if it is paid for an increase in the efficiency of the building structure or any one of its building systems (for example, the HVAC system).[24]

Reg. § 1.263(a)-3(j)(3) contains numerous examples that illustrate the betterment rules. The discussion that follows uses the examples to look at various categories of expenditures that have application to real property under the betterment rules.

[C] Building Refresh

Generally, simple cosmetic changes and general repairs and maintenance are not improvements and are deductible.

> ***Example 2:*** Every several years, a national retailer refreshes the look and layout of its stores to maintain their appearance and functionality. The work performed includes replacing and reconfiguring display tables and racks to provide better exposure of the merchandise, making corresponding lighting relocations and flooring repairs, moving a wall to accommodate the reconfiguration of tables and racks, patching holes in walls, repainting the interior

[21] Reg. § 1.263(a)-3(j)(2)(iv)(B).

[22] Reg. § 1.263(a)-3(j)(2)(iv)(C).

[23] Reg. § 1.263(a)-3(j)(2)(iii).

[24] Reg. § 1.263(a)-3(j)(2)(ii).

structure with a new color scheme to coordinate with new signage, replacing damaged ceiling tiles, cleaning and repairing wood flooring throughout the store building, and power washing building exteriors. The display tables and the racks are section 1245 property (depreciable personal property) and not part of the buildings. The work does not ameliorate any material conditions or defects that existed when the retailer acquired the store buildings, nor does it result in any material additions to the store buildings.

Considering the facts and circumstances including the purpose of the expenditure, the physical nature of the work performed, and the effect of the expenditure on the buildings' structure and systems, the amounts paid for the refresh of each building are not for any material additions to, or material increases in the capacity of, the buildings' structure or systems as compared with the condition of the structure or systems after the previous refresh. Moreover, the amounts paid are not reasonably expected to materially increase the productivity, efficiency, strength, quality, or output of any building structure or system as compared to the condition of the structures or systems after the previous refresh. Rather, the work performed keeps the store buildings' structures and buildings' systems in their ordinarily efficient operating condition. Therefore, the retailer is not required to treat the cost of the refresh as betterments. However, the retailer is required to capitalize the amounts paid to acquire and install each section 1245 property.

If in the course of refreshing a building, however, any additions or improvements must be capitalized. The refresh costs, however, continue to be deductible, provided the refresh is separate from the additions or improvements.

Example 3: Suppose that in the previous example the retailer, at the same time it performs the refresh of one of its buildings, also constructs an addition to the back of the store building, including adding a new overhead door and loading dock. The work also involves upgrades to the electrical system of the building, including the addition of a second service box with increased amperage and new wiring from the service box to provide lighting and power throughout the new space. Although the work is performed at the same time, the construction of the additions does not affect, and is not otherwise related to, the refresh of the retail space.

The cost of adding the storage space, loading dock, overhead door, and expanding the electrical system are for betterments to the building structure and to the electrical system because they are for material additions to, and a material increase in capacity of, the structure and the electrical system. The retailer must capitalize the cost improvements. The retailer is not required to capitalize the refresh costs because they do not directly benefit and are not incurred because of the additions to the building structure and electrical system.

Taxpayers in the retail and restaurant industries regularly incur expenditures to remodel or refresh and, along with the IRS, frequently encounter questions regarding whether the costs for a particular remodel-refresh project should be characterized as repairs, maintenance, or an improvement, causing taxpayers and the IRS to expend significant resources on this factually intensive issue. To simplify matters, the IRS has issued a safe harbor for the retail and restaurant industries for characterizing remodel-refresh costs as deductible expenses or capital costs.

Under the safe harbor, a qualified taxpayer treats 75 percent of its qualified costs as deductible under Code Sec. 162(a), and the remaining 25 percent of its qualified costs as costs for improvements to a building under Code Sec. 263(a) and for the production of property for use in a trade or business under Code Sec. 263A.[25]

[D] Building Remodel

Unlike a simple building refresh, however, a complete remodel most likely will require that the cost be capitalized as an improvement to the property.

> ***Example 4:*** A national retailer with a chain of stores determines that, because of changes in the retail market, it can no longer compete in its current store class and decides to upgrade its stores to offer higher end products to a different type of customer. The retailer replaces large parts of the exterior walls of its stores with windows, replaces the escalators with a monumental staircase, adds a new glass enclosed elevator, rebuilds the interior and exterior facades, replaces vinyl floors with ceramic flooring, replaces ceiling tiles with acoustical tiles, and removes and rebuilds walls to move changing rooms and create specialty departments. The work also includes upgrades to increase the capacity of the buildings' electrical system to accommodate the structural changes and the addition of new section 1245 property, such as new product information kiosks and point of sale systems. The work to the electrical system also involves the installation of new more efficient and mood enhancing lighting fixtures. In addition, the work includes remodeling all bathrooms by replacing contractor-grade plumbing fixtures with designer-grade fixtures that conserve water and energy. Finally, the retailer also pays to clean debris from construction during the remodel, patch holes in walls that were made to upgrade the electrical system, repaint existing walls with a new color scheme to match the new interior construction, and to power wash building exteriors to enhance the new exterior facade.
>
> Considering the facts and circumstances, including the purpose of the expenditure, the physical nature of the work performed, and the effect of the work on the buildings' structures and buildings' systems, the remodeling results in betterments to the buildings' structures and several of their systems. The retailer must capitalize the cost of the remodel. The cost of cleaning debris, patching and repainting existing walls with a new color scheme, and to power wash building exteriors, while not betterments by themselves, directly benefitted and were incurred because of the improvements to the buildings' structures and electrical systems and, therefore, must be capitalized as part of the remodel.

[25] 2015-49 IRB 827. For details on this safe harbor, *see* Rev. Proc. 2015-56, 2015-49 IRB 827.

[E] Amelioration of Pre-Existing Conditions

The amelioration or correction of a material defect or condition that existed before a taxpayer acquired the property is a betterment and subject to capitalization. On the other hand, simply correcting a problem that does not rise to the level of a material defect may not be considered a betterment. This somewhat nebulous statement is illustrated in the following three examples.

> ***Example 5:*** A taxpayer purchases a store located on land that contains underground gasoline storage tanks left by prior occupants. Assume that the parcel of land is the unit of property. The tanks had leaked before the taxpayer's purchase, causing soil contamination. The taxpayer is not aware of the contamination at the time of purchase. A year after the purchase, the taxpayer discovers the contamination and incurs costs to remediate the soil. The remediation costs are for a betterment to the land because the taxpayer incurred the costs to ameliorate a material condition or defect that existed before acquisition of the land.
>
> ***Example 6:*** A taxpayer owns an office building that was constructed with insulation that contained asbestos. Several years after the taxpayer placed the building into service, it determines that some areas of asbestos-containing insulation have begun to deteriorate and could eventually pose a health risk to employees. The taxpayer removes the asbestos-containing insulation from the building structure and replaces it with new insulation that is safer to employees, but no more efficient or effective than the asbestos insulation.
>
> Although the asbestos is unsafe under certain circumstances, the presence of asbestos insulation in a building, by itself, is not a preexisting material condition or defect of the building structure. In addition, the removal and replacement of the asbestos is not for a material addition to the building structure or a material increase in the capacity of the building structure when compared to the condition of the property before the deterioration of the insulation. Similarly, the removal and replacement of asbestos is not reasonably expected to materially increase the productivity, efficiency, strength, quality, or output of the building structure when compared to the condition of the property before the deterioration of the insulation. Therefore, the cost to remove and replace the asbestos insulation is not for a betterment to the building structure or an improvement to the building.
>
> ***Example 7:*** A health care provider acquires a building for use in its business of providing assisted living services. Before and after the purchase, the building functions as an assisted living facility. However, at the time of the purchase, the provider is aware that the building is in a condition that is below the standards that it requires for facilities used in its business. Immediately after the acquisition and during the following two years, while the health care provider continues to use the building as an assisted living facility, it pays for extensive repairs and maintenance, and the acquisition of new property to bring the facility into the high-quality condition for which its facilities are known. The work includes repairing damaged drywall, repainting, re-

wallpapering, replacing windows, repairing and replacing doors, replacing and regrouting tile, repairing millwork, and repairing and replacing roofing materials. The work also involves the replacement of section 1245 property, including window treatments, furniture, and cabinets.

Considering the purpose and the effect of the expenditures on the building structure, the amounts paid for repairs and maintenance to the building structure comprise a betterment to the building structure because the amounts ameliorate material conditions that existed before the health care provider's acquisition of the building. Therefore, the provider must treat the amount paid for the betterment to the building structure as an improvement to the building and must capitalize the cost. The health care provider also is required to capitalize the cost to acquire and install each section 1245 property, including each window treatment, each item of furniture, and each cabinet.

[F] Meeting Regulatory Requirements

That a government agency or regulatory authority requires a taxpayer to make changes to its property is not relevant in determining whether those changes amount to a capital improvement or deductible repair expense.

Example 8: A company owns a building that it uses in its business. The city passes an ordinance setting higher safety standards for buildings because of the hazardous conditions caused by earthquakes. To comply with the ordinance, the company adds expansion bolts to its building structure. These bolts anchor the wooden framing of the building to its cement foundation, provide additional structural support and resistance to seismic forces, and make the building more resistant to damage from lateral movement. The framing and foundation are part of the building structure. Before the ordinance, the old building was in good condition.

The addition of the expansion bolts meets the new requirements, but also materially increases the strength of the building structure. Therefore, the company must treat the addition of the expansion bolts as a betterment to the building structure and must capitalize the cost as an improvement to building. The city's new requirement that the company's building meet certain safety standards to continue to operate is not relevant in determining whether the cost incurred improved the building.

Example 9: After operating a meat processing plant for many years, a meat packer discovers that oil is seeping through the concrete walls of the plant. Federal inspectors advise the packer that it must correct the seepage problem or shut down its plant. To correct the problem, the packer adds a concrete lining to the walls from the floor to a height of about four feet and also adds concrete to the floor of the plant. Before the seepage, the walls did not leak and were functioning for their intended use.

The meat packer is not required to treat the changes as a betterment because they did not amount to a material addition to, or a material increase in the capacity of, the building's structure as compared to the condition of the structure before the seepage of oil. Moreover, the changes are not reasonably expected to materially increase the productivity, efficiency, strength, quality, or output of the building structure when compared to the condition of the structure before the seepage. The federal inspectors' requirement is not relevant in determining whether incurring the cost improved the plant.

[G] Increase in Efficiency, Capacity, Etc.

There are no hard and fast guidelines as to what amounts to a material increase in capacity, efficiency, productivity, strength, or quality, and how much of an increase in any of these attributes amounts to a betterment to property. The examples below, taken from the regulations, indicate a ten percent increase is not material, but a 50 percent increase is material. Another example, involving the dredging of a harbor channel, indicates a 25 percent increase may be sufficient in some cases.

> ***Example 10:*** A taxpayer owns an office building that it uses to provide services to customers. The building contains an HVAC system that incorporates ten roof-mounted units that provide heating and air conditioning for different parts of the building. When the taxpayer experiences climate control problems in various offices throughout the building, the taxpayer replaces two specified units. The two new units are expected to eliminate the climate control problems and to be ten percent more energy efficient than the replaced units in their original condition. No work is performed on the other roof-mounted heating/cooling units, the duct work, or the controls. The replacement of the two roof-mounted units is not a material addition to or a material increase in the capacity of the HVAC system when compared to the condition of the system before the climate control problems. In addition, given the ten percent efficiency increase in two units of the entire HVAC system, the replacement is not expected to materially increase the productivity, efficiency, strength, quality, or output of the HVAC system. Therefore, the taxpayer is not required to capitalize the amounts paid for these replacements as betterments to the building.
>
> ***Example 11:*** A taxpayer conducts an energy assessment and determines that it could significantly reduce its energy costs by adding insulation to its building that it uses in its service business. The taxpayer pays an insulation contractor to apply a combination of loose-fill, spray foam, and blanket insulation throughout the building structure, including within the attic, walls, and crawl spaces. The taxpayer reasonably expects the new insulation to make the building more energy efficient because the contractor indicated that it would reduce its annual energy and power costs by approximately 50 percent of its annual costs for the last five years. The taxpayer must capitalize as a betterment the cost to add the insulation because the insulation is reasonably expected to materially increase the efficiency of the building structure.
>
> ***Example 12:*** A manufacturer owns a factory building with a storage area on the second floor. The manufacturer reinforces the columns and girders supporting the second floor to permit storage of supplies with a gross weight 50 percent greater than the previous load-carrying capacity of the storage area.

The manufacturer must treat the changes as a betterment because they materially increases the load-carrying capacity and the strength of the building structure and must capitalize the cost of the improvement.

.03 Restoration of Property

An amount is paid to restore a unit of property only if it:

1. Is for the replacement of a component of a unit of property and the taxpayer has properly deducted a loss for that component (other than a casualty loss under Reg. § 1.165-7);
2. Is for the replacement of a component of a unit of property and the taxpayer has properly taken into account the adjusted basis of the component in realizing gain or loss resulting from the sale or exchange of the component;
3. Is for the repair of damage to a unit of property for which the taxpayer has properly taken a basis adjustment as a result of a casualty loss under Code Sec. 165 or relating to a casualty event described in Code Sec. 165 (the capitalization requirement is limited by adjusted basis before the casualty);
4. Returns the unit of property to its ordinarily efficient operating condition if the property has deteriorated to a state of disrepair and is no longer functional for its intended use;
5. Results in the rebuilding of the unit of property to a like-new condition after the end of its class life; or
6. Is for the replacement of a part or a combination of parts that comprise a major component or a substantial structural part of a unit of property.[26]

A taxpayer is not required to treat as a restoration amounts paid under 1 or 2, above, if the unit of property has been fully depreciated and the loss is attributable only to remaining salvage value as computed for federal income tax purposes.[27]

A unit of property is rebuilt to a like-new condition under 5, above, if it is brought to the status of new, rebuilt, remanufactured, or a similar status under the terms of any federal regulatory guideline or the manufacturer's original specifications. Generally, a comprehensive maintenance program, even though substantial, does not return a unit of property to a like-new condition.[28]

Of course, there still may be a restoration that must be capitalized even if property is not brought to a like-new condition. Under 4, above, returning a unit of property to its ordinary efficient use after it has deteriorated and is no longer functional is a restoration that must be capitalized.

Example 13: A farmer owns and operates a farm with several barns and outbuildings, but did not use or maintain one of the outbuildings on a regular basis, and the outbuilding fell into a state of disrepair. The outbuilding was used for storage but can no longer be used for that purpose because it is not structurally sound. The farmer shores up the walls and replaces the siding on

[26] Reg. § 1.263(a)-3(k).

[27] Reg. § 1.263(a)-3(k)(3).

[28] Reg. § 1.263(a)-3(k)(5).

the building. The farmer must treat shoring up the walls and replacing the siding as a restoration of the building structure because the work returns the building to its ordinarily efficient operating condition. Therefore, the farmer must treat the cost as an improvement to the building and must capitalize that cost.

[A] Restoration of Damage from Casualty

The entire cost of restoring property following a casualty may not have to be capitalized, if the cost of restoration exceeds the adjusted basis of the property before the casualty. The cost for restoration of damage to property that must be capitalized following a casualty is limited to the excess (if any) of:

- The amount of the adjusted basis of the single, identifiable property (under § 1.167-7(b)(2)(i)) for determining the loss allowable on account of the casualty, over
- The amount paid for restoration of damage to the unit of property that also constitutes an improvement under any other definition of a restoration.[29]

Any cost of the restoration that exceeds the limitation is treated under otherwise applicable IRC provisions and regulations.[30]

Example 14: A storm damages a building used in a taxpayer's business when the building has an adjusted basis of $500,000. The cost of restoring the property is $750,000, and the taxpayer deducts a $500,000 casualty loss and reduces the building's basis to $0. The restoration work involves replacing the building's entire roof at a cost of $350,000 and pumping water from the building, cleaning debris from the interior and exterior, and replacing areas of damaged dry wall and flooring at a cost of $400,000. The pumping, cleaning, and replacing damaged drywall and flooring results from the casualty, but does not directly benefit and is not incurred because of the roof replacement.

The taxpayer must capitalize as an improvement the $350,000 cost of replacing the roof because it is a major component and a substantial structural part of the building. The taxpayer also must treat as a restoration a portion of the remaining cost, limited to the excess of the adjusted basis of the building over the cost of the improvement, that is, $150,000 ($500,000 - $350,000). The taxpayer is not required to capitalize the remaining $250,000 repair and cleaning costs as a restoration following a casualty.

[B] Replacement of a Major Component or a Substantial Structural Part

The regulations state that whether the replacement of a part or a combination of parts comprise a major component or a substantial structural part of the property under paragraph 6, above, depends on all the facts and circumstances, including

[29] Reg. § 1.263 (a)-3(k)(4).

[30] *See*, for example, Reg. § 1.162-4 (repairs and maintenance); Reg. § 1.263(a)-2 (costs to acquire and produce units of property); and Reg. § 1.263(a)-3 (costs to improve units of property).

the quantitative and qualitative significance of the part or combination of parts in relation to the property.

A major component is a part or combination of parts that performs a discrete and critical function in the operation of the property. An incidental component of the property, even though it performs a discrete and critical function in the operation of the property, generally does not, by itself, constitute a major component. A substantial structural part is a part or combination of parts that comprises a large portion of the physical structure of the property.[31]

In the case of a building, an amount is for the replacement of a major component or a substantial structural part of the building unit of property if:

1. The replacement includes a part or combination of parts that comprise a major component, or a significant portion of a major component, of a building, condominium, cooperative, or leased building or leased portion of a building; or
2. The replacement includes a part or combination of parts that comprises a large portion of the physical structure of a building, condominium, cooperative, or leased building or portion of a building.[32]

Example 15: A taxpayer owns a building in which it provides medical services. The building contains one HVAC system comprised of three furnaces, three air conditioning units, and duct work that runs throughout the building. One furnace in the building breaks down, and the taxpayer replaces it with a new furnace. The three furnaces, together, perform a discrete and critical function in the operation of the HVAC system (providing heat) and are a major component of the HVAC system. The single furnace, however, is not a significant portion of this major component of the HVAC system or a substantial structural part of the HVAC system. The taxpayer is not required to treat the cost of replacing the furnace as a restoration of the building.

Example 16: A consulting firm provides consulting services from a large office building that it owns. The building contains one HVAC system comprised of one chiller unit, one boiler, pumps, duct work, diffusers, air handlers, outside air intake, and a cooling tower. The chiller unit includes the compressor, evaporator, condenser, and expansion valve, and it functions to cool the water used to generate air conditioning throughout the building. The firm replaces the chiller with a comparable unit.

The HVAC system, including the chiller unit, is a building system and the chiller unit performs a discrete and critical function in the operation of the HVAC system because it provides the cooling mechanism for the entire system. Therefore, the chiller unit is a major component of the HVAC system. Because the chiller unit comprises a major component of a building system, the firm must treat its replacement as a restoration to the building and must capitalize its cost as an improvement to the building.

[31] Reg. § 1.263(a)-3(k)(6)(i).

[32] Reg. § 1.263(a)-3(k)(6)(ii).

Example 17: A supply company owns a building from which it supplies its customers. The building contains a HVAC system that incorporates ten roof-mounted units that provide heating and air conditioning. The HVAC system also consists of controls for the entire system and duct work that distributes the heated or cooled air. After the company experiences climate control problems in various areas of the building, the company replaces three of the roof-mounted heating and cooling units. No work is performed on the other roof-mounted heating and cooling units, the duct work, or the controls.

The HVAC system, including the ten roof-mounted heating and cooling units, is a building system. As the components that generate the heat and the air conditioning in the HVAC system, the ten roof-mounted units, together, perform a discrete and critical function in the operation of the system and, therefore, are a major component of the system. The three roof-mounted heating and cooling units are not a significant portion or a substantial structural part of the 10-unit major component of the HVAC system. Accordingly, the company is not required to treat the replacement of the three roof-mounted heating and cooling units as a restoration of the building.[33]

[C] Previous Case Law

Prior to the adoption of the repair regulations, the replacement of major components of a building generally were treated as capital expenditures. With no bright-line tests in the regulations, case law before the adoption of the regulations may be helpful in determining whether "the facts and circumstances" point to the replacement of a major component or substantial structural part. For example, the replacement of attic beams and the installation of a support girder in a crawl space are capital expenditures.[34] Other examples of replacements as capital expenditures are:

- Carpet, drapery, and refrigerator replacements in rental property;[35]
- Electrical system replacement in an office building;[36]
- Flooring (new) laid on top of old flooring, lumber and labor;[37]
- Furnace and water heater (new) in rental property;[38]
- Roof, doors, and carpeting (all new) for an office building;[39]
- Sewer replacement and reconnection of the lines;[40]
- Windows (new);[41]

[33] Additional examples may be found in Reg. § 1.263(a)-3(k)(7).

[34] M. Mozayeny, 53 TCM 566, CCH Dec. 43,835(M), T.C. Memo. 1987-188.

[35] J.J. Otis, 73 TC 671, CCH Dec. 36,716.

[36] A.F. Harris, 55 TCM 769, CCH Dec. 44,751(M), T.C. Memo. 1988-195.

[37] Standard Fruit Product Co., 8 TCM 733, CCH Dec. 17,159(M).

[38] B. Davis, 37 TCM 42, CCH Dec. 34,914(M), T.C. Memo. 1978-12; C.M. Hill, Jr., 45 TCM 821, CCH Dec. 39,930(M), T.C. Memo. 1983-112.

[39] R.O. Watts, 34 TCM 613, CCH Dec. 33,184(M), T.C. Memo. 1975-131.

[40] Standard Fruit Product Co., 8 TCM 733, CCH Dec. 17,159(M).

[41] B.T. Wright, Inc., 12 BTA 1149, CCH Dec. 4200, *nonacq.* 1929-1 CB 62.

- Wooden floor replacement in an old building that was to be used for business purposes; and[42]
- Wooden stairway replacement with steel stairway.[43]

.04 Adaptation of Property

An amount is paid to adapt a unit of property to a new or different use if the adaptation is not consistent with the taxpayer's intended ordinary use of the unit of property at the time originally placed in service by the taxpayer.[44]

In the case of a building, an amount is paid to improve a building if it is paid to adapt to a new or different use a building, condominium, cooperative, or leased building or leased portion of a building. For instance, an amount is paid to improve a building if it is paid to adapt the building structure or any one of its buildings systems to a new or different use.[45]

Example 18: A manufacturing company owns a building that it has used for 30 years for manufacturing. The company now converts its manufacturing building into a showroom for its business. To convert the facility, the company removes and replaces various structural components to provide a better layout for the showroom and its offices. It also repaints the building interiors as part of the conversion. In the conversion, the company uses comparable and commercially available replacement materials as compared to the materials removed.

The conversion of the manufacturing building into a showroom adapts the building structure to a new or different use because the conversion to a showroom is not consistent with the company's ordinary use of the building when it was placed in service. Therefore, the company must capitalize the cost of converting the building into a showroom as an improvement.

Example 19: A developer owns and leases out space in a building consisting of twenty retail spaces. The space was designed to be reconfigured; that is, adjoining spaces could be combined into one space. One of the tenants expands its occupancy by leasing two adjoining retail spaces. To facilitate the new lease, the developer pays to remove the walls between the three retail spaces. Assume that the walls between spaces are part of the building and its structural components.

The conversion of three retail spaces into one larger space for an existing tenant does not adapt the developer's building structure to a new or different use because the combination of retail spaces is consistent with the developer's intended, ordinary use of the building. Therefore, the cost to remove the walls does not improve the building and is not required to be capitalized.[46]

---

[42] La France Wine Co., 33 TCM 1130, CCH Dec. 32,786(M), T.C. Memo. 1974-254.

[43] O.L. Thomas, 21 TCM 708, CCH Dec. 25,526(M), T.C. Memo. 1981-128.

[44] Reg. § 1.263(a)-3(l).

[45] Reg. § 1.263(a)-3(l)(2).

[46] Additional examples may be found in Reg. § 1.263(a)-3(l)(3).

.05 Abandonment of Improvement Plans

A loss incurred in a business or in a transaction entered into for profit and arising from the sudden termination of the usefulness of any nondepreciable property is allowed as a deduction under Code Sec. 165(a) for the taxable year in which the loss is actually sustained.[47]

For example, an architect's fees for a proposed building are a deductible loss for the taxable year in which the project is abandoned.[48] The same principle should apply to the abandonment of plans to improve or renovate an existing building. A current loss deduction should be available if it is clear that the plans have been completely abandoned and that the expense incurred has no further value to the taxpayer. In *R.B. Haspel*,[49] a loss deduction for the abandonment of an architect's plans was denied because the original plans were used or incorporated in part in later plans by a different architect.

In *Roux Laboratories, Inc.*,[50] an abandonment loss was allowed for the cost of plans drawn by an architectural firm for a building that was different from the one that the corporation eventually built. However, the corporation could not claim an abandonment loss for the cost of the materials handling consultant's report on which the original design was based because the report was of continued use to the corporation in making plans for its new building.

The cost of attempting to obtain a zoning change, if unsuccessful, also may be taken as an abandonment loss under Code Sec. 165.[51] But again, the project for which the zoning change is sought must be completely abandoned before there is a loss.[52]

When an improvement or replacement does not work out as intended, it does not mean that the cost of the improvement or replacement can be taken as an abandonment loss. For example, no loss was allowed for a marble floor that became defective and was covered with carpeting. The asset, which remained in the taxpayer's possession, was not completely abandoned but remained as a subfloor beneath the carpeting.[53] An abandonment loss has also been denied for one flooded apartment in an apartment complex that was converted to guestrooms and a clubhouse.[54]

¶ 802 SPECIAL AMORTIZATION PROVISIONS

Some capital expenditures, as permitted by the Internal Revenue Code, may be amortized rather than added to basis and recovered through depreciation or on the sale or other disposition of the property. Amortization, in this case, is the ratable writeoff or deduction of the costs involved over some specified period. In the case of real property, the special amortization provisions that may apply are those for the

[47] Reg. § 1.165-2(a).

[48] Western Wheeled Scraper Co., 14 BTA 496, CCH Dec. 4547, *acq.* and *nonacq.* 1929-1 CB 48, 61.

[49] 62 TC 59, CCH Dec. 32,549.

[50] DC Fla., 76-2 USTC ¶ 9751.

[51] Chevy Chase Land Co. of Montgomery County, Md., 72 TC 481, CCH Dec. 36,127.

[52] J.R. Clem, 10 TCM 1248, CCH Dec. 18,718(M); G. Weiss, CA-8, 55-1 USTC ¶ 9365, 221 F.2d 152.

[53] Wauwatosa Colony, Inc., 25 TCM 298, CCH Dec. 27,873(M), T.C. Memo. 1966-51.

[54] E.V. Scott, 38 TCM 115, CCH Dec. 35,839(M), T.C. Memo. 1979-29.

cost of pollution control facilities and for certain reforestation expenses. Soil and water conservation expenditures, although technically not subject to special amortization since they are eligible for an immediate, although limited, deduction, are also covered in this section.

.01 Pollution Control Facilities

Individuals and businesses may elect to amortize the cost of certified pollution control equipment over a period of 60 months.[55] The amortization deduction is available for treatment facilities that are used to abate or control water or air pollution in connection with any plant or other property.[56] In this regard, "plant or other property" includes any tangible property, whether or not the property is used in a trade or business or held for the production of income. For example, pollution control facilities or equipment installed in connection with paper mills, motor vehicles, or furnaces in an apartment house would all be eligible for the 60-month amortization.[57]

[A] Amortization Election Requirements

A taxpayer who wants to elect the 60-month amortization for pollution control facilities generally must meet the following requirements contained in Code Sec. 169(d):

1. The pollution control facility must abate or control water or air pollution or contamination by removing, altering, disposing, storing or preventing the creation or emission of pollutants, contaminants, wastes, or heat.
2. The pollution control facility must be new tangible property. Buildings and their structural components generally do not qualify as pollution control facilities. However, if a building is used exclusively as a treatment facility, it does qualify.
3. The pollution control facility must be used in connection with a plant or other property that was in operation before January 1, 1976.
4. The state certifying authority must certify that the pollution control facility is in conformity with the state program or requirements for pollution control.
5. The Environmental Protection Agency must certify the pollution control facility.[58]
6. The pollution control facility must not significantly increase the output or capacity, extend the useful life, or reduce the total operating costs of the plant or property to which it relates.
7. The pollution control facility must not alter the nature of the manufacturing or production process or facility.

The 60-month amortization period begins with the month following the month in which the pollution control facility is completed or acquired or with the first

---

[55] Code Sec. 169(a).

[56] Reg. § 1.169-2(a)(2).

[57] Reg. § 1.169-2(a)(4).

[58] The EPA issued regulations are at Reg. § 1.602-1—§ 1.602-10.

month of the next taxable year.[59] The procedure for filing the election is contained in Reg. § 1.169-4. An election to amortize pollution control costs may be discontinued or revoked at any time. Any unamortized pollution control facility cost that is unamortized when the election is discontinued is added to basis and recovered through normal depreciation rules.[60] A taxpayer may not renew the election to amortize pollution control facility costs once the original election has been terminated.

Corporations are subject to a 20 percent reduction in tax preferences under Code Sec. 291. Accordingly, only 80 percent of the cost of certified pollution control facilities may be amortized over 60 months by a corporation.[61] The 20 percent that is not eligible is recovered under the normal depreciation rules.

[B] Limitation for Longer-Lived Facilities

The amortizable cost of pollution control facilities is limited in the case of facilities that have a useful life for depreciation purposes of more than 15 years.[62] This limitation, therefore, affects only pollution control facilities that come within the 20-year class of depreciable property or residential rental property (27.5-year depreciation period) or nonresidential real property (39-year depreciation period).

Under the limitation, only the portion of the pollution control facility cost that bears the same ratio to total cost as 15 years bears to the depreciable life of the facility is eligible for the 60-month amortization. The excess cost that is not amortizable over 60 months is added to basis and recovered under the normal depreciation rules.[63] (Depreciation is the subject of Chapter 9.)

> ***Example 20:*** A corporation constructs a building that is used exclusively as a treatment facility and qualifies as a certified pollution control facility. The cost of the treatment facility is $100,000 and it has a depreciable life of 39 years.
>
> The amortizable basis of this pollution control facility is $38,462 ($100,000 × 15.0/39). This amount must be further reduced by 20 percent because the taxpayer is a corporation. This reduction is $7,692, leaving $30,770 to be amortized over 60 months at a rate of $512.83 per month. The $69,230 portion of the total cost of the pollution control facility that the corporation may not amortize over 60 months may be recovered under the normal depreciation rules over the 39-year depreciable life of the building.

[C] Special Rule for Air Pollution Control Facilities

A certified air pollution control facility placed in service after April 11, 2005, and used in connection with a coal-fired electric generation plant is eligible for amortization regardless of whether the associated plant or other property was in operation before 1976. In the case of a facility used in connection with a plant that was not in operation before 1976, however, the amortization period is 84 months

[59] Code Sec. 169(b).

[60] Code Sec. 169(c).

[61] Code Sec. 291(a)(5).

[62] Code Sec. 169(f)(2).

[63] Code Sec. 169(g).

rather than 60 months.[64] Further, the facility must be completed after April 11, 2005, or acquired after April 11, 2005, if the original use of the facility begins with the taxpayer after that date.

.02 Reforestation Expenses

Under Code Sec. 194, for expenses incurred before October 23, 2004, a taxpayer may, over a period of 84 months, amortize up to $10,000 ($5,000 in the case of a separate return) of reforestation expenses for qualified timber property incurred in a single tax year rather than adding the expenses to cost basis. The amortization period begins on the first day of the first month of the last half of the taxable year during which the taxpayer incurs the reforestation expenses.[65] If the taxpayer disposes of qualified timber property, the amortization deductions may be recaptured as ordinary income.[66]

For reforestation costs paid or incurred after October 22, 2004, a taxpayer may deduct up to $10,000 of qualified reforestation expenditures in the year paid or incurred.[67] Qualified reforestation expenditures above $10,000 in any one year may be amortized over 84 months.[68]

Qualified timber property for which reforestation expenses may be deducted or amortized over 84 months is property located in the United States which will contain trees in significant commercial quantities and which the taxpayer holds for the growing and cutting of trees for sale or use in the commercial production of timber products.[69] The property may be a woodlot or other site, but must consist of at least one acre that is planted with tree seedlings in the manner normally used in forestation or reforestation.[70] Allowable reforestation expenses are limited to the direct costs incurred to plant or seed for forestation or reforestation purposes. Qualifying expenditures include site preparation, seed or seedlings, and labor and tool costs, including depreciation on equipment used in the planting or seeding.[71] Only costs that must be capitalized and are included in the adjusted basis of the property qualify as reforestation expenditures. Costs that are otherwise currently deductible do not qualify.[72]

In the case of a partnership, the $10,000 limit applies at the partnership as well as the partner level.[73] Similar rules apply to S corporations.[74]

If a taxpayer is reimbursed under any governmental reforestation cost-sharing program, the expenditures do not qualify as reforestation expenses, unless the reimbursed amounts are included in the taxpayer's gross income.[75] The procedure for electing to amortize reforestation expenses is contained in Reg. § 1.194-4.

---

64 Code Sec. 169(d)(5).
65 Reg. § 1.194-1(b).
66 Reg. § 1.194-1(c).
67 Code Sec. 194(b).
68 Code Sec. 194(c)(2).
69 Code Sec. 194(c)(1).
70 Reg. § 1.194-3(a).
71 Code Sec. 194(c)(3).
72 Reg. § 1.194-3(c).
73 Reg. § 1.194-2(b)(5)(ii).
74 Reg. § 1.194-2(b)(6).
75 Code Sec. 194(c)(3)(B).

.03 Soil and Water Conservation Expenditures

A taxpayer engaged in the business of farming may treat expenditures for soil and water conservation or to prevent erosion or for endangered species recovery as current deductions rather than adding these costs to the basis of the land.[76] There is, however, an annual limit of 25 percent of the taxpayer's gross income from farming on the amount that the taxpayer can currently deduct.[77] Also, the expenditures that are eligible for this special treatment are limited to those that are consistent with a conservation plan approved by the Soil Conservation Service of the U.S. Department of Agriculture or the recovery plan approved under the Endangered Species Act of 1973 or, in the absence of a federally approved plan, a plan of a comparable state agency.[78]

The expenditures that are eligible for the special deduction include the cost of the treatment or moving of earth, such as leveling, grading, terracing, and contour furrowing, and the construction, control, and the protection of diversion channels, drainage ditches, earthen dams, watercourses, outlets, and ponds. The cost of eradicating brush and planting windbreaks is also eligible for the current deduction, as are expenditures to achieve site-specific management actions under endangered species recovery plans.[79]

The deduction for soil and water conservation and endangered species recovery expenditures, however, applies only to nondepreciable items. Taxpayers may not deduct expenditures for the purchase, construction, installation, or improvement of structures, appliances, or facilities subject to depreciation. The deduction is available for earthen items that are not subject to depreciation. For example, expenditures for structures such as tanks, reservoirs, pipes, conduits, canals, dams, wells, or pumps composed of masonry, concrete, tile, metal, or wood do not qualify, but expenditures for earthen terraces and dams that are nondepreciable do qualify.[80]

A taxpayer engaged in the business of farming may take a current deduction for the cost of fertilizer, lime, and similar items that are used to enrich, neutralize, or condition the land.[81] The current deduction is available for these items even though the effect on the land extends beyond one year and the cost would otherwise be treated as a capital expenditure.[82]

¶ 803 ENERGY EFFICIENT COMMERCIAL BUILDINGS DEDUCTION

A deduction is available for energy-efficient commercial building property expenditures.[83] The deduction applies to property placed in service after 2005 and before 2018 (unless again extended by Congress) and is limited to $1.80 per square foot of the property for which the expenditures are made. The deduction is allowed in the year in which the property is placed in service.[84] The deduction reduces the basis of the property.[85]

---

76 Code Sec. 175.

77 Code Sec. 175(b).

78 Code Sec. 175(c)(3).

79 Code Sec. 175(c)(3).

80 Reg. § 1.175-2(b).

81 Code Sec. 180.

82 *See*, for example, I.T. 3843, 1947-1 CB 12, holding that the cost of lime spread on farmland is a capital expenditure if the effectiveness of the lime extends substantially beyond the taxable year.

83 Code Sec. 179D.

84 Code Sec. 179D(b).

85 Code Sec. 179D(e).

To qualify for the deduction, the property must be:

1. Installed on or in any building located in the United States that is within the scope of Standard 90.1-2007 of the American Society of Heating, Refrigerating, and Air Conditioning Engineers and the Illuminating Engineering Society of North America (as in effect on the day before the adoption of Standard 90.1-2010);
2. Installed as part of the interior lighting systems, the heating, cooling, ventilation, and hot water systems, or the building envelope; and
3. Certified as being installed as part of a plan designed to reduce the total annual energy and power costs for the interior lighting systems, heating, cooling, ventilation, and hot water systems of the building by 50 percent or more in comparison to a reference building that meets the minimum requirements of Standard 90.1-2007.[86]

If a building does not meet the overall requirement of a 50 percent energy savings, a partial deduction is allowed for each separate building system certified by a qualified professional as meeting or exceeding the applicable system-specific savings targets established by the IRS. The maximum allowable deduction is $0.60 per square foot for each separate system.[87] Interim rules are provided for lighting systems until the IRS issues final regulations establishing system-specific targets.[88] Also, the IRS has issued Notice 2006-52[89] that sets forth a process that allows a taxpayer who owns, or is a lessee of, a commercial building and installs property as part of the commercial building's interior lighting systems, heating, cooling, ventilation, and hot water systems, or building envelope to obtain a certification that the property satisfies the energy efficiency requirements of Code Secs. 179D(c)(1) and (d). This notice also provides for a public list of software programs that must be used in calculating energy and power consumption for purposes of Code Sec. 179D.

¶ 804 TAX CREDITS FOR BUILDING REHABILITATIONS

Before 1986, an investment tax credit was available for the purchase or construction of tangible personal property for use in a trade or business. The credit of up to ten percent of the cost of qualifying property was not available for buildings or their structural components. In 1978, Congress expanded the investment credit to encourage the rehabilitation of existing commercial buildings and historic structures. When Congress repealed the regular investment credit in 1986, it largely left intact the credits for real estate rehabilitations. A ten percent credit is available generally for the rehabilitation of older commercial buildings before 2018, and a 20 percent credit is available for the rehabilitation of certified historic structures.[90] The Tax Cuts and Jobs Act[91] repealed the ten percent credit for the rehabilitation of older commercial buildings, and requires that the 20 percent credit for the rehabilitation of certified historic structures after 2017 be taken over a five-year period.

---

[86] Code Sec. 176D(c).
[87] Code Sec. 179D(d).
[88] Code Sec. 179D(f).
[89] 2006-26 IRB 1175.
[90] Code Sec. 47(a).
[91] P.L. 115-97.

The changes to the rehabilitation credit made by the Tax Cuts and Jobs Act generally apply to amounts paid or incurred after December 31, 2017. A transition rules provides that in the case of qualified rehabilitation expenditures (for either a certified historic structure or a pre-1936 building) for any building owned or leased by the taxpayer at all times on and after January 1, 2018, the 24-month period, or the 60-month period selected under the rule for phased rehabilitations, begins not later than the end of the 180-day period beginning on December 22, 2017. The changes made by the Tax Cuts and Jobs Act apply to rehabilitation expenditures paid or incurred after the end of the tax year in which the 24-month or 60-month period ends.

The investment credit for rehabilitation expenditures is included with other credits that make up the general business credit of Code Sec. 38 for purposes of applying the ceiling on credits measured by tax liability. The other tax credits that are combined with the investment credit (which is made up of the rehabilitation, energy, advanced coal project, the gasification project, advanced-energy project, and therapeutic discovery project credits) are: work opportunity credit, alcohol fuel credit, incremental research credit, low-income housing credit, enhanced oil recovery credit, disabled access credit, renewable electricity production credit, empowerment zone employment credit, Indian employment credit, credit for taxes on employee tips, orphan drug credit, new markets tax credit, small employer pension plan startup cost credit, employer-provided child care credit, railroad track maintenance credit, biodiesel fuel credit, low sulfur diesel fuel production credit, marginal oil and gas well production credit, distilled spirits credit, advanced nuclear power facility production credit, nonconventional source fuel production credit, energy efficient home credit, energy efficient appliance credit, alternative motor vehicle credit attributable to business property, alternative fuel vehicle refueling property credit attributable to business property, mine rescue team training credit, agricultural chemicals security credit, differential wage payment credit, carbon dioxide sequestration credit, plug-in electric drive motor vehicle credit, the small employer health insurance credit, and the paid family and medical leave credit.

The general business credit for any year (other than the empowerment zone employment credit) cannot be more than the taxpayer's net income tax over the greater of the tentative minimum tax for the tax year, or 25 percent of the taxpayer's net regular tax liability in excess of $25,000.[92] (The limitation for the empowerment zone employment credit and the portion of the work opportunity credit for the New York Liberty Zone are figured separately.) Unused credits are subject to carryback and carryover rules.[93]

The tentative minimum tax is treated as zero for purposes of determining the tax liability limitation for alcohol fuels credit, low-income housing credit, renewable electricity production credit, credit for taxes paid on employee tips, railroad track maintenance credit, small employer health insurance credit, work opportunity credit, and the energy and rehabilitation portions of the investment credit. In other words, these credits may offset the alternative minimum tax.[94]

---

[92] Code Sec. 38(c)(1).

[93] Code Sec. 39.

[94] Code Sec. 38(c)(4).

The rehabilitation credit is treated as a tax credit from real estate in which an investor actively participates, so that the limitation on passive losses does not apply, and an individual investor may use credit equivalents to shelter up to $25,000 of income per year from non-passive sources. This $25,000 allowance is phased out for investors with adjusted gross incomes of $200,000 or more at a rate of 50 cents to the dollar in excess of $200,000. See Chapter 11 for a discussion of the passive loss limitations.

The tax credits for rehabilitating qualifying buildings are substantial inducements to renovate rather than relocate. Also, in appropriate cases, the purchase of older buildings, rather than new construction, may be more attractive because of the credits. These important tax incentives are discussed in the following materials.

The IRS has provided a safe harbor for partnerships and their partners under which it will not challenge allocations of rehabilitation credits to the partners. The safe harbor provides a partnership and its partners with more certainty regarding allocation of rehabilitation credits.[95]

.01 Rehabilitation of Older Commercial Buildings

A tax credit of ten percent of the qualified rehabilitation expenditures paid or incurred before 2018 is available for buildings other than historic structures. A qualified rehabilitation is treated as an acquisition of new property, so that the used-property limitations that applied to the investment credit prior to 1991 do not apply to rehabilitation credits.[96] Should property that qualifies for the rehabilitation credit also qualify for energy credits, the energy credits may not be taken for the same expenditures.[97]

In order to qualify for the credit, the building that is being rehabilitated must have been originally placed in service before 1936.[98] In addition, the building must not be used for residential purposes other than on a transient basis.[99] This latter requirement excludes buildings such as apartment buildings from eligibility for the credit. Otherwise, all older buildings used for business or productive purposes qualify, including stores, warehouses, factories, hotels, and office buildings. The type of building is determined following the rehabilitation, so that an apartment building that was built before 1936 that is converted into an office building in a qualifying rehabilitation qualifies for the ten percent tax credit.

In addition to the requirement that the building have been first placed in service before 1936, a building must meet the following three additional requirements in order for rehabilitation expenditures to qualify for the credit:

1. The building must be substantially rehabilitated;[100]
2. The building must have been placed in service before the beginning of the rehabilitation, but not necessarily by the taxpayer claiming the credit;[101] and

[95] For the details regarding this safe harbor, *see* Rev. Proc. 2014-12, 2014-3 IRB 415, as modified by T.D. 9872.

[96] Former Code Sec. 48(g)(4), as in effect prior to 1991.

[97] Code Sec. 48(a)(2)(B).

[98] Code Sec. 47(c)(1)(B).

[99] Code Sec. 50(b)(2).

[100] Code Sec. 47(c)(1)(A)(i).

[101] Code Sec. 47(c)(1)(A)(ii).

3. The building must retain in place 50 percent or more of its existing external walls as external walls, 75 percent of its existing external walls as external or internal walls, and 75 percent of its existing internal structural framework.[102]

Expenditures that qualify for the credit are capital expenditures for depreciable property that is nonresidential real property, residential rental property (but only in the case of historic structures), real property with a class life of more than 12.5 years, and an addition or improvement to these classes of property.[103] The expenditures must be made in connection with the rehabilitation of a qualified rehabilitated building that meets all of the requirements set out above.[104] Expenditures for work done to various facilities related to a building, such as sidewalks, parking lots, and landscaping, are not treated as made in connection with the rehabilitation of a qualified rehabilitated building.[105]

[A] Substantial Rehabilitation Test

Rehabilitation expenditures do not qualify for the credit unless the building is "substantially rehabilitated." A building is substantially rehabilitated if the qualified rehabilitation expenditures for a 24-month period selected by the taxpayer and ending within the taxable year exceed the greater of (1) $5,000, and (2) the adjusted basis of the building and its structural components as of the first day of the 24-month period or of the holding period of the building, whichever is later.[106] Note that the adjusted basis used to determine whether a rehabilitation is substantial does not include the basis of land. Careful allocation of cost on the purchase of an older building and land may make it easier to obtain the rehabilitation credit at a later time.

The 24-month rehabilitation period may be extended to 60 months if the rehabilitation will be completed in phases. Architectural plans and specifications for the phased rehabilitation, however, must be completed before the rehabilitation begins for the 60-month period to apply.[107]

The substantial rehabilitation test is illustrated by the following example, adapted from Reg. § 1.48-12(b)(2)(x).

> ***Example 21:*** The Taxpayer who is on the calendar year purchases a building for $140,000 on January 1, 2014. The Taxpayer incurs qualified rehabilitation expenditures of $48,000 ($4,000 per month) in 2014, $100,000 in 2015, and $20,000 ($2,000 per month) in the first ten months of 2016. The rehabilitation does not qualify as a phased rehabilitation because plans did not exist before work began. The Taxpayer places the building in service on October 31, 2016.
>
> The Taxpayer may select any 24-month measuring period that ends in 2016 for purposes of meeting the substantial rehabilitation test. The Taxpayer

[102] Code Sec. 47(c)(1)(A)(iii). Requirements (1) and (3) are explored at ¶¶ 804.01[A] and 804.01[C].

[103] Code Sec. 47(c)(2)(A)(i).

[104] Code Sec. 47(c)(2)(A)(ii).

[105] Reg. § 1.48-12(c)(5).

[106] Code Sec. 47(c)(1)(C)(i); Reg. § 1.48-12(b)(2).

[107] Code Sec. 47(c)(1)(C)(ii); Reg. § 1.48-12(b)(2)(v).

selects the period that begins on February 1, 2014, and ends on January 31, 2016. The Taxpayer's basis in the building was $144,000 on February 1, 2014 ($140,000 plus $4,000 of rehabilitation expenditures incurred during January 2014). The amount of qualified rehabilitation expenditures incurred during the measuring period is $146,000 ($44,000 from February 1 to December 31, 2014, plus $100,000 in 2015, plus $2,000 in January 2016).

The building is treated as "substantially rehabilitated" for the Taxpayer's 2016 tax year because the $146,000 of expenditures incurred during the measuring period exceeded the taxpayer's adjusted basis of $144,000 at the beginning of the period. If the other requirements are met, the building is treated as a qualified rehabilitated building, and the Taxpayer has $168,000 of qualified rehabilitation expenditures ($146,000 incurred during the measuring period, $4,000 incurred before the beginning of the measuring period, and $18,000 incurred after the measuring period and during the year in which the measuring period ends).

The result would generally be the same if the property attributable to the rehabilitation expenditures were placed in service as the expenditures were incurred, but the Taxpayer would have $148,000 of qualified rehabilitation expenditures for 2015 and $20,000 for 2016.

[B] Expenditures Incurred by Predecessor

If rehabilitation expenditures are incurred for a building by a person other than the taxpayer and the taxpayer subsequently acquires the building or a portion of the building to which some or all of the expenditures are allocable (for example, a condominium unit), the taxpayer acquiring the property is treated as having incurred the rehabilitation expenditures actually incurred by the transferor if:

1. The building or portion of the building acquired by the taxpayer was not used or placed in service after the rehabilitation expenditures were incurred and prior to the date of acquisition, and
2. No credit for the qualified rehabilitation expenditures is claimed by anyone other than the taxpayer acquiring the property.[108]

How this rule affects the substantial rehabilitation requirement is illustrated in the following example.

Example 22: The Seller owns a building with a basis of $10,000, and the Seller incurs $5,000 of rehabilitation expenditures. Before completing the rehabilitation project, the Seller sells the building to the Buyer for $30,000. The Buyer is treated as having incurred the $5,000 of rehabilitation expenditures actually incurred by the Seller. Because the Buyer's basis in the building is $30,000, which includes the property attributable to the Seller's rehabilitation expenditures, the Buyer's basis for purposes of the substantial rehabilitation test is reduced to $25,000 ($30,000 cost basis less the $5,000 rehabilitation expenditure treated as incurred by the Buyer). The Buyer, therefore, would be required to incur more than $20,000 of rehabilitation expenditures, in addition

[108] Reg. § 1.48-12(c)(3)(ii).

to the $5,000 incurred by the Seller and treated as having been incurred by the Buyer, during a measuring period selected by the Buyer in order to satisfy the substantial rehabilitation test.

[C] The "Wall Test"

A building must meet the "wall test" in order to be considered a qualified rehabilitated building. This three-part test requires that 50 percent or more of the existing external walls be retained in place as external walls. Moreover, 75 percent of existing external walls must be retained as internal or external walls and 75 percent of the existing internal structural framework of the building must be retained in place.

The measurement of the walls is based on the total area of the walls, including both the supporting and nonsupporting elements. Therefore, a curtain, window, or door is counted in measuring the area of an external wall. An "external wall" is a wall that has one face exposed to the weather, earth, or an abutting wall of an adjacent building. A party wall, that is, a single wall shared with an adjacent building, also is considered an external wall, provided that the shared wall has no windows or doors in any portion of the wall that does not have one face exposed to the weather, earth, or an abutting wall.

External walls generally include only those walls that form part of the outline or perimeter of the building or that surround an uncovered courtyard. The walls of an uncovered internal shaft, such as a light well in the center of a building that is designed solely to bring light or air into the center of a building, which are completely surrounded by external walls and which enclose space not designed for use by people, are not considered external walls. Walls surrounding an outdoor space that is usable by people, however, such as a courtyard, are external walls.[109]

The "internal structural framework" includes all load-bearing internal walls and any other internal structural supports that are essential to the stability of the building. Internal supports include such things as columns, girders, beams, trusses, spandrels, and all other essential members.[110]

An external wall is retained in place even if it is covered with siding or is reinforced. Doors and windows may be replaced, enlarged, or eliminated. An existing curtain may be replaced, provided that the structural framework that supports the existing curtain is retained. The external wall may be disassembled and reassembled if the same supporting elements are used. For example, original bricks may be removed, cleaned and replaced to form the wall. An existing external wall is not retained in place, however, if the supporting elements of the wall are replaced by new supporting elements.[111]

> ***Example 23:*** The Taxpayer rehabilitated a building that has two external walls measuring 75' × 20' and two other external walls measuring 100' × 20'. The Taxpayer demolished one of the larger walls, including its supporting elements and constructs a new wall. Because one of the larger walls is more

[109] Reg. § 1.48-12(b)(3)(ii).

[110] Reg. § 1.48-12(b)(3)(iii).

[111] Reg. § 1.48-12(b)(3)(iv).

than 25 percent of the area of the building's external walls, the Taxpayer did not satisfy the requirement that 75 percent of external walls be retained and is not eligible for the rehabilitation credit.

Suppose, however, that the Taxpayer did not demolish the wall, but rather converted it into an internal wall by building a new external wall. In this case, the building would satisfy the external wall requirements and the building would qualify for the rehabilitation credit.

[D] Nonqualifying Expenditures

Certain expenditures are specifically excluded from the definition of qualified rehabilitation expenditures by Code Sec. 47(c)(2)(B). These nonqualifying expenditures are:

1. Expenditures for which straight line depreciation is not used, other than tax-exempt bond financed property and tax-exempt use property for which the alternative depreciation system must be used (depreciation is the subject of Chapter 9).
2. The cost of acquiring any building or an interest in any building.
3. Any expenditure attributable to the enlargement of an existing building. While rehabilitation includes renovation, restoration, or reconstruction, it does not include either enlargement or new construction. A building is enlarged if the total volume of the building is increased, but an increase in floor space that results from interior remodeling is not considered an enlargement.[112] When a new brick stair tower was attached to rehabilitated property, the IRS ruled that the outer wall of the stair tower became the outer wall for determining the volume. Because the total volume of the building was increased by the tower, the amount spent on the tower did not qualify for the credit.[113] If expenditures go to both enlargement and qualified rehabilitation, the expenditures must be apportioned between the original building and the enlargement.[114]
4. Any expenditure (with certain very limited exceptions) attributable to the rehabilitation of a certified historic structure or building in a registered historic district. These expenditures generally must qualify for the 20 percent credit discussed at ¶ 804.02.
5. Any expenditure by a lessee of a building if the remaining term of the lease is less than the depreciation period of the building when the rehabilitation is completed.[115]
6. Rehabilitation expenditures attributable to a building or portion of a building that is, or may reasonably be expected to be, tax-exempt use property. These expenditures, however, are considered in determining whether or not a building has been substantially rehabilitated.

---

[112] Reg. § 1.48-12(c)(10)(i).

[113] PLR 200518016.

[114] Reg. § 1.48-12(c)(10)(ii).

[115] *See* the discussion of investment credit considerations in connection with leasehold improvements and additions at ¶ 603.

[E] Basis Reduction by Credit Amount

The basis of rehabilitated property must be reduced by the full amount of any rehabilitation credit.[116] This basis reduction, of course, reduces future depreciation deductions that may be taken for the property.

.02 Rehabilitations of Certified Historic Structures

A taxpayer that rehabilitates an historic structure or building is entitled to a credit of 20 percent of the qualified rehabilitation expenditures.[117] This is a substantial tax incentive that has rather broad application. For historic rehabilitations after 2017, the 20 percent credit is taken over a period of five years. As long as the certification requirements are met, any type of building may qualify for the credit. Also, a certified historic structure does not have to be used for the same purpose after the rehabilitation as before the rehabilitation.

In general, the rehabilitation expenditures that qualify for the 20 percent credit are the same types of expenditures that qualified for the ten percent credit for older commercial buildings before 2018. The rehabilitation of an historic building, in addition to the certification requirements discussed below, must qualify under the same rules that applied to the ten percent credit, with the following three exceptions:

1. The building for which an historic rehabilitation credit is claimed does not have to have been originally placed in service before 1936. A building of any age qualifies, if it is a "certified historic structure."
2. The credit for the rehabilitation of historic structures is available even for residential property. An historic building may be used as an apartment building after the rehabilitation and still qualify for the credit.
3. The "wall test" for the rehabilitation of older commercial buildings does not apply. It is the opinion of Congress that the certifying procedure is sufficient to ensure that certified historic structures will be properly rehabilitated. The Senate Finance Committee, in repealing the wall test for historic structures, stated that it was expected that certification would be denied, however, when less than 75 percent of the external walls are retained.[118]

[A] Certification Requirements

The rehabilitation of an historic building or structure must be a certified rehabilitation in order to be eligible for the 20 percent credit. A certified rehabilitation is the rehabilitation of a "certified historic structure" which the Secretary of the Interior has certified to the Treasury Secretary as consistent with the historic character of the property or the district in which the property is located.[119] Taxpayers must submit plans and specifications in order to obtain the certification, and the

[116] Code Sec. 50(c).

[117] Code Sec. 47(a)(2).

[118] *See* the Senate Finance Committee Report on the Tax Reform Act of 1986.

[119] Code Sec. 47(c)(2)(C).

actual rehabilitation itself must be approved. At times, this certification process can be quite time-consuming.

A "certified historic structure" is a building and its structural components that is either (1) listed in the National Register of Historic Places or (2) located in a registered historic district and certified by the Secretary of the Interior as being of significance to the district.[120]

A registered historic district is any district that is (1) listed in the National Register of Historic Places, or (2) designated under a statute of a state or local government (if the statute is certified by the Secretary of the Interior as containing criteria that will substantially achieve the purpose of preserving and rehabilitating buildings of historic significance to the district) and is certified by the Secretary of the Interior as meeting substantially all of the requirements for the listing of districts in the National Register of Historic Places.[121]

[B] Nonqualified Buildings Credit Allowance

The ten percent credit for the rehabilitation of older commercial buildings generally was not available for certified historic structures or buildings in registered historic districts. The rehabilitation of these buildings generally must qualify for the 20 percent credit for historic rehabilitations. The ten percent rehabilitation credit, however, was available for a building in a registered historic district if the building did not qualify for the 20 percent credit, but only if the following conditions were met:

1. The building must not be a certified historic structure.[122]
2. The Secretary of the Interior must certify to the Treasury Secretary that the building is not of historic significance to the district.[123]
3. If the required certification in 2 occurs after the rehabilitation of the building begins, the taxpayer must certify to the Treasury Secretary that he or she in good faith was not aware of the certification requirement at the beginning of the rehabilitation.[124]

.03 Recapture of Rehabilitation Credits

The credits for the rehabilitation of older commercial buildings and historic structures are subject to recapture if a building for which a rehabilitation credit was taken is disposed of within five full years of the rehabilitation. Recapture also occurs if the Department of the Interior revokes or otherwise invalidates a certification after the property is placed in service or if a building, other than a historic structure, is moved from the place where it is rehabilitated after the property is placed in service. In addition, if all or a portion of a substantially rehabilitated building becomes tax-exempt use property for the first time within five years after the credit is claimed, the credit will be recaptured.[125]

[120] Code Sec. 47(c)(3)(A).

[121] Code Sec. 47(c)(3)(B).

[122] Code Sec. 47(c)(2)(B)(iv)(I).

[123] Code Sec. 47(c)(2)(B)(iv)(II).

[124] Code Sec. 47(c)(2)(B)(iv)(III).

[125] Reg. § 1.48-12(f)(3).

To the extent a credit is recaptured, it increases the taxpayer's tax liability for the year in which the recapture event occurs. The credit is recaptured on a sliding scale as provided in Code Sec. 50(a)(1). If the recapture event occurs within one year of the rehabilitation, 100 percent of the credit is recaptured; if the recapture event occurs within two years of the rehabilitation, 80 percent of the credit is recaptured; if within three years, 60 percent; if within four years, 40 percent; and if within five years, 20 percent. There is no recapture potential after five full years.

Any credit that is recaptured, in addition to increasing tax liability, is added to the basis of the property because the basis was reduced by the full amount of the credit at the time the credit was claimed.

¶ 805 LOW-INCOME HOUSING CREDIT

Over the years, Congress has provided various tax incentives to encourage the development and maintenance of low-income rental housing. Those incentives have included special accelerated depreciation, five-year amortization of rehabilitation expenses, exemption from the capitalization requirement for construction period interest and taxes, and tax-exempt bond financing for multi-family rental properties. In the Tax Reform Act of 1986, Congress repealed many of the then existing tax incentives for low-income housing and enacted a tax credit that may be claimed by owners of residential property used for low-income housing.[126]

The credit is available for the cost of new construction, the cost of rehabilitation, or the cost of acquiring existing buildings by purchase and their rehabilitation. Generally, only the cost of buildings attributable to low-income units qualifies for the credit. Cost attributable to residential units other than low-income units and cost attributable to land are not eligible for the credit. The low-income housing credit is included in the general business credit and is subject to the tax liability limitation of Code Sec. 38 and the carryback and carryover rules of Code Sec. 39.

The low-income housing credit is taken annually, generally for a period of ten years. New construction and rehabilitation expenditures for projects that were placed in service in 1987 were eligible for a credit equal to nine percent of the qualified cost each year for ten years. The acquisition cost of existing projects and the cost of newly constructed projects receiving other federal subsidies placed in service in 1987 were eligible for a credit equal to four percent of the qualified cost each year for ten years. For buildings placed in service after 1987, the credit percentages are adjusted figures. The exact percentages are redetermined each month in order to provide a total credit over the 10-year credit period equal to a present value of 70 percent of the qualified costs for new construction and rehabilitation. The credit rate is set to yield an amount with a present value equal to 30 percent of the cost if the construction or rehabilitation is financed with tax-exempt bonds or other federal subsidies. The lower credit is also available for the acquisition cost of low-income housing, whether or not construction or rehabilitation takes place.

[126] Code Sec. 42.

The low-income housing credit is treated as a tax credit from real estate in which an investor actively participates, so that the limitation on passive losses does not apply.[127]

The low-income housing credit does not reduce the basis of a project for purposes of depreciation.

.01 Overview of the Credit Process

The low-income housing credit program is jointly administered by the IRS and state tax credit allocation agencies. The following provides a brief overview of the process.

IRS Apportions Tax Credits. Code Sec. 42 directs the IRS to provide the tax credit allocating agencies of the states with information each year to compute the tax credits available to them for allocation. The allocation is limited annually to: (1) $1.75 per state resident or $2,000,000 if greater, as adjusted for inflation (for 2018, the amounts are $2.40 and $2,760,000[128]) (2) unused credits from the prior year, (3) credits initially allocated in previous years and returned in the current year, and (4) a portion of the unused tax credit returned to the IRS by other states. In calendar years 2018, 2019, 2020, and 2021, each of the inflation-adjusted dollar amounts used for computing the annual housing credit ceiling for each state is increased by multiplying the dollar amount by 1.125.[129] In effect, the otherwise applicable dollar amount for each of those four years is increased by 12.5 percent. For 2018, a state's inflation-adjusted ceiling is equal to the greater of $2.40 multiplied by a state's population or $2.76 million. With the increase of 12.5 percent, these dollar amounts are increased to $2.70 ($2.40 × 1.125) and $3.105 million ($2.76 million × 1.125).

The state allocating agencies have up to two years to award the credits to housing projects; after that time, they must return any unused credits to the IRS for reassignment to other states. When the credits have been awarded, they are usually available to the owners/investors annually for a ten-year period as long as the project continues to meet the statutory and regulatory requirements.

Developers Apply to the Allocating Agencies. To apply for low-income housing tax credits, a developer must submit a detailed proposal to an allocating agency. The proposal must describe the housing project, indicate how much it will cost, and identify the sources and uses of the funds available to finance the project's development and operations. In describing the project, the developer must identify the total number of units and the number of units expected to qualify for tax credits. To qualify for consideration, a project must:

1. Be residential rental property;
2. Maintain at least 20 percent of the available units for households earning up to 50 percent of the area's median gross income adjusted for family size, or at least 40 percent of the units for households earning up to 60 percent of the area's median gross income adjusted for family size; or at least 40

[127] *See* Chapter 11 for a discussion of the passive loss limitations.

[128] Rev. Proc. 2018-18, 2018-10 IRB 392.

[129] Code Sec. 42(h)(3)(I).

percent of the units in the project for households with income up to the imputed income limitation under the average income test;

3. Restrict the rents (including the utility charges) for tenants in low-income units to 30 percent of the 20-50, 40-60, or average income limitations;
4. Maintain habitability standards; and
5. Operate under the program's rent and income restrictions for 15 years for projects placed in service before 1990 and for 30 or more years for later projects pursuant to extended use agreements.

State Agencies Award Tax Credits. The state allocating agencies are responsible for:

1. Awarding their tax credits to qualifying projects that meet their state's qualified allocation plans; and
2. Controlling the value of the tax credits awarded to projects.

When selecting developers' proposals for tax credit awards, an allocating agency must evaluate the proposed projects against a qualified allocation plan developed in accordance with the Internal Revenue Code's requirements. The qualified allocation plan must establish a procedure for ranking the projects on the basis of how well they meet the state's identified housing priorities and meet selection criteria that are appropriate to local conditions. In addition, the plan must give preference to projects that serve the lowest income tenants and serve qualifying tenants for the longest period of time.

State housing credit agencies allocating low-income housing tax credit (LIHTC) are not required or encouraged to reject all proposals that do not obtain the approval of the locality where the project developer proposes to place the project.[130] Although Code Sec. 42 requires each local jurisdiction to have a reasonable opportunity to comment on any proposal to allocate a housing credit to a project within that jurisdiction, that requirement does not mean the locality must approve of the project. According to the IRS, the clear meaning of "reasonable opportunity to comment" is that the locality has a chance to weigh in, or even object; it does not authorize an allocating agency to abandon the responsibility to exercise its own judgment. In particular, it does not require or encourage allocating agencies to bestow veto power over projects either on local communities or on local public officials.

In awarding tax credits to a project, a state allocating agency may provide no more credits than it deems necessary to ensure the project's financial feasibility throughout the 15-year tax credit compliance period. An allocating agency must consider any proceeds or receipts expected to be generated through tax benefits, the percentage of housing credit dollar amounts used for project costs other than the cost of intermediaries, and the reasonableness of developmental and operational costs. In general, the agency must compare the proposed project's developmental costs with the nontax credit financing, both private and governmental. The difference between the development costs and the nontax credit financing is the

[130] Rev. Rul. 2016-29, 2016-2 CB 875.

financing gap. Tax credits are used to attract the equity investment needed to fill the gap, but are limited to a ceiling.

Under Code Sec. 42, the ceiling on tax credits limits the present value of the ten-year stream of tax benefits to: (1) 70 percent of the qualified basis for new construction or substantial rehabilitation of each qualified low-income building or (2) 30 percent of the qualified basis of acquired buildings that are substantially rehabilitated. To qualify as "substantial rehabilitation," the rehabilitation expenditures must equal at least ten percent of the building's cost or at least $3,000 per low-income unit, whichever is greater.

For buildings placed in service in 1987, the credit was taken at annual rates of nine percent (for the 70 percent value credit) and four percent (for the 30 percent value credit). Three types of credit are available for low-income buildings placed in service after 1987. The first type of credit is a nine percent annual credit for the cost of a new building or qualifying rehabilitation costs, without a "federal subsidy." The second type of credit is a four percent annual credit for the cost of a new building or substantial rehabilitation built with a "federal subsidy." The third type of credit is a four percent annual credit for the cost of buying an existing building for which substantial rehabilitation expenditures are also incurred. Although the three types of credits are called nine percent and nine percent credits, the nine percent and four percent figures are approximate. These figures are set each month by the IRS based upon fluctuating interest rates. A project can qualify for one of the three credits or a combination of the credits. For example, the same project can be eligible for the four percent credit, based on the cost of purchasing an existing building, and the nine percent credit, based on the amount spent to substantially rehabilitate that building.

Low-income housing tax credit amounts are based on the cost of a building and the portion of the project that low-income households occupy. The cost of acquiring, rehabilitating, and constructing a building constitutes the building's eligible basis. The portion of the eligible basis attributable to low-income units is the building's qualified basis. In general, the qualified basis excludes the costs of land, obtaining permanent financing, rent reserves, syndication, and marketing. The applicable percentage (described in the previous paragraph) of the qualified basis may be claimed annually for ten years as the low-income housing tax credit.

Low-income housing tax credit projects that use federal subsidies generally receive a smaller credit. If federally subsidized loans are used to finance substantial rehabilitation or new construction, either the eligible basis of the building must be reduced or the four percent credit must be used. Federally subsidized loans include below-market federal loans and tax-exempt financing. Projects funded by the Affordable Housing Program established under section 721 of the Financial Institutions Reform, Recovery, and Enforcement Act of 1989 (FIRREA), as well as Community Development Block Grants, are not treated as federally subsidized and, therefore, are eligible for the nine percent credit. Below-market loans made after August 10, 1993, with Homes Investment Partnership Act Funds may also qualify for the nine percent credit if 40 percent or more of the residential rental units in the building are occupied by individuals with income of 50 percent or less of the area median gross income.

State Agencies Monitor Compliance. A state agency cannot allocate low-income housing credits unless the state allocation plan contains a procedure that the agency (or an agent of, or private contractor hired by, the agency) will follow in monitoring compliance with the requirements of Code Sec. 42. The agency is required to notify the IRS of any noncompliance of which the agency becomes aware.

The requirement that a state agency monitor for compliance became effective on January 1, 1992, and applies to all buildings for which the low-income housing credit is, or has been, allowable at any time. Reg. § 1.42-5 provides the minimum standards for how a state agency must conduct its compliance monitoring activities. T.D. 8859 modified the regulations to reduce the inspection burden for new buildings and the changes were generally effective January 1, 2001. Further modifications regarding the selection of low-income units for inspection and low-income certifications for review were made in T.D. 9753, effective February 25, 2016. The temporary regulations in T.D. 9753 were finalized by T.D. 9848, effective February 26, 2019.

The compliance monitoring regulations require the owner of a project, at a minimum, to certify annually to the state agency that for the preceding 12-month period the project was in compliance with Code Sec. 42 requirements. The certification covers a variety of requirements including that the owner has received an annual income certification from each low-income tenant and documentation supporting that certification, and that each building in the project was suitable for occupancy, taking into account local health, safety, and building codes. Reg. § 1.42-5(c)(1) lists the annual certification requirements.

Owners of qualified low-income housing projects may obtain a waiver from the IRS of the annual recertification of tenant income for 100 percent low-income buildings.[131] The owner applying for the waiver for its 100 percent low-income building must: (1) complete and sign the applicable portions of Form 8877, Request for Waiver of Annual Recertification Requirement for the Low-Income Housing Credit; (2) have the state agency responsible for monitoring the building for compliance sign the applicable portion of the form; and (3) file the form with the IRS according to the instructions accompanying the form. The IRS will notify the owner whether the request for waiver has been approved or denied.

The compliance monitoring regulations require agencies to report noncompliance or failure to certify, and whether the noncompliance or failure to certify was corrected, to the IRS on Form 8823, Low-Income Housing Credit Agencies Report of Noncompliance.

Incentive for Investors. Syndicators (usually investment partnerships) are a primary source of equity financing for tax credit projects. They recruit investors who are willing to become partners (generally, limited partners) in housing projects

[131] Rev. Proc. 2004-38, 2004-2 CB 10.

that, because of rent restrictions, are generally not expected to return rental profits to investors. Rather, the investors expect, for ten years, to receive tax credits and other tax benefits, such as business loan deductions, that they can use to offset taxes. Those tax benefits (plus the possibility of cash proceeds from the sale of the project) represent the return on investment. The value of the tax benefits may vary from year to year, since the value of the tax credit depends on the number of habitable, rent-restricted units occupied by qualifying low-income households.

.02 Qualification for the Credit

The low-income housing credit is available on a per unit basis for units located in qualified buildings within qualified low-income housing projects. A low-income unit is one that is rent restricted and occupied by individuals with incomes that are 50 percent or 60 percent of the area's median gross income, depending on the minimum set-aside[132] elected by the owner of the project. A unit that is used on a transient basis does not qualify as a low-income unit. Also, a unit in a building that has four units or fewer does not qualify if the owner or a person related to the owner occupies one of the units.[133]

[A] Qualified Low-Income Building

A qualified low-income building is one that was part of a qualified low-income housing project for the 15 years beginning with the first tax year of the credit period.[134] After the end of the 15-year compliance period, the owner may elect to treat the building as not part of the project.[135]

[B] Qualified Low-Income Housing Project

The low-income housing credit is available to the owner of a qualified low-income housing project. Residential rental property qualifies as a low-income housing project for purposes of the credit if it meets all of the following requirements.

Minimum Set-Aside. To be a qualified low-income housing project, 20 percent or more of the units in the project must be occupied by tenants whose incomes are 50 percent or less of the area median gross income, adjusted for family size (the 20-50 test), or at least 40 percent of the units must be occupied by tenants whose incomes are 60 percent or less of the area median gross income, adjusted for family size (the 40-60 test).[136]

For elections made after March 23, 2018, a third test has been added for determining whether a low-income housing project qualifies for the low-income housing credit. The "average income test," is an alternative to the "20-50" test and "40-60" test for determining whether a project is a qualified low-income housing project. A project satisfies the average income test if 40 percent or more of the residential units in the project are both rent-restricted and occupied by individuals with income no greater than an "imputed income limitation" designated by the

[132] *See* ¶ 805.

[133] Code Sec. 42(i)(3).

[134] Code Sec. 42(c)(2) and 42(i)(1).

[135] Code Sec. 42(g)(5).

[136] Code Sec. 42(g)(1).

taxpayer for each unit.[137] Under this third test, the taxpayer designates an imputed income limitation for each unit taken into account in satisfying the average income test. The designated imputed income limitation for any unit must be set at 20, 30, 40, 50, 60, 70, and 80 percent of area median gross income. The average of the imputed income limitations for the units may not exceed 60 percent of the area median gross income.

The owner of the project must elect the applicable test by the due date of the tax return. A building is treated as a qualified low-income building only if the project of which it is a part meets the minimum set-aside requirement by the close of the first year of the credit period for the building.[138] A special rule is provided for multi-building projects to allow several buildings to be tested together under the minimum set-aside requirement.[139]

Income limits under the minimum set-aside requirement may be adjusted for areas with unusually low family incomes or high housing costs relative to family incomes. The designation of an insignificant portion of the gross rent of a low-income housing unit for use toward the purchase of the unit by the tenant at the end of the 15-year credit compliance period does not affect a unit's eligibility for the credit. Amounts paid to the lessor toward the purchase of a unit, however, are considered part of the gross rent in determining whether the unit meets the requirement that it be rent restricted.[140]

Rent Restriction. The gross rent charged to a tenant in a low-income unit must not exceed 30 percent of the qualifying income level for the tenant's family size in order for a project to qualify for the credit.[141] Gross rent includes utilities, other than telephone, paid by the tenant. Gross rent does not include payments under Section 8 of the U.S. Housing Act or similar rental assistance payments. A low-income tenant's payment (based on submetering) to a building owner for renewable resource energy acquired by the owner is treated as paid directly by the tenant to the person from whom the owner acquired the energy and is not considered a payment of gross rent to the owner. The gross rent paid by the tenant may exceed 30 percent of the income limit if required under the applicable federal housing program statute.[142]

State Credit Authority. Owners of qualified low-income projects may not claim a low-income housing credit without authorization by an appropriate state or local agency.[143] No credit authority is required, however, for projects financed by tax-exempt bonds subject to the private activity bond volume limitation of Code Sec. 146.

Generally, the owner of a project must obtain the allocation by the end of the calendar year in which a low-income building is placed in service.[144] A housing credit agency may authorize all or part of the credit to which the owner of a low-income project is otherwise entitled, and the owner may not claim a credit in excess

[137] Code Sec. 42(g)(1)(C).
[138] Code Sec. 42(g)(3)(A).
[139] Code Sec. 42(g)(3)(B).
[140] Code Sec. 42(g)(6).
[141] Code Sec. 42(g)(2).
[142] Code Sec. 42(g)(2)(E).
[143] Code Sec. 42(h)(1).
[144] Code Sec. 42(h)(1)(B).

of the credit dollar amount allocated to the project. State credit authority cannot increase the amount of the credit available to the owner of a low-income housing project above the amount calculated under the rules of Code Sec. 42. If the owner of a project does not use the full credit authority, the authority is lost.

Certification. The owner of a low-income housing project must certify certain information to the IRS within 90 days after the end of the first tax year for which the low-income housing credit is claimed. Certification is made on Form 8609, Low-Income Housing Credit Allocation.

.03 Calculation of the Low-Income Housing Credit

The owner of a qualified low-income housing project takes the low-income housing credit in each of ten years, beginning with the year the property is placed in service or the following tax year.[145] The amount of the credit in each year is determined by multiplying the applicable credit rate for the type of project by the qualified basis allocable to low-income units in each qualified low-income building.[146]

[A] Applicable Credit Rates

For newly constructed low-income units and rehabilitation expenditures that exceeded a specified minimum amount per unit[147] and were not federally subsidized, the credit rate for property placed in service in 1987 was nine percent. For projects placed in service after 1987, the credit rate is computed so that the present value of the ten annual credit amounts as of the beginning of the credit period equals 70 percent of the qualified basis of the low-income units. The applicable credit rates after 1987 are published monthly by the IRS and apply for the month in which the building is placed in service.[148]

For subsidized construction or rehabilitation and the acquisition of existing housing, the credit rate was four percent for 1987. After 1987, the credit rate is computed so that the present value of the ten annual credit amounts as of the beginning of the credit period equals 30 percent of the qualified basis of the low-income units.[149] A temporary minimum applicable percentage of nine percent applies for computing the low-income housing credit for newly constructed non-federally subsidized buildings placed in service after July 30, 2008, for which housing credit dollar amount allocations are made before January 1, 2014.[150]

The owner of a low-income project may elect to determine the low-income housing credit rate applicable to a building in advance of the date the building is placed in service. The election must be made when a binding commitment for the amount of housing credit allocated to the building is received from the state credit agency or when tax-exempt bonds are issued for building financed with the bonds for which no state credit authorization is required.[151]

---

145 Code Sec. 42(f)(1).

146 Code Sec. 42(a).

147 *See* ¶ 805.

148 Code Sec. 42(b)(1)(B).

149 Code Sec. 42(b)(1)(B)(ii).

150 Code Sec. 42(b)(2).

151 Code Sec. 42(b)(1)(A).

[B] Qualified Basis for Determination of Credit

Qualified basis, the amount to which the low-income housing credit rate is applied to determine the credit amount, is the portion of eligible basis allocable to low-income housing units in a building. To determine the qualified basis portion of the eligible basis of a building, multiply the eligible basis by the lesser of the "unit fraction" and the "floor space fraction."[152] The unit fraction is the number of low-income units in the building divided by the total number of residential units in the building.[153] The floor space fraction is the total floor space of the low-income units in the building divided by the total floor space of all residential units in the building.[154]

The eligible basis of a new building is its adjusted basis.[155] The eligible basis of an existing building is the sum of (1) the portion of its adjusted basis attributable to its acquisition cost, and (2) capital expenditures incurred by the owner before the end of the first tax year in the credit period for depreciable property, improvements or additions.[156] Also, an existing building must meet the following requirements:

1. The building must be acquired by purchase;
2. There must be at least ten years between the date of acquisition and the later of the date the building was last placed in service and the date of the most recent nonqualified substantial improvement of the building;
3. The building must not have been previously placed in service by the taxpayer or a related person as of the time previously placed in service; and
4. There must be a substantial rehabilitation, that is, rehabilitation expenditures during any 24-month period must equal the greater of $3,000 per low-income unit and ten percent of the building's unadjusted basis.[157]

For purposes of requirement 2 above, a nonqualified substantial improvement is a capital improvement, subject to five-year amortization as a low-income housing rehabilitation cost under Code Sec. 167(k), if the capital costs of the improvements made within a two-year period are at least 25 percent of the adjusted basis of the building as of the beginning of the 24-month period.[158] Other special rules are provided for transfers in which the buyer has a carryover basis and for certain other transfers.[159]

If non-low-income units in a building are above the average quality standard of the low-income units in the building, the portion of the adjusted basis allocable to the above-average units is not included in the eligible basis.[160] An exception is provided that includes a portion of the basis allocable to above-average units in eligible basis when the disparity is not too great.[161] Under this exception, the cost per square foot of the disproportionate unit may not exceed 15 percent of the

[152] Code Sec. 42(c).

[153] Code Sec. 42(c)(1)(C).

[154] Code Sec. 42(c)(1)(D).

[155] Code Sec. 42(d)(1).

[156] Code Sec. 42(d)(2)(A).

[157] Code Sec. 42(d)(2)(B).

[158] Code Sec. 42(d)(2)(D)(i).

[159] Code Sec. 42(d)(2)(D)(ii).

[160] Code Sec. 42(d)(3)(A).

[161] Code Sec. 42(d)(3)(B).

average cost per square foot of the low-income units. The cost of the entire disproportionate unit is excluded from eligible basis if this limit is exceeded.

The adjusted basis of any building generally is determined without regard to the basis of any property that is not residential rental property. However, the adjusted basis may include the basis of property used in common areas or provided as comparable amenities to all residential rental units in the building. Further, the adjusted basis of a building located in a qualified census tract may include the basis of property used throughout the tax year to provide a community service facility. A community service facility is one designed primarily to serve individuals whose income is 60 percent or less of area median income. Basis for a community service facility is limited to no more than ten percent of eligible basis.[162] A qualified census tract generally is one designated by HUD in which 50 percent or more of the households have an income which is less than 60 percent of the area median gross income or has a poverty rate of at least 25 percent.[163]

In Rev. Rul. 2003-77,[164] the IRS ruled that a portion of a building used throughout the year to provide services to residents as well as nonresidents is a community service facility. The facility includes a meeting room, an administrative office, a storage room, and several multi-purpose rooms. The services provided at the facility include day care, career counseling, literacy training, education (including tutorial services), recreation, and outpatient clinical health care. The services are provided free of charge or for a fee that is affordable to individuals whose income is 60 percent or less of area median income

A person who acquires an existing low-income building before the end of the prior owner's ten-year credit period generally cannot include the basis of the building in eligible basis. There is, however, an exception for the acquisition of an existing building before the end of the prior owner's 15-year compliance period for the building. In this case, the buyer steps into the shoes of the transferor and may take the credits to which the transferor would have been entitled had the transferor retained the property.[165] Under this exception, the three requirements that an existing building must meet to have eligible basis do not apply.

Special at-risk rules apply in determining qualifying basis for which a credit may be taken when the low-income housing is financed with nonrecourse financing.[166]

.04 Rehabilitation Expenditures

Expenditures to rehabilitate low-income housing are treated as separate new buildings and are eligible for the higher credit rate, if certain conditions are met.[167] The separate new building treatment applies only if the qualified basis attributable to the rehabilitation expenditures during any 24-month period is at least $6,000 per low-income unit or 20 percent of the unadjusted basis of the building, whichever is

[162] Code Sec. 42(d)(4).

[163] Code Sec. 42(d)(5).

[164] 2003-29 IRB 75.

[165] Code Sec. 42(d)(7).

[166] Code Sec. 42(k).

[167] Code Sec. 42(e).

greater.[168] The average expenditure per unit is determined at the end of the first tax year of the credit period for the expenditures.

Rehabilitation expenditures treated as a separate new building are considered placed in service at the end of the 24-month period used to compute average expenditures per unit. The requirements for an existing building to have an eligible basis do not apply when rehabilitation expenditures are treated as a new building. Rehabilitation expenditures eligible for treatment as a new building do not include:

1. Costs of acquiring property;
2. Expenditures for above-average quality units;
3. Expenditures that would not ordinarily be included in the adjusted basis of units for determining eligible basis; and
4. Cost of property that is not residential rental property.[169]

.05 Compliance and Recapture Provisions

The owner of a qualified low-income housing project is required to repay a portion of the credits taken on the project if the project ceases to meet the qualification requirements at any time during the 15-year period that begins with the first credit year.[170] If there is a reduction in the qualified basis, but the project remains a qualified low-income housing project, the recapture is limited to the portion of the credit attributable to the reduction in qualified basis.

The following are the events that trigger recapture of the low-income housing credit:

1. The project fails to meet the minimum set-aside requirements (the 20-50 or 40-60 tests);
2. The gross rent charged tenants of the low-income units exceeds 30 percent of the qualifying income levels;
3. The project obtains financing from federal subsidies or the proceeds of tax-exempt bonds;
4. The owner disposes of the interest in the project;[171] and
5. There is a decrease in the qualifying basis of the project, even though the minimum set-aside requirement continues to be met.

The first four events listed above require recapture of the credit taken for the entire project. The fifth event listed requires recapture only for the units that go out of compliance. Insignificant changes in qualified basis because of changes in the floor space of low-income housing units do not trigger recapture.[172]

[168] Code Sec. 42(e)(3).

[169] Code Sec. 42(e)(2)(B).

[170] Code Sec. 42(j).

[171] But recapture can be avoided if the owner furnishes a bond and it is expected that the building will continue to be operated as low-income housing for the remainder of the 15-year compliance period, *see* Code Sec. 42(j)(6).

[172] Code Sec. 42(j)(4)(F).

[A] Increases in Tenant Income

A low-income unit does not lose its status as a low-income unit solely because of an increase in the tenant's income. Once a unit qualifies as a low-income unit, it continues to qualify until the tenant's income exceeds 140 percent of the qualifying income level applicable to low-income units. Even after a tenant's income exceeds 140 percent of the qualifying income level, the unit continues to qualify as a low-income unit as long as the owner continues to fill vacancies in comparable or smaller units with tenants who qualify as low-income tenants.

In the case of a project for which the taxpayer has elected the average income method of qualification, if the income of the occupants of a unit increases to above 140 percent of the greater of 60 percent of area median gross income or the imputed income limitation designated for the unit, then the unit loses its status as a low-income housing unit when any residential rental unit (of a comparable or smaller size) within the same building is occupied by a new resident with income exceeding a prescribed limitation. If the newly occupied was taken into account as a low-income unit prior to becoming vacant, the limitation is the imputed income limitation designated for that unit. Otherwise the prescribed limitation is the imputed income limitation that would need to be designated for the newly occupied unit in order for the project to continue to meet the 60 percent of area median gross income requirement.

In the case of a "deep-rent skewing" set-aside, a unit is not disqualified as a low-income unit unless the tenant's income increases to more than 170 percent of the qualifying income level and a comparable unit in the project is rented to a tenant who does not qualify as a low-income individual. The owner may elect to have a qualified low-income housing project treated as a deep-rent skewed project if 15 percent or more of the low-income units in the project are occupied by tenants whose income is 40 percent or less of the area median gross income, gross rents are not more than 30 percent of the qualifying income level for the units, and the gross rent for each low-income unit does not exceed one-third of the average rent of units of comparable size that are not occupied by tenants who meet the applicable income limit.

For projects that elect the average income method for qualification, if the income of the occupants of a unit in a deep-rent skewed project increases to above 170 percent of the greater of 60 percent of area median gross income or the imputed income limitation designated for the unit, then the unit loses its status as a low-income housing unit when any low income unit in the building is occupied by a new resident with income exceeding the lesser of 40 percent of area median gross income or the imputed income limitation designated for the unit.

There is also the question of what happens when individuals move into a residential unit in an existing building on or after a taxpayer acquires the existing building for rehabilitation and their incomes increase before the beginning of the first tax year of the building's credit period. Some taxpayers have required that the individuals' incomes not exceed the income limitation at the beginning of the first tax year of the building's credit period, even though the individuals' income did not exceed the income limitation when the individuals moved into the unit. According to the IRS, this has resulted in some individuals being evicted, where permissible under local law, from low-income housing projects. As a result, the IRS has provided safe harbors under which it will treat a residential unit in a building as a low-income unit if the incomes of the individuals occupying the unit are at or below the income limitation before the beginning of the first tax year of the building's credit period, but their incomes exceed the income limitation at the beginning of the first tax year of the building's credit period. The safe harbors are spelled out in Rev. Proc. 2003-82.[173]

[B] Large Partnerships

A partnership with 35 or more partners (husband and wife count as one) is subject to recapture at the partnership level, unless the partnership elects not to have recapture apply at the partnership level.[174] Unless a partnership makes this election, no recapture event occurs because of a change in ownership unless more than 50 percent of the partnership interests (by value) change hands during a 12-month period. Should a partnership make the election not to have recapture apply at the partnership level, the disposition of a partnership interest by a partner will trigger recapture to the partner.

When recapture does occur at the partnership level, the increase in tax as a result of the recapture is allocated among the partners in the same manner as partnership taxable income.[175]

[C] Recapture Amount

When a recapture event occurs, the owner of a qualified low-income housing project is required to pay additional tax for the year in which the recapture event occurs. This additional tax is equal to the "accelerated portion" of the credit allowable in earlier years.[176] In addition, interest is assessed from the dates the recaptured credit was claimed at the overpayment rate fixed by Code Sec. 6621.[177]

The "accelerated portion" of a credit is the aggregate of the credit taken over the aggregate of the credit that would have been allowed if the credit had been spread over 15 years rather than ten years.[178] In the absence of previous recapture events, credits are recaptured in the following amounts:

Year of Recapture Event	*Recapture Fraction*
2 through 11	1/3
Year 12	4/15
Year 13	3/15
Year 14	2/15
Year 15	1/15

[173] 2003-47 IRB 1097.

[174] Code Sec. 42(j)(5).

[175] Code Sec. 42(j)(5)(A)(iv).

[176] Code Sec. 42(j)(2)(A).

[177] Code Sec. 42(j)(2)(B).

[178] Code Sec. 42(j)(3).

The credit for additions to the qualified basis after the first year of the credit period is computed at two-thirds the regular credit rate.[179] This means that there is no accelerated portion of the credit for additions, and there is no recapture when later reductions in qualifying basis occur except to the extent that reductions exceed the additions to qualified basis.

> ***Example 24:*** Low-Income Housing Corporation built and placed in service a low-income housing project in 2015. The corporation claimed low-income housing credits beginning in 2015 based on the allocation of 30 percent of the basis of the project to units that met the 20-50 test (30 percent of the units were occupied by tenants earning 50 percent or less of the area median income). In 2018, vacancies in some of the low-income units are filled with tenants with nonqualifying income and, as a result, only 25 percent of the basis of the project is allocable to units with tenants whose income is 50 percent or less of the area median. The project, nevertheless, continues to meet the 20-50 test, so full recapture is not required. One-third of the credit claimed for the years 2015 through 2017 which is allocable to the five percent of basis that is no longer eligible for the credit, however, must be recaptured with interest.
>
> In 2020, additional vacancies in the low-income units are filled with tenants with nonqualifying income and, as a result, only 15 percent of the basis of the project is now properly allocable to units whose tenants earn 50 percent or less of the area median income. The project no longer meets the 20-50 test of the minimum set-aside requirement, so full recapture is required. The recapture amount is one-third of the total of all credits taken for the years 2015 through 2019 which were allocable to the 25 percent of the basis of the project that represented units occupied by tenants with income of 50 percent or less of the area median up until 2020. The credits relating to the five percent of basis that were recaptured in 2018 are not taken into account again in 2020.
>
> ***Example 25:*** Low-Income Housing Corporation built and placed in service a qualifying low-income housing project in 2016, and 25 percent of the basis of the project was allocable to units whose tenants had income of 50 percent or less of the area median. In 2018, additional low-income tenants rented units in the project, so that 35 percent of the basis of the project was allocable to low-income units. Low-Income began to take an additional credit for the additional ten percent of qualified basis at two-thirds of the regular credit rate.
>
> In 2020, vacancies in the low-income units were filled with tenants who were not low-income tenants and, as a result, only 30 percent of the basis of the project is properly allocable to units whose tenants have incomes of 50 percent or less of the area median. Although there is a decrease in the qualified basis of five percent, there is no recapture in 2020 because that five percent is allocable to additions to qualified basis after the first credit year.
>
> Suppose, however, that qualified basis in 2020 falls to 20 percent of basis rather than 30 percent. In this case, one-third of the credit claimed for the

[179] Code Sec. 42(f)(3).

years 2016 through 2019 attributable to five percent of the qualified basis would be recaptured. The first ten percent of the reduction in qualified basis would be attributable to the additions to qualified basis which occurred after the first credit year and would not be subject to recapture.

If credits on a qualified low-income project could not be taken because of the limitations on the general business credit contained in Code Sec. 38, or because no tax was due against which the credit could be applied, no recapture is required.[180] An adjustment of carryovers, however, must be made.

[D] Casualty Losses

Recapture does not apply to a reduction in qualified basis that occurs because of a casualty loss to the extent the loss is restored by reconstruction or replacement within a reasonable period established by the Treasury Secretary.[181]

¶ 806 RENEWAL COMMUNITIES AND NEW YORK LIBERTY ZONE

As part of a series of tax incentives to assist economically depressed areas and New York City following the terrorist attacks of September 11, 2001, Congress included additional deductions for the acquisition or revitalization of qualifying property.

.01 Commercial Revitalization Deduction

For buildings placed in service before 2010, a taxpayer was able to elect either to deduct one-half of commercial revitalization expenditures for the tax year a building was placed in service or amortize all the expenditures ratably over the 120-month period beginning with the month the building was placed in service.[182]

A commercial revitalization expenditure is the cost of a new building or the cost of substantially rehabilitating an existing building. The building must be used for commercial purposes and be located in a renewal community. In the case of the rehabilitation of an existing building, the cost of acquiring the building is a qualifying expenditure only to the extent that cost does not exceed 30 percent of the other rehabilitation expenditures.[183] The qualifying expenditures for any building cannot exceed $10 million.[184]

Each state is permitted to allocate up to $12 million of commercial revitalization expenditures to each renewal community located within the state for each calendar year after 2001 and before 2010. A state agency makes the allocations under a qualified allocation plan.[185]

No depreciation is allowed for amounts deducted under Code Sec. 1400I. Adjusted basis is reduced by the amount of the commercial revitalization deduction, and the deduction is treated as a depreciation deduction in applying the deprecia-

[180] Code Sec. 42(j)(4)(B).
[181] Code Sec. 42(j)(4)(E).
[182] Code Sec. 1400I(a).
[183] Code Sec. 1400I(b).
[184] Code Sec. 1400I(c).
[185] Code Sec. 1400I(d).

tion recapture rules. The commercial revitalization deduction is allowed in computing alternative minimum taxable income.[186]

The commercial revitalization deduction is treated in the same manner as the low-income housing credit in applying the passive loss rules of Code Sec. 469. Up to $25,000 of deductions (together with the other deductions and credits not subject to the passive loss limitation under Code Sec. 469(i)) are allowed to an individual taxpayer regardless of the taxpayer's adjusted gross income.

.02 New York Liberty Zone

Code Sec. 1400L provided specific tax benefits for the area of New York City damaged by the terrorist attacks of September 11, 2001. The area was designated as the New York Liberty Zone and included the area on or south of Canal Street, East Broadway (east of its intersection with Canal Street), or Grand Street (east of its intersection with East Broadway) in the Borough of Manhattan in the City of New York, New York.

Among the benefits, Code Sec. 1400L(b) allowed an additional first-year depreciation deduction of 30 percent of the adjusted basis of qualified New York Liberty Zone property. The additional first-year depreciation deduction was allowed for both regular tax and alternative minimum tax purposes for the tax year in which the property was placed in service. The basis of the property and the depreciation allowances in the year of purchase and later years are adjusted to reflect the additional first-year depreciation deduction.

Nonresidential real property and residential rental property was eligible for the additional first-year depreciation only to the extent it rehabilitated real property damaged, or replaced real property destroyed or condemned as a result of the terrorist attacks of September 11, 2001. Property was treated as replacing destroyed property if, as part of an integrated plan, the property replaced real property that was included in a continuous area that included real property destroyed or condemned.

In addition, for property to qualify, the original use of the property in the New York Liberty Zone must have begun with the taxpayer on or after September 11, 2001 (except for some leased property). Also, the taxpayer must have purchased the property after September 10, 2001, and in the case of qualifying nonresidential real property and residential rental property, must have placed the property in service before January 1, 2010. Property did not qualify if a binding written contract for the acquisition of the property was in effect before September 11, 2001.

---

[186] Code Sec. 1400I(f).

Chapter 9
Depreciation

¶ 900 Overview of Chapter
¶ 901 MACRS Depreciation System
¶ 902 Alternative Depreciation System
¶ 903 Cost Segregation
¶ 904 ACRS Depreciation for Pre-1987 Property
¶ 905 Depreciation of Pre-1981 Property

¶ 900 OVERVIEW OF CHAPTER

Depreciation is a reasonable allowance for the exhaustion, wear and tear, and obsolescence of assets used to produce income. It is simply a deduction of a portion of the cost of an asset each year the asset is in use in recognition of the fact that income-producing assets gradually wear out or are used up. The deduction for depreciation is limited to property used in a trade or business or property held for the production of income.[1] Depreciation deductions are not available for the cost of property used purely for personal purposes, so depreciation is not available on a personal residence, for example.

The manner of computing depreciation for tax purposes spelled out in the Internal Revenue Code is subject to constant change as Congress responds to political, economic, and revenue pressures. The system in use today was adopted in the Tax Reform Act of 1986 and generally applies to property placed in service after 1987. The Accelerated Cost Recovery System (ACRS) applies to property placed in service after 1980 and before 1987, but the ACRS system itself was modified several times during the six years between 1980 and 1987. Depreciation for property placed in service before 1981 is based on the "useful life" of the property, and straight-line and accelerated methods of calculating the deduction were permitted.

Depreciation is available only for tangible property and only for that part of the property which is subject to wear and tear, to decay or decline from natural causes, to exhaustion, and to obsolescence. Land is not depreciable, although certain improvements to land may be depreciable.[2] See the discussion of allocating costs on the purchase of real estate at ¶ 102.02.

Depreciation begins when property is placed in service, and the deduction is available to the owner of the property who has made a capital investment in the property and who has the benefits and burdens of ownership. The person entitled

[1] Code Sec. 167(a).

[2] Reg. § 1.167(a)-2.

to depreciation deductions is not necessarily the owner of legal title to the property. See the discussion of ownership for tax purposes at ¶ 201.

While depreciation deductions are available for personalty, as well as realty, used in business or for the production of income, the discussion of depreciation in this chapter is essentially limited to the depreciation of real property. The cost of property that is not real property generally can be recovered over a much shorter period of time, and tax savings often result from a careful allocation of cost between realty and personalty on the purchase of a building.

¶ 901 MACRS DEPRECIATION SYSTEM

The depreciation deduction for property placed in service after 1986 is determined using the general depreciation system, also referred to as the Modified Accelerated Cost Recovery System (MACRS), unless the alternative depreciation system discussed at ¶ 902 applies. Depreciation rules for property placed in service before 1987 are taken up later in this chapter.

In some cases, property placed in service before 1991 may have been depreciated under the ACRS system, which allowed recovery of the cost of real estate over 19 years, rather than the much longer period of current law. Generally, property constructed, reconstructed, or acquired under a written contract that was binding as of March 1, 1986, could be depreciated under the pre-1987 rules, if it was placed in service before 1991. March 1, 1986, is also the critical date for other transitional rules that allowed the shorter recovery period for self-constructed property, equipped buildings, and plant facilities that were placed in service before 1991.[3]

Under a transition rule contained in Sec. 1315(b)(2) of the Omnibus Budget Reconciliation Act of 1993, nonresidential real property placed in service before January 1, 1994, may be treated as 31.5-year property (rather than the 39-year property of current law) if the taxpayer or a qualified person entered into a binding written contract to purchase or construct the property before May 13, 1993, or construction began for those persons before that date. A qualified person is a person who transfers rights in a contract or property to the taxpayer before the property is placed in service.

Depreciation is calculated on the tax basis of the depreciable property. The determination of basis is taken up in considerable detail at ¶ ¶ 101-101.01. Other areas related to depreciation include the treatment of additions and improvements to leased property by lessor (see ¶ 601) and lessee (see ¶ 602), the distinction between repairs and improvements (see ¶ 703.01[A]), special amortization provisions (see ¶ 802), and recapture of "accelerated depreciation" on the sale of property (see ¶ 1301.03).

---

[3] These transitional rules are explained in some detail in the Conference Committee Report on the Tax Reform Act of 1986 (P.L. 99-514).

.01 Computation of the Deduction

The depreciation deduction for property placed in service after 1986 is calculated by using the applicable depreciation method, the applicable recovery period, and the applicable convention.[4]

[A] Recovery Periods

Under the general depreciation system, there are eleven classes of property, and these are assigned recovery periods of from three to 50 years.[5] In the case of real property, residential rental property has a recovery period of 27.5 years and nonresidential real property has a recovery period of 39 years. The recovery periods are based on full 12-month periods and are not based on taxable years.

A building or structure is residential rental property only if 80 percent or more of the gross rental income from the building or structure is rental income from dwelling units. If any portion of a building or structure is occupied by the taxpayer as a residence, the gross rental income from the building or structure includes the rental value of the portion occupied by the taxpayer.[6] Hotels, motels, inns, and similar establishments are excluded from the residential rental property class if more than one-half of the units are used on a transient basis.

Nonresidential real property is real property that is not residential rental property and that does not have a class life of less than 27.5 years. The class life of property is the class life that would be applicable to the property as of January 1, 1986, under Code Sec. 167(m). The class lives of property are set out in Rev. Proc. 87-56.[7]

See ¶ 901.01[E] and ¶ 901.01[G] for shorter recovery periods for certain real property.

[B] Straight-Line Method

For residential rental and nonresidential real property, the applicable depreciation method is the straight-line method.[8] Salvage value is treated as zero.[9]

Under the straight-line method, the depreciation rate, in percentage terms, is determined by dividing one by the length of applicable recovery period remaining as of the beginning of the taxable year. The rate is applied to the unrecovered basis of the property, that is, the cost or other basis of the property adjusted for depreciation previously allowed or allowable and for all other adjustments to basis. If the remaining recovery period as of the beginning of any tax year is less than one year, the depreciation rate for that year is 100 percent.

The computation of depreciation rates must reflect a reasonable and consistent rounding convention that, in the case of real property, is exact to at least one-thousandth of a percent. Under any rounding convention, no taxpayer may recover more than 100 percent of the recoverable basis of the property.[10]

---

4 Code Sec. 168(a).

5 Code Sec. 168(c) and (j).

6 *See* Code Sec. 168(e)(2).

7 1987-2 CB 674.

8 Code Sec. 168(b)(3).

9 Code Sec. 168(b)(4).

10 Rev. Proc. 87-57, 1987-2 CB 687.

[C] Mid-Month Convention

A mid-month convention applies to most all residential rental and nonresidential real property.[11] The mid-month convention does not apply to any other classes of property. (See ¶ 901.01[E] for treatment of certain property with reduced recovery periods.)

Under the mid-month convention, property placed in service, disposed of, or retired during any month is treated as being placed in service, disposed of, or retired on the midpoint of the month. Therefore, regardless of when during the month a taxpayer places real property in service, the property is deemed to be placed in service on the midpoint of that month. Under the mid-month convention, depreciation is allowable for a fraction of a year for each property placed in service, disposed of, or retired during the year. The numerator of the fraction is equal to 0.5 plus the number of full months in the taxable year in which the property is in service. The denominator of the fraction is 12. Allowable depreciation for real property in a taxable year in which the mid-month convention applies is that fraction of the amount that would be allowable under the straight-line method for a full year. The remaining recovery period as of the beginning of the taxable year following a taxable year in which property is placed in service is equal to the property's applicable recovery period less the fraction of the first year for which depreciation is allowable.[12]

> ***Example 1:*** On March 1, 2019, the Taxpayer who is on the calendar year places in service residential rental property. For 2019, the Taxpayer is entitled to 9.5/12 of the amount of depreciation that would be allowable under the straight-line method for a full year. As of January 1, 2020, the remaining recovery period for the property is 26 years and 8½ months (that is, 27 years and six months less the 9½ months for which depreciation was allowable in 2019).

First-Year Depreciation for Residential Rental Property

The following table lists the percentages of the basis of 27.5-year residential rental property that may be taken as depreciation for the first year based on the month in which the property is placed in service:

Month	Percentage
January	3.4848%
February	3.1818%
March	2.8788%
April	2.5758%
May	2.2727%
June	1.9697%
July	1.6667%
August	1.3636%
September	1.0606%

[11] Code Sec. 168(d)(2).

[12] *See* Rev. Proc. 87-57, 1987-2 CB 687, as amplified and clarified by Rev. Proc. 89-15, 1989-1 CB 816.

October	0.7576%
November	0.4545%
December	0.1515%

First-Year Depreciation for Nonresidential Property

The following table lists the percentages of the basis of 39-year nonresidential property that may be taken as depreciation for the first year based on the month in which the property is placed in service:

January	2.4572%
February	2.2435%
March	2.0299%
April	1.8162%
May	1.6025%
June	1.3888%
July	1.1752%
August	0.9615%
September	0.7478%
October	0.5341%
November	0.3205%
December	0.1068%

The calculation of depreciation under the general depreciation system (MACRS) is illustrated in the following example.

Comprehensive Example 2: In July 2019, the Taxpayer who is on the calendar year purchases land and a building with a single storefront and six residential apartments. Of the total $240,000 purchase price, $200,000 is allocated to the building, and $40,000 is allocated to the land (how such an allocation might be made is discussed at ¶ 102.02[A]). The Taxpayer moves into one of the apartments and rents the others for $500 per month. The store rents for $700 per month.

Since the gross rental income from the apartments (including the apartment in which the owner lives) is more than 80 percent of the gross rental income from the building (6 × $500 = $3,000, which is more than 80 percent of $3,700), the building qualifies as residential rental real estate. If depreciation is allocated in proportion to rents, the Taxpayer's depreciation deduction for 2019 is $2,883. This figure is determined by computing a full year's depreciation ($200,000/27.5 = $7,273), dividing this full year figure by 12 to determine a full month's depreciation ($7,273/12 = $606), multiplying the full month's depreciation by 5.5 to reflect the number of months under the mid-month convention that the property is in service during 2019 ($606 × 5.5 = $3,333), and multiplying $3,333 by 32/37 ($3,200/$3,700) to limit depreciation to the portion of the building not used for personal purposes. (Note that the $3,333 figure could have been arrived at by multiplying $200,000 by 1.6667%, the percentage of basis for the first year when residential rental property is placed in service in July.)

Suppose, however, that the rental on the apartments was only $400 per month instead of $500. In this case, the building would not qualify as residential rental property because the gross rental from the apartments (6 × $400 = $2,400) is less than 80 percent of the gross rental income of the building ($2,400 + $700 = $3,100). As nonresidential real estate, depreciation must be based on a recovery period of 39 years. In this case, the Taxpayer's depreciation deduction for 2019 would be $2,045. This figure is determined by computing a full year's depreciation ($200,000/39 = $5,128), dividing this full year figure by 12 to determine a full month's depreciation ($5,128/12 = $427), multiplying the full month's depreciation by 5.5 to reflect the number of months under the mid-month convention that the property is in service during 2019 ($427 × 5.5 = $2,348), and multiplying $2,348 by 27/31 ($2,700/$3,100) to limit depreciation to the portion of the building not used for personal purposes. (Note that the $2,348 figure could have been arrived at by multiplying $200,000 by 1.1752%, the percentage of basis for the first year when nonresidential property is placed in service in July.)

[D] Use of Optional Tables

The IRS has provided optional depreciation tables that may be used to compute the annual depreciation allowance for most types of property.[13] The optional depreciation tables specify schedules of annual depreciation rates that are applied to the *unadjusted* basis of property in each taxable year. If a taxpayer uses a table to compute the annual depreciation deduction for any item of property, the table must be used to compute the depreciation deductions for the entire recovery period.

[13] Rev. Proc. 87-57, 1987-2 CB 687.

OPTIONAL TABLE FOR 27.5-YEAR RESIDENTIAL RENTAL PROPERTY UNDER GENERAL DEPRECIATION SYSTEM

If the Recovery Year is:	And the Month in the First Recovery Year the Property is Placed in Service is:											
	1	2	3	4	5	6	7	8	9	10	11	12
	the Depreciation Rate is:											
1	3.485	3.182	2.879	2.576	2.273	1.970	1.667	1.364	1.061	0.758	0.455	0.152
2	3.636	3.636	3.636	3.636	3.636	3.636	3.636	3.636	3.636	3.636	3.636	3.636
3	3.636	3.636	3.636	3.636	3.636	3.636	3.636	3.636	3.636	3.636	3.636	3.636
4	3.636	3.636	3.636	3.636	3.636	3.636	3.636	3.636	3.636	3.636	3.636	3.636
5	3.636	3.636	3.636	3.636	3.636	3.636	3.636	3.636	3.636	3.636	3.636	3.636
6	3.636	3.636	3.636	3.636	3.636	3.636	3.636	3.636	3.636	3.636	3.636	3.636
7	3.636	3.636	3.636	3.636	3.636	3.636	3.636	3.636	3.636	3.636	3.636	3.636
8	3.636	3.636	3.636	3.636	3.636	3.636	3.636	3.636	3.636	3.636	3.636	3.636
9	3.636	3.636	3.636	3.636	3.636	3.636	3.636	3.636	3.636	3.636	3.636	3.636
10	3.637	3.637	3.637	3.637	3.637	3.637	3.636	3.636	3.636	3.636	3.636	3.636
11	3.636	3.636	3.636	3.636	3.636	3.636	3.637	3.637	3.637	3.637	3.637	3.637
12	3.637	3.637	3.637	3.637	3.637	3.637	3.636	3.636	3.636	3.636	3.636	3.636
13	3.636	3.636	3.636	3.636	3.636	3.636	3.637	3.637	3.637	3.637	3.637	3.637
14	3.637	3.637	3.637	3.637	3.637	3.637	3.636	3.636	3.636	3.636	3.636	3.636
15	3.636	3.636	3.636	3.636	3.636	3.636	3.637	3.637	3.637	3.637	3.637	3.637
16	3.637	3.637	3.637	3.637	3.637	3.637	3.636	3.636	3.636	3.636	3.636	3.636
17	3.636	3.636	3.636	3.636	3.636	3.636	3.637	3.637	3.637	3.637	3.637	3.637
18	3.637	3.637	3.637	3.637	3.637	3.637	3.636	3.636	3.636	3.636	3.636	3.636
19	3.636	3.636	3.636	3.636	3.636	3.636	3.637	3.637	3.637	3.637	3.637	3.637
20	3.637	3.637	3.637	3.637	3.637	3.637	3.636	3.636	3.636	3.636	3.636	3.636

If the Recovery Year is:	And the Month in the First Recovery Year the Property is Placed in Service is:											
	1	2	3	4	5	6	7	8	9	10	11	12
	the Depreciation Rate is:											
21	3.636	3.636	3.636	3.636	3.636	3.636	3.637	3.637	3.637	3.637	3.637	3.637
22	3.637	3.637	3.637	3.637	3.637	3.637	3.636	3.636	3.636	3.636	3.636	3.636
23	3.636	3.636	3.636	3.636	3.636	3.636	3.637	3.637	3.637	3.637	3.637	3.637
24	3.637	3.637	3.637	3.637	3.637	3.637	3.636	3.636	3.636	3.636	3.636	3.636
25	3.636	3.636	3.636	3.636	3.636	3.636	3.637	3.637	3.637	3.637	3.637	3.637
26	3.637	3.637	3.637	3.637	3.637	3.637	3.636	3.636	3.636	3.636	3.636	3.636
27	3.636	3.636	3.636	3.636	3.636	3.636	3.637	3.637	3.637	3.637	3.637	3.637
28	1.970	2.273	2.576	2.879	3.182	3.485	3.636	3.636	3.636	3.636	3.636	3.636
29	0.000	0.000	0.000	0.000	0.000	0.000	0.152	0.455	0.758	1.061	1.364	1.667

OPTIONAL TABLE FOR 31.5-YEAR NONRESIDENTIAL REAL PROPERTY UNDER GENERAL DEPRECIATION SYSTEM

If the Recovery Year is:	And the Month in the First Recovery Year the Property is Placed in Service is:											
	1	2	3	4	5	6	7	8	9	10	11	12
	the Depreciation Rate is:											
1	3.042	2.778	2.513	2.249	1.984	1.720	1.455	1.190	0.926	0.661	0.397	0.132
2	3.175	3.175	3.175	3.175	3.175	3.175	3.175	3.175	3.175	3.175	3.175	3.175
3	3.175	3.175	3.175	3.175	3.175	3.175	3.175	3.175	3.175	3.175	3.175	3.175
4	3.175	3.175	3.175	3.175	3.175	3.175	3.175	3.175	3.175	3.175	3.175	3.175
5	3.175	3.175	3.175	3.175	3.175	3.175	3.175	3.175	3.175	3.175	3.175	3.175
6	3.175	3.175	3.175	3.175	3.175	3.175	3.175	3.175	3.175	3.175	3.175	3.175
7	3.175	3.175	3.175	3.175	3.175	3.175	3.175	3.175	3.175	3.175	3.175	3.175
8	3.175	3.174	3.175	3.174	3.175	3.174	3.175	3.175	3.175	3.175	3.175	3.175
9	3.174	3.175	3.174	3.175	3.174	3.175	3.174	3.175	3.174	3.175	3.174	3.175
10	3.175	3.174	3.175	3.174	3.175	3.174	3.175	3.174	3.175	3.174	3.175	3.174
11	3.174	3.175	3.174	3.175	3.174	3.175	3.174	3.175	3.174	3.175	3.174	3.175
12	3.175	3.174	3.175	3.174	3.175	3.174	3.175	3.174	3.175	3.174	3.175	3.174
13	3.174	3.175	3.174	3.175	3.174	3.175	3.174	3.175	3.174	3.175	3.174	3.175
14	3.175	3.174	3.175	3.174	3.175	3.174	3.175	3.174	3.175	3.174	3.175	3.174
15	3.174	3.175	3.174	3.175	3.174	3.175	3.174	3.175	3.174	3.175	3.174	3.175
16	3.175	3.174	3.175	3.174	3.175	3.174	3.175	3.174	3.175	3.174	3.175	3.174
17	3.174	3.175	3.174	3.175	3.174	3.175	3.174	3.175	3.174	3.175	3.174	3.175
18	3.175	3.174	3.175	3.174	3.175	3.174	3.175	3.174	3.175	3.174	3.175	3.174
19	3.174	3.175	3.174	3.175	3.174	3.175	3.174	3.175	3.174	3.175	3.174	3.175
20	3.175	3.174	3.175	3.174	3.175	3.174	3.175	3.174	3.175	3.174	3.175	3.174

If the Recovery Year is:	And the Month in the First Recovery Year the Property is Placed in Service is:											
	1	2	3	4	5	6	7	8	9	10	11	12
	the Depreciation Rate is:											
21	3.174	3.175	3.174	3.175	3.174	3.175	3.174	3.175	3.174	3.175	3.174	3.175
22	3.175	3.174	3.175	3.174	3.175	3.174	3.175	3.174	3.175	3.174	3.175	3.174
23	3.174	3.175	3.174	3.175	3.174	3.175	3.174	3.175	3.174	3.175	3.174	3.175
24	3.175	3.174	3.175	3.174	3.175	3.174	3.175	3.174	3.175	3.174	3.175	3.174
25	3.174	3.175	3.174	3.175	3.174	3.175	3.174	3.175	3.174	3.175	3.174	3.175
26	3.175	3.174	3.175	3.174	3.175	3.174	3.175	3.174	3.175	3.174	3.175	3.174
27	3.174	3.175	3.174	3.175	3.174	3.175	3.174	3.175	3.174	3.175	3.174	3.175
28	3.175	3.174	3.175	3.174	3.175	3.174	3.175	3.174	3.175	3.174	3.175	3.174

OPTIONAL TABLE FOR 39-YEAR NONRESIDENTIAL REAL PROPERTY UNDER GENERAL DEPRECIATION SYSTEM

If the Recovery Year is:	And the Month in the First Recovery Year the Property is Placed in Service is:											
	1	2	3	4	5	6	7	8	9	10	11	12
	the Depreciation Rate is:											
1	2.461	2.247	2.033	1.819	1.605	1.391	1.777	0.963	0.749	0.535	0.321	0.107
2-39	2.564	2.564	2.564	2.564	2.564	2.564	2.564	2.564	2.564	2.564	2.564	2.564
40	0.107	0.321	0.535	0.749	0.963	1.177	1.391	1.605	1.819	2.033	2.247	2.461

[E] Shorter Recovery Periods for Leasehold and Retail Improvements and Restaurant Property Before 2018

A 15-year recovery period applies to qualified leasehold improvement property and qualified restaurant property placed in service after October 22, 2004 and before 2018. A 15- year recovery period also applies to qualified retail improvement property placed in service after December 31, 2008 and before 2018.[14] Depreciation is calculated using the straight-line method (see ¶ 901.01[B]) and half-year convention, rather than the mid-month convention that applies to most real property (see ¶ 901.01[C]). A 39-year recovery period applies to these three types of property if depreciation is computed using the MACRS alternative depreciation system (see ¶ 902).[15] When the special 15-year recovery period does not apply, they are treated as any other building or structural component under MACRS.

For property placed in service before 2016, qualified restaurant property placed in service after 2008 and retail improvement property did not qualify for bonus depreciation. Qualified leasehold improvement property, however, did qualify for bonus depreciation. For property placed in service after 2015 and before 2018, qualified improvement property qualifies for bonus depreciation. See ¶ 901.03[B].

Qualified Leasehold Improvements

A qualified leasehold improvement is any improvement to an interior portion of nonresidential real property that satisfies the following requirements:[16]

1. The improvement is made under a lease by the lessee, lessor or any sublessee of the interior portion.
2. The improvement is section 1250 property, that is, a structural component and not section 1245 personal property that is eligible for a shortened recovery period under the cost segregation rules. (See ¶ 102.02[C])
3. The lease is not between related persons.

[14] Code Sec. 168(e)(3)(E).

[15] Code Sec. 168(g)(3)(B).

[16] Code Sec. 168(k)(3).

4. The interior portion of the building will be occupied exclusively by the lessee or any sublessee of that interior portion.
5. The improvement is placed in service more than three years after the date the building was first placed in service by any person.

Expenditures for the following are not qualified leasehold improvement property:[17]

1. The enlargement of the building.
2. Elevators and escalators.
3. Structural components that benefit a common area.
4. Internal structural framework.

Qualified Restaurant Property

Qualified restaurant property includes a building or an improvement to a building, if more than 50 percent of the building's square footage is devoted to preparation of, and seating for, on-premises consumption of prepared meals.[18]

For property placed in service after October 22, 2004, and before 2009, qualified restaurant property included only improvements to existing buildings that were made more than three years after the building was first placed in service by anyone. After 2008 and before 2018, qualified restaurant property includes a new building and improvements made to an existing building.

Qualified Retail Improvement Property

Qualified retail improvement property is an improvement made to the interior portion of nonresidential real property that meets the following requirements:[19]

1. The interior portion of the building must be open to the general public and used in the retail trade or business of selling tangible personal property to the general public.
2. The improvement must be placed in service more than three years after the building was first placed in service.
3. The improvement must be placed in service after December 31, 2008.

Qualified retail improvement property does not include the following:[20]

1. The enlargement of the building.
2. Elevators and escalators.
3. Structural components that benefit a common area.
4. Internal structural framework.

[F] Improvement Property After 2017

The Tax Cuts and Jobs Act (TCJA)[21] eliminated the classes for 15-year leasehold improvement property, retail improvement property, and restaurant improvements and buildings. The TCJA also, presumably, was to assign a 15-year recovery

[17] Code Sec. 168(k)(3)(B).
[18] Code Sec. 167(e)(7).
[19] Code Sec. 168(e)(8).
[20] Code Sec. 168(e)(8)(C).
[21] P.L. 115-97.

period for qualified improvement property placed in service after 2017. According to the Conference Report on the Tax Cuts and Jobs Act, a 15-year recovery period applies for qualified improvement property. The text of the final bill, however, while providing a definition of qualified improvement property, inadvertently omitted the provision which would give that property a 15-year recovery period. If this is not corrected, improvement property will be treated as 39-year nonresidential real property. Another consequence of failing to provide a 15-year recovery period for qualified improvement property placed in service after December 31, 2017, is that the property will not qualify for bonus depreciation.

On August 8, 2018, the IRS issued proposed regulations[22] on first-year bonus depreciation that reflect the TCJA with the 15-year recovery period for improvement property omitted. On August 16, 2018, members of the Senate Finance Committee attempted to clarify congressional intent and called on Treasury and the IRS to issue tax reform guidance consistent with the clarifications. The letter states that Congressional intent for Section 13204 of the TCJA was to provide a 15-year MACRS recovery period for qualified improvement property. The letter indicates that the new law should also provide a 20-year alternative deprecation system (ADS) recovery period for qualified improvement property. The Senators intend to introduce technical corrections legislation.

On September 16, 2019, the IRS issued final regulations[23] dealing with 100 percent bonus depreciation. Once again, the IRS declined to make qualified improvement property placed in service after 2017 eligible for bonus depreciation. According to the IRS, a technical correction must first be enacted to give this property its intended 15-year recovery period. With a 15-year recovery period, qualified improvement property will then qualify for bonus depreciation.

Assuming the technical correction is enacted, qualified improvement property will be assigned a recovery period of 15 years, effective for property placed in service after December 31, 2017. Qualified improvement property is depreciated using the straight-line method and half-year convention or, if applicable, the mid-quarter convention. The ADS recovery period for qualified improvement property is 20 years (assuming a correction).

The definition of qualified improvement property for purposes of the new 15-year recovery period is the same as the definition that has applied for bonus depreciation purposes. Specifically, qualified improvement property includes any improvement to an interior portion of a building that is nonresidential real property if the improvement is placed in service after the date the building was first placed in service by anyone.[24]

Qualified improvement property does not include expenditures attributable to:

- The enlargement of a building;
- Any elevator or escalator; or
- The internal structural framework of a building.[25]

---

[22] NPR REG-104397-18.

[23] T.D. 9874.

[24] Code Sec. 168(e)(6)(A).

[25] Code Sec. 168(e)(6)(B).

All improvements which previously qualified for a 15-year recovery period as qualified leasehold improvement property or qualified retail improvement property fall within the definition of qualified improvement property and have a 15-year recovery period, effective for property placed in service after December 31, 2017 (assuming the correction). Improvements to a restaurant will only qualify for the 15-year recovery period for qualified improvement property if the improvement is to the interior of the restaurant and does not relate to an enlargement or the internal structural framework of the building, or to an elevator or escalator. External improvements to a restaurant and restaurant buildings which did qualify as 15-year qualified restaurant property do not meet the requirements for qualified improvement property, are not eligible for the 15-year recovery period, and must be depreciated over 39 years, effective for property placed in service after December 31, 2017.

[G] Motorsports Entertainment Complexes

A seven-year recovery period applies to motorsports entertainment complexes and their related ancillary and support facilities placed in service after October 22, 2004, and before 2018 (unless once again extended by Congress). A motorsports entertainment complex is a racing track facility that is permanently situated on land, hosts at least one racing event for cars of any type, trucks, or motorcycles during the 36-month period following the first day of the month in which it is placed in service, and is open to the public for an admission fee.[26] Related facilities owned by the same taxpayer who owns the complex and that are provided for the benefit of patrons of the complex also qualify for a seven-year recovery period. Related facilities include:[27]

1. Ancillary facilities and land improvements in support of the complex's activities, including parking lots, sidewalks, waterways, bridges, fences, and landscaping.
2. Support facilities, including food and beverage retailing, souvenir vending, and other nonlodging accommodations.
3. Appurtenances associated with the facilities and related attractions and amusements, including ticket booths, race track surfaces, suites and hospitality facilities, grandstands and viewing structures, props, walls, facilities that support entertainment services delivery, other special purpose structures, facades, shop interiors, and buildings.

A motorsports entertainment complex does not include any transportation equipment, administrative services assets, warehouses, administrative buildings, hotels, or motels.[28]

[26] Code Sec. 168(i)(15).

[27] Code Sec. 168(i)(15)(B).

[28] Code Sec. 168(i)(15)(C).

.02 Depreciation of Additions and Improvements

Additions and improvements to property are treated as separate property items for purposes of computing depreciation.[29] The recovery period for any addition or improvement to property begins the later of (1) the taxable year in which the addition or improvement is placed in service, or (2) the taxable year in which the property to which the addition or improvement relates is placed in service. The applicable recovery period, applicable convention, and applicable depreciation method for an addition or improvement to property are the same as those that would be applicable to the underlying property if the underlying property were placed in service at the same time as the addition or improvement.

Accordingly, an addition or improvement to residential rental real estate is depreciated over 27.5 years using the straight line method and the mid-month convention. An addition or improvement to nonresidential real estate is depreciated over 39 years using the straight line method and the mid-month convention.

In view of the long recovery period for additions and improvements, a premium is placed on classifying as much work on property as possible as currently deductible repairs rather than as depreciable improvements. See the discussion of repairs at ¶ 703.01 and improvements at ¶ 801.

[A] Land Improvements

Generally, those land improvements that do not permanently improve the land but improve it only for use with a specific building are depreciable. As the IRS has put it, land improvement costs are depreciable if they are directly associated with buildings rather than inextricably associated with the land.[30]

Land improvements are subject to depreciation over a recovery period of 15 years using the 150-percent declining balance method of depreciation and a half-year convention (unless more than 40 percent of the basis of depreciable property placed in service during the year is placed in service during the last quarter, in which case a mid-quarter convention applies).[31]

In Rev. Rul. 65-265, the IRS ruled that the cost of general grading of the land is part of the cost basis of the land and is nondepreciable. The cost of the digging and the removing of the soil that is necessary for the proper setting of the buildings and paving of the roadways, however, is part of their cost and is depreciable. This ruling was further clarified by Rev. Rul. 68-193,[32] which allowed depreciation for certain grading costs for roads constructed to provide for movement of heavy materials between buildings in cases where the grading would be abandoned or replaced with the buildings with which it was directly associated.

Landscaping consisting of perennial shrubbery and ornamental trees adjacent to buildings was considered a depreciable land improvement when replacement of the buildings would require replacement of the landscaping. On the other hand, the

[29] Code Sec. 168(i)(6).

[30] Rev. Rul. 65-265, 1965-2 CB 52.

[31] *See* Rev. Proc. 87-56, 1987-2 CB 674, Asset Class 00.3, which specifies that land improvements have a class life of 20 years and a recovery period under the general depreciation system of 15 years and a recovery period under the alternative depreciation system of 20 years.

[32] 1968-1 CB 79.

cost of general landscaping of the grounds around the same buildings was considered a general land improvement cost and part of the basis of the nondepreciable land.[33]

Rev. Proc. 87-56[34] contains the class lives and recovery periods for computing depreciation deductions for various assets. Under this Revenue Procedure, land improvements include depreciable improvements such as sidewalks, roads, canals, waterways, drainage facilities, docks, bridges, fences, landscaping, and shrubbery.

[B] Property Under Construction

In regulations proposed on February 16, 1984, the IRS provided guidance on how to compute depreciation (cost recovery allowances) under ACRS for a building that is made available in stages.[35] Presumably the same principles apply to the calculation of depreciation under the general depreciation system (MACRS) using the applicable recovery period, depreciation method, and convention of current law.

Under Prop. Reg. § 1.168-2(e)(3), a building is considered placed in service only when a significant portion is made available for use in a finished condition—for example, when a certificate of occupancy is issued for the finished portion. If less than the entire building is made available, then the unadjusted basis that is taken into account for depreciation is the amount of the unadjusted basis of the building that is properly allocable to the portion made available. If another portion of the building is subsequently made available, then that amount of unadjusted basis that is properly allocable to the ensuing available portion is taken into account for depreciation when that portion becomes available. The taxpayer must use the same recovery period and method for all portions of the building.

The following example is based on Prop. Reg. § 1.168-2(e)(5), Examples (2) and (3).

> ***Comprehensive Example 3:*** The Taxpayer who is on the calendar year begins constructing a ten-story office building in 1982. All floors will have approximately the same amount of usable space. By 1983, the Taxpayer has paid $10 million for the building's shell, $4 million for work on the first three floors, and $5 million for work directly related to other floors. In March 1983, the Taxpayer receives a certificate of occupancy for the first three floors and begins offering those floors for rent to tenants. The building is considered placed in service in 1983, and no depreciation deductions are allowed for 1982.
>
> The Taxpayer's depreciation deduction for 1983 is the properly allocated unadjusted basis times the applicable percentage (which for 1983 was ten percent). The properly allocable unadjusted basis is $7 million, consisting of the amounts of unadjusted basis directly related to the portion of the building made available for use ($4 million) plus that amount of the unadjusted basis that is not directly related to any specific portion of the building ($10 million) properly allocable to the portion made available for use (that is, 3 floors/10

[33] Rev. Rul. 74-265, 1974-1 CB 56.

[34] 1987-2 CB 674.

[35] Prop. Reg. § 1.168-2(e)(3).

floors = 30% × $10 million = $3 million). No deduction is allowed for 1983 for the $5 million paid for work directly related to the top seven floors.

In January 1984, the Taxpayer receives a certificate of occupancy for the remaining seven floors and begins offering them for rent to tenants. The Taxpayer spent an additional $7 million to complete the building. In January 1984, the Taxpayer takes into account as basis for depreciation the $12 million not previously taken into account plus the $7 million of later expenditures. The Taxpayer begins depreciating the $19 million portion of the basis in January 1984.

[C] Zoning and Variances

Land generally is not depreciable because it has no limited useful life and is not subject to exhaustion or obsolescence. Also, the cost of obtaining a zoning change for land must be capitalized and is not depreciable if the benefits resulting from the zoning change are indefinite and undeterminable in duration.[36] But what of a variance as opposed to a zoning change? Generally, a variance covers only a particular structure and allows a building to be built that would otherwise not be permitted under the existing zoning.

In *Maguire/Thomas Partners*,[37] the owner of property argued that the cost of a variance should be depreciable in that it would give the owner no right to construct a replacement building on the property. If the owner were to replace the building constructed under the variance, the owner could not build another building outside the zoning rules governing the property without obtaining a second variance. Variances, the owner argued, do not automatically apply to buildings built after those already placed in service.

The Tax Court concluded that the cost of the variance is allocable to the building that is the subject of the variance and not to the land. Further, that the variance has a limited useful life that is equal to the depreciable life of the building, and the cost of the variance is includable in the depreciable basis of the building built under that variance.

.03 Expensing and Bonus Depreciation

A taxpayer may elect under Code Sec. 179 to expense all or a portion of a limited amount of property placed in service during the year rather than recover the cost over the usual recovery periods for that property. Also, a taxpayer may elect to take a bonus depreciation deduction for specified property placed in service during the year under Code Sec. 168(k). While these provisions generally apply to property that is not real property, their limited application to real property is discussed here.

---

[36] A.T. Galt, 19 TC 892, CCH Dec. 19,491, *rev'd in part and aff'd in part on other issues*, CA-7, 54-2 USTC ¶ 9457, 216 F.2d 41. *See also* Oliver, 35 TCM. 656, T.C. Memo. 1976-145, *aff'd*, CA-8, 77-1 USTC ¶ 9339, 553 F.2d 560; Ackerman Buick, Inc., 32 TCM 1061, T.C. Memo. 1973-224.

[37] 89 TCM 799, T.C. Memo. 2005-34.

[A] Expensing Election

A taxpayer may elect to treat the cost of qualifying section 179 property as an expense rather than a capital expenditure. Section 179 property is generally defined as new or used depreciable tangible section 1245 property that is purchased for use in the active conduct of a trade or business (property merely held for the production of income does not qualify).[38] The deduction is generally not available for real property, including buildings and their structural components. The deduction is limited to a maximum dollar amount, and further limited by the taxpayer's taxable income from the business.[39]

Limitations

For tax years beginning before 2018, the maximum amount of property eligible for the section 179 deduction in any year was $500,000 ($510,000 inflation adjusted for 2017). If the aggregate amount of property eligible for the section 179 deduction placed in service in any one year exceeded $2,000,000 ($2,030,000 inflation adjusted for 2017), the $500,000 limit was reduced by the excess over $2,000,000. The deduction, as determined after applying the $500,000 and $2,000,000 amounts, was further limited by the taxpayer's taxable income derived from the business for which the section 179 property was purchased.

For tax years beginning after 2017, the overall expensing dollar limitation is increased to $1 million, and the investment limitation is increased to $2.5 million.[40] These increases are permanent and are inflation-adjusted for tax years beginning after 2018. When adjusting the dollar limitation or the investment limitation for inflation, the resulting amount must be rounded to the nearest multiple of $10,000.

Qualified Real Property

Although most real property in not eligible for the section 179 deduction, qualified real property is eligible. Prior to 2018, qualified real property generally consisted of qualified leasehold improvements, qualified restaurant property, and qualified retail improvements.

For tax years beginning after 2017, the definition of qualified real property that taxpayers may elect to treat as section 179 property is significantly expanded. Effective for tax years beginning after 2017, qualified real property is defined as:

1. Qualified improvement property (see ¶ 901.01[F]); and
2. Any of the following improvements to nonresidential real property that are placed in service after the nonresidential real property was first placed in service:
    a. roofs;
    b. heating, ventilation, and air-conditioning property;
    c. fire protection and alarm systems; and
    d. security systems.[41]

---

[38] Code Sec. 179(d)(1).
[39] Code Sec. 179(b)(3)(A).
[40] Code Sec. 179(b).
[41] Code Sec. 179(f).

A taxpayer must elect to treat qualified real property as section 179 property.[42] A taxpayer may make or change an election to expense qualified real property placed in service in tax years beginning after 2017 on an original or amended return. A taxpayer may also increase the portion of the cost which it expensed by filing an amended return for the year in which the expense deduction was first claimed. Filing an amended return to increase the amount of qualified real property expensed is not considered a revocation of the prior election.[43]

If the election is made and the total cost of all section 179 property, including qualified real property, exceeds the investment limitation ($2.5 million in 2018), the dollar limitation ($1 million in 2018) is reduced by the excess.

Generally, the amount of the section 179 deduction disallowed because of the limitations may be carried over to following years. In the case of qualifying real property, however, disallowed amounts may not be carried over. Rather, the disallowed amount must be recovered through depreciation.[44]

Property Used in Connection with Lodging

Effective for property placed in service in tax years beginning after December 31, 2017, property that is used predominantly to furnish lodging or in connection with the furnishing of lodging qualifies for section 179 expensing.[45]

The primary impact of this provision is to allow expensing of section 1245 property purchased for use in connection with a residential rental building. Examples of property used in connection with the furnishing of lodging include lobby furniture, office equipment, and laundry and swimming pool equipment. Property used in furnishing electrical energy, water, sewage disposal services, gas, telephone service, or similar services are not used in connection with the furnishing of lodging.

[B] First-Year Bonus Depreciation

A taxpayer may take an additional first-year depreciation deduction of 100 percent for qualifying property acquired and placed in service after September 27, 2017, and before January 1, 2023. The rate phases down after 2022. Under prior law, the bonus depreciation rate was generally 50 percent. The additional first-year depreciation deduction is allowed for both regular tax and alternative minimum tax purposes for the tax year in which the property is placed in service. The basis of the property and the depreciation allowances in the year of purchase and later years are adjusted to reflect the additional first-year depreciation deduction. In addition, there is no adjustment to the allowable amount of depreciation for purposes of computing a taxpayer's alternative minimum taxable income for property to which bonus depreciation applies.[46]

The 100-percent allowance is phased down by 20 percent per calendar year for property placed in service after 2022.[47] In general, the bonus depreciation percentage rates are as follows:

---

[42] Code Sec. 179(d)(1)(B)(ii).

[43] Rev. Proc. 2019-8, 2019-3 IRB 347.

[44] Code Sec. 179(f)(4).

[45] Code Sec. 179(d)(1).

[46] Code Sec. 168(k).

[47] Code Sec. 168(k)(6)(A).

1. 100 percent for property placed in service after September 27, 2017, and before January 1, 2023;
2. 80 percent for property placed in service after December 31, 2022, and before January 1, 2024;
3. 60 percent for property placed in service after December 31, 2023, and before January 1, 2025;
4. 40 percent for property placed in service after December 31, 2024, and before January 1, 2026;
5. 20 percent for property placed in service after December 31, 2025, and before January 1, 2027; and
6. 0 percent (bonus expires) for property placed in service after December 31, 2026.

In the case of property with a longer production period and noncommercial aircraft, the placed-in-service deadlines for property acquired after September 27, 2017, are extended for one year.

Property acquired before September 28, 2017, is subject to prior law and a 50-percent rate if placed in service in 2017, a 40-percent rate if placed in service in 2018, and a 30-percent rate if placed in service in 2019. Property acquired before September 28, 2017, and placed in service after 2019 is not eligible for bonus depreciation. In the case of longer production property and noncommercial aircraft acquired before September 28, 2017, each of these placed-in-service dates are extended. The rates are 50 percent if placed in service in 2017 or 2018, 40 percent in 2019, and 30 percent in 2020, and 0 percent after 2020.[48]

Property subject to a binding written contract entered into before September 28, 2017, is not eligible for the 100-percent rate, and is subject to a 40-percent rate if placed in service in 2018 and a 30-percent rate if placed in service in 2019 (2019 and 2020 for longer production period property). The 50-percent rate applies if the property is placed in service in 2017 (2018 for longer production period property).

Election of 50-Percent Rate

A taxpayer may elect to apply the 50-percent rate instead of the 100-percent rate for qualified property placed in service during the taxpayer's first tax year ending after September 27, 2017.[49] For example, a calendar year taxpayer making this election can apply the 50-percent rate to all qualified property placed in service in 2017 and ignore the 100-percent rate that would otherwise apply to qualified property acquired and placed in service after September 27, 2017, and before January 1, 2018.

Qualified Improvement Property

Qualified improvement property has been removed as a specifically named category of property eligible for bonus depreciation, effective for property placed in service after December 31, 2017. However, all qualified improvement property remain eligible for bonus depreciation, provided a technical correction is enacted to

[48] Code Sec. 168(k)(8).

[49] Code Sec. 168(k)(10).

reflect congressional intent that qualified improvement property has a 15-year recovery period.

On August 8, 2018, the IRS issued proposed regulations[50] on first-year bonus depreciation that reflect the TCJA with the 15-year recovery period for improvement property omitted. On August 16, 2018, members of the Senate Finance Committee attempted to clarify congressional intent and called on Treasury and the IRS to issue tax reform guidance consistent with the clarifications. The letter states that Congressional intent for Section 13204 under the TCJA was to provide a 15-year MACRS recovery period for qualified improvement property. The letter indicates that the new law should also provide a 20-year ADS recovery period for qualified improvement property. The Senators intend to introduce technical corrections legislation.

On September 16, 2019, the IRS issued final regulations[51] dealing with 100 percent bonus depreciation. Once again, the IRS declined to make qualified improvement property placed in service after 2017 eligible for bonus depreciation. According to the IRS, a technical correction must first be enacted to give this property its intended 15-year recovery period. With a 15-year recovery period, qualified improvement property will then qualify for bonus depreciation.

It was previously necessary to list qualified improvement property as a separate category of property eligible for bonus depreciation because some types of improvements which met the definition of qualified improvement property had a recovery period of 39 years. Therefore, this 39-year qualified improvement property would not have been eligible for bonus depreciation without the separate category for qualified improvement property because bonus depreciation generally otherwise only applies to property with an MACRS recovery period of 20 years or less.[52] Assuming a technical correction is enacted, all qualified improvement property placed in service after December 31, 2017, will have. a standard 15-year recovery period. This means qualified improvement property will qualify for bonus depreciation because it has a recovery period of 20 years or less.

Qualified improvement property is defined as an improvement to the interior of nonresidential real property, but does not include improvements for expenditures attributable to the enlargement of a building, any elevator or escalator, or the internal structural framework of a building.[53]

Used Property Qualifies

Effective for property acquired and placed in service after September 27, 2017, property previously used by an unrelated person may qualify for bonus depreciation if it meets the following requirements:

1. The taxpayer did not use the property at any time before acquiring it; and
2. The taxpayer acquired the property by "purchase" within the meaning of Code Sec. 179.

---

[50] NPR REG-104397-18.

[51] T.D. 9874.

[52] Code Sec. 168(k)(2).

[53] Code Sec. 168(e)(6).

The acquisition is also subject to the cost requirements of Code Sec. 179, which excludes the portion of the basis of property that is determined by reference to the basis of other property held at any time by the person acquiring the property.[54] In the case of trade-ins, like-kind exchanges, or involuntary conversions, bonus depreciation only applies to any money paid in addition to the trade-in property or in excess of the adjusted basis of the replaced property. This limitation should only apply when the replacement property is used property. Bonus depreciation regulations currently in effect provide that bonus depreciation may be claimed on the carryover and excess basis of property acquired in a like-kind exchange if the property received in the exchange meets all other qualification requirements, including the original use requirement.

Late Elections for a Tax Year Including September 28, 2017

There are three elections that relate to bonus depreciation. Taxpayers may elect out of 100 percent bonus depreciation, elect the 50 percent rate in place of the 100 percent rate, and elect 100 percent bonus depreciation on specified plants in the year of planting or grafting. The IRS has provided procedures that allow taxpayers to make late elections or revoke prior elections for property acquired after September 27, 2017, in a tax year that includes September 28, 2017.[55]

A late election or revocation of an election may be made on an amended return for the 2016 or 2017 tax year that includes September 28, 2017. The taxpayer must file the amended return before filing a return for the first tax year succeeding the 2016 or 2017 tax year, and must include the adjustment directly related to the late election or revocation as well as any collateral adjustments.

A late election or revocation also may be made by filing Form 3115, Application for Change in Accounting Method. The Form 3115 must be filed with a timely filed federal tax return for the first, second, or third tax year succeeding the 2016 or 2017 tax year that includes September 28, 2017. The automatic consent procedures apply and no fee is required.

Taxpayers who filed a timely 2016 or 2017 return that includes September 28, 2017, without following formal election procedures, may be deemed to have made valid bonus depreciation elections. The deemed elections are based on how eligible property was treated on the timely filed tax return. Deemed elections also may be revoked by following the same procedures.

¶ 902 ALTERNATIVE DEPRECIATION SYSTEM

Under the alternative depreciation system,[56] annual depreciation allowances are lower than allowances under the general depreciation system. The alternative depreciation system must be used by corporations to compute earnings and profits for the purpose of applying the rules relating to corporate distributions.[57] Also, the alternative depreciation system must be used in place of the general depreciation system in order to compute depreciation for purposes of the alternative minimum

[54] Code Sec. 168(k)(2)(E).

[55] Rev. Proc. 2019-33, 2019-34 IRB 662.

[56] Code Sec. 168(g).

[57] Code Sec. 312(k)(3).

tax before 1999.[58] The alternative depreciation system also must be used for the following types of property (not all are real estate) to compute depreciation for regular tax purposes:

1. Tangible property that is used predominantly outside the United States during the taxable year;
2. Tax-exempt use property (discussed at ¶ 902.02[A]);
3. Tax-exempt bond-financed property (discussed at ¶ 902.02[B]);
4. Imported property covered by an Executive Order that finds that the country of origin is maintaining trade restrictions or engaging in discriminatory acts;
5. Plants and animals used in farming and placed in service during a taxable year in which the taxpayer elects not to have the uniform capitalization rules of Code Sec. 263A apply;[59] and
6. Property for which the taxpayer elects to have the alternative depreciation system apply (see ¶ 902.02).

A real property trade or business that elects out of the business interest deduction limits must use the alternative depreciation system for residential rental property, nonresidential real property, and qualified improvement property (see ¶ 303.02[D]).

.01 Calculation of Alternative Depreciation

Alternative depreciation, as with general depreciation, is calculated using an applicable method, convention, and recovery period. The residential rental property and nonresidential real property classes are defined in the same manner for the alternative depreciation system as for the general depreciation system discussed above. Alternative depreciation for both classes of real property is calculated using the straight line method and the mid-month convention, but the recovery period for nonresidential real property is 40 years, rather than the 39 years under the general depreciation system. For property placed in service after 2017, the alternative depreciation system recovery period for residential rental property is 30 years. For property placed in service before 2018, the alternative depreciation system recovery period for residential rental property is 40 years.[60]

Under a special rule, the recovery period under the alternative depreciation system for any leased tax-exempt use property must be at least 125 percent of the lease term.[61] For example, if nonresidential real property is leased to a tax-exempt entity under a 99-year lease, the recovery period for the property is 123.75 years, rather than the 39 years that applies to nonresidential real property under the general depreciation system.

---

[58] Code Sec. 56(a)(1)(A).

[59] Code Sec. 263A(d)(3) and (e)(2)(A).

[60] Code Sec. 168(g)(2).

[61] Code Sec. 168(g)(3)(A).

[A] Election of Alternative Depreciation

A taxpayer may irrevocably elect to use the alternative depreciation system in lieu of the general depreciation system.[62] In the case of residential rental property and nonresidential real property, the election to use the alternative depreciation system may be made separately for each property. In the case of other classes of property, the election applies to all property within the class placed in service during the taxable year.

The election to have the alternative depreciation system apply must be made by the due date, including extensions, of the tax return for the first taxable year for which the election is being made. A statement identifying the election by reference to the Internal Revenue Code or Act section and identifying the property for which the election is being made must accompany the tax return.[63]

Since the alternative depreciation system provides lower annual depreciation deductions, most taxpayers will not want to elect to have the alternative depreciation system apply.

The calculation of depreciation under the alternative depreciation system is illustrated in the following example.

> ***Comprehensive Example 4:*** In July, the Taxpayer who is on the calendar year purchases an office building for $250,000. Of the total purchase price, $200,000 is allocated to the building and $50,000 is allocated to the land (how such an allocation might be made is discussed in at ¶ 102.02[A]). The building is nonresidential real property for depreciation purposes. If the Taxpayer uses the general depreciation system, the Taxpayer's depreciation deduction for the year is $2,348. This figure is determined by computing a full year's depreciation ($200,000/39 = $5,128), dividing this full year figure by 12 to determine a full month's depreciation ($5,128/12 = $427), and multiplying the full month's depreciation by 5.5 to reflect the number of months under the mid-month convention that the property is in service during the year ($427 × 5.5 = $2,348). (Note that the $2,348 figure could have been arrived at by multiplying $200,000 by 1.1752%, the percentage of basis from the optional table for the first year when nonresidential real property is placed in service in July.)
>
> Suppose, however, that the Taxpayer elects to use the alternative depreciation system. In this case, depreciation must be based on a recovery period of 40 years, and the Taxpayer's depreciation deduction for the year would be $2,292. This figure is determined by computing a full year's depreciation ($200,000/40 = $5,000), dividing this full year figure by 12 to determine a full month's depreciation ($5,000/12 = $416.66), and multiplying the full month's depreciation by 5.5 to reflect the number of months under the mid-month convention that the property is in service during the year ($416.66 × 5.5 = $2,292). (Note that the $2,292 figure could have been arrived at by multiplying $200,000 by 1.1460, the percentage of basis from the optional table under the

[62] Code Sec. 168(g)(7).

[63] Temp. Reg. § 301.9100-7T.

alternative depreciation system for the first year when nonresidential real property is placed in service in July. The optional table is set out at ¶ 902.01[B].)

[B] Use of Optional Tables

The IRS has provided optional depreciation tables that may be used to compute the annual depreciation allowance under the alternative depreciation system for most types of property.[64] The optional depreciation tables specify schedules of annual depreciation rates that are applied to the *unadjusted* basis of property in each taxable year. If a taxpayer uses a table to compute the depreciation deduction for any item of property, the taxpayer generally must use the table to compute the depreciation deduction for the entire recovery period of the property. A taxpayer may not continue to use the table, however, if there are any adjustments to the basis of the property other than for depreciation or an addition or improvement that is subject to depreciation as a separate item of property.

OPTIONAL TABLE FOR NONRESIDENTIAL REAL PROPERTY (and RESIDENTIAL RENTAL PROPERTY PLACED IN SERVICE BEFORE 2018) UNDER ALTERNATIVE DEPRECIATION SYSTEM

If the Recovery Year is:	And the Month in the First Recovery Year the Property is Placed in Service is:					
	1	2	3	4	5	6
	the Depreciation Rate is:					
1	2.396	2.188	1.979	1.771	1.563	1.354
2 to 40	2.500	2.500	2.500	2.500	2.500	2.500
41	0.104	0.312	0.521	0.729	0.937	1.146

If the Recovery Year is:	And the Month in the First Recovery Year the Property is Placed in Service is:					
	7	8	9	10	11	12
	the Depreciation Rate is:					
1	1.146	0.938	0.729	0.521	0.313	0.104
2 to 40	2.500	2.500	2.500	2.500	2.500	2.500
41	1.354	1.562	1.771	1.979	2.187	2.396

[64] Rev. Proc. 87-57, 1987-2 CB 687; Rev. Proc. 2019-8, 2019-3 IRB 347.

OPTIONAL TABLE FOR RESIDENTIAL RENTAL PROPERTY PLACED IN SERVICE AFTER 2017 UNDER ALTERNATIVE DEPRECIATION SYSTEM

If the Recovery Year is:	And the Month in the First Recovery Year the Property is Placed in Service is:											
	1	2	3	4	5	6	7	8	9	10	11	12
	the Depreciation Rate is:											
Year												
1	3.204%	2.926%	2.649%	2.371%	2.093%	1.815%	1.528%	1.250%	0.972%	0.694%	0.417%	0.139%
2-30	3.333%	3.333%	3.333%	3.333%	3.333%	3.333%	3.333%	3.333%	3.333%	3.333%	3.333%	3.333%
31	0.139%	0.417%	0.694%	0.972%	1.250%	1.528%	1.815%	2.093%	2.371%	2.649%	2.926%	3.204%

.02 Real Property Subject to Alternative Depreciation

The alternative depreciation system must be used for property used predominantly outside the United States,[65] tax-exempt use property,[66] and tax-exempt bond financed property.[67] Also, the alternative depreciation system must be used before 1999 to compute alternative minimum taxable income.[68] A real property trade or business that elects out of the business interest deduction limits must use the alternative depreciation system for residential rental property, nonresidential real property, and qualified improvement property (see ¶ 303.02[D]). A farming business that elects out of the business interest deduction limits must use the alternative depreciation system for property with a MACRS recovery period of ten years or more. See Rev. Proc. 2019-8[69] for the procedures that apply to a business electing out of the business interest deduction limits and making the required switch to the alternative depreciation system.

[A] Tax-Exempt Use Property

Tax-exempt organizations and government units gain no benefit from depreciation or tax credits on property that they own or use. Through leasing from investors rather than buying and owning property, tax-exempt entities could obtain indirectly, through reduced rentals, the incentives intended for investments in property. The investors, because of the investment incentives of depreciation and tax credits, could offer the lower rentals.

Prior to the Tax Reform Act of 1984, the only limit on these mutually beneficial arrangements was a denial of the investment credit on property leased to or used by certain tax-exempt organizations and domestic government units. Sale-leasebacks involving almost every item of property that could be used by a tax-exempt organization or government unit, including the local town hall and city jail, were widespread and represented a severe drain on federal revenue. In 1984, Congress imposed a complicated series of restrictions on the tax advantages of leasing property to tax-exempt organizations and government units, including foreign governments. These restrictions included loss of the investment credit and accelerated depreciation, and longer recovery periods for property leased to or

[65] Code Sec. 168(g)(1)(A).
[66] Code Sec. 168(g)(1)(B).
[67] Code Sec. 168(g)(1)(C).
[68] Code Sec. 56(a)(1)(A).
[69] 2019-3 IRB 347.

used by a tax-exempt entity. The required use of the alternative depreciation system for tax-exempt use property reflects a continuation of this policy.

Disqualified Lease Defined

In general, in the case of real property, tax-exempt use property is the portion of nonresidential real property leased to a tax-exempt entity in a disqualified lease.[70] A disqualified lease is any lease to a tax-exempt entity that falls into one of the following categories:

1. All or part of the leased property is financed by a tax-exempt obligation, and the tax-exempt entity leasing the property, or a related entity, participates in the financing;
2. The lease includes a purchase or sale option at a fixed or determinable price which involves the tax-exempt entity, or there is the equivalent of such an option;
3. The lease term exceeds 20 years; or
4. The lease is made after a sale or other transfer of the property by, or lease of the property from, the tax-exempt entity or a related entity, and the property was used by the tax-exempt entity or a related entity before the sale or other transfer or lease.[71]

In the case of property leased to a partnership, whether the property is tax-exempt use property is determined at the partner level. Property leased to a partnership is treated as leased to the partners in proportion to their distributive share of partnership items. Similar rules apply to other pass-through entities.[72]

Exceptions from Definition

As is apparent from the definition of a disqualified lease, most commercial leases to tax-exempt entities will not be disqualified leases. Even when there is a disqualified lease, there are several exceptions that may prevent property leased to a tax-exempt entity from being subject to the alternative depreciation system.

Tax-exempt use property does not include any property if the portion of the property leased to tax-exempt entities in disqualified leases is 35 percent or less of the property.[73] The 35 percent is measured by the net rentable floor space in the property, computed without including any common areas. Tax-exempt use property does not include real estate that is leased to a tax-exempt entity for a period of less than three years.[74] Options to renew are included in the lease term, unless at fair market value at the date of renewal, and two or more successive leases that are part of the same transaction or series of transactions for the same or substantially similar property are treated as a single lease.[75]

[70] Code Sec. 168(h)(1)(B).
[71] Code Sec. 168(h)(1)(B)(ii).
[72] Code Sec. 168(h)(5).
[73] Code Sec. 168(h)(1)(B)(iii).
[74] Code Sec. 168(h)(1)(C).
[75] Code Sec. 168(i)(3).

Finally, tax-exempt use property does not include any portion of property predominantly used by the tax-exempt entity in an unrelated trade or business when the income from the trade or business is subject to tax under Code Sec. 511.[76]

Tax-Exempt Entities

Tax-exempt entities include: (1) The United States, any state or political subdivision, any possession of the United States, or agencies and instrumentalities of any of the foregoing; (2) An organization, other than a farmers' cooperative, that is exempt from income tax; (3) A foreign person or entity, unless the property used by the foreign person or entity is subject to U.S. taxation; and (4) any Indian tribal government.[77]

[B] Tax-Exempt Bond Financed Property

Tax-exempt bond financed property subject to the alternative depreciation system is property placed in service after 1986 to the extent it is financed directly or indirectly by bonds on which the income is exempt from tax under Code Sec. 103(a).[78] The extent to which property is considered financed by the proceeds of tax-exempt bonds is determined based on the order in which property is placed in service.[79]

Tax-exempt bond financed property does not include qualified residential projects.[80] These are low-income housing projects that meet the minimum set-aside requirements that apply for the low-income housing credit (see ¶ 805). These are projects in which 20 percent or more of the units are occupied by tenants whose incomes are 50 percent or less of the area median gross income or in which 40 percent or more of the units are occupied by tenants whose incomes are 60 percent or less of the area median gross income.

[C] Alternative Minimum Tax

The alternative depreciation system must be used for real estate to determine the depreciation deduction in computing alternative minimum taxable income before 1999 for purposes of the alternative minimum tax.[81] Since the basis of property for minimum tax purposes is adjusted under the alternative depreciation system, gain or loss on the sale of property may be different for regular tax and minimum tax purposes. For property placed in service after 1998, regular depreciation, not alternative depreciation, is used to compute alternative minimum taxable income.

For property placed in service before 1987, the excess of accelerated depreciation over straight-line depreciation for real estate is a tax preference item subject to the minimum tax.[82] This rule continues to apply for purposes of the minimum tax in the case of property placed in service before 1987.

[76] Code Sec. 168(h)(1)(D).
[77] Code Sec. 168(h)(2).
[78] Code Sec. 168(g)(5)(A).
[79] Code Sec. 168(g)(5)(B).
[80] Code Sec. 168(g)(5)(C).
[81] Code Sec. 56(a)(1).
[82] Code Sec. 57(a)(7).

¶ 903 COST SEGREGATION

As discussed at ¶ 901.01, taxpayers must use the correct method and proper recovery period for each asset or property owned to calculate depreciation for income tax purposes. Property, whether acquired or constructed, often consists of numerous asset types with different recovery periods. Thus, property must be separated into individual components or asset groups having the same recovery periods and placed-in-service dates in order to properly compute depreciation.

When the actual cost of each individual component is available, this is a rather simple procedure. However, when only lumpsum costs are available, cost estimating techniques may be required to segregate or allocate costs to individual components of property (for instance, land, land improvements, buildings, equipment, furniture and fixtures, etc.). This type of analysis is generally called a cost segregation study or cost allocation study. The most common situation is the allocation or reallocation of building costs to tangible personal property.

In addition to identifying specific components that qualify as personal property, cost segregation studies may treat portions of building components as personal property. For example, a study may conclude that 15 percent of a building's electrical system directly supports personal property, such as specialized kitchen equipment. Based on that conclusion, the study will then treat 15 percent of the electrical system as personal (Code Sec. 1245) property. The allocation of building components as personal property is often a contentious issue between the IRS and taxpayers. (See the discussion on cost allocation beginning at ¶ 102.02.)

.01 Recharacterizing Existing Property

Taxpayers may conduct a cost segregation study on property they already own and then recompute depreciation deductions for prior years. In general, the IRS takes the position that in the year an asset is placed in service, an accounting method is adopted relative to the depreciation method, recovery period, or convention for the depreciable property. In any later year, a change in depreciation method, recovery period, or convention resulting from a reclassification of that property results in a change in method of accounting that requires the consent of the IRS.[83]

The Fifth Circuit, affirming the Tax Court, however, has held that the reclassification of gas station properties as 15-year property for MACRS purposes was not a change in accounting method requiring the IRS's consent.[84] The Circuit Court agreed with the Tax Court that taxpayers should be allowed to make temporal changes in their depreciation schedules without the consent of the IRS. The Court also affirmed that Brookshire's change in the classification of its gas station properties from straight-line depreciation of non-residential real estate to declining balance depreciation of 15-year property was not a change in Brookshire's method of accounting under Code Sec. 446.

---

[83] *See* Rev. Rul. 90-38, 1990-1 CB 57.

[84] Brookshire Brothers Holding, Inc. & Subsidiaries, CA-5, 320 F.3d 507 (2003), *aff'g* T.C. Memo. 2001-150.

Green Forest Manufacturing Inc.[85] followed Brookshire by holding that a change in computing depreciation from the general depreciation system to the alternative depreciation system is not a change in method of accounting. *O'Shaughnessy*[86] also followed *Brookshire* by holding that a change in classification under MACRS is not a change in method of accounting.

The decision of the Fifth Circuit in Brookshire conflicts with the opinion of the Tenth Circuit in *Kurzet.*[87] In *Kurzet*, the taxpayer sought to change the classification of a reservoir from nonresidential real property with a 31.5 year recovery period to 15-year property. The taxpayer did not change the method of depreciation for the reservoir, which was the straight-line method. Although the Tenth Circuit found some persuasive value to the argument that a change in recovery period under MACRS should be treated like a change in useful life, the Court concluded that the IRS's interpretation of Reg. § 1.446-1(e)(2)(ii) as requiring a taxpayer to obtain permission for a change in recovery period was not plainly erroneous.

Following on the heels of the court decisions, the IRS issued new temporary regulations covering this issue, effective for tax years ending on or after December 30, 2003.[88] The regulations were made final, effective December 28, 2006.[89] The regulations provide that a change in the depreciation or amortization method, period of recovery, or convention of a depreciable or amortizable asset is a change in method of accounting. Example 9 of Reg. § 1.446-1(e)(2)(iii) specifically relates to changes based on a cost segregation study. However, for depreciable or amortizable property placed in service in tax years ending before the effective date of the new temporary regulations, the IRS will not assert that a change in computing depreciation is a change in method of accounting.[90] For example, if a taxpayer completed a cost segregation study in 2005 for its property placed in service in 2002 and, as a result, reclassified that property from nonresidential real property to 15-year property, the IRS will not assert that the change in computing depreciation resulting from the reclassification is a change in method of accounting. The taxpayer in this situation may file amended federal tax returns for 2002 and any affected later year to effect this change in computing depreciation.

For a detailed look at what IRS examiners will look for in a cost segregation study, see the IRS's Cost Segregation Audit Techniques Guide (Revised October 2016).

¶ 904 ACRS DEPRECIATION FOR PRE-1987 PROPERTY

For most property placed in service after 1980 and before 1987, the Economic Recovery Tax Act of 1981 allowed the cost of the property to be recovered under an accelerated schedule over much shorter periods than it was possible to recover this cost under the pre-1981 depreciation methods that were keyed to the property's useful life. While the Accelerated Cost Recovery System (ACRS) replaced the old depreciation system, the old system must continue to be used for property placed in

[85] T.C. Memo. 2003-75

[86] CA-8, 332 F.3d 1125 (2003), *rev'g in part* 2002-1 USTC ¶ 50,235 (D. Minn. 2001).

[87] CA-10, 222 F.3d 830 (2000).

[88] Reg. § 1.446-1T(e)(2).

[89] T.D. 9307; Reg. § 1.446-1(e)(2).

[90] CC-2004-007.

service before 1981. Similarly, ACRS must continue to be used for most property placed in service after 1980 and before 1987, even though ACRS was replaced by the general depreciation system or Modified Accelerated Cost Recovery System for property placed in service after 1986.

.01 Computation of Deduction

Under ACRS, as originally enacted, most real property was assigned a recovery period of 15 years. This recovery period applied to low-income housing and to all other real estate. The Tax Reform Act of 1984 extended the recovery period for real estate, other than low-income housing, from 15 to 18 years. Amendments in 1985 further extended the recovery period to 19 years.

The 18-year recovery period generally applies to property placed in service after March 15, 1984, and before May 9, 1985, although a separate schedule applies to 18-year property placed in service after June 22, 1984, to reflect the adoption of the mid-month convention. The 19-year recovery period generally applies to property placed in service after May 8, 1985 and before 1987.

Under the transition rules, the cost of property placed in service before 1987, however, may be recovered under the 15-year ACRS schedule if the taxpayer or qualified person entered into a binding contract to purchase or construct the property before March 16, 1984, or if construction of the property by or for the taxpayer or qualified person was begun before March 16, 1984. Similarly, the cost of property placed in service before 1987 may be recovered under the 18-year ACRS schedule if there was a binding contract to construct or acquire the property, or if construction was begun by or for the taxpayer after March 15, 1984, and before May 9, 1985. A qualified person is one who transfers his or her rights in the contract or the property to the taxpayer, but only if the property was not placed in service before the transfer to the taxpayer.

The IRS has issued depreciation (or cost recovery) schedules based on an 18-year period and a 19-year period using the 175 percent declining balance method of depreciation and a mid-month convention for most real property, other than low-income housing, acquired after June 22, 1984. There are separate schedules for 18-year property acquired after March 15, 1984, and before June 23, 1984, which do not reflect the use of the mid-month convention. A similar schedule, but based on a 15-year recovery period applies to real property, other than low-income housing, acquired after 1980 but prior to March 16, 1984. The ACRS schedule for pre-1987 low-income housing is based on a 15-year period and 200 percent declining balance depreciation.

Computing the proper ACRS depreciation deduction is simply a matter of applying the percentage specified in the appropriate schedule to the unadjusted basis of the property. The ACRS schedules for real property are set out below.

Extended recovery periods and less accelerated depreciation were required for property outside the United States. Schedules are also provided for property falling in this category.

[A] Straight-Line Election

Instead of using the percentages and recovery periods that reflect accelerated depreciation over the appropriate ACRS recovery period, a taxpayer could have elected straight-line depreciation over any one of three recovery periods. In the case of real estate, the straight-line election was available over the usual ACRS recovery period (*i.e.,* 15, 18, or 19 years) and over extended recovery periods of 35 or 45 years.

Since the straight-line election served to reduce depreciation deductions, at least in the initial years after the property was placed in service, the election was not often used. In the case of rehabilitated real estate, however, the tax credit for rehabilitation costs was available only if straight-line depreciation was used to recover costs. When the credit was a factor, the straight-line election was made.

[B] ACRS Schedules

The ACRS schedules are keyed to the year and to the month during the first year in which the property was placed in service. If ACRS property is sold before the end of the recovery period, the ACRS deduction for the year of disposition must be adjusted to reflect only the months during that year that the property was in service. Adjustments are also required in the case of short taxable years.

Accelerated Schedules

The ACRS schedules that apply when straight-line depreciation or optional longer recovery periods were not elected when the property was placed in service may be found as follows:

Table 1. 15-Year Real Property, other than low-income housing, placed in service after December 31, 1980, and before March 16, 1984. Notice 81-16, 1981 CB 545.

Table 2. 18-Year Real Property placed in service after March 15, 1984, and before June 23, 1984. Notice 84-16, 1984-52 IRB 64.

Table 3. 18-Year Real Property placed in service after June 22, 1984, and before May 9, 1985. Notice 84-16, 1984-2 CB 475.

Table 4. 19-Year Real Property placed in service after May 8, 1985, and before 1987. Rev. Proc. 86-14, 1986-1 CB 542.

Table 5. 15-Year Low-Income Housing placed in service after December 31, 1980, and before May 9, 1985). Notice 81-16, 1981-2 CB 545.

Table 6. 15-Year Low-Income Housing placed in service after May 8, 1985, and before 1987. Rev. Proc. 86-14, 1986-1 CB 542.

Table 7. Low-Income Housing Used Predominantly Outside the United States placed in service after December 31, 1980 and before May 9, 1985; 15-Year Real Property Used Predominantly Outside the United States placed in service after December 31, 1980 and before March 16, 1984; 18-Year Real Property Used Predominantly Outside the United States placed in service after March 15, 1984, and before June 23, 1984. Notice 84-16, 1984-52 IRB 64.

Table 8. 18-Year Real Property Used Predominantly Outside the United States placed in service after June 22, 1984, and before May 9, 1985. Notice 84-16, 1984-52 IRB 64.

Table 9. 19-Year Real Property Used Predominantly Outside the United States placed in service after May 8, 1985, and before 1987. Rev. Proc. 86-14, 1986-1 CB 542.

Table 10. Low-Income Housing Used Predominantly Outside the United States placed in service after May 8, 1985, and before 1987. Rev. Proc. 86-14, 1986-1 CB 542.

Optional Straight-Line Schedules

Depreciation schedules that applied when straight-line depreciation or optional longer recovery periods were elected when the property was placed in service may be found as follows:

Table 11. 15-Year Real Property placed in service after December 31, 1980, and before March 16, 1984; Low-Income Housing placed in service after December 31, 1980, and before March 16, 1984. Prop. Reg. § 1.168-2(c)(4)(ii)(A).

Table 12. 18-Year Real Property placed in service after March 15, 1984, and before June 23, 1984; Low-Income Housing placed in service after March 15, 1984, and before May 9, 1985. Notice 84-16, 1984-52 IRB 64.

Table 13. 18-Year Real Property, other than low-income housing, placed in service after June 22, 1984, and before May 9, 1985. Notice 84-16, 1984-52 IRB 64.

Table 14. 19-Year Real Property, other than low-income housing, placed in service after May 8, 1985, and before 1987. Announcement 86-5, 1986-3 IRB 43; Rev. Proc. 86-14, 1986-1 CB 542.

Table 15. Low-Income Housing placed in service after May 8, 1985. Rev. Proc. 86-14, 1986-1 CB 542.

Table 16. Low-Income Housing placed in service after December 31, 1980, and before May 9, 1985; 15-Year Real Property placed in service after December 31, 1980, and before March 16, 1984; 18-Year Real Property placed in service after March 15, 1984, and before June 23, 1984. Notice 84-16, 1984-52 IRB 64.

Table 17. 18-Year Real Property placed in service after June 22, 1984, and before May 9, 1985. Notice 84-16, 1984-2 CB 475.

Table 18. 19-Year Real Property placed in service after May 8, 1985, and before 1987. Rev. Proc. 86-14, 1986-1 CB 542.

Table 19. Low-Income Housing placed in service after May 8, 1985, and before 1987. Rev. Proc. 86-14, 1986-1 CB 542.

Table 20. Low-Income Housing placed in service after December 31, 1980; 15-Year Real property placed in service after December 31, 1980, and before March 16, 1984; 18-Year Real Property placed in service after March 15, 1984, and before June 23, 1984. Notice 84-16, 1984-2 CB 475.

Table 21. 18-Year Real Property placed in service after June 22, 1984, and before May 9, 1985. Notice 84-16, 1984-2 CB 475.

Table 22. 19-Year Real Property placed in service after May 8, 1985, and before 1987. Rev. Proc. 86-14, 1986-1 CB 542.

.02 Additions and Improvements

In the case of improvements and additions to pre-1987 ACRS property, different rules apply to additions and improvements that are merely components of the original property and additions and improvements that qualify as substantial improvements. In general, the deduction for any component of a building added to the building before 1987 must be computed in the same way as the deduction for the building itself.[91] This general rule, however, was modified by transition rules to reflect the changing recovery periods for real property between 1981 and 1987.

The ACRS recovery period for real property placed in service after 1980 and before March 16, 1984, is 15 years. This recovery period was changed to 18 years for most real property other than low-income housing placed in service after March 15, 1984, and before May 9, 1985. The first component added after March 15, 1984, and before May 9, 1985, must be treated as a separate building and depreciated using the 18-year cost recovery schedules, if the building was placed in service before March 16, 1984. The deduction for any subsequent components added to the building before May 9, 1985, must be calculated in the same way as the deduction for the first component added after March 15, 1984, and before May 9, 1985.

The ACRS recovery period for most real property placed in service after May 8, 1985, and before January 1, 1987, was extended to 19 years. Rules similar to those for the transition from a 15-year recovery period to an 18-year recovery period apply to the transition from an 18-year recovery period to a 19-year recovery period. The first component added after May 8, 1985, and before January 1, 1987, must be treated as a separate building and depreciated using the 19-year cost recovery schedules, if the building was placed in service before May 9, 1985. The deduction for any subsequent components added to the building before 1987 must be calculated in the same way as the deduction for the first component added after May 8, 1985, and before 1987.

[A] Substantial Improvements as Separate Property

An exception to the general rule that cost recovery deductions for pre-1987 additions and improvements to a building are computed in the same way as the deduction for the building (or, when the transition rules apply, the first component added after March 15, 1984, or May 9, 1985) applies to "substantial improvements" made three or more years after the building was placed in service. Under this rule, a substantial improvement is treated as a separate property for purposes of computing the ACRS deduction. As separate property, the various elections and options under the ACRS system were available for a substantial improvement.

[91] Former Code Sec. 168(f)(1) of the Internal Revenue Code of 1954.

[B] Qualification as Substantial Improvement

To qualify as a substantial improvement, the capital expenditures for improvements to the building during a 24-month period had to be at least 25 percent of the adjusted basis of the building as of the first day of the 24-month period. Adjusted basis for this purpose was calculated by ignoring any prior depreciation or cost recovery deductions.

¶ 905 DEPRECIATION OF PRE-1981 PROPERTY

Taxpayers that placed depreciable property in service before 1981 were generally free to use any reasonable method of computing depreciation, as long as the method chosen was used consistently throughout the life of the property. Depreciation deductions were spread over the useful life of the property. Useful life was based on how long the property could reasonably be expected to be used for the purpose in which it was employed. In many cases, the useful life of real property could be as long as 40 years or more.

While the consistent application of any reasonable method of depreciation was permitted for pre-1981 property, the Internal Revenue Code of 1954 specifically authorized three methods:

1. Straight-line method;
2. Declining-balance method; and
3. Sum-of-the-years digits method.

Also, in the case of real property, the use of accelerated methods of depreciation was limited.

.01 Calculation of Deduction for Real Property

Accelerated depreciation is a depreciation method other than the straight-line method. For real property placed in service before 1981, accelerated depreciation is limited. Property that was new commercial property when placed in service cannot be depreciated faster than the 150 percent declining-balance method permits, and used commercial property cannot be depreciated faster than the straight-line method permits.

Residential property placed in service before 1981 is subject to more liberal restrictions on the use of accelerated depreciation methods. Property that was new residential property when placed in service may be depreciated using the double (200%) declining-balance method or the sum-of-the-years digits method. Used residential property may be depreciated using the 125 percent declining-balance method.

[A] Depreciation Methods

Straight-line depreciation is simply the amount calculated by dividing the basis of property (less salvage value and prior depreciation) by the number of years remaining in the useful life of the property. The cost of any improvements are simply added to basis for purposes of computing depreciation. Property or improvements acquired, sold, or disposed of during a year are allowed a proportionate part of a full year's deduction.

The *declining-balance method* of depreciation provides greater depreciation deductions during the early years of a property's useful life and progressively smaller deductions in later years (hence the term "accelerated depreciation"). Under the declining-balance method, the deduction is calculated by applying a percentage of the straight-line rate to the property's adjusted basis. For instance, a building with a 50-year useful life would have a straight-line rate of two percent (100%/50 years). The double declining-balance (200 percent) rate for this building would be four percent (200% × 2%); the 150 percent declining-balance rate would be three percent; and the 125 percent declining-balance rate would be 2.5 percent. Property held for only part of the year is entitled to only a proportionate part of a full year's deduction.

The *sum-of-the-years digits method* of depreciation is also an accelerated method. Under this method, a fraction of the property's original basis (less salvage value) is deducted each year. The fraction for any year is set by adding the years of the property's useful life to determine the denominator and using the number of years left in the property's useful life for the numerator. For instance, if real property had a useful life of 40 years, the denominator of the fraction would be calculated by adding the digits 1 through 40 (1 + 2 + 3 + 4, etc.) to arrive at 820. The fraction to determine the deduction for this property for its first year (when there are 40 years in its useful life) would be 40/820; the fraction for the second year would be 39/820; for the third year, 38/820; etc. Property in service for only part of a year is entitled to only a proportionate part of a full year's deduction.

[B] Change of Depreciation Methods

A change in depreciation methods for property placed in service before 1981 is considered a change in accounting method that generally requires IRS consent. A change from a declining-balance method to the straight-line method, however, may be made without prior IRS consent.[92] It is often beneficial to switch to the straight-line method when the depreciation deductions from the declining-balance method are about to fall below the deductions that would be available if the remaining basis of the property were depreciated using the straight-line method.

.02 Anti-Churning Rules

When the ACRS system was adopted for assets placed in service after 1980, Congress moved to block attempts by taxpayers to get the more generous deductions under ACRS for property that they had already placed in service. The anti-churning rules, as they were called, prevented taxpayers from transferring property to related parties to gain the larger ACRS deductions. The same rules were adopted when the MACRS system was adopted for post-1987 property. However, these anti-churning rules do not apply to real property because the depreciation deductions for real property under the general depreciation system (MACRS) are much less generous than those that were available under ACRS.

---

[92] Rev. Rul. 74-324, 1974-2 CB 66.

[A] Real Property Rules

The anti-churning rules exclude certain property from the definition of recovery property under ACRS. In the case of real property, recovery property entitled to ACRS does not include any property that was:

1. Owned by the taxpayer or a related person at any time during 1980;
2. Leased to a person, or related person, who owned the property at any time during 1980; and
3. Acquired in a tax-free exchange or acquisition under Code Secs. 1031, 1033, 1038, or 1039 to the extent of the basis of the property given up in the transaction.[93]

[B] Related Party Transfers

The relationships that bring property within the ambit of the anti-churning rules are:

1. Family, which includes brothers, sisters, spouse, ancestors, and lineal descendants;
2. Fiduciary, which includes a trust, its grantor, trustee, and beneficiary;
3. Corporation and shareholder owning at least ten percent of the corporation;
4. Partnership and partner owning at least ten percent of the partnership; and
5. Corporations under 50 percent common control.

[C] Tax-Free Transfers

Restrictions are imposed on tax-free transfers of recovery property under ACRS. Transfers covered by this transferee rule include:

1. Liquidation of a subsidiary;
2. Transfer to a controlled corporation;
3. Tax-free reorganization;
4. Bankruptcy or receivership;
5. Contribution to a partnership; or
6. Distribution from a partnership.

In these transactions, the transferee must continue to use the transferor's depreciation recovery period and method in computing the ACRS deduction for the portion of the transferee's basis that does not exceed the transferor's adjusted basis. The transferee must, as a result, compute depreciation on the carried-over adjusted basis as if the transfer had not occurred. The transferee may, however, depreciate the excess basis as if it were newly acquired property.

[93] Former Code Sec. 168(e)(4) of the 1954 Internal Revenue Code and Code Sec. 168(f)(5) of the 1986 Internal Revenue Code.

Chapter 10
Development, Subdivision, and Sales in the Ordinary Course of Business

¶ 1000 Overview of Chapter
¶ 1001 Development Costs
¶ 1002 Dealer Status
¶ 1003 Subdivision by Investor

¶ 1000 OVERVIEW OF CHAPTER

The development, subdivision, and sale of real estate in the ordinary course of business involves tax questions and problems that are unique when compared to those involved in the one-time sale of either rental property or property used in a trade or business.

The cost or basis of the property must be apportioned among the parcels that are sold in order to determine income as the parcels are sold. Also, there are the development costs that must be included in the basis of the property and allocated among the parcels. In many cases, a developer will sell lots before all development costs have been incurred. In this case, the developer may estimate future development costs and allocate a share to the lots already sold in order to reduce the taxable income that the developer must report. (How basis is determined generally is considered at ¶ 101.01.) For home builders, there is also the question of whether their homes qualify for a special tax credit.

Apart from the amount of income that must be reported as subdivided property is sold, there is the question of the character of that income. The sale of property held for investment generally produces capital gain or loss, while property that is sold in the ordinary course of business produces ordinary income or loss. The distinction usually turns on whether the seller is considered a "dealer" in real property. Dealer sales generally produce the ordinary income or loss result. Of course, the distinction between capital gain and ordinary income is less important when the two types of income are subject to the same or nearly the same tax rates, but Congress is constantly changing the treatment of capital gain. Even when the two types of income are subject to the same tax rates, the distinction remains important because of the rules limiting deduction of capital losses. Capital losses can always offset capital gain, but the deduction of capital losses against ordinary income is severely limited.

At times, an investor may hold property that cannot be sold unless the property is subdivided. The subdivision and sale of separate parcels may create dealer status. There is, however, a statutory provision that allows an investor to realize capital gain when the investor must subdivide holdings for sale.

¶ 1001 DEVELOPMENT COSTS

In the early stages of development, a developer incurs costs and realizes no income as the property is readied for sale. During this time, some of the costs may qualify as ordinary and necessary business expenses which are currently deductible. Many costs, however, are expenditures that have to be capitalized as part of the cost of the property under the capitalization rules discussed at ¶ 103.01 or under those that apply to additions and improvements discussed at ¶ 801. Development costs are also capital expenditures. These capitalized costs can be recouped only as sales are made. The total cost of the property, including development costs, must be apportioned among units or parcels that are sold separately to determine the amount of income or loss on each unit or parcel.

.01 Equitable Apportionment Rule

Under the regulations, when part of a larger property is sold, the cost or other basis of the entire property must be equitably apportioned among the several parts, and the gain realized or loss sustained on the part of the entire property sold is the difference between the selling price and the cost or other basis allocated to the part sold.[1] The sale of each part is treated as a separate transaction and the gain or loss is computed separately on each part. The seller cannot defer reporting gain or loss until the entire property has been sold.

Even if the taxpayer did not contemplate subdivision at the time the real estate was purchased but intended to sell it as a whole, the subsequent sale of part of the property in separate tracts creates a series of separate transactions for purposes of accounting for gain or loss.[2]

The rule of equitable apportionment applies to condominiums. A taxpayer who purchases a rental apartment building, converts that building into condominiums, and then sells the units individually cannot use the cost recovery method of accounting for the income from the sales and thus defer reporting income until the taxpayer recovers the entire basis.[3] The equitable apportionment rule also applies to the subdivision and sale of cemetery lots.[4]

Development costs expended or to be expended are added to basis that is apportioned.[5] These costs include such items as the cost of water and sewer facilities, even though the facilities are transferred to a public service company without consideration.[6] Other costs added to basis include the cost of surveying

[1] Reg. § 1.61-6(a).

[2] F. Skinner, 20 BTA 491, CCH Dec. 6241, *acq.* 1931-1 CB 60.

[3] Rev. Rul. 79-276, 1979-2 CB 200.

[4] Cedar Park Cemetery Assn., Inc., CA-7, 50-2 USTC ¶ 9376, 183 F.2d 553, *cert. denied*, 292 U.S. 639, 54 S.Ct. 773.

[5] Colony, Inc., 26 TC 30, CCH Dec. 21,665, *acq.* 1958-1 CB 4, *aff'd*, CA-6, 57-1 USTC ¶ 9636, 244 F.2d 75.

[6] G.W. Offutt, CA-4, 64-2 USTC ¶ 9757, 336 F.2d 483.

boundaries and expenditures for platting, grading and cindering streets, and installing sidewalks.[7] The addition of development costs to the basis of subdivided real estate is considered further at ¶ 1001.02.

[A] Manner of Apportionment of Basis

The cost or other basis of property must be "equitably apportioned" among the parts that are sold separately. Equitable apportionment is not ratable apportionment. The apportionment of basis must reflect differences in the relative values of the parcels being sold, if such differences exist. Of course, when there is no difference in value, apportionment may be done on a pro rata basis. For instance, in *J.D. Byram*,[8] the Court of Appeals upheld an IRS determination to allocate the basis of a parcel of land that had been subdivided into two tracts on a pro rata basis. The taxpayer was unable to show that the value per acre of Tract One was greater than that of Tract Two on the date of purchase.

In many cases, however, there will be a difference in relative values because of size, location, or other factors, and the apportionment of basis must reflect this difference. There is an opportunity for tax planning in this. If more basis can be allocated to the earlier sales, income can be deferred until later sales. For example, in a housing subdivision, some lots may be located on a lake. These lots, most likely, will have a higher value than interior lots. If the lakefront lots are sold first, a greater portion of the total basis will be available to offset the selling price of these lots.[9]

In smaller subdivisions, apportioning basis may be a relatively simple matter, as illustrated in Reg. § 1.61-6(a), Example (2).

> ***Example 1:*** The Taxpayer purchases for $25,000 property consisting of a used car lot and an adjoining gas station. At the time of purchase, the fair market value of the gas station is $15,000 and the fair market value of the used car lot is $10,000. Five years later, the Taxpayer sells the gas station for $20,000 at a time when $2,000 has been properly allowed as depreciation. The Taxpayer's gain on the sale is $7,000 since $7,000 is the amount by which the selling price of the gas station ($20,000) exceeds the portion of the cost equitably allocable to the gas station at the time of purchase reduced by the depreciation ($15,000 - $2,000 = $13,000).

In larger projects and subdivisions, however, the apportionment of basis, which includes both on- and off-site development costs can become rather involved. The trick for the developer is to choose a method of equitable apportionment that results in the greatest possible portion of basis being allocated to the earlier sales in order to boost cash flow during those early critical stages of a development, but without having the method struck down by the IRS.

---

[7] Frishkorn Real Estate Co., 15 BTA 463, CCH Dec. 6588.

[8] CA-5, 77-2 USTC ¶ 9541, 555 F.2d 1234.

[9] *See* Biscayne Bay Islands, Co., 23 BTA 731, CCH Dec. 7030, *acq.* XI-1 CB 2, in which the total cost of a group of lots was partly allocated to interior lots as well as to waterfront lots, but on a ratio of one to three, and not on a ratable proportion.

[B] Methods of Apportionment of Basis

As a general proposition, the Tax Court has required that the allocation of basis be made at the time of purchase rather than at the time of sale.[10] Under this principle, the equitable apportionment may be based on an appraisal of the relative value of the different lots or other parcels before actual sales are made.

> ***Example 2:*** The Developer purchases a tract of land for $500,000 and subdivides this tract into 25 lots. The expected selling price of the lots ranges from $25,000 to $75,000 per lot, depending on size, location, etc. The total appraised price at which the Developer expects to sell the lots is $1,100,000. During the first year of sales, ten lots are sold for a total of $450,000. These sales represent lots that were originally appraised at $462,500. The Developer spent $50,000 in improving the ten lots that are sold and estimates further development costs for these lots at an additional $50,000.
>
> Since the initial appraisal would seem to be a method of equitably apportioning basis in this case, the Developer could assign about 42 percent (462,500/1,100,000) of the original cost basis to the ten lots sold, or $210,227.25. Adding the $100,000 in development costs for these lots to the $210,227.25 cost basis, gives the Developer a total basis for the ten lots sold of $310,227.25. Subtracting this basis from the actual sales price of the ten lots results in a gain of $139,772.75 ($450,000 - $310.227.25).

Use of the gross profit from sales has been approved in some cases, even though this method ignores the principle that the allocation should be made at the time the property is acquired. For instance, in *R. W. Ewing,*[11] the gross receipts from the lots sold were divided by the sum of the receipts and the tentative selling price of the unsold land. This fraction was multiplied by the total cost of the land, and the resulting figure was allocated to the lots sold.

In still other cases, the selling price has been used as the basis for equitable apportionment. The Tax Court has held that an IRS allocation of the cost based on selling price was reasonable when nothing had occurred from the date of purchase until the time of sale to alter the relative values.[12] The taxpayer had sought an allocation to two separate frontages in one parcel of 90 percent and ten percent, but the IRS allocation based on selling price was 65 percent and 35 percent.

Apportionment of cost to each lot sold on the basis of assessed valuation by the local property tax assessor has been approved in the absence of a better method.[13]

Considering the wide variety of methods available to equitably apportion the cost of property, it would seem that almost any method chosen should be acceptable, provided it fairly matches costs with revenues. A method that distorts the income realized by the developer when lots or other units are sold, however, would not be acceptable.

---

[10] W.A. Ayling, 32 TC 704, CCH Dec. 23,647, *acq.* 1959-2 CB 3.

[11] 17 TCM 626, CCH Dec. 23,042(M), T.C. Memo. 1958-115.

[12] R.M. Clayton, 15 TCM 105, CCH Dec. 21,537(M), T.C. Memo. 1956-21, *aff'd,* CA-6, 245 F.2d 238, 57-1 USTC ¶ 9447.

[13] J.S. Cullinan, 5 BTA 996, CCH Dec. 2041, *acq.* 1928-1 CB 8.

.02 Inclusion of Development Costs in Basis

The basis of subdivided lots generally includes a pro rata portion of the cost of developing the parcel and making it suitable for subdivision. A developer may add to the cost of the lots the cost of land set aside for streets[14] or the release of frontage for a road.[15]

The IRS has also ruled that a pro rata portion of the cost of water lines should be added to the basis of each lot in a subdivision.[16] The developer agreed to build water lines and convey them to a water utility company because the developer needed water service for the subdivision; but once the developer conveyed the water lines to the water company, the developer retained no rights to them.

Deposits required to have public utilities extended to subdivided real estate are added to the basis of the subdivided lots.[17] The cost of a sewage disposal system operated by a corporation was includible in the basis of lots sold by a real estate developer, even though he owned the corporation and therefore the plant.[18] The same result was reached when water and sewer facilities were conveyed to a utility company wholly owned by an individual who owned 40 percent of the stock in the development company.[19]

In Rev. Rul. 60-3,[20] the basis of each lot was held to include a pro rata portion of the payment for installing water lines in a subdivision, even though the developer might receive a repayment of all or part of the payment. See also *A. Gersten*,[21] in which it was held that allocable portions of the cost of extending water lines paid by the subdivider were properly added to the cost of the properties sold, even though all or part of the cost would be recovered over a 10-year period out of collections from the subdivision.

The value of lots donated to a recreation center increased the basis of the remaining lots when membership in the center would be open to purchasers of lots in the subdivision.[22] In *Country Club Estates, Inc.*,[23] the taxpayer, a corporation formed to develop a tract of land as a residential subdivision, donated a part of the land to a country club. Since the donation was intended as an inducement for people to buy nearby lots, the cost of the land donated was part of the cost basis of the lots sold. The IRS extended this position and ruled that the basis of subdivided lots includes a pro rata portion of the payments made for construction of a golf course, dam, lake, and related recreational facilities, as well as the cost of land donated to the nonprofit country club.[24]

In *Triumph Mixed Use Investments III, LLC*,[25] a developer transferred real property and development credits to a city in exchange for a development plan

[14] Laguna Land & Water Co., CA-9, 41-1 USTC ¶ 9302, 118 F.2d 112.

[15] Rev. Rul. 57-488, 1957-2 CB 157.

[16] Rev. Rul. 81-83, 1981-1 CB 434.

[17] T.M. Divine, Jr., DC Tenn., 62-2 USTC ¶ 9632.

[18] M.A. Collins Est., 31 TC 238, CCH Dec. 23,228, *acq.* 1959-2 CB 4.

[19] G.W. Offutt, CA-4, 64-2 USTC ¶ 9757, 336 F.2d 483.

[20] 1960-1 CB 284.

[21] 28 TC 756, CCH Dec. 22,466, *acq.* 1958-1 CB 4, *aff'd*, CA-9, 59-1 USTC ¶ 9303, 267 F. 2d 195.

[22] Sevier Terrace Realty Co., 21 TCM 1289, CCH Dec. 25,707(M), T.C. Memo. 1962-242, *aff'd*, CA-6, 64-1 USTC ¶ 9268, 327 F.2d 999.

[23] 22 TC 1283, CCH Dec. 20,575, *acq.* 1955-1 CB 4.

[24] Rev. Rul. 68-478, 1968-2 CB 330.

[25] 115 TCM 1329, CCH Dec. 61,175(M), T.C. Memo. 2018-65.

approval and the expectation of a future development plan approval. The developer sought a charitable deduction for the value of the transferred property and development credits. The Tax Court ruled that the transfer did not qualify as a charitable contribution because it was part of a quid pro quo arrangement and the developer did not prove that it had made any excess payment. Although not specifically mentioned, it would seem that the value of the property transferred would become part of the basis of the property the future development plan would benefit.

[A] Development Improvements as Separate Interest

While the cost of improvements such as streets, water, and sewage utilities and recreational facilities that benefit a real estate development as a whole may be added to the basis of the property sold, these same costs generally may not be added to basis when the developer retains ownership and control of the improvements and is able to commercially exploit them or operate them as a business separate from the subdivision.

In *Colony, Inc.*,[26] a developer applied the cost of a water supply system to the cost of lots sold. Water meters were installed, and the developer was paid for the water purchased by the consumers. In this situation, the Tax Court held that the cost of the system constructed by the developer was not a development expense that could be added to the developer's basis in the subdivision lots because the developer retained ownership of the system and did not part with the property for the benefit of the subdivided lots. A similar result was reached in *R.J. Sabinske*,[27] in which it was held that subdividers could not add the aliquot portion of the costs of water systems to the basis of each lot sold because the operation of the water systems was a separate business.

In *M.J. Noell*,[28] the taxpayer was not permitted to add the basis in an adjoining airport runway and taxiways to the basis in subdivided residential lots. The taxpayer retained sufficiently complete control and ownership over the landing facilities for ancillary but independent commercial exploitation. Accordingly, the facilities represented a separate asset and their cost was not properly allocable to the cost of the lots.

Even when the improvements are not commercially exploited on a separate basis, their cost may not be added to the basis of subdivided lots when they benefit some other enterprise of the developer and not just the subdivided lots. For instance, the cost of water systems that were constructed to benefit the developer's substantial recreational facilities and not merely to make lots more salable could not be included in computing the basis of subdivided lots.[29]

[B] Estimated Future Costs

Generally, before the economic performance rules of Code Sec. 461(h) were enacted, a subdivider that sold lots before completion of the development work was permitted to add to the actual cost or other basis of the property sold the estimated

[26] 26 TC 30, CCH Dec. 21,665, *acq.* 1958-1 CB 4, *aff'd*, CA-6, 244 F.2d 75, 57-1 USTC ¶ 9636.

[27] DC Tex., 62-1 USTC ¶ 9210.

[28] 66 TC 718, CCH Dec. 33,927, *acq.* 1977-2 CB 2.

[29] Bryce's Mountain Resort, Inc., 50 TCM 164, CCH Dec. 42,164(M), T.C. Memo. 1985-293.

costs of future common improvements to the property in determining the gain or loss from the sale of the lots.[30] Under Rev. Proc. 75-25, as amplified by Rev. Proc. 78-25,[31] the subdivider had to be contractually obligated to provide the common improvements and the costs of the common improvements could not be recoverable through depreciation. Following the enactment of the economic performance rules of Code Sec. 461(h), the IRS issued proposed regulations and noted that the economic performance requirement obsoleted Rev. Proc. 75-25. Subsequently, the IRS issued Rev. Proc. 92-29[32] that contains an alternative cost method for the treatment of common improvement costs and a streamlined procedure that taxpayers must follow to use the new rules.

Under the alternative cost method of Rev. Proc. 92-29, a developer is permitted to include in the basis of properties sold their allocable share of the estimated cost of common improvements without regard to whether economic performance has occurred under Code Sec. 461(h). Examples of common improvements include streets, sidewalks, sewer lines, playgrounds, clubhouses, tennis courts, and swimming pools that the developer is contractually obligated or required by law to provide. As of the end of any tax year, however, the total amount of common improvement costs included in the basis of the properties sold may not exceed the amount of common improvement costs that have been incurred under section 461(h) of the Code ("the alternative cost limitation"). If the alternative cost limitation precludes a developer from including the entire allocable share of the estimated cost of common improvements in the basis of the properties sold, the costs not included may be taken into account in a subsequent tax year to the extent additional common improvement costs are incurred under Code Sec. 461(h).

The alternative cost limitation is applied on a project-by-project basis. Thus, the common improvement costs incurred for one project may not be included in the alternative cost limitation of a second project. A developer may use any reasonable method to define a project in light of the common improvements to be provided.

The alternative cost method does not affect the application of general capitalization rules to developers of real estate. Thus, common improvement costs are allocated among the benefited properties and may provide the basis for additional computations (for example, interest capitalization under Code Sec. 263A(f)).

> ***Example 3:*** A developer will build ten houses of equal value on a tract of land. The developer is contractually obligated to provide common improvements that will benefit all the houses on the tract equally. The developer estimates that those common improvements will cost $500,000 (including the cost of the land associated with the common improvements). The cost of those common improvements is not recoverable through depreciation. Each house's allocable share of the estimated cost of the common improvements is $50,000 ($500,000/10 houses). During the first tax year, the developer sells four houses and incurs $250,000 of common improvement costs (including the cost of the land associated with the common improvements). In the second tax

[30] Rev. Proc. 75-25, 1975-1 CB 720.

[31] 1978-1 CB 505.

[32] 1992-1 CB 748.

year, the developer sells four houses and incurs $150,000 of common improvement costs. In the third tax year, the developer sells two houses and incurs $100,000 of common improvement costs. The developer receives permission from the IRS to use the alternative cost method.

In year 1, the developer may include $200,000 of common improvement costs in the aggregate bases of the four houses sold in determining the gain or loss from the sales. That amount represents the allocable share of the estimated cost of common improvements for the four houses (($500,000 / 10) × 4). That amount does not exceed the amount of common improvement costs incurred as of the end of the tax year ($250,000). (If the developer had not received permission to use the alternative cost method, the developer would include only $100,000 of common improvement costs in the aggregate bases of the four houses sold during the taxable year (($250,000 / 10) × 4)).

For year 2, the developer may include $200,000 of common improvement costs in the aggregate bases of the four houses sold during the tax year in determining the gain or loss from the sales. That amount represents the allocable share of the estimated cost of common improvements for the four houses (($500,000 / 10) × 4). That amount plus the amount of common improvement costs included in the aggregate bases of the four houses sold in the preceding year ($200,000) does not exceed the amount of common improvement costs incurred as of the end of the second tax year ($400,000).

In year 3, the developer may include $100,000 of common improvement costs in the aggregate bases of the two houses sold in determining the gain or loss from the sales. That amount represents the allocable share of the estimated cost of common improvements for the two houses (($500,000 / 10) × 2). That amount plus the amount of common improvement costs included in the aggregate bases of the eight houses sold in the preceding years ($200,000 + $200,000) does not exceed the amount of common improvement costs incurred as of the end of the third tax year ($500,000).

Example 4: Assume the same facts as in Example 3, except that the developer incurs $30,000 of common improvement costs in the second tax year and $220,000 of common improvement costs in the third tax year. The developer may include only $80,000 of common improvement costs in the aggregate bases of the four houses sold during the second tax year in determining the gain or loss from the sales. The alternative cost limitation precludes the developer from including the remaining $120,000 of the allocable share of the estimated cost of common improvements for the four houses in their aggregate bases. The developer may take into account the costs not included in basis because of the alternative cost limitation when the developer incurs the additional $220,000 of common improvement costs in the third tax year.

.03 Energy Efficient Home Credit

Eligible contractors may qualify for a tax credit for the construction of energy-efficient homes.[33] The eligible contractor is the person who constructs the home, or in the case of a manufactured home, produces the home.[34] The credit is $1,000 for a home that meets the 30 percent standard and $2,000 for a home that meets the 50 percent standard.[35]

An energy-efficient home is a dwelling certified to have a projected level of annual heating and cooling energy consumption that provides either a 30 percent or 50 percent reduction in energy usage compared to a comparable dwelling constructed following the standards of chapter 4 of the 2006 International Energy Conservation Code and any applicable Federal minimum efficiency standards for equipment. Only manufactured homes may qualify for the credit using the 30 percent standard and one-third of the energy savings must come from the building envelope. For other homes that meet the 50 percent standard, one-fifth of the energy savings must come from the building envelope.[36]

In addition to providing the energy savings, the dwelling must be located in the United States, substantially completed after August 8, 2005, and purchased after 2005 and before 2018 (unless again extended by Congress).[37]

The IRS has issued guidance on calculating heating and cooling energy and cost savings to determine the eligibility of dwelling units for the credit.[38] The Notices provide that calculations of heating and cooling energy and cost savings be done in accordance with Residential Services Network (RESNET) Publication No. 05-001. The Notices also provide that software would be included on the public list of software programs that may be used to calculate energy consumption only if the software developer certified that the program satisfied all tests required to conform to the software accreditation process prescribed in RESNET Publication No. 05-001. After the publication of the Notices, RESNET updated Publication No. 05-001 by issuing Publication No. 06-001, which is intended to provide more appropriate regional standards for calculating energy and cost savings. The IRS has announced that taxpayers may use either the prior RESNET standards in Publication No. 05-001 or the current standards in Publication No. 06-001.[39]

In Notice 2008-35[40] the IRS substantially republished the guidance in Notice 2006-27, but also clarified the meaning of the terms "equivalent rating network" and "eligible contractor". Notice 2008-35 also permits calculation of heating and cooling energy consumption in accordance with a calculation procedure equivalent to the procedures prescribed in RESNET Publication No. 05-001 or No. 06-001. The later notice also clarifies the process for removing software from the list of approved software.

---

[33] Code Sec. 45L.

[34] Code Sec. 45L(b)(1).

[35] Code Sec. 45L(a)(2).

[36] Code Sec. 45L(c).

[37] Code Sec. 45L(g).

[38] Notice 2006-27, 2006-11 IRB 626, and Notice 2006-28, 2006-11 IRB 628.

[39] Ann. 2006-88, 2006-46 IRB 910.

[40] 2008-12 IRB 647.

¶ 1002 DEALER STATUS

Property held primarily for sale to customers in the ordinary course of business is not a capital asset. In real estate, property held for sale is commonly called "dealer property," although a dealer in real property may still hold property for investment. The gain or loss on the sale of dealer property is ordinary income or loss, rather than a capital gain or loss. Also, real property held primarily for sale to customers in the ordinary course of business is not eligible for installment reporting, while the sale of real property used in a trade or business or held for investment may be reported on the installment method (see ¶ 1401.02).

The question of whether a particular piece of property is dealer property, that is, held primarily for sale, has been the source of a great deal of litigation. The reason for this is that the question of whether land or improved realty is held primarily for sale to customers in the ordinary course of a taxpayer's trade or business or for investment is one of fact, and is determined on a case-by-case, property-by-property basis.[41]

.01 Characterization of Dealer Property

The Supreme Court has interpreted the word "primarily" to mean "principally" or "of first importance."[42] According to the Court in *Malat*, the purpose of the "primarily" requirement is to distinguish between ordinary profits arising in the everyday operation of a business and the realization of appreciation in the value of an asset accrued over a substantial period of time. While *Malat* involved a dual purpose on the part of the taxpayer, investment or sale, other cases have held that the same principles are equally applicable when property is acquired with the single purpose of selling it sometime in the future.[43]

As a general matter, there does not seem to be any one single factor or combination of factors that controls the characterization of property as dealer property. For example, in *W.K. Dean Est.*,[44] a corporation treated certain parcels of real estate on its books and in every corporate audit report as current assets held primarily for sale to customers in the ordinary course of business. This practice was found not conclusive as to the status of the real estate because the purpose for holding real estate is subject to change based on a change in circumstances.

Dealer status does not automatically attach to a parcel of property merely because a substantial part of the owner's business is devoted to the business of selling real estate. Gain from the sale of an apartment house by a real estate broker was capital gain when the property was not held primarily for sale in the course of business.[45] See also *J.S. Murray*,[46] in which a real estate dealer was found to be an investor as to some properties sold and to be entitled to treat the proceeds from the sale of these properties as capital gain. As to other pieces of property, the dealer

---

[41] E.L. Freeland, CA-9, 68-1 USTC ¶ 9278, 393 F.2d 573, *cert. denied.* 393 U.S. 845, 89 S.Ct. 132.

[42] W. Malat v. Riddell, S.Ct., 66-1 USTC ¶ 9317, 393 U.S. 569, 86 S.Ct. 1030.

[43] *See*, for example, W.A. Scheuber, CA-7, 67-1 USTC ¶ 9219, 371 F.2d 996.

[44] 34 TCM 631, CCH Dec. 33,192(M), T.C. Memo. 1975-137.

[45] P.A. Miller, 20 BTA 230, CCH Dec. 6170, *acq.* 1931-1 CB 44.

[46] CA-4, 67-1 USTC ¶ 9181, 370 F.2d 568, *cert. denied*, 389 U.S. 834, 88 S.Ct. 38.

was found to be in the business of selling real estate, and sales proceeds were ordinary income.

In *Sugar Land Ranch Development, LLC,*[47] the Tax Court ruled that a partnership's income from the sale of two parcels of land was properly reported as capital gain, even though the partnership was formed to engage in real estate development and originally intended to be in the business of selling residential and commercial lots to customers. The partnership, however, ceased to hold its properties primarily for sale and began to hold them only for investment. The partnership sold two parcels in two separate transactions. When the parcels were sold, they were not sold in the ordinary course of business: the partnership did not market the parcels by advertising or other promotional activities, and it did not solicit purchasers for the parcels. The managers or members devoted no time or effort to selling the property. More importantly, sale of the parcels was essentially a bulk sale of a single, large, and contiguous tract of land to a single seller, clearly not a frequent occurrence in the partnership's ordinary business. Therefore, the gain from the sales was capital because the parcels were held for investment.[48]

[A] Tests Applied for Classification of Property

To aid in deciding whether property is held primarily for sale to customers in the ordinary course of business, the courts have developed several tests. Among these, one of the most frequently applied concerns the purpose or reason for the taxpayer's acquisition and disposition of the property. Real estate is not dealer property if the sales purpose is substantial but not dominant.[49]

The Tax Court applied the purpose test of the Eighth Circuit's *Municipal Bond* decision in the following fashion. If the rental of a piece of realty is merely incidental to its eventual sale, such as might be the case when the property is in a bad rental area, the principal purpose for which the property is held is sale. On the other hand, if the property is held for a long period of time, if no effort is made to sell it, and if the property is a good income producer, the principal purpose for holding the property is investment. In cases where sales are made reluctantly, such as when condemnation proceedings are threatened or actually commenced, the principal purpose for holding property is investment.

In *C.T. Au,*[50] the court held that a taxpayer did not hold property primarily for sale to customers in the ordinary course of business. The court noted that the taxpayer's stated purpose for acquiring the property was either the construction of a shopping center or its sale for a profit. In addition, the facts that the taxpayer was not a real estate dealer and that his entire income was derived from sources other than transactions in real estate suggested that the property was not held for sale. On the other hand, gain on the sale of six parcels of unimproved land from a larger

[47] 115 TCM 1078 CCH Dec. 61,126(M), T.C. Memo. 2018-21.

[48] *See also* Conner, 115 TCM 1013, CCH Dec. 61,109(M), T.C. Memo. 2018-6, in which the court held that a taxpayer's sale at a loss of all its property in a single sale produced a capital loss. The taxpayer held the property for many years without engaging in development activities and, other than securing permits and preparing design plans, did nothing to further the development of the property.

[49] Municipal Bond Corp., CA-8, 65-1 USTC ¶ 9247, 341 F.2d 683.

[50] Cls. Ct., 84-1 USTC ¶ 9256, 4 Cls. Ct. 441.

tract of land was taxable as ordinary income (dealer property) because the taxpayer was engaged in the business of selling real estate, the taxpayer had held the property for the purpose of selling it and had sold numerous other parcels of land from the property over a period of many years, and the profits realized from the sale were contemplated in the ordinary operation of the taxpayer's business.[51]

In addition to the purpose test, other tests applied by the courts in deciding whether property is dealer property are:

1. The continuity of sales or sales-related activity over a period of time;
2. The number and frequency of sales;
3. The extent of sales activities such as developing or improving the property, soliciting customers, and advertising;
4. The volume of sales in relation to the taxpayer's other sources of income;
5. The desire to liquidate land acquired unexpectantly, such as by inheritance;
6. Reluctance on the part of the taxpayer to sell the property; and
7. The amount of the gain obtained on the sale.

Frequent sales and continuity of sales effort are often enough to tip the scales in favor of classifying property as dealer property, even in the absence of many other factors indicating dealer property.[52] In *B.B. Margolis*,[53] an individual engaged in buying and selling real estate on a broad basis was found to have held residential lots for sale in the ordinary course of business, even though they were acquired with the intent of holding them for a substantial period before sale. In the same case, however, commercial lots were found to have been held as an investment because they were acquired with the intent of converting the lots into income-producing properties.

If sales are infrequent, result from unsolicited offers, or are required by a change in circumstances, property is more likely to be treated as investment property than as dealer property.[54] According to the Eleventh Circuit Court of Appeals, four sales over a twenty-year period clearly were not enough to make the owner a dealer for tax purposes.[55]

While normally adverse, an acquisition with the primary intent to resell may not result in the property's classification as dealer property if the taxpayer is not in the business of selling real estate.[56] Merely because the owner realizes at the outset that the property may be sold in the future does not mean that the property was

[51] Suburban Realty Co., CA-5, 80-1 USTC ¶ 9351, 615 F.2d 171, *cert. denied*, 449 U.S. 920, 101 S.Ct. 318.

[52] D.B. Goodman, Ct. Cls., 68-1 USTC ¶ 9171, 390 F.2d 915, *cert. denied*, 393 U.S. 824, 89 S.Ct. 87.

[53] CA-9, 64-2 USTC ¶ 9755, 337 F.2d 1001.

[54] W.E. Starke, CA-9, 63-1 USTC ¶ 9199, 312 F.2d 608. *See also* South Texas Properties Co., 16 TC 1003, CCH Dec. 18,267, *acq.* 1951-2 CB 4 (infrequent and unusual sales of unimproved property by a corporation organized to own and rent properties resulted in capital gain); H.C. Martin, DC Ga., 54-1 USTC ¶ 9157, 119 F. Supp. 468 (sales by a partnership engaged in the management and ownership of real estate were sales of capital assets where the property was sold only when it became unprofitable, the partnership wished to improve its holdings, or an unsolicited offer was too good to refuse).

[55] John Weller Wood, CA-11, 2005-1 USTC ¶ 50,434.

[56] G.W. Mitchell, 47 TC 120, CCH Dec. 28,177, *acq. in part, nonacq. in part.* 1970-2 CB xxii.

acquired for sale.[57] In *Biedenharn*, the Court of Appeals found that a realty company derived ordinary income, not capital gain, from the sale of certain subdivided lots. The property was originally acquired for investment but was transformed into ordinary business property as a result of the substantiality and frequency of the company's sales over an extended period of time, the improvements it made, its solicitation and advertising efforts, and brokers' activities.

[B] Subdivided Realty as Dealer Property

Often an investor or other taxpayer acquires unimproved real estate with the intention of holding it for investment purposes or for use in a trade or business other than a real estate business but then subdivides and sells the property in lots or parcels. Although the property was not dealer property when it was acquired, the later sales of the lots or parcels closely resemble the sale of property in the ordinary course of business. Code Sec. 1237 provides a precise set of circumstances under which subdivided realty will not be treated as dealer property solely because of the subdivision. This statutory "safe harbor" is discussed at ¶ 1003. When Code Sec. 1237 does not apply, however, the taxpayer is faced with a conflicting collection of cases and rulings as to whether the mere fact that property is subdivided for sale creates dealer status.

The IRS has ruled that when sizable improvements are made to facilitate the sale of lots, the property becomes dealer property.[58] When one portion of a tract is subdivided and the remaining part is not, however, the taxpayer is not in the business of selling real estate as to the unsubdivided part.[59] More recently, however, the Eleventh Circuit Court of Appeals ruled that taxpayers were liable for tax on ordinary income on the bulk sale of a parcel of land following its development. The taxpayers owned a real estate business and acquired nearly 1,900 acres of vacant real property. The taxpayers engaged in development activities related to the property, including submitting development plans, deducting business expenses related to the property, and selling several lots to buyers over a period of five years. The taxpayers sold the remaining property, nearly 1,100 acres, in a bulk sale to a development company. The Court ruled that income from the taxpayers' bulk sale of property resulted in ordinary income.[60]

In *R. Herndon*,[61] the sale of subdivided farm property used by a real estate dealer as his summer home and for farming after his wife's illness was the liquidation of a capital asset and not a sale to customers in the ordinary course of his real estate business. Similarly, dealer status did not arise on the sales by a trust to liquidate lands acquired by gift.[62] On the other hand, taxpayers' desire to liquidate their investment in repossessed lots and lands acquired on tax sales did

[57] Biedenharn Realty Co., CA-5, 76-1 USTC ¶ 9194, 526 F.2d 409, *cert. denied*, 429 U.S. 819, 97 S.Ct. 64.

[58] Rev. Rul. 59-91, 1959-1 CB 15.

[59] Rev. Rul. 57-565, 1957-2 CB 546. *See also* O. Patrick, 60-1 USTC ¶ 9334, CA-7, 275 F.2d 437 (lots were held to be for sale in the ordinary course of business where taxpayer originally acquired land for investment but later subdivided and built houses).

[60] G.G. Boree, CA-11, 2016-2 USTC ¶ 50,406.

[61] 27 TCM 662, CCH Dec. 29,028(M), T.C. Memo. 1968-135.

[62] A. Moore, 30 TC 1306, CCH Dec. 23,188, *acq*. 1959-1 CB 4.

not prevent the sales from being classified as sales in the ordinary course of business.[63]

Land acquired by an attorney as a fee was held to be for sale in the ordinary course of business after he engaged a real estate company to develop, subdivide, and sell the land.[64] But an attorney who subdivided land and sold several lots over a period of years was found not to have made the sales in the ordinary course of business.[65]

When a taxpayer abandoned farming because of a lack of farm labor and sold lots, it was held that such sales were not dealer sales.[66] The same result was reached when a doctor bought a 160-acre farm with the intention of going into the dairy business but sold subdivided lots after deciding to liquidate the farmland holdings because of a serious illness.[67]

On the other hand, the sales of lots from farm land that was held by the taxpayer for 27 years, during which he neither bought nor sold any other property, were treated as made in the ordinary course of business.[68] See also *J.W. Kelley*,[69] in which it was held that subdivision and sales activities, including substantial improvements, in connection with ranch land after the taxpayer's ranching business failed were sufficient to make the taxpayer a real estate dealer.

.02 Tax Effects of Classification as a Dealer

When property is classified as dealer property, that is, property held primarily for sale in the ordinary course of business, there are two important tax effects. First, dealer property produces ordinary income or loss, not capital gain or loss. Second, the sale of dealer property, with a limited exception, may not be reported on the installment basis. (Installment reporting for sales of real estate is considered in detail at ¶ 1401).

The lower tax rates generally applied to capital gain combined with increased regular tax rates increases the stakes in having gain property classified as nondealer property and loss property classified as dealer property.

[A] Dealer Installment Sales

In general, gain on any disposition of real property held for sale to customers in the ordinary course of business may not be reported under the installment method.[70] Certain exceptions, however, are provided, and installment reporting is permitted for sales to individuals in the ordinary course of business of:

1. Timeshare rights to use or timeshare ownership interests in residential real property for not more than six weeks, or rights to use specified campgrounds for recreational purposes; and

[63] W. Critzer Est., 13 TCM 1087, CCH Dec. 20,691(M), T.C. Memo. 1954-211; W.J. Lewis, Jr., 13 TCM 1161, CCH Dec. 20,724(M), T.C. Memo. 1954-232.

[64] W.N. Foster, 2 TCM 595, CCH Dec. 13,425(M).

[65] W.T. Minor, Jr., 18 TCM 14, CCH Dec. 23,404(M), T.C. Memo. 1959-4.

[66] R.L. Harcum, DC Va., 58-2 USTC ¶ 9684, 164 F. Supp. 650.

[67] T. Berberovich v. Menninger, DC Mich., 57-1 USTC ¶ 9390, 147 F. Supp. 890.

[68] M.A. Nieman Est., 17 TCM 105, CCH Dec. 22,851(M), T.C. Memo. 1958-24.

[69] CA-9, 60-2 USTC ¶ 9635, 281 F.2d 527.

[70] Code Sec. 453(b).

2. Residential lots, but only if the taxpayer (or any related person) is not to make improvements to the lots.[71]

Installment reporting is also available for sales of any property used or produced in the trade or business of farming.[72]

[B] Dealer Sales of Timeshares and Residential Lots

In the case of sales of timeshares and residential lots, installment reporting by a dealer is permitted only if the dealer elects to pay interest on the tax deferred by the use of the installment method.[73] This interest is added to the dealer's income tax. The amount of interest is based on the tax for the year attributable to installment payments received during the year and is calculated from the date of sale to the date the payments are received. The interest rate that is applied is the applicable federal rate, compounded semiannually, in effect at the time of the sale under the original issue discount rules (how this rate is set is explained at ¶ 304). No interest is assessed in the case of installment payments received in the year of sale. Any interest paid under this rule is treated as interest in determining the dealer's interest deduction.

¶ 1003 SUBDIVISION BY INVESTOR

Real estate that is held primarily for sale to customers in the ordinary course of business produces ordinary income on its sale. As discussed at ¶ 1002.01[B], this tax treatment may result when a larger parcel is subdivided and sold as separate lots or smaller parcels. There is, however, a special rule that assures an individual or taxpayer other than a C corporation capital gain treatment when a large tract is subdivided and sold.[74] This special rule is merely a safe harbor, and it does not determine whether or not real property is held primarily for sale in the ordinary course of business if its requirements are not met. Code Sec. 1237 does not apply to the conversion of rental units in an apartment building into condominiums and the sale of condominiums to the general public.[75]

When its conditions are met, Code Sec. 1237 provides that if there is no other substantial evidence that a taxpayer holds real estate primarily for sale to customers in the ordinary course of business, the taxpayer is not considered a real estate dealer holding it primarily for sale merely because the taxpayer has subdivided the tract into lots or parcels and engaged in advertising, promotion, selling activities, or the use of sales agents in connection with the sale of lots in the subdivision. The subdivision and selling activities are disregarded in determining the purpose for which a taxpayer held real property sold from a subdivision whenever these activities constitute the only substantial evidence that the taxpayer ever held the property primarily for sale to customers in the ordinary course of business.[76]

When other substantial evidence shows that the taxpayer held real property for sale to customers in the ordinary course of business, however, the taxpayer's activities in connection with the subdivision and sale of the property sold are taken

[71] Code Sec. 453(l)(2)(B).

[72] Code Sec. 453(l)(2)(A).

[73] Code Sec. 453(l)(3).

[74] Code Sec. 1237.

[75] Rev. Rul. 80-216, 1980-2 CB 239.

[76] Reg. § 1.1237-1(a)(2).

into account in determining the purpose for which the taxpayer held both the subdivided property and any other real property. For example, other evidence may consist of the taxpayer's selling activities in connection with other property in prior years during which the taxpayer was engaged in subdividing or selling activities in connection with the subdivided tract, the taxpayer's intention in prior years (or at the time the subdivided property was acquired) to hold the tract primarily for sale, subdivision of other tracts in the same year, holding other real property for sale in the same year, or construction of a permanent real estate office which could be used in selling other real property. On the other hand, if the only evidence of the taxpayer's purpose in holding real property consisted of not more than one of the following, that would not be considered substantial other evidence:

1. Holding a real estate dealer's license;
2. Selling other real property that was clearly investment property;
3. Acting as a salesman for a real estate dealer, but without any financial interest in the business; or
4. Mere ownership of other vacant real property without engaging in any selling activity whatsoever in connection with it.

If more than one of the above exists, the circumstances may or may not constitute substantial evidence that the taxpayer held real property for sale in the ordinary course of business, depending on the particular facts in each case.[77]

If a taxpayer meets the requirements of Code Sec. 1237, the gain on the sale of lots from a subdivision will be treated as capital gain except for up to five percent of the selling price, which is treated as ordinary income after five lots in the same tract have been sold.

.01 Qualification for Special Tax Treatment

Generally, any lot or parcel that is part of a tract of real property that is not owned by a C corporation (S corporations are eligible) is not treated as held primarily for sale to customers in the ordinary course of business at the time of sale merely because the owner subdivides the tract for sale or because of any activity incident to the subdivision, if the following requirements are met:

1. The tract or any part of the tract has not been held previously by the owner for sale in the ordinary course of business and, in the year of sale, the owner does not hold any other property for sale in the ordinary course of business (this automatically disqualifies real estate dealers);
2. No substantial improvements have been made by the owner while the property was held and no substantial improvements will be made under a contract of sale between the owner and the buyer; and
3. The property, except in the case of property acquired by inheritance, has been held by the owner for at least five years.[78]

If a taxpayer fails to meet the requirements of Code Sec. 1237, it does not necessarily imply that the taxpayer held property primarily for sale. Also, even if the

[77] Reg. § 1.1237-1(a)(3).

[78] Code Sec. 1237(a).

requirements are met, Code Sec. 1237 does not apply if the property sold would not have been considered real property held primarily for sale in the ordinary course of business. Code Sec. 1237 has no application to losses realized on the sale of realty from subdivided property.[79]

[A] Holding Period Rules

A taxpayer is considered as holding property that the taxpayer owns individually, jointly, or as a member of a partnership.[80] To apply Code Sec. 1237, the taxpayer must either have inherited the lot sold or have held it for five years. Generally, the holding period rules contained in Code Sec. 1223 apply to determine the period for which the taxpayer has held the property.

> ***Example 5:*** An individual held a tract of land for three years under circumstances that would otherwise qualify for capital gain treatment under Code Sec. 1237. The individual made a gift of the tract to the Taxpayer at a time when the fair market value of the tract exceeded the donor's basis for the tract. The Taxpayer held the tract for two more years under similar circumstances. The Taxpayer then sold four lots from the tract. The Taxpayer is entitled to the benefits of Code Sec. 1237 since the lots were held for five years[81] and all other requirements of Code Sec. 1237 are met.

Although an individual is not considered to hold property that is held by family members, a taxpayer is considered to have made improvements made by family members while the tract was held by the taxpayer.[82]

> ***Example 6:*** The Father held a tract of land for three years during which time he made substantial improvements that substantially enhanced the value of every lot on the tract. He then made a gift of the tract to his Son, who made no further improvements on the tract, but held it for three years and then sold several lots. The Son is not entitled to the benefits of Code Sec. 1237 because, under Code Sec. 1237(a)(2), the Son is deemed to have made the substantial improvements made by the Father, and under Code Sec. 1223(2) the Son is treated as having held the property for the period it was held by the Father. Accordingly, the disqualifying improvements are deemed to have been made by the Son while the tract was held by him. (Disqualifying improvements are discussed at ¶ 1003.01[B].)

[B] Improvements to Land Tracts

Sales of subdivided lots do not qualify under Code Sec. 1237 if the lots were substantially enhanced in value as a result of substantial improvements made anywhere on the tract by the taxpayer, or by anyone else pursuant to the contract of sale between the taxpayer and the buyer.[83] An improvement is considered to be made by the taxpayer if, while the tract is held by the taxpayer, the improvement is made by a family member, by a corporation controlled by the taxpayer, an S

[79] Reg. § 1.1237-1(a)(4). *See also* R.E. Gordy, 36 TC 855, CCH Dec. 24,982, *acq.* 1964-1 CB (Part 14).

[80] Reg. § 1.1237-1(b)(3).

[81] *See* Code Sec. 1223(2) which provides for the tacking of holding period in the case of a gift.

[82] Reg. § 1.1237-1(c)(2)(i)(a).

[83] Code Sec. 1237(a)(2); Reg. § 1.1237-1(c)(3).

corporation that includes the taxpayer as a shareholder, or by a partnership in which the taxpayer is a partner. Also, if an improvement is made by a lessee and the improvement is treated as rental income to the taxpayer, the improvement is deemed made by the taxpayer. If an improvement is made by the federal government, or a state or local government or political subdivision, and the improvement increases the taxpayer's basis (as in the case of a special assessment for a local benefit), the improvement is considered made by the taxpayer.[84]

Whether improvements substantially increase the value of a lot depends on the circumstances in each case. If improvements increase the value of a lot by ten percent or less, the increase is not considered substantial, but if the value of the lot is increased by more than ten percent, then all relevant factors are considered to determine whether the increase is substantial.[85] Improvements may increase the value of some lots in a tract without equally affecting other lots in the same tract. Only lots whose value is substantially increased are ineligible under Code Sec. 1237.[86] The improvement that enhances the value of the lots must itself be substantial to disqualify the lots under Code Sec. 1237. Among the improvements considered substantial are shopping centers, or other commercial or residential buildings, and the installation of hard surface roads or utilities such as sewers, water, gas, or electric lines. On the other hand, a temporary structure used as a field office, surveying, filling, draining, leveling and clearing operations, and the construction of minimum all-weather access roads, including gravel roads where required by the climate, are not substantial improvements.[87]

[C] Necessary Improvements to Property After Ten Years

After ten years, certain necessary improvements, such as water, sewer, roads, etc., may be made to the property without disqualifying the property under Code Sec. 1237. The owner, however, must elect not to add the cost of the improvements to the tax basis in the land. Also, the owner must show that the property could not be marketed at the prevailing local price for similar building sites without the improvements.[88]

> ***Example 7:*** The Taxpayer, an individual, purchased land 15 years ago for \$100 per acre and has just been offered \$500 per acre for a tract of the land without roads, water, or sewer facilities. An adjacent tract has been subdivided and improved with water facilities and roads, and has sold for \$4,000 per acre. The estimated cost of roads and water facilities on the tract under consideration is \$2,500 per acre. The prevailing local price for similar building sites in the vicinity is \$1,500 per acre (\$4,000 - \$2,500). If the Taxpayer installs roads and water at a cost of \$2,500 per acre, the tract would sell for about \$4,000 per acre rather than the \$500 that has been offered.
>
> In this case, the Taxpayer can add the roads and water facilities and still qualify under Code Sec. 1237. However, if the tract is sold for \$4,000 per acre, the Taxpayer's gain would be \$3,900 (\$4,000 - \$100 tax basis). The Taxpayer

[84] Code Sec. 1237(a)(2); Reg. § 1.1237-1(c)(2).

[85] Reg. § 1.1237-1(c)(3)(ii).

[86] Reg. § 1.1237-1(c)(3)(iii).

[87] Reg. § 1.1237-1(c)(4).

[88] Code Sec. 1237(b)(3); Reg. § 1.1237-1(c)(5).

cannot add the cost of the roads and water facilities to the tax basis and still qualify under Code Sec. 1237. If the Taxpayer does add the cost of the improvements to the basis, the property may be treated as property held for sale in the ordinary course of business (dealer property), and this would result in ordinary income in the amount of $1,400 per acre ($4,000 - $2,600 tax basis).

If the Taxpayer could sell the unimproved tract for $1,500 per acre without the improvements, rather than $500, any improvements would not be considered necessary improvements because the Taxpayer could obtain the prevailing local price without any improvement.

As can be seen from the example, qualifying under Code Sec. 1237 when substantial necessary improvements are made after ten years is not necessarily an advantage. The inability to offset sale proceeds by the cost of the improvements, in fact, can create a substantial tax disadvantage when the tax preference for capital gain is not enough to offset the increased taxable gain.

.02 Calculation of the Amount and Character of Gain

When a subdivision qualifies under Code Sec. 1237, gain realized on the sale of lots is all capital gain until the year in which the sixth lot is sold. For the year in which the sixth lot is sold and all subsequent years, five percent of the selling price of the lots is treated as gain from the sale of property held primarily for sale to customers in the ordinary course of business, that is, ordinary income.[89]

[A] Five-Percent Rule

Under this rule, a subdivider who sells or exchanges only five lots or less in the first taxable year of the subdivision sales realizes all capital gain. If the subdivider sells or exchanges more than five lots or parcels in the first taxable year, then the amount by which five percent of the selling price of each lot exceeds the expenses incurred in its sale is ordinary income to the extent it represents gain.[90] In computing the number of lots or parcels sold, two or more contiguous lots sold to a single buyer in a single sale is counted as only one parcel.[91]

Note that an exchange is counted as a sale or exchange for determining if five lots or parcels have been sold, even if gain or loss is not recognized on the exchange. The "selling price" in the case of an exchange is the fair market value of property received plus any money received in exchange for the lot.[92]

Application of the five-percent rule is illustrated in the following example taken from Reg. § 1.1237-1(e)(2).

Comprehensive Example 8: The selling price of the sixth lot of a tract is $10,000. The basis of the lot is $5,000, and the expenses of sale are $750. The sale is subject to Code Sec. 1237. On the sale, the subdivider realizes a gain of $4,250. The entire amount of this gain is capital gain, computed as follows:

[89] Code Sec. 1237(b)(1).

[90] Reg. § 1.1237-1(e)(2)(ii).

[91] Reg. § 1.1237-1(e)(2)(i).

[92] Reg. § 1.1237-1(e)(2)(iii).

Selling price		$10,000
Basis		5,000
Excess over basis		5,000
5% of selling price	$500	
Expenses of sale	750	
Ordinary income		0
Excess over basis		5,000
5% of selling price	500	
Excess expenses over 5% of selling price	250	750
Amount of gain from sale of property not held for sale in ordinary course of business		$4,250

Suppose, however, that the expenses of sale of the sixth lot were $300 rather than $750. In this case, the subdivider realizes a gain of $4,700 on the sale, and of this amount, $200 is ordinary income and $4,500 is gain from the sale of property not held for sale in the ordinary course of business, computed as follows:

Selling price		$10,000
Basis		5,000
Excess over basis		5,000
5% of selling price	$500	
Expenses of sale	300	
Ordinary income		200
Excess over basis		5,000
5% of selling price	500	
Excess expenses over 5% of selling price	0	500
Amount of gain from sale of property not held for sale in ordinary course of business		$4,500

[B] Five-Year Rule

If a subdivider does not sell or exchange any lots from the tract for a period of five years after the sale or exchange of at least one lot in the tract, then the remainder of the tract is treated as a new tract when counting the number of lots sold from the same tract under Code Sec. 1237(b)(1). The pieces in the new tract need not be contiguous, and the five-year period is measured between the dates of the sales or exchanges.[93] In other words, if five years elapse after the last sale of a

[93] Reg. § 1.1237-1(g)(2).

lot, any new sales after the end of the five-year period are treated as if they are being made from a tract that is newly subdivided.

A "tract" is either a single piece of real property or two or more pieces of real property if they were contiguous at any time while held by the taxpayer, or would have been contiguous but for the interposition of a road, street, railroad, stream, or similar property. Properties are contiguous if their boundaries meet at one or more points. The single piece or contiguous properties need not have been conveyed by a single deed. The taxpayer may have assembled them over a period of time and may hold them separately, jointly, or as a partner, or in any combination of these forms of ownership.[94]

A subdivider selling lots in separate tracts applies the "sixth-lot rule" and the "five-year rule" to each tract independently of the sales or exchanges of lots from the other tract.

[94] Reg. § 1.1237-1(g)(1).

Chapter 11
Passive Activity Loss Rules

¶ 1100 Overview of Chapter
¶ 1101 General Provisions
¶ 1102 Identification of Separate Activities
¶ 1103 Limits on Rental Activities
¶ 1104 Tax Treatment of Passive Losses and Credits
¶ 1105 Publicly Traded Partnerships

¶ 1100 OVERVIEW OF CHAPTER

Before the Tax Reform Act of 1986, there were no general limitations placed on the ability of a taxpayer to use tax deductions from a particular activity to offset income from other activities. Also, most tax credits could be used to offset tax attributable to income from any of a taxpayer's activities. Without such limitations, taxpayers with substantial sources of income frequently invested in tax shelters that offered the opportunity to reduce or avoid tax liability by making available deductions and credits, often exceeding real economic costs, in advance of the income from the tax shelters.

In the wisdom of Congress, the passive activity loss rules[1] were adopted to limit sheltering activities. The passive activity loss rules, however, went beyond limiting traditional tax sheltering activities by limiting deductions for actual out-of-pocket expenses as well as deductions for noncash items such as depreciation and accrued but unpaid expenses. As they stand today, the passive activity loss rules may prevent the current recognition of real cash losses, as well as paper losses.

In concept, the passive activity loss rules are simple. Generally, under the rules, losses from "passive activities" can be used only to offset income from passive activities. Similarly, a tax credit generated by a passive activity can be used only to offset a tax liability attributable to a passive activity. Any loss or credit that cannot be used by a taxpayer because of the rules may be carried over to future years and applied to passive income (or tax liability attributable to passive income in the case of credits) in subsequent years. A loss attributable to a passive activity that remains unused at the time the taxpayer disposes of that activity may be deducted at that time.

While the concept of the passive activity loss rules may be simple to state, there is certainly no simplicity in their application, nor in the several hundred pages of Internal Revenue Code and Income Tax Regulations (with more to come) that

[1] Code Sec. 469.

attempt to explain the rules. Moreover, tracking losses and making sure disallowed losses are tied to the right activity to figure the proper deduction when a taxpayer disposes of a passive activity creates a recordkeeper's nightmare. In any event, taxpayers must deal with these rules. The material in this chapter tries to explain the important aspects of the passive loss rules as they might apply to the owner of real property, whether the real property is held for investment, as rental property, or for use in a trade or business.

¶ 1101 GENERAL PROVISIONS

In order to apply the passive activity loss rules, it is necessary to know what taxpayers are subject to the rules, the activities that are covered by the rules, and the concept of "material participation" that applies to most activities other than rental activities. It is generally the material participation by the taxpayer in an activity that separates a passive activity from a nonpassive activity.

Whenever the passive activity loss rules apply to an activity of a taxpayer, the taxpayer may lose the current benefit of any tax deductions and tax credits to which the taxpayer is entitled under other provisions of the Internal Revenue Code. These rules must be kept in mind whenever a taxpayer attempts to determine the value of a tax deduction or credit.

.01 Taxpayers Subject to the Rules

The passive activity loss rules apply to the following taxpayers:

1. Noncorporate taxpayers, including individuals, trusts (except to the extent governed by the grantor trust rules), and estates;
2. Closely held regular C corporations; and
3. Personal service corporations.[2]

The rules apply at the taxpayer level. Therefore, income, deductions, and credits from passthrough entities (partnerships and S corporations) are subject to the passive activity loss rules at the individual partner or shareholder level.

[A] Closely Held C Corporations

A closely held C corporation is subject to the passive activity loss rules, but a less stringent version applies if the corporation is not also a personal service corporation. A regular C corporation is closely held if, at any time during the last half of the tax year, more than 50 percent in value of the corporation's stock is owned by five or fewer individuals.[3]

Under a limited exception to the passive loss rules, a closely held C corporation, other than a personal service corporation, may use passive activity losses and credits to offset income from business operations, but not from portfolio income. Portfolio income is generally income from dividends, interest, annuities, and royalties, and is not considered passive income under the passive loss rules.[4]

[2] Code Sec. 469(a)(2).

[3] Code Sec. 469(j)(1).

[4] Code Sec. 469(e)(1).

The limited exception may be important for corporations that can take advantage of investments to produce passive losses for offsetting operating income. Closely held corporations, in the past, often served as tax shelters for their shareholders. Now, however, the top tax rate for corporations exceeds the top rate for individuals. Also, to get money out of a corporation now usually requires payment of a double tax, once at the corporate level and again at the shareholder level, and this further reduces the tax shelter potential of a closely held corporation. In this climate, many closely held corporations may find that passive activity investments are viable parking places for corporate funds that are not needed as working capital.

[B] Personal Service Corporations

Personal service corporations are subject to the passive activity loss rules. A corporation may be subject to the rules as both a closely held corporation and a personal service corporation. If this is the case, the limited exception to the rules that permits passive losses to offset operating income does not apply. A personal service corporation is a corporation that meets the following requirements:

1. It is a regular C corporation and not an S corporation;
2. The principal activity of the corporation is the performance of personal services;
3. The personal services are substantially performed by employee-owners; and
4. Employee-owners, in the aggregate, own more than ten percent of the stock of the corporation.[5]

A person is an employee-owner of a personal service corporation if the person is an employee of the corporation and owns any of the outstanding stock of the corporation. Ownership of stock is determined under the constructive ownership rules of Code Sec. 318. Personal services include only services performed in the fields of health, law, engineering, architecture, accounting, actuarial science, performing arts, and consulting. Personal services are substantially performed by employee-owners if the corporation's compensation cost for personal services performed by employee-owners is more than 20 percent of the corporation's total compensation cost for personal services.[6]

.02 Activities Subject to the Rules

Passive activities, that is, those subject to the passive activity loss rules, in most cases depend for their classification on the relationship of the taxpayer to the activities. It is quite possible for an activity conducted through a partnership to be a passive activity for some of the partners and an active or nonpassive activity for other partners. Under the general rule, an activity is passive if it involves a trade or business in which the taxpayer does not materially participate.[7]

---

[5] Code Sec. 469(j)(2).

[6] Temp. Reg. § 1.469-1T(g)(2) and Reg. § 1.441-3(c).

[7] Code Sec. 469(c)(1).

Rental activities are subject to a special rule and are automatically classified as passive activities,[8] but there are two exceptions for rental real estate activities that may permit deductions generated by rental real estate to offset nonpassive activity income. First, a limited exception is provided in Code Sec. 469(i) for real estate activities in which a taxpayer actively participates, as discussed at ¶ 1103.05. Second, as discussed at ¶ 1103.06, the rental activities rule does not apply to any rental real estate activity of a taxpayer in the real property business as defined in Code Sec. 469(c)(7).

[A] Limited Partnership Interests

A limited partner, generally, does not take part in the management of the partnership and cannot actively participate in the limited partnership activity. Therefore, the ownership of a limited partnership interest is generally treated as a passive activity.[9] There are, however, four exceptions to the general rule provided by the regulations:

1. If the limited partner participates in the limited partnership activity for more than 500 hours during the year, the activity is not a passive activity;
2. If the limited partner materially participated in the activity for any five tax years, whether or not consecutive, during the ten tax years immediately preceding the current tax year, the activity is not a passive activity;
3. If the activity of the partnership is a personal service activity and the limited partner materially participated in the activity for any three tax years, whether or not consecutive, preceding the current tax year, the activity is not a passive activity; and
4. If the limited partner is also a general partner, the partner is not treated as a limited partner and the limited partnership rule does not apply.[10]

A special version of the passive activity loss rules applies to publicly traded partnerships and is discussed at ¶ 1105.

[B] Oil and Gas Property Working Interests

A working interest in an oil and gas property is not a passive activity if the taxpayer holds the interest directly or through an entity that does not limit the taxpayer's liability.[11] It does not matter whether or not the taxpayer materially participates. A working interest is a working or operating mineral interest in any tract or parcel of land within the meaning of Reg. § 1.612-4(a).[12]

The working interest exception to the passive activity rules does not apply to a working interest held through an entity that limits the taxpayer's liability. Holding an interest through the following forms of ownership will be considered an interest in an entity that limits the taxpayer's liability:

---

[8] Code Sec. 469(c)(2).
[9] Temp. Reg. § 1.469-5T(e)(1).
[10] Temp. Reg. § 1.469-5T(e)(2).
[11] Code Sec. 469(c)(3)(A).
[12] Reg. § 1.469-1(e)(4)(iv).

1. A limited partnership interest in a partnership in which the taxpayer is not a general partner;
2. Stock in a corporation; or
3. An interest in any entity other than a limited partnership or corporation that, under state law, limits the potential liability of the holder of an interest for all obligations of the entity to a determinable fixed amount, such as the amount of the holder's capital contributions.[13]

Protection against loss through an indemnification agreement, a stop-loss agreement, insurance, or any similar arrangement is not considered in determining whether a taxpayer holds a working interest through an entity that limits the taxpayer's liability.[14]

.03 Material Participation

In many cases, material participation in an activity determines whether or not the activity is subject to the passive activity loss rules. Material participation, however, is not relevant in many rental activities (see ¶ 1103) or when the activity involves a working interest in oil and gas property as discussed at ¶ 1101.02[B]. A limited partner may or may not be affected by the material participation standard, as discussed at ¶ 1101.02[A]. Generally, a trade or business in which a taxpayer materially participates is not an activity subject to the passive loss rules.[15]

[A] Material Participation by an Individual

The regulations provide seven tests for determining material participation.[16] Material participation is established if the individual satisfies any one of the following tests:

1. The individual participates in the activity for more than 500 hours during the tax year.
2. The individual's participation in the activity for the tax year constitutes substantially all of the participation in the activity of all individuals, including individuals, such as employees, who are not owners (this test covers activities that do not require 500 hours to operate).
3. The individual participates in the activity for more than 100 hours during the tax year and the individual's participation in the activity is not less than the participation of any other individual, including individuals who are not owners (this test covers activities that do not require more than 500 hours by any one individual to operate).
4. The activity is a significant participation activity (the individual participates in the activity for more than 100 hours during the tax year but fails to satisfy any other test for material participation) and the individual's aggregate participation in all significant participation activities during the tax year exceeds 500 hours (this test treats individuals who participate in multiple activities equally with those who devote the same amount of time to one activity).

---

[13] Temp. Reg. § 1.469-1T(e)(4)(v)(A).

[14] Temp. Reg. § 1.469-1T(e)(4)(v)(B).

[15] Code Sec. 469(c)(1).

[16] Temp. Reg. § 1.469-5T(a).

5. The individual materially participated in the activity for any five tax years, whether or not consecutive, during the ten tax years immediately preceding the current tax year (this test recognizes that material participation over a long period of time usually represents more than a mere passive investment).
6. The activity involves the performance of personal services in the fields of health, law, engineering, architecture, accounting, actuarial science, performing arts, consulting, or any other trade or business in which capital is not a material income-producing factor, and the individual materially participated in the activity for any three tax years, whether or not consecutive, preceding the current tax year (this test recognizes that a personal service business in which the taxpayer materially participates over a period of time is likely to be the taxpayer's livelihood rather than a mere investment).
7. Based on all of the facts and circumstances, the individual participates in the activity on a regular, continuous, and substantial basis during the tax year. Under this test, an individual's management services are not considered if a paid manager participates in the activity or if someone else performs management services that exceed (based on hours) those performed by the individual.[17] Also, the test does not apply if an individual participates in an activity for less than 100 hours during the tax year.[18]

Generally, any work done by an individual in connection with an activity in which the individual owns an interest is considered participation in the activity. It does not matter in what capacity the individual does the work.[19] However, work done in connection with an activity is not counted as participation if the work is not the type that is customarily done by an owner and one of the principal purposes for doing the work is to avoid disallowance of a loss or credit under the passive activity loss rules.[20]

Work done in the capacity of an investor in an activity is not counted as participation in the activity. This type of work includes studying and reviewing financial statements or reports on operations of the activity, preparing or compiling summaries or analyses of the finances or operations of the activity for the individual's own use, and monitoring the finances or operations of the activity in a nonmanagerial capacity.[21]

The participation of an individual's spouse is combined with that of the individual in determining material participation by the individual. It does not matter whether the participating spouse owns an interest in the activity or whether the spouses file a joint return.[22]

[B] Material Participation by a Corporation

A closely held C corporation or personal service corporation materially participates in an activity if and only if:

[17] Temp. Reg. § 1.469-5T(b)(2)(ii).
[18] Temp. Reg. § 1.469-5T(b)(2)(iii).
[19] Reg. § 1.469-5(f)(1).
[20] Temp. Reg. § 1.469-5T(f)(2)(i).
[21] Temp. Reg. § 1.469-5T(f)(2)(ii).
[22] Temp. Reg. § 1.469-5T(f)(3).

1. One or more individuals, each of whom materially participates in the activity for the year, directly or indirectly hold in the aggregate more than 50 percent in value of the outstanding stock of the corporation, or
2. In the case of a closely held corporation, the corporation is considered an active business as defined for purposes of the at-risk rules in Code Sec. 465(c)(7)(C).[23]

In order to apply the significant participation test for determining material participation by a corporation in an activity, an activity is treated as a significant participation activity only if the corporation is not treated as materially participating in the activity for the tax year, and one or more individuals, each of whom significantly participates in the activity, directly or indirectly hold in the aggregate more than 50 percent in value of the outstanding stock of the corporation.[24] An individual is treated as materially participating or significantly participating in an activity for purposes of determining a corporation's material participation if the individual meets one of the seven tests set out above for individual material participation. In applying these tests, however, the following factors apply:

1. All activities of the corporation must be treated as activities in which the individual holds an interest to determine whether the individual participates in an activity of the corporation; and
2. The individual's participation in all activities other than activities of the corporation must be disregarded to determine whether the individual's participation in an activity of the corporation is material participation under the test for significant participation in multiple activities.[25]

¶ 1102 IDENTIFICATION OF SEPARATE ACTIVITIES

To apply the passive activity loss rules, taxpayers must determine just what constitutes an activity. The material participation standard is applied to each "activity." If several undertakings of the taxpayer are one activity, then the taxpayer must establish material participation only for the activity as a whole to avoid the passive loss rules. On the other hand, if several undertakings are separate activities, then the taxpayer must establish material participation for each separate activity. Also, knowing what constitutes an activity is important in determining whether a taxpayer has disposed of his entire interest or only a portion of an activity.

The IRS has issued regulations that define an activity for purposes of the passive activity loss rules.[26] The following discussion is based on those regulations and summarizes their application.

.01 General Rule

One or more trade or business activities or rental activities may be treated as a single activity if the activities are an appropriate economic unit for the measurement of gain or loss under the passive activity loss rules.[27] Trade or business

[23] Temp. Reg. § 1.469-1T(g)(3)(i).
[24] Temp. Reg. § 1.469-1T(g)(3)(ii).
[25] Temp. Reg. § 1.469-1T(g)(3)(iii).
[26] Reg. § 1.469-4.
[27] Reg. § 1.469-4(c)(1).

activities are activities, other than rental activities or activities that are treated under Reg. § 1.469-1T(e)(3)(vi)(B) (see ¶ 1103.01) as incidental to holding property for investment, that:

1. Involve the conduct of a trade or business;
2. Are conducted in anticipation of the beginning of a trade or business; or
3. Involve research or experimental expenditures that are deductible under Code Sec. 174 (or would be deductible if the taxpayer adopted the current expense method for R&E costs).[28]

An activity is a rental activity if tangible property held in connection with the activity is used by, or held for use by, customers, and the gross income from the activity represents amounts paid or to be paid primarily for the use of property.[29]

A taxpayer may use any reasonable method of applying relevant facts and circumstances in grouping activities. The IRS gives the factors listed below the greatest weight in determining whether activities are an appropriate economic unit for the measurement of gain or loss under the passive activity loss rules:

1. Similarities and differences in types of trades or businesses;
2. The extent of common control;
3. The extent of common ownership;
4. Geographical location; and
5. Interdependencies between or among the activities (for example, the extent to which the activities purchase or sell goods between or among themselves, involve products or services that are normally provided together, have the same customers, have the same employees, or are accounted for with a single set of books and records).[30]

> ***Example 1:*** Taxpayer has a significant ownership interest in a bakery and a movie theater at a shopping mall in Baltimore and in a bakery and a movie theater in Philadelphia. After taking into account all the relevant circumstances, there may be more than one reasonable method for grouping Taxpayer's activities. For instance, depending on the circumstances, the following groupings may or may not be allowed: a single activity; a movie theater activity and a bakery activity; a Baltimore activity and a Philadelphia activity; or four separate activities. Also, once Taxpayer groups the activities into appropriate economic units, Taxpayer generally must continue to use that grouping in later tax years unless a material change in circumstances makes it clearly inappropriate.

.02 Limitations on Grouping

The grouping of activities for the passive activity loss rules is subject to several limitations.

---

[28] Reg. § 1.469-4(b)(1).

[29] Reg. § 1.469-4(b)(2).

[30] Reg. § 1.469-4(c)(2).

A rental activity may not be grouped with a trade or business activity unless the activities being grouped together are an appropriate economic unit (see ¶ 1102.01) and:

1. The rental activity is insubstantial in relation to the trade or business;
2. The trade or business is insubstantial in relation to the rental activity; or
3. Each owner of the trade or business has the same proportionate ownership interest in the rental activity, in which case the portion of the rental activity that involves the rental of items of property for use in the trade or business may be grouped with the trade or business.[31]

Example 2: Attorney is a sole practitioner in his hometown. Attorney also owns residential real estate in the town that he rents to third parties. Attorney's law practice is a trade or business and the residential real estate is a rental activity and is insubstantial in relation to Attorney's law practice. Under the circumstances, the law practice and the residential real estate are not an appropriate economic unit and Attorney may not treat the law practice and real estate as a single activity.

Example 3: Husband and Wife are married and file a joint return. Husband is the sole shareholder of an S corporation that runs a grocery store business. Wife is the sole shareholder of an S corporation that owns and rents out a building. Part of the building is rented to Husband's grocery store. The grocery store rental and the grocery store business are not insubstantial in relation to each other.

Because they file a joint return, Husband and Wife are considered one taxpayer for the passive activity loss rules. The sole owner of the trade or business activity (the married couple) is also the sole owner of the rental activity. Each owner of the trade or business activity has the same proportionate ownership interest in the rental activity and the grocery store rental and the grocery store business may be grouped together into a single trade or business activity, if the grouping is otherwise appropriate (see ¶ 1102.01).

An activity that involves the rental of real property and an activity that involves the rental of personal property (other than personal property provided in connection with the real property or real property provided in connection with the personal property) may not be treated as a single activity.[32]

A taxpayer who owns an interest as a limited partner or limited entrepreneur in an activity described in Code Sec. 465(c)(1), which deals with the at-risk rules (see ¶ 302), may not group that activity with any other activity. A taxpayer who owns an interest as a limited partner or a limited entrepreneur in a Code Sec. 465(c)(1) activity may group that activity with another activity in the same type of business if the grouping is otherwise appropriate as discussed at ¶ 1102.01.[33]

Example 4: Individual owns and operates a farm. Individual is also a member of a limited liability company (LLC) that conducts a cattle-feeding

[31] Reg. § 1.469-4(d)(1).

[32] Reg. § 1.469-4(d)(2).

[33] Reg. § 1.469-4(d)(3).

business, but does not actively participate in the management of the LLC. Individual is also a limited partner in an oil and gas production limited partnership.

Because Individual does not actively participate in the management of the LLC, Individual is a limited entrepreneur in the LLC's activity. The cattle-feeding business is described in Code Sec. 465(c)(1)(B) and may not be grouped with any other activity that does not involve farming. Further, Individual's farm may not be grouped with the cattle-feeding activity unless the grouping is an appropriate economic unit for the measurement of gain or loss.

Because Individual is a limited partner and the partnership's oil and gas activity is described in Code Sec. 465(c)(1)(D), Individual may not group the partnership's oil and gas activity with any other activity that does not involve oil and gas. The partnership's activity may not be grouped with Individual's farm or with LLC's cattle-feeding business.

A C corporation subject to the passive activity loss rules, an S corporation, or a partnership (a Sec. 469 entity) must group its activities under the grouping rules. Once the Sec. 469 entity groups its activities, a shareholder or partner may group those activities with each other, with activities conducted directly by the shareholder or partner, and with activities conducted through other Sec. 469 entities under the grouping rules. A shareholder or partner may not treat activities grouped together by a Sec. 469 entity as separate activities.[34]

.03 Regrouping

Once a taxpayer has grouped activities for the passive activity loss rules, the taxpayer generally may not regroup those activities in later tax years. Taxpayers must comply with disclosure requirements that the IRS may prescribe for both their original groupings and the addition and disposition of specific activities within those chosen groupings in later tax years. If a taxpayer determines that the original grouping clearly was inappropriate or if a material change in circumstances occurs that makes the original grouping clearly inappropriate, however, the taxpayer must regroup the activities and must comply with disclosure requirements that the IRS may prescribe.[35]

The IRS may regroup a taxpayer's activities if any of the activities resulting from the grouping is not an appropriate economic unit and a principal purpose of the taxpayer's grouping, or failure to regroup, is to circumvent the underlying purposes of the passive activity loss rules.[36]

For the tax year in which there is a disposition of substantially all of an activity, a taxpayer may treat the part disposed of as a separate activity, but only if the taxpayer can establish with reasonable certainty: (1) the amount of deductions and credits allocable to that part of the activity for the tax year under Reg. § 1.469-1(f)(4), and (2) the amount of gross income and of any other deductions and credits allocable to that part of the activity for the tax year.[37]

---

[34] Reg. § 1.469-4(d)(5).

[35] Reg. § 1.469-4(e).

[36] Reg. § 1.469-4(f).

[37] Reg. § 1.469-4(g).

.04 Reporting Requirements for Grouping

The IRS requires taxpayers to report their groupings and regroupings of activities under the passive activity loss rules. Taxpayers also must report the addition of specific activities within their current grouping of activities. A taxpayer is not required to report the grouping of activities made before January 25, 2010, until the taxpayer makes a change to the grouping. If a taxpayer fails to report whether activities have been grouped as a single activity, the unreported activities generally are treated as separate activities. The reporting requirements apply to tax years beginning after January 24, 2010.[38] The requirements, however, do not apply to rental real estate activities subject to the real property business exception if the qualifying taxpayer elects to treat all interests in real estate as a single activity as discussed at ¶ 1103.06.

New Groupings

A taxpayer must file a written statement with the original income tax return for the first tax year in which two or more trade or business activities or rental activities are originally grouped as a single activity. This statement must identify the names, addresses, and employer identification numbers for the trade or business activities or rental activities that are being grouped as a single activity. In addition, any statement reporting a new grouping of two or more trade or business activities or rental activities as a single activity must contain a declaration that the grouped activities constitute an appropriate economic unit for the measurement of gain or loss.

Addition of New Activities to Existing Groupings

If a taxpayer adds a new trade or business activity or a rental activity to an existing grouping for a tax year, the taxpayer must file a written statement with the original income tax return for that tax year. This statement must identify the names, addresses, and employer identification numbers for the new trade or business activity or rental activity added to the existing grouping, as well as the names, addresses, and employer identification numbers for the activity or activities within the existing grouping. In addition, the statement reporting an addition to an existing grouping must contain a declaration that the activities constitute an appropriate economic unit for the measurement of gain or loss.

Regroupings

If a taxpayer's original grouping was clearly inappropriate or a material change occurs that makes the original grouping clearly inappropriate and the taxpayer must regroup the activities as discussed at ¶ 1102.03, the taxpayer must file a written statement with the original income tax return for the tax year in which the trade or business activities or rental activities are regrouped. This statement must identify the names, addresses, and employer identification numbers for the trade or business or rental activities that are being regrouped. If two or more activities are regrouped into a single activity, the statement reporting the regrouping also must contain a declaration that the regrouped activities constitute an appropriate eco-

[38] Rev. Proc. 2010-13, 2010-4 IRB 329.

nomic unit for the measurement of gain or loss. Furthermore, the taxpayer must include an explanation of why the original grouping was clearly inappropriate or the nature of the material change that makes the original grouping clearly inappropriate.

Groupings by Partnerships and S Corporations

Although partnerships and S corporations must group their activities (see ¶ 1102.02) they are not subject to the reporting requirements set out above. Rather, partnerships and S corporations must comply with the disclosure instructions for grouping activities provided for on the Partnership (Form 1065) or S Corporation (Form 1120S) income tax return. Generally, this requires disclosing the entity's groupings to the partners or shareholders by separately stating the amounts of income and loss for each grouping conducted by the entity on attachments to the entity's annual Schedule K-1. A partner or shareholder is not required to make a separate disclosure of the groupings disclosed by the entity unless the partner or shareholder (1) groups together any of the activities that the entity does not group together, (2) groups the entity's activities with activities conducted directly by the partner or shareholder, or (3) groups the entity's activities with activities conducted through other entities. A shareholder or partner may not treat activities grouped together by a Code Sec. 469 entity as separate activities.

¶ 1103 LIMITS ON RENTAL ACTIVITIES

A rental activity generally is classified as a passive activity regardless of the taxpayer's level of participation in the activity.[39] This sometimes, but not always, makes classification of an activity as a rental activity disadvantageous for a person who participates in the activity. There are, however, occasions when classification of an activity as a rental activity producing passive income may be advantageous: for instance, when a taxpayer has passive losses that may be used to offset the income. In these situations, taxpayers would be inclined to rearrange their business or investment holdings in an effort to produce passive income. So, in addition to the rules defining rental activities as passive activities, there are rules that block such a classification in certain situations and require that the income produced be treated as income that is not from a passive activity.

In the case of real estate, there are special rules that create two exceptions to the general rule that all rental activities are passive activities. First, a limited exception is provided in Code Sec. 469(i) for real estate activities in which a taxpayer actively participates, as discussed at ¶ 1103.05. Second, as discussed at ¶ 1103.06, the rental activities rule does not apply to any rental real estate activity of a taxpayer in the real property business as defined in Code Sec. 469(c)(7). In other situations, even if a taxpayer can show that a particular activity is not a rental activity, the taxpayer still must show material participation, as discussed at ¶ 1101.03[A], to avoid the passive activity loss rules.

[39] Code Sec. 469(c)(2).

.01 Rental Activity Defined

An activity is considered a rental activity if tangible property held in connection with the activity is used by, or held for use by, customers, and the gross income from the activity represents amounts paid or to be paid primarily for the use of property.[40] If any one of the following six tests is met, the activity will not be considered to be a rental activity:

1. The average period of customer use of the rental property is seven days or less. This test excludes short-term use of hotel and motel rooms from the passive loss rules.
2. The average period of customer use is 30 days or less and significant personal services are provided by or on behalf of the owner. Whether services are significant is based on factors such as their frequency, their value relative to the amount charged for the use of the property, and the type and amount of labor required. Services are not significant if they (a) are necessary to permit lawful use of the property, (b) are for construction, improvements or repairs that extend the life of the property substantially beyond the average period customers use the property, or (c) are similar to those commonly provided in connection with long-term rentals of high-grade commercial or residential real property, such as cleaning of common areas, routine repairs, trash collection, elevator service, and entrance or perimeter security.[41]
3. Extraordinary personal services are provided by or on behalf of the owner, even if the average period of customer use is greater than 30 days. Services are extraordinary only if they are performed by individuals and the use of the property by customers is incidental to the services. For example, boarding facilities at a hospital are incidental to the personal services of the hospital staff, or boarding facilities at a school are incidental to the services of the teaching staff.[42]
4. The rental of the property is treated as incidental to a nonrental activity. This test applies to rentals of property that are incidental to the holding of property for investment, the use of property in a trade or business activity, or the holding of property for sale to customers in the ordinary course of business. (See further discussion at ¶ 1103.01[A].)
5. The property is customarily made available during defined hours of business for the nonexclusive use of customers. This test excludes the operation of facilities such as golf courses that are used by customers.
6. Property is provided to a partnership, S corporation, or joint venture in which the taxpayer holds an interest, if the property is provided in the taxpayer's capacity as owner rather than rented to the entity. (See further discussion at ¶ 1103.01[B].)

[40] Temp. Reg. § 1.469-1T(e)(3).

[41] Temp. Reg. § 1.469-1T(e)(3)(iv).

[42] Temp. Reg. § 1.469-1T(e)(3)(v).

The following example illustrates the application of the significant services and extraordinary services tests (see tests 2 and 3 above).

> ***Example 5:*** The Taxpayer is engaged in an activity of owning and operating a residential apartment hotel. For the taxable year, the average period of customer use for apartments exceeds seven days but does not exceed 30 days. In addition to cleaning public entrances, exits, stairways, and lobbies, and collecting and removing trash, the Taxpayer provides a daily maid and linen service at no additional charge. All of the services, other than the maid and linen services, are similar to those commonly provided in connection with long-term rentals of high-grade residential real property. The value of the maid and linen services, measured by the cost to the Taxpayer of employees performing these services, is less than ten percent of the amount charged to tenants for occupancy of apartments. Under these facts, the Taxpayer provides neither significant personal services (test 2) nor extraordinary personal services (test 3) in connection with making the apartments available for use by customers. Accordingly, the activity is a rental activity.

Additional examples may be found in the regulations at Temp. Reg. § 1.469-1T(e)(3)(viii).

[A] Rentals Incidental to Nonrental Activities

The rental of property that is incidental to a nonrental activity is not considered a rental activity. This exception applies to rentals of property that are incidental to holding property for investment, the use of property in a trade or business activity, or holding property for sale to customers in the ordinary course of business.[43]

The rental of property is incidental to the activity of holding the property for investment only if:

1. The principal purpose for holding the property is to realize gain from the appreciation of the property; and
2. The gross rental income from the property for the taxable year is less than two percent of the unadjusted basis of the property or the fair market value of the property, whichever is less.

The rental of property is incidental to a trade or business activity only if:

1. The taxpayer owns an interest in the trade or business during the taxable year;
2. The property was predominantly used in the trade or business during the taxable year or during at least two of the five tax years immediately preceding the current year; and
3. The gross rental income from the property for the taxable year is less than two percent of the unadjusted basis of the property or the fair market value of the property, whichever is less.

[43] Temp. Reg. § 1.469-1T(e)(3)(vi).

Lodging provided to an employee or an employee's spouse or dependents for the convenience of the employer (within the meaning of Code Sec. 119) is incidental to the activity of the taxpayer in which the employee performs services.[44]

Example 6: The Taxpayer owns 1,000 acres of unimproved land with a fair market value of $350,000 and an unadjusted basis of $210,000. The Taxpayer holds the land for the principal purpose of realizing gain from appreciation. In order to defray the cost of carrying the land, the Taxpayer leases the land to a rancher for grazing cattle. The rancher pays $4,000 per year as rent. The gross rental income from the land is less than two percent of the lesser of the fair market value and the unadjusted basis of the land (2% × $210,000 = $4,200). The rental of the land is not a rental activity because the rental is incidental to holding the property for investment.

Example 7: In 2019, the Taxpayer acquires vacant land for the purpose of constructing a shopping mall. Before beginning construction, the Taxpayer leases the land under a one-year lease to an automobile dealer who uses the land to park cars held in inventory. The Taxpayer begins construction in 2020.

The Taxpayer acquired the land for the principal purpose of constructing the shopping mall, not for the principal purpose of realizing gain from the appreciation of the property. The rental of the property in 2019 is not incidental to holding the property for investment. Also, since the land has not been used in any trade or business of the Taxpayer, the rental of the property in 2019 is not treated as incidental to a trade or business activity. Since the rental of the property in 2019 is not incidental to a nonrental activity of the Taxpayer, the rental of the land in 2019 is a rental activity.

A special rule relating to the treatment of income from the rental of nondepreciable property is discussed at ¶ 1103.04.

[B] Property Provided to a Partnership, Joint Venture, or S Corporation

Providing property to a partnership, joint venture, or S corporation conducting an activity other than a rental activity in which the taxpayer holds an interest is not a rental activity if the property is provided in the taxpayer's capacity as owner rather than rented to the entity.[45] For instance, if a partner contributes the use of property to a partnership, none of the partner's distributive share of partnership income is income from a rental activity unless the partnership is engaged in a rental activity. In addition, a partner's gross income attributable to a guaranteed payment is not income from a rental activity under any circumstances.[46] The determination of whether property used in an activity is provided by the taxpayer in the capacity as owner of an interest in a partnership, S corporation, or joint venture is made on the basis of all of the facts and circumstances.

Example 8: The Taxpayer makes farmland available to a tenant farmer under an arrangement designated a "crop-share lease." Under the arrange-

---

[44] Reg. § 1.469-1(e)(3)(vi)(D).

[45] Temp. Reg. § 1.469-1T(e)(3)(vii).

[46] Temp. Reg. § 1.469-2T(e)(2).

ment, the tenant is required to use his best efforts to farm the land and produce marketable crops. The Taxpayer is obligated to pay 50 percent of the costs incurred in the activity, regardless of whether crops are successfully produced or marketed, and is entitled to 50 percent of the crops produced or 50 percent of the proceeds from marketing the crops. The Taxpayer is providing the farmland for use in a farming activity conducted by a joint venture in the capacity as an owner of an interest in the joint venture. The Taxpayer is not engaged in a rental activity, regardless of whether the Taxpayer performs any services in the farming activity.

.02 Self-Rented Property

An amount of the taxpayer's gross rental activity income for the taxable year from an item of property equal to the net rental activity income for the year from the property is treated as not from a passive activity if the property is rented for use in a trade or business activity in which the taxpayer materially participates and the property is not rented incident to development as discussed below.[47] This rule is aimed primarily at situations in which a taxpayer conducts a trade or business that must make use of property, typically real estate, that may be owned or leased. For instance, an individual may run a retail operation as a corporation, but own the store from which the operation is conducted in the individual's name. If the rental of the store to the corporate business produced passive income, the taxpayer would be able to offset that income with passive losses. At the same time, the rent deduction for the corporation would reduce its regular taxable operating income. Reg. § 1.469-2(f)(6) prevents this by, in effect, converting the otherwise passive income from the rental into nonpassive income so that the taxpayer cannot shelter this rental income with passive losses from other activities.

.03 Rental Incident to Development

Generally, a rental activity is a passive activity and gain from the sale or disposition of property used in a passive activity is treated as passive activity income.[48] A taxpayer that materially or significantly participates in the development of property that is rented during the year of its sale, however, may have nonpassive income in the year of the sale.[49] Net rental activity income from the rental or sale of property used in a rental activity for the taxable year is not treated as passive income if the following three conditions are met:

1. The taxpayer recognizes gain from the sale, exchange, or other disposition of the property for the taxable year;
2. The use of the property in a rental activity began less than 24 months before the date of disposition of the property;[50] and
3. The taxpayer materially participated or significantly participated (as defined at ¶ 1101.03 above) for any taxable year in an activity that involved the performance of services for the purpose of enhancing the value of the property.

---

[47] Reg. § 1.469-2(f)(6).

[48] Temp. Reg. § 1.469-2T(c)(2).

[49] Reg. § 1.469-2(f)(5).

[50] Rental begins when substantially all of the property is first held out for rent and is in a state or readiness for rental; Reg. § 1.469-2(f)(5)(ii).

Services that enhance the value of property include, but are not limited to, construction, renovation, and lease-up as long as the taxpayer acquires an interest in the property before a substantial portion of the property is leased.[51]

Example 9: The Taxpayer, a calendar-year individual, is a partner in Partners, a calendar-year partnership which develops commercial real estate. In 2017, Partners acquires undeveloped land and arranges for the financing and construction of an office building on the land. Construction is completed in February 2019, and substantially all of the building is held out for rent and is in a state of readiness for rental beginning on March 1, 2019.

Partners holds the building for rent for the remainder of 2019 and all of 2020, and sells the building on January 15, 2021, under a contract that was signed on January 15, 2020. Partners did not hold out the office building or any other building for sale to customers in the ordinary course of business. The Taxpayer's share of Partners' taxable losses from the rental of the building is $50,000 for 2019 and $30,000 for 2020. All of the Taxpayer's losses from the rental building are disallowed passive activity losses. The Taxpayer's share of the gain recognized by Partners on the sale of the building is $150,000. The Taxpayer has no other income or deductions from the activity of renting the building.

In 2017, 2018, and 2019, the real estate development activity that the Taxpayer holds through Partners involves the performance of services for the purpose of enhancing the value of the building. The date on which the use of the building in the rental activity began was less than 12 months before the date on which a binding contract for the sale was executed. If the Taxpayer materially participated in the real estate development activity in 2017, 2018, and 2019, regardless of whether the Taxpayer materially participated in the activity in more than one of those years, an amount of the Taxpayer's gross rental activity income for 2021 from the building equal to the Taxpayer's net rental activity income for 2021 from the building ($150,000 - $80,000 of previously disallowed losses = $70,000) is gross income that is not from a passive activity.

.04 Rental of Nondepreciable Property

Income from the rental of nondepreciable property is not treated as passive activity income but as portfolio income. Property is nondepreciable if less than 30 percent of its unadjusted basis is subject to depreciation. Unadjusted basis is adjusted basis determined without regard to any adjustments under Code Sec. 1016 that decrease basis.[52] This rule primarily affects ground rents and other rentals of undeveloped land.

Example 10: The Taxpayer is a limited partner in a partnership. The partnership acquires vacant land for $300,000, constructs improvements on the land at a cost of $100,000, and leases the land and improvements to a tenant.

[51] Reg. § 1.469-2(f)(5)(iii).

[52] Temp. Reg. § 1.469-2T(f)(3).

The partnership then sells the land and improvements for $600,000, thereby realizing a gain on the disposition. The unadjusted basis of the improvements ($100,000) equals 25 percent of the unadjusted basis of all property ($400,000) used in the rental activity. Therefore, an amount of the Taxpayer's gross income from the activity equal to the net passive income from the activity, which is computed by taking into account the gain from the disposition including gain allocable to the improvements, is treated as not from a passive activity.

.05 Active Participation in Rental Real Estate

A limited exception to the passive activity loss rules is available to an individual taxpayer for rental real estate in which the individual "actively participates."[53] The active participation standard requires much less participation on the part of the taxpayer than the material participation standard that generally applies under the passive loss rules. The taxpayer, however, must participate in the making of management decisions or arrange for others to provide services such as repairs in a significant and bona fide sense. The active participation requirement does not apply, however, to rehabilitation and low-income housing tax credits.[54]

An individual is not considered to actively participate, regardless of the actual level of participation, if the individual and spouse together own less than ten percent of the value of all interests in the activity (Code Sec. 469(i)(6)). Also, the active participation requirement precludes investing as a limited partner in order to realize tax deductions in excess of income from passive activities. The exception does permit deductions from real estate against nonpassive income for individual owners and investors who participate in the rental activity through a general partnership or S corporation, provided they meet the ten percent ownership requirement.

[A] $25,000 Limit

Under the exception to the passive activity loss rules for rental real estate in which an individual actively participates, up to $25,000 of losses and credits, in a deduction equivalent sense, may be used to offset nonpassive income.[55] The $25,000 amount is applied by first netting income and loss from all real estate activities in which the taxpayer actively participates. If there is a net loss from these activities, net passive income, if any, from other activities is then applied against the net loss in determining the amount eligible for the $25,000 deduction.

[B] Filing Status

The exception is generally available to single individuals and married taxpayers who file joint returns. Married individuals who file separate returns are not eligible for the exception, unless they lived apart at all times during the tax year. Married individuals living apart and filing separate returns each may qualify for up to $12,500 in deductions.[56]

---

[53] Code Sec. 469(i).

[54] Code Sec. 469(i)(6)(B).

[55] Code Sec. 469(i)(2).

[56] Code Sec. 469(i)(5).

[C] Phase-Out of Deduction

The maximum $25,000 deduction under the exception to the passive activity loss rules for rental real estate is reduced for higher income individuals. The $25,000 amount is reduced by 50 cents for each dollar of adjusted gross income in excess of $100,000. Individuals with incomes in excess of $150,000, therefore, cannot benefit from the exception to the passive activity loss rules for active participation in rental real estate.[57] The dollar amounts for the phase-out, as with the $25,000 limit itself, are cut in half for married individuals living apart who file separate returns.

In the case of a rehabilitation credit determined under Code Sec. 47, the phase-out starts at $200,000 rather than $100,000. Further, there is no phase-out for a passive activity loss attributable to the commercial revitalization deduction under Code Sec. 1400I or the low-income housing credit under Code Sec. 42. Ordering rules to reflect those exceptions and separate phase-out are contained in Code. Sec. 469(i)(3)(E).

For purposes of computing the reduction in the $25,000 limit for individuals with adjusted gross income in excess of $100,000, adjusted gross income is computed without regard to any passive activity loss, taxable social security or railroad retirement benefits, the exclusion for qualified U.S. savings bonds used to pay higher education expenses, the exclusion for employer adoption assistance payments, any overall loss from a publicly traded partnership, rental real estate losses allowed to real estate professionals, the deduction for contributions to IRAs and pension plans, the deduction for one-half of self-employment tax, the deduction for interest on student loans, the deduction for tuition and fees, the domestic production activities deduction for tax years beginning before 2018, and the foreign-derived intangible income deduction for tax years beginning after 2017.[58]

.06 Real Property Business Exception

Rental real estate activities of qualifying taxpayers, generally those in a real property business, are not subject to the rule that treats all rental activities as passive.[59] As a result, a real estate activity of a qualifying taxpayer is not passive if the taxpayer materially participates in the activity. Further, each of a qualifying taxpayer's interests in rental real estate is treated as a separate activity unless the taxpayer elects to treat all interests in real estate as a single activity.[60]

To qualify for the real property business exception to the rule that treats all rental activities as passive, a taxpayer must perform:

1. More than one-half of the personal services performed in trades or businesses during the tax year in real property trades or businesses in which the taxpayer materially participates; and
2. More than 750 hours of services during the tax year in real property trades or businesses in which the taxpayer materially participates.[61]

---

[57] Code Sec. 469(i)(3).

[58] Code Sec. 469(i)(3)(D).

[59] Code Sec. 469(c)(7).

[60] Code Sec. 469(c)(7)(A)(ii).

[61] Code Sec. 469(c)(7)(B).

In the case of a joint return, the requirements are satisfied if and only if either spouse separately satisfies the requirements. For a closely held C corporation, the requirements are met if more than 50 percent of the gross receipts of the corporation are derived from real property trades or businesses in which the corporation materially participates.[62] Personal services performed as an employee do not count, unless the employee is a five-percent owner.

As to establishing an individual's participation in an activity, the regulations provide that participation may be established by any reasonable means. Contemporaneous daily time reports, logs, or similar documents are not required if the extent of participation may be established by other reasonable means. Reasonable means may include, but are not limited to, the identification of services performed over a period of time and the approximate number of hours spent performing the services during that period, based on appointment books, calendars, or narrative summaries.[63] The Tax Court, however, has ruled that the regulations do not allow a post-event "ballpark guesstimate."[64]

Despite IRS arguments to the contrary, the Tax Court has held that a trust that owned real estate rental property and engaged in other real estate activities qualified as a real estate professional and was exempt from the passive activity loss rules.[65] In determining whether the trust materially participated in its real estate activities, the Court looked to the participation of individuals who served both as trustees and employees of the trust's wholly owned limited liability company charged with managing its rental activities, and of individual trustees who served as employees of other entities in which the trust had a majority interest and the employees a minority interest.

An individual apparently can be a real estate professional and exempt from the passive loss rules, even if real estate is a second profession for the individual. In *Windham*,[66] a stock broker was entitled to deduct rental real estate losses because she was a real estate professional who materially participated in the real estate activity. Although, the taxpayer did not make an election to group her 12 rental properties together, the taxpayer's testimony and logs showed that she spent more than 850 hours on the real estate activities, which was more than one-half of the total time she spent on all of her business activities. The taxpayer spent a considerable amount of time and money to keep her rental real estate activities viable and handled all aspects of the business from collecting rent to overseeing the work of repairmen, meeting prospective buyers, and handling problems with utility and service companies.

The same logic was applied to a dentist in *Zarrinnegar and Dini*.[67] The Tax Court ruled the dentist was entitled to deduct rental real estate losses because he was a real estate professional. The dentist's testimony and logs showed that he

[62] Code Sec. 469(c)(7)(D).

[63] Reg. § 1.469-5T(f)(4).

[64] Bailey, CCH Dec. 54,541(M), T.C. Memo. 2001-296; Goshorn, CCH Dec. 49,453(M), T.C. Memo. 1993-578; *see also* Birdsong, 116 TCM 274, CCH Dec. 61,262(M), T.C. Memo. 2018-148.

[65] *Frank Aragona Trust*, 142 TC 165.

[66] 113 TCM 1318, CCH Dec. 60,882(M), T.C. Memo. 2017-068.

[67] 113 TCM 1148, CCH Dec. 60,838(M), T.C. Memo. 2017-034.

spent more than 1,000 hours per year on the real estate activities, which was more time than he spent working as a dentist. The dentist credibly testified that the logs had been prepared contemporaneously and provided specific details about the logs' contents. The dentist also offered the testimony of several other witnesses, including his wife, that was credible and tended to corroborate the dentist's logs and testimony.

Failure to aggregate may be another problem for a real estate professional who manages several properties. In *Ramirez*,[68] the Tax Court said that even if they found an individual was a real estate professional, not electing to treat all rental properties as a single activity could prevent the individual from qualifying for the real property business exception. When a taxpayer who owns more than one rental property does not make the aggregation election, the default rule is to treat each rental property as a separate activity. Under this reading, presumably the court would treat each activity as a separate business to which the 750-hour requirement applies.

A real property trade or business is any real property development, redevelopment, construction, reconstruction, acquisition, conversion, rental, operation, management, leasing, or brokerage trade or business.[69]

For any tax year in which a qualifying taxpayer materially participates in a rental real estate activity, that activity is treated as a former passive activity if disallowed deductions or credits are allocated to the activity.[70]

[A] Grouping Rental Real Estate Activities

A taxpayer who qualifies for the real estate business exception to the passive activity loss rules may not group a rental real estate activity with any other activity. For instance, if a qualifying taxpayer develops real property, constructs buildings, and owns an interest in rental real estate, the taxpayer's interest in rental real estate may not be grouped with the taxpayer's development activity or construction activity. This means that only the participation of the taxpayer as to the rental real estate may be used to determine if the taxpayer materially participates in the rental real estate activity.[71]

A qualifying taxpayer may participate in a rental real estate activity through participation in the management of rental real estate, even if this management activity is conducted through a separate entity. In determining whether the taxpayer materially participates in the rental real estate activity, however, work the taxpayer performs in the management activity is taken into account only to the extent it is performed in managing the taxpayer's own rental real estate interest.[72]

> ***Example 11:*** Taxpayer owns interests in three rental buildings, X, Y, and Z. In 2019, Taxpayer has $30,000 of disallowed passive losses allocable to building X, and $10,000 allocable to building Y. In 2020, Taxpayer has $5,000 of net income from building X, $5,000 of net losses from building Y, and $10,000 of net income from building Z. In 2020, Taxpayer is a qualifying taxpayer for

[68] 116 TCM 517, CCH Dec. 61,316(M), T.C. Memo. 2018-196.

[69] Code Sec. 469(c)(7)(C).

[70] Reg. § 1.469-9(e)(2).

[71] Reg. § 1.469-9(e)(3)(i).

[72] Reg. § 1.469-9(e)(3)(ii).

the real property business exception. Each building is treated separately unless Taxpayer elects to treat them as a single rental real estate activity. If the buildings are treated as separate activities, material participation is determined separately for each building. If Taxpayer elects to treat the buildings as a single activity, all participation relating to the buildings is aggregated to determine whether Taxpayer materially participates in the combined activity.

Assume Taxpayer elects to treat the buildings as a single activity in 2020 and works full-time managing the buildings so that he materially participates in the combined activity. The combined activity is not a passive activity in 2020, and the disallowed passive losses from 2019 of $40,000 are allocated to the combined activity. Taxpayer's net income from the rental real estate activity for 2020 is $10,000, and this net income is nonpassive income. Because the three buildings are treated as one activity and this activity is a former passive activity, however, Taxpayer may offset the $10,000 of net income from the buildings with an equal amount of disallowed passive losses allocable to the buildings, regardless of which building produced the income or losses. Taxpayer has $30,000 of disallowed passive losses remaining from the buildings after 2020.

[B] Limited Partnership Interests

If a taxpayer elects to treat all interests in rental real estate as a single rental activity, and at least one interest is held as a limited partnership interest, the combined rental real estate activity is treated as a limited partnership interest in order to determine material participation.[73] What this means is that the taxpayer will not be treated as materially participating in the combined rental real estate activity unless the taxpayer materially participates in the activity under the tests for determining material participation by a limited partner and set out at ¶ 1101.02[A].

If a taxpayer elects to treat all interests in rental real estate as a single rental activity, and the taxpayer's share of gross rental income from all of the taxpayer's limited partnership interests in rental real estate is less than ten percent of the taxpayer's share of gross rental income from all interests in rental real estate, the taxpayer may determine material participation under any of the tests that apply to rental real estate activities.[74]

[C] Coordination with Active Participation Exception

Passive losses and credits from rental real estate activities are allowed to a limited extent when the taxpayer actively participates in the activity (see ¶ 1103.05). The amount of losses or credits that are allowed under that exception is determined after the exception for a rental real estate business is applied. Losses allowed by the rental real estate business exception, however, are not taken into account to determine adjusted gross income for the phase-out of the limited $25,000 exception for active participation (see ¶ 1103.05[C]).[75]

[73] Reg. § 1.469-9(f)(1).

[74] Reg. § 1.469-9(f)(2).

[75] Reg. § 1.469-9(j).

Example 12: Taxpayer owns two rental buildings, X and Y. In 2020, Taxpayer qualifies for the rental real estate business exception to the passive activity loss rules, but does not elect to treat the two buildings as a single activity. Taxpayer materially participates in building X that has \$100,000 of disallowed losses from prior years and produces \$20,000 of losses in 2020. Taxpayer does not materially participate in building Y that produces \$40,000 of income in 2020. Taxpayer also has \$50,000 of nonpassive income from other sources in 2020.

For 2020, Taxpayer may use the \$20,000 of losses produced by building X to offset part of the \$50,000 of nonpassive income. This leaves Taxpayer with \$30,000 of nonpassive income. Also, Taxpayer may offset the \$40,000 of passive income from building Y with \$40,000 of the prior years' \$100,000 of disallowed passive losses from building X. Because Taxpayer still has \$60,000 of passive losses remaining from building X and meets the requirements for the exception for active participation in rental real estate, Taxpayer may offset up to \$25,000 of nonpassive income (the limit under the active participation exception) with passive losses from building X. The final result leaves Taxpayer with \$5,000 of nonpassive income and disallowed passive losses from building X of \$35,000 in 2020.

¶ 1104 TAX TREATMENT OF PASSIVE LOSSES AND CREDITS

If the passive activity loss rules apply to one or more activities, the taxpayer faces the hurdle of computing the deductible loss, if any, and the extent to which any tax credit generated by a passive activity may be used to offset tax liability. Generally, losses from passive activities can be used only to offset income from passive activities and a tax credit generated by a passive activity can be used only to offset tax liability attributable to a passive activity.

.01 Computation of Deductible Loss

A passive activity loss is not deductible.[76] A passive activity loss, in the case of a taxpayer other than a closely held corporation, is the amount by which the passive activity deductions exceed the passive activity gross income for the taxable year.[77] In order to compute the passive activity loss, then, it is necessary to first compute passive activity gross income and passive activity deductions. Since a closely held corporation may use passive losses to offset operating income, a modified computation, as discussed below, is required.

[A] Passive Activity Gross Income

Passive activity gross income for a taxable year includes an item of gross income only if the income is from a passive activity.[78]

---

[76] Code Sec. 469(a)(1)(A).

[77] Temp. Reg. § 1.469-2T(b)(1).

[78] Temp. Reg. § 1.469-2T(c)(1).

Portfolio Income

Passive activity income does not include portfolio income.[79] Portfolio income is all gross income, other than income derived in the ordinary course of business, that is derived from the following sources:

1. Interest, annuities, royalties, dividends on C corporation stock, and income from a real estate investment trust, regulated investment company, real estate mortgage investment conduit, common trust fund, controlled foreign corporation, qualified electing fund (described in Code Sec. 1295(a)), or cooperative;
2. Dividends on S corporation stock that exceed the corporation's accumulated adjustment account but not earnings and profits;
3. Gain or loss attributable to the disposition of any property that produces income of the types described in 1, and
4. Gain or loss on the disposition of property held for investment.

If income falls into any of the classifications above but is derived in the ordinary course of a trade or business, it is not considered portfolio income. Gross income derived in the ordinary course of a trade or business includes only the following:

1. Interest income on loans and investments made in the ordinary course of a trade or business. For example, interest on mortgage loans received by a mortgage company would not be portfolio income.
2. Interest on accounts receivable arising from the performance of services or the sale of property in the ordinary course of a trade or business of performing the services or selling the property, but only if credit is customarily offered to customers of the business.
3. Income from investments made in the ordinary course of a trade or business of furnishing insurance or annuity contracts or reinsuring risks underwritten by insurance companies.
4. Income or gain derived in the ordinary course of an activity of trading or dealing in any property if the activity constitutes a trade or business. A dealer's income or gain is not business income, and is therefore portfolio income, however, if the income or gain is from property that the dealer held for investment at any time before the income or gain is recognized.
5. Royalties derived by the taxpayer in the ordinary course of a trade or business of licensing intangible property, but only if the taxpayer created the property or performed substantial services or incurred substantial costs to develop or market the property.[80]
6. Amounts included in the gross income of a patron of a cooperative for any payment or allocation to the patron based on patronage occurring with respect to a trade or business of the patron.
7. Other income identified by the IRS as income from a trade or business.

See Temp. Reg. § 1.469-2T(c)(3)(ii).

[79] Temp. Reg. § 1.469-2T(c)(3)(i).

[80] Temp. Reg. § 1.469-2T(c)(3)(iii)(B).

Example 13: A partnership operates a rental apartment building for low-income tenants. Under local law, the partnership is required to maintain a reserve fund to pay for the maintenance and repair of the building. The partnership invests the reserve fund in short-term interest-bearing deposits. The interest the partnership receives from investing this reserve fund is not derived in the ordinary course of a trade or business under the rules set out above. Therefore, the partnership's interest income from the deposits is portfolio income.

Example 14: An individual engaged in the trade or business of farming sells farmland in an installment sale. The individual is not engaged in the trade or business of selling farmland. In this situation, the individual's interest income from the installment sale is portfolio income since it is not derived in the ordinary course of a trade or business.

Gain on Sale or Disposition

Generally, gain recognized on the sale, exchange, or other disposition of an interest in property used in an activity or of an interest in an activity held through a partnership or S corporation is treated as passive activity gross income for the tax year or years in which it is recognized if the activity is a passive activity for the tax year of disposition.[81] Any material portion of property that was used in any activity at a time when the remainder of the property was not used in the activity is treated as a separate interest in property and the amount realized from the disposition and the adjusted basis of the property must be allocated among the separate interests in a reasonable manner.[82]

Example 15: The Taxpayer sold a 10-floor office building that the Taxpayer had owned for three years. For the entire time the building was held, the Taxpayer used seven floors of the building in a trade or business activity and three floors in a rental activity. The fair market value per square foot is substantially the same throughout the building, and the Taxpayer did not maintain a separate adjusted basis for any part of the building.

The seven floors used in the trade or business activity and the three floors used in the rental activity are treated as separate interests in property. The amount realized and the adjusted basis of the building must be allocated between the separate interests in a reasonable manner. Accordingly, an allocation based on the square footage of the parts of the building used in each activity would be reasonable.

If an interest in property is used in more than one activity during the 12 months before its disposition, the amount realized and the adjusted basis of the interest must be allocated among the activities in a manner that reasonably reflects the use of the interest in property during that 12-month period. An allocation of the amount realized and the adjusted basis solely to the activity in which an interest in property is predominantly used during the 12-month period reasonably reflects the

[81] Temp. Reg. § 1.469-2T(c) (2) (i) (A).

[82] Temp. Reg. § 1.469-2T(c) (2) (i) (C).

use of the interest in property, if the fair market value of the interest does not exceed $10,000 or ten percent of the sum of the fair market value of the interest and the fair market value of all other property used in the activity immediately before the disposition, whichever is less.[83]

> ***Example 16:*** Assume the same facts as in Example 15, except that two of the seven floors used in the trade or business activity were used in the rental activity until five months before the sale. The five floors used exclusively in the trade or business activity and the two floors used first in the rental activity and then in the trade or business activity are treated as separate interests in property.
>
> For the amount realized and the adjusted basis of the building, the Taxpayer allocates 30 percent to the three floors used exclusively in the rental activity, 50 percent to the five floors used exclusively in the trade or business activity, and 20 percent to the two floors used first in the rental activity and then in the trade or business activity. The amount realized and the adjusted basis allocated to the two floors that were used in both activities during the 12 months before the sale must also be allocated between the activities. Under these facts, an allocation of 7/12 to the rental activity and 5/12 to the trade or business activity would reasonably reflect the use of the two floors during the 12-month period.

If an interest in property used in an activity is substantially appreciated at the time of its disposition, any gain from the disposition is treated as not from a passive activity, unless the interest was used in a passive activity for either 20 percent of the time the taxpayer held the interest or the entire 24 months before the disposition.[84] An interest in property is substantially appreciated if the fair market value of the interest exceeds 120 percent of the adjusted basis of the interest.[85]

> ***Example 17:*** The Taxpayer acquired a building on January 1, 2008, and uses the building in a trade or business activity in which the Taxpayer materially participates until March 31, 2019. On April 1, 2019, the Taxpayer leases the building. On December 31, 2020, the Taxpayer sells the building when the interest is substantially appreciated. Assuming the Taxpayer's lease of the building is a rental activity, the building is used in a passive activity for 21 months (April 1, 2019, through December 31, 2020). The building was not used in a passive activity for the entire 24 months before its sale. In addition, the 21-month period during which the building was used in a passive activity is less than 20 percent of the Taxpayer's holding period of 13 years for the building. Therefore, the gain from the sale is not treated as passive activity income.

Special rules apply to dealer property (held primarily for sale to customers in the ordinary course of business) used in a nondealer activity. Holding an interest in property in a dealing activity (the marketing of the property) is treated as the use of the interest in a nondealing activity if the marketing of the property is incidental to

---

[83] Temp. Reg. § 1.469-2T(c)(2)(ii).

[84] Reg. § 1.469-2(c)(2)(iii)(A).

[85] Reg. § 1.469-2(c)(2)(iii)(C).

the nondealing use. When these rules apply, the interests in property are treated as used in the last nondealing activity in which they were used prior to their disposition. The marketing of the property is treated as incidental to the nondealing use if the interest in the property was used in nondealing activities for more than 80 percent of the taxpayer's holding period in the property and the taxpayer did not acquire and hold the interest for the principal purpose of selling it to customers in the ordinary course of a trade or business.[86]

A taxpayer is rebuttably presumed to have a dealing purpose unless the interest in property was used in nondealing activities for more than 24 months or 20 percent of the property's recovery period, whichever is less. The same presumption applies if the interest in property was offered for sale to customers during more than 25 percent of the period in which the interest was held in nondealing activities.[87]

Personal Service Income

Passive activity gross income does not include compensation paid to or on behalf of an individual for personal services performed or to be performed by the individual at any time. Compensation for personal services includes only:

1. Earned income, including payments by a partnership to a partner that represent compensation for services by the partner;
2. Amounts includible in income as property transferred for services under Code Sec. 83;
3. Distributions from qualified retirement plans;
4. Payments under deferred compensation arrangements other than qualified plans;
5. Social security benefits included in gross income; and
6. Other income that the IRS designates as income derived from personal services.

A partner's distributive share of partnership income or a shareholder's pro rata share of income from an S corporation, however, cannot be treated as compensation for personal services.[88]

Change of Accounting Method

If a change in accounting method results in an increase in income from an activity as a result of the adjustments required by Code Sec. 481, a ratable portion of the amount taken into account for a tax year as a result of the adjustment is treated as gross income from the activity for the tax year. This income is passive activity gross income only if the activity is a passive activity for the year of the change in accounting method.[89]

[86] Reg. § 1.469-2(c)(2)(v).

[87] Reg. § 1.469-2T(c)(2)(v)(A)*(1)(ii)*.

[88] Temp. Reg. § 1.469-2T(c)(4).

[89] Temp. Reg. § 1.469-2T(c)(5).

Other Income Items

Passive activity gross income does not include the following items:

1. Gross income from intangible property, such as a patent, copyright, or literary, musical, or artistic composition, if the individual's personal efforts significantly contributed to the creation of the property;
2. Gross income from a qualified low-income housing project, as defined in Sec. 502 of the Tax Reform Act of 1986, for any taxable year in the relief period;
3. Gross income from a refund of any state, local, or foreign income, war profits, or excess profits tax;
4. Gross income from a covenant not to compete; and
5. Gross income that is treated as not from a passive activity under the Code Sec. 469 regulations.

[B] Passive Activity Deductions

Passive activity deductions are the deductions that may be taken against passive activity gross income in order to compute passive activity income or loss. Generally, a deduction is a passive activity deduction for a tax year only if the deduction arises in connection with the conduct of a passive activity for the tax year or is a carryover deduction from a prior year.[90]

Exceptions

Passive activity deductions do not include the following:

1. A deduction for an expense item, other than interest, that is clearly and directly allocable to portfolio income;
2. A deduction for dividends received by a corporation if the dividends are not included in passive activity gross income;
3. Interest expense, but only if it is allocated to a passive activity expenditure and is not a qualified residence interest or capitalized under a capitalization provision;
4. A deduction for a loss from the disposition of property that produces portfolio income;
5. A deduction that is allowed on the disposition of a passive activity;
6. A deduction for any state, local, or foreign income, war profits, or excess profits tax;
7. A miscellaneous itemized deduction that is subject to the two-percent floor;
8. A charitable contribution deduction;
9. Net operating loss, depletion allowance, or capital loss that is carried over to the tax year;
10. An item of loss or deduction that would have been allowed for a tax year before 1987, had it not been subject to the at-risk rules;

[90] Temp. Reg. § 1.469-2T(d)(1).

11. A casualty or theft loss deduction if losses that are similar in cause and severity do not recur regularly in the activity; and
12. A deduction or loss allocable to business or rental use of a dwelling when deduction or loss is limited to the income from the business or rental use under Code Sec. 280A(c)(5).[91]

An expense is clearly and directly allocable to portfolio income only if the expense is incurred as a result of, or incident to, an activity in which the portfolio income is derived or in connection with property from which the portfolio income is derived. For example, general and administrative expenses and compensation paid to officers attributable to the performance of services that do not directly benefit or are not incurred because of a particular activity or particular property are not clearly and directly allocable to portfolio income.[92]

Loss on Sale or Disposition

Generally, loss recognized on the sale, exchange, or other disposition of an interest in property used in an activity or of an interest in an activity held through a partnership or S corporation, and any deduction allowed because of the abandonment or worthlessness of the interest, is treated as a deduction from a passive activity if the activity is a passive activity for the tax year of disposition.[93]

Generally, the rules discussed above in connection with the discussion of when gain on a sale or disposition is treated as passive activity gross income apply to deductions. This includes all the allocation rules for separate interests and the use of property in more than one activity during the 12 months before the sale or disposition.

Change of Accounting Method

If a change in accounting method results in a decrease in income from an activity as a result of the adjustments required by Code Sec. 481, a ratable portion of the amount taken into account for a tax year as a result of the adjustment is treated as a deduction from the activity for the tax year. This deduction is a passive activity deduction only if the activity is a passive activity for the year of the change in accounting method.[94]

[C] Partners and S Corporation Shareholders

Partners and S corporation shareholders determine the character of items from these passthrough entities as passive activity income and deductions, when participation is relevant, based on their participation in the activities generating the income or deduction items. Participation is determined for the tax year of the passthrough entity and not the partner or shareholder.[95]

> ***Example 18:*** The Taxpayer is a calendar-year taxpayer and a partner in a partnership that has a tax year ending January 31. During the partnership year ending January 31, 2020, the partnership engages in only one trade or business

[91] Temp. Reg. § 1.469-2T(d)(2) and Reg. § 1.469-2(d)(2).

[92] Temp. Reg. § 1.469-2T(d)(4).

[93] Temp. Reg. § 1.469-2T(d)(5).

[94] Temp. Reg. § 1.469-2T(d)(7).

[95] Temp. Reg. § 1.469-2T(e)(1).

activity and the Taxpayer does not materially participate in this activity during the partnership's tax year. On the Taxpayer's return for the calendar year 2020, the Taxpayer's share of the partnership's gross income and deductions from the activity are passive activity gross income and passive activity deductions. This would be the case even if the Taxpayer materially participated in the activity from February 1, 2020, through December 31, 2020.

Payments to Partners

Partners may receive payments that are not distributions of the partners' shares of income. These payments are subject to special rules.[96]

Any income or deductions attributable to a transaction between a partner and a partnership that is treated as occurring between the partnership and an outsider is characterized under the passive activity loss rules in a manner that is consistent with the treatment of the transaction under Code Sec. 707(a).[97]

In the case of a guaranteed payment made to a partner for services or capital under Code Sec. 707(c), the payment is characterized as a payment for services or as the payment of interest and not as a distributive share of partnership income.[98]

Any gain or loss taken into account by a retiring partner or a deceased partner's successor in interest as a result of a payment under Code Sec. 736(b) for the deceased or retiring partner's interest in the partnership is treated as passive activity gross income or a passive activity deduction only to the extent that the gain or loss would have been passive income or a passive deduction of the retiring or deceased partner if it had been recognized at the time the liquidation of the partner's interest began.[99] Payments made to a retiring partner or a deceased partner's successor in interest under Code Sec. 736(a) for unrealized receivables and goodwill are passive activity income only in the same percentage as the percentage that the retiring or deceased partner would have recognized as passive activity income if the unrealized receivables and goodwill had been sold at the time that the liquidation of the partner's interest began.[100]

Sale or Exchange of Interest in Entity

If a partner or S corporation shareholder disposes of an interest in the passthrough entity, a ratable portion of any gain or loss from the disposition is treated as gain or loss from the disposition of an interest in each trade or business, rental, or investment activity in which the passthrough entity owns an interest on the applicable valuation date.[101]

The applicable valuation date is the beginning of the taxable year of the partnership or S corporation, or the date on which the disposition occurs, depending on which date is selected by the passthrough entity. However, the applicable valuation date is the date immediately preceding the date of disposition if any of the following occur between the beginning of the entity's tax year and the date of disposition of the interest by the partner or shareholder:

---

[96] Temp. Reg. § 1.469-2T(e)(2).

[97] Temp. Reg. § 1.469-2T(e)(2)(i).

[98] Reg. § 1.469-2(e)(2)(ii).

[99] Reg. § 1.469-2(e)(2)(iii)(A).

[100] Reg. § 1.469-2(e)(2)(iii)(B).

[101] Temp. Reg. § 1.469-2T(e)(3)(ii)(A).

1. The passthrough entity disposes of more than ten percent of its interest, measured by value as of the beginning of the taxable year, in any activity;
2. More than ten percent of the property, by value as of the beginning of the taxable year, used in any activity of the passthrough entity is disposed of; or
3. The holder of the interest contributes substantially appreciated property or substantially depreciated property to the entity, and the total fair market value of appreciated property or adjusted basis of depreciated property exceeds ten percent of the total fair market value of the holder's interest in the passthrough entity as of the beginning of the taxable year.[102]

Examples of the application of these rules may be found in Temp. Reg. § 1.469-2T(e)(3)(vii).

.02 Closely Held Corporation's Passive Activity Loss

The manner of computing a closely held corporation's passive activity loss is slightly different because closely held corporations may use deductions generated by passive activities to offset certain operating income as well as income from passive activities. A closely held corporation's passive activity loss for the taxable year is the amount by which the corporation's passive activity deductions for the taxable year exceed the sum of the corporation's passive activity gross income and its net active income for the taxable year.[103] Passive activity gross income and passive activity deductions are determined in the same fashion as discussed above for other taxpayers subject to the passive activity loss rules.

A corporation's net active income is the corporation's taxable income computed without regard to the following items:

1. Passive activity gross income;
2. Passive activity deductions;
3. Portfolio income;
4. Income from working interests in oil and gas properties which is not subject to the passive activity loss rules;
5. Income and deductions from a trade or business activity of trading personal property, but only if the corporation did not materially participate in the activity;
6. Deductions attributable to portfolio income; and
7. Interest expense that is allocable to a portfolio expenditure.[104]

The following examples illustrate the computation of a closely held corporation's passive activity loss.

Comprehensive Example 19: Closely Held Corporation (CHC) is engaged in two activities for 2019. One is a trade or business activity in which CHC materially participates for 2019, and the other is a rental activity. CHC also holds portfolio investments. CHC's gross income and deductions for 2019 are:

---

[102] Temp. Reg. § 1.469-2T(e)(3)(ii)(D)(*1*).

[103] Temp. Reg. § 1.469-1T(g)(4)(i).

[104] Temp. Reg. § 1.469-1T(g)(4)(ii).

Gross Income:	
Rents	$ 60,000
Business income	100,000
Portfolio income	35,000
Total	$195,000
Deductions:	
Rental deductions	$100,000
Business deductions	80,000
Interest expense allocable to portfolio expenditures	10,000
Deductions allocable to portfolio income	5,000
Total	$195,000

CHC's net active income for 2019 is $20,000, computed as follows:

Gross income		$195,000
Amounts not included in net active income:		
Rents	$ 60,000	
Portfolio income	35,000	
	$ 95,000	95,000
Gross active income		$100,000
Deductions		$195,000
Amounts not included in net active income:		
Rental deductions	$100,000	
Interest expense for portfolio income	10,000	
Other deductions for portfolio income	5,000	
	$115,000	115,000
Deductions from active income		$ 80,000
Gross active income		$100,000
Deductions from active income		80,000
Net active income		$ 20,000

CHC's passive activity loss for 2019 is $20,000, the amount by which the passive activity deductions ($100,000) exceed the sum of the passive activity gross income ($60,000) and the net active income ($20,000). The $20,000 of deductions from CHC's rental activity that are disallowed for 2019 are treated as deductions from the rental activity for 2020 (see the discussion of disallowed losses below). If computed without regard to the net active income, CHC's passive activity loss would be $40,000 ($100,000 of rental deductions minus

$60,000 of rental income). The effect of including active income in the computation of passive activity loss is to reduce CHC's passive activity loss for the year by the amount of CHC's net active income for the year.

Under these facts, CHC's taxable income for 2019 is $20,000, computed as follows:

Gross income		$195,000
Deductions:		
Total deductions	$195,000	
Passive activity loss	20,000	
Allowable deductions	$175,000	175,000
Taxable income		$ 20,000

Comprehensive Example 20: Assume the same facts as in Comprehensive Example 19, except that in 2020, CHC has a loss from the trade or business activity, and a net operating loss (NOL) of $15,000 that is carried back to 2019. Since NOL carrybacks are taken into account in computing net active income, CHC's net active income for 2019 must be recomputed as follows:

Net active income before NOL carryback	$20,000
Less: NOL carryback	15,000
Net active income	$5,000

Under these facts, CHC's disallowed passive activity loss for 2019 is $35,000, the amount by which the passive activity deductions for the taxable year ($100,000) exceed the sum of the passive activity gross income for the taxable year ($60,000) plus the net active income for the taxable year ($5,000).

The $35,000 of deductions for CHC's rental activity that are disallowed for 2019 are treated as deductions from the rental activity for 2020. CHC's taxable income for 2019 is $20,000, computed as follows:

Gross income		$195,000
Deductions:		
Total deductions	$210,000	
Passive activity loss	35,000	
Allowable deductions	$175,000	175,000
Taxable income		$20,000

Taking the NOL carryback into account in computing net active income for 2019 does not affect CHC's taxable income for 2019, but increases the deductions from CHC's rental activity for 2020 and decreases CHC's NOL carryover to years other than 2019.

.03 Disallowed Losses

Generally, losses from passive activities can be used only to offset income from passive activities. Any loss that cannot be used by a taxpayer because of the passive activity loss rules may be carried over to future years and applied to passive income in subsequent years.[105] A loss that remains unused as of the time the taxpayer disposes of the passive activity that generated the loss may be deducted at that time.[106] These rules require that disallowed passive activity losses be allocated among activities.

[A] Allocation of Disallowed Loss

If any portion of a taxpayer's passive activity loss is disallowed for the taxable year, a ratable portion of the loss, if any, from each passive activity of the taxpayer is disallowed. The ratable portion of a loss from an activity is computed by multiplying the passive activity loss that is disallowed for the taxable year by the fraction that is obtained by dividing:

1. The loss from the activity for the taxable year; by
2. The sum of the losses for the taxable year from all activities having losses for the year.[107]

The allocation may be computed using the worksheets that accompany the instructions to Form 8582, Passive Activity Loss Limitations.

Example 21: An individual holds interests in three passive activities, A, B, and C. For the taxable year, activity A produces $7,000 of gross income and $16,000 in deductions, activity B produces gross income of $4,000 and deductions of $20,000, and activity C produces gross income of $12,000 and deductions of $8,000.

The individual's passive activity loss for the taxable year in the amount of $21,000 ($23,000 total income less $44,000 total deductions) is disallowed. Therefore, a ratable portion of the losses from activities A and B is disallowed. The disallowed portion for each activity is calculated by multiplying the passive loss by a fraction which has the net loss from the activity as its numerator and total net losses from all loss activities as its denominator. In this case, the results are as follows:

For A: $21,000 × $ 9,000/$25,000 = $ 7,560.

For B: $21,000 × $16,000/$25,000 = $13,440.

A special allocation rule applies to significant participation activities when passive activity gross income from these activities exceeds the passive activity deductions attributable to these activities. In this case, the significant participation activities are treated as a single activity that does not have a loss for the taxable year.[108] This rule allows all significant participation activities to be treated as one activity only for purposes of allocating the loss among activities and allows a

---

[105] Code Sec. 469(b).

[106] Code Sec. 469(g).

[107] Temp. Reg. § 1.469-1T(f)(2)(i)(A).

[108] Temp. Reg. § 1.469-1T(f)(2)(i)(C).

taxpayer to avoid piecemeal allocation to significant participation activities when the net result of all significant participation activities is passive income rather than loss.

Example 22: An individual holds interests in four passive activities, A, B, C, and D. Activity A produces gross income of $15,000 and deductions of $5,000, or net income of $10,000. Activity B produces gross income of $5,000 and deductions of $10,000, or a net loss of $5,000. Activity C produces $10,000 of gross income and deductions of $20,000, or a net loss of $10,000. Activity D produces $10,000 of gross income, and $8,000 of deductions, or net income of $2,000. The total result of all of the individual's passive activities is gross income of $40,000, deductions of $43,000, and a net loss of $3,000.

Activities A and B are significant participation activities. The gross income from these activities for the taxable year ($20,000) exceeds the passive activity deductions from these activities for the taxable year ($15,000) by $5,000. Solely for applying the allocation rule, activities A and B are treated as a single activity that does not have a loss for the taxable year. The individual's passive activity loss for the taxable year is $8,000 ($43,000 of passive activity deductions minus $35,000 of passive activity gross income). The result of treating activities A and B as a single activity that does not have a loss for the year is that none of the $8,000 passive activity loss is allocated to activity B, even though the individual incurred a loss in that activity.

[B] Allocation Within Loss Activities

Once a taxpayer allocates the passive activity loss among all the passive activities that produced a loss, the taxpayer must then allocate the ratable portion applied to each loss among the deductions from the activity that produced the loss. A ratable portion of each passive activity deduction, other than an excluded deduction, from the activity is disallowed. The ratable portion of a passive activity deduction is the amount of the disallowed portion of the loss from the activity multiplied by the fraction obtained by dividing:

1. The amount of the deduction; by
2. The sum of all passive activity deductions, other than excluded deductions, from the activity.[109]

An excluded deduction is any passive activity deduction that is taken into account in computing the taxpayer's net income from an item of property in which an amount of the gross income from the item of property is treated as not being from a passive activity.[110]

[C] Carryover of Disallowed Deductions

If any deductions are disallowed for a taxable year under the passive activity loss rules, the disallowed deductions must be allocated among the taxpayer's activities for the succeeding taxable year in a manner that reasonably reflects the extent to which each activity continues the business and rental operations that

[109] Temp. Reg. § 1.469-1T(f)(2)(ii).

[110] Temp. Reg. § 1.469-1T(f)(2)(ii)(B).

constituted the loss activity. Also, the disallowed deductions allocated to an activity are treated as deductions from the activity for the succeeding year.[111]

> ***Example 23:*** The Taxpayer owns interests in a convenience store and an apartment building that are treated as interests in two separate passive activities. A $5,000 loss from the convenience store and a $3,000 loss from the apartment building are disallowed for 2019.
>
> The $5,000 loss from the convenience store is allocated among the passive activity deductions from that activity for 2019, and the $3,000 loss from the apartment building is treated similarly. In 2020, the business and rental operations that constituted the convenience store activity are continued in a single activity, and the business and rental operations that constituted the apartment building activity are similarly continued in a separate activity.
>
> The disallowed deductions from the convenience store for 2019 must be allocated to the Taxpayer's convenience store activity in 2020. Similarly, the disallowed deductions from the apartment building for 2019 must be allocated to the Taxpayer's apartment building activity in 2020. The disallowed deductions allocated to the convenience store in 2020 are treated as deductions from that activity for 2020, and the disallowed deductions allocated to the apartment building for 2020 are treated as deductions from that activity for 2020.

If a taxpayer continues part or all of the business and rental operations that constitute a loss activity through a C corporation or similar entity, the taxpayer's interest in the entity is treated for purposes of the carryover of disallowed deductions as an interest in a passive activity that continues the business and rental operations. An entity is similar to a C corporation if the owners of interests in the entity derive only portfolio income from the ownership interests.[112]

> ***Example 24:*** The Taxpayer owns stock in an S corporation for the taxable year 2019. After 2019, the S corporation is a C corporation. For 2019, the Taxpayer's pro rata share of the corporation's loss from a rental activity is $5,000, and the entire loss is disallowed under the passive activity loss rules.
>
> The Taxpayer's $5,000 loss from the rental activity is allocated among the deductions from that activity for 2019. In 2020, the business and rental operations that constituted the rental activity are continued through the C corporation, and the Taxpayer's interest in the C corporation is treated as a passive activity that continues the rental operations. The Taxpayer must allocate the disallowed deductions from the rental activity for 2019 to the C corporation activity in 2020 and treat them as deductions from the C corporation activity for 2020.
>
> The Taxpayer's treatment of the interest in the C corporation as an interest in a passive activity that continues the operations of the rental activity does not change the character of the dividend income from the C corporation.

---

[111] Reg. § 1.469-1(f)(4)(i).

[112] Temp. Reg. § 1.469-1T(f)(4)(ii)(A).

The Taxpayer's dividend income is portfolio income and is not included in passive activity gross income. The Taxpayer's loss from the C corporation activity for 2020 is $5,000.

[D] Disposition of a Passive Activity

If a taxpayer disposes of the entire interest in a passive activity or former passive activity in a taxable transaction, any passive activity loss on that activity that has been carried over from prior years, as well as any loss for the current year, becomes deductible as a nonpassive activity loss to the extent it exceeds passive income from other activities for the year. If the taxpayer realizes income or gain from the passive activity in the year of its disposition, the suspended losses from prior years must be used first to offset this gain. Any loss in excess of this gain is then used to offset passive income for the year from other activities. Only then may the taxpayer use the loss to offset nonpassive income or gain.[113] This rule does not apply, however, if the taxpayer and transferee of the passive activity are related. In this case, the suspended loss remains suspended until the passive activity is acquired by another person who is not related to the taxpayer.[114]

Transfer at Death

A similar rule applies to the transfer of a passive activity on the death of a taxpayer. In this case, however, a suspended loss may be deducted from the deceased taxpayer's other income for the year of death only to the extent the loss exceeds any increase in the basis of the interest in the passive activity that occurs as a result of the transfer (the step-up in basis).[115]

Installment Sale

If the taxpayer disposes of the entire interest in a passive activity through an installment sale, the suspended loss may not be deducted in full in the year of sale. Rather, the taxpayer deducts the loss as the income from the sale is reported, that is, the taxpayer deducts the loss in the same ratio as the income from the installment sale is reported.[116]

Income realized after 1986 as a result of an installment sale that occurred before 1987 is passive income if the activity from which the sale arose would have been a passive activity in the year of sale had the passive activity loss rules applied.[117]

.04 Passive Activity Credits

Tax credits generated by passive activities (passive activity credits) generally may not be used to offset income tax liability attributable to nonpassive activities. A taxpayer's passive activity credit for a taxable year is the amount by which the sum of all tax credits that are subject to the passive activity loss rules for the year exceeds the taxpayer's regular tax liability allocable to all passive activities for the year.[118] The tax credits that are subject to the passive activity loss rules are:

[113] Code Sec. 469(g)(1)(A).

[114] Code Sec. 469(g)(1)(B).

[115] Code Sec. 469(g)(2).

[116] Code Sec. 469(g)(3).

[117] Technical and Miscellaneous Revenue Act of 1988, Sec. 1005(a)(10).

[118] Code Sec. 469(d)(2).

1. Investment credit under Code Sec. 46, made up of the rehabilitation credit, the energy credit, the advanced coal project credit and the gasification project credit;
2. All other credits that make up the general business credit, see ¶ 804;
3. Alcohol fuels credit;
4. Research credit;
5. Refined coal production credit;
6. Indian coal production credit;
7. Disabled access credit;
8. Renewable community employment credit; and
9. Electric vehicle credit.[119]

A taxpayer's regular tax liability allocable to all passive activities, against which credits from passive activities may be used, is the excess of the taxpayer's regular tax liability over the amount of tax that the taxpayer would pay if taxable income were reduced by passive activity gross income in excess of passive activity deductions.[120]

The application of the rule limiting the use of credits is illustrated by the following example. In any calculation involving the determination of tax liability, the tax rates in effect for the 2016 tax year have been used.

Comprehensive Example 25: A single individual acquires an interest in a partnership that rehabilitates a building and places it in service in a trade or business activity in which the individual does not materially participate. For the year in which the building is placed in service, the individual has the following items of gross income, deductions, and credits:

Gross Income:		
Nonpassive income	$110,000	
Passive activity income	20,000	$130,000
Deductions:		
Nonpassive deductions	$23,950	
From passive activities	18,000	41,950
Taxable income		$88,050
Credits:		
Rehabilitation credit from passive activity		$8,000

The amount by which the individual's passive activity gross income exceeds the passive activity deductions (the individual's net passive income) is $2,000. The individual's regular tax liability allocable to passive activities is determined as follows:

[119] Code Sec. 469(d)(2).

[120] Temp. Reg. § 1.469-3T(d).

Taxable income	$88,050	
Regular tax liability		$17.784
Taxable income less net passive income	86,050	
Tax liability on income of $86,050		17,284
Regular tax liability allocable to passive activities		$500

The individual's passive activity credit is the amount by which credits from passive activities for the year ($8,000) exceed regular tax liability allocable to passive activities ($500). Therefore, the individual's passive activity credit that is suspended and carried over to future years is $7,500.

Suppose, however, that the individual had an additional $100,000 in deductions from a trade or business in which the individual materially participated. This would produce a taxable loss for the individual in the amount of $11,950, rather than taxable income of $88,050.

In this case, since regular tax liability cannot exceed the tax imposed, the individual's regular tax liability allocable to passive activities is zero. Although the net operating loss is reduced by net passive income and regular tax liability for other taxable years may increase as a result of the reduction, the increase does not change regular tax liability allocable to passive activities for the current year. Therefore, the individual's passive activity credit that is suspended is the full $8,000 credit attributable to passive activities.

[A] Closely Held Corporation

A closely held corporation that is subject to the passive activity loss rules may use losses from passive activities to offset operating income as well as passive income. Similarly, these corporations may use tax credits generated by a passive activity to offset tax liability attributable to operating income as well as passive income. Under Temp. Reg. § 1.469-1T(g)(5), a closely held corporation's passive activity credit for the taxable year (the amount of the credit that is suspended) is reduced by the corporation's net active income tax liability for the year.

A corporation's net active income tax liability is the amount by which:

1. The corporation's regular tax liability for the taxable year, determined by reducing the corporation's taxable income by an amount equal to the excess, if any, of the corporation's passive activity gross income over the corporation's passive activity deductions; exceeds

2. The sum of (a) the corporation's regular tax liability determined by reducing the corporation's taxable income by an amount equal to the excess, if any, of the sum of the corporation's net active income (as defined above in connection with the discussion of a corporation's passive activity loss) and passive activity gross income over the corporation's passive

activity deductions, plus (b) the corporation's credits, other than credits from passive activities, that are allowable for the taxable year.[121]

Special rules apply in the case of affiliated groups filing consolidated returns.[122]

[B] Carryover of Suspended Credit

If a taxpayer's passive activity credit is disallowed for the taxable year under the passive activity loss rules, a ratable portion of each credit from each passive activity is disallowed.[123] A taxpayer need not account separately for any credit unless the credit may, if separately taken into account, result in an income tax liability for any year other than that which would result were the credit not taken into account separately. Credits that must be accounted for separately include, but are not limited to:

1. Credits, other than the low-income housing and rehabilitation credits, from a rental real estate activity in which the taxpayer actively participates;
2. Credits, other than low-income housing and rehabilitation credits, from a rental real estate activity in which the taxpayer does not actively participate; and
3. Low-income housing and rehabilitation credits from a rental real estate activity.[124]

If any credits from an activity are disallowed under the passive activity loss rules, the disallowed credits are allocated among the taxpayer's activities for the succeeding year in a manner that reasonably reflects the extent to which each activity continues the business and rental operations that constituted the loss activity, and the disallowed credits allocated to an activity are treated as credits from the activity for the succeeding taxable year.[125] This is the same rule that applies to disallowed deductions from passive activities, as discussed above.

While credits that are disallowed under the passive loss rules are suspended and carried over to succeeding years, just as disallowed losses are suspended and carried over to succeeding years, there is no provision that allows a taxpayer to take suspended credits when the taxpayer sells or otherwise disposes of the entire interest in a passive activity that gave rise to the suspended credit. Once a suspended credit becomes allowable under the passive loss rules, because of the tax liability attributable to passive income or under the limited exception for real estate activities in which the taxpayer actively participates, the credits are then aggregated with credits from nonpassive activities in order to apply the various other limitations on tax credits, such as the tax-liability limitation and the limitation on the use of credits to reduce alternative minimum tax.

¶ 1105 PUBLICLY TRADED PARTNERSHIPS

In response to the growing use of publicly traded partnerships to combine the organizational and operational advantages of a corporation with the tax advantages

[121] Temp. Reg. § 1.469-1T(g)(5)(ii).
[122] Temp. Reg. § 1.469-1T(h).
[123] Temp. Reg. § 1.469-1T(f)(3)(i).
[124] Temp. Reg. § 1.469-1T(f)(3)(iii).
[125] Reg. § 1.469-1(f)(4)(i).

of a partnership, Congress enacted Code Sec. 7704, which treats certain publicly traded partnerships as corporations for federal income tax purposes. A publicly traded partnership is defined by Code Sec. 469(k) as a partnership in which interests are traded on an established securities market or are readily tradable on a secondary market, or the substantial equivalent of a secondary market.

While many publicly traded partnerships are now treated as corporations under this rule, those publicly traded partnerships that are not, such as real estate partnerships, are subject to a special passive activity loss rule. This rule, generally, isolates losses from publicly traded partnerships and bars their use to offset other passive income. This special rule for publicly traded partnerships under the passive loss rules also applies to a Regulated Investment Company (RIC) that holds an interest in a publicly traded partnership as to items attributable to that interest in the partnership.[126] Publicly traded partnerships treated as corporations and public limited partnerships in general are considered further in Chapter 21. The following discussion focuses on the special passive activity loss rule that applies to publicly traded partnerships that are not treated as corporations.

.01 Partnerships Subject to the Rule

The treatment of publicly traded partnerships as corporations is subject to some very important exceptions, primarily for partnerships engaged in real estate and natural resource (such as oil and gas) operations.[127] A publicly traded partnership is not treated as a corporation, and the special passive activity loss rule for publicly traded partnerships applies, if 90 percent or more of the partnership's gross income is qualifying income. Qualifying income includes the following:

1. Interest, but this category does not include amounts contingent on profits or interest earned in the course of a financial or insurance business;
2. Dividends;
3. Rents from real property, including real property rents based on a fixed percentage of receipts or a fixed percentage of gross sales, but not amounts contingent on profits;
4. Gain from the disposition of real property (gross income is not reduced by the inventory costs of property taken into account in determining gain from the sales in the case of real property sold to customers in the ordinary course of business);
5. Income and gains from natural resource activities (natural resources include fertilizer, geothermal energy, and timber, as well as oil and gas and products of oil and gas);
6. Any gain from the disposition of a capital asset or asset held for the production of income that falls within the first five categories; and
7. Income and gains from commodities (other than those held for sale to customers in the ordinary course of business), futures, options, or forward contracts on commodities (including foreign currency transactions of a

[126] Code Sec. 469(k)(4).

[127] Code Sec. 7704(c).

commodity pool), but only if the principal activity of the partnership is the buying and selling of the commodities, futures, options, or forward contracts (this category of qualifying income excludes typical commodity pools from treatment as corporations).[128]

.02 Partnerships Subject to Grandfather Rule

In addition to the exception to treating publicly traded partnerships as corporations based on qualifying income, there is another exception for partnerships that were in existence on December 17, 1987. These publicly traded partnerships are not treated as corporations until after December 31, 1997. After 1997, a publicly traded partnership that was in existence on December 17, 1987, and to which the grandfather rule applied through 1997, may elect to continue to be subject to the grandfather rule at a tax cost of 3.5 percent of its gross income.[129] Publicly traded partnerships not treated as corporations under the grandfather rule are subject to the special passive activity loss rule.

.03 Application of the Special Passive Activity Loss Rule

Generally, as discussed above, an interest in a limited partnership as a limited partner is considered a passive activity. Publicly traded partnerships that are not treated as corporations because they have qualifying income or are subject to the ten-year grandfather rule for partnerships in existence on December 17, 1987, however, are subject to a special passive activity loss rule.[130] The thrust of the rule is to block the use of income or loss generated by a publicly traded partnership to offset passive income or loss from other passive activities, as well as income and loss from other sources.

Each partner in a publicly traded partnership treats a loss, if any, from the partnership as separate from income and loss from any other publicly traded partnership and also as separate from income or loss from other passive activities. Net income from a publicly traded partnership is treated as portfolio income under the passive activity loss rules. A net loss attributable to an interest in a publicly traded partnership may not be deducted against the partner's other income but must be suspended and carried forward. These net losses can be applied against net income from the partnership in future years. When a partner disposes of the entire interest in a publicly traded partnership, any remaining suspended losses may be deducted against other income at that time.[131]

There is an exception that allows a partner to use his or her share of low-income housing credits and rehabilitation credits from a publicly traded partnership against tax liability attributable to nonpartnership income to the extent of the unused $25,000 deduction-equivalent allowance. The credits are allowable under the partner's $25,000 allowance to the extent that the partner has not fully utilized the allowance for losses and credits otherwise allowed under the regular passive activity loss rules.[132]

---

[128] Code Sec. 7704(c).
[129] Code Sec. 7704(g).
[130] Code Sec. 469(k).
[131] Code Sec. 469(k)(3).
[132] Code Sec. 469(k)(1).

The application of the passive activity loss rule to publicly traded partnerships that are not treated as corporations is illustrated by the following example.

Comprehensive Example 26: The Taxpayer owns limited partnership interests in two limited partnerships, A and B, but owns no interest in any other passive activity. Limited partnership A is a publicly traded limited partnership but is not subject to being treated as a corporation because 90 percent of its gross income is from real estate activities. Limited partnership B is not a publicly traded partnership.

For the current tax year, partnership A produced a net loss passed through to the Taxpayer in the amount of $1,000. Partnership B produced net income passed through to the Taxpayer in the amount of $1,500. The income from B was not portfolio income to the partnership. Neither partnership produced income or loss for the Taxpayer in any prior tax year. The Taxpayer cannot use the $1,000 loss from partnership A to offset the $1,500 of income from partnership B. The Taxpayer must report the $1,500 of passive activity income from partnership B, which is not a publicly traded partnership. The Taxpayer's loss from publicly traded partnership A is suspended, and the Taxpayer may carry this amount forward to offset income that may eventually be realized from partnership A. If the loss is still unused when the Taxpayer disposes of the entire interest in partnership A, the Taxpayer may take a deduction for the unused loss at that time.

Suppose, however, the situation were reversed. Assume that partnership A, the publicly traded partnership, produces net income for the Taxpayer in the amount of $1,500 and that partnership B, the partnership that is not publicly traded, produces a net loss for the Taxpayer in the amount of $1,000. In this situation, the Taxpayer cannot use the loss from partnership B to offset the $1,500 of income from partnership A. The $1,500 of income realized by the Taxpayer from partnership A is treated as portfolio income under the passive activity loss rules. The $1,000 loss from partnership B, however, is a passive loss under the passive activity loss rules. If the Taxpayer realized income from other passive activities, this loss could be used to offset that passive income. In the absence of income from passive sources, the $1,000 loss is suspended and carried over to future years under the regular passive activity loss rules, and the Taxpayer may deduct this loss against income realized in the future from any passive activity, not just partnership B.

If neither limited partnership A nor limited partnership B were a publicly traded partnership, the Taxpayer could deduct the $1,000 loss realized from one partnership against the $1,500 in income realized from the other partnership under the usual passive activity loss rules. The net result for the Taxpayer in this case would be taxable income from the partnerships in the amount of $500.

Chapter 12
Troubled Financings

¶ 1200 Overview of Chapter
¶ 1201 Settlement of Debt at Discount
¶ 1202 Foreclosure
¶ 1203 Conveyance and Abandonment of Mortgage
¶ 1204 Repossession of Seller-Financed Property

¶ 1200 OVERVIEW OF CHAPTER

While owners of real estate may be reluctant to admit it, there are times when real estate cannot support the debt incurred to finance its purchase or support the debts incurred for other purposes and secured by the real estate. Troubled real estate financings may develop in the course of holding real estate for investment, for the production of rental income, or for use in a trade or business. As the mortgagor tries to meet payments, the mortgagor may seek ways to get out from under the burden that the real estate now represents. The mortgagee who sees late payments and, finally, a default in payments may take steps to realize as much as possible on the value represented by the real estate.

The first course of action for the mortgagee, assuming the mortgagor wants to continue ownership of the property, may be an attempt at some compromise or settlement of the debt at a discount. This is most likely if a decline in value, through no fault of the mortgagor, means that the real estate is no longer worth as much as the debt secured by the real estate and cannot generate the cash flow necessary to meet the payment obligations. Settlement of a mortgage debt at a discount has tax consequences for both the mortgagor and the mortgagee.

When the mortgagor wants out, or the mortgagee is unwilling to compromise or wait for payments, foreclosure looms. From the mortgagor's point of view, a foreclosure is essentially a sale on which he or she may realize gain or loss, even though the sale may not be voluntary. For the mortgagee, a foreclosure may have more complicated consequences, depending on whether the foreclosure results in a sale to a third party or whether the mortgagee is forced to bid because of the lack of acceptable bids from third parties.

To avoid foreclosure, a mortgagor may convey the property to a creditor. Again, there are tax consequences to both debtor and creditor. In the rare case when real estate has declined in value so much that neither the mortgagor nor the mortgagee wants the property, the mortgagor may simply walk away from the property and abandon it. When this occurs, there is a question of whether the abandonment generates a deductible loss for tax purposes.

Finally, special considerations arise when the troubled financing is seller financing in the form of a purchase-money mortgage. Is a reduction in the debt merely a reduction in the selling price, or does it produce a deductible loss? And what if the seller reacquires the property through foreclosure or conveyance from the purchaser? Here, too, there are special tax considerations that come into play.

¶ 1201 SETTLEMENT OF DEBT AT DISCOUNT

In the normal course of events, when a debtor satisfies the debt at its face amount, there are no tax consequences for either the debtor or the creditor. There is no economic benefit to either party in addition to the original bargain that gave rise to the debt. The same cannot be said, however, when a mortgage debt is satisfied at less than face value. In this case, the borrower may be receiving an economic benefit, and the lender may be suffering an economic detriment. Generally, the tax law recognizes this and taxes the benefit realized by the borrower and allows the lender a deduction for the economic loss.

.01 Tax Treatment of Debtor

While the tax law does tax the debtor on the benefit received from the discharge of a debt at a discount, the timing of that tax is another matter. The actual treatment of the debtor who satisfies the debt at a discount hinges on the status of the debtor at the time. The solvent debtor, who presumably would have no problem meeting a current tax payment for the benefit of the discharged debt, generally is subject to an immediate tax on income from the discharge of indebtedness.[1] Insolvent and bankrupt debtors, however, may escape an immediate tax under the rules of Code Sec. 108 (see ¶ 1201.01[B]). There also are special rules that allow income from the discharge of "qualified real property business indebtedness" (see ¶ 1201.01[C]) and "qualified principal residence indebtedness" (see ¶ 1201.01[D]) to escape current tax. Special rules in Code Sec. 108(g) apply to the discharge of qualified farm indebtedness.

[A] Solvent Debtor

At one time, solvent debtors were able to defer the tax on income from the discharge of indebtedness. This rule was repealed in the Tax Reform Act of 1986 on the theory that a solvent debtor had the capacity to pay the tax currently and there was no reason to permit a deferral. Of course, the reduction of a mortgage debt does not produce any immediate cash flow with which to fund the tax payment and, if the value of the property has declined, may never produce a cash amount corresponding to the "benefit" of the debt reduction. Nevertheless, in the case of a solvent debtor, other than in the case of qualified real property business indebtedness and qualified farm indebtedness, gross income includes income from the discharge of indebtedness.[2]

The term "income from discharge of indebtedness" is broad and seems to encompass any debt reduction. The IRS has ruled that an individual taxpayer realizes income from the discharge of indebtedness under Code Sec. 61(a)(12) on

[1] Code Sec. 61(a)(12).

[2] Code Secs. 61(a)(12) and 108(a)(1).

the discounted prepayment to a lender of all or a portion of mortgage indebtedness. Further, according to the IRS, the amount of the discount is includible whether the mortgage note is recourse or nonrecourse,[3] and whether or not the fair market value is more or less than the amount of debt.[4] Also, if the nonrecourse debt does exceed the fair market value of the property, the excess is taken into account in determining whether and to what extent the taxpayer is insolvent, but only to the extent that the excess nonrecourse debt is discharged.[5]

Debt Forgiveness as Gift

One exception to this rule would be when the forgiveness or reduction of the debt is really a gift from the creditor to the debtor. Whether the reduction or cancellation of the debt is voluntary or involuntary does not matter. Simply because a debt is reduced or cancelled on a voluntary basis does not establish a gift. Rather, a gift depends on donative intent. As the Supreme Court has put it, "the transfer of something for the best price available" does not amount to a gift.[6] In *W. DiLaura,*[7] the discharge of a mortgage for an amount less than the principal balance due was taxable as income to the mortgagor because the mortgagee did not act with disinterested generosity but was motivated by the sound economic reason of ridding itself of a low-interest mortgage.[8]

For the treatment of a reduction in a purchase-money mortgage as a reduction in the selling price in the case of seller financing, see ¶ 1201.01[E].

Acquisition of Debt by Related Parties

Forgiveness of the debt by the creditor is not the only way in which a debtor can be relieved of the obligation to repay the debt. The Internal Revenue Code recognizes this in Code Sec. 108(e), which provides some general rules for the discharge of indebtedness, including discharges outside of bankruptcy or insolvency. Under Code Sec. 108(e)(4), an outstanding debt acquired from an unrelated creditor by a person related to the debtor is treated as if the debtor had acquired the debt. To the extent provided in Reg. § 1.108-2(f), this gives rise to income from the discharge of indebtedness. Parties related to the debtor that trigger this rule are:

1. Members of a controlled group of corporations of which the debtor is also a member;
2. Trade or business under common control;
3. Partner in a partnership controlled by the debtor of a controlled partnership, as defined in Code Sec. 707(b)(1); and
4. Family members, that is, an individual's spouse, children, grandchildren, parents, and a spouse of the individual's children or grandchildren.

---

[3] Rev. Rul. 82-202, 1982-2 CB 35.

[4] Rev. Rul. 91-31, 1991-1 CB 19.

[5] Rev. Rul. 92-53, 1992-2 CB 48.

[6] American Dental Co., S.Ct., 43-1 USTC ¶ 9318, 318 U.S. 322, 63 S.Ct. 577.

[7] 53 TCM 1077, CCH Dec. 43,973(M), T.C. Memo. 1987-291.

[8] *See also* M.H. Juister, Jr., 53 TCM 1079, CCH Dec. 43,974(M), T.C. Memo. 1987-292; J.H. Sutphin, Cls. Ct., 88-1 USTC ¶ 9269, 14 Cls. Ct. 545.

[B] Insolvent or Bankrupt Debtor

Prior to the Bankruptcy Tax Act of 1980, there were exceptions to the general rule that gross income includes income from the discharge of indebtedness. Under a judicially developed insolvency exception, no income arose from discharge of indebtedness if the debtor were insolvent both before and after the transaction.[9] If the transaction left the debtor with assets whose value exceeded the remaining liabilities, however, income was realized, but only to the extent of the excess.[10] The old Bankruptcy Act (repealed in 1979 by P.L. 95-598) provided that no income was recognized on cancellation of indebtedness in an insolvency reorganization under Chapter X. The debtor corporation would reduce the basis of its assets by the amount of the indebtedness discharged. Similar rules applied to arrangements under Chapter XI, real property arrangements under Chapter XII, and wage earner plans under Chapter XIII of the old Bankruptcy Act.

When the old Bankruptcy Act was repealed, the tax provisions contained in that Act also were repealed. This led to the passage of the Bankruptcy Tax Act of 1980, which provided tax rules in Code Sec. 108 that apply to debt discharge in the case of bankrupt or insolvent debtors. The 1980 Act also made related changes to existing law applicable to solvent debtors outside of bankruptcy and codified them in Code Sec. 108. Now, there is no insolvency exception, other than that in Code Sec. 108, from the general rule that gross income includes income from the discharge of indebtedness.[11]

Insolvent Debtor

An insolvent debtor who has a debt discharged or cancelled outside of bankruptcy does not recognize income from the discharge of indebtedness.[12] The exclusion, however, is limited to the amount of the debtor's insolvency.[13] The amount of the debtor's insolvency is measured by the excess of the debtor's liabilities over the assets immediately before the discharge.[14] The excluded amount of an insolvent debtor's income from the discharge of indebtedness is used to reduce tax attributes, as discussed below. The amount of the debt that is not excluded from income because it exceeds the debtor's insolvency is subject to the rules discussed at ¶ 1201.01[A] that apply to the discharge of a solvent debtor.

Bankrupt Debtor

If the discharge of debt occurs in a bankruptcy proceeding, the debtor excludes the amount of the discharged debt from income[15] and reduces tax attributes by the amount of the debt discharged.[16] To benefit from this exclusion, the debtor must be under the jurisdiction of the court in a bankruptcy case,[17] and the discharge of indebtedness must be granted by the court or carried out under a plan approved by the court.[18]

---

[9] Dallas Transfer & Terminal Warehouse Co., CA-5, 4 USTC ¶ 1270, 70 F.2d 95; Reg. § 1.61-12(b)(1).

[10] Lakeland Grocery Co., 36 BTA 289, CCH Dec. 9707.

[11] Code Sec. 108(e)(1).

[12] Code Sec. 108(a)(1)(B).

[13] Code Sec. 108(a)(3).

[14] Code Sec. 108(d)(3).

[15] Code Sec. 108(a)(1)(A).

[16] Code Sec. 108(b)(1).

[17] Title 11 of the United States Code.

[18] Code Sec. 108(d)(2).

Reduction of Tax Attributes

Income from the discharge of indebtedness that is excluded from the income of an insolvent or bankrupt debtor under Code Sec. 108(a) is not forgiven, but merely deferred through the mechanism of reductions in the taxpayer's "tax attributes."[19] The excluded amount reduces the following tax attributes in the order shown:

1. Any net operating loss for the taxable year of the discharge, and any net operating loss carryover to that year;
2. Carryovers of the general business credit;
3. The minimum tax credit as of the beginning of the tax year following the year of discharge;
4. Any net capital loss for the taxable year of the discharge, and any capital loss carryover to that year;
5. The basis of depreciable and nondepreciable property;
6. Any passive activity loss or credit carryover from the year of the discharge; and
7. Foreign tax credit carryovers.[20]

Tax attributes, other than credit carryovers, are reduced one dollar for each dollar of discharged debt that is excluded from income.[21] The reduction in credit carryovers is 33 ⅓ cents for each dollar of excluded discharged debt.[22] The required reductions are made in the order of tax years in which the items would be used, without regard to the exclusion from income of the debt discharged or to the limitations on the use of credits. The excluded amount of discharged debt first reduces the current year's loss and then reduces the loss carryovers in the order in which they arose, and the credit carryovers are reduced in the order in which they would be used against taxable income.[23]

Election to Reduce Basis

An insolvent or bankrupt debtor may take advantage of a special election to reduce the basis of the depreciable property first, rather than apply the excluded discharged debt to reduce tax attributes in the order listed above. The debtor applies the reduction in basis to the property held at the beginning of the taxable year following the year in which the discharge occurs.[24] In an election within an election, this basis reduction may include real property that is dealer property, that is, real property held for sale in the ordinary course of business.[25] If the amount of discharged debt that is excluded from income exceeds the aggregate adjusted basis of depreciable or dealer real property, the excess is then applied to reduce tax attributes in the order specified above.

[19] Code Sec. 108(b)(1).

[20] *See* Code Sec. 108(b)(2).

[21] Code Sec. 108(b)(3)(A).

[22] Code Sec. 108(b)(3)(B).

[23] Code Sec. 108(b)(4).

[24] Code Sec. 1017(a).

[25] Code Sec. 1017(b)(3)(E).

Reg. § 1.1017-1 provides ordering rules for reducing the basis of property in the context of both the reduction of tax attributes and the election to first reduce basis before reduction of other tax attributes.

The election to reduce the basis of depreciable and dealer property gives a debtor flexibility to account for a debt discharge amount in a way that is most favorable to the debtor's tax situation. For example, a bankrupt or insolvent debtor who wishes to retain net operating losses and other carryovers is able to elect to reduce the basis of depreciable assets and real property held for sale in the ordinary course of business. On the other hand, a debtor with an expiring net operating loss that would otherwise be "wasted" is able to apply the excluded amount of the discharged debt first against the net operating loss.

To insure that income from the discharge of indebtedness that is excluded under Code Sec. 108 eventually does result in ordinary income and cannot be converted into capital gain, Code Sec. 1017(d) provides that any gain on a subsequent disposition of the reduced-basis property is subject to recapture as ordinary income.

[C] Qualified Real Property Business Debt

A taxpayer other than a C corporation can elect to exclude from income the discharge of qualified real property business debt.[26] A taxpayer who makes this election must reduce the basis of depreciable real property by the excluded amount.[27]

Qualified real property business debt is debt, other than qualified farm debt, that was:

1. Incurred or assumed in connection with real property used in a trade or business;
2. Secured by the real property; and
3. Incurred or assumed before January 1, 1993, or incurred or assumed to acquire, construct, or substantially improve the real property.

The taxpayer must elect to apply the rules to the property. Qualified real property business debt includes refinancing of debt described in 3 above, but only to the extent it does not exceed the debt being refinanced.[28]

A taxpayer cannot exclude more than either:

1. The excess of outstanding principal of the debt before the discharge over the fair market value before the discharge of the business real property reduced by the outstanding amount of any other qualified real property business debt secured by the property before the discharge, or
2. The total adjusted bases of depreciable real property held immediately before the discharge. (The bases are determined after any basis reduction due to a discharge in bankruptcy, insolvency, or of qualified farm debt.)[29]

[26] Code Sec. 108(a)(1)(D).

[27] Code Sec. 108(c)(1).

[28] Code Sec. 108(c)(3).

[29] Code Sec. 108(c)(2) and Reg. § 1.108-6.

In Rev. Proc. 2014-20,[30] the IRS has provided a safe harbor that treats indebtedness secured by 100 percent of the ownership interest in a disregarded entity (for example, a single member LLC) holding real property as indebtedness that is secured by real property. The borrower (taxpayer or disregarded entity of the taxpayer) meets the requirements of the safe harbor if:

1. Borrower directly or indirectly owns 100% of the ownership interest in a separate disregarded entity that owns real property.
2. Borrower pledges to the lender a first priority security interest in its ownership interest in the entity.
3. At least 90 percent of the fair market value of the total assets (immediately before the discharge) directly owned by the disregarded entity must be real property used in a trade or business and any other assets held by the entity must be incidental to the entity's acquisition, ownership, and operation of the real property.
4. On default and foreclosure, the lender will replace the borrower as the sole member of the disregarded entity.

[D] Qualified Principal Residence Debt

The exclusion for qualified principal residence indebtedness applies to discharges after 2007 and before 2018 (unless again extended by Congress). Any exclusion reduces the basis of the residence.[31]

Qualified principal residence indebtedness is debt incurred in acquiring, constructing, or substantially improving the taxpayer's principal residence (or adjoining land) that is secured by the residence. The aggregate amount of debt that may be treated as principal residence indebtedness for any period may not exceed $2 million ($1 million for a married individual filing a separate return).[32] The exclusion does not apply if the debt discharge is for services performed for the lender or any other factor not directly related to a decline in value of the residence or the financial condition of the homeowner.[33]

If all or part of a loan is discharged and only a portion of the loan is qualified principal residence indebtedness, the exclusion applies only to the amount discharged that exceeds the amount of the loan that is not qualified principal residence indebtedness.[34] The insolvency exclusion (see ¶ 1201.01[B]) does not apply if the qualified principal residence exclusion applies, unless the taxpayer elects otherwise.[35]

Home Affordable Modification Program

To help financially distressed homeowners lower their monthly mortgage payments, Treasury and HUD established the Home Affordable Modification Program (HAMP). Under the Principal Reduction Alternative (PRA) within HAMP, the principal of a borrower's mortgage may be reduced by a predetermined amount

[30] 2014-9 IRB 614.

[31] Code Sec. 108(h)(1).

[32] Code Sec. 108(h)(2).

[33] Code Sec. 108(h)(3).

[34] Code Sec. 108(h)(4).

[35] Code Sec. 108(a)(2)(C).

called the PRA Forbearance Amount if the borrower satisfies certain conditions during a trial period. The principal reduction occurs over three years.

More specifically, if the loan is in good standing on the first, second, and third annual anniversaries of the effective date of the trial period, the loan servicer reduces the unpaid principal balance of the loan by one-third of the initial PRA Forbearance Amount on each anniversary date. This means that if the borrower continues to make timely payments on the loan for three years, the entire PRA Forbearance Amount is forgiven. To encourage a mortgage loan holder to participate in HAMP-PRA, the HAMP program administrator makes an incentive payment to the loan holder (called a PRA investor incentive payment) for each of the three years in which the loan principal balance is reduced.

PRA investor incentive payments made by the HAMP program administrator to mortgage loan holders are treated as payments on the mortgage loans by the United States government on behalf of the borrowers. These payments are generally not taxable to the borrowers under the general welfare doctrine.[36]

If the principal amount of a mortgage loan is reduced by an amount that exceeds the total amount of the PRA investor incentive payments made to the mortgage loan holder, the borrower may be required to include the excess amount in gross income as income from the discharge of indebtedness. However, a borrower may be eligible to exclude the discharge of indebtedness income from gross income if the discharge applies to indebtedness that is qualified principal residence indebtedness. A discharge under HAMP-PRA may also qualify for exclusion if the borrower is insolvent (see ¶ 1201.01[B]).

Borrowers who receive aid under the HAMP-PRA program may report any discharge of indebtedness income, whether or not excluded from income, either in the year of the permanent modification of the mortgage loan or ratably over the three years in which the mortgage loan principal is reduced on the servicer's books. Borrowers who exclude the discharge of indebtedness income must report both the amount of the income and any resulting reduction in basis or tax attributes on Form 982.

Mortgage loan holders must file a Form 1099-C for a borrower who realizes discharge of indebtedness income of $600 or more for the year in which the permanent modification of the mortgage loan occurs. This rule applies regardless of whether the borrower chooses to report the income in the year of the permanent modification or one-third each year as the mortgage loan principal is reduced and regardless of whether the borrower excludes some or all of the amount from gross income.

[E] Purchase-Money Mortgage Reduction

When the seller of real estate provides financing to the purchaser in the form of a purchase-money mortgage, two relationships are created. There is, of course, the buyer-seller relationship. Buyers and sellers may negotiate over the purchase price and increase or decrease that price based on a number of factors, including

[36] Rev. Proc. 2013-16, 2013-7 IRB 488.

their relative bargaining powers. There is also a debtor-creditor relationship created. This dual relationship can create a question when, after the sale is complete and the financing is arranged, the parties agree to reduce the amount of the debt. Is the reduction one that flows from the debtor-creditor relationship so that the reduction produces discharge of indebtedness income for the buyer-debtor? Or does the reduction flow from the buyer-seller relationship, so that the reduction is nothing more than a reduction in the purchase price paid by the buyer-debtor?

Congress enacted Code Sec. 108(e)(5) to eliminate disagreements between the IRS and debtors as to whether, in a particular case to which the provision applies, the debt reduction should be treated as income from the discharge of indebtedness or a true price adjustment. If the seller of specific property reduces the debt of the purchaser which arose out of the purchase, and the reduction to the purchaser does not occur in a bankruptcy case or when the purchaser is insolvent, then the reduction to the purchaser of the purchase-money mortgage is treated as a purchase price adjustment on the property. This rule applies only if the amount of the reduction otherwise would be treated as income from the discharge of indebtedness.[37]

The treatment of a reduction in the amount of a purchase-money mortgage as a price adjustment only applies when it occurs between the original buyer and original seller of the property. If the debt is transferred by a seller to a third party, even a party related to the seller, or if the property is transferred by the buyer to a third party, even a party related to the buyer, Code Sec. 108(e)(5) does not apply to determine whether a reduction in the amount of a purchase-money mortgage should be treated as income from the discharge of indebtedness or a true price adjustment. Also, Code Sec. 108(e)(5) does not apply if the debt is reduced because of factors that do not involve direct agreements between the buyer and seller, such as the running of the statute of limitations on the enforcement of the obligation.

.02 Tax Treatment of Creditor

In the typical case, the mortgagee lends the mortgagor the face amount of the debt. The amount of the loan becomes the mortgagee's basis for the loan. As the mortgagor pays off the loan, the mortgagee is merely recovering the basis and there are no tax consequences. However, if the mortgagee receives less than the face amount of the debt or the basis, then the mortgagee obviously realizes a loss. This loss may be deductible simply as a loss under Code Sec. 165, or as a bad debt under Code Sec. 166.

If the mortgage is a purchase-money mortgage provided by the seller of property to the buyer, the rule that treats a reduction in the amount of the mortgage as a reduction in the purchase price (discussed at ¶ 1201.01[E] in connection with the tax treatment of the debtor) applies equally to the creditor. Therefore, if the conditions of Code Sec. 108(e)(5) are met, the creditor must treat a reduction of a purchase-money mortgage as a reduction of the selling price rather than as a loss or bad debt.

[37] Code Sec. 108(e)(5)(C).

[A] Loss on Discount

Generally, a loss that is not compensated for by insurance or otherwise is deductible in full for the year in which it is sustained.[38] In the case of individuals, losses are deductible under Code Sec. 165 only if they are incurred in a trade or business or in a transaction entered into for profit.[39] Since a loss on a mortgage loan will be from a transaction entered into for profit, if not actually a trade or business, most taxpayers would benefit from being able to deduct the reduction in a mortgage loan as a loss under Code Sec. 165, rather than a bad debt under Code Sec. 166. Only "business bad debts" are deductible in full. Other bad debts are treated as capital losses (see ¶ 1201.02[B]).

The distinction between a loss under Code Sec. 165 and a bad debt deduction under Code Sec. 166 for a mortgagee evidently turns on the reason for the reduction in the amount of debt and the financial status of the debtor. If a mortgagee agrees to settle a debt at a discount because the mortgagor is unable to pay, or refuses to pay because the property has declined in value, the situation obviously involves a bad debt. But what if the mortgagor is able and willing to pay, but only according to the terms of the mortgage loan? How can there be a "bad debt" in this situation?

The obvious answer to these questions is that there really is no bad debt. The mortgagee may want to eliminate a loan that carries a low interest rate and be willing to accept less than the basis and take the loss in order to obtain cash that can be put to better use. The mortgagee also simply may need the cash and cannot wait for the mortgagor to make the agreed payments. When the mortgagee offers and accepts less than the remaining balance on the mortgage in these situations, the loss should be deductible under Code Sec. 165. The deduction would be the difference between the amount received and the remaining basis for the mortgage.

While there is limited authority for this viewpoint, it is not without some support. In Letter Ruling 8547001, June 26, 1985, the IRS permitted a cash method domestic federal savings and loan association to deduct a loan discount that was used to encourage an early payoff of a low-interest mortgage as an ordinary loss in the year that the mortgage was repaid.[40] Loss due to compromise of debt is not deductible as a bad debt if the debtor is solvent.[41]

A mortgagee must not assume that discounting a mortgage and assigning the mortgage to a third party will produce the same tax result as discounting the mortgage on behalf of the mortgagor. While the economic results are essentially the same, that is, the mortgagee receives less than the remaining basis in the mortgage note, the assignment of the mortgage to a third party is a sale or exchange of the mortgage rather than the compromise of a debt. If the mortgage debt is a capital asset in the hands of the mortgagee, the assignment means that the loss is subject to the limits on the deduction of capital losses. For instance, in *Yates*

[38] Code Sec. 165(a).

[39] Code Sec. 165(c).

[40] *See also* I.T. 4018, 1950-2 CB 20; *but see also* Rev. Rul. 69-43, 1969-1 CB 310.

[41] G.C. Peterson Co., 1 BTA 690, CCH Dec. 259, *acq.* 1925-1 CB 3; Raffold Process Corp., 3 TCM 1050, CCH Dec. 14,170(M), *aff'd*, CA-1, 153 F.2d 168, 52-1 USTC ¶ 9359.

Holding Corp.,[42] the taxpayer's assignment of a mortgage to a partnership formed by certain members of the mortgagor was held to be the sale of a capital asset and not a compromise of debt because the transaction took place between the taxpayer and the partnership, rather than between the taxpayer and the mortgagor. In this case, the taxpayer was allowed only a capital loss on the transaction.

[B] Bad Debt Deduction

A mortgagee who is unable to collect on a mortgage note is entitled to a bad debt deduction under Code Sec. 166. The deduction is taken in the year the debt becomes worthless.[43] If the mortgagee can show that the debt is recoverable only in part, a deduction may be allowed for the part that cannot be collected.[44] The deduction for a corporate mortgagee is always an ordinary deduction that is deductible in full against ordinary income. The deduction for a noncorporate taxpayer, however, hinges on whether the debt is considered a business bad debt or a nonbusiness bad debt. Business bad debts are deductible in full, but nonbusiness bad debts are treated as capital losses subject to the limits on the deduction of capital losses.[45]

The sale of mortgaged property in a foreclosure for less than the amount of the mortgage debt may establish the amount of the worthless debt (see discussion at ¶ 1202 in connection with foreclosure). Otherwise, in determining whether a debt is worthless in whole or only in part, the IRS considers "all pertinent evidence, including the value of the collateral, if any, securing the debt and the financial condition of the debtor."[46]

Going to the expense and trouble of reducing a debt to judgment and showing that it is uncollectible is not always necessary. Reg. § 1.166-2(b) provides that if the surrounding circumstances indicate that a debt is worthless and uncollectible and that legal action to enforce payment would in all probability not result in the satisfaction of execution on a judgment, this is sufficient to establish the bad debt deduction. However, a taxpayer who makes what he or she considers a bona fide loan cannot refrain from pressing for collection of the full amount from a solvent debtor simply because the taxpayer is faced with the necessity of litigation and then deduct the difference between what the debtor is willing to pay and the face amount of the loan as a "loss."[47]

Bankruptcy, generally, is proof of worthlessness of at least a part of an unsecured and unpreferred debt.[48] In bankruptcy cases, a debt may become worthless before settlement in some instances, while in others, it may become worthless only when a settlement in bankruptcy is reached. This may make it difficult to decide when a bad debt deduction should be taken. In the usual situation, a mortgagor does not fall into financial straits overnight, but gradually slips into financial difficulty. This makes establishing the worthlessness of a debt at a particular time extremely difficult.

[42] 39 TCM 303, CCH Dec. 36,373(M), T.C. Memo. 1979-416.

[43] Code Sec. 166(a)(1).

[44] Code Sec. 166(a)(2).

[45] Code Sec. 166(d).

[46] Reg. § 1.166-2(a).

[47] N. D'Alonzo, 10 TCM 817, CCH Dec. 18,509(M).

[48] Reg. § 1.166-2(c).

A mere refusal of a debtor to pay its debt does not warrant the debt's deduction as a bad debt,[49] nor does the refusal to pay combined with the creditor's belief that collection might be barred by the statute of limitations;[50] but the creditor is not required to be an "incorrigible optimist."[51] Generally, there must be some identifiable events that form a basis for abandoning hope of recovery.[52] An attorney's unsuccessful attempts to collect on accounts turned over to the attorney for collection was held to be sufficient proof of the worthlessness of the debts.[53]

[C] Nonbusiness Bad Debts

Unlike "business bad debts," nonbusiness bad debts are not deductible in full, but are subject to the limitations on the deduction of capital losses. Moreover, no deduction is allowed for the partial worthlessness of a nonbusiness bad debt.[54] This places a premium on classifying a bad debt as a business bad debt. A business bad debt is a debt (1) that is created or acquired in connection with a taxpayer's trade or business, or (2) whose worthlessness results in a loss which is incurred in the taxpayer's trade or business. Any other debt is a nonbusiness debt.[55]

The use to which the borrowed funds are put by the debtor is of no consequence in determining whether a debt is a business or nonbusiness debt. The character of the debt is determined by the relation which the loss resulting from the debt's becoming worthless bears to the trade or business of the taxpayer. If that relation is a proximate one in the conduct of the trade or business in which the taxpayer is engaged at the time the debt becomes worthless, the debt is a business debt and not a nonbusiness debt.[56] The settlement of a mortgage at a discount resulted in a business bad debt when the mortgage was held for sale in the ordinary course of the taxpayer's real estate business.[57] An individual with extensive investments in real estate and stocks and bonds, however, was not entitled to a business bad debt since his activities consisted solely of keeping records of investments and collecting dividends and interest.[58]

¶ 1202 FORECLOSURE

When a mortgagor fails to make payments on a mortgage note and a settlement or compromise cannot be reached, the mortgagee is likely to take steps to secure payment of the debt through a foreclosure and sale of the property. In the case of a deed of trust, as opposed to a mortgage, the trustee sells the property under the powers contained in the deed of trust. In the usual case, a foreclosure sale is simply the sale of the property securing the mortgage debt to a third party. The sale proceeds are then turned over to the mortgagee in full or partial satisfac-

---

[49] P.C. Hughes, 10 TCM 204, CCH Dec. 18,180(M).

[50] C.C. Cooke, 10 TCM 881, CCH Dec. 18,556(M), *aff'd and rev'd*, CA-10, 203 F.2d 258.

[51] Home Agency Co., 25 TCM 272, CCH Dec. 27,868(M), T.C. Memo. 1966-48.

[52] W. Ockrant, 25 TCM 333, CCH Dec. 27,885(M), T.C. Memo. 1966-60.

[53] J.M. Clarkston, 17 TCM 446, CCH Dec. 22,986(M), T.C. Memo. 1958-91.

[54] Code Sec. 166(d).

[55] Code Sec. 166(d)(2).

[56] Reg. § 1.166-5(b).

[57] Theodore Gutman Est., 18 TC 112, CCH Dec. 18,923, *acq.* 1952-2 CB 2; R.E. Keller, 29 TCM 369, CCH Dec. 30,043(M), T.C. Memo. 1970-79.

[58] E. Higgins, S.Ct., 41-1 USTC ¶ 9233, 312 U.S. 312, 61 S.Ct. 475.

tion of the debt, and neither the mortgagee nor mortgagor has any further interest in the property, unless the mortgagor retains a right of redemption under local law.

For the mortgagor, the foreclosure is simply a sale for tax purposes on which gain or loss is realized. The mortgagee who receives payment in full as a result of the foreclosure merely receives back the basis in the mortgage debt, and there are no further tax consequences. If the foreclosure results in less than full satisfaction of the debt, however, the mortgagee may have a bad debt or loss deduction. A bad debt deduction may be available to the mortgagee, even if it is the mortgagee who purchases the property in the foreclosure.

.01 Tax Treatment of the Debtor

A foreclosure is a "sale" for tax purposes.[59] It is immaterial whether the taxpayer is personally liable on the mortgage.[60] See also Rev. Rul. 78-164,[61] in which the IRS ruled that a voluntary conveyance of real property to a mortgagee by a mortgagor who was not personally liable on the mortgage was a sale. Nor does the "involuntary" nature of a foreclosure make the foreclosure an involuntary conversion that would allow postponement of tax under Code Sec. 1033.[62]

Since the foreclosure is a sale of the property, the mortgagor realizes gain or loss on the sale as measured by the difference between the adjusted basis for the property and the amount realized on the foreclosure sale.[63]

[A] Calculation of Gain or Loss

When a foreclosure sale produces proceeds that, after the expenses of sale, exceed the amount of the mortgage, the net proceeds are the amount realized by the mortgagor. This is fairly easy to see, since the proceeds are applied first to the unpaid mortgage, and any excess then is paid to the mortgagor.

> ***Example 1:*** The Mortgagor purchased real property for $50,000, paying $5,000 in cash and financing the balance with a $45,000 mortgage. After amortizing $1,000 of the outstanding mortgage debt, the Mortgagor experiences financial difficulty and stops making payments on the debt. The mortgagee forecloses and the real property is sold for $49,000 after sale expenses. Up to the time of the foreclosure, the Mortgagor had taken $3,000 in depreciation deductions on the property, so that the adjusted basis at the time of the foreclosure was $47,000.
>
> In this case, the $49,000 sale proceeds are applied first to the $44,000 of outstanding mortgage debt. The balance of $5,000 belongs to the Mortgagor and is paid to the Mortgagor. The Mortgagor realizes a gain of $2,000 on this sale, measured by the difference between the adjusted basis and the net proceeds of the sale ($49,000 – $47,000 = $2,000).

[59] G. Hammel, S.Ct., 41-1 USTC ¶ 9169, 311 U.S. 504, 61 S.Ct. 368.

[60] E.F.C. McLaughlin, 43 BTA 528, CCH Dec. 11,642; J.G. Abramson, CA-2, 42-1 USTC ¶ 9200, 124 F.2d 416.

[61] 1978-1 CB 264.

[62] Cooperative Publishing Co., CA-9, 40-2 USTC ¶ 9823, 115 F.2d 1017; J.A. Woolf, 42 TCM 63, CCH Dec. 37,970(M), T.C. Memo. 1981-286.

[63] Code Sec. 1001(a).

A foreclosure can also produce a loss for the mortgagor, even if the net proceeds of the foreclosure exceed the outstanding balance of the mortgage debt.

> ***Example 2:*** Assume the same facts as in Example 1, except that the net proceeds from the foreclosure sale are $45,000, rather than $49,000.
>
> In this case, the $45,000 sale proceeds are applied first to the $44,000 of outstanding mortgage debt. The balance of $1,000 belongs to the Mortgagor and is paid to the Mortgagor. The Mortgagor realizes a loss of $2,000 on this sale, measured by the difference between the adjusted basis and the net proceeds of the sale ($45,000 - $47,000 = ($2,000)).

A situation that is less easy to see arises when the proceeds of the foreclosure sale are not sufficient to pay off the outstanding mortgage debt. In this situation, is the amount realized by the mortgagor limited to the proceeds of the sale? The answer to this is "no," based on the principle established in *B.B. Crane*[64] and discussed at ¶ 101.02.

While this result is clearly called for when the mortgagor is not personally liable for the mortgage debt, there may be some question as to whether this rule should apply when the mortgagor remains liable for the deficiency. In any event, the case law seems to support the proposition that the amount realized includes the entire mortgage, not just the net proceeds of the foreclosure sale. The theory seems to be that any deficiency payment made at a later time is merely part of the mortgagor's cost that had been fully accounted for in the basis at the time of the foreclosure. This result applies regardless of whether the mortgagor realizes a gain or loss on the foreclosure and sale for less than the outstanding mortgage debt.

When a taxpayer acquired mortgaged property in a tax-free exchange and subsequently the mortgagee foreclosed and bought the property for a nominal sum, the foreclosure was held a "disposition," and the amount realized was the amount of the mortgage. Treating the amount of the mortgage as the amount realized resulted in a gain to the taxpayer measured by the difference between the mortgage and the taxpayer's adjusted basis.[65] In Rev. Rul. 73-36,[66] a foreclosure resulted in a loss. The mortgage foreclosure was ruled a sale of real estate in consideration of the cancellation of the mortgage debt, and the taxpayer sustained a loss equal to the excess of the adjusted basis of the property over the amount of the cancelled mortgage.[67]

> ***Example 3:*** The Mortgagor purchased real property for $50,000, paying $5,000 in cash and financing the balance with a $45,000 mortgage. After amortizing $1,000 of the outstanding mortgage debt, the Mortgagor experiences financial difficulty and stops making payments on the debt. The mortgagee forecloses and the real property is sold for $43,000 after sale expenses. The Mortgagor remains liable for the $1,000 deficiency between the outstanding mortgage balance of $44,000 and the $43,000 sale proceeds. Up to the time

[64] 47-1 USTC ¶ 9217, 333 U.S. 1, 67 S.Ct. 1047.

[65] Woodsam Associates, Inc., CA-2, 52-2 USTC ¶ 9396, 198 F.2d 357.

[66] 1973-1 CB 372.

[67] *See also* E. Harris, 34 TCM 597, CCH Dec. 33,173(M), T.C. Memo. 1975-125.

of the foreclosure, the Mortgagor had taken $3,000 in depreciation deductions on the property, so that the adjusted basis at the time of the foreclosure was $47,000.

In this case, the $43,000 sale proceeds are insufficient to pay in full the $44,000 of outstanding mortgage debt. The balance of $1,000 is eventually paid to the mortgagee by the Mortgagor. The Mortgagor realizes a loss of $3,000 on this sale, measured by the difference between the adjusted basis and the amount of the outstanding mortgage debt ($44,000 - $47,000 = ($3,000)). When the Mortgagor eventually pays the $1,000 deficiency, there are no further tax consequences and no loss to the Mortgagor because that portion of the debt, as well as the portion paid with the foreclosure proceeds, was reflected in the adjusted basis for purposes of computing the gain or loss on the foreclosure sale.

Suppose, however, that the Mortgagor had taken $8,000 in depreciation deductions prior to the foreclosure so that the adjusted basis at the time of the foreclosure is $42,000. In this case, the Mortgagor realizes a gain of $2,000 on this sale, measured by the difference between the adjusted basis and the outstanding mortgage balance ($44,000 - $42,000 = $2,000). Again, when the Mortgagor eventually pays the $1,000 deficiency, there are no further tax consequences and no loss to the Mortgagor because that portion of the debt, as well as the portion paid with the foreclosure proceeds, was reflected in the adjusted basis for purposes of computing the gain or loss on the foreclosure sale.

Sometimes, the holder of a second or subordinate mortgage on real estate will make payments to the holder of the first mortgage in order to protect the interest when the mortgagor defaults. When this occurs, the mortgagor becomes indebted to the second mortgagee for the amount of the payments in addition to the amount of the second mortgage. The payments made by the holder of the second mortgage are added to the amount of the second mortgage to determine the amount of cancelled mortgage debt on a foreclosure of the second mortgage.[68]

Generally, the mortgagor reports the gain or loss from the foreclosure sale in the year in which the foreclosure occurs. The definitive event fixing the amount of gain or loss is the foreclosure sale, not the foreclosure decree that orders and precedes the sale.[69] When the mortgagor retains a right of redemption under local law, however, the gain or loss is not reportable until that right expires.[70] If the mortgagor releases the right to redeem prior to the expiration of the redemption period, however, the mortgagor reports gain or loss on release of the redemption right.[71] Essentially, a mortgagor in a jurisdiction that grants a right of redemption may choose the year in which to report the gain or loss. If the mortgagor wants to delay, the mortgagor merely allows the redemption period to run its course. To accelerate the gain or loss, the mortgagor merely releases the redemption right early.

[68] E. Harris, 34 TCM 597, CCH Dec. 33,173(M), T.C. Memo. 1975-125.

[69] G. Hammel, S.Ct., 41-1 USTC ¶ 9169, 311 U.S. 504, 61 S.Ct. 368.

[70] J.C. Hawkins, CA-5, 37-2 USTC ¶ 9412, 91 F.2d 354; G.J. Kolowich, 1 TCM 416, CCH Dec. 12,936-C.

[71] Atmore Realty Co., BTA Memo., CCH Dec. 12,517-A; S.A. Hill, Admr., 40 BTA 376, CCH Dec. 10,796, *nonacq.* 1939-2 CB 53.

[B] Character of Gain or Loss

Since a foreclosure is a sale for tax purposes, the character of the gain or loss realized by the mortgagor on a foreclosure depends on the nature of the property. If the foreclosed property is a capital asset, the gain or loss resulting from the foreclosure is a capital gain or loss.[72] A taxpayer realized a capital loss when real estate that had been purchased in a joint venture was sold at a foreclosure sale because the joint venture did not hold the real estate primarily for sale to customers in the ordinary course of business.[73]

The gain or loss on foreclosed property may also be an ordinary gain or loss[74] or a Section 1231 gain or loss.[75] In Rev. Rul. 67-188, the IRS ruled that if a general partner is engaged in the real estate business individually as a dealer, and the partnership operates a hotel, the general partner's share of the partnership loss resulting from the foreclosure of a mortgage on the hotel property is a Section 1231 loss. The individual business activities of the partner were not taken into account in determining the nature of the partner's share of partnership gains or losses.

For more on the treatment of the sale of real estate other than in the ordinary course of business, see ¶ 1301. For a discussion of the sale of real property in the ordinary course of business, see Chapter 10.

.02 Tax Treatment of the Creditor

A foreclosure may result in the sale of the mortgaged property to a third party or to the mortgagee. When the sale is to a third party, the tax consequences are fairly straightforward since the mortgagee has no further interest in the property and merely receives whatever proceeds are available to fully or partially satisfy the mortgage debt. If no third party comes forward with a reasonable bid in the foreclosure, however, the property may be purchased by the mortgagee in order to protect the mortgagee's interest. When this occurs, the mortgagee is placed in the role of both creditor and purchaser. As a creditor, the mortgagee may have a bad debt loss, and, as a purchaser, the mortgagee may realize a gain or loss. Whatever the final results of the foreclosure, however, the mortgagee can be sure that expenses will be incurred in protecting the property before the foreclosure, for the foreclosure itself, and, if the mortgagee acquires the property, for charges that have accumulated against the property.

[A] Foreclosure Expenses

The costs of the foreclosure itself borne by the mortgagee, such as legal fees and court costs, reduce the proceeds of the foreclosure.[76] These expenses, therefore, may increase the mortgagee's loss from the foreclosure or decrease any gain the mortgagee might realize if the mortgagee reacquires the property as a result of the foreclosure.

[72] G. Hammel, S.Ct., 41-1 USTC ¶ 9169, 311 U.S. 504, 61 S.Ct. 368; Electro-Chemical Engraving Co., Inc., S.Ct., 41-1 USTC ¶ 9170, 311 U.S. 513, 61 S.Ct. 372.

[73] K.R. Terry, 48 TCM 906, CCH Dec. 41,431(M), T.C. Memo. 1984-442.

[74] H. Rothschild v. H.A. Berliner, DC Cal., 50-2 USTC ¶ 9521.

[75] Rev. Rul. 67-188, 1967-1 CB 216.

[76] G.C.M. 19573, 1938-1 CB 214.

Taxes and water rates against property that are paid by the mortgagee prior to acquiring title on foreclosure increase the amount of mortgage debt and, as a result, are recognized in determining gain or loss from the foreclosure.[77] The same rule would apply to any other charges against the property that the mortgagee pays prior to the foreclosure proceedings.

On the other hand, if the mortgagee acquires the property in the foreclosure and pays charges against the property at the time of foreclosure or afterwards, these charges are part of the mortgagee's basis for the acquired property. In *Schieffelin*, the taxpayer purchased other mortgaged property at the foreclosure sale, with taxes and water rates outstanding against the property. The court ruled that payment of these charges in the year after the foreclosure was an additional capital investment in the property and did not enter into the calculation of gain or loss on the foreclosure. See also *M.S. Rogers,*[78] in which taxes paid by the mortgagee as a condition precedent to the acquisition of title by foreclosure increased the basis for depreciation of the buildings on the foreclosed realty. If the mortgagee does not acquire the property, these charges would presumably be added to the mortgage debt and increase the mortgagee's basis for the debt in the same fashion as charges incurred prior to the foreclosure.

[B] Purchase by Third Party

If the proceeds of the foreclosure sale are less than the amount of the debt, and the portion of the mortgage debt that remains unsatisfied after the sale is wholly or partially uncollectible, the mortgagee is entitled to a bad debt deduction for the taxable year in which it becomes wholly worthless or is charged off as partially worthless.[79] The mortgagee may also include accrued and unpaid interest on the mortgage as part of the bad debt deduction, but only if the mortgagee previously reported the accrued interest as income.[80] Generally, if the mortgagee obtains a deficiency judgment for the amount of the mortgage debt that is not covered by the proceeds of the foreclosure sale, a bad debt deduction cannot be taken until the judgment becomes uncollectible.

For the treatment of a bad debt as a business bad debt or a nonbusiness bad debt, and the determination of when a debt becomes worthless, see the discussion of the bad debt deduction at ¶ 1201.02[B].

> ***Example 4:*** The Mortgagor defaults when a balance of $52,000 is owed on the mortgage obtained to finance the purchase of a parcel of real estate. In order to protect the interest before foreclosure, the Mortgagee pays real estate taxes on the parcel in the amount of $2,500. The real estate taxes paid by the Mortgagee are considered an additional loan and increase the Mortgagee's basis for the debt to $54,500 ($52,000 + $2,500).

[77] L.S. Schieffelin Est., 44 BTA 137, CCH Dec. 11,752, *acq.* 1941-1 CB 9.

[78] DC Conn., 46-2 USTC ¶ 9361, 69 F. Supp. 8.

[79] Reg. § 1.166-6(a)(1).

[80] Reg. § 1.166-6(a)(2).

In the foreclosure sale, the parcel is sold for $49,000. The expenses of the foreclosure, including legal fees and court costs, are $3,600. These expenses reduce the proceeds of the foreclosure sale to $45,400 ($49,000 - $3,600). The Mortgagee's bad debt deduction therefore is $9,100. This is the Mortgagee's basis in the debt of $54,500, less the net proceeds of the foreclosure of $45,400 ($54,500 - $45,400 = $9,100).

[C] Purchase by Mortgagee

Just as with a purchase by a third party, if the proceeds, or in this case the amount bid by the mortgagee, are less than the amount of the debt, and the portion of the mortgage debt that remains unsatisfied after the sale is wholly or partially uncollectible, the mortgagee is entitled to a bad debt deduction for the taxable year in which the debt becomes wholly worthless or is charged off as partially worthless. Thus, the mortgagee realizes a bad debt loss measured by the difference between the bid price and the amount of the outstanding mortgage debt whenever the bid price is less than the outstanding debt.[81]

A mortgagee who bids for and acquires the property in a foreclosure sale, however, wears a second hat in addition to that of a creditor. The mortgagee is also a purchaser of the property and, in this role, may realize a gain or loss on the transaction, in addition to any possible bad debt loss. This gain or loss is measured by the difference between the amount of the obligations of the debtor that are applied to the purchase or bid price of the property and the fair market value of the property.[82] The fair market value of the property is presumed to be the amount for which it is bid in by the mortgagee, in the absence of clear and convincing proof to the contrary.[83]

The effect of these rules is that the mortgagee realizes no gain or loss, apart from any bad debt loss, if the bid price is equal to the fair market value of the property. If the bid price is less than the fair market value of the property, however, any bad debt loss is offset by the gain realized, so that the actual economic gain or loss realized by the mortgagee is reflected in his taxable income or loss. Similarly, if the bid price is more than the fair market value of the property, the additional economic loss is added to the bad debt loss. While this might give a mortgagee an incentive to bid low if the gain would be treated as a capital gain, the IRS has ruled that if a taxpayer receives an ordinary deduction on foreclosure, any offsetting gain is taxable as ordinary income.[84] The ruling involved a real estate investment trust that engaged primarily in short-term financing activities. The trust had made a construction loan on which it later foreclosed and bid in the property for less than its fair market value. Since the trust's basis in the mortgage note exceeded the property's value, and the balance due on the note was wholly uncollectible, the trust sustained an ordinary bad debt loss. The gain realized by the trust as a result of the bid on the property at less than fair market value was ruled to be ordinary income.

As to the presumption in Reg. § 1.166-6(b)(2) that the bid price is equal to the fair market value of the property, the Tax Court has defined the workings of the

[81] Reg. § 1.166-6(a)(1).

[82] Reg. § 1.166-6(b)(1).

[83] Reg. § 1.166-6(b)(2).

[84] Rev. Rul. 80-56, 1980-1 CB 154.

presumption in the following manner. The fair market value is presumed to be the bid price absent clear and convincing proof to the contrary. Upon proof of the bid price, the mortgagee comes within the presumption and meets the burden of proof as to the fair market value of the property. The presumption applies even when the value of the property is greater than the bid price and the presumption is not limited to cases in which the alleged fair market value is lower than the bid price. The IRS cannot disregard the presumption without producing evidence to indicate that the bid price is not representative of the fair market value.[85] The IRS, however, may use evidence to prove that the fair market value is different than the bid price, even if state law provides that a successful bid price at a foreclosure proceeding determines the fair market value of real property.[86] The IRS may use an expert witness to rebut the presumption and establish a fair market value other than the bid price.[87]

Example 5: The Mortgagor owes a balance of $53,000 on a parcel of real estate when the Mortgagee acquires the property in a foreclosure by bidding in $50,000. The remaining amount of the debt is uncollectible. The Mortgagee's bad debt deduction is $3,000 ($53,000 basis of debt - $50,000 bid = $3,000 bad debt loss). If the fair market value of the property is $50,000, or if there is no clear and convincing evidence that the fair market value is anything other than the bid price, the Mortgagee would realize no further gain or loss as a result of the purchase of the property in the foreclosure.

Suppose, however, that the fair market value of the property is $45,000. In this case, in addition to the bad debt loss, the Mortgagee would realize an additional loss of $5,000 ($50,000 obligations of debtor applied to bid price - $45,000 fair market value = $5,000 loss on purchase). This loss may be a capital loss if the debt is a capital asset in the hands of the Mortgagee.

If the fair market value of the property is $55,000, however, the Mortgagee would realize a gain on the purchase of $5,000 ($55,000 fair market value - $50,000 obligations of debtor applied to bid price = $5,000 gain on purchase). The gain may be capital gain if the debt is a capital asset. However, as noted above, the IRS applies tax benefit principles to treat gain offsetting a deduction from ordinary income as ordinary income (Rev. Rul. 80-56, 1980-1 CB 154). Therefore, if the $3,000 bad debt loss produces an ordinary loss deduction for the Mortgagee, $3,000 of the $5,000 gain on the purchase transaction would be ordinary income, even if the debt qualified as a capital asset in the hands of the Mortgagee.

In Rev. Rul. 72-238,[88] the IRS ruled that gain realized in a foreclosure proceeding by a bank that purchases mortgaged property at a bid price less than the fair market value of the property is ordinary income. The loan is not a capital asset in the hands of a bank originating the loan.

---

[85] Community Bank, 62 TC 503, CCH Dec. 32,679, *acq.* 1975-1 CB 1.

[86] Community Bank, 79 TC 789, CCH Dec. 39,481, *aff'd*, CA-9, 87-2 USTC ¶ 9379.

[87] *See*, for example, C.J. Heath, 30 TCM 545, CCH Dec. 30,812(M), T.C. Memo. 1959-80.

[88] 1972-1 CB 65.

As a general rule, a mortgagee will want to bid as low as possible in order to produce the greatest bad debt deduction on a foreclosure. The lower bounds, taking into account the bid necessary to acquire the property, should be such as to come within the presumption that the bid price is equal to fair market value, that is, not so low as to invite a challenge. The mortgagee can support the position taken with appraisals or other evidence showing that the bid price is equal to fair market value. While a bid that is lower than fair market value would produce an even larger bad debt loss, the additional loss would be offset by the gain realized on the purchase transaction.

The mortgagee's basis for property bid in at a foreclosure sale is the fair market value of the property.[89] The fair market value of the property, rather than the bid price, is used to fix the mortgagee's basis because any difference between the bid price and the fair market value of the property is reflected in the mortgagee's income at the time of the foreclosure. If the mortgagee pays charges against the property at the time of foreclosure or afterwards, these charges are added to the mortgagee's basis for the acquired property (see further discussion of expenses of foreclosure, at ¶ 1202.02[A]).

For the special rules that apply when the seller reacquires property subject to a purchase-money mortgage, see the discussion at ¶ 1204.

¶ 1203 CONVEYANCE AND ABANDONMENT OF MORTGAGE

The settlement of the mortgage debt at a discount or foreclosure are not the only options open to the parties when a mortgage loan is in trouble. A mortgagee may be willing to accept the conveyance of the mortgaged property in full satisfaction of the mortgage debt. This course may appeal to the mortgagee who wants to avoid the time-consuming and costly process of foreclosure. It is also likely to appeal to a mortgagee who foresees an unnecessary loss on a foreclosure sale because of market or other conditions that may improve with time.

A mortgagor who is unable to meet mortgage obligations on the property may be willing to simply "walk away" from the property. Whether such an abandonment produces tax results that differ from foreclosure or conveyance to the mortgagee is a question that has troubled the courts for years. Earlier cases indicate that when there is an abandonment there is no sale or exchange necessary to support capital loss treatment and, therefore, abandonment automatically produces an ordinary loss. More recent cases, however, do not accept this notion.

.01 Conveyance to Mortgagee

A mortgagee may be willing to accept the mortgaged property in full satisfaction of the mortgage debt in some cases when the mortgagor is no longer able to make the required payments. The conveyance of the mortgaged property to the mortgagee has tax consequences for both parties to the mortgage loan.

[89] Reg. § 1.166-6(c).

[A] Tax Treatment of Mortgagor

The transfer of the mortgaged property by the mortgagor to the mortgagee in satisfaction of the mortgage debt is treated as a sale of the mortgaged property. The outstanding mortgage debt is the amount realized from the sale, and if this is less than the mortgagor's basis for the property, the mortgagor realizes a loss.[90] However, regulations issued under Code Sec. 1001 may require the mortgagor to recognize income from the discharge of indebtedness in the case of a recourse mortgage which exceeds the fair market value of the property. If the mortgage debt is greater than the mortgagor's basis for the property, the mortgagor realizes a gain, regardless of whether the mortgagor is personally liable on the debt.[91]

The general rule is that the amount realized from a sale or other disposition of property includes the amount of liabilities from which the transferor is discharged as a result of the sale or disposition.[92] However, the amount realized on a sale or other disposition of property that secures a recourse liability does not include amounts that are or would be, if realized and recognized, income from the discharge of indebtedness.[93] This rule applies only if the amount of debt were included in the basis of the property.[94]

> ***Example 6:*** The Mortgagor transfers to the mortgagee property with a fair market value of $60,000, and the mortgagee discharges a $75,000 mortgage for which the Mortgagor was personally liable. The amount of the mortgage was included in the Mortgagor's basis for the property. The amount realized by the Mortgagor on the transfer of the property is its fair market value of $60,000. In addition, the Mortgagor has income from the discharge of indebtedness of $15,000 ($75,000 - $60,000 = $15,000).

Under the regulations, a disposition of property includes a transfer of the property in satisfaction of liabilities to which it is subject.[95] The sale or other disposition of property that secures a recourse liability discharges the transferor from liability if another person agrees to pay the liability, regardless of whether the transferor is in fact released from liability.[96] The sale or other disposition of property that secures a nonrecourse liability discharges the transferor from liability.[97]

[B] Tax Treatment of Mortgagee

The mortgagee realizes a loss when the mortgaged property is accepted in satisfaction of the mortgage debt if the value of the property is less than the mortgagee's basis for the debt. This loss is deductible as a bad debt since there is no sale or exchange of the mortgage notes.[98] See also *National Bank of Commerce of San Antonio,*[99] in which the court ruled that a bank had a deductible bad debt loss, not a capital loss, equal to the difference between the amount of its loans to an

[90] A.A. Kaufman, CA-9, 41-1 USTC ¶ 9468, 119 F.2d 901.

[91] Lutz & Schramm Co., 1 TC 682, CCH Dec. 13,014, *nonacq.* 1943 CB 35.

[92] Reg. § 1.1001-2(a)(1).

[93] Reg. § 1.1001-2(a)(2).

[94] Reg. § 1.1001-2(a)(3).

[95] Reg. § 1.1001-2(a)(4)(iii).

[96] Reg. § 1.1001-2(a)(4)(ii).

[97] Reg. § 1.1001-2(a)(4)(i).

[98] H.P. Bingham, CA-2, 39-2 USTC ¶ 9636, 105 F.2d 971; A.B. Spreckles, CA-9, 41-2 USTC ¶ 9546, 120 F.2d 517.

[99] CA-5, 40-2 USTC ¶ 9550, 112 F.2d 946.

estate and the value of property conveyed to it by the debtor in settlement of the loans—the transaction was not a sale.

If the value of the mortgaged property exceeds the mortgagee's basis for the debt, the mortgagee realizes a gain. If there is accrued but unreported interest on the debt, or if the excess represents discount, to this extent the gain is ordinary income. Interest income cannot arise, however, if the value of the property does not exceed the principal of the mortgage loan.

Special rules apply when a mortgagee reacquires property that was sold subject to a purchase-money mortgage. These rules are discussed at ¶ 1204.

Mortgaged property may be conveyed to the mortgagee in full satisfaction of the mortgage debt under court order in foreclosure. The tax consequences to the mortgagee of such an involuntary conveyance are the same as those discussed at ¶ 1203.01[A] that apply in the case of a voluntary transfer by the mortgagor. If the fair market value of the property exceeds the mortgagee's basis for the debt, the mortgagee realizes gain. If the basis of the debt is greater than the fair market value of the property, the mortgagee realizes a bad debt loss. If the mortgagor retains a right of redemption, however, the deduction for the bad debt loss may be delayed until the right expires or is released or abandoned.

.02 Abandonment by Mortgagor

The abandonment of property by the mortgagor leaves the mortgagor in essentially the same economic position the mortgagor would be in had the property been conveyed to the mortgagee or had the mortgagee foreclosed. Nevertheless, early case law looked upon abandonment as producing a different tax result, at least if the mortgagor were not personally liable on the debt. If a taxpayer did not assume the mortgage on property at the time of purchase, notice to the mortgagee of abandonment of all rights in the property resulted in an ordinary loss.[100] The theory behind these decisions was that there was no sale or exchange when the property was abandoned, and, therefore, without a sale or exchange, gain or loss would not be a capital gain or loss.

If the mortgagor was personally liable on the mortgage debt, however, the early cases did recognize that a sale or exchange took place, with the discharge of the debt treated as property received by the mortgagor.[101] Also, the early cases found a sale or exchange rather than an abandonment whenever any consideration at all flowed to the mortgagor. For instance, a capital loss resulted after a mortgagor decided to abandon property and then directed a conveyance of the title for nominal consideration, which he never received.[102] In *H.C. Aberle,*[103] there was a sale resulting in a capital loss when the owner of property subject to a mortgage on which he was not personally liable conveyed the property to the mortgagee in consideration for the mortgagee's agreement to pay real property taxes which were the personal liability of the owner.

---

[100] W.W. Hoffman, CA-2, 41-1 USTC ¶ 9280, 117 F.2d 987. *See also* T. Stokes, CA-3, 41-2 USTC ¶ 9770, 124 F.2d 335; Realty Operators, Inc., 40 BTA 1051, CCH Dec. 19,914, *nonacq.* 1940-1 CB 8.

[101] *See*, for example, P. Green, CA-3, 42-1 USTC ¶ 9277, 126 F.2d 70.

[102] A. Blum, CA-2, 43-1 USTC ¶ 9283, 133 F.2d 447.

[103] CA-3, 41-2 USTC ¶ 9558, 121 F.2d 726.

More recently, however, the Tax Court has found that a sale or exchange can occur when property is abandoned and that a capital loss, rather than an ordinary loss, is the result for the mortgagor (assuming, of course, that the property is a capital asset in the hands of the mortgagor). This more recent line of decisions is based on the Tax Court's decision in *E.L. Freeland,*[104] in which the Court ruled that a transaction in which the purchaser of real property reconveyed the property to the mortgagee without consideration, when the fair market value of the property was less than the unpaid mortgage principal, was the sale of a capital asset, and thus the loss was capital rather than ordinary.

While *E.L. Freeland* did not deal directly with abandonment, the same principle was soon extended to the abandonment of property by a mortgagor who was not personally liable on the mortgage debt. When a partnership that held real property subject to nonrecourse mortgages in excess of the fair market value of the property abandoned the property, the Tax Court held that the losses from the abandonment were capital losses, not ordinary losses.[105] The Tax Court specifically followed its decision in *E.L. Freeland* and ruled that to the extent *W.W. Hoffman* held to the contrary, it was no longer controlling. Other decisions soon followed.

In *L.J. Arkin,*[106] the taxpayer's abandonment of the interest in a land trust was ruled a sale or exchange of a capital asset, and the loss deductible as a capital loss rather than an ordinary loss. The taxpayer's interest was admittedly a capital asset, and the relinquishment of the bundle of rights constituting the interest in the land trust in return for being relieved of the obligation to bear a proportionate share of the costs of the mortgage payment, trustee's fees, insurance costs, taxes, and tort or contract liability constituted a sale or exchange, regardless of whether a technical abandonment also occurred under state law.

A taxpayer, a member of a joint venture that held unimproved property subject to a nonrecourse mortgage in excess of the property's fair market value, sustained a long-term capital loss from the sale or exchange of a capital asset at the time the joint venture abandoned the property. The Tax Court's characterization of the loss from the abandonment of unimproved real estate as a long-term capital loss, rather than an ordinary loss, was affirmed on appeal.[107] According to the appellate court, the abandonment of unimproved real estate held subject to a nonrecourse mortgage exceeding its fair market value constituted a "sale or exchange" because the taxpayer received the benefit of being relieved of the obligation to pay the debt and taxes and assessments against the property.[108]

What the recent decisions have done is to bring the tax treatment of abandonment into conformity with the treatment of foreclosure and voluntary conveyance as a means of dealing with troubled real estate financings. Considering the economic equivalence of these transactions from the mortgagor's point of view, the uniform treatment seems justified.

---

[104] 74 TC 970, CCH Dec. 37,127.

[105] M.L. Middleton, 77 TC 310, CCH Dec. 38,124, *aff'd per curiam* CA-11, 693 F.2d 124, 82-2 USTC ¶ 9713.

[106] 76 TC 1048, CCH Dec. 38,017.

[107] J.W. Yarbo, CA-5, 84-2 USTC ¶ 9691, *aff'g* 45 TCM 170, CCH Dec. 39,513(M), T.C. Memo. 1982-675.

[108] *See also* F.L. LaPort, CA-7, 82-1 USTC ¶ 9230, 671 F.2d 1028, *aff'g* 40 TCM 1134, CCH Dec. 37,202(M), T.C. Memo. 1980-355.

¶ 1204 REPOSSESSION OF SELLER-FINANCED PROPERTY

When the seller of real property provides financing to the purchaser through a purchase-money mortgage, a foreclosure puts the mortgagee (seller) in the position of reacquiring property that he previously owned. This situation differs from third-party financing, and the tax law recognizes this difference. Generally, under Code Sec. 1038, the mortgagee recognizes neither gain nor loss on the reacquisition of seller-financed property, except to the extent of payments received in excess of gain reported on the original sale.

In the case of an all-cash sale, or when there is third-party financing, Code Sec. 1038 does not apply. If the seller of property receives the entire purchase price and then accepts a reconveyance of the property and returns the buyer's funds in the same taxable year, no gain is recognized by the seller on the sale. If the reconveyance occurs after the taxable year of the sale, the seller reports the sale in the tax year of the sale and acquires a new basis in the property when it is reconveyed equal to the amount paid for the reconveyance.[109]

.01 Nonrecognition of Gain or Loss

The general rule of Code Sec. 1038 is that if the sale of real property gives rise to indebtedness to the seller which is secured by the real property that is sold, and the seller of the property reacquires the property in full or partial satisfaction of the indebtedness, then the seller recognizes neither gain nor loss as a result of the reacquisition.[110] The property need not be reacquired from the purchaser, but may be reacquired from the purchaser's transferee or assignee, as long as the indebtedness that is partially or completely satisfied in the reacquisition arose in the original sale and was secured by the property.[111]

The mortgagee reacquiring the property must have been the seller of the property for the nonrecognition provisions to apply. When a taxpayer acquired real property on the foreclosure of a mortgage, but had obtained the mortgage for a note that had been acquired as part payment for the sale of stock, Code Sec. 1038 did not apply to the gain attributable to the acquisition of the real property through the foreclosure. Code Sec. 1038 applies only when the reacquired property was previously sold by the mortgagee.[112] Similarly, the IRS has ruled that the nonrecognition provisions do not apply to a former shareholder who has received an installment obligation in a corporation's liquidation when that shareholder, on the buyer's default, receives the real property used to secure the debt. In this case, the liquidated corporation, not the former shareholder, is the seller of the property.[113]

The nonrecognition provision applies regardless of whether the seller realized a gain or loss on the sale of the property. Also, it does not matter what method of accounting the seller used to report gain or loss from the sale or whether at the time of reacquisition the property has appreciated or depreciated since the original sale.[114] The nonrecognition provision even applies on the repossession of improved

[109] Rev. Rul. 80-58, 1980-1 CB 181.

[110] Code Sec. 1038(a).

[111] Reg. § 1.1038-1(a)(4).

[112] E.R. Held, DC Ala., 75-2 USTC ¶ 9678.

[113] Rev. Rul. 86-120, 1986-2 CB 145.

[114] Reg. § 1.1038-1(a)(1).

property in satisfaction of an obligation resulting from the sale of the same property prior to the improvements.[115] The only gain that must be recognized is that from payments received that exceed previously reported gain, as discussed below.

Title does not have to pass to the purchaser in order for there to be a sale, so that the nonrecognition provision applies on a repossession in a contract-type sale. If the purchaser has a contractual right to retain possession of the property as long as the obligations under the contract are performed and to obtain title on the completion of the contract, a sale has taken place for purposes of Code Sec. 1038. A sale may have occurred even if the purchaser does not have the right to possession until the purchaser partially or fully satisfies the terms of the contract.[116]

Code Sec. 1038 applies only when the seller reacquires the property in partial or full satisfaction of the indebtedness to the seller that arose from the sale of the real property and that was secured by the property. It is not necessary, however, that the purchaser default or that default be imminent. As long as the seller is reacquiring the property only in exchange for the discharge of the purchaser's obligation to the seller, and does not pay any additional consideration, the nonrecognition provision applies.[117] If additional consideration is paid by the seller on the reacquisition, the reacquisition and additional consideration must be provided for in the original sale contract or the purchaser must be in default or default must be imminent. For example, if the purchaser is in arrears on the payment of interest or principal or has in any other way defaulted on the contract for the purchase of the property, or if the facts indicate that the purchaser is unable to perform the obligations satisfactorily under the contract, and the seller reacquires the property from the purchaser for consideration in addition to discharging the purchaser's indebtedness to the seller which arose from the sale and was secured by the property, Code Sec. 1038 applies to the reacquisition.

[A] Prior Bad Debt Deductions

A bad debt deduction is not allowed on the reacquisition of property under Code Sec. 1038.[118] If the seller-mortgagee previously took a bad debt deduction for the partial or complete worthlessness of the debt secured by the property, the seller must report an equal amount of income on the reacquisition of the property under Code Sec. 1038. Income inclusion is not required, however, to the extent the seller-mortgagee did not receive a tax benefit from the prior bad debt deduction.[119]

[B] Holding Period of Reacquired Property

Since the reacquisition of seller-financed property is essentially a nullification of the original sale of the property, the holding period of the property after its reacquisition includes the period the seller held the property prior to its original sale. The holding period does not include the period of time beginning with the date following the date on which the property is originally sold and ending with the date on which the seller reacquires the property.[120]

---

115 R.R. Connners, 88 TC 541, CCH Dec. 43,750.

116 Reg. § 1.1038-1(a)(2).

117 Reg. § 1.1038-1(a)(3).

118 Code Sec. 1038(a).

119 Reg. § 1.1038-1(f)(2).

120 Reg. § 1.1038-1(g)(3).

[C] Basis of Reacquired Property

In order to preserve any gain or loss that goes unrecognized under Code Sec. 1038 on the disposition of the mortgage, the seller-mortgagee's basis for the reacquired property is a substituted basis, *i.e.,* the property generally takes the basis the seller-mortgagee had in the mortgage debt prior to the reacquisition of the property securing that debt.[121] This basis is adjusted for any gain recognized, as discussed below, and for any extra consideration paid by the seller in reacquiring the property. Specifically, Reg. § 1.1038-1(g)(1) provides that the basis of any real property acquired in a reacquisition to which Code Sec. 1038 applies is the sum of the following amounts:

1. The adjusted basis of all indebtedness of the purchaser to the seller which is secured by the property at the time of reacquisition;
2. The amount of gain that results because payments received by the seller exceed the amount of gain previously reported; and
3. The amount of money and the fair market value of other property paid by the seller in connection with the reacquisition of the real property.

The calculation of basis is illustrated in the examples below dealing with the recognition of gain.

.02 Recognition of Gain

Although the general rule provides that gain or loss is not recognized when seller-financed real property is reacquired by the seller, an exception applies when the seller has received money or other property from the purchaser in excess of gain reported on the sale of the property for periods prior to the reacquisition.[122] This may occur if the seller is reporting the original sale on the installment basis or if the seller elected out of installment reporting.

In either case, the gain reported under Code Sec. 1038 is limited to the potential gain on the original sale (selling price less adjusted basis), reduced by the sum of: (1) the amount of gain reported by the seller prior to the reacquisition, and (2) the expenses and other costs incurred by the seller in the reacquisition. In determining the potential gain from the original sale, the gross sales price is reduced by the selling commissions, legal fees, and other expenses incident to the sale of the property which are properly taken into account in determining gain or loss on the sale.[123]

To determine the amount of gain reported as income prior to the reacquisition, the seller includes gain resulting from payments received in the taxable year in which the reacquisition occurs, if the payments are received prior to the reacquisition.[124]

Example 7: The Seller, a calendar year taxpayer, sells property with an adjusted basis of $15,000 to the Purchaser for $50,000. The sale takes place in 2018, and the Seller elects to report the gain from the sale under the install-

[121] Code Sec. 1038(c).

[122] Code Sec. 1038(b)(1).

[123] Code Sec. 1038(b)(2).

[124] Reg. § 1.1038-1(b)(1)(ii).

ment method. During 2018 and 2019, the Seller receives a total of $20,000 on the contract. On May 15, 2020, the Seller receives $5,000 on the contract. After this payment, the Purchaser defaults and the Seller reacquires the property on October 1, 2020. The gain the Seller reported as income prior to the reacquisition includes gain attributable to the payment received in 2020, as well as the payments received in 2018 and 2019. Under the installment method, of the $25,000 in payments received prior to the reacquisition, 70 percent ($35,000 gain/$50,000 contract price), or $17,500, would have been reported as gain. The Seller would report the remaining $7,500 in payments received prior to the reacquisition as gain under Code Sec. 1038. (Installment sales are considered in Chapter 14.)

In determining the amount of payments and other property received prior to the reacquisition, the seller includes payments made by the purchaser for the purchaser's benefit, as well as payments made and other property transferred directly to the purchaser. If the purchaser makes payments on a mortgage or other indebtedness to which the property was subject at the time of the sale, or on which the seller was personally liable at the time of the sale, the seller includes these amounts as payments received prior to the reacquisition. If after the sale the purchaser borrows money and uses the property as security for the loan, however, payments by the purchaser in satisfaction of this indebtedness are not considered amounts received by the seller from the sale of the property, even though the seller does benefit indirectly when the purchaser makes these payments.[125]

Payments received by the seller also include payments made by the purchaser at the time of the reacquisition which are attributable to the original sale of the property.[126] For instance, if the purchaser makes a payment in partial or complete satisfaction of the original purchase-money mortgage when the seller reacquires the property, the seller treats the payment as received prior to the reacquisition with respect to the original sale. Interest, stated or unstated, is excluded from the computation of gain on the sale of the property and is not considered money or other property received with respect to the sale.[127]

[A] Reacquisition Following Installment Sale

The seller who makes an installment sale of property and later repossesses the property is subject to Code Sec. 1038. The determination of the amount of gain that the seller must report on the reacquisition of the property, as well as the basis for the reacquired property, is illustrated by the following example.

Example 8: The Seller purchased real property for $80,000 and later sold that property to the Purchaser for $100,000. At the time of the sale to the Purchaser, there was no existing mortgage on the property. Under the contract of sale from the Seller to the Purchaser, the Purchaser paid $10,000 down and executed a note for the balance of $90,000, with interest at the current market rate. The principal, together with accrued interest, was to be paid in nine annual installments. The Seller elected to report the gain from the sale on

[125] Reg. § 1.1038-1(b)(2)(i).

[126] Reg. § 1.1038-1(b)(2)(ii).

[127] Reg. § 1.1038-1(b)(2)(iii).

the installment method. After the second $10,000 annual payment, the Purchaser defaults and the Seller accepts a voluntary reconveyance of the property in complete satisfaction of the purchase-money debt. The Seller incurs $5,000 in expenses in connection with the reacquisition of the property. At the time of the reacquisition, the property is worth $110,000.

The gain the Seller reports as a result of the reacquisition of the property is $9,000, determined as follows:

Gain before limitation:		
Money received prior to reacquisition		$30,000
Less gain previously reported as income ($30,000 × $20,000/$100,000)		6,000
Gain before limitation		$24,000
Limitation on reportable gain:		
Sales price		$100,000
Less:		
Basis at time of sale	$80,000	
Gain reported prior to reacquisition	6,000	
Expense of reacquisition	5,000	91,000
Limitation on amount of gain		$9,000

The basis of the reacquired property at the time of reacquisition by the Seller is $70,000, determined as follows:

Adjusted basis of indebtedness ($70,000 – ($70,000 × $20,000/$100,000))	$56,000
Gain from reacquisition	9,000
Expense of reacquisition	5,000
Basis of reacquired property	$70,000

[B] Reacquisition Following Election Out of Installment Reporting

If the seller does not report the gain from the original sale on the installment method, the taxable gain on the reacquisition of the property depends on whether the seller valued the purchaser's obligation at face value or less than face value.

Example 9: The Seller purchased real property for $80,000 and later sold that property to the Purchaser for $100,000. At the time of the sale to the Purchaser, there was no existing mortgage on the property. Under the contract of sale from the Seller to the Purchaser, the Purchaser paid $10,000 down and executed a note for the balance of $90,000, with interest. The principal, together with accrued interest, was to be paid in nine annual installments. At the time of sale, the Purchaser's note had a fair market value of $90,000. The

Seller elected not to report the gain from the sale on the installment method, but to treat the transaction as a deferred-payment sale. After the third $10,000 annual payment, the Purchaser defaults and the Seller forecloses. Under the foreclosure sale, the Seller bids in the property at $70,000 (its fair market value at the time), cancels the Purchaser's outstanding obligation of $60,000, and pays $10,000 to purchaser. The Seller incurs no additional expenses in connection with the reacquisition of the property.

The gain the Seller reports as a result of the reacquisition of the property is zero, determined as follows:

Gain before limitation:		
Money received prior to reacquisition		$40,000
Less gain previously reported as income (($10,000 + $90,000) - $80,000)		20,000
Gain before limitation		$20,000
Limitation on reportable gain:		
Sales price		$100,000
Less:		
Basis at time of sale	$80,000	
Gain reported prior to reacquisition	20,000	
Expense of reacquisition	10,000	110,000
Limitation on amount of gain (not less than zero)		$0

The basis of the reacquired property at the time of reacquisition by the Seller is $70,000, determined as follows:

Adjusted basis of indebtedness (face value at time of reacquisition)	$60,000
Gain from reacquisition	0
Expense of reacquisition	10,000
Basis of reacquired property	$70,000

Suppose that the Purchaser's note at the time of sale was valued at $75,000, instead of $90,000, by the Seller. In this case, the gain the Seller would report as a result of the reacquisition of the property would be $5,000, determined as follows:

Gain before limitation:		
Money received prior to reacquisition		$40,000
Less:		
Gain previously reported as income (($10,000 + $75,000) - $80,000)		5,000
Gain before limitation		$35,000
Limitation on reportable gain:		
Sales price		$100,000
Less:		
Basis at time of sale	$80,000	
Gain reported prior to reacquisition	5,000	
Expense of reacquisition	10,000	95,000
Limitation on amount of gain		$5,000

The basis of the reacquired property at the time of reacquisition by the Seller in this case would be $60,000, determined as follows:

Adjusted basis of indebtedness	$45,000
Gain from reacquisition	5,000
Expense of reacquisition	10,000
Basis of reacquired property	$60,000

[C] Third-Party Mortgages

In the examples above, it was assumed that the only indebtedness on the property reacquired by the seller was the original purchase-money mortgage. This may not always be the case. For example, the purchaser may obtain a first mortgage from a bank and a second mortgage from the seller. When the seller reacquires the property and assumes a debt to a third party secured by the property, or takes the property subject to an indebtedness that is not owed by the purchaser to the seller, the seller treats the amount of the outstanding third-party debt as money paid him by the seller in connection with the reacquisition of the property.[128] In effect, regardless of whether the seller assumes a third-party mortgage or takes the property subject to the third-party mortgage, the existence of such a mortgage reduces the amount of gain the seller reports as a result of the reacquisition and increases the seller's basis for the reacquired property.

[D] Character of Gain

Logically, it would seem reasonable to characterize gain realized on the reacquisition of property under Code Sec. 1038 in the same fashion as the gain realized from the original sale; that is, if the original sale produced capital gain, gain

[128] Reg. § 1.1038-1(c)(4)(ii).

on repossession also would be capital gain. This simple and logical approach is denied by the regulations, which provide a rather complicated rule for determining the character of gain realized on the reacquisition of seller-financed real property.

Under Reg. § 1.1038-1(d), the character of the gain resulting from the reacquisition depends on whether the gain on the original sale was reported on the installment method, or, if not, on whether title to the real property was transferred to the purchaser and whether the reconveyance of the property to the seller was voluntary.

If the gain on the original sale of the reacquired property was reported on the installment method, the character of the reacquisition gain is determined under Reg. § 1.453-9. This means that if the property were a capital asset, the reacquisition gain would be a capital gain. Similarly, a Section 1231 asset would produce a Section 1231 gain on reacquisition.

If the original sale was not on the installment method but was a deferred-payment sale, the reacquisition gain is ordinary income if title to the real property was transferred to the purchaser and the seller accepts a voluntary reconveyance of the property. If the purchaser was a corporation, however, and the obligations of the corporation satisfied on the reacquisition are securities, reacquisition gain is capital gain.

Part IV

DISPOSITION OF REAL ESTATE

Introduction to Part IV

Part IV examines the disposition of real estate through various taxable and nontaxable transactions. Chapter 13 focuses on sales and exchanges of real estate, both taxable and nontaxable. Generally, the sale or exchange of real estate is treated in much the same fashion as the sale or exchange of other assets, and the basic rules for computing taxable gain or loss apply equally to both sales and exchanges. The tax on the gain from an exchange of property, however, may be deferred if certain requirements are met. The all-important like-kind exchange rules for two-way, three-way, even four-way exchanges are explained in some detail. There is also a discussion of the reduced or zero tax rates for the sale of qualifying property in designated depressed areas.

Although a seller generally must report recognized gain from the sale of real estate in the year of the sale, an important exception to this rule applies when the seller does not receive the full purchase price in the year of sale. This is most likely to occur when the seller provides financing to the buyer in the form of a purchase money mortgage. Seller financed sales and installment reporting are the subject of Chapter 14. Also included in this chapter is a discussion of the tax consequences of a disposition or pledge of installment obligations received by the seller of real estate.

The tax consequences of the involuntary disposition of real estate are explored in Chapter 15. Casualties and condemnations may produce either a gain or loss, much like a sale. Timely reinvestment of the proceeds of an involuntary conversion can avoid a current tax on a gain. Finally, the income tax consequences of a gratuitous transfer of real estate, whether as a gift to charity or family members, is the subject of Chapter 16.

Chapter 13
Sales and Exchanges

¶ 1300 Overview of Chapter
¶ 1301 Sale of Real Estate
¶ 1302 Tax-Free Exchange of Property
¶ 1303 Reporting Requirements
¶ 1304 Qualified Opportunity Zones
¶ 1305 Reduced Taxes on Depressed Area Property

¶ 1300 OVERVIEW OF CHAPTER

In this chapter, the basic rules for determining the amount of gain or loss on the sale or exchange of real estate are considered. For the most part, the sale or exchange of real estate is treated in the same fashion as the sale or exchange of other assets. While there may be a gain or loss on the transfer of an asset not all transfers produce immediate tax consequences. Generally, the first requirement for a taxable transaction is that there be a sale or exchange. A sale is the transfer of property for money or a promise to pay money, such as a mortgage or note. An exchange is the transfer of property for other property or services.

The basic rules for computing taxable gain or loss apply equally to both sales and exchanges, but not all exchanges that produce a gain are immediately taxable. The tax on the gain produced by the exchange of like-kind property may be deferred, if certain requirements of the Internal Revenue Code are met.

While the basic rules for sales and exchanges are covered in this chapter, special situations involving the sale, exchange or transfer of real estate are considered in other chapters. The distinction between a lease and a sale is explained in Chapter 3. The sale of real estate in the ordinary course of business by real estate dealers, as well as the subdivision and sale of real estate, is the subject of Chapter 10. The rules governing the transfer of real estate in satisfaction of a debt or in bankruptcy are covered in Chapter 12. The special rules governing installment sales are the subject of Chapter 14, while the loss or transfer of real estate assets as the result of casualty or condemnation is considered in Chapter 15.

The gain on the sale of a personal residence, subject to limitations, may not be subject to tax. The special rules relating to the sale of a personal residence are the subject of Chapter 20.

¶ 1301 SALE OF REAL ESTATE

In order to determine the proper tax treatment for the sale of real estate, the amount of gain or loss, of course, must be computed. But knowing the amount of gain or loss is only a beginning. The character of that gain or loss, that is, ordinary or capital, must be determined from the character of the property in the hands of the seller prior to the sale. In some cases, the character of any gain or loss may depend on the length of time the seller held the property. Also, various "recapture" provisions may convert an otherwise capital gain into ordinary income.

.01 Computation of Gain or Loss

Computing the gain or loss on an item or parcel of real estate requires two figures—the "adjusted basis" for the property sold and the "amount realized" from the sale. Gain is simply the excess of the amount realized from the sale over the adjusted basis of the property. Similarly, loss is the excess of the adjusted basis for the property over the amount realized.[1]

[A] Adjusted Basis

A taxpayer's adjusted basis for real estate is the property's original basis to the taxpayer as affected by events occurring while the taxpayer held the property.[2] As more fully explained at ¶ 101.01, the original basis for real estate is determined by the manner in which the taxpayer acquired the property. The most common adjustments to the original basis in the case of real estate are increases for capital improvements or additions and decreases for depreciation, amortization, and casualty losses.

The following chart summarizes the method of determining basis for property acquired through various transactions. The adjustments to basis are discussed throughout this volume in connection with the specific activities or events that give rise to the adjustments.

BASIS OF PROPERTY ACQUISITIONS

Acquisition	*Basis*
Arm's-length purchase	Cost
Bargain purchase	Cost, unless saving is gift, compensation, dividend, or other
Bequest	Generally, fair market value at date of decedent's death, but value assigned at settlement in the case of property acquired in lieu of specific amount of bequest (see ¶ 101.01[F])
Cash purchase	Cost
Cash purchase plus mortgage assumed or given	Full purchase price including the amount of the mortgage
Cash purchase plus redeemable ground rent assumed or property taken subject to ground rent	Full purchase price including amount of redeemable ground rent

[1] Code Sec. 1001(a).

[2] Code Sec. 1011; Reg. § 1.1011-1.

Acquisition	*Basis*
Corporate property acquired for stock by controlled corporation	Transferor's basis for property
Corporate property acquired for stock in taxable transaction	Fair market value of stock at time of exchange
Corporate property contributed by nonstockholders	Zero
Corporate property acquired as paid-in surplus	Transferor's basis
Dividend	Fair market value
Divorce or separation agreement	Same as gift
Gift	Donor's basis plus gift tax, but basis for loss limited to lesser of donor's basis or fair market value at time of gift (see ¶ 101.01[E])
Lessor's acquisition of lessee's improvements	Zero, if excluded from income
Mortgaged property or property subject to redeemable ground rent	Basis includes mortgage or ground rent
Partnership property received as contribution for interest	Partner's adjusted basis for property contributed
Partnership property received in distribution from partnership	Partnership's adjusted basis, limited to partner's basis for his interest
Partnership property received in liquidation of partnership	Adjusted basis of partnership interest less cash received
Purchase for more than fair market value	Cost, but may be limited to fair market value if excess is a gift
Repossessed real property reacquired in satisfaction of purchaser's debt secured by the property	Adjusted basis of debt plus gain from the reacquisition and reacquisition costs
Residence	Cost minus gain not recognized
Transfer in trust	Grantor's basis, plus gain or minus loss recognized by grantor on transfer

[B] Amount Realized

The amount realized on the sale of real estate is the total of all money received plus the fair market value of all property or services received.[3]

Mortgages and Other Liabilities

The amount realized by the seller of property includes any liabilities that are assumed by the buyer and any liabilities to which the property sold is subject.[4] Therefore, the seller of real estate must include the face amount of any mortgage on the property in the "amount realized" for the purpose of determining the gain or

[3] Code Sec. 1001(b).

[4] Reg. § 1.1001-2.

loss. This rule applies regardless of whether the seller is personally liable on the mortgage or whether the buyer actually assumes the mortgage or merely purchases the property subject to the mortgage.

See *B.B. Crane*[5] and the discussion of mortgage and basis at ¶ 101.02

Selling Expenses

Generally, the amount realized on a sale is the selling price of the property reduced by any selling expenses. Except for property sold by dealers (see ¶ 1002.01), fees and commissions paid by the seller to brokers or others are offset against the selling price to determine the amount realized from the sale and are not taken as separate deductions.[6]

State and local taxes, such as state stamp taxes, mortgage recording taxes, and other transfer taxes, paid by the seller in connection with the sale of real estate also are treated as reductions in the amount realized.[7] State, local, and foreign income taxes imposed on the seller, however, are deductible from income and are not treated as reductions in the selling price or amount realized.[8] According to the IRS, the Vermont land gains tax is not an income tax and is, therefore, an offset to the selling price and cannot be taken as a separate deduction from income.[9]

Example 1: The Taxpayer bought an apartment building for $350,000. As owner of the building, the Taxpayer made improvements that cost $100,000 and claimed depreciation deductions in the amount of $50,000. The Taxpayer sold the building for $500,000 in cash, plus property with a fair market value of $100,000. The Buyer assumed the current real estate taxes of $15,000 (a liability of the Taxpayer) and a mortgage of $85,000. The selling expenses of the Taxpayer in connection with the sale of this property are $20,000. The gain on the property is computed as follows:

Amount Realized:

Cash	$500,000
Property received	100,000
Taxes assumed by buyer	15,000
Mortgage assumed by buyer	85,000
	$700,000
Less: Selling expenses	20,000

[5] S.Ct., 47-1 USTC ¶ 9217, 331 U.S. 1, 67 S.Ct. 1047.

[6] Reg. § 1.263(a)-2(f); *see also* the discussion of expenses at ¶ 703.05.

[7] Code Sec. 164(a).

[8] Code Sec. 164(a)(3).

[9] Rev. Rul. 80-121, 1980-1 CB 43.

Amount Realized		$680,000
Adjusted Basis:		
Cost	$350,000	
Improvements	100,000	
	$450,000	
Less: Depreciation	50,000	
Adjusted Basis		400,000
Gain Realized		$280,000

Sale on Contract for Deed

A cash basis taxpayer who sells property on contract without receiving a note or similar obligation of the purchaser may not be taxable until the receipts exceed the adjusted basis for the property.[10] By contrast, a seller on the accrual basis is taxable on the amount owed under a contract for sale as soon as the purchaser becomes unconditionally obligated to pay for the property. This obligation may arise on transfer of title or possession, whichever occurs earlier. Therefore, an accrual basis seller who sells property under a contract for deed realizes gain on the execution of the contract under which the buyer takes possession.[11] For both cash and accrual taxpayers, loss on a sale is deductible in the year of sale, regardless of when the consideration is to be paid under the contract.

The IRS has taken the position, however, that contracts must be valued, and only in rare circumstances will a contract be one that cannot be valued for purposes of "closing" a transaction for tax purposes.[12] Later cases lean to this view and support the idea that even a cash basis taxpayer must report the gain from a sale contract when the contract is executed. In *Warren Jones Co.*,[13] the fair market value of a real estate sales contract was treated as an amount realized in the year of sale by a cash basis seller even though payments were to be received over a 15-year period and even though the contract could not have been sold without a discount of the sales price.[14]

Sale of Easement

Granting or selling an easement usually is not a taxable sale of property. Rather, the amount received for the easement is subtracted from the basis of the property. If only a part of the entire tract of property is permanently affected by the easement, only the basis of that part is reduced by the amount received, unless it is impossible or impractical to separately determine the basis of the part of the property on which the easement is granted.

---

[10] *See, for example,* N.J. Ennis, 17 TC 465 CCH Dec. 18,543; C. Hurlburt Est., 25 TC 1286, CCH Dec. 21,637, *nonacq.* 1956-2 CB 10; R.W. Ewing, 17 TCM 626, CCH Dec. 23,042(M), T.C. Memo. 1958-115.

[11] North Texas Lumber Co., S.Ct., 2 USTC ¶ 484, 281 US 11, 50 S. Ct. 184.

[12] Rev. Rul. 58-402, 1958-2 CB 15.

[13] CA-9, 75-2 USTC ¶ 9732, 524 F.2d 788.

[14] *See also* D.J. Corley, 51 TCM 280, CCH Dec. 42,818(M), T.C. Memo. 1986-17; J.M. Smith, CA-9, 424 F.2d 219, 70-1 USTC ¶ 9327; W.A. Ehlers v. R.P. Vinal, CA-8, 67-2 USTC ¶ 9612, 382 F.2d 58.

If the amount received for an easement is more than the basis of the property to which the easement relates, the excess is a taxable gain. In this case, the granting of the easement is reported as if it were a sale of property.

[C] Disallowed Losses

A loss on the sale or exchange of property is not deductible if the transaction is between certain specified related parties.[15] The relationships that trigger the loss disallowance rule are listed in Code Sec. 267(b) and include the following:

1. Members of the same immediate family, including brothers and sisters, half-brothers and half-sisters, spouse, ancestors, and lineal descendants;[16]
2. An individual and a corporation, if the individual owns, directly or indirectly, more than 50 percent in value of the outstanding stock of the corporation;
3. Two corporations that are members of the same controlled group as defined in Code Sec. 1563(a), except that "more than 50 percent" is substituted for "at least 80 percent" in the definition[17] (controlled group does not include a DISC for this purpose, nor does loss disallowance apply to redemption by fund-of-funds regulated investment companies);[18]
4. A trust fiduciary and a corporation, if the trust or the grantor of the trust owns, directly or indirectly, more than 50 percent in value of the outstanding stock of the corporation;
5. A grantor and fiduciary, and the fiduciary and beneficiary, of any trust;
6. A fiduciary and beneficiary of two different trusts, if the same person is the grantor of both trusts;
7. A tax-exempt educational or charitable organization and a person who, directly or indirectly, controls the organization, or a member of that person's family;
8. Fiduciaries of two different trusts, if the same person is the grantor of both trusts;
9. A corporation and a partnership if the same persons own more than 50 percent in value of the outstanding stock of the corporation and more than 50 percent of the capital interest or the profits interest in the partnership;
10. Two S corporations if the same persons own more than 50 percent in value of the outstanding stock of each corporation;
11. Two corporations, one of which is an S corporation, if the same persons own more than 50 percent in value of the outstanding stock of each corporation; and
12. An executor and beneficiary of an estate, except in the case of a sale or exchange in satisfaction of a pecuniary bequest.

---

[15] Code Sec. 267(a).

[16] Code Sec. 267(c)(4).

[17] Code Sec. 267(f)(1).

[18] Code Sec. 267(f)(3).

If a sale or exchange is between any of the related parties listed above and involves the sale of a number of parcels of real estate, the gain or loss must be computed separately for each parcel. The gain on each parcel is taxable, but the loss on any parcel is not deductible. Also, gains from the sales of any of the parcels may not be reduced by losses on the sales of any of the other parcels.[19]

Controlled Group Loss Deferral

Losses on transactions between members of the same controlled group are deferred rather than denied. The losses are deferred until the property is transferred outside and the loss recognized under consolidated return principles or until such other time as may be prescribed in regulations.[20]

Constructive Ownership Rules

In determining whether an individual directly or indirectly owns any of the outstanding stock of a corporation in applying the loss disallowance rules, the following rules of constructive ownership apply:[21]

1. Stock owned directly or indirectly by or for a corporation, partnership, estate, or trust is considered to be owned proportionately by or for its shareholders, partners, or beneficiaries.
2. An individual is considered to own the stock owned directly or indirectly by or for the family (brothers and sisters, half-brothers and half-sisters, spouse, ancestors, and lineal descendants).
3. An individual who owns (other than by constructive ownership from a family member) any stock in a corporation is considered to own the stock owned directly or indirectly by or for a partner.
4. For purposes of applying the first three rules, stock constructively owned by a person under rule 1 is treated as actually owned by that person, but stock constructively owned by an individual under rule 2 or 3 is not treated as owned by the individual for again applying either rule 2 or 3 to make another person the constructive owner of the stock.

Tax Treatment of Disallowed Losses

If a taxpayer sells or exchanges at a gain property received from a related party, the taxpayer recognizes the gain only to the extent that it is more than the loss previously disallowed to the transferor-related party.[22] This rule applies only to the original transferee.

> ***Example 2:*** A sells a parcel of real estate to his brother B for $76,000. The adjusted basis of the real estate in A's hands was $100,000. Under Code Sec. 267, A's loss of $24,000 is not deductible. Later, B sells the property to an unrelated person for $105,000. B's gain is $29,000 ($105,000 amount realized - $76,000 adjusted cost basis), but B's reportable gain is only $5,000. This is the excess of B's gain of $29,000 over the amount of the loss that was previously disallowed to A of $24,000.

[19] Reg. § 1.267(d)-1(b).
[20] Code Sec. 267(f)(2).
[21] Code Sec. 267(c).
[22] Code Sec. 267(d).

Suppose, however, that B sells the property to an unrelated person for $69,000 rather than $105,000. In this case, B's reportable loss is $7,000 ($76,000 adjusted basis - $69,000 loss realized). B cannot deduct the loss of $24,000 that was previously disallowed to A.

[D] Sale Between Spouses and Former Spouses

Whenever property is transferred from one spouse to another, or from one spouse to a former spouse incident to a divorce, the transfer is a tax-free event and no gain or loss is realized by the transferor spouse.[23] The transferee spouse's basis for the property is the adjusted basis the property had in the hands of the transferor spouse.[24] The transfer of property from a spouse to a former spouse is considered incident to a divorce if the transfer takes place within one year after the date on which the marriage ends or is related to the cessation of the marriage.

[E] Partial Dispositions

Taxpayers may make an annual partial disposition election to recognize the disposition of a portion of a building, including its structural components, in tax years beginning after 2013.[25] The election is made by reporting the gain or loss on a timely filed original tax return, including extensions, for the tax year in which the portion of the building is disposed. No specific form or election statement is required to be attached to the return. The election may be made by any taxpayer having a depreciable interest in a building or its structural components. Electing a partial disposition of a building will generally result in a loss recognized on the tax return.

The regulations on partial dispositions only apply to MACRS property. If a partially disposed asset was depreciated under a pre-MACRS method, a loss cannot be recognized on the partial disposition. Prior to the partial disposition regulations, recognizing a loss on a disposed portion of an asset was generally prohibited, requiring taxpayers to continue depreciating the basis associated with the disposed portion. For example, a loss could not be recognized when an old roof was disposed and replaced with a new roof.

The IRS Large Business and International Division has issued a Practice Unit that focuses on identifying when taxpayers elect a partial disposition of a building or its structural components.[26] While Practice Units are not official pronouncements of law or directives, they do provide IRS staff with explanations of general tax concepts and information on specific types of transactions, and, in this regard, are useful to taxpayers and tax professionals.

The Unit states that the identification of a partial disposition occurs through a review of taxpayer documents and tax return information during an examination. After a positive identification, the IRS examiner can determine if there is a risk of noncompliance in recognizing the partial disposition. Since no specific form is filed in making the election, identification of a partial disposition election for a building, including its structural components, occurs through a review of the following documents and tax return information during an examination:

---

[23] Code Sec. 1041(a).

[24] Code Sec. 1041(b).

[25] Reg. § 1.168(i)-8(d)(2).

[26] Document Control Number DCE/P/252_04_-02.

1. Annual Reports and Forms 10-K.
2. Depreciation tax asset detail schedules.
3. Tax return for specific forms filed related to asset dispositions.

The Unit also notes that the Tangible Property Regulations under Reg. § 1.263(a)-3 (also known as the repair regs, see ¶ 801) provide rules for improvements to buildings, including their structural components, and that those regulations and the disposition regulations under Reg. § 1.168(i)-8 interact with each other. In some cases, capitalization of the replacement costs is required on the partial disposition of an asset or portion of an asset. A review of the Annual Report or 10-K may help determine if there was a partial disposition of a building or its structural components that required the taxpayer to capitalize the replacement of the disposed portion of the asset.

.02 Character of Gain or Loss

Once the amount of any recognizable gain or loss for tax purposes is determined following the sale or exchange of real estate, it still is necessary to fix the character of that gain or loss as either capital or ordinary. In some cases, especially for property used in a trade or business, the character of the gain or loss may be either capital or noncapital, depending on the taxpayer's particular circumstances.

[A] Capital Gains and Losses

Generally all property is classified as one of three types by the Internal Revenue Code:

1. Capital asset, which produces capital gain or loss on its sale or exchange;
2. Noncapital asset, which produces ordinary income or loss on its sale or exchange; or
3. Section 1231 asset used in a trade or business, which may produce capital or ordinary gain or loss, depending upon whether sales and exchanges of all such assets produce a net gain or loss for the year.

For the most part, all personal and investment assets are capital assets. In fact, the Internal Revenue Code, in defining capital assets, takes a negative approach by listing those assets that are *not* capital assets rather than attempting to list those assets that are capital assets. According to Code Sec. 1221(a), a capital asset is any property except:

1. Property held mainly for sale to customers or property that will actually become part of merchandise or property that is for sale to customers (these assets are essentially "inventory" assets);
2. Depreciable property used in a trade or business;
3. Real property used in a trade or business;
4. Accounts or notes receivable acquired in the ordinary course of business, for services rendered as an employee, or from the sale of inventory assets;
5. Copyright, literary, musical, or artistic composition, letter or memorandum or similar property created by the holder or, in the case of a letter or

memorandum or similar property, held by the person for whom the asset in question was produced (these assets remain noncapital assets in the hands of a transferee who acquires them from the creator or the one for whom produced, if they have the same basis as in the hands of the transferor);

6. U.S. government publications received for free or for less than the normal sales price;
7. Commodities derivative financial instruments held by a commodities derivatives dealer;
8. Hedging transactions that are clearly identified as such before the close of the day on which acquired, originated, or entered into; and
9. Supplies of a type regularly used or consumed by the taxpayer in the ordinary course of a trade or business.

Investment property is a capital asset, and a gain or loss on its sale is a capital gain or loss. Rental property, however, is treated as business property. Real property used in a trade or business is subject to the special capital gain/ordinary loss treatment of Code Sec. 1231 discussed at ¶ 1301.02[B]. Note that while real property used for personal purposes, such as a personal residence or vacation home, is a capital asset and gain from its sale is a capital gain, losses from sales and exchanges of such property are not deductible unless they result from a casualty. Of course, if real estate is held for sale in the ordinary course of business, it is not a capital or Section 1231 asset but is "dealer" property. Dealer property and sales of real property in the ordinary course of business are discussed at ¶ 1002.01.

Gain on Related Party Sales

Capital gain treatment is denied, and any gain recognized is ordinary income, for the sale or exchange of property, including leaseholds, if the property is depreciable property in the hands of the buyer and if the buyer and seller are related.[27] Related parties that bring this rule into play are:

1. A person and an entity controlled by that person[28] (what constitutes a controlled entity is discussed below);
2. A taxpayer and any trust in which the taxpayer (or spouse) is a beneficiary, unless the beneficiary's interest in the trust is a remote contingent interest, that is, the value of the interest computed actuarially is five percent or less of the value of the trust property;[29]
3. An employer and any person related to the employer under rules 1 and 2, above;[30]
4. A welfare benefit fund (as defined in Code Sec. 419(e)) that is controlled directly or indirectly by persons related to the employer under rules 1 and 2, above;[31] and
5. An executor and beneficiary of an estate, except in the case of a sale or exchange in satisfaction of a pecuniary bequest.[32]

---

[27] Code Sec. 1239(a).
[28] Code Sec. 1239(b)(1).
[29] Code Sec. 1239(b)(2).
[30] Code Sec. 1239(d)(1).
[31] Code Sec. 1239(d)(2).
[32] Code Sec. 1239(b)(3).

A "controlled entity" is defined by Code Sec. 1239(c)(1) and includes:

1. A corporation in which more than 50 percent of the value of all outstanding stock, or a partnership in which more than 50 percent of the capital interest or profit interest, is owned directly or indirectly by or for one person;
2. A corporation and a partnership, if the same persons own more than 50 percent in value of the outstanding stock of the corporation and more than 50 percent of the capital interest or profits interest in the partnership;
3. Two corporations that are members of the same controlled group;
4. Two S corporations if the same persons own more than 50 percent in value of the outstanding stock of each corporation; and
5. Two corporations, one of which is an S corporation, if the same persons own more than 50 percent in value of the outstanding stock of each corporation.

Control is based on constructive, as well as actual, ownership.[33] In figuring stock ownership for purposes of determining control:

1. Stock owned directly or indirectly by or for a corporation, partnership, estate, or trust is treated as owned proportionately by or for its shareholders, partners, or beneficiaries;
2. An individual is treated as owning stock that is directly or indirectly by or for the individual's family, including only brothers and sisters, half-brothers and half-sisters, spouse, ancestors, and lineal descendants; and
3. Stock that is constructively owned by a person under rule 1 is treated as actually owned by that person for applying rules 1 and 2, but stock that is constructively owned by an individual under rule 2 is not treated as owned by that individual for again applying rule 2 to make another person the constructive owner of that stock.

Tax Treatment of Individual Capital Gains and Losses

The tax treatment of capital gains and losses differs depending on whether the taxpayer is an individual or corporate taxpayer. In either case, however, short-term gains and losses must be separated from long-term gains and losses. The long-term holding period is more than one year (see ¶ 1301.02[C]). For capital assets held more than one year the maximum tax rate on most capital gains is 15 percent. A zero percent rate generally applies to capital gain otherwise taxed under the regular tax rates at a 15 percent or lower rate. A 20 percent rate, however, generally applies to individuals if the gain would be subject to the 35 percent regular tax rate. Note that the top rate on real property gain attributable to depreciation not already recaptured (that is, taxed at ordinary income rates) is 25 percent (see ¶ 1301.03[B]).

[33] Code Sec. 1239(c)(2).

In the case of an individual, short-term capital gains and losses realized during the year are combined to compute a net short-term capital gain or loss. Similarly, long-term capital gains and losses realized during the year are combined to compute a net long-term capital gain or loss. If net long-term gain exceeds net short-term loss, the net gain is eligible for the lower tax rates on net capital gain. If the individual realizes a net loss, the loss is deductible, subject to the limitation discussed immediately below.

An individual with a net capital loss for a year may deduct that loss against ordinary income only to the extent of $3,000 or the net capital loss, whichever is less. In the case of married taxpayers filing separate returns, the limit is $1,500 rather than $3,000.[34] Note that an individual must deduct a net capital loss up to the $3,000 limit, even if the individual has no ordinary income to offset the loss.

The limitation on the deduction of a net capital loss is mitigated by the carryover provision found in Code Sec. 1212. An individual with a net capital loss in excess of the deduction limit may carry over the excess to later years until it is completely used up. The unused loss is carried over as a short-term or long-term loss, as the case may be.[35]

> ***Example 3:*** A married couple sold property in 2019. The sale resulted in a capital loss of $7,000, and the couple had no other capital transactions in 2019. On their joint return, the couple deducts $3,000, the lower of $3,000 or $7,000. The unused part of the loss, $4,000 ($7,000 - $3,000) is carried over to 2020. If this couple had no taxable income in 2019, the carryover to 2020 would still be $4,000. The allowable $3,000 deduction is considered used, even if they had no income against which the deduction could be taken to produce a tax benefit.
>
> If the couple had incurred a $2,500 loss rather than a $7,000 loss in 2019, their deduction for 2019 would have been $2,500 and they would have no carryover to 2020. In computing a capital loss carryover, short-term losses are deducted before long-term losses.

Tax Treatment of Corporate Capital Gains and Losses

Generally, after 2017, a corporation's net capital gain is taxed at the same rates as other corporate income. Prior to 2018, if the corporate tax rate exceeds 35 percent, a corporation's net capital gain is taxed at 35 percent.[36] A corporation's net capital gain is "the excess of the net long-term capital gain for the taxable year over the net short-term capital loss for such year".[37] A corporation's capital losses, unlike an individual's, may be deducted only to the extent of capital gains. A corporation cannot use capital losses to offset ordinary income.[38] An unused capital loss may be carried back three years and carried forward five years and used to offset capital gains in those years until used up. The unused loss generally must be carried to the earliest year in which it can be used. Any capital loss carryback or capital loss carryforward is treated as a short-term loss in the year(s) to which it is carried.[39]

---

[34] Code Sec. 1211(b).
[35] Code Sec. 1212(b).
[36] Code Sec. 1201(a).
[37] Code Sec. 1222(11).
[38] Code Sec. 1211(a).
[39] Code Sec. 1212(a).

[B] Property Used in a Trade or Business: Section 1231 Assets

Real property used in a trade or business and depreciable business property are given special capital gain/ordinary loss treatment in Code Sec. 1231. The split treatment came about as a result of pressure from business, which was not happy with the exclusion of most business property from the definition of capital assets when these assets were sold at a gain, but did not want to give up the benefit of ordinary loss treatment when these assets were sold at a loss. Generally, all gains and losses for the year on Section 1231 assets are combined. If the net result is a loss, then all Section 1231 gains and losses are treated as ordinary gains and losses. If the net result is a gain, then all Section 1231 gains and losses are treated as capital gains and losses.

Keep in mind that Code Sec. 1231 only serves to characterize the nature of gain or loss as capital or ordinary. The section has no other function.

When gain is treated as a capital gain under Code Sec. 1231, other Internal Revenue Code provisions may convert that gain into ordinary income. The depreciation recapture provisions (Code Secs. 1245 and 1250, discussed at ¶ 1301.03[A] and ¶ 1301.03[B]) take precedence over Code Sec. 1231. Also, prior Section 1231 losses are subject to recapture when Section 1231 gains are realized in later years.

Section 1231 Assets

Code Sec. 1231 requires combining gains and losses on all Section 1231 assets, not just real property used in a trade or business. Code Sec. 1231(b) requires taxpayers to take the following assets into account:

1. Depreciable personal property used in a trade or business and held for more than one year.
2. Real property used in a trade or business and held for more than one year.
3. Property held for the production of rents or royalties and held more than one year.
4. Leaseholds used in a trade or business and held more than one year.
5. Timber, coal, and iron ore to which Code Sec. 631 applies.
6. Cattle and horses held for draft, breeding, dairy, or sporting purposes and held for two years or more from the acquisition date.
7. Livestock, other than cattle, horses, and poultry, held for draft, breeding, dairy, or sporting purposes and held for more than one year.
8. Unharvested crops on land used in farming, if the crop and land are sold, exchanged, or involuntarily converted at the same time and to the same person, and if the land has been held more than one year.[40]
9. Compulsory conversions (*i.e.,* condemnations, eminent domain, etc.) and involuntary conversions through casualty or theft of business property, property held for the production of rents and royalties, and investment property, but only if total compulsory and involuntary conversion gains exceed total compulsory and involuntary conversion losses.[41]

[40] Code Sec. 1231(b)(4).

[41] Code Sec. 1231(a)(4)(C).

Inventory and property held for sale to customers in the ordinary course of business, "dealer" property, is excluded from Code Sec. 1231. Apartments, office buildings, and other income-producing real estate generally qualify as Section 1231 assets. A leasehold of land with improvements used in the taxpayer's trade or business also qualifies as a Section 1231 asset, provided the taxpayer is not a "dealer" in leases.[42]

Growing crops sold with a lease on the land, even though to the same person in the same transaction, are not considered Section 1231 assets. Reg. § 1.1231-1(f) says a leasehold or estate for years is not "land" for Code Sec. 1231 purposes.[43] Also, a sale, exchange, or involuntary conversion of an unharvested crop with land is not included in Code Sec. 1231 if the taxpayer keeps any right or option to reacquire the land, directly or indirectly, other than a right customarily incident to a mortgage or other security interest.[44]

Tax Treatment of Section 1231 Gains and Losses

In order to apply Code Sec. 1231, combine all gains and losses from the sales and dispositions of all Section 1231 property for the tax year. If the Section 1231 gains exceed the Section 1231 losses, there is a net Section 1231 gain and all the Section 1231 gains and losses are treated as long-term capital gains or long-term capital losses, as the case may be.[45] On the other hand, an excess of Section 1231 losses over Section 1231 gains results in a net Section 1231 loss. If the Section 1231 losses equal or exceed the Section 1231 gains, then each item is treated as an ordinary gain or loss.[46]

> ***Example 4:*** An individual taxpayer sells two Section 1231 assets during 2019. Asset #1 has an adjusted basis of $100,000 and is sold for $120,000. Asset #2 has an adjusted basis of $60,000 and is sold for $20,000. Since the net result is a $20,000 loss ($20,000 gain on Asset #1 and $40,000 loss on Asset #2), the $20,000 gain on Asset #1 is ordinary income and the $40,000 loss on Asset #2 is a fully deductible ordinary loss which, when combined, result in a fully deductible $20,000 loss.
>
> Suppose, however, that the individual sells Asset #1 for $140,000 and Asset #2 for $40,000, instead of the selling prices assumed above. In this case, the individual realizes a net gain of $20,000 ($40,000 gain on Asset #1 and a $20,000 loss on Asset #2). If the individual did not realize a net loss on Section 1231 property in 2014 through 2018, the $40,000 gain on Asset #1 would be a capital gain and the $20,000 loss on Asset #2 would be a capital loss which, when combined, result in a $20,000 net capital gain.

Generally speaking, it is better to have ordinary losses rather than capital losses, and capital gain rather than ordinary income. Therefore, the usual strategy

[42] Rev. Rul. 72-85, 1972-1 CB 234.

[43] Bidart Bros., CA-9, 59-1 USTC ¶ 9193, 262 F.2d 607, *cert. denied*, 359 U.S. 1003, 79 S.Ct. 1141.

[44] J.F. Nutt Est., CA-9, 71-2 USTC ¶ 9607, 447 F.2d 1109.

[45] Code Sec. 1231(a)(1).

[46] Code Sec. 1231(a)(2).

for tax savings under Code Sec. 1231 is to segregate gains and losses into different tax years. Keep in mind, however, that the Section 1231 recapture rule can convert current capital gains into ordinary income.

Recapture of Prior Section 1231 Losses

The relatively straightforward rule for Section 1231 assets and the opportunities for tax planning through segregating sales at a gain and loss sales into different tax years were complicated by a recapture rule introduced by the Tax Reform Act of 1984. Generally, a net Section 1231 gain is not automatically treated as capital gain. It is necessary to "look back" to the preceding five years to see if sales of Section 1231 property in any of those years produced a net loss deducted from ordinary income. If there was a net loss in any of those years, a net gain in the current year must be treated as ordinary income to the extent any prior net losses exist which have not been used already to convert otherwise capital gain into ordinary income on the sale or other disposition of Section 1231 property.[47]

> ***Example 5:*** The calendar-year Corporation had a net Section 1231 loss of $12,000 in 2015. The Corporation had no net Section 1231 losses in 2016, 2017, or 2018. The Corporation had a net Section 1231 gain of $7,750 in 2019 and has a net Section 1231 gain of $6,900 in 2020. In computing its taxable income for 2019, the Corporation treated its net Section 1231 gain of $7,750 as ordinary income by recapturing $7,750 of its $12,000 net Section 1231 loss from 2015. Then in 2020, the Corporation applies the remaining net Section 1231 loss of $4,250 ($12,000 - $7,750) against its net Section 1231 gain of $6,900. The Corporation reports $4,250 as ordinary income and also reports $2,650 ($6,900 - $4,250) as long-term capital gain.

Despite the Section 1231 recapture rule, planning the sale or disposition of Section 1231 property remains a matter of timing. Section 1231 gains are recaptured as ordinary income only if they *follow* Section 1231 losses. If several Section 1231 assets are to be sold within a relatively short period of time, dividing the sales between two tax years will still produce the capital gain/ordinary loss advantage if the sales at a gain are made in the year *before* the loss sales.

[C] Holding Period

The holding period for an asset is the length of time a taxpayer owns the asset before disposing of it. If a capital asset is held for one year or less, the gain or loss from its disposition is short term. If the capital asset is held longer than one year, the gain or loss on its disposition is long term.[48] Also, application of Code Sec. 1231 to the sale or disposition of business property depends on the holding period for the property. Generally, property must be held for "more than one year" for Code Sec. 1231 to apply.

The holding period for property generally begins on the day following the day the property is acquired and includes the day the property is disposed of or sold.[49] For example, if a taxpayer purchases an asset on July 19, 2018, the taxpayer begins

[47] Code Sec. 1231(c).

[48] Code Sec. 1222.

[49] Rev. Rul. 66-7, 1966-1 CB 188; H.M. Hooper, 26 BTA 758, CCH Dec. 7689.

counting the holding period on July 20, 2018. If the taxpayer sells the property on July 19, 2019, the holding period is not more than one year, but if the taxpayer sells on July 20, 2019, the holding period is more than one year.

While the passing of title generally indicates when a sale has taken place and when a new owner's holding period begins, a taxpayer's holding period may begin before title passes. The holding period of property that is the subject of an unconditional contract of sale begins on the day following that on which title passes, or on the day following that on which delivery of possession is made and the burdens and benefits of ownership are assumed by the purchaser, whichever occurs first.[50] However, taking delivery of possession of real property under an option agreement is not enough to start the holding period. The holding period cannot start until there is an actual contract of sale. The holding period of the seller cannot end before that time.[51]

In *Edwards Industries, Inc.*,[52] the holding period of real estate began when the purchase price was paid under an escrow agreement. This was the time when the parties intended the burdens and benefits of ownership to shift to the purchaser. The period during which the purchaser held an option on the property was not included in the holding period.

When land is acquired and a building or other improvement is constructed upon it, there may be more than one holding period. The holding period of a newly constructed building does not begin with the date of acquisition of the land.[53] The IRS has ruled that the holding period of an office building which was constructed for use in the taxpayer's business and which was sold shortly after completion to an unrelated party began progressively as the building was being constructed. The portion of the building actually completed more than one year before the date of sale is considered held for more than one year for purposes of Code Sec. 1231.[54]

When property is acquired other than by purchase, the holding period does not necessarily begin on the date the property is acquired. Under Code Sec. 1223, the holding period of newly acquired property may include the holding period of other property which is "tacked on" to the holding period of the newly acquired property.

The most usual situation in which an additional period is tacked on to the holding period of property is following a nontaxable exchange. If a taxpayer acquired an asset in exchange for another asset and the basis for the new asset is figured, in whole or in part, by the taxpayer's basis in the old property, the holding period of the new property includes the holding period of the old property.[55]

The holding period of property acquired by gift includes the donor's holding period if basis is determined using the donor's basis.[56] Property acquired from a decedent automatically has a long-term holding period.[57]

---

[50] Rev. Rul. 54-607, 1954-2 CB 177.

[51] V. Hoven, 56 TC 50, CCH Dec. 30,721, *acq.* 1971-2 CB 3.

[52] 33 TCM 569, CCH Dec. 32,581(M), T.C. Memo. 1974-120.

[53] M.A. Paul, CA-3, 53-2 USTC ¶ 9527, 206 F.2d 763.

[54] Rev. Rul. 75-524, 1975-2 CB 342.

[55] Reg. § 1.1223-1(a).

[56] Reg. § 1.1223-1(b).

[57] Code Sec. 1223(9); Reg. § 1.1223-1(j).

.03 Depreciation Recapture

The good, or positive, side of depreciation is presented in Chapter 9. Depreciation, as a "noncash" expense, can shelter from taxation the income generated by real estate. Of course, as depreciation deductions are taken on property, the adjusted basis of that property is reduced. This reduction in basis for depreciation means that the shelter will be reversed and that any depreciation deductions in excess of actual economic depreciation (or loss in value) will be taxed as gain on the sale or other taxable disposition of the property.

Although depreciation in excess of any real decline in value would eventually be recovered by the government because of the basis mechanism, one problem remains. Depreciation could convert ordinary income into capital gain, that is, the deductions for depreciation would offset ordinary taxable income, but any later gain on the sale of the property resulting from the prior depreciation deductions would be taxed only as capital gain under the characterization rule of Code Sec. 1231. This is where the recapture rules of Code Secs. 1245 and 1250 come into play. It is this conversion of ordinary income into capital gain that the recapture rules are designed to prevent.

While the principle of depreciation recapture is easy enough to state, the application of the recapture mechanism is complicated by two sets of rules that apply to two different types of property, that is, Section 1245 property and Section 1250 property. Generally, the dividing line between Section 1245 and Section 1250 property is that between "personalty" (Code Sec. 1245) and "realty" (Code Sec. 1250), but the line is not completely clear cut. Further complication is added because different recapture rules may apply to the same property for depreciation taken over different periods of time.

[A] Section 1245 Property Recapture

Under Code Sec. 1245, all prior depreciation and amortization deductions, plus any basis reduction as a result of an investment credit taken on the property, are recaptured as ordinary income to the extent of any gain realized on the disposition of the property. The Internal Revenue Code achieves this result by requiring that gain be treated as ordinary income on the sale, exchange, or involuntary conversion of Section 1245 property, including a sale and leaseback transaction, to the extent of the lesser of:

1. The recomputed basis of the property minus the adjusted basis of the property, or
2. The amount realized from the sale minus the adjusted basis of the property.[58]

The recomputed basis of Section 1245 property is the adjusted basis of the property plus all adjustments reflected in that adjusted basis because of deductions allowed *or allowable* for depreciation or amortization.[59] Depreciation includes the amount allowed or allowable based on useful life for depreciable property and the

[58] Code Sec. 1245(a)(1).

[59] Code Sec. 1245(a)(2).

regular or alternate ACRS deductions for recovery property. Amortization includes any first-year expense deduction under Code Sec. 179 and deductions for clean-fuel vehicles, complying with EPA sulfur regulations, the removal of barriers for the handicapped and elderly, child-care facilities, on-the-job training facilities, pollution control facilities, reforestation expenditures, advanced mine safety equipment costs, expensed refinery costs, energy efficient building costs, and certain expenditures for historic structures.

Property subject to Code Sec. 1245 recapture includes any property that is or has been subject to an allowance for depreciation and that is:

1. Personal property, both tangible and intangible.[60]
2. Tangible depreciable property, except a building or its structural components, that is or has been an integral part of manufacturing, production, or extraction, or an integral part of the furnishing of transportation, communication, electrical energy, gas, water, or sewage disposal services. Also included are research facilities or storage facilities used in connection with any of these activities.[61]
3. Single-purpose agricultural or horticultural structures.[62]
4. Storage facilities used in connection with the distribution of petroleum or any primary product of petroleum.[63]
5. Real property, not included in 2, 3, or 4, above, to the extent its adjusted basis has been reduced by certain amortization deductions, including those for certified pollution control facilities, on-the-job training and child-care facilities, removal of architectural barriers to the handicapped and elderly, clean-fuel vehicle refueling property, the cost of complying with EPA sulfur regulations, advanced mine safety equipment costs, expensed refinery costs, energy efficient building costs, and reforestation expenditures, or by a first-year expense deduction under Code Sec. 179.[64]
6. Railroad grading or tunnel bore.[65]

Improvement Property

The cost of improvement property, in some cases, may be expensed under Code Sec. 179 (see ¶ 901.03[A]). If the Code Sec. 179 allowance is claimed, the entire section 179 allowance is subject to recapture as ordinary income under the section 1245 recapture rules. Also, qualified improvement property may be eligible for first-year bonus depreciation (see ¶ 901.03[B]).

Qualified improvement property does not lose its status as section 1250 property because of its status as MACRS 15-year property. Thus, any bonus deduction is subject to recapture as ordinary income to the extent the bonus allowance exceeds the straight-line depreciation that would have been allowed. (See ¶ 1301.03[B].)

---

[60] Code Sec. 1245(a)(3)(A); Reg. § 1.1245-3(b).
[61] Code Sec. 1245(a)(3)(B); Reg. § 1.1245-3(c).
[62] Code Sec. 1245(a)(3)(D).
[63] Code Sec. 1245(a)(3)(E).
[64] Code Sec. 1245(a)(3)(C).
[65] Reg. § 1.1245-3.

Bonus depreciation and recapture of Code Sec. 179 deductions are limited to the gain recognized on a disposition. No recapture is required if the property is disposed of after the end of its 15-year recovery period.

[B] Section 1250 Property Recapture

Section 1250 property generally includes all buildings and other improvements to land that are not Section 1245 property and that were placed in service before 1981. For property placed in service after 1980, Section 1250 property includes:

1. Residential real property;
2. Real property located outside the United States;
3. Any real property depreciated on a straight-line basis; and
4. Low-income housing.[66]

Note that, since most real property placed in service after 1986 must be depreciated using the straight-line method, it generally will be Section 1250 property. Also, since only "excess" depreciation generally is subject to recapture in the case of Section 1250 property, as discussed below, there will be no recapture on most real property that was placed in service after 1986. Qualified leasehold improvement property placed in service before 2016 and all qualified improvement property placed in service after 2015 are eligible for first-year bonus depreciation (see ¶ 901.03[B]), and any bonus deduction is subject to recapture to the extent the bonus allowance exceeds the straight-line depreciation that would have been allowed.

Reduced Capital Gain Preference

Although there is no recapture for straight-line depreciation on real estate under Code Sec. 1250, gain from the sale of depreciable property by a noncorporate taxpayer may not be eligible for the most favorable capital gain tax rates. Gain on real property held for more than one year and not recaptured under Code Sec. 1250 is subject to a 25 percent maximum capital gain tax rate, rather than the lower maximum rates that apply to most other assets.[67]

Gain Subject to Recapture

The amount of gain that is subject to recapture on the sale or disposition of Section 1250 property is determined as follows:

1. Determine the excess of the amount realized over the adjusted basis of the property in a sale, exchange, or involuntary conversion or the excess of fair market value over adjusted basis in the case of any other disposition,
2. Determine any "excess" depreciation for periods after 1975, and
3. Multiply the lesser of 1 or 2 by the applicable percentage for the particular type of property involved.[68] (The applicable percentage for various types of properties is discussed below.)

---

[66] Code Sec. 1250(c).

[67] Code Sec. 1(h)(1)(D). *See* the discussion under "Tax Treatment of Individual Capital Gains and Losses" at ¶ 1301.02[A].

[68] Code Sec. 1250(a)(1)(A).

4. Determine the "excess" depreciation for periods after 1969 but before 1976,
5. Multiply the lesser of the remaining gain (1 less 2 or 4) by the applicable percentage for the particular type of property involved.[69]
6. Add the results from 3 and 5 to figure the gain subject to recapture as ordinary income, in the case of taxpayers other than corporations. In the case of corporations, an additional amount is subject to recapture, as discussed below.

"Excess" depreciation is the amount by which depreciation deductions exceed the amount of the deductions that would be available if depreciation were figured under the straight-line method for the same period.[70] If property is held less than 12 months, however, all depreciation is treated as excess depreciation. Also, any reduction in basis for investment credit is treated as a deduction for depreciation. Generally, recapture can arise if Section 1250 property has been depreciated under the regular ACRS method, the declining-balance method, the sum-of-the-years digits method, the units-of-production method, or any other method of rapid or accelerated depreciation. The 60-month write-off for the rehabilitation of low-income housing before 1987 also may produce excess depreciation subject to recapture.

The amount of excess depreciation that is subject to recapture (the "applicable percentage") depends on the type of property that is disposed of in the sale, exchange, or other transaction.

Nonresidential Real Property

For real property that is neither residential real property nor low-income housing, the applicable percentage of excess depreciation that is subject to recapture is 100 percent for periods after 1969.[71] There is no recapture of depreciation for excess depreciation attributable to periods before 1970.

Residential Real Property

For residential real property, other than low-income housing, the applicable percentage of excess depreciation that is subject to recapture is 100 percent for periods after 1975.[72] For periods after 1969 and before 1976, the applicable percentage of excess depreciation that is subject to recapture is 100 percent minus one percent for each full month the property was held in excess of 100 months. There is no recapture of depreciation for periods before 1970. Because of the one percent per month reduction in excess depreciation for periods before 1976, anyone now holding property held before 1976 will not be subject to depreciation recapture, although noncorporate taxpayers will be subject to the 25 percent maximum capital gain tax rate rather than the lower rates generally applicable to capital gains other than real property gains.

For periods after 1975, 85 percent of the gross income from the property must be from dwelling units in order for the property to be considered residential

[69] Code Sec. 1250(a)(2)(A).

[70] Code Sec. 1250(b)(1).

[71] Code Sec. 1250(a)(1)(B)(v) and (a)(2)(B)(v).

[72] Code Sec. 1250(a)(1)(B)(v).

property. For periods before 1976, only 80 percent of the gross income had to be from dwelling units to be considered residential property.

Low-Income Housing

Low-income housing includes the following types of property:

1. Federally assisted housing projects, if the mortgage is insured under Sections 221(d)(3) or 236 of the National Housing Act, or housing financed or assisted by a direct loan or tax abatement under similar provisions of state or local laws;[73]
2. Low-income rental housing for which a depreciation deduction for rehabilitation expenditures is allowed;[74]
3. Low-income rental housing held for occupancy by families or individuals who are eligible to receive subsidies under Section 8 of the United States Housing Act of 1937, or under the provisions of state or local laws that authorize similar subsidies for low-income families;[75] and
4. Housing financed or assisted by direct loan or insured under Title V of the Housing Act of 1949.[76]

The applicable percentage of excess depreciation subject to recapture for periods after 1975 for low-income housing is 100 percent minus one percent for each full month the property was held in excess of 100 months.[77] For low-income housing described in categories 2, 3, and 4, above, the applicable percentage for periods after 1969 and before 1976 is 100 percent minus one percent for each full month the property is held over 100 months. For low-income housing in category 4 above, however, the applicable percentage is 100 percent minus one percent for each full month the property was held over 20 full months.[78] There is no recapture for periods before 1970.

Summary of Section 1250 Recapture

The following charts summarize the recapture rules for real property for the periods 1970-1975, 1975-1980, and post-1980, based on the type of property involved and the holding period for the property.

DEPRECIATION AFTER 1969 AND BEFORE 1976

Type of Property	*Holding Period*	*Recapture*
Nonresidential	Not more than 12 months	All depreciation is subject to recapture.
	More than 12 months	All excess depreciation; that is, all depreciation in excess of what would have been allowed under the straight-line method.

[73] Code Sec. 1250(a)(1)(B)(i) and (a)(2)(B)(ii).

[74] Code Sec. 1250(a)(1)(B)(iii) and (a)(1)(B)(iv).

[75] Code Sec. 1250(a)(1)(B)(ii).

[76] Code Sec. 1250(a)(1)(B)(iv).

[77] Code Sec. 1250(a)(1)(B).

[78] Code Sec. 1250(a)(2)(B).

Type of Property	*Holding Period*	*Recapture*
Residential other than low-income housing	Not more than 12 months	All depreciation is subject to recapture.
	More than 12 months but not more than 100 months	All excess depreciation; that is, all depreciation in excess of what would have been allowed under the straight-line method.
	More than 100 months but not more than 200 months	All excess depreciation less 1% per month for each full month property held over 100 months.
	More than 200 months (16 ⅔ years)	No recapture.
Low-income housing with federally insured mortgage or direct loan or tax abatement	Not more than 12 months	All depreciation is subject to recapture.
	More than 12 months but not more than 20 months	All excess depreciation; that is, all depreciation in excess of what would have been allowed under the straight-line method.
	More than 20 months but not more than 120 months	All excess depreciation less 1% per month for each full month property held over 20 months.
	Over 120 months	No recapture.
Other low-income housing	Not more than 12 months	All depreciation is subject to recapture.
	More than 12 months but not more than 100 months	All excess depreciation; that is, all depreciation in excess of what would have been allowed under the straight-line method.
	More than 100 months but not more than 200 months	All excess depreciation less 1% per month for each full month property held over 100 months.
	More than 200 months	No recapture.

DEPRECIATION AFTER 1975 AND BEFORE 1981

Type of Property	*Holding Period*	*Recapture*
Nonresidential and residential other than low-income housing	Not more than 12 months	All depreciation is subject to recapture.
	More than 12 months	All excess depreciation; that is, all depreciation in excess of what would have been allowed under the straight-line method.
Low-income housing	Not more than 12 months	All depreciation is subject to recapture.
	More than 12 months but not more than 100 months	All excess depreciation; that is, all depreciation in excess of what would have been allowed under the straight-line method.
	More than 100 months but not more than 200 months	All excess depreciation less 1% per month for each full month property held over 100 months.
	More than 200 months	No recapture.

DEPRECIATION AFTER 1980

Type of Property	*Holding Period*	*Recapture*
Nonresidential depreciated under the accelerated schedules (Section 1245 property)		All depreciation is subject to recapture.
Residential other than low-income housing	Not more than 12 months	All depreciation is subject to recapture.
	More than 12 months	All excess depreciation; that is, all depreciation in excess of what would have been allowed under the straight-line method.
Low-income rental housing	Not more than 12 months	All depreciation is subject to recapture.
	More than 12 months but not more than 100 months	All excess depreciation; that is, all depreciation in excess of what would have been allowed under the straight-line method.

Type of Property	*Holding Period*	*Recapture*
	More than 100 months but not more than 200 months	All excess depreciation less 1% per month for each full month property held over 100 months.
	More than 200 months	No recapture.
Property located outside the United States	Not more than 12 months	All depreciation is subject to recapture.
	More than 12 months	All excess depreciation; that is, all depreciation in excess of what would have been allowed under the straight-line method.
All real property depreciated on a straight-line basis	Not more than 12 months	All depreciation is subject to recapture.
	More than 12 months	No recapture.

Substantial Improvements

Substantial improvements to Section 1250 property may be treated separately for purposes of determining recapture.[79] To be considered a separate element, the cost of improvements added to the capital account for the property during a 36-month period ending on the last day of a taxable year must exceed the greatest of:

1. 25 percent of the adjusted basis of the property;
2. Ten percent of the original basis of the property, plus the cost of any improvements made prior to the current improvements, less the cost of retired components; or
3. $5,000.

Improvements in any one year are not counted under the rule if they are (a) $2,000 or less, or (b) one percent or less of the basis in 2, above, whichever is greater.

The amount of depreciation subject to recapture when substantial improvements are treated as separate properties is the sum of the recapture amounts applicable to each separate element of the property.

Additional Recapture for Corporations

If a corporation disposes of property subject to Section 1250 recapture, an extra amount must be recaptured as ordinary income in addition to the recapture called for by the Section 1250 rules. Generally, the corporation determines Section 1250 recapture in the normal fashion. To this amount, the corporation adds 20 percent of

[79] Code Sec. 1250(f).

the difference between the normal Section 1250 recapture amount and the amount that the corporation would have had to recapture had the Section 1250 property been Section 1245 property.[80]

> ***Example 6:*** Several years ago, a corporation purchased real property for use in its trade or business. The corporation claimed depreciation deductions on this property in the amount of $50,000 and recently sold this property for $60,000 in excess of its adjusted basis. If the corporation had used straight-line depreciation, its depreciation deductions would have been $32,000 instead of $50,000.
>
> Under Code Sec. 1250, the normal recapture amount for this property is the amount of excess depreciation, or $18,000 ($50,000 - $32,000). To this amount, the corporation must add 20 percent of the difference between the Section 1250 recapture and the amount that would have been recaptured if the property were Section 1245 property. Under Code Sec. 1245, all depreciation to the extent of gain is recaptured, in this case $50,000. The difference between $50,000 and the Section 1250 recapture amount of $18,000 is $32,000. The corporation must add 20 percent of $32,000, or $6,400, to its normal Section 1250 recapture. Total depreciation subject to recapture, therefore, is $24,400 ($18,000 + $6,400).

Rehabilitated Buildings

If certain requirements are met as discussed in Chapter 8, the cost of rehabilitating older commercial buildings and historic structures is eligible for a tax credit. Generally, straight-line depreciation applies to the rehabilitation costs (even for property placed in service before 1987), and the amount of the credit reduces the basis for depreciation. In most cases, straight-line depreciation for real property eliminates future recapture under Code Sec. 1250. This, however, is not the case if the rehabilitation tax credit was taken for the property.

The reduction in adjusted basis as a result of the rehabilitation tax credit is treated as a deduction for depreciation for purposes of the depreciation recapture provisions.[81] Furthermore, in the case of Section 1250 property, recapture applies to deductions in excess of those that would have been allowed under the straight-line method on the basis of the property unreduced by the rehabilitation tax credit.[82] In other words, the tax credit for rehabilitation expenses produces excess depreciation subject to recapture under Code Sec. 1250. Note that if a building is held less than five years following a rehabilitation eligible for a tax credit, some or all of the tax credit is recaptured (see discussion at ¶ 804.03). This credit recapture would increase the basis of the building and also reduce the amount of the basis reduction treated as depreciation for Section 1250 recapture purposes.

.04 Alternative Minimum Tax

The alternative minimum tax (AMT) imposed by Code Sec. 55 is designed to assure that everyone with income pays at least some tax. Although it is not directed

[80] Code Sec. 291(a)(1).

[81] Code Sec. 50(c)(4)(A).

[82] Code Sec. 50(c)(4)(B).

particularly at the owners of real estate, the workings of the alternative minimum tax frequently bring real estate owners within its grasp. The alternative minimum tax applies to individuals and, in the case of tax years beginning before 2018, corporations. Corporations are not subject to the alternative minimum tax in tax years beginning after 2018. There are some differences in the required adjustments and preferences for corporations as compared to other taxpayers. The following discussion is not meant to be a complete exposition of all the intricacies involved in the calculation of the alternative minimum tax. It is meant to bring the possible effects of this tax on the ownership, operation, and sale of real estate to the attention of those taxpayers who might be affected by the tax. Also, while the following discussion generally applies to all taxpayers, some of the preferences and adjustments that apply only to corporations are not considered.

[A] Basic Computation

Essentially, taxpayers must compute their tax liability for the regular tax and the alternative minimum tax. Once this is done, a taxpayer simply pays the higher of the two, although technically it is the difference between the tentative minimum tax and the regular tax that is added to the regular tax if the alternative minimum tax figure is the higher of the two.[83] Taxpayers must consider any possible alternative minimum tax in making estimated tax payments since estimated tax payments are required against the alternative minimum tax as well as the regular income tax.

In order to compute the alternative minimum tax, a taxpayer begins with taxable income, computed in the usual fashion, makes certain adjustments, and then adds tax preferences. This new figure is known as the alternative minimum taxable income.[84] In the case of noncorporate taxpayers, the amount to which the 26 percent rate applies, the exemption amounts, and the exemption phaseout thresholds listed below apply for 2018 through 2025. These amounts are adjusted for inflation for tax years beginning after 2018 and, therefore, may change from one year to the next.

For taxpayers other than corporations, the rate is 26 percent of the first $175,000 ($87,500 in the case of married individuals filing separately) of alternative minimum taxable income in excess of the exemption amount, plus 28 percent of any additional alternative minimum taxable income. In the case of noncorporate taxpayers, the exemption is based on filing status as follows:[85]

Married taxpayers filing a joint return . .	$109,400
Single or head-of-household filers	$70,300
Married taxpayers filing separate returns	$54,700
Estates and trusts	$22,500

For noncorporate taxpayers, the exemption amounts are phased out or reduced as alternative minimum taxable income rises above a certain level. The

[83] Code Sec. 55(a).

[84] Code Sec. 55(b)(2).

[85] Code Sec. 55(d)(1).

exemption is reduced by 25 percent of alternative minimum taxable income in excess of the following amounts, based on filing status:[86]

Married taxpayers filing a joint return . .	$1,000,000
Single or head-of-household filers	$500,000
Married taxpayers filing separate returns	$500,000
Estates and trusts	$75,000

For corporate taxpayers before 2018, a tax rate of 20 percent is applied to alternative minimum taxable income in excess of a $40,000 exemption.[87]

The only tax credit that has been generally allowed against the alternative minimum tax is the alternative minimum tax foreign tax credit.[88]

The amount of general business credit that a taxpayer can claim during a tax year may not exceed the sum of the taxpayer's combined regular tax liability and AMT liability, less nonrefundable personal tax credits, and less the greater of (1) the taxpayer's tentative minimum tax, or (2) 25 percent of the taxpayer's net regular tax liability over $25,000.[89]

Over a period of years, Congress has allowed several specified credits to offset combined regular tax and AMT liability in full, although some may be subject to particular limitations specific to the individual credit. These credits include the alcohol fuels credit, the low-income housing credit, the renewable electricity production credit, the employer cash tip credit, the railroad track maintenance credit, the small employer health insurance credit, employer credit for paid family and medical leave, the rehabilitation credit, the business energy credit, the work opportunity credit, and certain eligible small business credits. The limitation is applied separately for the empowerment zone employment credit, substituting 75 percent of tentative AMT for 100 percent of AMT.[90]

For tax years beginning after December 31, 2011, all nonrefundable personal tax credits are allowed to the full extent of the taxpayer's regular tax and AMT liability. For this purpose, the taxpayer's regular tax liability is first reduced by the amount of any applicable foreign tax credit.[91] The nonrefundable personal tax credits include: the dependent care credit, the credit for the elderly and disabled, the adoption credit, the child tax credit, the credit for interest on home mortgages, the Hope Scholarship and Lifetime Learning credits (including the American Opportunity tax credit), the retirement savings contributions credit, the credit for certain nonbusiness energy property, the credit for residential energy efficient property, the plug-in electric drive motor vehicle credit, the new qualified plug-in electric drive motor vehicle credit, the alternative motor vehicle credit, and the District of Columbia first-time homebuyer credit.

[86] Code Sec. 55(d)(3).

[87] Code Sec. 55(d)(2).

[88] Code Secs. 55(b), 59(a).

[89] Code Sec. 38(c).

[90] Code Sec. 38(c)(4).

[91] Code Sec. 26(a).

To prevent capital gain from aggravating alternative minimum tax problems, Code Sec. 55(b)(3) applies the same preferential rates that apply for regular tax purposes to capital gains realized by noncorporate taxpayers for alternative minimum tax purposes (see ¶ 1301.02[A]).

[B] Small Business Exception

For tax years beginning before 2018, a small business corporation is exempt from the alternative minimum tax if the corporation had average annual gross receipts of $7.5 million or less for all three-tax-year periods before the current year. For the first three-year period, the amount is $5 million.[92] Qualifying corporations with unused minimum tax credits after 1997 that would otherwise be available to offset regular tax in excess of tentative minimum tax, may use the credit to offset 75 percent of regular tax.[93]

All corporations, including small business corporations, are not subject to the alternative minimum tax after 2017.

[C] Adjustments to Taxable Income

Part of the process of going from regular taxable income to alternative minimum taxable income involves making adjustments to the way certain deductions and other items are treated for alternative minimum tax purposes as opposed to the regular tax. To compute alternative minimum taxable income, the following items are treated in the manner indicated.

Depreciation

Depreciation on property placed in service after 1986 and before 1999 must be redetermined using the alternative depreciation system (see Chapter 9) for alternative minimum tax purposes.[94] Generally, the alternative depreciation system provides for smaller deductions through longer depreciation periods and, in the case of personal property, a less accelerated method of calculating deductions. For real property placed in service after 1998, there is no alternative minimum tax adjustment. For personal property placed in service after 1998, the adjustment is still required, but it is computed using regular tax depreciation lives. For property placed in service before 1987, accelerated depreciation (excess of depreciation over the straight-line amount) is a tax preference that is added to alternative minimum taxable income.[95]

Another aspect of depreciation and the alternative minimum tax is that the alternative depreciation system also must be used to calculate the adjusted basis of property for minimum tax purposes.[96] This means that on the sale or exchange of property, the property may have a different adjusted basis for minimum tax purposes than for regular tax purposes and, accordingly, the amount of gain for minimum tax purposes may be different than for regular tax purposes.

[92] Code Sec. 55(e).

[93] Code Sec. 55(e)(5).

[94] Code Sec. 56(a)(1).

[95] Code Sec. 57(a)(6).

[96] Code Sec. 56(a)(6).

Mining Exploration and Development Costs

The deduction for mining exploration and development costs must be redetermined for minimum tax purposes based on the capitalization of these costs and ten-year amortization.[97]

Long-Term Contracts

Income from long-term contracts must be redetermined for minimum tax purposes using the percentage-of-completion method of accounting if the completed-contract method of accounting is used for regular tax purposes.[98]

Net Operating Loss

Any net operating loss deduction must be redetermined using the rules contained in Code Sec. 56(d) to determine the alternative tax net operating loss deduction.[99] The net operating loss cannot offset more than 90 percent of alternative minimum taxable income.

Pollution Control Facilities

Deductions for pollution control facilities placed in service after 1986 must be calculated using the alternative depreciation system for minimum tax purposes.[100] This makes pollution control facilities subject to the same depreciation rules as other property in computing the alternative minimum tax. For property placed in service after 1998, the deduction is determined under Code Sec. 168 using the straight-line method.

Miscellaneous Itemized Deductions

Deductions for miscellaneous itemized expenses (except as noted below) or for state and local taxes are not allowed in computing alternative minimum taxable income.[101] Medical expenses are deductible for alternative minimum tax purposes only to the extent they exceed ten percent of the taxpayer's adjusted gross income (7.5 percent for 2017 and 2018).[102] The deduction for interest is generally allowed to the same extent as for regular tax purposes, but there is a special limitation put on the deduction of interest on a refinanced home mortgage. In this latter case, the interest deduction for alternative minimum tax purposes is limited to the amount of the debt prior to the refinancing.[103]

Circulation Expenditures

Circulation expenditures of periodicals must be amortized over three years for alternative minimum tax purposes.[104]

Research and Experimental Expenditures

R&D expenses must be amortized over ten years for alternative minimum tax purposes, unless the taxpayer materially participates in the R&D activity.[105]

[97] Code Sec. 56(a)(2).
[98] Code Sec. 56(a)(3).
[99] Code Sec. 56(a)(4).
[100] Code Sec. 56(a)(5).
[101] Code Sec. 56(b)(1)(A).
[102] Code Sec. 56(b)(1)(B).
[103] Code Sec. 56(b)(1)(C) and (e).
[104] Code Sec. 56(b)(2)(A)(i).
[105] Code Sec. 56(b)(2)(A)(ii).

Passive Farm Losses

Losses from farming activities in which the taxpayer does not materially participate are generally not allowed in computing alternative minimum taxable income.[106]

Passive Activity Losses

Generally, the passive activity loss rules (see Chapter 11) apply in determining alternative minimum taxable income as well as regular taxable income. The various adjustments for the alternative minimum tax apply.[107] Any deduction that is a tax preference under the minimum tax is not taken into account under the passive loss rules.[108]

[D] Tax Preferences

After a taxpayer makes the adjustments listed above to regular taxable income, tax preferences are added to arrive at alternative minimum taxable income. Tax preferences for noncorporate taxpayers include the following items:

Depletion

Percentage depletion in excess of the basis of the property at the end of the year is a tax preference.[109]

Intangible Drilling Costs

The tax preference for intangible drilling costs is the amount by which the deduction for such costs on successful wells exceeds the amount that could be deducted if the costs were amortized over ten years, but only to the extent that this amount exceeds 65 percent of the taxpayer's net income from oil, gas, and geothermal wells for the year.[110]

Tax-Exempt Interest

The interest on certain private activity bonds issued after August 7, 1986, which continues to be exempt from regular tax, is a tax preference for minimum tax purposes.[111] Private activity bonds are bonds issued by government for nonessential functions.

Small Business Stock Gain

Seven percent of gain from the sale of small business stock that is excluded from income under Code Sec. 1202 is a tax preference.[112]

Accelerated Depreciation

The excess of accelerated depreciation, including the amortization of certified pollution control facilities, over the straight-line amount for property placed in service before 1987 is a tax preference.[113]

---

106 Code Sec. 58(a).
107 Code Sec. 58(b)(1).
108 Code Sec. 58(b)(2).
109 Code Sec. 57(a)(1).
110 Code Sec. 57(a)(2).
111 Code Sec. 57(a)(5).
112 Code Sec. 55(a)(7).
113 Code Sec. 57(a)(6).

[E] Optional Ten-Year Writeoff

Taxpayers may elect to amortize certain costs in order to avoid adjustments or preferences for alternative minimum tax purposes.[114] Generally, if the following are amortized over ten years, they are not considered in computing alternative minimum taxable income:

1. Research and experimental expenditures;
2. Intangible drilling costs;
3. Mine exploration expenses; and
4. Mine development expenses.

Circulation expenditures that are amortized over three years do not enter into the alternative minimum taxable income calculation.[115] Also, the adjustment for depreciation on property placed in service after 1986 is avoided if the alternative depreciation system is used for regular tax purposes.

[F] Alternative Minimum Tax Credit

In order to prevent the double taxation of certain amounts that may show up in alternative minimum taxable income in one year and in regular taxable income in another year, the alternative minimum tax paid may be used as a tax credit against regular tax, but not alternative minimum tax, in future years.[116] The credit is allowed to the extent that alternative minimum tax results from "deferral" preferences and adjustments. Only alternative minimum tax that results from "exclusion" preferences and adjustments may not be used to offset future regular tax in excess of alternative minimum tax. The exclusion preferences and adjustments include:

1. Individual itemized deductions;
2. Depletion;
3. Tax-exempt interest; and
4. Exclusion for gain on small business stocks.[117]

Corporate Minimum Tax Credit Refundable

The corporate minimum tax was repealed for tax years beginning after 2017. A corporation's tentative minimum tax is zero ($0) for purposes of the minimum tax credit beginning in 2018. As a result, a minimum tax credit claimed by a corporation after 2017 is generally limited to the taxpayer's regular tax liability, reduced by other nonrefundable credits. The minimum tax credit is the corporation's AMT liability from tax years prior to its repeal and carried over to tax years after 2017. Any minimum tax credit carryover from a C corporation tax year may continue to offset the built-in gain tax of an S corporation until tax years beginning after December 31, 2021.

Any unused minimum tax credit is refundable for tax years beginning in 2018, 2019, 2020, and 2021. The refundable credit amount is equal to 50 percent (100 percent for tax years beginning in 2021) of the excess of the minimum tax credit for

[114] Code Sec. 59(e).

[115] Code Sec. 59(e)(1).

[116] Code Sec. 53.

[117] Code Sec. 53(d).

the tax year, over the amount allowable for the year against regular tax liability. This means that any minimum tax credit carried over from years before repeal will be allowed in full by 2022. If a corporation has a short tax year, then the refundable credit amount for that year is prorated based on the number of days in the short year compared to 365 days.

The annual election provided to corporations to claim unused minimum tax credits in place of bonus depreciation on property placed in service during the tax year of the election does not apply for tax years beginning after December 31, 2017.

¶ 1302 TAX-FREE EXCHANGE OF PROPERTY

Under the general rules of Code Secs. 1001 and 1002, an exchange of one parcel of real estate for another parcel of real estate is taxable to the same extent as a cash sale. The fair market value of the property received in the exchange is the "amount realized," and the difference between this figure and the adjusted basis of the property given up is the amount of gain or loss realized.

The Internal Revenue Code, however, recognizes that when a taxpayer gives up property in exchange for similar property, the taxpayer has not effectively "realized" a profit on the transaction. Rather, the exchange of similar properties actually represents a continued investment on the part of the taxpayer, and it is inappropriate to impose a tax at this point. Practical considerations also may have played a part in Congress's decision to exempt various exchange transactions from current taxation. From an administrative standpoint, it may be difficult to value property that is exchanged solely or primarily for similar property. Even more importantly, in a pure exchange of one property for another, no cash is generated with which to pay a tax. Accordingly, Code Sec. 1031(a)(1) provides that:

> No gain or loss shall be recognized on the exchange of real property held for productive use in a trade or business or for investment if such real property is exchanged solely for real property of like kind which is to be held either for productive use in a trade or business or for investment.

The tax consequences from any potential gain or loss on property, however, are not completely avoided. The nonrecognition rule is coupled with a basis rule in Code Sec. 1031(d) that preserves any unrecognized gain or loss in the adjusted basis of the replacement property. A future taxable disposition of the replacement property ultimately results in the recognition of this previously unrecognized gain or loss.

The nonrecognition rule of Code Sec. 1031, as noted, applies to losses as well as to gains. Moreover, the nonrecognition provisions are not elective. If the requirements are met, Code Sec. 1031 applies. In cases where there is a potential loss on real estate, it may be better to sell the property, recognize the loss, and use the proceeds to purchase replacement property.

.01 Like-Kind Exchange Requirements

Prior to 2018, the like-kind exchange rules generally applied to all tangible property used in a trade or business, not just to real property. After 2017, the requirements for a tax-free exchange of real property under Code Sec. 1031 remain largely unchanged from those in effect before 2018. In order for an exchange of properties to qualify as a tax-free like-kind exchange under Code Sec. 1031, six basic requirements or conditions must be satisfied:

1. The property received and the property given up in the exchange must be business or investment property.

Business property may be exchanged for investment property or investment property for business property.[118] The use of either the property given up or the property received for personal purposes takes the transaction out of the like-kind exchange provisions and results in current taxation. For instance, the exchange of business or investment property for property that will be used as a personal residence does not qualify as a tax-free exchange.[119]

2. The property must not be property held for sale.

Neither the property received nor the property given up in the exchange may be property that is sold to customers.[120] Real estate that dealers hold for sale to customers does not qualify for like-kind exchange treatment.[121] A corporation engaged in the business of real estate development and sale was not entitled to nonrecognition of gain on the exchange of an orange grove for grazing land when the grazing land was held primarily for sale rather than for investment.[122]

3. There must be an exchange of like property.

An exchange occurs when there is a reciprocal transfer of property, as distinguished from a transfer of property for money consideration only.[123] The transfer of money along with qualifying property, however, does not completely disqualify the exchange. Money received in addition to like-kind property results in the recognition of gain, but only to the extent of the money received.[124] Also, a transaction that appears to be an "exchange" may, in fact, be a sale. For instance, a company transferred its old plant to a contractor, who accepted the property to apply to the construction cost of a new building for the company. The contractor did not own the land on which the building was constructed, nor did the contractor own the building he was constructing. In this situation, the contractor was not exchanging property that he owned, and the transaction was a sale with the old plant serving as part of the consideration.[125]

4. Prior to 2018, the property must be tangible property.

This requirement is not a problem in the case of real estate, which is tangible property. Code Sec. 1031(a)(2), as in effect before 2018, specifically excludes the following from the like-kind exchange provision: (a) stocks, bonds, and notes, (b) other securities and evidences of indebtedness or interest, (c) interests in a partnership, (d) certificates of trust and beneficial interest, and (e) choses in action.

[118] Reg. § 1.1031(a)-1(a).

[119] D.H. Click, 78 TC 225, CCH Dec. 38,790.

[120] Code Sec. 1031(a)(2).

[121] California Delta Farms, Inc., 6 BTA 1301, CCH Dec. 2455, *acq.* 1928-1 CB 5.

[122] Land Dynamics, 37 TCM 1119, CCH Dec. 35,263(M), T.C. Memo. 1978-259.

[123] Reg. § 1.1002-1(d).

[124] Code Sec. 1031(b). *See* the discussion of partially tax-free exchanges at ¶ 1302.02.

[125] Bloomington Coca-Cola Bottling Co., CA-7, 51-1 USTC ¶ 9320, 189 F.2d 14.

5. The property to be exchanged must be identified within 45 days.

Property to be received in a like-kind exchange must be identified on or before the day which is 45 days after the date on which the taxpayer transfers the property given up in the exchange.[126] This identification requirement may be met by designating the property in the contract between the parties. The requirement is also met if the contract specifies a limited number of properties that may be transferred and the particular property to be transferred is determined by contingencies beyond the control of both parties. For instance, if A transferred real estate in exchange for a promise by B to transfer Property #1 to A if zoning changes were approved and Property #2 if they were not, the exchange would qualify for like-kind treatment, provided the other requirements were met.

6. There must be a completed transaction.

Property to be received in a tax-free like-kind exchange must be received on or before the earlier of (a) the 180th day after the date on which the taxpayer transfers the property given up, and (b) the due date, including extensions, for the taxpayer's return for the tax year in which the transfer of the property given up occurs.[127]

[A] Like-Kind Real Estate Defined

The tax-free exchange provision of Code Sec. 1031 applies only to exchanges of properties that are of a "like kind." Like kind refers to the nature or character of the property, not to its grade or quality. That real estate involved in an exchange is improved or unimproved is not material because that relates only to the grade or quality of the property, to its kind or class.[128] Real property in the United States and foreign real property are not like-kind.[129]

Whether property is new or used does not affect a like-kind exchange. The distinction between new and used property is one of grade or quality, not one of kind. City real estate may be exchanged tax-free for a farm or ranch. A leasehold with 30 years or more to run may be exchanged for a fee interest in real estate.[130]

The Tax Court has listed several factors to consider in determining whether property is of a like kind:

1. Respective interests in the physical properties;
2. Nature of title conveyed;
3. Rights of the parties;
4. Duration of the interests; and
5. Any other factor bearing on the nature or character of the properties as distinguished from their grade or quality.

Applying these factors and pointing out that "like kind" does not mean "identical," the Court held that taxpayers who exchanged fee interests in unimproved real estate for the fee interest in improved property were entitled to like-kind exchange

[126] Code Sec. 1031(a)(3)(A).

[127] Code Sec. 1031(a)(3)(B).

[128] Reg. § 1.1031(a)-1(b).

[129] Code Sec. 1031(h).

[130] Reg. § 1.1031(a)-1(c).

treatment, even though the property they received was subject to a long-term lease.[131]

Mineral rights are interests in real property, and the transfer of an undivided interest in oil, gas and other minerals for an undivided interest in a city lot is a nontaxable exchange.[132] The IRS has ruled that an exchange of a producing oil lease extending until exhaustion of the deposit for a fee interest in an improved ranch is a like-kind exchange.[133] Similarly, if water rights are considered real property rights under state law, the exchange of water rights for a fee interest in land may qualify as a like-kind exchange.[134]

The exchange of leaseholds may qualify for like-kind exchange treatment.[135] However, the transfer of a lot for the execution of a leasehold interest in the lot and in other properties was not a like-kind exchange on the part of the transferee-lessor, although it was for the transferor-lessee. The lot received by the transferee-lessor was an advance rental.[136]

An exchange of one remainder interest in real property for a remainder interest in another parcel of real property qualifies as a like-kind exchange.[137] The exchange of a life estate in real property owned by a son for a remainder interest in real property owned by his 70-year-old father, however, was ruled not to be a like-kind exchange.[138]

In a private letter ruling,[139] the IRS has approved like-kind treatment for an investor-shareholder's exchange of stock in a cooperative for a condominium interest. Although stock is explicitly excluded from the like-kind exchange rules under Code Sec. 1031(a)(2)(B), the IRS noted that the investor-shareholder in a cooperative was in a unique position that called for different treatment than the normal shareholder in a corporation. In the ruling, the IRS pointed to the regulation (Reg. § 1.1031(a)-1(c)) that treats a leasehold interest with 30 years or more to run as an interest in real estate (the lease on the cooperative had 92 years to run). Also, the investor-shareholder's interest was characterized as real estate under the laws of California, where the cooperative was located.

The exchanging taxpayer must hold both the property transferred and the property received for business or investment use in order for the nonrecognition provision to apply. Accordingly, the IRS has ruled that when an individual exchanged land and buildings used in a business for land and an office building and immediately thereafter, in a prearranged plan, transferred the land and office building to a newly created corporation, there was no like-kind exchange.[140] Similarly, the IRS has also ruled that an individual's prearranged transfer of a shopping center, received from the liquidation of the individual's wholly owned corporation

---

[131] C.E. Koch, 71 TC 54, CCH Dec. 34,062, *acq.* 1980-2 CB 1.

[132] W. Fleming v. Campfield, CA-5, 53-2 USTC ¶ 9469, 205 F.2d 549.

[133] Rev. Rul. 68-331, 1969-2 CB 352.

[134] Rev. Rul. 55-749, 1955-2 CB 295; *see also* PLR 200404044.

[135] Rev. Rul. 76-301, 1976-2 CB 241.

[136] Rev. Rul. 66-209, 1966-2 CB 299.

[137] Rev. Rul. 78-4, 1978-1 CB 256.

[138] Rev. Rul. 72-601, 1972-2 CB 467.

[139] Ltr. Rul. 8810034, December 10, 1987.

[140] Rev. Rul. 75-292, 1975-2 CB 333.

and immediately exchanged for like-kind property held by an unrelated party, did qualify for nonrecognition of gain or loss under Code Sec. 1031.[141]

The Tax Court and the Ninth Circuit Court of Appeals, however, have disagreed with Rev. Rul. 77-337. These courts have held that an exchange of real property which was acquired as a corporate liquidating distribution for three parcels of realty qualified for nonrecognition of gain as a like-kind exchange of property "held for investment," even though the exchange was contemplated before the liquidating distribution occurred. The realty received as a liquidating distribution did not have to be held, even briefly, with the intention of keeping it indefinitely in order to qualify as being "held for investment." The requirement that the property be held for investment was satisfied because the property was not acquired with the intention of liquidating it or using it for personal pursuits.[142]

Related Parties

If a taxpayer exchanges property with a related party (as defined in Code Sec. 267, relating to disallowed losses as discussed at ¶ 1301.01[C]) and the taxpayer would otherwise be eligible for nonrecognition treatment under Code Sec. 1031, the exchange does not qualify for nonrecognition if either the related party disposes of the property received or the taxpayer disposes of the like-kind property within two years of the exchange.[143] This related party rule generally applies to exchanges after July 10, 1989. Any gain or loss not recognized by the taxpayer as of the date of the original exchange is recognized as of the date of the subsequent disposition, subject to the disallowed loss rules of Code Sec. 267. Adjustments to the basis of the properties involved in the exchange also are made as of the date of the subsequent disposition.

A disposition of the property exchanged by related parties does not invalidate the nonrecognition treatment of the original exchange if the subsequent disposition is due to the death of either party or the involuntary conversion of the property, provided that the original exchange occurred before the threat or imminence of the conversion.[144] A disposition also does not invalidate the nonrecognition treatment of the original exchange if it is established that neither the exchange nor the subsequent disposition had as one of its principal purposes the avoidance of Federal income tax.[145] According to the Senate Committee Report on the Revenue Reconciliation Act of 1989, it is intended that the non-tax avoidance exception generally will apply to the following:

1. Transactions involving an exchange of undivided interests in different properties that results in each taxpayer's holding the entire interest in a single property or a larger undivided interest in any of the properties;
2. Dispositions of property in nonrecognition transactions; and
3. Transactions that do not involve the shifting of basis between properties.

---

[141] Rev. Rul. 77-337, 1977-2 CB 305.

[142] J.R. Bolker, CA-9, 85-1 USTC ¶ 9400, 760 F.2d 1039, *aff'g* 81 TC 782, CCH Dec. 40,558.

[143] Code Sec. 1031(f)(1).

[144] Code Sec. 1031(f)(2).

[145] Code Sec. 1031(f)(2)(C).

A disposition includes indirect dispositions of the property, such as by means of the disposition of the stock of a corporation or interests in a partnership that owns the property.

Nonrecognition of gain or loss under Code Sec. 1031 is not available for any exchange which is part of a transaction or series of transactions structured to avoid the purpose of the related party rules.[146] For example, if a taxpayer, under a prearranged plan, transfers property to an unrelated party who then exchanges the property with a party related to the taxpayer within two years of the previous transfer in a transaction otherwise qualifying under Code Sec. 1031, the related party will not be entitled to nonrecognition treatment under Code Sec. 1031.

The IRS has ruled that a taxpayer who transfers property to a qualified intermediary in exchange for replacement property formerly owned by a related party is not entitled to nonrecognition treatment under Code Sec. 1031 if, as part of the transaction, the related party receives cash or other non-like-kind property for the replacement property.[147] The facts of the ruling involved an individual who owned high value, low basis property and a related party with high value, high basis property. The individual transferred the low basis property to a qualified intermediary who sold the property to another. The intermediary then acquired the high basis property from the related party for cash and transferred the high basis property to the individual as replacement property.

The Tax Court has reached a similar conclusion under similar facts.[148] The court inferred that the qualified intermediary was interposed in an attempt to circumvent the related party limitations that would have applied to exchanges directly between related persons. The court concluded that the transactions were structured to avoid the purposes of the related party rules and, consequently, the transferor could not take advantage of the nonrecognition rules of Code Sec. 1031.

Delayed Exchanges

The requirement that property to be exchanged be identified within 45 days and that the exchange be completed within 180 days were added to the like-kind exchange requirements in 1984. Prior to that, delayed or nonsimultaneous exchanges were possible, although they did risk challenge from the IRS. In *T.J. Starker*,[149] however, the court held that an exchange qualified for like-kind treatment, even though the property to be exchanged could be designated by the transferor for up to five years after the transaction and even though the transferor could have ultimately received cash rather than like-kind property if suitable property could not be found to complete the exchange. It was in response to *Starker* that Congress enacted the 45-day identification requirement and 180-day completed transaction requirement for like-kind exchanges.

Of course, nonsimultaneous exchanges remain possible within the confines of the identification and completed transaction time limits. Generally, the contract

---

146 Code Sec. 1031(f)(4).

147 Rev. Rul. 2002-83, 2002-49 IRB 927.

148 Teruya Brothers, Ltd., 124 TC No. 4; *see also* The Malulani Group, Limited, 112 TCM 530, T.C. Memo. 2016-209.

149 CA-9, 79-2 USTC ¶ 9541, 602 F.2d 1341.

between a seller who wants like-kind treatment and a purchaser will provide that the purchaser is to deliver the purchase price to the owner of the property that is desired by the seller and that the owner of that property will convey it to the seller (a form of a multi-party exchange, see ¶ 1302.03). If suitable property cannot be found within the time limits, the purchase price is delivered to the seller and the transaction becomes a taxable sale. The contract to pay cash if suitable exchange property cannot be located within the necessary time limits does not destroy a tax-free exchange if suitable property is found.

On a delayed exchange, the taxpayer must of course take care that any security arrangement not result in the actual or constructive receipt of cash that is then used to purchase replacement property. That would destroy the like-kind exchange. The IRS has provided four safe harbors to secure a delayed exchange that will not result in actual or constructive receipt of money or other property for purposes of Code Sec. 1031.[150] More than one safe harbor can be used in the same deferred exchange, but the terms and conditions of each must be separately satisfied. The safe harbors spelled out in the regulations are:

1. Security or guarantee arrangements by which the taxpayer's right to receive the replacement property is secured by a mortgage, deed of trust, or other security interest in property (other than cash or a cash equivalent), a standby letter of credit, or guarantee of a third party.
2. Escrow accounts and trusts by which the transfer of the replacement property to the taxpayer is secured by cash or a cash equivalent if the cash or cash equivalent is held in a qualified escrow account or in a qualified trust as spelled out in the regulations.
3. Qualified intermediaries if the intermediary is not the agent of the taxpayer.
4. Interest or growth factors may be paid to the taxpayer for the time the exchange is delayed.

Suppose, however, that the prospective parties to a like-kind exchange need more time than that provided by the identification and completed transaction requirements. Is it possible to have the equivalent of an exchange that exceeds the time limits yet still qualifies as a tax-free exchange?

The IRS has ruled on the tax consequences of an option to purchase real property that permitted the option price to be paid in either cash or other real property. When the option was ultimately exercised by the purchaser by acquiring property equal in value to the option price and transferring that property to the seller, the seller was given tax-free like-kind exchange treatment on the exercise of the option by the purchaser.[151] Only the cash originally received for the option was taxable.

While a simple option does permit a delayed like-kind exchange, what if the purchaser wants immediate possession of the property? In this case, it may be possible for the seller, who wants to achieve a like-kind exchange, to lease the

[150] Reg. § 1.1031(k)-1(g).

[151] Rev. Rul. 84-121, 1984-2 CB 168.

property to the purchaser in connection with the purchase option. Under this strategy, the purchaser receives immediate use of the property to be given up by the seller in the exchange but does not have to find suitable replacement property until it is time to exercise the option. The danger in this strategy is that the IRS may insist that when the purchaser takes possession under the lease a "transfer" has occurred that triggers the running of the 45-day and 180-day requirements for a like-kind exchange. Retention of ownership by the seller and a contract that does not actually bind the purchaser to purchase the property until the option is exercised may minimize the danger of such an IRS attack.

Parking Transactions

Parking transactions typically are designed to "park" desired replacement property with an accommodation party until the taxpayer arranges for the transfer of the relinquished property to the ultimate transferee in a simultaneous or deferred exchange. Once the transfer is arranged, the taxpayer transfers the relinquished property to the accommodation party in exchange for the replacement property, and the accommodation party transfers the relinquished property to the ultimate transferee. In other situations, an accommodation party may acquire the desired replacement property on behalf of the taxpayer and immediately exchange that property with the taxpayer for the relinquished property, thereafter holding the relinquished property until the taxpayer arranges for a transfer of the property to the ultimate transferee.

The IRS has provided procedures for qualifying parking transactions as like-kind exchanges when the taxpayer has a genuine intent to accomplish a like-kind exchange at the time that the taxpayer arranges for the acquisition of the replacement property and actually accomplishes the exchange within a short time thereafter. The IRS will not challenge the qualification of property held in a qualified exchange accommodation arrangement (QEAA) as either replacement property or relinquished property, or the treatment of the exchange accommodation titleholder as the beneficial owner of such the property.[152] Taxpayers are not required to establish that the exchange accommodation titleholder bears the economic benefits and burdens of ownership and is the owner of the property. Rev. Proc. 2000-37 does not apply if the taxpayer owns the property intended to qualify as replacement property before initiating a QEAA.[153]

Build-to-Suit Exchange

The owner/seller of property may find a purchaser who is willing to construct new facilities for the seller so that the seller can take advantage of the like-kind exchange provision. The IRS has approved such a build-to-suit arrangement in Rev. Rul. 75-291.[154]

---

[152] Rev. Proc. 2000-37, 2000-2 CB 308.

[153] Rev. Proc. 2004-51, 2004-33 IRB 294. *But see* AOD 2017-6, in which the IRS announced its nonacquiescence to the decision in *Bartell Est.*, 147 TC 140 (2016), "relating to the holding that a taxpayer's sale and acquisition of business property qualifies as a like-kind exchange even though 17 months before the purported exchange, an accommodating party facilitating the transaction acquired title to the replacement property and the taxpayer acquired the benefits and burdens of ownership of the property."

[154] 1975-2 CB 332.

In the ruling, the purchaser wanted to acquire the seller's land and factory, but the seller wanted a tax-free exchange. The parties agreed for the purchaser to buy land and construct a new factory to the seller's specifications. The contract allowed the purchaser to cancel if the cost of buying the replacement land and constructing the new factory exceeded a specified amount. The purchaser ultimately bought land, constructed the factory, and exchanged properties with the seller. The IRS ruled that the transaction qualified as a like-kind exchange for the seller under Code Sec. 1031, even though the property received in the exchange was acquired by the purchaser solely to complete the exchange. The IRS emphasized that the purchaser had to act on the purchaser's own behalf, and not as agent for the seller, in buying the land and constructing the new factory. The purchaser was not eligible for like-kind exchange treatment, however, because the land and factory exchanged were not held for business or investment purposes. In most cases, this would not matter to a prospective purchaser.

[B] Basis Rule

In order to preserve the potential gain or loss when property is exchanged in a like-kind exchange under Code Sec. 1031, the basis of the property acquired in the exchange is the same as the adjusted basis of the property transferred at the time of the exchange.[155] This basis is known as a "substituted basis." A cash payment or the value of other consideration given in connection with a tax-free like-kind exchange is added to the substituted basis of the acquired property.[156]

> ***Example 7:*** The Taxpayer exchanges land and a building worth $100,000, but with an adjusted basis of $60,000, for land worth $100,000. The exchange qualifies for like-kind treatment. The Taxpayer's basis for the land received is $60,000 and the potential gain of $40,000 on the land and building given up is preserved.
>
> If the land received by the Taxpayer was worth $110,000, the Taxpayer may have completed the exchange by paying $10,000 cash in addition to the land and building given up in the exchange. In this case, the Taxpayer's basis for the land received would be $70,000 ($60,000 adjusted basis of the property given up + $10,000 cash paid).

Generally, if a taxpayer receives money or nonqualifying property in an otherwise tax-free like-kind exchange, the taxpayer is taxed on any gain up to the amount of money or other property received (see partially tax-free exchanges, at ¶ 1302.02). In this case, the basis of the acquired property is the adjusted basis of the property given up, decreased by the amount of money or value of other property received and increased by the amount of gain recognized on the exchange.[157] Application of this rule is illustrated at ¶ 1302.02[C] in connection with the discussion of partially tax-free exchanges.

---

[155] Code Sec. 1031(d).

[156] Reg. § 1.1031(d)-1(a).

[157] Code Sec. 1031(d); Reg. § 1.1031(d)-1(b).

[C] Basis Allocation Among Multiple Properties

If more than one property is received in a like-kind exchange, the adjusted basis of the property given up must be allocated among the properties received according to their fair market values on the date of the exchange.[158] When multiple properties are received, appraisals of the fair market values of the properties should be obtained to facilitate this allocation. Allocation of basis also is required when land and a building are acquired in the exchange, since the land and building are two separate properties (see allocation of costs at ¶ 102.02).

Example 8: A corporation exchanges land and buildings with a total adjusted basis of $110,000 ($100,000 is the basis of the land and $10,000 is the basis of the buildings) for two lots, A and B. Each of the lots received has a building on it. The fair market values of these properties received by the corporation are:

Lot A:	
Land	$20,000
Building	80,000
Total	$100,000

Lot B:	
Land	$30,000
Building	120,000
Total	$150,000

The basis of the property given up is allocated to the land and building for each lot received in proportion to its fair market values. Accordingly, 2/5 ($100,000/$250,000) of the $110,000 adjusted basis of the property given up is allocated to property A, and 3/5 ($150,000/$250,000) is allocated to property B:

Property A: 2/5 × $110,000 = $44,000.

Property B: 3/5 × $110,000 = $66,000.

The basis allocated to property A and property B must then be allocated between the land and building. Since the building on lot A represents 4/5 of the total value of A ($80,000/$100,000) and the land represents 1/5 of the total value of A ($20,000/$100,000), 4/5 of the basis allocated to A is allocated to the building and 1/5 to the land:

Building A: 4/5 × $44,000 = $35,200.

Land A: 1/5 × $44,000 = $8,800.

A similar allocation is made between the land ($30,000/$150,000 = 1/5) and building ($120,000/$150,000 = 4/5) located on lot B based on their relative fair market values:

[158] Rev. Rul. 68-36, 1968-1 CB 357.

Building B: 4/5 × $66,000 = $52,800.

Land B: 1/5 × $66,000 = $13,200.

The basis to the corporation for the two acquired properties is, therefore, $44,000 for lot A (with $8,800 allocated to the land and $35,200 allocated to the building) and $66,000 for lot B (with $13,200 allocated to the land and $52,800 allocated to the building).

[D] Exchange as Part of Business Acquisition

Under Code Sec. 1060, the purchase price of assets, including real estate, that constitute a trade or business generally must be allocated for tax purposes using the residual method (see ¶ 102.02[D]). However, like-kind property and other property or money that are treated as transferred in exchange for like-kind property under Code Sec. 1031 are excluded from the allocation rules of section 1060 when the properties exchanged are part of a group of assets that constitute a trade or business under section 1060. Code Sec. 1060 does apply to property that is not like-kind property or other property or money treated as transferred in exchange for the like-kind property.[159] For an example, see Reg. § 1.1060-1(d).

.02 Partially Tax-Free Exchanges

It is the rare exchange of properties that does not require some payment or other consideration to equalize the values of the properties. An exchange of real estate is only partially tax free for the party who receives money or other property, often called "boot," in addition to the like-kind property. The tax-free status of an exchange is not affected by the giving of boot, only by its receipt.[160] While the receipt of boot will trigger the recognition of gain, the receipt of boot does not permit the recognition of any loss realized on the exchange.[161]

[A] Other Property or Money

The receipt of money or other unlike property, in addition to property that may be received tax free in a like-kind exchange, is taxable to the party receiving it if the recipient realizes a gain on the exchange. The recipient of the boot pays a tax on gain, but only to the extent of the money and fair market value of the other property received.[162]

Example 9: The Taxpayer, who is not a dealer in real estate, exchanges real property held for investment, which was acquired several years before and which has a basis of $50,000, for other real estate to be used in a trade or business and $20,000 in cash. The value of the real estate received is $60,000. The Taxpayer's amount realized is $80,000 ($20,000 cash plus $60,000 like-kind property). The Taxpayer's gain from the transaction is, therefore, $30,000 ($80,000 amount realized less $50,000 basis), but the gain is recognized only to the extent of the cash received of $20,000.[163]

[159] Reg. § 1.1031(d)-1T.

[160] Reg. § 1.1031(a)-1(c).

[161] Code Sec. 1031(c).

[162] Code Sec. 1031(b); Reg. § 1.1031(b)-1(a).

[163] Reg. § 1.1031(b)-1(b).

The disposition of property in a like-kind exchange transaction is subject to the depreciation recapture provisions as discussed at ¶ 1301.03. However, income results from the recapture of depreciation on a like-kind exchange only to the extent gain is otherwise recognized[164] or if the amount of recapture on the property exchanged exceeds the value of the depreciable property received.[165]

Gain recognized in a like-kind exchange may be reported on the installment method if the transaction otherwise qualifies as an installment sale.[166]

[B] Mortgages and Other Liabilities

The assumption of liabilities by the other party to the exchange, or the other party's acquisition of property subject to a liability, is treated as money received by the taxpayer on the exchange.[167] It does not matter whether the taxpayer is personally liable for the debt or whether the other party actually assumes the debt.[168] An individual who made a like-kind exchange of investment real property for other investment real property, cash, and the transferee's assumption of a liability on the transferred property was required to recognize gain to the extent of the cash received and the liability assumed.[169]

> ***Example 10:*** Individual B owns an apartment house which has an adjusted basis in B's hands of $500,000, but which is subject to a mortgage of $150,000. B transfers the apartment house to individual C in exchange for $50,000 in cash and another apartment house with a fair market value on the date of the transfer of $600,000. The transfer to C is subject to the $150,000 mortgage. B realizes a gain of $300,000 on the exchange, computed as follows:

Value of property received	$600,000
Cash	50,000
Liabilities transferred	150,000
Amount realized	$800,000
Less: Basis of property transferred	500,000
Gain realized	$300,000

> Under Code Sec. 1031(b), B's recognized gain is limited to $200,000 of the $300,000 total gain. This is the amount of boot received by taxpayer, consisting of the $50,000 cash and the $150,000 of mortgage debt to which the transferred property was subject.

When a taxpayer exchanges mortgaged property for other mortgaged property and each party to the exchange assumes the mortgage of the other, a balancing of the liabilities takes place.[170] Only the net reduction of the taxpayer's mortgage debt, if any, is treated as money received. According to the regulations:

---

[164] Code Sec. 1250(d)(4)(A)(i).

[165] Code Sec. 1250(d)(4)(C).

[166] Rev. Rul. 65-155, 1965-1 CB 356. *See* the discussion of installment reporting at ¶ 1401.02.

[167] Code Sec. 1031(d); Reg. § 1.1031(b)-1(c).

[168] G.P. Allen, 10 TC 413, CCH Dec. 16,288.

[169] D.W. Westall, 56 TCM 66, CCH Dec. 45,040(M), T.C. Memo. 1988-421.

[170] Rev. Rul. 59-229, 1959-2 CB 180.

> Where, on an exchange described in section 1031(b), each party to the exchange either assumes a liability of the other party or acquires property subject to a liability, then, in determining the amount of "other property or money" for purposes of section 1031(b), consideration given in the form of an assumption of liabilities (or a receipt of property subject to a liability) shall be offset against consideration received in the form of an assumption of liabilities (or a transfer subject to a liability).[171]

Example 11: D, an individual, owns an apartment house with an adjusted basis in D's hands of $100,000. The fair market value of this apartment house is $220,000, but it is subject to a mortgage of $80,000. D transfers the apartment house to E, also an individual, in exchange for $40,000 in cash and another apartment house. The apartment house owned by E before the exchange has an adjusted basis in E's hands of $175,000 and a fair market value of $250,000, but it is subject to a mortgage of $150,000. As part of the exchange, each apartment house is transferred subject to the mortgage on it.

D realizes a gain of $120,000 on the exchange, computed as follows:

Value of property received	$250,000
Cash	40,000
Liabilities transferred	80,000
Amount realized	$370,000
Less: Basis of property transferred	100,000
	$270,000
Less: Liabilities received	150,000
Gain realized	$120,000

For purposes of Code Sec. 1031(b), the amount of "other property or money" received by D is $40,000. Consideration received by D in the form of a transfer subject to a liability of $80,000 is offset by consideration given in the form of a receipt of property subject to a $150,000 liability. Accordingly, only the consideration received in the form cash, $40,000, is treated as boot, and D recognizes only $40,000 of the $120,000 gain.

As for the other side of the exchange, E realizes a gain of $75,000 on the exchange, computed as follows:

Value of property received	$220,000
Liabilities transferred	150,000
Amount realized	$370,000
Less: Basis of property transferred	175,000
	$195,000

[171] Reg. § 1.1031(b)-1(c).

Less: Cash paid	40,000
	$155,000
Less: Liabilities received	80,000
Gain realized	$75,000

For purposes of Code Sec. 1031(b), the amount of "other property or money" received by E is $30,000. Consideration received by E in the form of a transfer subject to a liability of $150,000 is offset by consideration given in the form of a receipt of property subject to an $80,000 liability and by the $40,000 cash paid by E. Although consideration received in the form of cash or other property is not offset by consideration given in the form of an assumption of liabilities or a receipt of property subject to a liability, consideration given in the form of cash or other property is offset against consideration received in the form of an assumption of liabilities or a transfer of property subject to a liability. Accordingly, E recognizes only $30,000 of the total gain of $75,000.

[C] Basis in Partially Tax-Free Exchanges

The application of the substituted basis rule to a like-kind exchange is complicated by adjustments when the exchange is only partially tax free, or if a loss is recognized because unlike property is transferred in the exchange along with the like-kind property.

When boot is received in a like-kind exchange, the basis of the like-kind property acquired is the basis of the property transferred, decreased by the amount of money received and increased by the amount of gain recognized on the exchange.[172] The basis of the "other" or unlike property received in an otherwise tax-free exchange is its fair market value on the date of the exchange.[173]

Example 12: The Taxpayer trades an apartment building worth $230,000 for another apartment building worth $190,000 and $15,000 in cash and stock with a fair market value of $25,000. The Taxpayer's adjusted basis at the time of the exchange for the building being given up is $150,000. The Taxpayer realizes a gain on the exchange of $80,000, but only $40,000 (the amount of boot received) is recognized. The Taxpayer's basis for the property received in the exchange is computed as follows:

Basis of property given up	$150,000
Less: Money received	15,000
	$135,000
Plus: Gain recognized	40,000
	$175,000
Less: Basis of stock (fair market value)	25,000
Basis of property received	$150,000

172 Code Sec. 1031(d); Reg. § 1.1031(d)-1(b).

173 Reg. § 1.1031(d)-1(c).

If a loss is recognized on a partially tax-free exchange because the taxpayer transfers unlike property to the other party to the exchange, the recognized loss decreases the basis of the property received in the exchange. The amount received for the other property given up is considered to be its fair market value on the date of the exchange.[174]

> ***Example 13:*** The Taxpayer exchanges a building with an adjusted basis of $150,000 and equipment worth $20,000 (but with a basis of $30,000) for land worth $170,000. The Taxpayer's $10,000 loss is recognized because the loss is on "unlike" property. The Taxpayer's basis for the land received is $170,000, that is, the basis of the properties transferred ($150,000 building + $30,000 equipment = $180,000) - the $10,000 loss recognized.

The amount of any liabilities of the taxpayer assumed by the other party to the exchange, or of any liabilities to which the property exchanged by the taxpayer is subject, is treated as money received by the taxpayer on the exchange. The amount of the liability, therefore, decreases the basis of the property acquired by the taxpayer.[175] The following examples illustrate these rules and are continuations of the examples set out above illustrating the effect of mortgages on the amount of gain recognized.

> ***Example 14:*** Individual B owns an apartment house which has an adjusted basis in B's hands of $500,000, but which is subject to a mortgage of $150,000. B transfers the apartment house to individual C in exchange for $50,000 in cash and another apartment house with a fair market value on the date of the transfer of $600,000. The transfer to C is subject to the $150,000 mortgage. B realizes a gain of $300,000 on the exchange, but the recognized gain is limited to $200,000. The basis of the apartment house acquired by B is $500,000, computed as follows:

Basis of property transferred	$500,000
Less: Cash received	50,000
	$450,000
Less: Liabilities transferred	150,000
	$300,000
Plus: Gain recognized	200,000
Basis of property acquired	$500,000

If both the property given up and the property received in a like-kind exchange are subject to liabilities, a balancing or netting of the liabilities is permitted. If the mortgage or liability on the property received is at least as much as the liability on the property transferred, there is no "money" received for purposes of determining the basis of the property received.[176]

---

[174] Reg. § 1.1031(d)-1(e).

[175] Code Sec. 1031(d); Reg. § 1.1031(d)-2.

[176] Rev. Rul. 59-229, 1959-2 CB 180; Reg. § 1.1031(d)-2.

Example 15: D, an individual, owns an apartment house with an adjusted basis in the individual's hands of $100,000. The fair market value of this apartment house is $220,000, but it is subject to a mortgage of $80,000. D transfers the apartment house to E, also an individual, in exchange for $40,000 in cash and another apartment house. The apartment house owned by E before the exchange has an adjusted basis in E's hands of $175,000, a fair market value of $250,000, but it is subject to a mortgage of $150,000. As part of the exchange, each apartment house is transferred subject to the mortgage on it.

D realizes a gain of $120,000 on the exchange, but recognizes only $40,000 of the gain. The basis of the apartment house acquired by D is $170,000, computed as follows:

Basis of property transferred	$100,000
Liabilities received	150,000
	$250,000
Less: Money received	40,000
	$210,000
Less: Liabilities transferred	80,000
	$130,000
Plus: Gain recognized	40,000
Basis of property acquired	$170,000

As for the other side of the exchange, E realizes a gain of $75,000 on the exchange, but recognizes only $30,000 of the gain. The basis of the apartment house acquired by E is $175,000, computed as follows:

Basis of property transferred	$175,000
Money paid	40,000
Liabilities received	80,000
	$295,000
Less: Liabilities transferred	150,000
	$145,000
Plus: Gain recognized	30,000
Basis of property acquired	$175,000

[D] Commissions and Other Expenses

Money paid in connection with a like-kind exchange for commissions, legal fees, and similar expenses is offset against money received in computing realized and recognized gain, and is added in determining the basis of property received.[177]

[177] Rev. Rul. 72-456, 1972-2 CB 468.

The following examples taken from Rev. Rul. 72-456 illustrate the effect of commissions on realized gain and basis of property received in connection with like-kind exchanges.

Example 16: The Taxpayer exchanged investment real estate with an adjusted basis of $120,000 for investment real estate with a fair market value of $200,000 and $100,000 in cash. The Taxpayer paid commissions and fees of $20,000 in connection with the exchange.

Received:	
Land—F.M.V.	$200,000
Cash	100,000
	$300,000
Less: Commissions and fees	20,000
Amount realized	$280,000
Given up:	
Land—basis	120,000
Realized gain (loss)	$160,000
Recognized gain (lesser of realized gain or net cash received)	$80,000
Basis:	
Land given up—basis	$120,000
Less: Cash received	100,000
Plus: Recognized gain	80,000
Plus: Commissions and fees	20,000
Basis of land received	$120,000

Example 17: The Taxpayer exchanged investment real estate with an adjusted basis of $295,000 for investment real estate with a fair market value of $200,000 and $100,000 in cash. The Taxpayer paid commissions and fees of $20,000 in connection with the exchange.

Received:	
Land—F.M.V.	$200,000
Cash	100,000
	$300,000
Less: Commissions and fees	20,000
Amount realized	$280,000
Given up:	
Land—basis	295,000
Realized gain (loss)	($15,000)
Recognized gain (lesser of realized gain or net cash received)	$-0-

Basis:

Land given up—basis	$295,000
Less: Cash received	100,000
Plus: Recognized gain	-0-
Plus: Commissions and fees	20,000
Basis of land received	$215,000

Example 18: The Taxpayer exchanged investment real estate with an adjusted basis of $100,000 for investment real estate with a fair market value of $200,000. The Taxpayer paid commissions and fees of $20,000 in connection with the exchange.

Received:	
Land—F.M.V.	$200,000
Cash	-0-
	$200,000
Less: Commissions and fees	20,000
Amount realized	$180,000
Given up:	
Land—basis	100,000
Realized gain (loss)	$80,000
Recognized gain (lesser of realized gain or net cash received)	$-0-
Basis:	
Land given up—basis	$100,000
Less: Cash received	-0-
Plus: Recognized gain	-0-
Plus: Commissions and fees	20,000
Basis of land received	$120,000

.03 Multi-Party Exchanges

The tax-free, like-kind exchange provisions also apply to property exchanges that involve three-party and four-party transactions. Any part of these multi-party exchanges may qualify as a like-kind exchange if it generally meets the requirements discussed above for such an exchange. Also, if the like-kind exchange includes money or unlike property, in addition to like-kind property, gain realized is taxed to the extent of the money and fair market value of the unlike property.[178]

[178] *See, for example,* Rev. Rul. 57-244, 1957-1 CB 247, which involved a triangular exchange among three lot owners.

[A] Three-Way Exchange

A problem frequently faced by the owner of business or investment property who would like to exchange it in a tax-free exchange is that the other party does not want the owner's property or wants only cash for the property. Another problem arises when the owner of property has a potential purchaser for the property, but wants to acquire property that the potential purchaser does not own. In these situations, it may be possible to work out a three-way exchange.

> ***Example 19:*** Individual A owns land held for investment and wishes to exchange it for improved business property owned by B. B does not want A's land but is willing to sell the business property. If A can find a buyer for the land, an exchange can be worked out. This third party may be a buyer who actually wants A's land, or an intermediary or broker who will arrange an exchange on behalf of A and ultimately resell A's land. The third party purchases B's business property and acquires title. The third party then exchanges the business property for A's land. In this case, A has a tax-free, like-kind exchange. Neither B nor the third party, however, qualify for like-kind exchange treatment. B does not qualify because the property was sold, and the third party does not qualify because the business property was never held by the third party for use in a trade or business or for investment.

In a three-way exchange, it is not necessary that the person receiving replacement property have that property deeded directly from the person to whom he transfers the relinquished property. For instance, if A transfers property to B in exchange for property of a like kind, the exchange as to A will qualify for nonrecognition under Code Sec. 1031, even though legal title to the property received by A is never held by B.[179]

While there are many possible variations of the three-party exchange, the taxpayer who directs the other party to purchase like-kind property in a three-way exchange generally must show that there was no intent to sell the property that was transferred in the exchange. The agreement must show an intent to make an exchange rather than a sale for cash.[180] A provision for alternative sale possibilities or the receipt of cash if the exchange is not completed, or the existence of a sales contract, however, does not destroy an otherwise tax-free exchange if the parties exhibited an intent to exchange properties and if the exchange actually occurs. For instance, when a taxpayer who was holding business property originally entered into an agreement to sell the property for cash but arranged to exchange the property with his purchaser for like-kind property before the sales contract was implemented, the exchange qualified as a like-kind exchange.[181]

Generally, the property transfers in a three-way exchange must be part of an integrated plan, although contractual interdependence between the taxpayer's

[179] Rev. Rul. 90-34, 1990-1 CB 154.

[180] J. Alderson, CA-9, 63-2 USTC ¶ 9499, 317 F.2d 790.

[181] L.Q. Coupe, 52 TC 394, CCH Dec. 29,610, *acq.* 1970-2 CB xix. *See also* Coastal Terminals, Inc., CA-4, 63-2 USTC ¶ 9623, 320 F.2d 333; F.B. Biggs, CA-5, 81-1 USTC ¶ 9114, 632 F.2d 1171.

transfer and the receipt of properties is not necessary for tax-free treatment.[182] The taxpayer may undertake to locate the exchange property and negotiate with the third party for its acquisition by the purchaser.[183]

[B] Four-Way Exchange

If a taxpayer wants to make a tax-free exchange and the prospective purchaser does not want to take title to the taxpayer's property, they may be able to work out a four-way exchange. Generally, a four-way exchange involves a taxpayer who wants the exchange property, a prospective purchaser of the taxpayer's property, a prospective seller of the property that the taxpayer wants to receive in the exchange, and a fourth party. The fourth party receives the taxpayer's property and sells that property to the prospective purchaser. The fourth party then purchases the prospective seller's property and transfers that property to the taxpayer, who wants like-kind exchange treatment. The fourth party ends up holding no property other than whatever compensation for facilitating the transaction was agreed to among the parties.

The fourth party to a four-way exchange may be an agent of one of the parties. In one case upholding like-kind exchange treatment, the fourth party was the prospective purchaser's agent,[184] and in another case, the fourth party was the taxpayer's bank, which the taxpayer controlled as majority shareholder.[185] The IRS's argument that the purchaser must have title to the exchange property as a prerequisite for a tax-free like-kind exchange has been rejected by the Fifth Circuit Court of Appeals.[186]

¶ 1303 REPORTING REQUIREMENTS

Code Sec. 6045(e)(1) provides that the "real estate reporting person" must file a return and statement in the case of a "real estate transaction." This provision was added to the Internal Revenue Code by the Tax Reform Act of 1986 in order to prevent sellers of real estate from avoiding tax on gain by not reporting the transaction on their tax returns. The IRS has issued regulations that spell out the details of the reporting requirement.[187]

Reporting is not required on the sale of a personal residence for $250,000 ($500,000 in the case of married taxpayers) or less, if the residence is a principal residence and the gain is not subject to tax under Code Sec. 121.[188] The reporting person must obtain "written assurances" from the seller of the personal residence for this exception to apply. The necessary written assurances and a sample form are set out in Rev. Proc. 2007-12.[189]

---

[182] A.E. Brauer, 74 TC 1134, CCH Dec. 37,200.

[183] J. Alderson, CA-9, 63-2 USTC ¶ 9499, 317 F.2d 790. *See also* Coastal Terminals, Inc., CA-4, 63-2 USTC ¶ 9623, 320 F.2d 333; L.A. Woodbury, 49 TC 180, CCH Dec. 28,696, *acq.* 1969-2 CB xxv.

[184] L.Q. Coupe, 52 TC 394, CCH Dec. 29,610, *acq.* 1970-2 CB xix.

[185] H. Rutland, 36 TCM 40, CCH Dec. 34,215(M), T.C. Memo. 1977-8.

[186] F.B. Biggs, CA-5, 81-1 USTC ¶ 9114, 632 F.2d 1171.

[187] Reg. § 1.6045-4.

[188] Code Sec. 6045(e)(5). *See* ¶ 2002.

[189] 2007-4 IRB 354.

.01 Transactions Subject to Reporting

Sales or exchanges of real estate for money, indebtedness, property other than money, or services are subject to the information reporting requirements.[190] Real estate subject to reporting includes land, including air space; any inherently permanent structure, including residential, commercial, or industrial buildings; any condominium unit, including appurtenant fixtures and common elements; any stock in a cooperative housing corporation; or any non-contingent interest in standing timber.[191]

A gift or a financing or refinancing that is not related to the acquisition of real estate is not subject to reporting.[192] Involuntary conversions also are not subject to reporting, but other tax-free sales or exchanges are subject to the reporting requirements.[193]

[A] Reporting Person

The person who is required to report real estate transactions under Code Sec. 6045(e) is generally the person responsible for closing the transaction.[194] If no person is responsible for closing the transaction,[195] the person who must report is the first-listed of the following who participates in the transaction as:

1. Mortgage lender;
2. Seller's broker;
3. Buyer's broker; or
4. Transferee of the property.[196]

To avoid any uncertainty as to who is responsible for reporting a real estate transaction, a designation agreement may be used. The agreement must be in writing and must be between the designated person and the person who would otherwise be treated as the real estate broker.[197] The person designated by the agreement must be an eligible person. Eligible persons are:

1. Persons responsible for closing the transaction described above;
2. Transferee's attorney, the transferor's attorney, or the title or escrow company, regardless of whether responsible for the closing; or
3. Mortgage lender.[198]

[B] Multiple Transferors

If more than one person is transferring an interest in the same one-to-four family real estate, the reporting person must make a separate information return for each transferor. A husband and wife who hold the real estate as tenants in common, joint tenants, tenants by the entirety, or community property, however, are treated as a single transferor.[199] If there are multiple transferors, the reporting person must

[190] Reg. § 1.6045-4(b)(1).

[191] Reg. § 1.6045-4(b)(2).

[192] Reg. § 1.6045-4(c).

[193] Reg. § 1.6045-4(b)(1).

[194] Reg. § 1.6045-4(e)(1).

[195] Reg. § 1.6045-4(e)(3).

[196] Reg. § 1.6045-4(e)(4).

[197] Reg. § 1.6045-4(e)(5)(i).

[198] Reg. § 1.6045-4(e)(5)(ii).

[199] Reg. § 1.6045-4(f).

request the transferors to provide an allocation of the gross proceeds among themselves at or prior to the closing.[200] The request or the response does not have to be in writing.

.02 Information Return and Statement

The real estate broker in a real estate transaction subject to the reporting requirements must file an information return with the IRS[201] and furnish the transferor with a statement.[202]

[A] Form and Content of Return

Unless filing is done on magnetic media,[203] the information is filed using Form 1099. The form must contain the following information:[204]

1. The name, address, and taxpayer identification number of the transferor. The transferor is required by law to furnish the reporting person with his or her TIN.[205]
2. A general description of the real estate transferred. This includes the complete address of the property and a legal description if the address would not be sufficient to identify the property.[206]
3. The date of closing, which is the date described as the Settlement Date if a Uniform Settlement Statement is used, or the earlier of the date on which the title is transferred and the date on which the burdens and benefits of ownership shift to the transferee.[207]
4. The gross proceeds, which are generally the total cash received or to be received by the transferor. Gross proceeds do not include the value of any property other than cash transferred as part of the transaction. Liabilities transferred with the property as assumed by the transferee are included in the gross proceeds.[208]
5. If the transferor received or will receive property other than cash and consideration treated as cash in computing gross proceeds, or services, as part of the consideration for the transaction, an indication that such property or services were or will be received.
6. The real estate reporting person's name, address, and TIN.
7. Any other information required by Form 1099 or its instructions.

[B] Statement for Transferor

The reporting person who is required to file the information return must furnish a written statement to the transferor, whose TIN must be shown on the information return. The written statement must contain the legend on the recipient copy of Form 1099 or the following:

---

200 Reg. § 1.6045-4(i)(5).

201 Code Sec. 6045(a).

202 Code Sec. 6045(b).

203 Reg. § 1.6045-4(k).

204 Reg. § 1.6045-4(h)(1).

205 Reg. § 1.6045-4(l).

206 Reg. § 1.6045-4(h)(2)(i).

207 Reg. § 1.6045-4(h)(2)(ii).

208 Reg. § 1.6045-4(i).

> This is important tax information and is being furnished to the Internal Revenue Service. If you are required to file a return, a negligence penalty or other sanction will be imposed on you if this item is required to be reported and the IRS determines that it has not been reported.[209]

The requirement that the reporting person furnish the transferor with a statement may be satisfied by giving the transferor a recipient copy of a completed Form 1099. In the case of a real estate transaction for which a Uniform Settlement Statement is used, the requirement is also satisfied by giving the transferor a copy of a completed statement in compliance with Reg. § 1.6045-4(m) and by designating on the Uniform Settlement Statement the items of information required on Form 1099. The statement may be given to the transferor in person, either at or after the closing, or mailed to the transferor at the transferor's last known address. A reporting person may use a truncated taxpayer identification number in statements furnished the transferor.

The statement for the transferor must be given to the transferor on or after the date of closing and before February 15 of the following calendar year.[210]

.03 Penalties

A responsible person who fails to file the necessary information return or furnish the transferor with the required statement may be subject to one or more of the following penalties:

1. Failure to file an information return (Code Sec. 6721);
2. Failure to furnish a statement to the transferor (Code Sec. 6722);
3. Failure to include correct information (Code Sec. 6723); and
4. Willful failure to supply information (Code Sec. 7203).

¶ 1304 QUALIFIED OPPORTUNITY ZONES

Qualified opportunity zones are low-income community population census tracts designated as opportunity zones by the governors of the various states. There are two main tax incentives to encourage investment in qualified opportunity zones. First, there is a temporary deferral of inclusion in gross income for capital gains that are reinvested in a qualified opportunity fund. Second, there is an exclusion from gross income for the post-acquisition capital gains on investments in opportunity zone funds. In the case of the sale or exchange of an investment in a qualified opportunity zone fund held for more than ten years, at the election of the taxpayer the basis of the investment in the hands of the taxpayer is the fair market value of the investment at the date of the sale or exchange. Taxpayers can continue to recognize losses associated with investments in qualified opportunity zone funds as under current law.[211]

Qualified opportunity zones have been designated by the governors of all 50 states. All population census tracts in Puerto Rico that are low-income communities are deemed to be certified and designated as qualified opportunity zones.[212] The

[209] Reg. § 1.6045-4(m)(1).

[210] Reg. § 1.6045-4(m)(2).

[211] Code Sec. 1400Z-2.

[212] Code Sec. 1400Z-1(b).

IRS has provided a final list of population census tracts that were nominated and have been designated as qualified opportunity zones in Notice 2018-48[213] and Notice 2019-42.[214]

The designation of a population census tract as a qualified opportunity zone remains in effect for the period beginning on the date of the designation and ending at the close of the tenth calendar year beginning on or after the date of designation.[215]

Note on Proposed Regulations

The discussion of qualified opportunity funds (QOF) and the deferral of capital gains in this ¶ 1304 is not intended to be a complete discussion of all the rules that apply. The IRS has issued two sets of proposed regulations to provide guidance on the deferral of gains as a result of an investment in a QOF. Specifically, the proposed regulations address the type of gains that may be deferred, the time by which corresponding amounts must be invested, and the manner in which investors may elect to defer specified gains. The proposed regulations also contain rules that apply to QOFs, including those for self-certification, valuation of QOF assets, and qualified opportunity zone businesses.[216] Taxpayers generally may rely on the proposed regulations, provided they are applied in their entirety and in a consistent manner.

.01 Opportunity Fund

A qualified opportunity fund (QOF) is an investment vehicle organized as a corporation or a partnership for the purpose of investing in qualified opportunity zone property (other than another QOF) and holds at least 90 percent of its assets in qualified opportunity zone property.[217] The corporation or partnership self-certifies by attaching Form 8996 to its return for each year it is a QOF.[218]

The draft Form 8996 for the 2019 tax year requires QOFs to report the following:

- The Employer Identification Number of each business in which the QOF has an ownership interest;
- The census tract location of the tangible property of the business;
- The value of the QOF's investment; and
- The value and census tract location of qualified business property directly owned or leased.

The corporation or partnership must be organized in the United States or a U.S. possession.[219]

---

[213] 2018-28 IRB 9.

[214] 2019-29 IRB 352.

[215] Code Sec. 1400Z-1(f).

[216] NPRM REG-115420-18 and NPRM REG-120186-18.

[217] Code Sec. 1400Z-2(d)(1).

[218] *See* Prop. Reg. § 1.1400Z-2(d)-1(a).

[219] *See* Prop. Reg. § 1.1400Z-2(d)-1(e).

[A] *Opportunity Zone Property*

Qualified opportunity zone property includes:

1. Any qualified opportunity zone stock,
2. Any qualified opportunity zone partnership interest, and
3. Any qualified opportunity zone business property.[220]

Qualified Opportunity Zone Stock

Qualified opportunity zone stock is stock in a domestic corporation that is acquired by the QOF after December 31, 2017, at its original issue (directly or through an underwriter) from the corporation solely in exchange for cash. At the time the stock is issued to the QOF, the corporation must be a qualified opportunity zone business (or, in the case of a new corporation, the corporation is being organized for purposes of being a qualified opportunity zone business). During substantially all of the QOF's holding period of the stock, the corporation must be a qualified opportunity zone business.[221]

Qualified Opportunity Zone Partnership

A qualified opportunity zone partnership interest is a capital or profits interest in a domestic partnership acquired by the QOF after December 31, 2017, from the partnership solely in exchange for cash. At the time the interest is acquired, the partnership must be a qualified opportunity zone business (or, in the case of a new partnership, the partnership is being organized for purposes of being a qualified opportunity zone business). During substantially all of the QOF's holding period of the partnership interest, the partnership must be a qualified opportunity zone business.[222]

Qualified Opportunity Zone Business

A qualified opportunity zone business is a trade or business in which at least 70 percent of the tangible property owned or leased by the business is qualified opportunity zone business property.[223] Qualified opportunity zone business property is tangible property used in a trade or business of the QOF (or in the trade or business of the qualified opportunity zone partnership issuing qualified partnership interests or the corporation issuing qualified opportunity zone stock). The property must be acquired by purchase after December 31, 2017. The original use of the property must begin in the qualified opportunity zone with the QOF (or with the partnership or corporation issuing the qualified partnership interest or qualified opportunity zone stock), or the property must be substantially improved by the fund (or zone partnership or corporation).[224]

[B] *90 Percent Test*

If a QOF fails to meet the 90 percent requirement and unless the fund establishes reasonable cause, the fund is required to pay a monthly penalty of the

[220] Code Sec. 1400Z-2(d)(2)(A).
[221] Code Sec. 1400Z-2(d)(2)(B).
[222] Code Sec. 1400Z-2(d)(2)(C).
[223] Code Sec. 1400Z-2(d)(2)(D).
[224] Code Sec. 1400Z-2(d)(3).

excess of the amount equal to 90 percent of its aggregate assets, over the aggregate amount of qualified opportunity zone property held by the fund multiplied by the underpayment rate in the Code. If the fund is a partnership, the penalty is taken into account proportionately as part of each partner's distributive share. The computation of the penalty does not take into account any months before the first month in which the entity is a QOF.[225]

The 90 percent test is based on the average of the percentage of qualified zone property held by the fund on the last day of the first six-month period of the fund's tax year and on the last day of the fund's tax year.[226] The fund's tax year for this purpose begins in the month in which it certifies as a QOF. The self-certification may identify the first month (in that initial tax year) in which the eligible entity wants to be a QOF. If the self-certification fails to specify the month in the initial tax year that the eligible entity first wants to be a QOF, then the first month of the eligible entity's initial taxable year as a QOF is the first month that the eligible entity is a QOF. If an investment occurs before the first month of QOF status, any election to defer gain for that investment is invalid.[227]

If a partnership or corporation becomes a QOF in the seventh or later month of a 12-month tax year, the 90 percent test takes into account only the QOF's assets on the last day of the tax year.[228]

A QOF with an applicable financial statement (as defined in Reg. § 1.475(a)-4(h)) may value its assets using the "applicable financial statement method" or the "alternative valuation method." Only one method may be used for valuing assets during the tax year. A QOF without an applicable financial statement must use the alternative valuation method. For details on the valuation of a QOF's assets, see Prop. Reg. § 1.1400Z-2(d)-1(b). The proposed regulations also contain safe harbors for inventory in transit and certain levels of working capital.

.02 Tax Deferral

A taxpayer generally may elect to exclude from income capital gain from the sale or exchange of any property to an unrelated party to the extent the gain is reinvested in a QOF within 180 days of the sale or exchange. The maximum amount of the deferred gain is equal to the amount invested in a QOF. For any gain that exceeds the maximum deferral amount, the gain must be recognized and included in gross income.[229] A taxpayer may not elect to defer capital gain from any sale or exchange that occurs after 2026.[230]

The deferral for gain reinvested in a QOF is available to any taxpayer that recognizes capital gains. Eligible taxpayers include individuals; C corporations, including regulated investment companies (RICs) and real estate investment trusts (REITs); partnerships; S corporations; and trusts and estates.[231]

The election to defer eligible gain is made on Form 8949, *Sales and Other Dispositions of Capital Assets*, attached to the tax return for the year in which the gain otherwise would have been recognized. Form 8949 is also used to report gain from the disposition of an interest in a QOF.

[225] Code Sec. 1400Z-2(f).
[226] Code Sec. 1400Z-2(d)(1).
[227] Prop. Reg. § 1.1400Z-2(d)-1(a)(1).
[228] Prop. Reg. § 1.1400Z-2(d)-1(a)(2).
[229] Code Sec. 1400Z-2(a).
[230] Code Sec. 1400Z-2(e)(2).
[231] Prop. Reg. § 1.1400Z-2(a)-1(b)(1).

[A] *Eligible Gain*

Eligible gains generally include capital gain from an actual or deemed sale or exchange, or any other gain that a taxpayer is required to include in the computation of capital gain.[232] Capital gain from a sale or exchange with a related person (as defined in Code Secs. 267(b) and 707(b)(1), but using 20 rather than 50 percent) does not qualify. A taxpayer who makes a deferral election with respect to some but not all of an eligible capital gain, may make a separate election for the portion to which the prior election did not apply. Both elections are subject to the same 180-day reinvestment period since the gain arose from the same sale or exchange.

Gain is not eligible for deferral if the gain is realized from the sale or transfer of property to a QOF or the transfer of property to another person in exchange for that person's interest in a QOF.[233]

Capital gain net income from Section 1231 property (see ¶ 1301.02[B]) is eligible for deferral. Gains and losses on all of a taxpayer's Section 1231 property for the tax year are netted. Netting is not required in the case of non-Section 1231 gain. The 180-day period for reinvesting any net income from the netted Section 1231 gains and losses in a QOF begins on the last day of the tax year.[234]

Mixed Investments

If a taxpayer invests more in a QOF than the capital gain from the sale or exchange that it wishes to defer, the investment in the QOF is treated as two separate investments. The gain deferral rules apply only to the portion of the investment attributable to the gain that is deferred.[235]

Pass-Through Entities

A partnership may make an election to defer recognition of eligible gain by investing in a QOF. Deferred gain is not included in the distributive shares of the partners until the deferred gain is recognized and no basis adjustments to the partner's interest are made until the deferred gain is recognized.[236]

If a partner's distributive share includes capital gains, the partner may elect to defer some or all of the gains. The gain must be an eligible gain for the partnership and the gain may not be from a sale or exchange with a person related to the partner. The 180-day period generally begins on the last day of the partnership tax year in which the partner's allocable share of the partnership's eligible gain is taken into account. However, a partner may elect to treat the partner's 180-day period as the same 180-day period that would apply to the partnership if it had instead made the deferral election.[237]

If an S corporation, a trust, or a decedent's estate recognizes an eligible gain, or would recognize an eligible gain if it did not elect to defer recognition of the gain,

[232] Prop. Reg. § 1.1400Z-2(a)-1(b)(2).

[233] Prop. Reg. § 1.1400Z-2(a)-1(b)(2).

[234] Prop. Reg. § 1.1400Z-2(a)-1(b)(2).

[235] Code Sec. 1400Z-2(e)(1); Prop. Reg. § 1.1400Z-2(e)-1(a)(1).

[236] Prop. Reg. § 1.1400Z-2(a)-1(c)(1).

[237] Prop. Reg. § 1.1400Z-2(a)-1(c)(2).

then rules analogous to the rules for partnerships and partners apply to that entity and to its shareholders or beneficiaries.[238]

[B] *Gain Recognition*

The amount of gain that is deferred when a taxpayer makes an equity investment in a QOF is included in the taxpayer's income in the tax year that includes the earlier of:

a. the date on which the qualifying investment is sold or exchanged, or

b. December 31, 2026.[239]

In general, any disposition of the owner's qualifying investment is an "inclusion event" triggering recognition of gain. The proposed regulations cover certain specific types of inclusion events such as gifts, charitable contributions, abandonments, and corporate and partnership transactions that occur before 2027.[240] An inclusion event also generally occurs when a taxpayer transfers a qualifying investment in a transaction that reduces the taxpayer's equity interest in the QOF. Subject to exceptions, transfers at death generally are not inclusion events.[241]

The basis of an investment in a QOF immediately after its acquisition is zero.[242] Basis is increased if the QOF is held at least five years with the following results:

- If the taxpayer's interest in the qualified opportunity fund is sold or disposed of in an inclusion event before five years have expired, the basis of the interest in the QOF is $0. Therefore, the entire deferred gain is recognized, assuming the entire investment is sold or disposed of.[243]
- If the fund is held for at least five years but less than seven years, the zero basis is increased by 10 percent of the deferred gain and, therefore, 90 percent of the deferred gain is recognized.[244]
- If the fund is held for at least seven years but less than 10 years, the zero basis is increased by 15 percent of the investment and, therefore, 85 percent of the deferred gain is recognized.[245]

Any deferred gain is recognized as income on December 31, 2026, if the fund has not been sold or disposed of by that date. The zero basis is increased by 10 percent if the fund was held for at least five years but less than seven years and by 15 percent if the fund was held for at least seven years.

Tax-Free Appreciation

If an investment in a QOF is held for at least ten years, any appreciation in the value of the investment attributable to the deferred gain may escape tax. The taxpayer may elect to treat the basis on the date of sale as the fair market value of the QOF on the date of its sale or exchange.[246] If the value of the fund has increased beyond the initial amount of invested deferred gain and the taxpayer makes the

[238] Prop. Reg. § 1.1400Z-2(a)-1(c)(3).

[239] Code Sec. 1400Z-2(b)(1).

[240] *See* Prop. Reg. § 1.1400Z-2(b)-1(b).

[241] *See* Prop. Reg. § 1.1400Z-2(b)-1(c).

[242] Code Sec. 1400Z-2(b)(2)(B)(i).

[243] Code Sec. 1400Z-2(b)(2)(B)(ii).

[244] Code Sec. 1400Z-2(b)(2)(B)(iii).

[245] Code Sec. 1400Z-2(b)(2)(B)(iv).

[246] Code Sec. 1400Z-2(c).

election, gain on the appreciation of the invested deferred gain in the fund is not recognized. In the case of an investment in excess of deferred gain (i.e., a mixed investment), gain is not recognized only to the extent attributable to the deferred gain that was invested.[247]

The election for investments held for at least ten years may be made for a sale that occurs after a qualified opportunity zone automatically loses its status at the close of the tenth calendar year beginning on or after the date of designation as a qualified opportunity zone. The election, however, has to be made for a disposition that occurs before 2048.[248]

> ***Example 20:*** Taxpayer, who holds a commercial building for rent, sells the building on January 15, 2019, to an unrelated person at a gain of $500,000. This is the only Section 1231 gain or loss the taxpayer realizes that year. The taxpayer then reinvests the full amount of that gain in a QOF on April 1, 2019. The taxpayer sells its investment in the QOF on April 15, 2022, for $750,000. Because the taxpayer held its QOF investment for less than five years, the QOF basis is $0. For the 2022 tax year, the taxpayer must recognize the deferred gain of $500,000 as well as the $250,000 in appreciation.

> ***Example 21:*** Assume same facts as in Example 20, except that the taxpayer sells the QOF investment in May 2026. Because the taxpayer held the QOF investment for more than seven years, the basis increases from $0 to $75,000 (15 percent of the deferred gain of $500,000). This reduces the amount of deferred gain the taxpayer must include in income from $500,000 to $425,000. The taxpayer must also recognize the additional $250,000 in appreciation.

> ***Example 22:*** Taxpayer, who holds a commercial building for rent, sells the building on January 15, 2025, to an unrelated person at a gain of $500,000. This is the only Section 1231 gain or loss the taxpayer realizes that year. The taxpayer then reinvests the full amount of that gain in a QOF on January 31, 2024. On December 31, 2026, the taxpayer must recognize the entire $500,000 deferred gain (QOF basis is zero) even though the taxpayer has not sold the QOF investment. The taxpayer does not increase the zero basis in the QOF because the taxpayer has not owned the fund for at least five years. On January 1, 2037, the taxpayer sells its interest in the QOF for $675,000. Because the taxpayer has held the QOF investment for ten or more years, the taxpayer may elect to treat the basis as $675,000 and the taxpayer recognized no additional gain. If the taxpayer does not make the election, basis would be $500,000 (the deferred gain that the taxpayer recognized on December 31, 2026, increases basis) and the taxpayer would recognize the $175,000 appreciation for 2037.

> ***Example 23:*** Assume the same facts as in Example 22, except that the value of the QOF has decreased to $400,000. The taxpayer should avoid making the fair market value election and recognize a $100,000 loss ($400,000 less $500,000 previously recognized gain).

---

[247] *See* Prop. Reg. §§1.1400Z-2(c)-1(a) and 1.1400Z-2(e)-1(a)(1).

[248] Prop. Reg. §1.1400Z-2(c)-1(b).

¶ 1305 REDUCED TAXES ON DEPRESSED AREA PROPERTY

To encourage investment in various depressed areas before the creation of opportunity zones, Congress enacted a series of incentives. Among those incentives are reduced or zero tax rates when qualifying property within one of the designated areas is sold.

.01 Rollover of Empowerment Zone Investment

A taxpayer can elect to roll over capital gain from the sale or exchange of any qualified empowerment zone asset purchased after December 21, 2000, and held for more than one year if the taxpayer uses the proceeds to purchase other qualifying empowerment zone assets in the same zone.[249] The taxpayer must purchase the replacement property within 60 days of the sale of the asset.[250]

A qualified empowerment zone asset is an asset that would be a qualified community asset under Code Sec. 1400F (see ¶ 1305.02), if the empowerment zone were a renewal community and the asset is acquired after December 21, 2000.[251] Assets in the D.C. Enterprise Zone (see ¶ 1305.03) are not eligible for the tax-free rollover treatment.[252]

The holding period of the replacement asset includes the holding period of the original asset, except that the replacement asset must actually be held for more than one year to qualify for another tax-free rollover.[253] The basis of the replacement asset is reduced by the gain not recognized on the rollover. However, if the replacement asset is qualified small business stock (as defined in Code Sec. 1202), the exclusion in that section does not apply to gain accrued on the original zone asset.[254]

.02 Renewal Community Capital Gain

A zero percent capital gain tax rate applies to gain from the sale of a qualified community asset acquired after December 31, 2001, and before January 1, 2010, and held for more than five years.[255] Gain attributable to periods after December 31, 2014, does not qualify.[256] A qualified community asset includes:

1. original-issue stock in a renewal community business purchased for cash;
2. a partnership interest in a renewal community business acquired for cash; and
3. tangible property originally used in a renewal community business by the taxpayer and that is purchased or substantially improved after December 31, 2001.

---

[249] Code Sec. 1397B.
[250] Code Sec. 1397B(a).
[251] Code Sec. 1397B(b)(1).
[252] Code Sec. 1397B(b)(1)(B).
[253] Code Sec. 1397B(b)(5).
[254] Code Sec. 1397B(b)(4).
[255] Code Sec. 1400F.
[256] Code Sec. 1400F(c)(2).

.03 D.C. Zone Capital Gain

Economically depressed census tracts in the District of Columbia are designated as the D.C. Enterprise Zone. Businesses and individual residents in the zone are eligible for special tax incentives. Under Code Sec. 1400B, a zero percent capital gain tax rate applies to capital gains from the sale of qualified District of Columbia zone assets held for more than five years. Qualified D.C. zone assets include D.C. zone business stock, D.C. zone partnership interests, and D.C. zone business property.

Qualified capital gain eligible for the zero percent rate does not include any gain attributable to periods before January 1, 1998, or after December 31, 2016. It also doesn't include any gain that would be treated as ordinary income because of recapture under Code Sec. 1245 or under Code Sec. 1250 if Code Sec. 1250 applied to all depreciation rather than the additional depreciation. Further, qualified capital gain doesn't include any gain that's attributable to real property, or an intangible asset, that is not an integral part of a D.C. zone business. Finally, qualified capital gain doesn't include any gain attributable to a transaction with a related person.

In general, D.C. zone business stock is stock in a U.S. corporation originally issued after December 31, 1997, if (1) the stock is acquired by the taxpayer before January 1, 2012, at its original issue solely for cash; (2) at the time the stock was issued, the corporation was a D.C. zone business; and (3) during substantially all of the taxpayer's holding period for the stock, the corporation qualified as a D.C. zone business.

A D.C. zone partnership interest is a capital or profits interest in a U.S. partnership originally issued after December 31, 1997, if (1) the interest is acquired by the taxpayer before January 1, 2012, from the partnership solely for cash; (2) at the time the interest was acquired, the partnership was a D.C. zone business; and (3) during substantially all of the taxpayer's holding period for the interest, the partnership qualified as a D.C. zone business.

In general, D.C. zone business property is tangible property if (1) the property was acquired by the taxpayer by purchase after December 31, 1997, and before January 1, 2012; (2) the original use of the property in the D.C. zone begins with the taxpayer; and (3) during substantially all of the taxpayer's holding period for the property, substantially all of the use of the property was in a D.C. zone business of the taxpayer. A special rule applies for buildings that are substantially improved. A D.C. zone business is any enterprise zone business (as defined in Code Sec. 1397C), subject to some modifications.

Chapter 14
Seller-Financed Sales

¶ 1400 Overview of Chapter
¶ 1401 Installment Sales
¶ 1402 Disposition or Pledge of Installment Obligations

¶ 1400 OVERVIEW OF CHAPTER

Chapter 13 examined the basic tax rules that affect the sale or exchange of real estate, including the manner of computing gain or loss and the character of the gain or loss. A taxpayer generally must report any recognized gain from the sale or exchange of real estate for the tax year in which the sale or exchange occurs, which is generally when title passes or the burdens and benefits of ownership shift from the seller to the buyer. An exception to this rule applies, however, when the seller does not receive the full purchase price in the year of sale.

The acquisition of real property usually is financed by a mortgage loan from a third-party lender (see Chapter 3). In this case, the general rule of reporting recognized gain in full in the year of sale generally does not impose an undue burden on the seller since the seller receives the full purchase price immediately, even though the buyer makes payments over a period of time to the holder of the mortgage. However, the seller of real estate may be willing to assist in the financing when adequate financing cannot be obtained from a third-party lender or if the seller's financing of the sale will provide the seller with tax or financial advantages. When the seller finances the sale, the seller typically takes back a purchase-money mortgage from the buyer to secure the future payment of the full purchase price. If the seller-financed sale qualifies as an installment sale under Code Sec. 453, then the seller may report gain from the sale as payments actually are received.

¶ 1401 INSTALLMENT SALES

When the seller finances the sale of real property, the seller's receipt of the buyer's note would require the seller to report the entire gain in the year of sale if there were no Internal Revenue Code provision for installment reporting. Absent installment reporting, the seller could face the undesirable prospect of paying tax on gain the seller has not actually received and, possibly, might never receive.

The installment method permits the seller to report the gain in excess of any amount of depreciation recapture as payments from the buyer actually are received. When installment reporting is available, it can be an important tax and financial planning tool for both the seller and the buyer. The seller is able to pay the tax from the sale proceeds and may retain a larger portion of the buyer's down payment for reinvestment or other purposes. Tax savings to the seller also may result if the gain from the sale would place the seller in a higher tax bracket for the year of sale. Gain spread out over more than one year may result in a lower total tax on the gain.

Of course, an installment sale is not right in every situation. In some cases, the seller may have losses from other sources that would wholly or partially offset the gain on the sale. In such cases, it may be advisable for the seller to elect out of installment reporting. An election out also may be warranted if tax rates will increase or the seller's tax bracket will be higher in future years when the installment payments are received. The tax on each payment received in future years is at the rate in effect in the year of receipt.

If depreciation recapture is significant, the seller may not be inclined to make an installment sale and may insist on full payment up front, either through a cash sale or third-party financing. Recapture income, as discussed at ¶ 1401.02[B], is currently taxable whether payments are received or not. At a minimum, the seller may want to consider recapture in setting the down payment or other payments to be received in the year of sale. The seller may want to insist that these initial payments be at least sufficient to cover the projected tax liability from recapture.

In general, the regular tax rules that apply in the case of loans from third-party lenders, as discussed at ¶ 1301, also apply to determine the effect of a purchase-money mortgage given by the seller on basis, income, and the amount realized on the sale of the property. Also, as a general proposition, the treatment of interest, discount, and costs associated with a purchase-money mortgage given by the seller is the same as third-party loans, as discussed at ¶ 301. The ability of sellers and buyers to manipulate tax consequences by varying interest and discount terms in seller-financed transactions, however, is limited by the imputed interest and the original issue discount rules. These rules are discussed at ¶ 304.

.01 Sales that Qualify as Installment Sales

An installment sale is simply the disposition of property when at least one payment is to be received by the seller after the close of the taxable year in which the disposition occurs.[1] Generally speaking, if the seller finances the buyer's purchase of the property, the transaction probably is an installment sale for tax purposes. The buyer's obligation to make future payments may be in the form of a deed of trust, a note, a land contract, a mortgage, or some other evidence of the buyer's indebtedness to the seller. Installment reporting is permitted, regardless of the amount of payments received in the year of sale, as long as at least one payment is to be received in a subsequent taxable year. Also, installment reporting is permitted even if the entire purchase price is to be received in a lump sum in a taxable year subsequent to the year of sale.[2] The installment sales provisions also permit installment reporting when the sales price is contingent.[3] This may facilitate some transactions and is discussed further below. These provisions allow the parties to control the amount and timing of payments to suit their individual financial and tax positions.

---

[1] Code Sec. 453(b)(1).

[2] Reg. § 15A.453-1(b).

[3] Code Sec. 453(f)(8)(B).

The installment sales provisions do not apply when the sale of property results in a loss. Losses are always reported in full for the year of sale. Also, installment reporting is not permitted if the sale is between certain related persons, as discussed further at ¶ 1401.03.[4]

[A] Dealer Sales

In the Omnibus Budget Reconciliation Act of 1987, Congress repealed the installment method of reporting income for dealers in property.[5] The apparent rationale, other than a need to raise revenue, was that dealers do not need the benefits of installment reporting since they generally are able to finance their receivables and frequently do. Thus payment of tax for the year of sale by a dealer does not create the cash flow problem that occurs in the case of non-dealers.

In general, gain on any disposition of personal property by a person who regularly sells or disposes of property on the installment plan, and gain on the sale or disposition of real property held for sale to customers in the ordinary course of business, subject to some limited exceptions, may not be reported under the installment method.[6] The ban on the use of the installment method does not affect the treatment of installment obligations that arose out of dispositions before March 1, 1986.

Despite the general disallowance of installment reporting for dealer sales, installment reporting remains available for sales or dispositions of any property used or produced in the trade or business of farming.[7] Also, installment reporting is permitted for sales to individuals in the ordinary course of business of:

1. Time-share rights to use, or time-share ownership interests in, residential real property for not more than six weeks, or rights to use specified campgrounds for recreational purposes, and
2. Residential lots, but only if the taxpayer (or any related person) is not to make any improvements to the lots.[8]

In the case of sales of timeshares and residential lots, installment reporting by dealers is permitted only if the dealer elects to pay interest on the tax deferred by the use of the installment method.[9] This interest is added to the dealer's income tax.[10] The amount of interest is based on the tax for the year attributable to installment payments received during the year and is calculated from the date of sale to the date the payments are received.[11] The interest rate that is applied is the applicable federal rate, compounded semiannually, in effect at the time of the sale under the original issue discount rules.[12] No interest is assessed in the case of

[4] Code Sec. 453(g).

[5] Code Sec. 453(b)(2).

[6] Code Sec. 453(l)(1). For a discussion of who is a dealer and what constitutes "dealer property," *see* ¶ 1002.01.

[7] Code Sec. 453(l)(2)(A).

[8] Code Sec. 453(l)(2)(B).

[9] Code Sec. 453(l)(3).

[10] Code Sec. 453(l)(3)(A).

[11] Code Sec. 453(l)(3)(B)(i).

[12] Code Sec. 453(l)(3)(B)(i)(III). For an explanation of how this rate is set, *see* the discussion of the original issue discount rules at ¶ 304.

installment payments received in the year of sale.[13] Any interest paid under this rule is treated as interest in determining the dealer's interest deduction.[14]

[B] Escrow Arrangements

In some cases, a sales agreement may require the buyer to establish an escrow account, out of which the installment payments are to be made. Generally, if there is no restriction on the seller's right to receive payments from the escrow account, other than the passage of time, the sale will not qualify for installment reporting. In this situation, the IRS views the buyer's obligation as paid in full when the purchase price is deposited into the escrow account. With the escrow account, the seller is no longer relying on the buyer for the rest of the payments, but on the escrow arrangement.[15]

Substitution of an escrow agreement as security following an installment sale also ends the seller's right to report the transaction on the installment basis. The IRS has ruled that an agreement to sell real property did not qualify for installment reporting when the installment obligations were secured by a deed of trust and the sales agreement was changed in the year of sale by a later agreement that required the seller to cancel the deed of trust in exchange for the buyer's deposit of the balance of the purchase price to an irrevocable escrow account. Under the new agreement, the buyer continued to be liable for the note payments, but the annual payments were made by the escrow agent from the escrow account.[16]

A similar result occurs when the escrow arrangement is established in a year after the sale. For instance, a sale of realty ceased to qualify for installment reporting when the purchaser made an escrow deposit in exchange for the release of the seller's security interest and the payment schedule was the only restriction on the seller's right to receive the total sales proceeds.[17]

On the other hand, if an escrow arrangement imposes a substantial restriction on the seller's right to receive the sale proceeds, the sale may be reported on the installment method, provided the sale otherwise qualifies for installment reporting. In order for an escrow arrangement to impose a substantial restriction, it must serve a bona fide purpose of the buyer, that is, a real and definite restriction placed on the seller or a specific economic benefit conferred on the buyer. For instance, an escrow agreement that secures the seller's agreement not to compete with the buyer following the sale, as well as securing the buyer's payments, would impose a definite restriction on the seller and would not defeat installment reporting. In *R.J. Murray*,[18] more than 75 percent of the purchase price was placed in escrow as security for the seller's agreement not to compete, and the escrow agent was to release one-fifth of the escrow funds each year provided the seller had not entered

---

[13] Code Sec. 453(l)(3)(B)(iii).

[14] Code Sec. 453(l)(3)(C).

[15] Rev. Rul. 73-451, 1973-2 CB 158. *See also* E. Pozzi, 49 TC 119, CCH Dec. 30,842; J.E. Oden, 56 TC 569, CCH Dec. 28,681. *But see* E. Grannemann, DC Mo., 87-1 USTC ¶ 9287, 649 F.Supp. 949, in which the district court held that sellers were entitled to choose not to accept the buyer's offer to pay the full purchase price in cash and could insist on installment payments using an escrow arrangement solely to reduce the tax consequences of the sale.

[16] Rev. Rul. 77-294, 1977-2 CB 173.

[17] Rev. Rul. 79-91, 1979-1 CB 179.

[18] 28 BTA 624, CCH Dec. 8151, *acq.* 1933-2 CB 10.

a competing business. In this situation, the receipt of the purchase price by the escrow agent was not constructive receipt by the seller and the sale could be reported on the installment method.

[C] Election out of Installment Reporting

Under current law, use of the installment method is automatic for any sale that qualifies as an installment sale.[19] The seller, however, may elect not to have the installment sale rules apply.[20] A seller who makes this election must recognize gain on the sale in accordance with the seller's regular method of accounting, which, in the case of a cash method taxpayer, means that the seller must report the entire gain from the sale for the year of the sale even though the seller will not be paid all of the selling price until later.

In determining the amount realized on the sale, the seller must include the buyer's notes or obligations to make the future payments at their fair market value. In making the fair market value determination, any provision of contract or local law restricting the transferability of the installment obligations is disregarded.[21] Notes, mortgages, land contracts, and even an oral promise enforceable under local law are examples of obligations that must be included in the seller's amount realized at their fair market value when the seller elects not to report on the installment method.

Example 1: The Taxpayer, a cash method, calendar year taxpayer, sold a parcel of land to the Buyer for $50,000, payable $10,000 down with the balance over a period of ten years at $4,000 per year plus 12 percent interest. The Buyer gave the Taxpayer a note for $40,000, and the note had a fair market value of $30,000. The Taxpayer's basis for the land at the time of the sale was $25,000, and the Taxpayer paid a commission of $3,000 in connection with the sale. The Taxpayer elects out of installment reporting. The Taxpayer's recognized gain for the year of sale is $12,000, computed as follows:

Cash		$10,000
Market value of note		30,000
Amount realized		$40,000
Less:		
Basis of property	$25,000	
Commission	3,000	28,000
Gain realized and recognized in the year of sale		$12,000

Provided the land was a capital asset in the Taxpayer's hands, the $12,000 gain would be a capital gain. However, since the Taxpayer included only the fair market value of the note (75 percent of its face value in this case) in the amount realized in the year of sale, the Taxpayer must report 25 percent of

[19] Code Sec. 453(a).

[20] Code Sec. 453(d)(1).

[21] Reg. § 15A.453-1(d)(2)(i).

each payment of principal received in later years as ordinary income. Of course, the Taxpayer must also report the interest on the note as ordinary interest income.

Determination of Fair Market Value

The regulations provide guidelines for determining the fair market value of the buyer's obligations when the seller elects out of installment reporting. If the amount payable under the buyer's obligation is fixed, the fair market value of the obligation to a cash method seller can never be less than the fair market value of the property sold (minus any other consideration received by the seller on the sale). An accrual method seller treats as an amount realized in the year of sale the total amount payable under the installment obligation.[22] Under no circumstances does the IRS allow an installment sale for a fixed amount obligation to be treated as an "open" transaction in which the seller reports income only as payments are received.

The fair market value of a contingent payment obligation may be determined from, and in no event will be considered less than, the fair market value of the property sold (less the amount of any other consideration received in the sale). A cash method taxpayer must include the fair market value of the contingent payment obligation in the amount realized for the year of sale. An accrual method taxpayer reports the amount realized from a contingent obligation in the year of sale in accordance with the accrual method of accounting, but in no event can the amount realized be less than the fair market value of the contingent payment obligation.[23]

Unlike a sale involving fixed payment obligations, the IRS has left the door open for reporting installment sales involving contingent payment obligations as open transactions when the seller elects out of installment reporting. Reg. § 15A.453-1(d)(2)(iii) provides:

> Only in those rare and extraordinary cases involving sales for a contingent payment obligation in which the fair market value of the obligation cannot reasonably be ascertained will the taxpayer be entitled to assert that the transaction is "open." Any such transaction will be carefully scrutinized to determine whether a sale in fact has taken place.

Making the Election

A seller makes the election not to report a qualifying installment sale under the installment method by reporting the entire gain on a timely filed tax return for the year of sale.[24] Late elections are generally not permitted, unless the IRS concludes that the taxpayer had good cause for failing to make a timely election. A recharacterization of a transaction as a sale in a taxable year subsequent to the taxable year in which the transaction occurred does not justify a late election.[25] For example, a transaction initially reported as a lease that is later determined to be an installment sale would not be good cause that would permit a late election out of installment reporting. A valid election out of installment reporting can be revoked only with the consent of the IRS.[26]

[22] Reg. § 1.15A.453-1(d)(2)(ii)(A).

[23] Reg. § 15A.453-1(d)(2)(iii).

[24] Reg. § 15A.453-1(d)(3)(i).

[25] Reg. § 15A.453-1(d)(3)(ii).

[26] Reg. § 15A.453-1(d)(4).

.02 Reporting Installment Income

If a sale qualifies as an installment sale, the taxpayer must report the sale on the installment method unless, as discussed above, the taxpayer elects out of installment reporting.[27] Generally, each installment payment consists of three parts: the return of the seller's basis in the property sold, the gain on the sale, and interest. A sale that results in a loss cannot be reported under the installment method, and the loss, if it is otherwise deductible, must be taken for the year of the sale.

[A] General Rules

Each year that a seller receives payments following an installment sale, the seller must report as income the portion of the payments that represents gain from the sale and must also report the interest portion of each payment as interest income (see the discussion of unstated interest, below). As with any sale, the seller does not report as income the portion of the amount realized that represents a return of the seller's basis in the property.

Under the installment method, gain is reported ratably as each installment payment is received. The amount of each payment treated as income is determined by multiplying the payment received by a fraction known as the "gross profit ratio." The gross profit ratio is simply the ratio of the gross profit realized (or to be realized) to the total contract price.[28] To convert this ratio or fraction into numbers, it is necessary to deal with several definitions.

"Gross profit," the numerator of the fraction, is the selling price of the property less its adjusted basis. Commissions and selling expenses are added to basis in order to determine the gross profit.[29] If any gain from the sale may be postponed or excluded from income (*e.g.*, gain on the sale of a personal residence by a taxpayer over 55 years of age), this gain is subtracted from the gross profit. The selling price that is included in the gross profit is the gross selling price without reduction to reflect any existing mortgage or other encumbrance on the property, regardless of whether the obligation is assumed or taken subject to by the buyer, and without reduction for selling expenses. Also, interest, whether stated or unstated, or original issue discount is not part of the selling price.[30]

The "total contract price," the denominator of the gross profit ratio, is the selling price reduced by any debt assumed or taken subject to by the buyer which does not exceed the seller's basis in the property adjusted for commissions and other selling expenses.[31] If the amount of any mortgage or other debt assumed or taken subject to by the buyer exceeds the seller's basis for the property, the excess does not reduce the selling price in determining the contract price.

The following worksheet outlines the basic method of determining the seller's gross profit ratio following an installment sale:

---

[27] Code Sec. 453(a); Reg. § 15A.453-1(a).

[28] Code Sec. 453(c); Reg. § 15A.453-1(b)(2)(i).

[29] Reg. § 15A.453-1(b)(2)(v).

[30] Reg. § 15A.453-1(b)(2)(ii).

[31] Reg. § 15A.453-1(b)(2)(iii).

1. Selling Price . . . . ______
2. Minus the sum of:
   Basis of property sold . . . . ______
   Selling expenses . . . . ______ ______
3. Gross Profit (Line 1 minus Line 2) . . . . ______
4. Contract Price . . . . ______
5. Gross Profit Ratio (Line 3 divided by Line 4) . . . . ______

Example 2: A, a calendar year taxpayer, sells Blackacre, an unencumbered capital asset in A's hand, to B for $100,000 on the following terms: $10,000 down and the remainder payable in equal annual installments over the next nine years, together with adequate stated interest. A's basis in Blackacre, exclusive of selling expenses, is $38,000. Selling expenses paid by A are $2,000.

The gross profit is $60,000 ($100,000 selling price - $40,000 basis inclusive of selling expenses). The gross profit ratio is 3/5 (gross profit of $60,000 divided by $100,000 contract price). Therefore, $6,000 (3/5 of $10,000) of each $10,000 payment is gain from the sale and $4,000 ($10,000 - $6,000) is recovery of basis. A also must report the interest received each year as ordinary interest income.

Depreciation Recapture

When property sold on the installment basis is subject to depreciation recapture (see discussion at ¶ 1301.03), the recapture must be reported in full for the year of the sale. This provision was added to the Internal Revenue Code by the Tax Reform Act of 1984, which provided that ". . . any recapture income shall be recognized in the year of the disposition and any gain in excess of the recapture income shall be taken into account under the installment method."[32] Current regulations do not specify how the gain in excess of recapture should be calculated for installment reporting purposes. Presumably, the recapture income reported in the year of sale reduces the gross profit in the gross profit ratio. This can be accomplished by simply adding the recapture amount to the adjusted basis of the property for purposes of determining gross profit for installment reporting purposes.

Example 3: Assume the same facts as in the example above, except that the sale of Blackacre is subject to depreciation recapture in the amount of $20,000. A must report the $20,000 recapture income for the year of sale, even though A receives only $10,000 on the purchase price in that year. A then reports the gain in excess of recapture on the installment basis. The gross profit is $40,000 ($100,000 selling price - $60,000 basis inclusive of selling expenses and depreciation recapture). The gross profit ratio is ⅖ (gross profit of $40,000 divided by $100,000 contract price). Therefore, $4,000 (⅖ of

[32] Code Sec. 453(i).

$10,000) of each $10,000 payment is gain from the sale and $6,000 ($10,000 - $4,000) is recovery of basis and previously reported recapture income.

Reduced Selling Price

If the parties to an installment sale later agree to reduce the selling price, the gross profit on the sale changes. The seller must then refigure the gross profit ratio for the remaining payments. The seller cannot go back and refigure the gain reported in earlier years.

> ***Example 4:*** In 2018, A sold land with a basis (inclusive of selling expenses) of $40,000 for $100,000. A received $20,000 as a down payment and the buyer's note for $80,000. Payments of $20,000 each plus adequate stated interest are due on each July 1 beginning in 2019. A's gross profit was $60,000 and his gross profit ratio was 3/5 ($60,000 divided by $100,000). On each of the payments received in 2018 and 2019, A reported a gross profit of $12,000 (3/5 of $20,000).
>
> In 2020, A and the buyer agree to reduce the selling price of the property to $85,000 and the payments in 2020, 2021, and 2022 to $15,000. A's adjusted gross profit on the sale is now $45,000, and the total amount of profit remaining to be reported is $21,000 ($45,000 gross profit - $24,000 profit already reported in 2018 and 2019). The remaining profit to be received by A of $21,000 is divided by the remaining selling price to be received by A of $45,000 ($85,000 adjusted selling price - $40,000 of selling price received in 2018 and 2019), to determine the new gross profit ratio of 7/15. A reports a gross profit of $7,000 (7/15 of $15,000) on each of the $15,000 payments due in 2020, 2021, and 2022.

[B] Payments

The seller of property under the installment method applies the gross profit ratio to "payments" received, including any down payment and each later payment of principal.[33] While the term "payment" usually denotes a cash payment, the term has much broader meaning when applied to installment reporting for federal income tax purposes. Payments include amounts actually or constructively received.[34] For example, if the buyer assumes and pays expenses of the seller in connection with the sale, it is considered a payment to the seller. The expenses also are included in both the selling price and the contract price when computing the gross profit ratio.

Receipt of the purchaser's evidence of indebtedness, such as the buyer's note, generally does not constitute a payment.[35] Even if the buyer's evidence of indebtedness comes with a third-party guarantee, it is not a payment. Receipt of an evidence of indebtedness that is secured directly or indirectly by cash or a cash equivalent, such as a bank certificate of deposit or treasury note, however, is treated by the regulations as the receipt of a payment.[36] Debt secured by a standby letter of credit, that is, a nonnegotiable, nontransferable letter of credit issued by a bank or other

[33] Code Sec. 453(c).

[34] Reg. § 15A.453-1(b)(3)(i).

[35] Code Sec. 453(f)(3).

[36] Reg. § 15A.453-1(b)(3)(i).

financial institution, is not treated as a payment. A letter of credit is not a standby letter of credit if it may be drawn upon in the absence of default in payment of the underlying debt.[37]

Mortgages and Other Debts Assumed

If the buyer assumes a mortgage on the property or otherwise takes the property subject to a mortgage, it is generally not treated as a payment. Also, other indebtedness not secured by the property but incurred or assumed by the buyer incident to the buyer's acquisition, holding, or operation in the ordinary course of business of the property generally is not treated as a payment for installment sale purposes.[38] These rules apply to qualifying indebtedness so long as the debt assumed or taken subject to by the buyer does not exceed the seller's basis in the property.

> ***Example 5:*** C sells Whiteacre to D for a selling price of $160,000. Whiteacre is encumbered by a longstanding mortgage in the amount of $60,000. D assumes the $60,000 mortgage and pays the remaining $100,000 in ten equal annual installments together with adequate stated interest. C's basis in Whiteacre is $90,000 and there are no selling expenses in connection with this sale.
>
> The contract price is $100,000, the $160,000 selling price reduced by the mortgage of $60,000. Gross profit is $70,000 ($160,000 selling price less C's basis of $90,000). C's gross profit ratio is 7⁄10 (gross profit of $70,000 divided by contract price of $100,000). Therefore, C must report $7,000 (7⁄10 of $10,000) of each $10,000 annual payment as gain from the sale and $3,000 as return of basis.

If the buyer assumes a mortgage or other qualifying debt and the debt exceeds the seller's basis for the property, the portion of the debt assumed in excess of basis is treated as a payment.[39] Also, if the debt assumed or taken subject to by the buyer exceeds the seller's basis, the seller recovers the entire basis in the year of sale and the seller's gross profit ratio will always be 1:1.

> ***Example 6:*** Assume the same facts as in the example above, except that C's basis in Whiteacre is $40,000 rather than $90,000.
>
> In this case, C is treated as receiving a payment of $20,000, the amount by which the mortgage assumed by D ($60,000) exceeds C's basis in the property ($40,000). Since C has fully recovered basis in the year of sale, the gross profit ratio is one (gross profit of $120,000 divided by contract price of $120,000), and C must report 100 percent of the $20,000 payment from the assumption of the mortgage in excess of basis and each $10,000 annual payment as gain from the sale of Whiteacre.

If the buyer assumes any type of debt other than qualifying indebtedness in connection with the sale, the full amount of the debt is treated as a payment in the year of sale. Qualifying indebtedness does not include an obligation of the seller incurred incident to the disposition of the property, such as legal fees relating to the

[37] Reg. § 15A.453-1(b)(3)(iii).

[38] Reg. § 15A.453-1(b)(2)(iv).

[39] Reg. § 15A.453-1(b)(3)(i).

sale, or an obligation unrelated to the acquisition, holding, or operation of the property, such as the seller's medical bills or a personal loan.

In an attempt to frustrate last minute borrowing on the property by the seller just prior to a sale in order to pull cash out without having a taxable payment, the regulations provide the following: "Any obligation created subsequent to the taxpayer's acquisition of the property and incurred or assumed by the taxpayer or placed as an encumbrance on the property in contemplation of disposition of the property is not qualifying indebtedness if the arrangement results in accelerating recovery of the taxpayer's basis in the installment sale."[40] While this rule leaves open the question of when a debt is incurred "in contemplation of the disposition of the property," it is unlikely that the IRS could successfully challenge a mortgage placed on property before any offer is made to buy or sell the property.

Wraparound mortgages have presented a special problem when it comes to determining the amount of payments received by the seller in connection with an installment sale. A wraparound mortgage is an agreement in which the buyer issues to the seller an installment obligation in an amount that equals or exceeds the seller's outstanding mortgage or other debt on the property (the wrapped debt), but the existing mortgage or other debt is neither paid off nor assumed by the buyer. In the usual case, the seller uses payments received from the buyer on the wraparound mortgage to make payments on the wrapped debt.

Under the regulations, use of a wraparound mortgage is treated as a sale in which the buyer takes the property subject to the seller's outstanding mortgage.[41] This is the case, according to the regulations, even though the seller remains liable for the wrapped debt and the buyer does not assume the seller's debt, and even though title to the property does not actually change hands. If the wrapped debt exceeds the seller's basis, then, under the regulations, the portion of the wrapped debt in excess of the seller's basis is a payment. The Tax Court, however, has held that the treatment of wraparound mortgages under the regulations is invalid.[42] According to the Tax Court, the buyer should not be treated as taking the property subject to or having assumed the existing mortgage when there is an installment sale of property with a wraparound mortgage, and the seller should not have to reduce the total contract price by the amount of the wrapped debt.

The IRS has acquiesced to the decision of the Tax Court.[43] Although the IRS has not withdrawn or modified the regulations dealing with wraparound mortgages, in its Action on Decision[44] it did say it does not intend to follow the approach of the regulation in view of an inconsistency with the specific language of the Code. According to the IRS, in the absence of revised regulations governing wrap around real estate transactions, it will litigate cases involving those transactions in accordance with the case law, in particular, *Stonecrest Corporation, Inc.*[45] *Stonecrest* held that there was no justification for reducing the sales price by the amount of any underlying indebtedness in determining the contract price in the installment sale

[40] Reg. § 15A.453-1(b)(2)(iv).

[41] Reg. § 15A.453-1(b)(3)(ii).

[42] Professional Equities, Inc., 89 TC 165, CCH Dec. 44,064, *acq*. 1988-2 CB 1.

[43] 1988-2 CB 1.

[44] CC-1988-023.

[45] 24 TC 659 (1959).

because the buyer neither assumed nor took subject to the underlying indebtedness.

If the buyer of the property in an installment sale is the holder of an existing mortgage on the property or other qualifying indebtedness, the seller's debt is not assumed on the sale but is cancelled.[46] In this case, the seller is treated as receiving a payment equal to the outstanding amount of the cancelled debt.

Demand and Readily Tradable Obligations

If the seller can immediately convert an obligation received into cash, there is really no reason to postpone tax through installment reporting. After all, installment reporting is designed to avoid the difficulties or "cash crunch" that might occur when a tax liability arises from a transaction that does not generate the funds with which to pay the tax. Accordingly, the installment sale provisions provide that those obligations which the holder can convert to cash at will must be treated as payments rather than as installment obligations subject to installment reporting.

A bond or other evidence of indebtedness issued by any person and payable on demand is a payment in the year received under the installment sale rules.[47] Also, an obligation that is readily tradeable is a payment under the installment sale rules and not an installment obligation payable in future years. An obligation is readily tradeable if it is issued:

1. With interest coupons attached (whether or not the obligation is readily tradable in an established securities market);
2. In registered form (other than an obligation issued in registered form which the taxpayer establishes will not be readily tradable in an established securities market); or
3. In any other form designed to render the obligation readily tradable in an established securities market.[48]

An obligation is considered to be in registered form if it is registered as to principal, interest, or both and if its transfer must be effected by the surrender of the old instrument and either reissuance of the old instrument to the new holder or the issuance of a new instrument to the new holder.[49] The definition of the terms "designed to be readily tradable in an established securities market," "readily tradable in an established securities market," "readily tradable," and "established securities market" may be found in Reg. § 15A.453-1(e)(4).

The seller reports a payment in the form of a demand or readily tradable obligation under his normal accounting method. If the seller is a cash method taxpayer, the amount realized on the payment in the form of a demand or readily tradable obligation is the fair market value of the obligation. If the seller uses the accrual method of accounting, the amount realized on receipt of a demand obligation is the face amount of the obligation, and the amount realized on receipt of a readily tradable obligation is the stated redemption price at maturity less any

[46] Reg. § 15A.453-1(b)(3)(i).

[47] Code Sec. 453(f)(4)(A).

[48] Code Sec. 453(f)(4)(B) and (f)(5).

[49] Reg. § 15A.453-1(e)(1)(i).

original issue discount or, if there is no original issue discount, the stated redemption price at maturity appropriately discounted to reflect total unstated interest, if any.[50]

Example 7: Several individuals owning equal interests in a tract of land with a fair market value of $1 million sell the land to C Corporation. The $1 million sales price is paid with bonds issued by C to the individuals. The bonds are not in registered form and do not have interest coupons attached. The bonds are payable in 120 equal installments, each due on the first day of each month over the next ten years. The bonds are negotiable and may be assigned by the holder to any other person, but the bonds are not quoted by any brokers or dealers who deal in corporate bonds and there are no comparable obligations of C which are so quoted.

In this case, the bonds are not treated as readily tradable in an established securities market. Also, under these particular facts, the bonds will not be considered to be in a form designed to render them readily tradable in an established securities market. The receipt of the bonds by the sellers of the land is not treated as payment under the sale provisions, even though the bonds are freely assignable.[51]

[C] Sale of Multiple Assets

When a taxpayer sells two or more assets in a single installment sale to one buyer and there is more than one type or class of asset, the taxpayer must apportion the selling price and payments among the assets sold.[52] Generally, an arm's-length allocation of the selling price and of the payments received in the year of sale made by the parties to the sale is acceptable to the IRS. In the absence of a specific arm's-length allocation, the seller must allocate selling price and payments among the assets sold according to their respective net fair market values.[53] The net fair market value of any asset is its fair market value reduced by any debt on the asset that the buyer assumes or takes the asset subject to.

If the selling price, the down payment, or both are separately stated for different assets in the sale of a going business, there must be an allocation of the selling price and the payments received in the year of sale to the following:

1. Inventory assets which the seller may not report on the installment method;
2. Assets sold at a loss which the seller must report in full in the year of sale;
3. Depreciable assets sold at a gain, part or all of which the seller must report in the year of sale because of depreciation recapture;
4. Real property sold at a gain which the seller may report on the installment method; and
5. Personal property sold at a gain which the seller may report on the installment method.[54]

[50] Reg. § 15A.453-1(e)(2). Original issue discount and unstated interest are considered at ¶ 304.

[51] Reg. § 15A.453-1(e)(4)(v), Example (1).

[52] Rev. Rul. 55-79, 1955-1 CB 370.

[53] Rev. Rul. 55-79; *see also* J.A. Johnson, 49 TC 324, CCH Dec. 28,802.

[54] Rev. Rul. 68-13, 1968-1 CB 195.

Since some gains reported on the installment method may be ordinary income and others capital gain, the seller may have to make separate computations to report the gain properly for each asset.

Example 8: The Taxpayer sells a business in an arm's-length transaction for $350,000 and receives $100,000 as a down payment in the year of sale. The Seller receives no other payments in the year of sale. The price of the inventory included in the sale is 40 percent of the total selling price, or $140,000. The balance of the selling price of $210,000 is for noninventory property.

In the absence of bona fide arm's-length allocation of the down payment, it must be ratably allocated to the inventory and noninventory property. Forty percent of the down payment ($40,000) is allocable to inventory property and 60 percent ($60,000) is allocable to noninventory property. The Seller may report gain from the sale of the noninventory property, other than depreciation recapture, on the installment method. The Seller must report any gain on the inventory property in full for the year of sale.

A taxpayer who sells separate and unrelated assets of the same type under a single contract may report the sale as a single transaction for installment sale purposes. If the taxpayer has a loss on one or more of the assets, however, the taxpayer may not report the sales at a loss on the installment method but must report the loss sales separately. The taxpayer may report only the assets sold at a gain together on the installment method.[55]

Example 9: The Taxpayer sold three separate and unrelated parcels of real property, A, B, and C, under a single contract. The total selling price for all three properties of $260,000 consisted of a cash down payment of $40,000, the buyer's assumption of a $60,000 mortgage on parcel B, and an installment obligation of $160,000 payable in eight annual installments with adequate stated interest. The sales contract did not allocate the selling price or the down payment among the individual parcels. The fair market value of parcels A and B was $120,000 each. The fair market value of parcel C was $20,000. The Taxpayer's basis for each parcel was $30,000, so the net gain was $170,000 ($260,000 amount realized - $90,000 basis). The Taxpayer decides to report the gain on the installment method and not to elect out of installment reporting.

Since the basis of parcel C was more than its fair market value, parcel C was sold at a loss and must be treated separately. The Taxpayer must allocate the total selling price and the amounts received in the year of sale between parcel C and the other two parcels. The total selling price of $260,000 is allocated as $240,000 for parcels A and B together and $20,000 for parcel C. The cash payment of $40,000 received in the year of sale and the buyer's note are allocated on the basis of the proportionate net fair market value of the properties. The net fair market value is the fair market value minus any debt assumed or which the property is taken subject to. The allocation is:

[55] Rev. Rul. 76-110, 1976-1 CB 126.

	A and B	*C*
Net fair market value:		
Fair market value	$240,000	$20,000
Less: Mortgage assumed	60,000	0
Net fair market value	$180,000	$20,000
Proportionate net FMV:		
Percentage of total	90%	10%
Payments in year of sale:		
$40,000 × 90%	$36,000	
$40,000 × 10%		$4,000
Excess of mortgage assumed over basis—parcel B .	30,000	
Allocation of payments in year of sale	$ 66,000	$ 4,000

The Taxpayer may not report the sale of parcel C on the installment method because the sale results in a loss. The Taxpayer reports this loss of $10,000 ($20,000 selling price - $30,000 basis) in full for the year of sale, unless the Taxpayer held parcel C for personal purposes.

The buyer's installment obligation of $160,000 is allocated to the properties sold according to their proportionate net fair market values. Ninety percent of each payment received is from parcels A and B, and ten percent of each payment is a return of basis from parcel C. If the Taxpayer receives any payments on the buyer's installment obligation in the year of sale, the Taxpayer includes them with the other payments received in the year of sale.

[D] Like-Kind Exchanges

Gain on property that is exchanged for "like-kind" property may be deferred under Code Sec. 1031, as discussed at ¶ 1302.01. Essentially, gain attributable to the receipt of the like-kind property is deferred, but gain attributable to money or other property received as part of the exchange is currently taxed. If, in addition to like-kind property, a taxpayer receives an obligation of the buyer that may be reported on the installment method, the following rules apply:

1. The contract price does not include the fair market value of the like-kind property the taxpayer receives in the trade.[56]
2. The gross profit is reduced by any gain on the exchange that can be postponed.[57]
3. Like-kind property received in the trade is not considered a payment on the installment obligation.[58]

Accordingly, in reporting the gain on the exchange under the installment method when an installment obligation is received in addition to the like-kind

[56] Code Sec. 453(f)(6)(A).

[57] Code Sec. 453(f)(6)(B).

[58] Code Sec. 453(f)(6)(C).

property, the gross profit is the amount of gain that will be recognized on the exchange if the installment obligation is satisfied in full at its face amount. Also, the total contract price does not include the value of the like-kind property, but consists solely of the sum of the money and fair market value of other property received plus the face amount of the installment obligation.

The basis of the like-kind property received is determined as if the obligation were satisfied at its face amount.[59] Thus, the taxpayer's basis in the property given up in the exchange is first allocated to the like-kind property received, but not in excess of the property's fair market value, and any remaining basis is used to determine the gross profit ratio.

> ***Example 10:*** The Taxpayer exchanges property with a basis of $400,000 for like-kind property worth $200,000. The Taxpayer also receives an installment note for $800,000. The note is payable $100,000 (plus interest) one year after the exchange and $700,000 (plus interest) two years after the exchange.
>
> The Taxpayer's gross profit is $600,000 ($1,000,000 selling price - $400,000 basis). The contract price is $800,000 ($1,000,000 - $200,000 fair market value of property received). The gross profit ratio is 3/4 or 75 percent ($600,000 divided by $800,000). The Taxpayer reports no gain in the year of the exchange because the like-kind property received is not treated as a payment. The Taxpayer reports $75,000 gain when the $100,000 installment (75% × $100,000) is received and $525,000 gain when the $700,000 installment (75% × $700,000) is received. The Taxpayer's basis for the like-kind property received in the exchange is $200,000.

[E] Contingent Sales

A contingent sale is one in which the total selling price cannot be determined by the end of the tax year in which the sale occurs. Generally, contingent sales must be reported on the installment basis, unless the seller elects out of installment reporting.[60] In directing the IRS to issue rules for reporting contingent payment sales on the installment method, Congress wanted to reduce the justification for treating transactions as "open" transactions. In an open transaction, the taxpayer may first recover basis before reporting any gain, and thus defer taxes. The cost-recovery method of reporting open transactions was sanctioned by the Supreme Court in 1931.[61]

With a contingent payment sale, since the selling price cannot be determined by the end of the year, the contract price and the gross profit ratio cannot be determined using the same rules that apply to an installment sale that has a fixed selling price. The regulations provide rules for allocating the seller's basis to payments received and to be received so that contingent sales may be reported on the installment basis. The rules distinguish contingent payment sales for which a maximum selling price can be determined, sales for which a maximum selling price

[59] Rev. Rul. 65-155, 1965-1 CB 356.

[60] Code Sec. 453(j)(2); Reg. § 15A.453-1(c)(1).

[61] D. Burnet v. E.A. Logan, S.Ct., 2 USTC ¶ 736, 283 US 404, 51 S.Ct. 550.

cannot be determined but the time over which payments will be received can be determined, and sales for which neither a maximum selling price nor a definite payment term can be determined.

Stated Maximum Selling Price

A contingent payment sale has a stated maximum selling price if the seller can determine the maximum proceeds from the sale by the end of the year in which the sale occurs. The seller must determine the stated maximum selling price by assuming that all of the contingencies contemplated by the agreement are met or otherwise resolved in a way that maximizes the selling price and accelerates the payments to the earliest date or dates permitted by the agreement. The seller treats the stated maximum selling price as the selling price for installment reporting purposes unless and until that maximum amount is reduced. If the maximum amount is reduced, the seller recomputes the gross profit ratio for payments received in or after the year in which the event requiring the reduction occurs.[62]

> ***Example 11:*** C owns Blackacre, which is encumbered by a long-standing mortgage of $100,000. C sells Blackacre to D under the following payment arrangement: $100,000 in cash on closing; nine equal annual payments of $100,000 beginning in the year after the sale; and nine annual payments equal to five percent of the gross annual rental receipts from Blackacre generated during the preceding calendar year. The agreement also calls for adequate stated interest on the deferred payments and limits the maximum amount payable to C, exclusive of interest, to $2,100,000. Also, D assumes the existing mortgage on Blackacre. C's basis in Blackacre plus the selling expenses total $300,000.
>
> The selling price is $2,100,000 and the contract price is $2,000,000 (selling price of $2,100,000 less the $100,000 existing mortgage assumed by the buyer). The gross profit ratio is 9/10 (gross profit of $1,800,000 divided by the $2,000,000 contract price). C reports $90,000 of the $100,000 payment received in the year of sale as gain attributable to the sale of Blackacre, and $10,000 is recovery of basis.[63]

Fixed Period

If a stated maximum selling price cannot be determined, but the maximum period over which the seller may receive payments under the contingent sale price agreement is fixed, the seller recovers the basis, including selling expenses, in equal annual increments over the fixed period. If payments in any year are less than the portion of basis allocated to that year, unrecovered basis allocated to that year is carried over to the following year. No loss is allowed until the final payment year, unless future payment obligations under the agreement have become worthless.[64]

The following examples from Reg. § 15A.453-1(c)(3)(ii) illustrate the rules for recovery of basis in a contingent payment sale in which stated maximum selling price cannot be determined but the period over which payments are to be received under the agreement is fixed.

---

[62] Reg. § 15A.453-1(c)(2)(i).

[63] Reg. § 15A.453-1(c)(2)(i)(B), Example (2).

[64] Reg. § 15A.453-1(c)(3)(i).

Example 12: A sells Blackacre to B for ten percent of Blackacre's gross yield for each of the next five years. A's basis in Blackacre is $5 million. Since the sales price is indefinite and the maximum selling price is not ascertainable from the terms of the contract, basis is recovered ratably over the period during which payment may be received under the contract. Thus, assuming A receives the payments, exclusive of interest, listed in the following table, A will report the following:

Year	*Payment*	*Basis Recovered*	*Gain Attributable to the Sale*
1	$1,300,000	$1,000,000	$ 300,000
2	$1,500,000	$1,000,000	$ 500,000
3	$1,400,000	$1,000,000	$ 400,000
4	$1,800,000	$1,000,000	$ 800,000
5	$2,100,000	$1,000,000	$1,100,000

Example 13: The facts are the same as in Example 12, except that the payment in Year 1 is only $900,000. Since the installment payment is less than the amount of basis allocated to that year, the unrecovered basis, $100,000, is carried forward to Year 2.

Year	*Payment*	*Basis Recovered*	*Gain Attributable to the Sale*
1	$ 900,000	$ 900,000	$ -0-
2	$1,500,000	$1,100,000	$ 400,000
3	$1,400,000	$1,000,000	$ 400,000
4	$1,800,000	$1,000,000	$ 800,000
5	$2,100,000	$1,000,000	$1,100,000

Fifteen-Year Basis Recovery

If a contingent price sale agreement neither specifies a maximum selling price nor limits payments to a fixed period, the seller recovers basis in equal amounts over a 15-year period, provided the agreement is, in fact, a sale. The regulations point out that when terms are so indefinite, "a question arises [as to] whether a sale realistically has occurred or whether, in economic effect, payments received under the agreement are in the nature of rent or royalty income." The regulations go on to warn that the IRS will closely scrutinize arrangements of this sort.[65]

Income Forecast Method

The IRS recognizes that there are cases in which the failure to take account of the nature or productivity of the property sold in a contingent payment sale may result in a distortion of the taxpayer's income over time because payments will be greater in earlier years and decline over time. Such cases involve property qualifying for depreciation under the income forecast method, such as movies, mineral

[65] Reg. § 15A.453-1(c)(4).

rights when the selling price is based on production, a sale under which the amount payable is based on a declining percentage of the buyer's revenues, and similar sales. In these cases, the seller may recover basis using an income forecast method of basis recovery.[66]

[F] Unstated Interest

Generally, the parties to an installment sale provide that each deferred payment on the sale will include interest or that there will be an interest payment in addition to the principal payment. Interest that is provided for by the parties is "stated interest." If an installment sale with some or all of the payments due more than one year after the date of sale does not provide for interest, a part of each payment due more than six months after the date of sale is treated as interest. The amount treated as interest is "unstated interest" or "imputed interest." When stated interest is under the rate specified by the Internal Revenue Code, the unstated interest is the difference between the specified rate of interest and the stated interest. Imputed interest on deferred payment sales is considered in some detail at ¶ 304.01.

In an installment sale, imputed interest affects the selling price and the contract price. It also affects the amount of gain on the sale, whether the seller reports on the installment method or elects out. For installment reporting, both the selling price and the contract price must be reduced by any imputed interest. If the seller elects out of installment reporting, imputed interest reduces the selling price before the seller computes gain or loss. For the rules on determining whether unstated interest exists and for imputing interest when a contract calls for less than the required amount of interest, see ¶ 304.01[A].

.03 Sales to Related Party

Two special rules apply to installment sales between related persons. First, installment reporting is not permitted in the case of sales of depreciable property between specified related persons.[67] Second, in the case of installment sales to family members and other related persons, a resale by the related person may trigger recognition of gain to the original installment seller.[68] The first rule prevents a sale to a related person to obtain the benefits of a stepped-up basis for depreciation without a concurrent reporting of income by the related seller. The second rule prevents the use of a related person to obtain the economic benefit of the full sales price while deferring the recognition of gain attributable to that sales price. While both rules apply to what are termed "related persons," the definition of "related persons" is not the same for both rules.

[A] Sales of Depreciable Property

A taxpayer who sells depreciable property (depreciable by the buyer) to certain related persons may not report the sale using the installment method.[69] Rather, the seller treats all payments to be received as received in the year of sale.[70]

[66] Reg. § 15A.453-1(c)(6).

[67] Code Sec. 453(g).

[68] Code Sec. 453(e).

[69] Code Sec. 453(g)(1)(A).

[70] Code Sec. 453(g)(1)(B)(i).

Payments to be received include the total amount of all payments that are not contingent and the fair market value of any payment that is contingent as to amount. If the fair market value of contingent payments is not reasonably ascertainable, the seller recovers basis ratably and the buyer may not increase the basis of any property acquired in the sale by any amount before the seller includes the amount in income.[71]

Related Persons

The following are "related persons" for purposes of the rule denying installment reporting in the case of sales of depreciable property to related persons.[72]

1. The seller and a controlled entity. A controlled entity is a partnership in which the seller owns, directly or indirectly, more than 50 percent of interest in its capital or profits, or a corporation in which the seller owns, directly or indirectly, more than 50 percent of the value of the outstanding stock.
2. The seller and any trust in which the seller or the seller's spouse is a beneficiary unless the interest is a remote contingent interest. A beneficiary's contingent interest in a trust is remote if, under the maximum exercise of discretion by the trustee for the beneficiary, the value of the interest is five percent or less of the value of the trust property.
3. An executor and beneficiary of an estate, except for sales and exchanges to satisfy a pecuniary bequest.
4. Two corporations that are members of the same controlled group.
5. Two S corporations if the same persons own more than 50 percent in value of the outstanding stock of each corporation.
6. An S corporation and a corporation that is not an S corporation if the same persons own more than 50 percent in value of the outstanding stock of each corporation.
7. A corporation and a partnership if the same persons own more than 50 percent in value of the outstanding stock of the corporation and more than 50 percent of the capital interest or profit interest in the partnership.
8. Two or more partnerships if the same persons own, directly or indirectly, more than 50 percent of the capital interest or profit interest in each partnership.

Constructive Ownership

Rules of constructive ownership are applied to determine indirect ownership interests:[73]

1. Stock owned by or for a corporation, partnership, estate, or trust is constructively owned proportionately by or for its shareholders, partners, or beneficiaries, and

[71] Code Sec. 453(g)(1)(B)(ii).

[72] The definition of "related person" for this rule is borrowed from Code Sec. 1239(b).

[73] The constructive ownership rules are borrowed from Code Sec. 267(c), other than paragraph (3). *See* Code Sec. 1239(c)(2).

2. An individual constructively owns the stock owned by or for the individual's spouse, brothers and sisters (whether by whole or half blood), lineal descendants, and ancestors.

In applying the constructive ownership rules, an individual's constructive ownership of stock under 1 is considered to be actual ownership of that stock and the individual's ownership may be attributed to a member of that individual's family. An individual's constructive ownership under 2, however, is not considered to be actual ownership and the individual's ownership may not be attributed to another member of the individual's family.

Exception to Reporting Rule

A sale of depreciable property to a related person may be reported on the installment method if the seller can show, to the satisfaction of the IRS, that avoidance of federal income taxes was not one of the principal purposes of the sale.[74] Installment reporting may also be allowed if the seller will derive no significant tax deferral benefits from the sale.

[B] Resale by Related Purchaser

Generally, if a taxpayer makes an installment sale of property (a "first disposition") to a related person, as defined below, who resells the property (a "second disposition") within two years of the first disposition, and before all payments are made under the first disposition, a special rule may come into play. Under this rule, part or all of the amount the related person realizes as a result of the second disposition is treated by the taxpayer as if it had been received from the first disposition at the time of the second disposition.[75]

A second disposition generally is a disposition of the property by the related person and includes a sale, exchange, gift, or cancellation of the installment note. If the second disposition is not a sale or exchange, the amount realized is equal to the fair market value of the property disposed of at the time of the second disposition. A transfer of the property after the death of the person making the first disposition or the related person's death, whichever is earlier, and any later transfer is not a second disposition.[76] Also, an involuntary conversion is not a second disposition if the taxpayer made the first disposition before any knowledge of the possibility that the property would be subject to an involuntary conversion.[77]

Related Person

The following are "related persons" for purposes of applying the rule that taxes the installment seller of property to a related person on a second disposition by the related person:[78]

1. Members of the seller's family, defined to include a spouse, brother, sister, half-brother, half-sister, or any ancestor or lineal descendant;
2. Partnership in which the seller is a partner;

[74] Code Sec. 453(g)(2).

[75] Code Sec. 453(e)(1).

[76] Code Sec. 453(e)(6)(C).

[77] Code Sec. 453(e)(6)(B).

[78] *See* Code Sec. 453(f)(1), which borrows the definition of "related person" from Code Secs. 318(a) and 267(b).

3. Estate in which the seller is a beneficiary;
4. Trust in which the seller is a beneficiary or of which the seller is treated as an owner;
5. Corporation (other than an S corporation) in which the seller owns 50 percent or more in value of the stock;
6. S corporation in which the seller is a shareholder;
7. Corporation and an individual who owns directly or indirectly more than 50 percent of the value of the outstanding stock of that corporation;
8. Two corporations that are members of the same controlled group;
9. Fiduciary of a trust and a corporation, if more than 50 percent of the value of the outstanding stock is owned directly or indirectly by or for the trust or by or for the grantor of the trust;
10. Grantor and fiduciary of any trust, and the fiduciary and beneficiary of any trust;
11. Fiduciaries of two different trusts, and the fiduciaries and beneficiaries of two different trusts, if the same person is the grantor of both trusts;
12. Certain educational and charitable organizations and any person (in the case of an individual, including the members of the individual's family) who directly or indirectly controls the organization;
13. Two S corporations if the same persons own more than 50 percent in value of the outstanding stock of each corporation;
14. S corporation and a corporation that is not an S corporation if the same persons own more than 50 percent in value of the outstanding stock of each corporation;
15. A corporation and a partnership if the same persons own more than 50 percent in value of the outstanding stock of the corporation and more than 50 percent of the capital interest, or profits interest, in the partnership; and
16. An executor and beneficiary of an estate, except for sales and exchanges to satisfy a pecuniary bequest.

The constructive ownership rules discussed at ¶ 1401.03[A] in connection with an installment sale of depreciable property to a related person also apply in the case of the related party resale rule.

Limit on Amount Treated as Received

There is a limit on the amount the installment seller is treated as receiving in a tax year as a result of a second disposition by a related person.[79] To compute this limit:

1. Take the lesser of (a) the total amount realized from any second disposition of the property that occurred before the close of the tax year, or (b) the total contract price for the first disposition.

[79] Code Sec. 453(e)(3).

2. Add (a) the total of all payments received by the end of the tax year from the first disposition to (b) the total of all amounts treated as received in earlier tax years as a result of a second disposition.
3. The limit is (1) minus (2). If less than zero, the installment seller does not treat any amount realized from the second disposition by a related person as if it were received from the first disposition.

The total amount realized from a second disposition is reduced by any amount attributable to improvements made by the related person while the related person held the property.[80]

Two-Year Cutoff

Except for marketable securities, the rules that apply to second dispositions by related persons apply only if the second disposition occurs within two years of the first disposition.[81] This two-year period is extended for any property by any period in which the related person's risk of loss is substantially reduced by:

1. The holding of a put on the property or similar property;
2. Another person holding a right to acquire the property; or
3. A short sale or any other transaction.[82]

An option does not significantly reduce the risk of loss if the option price is determined by the fair market value of the property at the time the option is exercised.

Payments After Second Disposition

Under the related party resale rule, the tax treatment of the initial installment seller does not turn on the strict chronological order in which resales or payments are made. If the initial seller must recognize gain as a result of the resale of the property by a related person, subsequent payments actually received by the initial seller as a result of the installment sale are tax-free until they equal the amount realized as a result of the second disposition by the related person.[83]

The following examples illustrate the tax treatment of an installment seller when the sale is made to a related party and the related party resells the property within two years.

Comprehensive Example 14: In 2018, Larry Brown sold farmland to his son Dan for $500,000. The sale price is to be paid in five equal installments over five years, plus adequate stated interest on the unpaid balance. Larry's installment sale basis for the land was $250,000 and the property was not subject to any outstanding liens or mortgages.

Larry's gross profit ratio is 50 percent or ½ ($250,000 gross profit divided by $500,000 contract price). Larry received $100,000 in 2018 and included $50,000 in his income for that year ($100,000 × 50 percent). Dan made no improvements to the property and sold it for $600,000 to the ABC Corporation

[80] *See* the Senate Finance Committee Report on P.L. 96-471.

[81] Code Sec. 453(e)(2)(A).

[82] Code Sec. 453(e)(2)(B).

[83] Code Sec. 453(e)(5).

in 2019. This $600,000 is the amount realized from the second disposition. Larry computes his installment sale income for 2019 as follows:

Lesser of amount realized on land sold by Dan or contract price	$500,000
Minus: Total payments from Dan in 2018 and 2019	200,000
Amount treated as payment because of second disposition . .	$300,000
Plus: Payment from Dan in 2019	100,000
Total payment received and treated as received for 2019	$400,000
Multiply by gross profit ratio	.50
Installment sale income for 2019	$200,000

Larry does not include in income from installment sales any principal payments he receives on Dan's installment obligation for 2020, 2021, and 2022, because Larry has already reported the entire amount of the payments from the first disposition of $500,000 ($100,000 in 2018 and $400,000 in 2019).

Comprehensive Example 15: Assume the same facts as in Example 14, except that Dan resells the farmland for $400,000 rather than $600,000. Larry computes his gain for 2019 as follows:

Lesser of amount realized on land sold by Dan or contract price	$400,000
Minus: Total payments from Dan in 2018 and 2019	200,000
Amount treated as payment because of second disposition . .	$200,000
Plus: Payment from Dan in 2019	100,000
Total payment received and treated as received for 2019	$300,000
Multiply by gross profit ratio	.50
Installment sale income for 2019	$150,000

In 2020, Larry receives a payment of $100,000 from Dan which is not taxed. It is recovered tax free, because Larry already has reported the payment and gain in 2019 as a result of the $200,000 that he treated as a payment even though he did not actually receive that payment. Larry would apply the $100,000 payment in 2020 against the $200,000 reported in 2019. Larry also is not taxed on the payment he receives in 2021, and he would apply this payment against the $200,000 treated as a payment in 2019. In 2022, Larry receives the final $100,000 payment and computes the amount of gain he must recognize in 2022 from the installment sale as follows:

Total of payments actually received as of the end of 2022 from first disposition		$500,000
Minus the sum of:		
Payment from 2018	$100,000	
Payment from 2019	100,000	
Amount treated as payment in 2019	200,000	
Total of amounts on which gain was previously recognized		400,000
Amount of payment on which gain is recognized for 2022		$100,000
Multiply by gross profit ratio		.50
Installment sale income for 2022		$ 50,000

Exception to Related Party Resale Rule

An installment seller is not treated as receiving a payment on a second disposition of the property by a related person if it is established to the satisfaction of the IRS that neither the first disposition nor the second disposition had as one of its principal purposes the avoidance of federal income taxes.[84] Guidance on when the nonavoidance exception may apply is provided in the Senate Finance Committee Report on P.L. 96-471.

The Senate Finance Committee Report anticipates that regulations and rulings under the nontax avoidance exception will deal with certain tax-free transfers that normally would not be treated as a second disposition of the property, for example, charitable transfers, like-kind exchanges, gift transfers, and transfers to a controlled corporation or partnership. The Finance Committee also intends for a second disposition to qualify under the nontax avoidance exception when it is an involuntary disposition, for example, foreclosure by a creditor of the related purchaser or bankruptcy of the related purchaser. The Finance Committee recommends that the exception also apply in the case of a second disposition that is also an installment sale if the terms of payment under the installment resale are substantially equivalent to, or longer than, those for the first installment sale. The exception would not apply, however, if the resale terms would permit significant deferral of recognition of gain from the initial sale when proceeds from the resale are being collected sooner.

Statute of Limitations Extension

The period for assessing a deficiency in tax attributable to a second disposition by the related purchaser does not expire until the day which is two years after the date the initial installment seller furnishes a notice to the IRS that there was a second disposition of the property. The initial seller provides this notice by answering questions 3 and 4 and completing Part III of Form 6252, Installment Sale Income, and attaching this form to the tax return for the year in which the second

[84] Code Sec. 453(e)(7).

disposition takes place. A protective notice may be filed to prevent the tolling of the statute of limitations when there are questions as to whether a second disposition has occurred or when there is a principal purpose of tax avoidance.

.04 Interest on Deferred Tax

In the case of a sale of property on the installment method for more than $150,000 by a non-dealer, the seller must pay interest on the deferred tax attributable to the installment obligation if the aggregate face amount of all the outstanding installment obligations held by the seller as of the end of the year exceeds $5,000,000.[85] Amounts treated as a payment because of a pledge of an installment obligation, as discussed at ¶ 1402, reduce the face amount of outstanding installment obligations for purposes of this rule. If interest must be paid on an installment obligation that arises during any year, interest must be paid for any subsequent year as long as any portion of that installment obligation remains outstanding.[86] Interest does not have to be paid on the deferred tax that arises from the installment sale of personal use or farm property.[87]

The amount of interest payable on the deferred tax arising from an installment obligation covered by the interest rules is determined by multiplying the "applicable percentage" of the deferred tax liability by the interest rate applied to tax deficiencies for the month in which the taxable year ends.[88] For any taxable year, the deferred tax liability from an installment obligation equals the amount of gain under the obligation that has not been recognized as of the close of the tax year multiplied by the maximum rate of tax in effect for the year[89] (if gain will be capital gain when recognized, the maximum rate of tax is the maximum rate on net capital gain under Code Sec. 1(h), or, in the case of a corporation before 2018, under Code Sec. 1201). This tax rate varies depending on whether the taxpayer is a corporation or is an individual, estate or trust.

The "applicable percentage" for an installment obligation arising in a taxable year is the percentage determined by dividing:

1. The portion of the aggregate face amount of installment obligations outstanding as of the close of the tax year in excess of $5 million, by
2. The aggregate face amount of the installment obligations outstanding as of the close of the tax year.

This applicable percentage does not change as payments are made on the installment obligation in subsequent tax years.[90]

The interest on deferred taxes arising from installment obligations for any tax year is payable as an additional tax.[91] The interest payable, however, is treated as interest that is subject to the general rules regarding the deductibility of interest on an underpayment of tax.[92]

---

[85] Code Sec. 453A.
[86] Code Sec. 453A(b)(2).
[87] Code Sec. 453A(b)(3).
[88] Code Sec. 453A(c)(2).
[89] Code Sec. 453A(c)(3).
[90] Code Sec. 453A(c)(4).
[91] Code Sec. 453A(c)(1).
[92] Code Sec. 453A(c)(5).

Example 16: In year 1, the Taxpayer, an individual who is not a dealer, sells property for $250,000, on which gain of $200,000 is realized. The Taxpayer receives $100,000 down and takes back the buyer's note for the $150,000 balance of the purchase price. The Taxpayer makes no other installment sales in year 1 but has $5,350,000 of installment obligations outstanding from sales in prior years. The Taxpayer receives no payments on the $150,000 note during year 1, so that the Taxpayer's outstanding installment obligations as of the end of year 1 total $5,500,000. Assume that the maximum tax rate imposed on individuals in year 1 is 28 percent and the interest rate on tax deficiencies as of the end of year 1 is ten percent (also assume simple interest rather than daily compounding for purposes of the example).

As of the end of year 1, the gain still to be reported by the Taxpayer as a result of the year 1 installment sale is $120,000 (the gross profit ratio of 80 percent × $150,000). The deferred tax liability on this gain is $33,600 ($120,000 × 28 percent). The applicable percentage applied to the deferred tax liability is 9.09 percent ($500,000/$5,500,000). Accordingly, the interest on the Taxpayer's deferred tax liability for year 1 arising from the year 1 installment obligations is $303.60, which is the ten percent interest rate on tax deficiencies applied to the applicable percentage of the Taxpayer's deferred tax liability of $3,036 ($33,600 × 9.09 percent).

In year 2, the Taxpayer receives no payments on the installment obligation from year 1 but receives other payments which reduce the amount of the outstanding installment obligations as of the end of year 2 to $4,800,000. Assume that the interest rate on tax deficiencies as of the end of year 2 is 12 percent (again, assume simple interest), and that the maximum tax rate on individuals remains at 28 percent. Even though the Taxpayer's outstanding installment obligations have fallen below $5 million, the Taxpayer still must pay interest on the deferred tax from the year 1 installment obligation. The amount of this interest is computed in the same fashion as the interest for year 1, with the exception of the interest rate on tax deficiencies. The applicable percentage remains the same, despite the reduction in the Taxpayer's aggregate outstanding installment obligations. Accordingly, the interest on the deferred tax for year 2 stemming from the year 1 installment obligation is $364.32, calculated as follows:

Gain to be reported		$120,000
Maximum tax rate	×	.28
Deferred tax		$ 33,600
Applicable percentage	×	.0909
		$ 3,036
Rate on deficiencies	×	.12
		$ 364.32

¶ 1402 DISPOSITION OR PLEDGE OF INSTALLMENT OBLIGATIONS

If the holder of an installment obligation disposes of that obligation, the holder usually will have a gain or loss to report. The gain or loss is considered to be gain or loss from the sale of the property for which the holder received the installment obligation.[93] Also, if an installment seller uses an installment obligation from a sale of business or rental real property for more than $150,000 to secure any debt, the net proceeds from the debt are treated as a payment on the installment obligation.[94] Repossession of property can also trigger a gain or loss for the installment seller.[95]

.01 Sale or Satisfaction at Less than Face Value

If an installment obligation is satisfied for an amount other than its face value or if an installment obligation is distributed, transmitted, sold, or otherwise disposed of, gain or loss may result. The gain or loss is measured by the difference between the basis of the obligation and the amount realized, in the case of satisfaction at other than face value or a sale or exchange.[96] In the case of some other disposition of the installment obligation, gain or loss is measured by the difference between basis and the fair market value of the obligation at the time of the disposition.[97]

The basis of an installment obligation is the difference between the face value of the obligation and the amount of income that would be returnable if the obligation were satisfied in full.[98]

> ***Example 17:*** Several years ago, the Taxpayer sold some property on the installment method. The buyer still owes the taxpayer $10,000 of the sales price. Assuming the Taxpayer's gross profit ratio is 60 percent, $6,000 (60% × $10,000) is the gain the Taxpayer still has to report. The balance of the unpaid obligation, $4,000, is the Taxpayer's basis in the installment obligation.

Any gain or loss resulting from the sale or disposition of an installment obligation is treated as if it resulted from the sale or exchange of property for which the installment obligation was received.

[A] Exceptions to Rule for Recognition of Gain

Exceptions to the requirement that gain or loss be recognized on the disposition of an installment obligation apply in the case of the transfer of the obligation at death and for transfers as part of the complete liquidation of a subsidiary corporation. Also, the sale or transfer of an installment obligation to a spouse or incident to a divorce does not result in gain or loss.

---

93 Code Sec. 453B(a).
94 Code Sec. 453A(d).
95 Code Sec. 1038.
96 Code Sec. 453B(a)(1).
97 Code Sec. 453B(a)(2).
98 Code Sec. 453B(b).

Transfer at Death

The transfer of an installment obligation as a result of the death of the seller or other holder of the obligation is not a disposition. Unreported gains from installment obligations are treated as items of gross income in respect of a decedent. This means that whoever receives the installment obligation as a result of the holder's death is taxed on the installment payments in the same way as the holder would have been if the holder had lived to receive the payments.[99] If an installment obligation is cancelled or transferred to the buyer because of the death of the holder of the obligation, however, it is a taxable disposition.

Liquidation of Subsidiary

If a parent corporation receives an installment obligation as part of the tax-free liquidation of its subsidiary corporation under Code Sec. 332 and the basis of the obligation to the parent is the same as the subsidiary's basis, the subsidiary does not recognize gain or loss on the distribution of the installment obligation.[100]

Transfer Between Spouses

No gain or loss is recognized on the transfer of an installment obligation between a husband and wife or former husband and wife if incident to a divorce. Rather, the transferor spouse merely takes the place of the transferee spouse and continues to report gain as payments are received just as the transferor spouse would have done if the obligation had not been transferred. The basis of the obligation to the transferee spouse (or former spouse) is the adjusted basis of the transferor spouse.[101]

A transfer of an installment obligation between former spouses is incident to a divorce if it occurs within one year after the date on which the marriage ends, or is related to the end of the marriage.

The nonrecognition rule does not apply if the spouse receiving the obligation is a nonresident alien.

Nonrecognition Transactions

Reg. § 1.453B-1(c) provides that if the Internal Revenue Code provides an exception to the recognition of gain or loss for a disposition, no gain or loss is recognized under Code Sec. 453B on the disposition of an installment obligation within that exception. The exceptions include:

1. Transfers to corporations under Code Secs. 351 and 361;
2. Contributions to a partnership under Code Sec. 721; and
3. Distributions by a partnership to a partner under Code Sec. 731 (except as provided by Code Secs. 704(c)(1)(B), 736, 737, and 751(b)).

This exception does not apply to a disposition that results in a satisfaction of an installment obligation, regardless of whether the disposition occurs as part of a

[99] Code Sec. 453B(c).

[100] Code Sec. 453B(d).

[101] Code Sec. 453B(g).

transaction for which the Internal Revenue Code provides an exception to the recognition of gain or loss. These dispositions include, but are not limited to:

1. The receipt of stock of a corporation from the corporation in satisfaction of an installment obligation of the corporation; and
2. The receipt of an interest in a partnership from the partnership in satisfaction of an installment obligation of the partnership.

[B] Cancellation of Installment Obligations

If the holder of an installment obligation cancels the obligation or if the obligation otherwise becomes unenforceable, it is treated as a disposition of the obligation other than a sale or exchange.[102] Gain or loss is the difference between the holder's basis in the obligation and the fair market value of the obligation at the time it is cancelled.

If the holder of the obligation accepts partial payment on the balance of the installment obligation and forgives the rest of the debt, the settlement is a disposition. Gain or loss is the difference between the holder's basis in the obligation and the amount realized on settlement.[103]

.02 Pledge of Installment Obligations

While an installment sale permits the tax on gain in excess of depreciation recapture to be deferred to future years, it also defers the receipt of the cash payments. At one time, it was possible to borrow against installment obligations to obtain cash without triggering the deferred tax. This strategy, however, was eliminated for pledges of installment obligations arising from the sale of property, other than personal use and farm property, for more than $150,000.[104]

If an installment obligation covered by Code Sec. 453A(d) is pledged by the holder as security for a debt, the net proceeds of the loan are treated as a payment on the installment obligation as of the later of the date that the debt is secured or the date the proceeds are received by the holder.[105] The "net proceeds" are the amount of the loan secured by the installment obligation less the direct expenses of obtaining the loan. To determine the amount of gain the holder must recognize on the pledge of an installment obligation, the gross profit ratio applicable to the installment obligation is applied to the net loan proceeds, just as it is applied to an actual payment to determine taxable gain.

A debt of a holder of an installment obligation is treated as secured by the installment obligation to the extent that the payment of principal or interest on the debt is directly secured, either under the terms of the debt or any other arrangement, by an interest in the installment obligation.[106]

---

[102] Code Sec. 453B(f).

[103] *See* the discussion of settlement of debt at a discount at ¶ 1201. *See also* the discussion of reduced selling price under the discussion of the general rules applicable to installment sales at ¶ 1401.02[A].

[104] Code Sec. 453A(d).

[105] Code Sec. 453A(d)(1).

[106] Code Sec. 453A(d)(4).

Receipt of payments on an installment obligation after it has been pledged as security for a debt of the holder generally does not result in recognition of additional gain.[107] If gain that otherwise would be recognized on account of the payment exceeds the gain recognized as a result of the pledge, however, this additional gain is recognized. The total amount of gain that can be recognized on an installment obligation as a result of secured loans and the receipt of actual payments can never exceed the total gain from the installment sale.

.03 Repossession of Property

Although the general rule provides that gain or loss is not recognized when seller-financed real property is reacquired by the seller, an exception applies when the seller has received money or other property from the purchaser in excess of gain reported on the sale of the property for periods prior to the reacquisition.[108] This may occur if the seller is reporting the original sale on the installment basis or if the seller elected out of installment reporting.

For a full discussion of the tax effects of the repossession of seller-financed property, see ¶ 1204.

[107] Code Sec. 453A(d)(3).

[108] Code Sec. 1038(b)(1).

Chapter 15
Casualty, Condemnation, and Demolition

¶ 1500 Overview of Chapter
¶ 1501 Business Casualty
¶ 1502 Condemnations
¶ 1503 Tax-Free Replacement of Property
¶ 1504 Demolition and Abandonment

¶ 1500 OVERVIEW OF CHAPTER

Not all real estate dispositions are voluntary. A variety of factors may force the owner of real estate to part with all or a part of his property. These "involuntary conversions," for the most part, arise from some sort of casualty. In other cases, an involuntary conversion may be the result of deliberate government action.

When property is damaged or destroyed by fire, flood, wind, vandalism, or similar events, there is a casualty. A casualty to business or investment property may produce a deductible loss, but not all casualties result in losses. If the owner is reimbursed through insurance or some other arrangement, the casualty can produce a taxable gain, if the reimbursement for the loss exceeds the basis of the property.

When the federal, state, or local government takes business or investment property for public use without the owner's consent, a condemnation of the property occurs. Since the owner of condemned property is compensated for the taking, the owner may realize a taxable gain or loss as a result of the condemnation.

Regardless of the reason for an involuntary conversion of business or investment property, if the conversion results in a gain, the owner may avoid current tax by timely reinvesting the proceeds from the involuntary conversion in qualifying replacement property.

The deduction for casualty losses to personal use property, such as a personal residence, is considered in Chapter 17. Losses from condemnation of property held for personal use, such as a personal residence, are not deductible.

¶ 1501 BUSINESS CASUALTY

Losses to business or investment real estate as a result of a casualty are deductible.[1] Unlike casualty losses to personal use property, discussed at ¶ 1703,

[1] Code Sec. 165(a).

the loss deduction for a business casualty is not subject to the "$100 deductible" or gross income limitations. Business casualty gains and losses are subject to the characterization rule of Code Sec. 1231, as discussed at ¶ 1301.02[B]. When property is used partly for business and partly for personal purposes, a casualty loss is treated as two separate casualties—one to business property and one to personal use property.

.01 Casualty Defined

Generally speaking, a casualty (other than a fire or storm, which are specifically mentioned in Code Sec. 165) is an identifiable event that is sudden, unexpected, or unusual.[2] A "sudden" event is one that is unanticipated and unintentional on the part of the one suffering the casualty, and an "unusual" event is one that is not typical for the property or activity involved. Under this definition, the term casualty embraces hurricanes,[3] floods,[4] vandalism,[5] sonic booms,[6] earthquakes or earthslides.[7]

Generally, there is no casualty when damage or destruction is a result of progressive deterioration, such as from a steadily operating cause or normal process of deterioration. The IRS has ruled that the death of trees caused by a massive attack of insects was sufficiently "sudden," however, when the death occurred within ten days after the infestation.[8] On the other hand, the loss of trees due to Dutch elm disease spread by insects was held not to be a casualty because of the progressive nature of the disease.[9] Also, in Rev. Rul. 87-59,[10] the IRS ruled that loss of timber over nine months caused by a combination of events, first an attack of pine beetles, followed by wood-destroying organisms to which the timber became susceptible because of the beetle attack, was not sudden enough to be labeled a casualty.[11]

The loss of shoreline buildings from battering by waves and winds or flooding of buildings is a casualty, but damage from gradual erosion or inundation is not.[12] Damage or loss to property from an unusual and unprecedented drought also may be a casualty.[13]

.02 Casualty Gains and Losses

In the absence of insurance or other reimbursement, a casualty to business or other income-producing property will result in a deductible loss. How this loss is measured depends on whether there was a complete or total destruction of prop-

[2] Rev. Rul. 76-134, 1976-1 CB 54.

[3] Western Products Co., 28 TC 1196, CCH Dec. 22,582, *acq.* 1958-1 CB 6; Rev. Rul. 70-164, 1970-1 CB 37.

[4] W.M. Ferguson Jr., CA-10, 3 USTC ¶ 975, 59 F.2d 893.

[5] B.E. Davis, 34 TC 586, CCH Dec. 24,246, *acq.* 1963-2 CB 4; C. Gutwirth, 40 TC 666, CCH Dec. 26,198, *acq.* 1966-2 CB 5.

[6] Rev. Rul. 60-329, 1960-2 CB 67.

[7] P. Abrams, 41 TCM 1459, CCH Dec. 37,892(M), T.C. Memo. 1981-231 (earthquake); R. Tank, CA-6, 59-2 USTC ¶ 9673, 270 F.2d 477 (earthslide).

[8] Rev. Rul. 79-174, 1979-1 CB 99.

[9] H.F. Burns, CA-6, 61-1 USTC ¶ 9127; 284 F.2d 436; *see also* W.R. Miller, 29 TCM 741, CCH Dec. 30,196(M), T.C. Memo. 1970-167, and D.W. Forrest, 45 TCM 1156, CCH Dec. 40,006(M), T.C. Memo. 1983-177, in which losses to trees from root suffocation and rain and snow damage were not sudden enough to qualify as casualties.

[10] 1987-2 CB 59.

[11] *See also* Rev. Rul. 90-61, 1990-2 CB 39.

[12] Rev. Rul. 76-134, 1976-1 CB 54.

[13] Rev. Rul. 76-521, 1976-2 CB 44; Rev. Rul. 77-490, 1977-2 CB 64.

erty or only a partial loss. Reimbursements, whether through insurance or other means, reduce the amount of the deductible loss or, if they exceed the basis of the property suffering the casualty, produce a gain.

[A] Casualty Losses

A taxpayer whose business or income-producing property is totally destroyed as a result of a casualty has a deductible loss equal to the adjusted basis of the property minus any salvage value and any insurance or other reimbursement. A taxpayer whose business or income-producing property is damaged but not completely destroyed as a result of a casualty has a deductible loss equal to the lesser of the adjusted basis of the property or the decrease in the fair market value of the property as a result of the casualty, less any insurance or other reimbursement.[14]

> ***Example 1:*** The Taxpayer owned a building that was used in a trade or business and was worth $100,000 when a fire totally destroyed the building. At the time of the fire, the Taxpayer's adjusted basis for the building was $40,000. The building was not insured and the Taxpayer expects no other reimbursement for the loss. The Taxpayer's deductible casualty loss is $40,000, the adjusted basis for the building at the time of its complete destruction.
>
> Suppose, however, that the Taxpayer's building was not completely destroyed but only partially damaged by the fire. Further suppose that after the fire, the building was worth $80,000. In this case, the Taxpayer's casualty loss is $20,000, the difference between the fair market value of the building before the casualty and its fair market value after the casualty ($100,000 - $80,000 = $20,000). If the building were worth only $50,000 after the fire, the Taxpayer's casualty loss would be limited to $40,000, the lesser of the adjusted basis of the building ($40,000) or the decline in fair market value ($100,000 - $50,000 = $50,000) as a result of the casualty.

Measuring the Decline in Fair Market Value

According to the IRS, the difference between the fair market value of property immediately before and immediately after a casualty should be determined by a "competent appraisal."[15] Competent appraisal means that the appraiser should have knowledge of sales of comparable property and conditions in the area and knowledge of the specific property involved, both before and after the casualty. The cost of cleaning up or repairing damaged property after a casualty may be used as a measure of the loss of value if:

1. The repairs are needed to bring the property back to its condition before the casualty,
2. The cost of repairs is not excessive,
3. The repairs do no more than take care of the damage, and
4. The value of the property after the repairs is no more than its value before the casualty.[16]

---

[14] Reg. § 1.165-7(b)(1).

[15] Reg. § 1.165-7(a)(2)(i).

[16] Reg. § 1.165-7(a)(2)(ii).

Separate Components

The casualty loss to business or income-producing property must be computed separately for each item that is damaged or destroyed.[17] Separate items in the case of business or income-producing real estate might include a building, the land under the building, and landscaping or other improvements to the land separate and apart from the building.

> ***Example 2:*** The Taxpayer owned rental property for which the Taxpayer paid $45,000. Of the total cost, $8,000 was allocated to the land, $35,000 to the building, and $2,000 to the landscaping. Before the building and landscaping were badly damaged by a fire, the Taxpayer had taken depreciation deductions for the building of $18,550.
>
> After the fire, competent appraisers determined that the building was worth $43,500 before the fire and only $13,000 after the fire. They also said that the landscaping (trees and shrubs) were worth $2,500 before the fire and only $1,500 after the fire. The landscaping was not covered by the Taxpayer's insurance, but the insurance company did pay the Taxpayer $30,500 for the damage to the building.
>
> The Taxpayer has a deductible casualty loss as a result of the damage to the landscaping. This loss is $1,000, the lesser of the basis of the landscaping ($2,000) or the decrease in the landscaping's fair market value ($2,500 - $1,500 = $1,000) as a result of the casualty.
>
> The Taxpayer does not have a deductible casualty loss because of the fire damage to the building. In the absence of insurance reimbursement, the Taxpayer's loss would be limited to the adjusted basis for the building or $16,450 ($35,000 original cost less $18,550 depreciation). Since the insurance reimbursement exceeds the Taxpayer's basis for the building, the Taxpayer has a casualty gain of $14,050 ($30,500 amount realized less $16,450 adjusted basis) as a result of the fire damage to the building.

[B] Casualty Gains

Reimbursement for a casualty that exceeds the adjusted basis of the damaged or destroyed property results in a gain equal to the difference between the adjusted basis of the property and the reimbursement.[18] This rule applies even if the decrease in value to the property is more than its adjusted basis. Also, while the intentional destruction of property, such as by arson, cannot produce a casualty loss, it can produce a casualty gain. The IRS has ruled that insurance proceeds received by a taxpayer who paid a third party to burn down a building represent gain includible as ordinary income in the taxpayer's gross income.[19]

A taxpayer can postpone recognition of gain realized as a result of a casualty to business or income-producing real estate by replacing the damaged or destroyed property with property that is similar or related in service or use (see

[17] Reg. § 1.165-7(b)(2)(i).

[18] Code Sec. 1001.

[19] Rev. Rul. 82-74, 1982-1 CB 110.

¶ 1503.02[A]). Gain realized as a result of a casualty is characterized as ordinary or capital under the rules of Code Sec. 1231, as discussed at ¶ 1301.02[B].

[C] Insurance and Other Reimbursements

Insurance or other types of reimbursement for a casualty reduce the amount of deductible casualty loss. No deduction is allowed to the extent a casualty loss is compensated for by insurance or otherwise.[20] Also, if a claim for reimbursement exists and the taxpayer reasonably expects to recover on the claim, the casualty loss is reduced by the expected recovery, even though the taxpayer has not actually received payment. If the taxpayer later determines with reasonable certainty that there will be no reimbursement, the taxpayer takes the casualty loss at that time for the amount of the loss that is not reimbursed.[21]

> ***Example 3:*** The Taxpayer owned business property with an adjusted basis of $100,000 which was completely destroyed by a fire in 2019. In 2019, the Taxpayer had a claim for insurance against the loss in the amount of $80,000 but did not receive any payment from the insurance in 2019. The Taxpayer's casualty loss deduction from this casualty for 2019 is $20,000.
>
> In 2020, the insurance company offered to settle the Taxpayer's claim for $70,000, and the Taxpayer accepted this offer. The Taxpayer may take a casualty loss deduction of $10,000 for 2020 as a result of the 2019 fire. This amount is the Taxpayer's loss of $30,000 ($100,000 basis - $70,000 insurance reimbursement) less the $20,000 the Taxpayer deducted for 2019.

Although insurance is the most common reimbursement for a casualty, reimbursement may come in other forms. For example, the following have been held reimbursement that reduces the amount of an otherwise deductible casualty loss:

1. If part of a federal disaster loan under the Disaster Relief Act is forgiven, the forgiven amount is a reimbursement.[22]
2. If a lessee must make repairs or repay the lessor for any part of the loss, the repayment and cost of repairs are considered a reimbursement to the lessor of the property.[23]
3. Court awards for damage or theft loss, less attorneys' fees and other necessary expenses, are reimbursements.[24]
4. Repairs, restoration, or cleanup services provided by a relief agency, such as the Red Cross, are reimbursements, but not food, medical supplies and similar items.[25]

[D] Basis After Casualty

A casualty loss deduction reduces the basis of the property damaged or destroyed by the casualty. Insurance or other reimbursements also reduce basis.[26]

---

[20] Code Sec. 165(a).

[21] Reg. § 1.165-1(d)(2).

[22] Rev. Rul. 71-160, 1971-1 CB 75.

[23] J.R. Hamilton, 29 TCM 97, CCH Dec. 29,949(M), T.C. Memo. 1970-34.

[24] H.L. Jackson, 29 TCM 980, CCH Dec. 30,281(M), T.C. Memo. 1970-227.

[25] Special Ruling, May 11, 1952, 525 CCH ¶ 6196.

[26] Code Sec. 1016(a).

Example 4: Before being partly destroyed by a fire, the Taxpayer's building had an adjusted basis of $150,000. Just before the fire, the building was worth $300,000. After the fire, the building was worth $200,000. The Taxpayer collected $100,000 from insurance on the building as a result of the fire. Since the insurance fully compensated the Taxpayer for the loss, the Taxpayer has no casualty loss deduction. The $100,000 insurance recovery reduces the Taxpayer's adjusted basis for the building from $150,000 to $50,000.

If the Taxpayer's building was not insured, the $100,000 loss would be deductible as a casualty loss. If this were the case, the $100,000 casualty loss would reduce the adjusted basis of the building by $100,000, from $150,000 to $50,000.

.03 Disaster Area Losses

A taxpayer that suffers a deductible loss from a disaster in a federally declared disaster area may elect to deduct that loss on the tax return for the year immediately preceding the tax year of the disaster.[27] If a taxpayer makes this election, the loss is treated as if it occurred in the preceding year.[28] The purpose of this election is to provide taxpayers who are affected by a major disaster immediate relief in the form of a tax refund or reduced tax liability. An affected taxpayer who chooses not to make the election simply deducts any casualty loss under the normal rule, that is, on the return for the tax year in which the loss actually occurs.

Example 5: A calendar year Taxpayer's office building is damaged by a flood in June of 2020, and the town in which the flood occurred is declared a federal disaster area. The Taxpayer may deduct the casualty loss as a result of the flood for the 2019 tax year.

[A] Method of Taking Earlier Deduction

A taxpayer who wants to deduct a disaster area loss for the preceding year must write and sign a statement saying that this is what the taxpayer wants to do. The statement should specify the date or dates of the disaster and the city, town, county, and state where the damaged or destroyed property was located. This statement must be filed with the taxpayer's return or amended return for the year in which the taxpayer is taking the deduction.[29] Generally, an affected taxpayer must file the required statement by the due date, without extensions, for filing the tax return for the year in which the disaster actually occurred or the due date, with extensions, for the return for the preceding tax year.

[B] Revocation of Election

Under the regulations, a taxpayer may revoke an election to claim a disaster area loss for the preceding tax year within 90 days of making the election by returning any refund or credit received as a result of the election to the IRS. If the taxpayer revokes the election before receiving a refund, the refund must be

[27] Code Sec. 165(i)(1).
[28] Code Sec. 165(i)(2).
[29] Reg. § 1.165-11(e).

returned within 30 days following its receipt.[30] However, a taxpayer who claimed a 1976 disaster loss on the 1975 return, subsequently revoked the election on an amended 1975 return, and took the loss on a timely filed 1976 return was permitted to claim the loss on his 1976 return. The Tax Court held that Reg. § 1.165-11(e) was invalid to the extent it imposed the 90-day period for revoking an election under these circumstances. According to the Court, although the intent of the legislature was to give taxpayers immediate help, a comparison of the relative tax benefits might not be possible until the time arrives for filing their return for the year of the loss.[31]

¶ 1502 CONDEMNATIONS

The condemnation of property by federal, state or local government is, essentially, a forced sale of the condemned property. As a sale, gain or loss, generally must be recognized for tax purposes in the same fashion as any other sale. As with other involuntary conversions, however, a taxpayer may postpone recognition of gain from a condemnation by the timely replacement of the condemned property (see ¶ 1503).

.01 Condemnation Defined

Condemnation is the process by which private property is legally taken, without the owner's consent, for public use. Since the owner receives money or property in exchange for the taken property, a condemnation is like a forced sale by the owner to the condemning authority.

In addition to actual condemnation, an involuntary conversion also occurs if property is sold under the threat or imminence of condemnation.[32] A taxpayer is under threat of condemnation if a representative of a government body or a public official authorized to acquire property for public use tells the taxpayer that the government body or official has decided to acquire the taxpayer's property. From this communication, the taxpayer would have reasonable grounds to believe that if the taxpayer did not sell voluntarily the property would be condemned.[33] Also, a taxpayer is under threat of condemnation if the taxpayer sells the property to someone other than the condemning authority and the taxpayer has reasonable grounds to believe that the property will be condemned. If the buyer of the property knows it is under threat of condemnation in this situation and sells the property to the condemning authority, the buyer's sale also is a condemnation.[34]

The IRS also has ruled that a taxpayer is under threat of condemnation if the taxpayer learns of a decision to acquire the property for public use through newspaper reports or other news media and this report is confirmed by a representative of the government body or public official involved. The taxpayer must have reasonable grounds to believe that the property will be condemned if the taxpayer

[30] Reg. § 1.165-11(e).

[31] C. Matheson, 74 TC 836, CCH Dec. 37,093, *acq.* 1981-2 CB 2.

[32] Reg. § 1.1033(a)-2(a).

[33] Rev. Rul. 74-532, 1974-2 CB 270.

[34] Rev. Rul. 81-181, 1981-2 CB 162.

does not sell voluntarily. If the taxpayer relies on oral statements by government representatives or officials, the IRS may ask for written confirmation of the statements.[35]

.02 Gain or Loss from Condemnation

A taxpayer whose business or income-producing property is condemned, or sold under threat of condemnation, computes the gain or loss in a fashion similar to the computation of gain or loss in the case of an ordinary sale. Gain or loss is the net condemnation award (the condemnation award minus the expenses of obtaining the award), less the adjusted basis of the condemned property.

> ***Example 6:*** The Taxpayer owned property with an adjusted basis of $87,000. The state highway authority acquired the property under threat of condemnation. The Taxpayer received $94,000 for the property and spent $2,000 to obtain the award. The Taxpayer realized a gain of $5,000 as a result of the involuntary conversion of the property ($94,000 award - $2,000 expenses = $92,000 - $87,000 adjusted basis = $5,000 gain).

Gain or loss from a condemnation is characterized under the rules of Code Sec. 1231, as discussed at ¶ 1301.02[B]. Recognition of gain from a condemnation may be postponed, as discussed below, if the condemned property is replaced with like-kind property. The condemnation of property that is used partly for business purposes and partly for personal purposes is treated as the condemnation of separate properties. Note that unlike casualty losses, no deduction is allowed for losses resulting from the condemnation of personal-use property.

.03 Determination of the Condemnation Award

A condemnation award is the money or value of other property given to a taxpayer for the taxpayer's condemned property or the proceeds from the sale of property under threat of condemnation. Amounts withheld from the award by the government to pay off liens against the property, such as a mortgage, or other debts of the property owner are part of the amount realized by the owner. This is the rule even if the owner of the property is not personally liable for a mortgage debt against the property.[36] For instance, if a taxpayer has acquired property worth $100,000 subject to a $50,000 mortgage (regardless of whether or not the taxpayer was personally liable for the mortgage debt) and, in a condemnation proceeding, the government awards the taxpayer $60,000 and awards the mortgagee $50,000 in satisfaction of the mortgage, the entire $110,000 is considered to be the condemnation award and the amount realized by the taxpayer.

Before determination of the amount of gain or loss from a condemnation, the gross amount of the award is reduced by the expenses of obtaining the award. Also, if only part of a taxpayer's property is taken, the gross award is reduced by any severance damages and any special assessments levied against the property.[37] Interest paid on an award for a delay in payment is, of course, interest income and is not treated as part of the condemnation award itself.

---

[35] Rev. Rul. 63-221, 1963-2 CB 332. *See also* Rev. Rul. 74-8, 1974-1 CB 200.

[36] Reg. § 1.1033(a)-2(c)(11).

[37] Reg. § 1.1033(a)-2(c)(10).

[A] Severance Damages

Severance damages are compensation paid to a taxpayer when part of the property is condemned and the value of the remaining property is decreased as a result of the condemnation. For example, a taxpayer may receive severance damages if the property retained after the condemnation is subject to flooding, or if the taxpayer must replace fences, dig new wells or ditches, or plant trees to restore the remaining property to the same usefulness it had before the condemnation.

Severance damages are distinct from the condemnation award. The condemnation award is compensation for the property taken, and severance damages are compensation for the injury to the property retained. The IRS has ruled that severance damages exist only when the designation has been stipulated by both contracting parties.[38] The amount of severance damages paid in connection with the purchase of property by a condemning authority is considered stipulated between the parties and clearly shown, although the contract executed by the parties does not refer to severance damages as such, if the property owner is furnished an itemized statement or closing sheet at settlement and payment by the condemning authority, which indicates the specific amount allocable for severance damages.[39] At the least, the owner of the condemned property must be able to show that a portion of the payment received represents severance damages to remaining property or the entire payment will be treated as a condemnation award paid for the condemned property.[40]

A taxpayer who receives severance damages in connection with the condemnation of a portion of the property reduces the severance damages by the expenses of obtaining the damages and then by any special assessment levied against the remaining part of the property if the assessment was withheld from the award by the condemning authority.[41] The taxpayer then applies the remaining net severance damages against the basis of the remaining property. If the severance damages are based on damage to a specific part of the remaining property, only the basis of that portion of the retained property damaged as a result of the condemnation is reduced by the net severance damages.[42]

If net severance damages exceed the basis of the property damaged and retained by the owner, the owner has a taxable gain. Recognition of this gain may be postponed by the purchase of replacement property.[43] If the owner restores the remaining property to its former use, the owner may treat the restoration cost as the cost of replacement property. The owner also may elect to postpone gain if the severance damages, together with the money received for the condemned property, are used to acquire nearby property so that the owner can continue the

---

[38] Rev. Rul. 59-173, 1959-1 CB 201.

[39] Rev. Rul. 64-183, 1964-1 CB (Part 1) 297.

[40] L.A. Beeghly, 36 TC 154, CCH Dec. 24,797, *acq.* 1962-1 CB 3; A.B. Johnson, 42 TC 880, CCH Dec. 26,920, *acq.* 1965-2 CB 5.

[41] C.C. Green, 37 BTA 25, CCH Dec. 9905, *acq.* 1938-2 CB 13; Pioneer Real Estate Co., 47 BTA 886, CCH Dec. 12,854, *acq.* 1943 CB 18.

[42] Rev. Rul. 68-37, 1968-1 CB 359.

[43] Rev. Rul. 73-35, 1973-1 CB 367.

business, even if the owner retains the damaged property for which the owner received the severance damages.[44]

The expenses of obtaining a condemnation award and severance damages must be allocated between the two when the expenses cannot be specifically allocated to one or the other.

> ***Example 7:*** The Taxpayer receives a condemnation award. One-fourth of it was stated in the award as severance damages. The Taxpayer incurred legal expenses in connection with the entire condemnation proceeding. The Taxpayer must allocate one-fourth of the legal expenses to the severance damages and the other three-fourths to the award for the condemned property. On the other hand, if the Taxpayer incurred the legal expenses only to collect the severance damages, the legal expenses would reduce the amount of the severance damages. In this case, the Taxpayer could not use the legal expenses to reduce the amount of the condemnation award.

[B] Special Assessments

A special assessment may be levied against the remaining property when only part of an owner's property is taken in a condemnation and the remaining portion of the property is benefited by the improvement resulting from the condemnation. Examples of such improvements may be a widening of a street or the installation of a sewer. Special assessments levied against the remaining property and withheld from the condemnation award are not treated as part of the condemnation award and so reduce the gain or increase the loss that the owner realizes as a result of the condemnation.[45] The assessment must be withheld from the award.[46] If severance damages are included in the award, special assessments must be used first to reduce the severance damages before applying any excess to the condemnation award.

> ***Example 8:*** The city acquired 25 feet of the Taxpayer's land in order to widen the street in front of the property. The Taxpayer was awarded $5,000 for this and spent $300 to obtain the award. The city levied a special assessment against the Taxpayer's remaining property for the street improvement and then paid the Taxpayer $4,200. The Taxpayer's net award is $3,900 ($5,000 gross award – $300 expenses = $4,700 – $800 special assessment = $3,900). If the $800 special assessment were not withheld from the award and the Taxpayer were paid $5,000, the net award would be $4,700, even if the Taxpayer later paid the special assessment of $800.
>
> Suppose, however, that the $5,000 awarded to the Taxpayer was divided, $4,000 for the condemned property and $1,000 for severance damages, and the Taxpayer's expenses were solely allocable to obtaining the severance damages. In this case, the $1,000 in severance damages are reduced to zero by first subtracting the $300 expenses and then $700 of the special assessment. The

[44] Rev. Rul. 80-184, 1980-2 CB 232. *See* the discussion of the tax-free replacement of property at ¶ 1503.

[45] C.C. Green, 37 BTA 25, CCH Dec. 9905, *acq.* 1938-2 CB 13; Pioneer Real Estate Co., 47 BTA 886, CCH Dec. 12,854, *acq.* 1943 CB 18.

[46] Reg. § 1.1033(a)-2(c)(10).

Taxpayer's award for the condemned property, $4,000, is reduced by the $100 balance of the special assessment, leaving a net condemnation award of $3,900.

The following examples were prepared by the IRS to illustrate how severance damages and special assessments affect gain or loss from a condemnation. In all of the following examples, these facts are assumed.

Comprehensive Examples—Facts:

The Taxpayer bought 640 acres of farmland for $128,000 ($200 per acre). The land has a grove of trees and a natural spring that livestock use for shade and water. There were no improvements on the land when the Taxpayer bought it, but the Taxpayer later built storage sheds on the land at a cost of $3,000.

The city condemned a ten-acre strip of land through the property. The condemned strip included the land on which the Taxpayer built the sheds and keeps the livestock from using the grove of trees or the spring on the other side of the property. Before the condemnation, the Taxpayer took $400 depreciation on the sheds and had deducted a $250 casualty loss for fire damage to one of the sheds in the previous year. The Taxpayer's total condemnation award was $12,000, and the Taxpayer spent $600 for legal and appraisal fees to obtain the award.

Comprehensive Example 9—No special assessment or severance damages: No special assessment was levied against the Taxpayer's remaining property and the Taxpayer did not receive any severance damages. The Taxpayer's gain from the condemnation is $7,050, computed as follows:

Total award		$12,000
Less: Legal and appraisal fees		600
Net condemnation award		$11,400
Less:		
10 acres @ $200	$2,000	
Cost of sheds	3,000	
	$5,000	
Less: Depreciation and casualty loss deduction	650	
Adjusted basis of condemned property		4,350
Gain realized		$7,050

Comprehensive Example 10—Special assessment but no severance damages: Before paying the Taxpayer the award, the city levied an assessment of $1,600 against the property the Taxpayer retained for benefits received from the public improvement fund. The city withheld the assessment from the Taxpayer's award, and the Taxpayer received only $10,400. The Taxpayer's gain is $5,450, computed as follows:

Total award		$12,000
Less: Legal and appraisal fees		600
		$11,400
Less: Special assessment		1,600
Net condemnation award		$9,800
Less:		
10 acres @ $200	$2,000	
Cost of sheds	3,000	
	$5,000	
Less: Depreciation and casualty loss deduction	650	
Adjusted basis of condemned property		4,350
Gain realized		$5,450

Comprehensive Example 11—Severance damages but no special assessment: Of the Taxpayer's $12,000 award, $2,000 was stated in the award as severance damages and $10,000 for the condemned property. No special assessment was levied against the retained property. The Taxpayer's $600 expense for obtaining the award applies to the entire $12,000. The Taxpayer's gain is $5,150, computed as follows:

Severance damages	$2,000	
Condemnation award		$10,000
Less: Legal and appraisal fees		
$600 × ($2,000/$12,000)	100	
$600 × ($10,000/$12,000)		500
Net severance damages	$1,900	
Basis of remaining property (630 acres @ $200)	$126,000	
Less: Net severance damages	1,900	
New basis of remaining property	$124,100	
Net condemnation award		$9,500
Less:		
10 acres @ $200	$2,000	
Cost of sheds	3,000	
	$5,000	
Less: Depreciation and casualty loss deduction	650	
Adjusted basis of condemned property		4,350
Gain realized		$5,150

Comprehensive Example 12—Severance damages and special assessment: Of the Taxpayer's $12,000 award, $2,000 was stated in the award as severance damages and $10,000 for the condemned property. The city levied a special assessment of $1,600 against the remaining property. The city withheld the $1,600 from the award paid the Taxpayer. The Taxpayer's $600 expense of obtaining the award applies to the entire $12,000. The Taxpayer's gain is $5,150, computed as follows:

Severance damages	$2,000	
Condemnation award		$10,000
Less: Legal and appraisal fees		
$600 × ($2,000/$12,000)	100	
$600 × ($10,000/$12,000)		500
	$1,900	
Less: Special assessment	1,600	
Net severance damages	$300	
Basis of remaining property		
(630 acres @ $200)	$126,000	
Less: Net severance damages	300	
New basis of remaining property	$125,700	
Net condemnation award		$9,500
Less:		
10 acres @ $200	$2,000	
Cost of sheds	3,000	
	$5,000	
Less: Depreciation and casualty loss deduction	650	
Adjusted basis of condemned property		4,350
Gain realized		$5,150

Comprehensive Example 13—Special assessment exceeds severance damages: Of the Taxpayer's $12,000 award, $2,000 was stated in the award as severance damages and $10,000 for the condemned property. The city levied a special assessment of $2,250 against the remaining property. The city withheld the $2,250 from the award paid the Taxpayer. The Taxpayer's $600 expense of obtaining the award applies to the entire $12,000. The Taxpayer's gain is $4,800, computed as follows:

Severance damages	$2,000	
Condemnation award		$10,000
Less: Legal and appraisal fees		
$600 × ($2,000/$12,000)	100	
$600 × ($10,000/$12,000)		500
Severance damages minus expenses	$1,900	
Condemnation award minus expenses		$9,500
Less: Special assessment:		
Subtracted from severance damages	1,900	
Subtracted from condemnation award		350
Net severance damages	$-0-	
Net condemnation award		$9,150
Less:		
10 acres @ $200	$2,000	
Cost of sheds	3,000	
	$5,000	
Less: Depreciation and casualty loss deduction	650	
Adjusted basis of condemned property		4,350
Gain realized		$4,800

If the Taxpayer's net severance damages exceeded the basis in the remaining property, the new basis of the remaining property would be reduced to zero.

¶ 1503 TAX-FREE REPLACEMENT OF PROPERTY

The involuntary conversion of property through casualty, theft, condemnation or threat of condemnation may result in either gain or loss, as discussed at ¶ 1501.02 and ¶ 1502.02. A loss from an involuntary conversion of real estate used for a business or income-producing activity is deductible under the usual rules that apply to business losses.[47] When an involuntary conversion results in a gain, the usual rules affecting the sale or exchange of property generally would require that the owner recognize the gain and pay a tax. Involuntary conversion gains, however, may escape current tax under the nonrecognition provision contained in Code Sec. 1033. For purposes of Code Sec. 1033, involuntary conversions include sales or transfers to federal, state, local, or Indian tribal goverments to implement hazard mitigation under the Robert T. Stafford Disaster Relief and Emergency Assistance Act or the National Flood Insurance Act.[48]

The taxpayer who receives insurance or other compensation for the involuntary conversion of the property in excess of the basis of the property realizes a gain.

[47] Code Sec. 165.

[48] Code Sec. 1033(k).

This gain is not recognized if the property is directly replaced, for example, by the insurer, with property that is "similar or related in service or use" to the converted property.[49] In this case, the nonrecognition treatment is mandatory and the replacement property simply takes as its basis the adjusted basis of the involuntarily converted property.[50]

Direct conversion into similar property, however, is unusual. In the usual case, the owner of involuntarily converted property will receive cash compensation, through insurance in the case of a casualty, the condemnation award in the case of an actual condemnation, or sales proceeds in the case of a sale under threat of condemnation. The owner of property that is involuntarily converted at a gain into money or dissimilar property must recognize that gain unless the owner replaces the property with similar property within a specified period and elects not to recognize the gain.[51]

.01 Election to Postpone Gain

The owner of involuntarily converted property can elect to postpone reporting the gain from the conversion if the owner purchases property that is similar or related in service or use to the condemned, damaged, destroyed, or stolen property. Nonrecognition also applies if the owner purchases a controlling interest in a corporation that owns similar property.[52] The cost of replacement property must at least equal the proceeds from the involuntary conversion for complete nonrecognition. The owner must recognize gain to the extent the amount realized from the involuntary conversion exceeds the cost of the replacement property.[53]

In order for the nonrecognition provision to apply, it must be the owner of the property who replaces the converted property and takes ownership of the replacement property. For instance, when a corporation's property is condemned, the corporation is the taxpayer that must make the replacement. A sole shareholder to whom all the corporate assets are distributed in complete liquidation following the condemnation is not entitled to purchase replacement property.[54] Similarly, a wife who purchases replacement property, after her husband's death, from funds that pass to her absolutely under state law upon his death is not a taxpayer who can replace condemned property owned solely by the husband during his lifetime.[55]

In a private letter ruling,[56] a wife was required to recognize gain from real estate held by her and her husband as tenants by the entirety when real estate was sold under threat of condemnation and the proceeds were reinvested in replacement property with the title held solely in the husband's name.

Grantors and grantor trusts, however, may be treated as the same taxpayer for the tax-free replacement of involuntarily converted property. For instance, the grantor of a trust, the corpus of which would revert to the grantor at a later date, was the taxpayer who could elect nonrecognition of gain from the sale of con-

[49] Code Sec. 1033(a)(1).

[50] Reg. § 1.1033(a)-2(b).

[51] Code Sec. 1033(a)(2).

[52] Code Sec. 1033(a)(2)(A).

[53] Reg. § 1.1033(a)-2(c)(7).

[54] Rev. Rul. 73-72, 1973-1 CB 368.

[55] G.W. Jayne Est., 61 TC 744, CCH Dec. 32,497.

[56] IRS Letter Ruling 8429004, March 22, 1984.

demned trust property that was required to be added to the trust corpus.[57] Also, if a taxpayer's grantor trust purchases replacement property for property of the taxpayer that has been involuntarily converted into money, the purchase can qualify the taxpayer's gain for nonrecognition under Code Sec. 1033.[58]

It had been the position of the IRS that there had to be an actual reimbursement in order for the owner of damaged or destroyed property to obtain nonrecognition benefits. For instance, if a hurricane uprooted trees and the timber were not insured, the sale of the downed or damaged timber and the use of the proceeds to buy replacement timber would not be eligible for nonrecognition.[59] The IRS later reversed itself, however, and now holds that the nonrecognition of gain provision of Code Sec. 1033 is applicable to proceeds received from the voluntary sale of timber downed by high winds, earthquake, or volcanic eruption when the proceeds are used to purchase other standing timber.[60]

[A] Advantages and Disadvantages of the Election

Because of the preferential treatment afforded capital gain, the decision on whether to elect nonrecognition requires some careful calculations.

Gain recognized on involuntary conversions is subject to the characterization rules of Code Sec. 1231, as discussed at ¶ 1301.02[B]. Gain from involuntary conversions is also subject to the recapture rules, also discussed at ¶ 1301.03. This means that gain from an involuntary conversion may qualify as capital gain. If gain is recognized and replacement property is purchased, the replacement property has a basis equal to its full cost.

On the other hand, if gain is not recognized, the basis of the replacement property is the adjusted basis of the involuntarily converted property, as discussed at ¶ 1503.03. A lower basis, in turn, means lower or reduced depreciation deductions. In short, increased depreciation deductions are purchased at the cost of a current tax if the taxpayer chooses not to elect the tax-free replacement provision. This can be a benefit when capital gain generated on an involuntary conversion is subject to a lower tax rate than the income that will be offset by future depreciation deductions.

[B] Method of Election

A taxpayer elects not to recognize gain on an involuntary conversion under Code Sec. 1033 by not reporting the gain for the year in which it is realized. In addition, the taxpayer must file a statement that supports nonrecognition with the tax return for each year gain is realized as a result of the involuntary conversion. This statement should contain all of the details of the involuntary conversion at a gain, including the details that relate to the replacement of the property, such as a description of the property, date and type of conversion, computation of the gain, and decision to replace.

---

[57] Rev. Rul. 70-376, 1970-2 CB 164.

[58] Rev. Rul. 88-103, 1988-2 CB 304.

[59] Rev. Rul. 72-372, 1972-2 CB 471.

[60] Rev. Rul. 80-175, 1980-2 CB 230, *revoking* Rev. Rul. 72-372, 1972-2 CB 471.

If a taxpayer makes the election not to recognize gain from an involuntary conversion and does not acquire replacement property within the required time period, spends less on the replacement property than was realized from the involuntary conversion, or decides not to replace the converted property, the taxpayer must file an amended return for the year in which the election was made not to recognize gain and must recompute the tax liability for that year.[61]

If a taxpayer who realizes a gain from an involuntary conversion does not elect nonrecognition on the return for the year in which the taxpayer realizes the gain, and subsequently purchases replacement property within the required replacement period, the taxpayer may file a claim for a credit or refund.[62]

[C] Replacement Period

The replacement period for property damaged or destroyed by a casualty begins on the date the property is damaged or destroyed.[63] The replacement period ends two years after the close of the tax year in which the taxpayer realized any part of the gain on the casualty.[64]

In the case of a condemnation, the replacement period begins on the earliest of:

1. Actual condemnation or seizure of the property;
2. Threat or imminence of condemnation or seizure; or
3. Sale or exchange of the property under threat or imminence of condemnation or seizure.[65]

The replacement period ends three years after the close of the first tax year in which the taxpayer realizes any part of the gain on the condemnation, if the property condemned or sold under threat of condemnation is real property held for use in a trade or business or for investment (but not property held primarily for sale).[66] For any property other than real property held for use in a trade or business or investment, the replacement period following an involuntary conversion as a result of condemnation or threat of condemnation is two years.[67]

As discussed at ¶ 1502.01, a threat or imminence of condemnation occurs when the owner of the property is informed by a public official or government body that is authorized to acquire the property that a decision has been made to acquire the property and it is reasonable to believe that the property will be taken. The communication may be either oral or written.

> ***Example 14:*** A calendar-year Taxpayer is notified on August 2, 2019, by the city in which the business is located that the city intends to acquire the Taxpayer's business real property by negotiation or by condemnation. On May 5, 2020, the city condemns the property and pays the Taxpayer $110,000 for the property, which had an adjusted basis at that time of $85,000. The replacement period for this property began on August 2, 2019, the date the Taxpayer was

[61] Reg. § 1.1033(a)-2(c)(2).

[62] Rev. Rul. 63-127, 1963-2 CB 333.

[63] Code Sec. 1033(a)(2)(B).

[64] Code Sec. 1033(a)(2)(B)(i).

[65] Code Sec. 1033(a)(2)(B).

[66] Code Sec. 1033(g)(4).

[67] Code Sec. 1033(a)(2)(B)(i).

notified of the intent to condemn the property, and the replacement period ends on December 31, 2023, three years after the last day of the year in which the taxpayer realized gain from the condemnation.

Once the threat or imminence of condemnation exists, the owner may purchase replacement property, as long as the owner continues to hold the replacement property at the time of the actual conversion.[68] Property acquired before there is a threat of condemnation does not qualify as replacement property because it is not property that is acquired during the replacement period.

The replacement property actually must be acquired during the replacement period in order for the nonrecognition provision to apply. For instance, an advance payment from the proceeds of property that is involuntarily converted to a contractor for the construction of replacement property is not a purchase of replacement property when the replacement property actually does not exist prior to the end of the replacement period.[69]

Extension of Replacement Period

In the case of other property, the replacement period may be extended if the owner of involuntarily converted property can show reasonable cause for not being able to make the replacement within the normal replacement period. A taxpayer in need of an extension should apply to the District Director for the IRS district in which the taxpayer filed the return containing the election to postpone the gain. The application should contain all the details about the need for the extension and should be filed before the end of the replacement period, although a taxpayer may file an application within a reasonable time after the replacement period if the taxpayer can show reasonable cause for the delay.[70]

Ordinarily, the IRS grants requests for extensions near the end of the replacement period or the extended replacement period. The IRS usually limits extensions to a period of one year or less. The high market value or scarcity of replacement property is not a sufficient reason for granting an extension. If a taxpayer's replacement property is under construction and the taxpayer can clearly show that the replacement or restoration cannot be made within the replacement period, the IRS generally will grant an extension of the replacement period.

Deficiency Assessments

If a taxpayer elects not to recognize gain from an involuntary conversion, the IRS may assess a deficiency for any tax year in which the taxpayer realizes any part of the gain within three years of the date the taxpayer notifies the District Director that the taxpayer is replacing the involuntarily converted property, or intends not to replace, within the replacement period.[71]

---

[68] Real Estate Corp., Inc., 22 TCM 654, CCH Dec. 26,135(M), T.C. Memo. 1963-138.

[69] Rev. Rul. 56-543, 1956-2 CB 521.

[70] Code Sec. 1033(a)(2)(B)(ii); Reg. § 1.1033(a)-2(c)(3).

[71] Code Sec. 1033(a)(2)(C).

.02 Replacement Property

Generally, involuntarily converted property must be replaced with property that is similar or related in service or use to the converted property in order for the nonrecognition provision of Code Sec. 1033 to apply.[72] A special rule, however, applies to condemned business or investment real property.[73] Other special rules apply to property damaged by federally declared disasters.[74] There is also a requirement that replacement property be acquired from an unrelated person in several situations.[75]

[A] Similar Property

The only statement in the regulations regarding what constitutes similar property is the following:[76]

> There is no investment in property similar in character and devoted to a similar use if—
>
> (i) The proceeds of unimproved real estate, taken upon condemnation proceedings, are invested in improved real estate.
>
> (ii) The proceeds of conversion of real property are applied in reduction of indebtedness previously incurred in the purchase of a leasehold.
>
> (iii) The owner of a requisitioned tug uses the proceeds to buy barges.

The IRS had applied a very strict test to determine whether replacement property was similar or related in service or use for all property. Under this test, the replacement property had to be functionally the same as the converted property. A series of appellate court decisions, however, held that this test was not correct when applied to owner-investors rather than owner-users.[77] Accordingly, the meaning of similar or related in service or use depends on whether the taxpayer is an owner-user or an owner-investor.[78]

Owner-User

For property used by the owner, replacement property is similar or related in service or use only if it is functionally the same as the converted property. Property is not considered similar or related in service or use to the converted property unless the physical characteristics and end uses of the replacement and converted properties are closely related. Under this strict function test, the IRS has ruled that a recreational billiards center is not sufficiently similar to bowling alleys destroyed by fire.[79] Also, a floating seafood processing plant in which the taxpayer invested insurance proceeds from a land-based seafood processing plant that was destroyed by fire is not similar or related in service or use and does not qualify as replacement property.[80]

---

[72] Code Sec. 1033(a)(2)(A).

[73] Code Sec. 1033(g). *See* ¶ 1503.02[C].

[74] Code Sec. 1033(h). *See* ¶ 1503.02[D].

[75] Code Sec. 1033(i). *See* ¶ 1503.02[B].

[76] Reg. § 1.1033(a)-2(c)(9).

[77] Liant Record, Inc., CA-2, 62-1 USTC ¶ 9494, 303 F.2d 326; Capitol Motor Car Co., CA-6, 63-1 USTC ¶ 9344, 314 F.2d 469; Steuart Bros., Inc., CA-4, 59-1 USTC ¶ 9143, 261 F.2d 580.

[78] Rev. Rul. 64-237, 1964-2 CB 319.

[79] Rev. Rul. 76-319, 1976-2 CB 242.

[80] Rev. Rul. 77-192, 1977-1 CB 249.

Although it did not specifically state, the IRS also followed the stricter test imposed on owner-users in a ruling involving a bank that had a building destroyed by a tornado. Before it was destroyed, the bank's building was leased for the production of rental income. The replacement building, in addition to being leased, was used by the bank for its banking operations. The part of the replacement building occupied by the bank was not similar or related in service or use to the converted property, and only the tenant-occupied part of the building qualified as replacement property.[81]

Owner-Investor

In considering whether replacement property acquired by an investor is similar or related in service or use, the IRS looks to the similarity in the relationship of the services or uses that the converted and replacement properties have to the owner. Whether replacement property has the same relationship of services or uses as the property it replaces is determined by the following factors:

1. Whether the properties are of similar service to the taxpayer;
2. The nature of the business risks connected with the properties; and
3. What the properties demand of the taxpayer in the way of management, service, and relations to the owner's tenants.

Under this test, the IRS has ruled that the investment of proceeds from condemnation of land and a warehouse held for rental purposes in constructing, on other land owned by the taxpayer, a gas station held for rental purposes was a replacement of property similar or related in service or use.[82] On the other hand, a hotel of which the taxpayer was the owner-lessor under a net lease was not similar to a hotel of which the taxpayer was owner-operator. As lessor, the taxpayer had a fixed return not dependent on economic fluctuations and risks of liability to guests. As operator, the taxpayer had to deal directly with guests. Thus, the nature of the taxpayer's relationship to the property was substantially changed.[83]

[B] Required Replacement from Unrelated Person

Some taxpayers cannot take advantage of the nonrecognition provisions of Code Sec. 1033 if they acquire the replacement property from related persons (as defined in Code Secs. 267(b) or 707(b)(1)). The rule does not apply if the related person acquired the property from an unrelated person within the replacement period.[84] The taxpayers affected by this rule are:

1. C corporations;
2. Partnerships in which one or more C corporations own more than 50 percent of the capital or profits interest at the time of the involuntary conversion; and
3. Any other taxpayer if the aggregate amount of realized gain on involuntarily converted property during the year exceeds $100,000.

---

[81] Rev. Rul. 79-261, 1979-2 CB 295.

[82] Rev. Rul. 71-41, 1971-1 CB 223.

[83] Rev. Rul. 70-399, 1970-2 CB 164.

[84] Code Sec. 1033(i).

[C] Special Rule for Condemned Property

A special rule applies to the replacement of real property used in a trade or business or held for investment if the property is condemned or sold under threat of condemnation. This special rule does not apply to real property held for sale. Under the special rule, nonrecognition of gain is available if the taxpayer replaces the condemned property, or property sold under threat of condemnation, with like-kind property.[85] This is the same like-kind test that applies to tax-free exchanges under Code Sec. 1031 as discussed at ¶ 1302. The like-kind test for replacement of condemned realty applies only to direct replacement and not to replacement through acquisition of corporate control, as discussed at ¶ 1503.02[F].[86]

Replacement of condemned property that does not qualify under the like-kind test of Code Sec. 1033(g) may still qualify for nonrecognition under Code Sec. 1033(a), if the replacement property is similar or related in service or use to the condemned property.[87] The IRS has ruled that condemnation proceeds received for property containing both the taxpayer's residence and business qualified for nonrecognition when similar amounts were spent to purchase new residential property and an apartment building. The new residential property was similar or related in service or use to the replaced residence, while the apartment building was like-kind property as to the converted business property.[88]

Replacement of Leased Property

Under the like-kind test, a leasehold of 30-year duration is of like-kind to a fee interest. When property under a lease is condemned, the lessee cannot rely on the like-kind test if the lessee replaces a leasehold of less than 30 years with a fee interest. The IRS has indicated, however, that a leasehold interest may be similar or related in service or use to a fee interest.[89] Accordingly, a lessee who receives payment when the leased property is condemned may purchase replacement property in fee under the stricter similar or related in service or use test and avoid recognition of income as a result of the payment. As long as the property purchased will be used for the identical purpose for which the converted leasehold was used, the former lessee does not have to recognize gain under Code Sec. 1033.

Of course, the lessee must actually give up the leasehold interest either by actual condemnation or by sale under threat of condemnation. In *Woodall,*[90] the taxpayers were partners who operated a nightclub on leased premises. The partnership was required under the lease to carry insurance coverage for the leased property. The property was damaged by fire and the partnership received insurance proceeds. The partnership repaired the premises, and later decided to buy the premises. The partnership claimed non-recognition of gain on the receipt of the insurance proceeds on the theory that the fee interest in the property purchased qualified as replacement property under Code Sec. 1033. Both the Tax Court and

[85] Code Sec. 1033(g).

[86] Code Sec. 1033(g)(2).

[87] Rev. Rul. 71-41, 1971-1 CB 223; Westchester Development Co., 63 TC 198, CCH Dec. 32,843, *acq.* 1975-2 CB 2.

[88] Rev. Rul. 72-424, 1972-2 CB 469.

[89] G.C.M. 38975, June 15, 1982; Rev. Rul. 83-70, 1983-1 CB 189.

[90] T.C. Memo. 1991-15, *aff'd,* 964 F.2d 361 (5th Cir. 1992).

Circuit Court held that *Woodall* was factually distinguishable from Rev. Rul. 83-70 because in the earlier ruling, the taxpayers gave up their leasehold interest. In contrast, in *Woodall*, the taxpayers did not suffer an involuntary conversion of their leasehold. The loss was only to the taxpayer's improvements. The purchase of the building replaced no damaged property and the funds used for its purchase did not fall under Code Sec. 1033.[91]

Severance Damages

Severance damages are compensation for the reduced value of remaining property after a portion of the owner's property is taken in condemnation. Severance damages are payments in addition to the condemnation award, and, as discussed above, the usual way to handle severance damages is to treat them as a reduction in the basis of the remaining property. If severance damages exceed remaining basis, the excess is a taxable gain.

Gain from severance damages may be reinvested under Code Sec. 1033 to avoid current tax on the gain.[92] At one time, the IRS asserted that the reinvestment had to be in property similar or related in service or use, rather than like-kind property, which allows nonrecognition in the case of a condemnation award. For instance, in Rev. Rul. 80-184,[93] part of a severance damage award was used to demolish a building leased to retail stores and to construct a warehouse for lease in its place. The remaining part of the award was used to purchase another parcel of land and construct an office building. The IRS ruled that the reinvestments were in property similar or related in service or use, and the taxpayer could defer the recognition of gain realized as a result of the severance damage award. Later, however, the IRS recognized that severance damages and condemnation awards should be treated in the same fashion and ruled that severance damages may be accorded nonrecognition treatment under Code Sec. 1033(g)(1), even though the taxpayer reinvests the severance damages in property that is not similar or related in service or use to the condemned property.[94]

[D] Federally Declared Disasters

If property held for productive use in a trade or business or for the production of income is involuntarily converted as a result of a federally declared disaster, tangible property of a type held for productive use in a trade or business is treated as property that is similar or related in service or use.[95] In the case of the loss of a principal residence, no gain is recognized on insurance proceeds received for unscheduled property and other insurance proceeds are treated as received for a single item of property. Any property that is similar or related in service or use to the converted residence is treated as similar or related in service or use to the single item of property.[96]

[91] *See also* FSA 200127001.

[92] Rev. Rul. 72-433, 1972-2 CB 470; Rev. Rul. 72-549, 1972-2 CB 472.

[93] 1980-2 CB 232.

[94] Rev. Rul. 83-49, 1983-1 CB 191, *modifying* Rev. Rul. 80-184, 1980-2 CB 232.

[95] Code Sec. 1033(h)(2).

[96] Code Sec. 1033(h)(1).

[E] Outdoor Advertising Displays

A taxpayer may elect to treat a qualifying outdoor advertising display as real property if the taxpayer did not claim a Code Sec. 179 deduction for the display or take an investment credit in a previous year.[97] An outdoor advertising display is a sign or device that is rigidly assembled and permanently attached to the ground, a building, or any other permanent structure that is used for commercial or other advertisement to the public.[98]

An election to treat an outdoor advertising display as real property for purposes of tax-free replacement under Code Sec. 1033 cannot be revoked without the consent of the IRS.[99] If a taxpayer makes this election and replaces an involuntarily converted outdoor advertising display with real property in which the taxpayer holds a different kind of interest, the replacement property may qualify as like-kind property.[100] For instance, real property purchased to replace a destroyed billboard and leased property on which the billboard was located qualify as property of a like kind.

[F] Acquisition of Corporate Control

A taxpayer may replace property by acquiring control of a corporation that owns property that is similar or related in service or use to the involuntarily converted property.[101] If the owner of involuntarily converted property does this, gain is recognized only to the extent it exceeds the cost of the stock of the corporation. Control is defined as stock having at least 80 percent of the combined voting power of all classes of voting stock and at least 80 percent of the total number of shares of all other classes of stock.[102]

> ***Example 15:*** The Taxpayer owned property with an adjusted basis of $175,000 that the Taxpayer used in the business. The property was destroyed by fire and the taxpayer received $200,000 from the insurer. The Taxpayer was unable to find suitable replacement property, but did buy, for $200,000, control of a corporation that owns property similar or related in service or use to the destroyed property. If the Taxpayer purchased the stock within the replacement period, the Taxpayer can postpone the tax on the $25,000 gain realized as a result of the involuntary conversion.

It is the position of the IRS that the corporation must own the similar or related in service or use property at the time the taxpayer acquires control in order for Code Sec. 1033 to apply.[103] In other words, the taxpayer cannot use the proceeds of an involuntary conversion to acquire control of a corporation by transferring the proceeds to the corporation and then having the corporation purchase the replacement property. The Tax Court, however, has held otherwise.

---

[97] Code Sec. 1033(g)(3)(A).

[98] Code Sec. 1033(g)(3)(C).

[99] Code Sec. 1033(g)(3)(B).

[100] Code Sec. 1033(g)(3)(D).

[101] Code Sec. 1033(a)(2)(A).

[102] Code Sec. 1033(a)(2)(E)(i).

[103] Rev. Rul. 77-422, 1977-2 CB 307.

In *John Richard Corp.*,[104] the taxpayer purchased control of a newly formed corporation in order to replace involuntarily converted property. On the following day, the corporation purchased property similar or related in service or use to the taxpayer's converted property. The Tax Court ruled that the taxpayer was entitled to the nonrecognition of gain provision when the organization of the new corporation, the taxpayer's acquisition of its stock and the purchase of replacement property by the corporation were merely steps in an integrated transaction designed to replace the taxpayer's involuntarily converted property. The Court went on to say that any distinction in the application of Code Sec. 1033 under these circumstances and in the case of a purchase of stock in a corporation that previously owned the property was not justified.

Although the IRS does not approve, the use of a newly formed corporation to acquire replacement property may offer substantial tax savings. As discussed below, replacement property generally takes the same basis as the involuntarily converted property. The owner of involuntarily converted property who acquires stock of a new corporation with the proceeds of an involuntary conversion has a basis for the stock equal to the basis of the converted property. When the new corporation uses the proceeds of the involuntary conversion to purchase replacement property, the corporation's basis is the cost of the property. The new corporation, therefore, may have substantially larger depreciation deductions than would be available to the owner if he had directly purchased the replacement property.

.03 Basis of Replacement Property

The basis of property acquired as replacement property following an involuntary conversion into money is its cost, decreased by the amount of gain that is not recognized on the conversion.[105]

> ***Example 16:*** The Taxpayer's store was destroyed by a fire. At the time of the casualty, the Taxpayer's adjusted basis for the store was $126,000. The Taxpayer's fire insurer paid the Taxpayer $136,000 as compensation for the loss and the Taxpayer spent $132,000 to build a new store on the land. The Taxpayer's gain as a result of the involuntary conversion of the store is $10,000, but the Taxpayer reports only $4,000, the amount of gain that was not reinvested in the new store. The Taxpayer's basis for the new store is $126,000, the $132,000 cost less the $6,000 of gain that was not recognized following the involuntary conversion. If the Taxpayer had spent the entire $136,000 to rebuild, the basis would still be $126,000 ($136,000 - $10,000 gain not recognized).

If the replacement property consists of more than one piece of property, the basis must be allocated to the properties in proportion to their costs.[106] This allocation rule also applies to the allocation of basis between land and improvements.[107]

---

[104] 46 TC 41, CCH Dec. 27,915, *nonacq.* 1974-2 CB 5 and *acq.* 1967-2 CB 3.

[105] Code Sec. 1033(b).

[106] *Id.*

[107] Rev. Rul. 73-18, 1973-1 CB 368.

Example 17: The Taxpayer owned land on which a warehouse had been built for use in the Taxpayer's business. When the Taxpayer's basis for the land and building was $500,000, the city condemned the property for public purposes and paid the Taxpayer $800,000 as a condemnation award. The Taxpayer used the $800,000 award to purchase new land for $200,000 and to construct a new warehouse for $600,000.

The Taxpayer's gain from the involuntary conversion of the land and warehouse is $300,000. This gain is not recognized, however, since the Taxpayer purchased replacement property within the required time period. The Taxpayer's basis for the new land and warehouse is $500,000, the $800,000 cost decreased by the $300,000 of gain that was not recognized. This $500,000 basis is apportioned between the land and warehouse according to cost as follows:

Basis of land: $500,000 × $200,000/$800,000 = $125,000.

Basis of warehouse: $500,000 × $600,000/$800,000 = $375,000.

Gain that is not recognized following the involuntary conversion and replacement of property must be used to reduce the basis of replacement property as a whole. When a taxpayer who elected not to recognize the gain realized on the involuntary conversion of unimproved land subsequently acquired improved land, he selected only the land as replacement property so that the unrecognized gain would only reduce the basis of the land and the taxpayer would have a higher basis for the improvements. The IRS, however, ruled that the taxpayer must apply the unrecognized gain to reduce the basis of the replacement property as a whole, and the remaining basis must be allocated to the land and improvements in proportion to their costs.[108]

[A] Replacement with Corporate Stock

If the basis of corporate stock acquired as replacement property (see ¶ 1503.02[F]) is reduced by unrecognized gain, an equal amount also must be applied to reduce the basis of property held by the corporation at the time the taxpayer acquired control of the corporation. The reduction is limited so as not to reduce the basis of the corporation's property below the taxpayer's adjusted basis for the corporation stock. The decrease in the basis of the corporation's property is applied first to property that is similar or related in service or use to the converted property, then to depreciable property, and finally to any other corporate property.[109]

[B] Direct Conversion to Replacement Property

If property is involuntarily converted directly into other property, the basis of the replacement property is the same as that of the converted property, decreased by any money received and not expended for replacement property, and increased by any gain or decreased by any loss recognized on the conversion.[110]

[108] Rev. Rul. 79-402, 1979-2 CB 297.

[109] Code Sec. 1033(b)(3).

[110] Code Sec. 1033(b)(1).

¶ 1504 DEMOLITION AND ABANDONMENT

At times, a taxpayer may dispose of real property by demolishing the property in order to clear the land on which it stands for other uses. In rare cases, a taxpayer may decide to simply walk away from real property and abandon it. While demolition cannot produce a loss deduction, abandonment may.

.01 Demolition

Before 1984, the costs of demolishing an historic structure and the adjusted basis of the structure at the time of demolition had to be added to the basis of the land on which the structure was located. For all other improvements, however, the tax treatment of demolition depended on whether the property was acquired with an intent to demolish it. If the owner acquired property with an intent to demolish it, costs and other losses were added to the basis of the land. If the owner did not have the intent to demolish at the time of purchase, the owner could deduct the cost and other losses as a result of a later demolition. Needless to say, the question of intent led to a great deal of litigation.

Since 1984, however, the Internal Revenue Code has eliminated all controversy. The owner of property must add the costs and other losses incurred in connection with the demolition of all buildings, including certified historic structures, to the basis of the land on which the demolished buildings were located.[111] A current deduction is not permitted for demolition losses.

.02 Abandonment

If nondepreciable property, such as land, is permanently retired from use in business or a transaction entered into for profit and physically abandoned, an abandonment loss deduction may be available under Code Sec. 165(a).[112] The deduction is the adjusted basis of the nondepreciable property when abandoned. Similarly, an abandonment loss deduction may be available when depreciable property is abandoned. The regulations provide:

> Where an asset is retired by actual physical abandonment (as, for example, in the case of a building condemned as unfit for further occupancy or other use), loss will be recognized measured by the amount of the adjusted basis of the asset abandoned at the time of such abandonment. In order to qualify for the recognition of loss from physical abandonment, the intent of the taxpayer must be irrevocably to discard the asset so that it will neither be used again by him nor retrieved by him for sale, exchange, or other disposition.[113]

[A] Abandonment of Land

Since land cannot be physically picked up and tossed away, proving an actual physical abandonment of land may be a difficult task. Generally, nonpayment of taxes is an important factor in proving the abandonment of land, especially when supported by other factors. In *Enid Ice & Fuel Co.*,[114] the Court sustained an

---

[111] Code Sec. 280B.

[112] Reg. § 1.165-2(a).

[113] Reg. § 1.167(a)-8(a)(4).

[114] DC Okla., 56-2 USTC ¶ 9665, 142 F. Supp. 486.

abandonment loss when, in addition to not paying real estate taxes, the corporate owner charged the property off on its books, had no intent to claim a right of redemption against the property, and held a worthless redemption right because the property was worth less than the unpaid taxes.[115]

[B] Abandonment of Improvements

An interesting question is whether improvements or buildings can be abandoned without also abandoning the land on which they sit. The Tax Court has allowed an abandonment loss for a building, even though the owner retained the land. In *H.R. Hanover,*[116] a partnership claimed an abandonment loss for a hotel equal to its adjusted basis of $260,000. The Court looked for three points to sustain an abandonment loss:

1. The intent to irrevocably discard the property so that it would be neither reused nor retrieved;
2. An affirmative act that establishes this intent; and
3. The complete elimination of all value of the property and recognition by the owner that the property no longer possesses any utility.

The Tax Court held that these conditions were met and that it was not impossible for an owner to physically abandon improvements to land and claim a loss deduction, even though the underlying land is retained. Once the owner established that the building had no value to it, based on the cost involved in reopening the hotel, the Tax Court saw the following as indicating an intent to abandon as well as affirmative acts of abandonment:

1. Business records stated that economic conditions required abandoning the hotel;
2. Building was locked and boarded;
3. Barricade was placed around the building to protect passers-by from falling masonry and stone;
4. Utilities were terminated;
5. Insurance was terminated;
6. Maintenance was discontinued;
7. Building was not held for sale.

The hotel in the *Hanover* case would have been demolished had it not been for the cost involved. Under current law, if a building is abandoned and then demolished, Code Sec. 280B, as discussed at ¶ 1504.01, would require that the basis of the building and the cost of demolition be added to the basis of the land.

---

[115] *See also* J.R. Hopkins, 15 TC 160, CCH Dec. 17,811, *acq.* 1951-1 CB 2, in which it was held that the existence of back taxes equal to market value of property does not prove that all equity has been lost, but when tax arrearages greatly exceed the value and the owner recognizes loss of his equity, a deductible loss is sustained.

[116] 38 TCM 1281, CCH Dec. 36,262(M), T.C. Memo. 1979-332.

Chapter 16
Contributions and Gifts

¶ 1600 Overview of Chapter
¶ 1601 Charitable Gifts
¶ 1602 Gifts and Contributions of Mortgaged Property
¶ 1603 Gifts of Loss Property

¶ 1600 OVERVIEW OF CHAPTER

In addition to a sale, exchange, involuntary conversion, or abandonment of property, the owner of real estate may make a gift of the property to family, friends, charities, government, or other entities. Obviously, family and charitable giving have many estate planning implications that are beyond the scope of this work. Also, lifetime gifts may produce gift tax consequences and affect future estate taxes. Neither gift nor estate taxes are properly the subject of this chapter or, for that matter, this book. Rather, the focus here is on the income tax consequences of gratuitous real estate transfers.

¶ 1601 CHARITABLE GIFTS

Real estate donated to charity or governmental units may provide the donor with a charitable deduction, subject to the limits on charitable deductions contained in Code Sec. 170. To qualify as a charitable contribution, the donor must transfer the property without receiving or expecting financial or economic benefit equal to the value of the property transferred. If the donor does receive, or can reasonably expect to receive, "substantial benefits" that are greater than those that would inure to the general public from a transfer for charitable purposes, a charitable deduction is not allowed.[1]

Generally speaking, an individual's deduction for charitable contributions in any one year is limited to 50 percent of the individual's adjusted gross income for the year.[2] A 60 percent limit applies to an individual's cash contributions to public charities, operating foundations, and certain government units.[3] A 30 percent limit may apply to gifts of certain capital gain property,[4] and also to gifts of ordinary income property to nonoperating foundations and certain other organizations.[5] A corporation's deduction is generally limited to 10 percent of its taxable income for the year.[6] A five-year carryover period is provided for contributions in excess of

[1] Rev. Rul. 76-185, 1976-1 CB 60. *See* the discussion of gifts with mixed motives at ¶ 1601.02.
[2] Code Sec. 170(b)(1)(A).
[3] Code Sec. 170(b)(1)(G).
[4] Code Sec. 170(b)(1)(C).
[5] Code Sec. 170(b)(1)(D).
[6] Code Sec. 170(b)(2).

these limits.[7] The special rules that affect charitable gifts of appreciated property are discussed at ¶ 1601.03.

.01 Valuation of Real Estate Gifts

The first step in determining the charitable contribution deduction for gifts of real property is to determine the fair market value of the property on the date of the contribution. Fair market value is defined as the price at which a willing buyer and a willing seller agree, neither being under any compulsion to buy or sell, and both having reasonable knowledge of the relevant facts.[8] If there is a restriction on the use of the donated property, the fair market value must reflect that restriction. For example, if a taxpayer donates land and restricts its use to agricultural uses, the taxpayer must value the land at its value for agricultural purposes, even if it would have a higher fair market value if it were not restricted.

Because each piece of real estate is unique and its valuation is complicated, a detailed appraisal by a professional appraiser is usually necessary to establish fair market value. A qualified appraisal is required, as discussed at ¶ 1601.01[B], for gifts of property that exceed $5,000. The weight given an appraisal depends on the completeness of the report, the qualifications of the appraiser, and the appraiser's demonstrated knowledge of the donated property. An appraisal must give all the facts on which to base an intelligent judgment of the value of the property. An appraiser's opinion is never more valid than the facts on which it is based.

[A] Types of Appraisals

In general, there are three main approaches to the valuation of real estate. An appraisal may involve the combined use of two or three methods rather than only one method.

Comparable Sales

The best indicator of value is, of course, an actual sale of the property on the date it is being valued. The next best indicator is a sale of the property reasonably close to the valuation date. Intervening factors which would affect value and which occur between the sale date and the valuation date must be identified and considered. Examples of such factors include a change in zoning, eminent domain, improvements built near the property, or a change in the neighborhood.

Absent a recent sale of the property being valued, the next best indicator of value is comparable sales. The comparable sales method of valuing property compares the donated property with several similar properties that have been sold. The selling prices, after adjustments for differences in date of sale, size, condition, and location, indicate the estimated fair market value of the donated property. If the comparable sales method is being applied to unimproved real estate, the appraiser

[7] Code Sec. 170(d).

[8] *See* the IRS Valuation Guide for Income, Estate and Gift Taxes. The Guide is designed primarily to benefit IRS officials who negotiate settlements of income, estate and gift tax cases in which valuation of real or personal property is necessary, but it also gives taxpayers and tax advisors insight into the major valuation problems and the accepted methods and approaches applied by IRS Appeals Officers in considering valuation questions. The material here on valuing real estate is based on this Guide and IRS Publication 561, "Determining the Value of Donated Property."

should consider the following factors when comparing the potential comparable property and the donated property:

1. Location, size, and zoning use or restrictions;
2. Accessibility and road frontage, and available utilities and water rights;
3. Riparian rights and existing easements, rights-of-way, leases, etc.;
4. Soil characteristics, vegetative cover, and status of mineral rights; and
5. Any other factors affecting value.

Comparable selling prices must be adjusted to reflect any differences between the sale property and the donated property. Because differences of opinion may arise between appraisers as to the degree of comparability and the amount of adjustment considered necessary for comparison purposes, an appraiser should document each item of adjustment. Only comparable sales having the least adjustments in terms of items and/or total dollar adjustments should be considered as comparable to the donated property.

Capitalization of Income

The capitalization of income method of valuing donated property capitalizes the net income from the property at a rate that represents a fair return on the particular investment at the particular time, considering the risks involved. This method is particularly useful for the appraisal of business or rental properties. The income flow should take into account the future demand for space, the vacancy rate, the cost of labor, maintenance, real estate taxes, and utilities. The key elements in this approach to valuing real estate are the determination of the income to be capitalized and the rate of capitalization.

In determining the income to be capitalized, the appraiser should consider actual income from the property, as well as potential income from the property's highest and best use. The usual method of determining income is to reduce gross income by certain expenses, including interest, because of the different financing choices that are available, and depreciation, which can be accounted for in the capitalization rate. Generally, a reduction for prospective income taxes is not taken because it is too speculative.

There are several methods for determining a proper capitalization rate to apply to the income stream in order to determine value. One is the direct capitalization rate, which is the rate derived by dividing the selling price into net income for comparable properties. With the residual method, a capitalization rate is built based on what a hypothetical willing buyer would want as a rate of return, considering liquidity, risk, safety, and depreciation. Since a common problem in real estate valuation is the allocation of cost to land and buildings, the method often used to separate land and building value is the building residual method. The building residual method is considered the most helpful of the several methods of determining a capitalization rate because it uses land, which can be valued more accurately in most cases, as a basis for the first step in the valuation process.

Still another method of determining a capitalization rate is the band of investment method. Under this method, a capitalization rate is derived by considering the rate for financing, the rate for equity, and the rate for depreciation.

Replacement Cost

This method of real estate valuation, used alone, usually does not result in a determination of fair market value, unless the property has only a special or limited use. Rather, replacement cost generally sets the upper limit of value, particularly in periods of rising costs, because it is reasonable to assume that an informed buyer will not pay more for the real estate than it would cost to reproduce a similar property. Of course, this reasoning does not apply if a similar property cannot be created because of location, unusual construction, or some other reason. Generally, this method of valuation serves to support the value determined from other methods. When the replacement cost method is applied to improved real estate, the land and improvements are valued separately.

The replacement cost of a building is determined from the materials, quality of workmanship, and the number of square or cubic feet in the building. This cost represents the total cost of labor and materials, overhead, and profit. After the replacement cost is determined, the following factors must be considered:

1. Physical deterioration—the wear and tear on the building itself;
2. Functional obsolescence—usually in older buildings with, for example, inadequate lighting, plumbing, or heating, small rooms, or a poor floor plan; and
3. Economic obsolescence—outside forces causing the whole area to become less desirable.

[B] Required Appraisal

Generally, if a claimed deduction for an item of donated property is more than $5,000, the taxpayer must obtain a qualified appraisal made by a qualified appraiser and must attach an appraisal summary (Section B, Form 8283) to the tax return.[9] This rule applies to charitable contributions made by individuals, partnerships, and corporations. The appraisal itself must be attached to the tax return in the case of a contribution exceeding $500,000.[10]

A qualified appraisal is an appraisal document that:

1. Relates to an appraisal made not earlier than 60 days before the contribution of the appraised property;
2. Does not involve a prohibited appraisal fee;
3. Includes certain information (detailed below); and
4. Is prepared, signed, and dated by a qualified appraiser.[11]

The taxpayer must receive the qualified appraisal before the due date, including extensions, of the return on which a charitable contribution deduction is first

[9] Reg. § 1.170A-13(c)(2).

[10] Code Sec. 170(f)(11).

[11] Reg. § 1.170A-13(c)(3).

claimed for the donated property. If the taxpayer first claims the deduction on an amended return, the qualified appraisal must be received before the date on which the return is filed.[12]

Prohibited Appraisal Fee

No part of the fee arrangement for a qualified appraisal can be based on a percentage of the appraised value of the property.[13] This rule does not apply to a fee paid to a generally recognized association that regulates appraisers if:

1. The association is not organized for profit and no part of the net earnings benefits any private shareholder or individual;
2. The appraiser does not receive any compensation from the association or any other persons for making the appraisal; and
3. The fee arrangement is not based in whole or in part on the amount of the appraised value that is allowed as a deduction after an IRS examination or otherwise.

A fee arrangement based on what is allowed as a deduction, after IRS examination or otherwise, generally is treated as a fee based on a percentage of appraised value.

Required Information

A qualified appraisal must include the following information:[14]

1. A description of the property in sufficient detail for a person who is not generally familiar with the type of property to determine that the property appraised is the property that was or will be contributed;
2. The physical condition of the property;
3. The date or expected date of contribution;
4. The terms of any agreement or understanding entered into (or expected to be entered into) by or on behalf of the donor;
5. The name, address, and taxpayer identification number of the qualified appraiser and, if the appraiser is a partner, an employee, or an independent contractor engaged by a person other than the donor, the name, address, and taxpayer identification number of the partnership or the person who employs or engages the appraiser;
6. The qualifications of the qualified appraiser who signs the appraisal, including the appraiser's background, experience, education, and any membership in professional appraisal associations;
7. A statement that the appraisal was prepared for income tax purposes;
8. The date or dates on which the property was valued;
9. The appraised fair market value on the date or expected date of contribution;

[12] Reg. § 1.170A-13(c)(3)(iv)(B).

[13] Reg. § 1.170A-13(c)(6).

[14] Reg. § 1.170A-13(c)(3)(ii).

10. The method of valuation used to determine fair market value, such as the capitalization of income approach, the comparable sales or market data approach, or the replacement cost less depreciation approach;
11. The specific basis for the valuation, such as any specific comparable sales transaction; and
12. A description of the fee arrangement between the donor and appraiser.

Qualified Appraiser

A qualified appraiser is an individual who declares on the appraisal summary (Section B, Form 8283) that he or she:

1. Is publicly acknowledged as an appraiser or performs appraisals on a regular basis;
2. Is qualified to make appraisals of the type of property being valued;
3. Is not an excluded individual; and
4. Understands the penalty for aiding and abetting an understatement of tax liability.[15]

An appraiser must complete Part IV of Section B, Form 8283 to be considered a qualified appraiser. More than one appraiser may appraise the property, provided that each complies with the requirements, including signing the qualified appraisal and appraisal summary.

The following persons cannot be qualified appraisers with respect to particular property:[16]

1. The donor of the property.
2. The donee of the property.
3. A party to the transaction in which the donor acquired the property being appraised, unless the property is donated within two months of the date of acquisition and its appraised value does not exceed its acquisition price. This applies to the person who sold, exchanged, or gave the property to the donor, or any person who acted as an agent for the transferor or donor in the transaction.
4. Any person employed by, or related (or married to a person who is related) under Code Sec. 267(b) to, any of the above persons. For example, if the donor acquired property from a dealer, neither the dealer nor persons employed by the dealer can be qualified appraisers for that property.
5. An appraiser who is regularly used by a person in 1, 2, or 3 and who does not perform a majority of the appraisals made during the tax year for other persons.

In addition, a person is not a qualified appraiser for a particular donation if the donor had knowledge of facts that would cause a reasonable person to expect the

[15] Reg. § 1.170A-13(c)(5).

[16] Reg. § 1.170A-13(c)(5)(iv).

appraiser to falsely overstate the value of the donated property.[17] For example, if a donor makes an agreement with the appraiser that the property will be valued at more than its fair market value, the appraiser is not a qualified appraiser for the donation.

.02 Gifts with Mixed Motives

As noted at ¶ 1601, if the donor of property receives or expects to receive substantial benefits that are greater than those than inure to the general public as a result of the contribution, a charitable deduction is not allowed. When the donor is a business, however, the donor may be entitled to a business expense deduction when it expects a benefit in return for its "contribution." The best treatment depends on the property involved and the various limitations on charitable and business expense deductions. A gift that would exceed the charitable contribution limit may have a business seeking an expense deduction. On the other hand, since the applicable business expense deduction for appreciated property is its cost, a charitable deduction measured by fair market value may be preferred. Also, if the expected benefit has a long life or adds to the value of other property, the cost of the benefit may have to be capitalized.

A charitable deduction was disallowed for the contribution of a school site located on a large tract of land that the taxpayer intended to develop when the school site became accessible after construction by the government of two new access roads. The taxpayer's remaining property was also relatively inaccessible and would have benefited greatly from the construction of the new roads. The contribution of the school site was made with the expectation of receiving "a significant economic benefit."[18]

In another case, however, the taxpayer obtained a charitable deduction for land donated as a school site as a condition of obtaining a zoning change.[19] The taxpayer was under no obligation to make the contribution gratuitously and the local government would have had to purchase or condemn the land if the taxpayer had not donated it.

In a private letter ruling, the IRS allowed a company a charitable contribution deduction for an overpass and a private frontage road donated to local government.[20] The company was located on a limited access highway and could be reached from either of two interchanges along a private frontage road that it owned or from a private overpass that it owned. The company built an interchange to connect with its overpass and then donated the new interchange and its frontage roads to the local government. The IRS concluded that the company would not receive "a substantial benefit," even though the interchange would make it easier for employees, visitors, and others to reach the company. These were incidental benefits in light of the improved traffic patterns that would be of public benefit. The "incidental benefits" realized by the company included improved road connections

[17] Reg. § 1.170A-13(c)(5)(ii).

[18] Ottawa Silica Co., CA FC, 83-1 USTC ¶ 9169, 699 F.2d 1124.

[19] J. Scheffres, 28 TCM 234, CCH Dec. 29,472(M), T.C. Memo. 1969-41.

[20] IRS Letter Ruling 8421018, February 15, 1984.

for access to its facilities, an immediate deduction for the cost of improvements that would otherwise be recoverable through depreciation, and removal of the donated property from the tax roles and the expense of local property taxes.

.03 Gifts of Appreciated Property

As noted above, the deduction for charitable gifts of property generally is measured by the fair market value of the property. There are, however, limitations that may apply in the case of a contribution of appreciated property, and the amount of the charitable deduction for gifts of such property may have to be reduced.[21] Whether a reduction is necessary and the amount of the reduction depends on the type of property given, the recipient of the property, and the use to which the recipient puts the property. Any reduction in the contribution of appreciated property is applied before the percentage of income limitations contained in Code Sec. 170(b).

[A] Ordinary Income Property

In the case of a contribution by an individual or by a corporation of ordinary income property, the charitable contribution deduction must be reduced by the amount of gain that would not have been long-term capital gain if the property had been sold by the donor at its fair market value at the time of its contribution.[22] "Ordinary income property" is property that would produce gain that is not long-term capital gain if sold at its fair market value.[23] In short, the charitable contribution deduction for ordinary income property is limited to the adjusted basis of the property at the time of the gift. The nature of the recipient has no effect on the amount of the allowable deduction.

In the case of real property, ordinary income property would include dealer property (see ¶ 1002.01), depreciable property that is subject to recapture (see ¶ 1301.03), and any other property subject to various recapture provisions, including mining and farm property. A real estate broker's charitable contribution deduction for parcels of real estate donated to churches was disallowed because the broker failed to prove the basis in the parcels. The broker's deduction, if allowed, would have been limited to the basis in the parcels because they were part of the real estate business and, if sold at the time of the contribution, would have produced ordinary income as dealer property.[24]

[B] Capital Gain Property

Capital gain property includes any property on which the taxpayer would realize long-term capital gain if the taxpayer sold the property for its fair market value on the date of the contribution. It also includes property used in a trade or business under Code Sec. 1231(b), to the extent recapture provisions do not apply to convert otherwise capital gain into ordinary income.[25] As a general rule, a taxpayer's deduction for a charitable gift of capital gain property is equal to the

[21] Code Sec. 170(e).

[22] Code Sec. 170(e)(1)(A).

[23] Reg. § 1.170A-4(b)(1).

[24] E.B. Lindsley, Jr., 47 TCM 540, CCH Dec. 40,652(M), T.C. Memo. 1983-729.

[25] Code Sec. 170(e)(1)(B).

property's fair market value. An individual, however, must reduce the charitable contribution deduction for capital gain real property by the amount that would be long-term gain if the real property were sold if:

1. The individual contributes the property to certain private nonoperating foundations,[26] or
2. The individual elects to disregard the special 30 percent of adjusted gross income limitation for capital gain property in favor of the 50 percent limitation.[27]

A corporation that makes a charitable gift of real property to a private nonoperating foundation also must reduce its deduction by the amount that would be long-term gain if the property were sold.

Private nonoperating foundations that require a reduction of charitable gifts of capital gain property by the amount of appreciation include any organization, other than a public charity or a private operating foundation, exempt from tax under Code Sec. 501(c)(3).[28]

[C] Mixed Property

If a taxpayer gives property to charity that would produce both ordinary income and long-term capital gain if sold, then both rules affecting the charitable contribution of appreciated property apply. To determine the deduction, the taxpayer must first reduce the fair market value of the property by the amount that would be ordinary income, then apply the capital gain appreciated property rule.

Example 1: The Taxpayer, an individual, donates a building with a fair market value of $100,000 to a private nonoperating foundation. At the time of the contribution, the Taxpayer's adjusted basis for the building is $40,000, and there is $12,000 in prior depreciation deductions subject to recapture as ordinary income. The Taxpayer figures the amount of the contribution as follows:

Fair market value		$100,000
Less:		
Ordinary income	$12,000	
Capital gain	48,000	60,000
Contribution		$40,000

The capital gain portion of the contribution equals the fair market value of the property less the Taxpayer's adjusted basis and gain subject to recapture ($100,000 - $40,000 - $12,000 = $48,000). Since the Taxpayer's contribution is of capital gain property to a private nonoperating foundation, the Taxpayer could deduct the $40,000 contribution for the current year only to the extent that it did not exceed 20 percent of adjusted gross income,[29] rather than the 50 percent of adjusted gross income limitation that generally applies to individual charitable contributions.

[26] Code Sec. 170(e)(1)(B)(ii).

[27] Code Sec. 170(b)(1)(C)(iii).

[28] Code Sec. 170(b)(1)(B).

[29] Code Sec. 170(b)(1)(D).

.04 Gifts of Partial Interests

If a taxpayer gives less than the entire interest in property to charity, the taxpayer generally is not entitled to a charitable deduction for the contribution.[30] Exceptions apply to transfers in trust that meet special requirements,[31] and to transfers not in trust to the extent that the value of the interest would be deductible if the interest had been transferred in trust.[32] A contribution of the right to use property that the taxpayer owns, for instance, the rent-free use of an office, is treated as a contribution of less than the taxpayer's entire interest in property.[33]

The purpose of the rule is to prevent a double tax benefit that might occur in certain situations when a taxpayer gives less than the entire interest in property. For instance, if a taxpayer let a charity use an office in a building rent free, the taxpayer's gross income would be reduced by the rent the taxpayer does not collect on the office and, if a charitable deduction were allowed, by the charitable deduction for the value of the office. Compare this to a cash contribution equal to the value of the rental which produces but a single tax benefit.

There are, however, exceptions to the general rule that denies a charitable deduction for gifts of partial interests not in trust.[34] Specifically, a charitable deduction is allowed for contributions of:

1. An undivided portion of an entire interest in property;
2. A remainder interest in a personal residence or farm; and
3. Qualified real property interests for conservation purposes.

Each of these exceptions is discussed further below.

The deduction for a charitable contribution of a partial interest in property covered by the exceptions is the fair market value of the partial interest at the time of the contribution.[35] If the contribution is of a remainder interest in real property, straight-line depreciation and depletion must be taken into account in determining value, and the value must be determined using actuarial tables as spelled out in the regulations.[36]

[A] Undivided Portion

A charitable deduction is allowed for contributions not in trust of an undivided portion of the donor's entire interest in property. An undivided portion of a donor's entire interest in property must consist of a fraction or percentage of each and every substantial interest or right owned by the donor in the property and must extend over the entire term of the donor's interest.[37]

> ***Example 2:*** The Taxpayer contributes to a charitable organization an undivided one-half interest in 100 acres of land, whereby as tenants in common they share in the economic benefits from the property. The present value of the contributed property is $50,000. The Taxpayer's contribution consists of an

[30] Code Sec. 170(f)(3).

[31] Code Sec. 170(f)(2); Reg. § 1.170A-6.

[32] Code Sec. 170(f)(3)(A).

[33] Reg. § 1.170A-7(a)(1).

[34] Code Sec. 170(f)(3)(B).

[35] Reg. § 1.170A-7(c).

[36] Reg. § 1.170A-12.

[37] Reg. § 1.170A-7(b)(1)(i).

undivided portion of the entire interest in the property and, therefore, the Taxpayer is entitled to a charitable deduction of $50,000.

If the Taxpayer had given the charity 50 of the 100 acres instead of an undivided interest in the entire 100 acres, the Taxpayer also would be entitled to a charitable deduction.

Suppose, however, that the Taxpayer only had a life estate in the 100 acres rather than owning the 100 acres outright. In this case, a gift of a one-half interest in the life estate would also qualify for a charitable contribution deduction since the Taxpayer would be giving a undivided portion of the entire interest (a life estate) in the property.

[B] Remainder Interest

The Internal Revenue Code generally does not permit a charitable contribution deduction for remainder interests unless a charitable deduction would be allowed if the charitable gift were given in trust. The only transfers of remainder interests in trust that qualify for a charitable contribution deduction are those in which the annual dollar-amount income interest is payable as a fixed annuity or payable under a trust instrument that provides for the income beneficiaries to receive payments annually, based on a fixed percentage of the net fair market value of the trust's assets—a charitable remainder annuity trust, a unitrust, or a pooled income fund.[38] Charitable gifts of remainder interests in personal residences and farms, however, are specifically excluded from this rule and a charitable deduction is available for gifts of remainder interests in these properties.[39]

Personal Residence

A charitable deduction is allowed for the value of a charitable contribution of an irrevocable remainder interest in a personal residence that is not the donor's entire interest in the property. For example, if a taxpayer contributes a remainder interest in a personal residence to a charitable organization and retains an estate for life or for a term of years in the residence, the taxpayer may take a charitable deduction for the value of the remainder interest.[40]

A "personal residence" is any property used by the taxpayer as a personal residence, even if it is not used as the taxpayer's principal residence. A contribution of a remainder interest in a vacation home qualifies for a charitable deduction. The term "personal residence" also includes stock owned by a taxpayer as a tenant-stockholder in a cooperative housing corporation if the dwelling which the taxpayer is entitled to occupy as such stockholder is used by the taxpayer as a personal residence.

Farm

A "farm" is any land used by the taxpayer or a tenant for the production of crops, fruits, or other agricultural products or for the sustenance of livestock. Livestock includes cattle, hogs, horses, mules, donkeys, sheep, goats, captive fur-

[38] Code Sec. 170(f)(2)(A); Reg. § 1.170A-6.

[39] Code Sec. 170(f)(3)(B)(i).

[40] Reg. § 1.170A-7(b)(3).

bearing animals, chickens, turkeys, pigeons, and other poultry. A farm also includes the improvements located on the land.[41]

A charitable deduction is allowed for the value of a charitable contribution of an irrevocable remainder interest in a farm that is not the donor's entire interest in the property. For example, if a taxpayer contributes a remainder interest in a farm to a charitable organization and retains an estate for life or for a term of years in the farm, the taxpayer may take a charitable deduction for the value of the remainder interest. The remainder interest does not have to be in the entire farm. The IRS has ruled that a charitable deduction is allowed for a charitable transfer of a remainder interest in part of the donor's pastureland leased to a tenant farmer, even though the donor retained a life interest in the portion donated and in the entire balance of the farm property.[42]

[C] Conservation Purposes

A taxpayer who contributes a qualified real property interest to a qualified organization exclusively for a conservation purpose may take a charitable contribution deduction for the interest.[43] Qualified real property interests include:

1. The entire interest of the donor other than a qualified mineral interest,
2. A remainder interest, and
3. A restriction, granted in perpetuity, on the use which may be made of the real property.[44]

If a donor transfers part of an interest in the property to a related person in order to reduce the interest donated or to retain control over more than a qualified mineral interest, the transfer does not qualify as a transfer of the entire interest.[45] Easements and other interests in real property that, under state laws, have similar attributes, such as restrictive covenants, may qualify as restrictions on the use which may be made of the property. The IRS has recognized that a property right exists in air space adjacent to real property. A restrictive easement that limits the height of buildings, if granted in perpetuity and for conservation purposes to a qualified organization, may qualify for a charitable deduction.[46]

After a long-term lessee and the lessor-owner of a historical building joined to grant a conservation easement, the lessee claimed a large charitable deduction. The Tax Court denied the lessee a charitable deduction because the lessee did not hold a fee interest in the property subject to the facade easement and had nothing to contribute.[47] According to the Court, the leasehold was personal property, not realty, under state (Massachusetts) law, and the lessee's interest in the property was for a term of years and was not perpetual. Because the lessee did not have perpetual rights in the building to contribute, the lessee could not take a charitable contribution deduction for the easement.

[41] Reg. § 1.170A-7(e)(4).

[42] Rev. Rul. 78-303, 1978-2 CB 122.

[43] Code Secs. 170(f)(3)(B)(iii), 170(h).

[44] Code Sec. 170(h)(2).

[45] Reg. § 1.170A-14(b).

[46] Rev. Rul. 64-205, 1964-2 CB 62.

[47] Harbor Lofts Associates, CCH Dec. 61,249, 151 TC 17.

A donor who donates an easement with the expectation of receiving a substantial benefit may be denied the charitable contribution deduction. A partnership donated an easement of 125 acres out of 1,280 acres that it owned to a county for use as a park. On the unencumbered portion of the 1,280 acres, the partnership planned to create a master-planned community designed so that all of the clusters of residential areas would have access to the 125-acre park. As the seller of the residential lots in the clusters, the partnership would benefit from the increased value to the lots from the park as an amenity. The Tax Court upheld the IRS determination that the partnership could not take a charitable deduction for the donation of the conservation easement.[48]

The charitable deduction for contributions of real property interests for conservation purposes is limited to contributions to governments and publicly supported charities. Also, an organization that is not itself publicly supported is an eligible recipient if the organization is controlled by a government or publicly supported organization.[49] Generally, the recipient must have a commitment to protect the conservation purposes of the donation and have the resources to enforce the restrictions. Later transfers of the property interest must be to qualified organizations and must be conditioned on the continued use of the property interest for conservation purposes as originally intended.[50]

If rehabilitation credits (see ¶ 804) were claimed on the property before the qualified conservation contribution, the deduction is reduced by an amount that bears the same ratio to the fair market value of the contribution as the sum of the rehabilitation credits under Code Sec. 47 for the preceding five tax years for a building that is part of the contribution bears to the fair market value of the building on the date of the contribution.[51]

For conservation contributions after August 17, 2006, a charitable deduction may not be taken for a structure or land area located in a registered historic district because of the structure's or land's location in the district. A charitable deduction may be taken for buildings, but the qualified real property interest that relates to the exterior of the building must preserve the entire exterior of the building, including the space above the building, the sides, the rear, and the front of the building. Also, the qualified real property interest must provide that no portion of the exterior of the building may be changed in a manner inconsistent with the historical character of the exterior.[52]

A contribution made for any one of the following four purposes is made for a conservation purpose:[53]

1. The preservation of land areas for outdoor recreation by, or the education of, the general public. Property that is preserved for a water area, boating or fishing, or a nature or hiking trail for use by the public qualifies. The

[48] Wendell Falls Development, LLC, 115 TC 1197, CCH Dec. 61,153(M), T.C. Memo. 2018-45.

[49] Code Sec. 170(h)(3).

[50] Reg. § 1.170A-14(c).

[51] Code Sec. 170(f)(14).

[52] Code Sec. 170(h)(4)(B).

[53] Code Sec. 170(h)(4).

preservation of the area does not meet this test, however, unless the recreation or education is for the substantial and regular use of the general public.[54]

2. The protection of a relatively natural habitat of fish, wildlife, or plants, or similar ecosystem. A contribution qualifies if it operates to protect or enhance the viability of an area or environment in which a fish, wildlife, or plant community normally lives or occurs. This includes areas that have been somewhat altered by human activities if the fish, wildlife, or plants exist there in a relatively natural state. Limitations on public access to the habitat of a threatened species are permissible.[55]

3. The preservation of open space, including farmland and forest land, if the preservation is for the scenic enjoyment of the general public, or made under a clearly delineated federal, state, or local governmental conservation policy, and will yield a significant public benefit. Visual access is sufficient to satisfy the scenic enjoyment requirement. In determining whether the preservation of the open space will yield a significant public benefit, all relevant factors are considered, including: the uniqueness of the property; the intensity of past, present, and projected land development in the area; the consistency of the proposed open space use with public and private conservation programs in the area; the likelihood that development of the property would lead or contribute to degradation of the scenic, natural, or historic character of the area; and the opportunity for the general public to enjoy the use of the property or to appreciate its scenic values.[56]

4. The preservation of a historically important land area or certified historic structure. Historically important land areas include independently significant land areas, such as a Civil War battlefield, and historic sites and related land areas whose physical or environmental features contribute to the historic or cultural importance and continuing integrity of historic structures or districts. In order to deduct a contribution in this category, some visual public access is required. If it is not visible from a public way, the terms of an easement must be such that the general public is given the opportunity on a regular basis to view the property preserved by the easement.[57]

A contribution for conservation purposes must be *exclusively* for conservation purposes.[58] The conservation purpose must be protected in perpetuity and the contribution must involve legally enforceable restrictions on the interest in the property retained by the donor that would prevent uses inconsistent with the conservation purpose. A reservation of a right to use or develop limited, but unspecified, areas within the area of the easement may result in a denial of any

[54] Reg. § 1.170A-14(d)(3).

[55] *Id.*

[56] Reg. § 1.170A-14(d)(4).

[57] Reg. § 1.170A-14(d)(5).

[58] Code Sec. 170(h)(5).

deduction for the easement. Any such restrictions do not protect conservation purposes in perpetuity, because the property may be used in ways inconsistent with the conservation purposes.[59]

In the case of remainder interests, a contribution does not qualify if the beneficiary-tenants can use the property in a manner that diminishes the conservation values that are intended to be protected by the contribution.[60] Also, the exclusive conservation purpose requirement is not met if the contribution accomplishes one of the four purposes but also allows uses of the property that would be destructive of other significant conservation purposes.[61]

A taxpayer may not take a deduction for a property interest contributed for conservation purposes if the property is subject to a mortgage, unless the mortgagee subordinates its rights in the property to the right of the charitable organization to enforce the conservation purposes of the gift in perpetuity.[62] Retention of mineral rights, if surface mining may be permitted at any time, defeats the charitable deduction for conservation purposes, unless the method of mining has limited impact on the property and is not irremediably destructive of the conservation purpose.[63] A special rule applies, however, to allow a deduction for a contribution of property in which the ownership of the surface estate and mineral interests has been and remains separated, if the probability of surface mining occurring on the property is so remote as to be negligible.[64]

¶ 1602 GIFTS AND CONTRIBUTIONS OF MORTGAGED PROPERTY

When property subject to a mortgage or other liability is sold, the amount of the debt is treated as part of the amount realized, as discussed at ¶ 1301.01[B]. But what if the property subject to the mortgage or debt is given away to a family member or to charity? Does the amount of the mortgage constitute an amount realized that could trigger a tax on the donor if the debt exceeds the basis for the property? The answer is yes. When property subject to a debt is given away, the transaction is split for tax purposes into a sale part and a gift part.

The regulations provide that the amount realized from a sale or other disposition of property includes the amount of liabilities from which the transferor is discharged as a result of the sale or disposition.[65] Further, according to the regulations, a disposition of property includes a gift of the property or a transfer of the property in satisfaction of liabilities to which it is subject.[66] The same rationale has been applied in other situations involving the transfer of property without apparent consideration. For instance, a stockholder who conveyed a building to the corporation without consideration but subject to a mortgage in excess of the adjusted basis for the property realized a taxable gain. The mortgaging of the property and its conveyance to the corporation, taken together, constituted a sale.[67]

---

[59] *See* Pine Mountain Preserve, LLLP, CCH Dec. 61,337, 151 TC 247.

[60] Reg. § 1.170A-14(g).

[61] Reg. § 1.170A-14(e).

[62] Reg. § 1.170A-14(g)(2).

[63] Code Sec. 170(h)(5)(B); Reg. § 1.170A-14(g)(4).

[64] Code Sec. 170(h)(5)(B)(ii).

[65] Reg. § 1.1001-2(a)(1).

[66] Reg. § 1.1001-2(a)(4)(iii).

[67] J.B. Simon, CA-3, 61-1 USTC ¶ 9136, 285 F.2d 422.

While gifts of mortgaged property to family and gifts of mortgaged property to charity both can trigger taxable gain, calculation of that gain differs in each case. The difference turns on how basis is applied to reduce the amount realized as a result of the transfer of the mortgaged property.

.01 Gifts to Family

When the owner of real estate transfers that property subject to a debt, the IRS has substantial authority, in addition to the regulations cited above, for taxing the donor on the difference between the amount of the debts that are assumed by the donee and the donor's adjusted basis for the property, whether or not the donor is personally liable for the debts.

A donor mortgaged farm real estate, used the mortgage proceeds for other business purposes, then transferred the encumbered property to a trust for the benefit of the grandchildren, and the trust assumed primary liability for the unpaid mortgage at a time when the mortgage liability exceeded the donor's basis in the property. The transfer was held to be a gift to the extent of the difference between the value of the property and the amount of the debt, and a taxable sale to the extent of the difference between the mortgage debt and the donor's adjusted basis in the property. According to the court, a part-sale resulted because the donor received valuable consideration, that is, relief from the primary liability for the debt assumed by the trust.[68]

The same rule applies to transfers subject to nonrecourse liabilities. A donor transferred mortgaged real property to a trust as a gift for the benefit of the grandchildren. The Second Circuit ruled that the donor realized taxable income on the transfer. The taxable income was the difference between the taxpayer's adjusted basis for the real estate and the amount of the nonrecourse mortgages on the property that were transferred to the trust and the amount of liabilities attributable to the property for which the donor was personally liable. The income derived from the nonrecourse loans was taxable under the principles laid down by the Supreme Court in B.B. Crane.[69]

> ***Example 3:*** The Taxpayer owns real estate that is worth $90,000, but the real estate is subject to a $75,000 mortgage. The Taxpayer gives this property to a son when the adjusted basis for the property is $45,000. This "gift" is, in fact, treated as a part sale and a part gift for income tax purposes. The Taxpayer recognizes income to the extent the liability exceeds the adjusted basis:
>
> Sale Portion:
>
> | | |
> |---|---|
> | Amount realized (amount of mortgage) . . . . | $75,000 |
> | Less adjusted basis . . . . | 45,000 |
> | Gain realized . . . . | $30,000 |

[68] R.C. Malone, DC Miss., 71-1 USTC ¶ 9475, 326 F.Supp. 106, *aff'd per curiam*, CA-5, 72-1 USTC ¶ 9217, 455 F.2d 502.

[69] B.B. Crane, S.Ct. 47-1 USTC ¶ 9217, 331 U.S. 1, 67 S.Ct. 1047; A. Levine, Est., CA-2, 80-2 USTC ¶ 9549, 634 F.2d 12; *see also* the discussion of *Crane* and the discussion of mortgage and basis at ¶ 101.02.

In addition to the taxable gain, the Taxpayer has made a gift equal to the amount by which the value of the property exceeds the liability:

Gift Portion:

Fair market value	$90,000
Less mortgage	75,000
Gift for gift tax purposes	$15,000

Whether the Taxpayer would incur a gift tax liability depends, of course, on the annual and lifetime exclusions still available to the Taxpayer.

If the liability exceeded the value of the property, there would be no "gift" portion of the transfer. Taxpayer would still have taxable income measured by the difference between the adjusted basis and the amount of the liability.

.02 Charitable Gifts

A transfer of appreciated real property subject to nonrecourse liabilities to a charitable organization was in part a charitable contribution and in part a taxable sale of capital assets. Accordingly, the taxpayer was entitled to a charitable contribution deduction to the extent that the fair market value of the properties exceeded the remaining mortgage indebtedness, but was required to report as capital gain resulting from a bargain sale the amount by which the mortgage indebtedness exceeded the bases in the properties.[70]

The IRS has ruled that a bargain sale to charity occurred when a limited partner donated a partnership interest to charity. The value of the partnership assets at the time of donation exceeded the partner's share of partnership liabilities and a charitable contribution deduction was allowable. Under Code Sec. 1011(b), the amount of the partnership liabilities at the time of transfer constituted an amount realized by the partner. Thus, the partner had a recognized gain on the transfer equal to the excess of the amount realized over that portion of the adjusted basis of the interest allocable to the sale.[71]

Since the charitable donation of property subject to a mortgage or other debt is a bargain sale, the provisions of Code Sec. 1011(b) relating to bargain sales to charitable organizations apply. Under these rules, the donor's basis for the property must be allocated between the gift portion and the sale portion. The IRS explained the rationale in Rev. Rul. 81-163.[72] If property is transferred subject to an indebtedness, the amount of the indebtedness must be treated as an amount realized for determining whether there is a sale or exchange to which Code Sec. 1011(b) applies, even though the transferee does not agree to assume or pay the indebtedness. If a charitable deduction is allowed by reason of a sale, the adjusted basis for determining the gain from the sale is the portion of the adjusted basis of the entire

[70] W.F.C. Guest, 77 TC 9, CCH Dec. 38,037, *acq*. 1982-1 CB 1; *see also* L.G. Ebben, CA-9, 86-1 USTC ¶ 9250, 783 F.2d 906, in which a partnership that transferred encumbered appreciated property to a charitable organization was held to realize capital gain from the transaction equal to the amount by which the mortgage indebtedness exceeded the partnership's adjusted basis in the property. The Court held that, based on *Guest*, such a charitable contribution, which entailed relief from nonrecourse indebtedness, constituted a sale.

[71] Rev. Rul. 75-194, 1975-1 CB 80.

[72] 1981-1 CB 43.

property that bears the same ratio to the adjusted basis as the amount realized bears to the fair market value of the entire property.[73]

> ***Example 4:*** The Taxpayer owns real estate that is worth $90,000, but the real estate is subject to a $75,000 mortgage. The Taxpayer gives this property to a charitable organization when the adjusted basis for the property is $45,000. This charitable gift is treated as a part sale and a part gift, but the Taxpayer must allocate the $45,000 basis between the gift portion and the sale portion, based on the value of each. In this case, the gift portion is the $15,000 excess of the value of the property over the mortgage, and the sale portion is the amount of the mortgage, or $75,000. Accordingly, 1/6th of the basis is allocated to the gift portion ($15,000/$90,000 × $45,000 basis = $7,500), and 5/6ths of the basis is allocated to the sale portion ($75,000/$90,000 × $45,000 = $37,500).
>
> The Taxpayer's income from this charitable gift of mortgaged property is, therefore, $37,500 ($75,000 amount realized - $37,500 adjusted basis = $37,500). The gift portion, valued at $15,000 with a basis of $7,500, may result in a charitable contribution deduction. The amount of the deduction depends on the type of property, the type of charity, and the Taxpayer's income and other charitable gifts. In other words, the deduction is subject to the charitable deduction rules discussed at ¶ 1601.03 for charitable contributions that do not involve a bargain sale.

Formerly, the regulations required that the charitable deduction be reduced by 100 percent of the unrealized appreciation inherent in the entire property following a bargain sale when the rules applicable to charitable contributions of appreciated property, as discussed above, required such a reduction. The Tax Court, however, ruled that taxpayers who sold their interest in a medical center for less than its fair market value, and who applied the "appreciation reduction rules" with respect to the portion of the capital gain property contributed in the bargain sale, properly reduced their contribution deduction by the unrealized appreciation of only the contributed portion of the property.[74] According to the Court, the regulations, as they existed at that time, led to inequitable results. Not only did the regulations improperly reduce the contribution by 100 percent of the gain on the contributed property, but they put the taxpayer in a less favorable position than if the taxpayer had sold the property and then donated a portion of the proceeds. The regulations were amended as a result of the Tax Court decision.[75]

¶ 1603 GIFTS OF LOSS PROPERTY

Generally speaking, the Internal Revenue Code prevents taxpayers from making a gift of a loss to another taxpayer. Under the basis rules discussed at ¶ 101, the basis of property acquired by gift is generally the same basis that the property had in the hands of the donor immediately before the gift. This general rule, however, does not apply to gifts of property when the fair market value of the property is less than the donor's basis for the property. If the donor's basis is greater than the fair

[73] Code Sec. 1011(b); Reg. § 1.1011-2(b).

[74] P.E. Bullard Est., 87 TC 261, CCH Dec. 43,227.

[75] Reg. § 1.170A-4, *amended by* T.D. 8176, 1988-1 CB 94.

market value of the property at the time of the gift, then for the purpose of determining loss, the basis is the fair market value.[76]

As a result of this basis rule, a gift of loss property can be very costly from a taxpayer's point of view. Since the donee cannot benefit from the potential loss on the property in the hands of the donor, the gift of loss property results in the potential loss deduction simply vanishing. If a donor gives property worth less than its basis to a donee, the potential loss cannot be taken by the donor or the donee. A donor considering a gift of loss property should consider a sale of the property and a gift of the proceeds rather than a gift of the property. The sale of the property at a loss would allow the donor to benefit from the loss deduction. At the same time, the donee would receive the same benefit as if the donee had received the property and then sold it for its fair market value.

> ***Example 5:*** The Taxpayer owns land and a building in a declining part of town. The land and building are worth only $50,000, although the Taxpayer's adjusted basis for the property is $75,000. If the Taxpayer gives the property to a son and the son sells it for its fair market value of $50,000, the son has neither a gain nor a loss on the sale. Under the usual basis rule, the son's basis for the property would be $75,000, the same basis the Taxpayer had immediately before the gift. Use of this basis by the son would result in a loss, however, so the son must use the fair market value of the property on the date of the gift, or $50,000, as the basis. The Taxpayer's $25,000 potential loss on the building simply disappears when the Taxpayer makes a gift of the property to the son.
>
> On the other hand, if the Taxpayer sells the property for $50,000 and gives the proceeds of the sale to the son, the Taxpayer may benefit from the $25,000 loss. If the property qualifies as Code Sec. 1231 property, the Taxpayer may use the loss to offset ordinary income without limitation. Meanwhile, the son receives the same $50,000 he would get if the Taxpayer made a gift of the building rather than the proceeds of the sale of the building.

[76] Code Sec. 1015.

Part V

PERSONAL RESIDENCES

Introduction to Part V

Ownership of a personal residence is favored by the tax law. The owner of a home is afforded advantages not given to the occupant of a rented residential apartment. For example, the owner of a home may deduct property taxes and mortgage interest, within limits, on the personal income tax return. The renter, however, may not deduct any portion of the rental payments, even though some of the rent is used by the landlord to pay property taxes and interest on a mortgage.

The various itemized deductions to which a homeowner is entitled, however, are only one way in which a taxpayer's ownership of a personal residence affects taxes. The sale of a personal residence may produce gain. In most cases, however, the tax on all or part of this gain may be avoided altogether.

These, then, are the primary topics of the following four chapters of Part V. Chapter 17 examines the deductions, exclusions, and tax credits available to all homeowners. Chapter 18 looks at the additional deductions available when a homeowner uses a personal residence in part for business. Special considerations for cooperative and condominium ownership are found in Chapter 19. Finally, the sale of a personal residence, including the avoidance or postponement of tax, is the topic of Chapter 20.

Chapter 17
Deductions for Homeowners

¶ 1700 Overview of Chapter
¶ 1701 Mortgage Interest
¶ 1702 Real Estate Taxes
¶ 1703 Casualty Losses
¶ 1704 Disaster Relief Exclusion
¶ 1705 Moving Expenses
¶ 1706 District of Columbia Homebuyer Credit
¶ 1707 First-Time Homebuyer Credit
¶ 1708 Credits for Energy Savings

¶ 1700 OVERVIEW OF CHAPTER

Many homeowners find that it is advantageous to itemize deductions rather than to take the standard deduction. In most cases, the largest deductions occur in the early years of ownership, when the bulk of each mortgage payment is attributable to interest. Most homeowners may deduct for federal income tax purposes the full amount of interest on their home mortgages paid during the year. Also, local property tax on a personal residence is deductible; but if it is paid through an escrow or similar arrangement, it is deductible only when the money is actually turned over to the taxing authority. Homeowners also may deduct, within certain limitations, casualty losses to their homes. Finally, homeowners, whether or not they itemize deductions, may find tax benefits in making their homes more energy efficient.

¶ 1701 MORTGAGE INTEREST

Generally, a noncorporate taxpayer may not deduct personal interest.[1] Personal interest does not include any of the following:

1. Interest paid or accrued on debt allocable to a trade or business, other than performing services as an employee;
2. Investment interest;
3. Interest taken into account in computing income or loss from a passive activity;
4. Qualified residence interest;
5. Interest on the unpaid portion of the estate tax for the period during which there is an extension of time for payment on the value of a reversionary or

[1] Code Sec. 163(h)(1).

remainder interest in property or when the estate consists largely of an interest in a closely held business; and

6. Interest on a qualified education loan.[2]

The deduction of interest in connection with real estate other than a qualified personal residence is considered at ¶ 303. Also, interest on a personal residence that exceeds the limitations discussed at ¶ 1701.01[B] may be subject to the tracing rules discussed at ¶ 303.02[C] to determine whether or not it is deductible as some other category of interest.

.01 Qualified Residence Interest

In most cases, homeowners may deduct all of their home mortgage interest. Specifically, a homeowner may deduct interest on a home mortgage that falls within one or more of the following categories:[3]

1. Acquisition debt that does not exceed $1 million, including pre-October 14, 1987 debt ($500,000 in the case of married taxpayers filing separate returns);
2. Home equity debt, other than acquisition debt, that does not exceed $100,000 ($50,000 in the case of married taxpayers filing separate returns); and
3. Mortgages taken before October 14, 1987.

All of these categories are specifically discussed below.

Special Rules for 2018 Through 2025

The deduction for home mortgage interest is limited for tax years 2018 through 2025.[4] A taxpayer is limited to claiming the home mortgage interest deduction only for interest paid or accrued on acquisition debt during those years; the deduction of interest on home equity debt is suspended. Further, the aggregate amount of acquisition indebtedness for which a taxpayer may take an interest deduction is limited to $750,000 ($375,000 in the case of a married individual filing a separate return). The reduction from the limit of $1 million ($500,000 for married filing separately) generally applies to any acquisition debt incurred after December 15, 2017.

The maximum amount that may be treated as acquisition debt remains $1 million ($500,000 if married filing separately) for any acquisition debt incurred for the taxpayer's principal residence on or before December 15, 2017. The acquisition debt incurred on or before December 15, 2017, reduces the $750,000/$375,000 limit to any acquisition debt incurred after December 15, 2017. After 2025, the $1 million/$500,000 limit will apply regardless of when the acquisition debt was incurred.[5]

The $1 million ($500,000 if married filing separately) dollar limit continues to apply to a taxpayer who entered a binding written contract before December 16,

[2] Code Sec. 163(h)(2).

[3] Code Sec. 163(h)(3).

[4] Code Sec. 163(h)(3)(F).

[5] Code Sec. 163(h)(3)(F)(ii).

2017, to close on the purchase of a principal residence before January 1, 2018, so long as the residence is purchased before April 1, 2018.

Mortgage Insurance

Premiums for mortgage insurance in connection with acquisition indebtedness on a qualified personal residence are treated as qualified residence interest and are deductible.[6] The deduction is not available for mortgage insurance contracts issued before January 1, 2007. Further, the deduction is not available for amounts paid or accrued after December 31, 2017, or properly allocable to periods after December 31, 2017 (although Congress may extend this expiration date, as it has done repeatedly since the provision was enacted). The deduction is phased out by ten percent for each $1,000 of the taxpayer's adjusted gross income in excess of $100,000.

If a homeowner pays a mortgage insurance premium allocable to the payment of a mortgage that extends beyond the close of the tax year, the homeowner must allocate the premium ratably over the shorter of the stated term of the mortgage or 84 months, beginning with the month in which the homeowner obtains the insurance. If a homeowner satisfies a mortgage before the end of its stated term, the homeowner may not deduct any of the premiums allocated to periods after the homeowner satisfies the mortgage. The allocation requirement does not apply to mortgage insurance provided by the Department of Veterans Affairs or the Rural Housing Service.[7]

[A] Qualified Residence Defined

A taxpayer may deduct interest on a mortgage on a personal residence which falls within the three categories set out above only if the personal residence is a "qualified residence." A qualified residence is the taxpayer's principal residence and one other residence, such as a vacation home, selected by the taxpayer. The home that the taxpayer selects to treat as a second residence must be used by the taxpayer for personal purposes for 14 days during the year or, if greater, ten percent of the number of days that the second residence is rented.[8] If the taxpayer does not rent a dwelling unit at any time during the year, the unit may be treated as a residence even if it is not used by the taxpayer for 14 days.[9]

A taxpayer cannot have more than one principal residence and more than one second residence which qualifies for the interest deduction at one time.[10] Residence is broadly defined to include much more than the traditional single family home or condominium. According to the regulations, whether property is a residence is determined based on all the facts and circumstances, including the good faith of the taxpayer. A residence may be a house, condominium, mobile home, boat, or house trailer that contains sleeping space and toilet and cooking facilities.[11] Under this provision, many taxpayers are able to deduct interest paid on a boat loan or recreational vehicle loan.

[6] Code Sec. 163(h)(3)(E).

[7] Reg. § 1.163-11.

[8] Code Sec. 163(h)(4)(A).

[9] Code Sec. 163(h)(4)(A)(iii).

[10] Temp. Reg. § 1.163-10T(p)(1).

[11] Temp. Reg. § 1.163-10T(p)(3)(ii).

Residence Under Construction

A taxpayer may treat a residence under construction as a qualified residence for up to 24 months, but only if the residence becomes a qualified residence once it is ready for occupancy.[12]

> ***Example 1:*** The Taxpayer owns a residential lot on which a vacation home will be built. On April 20, 2019, the Taxpayer obtained a mortgage secured by the lot and the property to be constructed on the lot and began construction of the vacation home on August 9, 2019. The residence will be ready for occupancy on November 9, 2021, and the Taxpayer elects to treat this vacation home as a second qualified residence for the period November 9, 2021, through December 31, 2021.
>
> Since the residence under construction is a qualified residence as of the first day that it is ready for occupancy, the Taxpayer may treat the residence as a second residence for up to 24 months of the period during which the residence is under construction. If the Taxpayer treats the residence under construction as a qualified residence beginning with the date construction was started, August 9, 2019, the residence under construction would cease to be a qualified residence on August 8, 2021, until construction is complete and the Taxpayer elects to treat the completed vacation home as a qualified residence.

Married Individuals

If a married couple files separate returns, the couple is treated as one taxpayer for determining whether a residence is a qualified residence. Each may take into account only one of the two qualified residences permitted, unless both consent in writing to allow one spouse to take both the principal and the second residence into account.[13]

[B] Acquisition Indebtedness

Acquisition indebtedness is debt that is incurred to acquire, construct, or substantially improve a qualified residence and that is secured by the qualified residence.[14] The aggregate amount of acquisition indebtedness for which a taxpayer may take an interest deduction is limited, as discussed at ¶ 1701.01. As discussed at ¶ 1701.01[D], debt incurred and secured by a qualified residence before October 14, 1987, is not subject to the limitation, but the debt does reduce the amount of the limitation allowed for other acquisition debt.

In Notice 88-74,[15] the IRS has provided guidance on the home mortgage interest deduction for acquisition indebtedness. According to the IRS, regulations will provide two tests to determine if debt qualifies as acquisition indebtedness. First, debt may qualify as acquisition indebtedness to the extent that the proceeds are used, within the meaning of the tracing rules of Temp. Reg. § 1.163-8T, to acquire, construct, or substantially improve the residence.[16] Secondly, a debt may

---

[12] Temp. Reg. § 1.163-10T(p)(5).

[13] Code Sec. 163(h)(4)(A)(ii).

[14] Code Sec. 163(h)(3)(B)(i).

[15] 1988-2 CB 385.

[16] Temp. Reg. § 1.163-8T, is discussed in detail at ¶ 303.02[C].

qualify as acquisition indebtedness if it is incurred within a prescribed time period, that is, it meets the 90-day rules.[17]

Tracing Rules

In general, interest expense is allocated in the same manner in which the debt that gave rise to the payment or accrual of interest is allocated. Debt is allocated under a tracing method that links the debt proceeds to the types of expenditures for which the proceeds are used.[18]

90-Day Rules

Regardless of the tracing rules, debt may be treated as incurred to acquire a residence to the extent of expenditures to acquire the residence made within 90 days before or after the date that the debt is incurred.

In the case of construction or substantial improvement of a residence, debt incurred prior to the time the residence or improvements are complete may be treated as being incurred to construct or improve the residence to the extent that the expenditures were made no more than 24 months prior to the date that the debt is incurred. Debt incurred no later than the date 90 days after the residence or improvements are complete may be treated as qualified debt to the extent of any expenditures made within the 24-month period prior to the date of completion and ending on the date the debt is incurred.[19]

Debt is incurred on the date that the loan proceeds are disbursed to, or for the benefit of, the taxpayer, that is, generally on the loan closing date. A taxpayer, however, may treat the debt as incurred when written application is made to incur the debt, but only to the extent that the debt proceeds are actually disbursed within a reasonable time after approval of the application. Debt proceeds disbursed within 30 days after approval of the application are disbursed within a reasonable time. Regulations will provide that if a written application is made for a debt within the requisite time period and the application is rejected, a reasonable additional time period will be allowed to make a new application for the debt. The rule that a taxpayer may treat debt as incurred on the date that a written application for the loan is made does not apply, however, when determining whether a debt was incurred before October 13, 1987.

Refinancing

If a taxpayer incurs a debt that is treated as incurred to acquire, construct or substantially improve a residence under either the tracing rules or the 90-day rules, and later incurs a second debt, the second debt may be treated as incurred to acquire, construct or substantially improve the residence if the proceeds of the second debt are used to refinance the first debt. Whether the second debt is used to refinance the first debt is determined under the tracing rules of Temp. Reg. § 1.163-8T.

---

[17] Notice 88-74, 1988-2 CB 385.

[18] The tracing rules are discussed at ¶ 303.02[C].

[19] Notice 88-74, 1988-2 CB 385.

Under the special rules for 2018 through 2025, the higher $1 million/$500,000 limit on acquisition debt continues to apply to any debt incurred after December 15, 2017, to refinance existing acquisition debt on the taxpayer's principal residence to the extent the amount of the debt resulting from the refinancing does not exceed the amount of the refinanced debt. Thus, the maximum dollar amount that may be treated as acquisition debt on the taxpayer's principal residence will not decrease because of a refinancing. The exception for refinancing existing acquisition debt will not apply after: (1) the expiration of the term of the original debt; or (2) the earlier of the expiration of the first refinancing of the debt or 30 years after the date of the first refinancing.[20]

Debt Partially Acquisition and Equity Indebtedness

A single debt may qualify as partially acquisition and partially home equity indebtedness. For example, if a taxpayer incurs a debt secured by a qualified residence, uses a portion of the debt proceeds to refinance an existing acquisition indebtedness, and uses the remaining portion for purposes other than home improvement, the portion of the debt used to refinance the acquisition indebtedness will qualify as acquisition indebtedness, and the portion of the debt used for other purposes will generally qualify as home equity debt. The limitation on home equity debt is discussed at ¶ 1701.01[C].

The following examples illustrate the application of the rules on acquisition indebtedness.

Comprehensive Example 2: The Taxpayer incurs a debt of $100,000 and uses the proceeds under the tracing rules to purchase a residential lot on January 15, 2019. The debt is secured by the lot. On January 1, 2020, the Taxpayer begins construction of a residence on the lot and uses $250,000 of unborrowed funds to construct the residence. The residence is complete on December 31, 2021, and becomes the Taxpayer's principal residence at that time. On March 15, 2022, the Taxpayer incurs a debt of $300,000 secured by the residence. The lender on the second debt disburses $100,000 to pay off the existing debt and disburses the remaining $200,000 directly to the Taxpayer.

The $100,000 debt the Taxpayer incurred in 2019 was incurred to construct the residence because the proceeds of the debt are directly traceable to expenditures to construct the residence, that is, the purchase of the lot. From January 15, 2019, through December 31, 2019, the Taxpayer may not treat the debt as acquisition indebtedness because it is not secured by a qualified residence. From January 1, 2020, through December 30, 2021, the Taxpayer may treat the residence under construction as a qualified residence, and, therefore, the debt may qualify as acquisition indebtedness. From December 31, 2021, through March 15, 2022, the residence is a qualified residence and the debt qualifies as acquisition indebtedness.

The Taxpayer also incurred the $300,000 debt to construct the residence—$100,000 because the Taxpayer used this amount to refinance debt incurred to construct the residence, and the remaining $200,000 because the

[20] Code Sec. 163(h)(3)(F)(iii).

Taxpayer incurred the debt within 90 days after the residence was complete and incurred construction expenditures of at least this amount within the period beginning 24 months before the residence was complete and ending when the debt was incurred. The entire $300,000 debt is acquisition indebtedness because it is also secured by a qualified residence. Therefore, the Taxpayer may deduct all of the interest on the debt as qualified residence interest.

Comprehensive Example 3: Assume the same facts as in Example 2, except that rather than borrowing to purchase the lot, the Taxpayer uses cash to purchase the lot. In this case, since the Taxpayer did not use any of the $300,000 debt to refinance a debt incurred to construct a qualified residence, the Taxpayer may treat the debt as incurred to construct a qualified residence only to the extent of the $250,000 in expenditures incurred during the period beginning 24 months before the residence was complete and ending when the debt was incurred. The Taxpayer spent the $100,000 to purchase the lot before this period and, therefore, cannot treat the debt as incurred for this purpose.

Accordingly, the Taxpayer may treat $250,000 of the March 15, 2022, debt as incurred to construct the residence and as acquisition debt. Because the debt is secured by a qualified residence, the remaining $50,000 of the debt qualifies as home equity indebtedness. Therefore, before 2026, the taxpayer may deduct only the interest on the $250,000 acquisition debt as qualified residence interest. After 2025, the taxpayer may deduct all of the interest on the $300,000 qualified residence interest.

[C] Home Equity Debt

Home equity indebtedness is debt, other than acquisition indebtedness, that is secured by a taxpayer's qualified residence. Interest on qualifying home equity indebtedness is deductible regardless of the use made of the proceeds. Qualifying home equity indebtedness may not exceed the fair market value of the residence securing the debt reduced by any acquisition indebtedness on the residence.[21] For 2018 through 2025, the interest on home equity debt is not deductible. Also, the aggregate amount of home equity indebtedness for which interest is deductible before 2018 and after 2025 is limited to $100,000 ($50,000 in the case of married taxpayers filing separate returns).[22]

Debt incurred by a taxpayer to acquire, construct or substantially improve a qualified residence can be home equity debt to the extent it exceeds the limitation on acquisition debt,[23] but as home equity debt it is subject to the suspension of the deduction for home equity debt, the $100,000 limit before 2018 and after 2025, and the fair market value limitation.

Example 4: A homeowner purchased a principal residence for its fair market value of $1,500,000 on June 1, 2019. The owner paid $300,000 and financed the remainder by borrowing $1,200,000 through a loan secured by the

---

[21] Code Sec. 163(h)(3)(C)(i).

[22] Code Sec. 163(h)(3)(C)(ii).

[23] Rev. Rul. 2010-25, 2010-44 IRB 571.

residence. The homeowner paid the interest that accrued on the mortgage debt during the year. The homeowner has no other debt secured by the residence.

The homeowner may deduct, as interest on acquisition debt, the interest paid on $750,000 of the $1,200,000 debt used to acquire the principal residence. The $1,200,000 debt was incurred in acquiring a qualified residence and was secured by the residence. After 2025, the homeowner may deduct, as interest on acquisition debt, the interest paid on $1,000,000 of the $1,200,000 debt used to acquire the principal residence. The homeowner also may deduct, as interest on home equity debt, interest paid on $100,000 of the remaining $200,000 of debt. The $200,000 is secured by the qualified residence, is not acquisition debt, and does not exceed the fair market value of the residence reduced by the acquisition debt.

Because the interest on both the acquisition debt and the home equity debt is qualified residence interest after 2025, the homeowner may deduct interest paid on $1,100,000 of the $1,200,000 mortgage as qualified residence interest. The interest the homeowner pays on the remaining mortgage debt of $100,000 is nondeductible personal interest unless it can be traced to some other deductible category such as business or investment interest.

Under the tracing rules, if a mortgage is secured by a home of the taxpayer, but the proceeds are used to finance investment property or a business venture, then the interest on the loan is not residence interest. Rather, the debt would qualify as investment or business interest that is deductible outside the limits on home mortgage debt. Of course, the interest may be subject to other limits, including the limit on investment interest and the limit on business interest. See ¶ 303.

The IRS has advised taxpayers that in many cases they can continue to deduct interest paid on home equity loans in 2018 through 2025.[24] For example, interest on a home equity loan used to build an addition to an existing home is typically deductible, while interest on the same loan used to pay personal living expenses, such as credit card debts, is not. The limits on acquisition debt apply to the combined amount of loans used to buy, build or substantially improve the taxpayer's main home and second home regardless of how the loan is labeled.

IRS provided several examples to illustrate these points:

Example 5: In January 2018, a taxpayer takes out a $500,000 mortgage to purchase a main home with a fair market value of $800,000. In February 2018, the taxpayer takes out a $250,000 home equity loan to put an addition on the main home. Both loans are secured by the main home and the total does not exceed the cost of the home. Because the total amount of both loans does not exceed $750,000, all of the interest paid on the loans is deductible. However, if the taxpayer used the home equity loan proceeds for personal expenses, such as paying off student loans and credit cards, then the interest on the home equity loan would not be deductible.

[24] IR 2018-32.

Example 6: In January 2018, a taxpayer takes out a $500,000 mortgage to purchase a main home. The loan is secured by the main home. In February 2018, the taxpayer takes out a $250,000 loan to purchase a vacation home. The loan is secured by the vacation home. Because the total amount of both mortgages does not exceed $750,000, all of the interest paid on both mortgages is deductible. However, if the taxpayer took out a $250,000 home equity loan on the main home to purchase the vacation home, then the interest on the home equity loan would not be deductible.

Example 7: In January 2018, a taxpayer takes out a $500,000 mortgage to purchase a main home. The loan is secured by the main home. In February 2018, the taxpayer takes out a $500,000 loan to purchase a vacation home. The loan is secured by the vacation home. Because the total amount of both mortgages exceeds $750,000, not all of the interest paid on the mortgages is deductible. A percentage of the total interest paid is deductible.

[D] Pre-1987 Indebtedness

Debt that a taxpayer incurred before October 14, 1987, and that is secured by a qualified residence is treated as acquisition indebtedness that is not subject to the $1,000,000 limitation. Interest on these loans is deductible regardless of the amount of the loan.[25] The amount of pre-October 14, 1987 indebtedness, however, does reduce the amount of the $1,000,000 limitation on new acquisition debt.[26] Pre-October 14, 1987 debt includes debt incurred before that date that is secured by a qualified residence on October 13, 1987, and at all times thereafter before interest is paid or accrued.[27] It also includes debt incurred after October 13, 1987, that is used to refinance pre-October 14, 1987 debt.[28]

Refinancing

If a taxpayer had a mortgage on a qualified residence on October 13, 1987, and refinances it after that date for no more than the balance of the existing mortgage, the taxpayer may continue to treat all of the new mortgage as pre-October 14, 1987 indebtedness. However, if the refinancing is for more than the balance of the existing mortgage, only the part of the new mortgage equal to the balance of the old mortgage at the time of refinancing is treated as pre-October 14, 1987 debt. The amount of the new mortgage that is in excess of the balance of the existing mortgage is either acquisition indebtedness or home equity indebtedness, or a combination of the two, and subject to the limitations that apply to post-October 13, 1987 debt.

Any refinancing may not extend the term of the debt beyond the term of the debt immediately before the refinancing. If the principal amount of the old debt was amortized over its life, the taxpayer may deduct all of the interest paid during what would have been the life of the old debt. Any interest the taxpayer pays after this

[25] Code Sec. 163(h)(3)(D)(i).
[26] Code Sec. 163(h)(3)(D)(ii).
[27] Code Sec. 163(h)(3)(D)(iii)(I).
[28] Code Sec. 163(h)(3)(D)(iii)(II).

period is personal interest.[29] If the principal amount of the old debt was not amortized over the life of the debt (for example, a balloon mortgage) the taxpayer may deduct the interest paid during the life of the new debt, up to a maximum of 30 years.[30]

Line of Credit

A taxpayer who had a line-of-credit mortgage on a qualified residence on October 13, 1987, and who borrows additional amounts on the line of credit after that date, cannot treat the new amounts borrowed as pre-October 14, 1987 debt. The additional amounts borrowed against the line of credit are treated as debts incurred after October 13, 1987, and are subject to the $1,000,000 limitation on acquisition indebtedness and the $100,000 limitation on home equity indebtedness.

.02 Points

"Points" is the term generally applied to charges paid by a borrower at the inception of a loan. These charges may also be called loan origination fees, maximum loan charges, or premium charges. If the payment of points is only for the use of money, it is interest and is treated as such for federal tax purposes. Note that the term "points" also may be applied to fees that a seller of property must pay to arrange financing for a buyer. The seller does not treat these points as interest, but rather treats them as a selling expense that reduces the amount realized from the sale.[31]

When points qualify as interest, the amount is prepaid interest. As a general rule, prepaid interest may not be deducted in the year paid, but must be deducted over the life of the loan.[32] There is an exception, however, for points paid by a taxpayer in connection with a loan to buy or improve his principal residence.[33] In order for the exception to apply and for points to be currently deductible in full, all of the following conditions must be met:

1. The payment of points must be an established business practice in the area where the loan is made;
2. The points paid must not exceed the amount generally charged in the area where the loan is made; and
3. The funds provided by the buyer, plus any points the seller paid, are at least as much as the points charged. (The buyer's funds do not have to be applied to the points, but the buyer cannot borrow the funds from the lender.)

The exception does not apply to points paid in connection with a loan on a second or vacation home.

[A] Points Charged for Services

Points charged for specific services by the lender for the borrower's account are not interest. To be deductible as interest, points must be paid as compensation

[29] Code Sec. 163(h)(3)(D)(iv)(I).

[30] Code Sec. 163(h)(3)(D)(iv)(II).

[31] Rev. Rul. 68-650, 1968-2 CB 78.

[32] Code Sec. 461(g)(1).

[33] Code Sec. 461(g)(2).

to the lender solely for the use or forbearance of money.[34] Examples of fees for services not considered interest are the lender's appraisal fee, preparation costs for the mortgage note or deed of trust, settlement fees, and notary fees.[35] Points paid by the borrower to obtain a VA mortgage is a service charge and is not interest.[36]

> ***Example 8:*** The Taxpayer borrowed $96,000 to buy a $120,000 principal residence. The Taxpayer paid the lender, in addition to interest on the loan at five percent, a loan processing fee of $1,920 (two points). No portion of the fee was for specific services, charging points was an established local business practice, and the amount paid was not more than the fee customarily charged. If the Taxpayer paid the points from separate funds, $1,920 may be deducted as interest on the residence for the year of payment.

[B] Refinancing

Points paid in refinancing a mortgage are not deductible in full in the year paid, regardless of how the taxpayer arranges to pay them. According to the IRS, points paid to refinance an existing home mortgage are for repaying the taxpayer's existing indebtedness and are not paid in connection with the purchase or improvement of the home. Points paid on refinancing generally must be deducted ratably over the period of the loan.[37] The IRS has spelled out the method of ratable allocation of points over the life of a loan in Rev. Proc. 87-15.[38]

If part of the proceeds from a refinancing are used to improve a taxpayer's principal residence, the taxpayer may deduct a portion of the points for the tax year paid.[39]

> ***Example 9:*** In 2014, the Taxpayer secured a mortgage for the purchase of a home. On July 1, 2020, the Taxpayer, who uses the cash method of accounting, refinanced this mortgage with a 15-year $100,000 mortgage loan. In order to obtain this loan, the Taxpayer was required to pay three points ($3,000), consisting of two points ($2,000) for prepaid interest and one point ($1,000) for fees charged for the lender's services. The Taxpayer paid the $3,000 out of private funds. Payment of points was an established practice, and three points were generally charged in the area. The Taxpayer made six payments on the loan in 2020.
>
> The Taxpayer used the funds obtained from the new mortgage to repay an existing indebtedness. Although the new mortgage loan was incurred in connection with the Taxpayer's continued ownership of a principal residence, the new mortgage was not incurred in connection with the purchase or improvement of that residence. Therefore, the Taxpayer cannot deduct all of the points for 2020. The Taxpayer can deduct two points ($2,000) ratably over the life of the loan, which works out to $66.67 for 2020 ($2,000 divided by 180

[34] Rev. Rul. 69-188, 1969-1 CB 54, *as amplified by* Rev. Rul. 69-582, 1969-2 CB 29.

[35] L.E. Lay, 69 TC 421, CCH Dec. 34,782; R.C. Goodwin, 75 TC 424, CCH Dec. 37,502; D.L. Wilkerson, 70 TC 240, CCH Dec. 35,156, *acq.* 1982-2 CB 2 and *nonacq.* 1982-2 CB 2, *rev'd and rem'd on another issue,* 81-2 USTC ¶ 9657, 655 F.2d 980.

[36] Rev. Rul. 67-297, 1967-2 CB 87.

[37] IR-News Release 86-68, May 13, 1986.

[38] 1987-1 CB 248.

[39] Rev. Rul. 87-22, 1987-1 CB 196.

payments over the life of the loan times six payments in 2020). The other point ($1,000) is not deductible as a fee for services.

Example 10: Assume the same facts as in Example 9, except that the Taxpayer used $25,000 of the loan proceeds to improve the home. Because the Taxpayer paid the points in 2020, the Taxpayer is allowed to deduct 25 percent of the two points that represent prepaid interest attributable to the portion of the loan used for home improvement for 2020. This amount is $500 ($2,000 prepaid interest × $25,000/$100,000 = $500).

In addition, the Taxpayer can deduct for 2020 the ratable part of the $1,500 ($2,000 prepaid interest - $500 attributable to home improvement) that must be spread over the life of the loan. This amount is $50 (($1,500/180) × 6 = $50).

Example 11: Assume the same facts as in Example 10, except that the Taxpayer did not pay the points out of private funds. Rather, the lender deducted the points from the loan proceeds. Since the Taxpayer did not actually pay the points, the Taxpayer cannot deduct for 2020 the portion of the two points that is attributable to the part of the loan used for home improvement. The Taxpayer can deduct the entire amount of the two points ratably over the 15-year life of the loan.

.03 Special Mortgage Situations

Financing for a residence may take forms other than fixed or variable rate loans. Also, a homeowner may receive payments from others toward mortgage costs. These special situations may affect the amount and timing of the deduction for qualified residence interest.

[A] Redeemable Ground Rents

A redeemable ground rent is treated by the Internal Revenue Code as in the nature of a mortgage and real property held subject to liabilities under a redeemable ground rent is treated as held subject to liabilities under a mortgage.[40] Taxpayers who make annual or periodic payments on a redeemable ground rent treat those payments as interest.[41] Accordingly, the payments under a redeemable ground rent are subject to the rules on qualified residence interest.

A ground rent is a redeemable ground rent if:

1. There is a lease of land for a term of more than 15 years, including renewal periods, and the lease is assignable by the lessee without the consent of the lessor;
2. The lessee has a present or future right to, under state or local law, terminate the lease and buy the lessor's entire interest in the land by paying a specific amount; and
3. The lessor's interest in the land is primarily a security interest to protect the rental payments to which the lessor is entitled.[42]

---

[40] Code Sec. 1055(a).

[41] Code Sec. 163(c).

[42] Code Sec. 1055(c); Reg. § 1.1055-1(b).

The lessee's right to terminate the lease and acquire the lessor's interest must be granted by state or local law. If the right exists solely by virtue of a private agreement or privately created condition, the ground rent is not a "redeemable ground rent." Payments made by the lessee to terminate the lease and to actually acquire the land are not ground rents, and the lessee may not deduct them as interest.

Payments on a nonredeemable ground rent are not interest and are not deductible unless the rent is for property used in a trade or business or held for the production of income.

[B] Shared Appreciation Mortgage (SAM)

Under a shared appreciation mortgage, SAM for short, the borrower pays a fixed rate of interest plus contingent interest to the lender. The contingent interest is a percentage of any appreciation in the value of the property that secures the loan and is due when the SAM terminates. Generally, monthly payments under a SAM include interest at a fixed rate. The fixed interest portion is deductible when paid by a cash basis taxpayer, subject to the limitations on qualified residence interest. The contingent interest portion is also deductible for the year paid, again subject to the qualified residence limitations.[43]

If a cash basis borrower refinances a SAM with the same lender and the face amount of the new loan includes contingent interest, the contingent interest is not deductible at that time. Rather, the borrower may deduct the contingent interest as it is paid over the term of the new mortgage.

> ***Example 12:*** In 2012, the Taxpayer purchased a principal residence for \$125,000 and financed the purchase with a 30-year, \$100,000 SAM. Under the terms of the SAM, the Taxpayer must pay the lender 40 percent of the appreciation on the residence when the Taxpayer pays off the loan or sells the home, or in ten years, if earlier. The Taxpayer sells the residence in 2020 for \$155,000 and pays off the principal on the mortgage plus \$12,000 contingent interest (40 percent of the \$30,000 appreciation). The Taxpayer may deduct the \$12,000 paid in 2020 as qualified residence interest. The result is the same if the Taxpayer pays off the SAM with funds obtained from a source other than the original SAM lender. If the Taxpayer simply refinanced the SAM through the same lender, the contingent interest would not be deductible in 2020, but only as the new mortgage is paid off.

[C] Mortgage Interest Credit

Low-income homeowners who obtained qualified mortgage credit certificates from state or local government may claim a tax credit during any year for which the certificate is in effect for a portion of the interest paid on the mortgage. A mortgage credit certificate is in effect for interest from the date a certificate is issued until it is either revoked by the issuing authority or until the taxpayer sells the residence or

[43] Rev. Rul. 83-51, 1983-1 CB 48.

stops using it as a personal residence.[44] If a taxpayer takes this credit, the taxpayer must reduce the deduction for mortgage interest by the amount of the credit.[45]

[D] Housing Allowances and Assistance Payments

Ministers and military personnel may deduct home mortgage interest on their homes, subject to the limitations on qualified residence interest, even though they receive a parsonage or military allowance that they may exclude from gross income.[46] Military personnel include all branches of the armed forces, the National Oceanic and Atmospheric Administration, and the Public Health Service. Eligible members of these services are entitled to receive tax-free housing and subsistence allowances if they do not reside on a federal base.[47]

On the other hand, recipients of mortgage assistance payments under Section 235 of the National Housing Act do not include the payments in income,[48] and may not deduct interest on their mortgages to the extent it is paid for them.[49] These payments, however, do not reduce other deductions, such as for real estate taxes.

Down Payment Assistance

Various organizations, both charitable and noncharitable, provide down payment assistance to homebuyers. In the case of charitable organizations, their goals usually involve providing assistance to the poor or improving blighted communities. They generally conduct broad-based fundraising and receive support from a wide array of sources. Generally, the staff does not know the identity or contributor status of the home sellers or any other party who may receive a financial benefit from the home sales. In the case of organizations that are not charitable organizations, they generally rely on sellers and other real-estate related businesses that stand to benefit from the transactions for their funds. The staff knows the identity of the home seller and may also know the identities of other interested parties. The organizations generally receive a payment from the home seller corresponding to the amount of the down payment assistance in substantially all of the transactions.

In the case of assistance received from charitable organizations, the homebuyer may exclude the down payment assistance from gross income as a gift under Code Sec.102. The homebuyer also may include the down payment assistance in the cost basis of the home under Code Sec. 1012.

In the case of assistance received from the private organizations, the homebuyer may exclude the down payment assistance from income because it represents a rebate or purchase price reduction. The homebuyer, however, may not include the amount of the down payment assistance in the cost basis of the home because it does represent a rebate or purchase price reduction.[50]

---

[44] Code Sec. 25.

[45] Code Sec. 163(g).

[46] Code Sec. 265(a)(6).

[47] Reg. § 1.61-2(b).

[48] Rev. Rul. 75-271, 1975-2 CB 23.

[49] Reg. § 1.163-1(d).

[50] *See* Rev. Rul. 2006-27, 2006-21 IRB 915.

Hardest Hit Fund Participants

In Notice 2017-40,[51] the IRS provided a safe harbor method for computing the deductions for mortgage interest and real estate taxes on a principal residence for homeowners participating in a program designated by state housing finance agency (HFA) using funds allocated from the HFA Hardest Hit Fund. The IRS amplified that notice in Notice 2018-63[52] to provide that the safe harbor, as modified, is available even if the limitation on the deduction for state and local taxes precludes a homeowner from deducting all of the real property taxes imposed on the principal residence (see ¶ 1702).

For tax years 2010 through 2021, a homeowner may deduct on his or her federal income tax return (subject to the limitation on the deduction for state and local taxes) the lesser of:

1. The sum of all payments on the home mortgage that the homeowner actually makes during a taxable year to the mortgage servicer or the state HFA; or
2. The sum of amounts shown on Form 1098, *Mortgage Interest Statement*, for mortgage interest received, real property taxes, and mortgage insurance premiums (if deductible for the tax year).

This safe harbor method of computing a homeowner's deduction applies if:

1. The homeowner meets the requirements to deduct all of the mortgage interest relating to the principal residence,
2. The homeowner meets the requirements for deducting all the real property taxes (determined without regard to $10,000 limit that applies in 2018 through 2025), and
3. The homeowner participates in a state program in which the program payments can be used to pay interest on the home mortgage.

If the homeowner's deduction, as provided above, is the sum of all payments made by the homeowner during a tax year, then the homeowner may first allocate amounts paid to mortgage interest up to the amount shown on Form 1098. The homeowner may then use any reasonable method to allocate the remaining balance of the payments to real property taxes, mortgage insurance premiums, home insurance premiums, and principal. Regardless of how a homeowner determines the deductible amount under this safe harbor, any part of such amount that is allocated to state or local property taxes is subject to the $10,000 limit on the deduction for state and local taxes.

[E] Payment Penalties

A taxpayer who pays off a mortgage early may have to pay a prepayment penalty. Such a penalty is deductible as home mortgage interest if it otherwise qualifies.[53]

[51] 2017-32 IRB 190.

[52] 2018-34 IRB 318.

[53] Rev. Rul. 57-198, 1957-1 CB 97.

A taxpayer may deduct a late payment charge or penalty on a home mortgage as mortgage interest, provided the charge is not for specific services performed by the lender.[54]

¶ 1702 REAL ESTATE TAXES

Homeowners may deduct state and local real property taxes as an itemized deduction on their personal tax returns.[55] The term "real property taxes" means taxes imposed on interests in real property and levied for the general public welfare, but it does not include taxes assessed against local benefits or payments for specific services.[56]

Many homeowners pay their real property taxes through an escrow arrangement with their mortgage lender, that is, they make monthly payments to their lender that represent about 1/12th of the annual real estate taxes. The payment of these amounts in escrow is not the payment of the taxes themselves since the mortgagee is acting as the agent of the homeowner. The deduction for real estate taxes for a cash basis homeowner arises only when the mortgagee pays the money over to the taxing authority from the escrow account.[57]

Annual assessments paid to homeowners' associations to maintain common areas and to promote the welfare of residents are not deductible as real estate taxes.[58]

Limitation for 2018 through 2025

The itemized deduction by individuals for state, local, and foreign property taxes, and state and local income taxes and general sales taxes paid or accrued during the tax year is limited for tax years 2018 through 2025. An individual cannot deduct foreign real property taxes, but may still claim an itemized deduction of up to $10,000 ($5,000 for married taxpayer filing a separate return) for state and local property taxes, income taxes, and general sales taxes.[59] An individual may also still claim a deduction for state and local real or personal property taxes paid or accrued in carrying on a trade or business or income-producing activity.

The IRS has adopted regulations that provide rules governing the availability of charitable contribution deductions under Code Sec. 170 when a taxpayer receives or expects to receive a corresponding state or local tax credit. The regulations are designed to prevent taxpayers from circumventing the $10,000 limitation on the deduction for state and local taxes by substituting an increased charitable contribution deduction for a disallowed state and local tax deduction.[60]

According to the regulations, when a taxpayer receives or expects to receive a state or local tax credit in return for a payment or transfer to an entity listed in Code

[54] Rev. Rul. 74-187, 1974-1 CB 48; Rev. Rul. 67-297, 1967-2 CB 87.

[55] Code Sec. 164(a)(1).

[56] Reg. § 1.164-3(b). For a complete discussion of the differences between deductible real property taxes and assessments against local benefits, *see* ¶ 704. For the apportionment of real estate taxes on the purchase or sale of real estate, *see* ¶ 102.03.

[57] Rev. Rul. 78-103, 1978-1 CB 58; *see also* United Mercantile Agencies, Inc., 23 TC 1105, CCH Dec. 20,940, *acq.* 1955-2 CB 9, *rem'd sub nom* F.W. Drybrough, CA-6, 57-1 USTC ¶ 9212, 238 F.2d 735; F.J. Hradesky, 65 TC 87, CCH Dec. 33,461, *aff'd*, CA-5, 76-2 USTC ¶ 9703, 540 F.2d 821.

[58] Rev. Rul. 76-495, 1976-2 CB 43.

[59] Code Sec. 164(b)(6).

[60] Reg. § 1.170A-1.

Sec. 170(c), the receipt of this tax benefit is a *quid pro quo* that may preclude a full deduction under Code Sec. 170(a). Therefore, under the regulations, the amount otherwise deductible as a charitable contribution must generally be reduced by the amount of the state or local tax credit received or expected to be received, just as it is reduced for many other benefits.

The regulations include a *de minimis* exception under which a taxpayer may disregard a state or local tax credit if the sum of the credits does not exceed 15 percent of the taxpayer's payment or 15 percent of the fair market value of the property transferred by the taxpayer. The *de minimis* exception reflects that the combined value of a state and local tax deduction, that is the combined top marginal state and local tax rate, currently does not exceed 15 percent. Therefore, under the regulations, a state or local tax credit that does not exceed 15 percent does not reduce the taxpayer's federal deduction for a charitable contribution.

¶ 1703 CASUALTY LOSSES

Losses to a taxpayer's home, household goods, and personal property generally are deductible for federal tax purposes. For the most part, the rules that apply to business casualties as discussed at ¶ 1501 apply to nonbusiness casualties as well. These rules include those concerning:

1. The definition of a casualty loss;
2. The effect of a casualty loss on basis;
3. The determination of the amount of a casualty loss or gain;
4. The postponement of a taxable casualty gain through the purchase of replacement property; and
5. The early deduction of disaster area losses.

The nonbusiness casualty loss deduction, however, is subject to a $100 "deductible" and is further limited to 10 percent of a taxpayer's adjusted gross income.[61]

Deduction Limited for 2018 through 2025

For tax years beginning after December 31, 2017, and before January 1, 2026, the itemized deduction for personal casualty losses is limited to those attributable to federally declared disasters. A taxpayer may still claim personal casualty losses not attributable to federally declared disasters to offset any personal casualty gains during 2018 through 2025. Any personal casualty gains used to offset personal casualty losses attributable to a federally declared disaster, however, are not taken into account in determining the taxpayer's ten percent of AGI limitation.[62]

Additional Relief for 2016 and 2017

If an individual has a net disaster loss for tax years beginning in 2016 or 2017, the $100 limitation applicable to each casualty related to the disaster is increased to $500, and the ten percent adjusted gross income limitation is waived. For this purpose, a net disaster loss is the qualified disaster-related personal casualty losses, over any personal casualty gains. A qualified disaster-related personal loss means a

[61] Code Sec. 165(h).

[62] Code Sec. 165(h)(5).

personal casualty loss arising in a disaster area on or after January 1, 2016, that is attributable to a federally declared disaster. For an individual who does not itemize deductions, his or her standard deduction is increased by the amount of the casualty loss attributable to the disaster.[63]

.01 Limitations

The deduction of nonbusiness casualty and theft losses is subject to two limitations. The first $100 of a casualty or theft loss is not allowable as a deduction. A separate $100 reduction applies to each individual casualty. After the $100 reduction for each casualty, total nonbusiness casualty losses may be deducted only to the extent they exceed 10 percent of the taxpayer's adjusted gross income.

Note: The examples in the following paragraphs assume losses were incurred in a federally declared disaster for 2018 through 2025.

[A] Deductible for Losses

The first $100 ($500 for 2009 only) of a casualty or theft loss on nonbusiness property is not deductible.[64] This $100 reduction for each casualty applies after any reimbursement for the loss, such as from insurance, is taken into account.[65]

Example 13: The Taxpayer has a $250 deductible insurance policy on a home. The home is damaged in a windstorm and the insurance company pays the Taxpayer for the damage, less the $250 deductible. The Taxpayer's casualty loss deduction following the windstorm and insurance reimbursement is limited to $150 (before applying the 10 percent of adjusted gross income limitation discussed at ¶ 1703.01[B]). The first $100 of unreimbursed casualty loss on nonbusiness property is not deductible.

The $100 reduction applies to each individual casualty or theft, regardless of the number of items or parcels of property damaged or lost through the same casualty or theft. According to the regulations, events closely related in origin are considered a single event. There is a single casualty when the damage is from two or more closely related causes, such as wind and flood damage from the same hurricane. A single casualty may also damage two or more widely separated pieces of property, for instance, the same severe storm may damage a taxpayer's home and a personal auto that is parked at the taxpayer's place of employment many miles away.[66]

Example 14: Hurricane Donna damages the Taxpayer's home, which is located about 20 miles from the coast. The hurricane also destroys the Taxpayer's pleasure boat, which is kept at a marina in a resort town on the coast. The damage to the Taxpayer's home is $6,700, and insurance covers $5,100 of this loss. The boat cost $12,000 when it was purchased several years ago, but the fair market value was $7,000 when it was destroyed. The Taxpayer carried no insurance on the boat. The Taxpayer's total casualty loss from hurricane Donna is $8,600 ($1,600 unreimbursed damage to the home and the

[63] Sec. 11028, P.L. 115-97 (The Tax Cuts and Jobs Act).

[64] Code Sec. 165(h)(1).

[65] Reg. § 1.165-7(b)(4)(i).

[66] Reg. § 1.165-7(b)(4)(ii).

$7,000 loss on the boat). The Taxpayer's deductible casualty loss before application of the 10 percent of adjusted gross income limitation is $8,500. The $100 reduction applies to the Taxpayer's total loss from the single casualty.

If a taxpayer suffers more than one casualty or theft during the year, the taxpayer must reduce each loss by $100.[67]

Example 15: Assume the same facts as in Example 14, except that only the Taxpayer's boat is damaged by hurricane Donna. Four months before hurricane Donna, the Taxpayer's home was damaged by an early summer lightning storm. In this case, the Taxpayer's loss deduction before application of the ten percent of adjusted gross income limitation is $8,400. The $1,600 unreimbursed loss to the home must be reduced by $100 and the separate $7,000 casualty loss to the boat also must be reduced by $100.

Multiple Owners

If two or more individuals, other than a husband and wife filing a joint return, have losses from the same casualty, the $100 reduction applies separately to each. The same rule applies when two or more individuals, other than a husband and wife filing a joint return, have a loss on property that they own jointly.[68] For instance, if two sisters live in a home that they own jointly and that home is damaged by a fire, each must reduce her casualty loss by $100.

Married Couples

If a husband and wife suffer a casualty loss and they file a joint return, they are treated as one taxpayer in applying the $100 reduction, regardless of whether they own the property separately or jointly. If they file separate returns, however, each must reduce his or her casualty loss by $100, even if they own the property jointly.

If the damaged property is owned separately by one spouse, only that spouse can take the casualty loss on a separate return. If the damaged property is owned as tenants by the entirety, each spouse may deduct only one half of the loss on a separate return, neither spouse may deduct the entire loss on a separate return, and each must reduce his or her loss by $100.[69]

[B] Adjusted Gross Income Limitation

A taxpayer may deduct a casualty loss to nonbusiness property only to the extent the loss is more than 10 percent of the taxpayer's adjusted gross income.[70] This adjusted gross income limitation applies after any casualty loss is reduced by any reimbursements and by $100. A taxpayer with more than one casualty loss during the year reduces the total of all losses by 10 percent of adjusted gross income, after reducing each unreimbursed loss by $100.

If a taxpayer has casualty gains in addition to casualty losses, the taxpayer must compare total casualty gains to total casualty losses, after reducing each loss by $100 but before applying the ten percent of adjusted gross income limitation. If the losses exceed the gains, the casualty gains reduce the casualty losses before

[67] *Id.*

[68] Reg. § 1.165-7(b)(4)(iii).

[69] Code Sec. 165(h).

[70] Code Sec. 165(h)(2).

applying the ten percent of adjusted gross income limitation.[71] If the recognized casualty gains exceed the casualty losses, the difference is treated as a capital gain.[72] The ten percent of adjusted gross income limitation does not apply when a taxpayer's casualty gains exceed casualty losses.

Multiple Owners

When two or more individuals, other than a husband and wife filing a joint return, have a casualty loss on property that they own jointly, the ten percent of adjusted gross income limitation applies separately to each.

A husband and wife who file a joint return and have a loss from the same casualty are treated as one individual for purposes of the ten percent of adjusted gross income limitation, regardless of whether they own the property jointly or separately.

.02 Calculation of the Casualty Deduction

A taxpayer who suffers a casualty generally must determine the loss separately for each item or parcel of property lost or damaged by the casualty. Real estate that is not used for business or investment, however, is considered one item of property.

[A] Real Estate

To determine the loss on real estate that a taxpayer uses for personal purposes, all improvements, such as buildings, landscaping, etc., are considered together. The amount of the loss is the lesser of the decrease in value of the entire property or the adjusted basis of the property.[73] From this loss amount, the taxpayer must subtract insurance or other reimbursements received or expected and the $100 reduction required by Code Sec. 165. If this is the taxpayer's only casualty or theft loss, the taxpayer would also subtract ten percent of adjusted gross income. If the taxpayer had other casualty or theft losses, the ten percent of adjusted gross income would reduce the total of all losses. Any amount remaining after these reductions is the casualty loss deduction.

Example 16: The Taxpayer purchased a cottage several years ago for $44,800, including $4,500 for the land. During the current year, the cottage is damaged by a forest fire (federally declared disaster), resulting in the Taxpayer's only casualty or theft loss during the year. Immediately before the fire, the fair market value of the cottage and land was $50,000. After the fire, the fair market value of the property is $35,000. As a result of the fire, the Taxpayer collected $10,000 from the insurance company. Assuming that the Taxpayer's adjusted gross income for the current year is $40,000, the Taxpayer's casualty loss deduction as a result of the fire is $900, calculated as follows:

1. Adjusted basis of property	$44,800
2. Value before fire	$50,000
3. Value after fire	35,000
4. Decrease in value	$15,000

[71] Code Sec. 165(h)(2)(A)(i).

[72] Code Sec. 165(h)(2)(B) and (h)(4)(A).

[73] Reg. § 1.165-7(b)(2)(ii).

5. Amount of loss (lesser of 1 or 4)	$15,000
6. Less: Insurance reimbursement	10,000
7. Loss after reimbursement	$5,000
8. Less: $100 reduction	100
9. Loss after $100 rule	$4,900
10. Less: 10% of adjusted gross income	4,000
11. Casualty loss deduction	$900

Example 17: The Taxpayer purchased a personal residence several years ago for $50,000—$10,000 for the land and $40,000 for the house. The Taxpayer also spent $2,000 for landscaping. During the current year, the Taxpayer's home is totally destroyed by a forest fire (federally declared disaster). The fire also damaged the shrubbery and trees on the property. This was the Taxpayer's only casualty or theft loss during the year. Appraisals valued the property at $75,000 before the fire but at only $15,000 after the fire. An insurance company paid the Taxpayer $45,000 as a result of the loss. Assuming the Taxpayer's adjusted gross income for the current year is $48,000, the Taxpayer's casualty loss deduction is $2,100, calculated as follows:

1. Adjusted basis of property	$52,000
2. Value before fire	$75,000
3. Value after fire	15,000
4. Decrease in value	$60,000
5. Amount of loss (lesser of 1 or 4)	$52,000
6. Less: Insurance reimbursement	45,000
7. Loss after reimbursement	$7,000
8. Less: $100 reduction	100
9. Loss after $100 rule	$6,900
10. Less: 10% of adjusted gross income	4,800
11. Casualty loss deduction	$2,100

[B] Personal Property

Personal property includes any property that is not real property. When personal property is damaged or destroyed by a casualty, taxpayers must compute their loss separately for each item of property.[74]

The amount of the loss is the lesser of the decrease in fair market value or the adjusted basis of the property. From this amount, the taxpayer subtracts insurance

[74] Reg. § 1.165-7(b)(2)(i).

or other reimbursements and the $100 reduction required by Code Sec. 165. The loss is further reduced by ten percent of adjusted gross income, if the loss is the only loss during the year. If the taxpayer suffered several losses during the year, the ten percent of adjusted gross income limitation, of course, would apply to the total of all the losses. Any amount remaining after these reductions is the taxpayer's personal casualty loss deduction.

Example 18: The Taxpayer's pleasure boat, which cost $8,500, was lost in a storm (federally declared disaster) in August of the current year. This was the Taxpayer's only casualty or theft loss during the year. The value of the boat before the storm was $7,000. The Taxpayer had no insurance on the boat but was able to salvage the outboard motor and sell it for $200. Assuming the Taxpayer's adjusted gross income is $52,000, the Taxpayer's casualty loss deduction is $1,500, computed as follows:

1. Adjusted basis of property	$8,500
2. Value before storm	$7,000
3. Value after storm	200
4. Decrease in value	$6,800
5. Amount of loss (lesser of 1 or 4)	$6,800
6. Less: Insurance reimbursement	-0-
7. Loss after reimbursement	$6,800
8. Less: $100 reduction	100
9. Loss after $100 rule	$6,700
10. Less: 10% of adjusted gross income	5,200
11. Casualty loss deduction	$1,500

Example 19: During the year, the Taxpayer's family auto was lost in a flood (federally declared disaster). The auto was purchased two years before for $10,000. Also lost in the flood was the Taxpayer's watch, purchased one month before the flood for $250. The value of the car just before the flood was $7,500, and its value after the flood was $80 (scrap). Insurance reimbursed the Taxpayer $6,000 for the car, but the watch was not insured. Assuming the Taxpayer's adjusted gross income for the year is $31,000, the Taxpayer's casualty loss deduction is zero, calculated as follows:

Car:

1. Adjusted basis of property	$10,000
2. Value before flood	$7,500
3. Value after flood	80
4. Decrease in value	$7,420

5. Amount of loss (lesser of 1 or 4)	$7,420
6. Less: Insurance reimbursement	6,000
7. Loss after reimbursement	$1,420

Watch:

1. Adjusted basis of property	$250
2. Value before flood	$250
3. Value after flood	-0-
4. Decrease in value	$250
5. Amount of loss (lesser of 1 or 4)	$250
6. Less: Insurance reimbursement	-0-
7. Loss after reimbursement	$250

Total casualty loss:

1. Total loss (watch + car)	$1,670
2. Less: $100 reduction	100
3. Loss after $100 rule	$1,570
4. Less: 10% of adjusted gross income	3,100
5. Casualty loss deduction	$-0-

[C] Loss to Real and Personal Property

If a single casualty causes a loss to both real and personal property, the taxpayer must figure the loss separately for each type of property, as discussed above, but the $100 reduction is applied to the total loss, before the ten percent of adjusted gross income limitation is applied.

Example 20: The Taxpayer's home, which cost $64,000 including land, was partially damaged by a hurricane (federally declared disaster) in August of the current year. The value of the property before the storm was $70,000, and its value after the storm was $60,000. The Taxpayer's household furnishings were also damaged. The Taxpayer separately figured the loss on each damaged household item and arrived at a total of $600. The Taxpayer collected $5,000 from the insurance company for damage to the home, but nothing for the household items. Assuming the Taxpayer's adjusted gross income for the year is $44,000, the Taxpayer's casualty loss deduction as a result of the hurricane is $1,100, calculated as follows:

1. Adjusted basis of real property	$64,000
2. Value before storm	$70,000
3. Value after storm	60,000
4. Decrease in value	$10,000
5. Loss on real estate (lesser 1 or 4)	$10,000
6. Less: Insurance reimbursement	5,000
7. Loss after reimbursement	$5,000
8. Loss on furnishings	$600
9. Less: Insurance reimbursement	-0-
10. Loss after reimbursement	$600
11. Total loss (7 plus 10)	$5,600
12. Less: $100 reduction	100
13. Loss after $100 rule	$5,500
14. Less: 10% of adjusted gross income	4,400
15. Casualty loss deduction	$1,100

.03 Part Business and Part Personal-Use Property

If property is used partly for business purposes and partly for personal purposes, any casualty or theft loss deduction to that property must be calculated as though there were two separate casualties or thefts, that is, one affecting the personal-use property and one affecting the business property.[75] The reason for this is simply that the casualty loss to personal-use property must be reduced by the $100 reduction and ten percent of adjusted gross income limitation, while casualty losses to business property are deductible in full, as discussed at ¶ 1501.02[A].

Example 21: The Taxpayer owns a three-story building that was built on leased land. The Taxpayer uses two floors (2/3 of the building) in the business and lives on the third floor (1/3 of the building). The cost of the building was $140,000, and the Taxpayer made no additions or improvements to it since it was built. A flood (federally declared disaster) during the current year damaged the entire building. The fair market value of the building was $133,000 immediately before the flood and $120,000 after the flood. The Taxpayer collected $9,000 from the insurance company as a result of the flood damage. Before the flood, the Taxpayer had taken $8,400 in depreciation deductions for the business portion of the building. The Taxpayer has a business casualty loss for the current year of $2,267, and, assuming the Taxpayer's adjusted gross income is $50,000, no personal casualty loss deduction is available because of

[75] Reg. § 1.165-7(b)(4)(iv).

the $100 rule and 10 percent of adjusted gross income limitation. These deductions are computed as follows:

Business Loss:

1. Adjusted basis (⅔ total cost of $140,000 less $8,400 depreciation)	$84,933
2. Value before flood (⅔ total)	$88,667
3. Value after flood (⅔ total)	80,000
4. Decrease in value	$8,667
5. Amount of loss (lesser of 1 or 4)	$8,667
6. Less: Insurance reimbursement (⅔ total)	6,000
7. Loss after reimbursement	$2,667
8. Deductible business casualty	$2,667

Personal Loss:

1. Adjusted basis (⅓ total cost of $140,000)	$46,667
2. Value before flood (⅓ total)	$44,333
3. Value after flood (⅓ total)	40,000
4. Decrease in value	$4,333
5. Amount of loss (lesser of 1 or 4)	$4,333
6. Less: Insurance reimbursement (⅓ total)	3,000
7. Loss after reimbursement	$1,333
8. Less: $100 reduction	100
9. Loss after $100 rule	$1,233
10. Less: 10% adjusted gross income	5,000
11. Deductible personal casualty	$ -0-

¶ 1704 DISASTER RELIEF EXCLUSION

Code Sec. 139 provides a specific exclusion from income for qualified disaster relief payments. Qualified disaster relief payments include payments, from any source, to, or for the benefit of, an individual to reimburse or pay reasonable and necessary personal, family, living, or funeral expenses incurred as a result of a qualified disaster. Qualified disaster relief payments also include payments, from any source, to reimburse or pay reasonable and necessary expenses incurred for the repair or rehabilitation of a personal residence to the extent that the need for the repair, rehabilitation, or replacement is attributable to a qualified disaster. Payments for the repair or replacement of the contents of the residence also qualify. Qualified disaster relief payments do not include payments for any expenses compensated for by insurance or otherwise.

For purposes of determining the tax basis of a rehabilitated residence, qualified disaster relief payments are treated in the same manner as amounts received on an involuntary conversion of a principal residence under Code Sec. 121(d)(5) and Code Sec. 1033(b) and (h). A residence is not precluded from being a personal residence solely because the taxpayer does not own the residence; a rented residence can qualify as a personal residence.

Code Sec. 139 also provides for the exclusion from income of qualified disaster mitigation payments paid to or for the benefit of the owner of any property. Payments must be under the Robert T. Stafford Disaster Relief and Emergency Assistance Act or the National Flood Insurance Act. Payments received for the sale or disposition of the property do not qualify for the exclusion under Code Sec. 139. Further, no increase in basis may result from excluded amounts, and no deduction or credit is allowed for expenditures to the extent of any excluded amount.

¶ 1705 MOVING EXPENSES

An employee or self-employed person may deduct the expenses of moving from one location to another, provided the move is related to starting work at a new principal place of employment. The deduction is a deduction from gross income.[76]

.01 Deduction Suspended for 2018 through 2025

The deduction for moving expenses for tax years beginning after December 31, 2017, and before January 1, 2026 has been suspended. An employee or self-employed individual may not claim an above-the-line deduction in calculating adjusted gross income for moving expenses in 2018 through 2025.[77]

The special rules that apply to members of the Armed Forces of the United States continue to apply after 2017. A member of the Armed Forces may still claim a deduction for moving expenses and exclude from income in-kind moving and storage expenses, as well as reimbursement or allowance for those expenses. The member of the Armed Forces must be on active duty and move pursuant to a military order and incident to a permanent change of station.

The exclusion for qualified moving expense reimbursements for tax years 2018 through 2025 also is suspended (see ¶ 1705.03[A]). However, members of the U.S. Armed Forces on active duty who move pursuant to a military order and incident to a permanent change of station are still permitted to exclude qualified moving expense reimbursements from their income. Employers are required to report all payments and reimbursements of employee moving expenses after 2017 and before 2026 as wages subject to income tax and employment tax withholding.

The discussion of the moving expense deduction in the following paragraphs applies to those years when the deduction is in effect.

---

[76] Code Sec. 217.

[77] Code Sec. 217(k).

.02 Qualification for the Deduction

Generally, taxpayers may deduct moving expenses only if the expenses are related to the start of work at a new location. Moving expenses incurred within one year from the time a taxpayer first reports to work at the new location are considered closely related. If a taxpayer does not move within one year of starting work at a new location, moving expenses are not deductible unless circumstances existed which prevented the taxpayer from moving within the year.[78] For example, taxpayers may delay a move to allow a child to finish high school in the same school and deduct moving expenses incurred after the one-year period.

In addition to meeting the requirement that a move be job related, a taxpayer must also satisfy specific distance and length-of-employment tests to deduct moving expenses.

[A] Distance

To deduct moving expenses, a taxpayer must show that the new principal place of work is at least 50 miles farther from the old residence than the old residence was from the old place of work.[79] Note that the distance test does not apply to the location of the taxpayer's new home. Also, distance is measured by the shortest commonly traveled routes.

> ***Example 22:*** The Taxpayer moved to a new home that was 30 miles from the old home. The distance from the old residence to the new place of work is 52 miles. The distance from the old residence to the old place of work is one mile. Since the distance from the Taxpayer's old residence to the new place of work is at least 50 miles farther than the distance from the old residence to the old place of work, the Taxpayer may deduct moving expenses.

In the case of a taxpayer returning to full-time work after a period of unemployment or part-time work, or in the case of a taxpayer beginning a first full-time job, the taxpayer's place of work must be at least 50 miles from the taxpayer's old home in order for the taxpayer to deduct moving expenses.

The new job must be the taxpayer's principal or main job, that is, the place where the taxpayer spends the most working time. An employee who works for several employers through a union hall treats the union hall as the main job location. A taxpayer with more than one job determines the main job based on the time spent at the different locations, the amount of work done at each place, and the money earned at each job location.

[B] Length of Employment

If the taxpayer is an employee, the taxpayer must be employed full time at least 39 weeks during the first 12 months after his move in order to qualify for the moving expense deduction. The employee does not have to work for the same employer for those 39 weeks, nor does the employee have to work for 39 consecutive weeks. If the taxpayer is self-employed, the taxpayer must be employed full time for at least 78 weeks during the 24 months following the move, in addition to

[78] Reg. § 1.217-2(a)(3).

[79] Code Sec. 217(c)(1).

meeting the 39 weeks/12 months test.[80] The full-time work requirement is waived, however, if death, disability, involuntary separation from work (other than for misconduct), or transfer to another location for the benefit of the employer occurs.[81]

A taxpayer who moves during the year and deducts the expenses for the year of the move on the assumption that the taxpayer will meet the length-of-employment test and then fails the test must either report the previously deducted expenses as income for the year following the move or amend the earlier return.

.03 Deductible Costs

Only those expenses that are reasonable for the circumstances of the move are deductible. A taxpayer who meets the requirements for deducting moving expenses may deduct the following:[82]

1. The cost of packing, crating, and transporting household goods and personal effects from the taxpayer's former home to the taxpayer's new home. The cost of storing and insuring household goods and personal effects within any period of 30 consecutive days after things are moved from the former home and before they are delivered to the new home are deductible.
2. Any costs of connecting or disconnecting utilities required because the taxpayer is moving household goods, appliances, or personal effects.
3. The cost of shipping a car and household pets to the taxpayer's new home.
4. The cost of moving household goods and personal effects from a place other than the taxpayer's former home. The deduction is limited to the amount it would have cost to move them from the former home.
5. The cost of transportation and lodging for the taxpayer and members of the taxpayer's household while traveling from the former home to the new home.

The following items are not deductible as moving expenses (many of these items were deductible under the moving expense deduction rules in effect before 1994):

- Premove househunting expenses,
- Temporary living expenses,
- Meal expenses,
- Expenses of buying or selling a home,
- Expenses of getting or breaking a lease,
- Security deposits,
- Home improvements to sell the old home,
- Loss on the sale of a home,

[80] Code Sec. 217(c)(2).
[81] Code Sec. 217(d).
[82] Code Sec. 217(b).

- Mortgage penalties,
- Losses from disposing of club memberships,
- Any part of the purchase price of a new home,
- Real estate taxes,
- Car tags and driver's license fees, and
- Storage charges except for foreign moves.

[A] Reimbursements

A taxpayer reimbursed for moving expenses by the employer reports the payments as income.[83] These reimbursements are subject to withholding and information reporting requirements unless the taxpayer is entitled to a moving expense deduction for the amounts.[84]

[B] Foreign Moves

The moving expense deduction relating to the commencement of work outside the United States and its possessions is similar to the deduction for moves within the United States.

In addition, deductible amounts include the reasonable expenses of moving household goods and personal effects to and from storage, and of storing goods and effects for part or all of the period during which the new place of work continues to be the taxpayer's principal place of work.[85]

¶ 1706 DISTRICT OF COLUMBIA HOMEBUYER CREDIT

For property purchased after August 4, 1997, and before January 1, 2012, a first-time homebuyer in the District of Columbia was entitled to a tax credit of up to $5,000.[86]

The amount allowable as a credit is reduced by the amount that bears the same ratio to the credit allowable as the excess of the taxpayer's modified adjusted gross income for the tax year over $70,000 ($110,000 in the case of a joint return) bears to $20,000. Modified adjusted gross income is adjusted gross income increased by any amount excluded from gross income under Code Sec. 911 (foreign earned income exclusion), Code Sec. 931 (exclusion for possessions income), or Code Sec. 933 (exclusion for Puerto Rico income).

A first-time homebuyer is an individual who had no present ownership interest in a principal residence in the District of Columbia during the one-year period ending on the date of the purchase of the principal residence. If an individual is treated as a first-time homebuyer for any principal residence, that individual may not be treated as a first-time homebuyer for any other principal residence.

¶ 1707 FIRST-TIME HOMEBUYER CREDIT

A first-time homebuyer who purchased a principal residence after April 8, 2008, and before May 1, 2010, was allowed a refundable tax credit of ten percent of

83 Code Sec. 82.

84 Reg. § 31.3401(a)(15)-1.

85 Code Sec. 217(h).

86 Code Sec. 1400C.

the purchase price up to a maximum of $8,000 ($4,000 for a married individual filing separately). For purchases in 2008, however, the maximum credit was $7,500 ($3,750 for a married individual filing separately). Also, a recapture provision applies to purchases in 2008 and the credit for 2008 essentially amounts to an interest-free loan that must be repaid. The May 1, 2010 deadline was extended to July 1, 2010, in the case of a homebuyer who signed a written contract before May 1, 2010, to close on the purchase before October 1, 2010.[87]

For purchases before November 7, 2009, the credit was phased out for taxpayers with modified adjusted gross income between $75,000 and $95,000 ($150,000-$170,000 for joint filers) for the year of purchase. For purchases after November 6, 2009, the credit was phased out for taxpayers with modified adjusted gross income between $125,000 and $145,000 ($225,000 and $245,000 for joint filers) for the year of purchase.

An individual (and, if married, the individual's spouse) who had maintained the same principal residence for any five-consecutive year period during the eight-year period ending on the date of the purchase of a subsequent principal residence was treated as a first-time homebuyer for purchases after November 6, 2009. The maximum allowable credit for long-time homeowners was $6,500 ($3,250 for a married individual filing separately).

.01 Recapture of Credit

The first-time homebuyer credit for a home purchased in 2008 is recaptured ratably over fifteen years with no interest charge beginning in the second tax year after the year in which the home is purchased. A taxpayer who claimed the credit for 2008 must report the appropriate recapture amount (6-2/3 percent of the credit) as an additional tax on his or her tax return for each year in the repayment period. If the homeowner sells the home or ceases to use it as a principal residence before complete repayment, any remaining amount is due on the tax return for that year. The required repayment is limited to the amount of gain from the sale of the residence to an unrelated person. Recapture is not required on the death of the homeowner. In the case of an involuntary conversion of the home, recapture is not accelerated if a new principal residence is acquired within a two-year period. In the case of a transfer of the residence to a spouse or to a former spouse incident to divorce, the transferee spouse (and not the transferor spouse) is responsible for any future recapture.[88]

Although the recapture rule generally does not apply to a home purchased in 2009 or 2010, recapture does occur if the homeowner sells the home or ceases to use it as a principal residence within 36 months of its date of purchase.[89]

¶ 1708 CREDITS FOR ENERGY SAVINGS

In the Energy Policy Act of 2005, Congress recognized that residential energy use, including energy use for heating and cooling, represents a large share of national energy consumption. In the Act, Congress provided two separate tax

[87] Code Sec. 36.

[88] Code Sec. 39(f).

[89] Code Sec. 39(f)(4)(D)(ii).

credits as an incentive for homeowners to save energy. One provision provides a tax credit for the purchase of qualified energy efficiency improvements to existing homes.[90] The other provides a tax credit for the purchase of qualified solar electric property and qualified solar water heating property. Tax credits for fuel cells and wind and geothermal property were added later.[91]

.01 Nonbusiness Energy Property Credit

For property placed in service after 2010 and before 2018 (unless extended once more by Congress), there is a ten-percent nonrefundable credit for the purchase of energy efficiency building envelope components that meet or exceed the criteria of the 2009 International Energy Conservation Code as in effect on February 17, 2009 (or the Energy Star program requirements for roofs and roof products or version 6.0 Energy Star requirements for windows, skylights, and doors).[92] The credit is also available for other specified property.[93] The taxpayer's basis in the property is reduced by the amount of the credit.[94]

Building Envelope Components

For a building envelope component to qualify, it must be installed in or on a dwelling located in the United States that is owned and used by the taxpayer as the taxpayer's principal residence. Further, the original use of the component must begin with the taxpayer and the component must reasonably be expected to remain in use for at least five years.[95]

Building envelope components are:

1. Insulation materials or systems which are specifically and primarily designed to reduce the heat loss or gain for a dwelling;
2. Exterior windows (including skylights) and doors;
3. Metal roofs with appropriate pigmented coatings which are specifically and primarily designed to reduce the heat loss or gain for a dwelling; and
4. Asphalt roofs that have cooling granules which are specifically and primarily designed to reduce the heat loss or gain for a dwelling.[96]

Other Property

The credit also is available for advanced main air circulating fans, qualified natural gas, propane, or oil furnaces or hot water boilers, qualified energy efficient property, and stoves that burn biomass fuel to heat the home or hot water for the residence.[97]

Biomass fuel is any plant-derived fuel available on a renewable or recurring basis, including agricultural crops and trees, wood and wood waste and residues (including wood pellets), plants (including aquatic plants), grasses, residues, and fibers.[98]

---

[90] Code Sec. 25C.
[91] Code Sec. 25D.
[92] Code Sec. 25C(a)(1).
[93] Code Sec. 25C(a)(2).
[94] Code Sec. 25C(f).
[95] Code Sec. 25C(c)(1).
[96] Code Sec. 25C(c)(3).
[97] Code Sec. 25C(d).
[98] Code Sec. 25C(d)(6).

An advanced main air circulating fan is a fan used in a natural gas, propane, or oil furnace and that has an annual electricity use of no more than two percent of the total annual energy use of the furnace (as determined in the standard Department of Energy test procedures).[99]

A qualified natural gas, propane, or oil furnace or hot water boiler is a natural gas, propane, or oil furnace or hot water boiler with an annual fuel utilization efficiency rate of at least 95.[100]

Qualified energy-efficient property includes:

1. An electric heat pump water heater that yields an energy factor of at least 2.0 in the standard Department of Energy test procedure;
2. An electric heat pump that achieves the highest efficiency tier established by the Consortium for Energy Efficiency in effect on January 1, 2009;
3. A central air conditioner with an energy efficiency rating in the highest efficiency tier established by the Consortium for Energy Efficiency as in effect on January 1, 2009;
4. A natural gas, propane, or oil water heater that has an energy factor of at least 0.82 or a thermal efficiency of at least 90 percent); and
5. A biomass stove with a thermal efficiency rating of at least 75 percent.[101]

Limitations

The credit allowed for any year may not exceed $500 reduced by nonbusiness energy credits taken in all prior years after 2005, and no more than $200 dollars of the credit may be attributable to expenditures on windows. Further, the credit is limited to $50 for each advanced main air circulating fan, $150 for each qualified natural gas, propane, or oil furnace or hot water boiler, and $300 for each item of qualified energy efficient property.[102]

The IRS has issued Notice 2009-53[103] which provides procedures that manufacturers may follow to certify property as either an eligible building envelope component or qualified energy property. The Notice also discusses the conditions under which homeowners seeking to claim the credit may rely on a manufacturer's certification or an Energy Star label. The IRS provided further guidance in Q and A format in Notice 2013-70.[104]

[A] Energy Property Credit before 2011

For property placed in service in 2009 and 2010, there was a 30-percent nonrefundable credit for the purchase of energy efficiency building envelope components that meet or exceed the criteria of the 2000 International Energy Conservation Code as in effect on August 8, 2005 (or the Energy Star program requirements for metal roofs with pigmented coatings). The credit was also availa-

99 Code Sec. 25C(d)(5).

100 Code Sec. 25C(d)(4).

101 Code Sec. 25C(d)(2).

102 Code Sec. 25C(b).

103 2009-25 IRB 1095.

104 2013-47 IRB 528.

ble for other specified property. The taxpayer's basis in the property was reduced by the amount of the credit.[105]

Building Envelope Components

For a building envelope component to qualify, it must have been installed in or on a dwelling located in the United States that was owned and used by the taxpayer as the taxpayer's principal residence. Further, the original use of the component must have begun with the taxpayer and the component must reasonably have been expected to remain in use for at least five years.

Building envelope components were:

1. Insulation materials or systems which are specifically and primarily designed to reduce the heat loss or gain for a dwelling and meet the criteria of the International Energy Conservation Code as in effect on February 17, 2009;
2. Exterior windows (including skylights) and doors that have a U-factor at or below 0.30 and a seasonal heat gain coefficient (SHGC) at or below 0.30;
3. Metal roofs with appropriate pigmented coatings which are specifically and primarily designed to reduce the heat loss or gain for a dwelling; and
4. Asphalt roofs that have cooling granules that meet the Energy Star requirements.

Other Property

The credit also was available for advanced main air circulating fans, qualified natural gas, propane, or oil furnaces or hot water boilers, and energy-efficient building property.[106]

Qualified energy-efficient building property included:

1. An electric heat pump water heater that yields an energy factor of at least 2.0 in the standard Department of Energy test procedure;
2. An electric heat pump that achieves the highest efficiency tier of the Consortium for Energy Efficiency as in effect on January 1, 2009;
3. A central air conditioner with an energy efficiency rating in the highest efficiency tier established by the Consortium for Energy Efficiency as in effect on January 1, 2009;
4. A natural gas, propane, or oil water heater that has an energy factor of at least 0.82 or a thermal efficiency of at least 90 percent; and
5. A stove that burns biomass fuel to heat the taxpayer's residence or water and that has a thermal efficiency rating of at least 75 percent, measured using a lower heating value.

---

[105] Code Sec. 25C, as in effect before 2011.

[106] Code Sec. 25C(d)(2).

Limitations

The credit allowed could not exceed $1,500 in total in the case of property placed in service in 2009 and 2010.[107]

Pre-2009 Credit

The nonbusiness energy property credit after 2005 and before 2009 was similar to the credit now in effect for property placed in service after 2010.

.02 Residential Energy Efficient Property

A personal tax credit is available before 2022 for the purchase of qualified solar electric property and qualified solar water heating property used exclusively for purposes other than heating swimming pools and hot tubs. The maximum credit for any tax year before 2009 for each of these systems was $2,000. There also is a credit for the purchase of qualified fuel cell power plants. The credit for any fuel cell for any tax year may not exceed $500 for each 0.5 kilowatt of capacity per year. A credit also is available after 2007 for small wind energy property expenditures and geothermal heat pump systems. The credit for wind property is limited for tax years beginning before 2009 to $500 for each half kilowatt of capacity up to a maximum of $4,000. The credit for geothermal heat pumps is limited for tax years beginning before 2009 to $2,000.[108]

For property placed in service before 2020, the credit rate is 30 percent. For property placed in service in 2020, the rate is 26 percent. For property placed in service in 2021, the rate is 22 percent.[109]

The credit is nonrefundable, but credits that go unused because of the limitations may be carried over.[110] The amount of the credit reduces the basis of the property.[111]

Qualifying solar water heating property is property used to heat water for use in a dwelling unit in the United States and used as a residence if at least half of the energy is derived from the sun.[112]

Qualified solar electric property is property that uses solar energy to generate electricity for use in a dwelling unit.[113]

A qualified fuel cell power plant is an integrated system comprised of a fuel cell stack assembly and associated balance of plant components that converts a fuel into electricity using electrochemical means, has an electricity-only generation efficiency of greater than 30 percent, and generates at least 0.5 kilowatts of electricity. The qualified fuel cell power plant must be installed on or in connection with a dwelling unit in the United States and used by the taxpayer as a principal residence.[114]

---

[107] Code Sec. 25C(b), as in effect for those years.

[108] Code Sec. 25D.

[109] Code Sec. 25D(g).

[110] Code Sec. 25D(c).

[111] Code Sec. 25D(f).

[112] Code Sec. 25D(d)(1).

[113] Code Sec. 25D(d)(2).

[114] Code Sec. 25(d)(3).

Qualified small wind energy property is property that uses a wind turbine to generate electricity in connection with a dwelling used as a residence by the taxpayer in the United States.[115]

Qualified geothermal heat pump property is equipment that uses the ground or ground water as a thermal energy source to heat the taxpayer's dwelling, or as a thermal heat sink to cool the dwelling. The equipment must meet the Energy Star program requirements.[116]

Specified equipment safety requirements must be met to qualify for the credit. Special proration rules apply in the case of jointly owned property, condominiums, and tenant-stockholders in cooperative housing corporations. If less than 80 percent of the property is used for nonbusiness purposes, only that portion of expenditures that is used for nonbusiness purposes is taken into account.[117]

[115] Code Sec. 25D(d)(4).

[116] Code Sec. 25D(d)(5).

[117] Code Sec. 25D(e).

Chapter 18
Mixed-Use Residences

¶ 1800 Overview of Chapter
¶ 1801 Business Use of Home
¶ 1802 Rental of Part of Home
¶ 1803 Rental of Vacation or Other Residence
¶ 1804 Residence Converted to Investment

¶ 1800 OVERVIEW OF CHAPTER

Not every taxpayer limits the use of a personal residence to purely personal purposes. Frequently, a taxpayer will use a portion of the residence for income-producing activities or convert all or part of the residence to business or investment use. When this occurs, the taxpayer may take business expense deductions for some costs associated with the home that, if the home were used solely as a personal residence, would not be deductible.

Obviously, the benefit of converting otherwise nondeductible expenses into deductible ones has often led to disputes between the IRS and taxpayers who sought to deduct expenses far in excess of any income produced by the business use of the home. Also, the possible tax deductions have led other taxpayers to claim a "home office" even when they had a regular place of business outside the home and actually conducted very little business from the home. In response to the problem, Congress enacted a special set of rules that govern the business use of a taxpayer's residence and the rental of a taxpayer's personal residence on a part-time basis. These rules, which essentially limit deductions from the business use of the home to income produced by the business activity, are the primary focus of this chapter. Also considered is the effect of converting a personal residence to investment or income-producing property.

¶ 1801 BUSINESS USE OF HOME

Generally, Code Sec. 280A denies an individual or S corporation deductions for the business use of a dwelling that is used by the taxpayer as a residence, unless the deductions are allowed without regard to their connection with the taxpayer's trade or business or income-producing activities.[1] After setting the general rule, the statute goes on to provide the exceptions.

A taxpayer may be able to deduct some of the expenses of using part of a home for business, if specific tests are met. Also, the deduction must be limited to the

[1] Code Sec. 280A(a) and (b).

income produced by the at-home business activity.[2] The home to which the tests apply is the taxpayer's dwelling unit, which may be a house, apartment, condominium, mobile home, boat, or similar property, and all appurtenant property.[3] The tests and limitation do not apply, however, to any part of a home that is used exclusively as a hotel, motel, inn, or similar establishment.[4]

.01 Safe Harbor Calculation

The IRS has provided an optional safe harbor method that individuals may use to determine the amount of deductible expenses attributable to business use of a residence.[5] This safe harbor method is an alternative to the calculation, allocation, and substantiation of actual expenses for purposes of satisfying the requirements of Code Sec. 280A. This optional safe harbor method of calculating the deduction is effective for tax years beginning on or after January 1, 2013.

Individuals who use the safe harbor method to compute their deduction must continue to satisfy all requirements of Code Sec. 280A for determining their eligibility to claim a deduction. For example, an individual may claim a deduction for business use of a portion of a residence only if that portion is exclusively used on a regular basis for business purposes. Also, an individual who is an employee may deduct expenses attributable to a business use of a residence only if that use is for the convenience of his or her employer.[6]

To determine the amount of deductible expenses under the safe harbor method, multiply the allowable square footage by $5.00. This rate may be adjusted by the IRS from time to time. The allowable square footage is the portion of a home used in a qualified business use of the home, up to a maximum of 300 square feet. This makes the maximum deduction using the safe harbor $1,500 per year.

Generally, an individual who elects the safe harbor method for the year cannot deduct any actual expenses related to the qualified business use of that home for that year. An individual who itemizes deductions and uses the safe harbor method, however, may deduct any expense related to the home that is deductible without regard to whether there is a qualified business use of the home, for example, qualified residence interest, property taxes, and casualty losses. Individuals using the safe harbor method deduct these expenses as itemized deductions on Form 1040, Schedule A, and may not deduct any portion of these expenses from the income derived from the business use of the home to determining the net income from the business or the gross income limitation on the safe harbor deduction. Individuals with a qualified business use of their home who also have a rental use of the same home, however, must allocate a portion of otherwise deductible expenses (qualified residence interest, property taxes, and casualty losses) to the rental use as required by Code Sec. 280A.

---

[2] Code Sec. 280A(c)(5).

[3] Code Sec. 280A(f)(1)(A).

[4] Code Sec. 280A(f)(1)(B).

[5] Rev. Proc. 2013-13, 2013-6 IRB 478.

[6] *See* ¶ 1801.02.

Depreciation

An individual who uses the safe harbor method may not deduct any depreciation (including any additional first-year depreciation) or Code Sec. 179 expense for the portion of the home that is used for business (see ¶ 901.01 and ¶ 901.03). The depreciation deduction allowable for that portion of the home is deemed to be zero.

If an individual uses the safe harbor method for one year and calculates and substantiates actual expenses for any later year, the individual must calculate the depreciation deduction in the later year by using the appropriate optional depreciation table for the property, regardless of whether he or she used an optional depreciation table for the property in its placed-in-service year. See ¶ 901.01[D] for the optional tables. The individual uses the recovery year that corresponds with the current tax year based on the placed-in-service year of the property.

Limitations

In addition to meeting all requirements under Code Sec. 280A, the following limitations apply to the safe harbor method of calculating the deduction for business use of a home:

1. The amount of the deduction cannot exceed the gross income derived from the qualified business use of the home for the year reduced by the business deductions unrelated to the qualified business use of a home. Any amount in excess of the gross income limitation is lost and may not be carried over as a deduction for any other year.
2. An individual who uses the safe harbor method may not deduct any disallowed amount carried over from a prior year for which the individual calculated and substantiated actual expenses for the business use of the home. The individual, however, may deduct the disallowed amount in the next succeeding year in which he or she calculates and substantiates actual expenses.
3. An individual who uses a home for business for a portion of the year (for example, a seasonal business or a business that begins during the year), or an individual who changes the square footage used for business business during the year (for example, an increase or decrease in the square footage), must determine the average of the monthly allowable square footage for the year and use the average to determine the safe harbor deduction. An individual may take no more than 300 square feet into account for any one month and must use the home for business for 15 or more days in the month for that month to be counted. For example, a calendar year individual who begins using 400 square feet of his or her home for business on July 20 and continues that use until the end of the year, has an average monthly allowable square footage of 125 square feet (300 square feet for each of the five months August through December divided by the number of months in the tax year ((300 × 5)/12 = 125).
4. Individuals who share a home (such as roommates or spouses, regardless of filing status), may each use the safe harbor method if otherwise eligible, but not for business use of the same portion of the home. For example, a

husband and wife, if otherwise eligible and regardless of filing status, may each use the safe harbor method for business use of the same home for up to 300 square feet of different portions of the home.

5. An individual who has more than one qualified business use of the same home in the same year and who elects the safe harbor method must use the safe harbor method for each qualified business use of the home. An individual who has a qualified business use of a home and a rental use of the same home, however, cannot use the safe harbor method for the rental use. An individual who has more than one qualified business use of the same home is limited to a maximum of 300 square feet and must allocate the square footage among the qualified business uses of the home. The individual may allocate the square footage in any reasonable manner, but may not allocate more square footage to a qualified business use than is actually used in that business.
6. An individual with qualified business uses of more than one home for the same year may use the safe harbor method for only one home for that year. The individual, however, may calculate and substantiate actual expenses for the business use of any other homes for that year if otherwise eligible.

.02 Exclusive Use for Business Test

In order for a taxpayer to take a deduction for using part of a home in business, the taxpayer must use that part *exclusively* and *regularly* for one of the following:

1. As the principal place of business for any trade or business of the taxpayer;
2. As a place to meet or deal with patients, clients, or customers in the normal course of the taxpayer's trade or business; or
3. In connection with the taxpayer's trade or business if the taxpayer is using a separate structure that is not attached to the taxpayer's house or residence.[7]

The requirement that business use must be exclusive generally bars a deduction when the same space is used both for business and personal living purposes. While this does not require a separate room or other segregated area for business, showing exclusive business use for only part of a room is difficult.[8]

In *Anderson*,[9] the owners of a bed and breakfast argued that a structure that otherwise would fall within the definition of a dwelling unit, such as their inn, at some point may become so commercial in operation and so different from a personal residence that the general disallowance rule of Code Sec.280A(a) should not apply to the dual-use portion. They asserted that business expenses relating to the dual-use portion of the property, in this case the lobby, registration area, office, kitchen, and laundry, should be allowed as deductions. In effect, they argued that their inn had become so commercial that it should be treated the same as a large

---

[7] Code Sec. 280A(c)(1).

[8] *See*, for example, G.H. Weightman, 42 TCM 104, CCH Dec. 37,986(M), T.C. Memo. 1981-301.

[9] T.C. Memo 2006-33.

hotel. The Tax Court held, however, that because they use a portion of their bed and breakfast inn as their personal residence, the general disallowance rule of Code Sec. 280A(a) and the exclusive-use limitation of Code Sec. 280A(f)(1)(B) apply. Therefore, they may not deduct the expenses relating to the portion of the inn that is used for both business and personal purposes (i.e., the dual-use portion).

The requirement that business use be regular means that the part of the home used for business must be used on a continuing basis. Occasional or incidental use does not qualify for the deduction, even if the part of the home is used for no other purposes.

In the case of an employee, business use of part of the employee's home for one of the three purposes listed above must be for the convenience of the employer, in addition to meeting the exclusive use test.[10]

[A] Exceptions to Exclusive Use Test

There are two exceptions to the exclusive use test for a home office or other business use of part of a taxpayer's personal residence. The use of part of the home as a day-care center, discussed at ¶ 1801.04, does not have to meet the exclusive test. Also, use of part of a home for the storage of inventory or product samples may not be subject to the exclusive use test, if several requirements are met.[11]

A taxpayer may deduct expenses that relate to the use of part of his home for the storage of inventory if:

1. The taxpayer keeps the inventory for use in his trade or business;
2. The trade or business is the wholesale or retail sale of products;
3. The home is the only fixed location of the trade or business;
4. The taxpayer uses the storage space on a regular basis; and
5. The storage space comprises a separately identifiable space suitable for storage.[12]

[B] Principal Place of Business

Deductions for business use of the home are allowed for that part of the home used exclusively and regularly as the principal place of business of the taxpayer. Generally speaking, each trade or business may have a principal place of business. The deduction is permitted as long as the business part of the home is the principal place of business for any trade or business of the taxpayer.[13]

A taxpayer may have more than one business location, including the home, for a single trade or business. To deduct expenses for the business use of the home in this case, the taxpayer must show that the home is the principal place of business for that trade or business. Factors to consider in determining the principal place of business include:

1. The total time spent doing work at each location;
2. The facilities for doing the work at each location; and
3. The relative amount of income derived from each location.[14]

---

[10] Code Sec. 280A(c)(1); Prop. Reg. § 1.280A-2(g)(2).

[11] Code Sec. 280A(c)(2).

[12] Prop. Reg. § 1.280A-2(e).

[13] Code Sec. 280A(c)(1)(A).

[14] Prop. Reg. 1.280A-2(b)(3).

The IRS withdrew the proposed regulations relating to determining a taxpayer's principal place of business discussed above following the 1993 Supreme Court decision in *Soliman.*[15] In that decision, the Court restricted a taxpayer's ability to deduct home office expenses. Taxpayers who may have used the home office only for administrative or management functions and spent considerable time away from the home office were denied deductions because the home office was not the "principal place of business."

In response to the *Soliman* decision, Congress, in the Taxpayer Relief Act of 1997, amended Code Sec. 280A(c)(1) to define principal place of business to include a place of business that is used by the taxpayer for the administrative or management activities of any trade or business of the taxpayer if there is no other fixed location of the business where the taxpayer conducts substantial administrative or management activities.

> ***Example 1:*** The Taxpayer is an outside salesperson and has no office space except at home. The Taxpayer spends a substantial amount of time on paperwork at home. If the Taxpayer maintains an office in his home, the home may qualify as the Taxpayer's principal place of business under Code Sec. 280A(c)(1).

[C] Place to Meet Patients, Clients, or Customers

If a taxpayer meets or deals with patients, clients, or customers in the home in the normal course of business, even though the taxpayer also carries on business at another location, the taxpayer may deduct expenses for the part of the home that is used exclusively and regularly for this purpose. The home office must be visited by clients. The deduction is not permitted if the only client contact is by telephone.

The part of the home the taxpayer uses for meeting patients, clients, or customers does not have to be the taxpayer's principal place of business. The use of the home by the patients, clients, or customers, however, must be substantial and integral to the conduct of the taxpayer's business. Occasional meetings are not sufficient to justify a deduction.[16] Taxpayers who generally meet this requirement are doctors, dentists, attorneys, and other professionals who maintain offices in their homes.

[D] Separate Structures

The expenses for a separate free-standing structure that is next to the taxpayer's home are deductible if the taxpayer uses the structure exclusively and regularly for a business. The structure does not have to be the taxpayer's principal place of business or the place where the taxpayer meets patients, clients, or customers. An artist's studio, a florist's greenhouse, and a carpenter's workshop are examples of structures that may qualify for the deduction under this provision.[17]

---

[15] 93-1 USTC ¶ 50,014, 113 S.Ct. 701.

[16] Prop. Reg. § 1.280A-2(c).

[17] Prop. Reg. § 1.280A-2(d).

.03 Allocation of Deductions

A taxpayer who qualifies for deductions relating to the business use of a home must divide the expenses of operating the home between personal (nondeductible) and business (deductible) use. A taxpayer may use any method that is reasonable under the circumstances to make this allocation.[18] Generally, some expenses will be directly related to the business use of the home, some will be indirectly related, and still others will be completely unrelated. Expenses that are attributable only to certain portions of the home must be allocated in full to those portions. Expenses that are not related to the use of the residence for business purposes (for example, the cost of lawn care or repairs to personal areas of the home) are not deductible.

[A] Direct Expenses

Direct expenses that benefit only the business part of the home, such as the cost of painting or repairs to the specific area or room that the taxpayer uses for business purposes, are deductible without further allocation, subject to the limitation discussed at ¶ 1801.03.

[B] Indirect Expenses

Indirect expenses are those that relate to maintaining and running the taxpayer's entire home; that is, they benefit both the business and personal parts of the home. A taxpayer must allocate these expenses between the business and personal uses of the home. Only the percentage that relates to the business portion is deductible.

If the rooms in the taxpayer's home are of approximately equal size, the taxpayer ordinarily may allocate the general indirect expenses of the home between business and personal uses according to the number of rooms used for business purposes. The taxpayer may also allocate indirect expenses according to the total floor space in the home that is used for business purposes.[19]

> ***Example 2:*** The Taxpayer's home is 2,400 square feet and the Taxpayer uses a portion of the home that measures 12 feet by 20 feet for business purposes. Since the Taxpayer is using ten percent (240/2,400) of the total area of the home for business purposes, the Taxpayer may deduct ten percent of the indirect expenses of the home as a business expenses, subject to the limitation on the deduction discussed at ¶ 1801.03.
>
> If the rooms in the Taxpayer's home were about equal in size, the Taxpayer could allocate indirect expenses on the basis of the number of rooms. If the Taxpayer's home were a nine-room home and the Taxpayer used one room for business, the Taxpayer could deduct 1/9th of the indirect expenses. The Taxpayer should determine the proportion of the home used for business purposes under both methods, then use the method that produces the higher deductions.

---

[18] Prop. Reg. § 1.280A-2(i)(3).

[19] Prop. Reg. § 1.280A-2(i)(3).

Some examples of indirect expenses include:

Real Estate Taxes: The portion of real estate taxes paid allocated to the percentage of the home used for business is deductible as a business expense.

Deductible Mortgage Interest: The portion of any deductible mortgage interest allocated to the business portion of the home is deductible as a business expense.

Casualty Losses: A casualty loss may be an unrelated expense, direct expense, or indirect expense. If the loss does not affect the business portion of the home, there is no business deduction. If the loss only affects the business portion, the entire loss is a business deduction. If the loss affects both portions of the home the loss must be allocated between personal expenses and business expenses.

Rent: A taxpayer who rents rather than owns the home and uses a portion of the home for business purposes may deduct a portion of the rent as a business expense. The allocation is made based on the percentage of the rented property used for business purposes.

Utilities: Expenses for utilities and services, such as electricity, gas, trash removal, and cleaning services, are primarily personal expenses. However, an individual who uses part of a home for business can deduct the business part of these expenses. Generally, the business percentage for utilities is the same as the percentage of the home used for business.

Telephone: The basic local telephone service charge, including taxes, for the first telephone line into a home is a nondeductible personal expense.[20] Long-distance business phone calls, however, are direct expenses.

Insurance: The cost of insurance that covers the business portion of the home is deductible.

Repairs: Repairs and supplies that relate to the business are deductible. For instance, if a central air conditioning unit is repaired and ten percent of the taxpayer's home is used for business, the taxpayer may deduct ten percent of the cost of the repair.

Depreciation: When the taxpayer uses the home partly for business purposes and otherwise meets the requirements for deducting business expenses relating to that use, the portion of the home used for business may be depreciated as nonresidential real property under the depreciation rules as discussed at ¶ 901.01. Other business property used in the home is also subject to depreciation allowances or a deduction under Code Sec. 179.

Note that when property is converted from personal to business use, the basis for depreciation is the lower of the adjusted basis of the property or its fair market value on the date the property is converted to business use.

.04 Limitation on Deductions

Generally, the deductions for the business use of a home are limited to the gross income derived from the business use of the home.[21] There is no limit on the expenses a taxpayer may deduct for the business use of a home if the total

[20] Code Sec. 262(b).

[21] Code Sec. 280A(c)(5).

expenses are less than or equal to the taxpayer's gross income from that business use. Any amount otherwise deductible that is disallowed because of the gross income limitation may be carried over and deducted in the following year, subject to the gross income limitation, whether or not the taxpayer continues to use the home as a residence.

[A] Determination of Gross Income from Business Use of Home

In determining gross income from a business use of the home in order to apply the limitation on deductions relating to that use, a taxpayer may take into account only gross income from a business use that gives rise to deductions under the rules discussed at ¶ 1801.01.[22]

> ***Example 3:*** The Taxpayer is a teacher at a public school and also is engaged in a retail sales business. The Taxpayer uses a home office on a regular basis as the principal place of business for the retail sales business (a use that permits deductions) and makes no non-business use of the home office. In applying the limitation on deductions, the Taxpayer takes into account the gross income from the use of the home office for the retail sales business. Even if the Taxpayer also corrects student papers and prepares class presentations in the home office (a business use that does not permit deductions), the Taxpayer cannot take into account any portion of the gross income from teaching in applying the limitation on deductions for the business use of the home.

Multiple Locations

If part of the gross income from a taxpayer's trade or business is from the business use of part of the home and part is from the use of another place of business, the taxpayer must determine the part of the gross income that is attributable to the home in order to apply the limitation. The regulations provide that a taxpayer must allocate the gross income from the business to the different locations on a reasonable basis.[23] The regulations further provide that the taxpayer, in making this allocation, must take into account the amount of time that the taxpayer engages in activity related to the business at each location, the capital investment related to the business at each location, and any other facts and circumstances that may be relevant.

Business Expenses Unrelated to Use of Home

In determining gross income derived from the business use of a home, a taxpayer must reduce the gross income from the business activity in the home by expenditures required for the activity but not allocable to the use of the home itself, such as expenditures for supplies and compensation paid to employees.[24]

> ***Example 4:*** The Taxpayer, a physician, uses a portion of the home for treating patients. In computing gross income derived from the business use of

[22] Prop. Reg. § 1.280A-2(i)(2).

[23] Prop. Reg. § 1.280A-2(i)(2)(ii).

[24] Prop. Reg. § 1.280A-2(i)(2)(iii).

the home, the Taxpayer must subtract from the gross income attributable to the business activity in the home any expenditures for nursing, secretarial services, supplies, and similar items.

[B] Order of Deductions

Business deductions for the business use of a taxpayer's home are allowed in the following order and only to the following extent:[25]

1. The portions of amounts allowable as deductions for the home without regard to any use of the home in a trade or business are allowable as business deductions to the extent of the gross income derived from the business use of the home. For example, mortgage interest (within limits) and real estate taxes are deductible whether the home is used for business or not. Therefore, the portion of these items allocable to the business use of the home are business deductions and are applied first against gross income from the business use of the home. The balance of any deductible mortgage interest and real estate taxes are taken as itemized deductions.
2. Amounts otherwise allowable as deductions for the business use of the home, other than those that would result in an adjustment to the basis of the property, are allowable to the extent the gross income derived from the business use of the home exceeds the deductions under Category 1.
3. Amounts otherwise allowable as deductions for the business use of the home and which would result in an adjustment to the basis of the property are allowable to the extent the gross income derived from the business use of the home exceeds the deductions under Category 1 and Category 2.

Example 5: The Taxpayer uses an office in the home on a regular basis in order to meet with clients of the Taxpayer's consulting service. The Taxpayer makes no other use of this office, which is ten percent of the area of the home, and has no other location for the consulting business. The Taxpayer has a special telephone line for the office at a cost of $150 for the year. The Taxpayer also employs a secretary on an "as-needed" basis and a gardener to take care of the lawn. The Taxpayer paid the secretary $500 during the year and the gardener $720. Also during the year, the Taxpayer incurred and paid the following expenses: $200 for business supplies, $5,000 in mortgage interest, $2,000 for real estate taxes, $600 for insurance on the home, and $900 for utilities. If the Taxpayer's home were entirely business real estate, the Taxpayer would be entitled to a $3,200 deduction for depreciation for the year. The Taxpayer's gross income from the consulting service was $1,900 for the year. Under the limitation on the deduction of expenses relating to the business use of a home, the Taxpayer's allowable business deductions for the use of the home office cannot exceed $1,050, calculated as follows:

[25] Prop. Reg. § 1.280A-2(i)(5).

Gross income from consulting		$1,900
Less: Deductions unrelated to home:		
Secretary expense	$500	
Business telephone	150	
Supplies	200	850
Gross income attributable to use of home office		$1,050

The Taxpayer then takes additional deductions for the business use of the home in the following order:

1. Mortgage interest	$500
Real estate taxes	200
	$700

This leaves $350 available for deductions in Category 2:

2. Insurance	$ 60
Utilities	90
	$150

This now leaves the Taxpayer with $200 available for deduction under Category 3. The Taxpayer's deduction for depreciation, if there were no gross income limitation, would be $320. However, since only $200 of the Taxpayer's gross income from the use of the home for the consulting business remains after all other deductions, the Taxpayer's depreciation deduction is limited to $200. The remaining amount of this deduction ($120) is a carryover to the following year and the Taxpayer may deduct this amount in the following year, subject to the gross income limitation for that year.

No portion of the Taxpayer's lawn care expense is allocable to the business use of the home and no deduction is permitted for this expense. The Taxpayer may claim the remaining $4,500 paid for mortgage interest and $1,800 for real estate taxes as itemized deductions.

.05 Use of Home as Day-Care Facility

A taxpayer may deduct expenses for using part of the home on a regular basis to provide day-care services, if the taxpayer meets the following requirements:[26]

1. The taxpayer must be in the trade or business of providing day care for children, for persons 65 or older, or for persons who are physically or mentally unable to care for themselves; and
2. The taxpayer must have applied for, been granted, or be exempt from having a license, certification, registration, or approval as a day-care center or as a family or group day-care home under any applicable state law.

The second requirement is not met if the application has been rejected or the license or other authorization has been revoked.[27]

[26] Code Sec. 280A(c)(4).

[27] Code Sec. 280A(c)(4)(B).

A taxpayer who uses part of the personal residence as a day-care facility must compute the portion of the home used for the day-care business as discussed above for the business use of a home in general. If the part used for the day-care business is used exclusively for that purpose, the taxpayer may deduct all allocable expenses, subject to the gross income limitation discussed above. Unlike other business use of the home, however, use of part of the home as a day-care facility need not be exclusive in order for the taxpayer to deduct related expenses. When the use is not exclusive, an additional allocation of expenses must be made on the basis of the amount of time that part of the home is used in the day-care business.

[A] Allocation Formula

If a portion of a taxpayer's home used for providing day-care services is not used exclusively for that purpose, the amount of expenses attributable to that portion "shall not exceed an amount which bears the same ratio to the total amount of the items allocable to such portion as the number of hours the portion is used for such purpose bears to the number of hours the portion is available for use."[28] In other words, the taxpayer compares the total time of business use as a day-care facility to the total time that that portion of the home can be used for all purposes.

[B] Application of Formula

The taxpayer may make this comparison based on the number of hours the space is used for day care in a week with the number of hours in a week (168), or the hours used for day care during the year with the number of hours in the taxpayer's tax year (8,760 in the case of a 365-day year). The taxpayer then determines the amount deductible, before applying the gross income limitation, by multiplying the expenses allocable based on the amount of space used by the fraction of hours used for day care versus total hours available for use.[29]

> ***Example 6:*** The Taxpayer uses the basement to care for children an average of 12 hours per day, five days per week, for 50 weeks. The Taxpayer's family may use the basement at other times. During the year, the Taxpayer uses the basement as a day-care center for a total of 3,000 hours (5 days per week × 50 weeks = 250 days × 12 hours = 3,000 hours). Since the basement is available for use for 8,760 hours during the year, only 34.25 percent (3,000/8,760) of the expenses of the Taxpayer's basement are business expenses. The Taxpayer may deduct 34.25 percent of any direct expenses for the basement, but only 34.25 percent of the basement portion of indirect expenses. If the Taxpayer's basement is 20 percent of the total area of the Taxpayer's home, the Taxpayer may deduct 6.85 percent (34.25% × 20% = 6.85%) of the indirect expenses. (Direct and indirect expenses are discussed above at ¶ 1801.02[A] and ¶ 1801.02[B].)

¶ 1802 RENTAL OF PART OF HOME

When a taxpayer rents part of the property, the rent received is generally taxable income. As for expenses, the taxpayer generally must divide expenses between the part of the property that is rented and the part that is used for personal

[28] Code Sec. 280A(c)(4)(C).

[29] Prop. Reg. § 1.280A-2(i)(4).

purposes as if the taxpayer owned two separate parcels of property. Further, whenever real property is used for personal purposes, in addition to being rented out, there may be limits on the deduction for rental expenses.

.01 Rental Income

Rental income is any payment a taxpayer receives for the use or occupancy of property and, generally, is included in gross income. In addition to regular, periodic rents, rental income may include advance rents, security deposits retained by the landlord, payments for cancelling a lease, expenses paid by the tenant on behalf of the landlord, payments in property or services, and payments under a lease with an option to buy until the option is exercised by the tenant. These topics are all discussed in some detail in Part II, "Rental and Leasing Arrangements."

A taxpayer that rents property for a period of less than 15 days during the tax year and also uses that property as a residence during the year does not have to include the rent in income.[30]

.02 Allocation of Expenses

Taxpayers generally may deduct the expenses of renting property from the gross rental income from the property. In certain cases, deductions may exceed rental income. Expenses of operating rental property are discussed in some detail in Part III, "Real Estate Operation."

If the taxpayer rents part of the property, the taxpayer must divide expenses between the part that is rented and the part that is used for personal or other purposes. This division is made in the same fashion as the division of expenses when a taxpayer uses part of the home for business purposes, as discussed at ¶ 1801.02. The taxpayer does not have to divide expenses that relate only to the rented portion of the property. These items are rental expenses in full. For expenses that must be divided, the division usually also follows the methods used for dividing expenses when part of a home is used for business purposes, that is, by area or number of rooms.

In some cases, there may be other more appropriate methods of dividing expenses relating to the rental of part of a home between rental and personal expenses. For instance, in some cases, the number of people involved may be more appropriate, such as when tenants are provided board in addition to rooms. In such a case, the number of people may be an appropriate way to divide food costs between rental expense and personal expense.

The same provision that allows a taxpayer to avoid reporting rental income when property used as a residence by the taxpayer is rented for less than 15 days during the tax year also prohibits the taxpayer from taking any deductions for expenses relating to the production of that income.[31] Also, any time a taxpayer rents a residence that the taxpayer also uses for personal purposes during the year, the taxpayer's deductions for rental expenses are subject to the limitation discussed at ¶ 1803.02 in connection with the rental of vacation homes and other residences.

---

[30] Code Sec. 280A(g); *see also* the discussion at ¶ 1803.

[31] Code Sec. 280A(g).

¶ 1803 RENTAL OF VACATION OR OTHER RESIDENCE

If a taxpayer rents out part or all of a vacation home or other dwelling unit and also uses any part of the dwelling for personal purposes, the taxpayer must divide expenses between rental use and personal use.[32] The taxpayer may then be able to deduct some or all of the rental expenses, or the taxpayer may find that none of the rental expenses are deductible, depending on how the dwelling was used during the year.

.01 Dwelling Unit Classification

For purposes of the rules that apply to vacation homes and other dwelling units under Code Sec. 280A, a dwelling unit includes a house, apartment, condominium, mobile home, boat, or similar property.[33] The key to classification as a dwelling unit is whether the property provides basic living accommodations, which the regulations define to include sleeping space, toilet, and cooking facilities.[34] A single structure may contain more than one dwelling unit, such as is the case in an apartment building. Similarly, if the basement of a home contains basic living accommodations, the basement is a separate dwelling unit. Structures and property appurtenant to a dwelling which do not constitute a dwelling unit are considered part of the unit.

> ***Example 7:*** The Taxpayer rents space in a garage to another individual. The garage is appurtenant to the house which the Taxpayer owns and in which the Taxpayer lives. The Taxpayer may take deductions related to his rental of the garage only to the extent permitted by the provisions of Code Sec. 280A.

Dwelling units not covered by the rules of Code Sec. 280A are those used exclusively as a hotel, motel, inn, or similar establishment.[35] Property is used for these purposes only if it is regularly available for occupancy by paying customers and only if no person having an interest in the property is considered to have used the unit as a residence during the year.[36] This exception from the Code Sec. 280A rules may apply to a portion of a home used to furnish lodging to tourists or long-term boarders. The exception may also apply to a dwelling unit entered into a rental pool if the owner of the unit does not use it as a residence at any time during the year.[37]

[A] Use as a Residence

If a taxpayer does not use a dwelling unit as a residence at any time during the year, the taxpayer's deductible rental expense can be more than gross rental income from the property. On the other hand, if a taxpayer rents a dwelling unit and also uses the dwelling unit as a residence during the year, deductions for rental expenses are limited under Code Sec. 280A, as at ¶ 1803.02.

A taxpayer uses a dwelling unit as a residence during the tax year if the taxpayer uses it for personal purposes for more than 14 days or, if greater, more

---

32 Code Sec. 280A(e).

33 Code Sec. 280A(f)(1)(A).

34 Prop. Reg. § 1.280A-1(c)(1).

35 Code Sec. 280A(f)(1)(B).

36 Prop. Reg. § 1.280A-1(c)(2).

37 Prop. Reg. § 1.280A-3(e).

than ten percent of the number of days during the year that it is rented at a fair rental price. A unit is not treated as rented at a fair rental for any day on which it is used for personal purposes.[38]

Example 8: The Taxpayer owns a boat equipped with sleeping space, toilet, and cooking facilities. The Taxpayer uses the boat for personal purposes for 16 days during the year and rents the boat at fair rental for 163 days during the year. Since personal use does not exceed the greater of 14 days or ten percent of the days rented at fair rental (ten percent of 163 days is 16.3 days and the Taxpayer's personal use was for only 16 days), the Taxpayer has not used the boat as a residence for the year.

Suppose, however, that five of the days that the Taxpayer used the boat for personal purposes were included in the 163 days that the boat was rented at fair rental. In this case, those five days are not treated as part of the rental period, and only 158 days are counted. Since ten percent of 158 days is 15.8 days, the Taxpayer would be treated as using the boat as a residence during the year because personal use exceeded the greater of 14 days or ten percent of the days rented.

[B] Personal Use

In determining the days of personal use in order to determine whether a taxpayer used a dwelling unit as a residence during the year, count as personal use any day that:[39]

1. The taxpayer or any other person who has an interest in the unit uses the unit, unless the unit is rented at fair rental under a shared equity financing agreement for use as the person's principal residence;[40]
2. A brother, sister, spouse, ancestor, or lineal descendant of the taxpayer or any person who has an interest in the unit uses the unit, unless the rental to the family member is at a fair rental and the family member uses the unit as a principal residence;[41]
3. Anyone uses the unit under an arrangement that allows the taxpayer to use some other dwelling unit, whether or not a rental is charged for the use of the other unit and regardless of the length of time that the taxpayer uses the other unit;[42] and
4. Any individual uses the unit, other than an employee whose use is for the convenience of the employer under Code Sec. 119, unless the unit is rented for that day for a rental which, under the facts and circumstances, is fair rental.[43]

A shared equity financing agreement is any written agreement under which two or more persons acquire undivided interests for more than 50 years in an entire dwelling unit, including the land, and one or more of the co-owners are entitled to

[38] Code Sec. 280A(d)(1).

[39] Code Sec. 280A(d)(2).

[40] Code Sec. 280A(d)(3)(B).

[41] Code Sec. 280A(d)(3)(A).

[42] Prop. Reg. § 1.280A-1(e)(1)(iii).

[43] Prop. Reg. § 1.280A-1(e)(1)(iv).

occupy the unit as their principal residence upon payment of rent to the other co-owner or owners.[44]

> ***Example 9:*** The Taxpayer owns a vacation home which is rented to the Taxpayer's sister at a fair rental for ten days. The Taxpayer also rents the home to an unrelated individual for 11 days as part of an arrangement under which the Taxpayer is allowed to use another vacation home for six days. As a favor, the Taxpayer rents the vacation home to a friend for 15 days at a discount rate. Based on this rental activity, the Taxpayer has used the vacation home for personal purposes for a period of 36 days.

Maintenance and Repairs

A taxpayer is not treated as using a dwelling unit for personal purposes on any day on which the taxpayer's principal purpose for using the unit is to perform repair or maintenance work on the unit.[45] Factors that IRS considers in determining whether the principal purpose of use is maintenance or repairs include, but are not limited to, the amount of time devoted to repair and maintenance work, the frequency of the use for repair and maintenance purposes during a taxable year, and the presence and activities of companions. In no case, however, is a day on which a taxpayer engages in full-time repair or maintenance considered a day of personal use.[46]

> ***Example 10:*** The Taxpayer owns a lakefront vacation home that the Taxpayer rents during the summer season. The Taxpayer and spouse arrive at the home late on a Thursday evening before the start of the rental season to prepare the home. The couple do no work on the home on Thursday, but the Taxpayer does put in a normal work day on Friday and Saturday, performing necessary maintenance chores. The Taxpayer's spouse spends some time helping, but spends most of the time relaxing and enjoying the lake. The work is completed by Saturday night, so the couple do not work on the home on Sunday, but leave for their principal residence about noon on Sunday.
>
> The principal reason for this use of the Taxpayer's vacation home is maintenance. Therefore, the use of the vacation home during this period is not considered personal use by the Taxpayer.[47]

Rental of Principal Residence

A taxpayer who uses a dwelling unit as a principal residence before or after renting it, or trying to rent it, may not have to count the days the dwelling is used as the principal residence as days of personal use for determining whether the limitation on the deduction of rental expenses applies.[48]

If a taxpayer rents or tries to rent a dwelling unit at a fair rental for 12 or more consecutive months, the taxpayer need not count as personal use the days the dwelling is used as the taxpayer's principal residence during the year in which the taxpayer began renting it or trying to rent it, and which occur before the taxpayer

---

[44] Code Sec. 280A(d)(3)(C); *see also* Prop. Reg. § 1.280A-1(e)(3)(ii) and (iv).

[45] Code Sec. 280A(d)(2).

[46] Prop. Reg. § 1.280A-1(e)(6).

[47] Prop. Reg. § 1.280A-1(e)(7), Example (3).

[48] Code Sec. 280A(d)(4).

began renting it or trying to rent it. Also, if a taxpayer rents or tries to rent a dwelling unit at a fair rental for 12 or more consecutive months, the taxpayer need not count as personal use the days the dwelling is used as the taxpayer's principal residence during the year in which the taxpayer stopped renting it or trying to rent it, and which occur after the taxpayer stopped renting it or trying to rent it.[49]

> ***Example 11:*** On February 28, 2018, the Taxpayer, who uses the calendar year as the tax year, moves out of the house that the Taxpayer had lived in for six years in order to take a job in another town. The Taxpayer rents the home at a fair rental from March 15, 2018, until May 14, 2019. On June 1, 2019, the Taxpayer moves back into the old house. The Taxpayer's use of the house as the principal residence from January 1 to February 28, 2018, and from June 1 to December 31, 2019, is not counted as personal use by the Taxpayer.

A taxpayer who sells or exchanges a home after renting it or trying to rent it does not count as personal use the days the home is used as the taxpayer's principal residence during the year the taxpayer rented or tried to rent it and which occur before the taxpayer rented it or tried to rent it.[50]

> ***Example 12:*** On January 31 of the current year, the Taxpayer moved out of a principal residence. The Taxpayer offered the old home for rent at a fair rental beginning on February 1. The Taxpayer did not find a tenant until April 1, and then sold the old home on September 15. The Taxpayer's use of the home from January 1 until January 31 is not counted as personal use.

.02 Determination of Income and Deductions

When a taxpayer rents a dwelling that is also used as a residence during the year, as discussed at ¶ 1803.01[A], specific limitations apply to the expense deductions that the taxpayer may claim in regard to the rental of the dwelling unit.[51] The limitations are aimed at reducing the tax benefits available to taxpayers who rent out vacation and other homes in order to minimize personal expenses rather than to make a profit from the rental activity.

[A] Rental for Less Than 15 Days

If a taxpayer uses a home as a residence during the year and also rents out that home for less than 15 days during the year, the taxpayer does not include in income any of the rental income produced by this minimal rental. Also, the taxpayer may not take any deductions attributable to the rental, but may take deductions otherwise allowable in connection with ownership of the home, including mortgage interest, real estate taxes, and casualty losses.[52]

[B] Rental for 15 Days or More

If a taxpayer uses a home as a residence during the year and also rents out that home for 15 days or more during the year, and the taxpayer's use meets the

[49] Code Sec. 280A(d)(4)(B)(i); Prop. Reg. § 1.280A-1(e)(4)(i).

[50] Code Sec. 280A(d)(4)(B)(ii); Prop. Reg. § 1.280A-1(e)(4)(ii).

[51] Code Sec. 280A(e).

[52] Code Sec. 280A(g).

personal use requirements discussed at ¶ 1803.01[B], the taxpayer's deductions attributable to the rental activity may not exceed the amount by which the gross income from the rental activity exceeds the deductions otherwise allowable for the property, such as mortgage interest and taxes.[53]

Gross income from rental of a dwelling unit equals the gross receipts from the rental of the unit reduced by expenses to obtain a tenant, such as realtor's fees and advertising expenses. Gross rental income includes rental income from periods during which a unit is rented at less than fair rental, as well as periods during which the unit is rented at fair rental.[54]

Deductions relating to the rental are taken in the following order and only to the following extent:[55]

1. The portions of amounts allowable as deductions for the home without regard to any rental of the home are deductible as rental expenses to the extent of the gross rental income derived from the rental of the home. For example, mortgage interest (within limits) and real estate taxes are deductible whether the home is rented or not. Therefore, the portions of these items allocable to the rental of the home are rental expense deductions and are applied first against gross rental income. The balances of any deductible mortgage interest and real estate taxes are taken as itemized deductions.
2. Amounts otherwise allowable as deductions because of the rental of the home, other than those that would result in an adjustment to the basis of the property, are allowable to the extent the gross rental income exceeds the deductions under Category 1.
3. Amounts otherwise allowable as deductions because of the rental of the home and which would result in an adjustment to the basis of the property are allowable to the extent the gross rental income exceeds the deductions under Category 1 and Category 2.

IRS Allocation Formula

In Prop. Reg. § 1.280A-3(c)(2), the IRS specifies that the portion of any item which is allocable to the rental use of a dwelling unit during a taxable year is that amount which bears the same relationship to the total amount of the item as the number of days on which the unit is rented at a fair rental during the taxable year bears to the number of days on which the unit is used for any purpose, other than repair or maintenance, during the taxable year. In other words, the IRS allocation formula for all expenses is based on the ratio between the number of days rented at fair rental and the number of days used for any purpose other than repairs or maintenance, regardless of the number of days the unit is used during the year.

> ***Example 13:*** The Taxpayer owns a lakeside home that the Taxpayer rents at a fair rental for 90 days during the year. The Taxpayer uses the home for personal purposes on 20 other days during the year and also rents the

[53] Code Sec. 280A(e).

[54] Prop. Reg. § 1.280A-3(d)(2).

[55] Prop. Reg. § 1.280A-3(d)(3).

home to a friend at a discount for ten days. The home, therefore, is used for some purpose other than repair or maintenance on 120 days during the year and the rental expense allocation fraction is 90/120, or 75 percent. That is, 75 percent of the expenses attributable to the home are rental expenses.

Assume the Taxpayer's gross receipts from the rental of the home, including receipts from the rental at a discount, are $2,400, and that the Taxpayer incurred $200 in advertising expenses relating to the rental. Further assume that the Taxpayer's expenses for the home include $1,000 in mortgage interest, $800 in real estate taxes, $400 for insurance, $600 in utilities, and $1,500 for depreciation. Of these expenses, 75 percent are attributable to generating the rental income and may be taken up to the gross income limitation, or $2,200 ($2,400 receipts - $200 advertising). Applying this allocation in the order in which the deductions must be taken produces the following results:

Deductions permitted by Code Sec. 280A	$2,200
Otherwise allowable deductions:	
Mortgage interest ($1,000 × 90/120)	750
	$1,450
Real estate taxes ($800 × 90/120)	600
	$850
Other expenses that do not reduce basis:	
Insurance ($400 × 90/120)	300
	$550
Utilities ($600 × 90/120)	450
	$100

Expenses that reduce basis:

Depreciation ($1,500 × 90/120 = $1,125)

Since only $100 is left, the Taxpayer's depreciation deduction is limited to $100. The remaining $1,025 of depreciation expense attributable to generating the rental income may not be taken as a deduction under the limitation. The balance of the mortgage interest ($250) and real estate taxes ($200) may be taken as itemized deductions by the Taxpayer.[56]

Tax Court Allocation Formula

The Tax Court takes the position that in determining the amount of interest and real estate taxes allocable to the rental use of a vacation or other home, taxpayers are entitled to allocate an amount based on the approximate percentage of days during the year that the property was rented compared to the number of days in the year rather than the number of days that the home was occupied or used. The rationale for this position is that, unlike other expenses, interest and

[56] Prop. Reg. § 1.280A-3(d)(4).

property taxes are assessed on a yearly basis. This position has been sustained by two Circuit Courts of Appeals.[57] This can make a substantial difference in the total deductions a taxpayer may take.

Example 14: Assume the same facts as in Example 13 demonstrating the IRS allocation formula, except that mortgage interest and real estate taxes allocable to the rental of the home will be based on 90 days of rental out of a 360-day year. Using this allocation formula produces the following results:

Deductions permitted by Code Sec. 280A	$2,200
Otherwise allowable deductions:	
Mortgage interest ($1,000 × 90/360)	250
	$1,950
Real estate taxes ($800 × 90/360)	200
	$1,750
Other expenses that do not reduce basis:	
Insurance ($400 × 90/120)	300
	$1,450
Utilities ($600 × 90/120)	450
	$1,000

Expenses that reduce basis:

Depreciation ($1,500 × 90/120 = $1,125)

Since $1,000 is left, the Taxpayer's depreciation deduction is limited to $1,000, as compared to $100 using the IRS allocation formula. The balance of the mortgage interest ($750) and real estate taxes ($600) may be taken as itemized deductions by the Taxpayer. The overall result to the Taxpayer using the Tax Court allocation formula is deductions totaling $3,550 ($2,200 for rental expense and $1,350 in itemized deductions for mortgage interest and taxes). Under the IRS allocation formula, the Taxpayer's total deductions were only $2,650 ($2,200 for rental expense and $450 in itemized deductions for mortgage interest and taxes).

.03 Other Limitations on Rental Losses

In addition to the limitation on deducting expenses relating to the rental of vacation or other dwelling units contained in Code Sec. 280A, two other limitations may affect deductions attributable to rental property. The at-risk rules limit deductible losses to the amount a taxpayer has at risk in the activity producing the deductions. Also, taxpayers generally may not deduct losses from passive activities. The at-risk rules are treated in detail at ¶ 302, as are the passive activity loss rules at ¶ 1101.

[57] D.D. Bolton, CA-9, 82-2 USTC ¶ 9699, 694 F.2d 556; E.G. McKinney, CA FC, 83-2 USTC ¶ 9698, 721 F.2d 163.

It should also be noted that any rental that avoids the Code Sec. 280A limitations may be subject to the "hobby loss" rules of Code Sec. 183. Rentals subject to Code Sec. 280A, however, are not also subject to Code Sec. 183.[58]

¶ 1804 RESIDENCE CONVERTED TO INVESTMENT

If a taxpayer converts a personal residence to rental use, the taxpayer becomes entitled to treat the property as investment property and is entitled to all the deductions relating to the operation of real estate, as discussed in Part III. The conversion must be actual and there must be a genuine holding out of the property for rental. The effort to rent need not be successful, but it must be bona fide.[59]

If a residence is converted to rental use, depreciation is based on the adjusted basis of the property or its fair market value at the time of the conversion, whichever is lower.[60]

A taxpayer who converts property to rental use at any time other than at the beginning of the tax year must divide any annual expenses between the portion of the year the property was held for rental and the portion of the year held for personal or other purposes. Only the part of the expense attributable to the part of the year the property is held for rental may be deducted and, of course, the amount may be limited under the rules discussed at ¶ 1801.03.

---

58 Code Sec. 280A(f)(3).

59 *See*, for example, I. Meredith, 65 TC 34, CCH Dec. 33,457; D.L. Henry, 46 TCM 186, CCH Dec. 40131(M), T.C. Memo. 1983-277.

60 Reg. § 1.167(g)-1. *See* Chapter 9 for detailed discussion on depreciation.

Chapter 19
Cooperatives, Condominiums, and Associations

¶ 1900 Overview of Chapter
¶ 1901 Cooperative Housing Corporations
¶ 1902 Condominiums
¶ 1903 Homeowners Associations

¶ 1900 OVERVIEW OF CHAPTER

A personal residence may include a condominium or cooperative apartment. The tax treatment of these units is generally the same as that of any other type of home ownership.

In a condominium, the taxpayer owns outright a dwelling unit in a multi-unit structure. Each unit owner also owns a share of the common elements, such as land, lobbies, elevators, and service areas. Unit owners usually pay assessments or dues to an association or service corporation which is organized to take care of the common elements.

In a cooperative apartment, the taxpayer owns shares of stock in a corporation that owns or leases housing facilities. As a shareholder, the taxpayer is entitled to occupy a dwelling unit in the housing controlled by the corporation. The dwelling unit may be a house, an apartment, or a house trailer, but it must have the three facilities necessary to be classed as a dwelling—that is, cooking, sleeping, and toilet facilities.

Condominium management associations and residential real estate management associations are homeowners associations. Both may elect to be treated as associations that are exempt from tax on their exempt function income. Cooperative housing corporations may not qualify as homeowners associations.

¶ 1901 COOPERATIVE HOUSING CORPORATIONS

Generally speaking, shareholders in a cooperative housing arrangement enjoy the same tax benefits as any other homeowner; that is, they may deduct mortgage interest and real property taxes, as discussed at ¶ 1701 and ¶ 1702, and they may benefit from the provision to exclude gain on the sale of their homes, as discussed at ¶ 2003.02. The major difference is in the need for the cooperative housing corporation and the tenant stockholders to comply with the provisions of Code Sec. 216.

.01 Qualification as a Cooperative Housing Corporation

In order for a corporation to qualify as a cooperative housing corporation so that its tenant-stockholders may derive the tax benefits of home ownership, the corporation must meet the following requirements:[1]

1. The corporation must have one and only one class of stock;
2. Each of the stockholders of the corporation must be entitled, solely by reason of ownership of stock in the corporation, to occupy for dwelling purposes a house, or an apartment in a building, owned or leased by the corporation;
3. No stockholder of the corporation may be entitled, either conditionally or unconditionally, to receive any distribution not out of earnings and profits of the corporation except on a complete or partial liquidation of the corporation; and
4. 80 percent or more of the gross income of the corporation must be derived from tenant-stockholders, or alternatively, 80 percent or more of the total square footage of the corporation's property must be used or available for use by the tenant-stockholders for residential purposes, or 90 percent or more of the corporation's expenditures for the year must be for the acquisition, construction, management, maintenance, or care of the corporation's property for the benefit of the tenant-stockholders.

A tenant-stockholder is a person who is a stockholder in a cooperative housing corporation, and whose stock is fully paid up in an amount that the IRS considers reasonably related to the portion of the value of the corporation's equity in the houses or apartment building and the land that is attributable to the house or apartment that the person is entitled to occupy.[2]

[A] One Class of Stock Requirement

There is a limited exception to the one class of stock requirement that permits certain stock to be issued to government units for financing and other purposes.[3] Also, the rights of some tenant-stockholders to larger apartments or additional parking spaces under their proprietary leases does not create more than one class of stock.[4] However, debt issued by the corporation that takes on too many of the characteristics of stock may become a second class of stock that could disqualify the corporation.[5]

[B] Right of Occupancy

Each stockholder of a cooperative must be entitled to occupy for dwelling purposes an apartment in a building or unit in a development owned or leased by the corporation, regardless of whether the stockholder qualifies as a tenant-stockholder. The stockholder does not have to actually occupy a unit, but only needs to

[1] Code Sec. 216(b)(1).

[2] Code Sec. 216(b)(2).

[3] Reg. § 1.216-1(d)(1) and (f).

[4] Rev. Rul. 87-130, 1987-2 CB 68.

[5] *See* Code Sec. 385; *but see also* Rev. Rul. 72-404, 1972-2 CB 180, in which the IRS ruled that a purchase-money debt that carried no voting rights was treated as debt even though the debt was secured by the outstanding stock of the corporation.

have the right to occupy the premises as against the corporation. This right must be conferred on each stockholder because the stockholder's ownership of stock in the corporation. The right to actually occupy the unit may be conditioned on the payment of rentals or assessments to the corporation.[6]

The inability of a purchaser of stock in a cooperative housing corporation to obtain occupancy because an existing tenant is protected by local rent control laws does not end the corporation's qualification as a cooperative housing corporation.[7]

In three cases, occupancy may be conditioned on approval by the corporation without jeopardizing the corporation's status as a cooperative housing corporation:[8]

1. When a person acquires stock of the cooperative by operation of law, by inheritance, or by foreclosure;
2. When a person other than an individual acquires stock in the cooperative; and
3. When the person from whom the corporation has acquired the apartments or houses acquires any stock of the cooperative from the cooperative not later than one year after the date on which the apartments or houses are transferred to the cooperative by that person.

[C] Distributions

No distributions may be made to stockholders of a cooperative housing corporation other than out of earnings and profits except on the complete or partial liquidation of the corporation. A refund of an overassessment, however, is not considered a "distribution."[9]

Under the normal rules of corporate taxation, gain is recognized by a corporation when it distributes appreciated property to shareholders in a liquidating distribution. A special provision allows a cooperative housing corporation to escape recognition of this gain when property that qualifies as a principal residence is distributed to a tenant-stockholder in exchange for the tenant-stockholder's stock.[10] This special nonrecognition rule facilitates the conversion of a cooperative into a condominium.

[D] Gross Income of Cooperative Housing Corporation

Eighty percent or more of the gross income of the corporation for the taxable year of the corporation in which the taxes and interest are paid or incurred must be derived from the tenant-stockholders in order for the stockholder to claim deductions for these items. Gross income attributable to any house or apartment that a government unit is entitled to occupy under a lease or stock ownership is disregarded.[11]

Qualifying income includes amounts paid by tenant-stockholders for maid and secretarial services, parking or garage space, utilities, recreational facilities, clean-

[6] Reg. § 1.216-1(d)(2).

[7] Rev. Rul. 80-299, 1980-2 CB 82.

[8] Prop. Reg. § 1.216-1(e)(2).

[9] Rev. Rul. 56-225, 1956-1 CB 58.

[10] Code Sec. 216(e); the dwelling must be the stockholder's principal residence as defined in Code Sec. 121, which provides for the exclusion of gain on the sale of a principal residence. Code Sec. 121 is discussed at ¶ 2002.

[11] Reg. § 1.216-1(d)(4).

ing, and any related services.[12] On the other hand, qualifying income does not include any rent received for the lease of commercial space within a building owned by the cooperative housing corporation.[13] The cooperative must use care to restrict commercial rents so as not to endanger its status as a cooperative housing corporation and lose the tax benefits of home ownership for its tenant-stockholders.

To prevent the gross income test from forcing cooperatives to charge commercial tenants below-market rental rates, alternatives to the gross income test that are not based on income were provided by Congress, effective for tax years ending after December 20, 2007. Under the alternative tests, tenant-stockholders may claim deductions for taxes and interest if 80 percent or more of the total square footage of the corporation's property is used or available for use by the tenant-stockholders for residential purposes, or 90 percent or more of the corporation's expenditures for the year is for the acquisition, construction, management, maintenance, or care of the corporation's property for the benefit of the tenant-stockholders.

.02 Deductions by Tenant-Stockholders

A tenant-stockholder is entitled to deductions for real property taxes and mortgage interest.[14] Also, if the tenant-stockholder uses a unit in a trade or business or for the production of income, the stockholder is entitled to deduct depreciation on the unit, in addition to other business expenses.

[A] Interest and Taxes

A taxpayer who qualifies as a tenant-stockholder of a cooperative housing corporation may deduct from gross income amounts paid or accrued within the tenant-stockholder's taxable year to the cooperative which represent the tenant-stockholder's proportionate share of:

1. The real estate taxes allowable as a deduction to the corporation which are paid or incurred by the corporation during the tenant-stockholder's taxable year on the houses or apartment building and the land on which the houses or apartment building are situated, and
2. The interest allowable as a deduction to the corporation which is paid or incurred by the corporation during the tenant-stockholder's taxable year on its indebtedness contracted in the acquisition, construction, alteration, rehabilitation, or maintenance of the houses or apartment building, or in the acquisition of the land on which the units are situated.[15]

A tenant-stockholder's proportionate share of interest and taxes is calculated by the proportion of the stock owned by the tenant-stockholder in relation to all outstanding stock, including stock held by the corporation.[16]

In order to more accurately reflect the relative burdens of interest and taxes born by different tenant-stockholders, however, a cooperative housing corporation

---

[12] Rev. Rul. 68-387, 1968-2 CB 112.

[13] Rev. Rul. 79-137, 1979-1 CB 118.

[14] Code Sec. 216(a).

[15] Reg. § 1.216-1(a).

[16] Reg. § 1.216-1(b).

may elect to allocate interest and taxes to its tenant-stockholders in a manner that departs from strict proportionality, if two conditions are met. First, each dwelling unit must be separately allocated a share of the cooperative's interest or taxes. Second, the allocation must reasonably reflect the cost to the cooperative of the interest and taxes attributable to the tenant-stockholder's unit and the unit's share of common areas.[17]

Example 1: MM Corporation is a cooperative housing corporation. MM purchases a site and constructs a building with 10 apartments of equal value at a total cost of $2,000,000. On completion, the fair market value of the land and building is $2,000,000. MM mortgages the property for $1,000,000 and sells 1,000 shares of stock, its total authorized stock, for $1,000,000. Ten individuals purchased this stock, with each person buying 100 shares for $100,000. Each 100 share certificate entitles the holder to lease a particular apartment in the building for a specified number of years. Each lease provides that the lessee must pay a proportionate part of the corporation's expenses.

During the current year (both the corporation and its stockholders use the calendar year), MM incurred expenses totalling $138,000, including $40,000 for real estate taxes, $50,000 for interest on the mortgage, $30,000 for maintenance, and $18,000 for other expenses. Each tenant-stockholder pays MM $13,800 during the year as his or her proportionate part of the expenses of the corporation. The entire gross income of MM during the year was from tenant-stockholders. Each tenant-stockholder is entitled to a deduction of $9,000 in computing taxable income for the current year, calculated as follows:

Shares of stock owned by tenant-stockholder	100
Shares owned by other tenant-stockholders	900
Total shares outstanding	1,000
Proportion of outstanding stock held by tenant-stockholder = 1/10	
Expenses of MM:	
Real estate taxes	$40,000
Interest	50,000
Maintenance	30,000
Other	18,000
Total expenses	$138,000
Amount paid by tenant-stockholder equal to a proportionate part (1/10 × $138,000)	$13,800
Tenant's proportionate part of real estate taxes and interest (1/10 × $90,000)	$9,000
Tenant's proportionate part of total expenses based on stock ownership (1/10 × $138,000)	$13,800

[17] Code Sec. 216(b)(3); Reg. § 1.216-1(d)(2).

Amount of tenant's payment representing real estate taxes and interest (9,000/13,800 × $13,800)	$9,000
Tenant's allowable deduction	$9,000

Example 2: The facts are the same as in Example 1, except that the building MM constructs has business space on the ground floor in addition to the 10 apartments. During the current year, MM rented the business space for $24,000 and deducted the $24,000 from its expenses in determining the amount of the expenses to be prorated among its tenant-stockholders. Each tenant-stockholder paid $11,400 instead of $13,800. More than 80 percent of MM's gross income for the current year is derived from tenant-stockholders. Each tenant-stockholder is entitled to a deduction under Code Sec. 216 for the current year of $7,434.80, computed as follows:

Total expenses of MM	$138,000.00
Less rent from business space	24,000.00
Expenses to be prorated	$114,000.00
Amount paid by tenant-stockholder equal to a proportionate part (1/10 × $114,000)	$11,400.00
Tenant's proportionate part of real estate taxes and interest (1/10 × $90,000)	$9,000.00
Tenant's proportionate part of total expenses based on stock ownership (1/10 × $138,000)	$13,800.00
Amount of tenant's payment representing real estate taxes and interest (9,000/13,800 × $11,400)	$7,434.80
Tenant's allowable deduction	$7,434.80

Tenant-stockholders may not be entitled to a deduction for real estate taxes paid by a cooperative on a building that it leases from another because the payment of those taxes may be considered rent.[18] Similarly, if a cooperative constructs a building on leased land, taxes on the land may not be deductible by the tenant-stockholders, but the taxes on the building owned by the cooperative would be deductible by the tenant-stockholders.[19] Also, tenant-stockholders may not deduct their share of real estate taxes on recreational facilities that are available for their use but are owned by a corporation other than the cooperative.[20]

[B] Depreciation

Stock in a cooperative housing corporation owned by a tenant-stockholder who uses the proprietary lease or right of tenancy in a trade or business or for the production of income is treated as depreciable property.[21] Depreciation deductions cannot exceed the tenant-stockholder's basis in his or her stock.[22] Any depreciation deduction disallowed because it exceeds the tenant-stockholder's basis may be carried over as a deduction for depreciation in the following year.[23]

---

[18] Rev. Rul. 62-177, 1962-2 CB 89.
[19] Rev. Rul. 62-178, 1962-2 CB 91.
[20] Rev. Rul. 69-76, 1969-1 CB 56.
[21] Code Sec. 216(c)(1).
[22] Code Sec. 216(c)(2)(A).
[23] Code Sec. 216(c)(2)(B).

A tenant-stockholder's depreciation deduction when the unit is used in a trade or business or for the production of income is determined as follows:[24]

1. Compute the amount of depreciation allowable on the depreciable property owned by the cooperative in which the tenant-stockholder has a proprietary lease or right of tenancy;
2. Reduce the amount computed in Step 1 in the same ratio as the rentable space in the property which is not subject to a proprietary lease or right of tenancy by reason of stock ownership but which is held for rental purposes bears to the total rentable space in the property; and
3. Compute the tenant-stockholder's proportionate share of the depreciation deduction as adjusted in Step 2.[25]

The depreciation deduction determined in the manner set out above must be adjusted when only a portion of the property occupied under a proprietary lease or right of tenancy is used in a trade or business or for the production of income.[26]

¶ 1902 CONDOMINIUMS

A condominium is an interest in real property that consists of an undivided interest in common in a portion of a parcel of real property, which may be a fee interest or an estate for years, together with a separate interest in space in a building located on this parcel. The undivided interests in the common elements must be vested in the unit holders.[27] In other words, the owner of a condominium unit owns a cube of space within a building and shares common property with other unit owners.

.01 Tax Treatment of Unit Owner

Essentially, the owner of a condominium unit is treated as any other homeowner for tax purposes since the owner owns the unit outright and not indirectly through shares in a corporation. The condominium owner may deduct real estate taxes on the unit, and mortgage interest if the unit is mortgaged, to the same extent as the owner of a single family home (see ¶ 1701 and 1702).[28] If a condominium is damaged by fire, storm or other casualty, the owner may take a casualty loss deduction for the unreimbursed loss.[29] If a condominium owner uses part of the unit for business purposes, or rents the unit to others, the unit owner is entitled to related business or rental expense deductions (see ¶ 1801.02). Finally, at a sale, the condominium unit owner is entitled to the special tax breaks available to other homeowners (see ¶ 2002-2003.02).

Occasionally, condominium unit owners are assessed for repairs or replacement. Capital assessments against unit owners for repairs or replacements and proceeds from a suit for defective construction used for repairs, replacements, or

[24] Reg. § 1.216-2(b)(1).

[25] Examples of the depreciation calculation may be found in Reg. § 1.216-2(d).

[26] Reg. § 1.216-2(b)(1). The allocation of deductions when only part of a taxpayer's home is used for business purposes is covered at ¶ 1801.02.

[27] Reg. § 1.528-1(b).

[28] *See* Rev. Rul. 64-31, 1964-1 CB 300, dealing with the deduction of real estate taxes by condominium owners.

[29] The limitations on and method of calculating a casualty loss on a personal residence are also considered at ¶ 1703.01 and 1703.02.

improvements are added to the unit owners' bases for their units. Recovery in a suit for defective construction of common elements reduces unit owners' bases proportionately and is not income to either unit owners or the condominium association.[30]

.02 Tax Treatment of Condominium Association

A condominium management association may elect to be treated as a tax-exempt homeowners association. If this election is made, the association is not taxed on exempt function income.[31] The tax treatment of homeowners associations, including condominium associations, is considered at ¶ 1903.

¶ 1903 HOMEOWNERS ASSOCIATIONS

Under Code Sec. 528, a qualified homeowners association, which may be a condominium management association, a residential real estate management association, or a timeshare association, may elect to be treated as a tax-exempt organization. If an association makes this election, it is not taxed on its exempt function income, that is, membership dues, fees, and other assessments collected from persons who own units and who are members of the association. The association does pay a tax at a flat rate of 30 percent (32 percent in the case of a timeshare association) on any income that is not exempt function income.

A condominium management association is any organization that is organized and operated to provide for the acquisition, construction, management, maintenance, and care of a condominium project if substantially all of the units in the project are used by individuals as residences.[32] A residential real estate management association is any organization organized and operated to provide for the acquisition, construction, management, maintenance, and care of a subdivision, development, or similar area if substantially all of the lots or buildings within the area are used by individuals for residences.[33] A timeshare association is any organization, other than a condominium management association, that is organized and operated to provide for the acquisition, construction, management, maintenance, and care of association property, if any member holds a timeshare right to use, or a timeshare ownership interest in, association real property.[34]

.01 Qualification for Tax-Exempt Status

If an association elects to be taxed as a homeowners association, it is not taxed on its exempt function income. To qualify for this election, a homeowners association must:[35]

1. Be organized and operated to provide for the acquisition, construction, management, maintenance, and care of association property;
2. Obtain 60 percent or more of its gross income from exempt function income;
3. Have at least 90 percent of its expenses be for the acquisition, construction, management, maintenance, and care of association property and, in

[30] Rev. Rul. 81-152, 1981-1 CB 433.

[31] Code Sec. 528.

[32] Code Sec. 528(c)(2).

[33] Code Sec. 528(c)(3).

[34] Code Sec. 528(c)(4).

[35] Code Sec. 528(c)(1).

the case of a timeshare association, for activities provided to or on behalf of association members; and

4. Ensure that no part of its net earnings will be used to benefit any private shareholder or individual, except through the acquisition, construction, management, maintenance, or care of association property or through the rebate of excess membership dues, fees, or assessments.

These requirements are explored in more detail in the following paragraphs.

[A] Association Property

Association property includes property held by the organization, property held in common by the members of the organization, property within the organization held privately by its members, and property owned by a governmental unit and used for the benefit of residents of the unit. In the case of a timeshare association, association property includes property in which the association or members have rights from recorded easements, covenants, or other recorded instruments, to use property related to the timeshare project.[36]

Property held by the organization or held in common by the organization is association property if it is available for the common benefit of all organization members and tends to increase the enjoyment of the private residences by their owners. This type of association property might include swimming pools and tennis courts. Facilities or areas set aside for nonmembers, or used primarily by nonmembers, however, are not association property. For example, property that is owned by the association for the purpose of leasing it to groups of nonmembers for use as a meeting place is not association property.[37]

Property normally owned by a governmental unit is association property if it includes areas and facilities traditionally recognized as part of a governmental function. These areas and facilities include roads, parks, sidewalks, streetlights, and fire stations. This type of property is association property whether it is owned by the organization, by its members as tenants in common, or by a governmental unit and used for the benefit of the residents of the unit as well as members of the organization.[38]

Property held privately by members of the association is association property if:[39]

1. It affects the overall appearance or structure of the residential units;
2. There is an agreement relating to the appearance or maintenance that applies on the same basis to all such property in the project;
3. There are annual assessments on all members of the association for maintaining this property; and
4. Membership in the association is a condition of every person's ownership of such property in the project.

[36] Code Sec. 528(c)(4).

[37] Reg. § 1.528-3(a).

[38] Reg. § 1.528-3(b).

[39] Reg. § 1.528-3(c).

Example 3: A condominium association enforces covenants that affect the appearance of individual units and maintains the exterior walls and roofs of the individual units. Although the property the association maintains is private, its appearance may directly affect the condition of the entire condominium project. The exterior walls and roof are association property as long as requirements 3 and 4 described above are also met.

[B] Use as Residences

"Substantially all" the units within a condominium project, or lots or buildings within a subdivision or development, must be used as residences for a condominium management or residential real estate management association to qualify for tax-exempt status.

Substantially all of the units within a condominium are used by individuals for residences if at least 85 percent of the total square footage of the units in the project is used by individuals for residential purposes.[40] Areas used for residential purposes include the following:

1. A unit constructed for use as a residence but never occupied;
2. A unit that is not occupied but has been in the past, if it was constructed for use as a residence and the last individual to occupy it did use it as a residence; and
3. Units that are used for purposes that are auxiliary to residential use, such as laundry areas, swimming pools, tennis courts, storage rooms, and areas used by maintenance personnel.

Substantially all of the lots or buildings within a subdivision or development, including unimproved lots, are used by individuals for residences if at least 85 percent of the lots are zoned for residential purposes. Lots are considered zoned for residential purposes even if used for parking spaces, swimming pools, tennis courts, schools, fire stations, libraries, and churches. Commercial shopping areas and their parking spaces, however, are not lots zoned for residential purposes.[41]

A unit or building is not used for residential purposes for purposes of qualifying a homeowners association for tax-exempt status if it is occupied for over half of the days in the association's tax year by a person or series of persons who occupy the unit or building for less than 30 days each.[42]

[C] Exempt Function Income

At least 60 percent of an association's income must be exempt function income in order for the homeowners association to qualify for tax-exempt status. Exempt function income is any amount received by the association as membership dues, fees, or assessments from owners of condominium housing units in the case of a condominium management association, from owners of residential real property in the case of a residential real estate management association, or from owners of timeshare rights to use, or timeshare ownership interests in, real property in the

[40] Reg. § 1.528-4(b).

[41] Reg. § 1.528-4(c).

[42] Reg. § 1.528-4(d).

case of a timeshare association.[43] This income does not have to be labeled as membership dues, fees, or assessments, but it must come from members as owners, not as customers, of the association's services.[44]

Dues, fees, or assessments paid by a developer on unfinished or finished units or lots that remain unsold are exempt function income, even though the developer does not use the units or lots for residential purposes. Dues, fees, or assessments are not exempt function income unless each member's liability for payment arises solely from membership in the association. Amounts based on the value or size of property are considered a result of membership in the association, but amounts based on the extent to which a member makes use of any facility are not exempt function income.[45]

Excess assessments during a tax year that are rebated to members or applied to their future assessments are not exempt function income for that year, but if the excess assessments are applied to a future year's assessments, they are exempt function income in that future year.

Examples of exempt function income are assessments to:

1. Pay principal, interest, and real estate taxes on association property;
2. Maintain association property; and
3. Clean snow from public areas and remove trash.[46]

Examples of income that is not exempt function income are:

1. Amounts that are not includible in the association's gross income other than under Code Sec. 528 (for instance, tax-exempt interest);
2. Amounts received from nonmembers;
3. Amounts received from members for special use of the association's facilities which are not available to all members from paying dues, fees, or assessments required from all members;
4. Interest earned on amounts set aside in a sinking fund;
5. Amounts received for work done on privately owned property that is not association property; and
6. Amounts received from members in return for their transportation to or from shopping, work, etc.[47]

Amounts received from members or tenants of residential units owned by members for special use of an association's facilities are considered exempt function income if:

1. The amounts paid by members are not paid more than once in any 12-month period; and
2. The privilege obtained from the payment lasts for the entire 12-month period or portion of the period in which the facility is commonly in use.[48]

---

[43] Code Sec. 528(d)(3).

[44] Reg. § 1.528-9(a).

[45] Reg. § 1.528-9(a).

[46] Reg. § 1.528-9(b).

[47] Reg. § 1.528-9(c).

[48] Reg. § 1.528-9(d).

For example, amounts received from members for a yearly fee for use of tennis courts or a swimming pool are exempt function income. Amounts received for the use of a building for an evening, weekend, week, etc., however, are not considered exempt function income.

[D] Expenditures

An association cannot exclude exempt function income from gross income unless 90 percent or more of its expenditures for the tax year are for the acquisition, construction, management, maintenance, and care of association property or for activities provided to members of a timeshare association. The determination of whether an association meets this expenditure test is made after the close of the association's tax year. Investments or transfers of funds held to meet future costs are not treated as expenditures. For example, transfers to a sinking fund to replace a roof are not considered expenditures, even if the roof is association property. Also, excess assessments that are rebated to members or applied against future assessments are not considered expenditures.[49]

Expenditures counted in the 90-percent test are those to acquire, construct, manage, maintain, and care for association property. They include current operating and capital expenditures. They also include expenditures on association property, even if the property produces income that is not exempt function income.[50] For example, expenditures on a swimming pool are qualifying expenditures even though guests' fees are not exempt function income. Expenditures that apply to both association property and other property must be allocated on a reasonable basis.

Here are some examples of expenditures that are counted for purposes of the 90-percent test:

1. Salaries of an association manager and secretary;
2. Paving of streets;
3. Street signs;
4. Security personnel;
5. Legal and accounting fees;
6. Upkeep of tennis courts, swimming pools, and recreation halls;
7. Replacement of common buildings, facilities, and air conditioning;
8. Insurance premiums on association property; and
9. Real estate and personal property taxes imposed on association property.[51]

[E] Inurement

An organization cannot qualify as a homeowners association if any part of its net earnings inures (other than as a direct result of its engaging in one or more exempt functions) to the benefit of a private person. To the extent members receive a benefit from the general maintenance of association property, this benefit is not

[49] Reg. § 1.528-6(a).

[50] Reg. § 1.528-6(b).

[51] Reg. § 1.528-6(c).

an inurement. If an organization pays rebates from amounts other than exempt function income, however, the rebates are inurements. In general, in determining whether an organization is in violation of the restriction on inurements, the IRS applies the principles used in making similar determinations for charities and other Code Sec. 501(c)(3) organizations.[52]

.02 Taxation of Homeowners Association

If a homeowners association elects to exclude exempt function income, it must pay a tax at a flat rate of 30 percent (32 percent in the case of a timeshare association) on its taxable income.[53] Taxable income is the association's gross income for the tax year, other than its exempt function income, reduced by any deductions directly connected with the production of the gross income subject to tax.[54] Deductions are directly connected with the production of gross income if they have both proximate and primary relationship to the production of the income. Deductions attributable solely to items of taxable gross income are proximately and primarily related to that income.[55]

In computing taxable income, the association may not deduct net operating losses, special deductions for corporations, such as the dividends received deduction, or expenses connected with the production of exempt function income. The association is allowed a specific deduction of $100 so that associations with only a minimal amount of nonexempt income are not subject to tax.[56]

If facilities or personnel are used both for exempt functions of the association and for the production of nonexempt gross income, the expenses attributable to the facilities or personnel must be allocated between the two activities on a reasonable basis. The portion of the expenses allocated to the production of nonexempt gross income is directly connected with that income and is deductible in figuring the association's taxable income.[57]

> ***Example 4:*** The Homeowners Association pays its manager a salary of $20,000 per year, and it does realize income other than exempt function income. If 10 percent of the manager's time during the year is devoted to activities generating nonexempt income, a deduction of $2,000 (10% × $20,000) generally would be permitted in computing the Homeowners Association's taxable income.

Note that a homeowners association does not have to elect exempt status under Code Sec. 528. A homeowners association should compute its tax using the regular corporate rates and tax return. Although, as a regular corporation, the association is not eligible to exclude income, the tax may be lower because of the lower regular corporate rates and deductions, which reduce income that would be exempt under Code Sec. 528.

---

[52] Reg. § 1.528-7.
[53] Code Sec. 528(b).
[54] Code Sec. 528(d)(1).
[55] Reg. § 1.528-10(c)(1).
[56] Code Sec. 528(d)(2).
[57] Reg. § 1.528-10(c)(2).

.03 Election of Exempt Status

A homeowners association must elect the exclusion for exempt function income each year. The election is made by filing a properly completed Form 1120-H. Once made, the election is binding and may not be revoked without the consent of the IRS.[58] The IRS has indicated, however, that it will permit a revocation of the election when the election is made as a result of incorrect tax advice on the part of a professional tax advisor, if the revocation is requested promptly after the error is discovered.[59]

.04 Nonexempt Associations

If an association is not a tax-exempt organization or cannot exclude exempt function income from gross income, the association must file tax returns in the same manner as other corporations. Even if it is an unincorporated association, it is treated as a corporation for tax purposes.

[A] Tax-Exempt Status

A homeowners association formed to administer and enforce covenants for preserving the architecture and appearance of a development and to own and maintain common green areas, streets, and sidewalks that cannot exclude exempt function income from gross income under Code Sec. 528 generally cannot qualify as a tax-exempt organization (that is, as a civic league or social welfare organization).[60] It may qualify for that tax-exempt status, however, if it can show that the following conditions apply:

1. The community served by the association is a geographical unit reasonably related to a governmental subdivision;
2. The association does not maintain the exterior of private residences;
3. The association owns and maintains only areas and facilities of direct governmental concern, such as roads, parks, sidewalks, and streetlights which are available to the general public; and
4. The association owns and maintains recreational areas and facilities for the use and enjoyment of the general public (the association may not qualify if it owns and maintains parking facilities only for its members).[61]

If an association establishes a separate organization to own and maintain recreational facilities and restricts their use to members, and no part of its earnings benefits any member, it may be able to qualify for tax-exempt status as a social club. But a club that provides social and recreational facilities and limits their use to members is precluded from qualifying for tax-exempt status as a social club by owning and maintaining residential streets, enforcing restrictive covenants, or providing residential fire and police protection and trash collection.[62]

---

[58] Reg. § 1.528-8.

[59] Rev. Rul. 83-74, 1983-1 CB 112.

[60] Rev. Rul. 74-17, 1974-1 CB 130.

[61] Rev. Rul. 74-99, 1974-1 CB 131.

[62] Rev. Rul. 75-494, 1975-2 CB 214.

[B] Cooperative Organization

A condominium management corporation that cannot exclude exempt function income from gross income may operate in such a way as to qualify as a cooperative.[63] This would permit the corporation to retain for reasonable business purposes up to 80 percent of its otherwise taxable income received from unit owner-stockholders as regular assessments. This is done by distributing qualified patronage dividends for which the cooperative receives a deduction. The patronage dividends may be paid 20 percent in cash and 80 percent in qualified written notices of allocation. Therefore, up to 80 percent of otherwise taxable income accumulated from the regular assessments may be retained by the cooperative corporation for its reasonable business needs. Owner-stockholders who do not use their condominium units in their trade or business or for the production of income may exclude patronage dividends from their income under this arrangement.[64]

[C] Assessments

Regular assessments paid by condominium owners are income to the corporation for services rendered. The excess of this income over expenses is subject to tax. Excess assessments over the expenses for the year do not result in taxable income to the corporation if they are either refunded to the owner-stockholders or applied to the following year's regular assessments because of a specific vote of the membership at a membership meeting.[65]

A special assessment is not included in the gross income of a condominium management corporation that cannot exclude exempt function income from gross income under Code Sec. 528 if the assessment has been specifically voted on and approved by the stockholders, designated for specific capital expense, set aside in a special bank account, and not committed with the regular assessments of the management corporation. If the special assessment is to pay for services rendered by the corporation to the owner-stockholders, however, the funds collected from the special assessment are included in the gross income of the management association.[66]

> ***Example 5:*** A special assessment of $100 is levied and collected from the owner-stockholders of a condominium to pay for the unexpected cost of repairing the condominium's swimming pool filter and for the increased cost of maintaining the lawns of the condominium. Because the special assessment in this case is for services rendered by the management corporation to the owner-stockholders, it is included in the corporation's gross income.

A special assessment that owner-stockholders vote on and designate for the replacement of personal property in the common elements of the condominium is treated as a contribution to the capital of the management corporation. It is not included in gross income, provided that the funds collected are designated for a specific capital expense and kept in a separate bank account.

---

[63] Code Secs. 1381–1388.

[64] Rev. Rul. 75-371, 1975-2 CB 52.

[65] Rev. Rul. 70-604, 1970-2 CB 9.

[66] Rev. Rul. 75-371, 1975-2 CB 52.

> ***Example 6:*** The owner-stockholders in a condominium levy and collect a special assessment to be used exclusively to replace outdoor lawn furniture owned by the condominium management corporation. The money collected is deposited in a separate bank account specifically designated for this purpose. The special assessment is not included in the gross income of the condominium management association.

If the owner-stockholders of a condominium management corporation vote to levy and collect a special assessment for a specific capital expense in the common elements of the condominium's real property, the corporation does not include the assessment in gross income because it owns none of the property benefited. Each owner-stockholder owns an undivided interest in the common elements of the condominium's real property. If the funds are deposited in a separate bank account earmarked for a specific capital expense and may only be spent for that designated purpose, the management corporation is acting as an agent for the owner-stockholders because it may not use these funds to benefit any property that it owns.[67]

> ***Example 7:*** The owner-stockholders of a condominium decide to levy and collect from each owner a special assessment of $25 per month for 24 months. The condominium management corporation is directed to deposit these assessments into two separate bank accounts and not to combine these assessments with any regular assessment funds. The special assessments will pay for the replacement of the roof and elevator located in the common elements of the property. The special assessments are not included in the management corporation's gross income because the corporation is collecting these funds as an agent, for the benefit of the owner-stockholders who own undivided interests in the common elements of the property.

[67] Rev. Rul. 75-370, 1975-2 CB 25.

Chapter 20
Sale of Residence

¶ 2000 Overview of Chapter
¶ 2001 Gain or Loss on Sale of Residence
¶ 2002 Tax Exclusion for Principal Residence
¶ 2003 Tax-Free Rollover of Gain
¶ 2004 Exclusion of Gain for Taxpayer Over 55

¶ 2000 OVERVIEW OF CHAPTER

The sale of a taxpayer's residence is generally a taxable transaction. A residence is a capital asset and its sale at a gain produces capital gain. There are, however, special provisions in the tax law that allow the tax to be avoided or postponed if specified requirements are met. Generally, for home sales on or after May 7, 1997, gain of up to $250,000 ($500,000 for married taxpayers filing jointly) is not subject to tax. For home sales before May 7, 1997, the replacement of a principal residence with a new principal residence allowed the tax on any gain to be postponed until the new residence is ultimately sold. Also, again for sales before May 7, 1997, taxpayers over the age of 55 who sold their homes could exclude a portion of their gain from income. These old provisions may still have a limited affect on current home sales. The basis of a home sold today may have a basis determined under the old rules if it was purchased as replacement property under those rules. Also, the time a taxpayer owned and used a former residence is counted toward the ownership and use of a current residence if gain on the former residence was rolled over under the old rules into the current residence.

¶ 2001 GAIN OR LOSS ON SALE OF RESIDENCE

A taxpayer's home is a capital asset; thus, any gain on the sale is a capital gain, and, unless the special provisions discussed beginning at ¶ 2002 apply, the gain is subject to current tax. While any gain is subject to tax, a loss on the sale of a personal residence is generally not deductible. Personal, living, or family expenses are not deductible, and a loss on the sale of a personal residence falls into this category.[1]

The general rules for the calculation of gain and loss on the sale of real property are discussed at ¶ 1301.01. Of course, to calculate gain or loss, a taxpayer must know his or her adjusted basis.[2] Oftentimes, taxpayers are lax in keeping

[1] Code Sec. 262(a); Reg. § 1.262-1(b)(4); *see also* Code Sec. 165(c) and (f), which limit the losses allowed to individuals and for capital losses.

[2] Basis rules are covered in detail at ¶ 101.

records to establish the adjusted basis of a personal residence which includes capital improvements and additions. The Tax Court has indicated that it will consider a taxpayer's estimates of such costs based on recollection, but the better course is to maintain receipts and other documentation. The amount of weight the Tax Court gives to recollection will bear heavily against the taxpayer whose own fault is the reason for any "inexactitude."[3]

.01 Business or Rental Use

While the loss from the sale of a residence is generally not deductible, this is not the case if the residence was used as rental property or in a trade or business of the taxpayer. Even if a house was originally purchased as a personal residence, a loss on its sale is deductible if the house was converted to rental or business use before the sale. The basis for determining any loss in this situation is, of course, the cost of the property or its fair market value on the date of conversion, whichever is less.[4] When a residence was used partly as a personal residence and partly for business or rental, gain or loss is apportioned between the two uses. Any loss on the business or rental portion is deductible, while loss on the part used as a personal residence is not.[5]

.02 Residence Held for Gain

In rare cases, the holding of a residence, even though it is not held for rental, may be considered as the holding of property for the production of income so as to allow any loss on the sale to be deductible.

In *E.G. Lowry, Jr.*,[6] a taxpayer had stopped using a summer home that was offered for sale at a price in excess of the market value in the area. The taxpayer held out for six years until appreciation finally brought the asking price. While the taxpayer did not rent the property during the six years, maintenance costs were deducted by the taxpayer. The court ruled that these expenses were deductible because the taxpayer had converted the property into property held for the production of income (the appreciation) under Reg. § 1.212-1(b).

In another case,[7] a taxpayer was entitled to deduct a loss on a residence that was inherited from a spouse even though the taxpayer occupied it for a short period of time. The taxpayer was able to convince the court that from the moment the property was acquired the taxpayer never intended to occupy the house as a residence and that the ownership of the property was for the production of income, not for residence purposes.

¶ 2002 TAX EXCLUSION FOR PRINCIPAL RESIDENCE

Individuals can exclude from income up to $250,000 ($500,000 for married couples filing jointly) in gain from the sale or exchange of their principal residence on or after May 7, 1997.[8] Gain excluded under this provision is never subject to tax. This exclusion replaced the tax-free rollover provision (¶ 2003) and the exclusion

[3] R.C. Bayly, 42 TCM 1216, CCH Dec. 38,291(M), T.C. Memo. 1981-549.

[4] Reg. § 1.165-9(b).

[5] Rev. Rul. 286, 1953-2 CB 20.

[6] DC NH, 74-2 USTC ¶ 9821, 384 F. Supp. 257.

[7] H.V. Watkins, 32 TCM 809, CCH Dec. 32,070(M), T.C. Memo. 1973-167.

[8] Code Sec. 121.

for taxpayers over 55 (¶ 2004). Any gain in excess of the $250,000 or $500,000 exclusion is subject to tax as capital gain regardless of whether proceeds are reinvested in another residence or not.

Although the exclusion generally applies to sales or exchanges after May 6, 1997, homeowners could have elected the old tax-free rollover and exclusion for taxpayers over 55 for sales:

1. After May 6, 1997, and before August 5, 1997;
2. After August 5, 1997, if subject to a binding contract in effect on August 5, 1997;
3. After August 5, 1997, if a replacement residence under the tax-free rollover provision was acquired before August 6, 1997, either outright or under a binding contract, and the rollover provision would have applied under prior law.[9]

.01 Qualifications for Exclusion

To qualify for the $250,000 ($500,000 for joint returns) exclusion on the sale of a home, the taxpayer must have owned and used the home as a principal residence for at least two years out of the five years immediately preceding the sale.[10] Further, the exclusion does not apply to any sale or exchange if the taxpayer took advantage of the exclusion for another residence within the two years preceding the current home sale.[11] Under the latter rule, no sale before May 7, 1997, is taken into account.[12]

If a taxpayer cannot meet the requirements for the exclusion because of a job change or health reasons, or other unforeseen circumstances allowed by the IRS, a reduced exclusion is available. The IRS has ruled a pregnancy qualified as an unforeseen circumstance when an unmarried couple, no longer in a relationship, decided to sell their home seven months after its purchase.[13] According to the couple, the residence was not large enough to accommodate two adults and a child and neither of them could afford to make the monthly mortgage payments on the residence alone. The IRS has also ruled a marriage qualified as an unforeseen circumstance when the newlyweds sold the old homes after purchasing a home large enough to house their combined families.[14] The husband had three children from a previous marriage, and the wife had two children from a previous marriage. The new residence allowed the couple to provide suitable bedroom arrangements for their blended family, which included adolescent children of the opposite sex.

The reduced exclusion is determined by the ratio of the period of use as a personal residence during the previous five years (or the period since the last sale subject to the exclusion, if less) to two years.[15] For instance, if a single taxpayer fails

[9] Taxpayer Relief Act of 1997, Sec. 312(d).
[10] Code Sec. 121(a).
[11] Code Sec. 121(b)(3).
[12] Code Sec. 121(b)(3)(B).
[13] Ltr. Rul. 200652041.
[14] Ltr. Rul. 200725018.
[15] Code Sec. 121(c).

to qualify because he lived in the residence only one year before being relocated by his employer, the ratio would be ½ (one year to two years). His exclusion would be limited to $125,000 (½ × $250,000).

[A] Joint Returns

For a married couple to claim the $500,000 exclusion, the following requirements must be met:

1. They must file a joint return for the year of sale;
2. Either spouse may have owned the home in two out of five of the previous years;
3. Both spouses must have used the home as their principal residence in two out of five of the previous years; and
4. Neither spouse must have taken advantage of the exclusion in the previous two years.[16]

In the Conference Report to the Taxpayer Relief Act of 1997, the conferees clarified that "the provision limiting the exclusion to only one sale every two years by the taxpayer does not prevent a husband and wife filing a joint return from each excluding up to $250,000 of gain from the sale or exchange of each spouse's principal residence provided that each spouse would be permitted to exclude up to $250,000 of gain if they filed separate returns."

[B] Nonqualified Use

For home sales after 2008, gain allocated to periods of nonqualified use may not be excluded from income.[17] A period of nonqualified use is any period during which a taxpayer, or the taxpayer's spouse or former spouse, did not use the property as a principal residence. Periods of nonqualified use do not include any time before 2009, any period after the last date the taxpayer uses the property as his or her principal residence, and any period up to two years that the taxpayer is temporarily absent because of a change in place of employment, health, or unforeseen circumstances.[18] Gain is allocated to periods of nonqualified in the same ratio as the aggregate periods of nonqualified use during the period the property was owned by the taxpayer bears to the total period of time the property was owned by the taxpayer.[19]

> ***Example 1:*** An individual purchased a vacation home on January 1, 2007, and moved into that home as his principal residence on January 1, 2014. The individual sold the home on January 1, 2016. The individual meets the two-out-of-five year requirement for the gain exclusion, but five years of his ownership, 2009 through 2013, is not qualified use, so 5/8ths of his gain is not eligible for exclusion.
>
> Suppose instead that the individual bought the vacation home on January 1, 2010 and doesn't move into it as his principal residence until January 1, 2016. If he sells the home on January 1, 2018, he would meet the two-out-of-five year

[16] Code Sec. 121(b)(2).

[17] Code Sec. 121(b)(5).

[18] Code Sec. 121(b)(5)(C).

[19] Code Sec. 121(b)(5)(B).

requirement, but six of his eight years of ownership would be nonqualified use and 6/8ths of his gain would not be eligible for the exclusion.

The rule that prohibits the exclusion of gain taken on a home used for business attributable to depreciation applies before the rule on nonqualified use is applied. Gain attributable to depreciation is not taken into account in determining the amount of gain allocated to nonqualified use.[20]

[C] Special Situations

Cooperative Housing

A taxpayer who is a tenant-stockholder in a cooperative housing corporation can qualify to exclude gain on the sale of his co-op. The two-out-of-five-years ownership requirement is applied to the cooperative stock, and the two-out-offive-years use requirement is applied to the house or apartment that the taxpayer occupied as the tenant-stockholder.[21]

Deceased and Former Spouses

An unmarried individual whose spouse is deceased at the time of the sale or exchange can include the period the deceased spouse owned and used the property before death in the period the unmarried individual owned and used the property.[22]

A divorced individual who received the property from the former spouse in the divorce can include in the ownership period the period the former spouse owned the property. Also, an individual is treated as using property as a principal residence during any period of ownership while the spouse or former spouse is granted use of the property under a divorce or separation agreement.[23]

For home sales after 2007, the $500,000 (rather than the $250,000) exclusion is available to an unmarried individual whose spouse is deceased on the date of the sale provided the sale occurs within two years of the deceased spouse's death. The tests for the $500,000 exclusion for a joint return listed at ¶ 2002.01[A] must have been met immediately before the deceased spouse's death.[24]

Prior Tax-Free Rollover

Individuals who rolled over gain into a replacement residence under Code Sec. 1034 (see ¶ 2003) can count the time they owned and used the former residence toward the ownership and use requirements for the $250,000 ($500,000) exclusion.[25]

Business Use

If a person used a personal residence for business purposes and claimed depreciation deductions for the residence, gain attributable to the depreciation deductions cannot be excluded from income.[26]

[20] Code Sec. 121(b)(5)(D).
[21] Code Sec. 121(d)(4).
[22] Code Sec. 121(d)(2).
[23] Code Sec. 112(d)(3).
[24] Code Sec. 121(b)(4).
[25] Code Sec. 121(g).
[26] Code Sec. 121(d)(6).

Military, Foreign, or Intelligence Service

An individual may elect to suspend the five-year test period during which the individual must have owned and used the residence for two years for service in the uniformed services, Foreign Service of the United States, or intelligence community. The maximum suspension is for up to 10 years. Under the election, the five-year period before the sale or exchange does not include any period up to 10 years during which the individual or individual's spouse is on qualified official extended duty as a uniformed service member, member of the Foreign Service, or employee of the intelligence community. The election may be applied to only one property at a time, and it may be revoked at any time.[27]

Prior Like-Kind Exchange

For sales and exchanges of principal residences after October 22, 2004, the exclusion does not apply if the principal residence was acquired within the prior five years in a like-kind exchange in which any gain was not recognized.[28] Like-kind exchanges are considered at ¶ 1302. See ¶ 2002.02 for a discussion of the joint application of the home sale exclusion and the like-kind exchange rules when a property has been used consecutively or concurrently as a residence and for business or rental purposes.

Involuntary Conversions

An involuntary conversion of a residence, that is, its destruction, seizure, requisition, or condemnation, is treated as the sale of the residence for purposes of applying the home sale exclusion.[29] Code Sec. 1033 provides for nonrecognition of gain when involuntarily converted property is replaced (see ¶ 1503). In applying Code Sec. 1033, the amount realized from the sale or exchange of property is treated as the amount determined without regard to Code Sec. 121, reduced by the amount of gain excluded under Code Sec. 121. The amount realized from an exchange of a principal residence for purposes of applying the Code Sec. 1033 nonrecognition rules is the fair market value of the relinquished property reduced by the amount of the gain excluded under the home sale exclusion of Code Sec. 121.[30] The gain excluded under Code Sec.121 is then added in the calculation of the taxpayer's basis in the replacement property.[31]

In summary, when a personal residence is involuntarily converted and the homeowner meets the requirements of both the home sale exclusion of Code Sec. 121 and the nonrecognition rule of Code Sec. 1033:

1. The home sale exclusion is applied to gain from the exchange before the application of Code Sec. 1033,
2. For purposes of determining gain that may be deferred under Code Sec. 1033, the home sale exclusion is applied first against amounts received by the homeowner that are not reinvested in the replacement property

[27] Code Sec. 121(d)(9).

[28] Code Sec. 121(d)(10).

[29] Code Sec. 121(d)(5)(A).

[30] Code Sec. 121(d)(5)(B).

[31] Code Sec. 121(d)(5)(C).

(amounts that would result in gain recognition absent the application of the home sale exclusion), and

3. The basis of the homeowner in the newly acquired residence is his basis for the old residence increased by any gain excluded under the home sale exclusion of Code Sec. 121 that is reinvested in the new residence.

[D] Employer Relocation Assistance

Many employers provide help when they transfer an employee to a new work location. That help may come directly from the employer or indirectly through a relocation management company working for the employer. If the employer structures its relocation assistance program so that the employer purchases the transferring employee's home and then resells it, the employee gets home sale treatment for the assistance. The employer, however, acquires a capital asset in the home and does not get to deduct the costs as ordinary and necessary business expenses. On the other hand, if the employer structures its program so that the employee's sale of the home is to a third party buyer facilitated by the employer, the employer deducts its costs as any other employee compensation. The employee, however, has ordinary income for the amount of any employer-provided assistance.

In *Amdahl Corporation*,[32] the court considered whether payments made by an employer to relocation service companies to assist in the disposition of homes of relocated employees were deductible as ordinary expenses or as capital losses. The court ruled that the employer did not acquire ownership of the employees' homes, and that the payments were deductible as ordinary expenses. The court found that the most significant factors of the relocation programs demonstrated that the employees retained the benefits and burdens of ownership of the homes. The court emphasized that it was not the intent of the parties to transfer ownership of the homes and the contracts of sale did not create obligations on the relocation service companies and the employees to transfer ownership. Further, the employees received the profits from the subsequent sales of the homes by the employer to third parties.

The key, as *Amdahl* points out, is whether the benefits and burdens of ownership of the home are transferred from the employee to the employer through the relocation assistance program. The following factors generally determine whether the benefits and burdens of ownership are transferred: (1) whether legal title passes; (2) how the parties treat the transaction; (3) whether an equity was acquired in the property; (4) whether the contract creates a present obligation on the seller to execute and deliver a deed and a present obligation on the purchaser to make payments; (5) whether the right of possession is vested in the purchaser; (6) which party pays the property taxes; (7) which party bears the risk of loss or damage to the property; and (8) which party receives the profits from the operation and sale of the property.[33]

[32] 108 TC 507 (1997).

[33] *See also* ¶ 201.

More recently, the IRS applied the burdens and benefits analysis to three hypothetical situations.[34] The IRS ruled that under two of them, the burdens and benefits of ownership were transferred to the employer because the employer's agent had the sole right to possession of the home and bore the risk of loss. The employee's exercise of an amended value option did not change the result. In the third situation, the IRS ruled the employee transferred the burdens and benefits of ownership directly to the third-party buyer so that there was a single sale that was merely facilitated by the employer.

.02 Exclusion for Mixed-Use Residence

Generally, as discussed at ¶ 2002, a homeowner may exclude up to $250,000 ($500,000 for joint returns) of gain on the sale or exchange of a home. The homeowner must have owned and used the property as his or her principal residence, for periods aggregating two years or more, during the five-year period ending on the date of the sale or exchange, and must not have used the exclusion during the two-year period ending on that date. The home-sale exclusion may apply to a home office, or other business portion of a home, but not to depreciation from the business use.

In the case of business property, a property owner generally does not recognize gain under Code Sec. 1031 on the exchange of the business property for replacement property of a like kind (see ¶ 1302). The property owner, however, does recognize gain to the extent of cash or property received that is not of a like kind. Property used solely as a home is not business property and is not eligible for the like-kind exchange provisions.

When a homeowner uses his property consecutively or concurrently as both a personal residence and for business or rental purposes, the homeowner may benefit from both the home-sale exclusion and the like-kind deferral.[35] In Rev. Proc. 2005-14, the IRS provided rules for computing gain and basis in those situations that are similar to the rules when both Code Sec. 121 and Code Sec. 1033 apply to an involuntarily converted home. According to Rev. Proc. 2005-14, the home sale exclusion must be applied to gain realized before applying the like-kind exchange rules. While the home sale exclusion does not apply to gain attributable to depreciation deductions claimed for the business or rental portion of the residence, the like-kind exchange rules may apply to that gain. In applying the like-kind exchange rules, cash or other non-like kind property (boot) is taken into account only to the extent the boot exceeds the gain excluded under the home sale exclusion for the relinquished business property.

In determining the basis of the property received in the exchange that the homeowner will use in a trade or business or for rental (the replacement business property), any gain excluded under the home sale exclusion is treated as gain recognized by the homeowner. The basis of the replacement business property, therefore, is increased by any gain attributable to the relinquished business property that is excluded under the home sale exclusion.

---

[34] *See* Rev. Rul. 2005-74, 2005-51 IRB 1153.

[35] Rev. Proc. 2005-14, 2005-7 IRB 528.

Example 2: Homeowner bought a house for $210,000 that the homeowner uses as a principal residence from 2000 to 2004. From 2004 until 2006, the owner rents the house to tenants and claims depreciation deductions of $20,000. In 2006, the owner exchanges the house for $10,000 in cash and a townhouse with a fair market value of $460,000 that he intends to rent to tenants. The owner realizes a gain of $280,000 on the exchange.

The homeowner's exchange of a principal residence that he rents for less than three years for a townhouse intended for rental and cash satisfies the requirements of both the home sale exclusion and the like-kind exchange rules. The home sale exclusion does not require the property to be the owner's principal residence on the sale or exchange date. Because the homeowner owned and used the house as his principal residence for at least two years during the five-year period before the exchange, the homeowner may exclude gain under Code Sec. 121. Because the house is investment property at the time of the exchange, the homeowner may defer gain under the like-kind exchange rules of Code Sec. 1031.

The homeowner applies the home sale exclusion to exclude $250,000 of the $280,000 gain before applying the like-kind exchange rules. The homeowner may defer the remaining gain of $30,000, including the $20,000 gain attributable to depreciation, under Code Sec.1031. Although the homeowner receives $10,000 of cash (boot) in the exchange, the homeowner is not required to recognize gain because the boot is taken into account for purposes of the like-kind exchange rules only to the extent the boot exceeds the amount of excluded gain under the home sale exclusion.

The homeowner's basis in the replacement property is $430,000, which is equal to the adjusted basis of the relinquished property at the time of the exchange ($190,000) increased by the gain excluded under the home sale exclusion ($250,000), and reduced by the cash the homeowner received ($10,000).

Additional examples illustrating the simultaneous application of the home sale exclusion of Code Sec. 121 and the like-kind exchange provisions of Code Sec. 1031 may be found in Rev. Proc. 2005-14.

¶ 2003 TAX-FREE ROLLOVER OF GAIN

Before passage in 1997 of the $250,000 exclusion for gain on the sale of a principal residence (¶ 2002), a taxpayer could postpone the tax on the gain from the sale of a principal residence by buying a new principal residence that cost as much as the adjusted sales price of the old home.[36] The gain rollover provisions, however, continued to apply if the taxpayer sold his principal residence after August 5, 1997, but had acquired a replacement property within the replacement period (¶ 2003.01[A]) before August 6, 1997. Also, the old rollover provisions still

[36] Code Sec. 1034 as in effect before its repeal in the Taxpayer Relief Act of 1997.

determine the basis of a residence that is sold under the new rules if it was purchased as replacement property under the old rollover provisions.

.01 Postponement of Tax Requirements

In order to postpone the tax on the sale of a residence, the residence must have been the taxpayer's principal residence. Also, the replacement home, which must have been the taxpayer's principal residence, must have been acquired within two years of the sale of the old residence.[37]

[A] Replacement Period

The replacement period under Code Sec. 1034 was 48 months. The taxpayer who sold a principal residence must have bought or built and lived in the replacement house within two years before or two years after the date of sale to postpone tax on the gain from the sale of the old residence. The taxpayer must have physically lived in the replacement home as the principal residence within the required period.[38]

The replacement period was suspended for a taxpayer while the taxpayer serves on extended active duty in the armed forces. The replacement period also was suspended while a taxpayer was stationed outside the United States by the military.

If the taxpayer's spouse was in the armed forces and the taxpayer was not, the suspension for military service also applied to the taxpayer if the old home was jointly owned. Both individuals must have used the old home as their principal residence.

The replacement period after the sale of a taxpayer's old residence was suspended while the taxpayer had a tax home outside the United States. The suspension applied only if the taxpayer's stay overseas began before the end of the two-year replacement period following the sale of the old residence. The replacement period plus period of suspension was limited to four years.[39]

.02 Tax Treatment

A taxpayer who sold a principal residence and purchased a new principal residence within the replacement period postponed paying tax on some or all of the gain realized on the sale of the old residence.[40] The provision was not elective. The taxpayer, in effect, rolled over the gain into the new residence and had the untaxed gain reflected in the adjusted basis of the new residence.

If the purchase price of the taxpayer's new residence was at least as much as the adjusted sales price of the old residence, no gain was taxed. If the purchase price of the new residence was less than the adjusted sales price of the old residence, the gain taxed in the year of sale was the lesser of the gain on the sale of the old home or the excess of the adjusted sales price of the old residence over the purchase price of the new residence.[41]

---

[37] Code Sec. 1034(a).

[38] E.L. Sheahan, CA-5, 63-2 USTC ¶ 9720, 323 F.2d 383.

[39] Code Sec. 1034(k).

[40] Code Sec. 1034(a).

[41] Reg. § 1.1034-1(a).

[A] Gain on Old Residence

When a taxpayer sold a principal residence, the gain realized was calculated in the usual fashion, that is, amount realized less adjusted basis.[42] The adjusted sales price of the old residence was used to compute the part of the gain that was not recognized and that was rolled over into the new residence as mentioned above. Adjusted sales price is the amount realized less fixing-up expenses.[43]

Fixing-up expenses are decorating and repair expenses paid in order to sell the old residence. To qualify, the expenses must:

1. Be for work done during the 90-day period ending on the day the contract for the sale of the old home is signed;
2. Be paid within 30 days after the sale;
3. Not be deductible in computing taxable income;
4. Not be taken into account in determining the amount realized on the sale; and
5. Not be for capital improvements or additions (which, of course, are added to the basis of the property).

Fixing up expenses were used only to determine the gain on which the tax was postponed. They did not enter into the computation of the actual gain on the sale.[44]

A taxpayer who traded the old residence for a new residence treated the trade as a sale and purchase for purposes of Code Sec. 1034.[45]

[B] Gain on New Residence and Basis

The purchase price of a taxpayer's replacement home was used to find the amount of gain subject to tax and the amount of gain on which the tax was postponed following the sale of a principal residence under Code Sec. 1034. Purchase price included costs incurred within the 48-month replacement period for:

1. Buying or building the home;
2. Rebuilding the home; and
3. Capital improvements or additions.

The taxpayer could not consider any costs incurred before or after the 48-month period, other than those incurred during a suspension of the replacement period for service in the armed forces.[46]

If a taxpayer sold a principal residence and purchased a new one within the replacement period, the taxpayer's basis for the new residence was its cost reduced by the gain not recognized under Code Sec. 1034 on the sale of the old residence.[47]

Application of the rules under Code Sec. 1034 for the calculation of the amount of gain not recognized and the basis of the new residence is illustrated in the

[42] For the general rules on the computation of gain or loss on the sale of real estate, *see* ¶ 1301.

[43] Code Sec. 1034(b)(1).

[44] Reg. § 1.1034-1(b)(6).

[45] Code Sec. 1034(c)(1).

[46] Reg. § 1.1034-4.

[47] Code Sec. 1034(e).

following examples based on Reg. § 1.1034-1(c)(2). Assume the transactions all took place before May 7, 1997.

Comprehensive Example 3: The Taxpayer sold a residence, which had a basis of $17,500. To make it more attractive to buyers, the Taxpayer painted the outside at a cost of $300 in April. The Taxpayer paid for the painting when the work was finished. In May, the house was sold for $20,000. Brokers' commissions and other selling expenses were $1,000. In October, the Taxpayer bought a new residence for $18,000. The amount realized, the gain realized, the adjusted sales price, and the gain recognized are computed as follows:

Selling price	$20,000
Less: Commissions and selling expenses	1,000
Amount realized	$19,000
Less: Basis	17,500
Gain realized	$1,500
Amount realized	$19,000
Less: Fixing-up expenses	300
Adjusted sales price	$18,700
Less: Cost of new residence	18,000
Gain recognized	$700
Cost of new residence	$18,000
Less: Gain not recognized ($1,500 – $700)	800
Adjusted basis of new residence	$17,200

Comprehensive Example 4: The facts are the same as in Example 3, except that the selling price of the old residence was $18,500. The computations are as follows:

Selling price	$18,500
Less: Commissions and selling expenses	1,000
Amount realized	$17,500
Less: Basis	17,500
Gain realized	$-0-

Since no gain was realized, Code Sec. 1034 did not apply. It was unnecessary to compute the adjusted sales price of the old residence. No adjustment to the basis of the new residence was made.

Comprehensive Example 5: The facts are the same as in Example 3, except that the cost of purchasing the new residence was $17,000. The computations are as follows:

Selling price	$20,000
Less: Commissions and selling expenses	1,000
Amount realized	$19,000
Less: Basis	17,500
Gain realized	$1,500
Amount realized	$19,000
Less: Fixing-up expenses	300
Adjusted sales price	$18,700
Cost of new residence	17,000
Difference	$1,700

Since the adjusted sales price of the old residence exceeded the cost of purchasing the new residence by $1,700, which is more than the gain realized, all of the gain realized ($1,500) was recognized. Since none of the gain goes unrecognized, no adjustment to the basis of the new residence was made and its basis was its cost of $17,000.

Comprehensive Example 6: The facts are the same as in Example 3, except that fixing-up expenses were $1,100. The computations are as follows:

Selling price	$20,000
Less: Commissions and selling expenses	1,000
Amount realized	$19,000
Less: Basis	17,500
Gain realized	$1,500
Amount realized	$19,000
Less: Fixing-up expenses	1,100
Adjusted sales price	$17,900
Less: Cost of new residence	18,000
Gain recognized	$-0-
Cost of new residence	$18,000
Less: Gain not recognized	1,500
Adjusted basis of new residence	$16,500

[C] Joint Ownership

A taxpayer and spouse may have owned a residence separately but have taken title to a replacement residence jointly. Or, they may have owned the old residence jointly but taken title to the replacement separately. The postponed gain that reduces the basis of the new home could be divided between taxpayer and spouse if both met the following requirements:

1. They used the old residence and new residence as their principal residences; and
2. They signed a statement that said: "We agree to reduce the basis of the new home(s) by the gain from selling the old home." The statement may be on Form 2119 or a separate sheet attached to the tax return.[48]

Example 7: The Taxpayer sold a home that was separately owned by the Taxpayer, but both the Taxpayer and spouse used the home as their principal residence. The adjusted sales price was $48,000, its adjusted basis was $36,000, and the gain realized was $12,000. The Taxpayer and spouse bought a replacement home within the replacement period for $50,000. Each contributed $25,000 from separate funds, and the couple took title jointly. If they consented to reduce the basis of the new home, the Taxpayer's gain on the sale of the old residence was postponed as if they had owned both homes jointly. Each spouse has a basis of $19,000 in the new residence, that is, $25,000 less $6,000 postponed gain. If they did not sign the consent, the Taxpayer's entire $12,000 was subject to tax because the adjusted sales price of the old home of $48,000 was greater than the Taxpayer's share of the cost of the new residence, and each spouse would have a basis of $25,000 in the new residence.

Suppose, however, that the Taxpayer and spouse owned the old residence jointly, but the spouse used separate funds to purchase the new house and took title individually. In this case, signing the consent meant that the $12,000 gain was postponed and the spouse has an adjusted basis of $38,000 in the new home. If they did not sign the consent, the Taxpayer was taxed on the Taxpayer's share of the gain from the sale of the old residence ($6,000), but the spouse postponed tax on the spouse's share of the gain because it was reinvested in a new principal residence. The spouse's basis for the home in this case would be $44,000.

.03 Partial Business Use

If a taxpayer sold property that was used partly as a principal residence and partly for business or rental purposes, the transaction was treated as the sale of two properties. Under Code Sec. 1034, the tax on the gain attributable to the residence could have been postponed by reinvesting an equal amount in a new principal residence. Tax on the gain attributable to the business portion of the home could not have been postponed under Code Sec. 1034.

A similar rule applied if a replacement residence was used partly for residential and partly for business or rental use. Only the part of the purchase price allocable to the principal residence portion of the home could be counted as the cost of purchasing the replacement home under Code Sec. 1034.[49]

---

[48] Code Sec. 1034(g); Reg. § 1.1034-1(f).

[49] Reg. § 1.1034-1(c)(3)(ii). For further discussion on homes used partly for business or rental purposes, *see* ¶ 1801.

¶ 2004 EXCLUSION OF GAIN FOR TAXPAYER OVER 55

Under Code Sec. 121 before its amendment by the Taxpayer Relief Act of 1997 to provide for the exclusion discussed at ¶ 2002, a taxpayer could exclude from gross income part or all of the gain on the sale of a principal residence, up to $125,000, if the taxpayer met the age, ownership, and use tests at the time of the sale. (**Note**: References to Code Sec. 121 in this ¶ 2004 are to that Code Sec. as in effect prior to its amendment by the Taxpayer Relief Act of 1997.)

.01 Exclusion Amount and Qualification Requirements

A taxpayer could elect to exclude from income $125,000 ($62,500 in the case of a married individual filing a separate return)[50] on the sale of the taxpayer's principal residence if:

1. The taxpayer was 55 or older on the date of the sale;[51]
2. The taxpayer owned and lived in the home for at least three years out of the five-year period ending on the date of sale;[52] and
3. The taxpayer or the taxpayer's spouse never excluded gain on the sale of a home under Code Sec. 121 after July 26, 1978.[53]

The taxpayer must have been 55 by the time the home was sold to qualify for the exclusion. A sale in the year the taxpayer turns 55, but before the taxpayer's birthday, did not qualify.[54]

[A] Ownership and Use Requirements

The required three years of ownership and use during the five years before the sale did not have to be continuous. The test was met if the taxpayer owned and lived in the property as a principal residence for either 36 full months or 1,095 days during the five-year period. Short, temporary absences for vacations or other seasonal absences, even if the taxpayer rents the property while away, counted as periods of use.[55]

The ownership and use tests could have been met during different three-year periods, as long as both tests were met during the five years before the sale.[56]

> ***Example 8:*** In 1985, the Taxpayer was 50 years old and lived in a rented apartment. The apartment building was later changed to a condominium and the Taxpayer bought the apartment on December 1, 1988. In 1990, the Taxpayer became ill and, on April 15 of that year, moved to a daughter's home. On February 17, 1992, while still living in the daughter's home, the Taxpayer sold the apartment.
>
> The Taxpayer can exclude the gain on the sale of the apartment under Code Sec. 121 because the age, ownership, and use tests were met. The Taxpayer was over 55 at the time of the sale. The five-year period is from

[50] Code Sec. 121(b)(1).

[51] Code Sec. 121(a)(1).

[52] Code Sec. 121(a)(2).

[53] Code Sec. 121(b)(2) and (3).

[54] Reg. § 1.121-a(1).

[55] Reg. § 1.121-1(c).

[56] Rev. Rul. 80-172, 1980-2 CB 56.

February 18, 1987, to February 17, 1992, the date the Taxpayer sold the apartment. The Taxpayer owned the apartment from December 1, 1988, to February 17, 1992 (over three years). The Taxpayer lived in the apartment from February 18, 1987, to April 15, 1990 (over three years).

[B] Purchase of New Principal Residence

If a taxpayer had gain remaining after the application of the $125,000 exclusion under Code Sec. 121, the taxpayer may have been able to postpone the tax on this gain by purchasing a new principal residence as discussed above.[57] The amount that must have been invested in a new residence in order to fully satisfy the nonrecognition provision of Code Sec. 1034 was reduced by the amount of gain excluded by the election under Code Sec. 121.

Example 9: The Taxpayers, a married couple, sold their home on June 14, 1991, for $250,000. Both were 60 years old and had lived in the home as their principal residence for 20 years. The adjusted basis of their old home was $75,000 and they had selling expenses of $15,000. They bought a new principal residence for $110,000 and moved into it on July 20, 1991. Neither spouse has excluded gain on the sale of a home before, and they elected to exclude gain on the sale of their old home under Code Sec. 121.

Their gain was greater than $125,000, but because they purchased a new home that cost as much as the difference between the adjusted sales price of their old home and the exclusion claimed, they postponed the tax on part of the gain not excluded under Code Sec. 121. They figured the gain excluded and postponed as follows:

Gain realized:	
Selling price of old home	$250,000
Less: Selling expenses	15,000
Amount realized	$235,000
Less: Adjusted basis of old home	75,000
Gain realized	$160,000
Gain after exclusion:	
Gain realized	$160,000
Less: Exclusion (lesser of gain realized or $125,000)	125,000
Gain after exclusion	$35,000
Gain taxed in 1991:	
Amount realized	$235,000
Less: Cost of new home	110,000
	$125,000
Less: Exclusion	125,000

[57] Code Sec. 121(d)(7).

Gain taxed in 1991	$-0-
Gain postponed:	
Gain after exclusion	$35,000
Less: Gain taxed in 1991	0
Gain postponed	$35,000
Adjusted basis of new home:	
Cost of new home	$110,000
Less: Gain postponed	35,000
Adjusted basis of new home	$75,000

.02 Election and Revocation of Election

The election, or revocation of the election, to exclude gain under Code Sec. 121 had to be made before the latest of the following dates:

1. Three years from the due date of the return for the year of sale;
2. Three years from the date the return was filed; or
3. Two years from the date the tax was paid.[58]

[A] Election of the Exclusion

The election to exclude gain under Code Sec. 121 was made by attaching a completed Form 2119 to the income tax return for the year of sale or by attaching a signed statement to the return. The statement must have stated that the taxpayer was choosing to exclude from income gain from the sale and must have also included:[59]

1. The taxpayer's name, age, social security number, and marital status on the date of sale. If jointly owned, this information must be supplied for each owner.
2. The date home was bought and sold.
3. The adjusted sales price and the adjusted basis of the property on the date of sale.
4. The length of time taxpayer was away from the home during the five years before the sale, not including vacations and other seasonal absences even if the home was rented.
5. Whether the taxpayer or a joint owner ever elected to exclude gain under Code Sec. 121, and if so, when and where. If the election was revoked, give date of revocation.

The election could have been made even if the taxpayer originally included it on the tax return for the year of sale by filing an amended return.

---

[58] Reg. § 1.121-4(a).

[59] Reg. § 1.121-4(b).

[B] Revocation of the Election

A spouse (or personal representative of a deceased spouse) who joined in making an election must join in revoking the election. The revocation is made in a signed statement showing the taxpayer's name and social security number and identifying the year in which the election was made. The statement is sent to the appropriate IRS service center. If less than one year is left in the assessment period for the return on which the election was made, the taxpayer must consent to extend the assessment period until one year after the statement of revocation is filed.[60]

[60] Reg. § 1.121-4(c).

Part VI

SECURITIZED REAL ESTATE INVESTMENTS

Introduction to Part VI

The three chapters that follow (21-23) take a brief look at ownership interests in real estate that are indirect and mass-marketed. All three, real estate limited partnerships, real estate investment trusts (REITs), and real estate mortgage investment conduits (REMICs), offer interests that are securities under federal securities laws.

According to the Supreme Court, in *United Housing Foundation, Inc. v. Forman,* 421 U.S. 837, 95 S.Ct. 2051 (1975) and *Securities and Exchange Commission v. W.J. Howey Co.,* 328 U.S. 293, 66 S.Ct. 1100 (1946), an investment contract embodies the essential attributes that define a security, namely, the presence of an investment in a common venture premised on a reasonable expectation of profits to be derived from the entrepreneurial or managerial efforts of others. A limited partnership, REIT, or REMIC investment clearly meets this definition. Once an interest is classified as a security, the underlying entity, its sponsors and promoters, and everyone who has a part in organizing the entity and selling interests in it, as well as the interests themselves, become subject to the securities laws, including the Securities Act of 1933, the Securities Exchange Act of 1934, and the Investment Advisors Act of 1940. These laws and the many court decisions interpreting them are quite complex and are a very specialized area of law.

The treatment of these entities under the tax law also may be special. The chapters that follow provide a summary of how the tax law treats these entities and investors in these entities.

Chapter 21
Real Estate Limited Partnerships

¶ 2100 Overview of Chapter
¶ 2101 Development of Limited Partnerships
¶ 2102 Tax Treatment of Real Estate Limited Partnerships
¶ 2103 Master Limited Partnerships

¶ 2100 OVERVIEW OF CHAPTER

As its name implies, a limited partnership is first and foremost a *partnership*. This concept of "partnership" is extremely important, and, for the most part, limited partnerships are subject to the same tax rules as any other partnership. (The general tax rules affecting partnerships are considered in Chapter 2.) In a limited partnership, there must be at least one general partner. The general partner or partners manage the business and are personally liable for the obligations of the partnership. The rights and obligations of the general partners in a limited partnership are the same as those of the partners in a general partnership. The limited partners in a limited partnership are exempt from partnership liability for the debts, obligations, and losses of the partnership as long as they do not participate in the management of the partnership. In other words, the most a limited partner can lose in a partnership is the investment, just like a shareholder in a corporation. This limited liability is what makes the limited partnership attractive as an investment vehicle.

The growth and development of the limited partnership investment vehicle can be traced back to the first real mass marketing of tax shelters that occurred in the early 1970s. In a real sense, the early history of limited partnership investments is the history of tax shelters. Today, limited partnerships may still offer tax advantages in the right situations, but, due to voluminous tax reform legislation enacted over the years, the main emphasis of partnerships has shifted away from tax shelter and toward enhanced investment return in the form of current cash flow.

A relatively recent development in the limited partnership field has been the formation of what are termed "master limited partnerships." Essentially, a master limited partnership is a limited partnership in which interests are publicly traded through listings on a stock exchange or in the over-the-counter market. Investor interest in master limited partnerships skyrocketed following passage of the Tax Reform Act of 1986, and many new businesses were being formed as publicly traded limited partnerships rather than corporations. The tax incentives appeared very attractive. However, tax legislation at the end of 1987 took away the advantages for many newly formed master limited partnerships. A ten-year grace period was provided for existing partnerships, and certain partnerships, specifically those investing in real estate or oil and gas, were exempted from the new provisions. In any event, with the loss of tax benefits, interest in the formation of new businesses (other than those excepted) as master limited partnerships waned. (The special rules for publicly traded partnerships are considered at ¶ 1105.)

¶ 2101 DEVELOPMENT OF LIMITED PARTNERSHIPS

Many factors influence investments of all types. These factors include economic conditions, the rate of inflation, interest rates, and the tax rates applied by federal, state and local government on income of different types. Investors, of course, respond to the changes and seek investments that offer what they perceive to be the most advantageous benefits in light of existing economic conditions and their own personal financial situations.

The period encompassing the last half of the 1970s and the first half of the 1980s was a time of generally high tax rates and high inflation. It was during this time that tax shelters and tax-advantaged investments experienced explosive growth. Battered by high taxes and high inflation, investors naturally sought out those investments that promised them either tax savings or exceptionally high returns. In this environment, the limited partnership became the investment vehicle of choice. With the election of this form of business organization, the limited partnership could be used to acquire and operate those assets that were perceived (rightly or wrongly) to offer high returns in a period of high inflation, assets such as real estate. Further, since this form of business organization is considered a partnership under the tax law, the limited partnership could be used to pass tax benefits on to investors which they could not obtain through the corporate form of business organization.

.01 Limited Partnerships as Tax Shelters

Most tax shelters took the form of limited partnerships because this form of organization provided the combination of the tax benefits of a partnership and limited liability for investors. This was the right combination for an investor in a mass-marketed investment in which other participants were total strangers. As a partnership, the limited partnership could bring together an individual (or a corporation) that has expertise in a specific industry and investors seeking specific tax benefits or specific returns. The partner supplying the expertise would act as general partner, and the investors would be limited partners.

In a tax shelter limited partnership, the general partner would manage the business and assume general liability for the partnership's obligations. Of course, this general liability of the general partner was often more illusory than real since the general partner was more often than not a corporate entity. The general partner, as manager of the tax shelter activity, would gather the investors' capital, make investments, keep the partnership books, report results, and distribute any partnership profits to the limited partners. Note that while the general partner would make all decisions regarding partnership capital, the general partner itself would contribute little or none of the partnership's capital. Investors, as limited partners in a tax shelter limited partnership, would provide the necessary capital to acquire and operate the underlying assets of the partnership and, to the extent available, would receive the bulk of cash distributions from profits generated by the partnership. While supplying most, if not all, of the limited partnership's capital, the limited partners surrendered any right to participate in the management of the underlying assets of the partnership.

Tax shelter limited partnerships would provide tax benefits to investors because profits and losses arising from the operation of partnership assets would flow through to the individual limited partners. The activities of the limited partnership would be reflected on the personal returns of the limited partners in proportion to their interests in the partnership. In short, tax shelter limited partnerships permitted investors to share in tax benefits as well as profits generated by the underlying assets of the partnership, while allowing the investors to retain the limited liability enjoyed by corporate shareholders.

Like corporate shareholders, limited partners could realize any income generated by the assets and operations of the business entity, with one additional advantage. Income from the partnership would retain the character of that income when reported on the partner's tax return. For instance, if the partnership realized capital gain or tax-exempt income, the individual partners would report their share of that capital gain or tax-exempt income. If a corporation earned tax-exempt income, that income would lose its character as tax-exempt income and would be taxable as a dividend when distributed to the shareholders.

In most cases, however, the primary goal of a tax shelter limited partnership was not to generate taxable income from the outset of its operations. Rather, tax shelters generally would look to generate tax or paper losses (tax deductions) and various tax credits early in their operations. These tax deductions and credits would be available to the limited partners for use on their personal tax returns to offset highly taxed income from other sources and to reduce their individual income tax bills. The same underlying assets producing tax deductions or credits would not provide a direct tax benefit to investors if the assets were held by a corporate entity. Such tax deductions and credits would remain locked in the corporation and could be used only on the corporation's tax return.

The advantages offered by tax shelter limited partnerships, however, unfortunately led to abuses in two respects. Some promoters would misrepresent the value or extent of the underlying assets that would be acquired by a tax shelter limited partnership. Others would misrepresent or overstate the tax benefits that would be available to the investors. It was these abuses that, in large measure, finally influenced Congress to pass the legislation that severely curtailed the tax shelters available to passive investors.

.02 Real Estate Tax Shelters

Over time, real estate has proved to be an excellent investment. Inflation and the pressure of demand pushed up values for real estate of all types, albeit to varying degrees and at different times. Widespread home ownership also has made real estate an investment that more people are comfortable with, since they already have some familiarity with its potential advantages and disadvantages. Of course, the financial crisis of 2008 took the steam out of real estate for many. Signs by the beginning of 2013, however, were pointing to a resurgence with investment groups buying up distressed homes for rental.

The major tax shelter aspect of real estate is that rents may be sheltered from taxation by deductions for depreciation and, to some extent, by interest and other expense deductions attributable to the purchase and operation of a real estate investment. Since depreciation does not require a cash expenditure to produce a tax deduction, rents may produce a positive cash flow without a corresponding amount of taxable income.

In the heyday of tax shelters, another feature of real estate was its ability to produce significant tax losses in conjunction with a positive cash flow. These tax losses could be used to shelter an investor's income from other sources which might otherwise be taxed at rates as high as 70 percent on the federal level alone. Now, of course, this feature of real estate is generally not available through public partnerships. Now, if deductions exceed rents so that a tax loss is created by a real estate investment, the excess loss may not be used to shelter income from non-passive activities or income from portfolio investments such as stocks and bonds. Nevertheless, real estate remains an attractive investment in the right situations, and tax benefits may still enhance the return an investor receives from income-producing real estate.

.03 Real Estate Limited Partnerships

As noted above, most tax shelters took the form of limited partnerships because of the combination of the tax benefits of a partnership and limited liability for investors. As Congress has passed laws to curtail the effectiveness of tax shelters, the importance of tax shelter limited partnerships to investors, of course, has declined. This has not meant, however, that the limited partnership itself has disappeared as an attractive investment vehicle. The flexibility of this form of business organization permits investments to be structured to provide investors with the best possible return in the face of changing conditions.

The return from a limited partnership investment comes in three forms: cash flow, tax benefits, and appreciation. All successful limited partnership investments provide some combination of these three forms of investment return.

Cash flow is the actual after-tax cash distributed to or realized by the limited partner while holding the interest and upon its liquidation. Tax benefits are the tax savings generated by the underlying investment and passed through to the investor by the limited partnership. These tax benefits flow from initial deductions provided by many underlying investments and deductions generated over the life of the investment. Finally, appreciation is the actual rise in the value of an investment because of an increase in value over time, such as has occurred with real estate; because of growth, such as the increase in the value of a stand of timber; or because of the actual activity of the limited partnership, such as the collection of rents in a real estate limited partnership investing in rental property.

Although all limited partnership investments produce some combination of cash flow, tax benefits, and appreciation, they may not do so equally. The three forms of return are interrelated, so that an increase in one form of return is usually achieved to the detriment of the other two. For example, the tax benefits (deductions) from an investment may be increased through leverage (borrowing) or a higher purchase price. To the extent tax benefits are increased through borrowing, cash flow from the investment is reduced. More borrowing means higher payments of both principal and interest on the debt. Cash that would otherwise flow to the limited partners must be diverted to service the debt. To the extent tax benefits are increased through a higher purchase price, there is obviously less potential for appreciation.

Similarly, cash flow from an investment can be increased by reduced borrowing or reduced equity buildup in an investment. To the extent cash flow is increased by reduced borrowing, tax benefits are reduced. The lower debt service means lower deductions for interest payments and smaller "paper loss" deductions. To the extent cash flow is increased by reducing equity buildup, that is, by drawing out cash that would otherwise be working in the investment, the ultimate value of the investment is reduced. Finally, appreciation, or the buildup in value of a limited partnership investment, may be increased by sacrificing early tax benefits or by drawing less cash out during the course of an investment.

Essentially, the structure and type of a limited partnership investment determines the nature of the return to the investor. Accordingly, limited partnerships may be structured to yield greater cash flow with reduced tax benefits and appreciation; greater tax benefits with reduced cash flow and appreciation; or greater appreciation potential with reduced cash flow and tax benefits.

If a limited partnership is to attract investors, its structure, of course, must be responsive to investors' needs and the existing tax and economic conditions. The shift from a high tax rate, high-inflation environment to a lower tax rate, lower-inflation environment saw a corresponding shift in the structure of limited partnership investments. Instead of structuring investments for maximum tax benefits through artificial or paper losses created by large borrowing, sponsors shifted to investments with reduced borrowing that offered less in the way of tax benefits and appreciation potential, but much more in the way of immediate tax-sheltered cash flow.

¶ 2102 TAX TREATMENT OF REAL ESTATE LIMITED PARTNERSHIPS

The subject of the taxation of partners and partnerships, in general, is discussed in Chapter 2. Recall that the key feature of a partnership for federal income tax purposes is that it is not, in the usual case, a taxpaying entity. Rather, the nature of a partnership for tax purposes is one of a conduit through which tax consequences flow to the individual partners, and this is true regardless of whether the partnership in question is a general partnership or a limited partnership. It is around this core concept that the partnership tax rules are built.

.01 Restrictions on Partnership-Generated Tax Losses

While the government is more than willing to allow investors in limited partnerships to report and pay taxes on as much income from their investments as possible, it is somewhat stingy in allowing investor use of deductions or losses generated by limited partnerships. The use of tax deductions or losses flowing through the conduit of a limited partnership may be restricted or limited by three different tax rules.

One of the limitations was discussed in Chapter 2 in connection with the role of a partner's basis in the partnership interest. A tax loss generated by a partnership is deductible by a partner only to the extent of the partner's tax basis for the partnership interest as of the end of the tax year in which the loss arose. A loss that exceeds basis may be deducted to the extent of the basis, and the excess loss may be carried over to future years and deducted against any future increase in basis. If there is an unused loss at the time a partner disposes of his partnership interest through a sale, exchange, or liquidation, the loss may be deducted at that time. The loss in this latter case generally is considered a capital loss.

In addition to the basis limitation on the use of losses or deductions generated by a limited partnership, there are two other rules that may come into play. In both cases, the rules are not directed solely to limited partnerships but apply generally to many investment activities. Limited partnerships, however, are often especially vulnerable to their application.

[A] At-Risk Rules

Congress enacted the "at-risk" provisions to curb what were perceived to be abuses in the use of nonrecourse financing. In a nonrecourse loan, the lender can look only to the financed asset for repayment. Before the at-risk rule was enacted, an investor could purchase an asset with nonrecourse financing, or through a limited partnership in which the investor was shielded from liability for partnership borrowings, and still take deductions based on the amount the investor put up in cash plus the amount of the debt (for which the investor had no real liability), that is, the tax basis.

Now, under the at-risk provisions, deductions from an activity may be taken to the extent of income from the activity. Income includes gain on sale of assets used in the activity as well as gain from a sale of the investment itself. In other words, to the extent an activity produces income, there is no at-risk limit on the deductions generated by that activity which may be used to offset that income.

In addition to deductions equal to income from an activity, an investor may take deductions in excess of income to the extent the investor is at risk. Amounts at risk in an activity include the amount of money invested, the adjusted basis of any property contributed to the activity, and borrowed amounts for which the borrower is personally liable for repayment or has pledged property other than the property in the activity to secure payment. The amount considered at risk for subsequent years is reduced by any allowable loss for the current year. Prior loss deductions are recaptured, that is, are reportable as income, if an amount formerly at risk in an activity becomes nonrecourse.

The at-risk rules are considered in detail at ¶ 302.

[B] Passive Loss Rule

The Tax Reform Act of 1986 placed a major restriction on the use of certain types of investments as a means to defer tax on income from sources other than these investments. The passive loss rule essentially provides that losses from "passive activities" can be used only to offset income from passive activities. Similarly, a tax credit generated by a passive activity can be used only to offset tax liability attributable to a passive activity.

Generally speaking, a passive activity is any activity that involves the conduct of a trade or business in which the taxpayer does not materially participate. Also included are most activities involving the rental of real or personal property. Portfolio income, such as dividends, interest, and royalties, is not considered income from passive activities under the rule. Any loss or credit that cannot be used because of the rule may be carried over to future years and applied to passive income or tax liability attributable to passive income in subsequent years.

The passive loss rules are treated in detail in Chapter 11.

.02 Limited Partnership Interests

In the case of a limited partnership interest, special considerations apply in the application of the passive loss rule. Since a limited partner generally is precluded from participating in the partnership's business if the partner is to retain limited liability status, material participation is not possible and a limited partnership interest is automatically passive. This means that income, deductions, and tax credits passed through to a limited partner generally are considered passive income, deductions, and credits, subject to these important exceptions:

1. Portfolio income (dividends, interest, etc.) earned by a limited partnership and passed through to the partners is not passive income under the passive loss rule. Rather, this income remains portfolio income to the limited partners.
2. The IRS has been given the power to issue regulations permitting or requiring income from certain limited partnership interests to be classified as passive income, portfolio income, or income not arising from a passive activity. Exercise of this authority could affect the classification of income passed through to limited partners by a limited partnership.
3. The Revenue Act of 1987 provides special rules for "publicly traded partnerships." Net income from a publicly traded partnership that is not subject to corporate taxation is treated as portfolio income and net losses from a publicly traded partnership can be used only to offset future income from that partnership. These special rules for publicly traded partnerships are discussed in further detail at ¶ 1105.

¶ 2103 MASTER LIMITED PARTNERSHIPS

Just what is a Master Limited Partnership (or MLP)? The easy answer is simply that an MLP is a "publicly traded limited partnership," that is, a partnership that has ownership interests, generally referred to as "units," which are traded on a recognized securities exchange or in the over-the-counter market. In reality, the MLP is not a legally defined entity and the term may be a misnomer. Regardless, it is a useful shorthand reference to an entire special class of limited partnership investments.

.01 Origins of Master Limited Partnerships

The beginnings of the MLP investment vehicle can be found in the explosive growth of tax shelters and tax-advantaged investments during the late 1970s and early 1980s. For various reasons, but most importantly for the tax advantage, these investments, as discussed above, usually were structured as limited partnerships. In most cases, these investments offered little in the way of liquidity, and investors were locked-in for a period of years.

Of all the many different investments packaged in limited partnership form and offered to investors as tax shelters during this period, one of the most popular was certainly oil and gas. As the price of oil shot from little more than $2 per barrel to well over $30 per barrel, oil and gas seemed like the sure ticket to riches. Even better, the tax advantages available to oil and gas investments meant that investors could make relatively sizable investments at little or no immediate out-of-pocket cash cost.

Oil exploration companies and other sponsors of oil and gas programs saw a virtually unlimited supply of capital and launched one program after another in seemingly endless succession. Some of the programs were good, others not so good, and still others were outright frauds. Nevertheless, they all had one thing in common: there was no real secondary market for the interests in the various programs acquired by the investors.

One approach tried early on in the boom of syndicated oil and gas investments as a means of achieving liquidity for investors in oil and gas programs was to have the investors contribute their various limited partnership interests to a corporation. A corporation would be formed so that investors in oil and gas properties could transfer their interests to the corporation in a "tax-free" incorporation transaction. These corporations would provide liquidity because investors who took advantage of the swap opportunity would end up owning shares in a publicly traded corporation, rather than holding limited partnership interests.

Although the corporation could provide liquidity, it defeated the primary reasons for using the limited partnership form in the first place. Any deductions generated by the oil and gas investment that could provide a tax benefit to the investors were locked in the corporation. Moreover, to the extent oil and gas income was produced, it was subject to a double tax, that is, once when earned by the corporation as corporate income, and again as individual income when distributed to the investor-shareholders as dividends. The need for liquidity on the part of oil and gas investors, combined with the desire to retain to whatever extent possible the tax advantages of the partnership form of organization, led one sponsor, Apache Petroleum Company, to form one of the first, if not the first, investment packages that would later fall under the heading of "Master Limited Partnership."

In 1981, Apache Petroleum Company offered to exchange units in Apache Partners (an MLP) for the limited partnership interests held by investors in the various oil and gas programs sponsored by Apache Petroleum Company the past 20 years. About 85 percent of the investors accepted the offer.

The Apache MLP thus became an early illustration of one way in which a master limited partnership may be formed: a promoter may gather together units from various partnerships under one roof. This new entity, organized as a limited partnership, continues the benefits of the limited partnership form of organization. Interests in the new partnership, however, are listed on a stock exchange and the investors achieve a degree of liquidity that they did not have prior to the formation of the master limited partnership. This type of MLP is generally referred to today as a *roll-up* master limited partnership, since smaller existing partnerships are "rolled up" into one large partnership.

It is these roll-up MLPs that probably account for the use of the word "Master" in the term "Master Limited Partnership." The concept underlying the term being simply that a number of smaller partnerships have been combined into one "master" partnership. The publicly traded limited partnership form, however, soon was adopted for many uses beyond that of a mere vehicle to house other partnership entities and provide investors with liquidity. But the MLP name stuck and is now applied to any publicly traded limited partnership, even those that do not involve the combination of many sub-partnerships.

.02 Evolution and Growth of the MLP Concept

Once the idea of the publicly traded limited partnership was accepted, it was not long before promoters, sponsors, corporate finance experts, investment bankers, and others found many different ways to employ the concept. Although uses for MLPs other than roll-ups were emerging before the Tax Reform Act of 1986, it was this legislation, even before its passage and while it was under discussion in Congress, that spurred many to act. For the first time, individual tax rates would be below corporate tax rates, thus providing an incentive for moving income off a corporate tax return and onto an individual tax return. Also, the restrictions on passive losses would create a demand for income generated by MLPs, which was thought at the time to be passive income that could be offset by passive losses from other partnership investments.

In addition to the roll-up MLPs, new MLPs were formed in a variety of ways. A corporation with substantial assets, especially real estate assets, would spin off those assets to an MLP. Shareholders who then became partners in the MLP would realize the yield from the assets in the partnership without the layer of corporate taxation that existed when the assets were held within the corporation. These MLPs, formed by a corporation transferring some of its assets to a limited partnership, are referred to as *roll-out* MLPs. In some cases, a corporation might sell units in the roll-out MLP in addition to distributing the MLP units to its shareholders.

Mature companies, those generating substantial cash income without a need to reinvest a substantial portion of that income in operations, also looked to the MLP for its potential as a tax saver. A corporation, by converting entirely to partnership form, could eliminate the corporate tax and provide its shareholders with the benefit of the lower individual tax rates on former corporate income as well. MLPs formed as a result of an existing corporation transferring all of its assets to a limited partnership are called *roll-over* MLPs.

In addition to roll-ups, roll-outs and roll-overs, still other MLPs were formed: first, to attract investor dollars, and second, to acquire assets for the partnership. These MLPs formed, as it were, from scratch are often called *roll-in* MLPs to distinguish them from the MLPs formed by existing entities for purposes other than attracting new investors.

.03 Impact of Tax Legislation on MLPs

As discussed at ¶ 1105.01, tax legislation enacted at the end of 1987 was directed at "publicly traded limited partnerships." MLPs are just that—limited partnerships in which interests are traded on a recognized stock exchange or in the over-the-counter market. Although the tax definition of "publicly traded limited partnership" encompasses more than MLPs, it is without question that MLPs are subject to the 1987 legislation.

As a result of the tax changes, some MLPs are or will be treated as corporations for tax purposes, and those MLPs that are not so treated are subject to a special passive loss rule that prevents losses generated by an MLP from being used to offset income from sources other than that particular MLP. Also, income from MLPs that are not treated as corporations is considered portfolio income under the passive loss rules so that losses from nonpublicly traded limited partnerships and various tax shelters cannot be used to offset the MLP income (see ¶ 1105.03).

While the 1987 tax changes certainly had an effect on MLPs, it by no means meant the end of the MLP as an attractive investment in the right circumstances. The law, perhaps, is more important in what it does not do than in what it does. The law does not treat as corporations a wide range of MLPs, especially those engaged in real estate operations or natural resource operations (primarily oil and gas, although others are covered). Moreover, any MLP in existence on December 17, 1987, cannot be treated as a corporation if it elects to continue its partnership status and consents to pay a tax of 3.5 percent of its gross income from the active conduct of trades or businesses for tax years after 1997.[1]

As for the MLPs that are not treated as corporations, the special passive loss rule should have a limited impact. Most MLPs were designed as income generators rather than as vehicles for creating tax losses.

---

[1] *See* Code Sec. 7704(g).

In the long run, the economics of the investments that may be packaged as MLPs will outweigh whatever negative influence the tax law has. Of course, the conversion of operating corporations to MLPs to avoid the corporate tax is no longer a viable proposition. However, the transfer of real estate and natural resource assets to MLPs as a means to enhance asset values and eliminate the potential double tax of corporate operation should continue, provided the underlying economics of the specific situation warrant it. Existing partnerships that will be treated as corporations down the line may have prices depressed by this fact. Some investors may find bargains among these issues in this environment.

.04 Real Estate MLPs

As an investment, real estate generally has performed well over the years, offering competitive returns and a hedge against inflation unmatched by most other assets. Although most real estate limited partnerships are not publicly traded and therefore are not within our definition of an MLP, many real estate MLPs have been formed as either roll-in or roll-out partnerships. On some limited occasions, existing real estate limited partnership units have been rolled-up into an MLP, but roll-ups are unusual.

For the most part, a real estate MLP must invest in or own mature properties, that is, properties that are already fully developed and producing steady rental income. A steady and consistent cash flow is a prerequisite if the market is to fully value the partnership units to reflect the value of the underlying real estate. This applies to MLPs of both the roll-out and the roll-in variety. As an inducement to investors, the sponsor of a roll-in MLP may set some minimum cash return to investors and agree to forgo management and other fees if it is not met. The corporate sponsor of a roll-out MLP may offer a similar deal, at least for some limited period of time, in order to support the post-roll-out market value of the MLP units.

A roll-up real estate MLP may end up with mature properties, but very real problems associated with rolling-up existing real estate partnerships are usually too much to overcome. It is extremely difficult, if not well nigh impossible, to value different properties in different markets with different rental rates in order to set a fair exchange rate for investors who swap their existing partnership units for new MLP units. In addition, there are extremely complex tax and accounting issues that must be addressed and overcome. When a sponsor does attempt to roll-up existing partnership units, it is likely to be a last-ditch effort to save partnerships with troubled or distressed properties by combining them with healthy partnerships.

Still another type of real estate MLP is one formed to invest in real estate mortgages rather than in the actual real estate. Mortgage MLPs either buy existing mortgages or provide new financing to other real estate partnerships or other investors. Since the underlying assets of a mortgage MLP are mortgages and the income is derived from interest on the mortgages, the stability and safety of cash flow is usually greater than in a partnership investing in the real estate directly. Of course, this greater stability and safety should be reflected in somewhat lower returns to investors.

Mortgage MLPs, as well as other real estate MLPs, should avoid classification as corporations under the tax rules that treat many publicly traded partnerships as corporations because of the exceptions which treat interest income and any gains from the sale of assets held for the production of interest income, as well as real estate rentals and gains from real estate sales, as qualifying income. Recall that a publicly traded partnership is not treated as a corporation and that partnership tax rules apply, if 90 percent or more of the partnership's gross income is "qualifying income."

Chapter 22
Real Estate Investment Trusts

¶ 2200 Overview of Chapter
¶ 2201 Tax Treatment of REITs
¶ 2202 Tax Treatment of REIT Shareholders
¶ 2203 Qualifying as a REIT

¶ 2200 OVERVIEW OF CHAPTER

An entity that meets the requirements and elects to be treated as a real estate investment trust (REIT) generally is treated as a partial conduit. A REIT is generally subject to the regular corporate tax[1] but receives a deduction for dividends paid provided that the amount of the dividends paid is not less than 90 percent of its ordinary income.[2]

Note that unlike a partnership, a REIT cannot serve as a conduit for losses. Losses suffered by a REIT are not passed through to shareholders to be deducted by them as is the case for partnership losses, which are passed through to partners and deducted by partners on their own tax returns (subject to the various limits on passive activity loss deductions discussed at ¶ 1101.02[A]). In general, an entity (corporation, trust, or association) may qualify as a REIT if it is a trust or corporation with at least 100 different freely transferable interests and if it would be taxed as an ordinary domestic corporation if it did not meet the REIT requirements.[3] These requirements relate to the composition of the entity's assets, which must be substantially real estate assets, and the entity's income, which must be realized in a substantial part from certain real estate and real estate-related sources.[4]

Also, a 100 percent tax is imposed on income from the sale of property held for sale to customers in the ordinary course of trade or business, other than foreclosure property.[5]

¶ 2201 TAX TREATMENT OF REITS

A REIT is subject to regular corporate income tax rates on its taxable income.[6] A REIT's taxable income generally is computed in the same manner as an ordinary corporation with several important differences:

---

[1] Code Sec. 857(b)(1).
[2] Code Sec. 857(a)(1).
[3] Code Sec. 856(a).
[4] Code Sec. 856(c).
[5] Code Sec. 857(b)(6).
[6] Code Sec. 857(b).

1. A REIT may deduct dividends paid to shareholders, but dividends attributable to net income from foreclosure property are not included.
2. A REIT's net income from foreclosure property or a prohibited transaction is disregarded.
3. The special deductions available to corporations, including the dividends-received deduction, are not available to a REIT, but the deduction for organizational expenditures (see ¶ 204.02[A]) is allowed.
4. Any tax imposed on redetermined rents, redetermined deductions, and excess interest, and any tax imposed for failures to meet the income, asset, or other REIT qualification requirements (see ¶ 2203) are deducted.
5. Taxable income is not annualized in the case of a change in accounting periods.

.01 Dividends-Paid Deduction

The deduction for dividends paid reduces a REIT's taxable income.[7] For purposes of the dividends-paid deduction, dividends declared and payable in October, November, or December of a calendar year are treated as paid on December 31 of that year if they are actually paid in January of the following calendar year.[8] Dividends paid by a qualified REIT must equal at least:

- 90 percent of its taxable income, determined without taking the deduction for dividends paid, and by excluding the net capital gain; plus
- 90 percent of its after-tax net income from foreclosure property; less
- Any excess noncash income.[9]

Excess noncash income is the excess of the sum of the following items over five percent of taxable income, before deduction of dividends paid, and excluding any net capital gain:

- The excess of the amount the REIT is required to include in income under a deferred rental agreement over the amount that the REIT would recognize under its normal method of accounting;
- Any income from the disposition of a real estate asset in a transaction that does not qualify as a like-kind exchange, unless the failure to qualify was due to willful neglect;
- For all REITs, regardless of their method of accounting, the excess of the original issue discount and coupon interest on REMIC interests over the amount of money and the fair market value of other property received during the tax year on the debt or interest; and
- Amounts includable in income by reason of cancellation of indebtedness.[10]

[A] Foreclosure Property

The deduction for dividends paid does not include income attributable to foreclosure property.[11] If a REIT has net income from foreclosure property, the deduction for dividends paid is the amount that bears the same ratio to the total

[7] Code Sec. 857(b)(2) and (3).
[8] Code Sec. 857(b)(9).
[9] Code Sec.857(a)(1)(A).
[10] Code Sec. 857(e).
[11] Code Sec. 857(b)(2)(B).

dividends paid or considered paid during the tax year as the REIT's taxable income bears to the sum of taxable income and the excess of net income from foreclosure property over the tax imposed on it. For these purposes, dividends paid or considered paid includes subsequent deficiency dividends. In addition, taxable income is determined without regard to the deduction for dividends paid.[12]

Foreclosure property can be any real property, interests in real property or personal property incident to the real property acquired by the REIT in a foreclosure or by a deed in lieu of foreclosure following a default of a debt obligation or after termination of a defaulted lease.[13] The REIT must elect to treat this property as foreclosure property.[14] Foreclosure property does not include property acquired as a result of defaulted indebtedness that arose from the sale of dealer property. Property acquired as a mortgagee-in-possession is not foreclosure property.[15]

[B] Designation of Qualified Dividends

A portion of a REIT's distribution may be classified as qualified dividend income subject to capital gain rates if it is attributable to income that was subject to corporate tax at the REIT level or a corporate dividend received as investment income by the REIT (and was qualified dividend income when it was received by the REIT). The amount of dividends paid by a REIT that may qualify for the reduced rate may not exceed the amount of aggregate qualifying dividends received by the REIT, and the aggregate amount of qualifying dividends received by the REIT must be less than 95 percent of its gross income.[16]

[C] Capital Gains

A REIT may be subject to tax on capital gains, but to the extent the REIT pays dividends out of capital gains, the dividends are deductible and taxed to the shareholders as capital gains.[17] To the extent a REIT retains and pays tax on capital gains, the shareholders include a proportionate amount of the capital gain in income and receive a credit for the tax paid by the REIT.[18]

For tax years beginning after 2017, a REIT is subject to tax at a 21-percent rate on its undistributed capital gain. The undistributed capital gain is the excess of the net capital gain over the deduction for dividends paid for capital gain only. For tax years beginning before 2018, if a REIT had any net capital gains in the tax year, the tax imposed was the lesser of: (1) the regular corporate tax on REIT taxable income; or (2) the regular corporate tax on REIT taxable income, determined by excluding net capital gains and by computing the deduction for dividends paid without capital gain dividends, plus 35 percent on the excess of the net capital gain minus any capital gain dividends paid.[19]

If a REIT retains any capital gain, it may elect to designate to its shareholders some or all of those undistributed amounts and the tax it paid on those gains. For this purpose, undistributed capital gain is the excess of net capital gain over the

[12] Reg. § 1.857-2(a)(3)(ii).

[13] Code Sec. 856(e)(1).

[14] Code Sec. 856(e)(5).

[15] Reg. § 1.856-6(b)(1).

[16] Code Sec. 857(c).

[17] Code Sec. 857(b)(3)(B).

[18] Code Sec. 857(b)(3)(D).

[19] Code Sec. 857(b)(3).

deduction for dividends paid for capital gain dividends only. The REIT must make the designation in a written notice to its shareholders at any time before the end of the 60-day period after the close of its tax year, or mailed with its annual report for the tax year. The REIT must also report any undistributed long-term capital gain not designated to shareholders and any net short-term capital gain.

.02 Built-in Gains Tax

A REIT may be subject to a modified version of the built-in gains tax imposed on an S corporation (see ¶ 206.02[A]) if property owned by a C corporation becomes property of the REIT when the corporation qualifies as a REIT or is transferred to the REIT, or if a C corporation engages in a conversion transaction involving a REIT.[20]

Built-in gain treatment does not apply to any conversion transaction to the extent that gain or loss otherwise is recognized on such conversion transaction by the C corporation that either qualifies as a REIT or that transfers property to a REIT.[21]

The built-in gains tax also does not apply to any corporation that:

1. Immediately prior to qualifying to be taxed as a REIT was subject to tax as a C corporation for a period not exceeding two taxable years; and
2. Immediately prior to being subject to tax as a C corporation was subject to tax as a RIC or REIT for a period of at least one tax year.

However, this exception does not apply to property acquired by the corporation while it was subject to tax as a C corporation in a transaction that results in the acquirer's basis in the property being determined by reference to a C corporation's basis in the property. Nor does it apply to REITs previously subject to built-in gain treatment.[22]

Regulations provide additional exceptions to the built-in gains tax for transfers of built-in gain property by a C corporation to a REIT to the extent the C corporation does not recognize the gain under the like-kind exchange provisions of Code Sec. 1031 (see ¶ 1302) or the involuntary conversion provisions of Code Sec. 1033 (see ¶ 1503).[23]

.03 Other Taxes

In addition to the tax on its taxable income, a REIT may be subject to the following additional taxes:

- A tax for failure to meet the REIT asset or income requirements for the tax year (see ¶ 2203);
- A tax at the highest corporate rate on net income from foreclosure property;[24]

[20] Reg. § 1.337(d)-7.

[21] Reg. § 1.337(d)-7(d)(1).

[22] Reg. § 1.337(d)-7(d)(2).

[23] Reg. § 1.337(d)-7(d)(3).

[24] Code Sec. 857(b)(4).

- A 100-percent tax on the net income derived from a prohibited transaction (*e.g.*, disposition of property, other than foreclosure property, that is held for sale to customers in the ordinary course of business);[25]
- A four-percent excise tax on the amount of any taxable income that is undistributed at the end of the tax year;[26] and
- A 100-percent tax on the excess portion of rents, deductions, and interest that must be reduced to clearly reflect income when a REIT and taxable REIT subsidiary engage in other than arm's length transactions.[27]

.04 REIT Subsidiaries

A REIT may own a qualified REIT subsidiary and treat all of the subsidiary's assets, liabilities, and items of income, deduction, and credit as its own.[28] A qualified subsidiary is any corporation other than a taxable REIT subsidiary, all of the stock of which is held by the REIT. A taxable REIT subsidiary is any corporation that is owned, in whole or in part, by the REIT and that both entities jointly elect to treat as a taxable REIT subsidiary.[29]

A taxable REIT subsidiary can be used by the REIT to provide noncustomary services to its tenants or to manage and operate properties without causing the amounts received or accrued to be disqualified as rents from real property. The election to be treated as a taxable REIT subsidiary can only be revoked with the consent of both the REIT and the subsidiary.

¶ 2202 TAX TREATMENT OF REIT SHAREHOLDERS

Shareholders generally treat distributions received from a REIT that are not designated as capital gain dividends as ordinary income to the extent of the REIT's earnings and profits. However, all or a portion of the distribution of an ordinary dividend may be a qualified dividend subject to the same tax rates as capital gain. The amount that a REIT can designate as qualified dividend income is limited to the sum of:

1. The REIT's qualified dividend income for the tax year;
2. The excess of the sum of REIT taxable income for the preceding tax year and the income subject to tax as built-in gain for that preceding tax year, over the taxes payable by the REIT under the REIT rules (see ¶ 2201) and as built-in gains for that preceding tax year; and
3. The amount of earnings and profits that were distributed by the REIT for the tax year and accumulated in tax years in which the entity was not a REIT.

The amount of qualified dividends must be specified by the REIT in a written notice to shareholders no later than 60 days after the close of the tax year.[30]

When a publicly offered REIT distributes stock to shareholders who have the option to receive cash or stock, the distribution is a Code Sec. 301 distribution that

[25] Code Sec. 857(b)(6).
[26] Code Sec. 4981.
[27] Code Sec. 857(b)(7).
[28] Code Sec. 856(i).
[29] Code Sec. 856(l).
[30] Code Sec. 857(c)(2).

generally results in a dividend.[31] The treatment applies if, among other requirements, each shareholder has a cash or stock election for part or all of the distribution and at least 20 percent of the aggregate declared distribution consists of money. The value of the stock received by any shareholder in lieu of cash is considered to be equal to the amount of cash for which the stock is substituted. If a shareholder participates in a dividend reinvestment plan, the stock received by that shareholder pursuant to the reinvestment plan is treated as received in exchange for cash received in the distribution.

Distributions in excess of the REIT's earnings and profits (other than deficiency dividends, see ¶ 2203.04) are a return of the shareholder's basis.

Dividends received by a corporation from a REIT do not qualify for the dividends-received deduction for corporations.

.01 Capital Gain

Shareholders treat distributions designated as capital gain dividends as long-term capital gain, regardless of how long they held their interests in the REIT.[32] This includes any undistributed capital gains designated by the REIT (see ¶ 2201.01[C]).

Shareholders are entitled to a credit or refund for their portion of any capital gain taxes paid by the REIT on undistributed capital gain. In addition, a shareholder must increase the basis of his or her REIT shares by the difference between his or her portions of the undistributed capital gain and the deemed taxes paid.

If a shareholder sells shares in a REIT held six months or less, and the REIT had designated undistributed capital gain to the shares or the shareholder had received a capital gain dividend, then any loss on the sale of those shares is treated as a long-term capital loss to the extent of the long-term capital gain dividend.[33] This rule does not apply to losses on the disposition of REIT stock under a plan for the periodic liquidation of the stock.

The IRS has provided guidance that a REIT and its shareholders must use in applying the net capital gain tax rates to capital gain dividends.[34]

.02 After-Tax Year Distributions

A REIT that declares a dividend, including a capital gain dividend, before the due date for filing its return for a tax year (including extensions), but distributes the dividend after the close of the tax year, may treat the dividend as having been paid during the tax year if the entire declared dividend is paid within the 12-month period following the close of the tax year and no later than the date of the first regular dividend payment after the declaration.[35] The shareholder treats the dividend as received in the tax year in which the distribution is made. This rule does not apply, however, to dividends declared in October, November, or December that are treated as paid on December 31, even though they are actually paid in January of the following calendar year (see ¶ 2201.01).

[31] Rev. Proc. 2017-45, 2017-35 IRB 216.

[32] Code Sec. 857(b)(3).

[33] Code Sec. 857(b)(8).

[34] Notice 97-64, 1997-2 CB 323; Notice 2004-39, 2004-1 CB 982.

[35] Code Sec. 858.

¶ 2203 QUALIFYING AS A REIT

Under Code Sec. 856, a corporation, trust, or association that acts as an investment agent specializing in real estate and real estate mortgages may elect to be a REIT. An entity qualifies as a REIT if it makes an election and meets requirements as to ownership and organization, source of income, investment of assets, and distribution of income to shareholders. A REIT election may be revoked voluntarily, but the organization will be prohibited from making a new REIT election for the four tax years after revocation. An organization may elect REIT status even if it fails the ownership test in the first year.

If an entity fails to satisfy one or more requirements of REIT qualification other than the income tests (see ¶ 2203.02) or asset requirements (see ¶ 2203.03), then the entity may still retain REIT qualification if the failure is due to reasonable cause and not willful neglect. However, the REIT must pay a penalty of $50,000 for each failure.[36]

.01 Ownership and Organization Requirements

To be eligible for REIT status, an entity must be taxable as a domestic corporation.[37] Foreign entities (corporations, trusts, and associations) and financial institutions, such as banks or insurance companies, are not eligible.

A REIT cannot directly manage the properties that it owns rather, it must employ independent contractors. Operations of the REIT must be overseen by a board of trustees, of which a majority must be "outside" trustees under the North American Securities Administrators Association (NASAA) guidelines. These restrictions may help in protecting the interests of investors (who have ultimate control to the same extent as shareholders of a corporation), but they greatly limit the operating flexibility of a REIT.

A REIT must adopt a calendar year accounting period.[38] An entity making a REIT election may change its accounting period to a calendar year without first obtaining IRS approval.

Beneficial ownership in a REIT must be evidenced by transferable shares or certificates of interest. The REIT must have at least 100 beneficial owners for at least 335 days of a 12-month tax year.[39] Ownership cannot be closely held, but attribution to another partner in a partnership is ignored.[40] Also, a pension trust generally is not treated as a single owner, and any REIT shares or certificates of interest held by the trust are treated as directly held by its beneficiaries. This look-through rule for pensions does not apply if persons disqualified from dealings with the pension trust own five percent or more of the value of the REIT and the REIT has accumulated earnings and profits attributable to a year it did not qualify as a REIT.

---

[36] Code Sec. 856(g)(5).

[37] Code Sec. 856(a).

[38] Code Sec. 859.

[39] Code Sec. 856(a) and (b).

[40] Code Sec. 856(h).

A corporation that was either a distributing or controlled corporation in a Code Sec. 355 distribution after December 6, 2015, is not eligible to make a REIT election during the ten-year period after the date of distribution.[41]

.02 Income Requirements

An entity must satisfy the following income tests each tax year in order to qualify as a REIT:

1. At least 95 percent of the entity's gross income must be from rents from real property, gain from the disposition of real property, dividends, interest, gains from dispositions of stock and securities, abatements and refunds of real property taxes, income and gain from foreclosure property, consideration received or accrued for agreeing to make loans secured by real property mortgages or interests or to purchase or lease real property, and certain mineral royalty income earned from real property owned by a timber REIT;[42] and
2. At least 75 percent of the entity's gross income, excluding income from prohibited transactions, must be from real property sources, which include rents from real property, interest on real property mortgages, gain from the disposition of a real estate asset (other than a nonqualified publicly offered REIT debt instrument), dividends and gain from the disposition of shares in other qualifying REITs, abatements and refunds of real property taxes, income and gain from foreclosure property, consideration received or accrued for agreeing to make loans secured by real property mortgages or interests or to purchase or lease real property, and qualified temporary investment income.[43]

For both tests, an entity's gross income does not include the gross income from prohibited transactions, foreign currency gains in the form of passive foreign exchange gains, or real estate foreign exchange gains.[44] Gross income also does not include gain from hedging transactions to reduce the risk of debt incurred to acquire or hold real estate or to manage the risk of currency fluctuations.[45] The IRS may designate income as not constituting gross income for purposes of the REIT income tests. Alternatively, the IRS may designate nonqualified income as qualified income.[46]

Real property includes land, inherently permanent structures, and structural components of inherently permanent structures.[47]

Rents from real property generally include rents from interests in real property, amounts received for customary services (utilities, maintenance), even if separate charges are made for the services, and rent attributable to personal property incidental to rental of real property if the amount allocable to personal property is 15 percent or less of the total rent.[48] Rents from real property do not

[41] Code Sec. 856(c)(8).
[42] Code Sec. 856(c)(2).
[43] Code Sec. 856(c)(3).
[44] Code Sec. 856(n).
[45] Code Sec. 856(c)(5)(G).
[46] Code Sec. 856(c)(5)(J).
[47] Reg. § 1.856-10.
[48] Code Sec. 856(d).

include rents that depend on income or profits derived by any person from the property; exceptions exist to this general prohibition. Rents from real property also do not include amounts received from:

1. Any noncorporate person in which the REIT owns ten percent or more in that person's assets or profits;
2. A corporation, if the REIT owns ten percent or more of either the voting stock or the value of all shares issued by the corporation; or
3. Amounts received based on income or profits of a tenant or debtor (unless certain conditions are met).

Amounts paid to a REIT by a taxable REIT subsidiary (see ¶ 2201.04) are treated as rents from real property if at least 90 percent of the property at issue is rented to unrelated parties at rents comparable to those paid by other tenants for comparable space.[49] In addition, a taxable REIT subsidiary may lease a qualified lodging facility or a qualified health care property, and the rents paid are treated as rents from real property so long as the facility is operated by an eligible independent contractor for a fee.

An entity that fails to meet either of the income tests for any tax year may still qualify as a REIT if it identifies the failure on a separate schedule prescribed by the IRS and the failure is due to reasonable cause and not willful neglect.[50] The REIT also must pay a tax equal to the greater of the amount by which the entity fails to meet either the 95-percent or 75-percent income test, multiplied by the fraction of the REIT's taxable income over its gross income for the tax year.[51]

.03 Asset Requirements

A REIT must meet the following requirements regarding its assets at the close of each quarter of the tax year:

1. At least 75 percent of the value of its total assets must consist of real estate assets (including interests in a real estate mortgage investment conduit (REMIC) (see ¶ 2300), cash items (including receivables), and government securities;
2. No more than 25 percent of the value of its total assets can be invested in securities other than those representing real estate assets or government securities;
3. No more than 20 percent of the value of its total assets can be invested in securities of taxable REIT subsidiaries (25 percent for tax years beginning before 2018);
4. No more than 25 percent of the value of its total assets can be invested in nonqualified publicly offered REIT debt instruments, as defined under Code Sec. 856(c)(5)(L)(ii); and
5. Except for government securities and securities of taxable REIT subsidiaries (see ¶ 2201.04), no more than five percent of the value of its total assets

[49] Code Sec. 856(d)(8).

[50] Code Sec. 856(c)(6).

[51] Code Sec. 857(b)(5).

can be invested in the securities of any one issuer, and investment in the securities of any one issuer cannot exceed ten percent of the total value or voting power of that issuer's outstanding securities.[52]

For purposes of the limitation that a REIT may not hold more than ten percent of the value of the outstanding securities of a single issuer, certain obligations are not treated as securities of an issuer, including straight debt securities, loans to an individual or estate, Code Sec. 467 rental agreements (see ¶ 404.01), or any obligation to pay rents from real property.[53] A straight debt security is debt payable on demand or on a specified date where the interest rate and interest payments are not contingent on profits, the borrower's discretion, or similar factors, and there is no convertibility (directly or indirectly) into stock. However, special rules permit certain contingencies of straight debt.

[A] Failure to Meet Asset Requirements

An entity that fails to meet any of the asset requirements for a particular tax quarter (other than the five-percent and ten-percent asset tests) may still qualify as a REIT if:

- It identifies the failure on a separate schedule prescribed by the IRS;
- Failure is due to reasonable cause and not willful neglect;
- The assets causing the failure are disposed of within six months of the last day of the quarter in which the failure occurred; and
- The REIT pays an excise tax.[54]

The excise tax is the greater of $50,000 or the tax on the net income generated by the assets during the period of failure at the highest applicable corporate rate. A REIT will not lose its exempt status for a *de minimis* failure to meet the five-percent or ten-percent asset requirements if the total value of the assets causing the failure does not exceed the lesser of one percent of the total value of the REIT's assets at the end of a tax quarter or $10 million. The REIT must dispose of the assets causing the failure within six months of the last day of the quarter in which the failure occurred.

[B] Ancillary Personal Property

In tax years beginning after 2015, the 95-percent income test, the 75-percent asset test, and the 75-percent income test can include rents from personal property and gains from the distribution of personal property that is ancillary to real property as well as obligations secured by mortgages where no more than 15 percent of the total fair market value of all secured property is represented by personal property.[55]

.04 Deficiency Dividends

If there is a determination that adjustments are needed to certain amounts that a REIT reports for a tax year, and if the adjustments could cause the entity to lose its REIT status, the REIT may avoid disqualification by making deficiency dividend

[52] Code Sec. 856(c)(4).

[53] Code Sec. 856(m).

[54] Code Sec. 856(c)(7).

[55] Code Sec. 856(c)(9).

distributions, and may claim a deduction for the dividends paid.[56] For a REIT, an adjustment can be:

- An increase in the sum of its taxable income (determined without regard to its dividends-paid deduction and excluding any net capital gain), plus the excess of its net income from foreclosure property minus the tax on the foreclosure property net income;
- An increase in the amount of the excess of its net capital gain over its deduction for capital gain dividends paid; or
- A decrease in its dividends-paid deduction (determined without regard to capital gains dividends).

The deficiency dividend procedure for REITs is the same as that for regulated investment companies (RICs) or mutual funds.

[56] Code Sec. 860; Reg. § § 1.860-1 through 1.860-5.

Chapter 23
Real Estate Mortgage Investment Conduits

¶ 2300 Overview of Chapter
¶ 2301 Investor Interests
¶ 2302 Tax Treatment of REMICs

¶ 2300 OVERVIEW OF CHAPTER

In the Tax Reform Act of 1986, Congress provided special tax rules[1] for what it dubbed "real estate mortgage investment conduits" or "REMICs." In general, a REMIC is a fixed pool of mortgages with multiple classes of interests held by investors. Any entity, whether a corporation, partnership, or trust, that meets specified requirements may elect to be treated as a REMIC.[2] Also, a segregated pool of assets may qualify as a REMIC as if it were a legal entity, provided the necessary requirements are met. In short, the REMIC is a replacement entity for limited partnerships, REITS, and mutual funds that in the past have invested in real estate mortgages.

¶ 2301 INVESTOR INTERESTS

As long as the requirements now specified in the Internal Revenue Code for qualification as a REMIC are met, the REMIC is not treated as a separate taxable entity.[3] Rather, the income of the REMIC is allocated to, and taken into account by, the holders of interests in the REMIC.[4] These interests are divided into "regular interests," which can be further divided into more than one class, and the single class of "residual interests."

The terms of a regular interest in a REMIC must be fixed and unconditionally entitle the holder to receive a specified principal or similar amount and base interest or similar payments, if any, at or before maturity on a fixed rate. (A variable rate may be used under regulations specified by the Internal Revenue Service.) These regular interests may be issued in the form of debt, stock, partnership interests, interests in a trust, or any form of legal organization permissible under state law.[5]

[1] Code Secs. 860A–860G.
[2] Code Sec. 860D(a).
[3] Code Sec. 860A(a).
[4] Code Sec. 860A(b).
[5] Code Sec. 860G(a)(1).

A residual interest is any interest in the REMIC other than a regular interest, and which is so designated by the REMIC. There can be only one class of residual interests, and all distributions, if any, made to holders of residual interests must be made on a pro rata basis.[6]

¶ 2302 TAX TREATMENT OF REMICS

A REMIC is not a taxable entity for federal income tax purposes.[7] The income of a REMIC generally is taken into account by holders of regular and residual interests as briefly described below.[8] This conduit feature of the REMIC applies regardless of whether the REMIC otherwise would be treated as a corporation, partnership, trust, or any other legal entity. In enacting the REMIC provisions into the tax law, Congress wanted them to be the exclusive set of rules for the treatment of all transactions relating to the REMIC and holders of REMIC interests, if the requirements for REMIC status are met by the entity. For instance, a REMIC that is organized as a partnership and that would be treated as a partnership under the tax law if there were no special REMIC provisions is not treated as a partnership if the REMIC requirements are met and an election under Code Sec. 860D(b) is made for its first taxable year. In such a case, the partnership tax rules do not apply to any transaction involving the REMIC or to any holders of interests in the REMIC.

.01 Regular Interests

The holder of a regular interest generally is taxed as if the regular interest were a debt instrument to which the rules of taxation applicable to debt instruments apply,[9] except that the holder is required to report income attributable to the regular interest on the accrual method of accounting regardless of his regular method of accounting.[10] In the case of a regular interest that is not an actual debt instrument, the amount of the fixed unconditional payment is treated as the stated principal amount of the instrument, and the periodic payments, if any, that are based on the amount of the fixed unconditional payment are treated as stated interest payments.[11] In other words, consistent with the conduit nature of the REMIC, the holders of regular interests generally take into account that portion of the REMIC's income that would be taken into account by an accrual method holder of a debt instrument with terms equivalent to the terms of the regular interest.

.02 Residual Interests

The holder of a residual interest in a REMIC takes into account as ordinary income the daily portion of the taxable income or net loss of the REMIC for each day during the taxable year in which the interest was held.[12] The taxable income or net loss of the REMIC for determining this pass through is figured in the same way that a calendar year individual using accrual accounting would figure taxable income, but with certain modifications.[13] The most important modification is that

[6] Code Sec. 860G(a)(2).

[7] Code Sec. 860A(a).

[8] Code Sec. 860A(b).

[9] Code Sec. 860B(a).

[10] Code Sec. 860B(b).

[11] Code Sec. 860B(c).

[12] Code Sec. 860C(a).

[13] Code Sec. 860C(b).

the REMIC deducts amounts that would be deductible as interest if the regular interests were treated as indebtedness of the REMIC. This provision, in effect, prevents the holders of residual interests from being taxed on income allocable to the regular interests.

[A] Distributions

Actual distributions from the REMIC are not included in the income of a residual holder to the extent that distributions do not exceed the holder's adjusted basis for the interest.[14] Distributions in excess of basis are treated as income from the sale of the residual interest.[15] The amount of any net loss of the REMIC that may be taken into account by the holder of a residual interest is limited to the holder's adjusted basis. Any loss disallowed as a deduction because of this provision may be carried over and used in the future, but only to offset future income generated by the same REMIC.[16]

[B] Income and Basis

These rules on the treatment of the income and loss of a REMIC allocable to residual interests closely parallel those applicable to partnerships, as discussed at ¶ 203.02. The method of determining the adjusted basis of a residual interest is also similar to the method of determining the basis of a partnership interest. A holder's initial basis (cost) is increased by the amount of taxable income of the REMIC that is taken into account by the holder. The basis is decreased, but not below zero, by the amount of any distributions received from the REMIC and by the amount of any net loss of the REMIC that is taken into account by the holder.[17]

Essentially, what Congress said in passing the REMIC provisions is that, no matter how an investor makes an indirect investment in a pool of mortgages, the tax treatment will be the same. Regardless of whether an investor acquires an interest in a pool of mortgages through a real estate limited partnership, a REIT, or a mutual fund, if the investor's interest has the characteristics of debt, it will be treated as debt for tax purposes. On the other hand, if the investor's interest has the characteristics of a sharing of profits and losses, that is, an investment in which the investor is assuming a position closely akin to that of a limited partner, the interest in the REMIC will be treated in the same fashion as a partnership interest for tax purposes.

[14] Code Sec. 860C(c)(1).

[15] Code Sec. 860C(c)(2).

[16] Code Sec. 860C(e)(2).

[17] Code Sec. 860C(d).

Case Table

References are to paragraph (¶) numbers.

A

Aberle, H.C. 1203.02
Abrams, P. 1501.01
Abramson, J.G. 1202.01
Ackerman Buick, Inc. . . . . . . 901.02[C]
Akers, L.R. . . . . 102.02[A]
Alabama-Georgia Syrup Co. . 703.01[F]
Alaska Realty Co. 601.01
Alderson, J. . . . . 1302.03[A]
Allen, A.L. . . . . 703.01[F]
Allen, E.H. . . . . 302.03[A]
Allen, G.P. . . . . 1302.02[B]
Almac's, Inc. . . . . 703.01[F]
Amdahl Corporation. . . . . . . 2002.01[D]
American Dental Co. . . . . . . 1201.01[A]
American Spring & Wire Specialty Co. . . . . 502.02[A]
Ames, L.S. 601.02
Amey, E.S. 401.02
Anderson. 1801.02
Anderson, P.C. . . . . 701.02[B]
Anderson-Tully Co. 703.08
Anover Realty Corp. . . . . 301.01[A]
Aragona, Frank, Trust 1103.06
Arkin, L.J. 1203.02
Astor Holding Co. 406.02
Atmore Realty Co. . . . . 1202.01[A]
Au, C.T. . . . . 1002.01[A]
Ayling, W.A. . . . . 1001.01[B]

B

Bachman, C.F. . . . . 501.01[A]
Bailey 1103.06
Baldwin, C.E. . . . . 704.01[B]
Bank of Houston. . . . . 703.01[F]
Bardes, O.L. 602.02
Baron Est., S. . . . . 101.02[A]
Bartell Est. . . . . 1302.01[A]
Baton Coal Co. 402.01
Bayly, R.C., ... 2001
Beck, J.C. . . . . 101.02[C]
Bee Holding Co. . . . . 703.01[F]
Beecham, Inc. 601.02; 602.01
Beeghly, L.A. . . . . 1502.03[A]
Bell Electric Co. . . . . 602.02[A]
Bell, I.L. 703.06
Bellingham Cold Storage Co. . . . . 402.02[A]
Bender, H.G. 401.04
Berberovich, T. . . . . 1002.01[B]
Berliner, H.A. . . . . 1202.01[B]
Berry, M. 305.04
Best, L.J. . . . . 703.01[F]
Beus, E.H. 405.01
Bev Anderson Chevrolet, Inc. . . . . 703.04[A]
Bidart Bros. . . . . 1301.02[B]
Biedenharn Realty Co. . . . . . 1002.01[A]
Biggs, F.B. . . . 1302.03[A]; 1302.03[B]
Bingham, H.P. . . . . 1203.01[B]
Birdsong 1103.06
Biscayne Bay Island, Co. . . . 1001.01[A]
Bjerke, L.A. . . . . 302.03[A]
Bjornsen Investment Corp. 303.01
Black, L.C. 704.03
Blake, Jr., T.W., ... 201
Blatt Co., M.E. 602.01; 602.02
Bliss, A. 703.08
Bloomington Coca-Cola Bottling Co. 1302.01
Blum, A. 1203.02
Boddie, C.A. . . . . 703.01[F]
Boland, J.L. . . . . 703.01[F]
Bolker, J.R. . . . . 1302.01[A]
Bollinger, Jr., J.C. 201.02
Bolton, D.D. . . . . 1803.02[B]
Bonwit Teller & Co., ... 501
Boos, H. 502.03
Boree, G.G. . . . . 1002.01[B]
Bosch Est., H.J. 202.04

Boston Fish Market Corp. . . 502.01[B]; 602.02[B]
Botany Worsted Mills. . . . . . . 703.04[A]
Boyd Est., E.B. 202.02
Boylston Market Assn. 703.06
Bradford Hotel Operating Co. . . . . 502.01[B]
Brauer, A.E. . . . . 1302.03[A]
Breece Veneer & Panel Co. 305.04
Brookshire Brothers Holding, Inc. & Subsidiaries. 903.01
Brown, A.M. . . . . 701.02[B]
Brown, I. 602.01
Brown, K.A. . . . . 703.01[F]
Brown Printing Co. . . . . 401.01; 401.04; 401.04[B]
Bryce's Mountain Resort, Inc. . . . . 1001.02[A]
Buff, W. . . . . 704.01[B]
Bullard Est., P.E. 1602.02
Burden, I.T. . . . . 703.01[F]
Burgess Poultry Market, Inc. . . . 701.02
Burnet, D. . . . . 1401.02[E]
Burns, H.F. 1501.01
Bush Terminal Buildings Co. . . . 703.08
Byram, J.D. . . . . 1001.01[A]

C

Calcasieu Paper Co., Inc. 305.04
Caldwell Milling Co. 704.02
California Delta Farms, Inc. 1302.01
Campbell, T.O. . . . . 703.01[F]
Capitol Motor Car Co. . . . . . 1503.02[A]
Car-Ron Asphalt Paving Co. . . 703.05[B]
Casalina Corp. 703.08
Casey, G.B. . . . . 704.01[A]
Cedar Park Cemetery Assn., Inc. 1001.01
Century Electric Co. . . . . 305.01[B]
Chevy Chase Land Co. of Montogomery County, Md. 703.08; 801.05
Chevy Chase Motor Co., Inc. . . . . 703.04[A]
City National Bank. . . . . 703.01[F]
Clarkston, J.M. . . . . 1201.02[B]
Clayton, Jr., C.W. . . . . 703.04[A]
Clayton, R.M. . . . . 1001.01[B]
C.L. Baumann & Co. . . . . 502.01[A]
Clem, J.R. 801.05
Click, D.H. 1302.01
Clinton Hotel Realty Corp. 406.02
Coastal Terminals, Inc. . . . . 1302.03[A]
Cohn, B.W. . . . . 703.01[F]
Collins Est., M.A. 1001.02
Colony, Inc. . . . . . . 1001.01; 1001.02[A]
Colston, W.A. . . . . 704.01[B]
Comdisco, Inc. . . . . 603.02[A]
Community Bank. . . . . 1202.02[C]
Conners. 1002.01
Conners, R.R. 1204.01
Conte, J. 202.02
Cooke, C.C. . . . . 1201.02[B]
Cooper, R.D. . . . . 401.04[B]
Cooperative Publishing Co. 1202.01
Corley, D.J. . . . . 1301.01[B]
Cothran, J.D. 703.08
Country Club Estates, Inc. 1001.02
Coupe, L.Q. . . . . 703.08; 1302.03[A]; 1302.03[B]
Crane, B.B. . . . . 101.02; 1202.01[A]; 1301.01[B]; 1602.01
Creston Corp. . . . . 102.02[A]
Critzer Est., W. . . . . 1002.01[B]
Crowley, Milner & Co. . . . . . 305.01[B]
Cullinan, J.S. . . . . 1001.01[B]
Cunningham, G.H. 602.02

D

D'Alonzo, N. . . . . 1201.02[B]
Dallas Transfer & Terminal Warehouse Co. . . . . 1201.01[B]
Davis, B. . . . . 801.03[C]
Davis, B.E. 1501.01
Dawson-Spatz Packing Co. . . 602.02[A]
Dean Est., W.K. 1002.01
DeMatteo Construction Co., M. . 601.03
Detroit Consolidated Theatres, Inc. . . . . 301.01[A]
Diamond, S. . . . . 203.02[B]
DiLaura, W. . . . . 301.03[B]; 1201.01[A]
Divine, Jr., T.M. 1001.02

Dixie Manor, Inc. . . . . 102.02[C]
Drybrough, F.W., ... 1702
Duaine, L.A. . . . . 102.02[C]
Dumble Co., E. . . . . 703.01[F]

E

Ebben, L.G. 1602.02
Edwards Industries, Inc. . . . . 1301.02[C]
Ehlers, W.A. . . . . 1301.01[B]
Electro-Chemical Engraving Co., Inc. . . . . 1202.01[B]
Eller, W.E. . . . . 703.04[B]
Endres Floral Co. . . . . 102.02[C]
Enid Ice & Fuel Co. . . . . 1504.02[A]
Ennis, N.J. . . . . 1301.01[B]
Enright Est., J.M. . . . . 701.02[B]
Equitable Publishing Co. . . . . 401.04[B]
Ettle Co., Inc. . . . . 703.04[A]
Evans, S.C. . . . . 703.01[F]
Ewing, R.W. . . 1001.01[B]; 1301.01[B]
Exelon Corporation . . . . 305.01[A]

F

Farmers Creamery Corp. of Fredericksburg, Va. . . . . . 703.01[F]
Fegan, T.B. . . . . 401.04[B]
Ferguson, Jr., W.M. 1501.01
Fieland, L.C. 601.02
Fifth Avenue-14th Street Corp. . . . . 301.03[B]
Film N' Photos, Inc. . . . . 102.02[C]
First American National Bank Of Nashville. . . . . 703.01[F]
Fleming, J.E. . . . . 102.02[C]
Fleming, W. . . . . 1302.01[A]
Follender, D.B. . . . . 302.03[A]
Forrest, D.W. 1501.01
Foster, W.N. . . . . 1002.01[B]
Franklin Est., C.T. . . . . 101.02[C]
Freeland, E.L. 1002; 1203.02
Frick, C.F. . . . . 703.05[A]
Frishkorn Real Estate Co. 1001.01
Furmanski, A.R. . . . . 703.04[B]

G

Galt, A.T. . . . . 501.01[C]; 901.02[C]
Gem, Inc. . . . . 402.02[A]
General American Life Insurance Co. . . . . 301.03[A]; 303.01
Geneva Drive-In Theatre, Inc. . . . 601.03
Georgia Ry. & Electric Co. 601.01
Gersten, A. 1001.02
Gibbons, J.M. 704.03
Giffin, E.A. . . . . 703.05[A]
Gilbert, A.J. 201; . . . . 704.01[A]
Gladdings Dry Goods Co., ... 201
Goodman, D.B. . . . . 1002.01[A]
Goodwin, R.C. . . . . 1701.02[A]
Gordy, R.E. 1003.01
Gorod, G., ... 703
Gorod, G.C., ... 703
Goshorn 1103.06
Grannemann, E. . . . . 1401.01[B]
Gray, A.J. . . . . 502.02[B]
Green, C.C. . . . 1502.03[A]; 1502.03[B]
Green, P. 1203.02
Green Forest Manufacturing, Inc. 903.01
Grodt & McKay Realty, Inc., ... 201
Guelph Hotel Corp. 502.03
Guenther, H.W. 703.06
Guest, W.F.C. 1602.02
Gutwirth, C. 1501.01

H

Haag, W.J. 401.03
Haggard, D.M. 405.01
Hahn, L. 202.02
Hamilton & Main, Inc. . . . . . . 502.01[B]
Hamilton, J.R. . . . . 1501.02[C]
Hammel, G. . . . . . . 1202.01; 1202.01[A]; 1202.01[B]
Handlery Hotels, Inc. . . . . . . 502.02[A]
Hanover, H.R. . . . . 1504.02[B]
Harbor Lofts Associates . . . 1601.04[C]
Harcum, R.L. . . . . . . 406.02; 1002.01[B]
Harris, A.F. . . . . 801.03[C]
Harris, E. . . . . 1202.01[A]

Haspel, R.B. 801.05
Hawkins, J.C. . . . . 1202.01[A]
Heath, C.J. . . . . 1202.02[C]
Heer-Andres Investment Co., ... 403
Heininger, S.B. . . . . 703.05[B]
Held, E.R. 1204.01
Henry, D.L., ... 1804
Hensel Phelps Construction Co. . . . . 203.02[B]
Herndon, R. . . . . 1002.01[B]
Hibernia National Bank 601.01
Higgins, E. . . . . 1201.02[C]
Hill Admr., S.A. . . . . 1202.01[A]
Hill, Jr., C.M. . . . . 801.03[C]
Hirsch, K. . . . . 301.03[B]
Hirschel, J., ... 703
Hoffman, R.C. 701.02
Hoffman, W.W. 1203.02
Home Agency Co. . . . . 1201.02[B]
Home Trust Co. . . . . 502.01[A]
Hoopengarner, H.H. 402.01
Hooper, H.M. . . . . 1301.02[C]
Hopkins, J.R. . . . 704.01[B]; 1504.02[A]
Hort, W.M. . . . . 502.01[B]
Hospital Corporation of America . . . . 102.02[C]
Houston Chronicle Publishing Co. . . . . 502.02[A]
Hoven, V. . . . . 1301.02[C]
Hradesky, F.J., ... 1702
Huber, P.O. . . . . 703.01[F]
Hudlow, Jr., W.C. . . . . 703.01[F]
Hudson, L., ... 703
Hughes, P.C. . . . . 1201.02[B]
Human Engineering Institute. . . . . 703.01[F]
Hurd, P. . . . . 102.02[A]
Hurlburt Est., C. . . . . 1301.01[B]
Hyde Park Realty, Inc. 403.01

I

Idaho Power Co. 103.01
Imerman, S. 401.04
International Building Co. . . . 703.01[F]
Issac G. Johnson & Co. 703.08
Iske, J. 703.08

J

J.& E. Enterprises, Inc. . . 403.01; 406.02
Jackson, H.L. . . . . 1501.02[C]
Jacobson, R.V. . . . . . . 703.05[A]; 703.06
James v. U.S. . . . . 101.02[B]
James, W.A. . . . . 204.02[A]
Jayne Est., G.W. 1503.01
John Richard Corp. . . . . 1503.02[F]
John Weller Wood. . . . . 1002.01[A]
Johnson, A.B. . . . . 1502.03[A]
Johnson, J.A. . . . . 1401.02[C]
Jones, A.R. . . . . 703.01[F]
Jones, J.M. . . . . 703.01[F]
Jordan Marsh Co. . . . . 305.01[B]
Journal-Tribune Publishing Co. . . 601.01
Juister, Jr., M.H. . . . . 1201.01[A]

K

Kauai Terminal, Ltd. 703.06
Kaufman, A.A. . . . . 1203.01[A]
Keeling, G.W. 402.01
Keiler, II, J.W. . . . . 502.02[A]
Keller, R.E. . . . . 1201.02[C]
Keller Street Development Co. . . . . 703.04[A]
Kelley, J.W. . . . . 1002.01[B]
King Radio Corp. Inc. . . . . . . 102.02[C]
Knoxville Iron Co. . . . . 703.01[F]
Koch, C.E. . . . . 1302.01[A]
Kohler-Campbell Corp. 403.01
Kolowich, G.J. . . . . 1202.01[A]
Kummer Realty Co., P.E. . . . . 703.04[A]
Kurzet. 903.01

L

La France Wine Co. . . . . 801.03[C]
Laguna Land & Water Co. 1001.02
Lakeland Grocery Co. . . . . . 1201.01[B]
Land Dynamics. 1302.01
Lang Chevrolet Co. 703.07
Langley Park Apartments, Sec. C., Inc. . . . . 703.04[A]

Lansburgh, L. . . . . 302.03[B]
LaPort, F.L. 1203.02
Latter, H. . . . . 502.02[A]
Lay, L.E. . . . . 1701.02[A]
Lazarus & Co., ... 201
Leslie Co. . . . . 305.01[B]
Levenson & Klein, Inc. . . . . . 501.01[C]
Levine Est., A. 1602.01
Lewis, S.R. . . . . 301.03[A]
Lewis, Jr., W.J. . . . . 1002.01[B]
Liant Record, Inc. . . . . 1503.02[A]
Limericks, Inc. . . . . 401.04[B]
Lindsley, Jr., E.B. . . . . 1601.03[A]
L.L. Bean, Inc. . . . . 102.02[C]
Longview Hilton Hotel Co. . . 301.01[A]
Louisiana Land & Exploration Co. 703.08
Lovejoy, J.S. . . . . 301.01[A]
Lowry, Jr., E.G. 2001.02
Lutz & Schramm Co. . . . . . . 1203.01[A]
Lyon, B.D. 403.01
Lyon Co., F. . . . . 305.02[A]

M

M&W Gear Co. 305.04
Maguire/Thomas Partners. . . 901.02[C]
Main & McKinney Bldg. Co. of Houston, Texas. . . . . 402.02[A]
Malat, W. 1002.01
Mallinckrodt, Inc. . . . . 102.02[C]
Malone, R.C. 1602.01
The Malulani Group, Limited. . . . . 1302.01[A]
Mantell, J. 406.02
Marcus, S. 703.08
Margolis, B.B. . . . . 1002.01[A]
Markovitz, M. . . . . 703.01[F]
Marks, D.N. . . . . 102.02[A]
Marlo Coil Co. . . . . 703.04[A]
Martin, F.T.B. 602.01
Martin, H.C. . . . . 1002.01[A]
Matheson, C. . . . . 1501.03[B]
Mathews, C.J. . . . . 305.03[B]
McBride, B.E. 602.01
McKinney, E.G. . . . . 1803.02[B]
McLaughlin, E.F.C. 1202.01
Meiers, S.A. . . . . 102.02[A]
Mele, J.A. 303.01
Melvin W. Issacson Est. . . . . 101.02[C]
Meredith, I., ... 1804
Metropolitan Building Co., ... 503
Michaels, J.A. . . . . 301.03[B]
Middleton, M.L. 1203.02
Mid-State Products Co. . . . . . 502.02[A]
Miller, P.A. 1002.01
Miller, S.D., ... 503
Miller, W.R. 1501.01
Millinery Center Building Corp. . . . . 502.01[A]; 602.02[A]
Minor, W.T. . . . . 1002.01[B]
Minot Federal Savings & Loan Assn. . . . . 102.02[C]
Mitchell, G.W. . . . . 1002.01[A]
Moline Properties, Inc. 201.01
Montgomery Co. . . . . 502.02[A]
Moore, A. . . . . 1002.01[B]
Moss, J.S. . . . . 703.01[F]
Moss, S.J. . . . . 602.02[A]
Mountain Fuel Supply Co. . . . 703.01[F]
Mountain State Steel Foundries, Inc. . . . . 703.01[F]
Mt. Morris Drive-In Theatre Co. . . . . 703.01[F]
Mozayeny, M. . . . . 801.03[C]
Municipal Bond Corp. . . . . . 1002.01[A]
Murray, J.S. 1002.01
Murray, R.J. . . . . 1401.01[B]

N

Narver, Jr., D.L. . . . . 101.02[C]
National Bank of Commerce of San Antonio. . . . . 1203.01[B]
National Builders, Inc. 701.02
National Carbide Corp. 201.02
New Capital Hotel, Inc. 403.01
Nicoll Co., R.J. . . . . 703.04[A]
Nieman Est., M.A. . . . . 1002.01[B]
Noble, G.A. 704.02
Noell, M.J. . . . . 1001.02[A]
North Carolina Midland Ry. Co. . 601.01

North Texas Lumber Co.... 1301.01[B]
Nutt Est., J.F. .... 1301.02[B]
N.W. Pugh Co., Inc. .... 501.01[B]

O

Oberman Mfg. Co. .... 703.01[F]
Ockles, T.S. .... 302.03[A]
Ockrant, W. .... 1201.02[B]
Oden, J.E. .... 1401.01[B]
Odom, Jr., F.L. 704.01
Oesterreich, W. 405.01
Offshore Operations Trust. . . 102.02[A]
Offutt, G.W. 1001.01; 1001.02
Ohio Cloverleaf Dairy Co. 601.01
Oliver .... 901.02[C]
Oliver Iron Mining Co. 502.03
Oriole Homes Corp. 704.04
O'Shaughnessy 903.01
Otis, J.J. .... 801.03[C]
Ottawa Silica Co. 1601.02
Ourisman, F.R. 201.02

P

Parker v. Delaney 101.02
Patrick, O. .... 1002.01[B]
Paul, M.A. .... 1301.02[C]
Peabody, S. .... 502.01[A]
Pearson, H.B. 601.03
Peerless Steel Equipment Co. .... 502.02[B]
Peerless Weighing & Vending Corp.... .... 502.02[A]
Pensacola Greyhound Racing, Inc. .... 102.02[A]
Perlmutter, B. .... 703.04[A]
Peterson Co., G.C. .... 1201.02[A]
Phil Gluckstern's, Inc. ...... 502.01[A]; 502.03
Phillips & Easton Supply Co. . 703.01[F]
Pickard, A. .... 703.05[A]
Pig & Whistle Co. 502.03
Pine Mountain Preserve, LLLP .... 1601.04[C]
Pioneer Real Estate Co. ....1502.03[A]; 1502.03[B]
Plainfield-Union Water Co. . . 703.01[F]
Poe v. H.G. Seaborn 202.04
Ponderosa Mouldings, Inc. . . 102.02[C]
Porreca, J. .... 302.03[B]
Post, R.H. 502.03
Powell, L.L. 202.02
Pozzi, E. .... 1401.01[B]
Pratt, E.T. .... 703.04[E]
Price, J.D., ...503
Professional Equities, Inc. . . 1401.02[B]

R

Raffold Process Corp. ...... 1201.02[A]
Ramirez 1103.06
Ray, L.W. .... 502.02[B]
Raymond Bertolini Trucking Co. .... 703.05[B]
Real Estate Corp., Inc. ...... 1503.01[C]
Realty Operators, Inc. 1203.02
Reisinger, C.H., ...601
Renwick, E.A., ...501
Ritholz Est., S.J., ...201
Roberts, W.M. 303.02
Roccaforte, Jr., J.A. 201.02
Rod Realty Co., ...403
Rogers, M.S. .... 1202.02[A]
Rose, J.T. .... 703.01[F]
Roth Properties Co. .... 703.04[A]
Rothschild, H. .... 1202.01[B]
Roux Laboratories, Inc. 801.05
Royal St. Louis, Inc. 601.01
Rush, G.S. .... 501.01[A]
Rutland, H. .... 1302.03[B]
Ruttenberg, D.C. .... 703.01[F]
Rutter, J.H. .... 703.01[F]

S

S.& B. Realty Co. .... 703.04[A]
S & L Building Corp. .... 301.01[A]
Sabinske, R.J. .... 1001.02[A]
Safway Steel Scaffolds Co. of Georgia . . .. 401.04[B]
Sanders, L. 202.04
Satterfield, D.G. 601.02; 602.01
Scheffres, J. 1601.02

Scheuber, W.A. 1002.01
Schieffelin Est., L.S. . . . . 1202.02[A]
Scott, E.V. 801.05
Scott Paper Co. . . . . 102.02[C]
Securities and Exchange Commission
Part VI Intro. . . . .
Serbousek, R.A. . . . . 305.03[B]
Sevier Terrace Realty Co. 1001.02
Shainberg, H. 703.06
Sheahan, E. L. . . . . 2003.01[A]
Shirley Hill Coal Co. . . . . 502.02[A]
Shoney's South, Inc. . . . . 102.02[C]
Sickle, B.V. 703.08
Sieber, R.J. 703.07
Simmons & Hammond Mfg. Co. . . . . . .
. . . . 703.01[F]
Simon, J.B., ... 1602
Sirbo Holdings, Inc. . . . . 502.01[B]
Skinner, F. 1001.01
Smith, J.M. . . . . 1301.01[B]
Smith, N.B. 402.01
Soelling, W.M. 703.08
Soliman. . . . . 1801.02[B]
Sorrell, Jr., G.S. 402.01
South Texas Properties Co. . 1002.01[A]
Spitzer, S. . . . . 301.01[A]
Spreckles, A.B. . . . . 1203.01[B]
Standard Fruit Product Co. . . 801.03[C]
Starke, W.E. . . . . 1002.01[A]
Starker, T.J. . . . . 1302.01[A]
Steele-Wedeles Co. . . . . 502.02[A]
Steinway & Sons. 401.03
Steuart Bros., Inc. . . . . 1503.02[A]
Stewart Supply Co., Inc. . . . . 703.01[F]
Stickles, S.E. 703.08
Stokes, T. 1203.02
Stonecrest Corporation, Inc. . . . .
. . . . 1401.02[B]
Suburban Realty Co. . . . . . . 1002.01[A]
Sugar Land Ranch Development. . . . . .
. . . . 1002.01
Sutphin, J.H. . . . 301.03[B]; 1201.01[A]
Swoby Corp. 601.01

T

Tank, R. 1501.01
Tennyson, H.L. . . . . 102.02[C]
Terre Haute Electric Co. 601.01
Terry, K.R. . . . . 1202.01[B]
Teruya Brothers, Ltd. . . . . . 1302.01[A]
Theodore Gutman Est. . . . . 1201.02[C]
Thielking, P.W., ... 501
Third National Bank in Nashville . . . . .
. . . . 502.02[A]
Thomas, O.L. . . . . 801.03[C]
Thornbrough, M. 704.01
379 Madison Ave., Inc. . . . . . 501.01[A]
Tracy, W.R. . . . . 704.01[A]
Triumph Mixed Use Investments III,
LLC. 1001.02
Tschupp, C. . . . . 703.04[B]
12701 Shaker Blvd. Co. . . . . . 301.03[A]
1220 Realty Co. 501.03

U

Union Pacific Co., R.R. 703.01
United Housing Foundation, Inc. Part VI
Intro. . . . .
United Mercantile Agencies, Inc., . 1702

V

Voloudakis, S., ... 503

W

Wacker, O.C. . . . . 301.01[A]
Wallace, J.D. 703.08
Warren Jones Co. . . . . 1301.01[B]
Warren Service Corp. . . . . . . 502.01[B]
Washington Package Store, Inc. . . . . .
. . . . 501.01[B]
Watkins, H.V. 2001.02
Watson Land Co. 601.01
Watts, R.O. . . . . . 703.01[F]; 801.03[C]
Wauwatosa Colony, Inc. 801.05
WBSR, Inc. 305.04
W.E. Davis & Sons, Inc. . . . . 401.04[B]
Weightman, G.H. 1801.02
Weiss, G. 801.05

References are to paragraph (¶) numbers.

Weiss, H.W. 601.01
Wells. . . . . 703.01[F]
Wells Fargo Bank & Union Trust Co., Trustee. . . . . 502.02[A]
Wendell Falls Development, LLC. . . . . 1601.04[C]
Wentz, L.P. 401.02
Westall, D.W. . . . . 1302.02[B]
Westchester Development Co. . . . . 1503.02[C]
Western Products Co. 1501.01
Western Wheeled Scraper Co. . . 801.05
Whiteco Industries, Inc. . . . . 102.02[C]
Whitfield, Jr., L.B. . . . . 703.01[F]
Whitman, C. . . . . 703.05[A]
Wilensky & Sons Co. 102.01
Wilkerson, D.L. . . . . 1701.02[A]
Williams, W.B. 403.02
Wilshire Holding Corp. 405.01
Wilshire Medical Properties, Inc. . . . . 602.02[A]
Wilson, P., ... 601
Windham. 1103.06
Wolfsen Land & Cattle Co. . . 703.01[F]
Wood, H.L. 402.01
Woodall. . . . . 1503.02[C]
Woodbury, L.A. . . . . 1302.03[A]
Woodsam Associates, Inc. . . 1202.01[A]
Woolf, J.A. 1202.01
World Publishing Co. 601.03
Wright, Inc., B.T. . . . . 801.03[C]

Y

Yarbo, J.W. 1203.02
Yates Holding Corp. . . . . . . 1201.02[A]
Young, M.C., ... 501
Your Health Club, Inc. 602.01

Z

Zaninovich, M.J. 402.01
Zarrinnegar and Dini. 1103.06

Finding Lists

Internal Revenue Code Sections

Code Sec.	Par. (¶)
1	209.03
1(h)	1401.04
1(h)(1)(D)	1301.03[B]
1(h)(11)	209.04
11	204.02[B]
25	1701.03[C]
25(d)(3)	1708.02
25C	1708; 1708.01[A]
25C(a)(1)	1708.01
25C(a)(2)	1708.01
25C(b)	1708.01; 1708.01[A]
25C(c)(1)	1708.01
25C(c)(3)	1708.01
25C(d)	1708.01
25C(d)(2)	1708.01; 1708.01[A]
25C(d)(4)	1708.01
25C(d)(5)	1708.01
25C(d)(6)	1708.01
25C(f)	1708.01
25D	1708; 1708.02
25D(c)	1708.02
25D(d)(1)	1708.02
25D(d)(2)	1708.02
25D(d)(4)	1708.02
25D(d)(5)	1708.02
25D(e)	1708.02
25D(f)	1708.02
25D(g)	1708.02
26(a)	1301.04[A]
36	1707
38	804; 805; 805.05[C]
38(c)	1301.04[A]
38(c)(1)	804
38(c)(4)	804; 1301.04[A]
39	804; 805
39(f)	1707.01
39(f)(4)(D)(ii)	1707.01
42	104; 805; 805.01; 805.02[B]; 1103.05[C]
42(a)	805.03
42(b)(1)(A)	805.03[A]
42(b)(1)(B)	805.03[A]
42(b)(1)(B)(ii)	805.03[A]
42(b)(2)	805.03[A]
42(c)	805.03[B]
42(c)(1)(C)	805.03[B]
42(c)(1)(D)	805.03[B]
42(c)(2)	805.02[A]
42(d)(1)	805.03[B]
42(d)(2)(A)	805.03[B]
42(d)(2)(B)	805.03[B]
42(d)(2)(D)(i)	805.03[B]
42(d)(2)(D)(ii)	805.03[B]
42(d)(3)(A)	805.03[B]
42(d)(3)(B)	805.03[B]
42(d)(4)	805.03[B]
42(d)(5)	805.03[B]
42(d)(7)	805.03[B]
42(c)	805.04
42(e)(2)(B)	805.04
42(e)(3)	805.04
42(f)(1)	805.03
42(f)(3)	805.05[C]
42(g)(1)	805.02[B]
42(g)(2)	805.02[B]
42(g)(2)(E)	805.02[B]
42(g)(3)(A)	805.02[B]
42(g)(3)(B)	805.02[B]
42(g)(5)	805.02[A]
42(g)(6)	805.02[B]
42(h)(1)	805.02[B]
42(h)(1)(B)	805.02[B]
42(h)(3)(I)	805.01
42(i)(1)	805.02[A]

Code Sec.	Par. (¶)
42(i)(3)	805.02
42(j)	805.05
42(j)(2)(A)	805.05[C]
42(j)(2)(B)	805.05[C]
42(j)(3)	805.05[C]
42(j)(4)(B)	805.05[C]
42(j)(4)(E)	805.05[D]
42(j)(4)(F)	805.05
42(j)(5)	805.05[B]
42(j)(5)(A)(iv)	805.05[B]
42(j)(6)	805.05
42(k)	805.03[B]
45L	105; 1001.03
45L(a)(2)	1001.03
45L(b)(1)	1001.03
45L(c)	105; 1001.03
45L(g)	105; 1001.03
46	1104.04
47	1105.05[C]; 1601.04[C]
47(a)	804
47(a)(2)	804.02
47(c)(1)(A)(i)	804.01
47(c)(1)(A)(ii)	804.01
47(c)(1)(A)(iii)	804.01
47(c)(1)(B)	804.01
47(c)(1)(C)(i)	804.01[A]
47(c)(1)(C)(ii)	804.01[A]
47(c)(2)(A)(i)	804.01
47(c)(2)(A)(ii)	804.01
47(c)(2)(B)	804.01[D]
47(c)(2)(B)(iv)(I)	804.02[B]
47(c)(2)(B)(iv)(II)	804.02[B]
47(c)(2)(B)(iv)(III)	804.02[B]
47(c)(2)(B)(vi)	603.01
47(c)(2)(C)	804.02[A]
47(c)(3)(A)	804.02[A]
47(c)(3)(B)	804.02[A]
48(a)(2)(B)	804.01
48(d)	603.01; 603.02[A]
48(d)(1)(A)	603.02[A]
48(d)(1)(B)	603.02[A]
48(d)(2)	603.02[B]
48(d)(5)(A)	603.02[A]
48(d)(5)(B)	603.02[A]
48(g)(4)	804.01
50(a)(1)	603.02[B]; 804.03
50(b)(2)	804.01
50(c)	603.02[A]; 804.01[E]
50(c)(4)(A)	1301.03[B]
50(c)(4)(B)	1301.03[B]
50(d)(5)	603.01; 603.02[A]; 603.02[B]
53	1301.04[F]
53(d)	1301.04[F]
55	1301.04
55(a)	1301.04[A]
55(a)(7)	1301.04[D]
55(b)	1301.04[A]
55(b)(2)	1301.04[A]
55(b)(3)	1301.04[A]
55(d)(1)	1301.04[A]
55(d)(2)	1301.04[A]
55(d)(3)	1301.04[A]
55(e)	1301.04[B]
55(e)(5)	1301.04[B]
56(a)(1)	902.02[C]; 1301.04[C]
56(a)(1)(A)	902; 902.02
56(a)(2)	1301.04[C]
56(a)(3)	1301.04[C]
56(a)(4)	1301.04[C]
56(a)(5)	1301.04[C]
56(a)(6)	1301.04[C]
56(b)(1)(A)	1301.04[C]
56(b)(1)(A)(ii)	704
56(b)(1)(B)	1301.04[C]
56(b)(1)(C)	1301.04[C]
56(b)(2)(A)(i)	1301.04[C]
56(b)(2)(A)(ii)	1301.04[C]
56(d)	1301.04[C]
56(e)	1301.04[C]
57	302.02[A]

Code Sec.	Par. (¶)
57(a)(1)	1301.04[D]
57(a)(2)	1301.04[D]
57(a)(5)	1301.04[D]
57(a)(6)	1301.04[C]; 1301.04[D]
57(a)(7)	902.02[C]
57(c)(1)(B)	603.02[B]
58(a)	1301.04[C]
58(b)(1)	1301.04[C]
58(b)(2)	1301.04[C]
59(a)	1301.04[A]
59(e)	1301.04[E]
59(e)(1)	1301.04[E]
61	303.01; 303.03[A]
61(a)	703.04[E]
61(a)(5)	401; 403
61(a)(12)	301.03[B]; 1201.01; 1201.01[A]
62(a)	209.01
63(b)	209.01
63(d)	209.01
82	1705.03[A]
83	1104.01[A]
102	1701.03[D]
103(a)	902.02[B]
108	1201.01; 1201.01[B]
108(a)	1201.01[B]
108(a)(1)	1201.01[A]
108(a)(1)(A)	1201.01[B]
108(a)(1)(B)	1201.01[B]
108(a)(1)(D)	1201.01[C]
108(a)(2)(C)	1201.01[D]
108(a)(3)	1201.01[B]
108(b)(1)	1201.01[B]
108(b)(2)	1201.01[B]
108(b)(3)(A)	1201.01[B]
108(b)(3)(B)	1201.01[B]
108(b)(4)	1201.01[B]
108(c)(1)	1201.01[C]
108(c)(2)	1201.01[C]
108(c)(3)	1201.01[C]
108(d)(2)	1201.01[B]
108(d)(3)	1201.01[B]
108(e)	1201.01[A]
108(e)(1)	1201.01[B]
108(e)(4)	1201.01[A]
108(e)(5)	301.03[B]; 1201.01[E]; 1201.02
108(e)(5)(C)	1201.01[E]
108(g)	1201.01
108(h)(1)	1201.01[D]
108(h)(2)	1201.01[D]
108(h)(3)	1201.01[D]
108(h)(4)	1201.01[D]
109	401.04[B]; 602.02[B]
110	602
112(d)(3)	2002.01[C]
119	1103.01[A]; 1803.01[B]
121	1303; 1901.01[C]; 2002; 2002.01[C]; 2002.02; 2004; 2004.01; 2004.01[A]; 2004.01[B]; 2004.02; 2004.02[A]
121(a)	2002.01
121(a)(1)	2004.01
121(a)(2)	2004.01
121(b)(1)	2004.01
121(b)(2)	2002.01[A]; 2004.01
121(b)(3)	2002.01; 2004.01
121(b)(3)(B)	2002.01
121(b)(4)	2002.01[C]
121(b)(5)	2002.01[B]
121(b)(5)(B)	2002.01[B]
121(b)(5)(C)	2002.01[B]
121(b)(5)(D)	2002.01[B]
121(c)	2002.01
121(d)(2)	2002.01[C]
121(d)(4)	2002.01[C]
121(d)(5)	1704
121(d)(5)(A)	2002.01[C]
121(d)(5)(B)	2002.01[C]

Code Sec.	Par. (¶)
121(d)(5)(C)	2002.01[C]
121(d)(6)	2002.01[C]
121(d)(7)	2004.01[B]
121(d)(9)	2002.01[C]
121(d)(10)	2002.01[C]
121(g)	2002.01[C]
139	1704
146	805.02[B]
162	301.01[B]; 401.02; 703; 703.01; 703.05[A]; 703.08
162(a)	703.04[E]; 801.02[C]
162(a)(1)	703.04
162(a)(3)	401; 402; 405
163(a)	303.02; 702.01; 703.09
163(c)	303.02; 1701.03[A]
163(d)	303.02; 303.02[B]; 303.02[C]
163(d)(4)(D)	303.02[B]
163(e)	304
163(g)	1701.03[C]
163(h)	303.02; 303.02[C]
163(h)(1)	1701
163(h)(2)	1701
163(h)(3)	1701.01
163(h)(3)(B)(i)	1701.01[B]
163(h)(3)(C)(i)	1701.01[C]
163(h)(3)(C)(ii)	1701.01[C]
163(h)(3)(D)(i)	1701.01[D]
163(h)(3)(D)(ii)	1701.01[D]
163(h)(3)(D)(iii)(I)	1701.01[D]
163(h)(3)(D)(iii)(II)	1701.01[D]
163(h)(3)(D)(iv)(I)	1701.01[D]
163(h)(3)(D)(iv)(II)	1701.01[D]
163(h)(3)(E)	1701.01
163(h)(3)(F)	1701.01
163(h)(3)(F)(ii)	1701.01
163(h)(3)(F)(iii)	1701.01[B]
163(h)(4)(A)	1701.01[A]
163(h)(4)(A)(ii)	1701.01[A]
163(h)(4)(A)(iii)	1701.01[A]
163(j)	303.02; 303.02[C]; 303.02[D]
163(j)(1)	303.02[D]
163(j)(2)	303.02[D]
163(j)(3)	303.02[D]
163(j)(4)	303.02[D]
163(j)(4)(B)	303.02[D]
163(j)(5)	303.02[D]
163(j)(6)	303.02[D]
163(j)(7)(B)	303.02[D]
163(j)(7)(C)	303.02[D]
163(j)(8)(A)	303.02[D]
163(j)(8)(B)	303.02[D]
164	702.01; 704.01[C]; 704.02
164(a)	704; 704.01; 704.03; 1301.01[B]
164(a)(1)	1702
164(a)(3)	1301.01[B]
164(b)(6)	704; 1702
164(c)(1)	704.02
164(d)	101.01[A]; 102.03
164(d)(1)	102.03
165	102.01[A]; 103.01[B]; 702; 801.03; 801.05; 1201.02; 1201.02[A]; 1501.01; 1503; 1703.02[A]; 1703.02[B]
165(a)	801.05; 1201.02[A]; 1501; 1501.02[C]; 1504.02
165(b)	101
165(c)	1201.02[A]; 2001
165(f)	2001
165(h)	1703; 1703.01[A]
165(h)(1)	1703.01[A]
165(h)(2)	1703.01[B]
165(h)(2)(A)(i)	1703.01[B]

Code Sec.	Par. (¶)
165(h)(2)(B)	1703.01[B]
165(h)(4)(A)	1703.01[B]
165(h)(5)	1703
165(i)(1)	1501.03
165(i)(2)	1501.03
166	1201.02; 1201.02[A]; 1201.02[B]
166(a)(1)	1201.02[B]
166(a)(2)	1201.02[B]
166(d)	1201.02[B]; 1201.02[C]
166(d)(2)	1201.02[C]
167(a)	900
167(e)(7)	901.01[E]
167(k)	805.03[B]
167(m)	901.01[A]
168	404.02; 601.01; 601.02; 1301.04[C]
168(a)	601.01; 901.01
168(b)(3)	901.01[B]
168(b)(4)	901.01[B]
168(c)	901.01[A]
168(d)(2)	901.01[C]
168(e)(2)	901.01[A]
168(e)(3)(E)	901.01[E]
168(e)(4)	905.02[A]
168(e)(6)	901.03[B]
168(e)(6)(A)	901.01[F]
168(e)(6)(B)	901.01[F]
168(e)(8)	901.01[E]
168(e)(8)(C)	901.01[E]
168(f)(1)	904.02
168(f)(5)	905.02[A]
168(g)	902
168(g)(1)(A)	902.02
168(g)(1)(B)	902.02
168(g)(1)(C)	902.02
168(g)(1)(F)	303.02[D]
168(g)(2)	902.01
168(g)(3)(A)	902.01
168(g)(3)(B)	901.01[E]
168(g)(5)(A)	902.02[B]
168(g)(5)(B)	902.02[B]
168(g)(5)(C)	902.02[B]
168(g)(7)	902.01[A]
168(h)(1)(B)	902.02[A]
168(h)(1)(B)(ii)	902.02[A]
168(h)(1)(B)(iii)	902.02[A]
168(h)(1)(C)	902.02[A]
168(h)(1)(D)	902.02[A]
168(h)(2)	902.02[A]
168(h)(5)	902.02[A]
168(i)(3)	902.02[A]
168(i)(6)	901.02
168(i)(8)	501.03; 601.02; 602.02
168(i)(15)	901.01[G]
168(i)(15)(B)	901.01[G]
168(i)(15)(C)	901.01[G]
168(j)	901.01[A]
168(k)	901.03; 901.03[B]
168(k)(2)	901.03[B]
168(k)(2)(E)	901.03[B]
168(k)(3)	901.01[E]; 901.03[B]
168(k)(3)(B)	901.01[E]
168(k)(6)(A)	901.03[B]
168(k)(8)	901.03[B]
168(k)(10)	901.03[B]
169(a)	802.01
169(b)	802.01[A]
169(c)	802.01[A]
169(d)	802.01[A]
169(d)(5)	802.01[C]
169(f)(2)	802.01[B]
169(g)	802.01[B]
170	1601
170(b)	1601.03
170(b)(1)(A)	1601
170(b)(1)(B)	1601.03[B]
170(b)(1)(C)	1601
170(b)(1)(C)(iii)	1601.03[B]
170(b)(1)(D)	1601; 1601.03[C]

Code Sec.	Par. (¶)
170(b)(1)(G)	1601
170(b)(2)	1601
170(d)	1601
170(e)	1601.03
170(e)(1)(A)	1601.03[A]
170(e)(1)(B)	1601.03[B]
170(e)(1)(B)(ii)	1601.03[B]
170(f)(2)	1601.04
170(f)(2)(A)	1601.04[B]
170(f)(3)	1601.04
170(f)(3)(A)	1601.04
170(f)(3)(B)	1601.04
170(f)(3)(B)(i)	1601.04[B]
170(f)(3)(B)(iii)	1601.04[C]
170(f)(11)	1601.01[B]
170(f)(14)	1601.04[C]
170(h)	1601.04[C]
170(h)(2)	1601.04[C]
170(h)(3)	1601.04[C]
170(h)(4)	1601.04[C]
170(h)(4)(B)	1601.04[C]
170(h)(5)	1601.04[C]
170(h)(5)(B)	1601.04[C]
170(h)(5)(B)(ii)	1601.04[C]
174	702.01; 1102.01
175	802.03
175(b)	802.03
175(c)(3)	802.03
176D(c)	803
178	501.02; 602.02[A]
179	703.01[C]; 901.03; 901.03[A]; 1301.03[A]; 1503.02[E]; 1801.01; 1801.03[B]
179(b)	901.03[A]
179(b)(3)(A)	901.03[A]
179(d)(1)	901.03[A]
179(d)(1)(B)(ii)	901.03[A]
179(f)	901.03[A]
179(f)(4)	901.03[A]

Code Sec.	Par. (¶)
179D	803
179D(b)	803
179D(c)(1)	803
179D(d)	803
179D(e)	803
179D(f)	803
180	802.03
183	1803.03
189	103.02
189(e)(1)	103.02
190	703.02
194	802.02
194(b)	802.02
194(c)(1)	802.02
194(c)(2)	802.02
194(c)(3)	802.02
194(c)(3)(B)	802.02
195	702; 702.01; 702.01[A]; 702.01[B]; 702.01[C]; 702.02
195(b)(1)	702
195(b)(2)	702
195(b)(3)	702
195(c)(1)(A)	702.01
195(c)(1)(B)	702.01
197	102.02[D]; 901.03[B]
199	209.01; 209.05
199(g)(1)	209.05
199(g)(2)(E)	209.05
199A	209; 209.04; 209.05
199A(a)	209.01; 209.04
199A(b)	209.01; 209.05
199A(b)(1)	209.04
199A(b)(2)	209.04
199A(b)(3)(A)	209.04
199A(b)(3)(B)(i)	209.04
199A(b)(3)(B)(ii)	209.04
199A(b)(3)(B)(iii)	209.04
199A(b)(7)	209.05
199A(c)	209.03

Code Sec.	Par. (¶)
199A(c)(2)	209.03
199A(c)(3)(A)	209.03
199A(c)(3)(A)(i)	209.03
199A(c)(3)(B)	209.03
199A(d)(1)	209.02
199A(d)(2)	209.02[A]
199A(d)(3)	209.02[A]
199A(d)(3)(B)	209.02[A]
199A(e)(2)(A)	209.04
199A(e)(3)	209.04
199A(e)(5)	209.04
199A(f)(1)(A)	209.01
199A(f)(1)(B)	209.01
199A(f)(1)(C)(i)	209.03
199A(f)(2)	209.03
199A(g)	209.05
199A(g)(1)(B)	209.05
199A(g)(2)(A)	209.05
199A(g)(2)(B)	209.05
199A(g)(4)	209.05
212	702.02; 703; 703.01; 703.08
216	1901; 1901.02[A]
216(a)	1901.02
216(b)(1)	1901.01
216(b)(2)	1901.01
216(b)(3)	1901.02[A]
216(c)(1)	1901.02[B]
216(c)(2)(A)	1901.02[B]
216(c)(2)(B)	1901.02[B]
216(e)	1901.01[C]
217	1705
217(b)	1705.03
217(c)(1)	1705.02[A]
217(c)(2)	1705.02[B]
217(d)	1705.02[B]
217(h)	1705.03[B]
217(k)	1705.01
248	204.02[A]; 702.01
262	402
262(a)	2001
262(b)	1801.03[B]
263	102.01; 103; 502.02; 704.04
263(a)	703.01[A]; 801.02[C]
263(a)(1)	801
263(a)(2)	801
263A	101.01[B]; 103.01; 303.02; 703.01[B]; 703.03; 703.06; 704.04; 801.02[C]; 902
263A(a)(2)	103.01[B]
263A(b)	103.01[B]
263A(c)	103.01[B]
263A(d)(3)	902
263A(e)(2)(A)	902
263A(f)	1001.02[B]
263A(f)(1)(A)	103.01[C]
263A(f)(1)(B)	103.01[C]
263A(i)	103.01[A]
263A(f)	103.01[C]
265(a)(6)	1701.03[D]
266	103.03; 303.02
267	303.02; 305.03[B]; 401.04[C]; 701.04; 701.04[A]; 701.04[C]; 1301.01[C]; 1302.01[A]
267(a)	701.04[A]; 1301.01[C]
267(a)(1)	701.04[A]
267(a)(2)	401.04[C]; 701.04[B]
267(b)	303.02; 303.02[D]; 401.04[C]; 701.04[A]; 701.04[C]; 1301.01[C]; 13.04.02[A]; 1401.03[B]; 1503.02[B]; 1601.01[B]

Code Sec.	Par. (¶)
267(c)	701.04[C]; 1301.01[C]; 1401.03[A]
267(c)(4)	1301.01[C]
267(d)	701.04[A]; 1301.01[C]
267(e)	701.04[C]
267(e)(1)	701.04[B]
267(e)(1)(C)	701.04[B]
267(e)(3)	701.04[B]
267(f)	401.04[C]; 701.04[C]
267(f)(1)	1301.01[C]
267(f)(2)	1301.01[C]
267(f)(3)	1301.01[C]
280A	1801; 1801.01; 1803.01; 1803.01[A]; 1803.02[B]; 1803.03
280A(a)	1801; 1801.02
280A(b)	1801
280A(c)(1)	1801.02; 1801.02[B]
280A(c)(1)(A)	1801.02[B]
280A(c)(2)	1801.02[A]
280A(c)(4)	1801.05
280A(c)(4)(B)	1801.05
280A(c)(4)(C)	1801.05[A]
280A(c)(5)	1104.01[B]; 1801; 1801.04
280A(d)(1)	1803.01[A]
280A(d)(2)	1803.01[B]
280A(d)(3)(A)	1803.01[B]
280A(d)(3)(B)	1803.01[B]
280A(d)(3)(C)	1803.01[B]
280A(d)(4)	1803.01[B]
280A(d)(4)(B)(i)	1803.01[B]
280A(d)(4)(B)(ii)	1803.01[B]
280A(e)	1803; 1803.02; 1803.02[B]
280A(f)(1)(A)	1801; 1803.01
280A(f)(1)(B)	1801; 1801.02; 1803.01
280A(f)(3)	1803.03
280A(g)	1802.01; 1802.02; 1803.02[A]
280B	102.02[A]; 1504.01; 1504.02[B]
280H	701.01[B]
291	802.01[A]
291(a)(1)	1301.03[B]
291(a)(5)	802.01[A]
311(b)	204.02[C]; 206.02[A]
312(k)(3)	902
318	1101.01[B]
318(c)	1401.03[B]
331	204.02[C]
332	1402.01[A]
336	204.02[C]
351	204.02[A]; 1402.01[A]
357(b)	204.02[A]
357(c)	204.02[A]
358	204.02[A]
361	1402.01[A]
362	204.02[A]
368(c)	204.02[A]
385	1901.01[A]
419(e)	1301.02[A]
441(i)	701.01[A]
441(i)(1)	701.01[A]
444	701.01[A]; 701.01[B]
444(b)(4)	701.01[B]
444(d)(2)(B)	701.01[B]
444(d)(3)	701.01[B]
446	303.02; 304; 701.02; 903.01
446(c)	701.02
446(d)	701.02
447	701.02[A]
447(c)	701.02[A]
448	701.02[A]
448(b)(1)	701.02[A]

Code Sec.	Par. (¶)
448(b)(3)	701.02[A]
448(c)	701.02[A]
448(d)(1)	701.02[A]
448(d)(2)	701.02[A]
448(d)(6)	701.02[A]
451	303.01; 403.01; 701.02[B]
451(b)	701.02[B]
451(c)	701.02[B]
453	1400
453(a)	1401.01[C]; 1401.02
453(b)	1002.02[A]
453(b)(1)	1401.01
453(b)(2)	1401.01[A]
453(c)	1401.02[A]; 1401.02[B]
453(d)(1)	1401.01[C]
453(e)	1401.03
453(e)(1)	1401.03[B]
453(e)(2)(A)	1401.03[B]
453(e)(2)(B)	1401.03[B]
453(e)(3)	1401.03[B]
453(e)(5)	1401.03[B]
453(e)(6)(B)	1401.03[B]
453(e)(6)(C)	1401.03[B]
453(e)(7)	1401.03[B]
453(f)(1)	1401.03[B]
453(f)(3)	1401.02[B]
453(f)(4)(A)	1401.02[B]
453(f)(4)(B)	1401.02[B]
453(f)(5)	1401.02[B]
453(f)(6)(A)	1401.02[D]
453(f)(6)(B)	1401.02[D]
453(f)(6)(C)	1401.02[D]
453(f)(8)(B)	1401.01
453(g)	1401.01; 1401.03
453(g)(1)(A)	1401.03[A]
453(g)(1)(B)(i)	1401.03[A]
453(g)(1)(B)(ii)	1401.03[A]
453(g)(2)	1401.03[A]
453(i)	1401.02[A]
453(j)(2)	1401.02[E]
453(l)(1)	1401.01[A]
453(l)(2)(A)	1002.02[A]; 1401.01[A]
453(l)(2)(B)	1002.02[A]; 1401.01[A]
453(l)(3)	1002.02[B]; 1401.01[A]
453(l)(3)(A)	1401.01[A]
453(l)(3)(B)(i)	1401.01[A]
453(l)(3)(B)(i)(III)	1401.01[A]
453(l)(3)(B)(iii)	1401.01[A]
453(l)(3)(C)	1401.01[A]
453A	1401.04
453A(b)(2)	1401.04
453A(b)(3)	1401.04
453A(c)(1)	1401.04
453A(c)(2)	1401.04
453A(c)(3)	1401.04
453A(c)(4)	1401.04
453A(c)(5)	1401.04
453A(d)	1402; 1402.02
453A(d)(1)	1402.02
453A(d)(3)	1402.02
453A(d)(4)	1402.02
453B	1402.01[A]
453B(a)	1402
453B(a)(1)	1402.01
453B(a)(2)	1402.01
453B(b)	1402.01
453B(c)	1402.01[A]
453B(d)	1402; 1402.01[A]
453B(f)	1402.01[B]
453B(g)	1402.01[A]
460	701.02[C]
460(a)	701.02[C]
460(b)	701.02[C]
460(c)	701.02[C]
460(e)	701.02[C]
460(e)(1)(A)	701.02[C]
460(e)(1)(B)	701.02[C]
460(e)(2)	701.02[C]
460(e)(4)	701.02[C]

Code Sec.	Par. (¶)
460(e)(5)	701.02[C]
460(e)(5)(B)	701.02[C]
461(c)	102.03; 701.02[B]
461(g)	303.02; 303.02[A]
461(g)(1)	1701.02
461(g)(2)	303.02[A]; 1701.02
461(h)	701.02[B]; 1001.02[B]
461(h)(3)	701.02[B]
461(h)(4)	701.02[B]
461(i)	701.02[B]
461(l)	705
461(l)(3)	705.01
461(l)(4)	705.02
465	302; 303.02
465(a)(1)	302.01
465(b)(2)	302.03[A]
465(b)(3)	302.03[A]
465(b)(4)	302.03
465(b)(5)	302.03
465(b)(6)	302.04
465(c)(1)	1102.02
465(c)(1)(B)	1102.02
465(c)(1)(D)	1102.02
465(c)(2)(B)(i)	302.01
465(c)(3)(B)(i)	302.01
465(c)(3)(B)(ii)	302.01
465(c)(4)	302.01
465(c)(7)	302.01
465(c)(7)(C)	1101.03[B]
465(e)	302.02[B]
467	402.02[A]; 402.02[B]; 403.01; 404; 404.01; 404.02; 404.02[A]; 404.02[B]; 406.02; 602.01
467(a)(2)	404.01
467(b)(1)	404.01
467(b)(2)	404.02
467(b)(4)	404.02
467(b)(5)	404.02[A]
467(c)(1)	404.02[B]
467(c)(2)(B)	404.02[B]
467(c)(3)	404.02[B]
467(d)	404.01
467(e)(1)	404.02
467(e)(3)	404.02
467(e)(4)	404.01
467(f)	402.02[A]; 404.01
469	303.02; 303.02[C]; 806.01; 1100; 1102.02; 1102.04; 1104.01[A]
469(a)(1)(A)	1104.01
469(a)(2)	1101.01
469(b)	1104.03
469(c)(1)	1101.02; 1101.03
469(c)(2)	1101.02; 1103
469(c)(3)(A)	1101.02[B]
469(c)(7)	1101.02; 1103; 1103.06
469(c)(7)(A)(ii)	1103.06
469(c)(7)(B)	1103.06
469(c)(7)(C)	1103.06
469(c)(7)(D)	1103.06
469(d)(2)	1104.04
469(e)(1)	1101.01[A]
469(g)	1104.03
469(g)(1)(A)	1104.03[D]
469(g)(1)(B)	1104.03[D]
469(g)(2)	1104.03[D]
469(g)(3)	1104.03[D]
469(i)	806.01; 1101.02; 1103; 1103.05
469(i)(2)	1103.05[A]
469(i)(3)	1103.05[C]
469(i)(3)(D)	1103.05[C]
469(i)(3)(E)	1103.05[C]
469(i)(5)	1103.05[B]
469(i)(6)	1103.05
469(i)(6)(B)	1103.05

Code Sec.	Par. (¶)
469(j)(1)	1101.01[A]
469(j)(2)	1101.01[B]
469(k)	1105; 1105.03
469(k)(1)	1105.03
469(k)(3)	1105.03
469(k)(4)	1105
481	1104.01[A]; 1104.01[B]
481(a)	103.01[C]
482	304; 401.04[B]
483	304; 304.01; 304.01[A]; 304.02[B]
483(b)	304.01[A]
483(c)	304.01[A]
483(c)(1)	303.03
483(d)(1)	304.01
483(d)(2)	304.01[A]
483(e)	304.01; 304.01[B]
501(c)(3)	1601.03[B]; 1903.01[E]
511	902.02[A]
528	1902.02; 1903; 1903.01[C]; 1903.02; 1903.04[A]; 1903.04[C]
528(b)	1903.02
528(c)(1)	1903.01
528(c)(2)	1903
528(c)(3)	1903
528(c)(4)	1903; 1903.01[A]
528(d)(1)	1903.02
528(d)(2)	1903.02
528(d)(3)	1903.01[C]
531–537	204.02[B]
541–547	204.02[B]
631	1301.02[B]
641–683	207.01
643(f)	209
704(b)	203.02[C]
704(c)(1)	203.02[B]
704(c)(1)(B)	1402.01[A]
704(c)(2)	203.02[B]
705	203.02[A]
705(a)	203.02[A]
706	205.02
706(b)	701.01[A]
706(b)(1)(B)(i)	701.01[A]
706(b)(1)(B)(ii)	701.01[A]
706(b)(1)(B)(iii)	701.01[A]
706(b)(2)	701.01[A]
707(a)	209.03; 703.04[E]; 1104.01[C]
707(a)(2)	203.02[B]; 203.02[C]
707(a)(2)(A)	703.04[E]
707(b)	303.02[D]
707(b)(1)	1201.01[A]; 1304.02[A]; 1503.02[B]
707(c)	203.02[E]; 703.04[E]; 1104.01[C]
708	205.02
709	203.02[C]; 702.01
721	203.02[B]; 1402.01[A]
722	203.02[A]
723	203.02[A]
731	1402.01[A]
731(a)	203.02[D]
731(b)	203.02[D]
732	203.02[D]
736	1402.01[A]
736(a)	1104.01[C]
736(b)	1104.01[C]
737	1402.01[A]
742	203.02[A]
751(b)	1402.01[A]
752(b)	203.02[B]
761(f)	203.01[C]
771–777	203.02[F]
776	203.02[F]

Code Sec.	Par. (¶)
856(a)	2200; 2203.01
856(b)	2203.01
857(b)(5)	2203.02
856(c)	2200
856(c)(2)	2203.02
856(c)(3)	2203.02
856(c)(4)	2203.03
856(c)(5)(G)	2203.02
856(c)(5)(J)	2203.02
856(c)(5)(L)(ii)	2203.03
856(c)(6)	2203.02
856(c)(7)	2203.03[A]
856(c)(8)	2203.01
856(c)(9)	2203.03[B]
856(d)	2203.02
856(d)(8)	2203.02
856(e)(1)	2201.01[A]
856(e)(5)	2201.01[A]
856(g)(5)	2203
856(h)	2203.01
856(i)	2201.04
856(l)	2201.04
856(m)	2203.03
856(n)	2203.02
857(a)(1)	2200
857(a)(1)(A)	2201.01
857(b)(1)	2200
857(b)(2)	2201
857(b)(2)(B)	2201.01[A]
857(b)(3)	2201, 2201.01[C]; 2202.01
857(b)(3)(B)	2201.01[C]
857(b)(3)(D)	2201.01[C]
857(b)(4)	2201.03
857(b)(6)	2200; 2201.03
857(b)(7)	2201.03
857(b)(8)	2202.01
857(b)(9)	2201.01
857(c)	2201.01[B]
857(c)(2)	2202
857(e)	2201.01
858	2202.02
859	2203.01
860	2203.04
860A–860G	2300
860A(a)	2301; 2302
860A(b)	2301; 2302
860B(a)	2302.01
860B(b)	2302.01
860B(c)	2302.01
860C(a)	2302.02
860C(b)	2302.02
860C(c)(1)	2302.02[A]
860C(c)(2)	2302.02[A]
860C(d)	2302.02[B]
860C(e)(2)	2302.02[A]
860D(a)	2300
860D(b)	2302
860G(a)(1)	2301
860G(a)(2)	2301
897	102.04
897(c)(1)(B)	102.04
897(i)	102.04
911	1706
931	1706
933	1706
988	209.03
1001	304; 1203.01[A]; 1302; 1501.02[B]
1001(a)	1202.01; 1301.01
1001(b)	1301.01[B]
1002	1302
1011	101; 1301.01[A]
1011(b)	1602.02
1012	101.01[A]; 101.01[B]; 102.03; 209.04; 304; 703.01[C]; 1701.03[D]
1014	101.01[F]
1014(e)	101.01[F]
1015	101.01[E]; 1603
1016	1103.04
1016(a)	1501.02[D]

Code Sec.	Par. (¶)
1017(a)	1201.01[B]
1017(b)(3)(E)	1201.01[B]
1017(d)	1201.01[B]
1019	602.02[B]
1022	101.01[F]
1031	101.01[C]; 102.01[A]; 203.02[B]; 209.04; 305.01[B]; 905.02[A]; 1302; 1302.01; 1302.01[A]; 1302.01[B]; 1302.01[D]; 1302.03[A]; 1401.02[D]; 1503.02[C]; 2002.02; 2201.02
1031(a)(1)	1302
1031(a)(2)	1302.01
1031(a)(2)(B)	1302.01[A]
1031(a)(3)(A)	1302.01
1031(a)(3)(B)	1302.01
1031(b)	1302.01; 1302.02[A]; 1302.02[B]
1031(c)	1302.02
1031(d)	101.01[C]; 1302; 1302.01[B]; 1302.02[B]; 1302.02[C]
1031(f)(1)	1302.01[A]
1031(f)(2)	1302.01[A]
1031(f)(2)(C)	1302.01[A]
1031(f)(4)	1302.01[A]

Code Sec.	Par. (¶)
1033	905.02[A]; 1202.01; 1503; 1503.01; 1503.01[B]; 1503.02; 1503.02[B]; 1503.02[C]; 1503.02[E]; 1503.02[F]; 2002.01[C]; 2002.02; 2201.02
1033(a)	1503.02[C]
1033(a)(1)	1503
1033(a)(2)	1503
1033(a)(2)(A)	1503.01; 1503.02; 1503.02[F]
1033(a)(2)(B)	1503.01[C]
1033(a)(2)(B)(i)	1503.01[C]
1033(a)(2)(B)(ii)	1503.01[C]
1033(a)(2)(C)	1503.01[C]
1033(a)(2)(E)(i)	1503.02[F]
1033(b)	1503.03; 1704
1033(b)(1)	1503.03[B]
1033(b)(3)	1503.03[A]
1033(g)	1503.02; 1503.02[C]
1033(g)(1)	1503.02[C]
1033(g)(2)	1503.02[C]
1033(g)(3)(A)	1503.02[E]
1033(g)(3)(B)	1503.02[E]
1033(g)(3)(C)	1503.02[E]
1033(g)(3)(D)	1503.02[E]
1033(g)(4)	1503.01[C]
1033(h)	1503.02; 1704
1033(h)(1)	1503.02[D]
1033(h)(2)	1503.02[D]
1033(i)	1503.02; 1503.02[B]
1033(k)	1503
1034	2002.01[C]; 2003; 2003.01[A]; 2003.02[A]; 2003.02[B]; 2003.03; 2004.01[B]
1034(a)	2003.01; 2003.02
1034(b)(1)	2003.02[A]

Code Sec.	Par. (¶)
1034(c)(1)	2003.02[A]
1034(e)	2003.02[B]
1034(g)	2003.02[C]
1034(k)	2003.01[A]
1038	905.02[A]; 1204; 1204.01; 1204.01[A]; 1204.01[C]; 1204.02; 1204.02[A]; 1204.02[D]; 1402
1038(a)	1204.01; 1204.01[A]
1038(b)(1)	1204.02; 1402.03
1038(b)(2)	1204.02
1038(c)	1204.01[C]
1039	905.02[A]
1041	202.03
1041(a)	101.01[G]; 1301.01[D]
1041(b)	101.01[G]; 1301.01[D]
1055(a)	1701.03[A]
1055(c)	1701.03[A]
1060	102.02[D]; 102.02[E]; 1302.01[D]
1201	1401.04
1201(a)	1301.02[A]
1202	1301.04[D]; 1305.01
1211(a)	1301.02[A]
1211(b)	1301.02[A]
1212	1301.02[A]
1212(a)	1301.02[A]
1212(b)	1301.02[A]
1221(a)	1301.02[A]
1222	1301.02[C]
1222(11)	1301.02[A]
1223	1003.01[A]; 1301.02[C]
1223(2)	1003.01[A]
1223(9)	1301.02[C]
1231	302.02[A]; 502.02[B]; 503; 602.02[B]; 702.02; 1202.01[B]; 1204.02[D]; 1301.02[A]; 1301.02[B]; 1301.02[C]; 1301.03; 1304.02[A]; 1304.02[B]; 1501; 1501.02[B]; 1502.02; 1503.01[A]; 1603
1231(a)(1)	1301.02[B]
1231(a)(2)	1301.02[B]
1231(a)(4)(C)	1301.02[B]
1231(b)	1301.02[B]; 1601.03[B]
1231(b)(4)	1301.02[B]
1231(c)	1301.02[B]
1237	1002.01[B]; 1003; 1003.01; 1003.01[A]; 1003.01[B]; 1003.01[C]; 1003.02; 1003.02[A]
1237(a)	1003.01
1237(a)(2)	1003.01[A]; 1003.01[B]
1237(b)(1)	1003.02; 1003.02[B]
1237(b)(3)	1003.01[C]
1239(a)	1301.02[A]
1239(b)	1401.03[A]
1239(b)(1)	1301.02[A]
1239(b)(2)	1301.02[A]
1239(b)(3)	1301.02[A]
1239(c)(1)	1301.02[A]
1239(c)(2)	1301.02[A]; 1401.03[A]
1239(d)(1)	1301.02[A]
1239(d)(2)	1301.02[A]
1241	502.02; 502.02[B]; 502.04; 503
1244(c)(3)	304.01

Code Sec.	Par. (¶)
1245	102.02[C]; 801.02[C]; 801.02[D]; 801.02[E]; 901.01[E]; 901.03[A]; 903; 1301.02[B]; 1301.03; 1301.03[A]; 1301.03[B]; 1305.03
1245(a)(1)	1301.03[A]
1245(a)(2)	1301.03[A]
1245(a)(3)(A)	1301.03[A]
1245(a)(3)(B)	1301.03[A]
1245(a)(3)(C)	1301.03[A]
1245(a)(3)(D)	1301.03[A]
1245(a)(3)(E)	1301.03[A]
1250	102.02[C]; 901.01[E]; 1301.02[B]; 1301.02[B]; 1301.03; 1301.03[A]; 1301.03[B]; 1305.03
1250(a)(1)(A)	1301.03[B]
1250(a)(1)(B)	1301.03[B]
1250(a)(1)(B)(i)	1301.03[B]
1250(a)(1)(B)(ii)	1301.03[B]
1250(a)(1)(B)(iii)	1301.03[B]
1250(a)(1)(B)(iv)	1301.03[B]
1250(a)(1)(B)(v)	1301.03[B]
1250(a)(2)(A)	1301.03[B]
1250(a)(2)(B)	1301.03[B]
1250(a)(2)(B)(ii)	1301.03[B]
1250(a)(2)(B)(iv)	1301.03[B]
1250(a)(2)(B)(v)	1301.03[B]
1250(b)(1)	1301.03[B]
1250(c)	1301.03[B]
1250(d)(4)(A)(i)	1302.02[A]
1250(d)(4)(C)	1302.02[A]
1250(f)	1301.03[B]
1271	304
1272	304; 304.02[A]
1273	304
1274	101.02[C]; 304; 304.01; 304.02; 304.02[A]; 304.02[B]; 304.03[D]
1274(b)(3)	101.02[C]; 304.03[E]
1274(c)	304.02
1274(c)(1)	303.03
1274(c)(3)(A)	304.01
1274(c)(3)(B)	304.01
1274(c)(3)(C)	304.01
1274(c)(3)(F)	304.01
1274(c)(4)	304.02[B]
1274(d)	303.03; 304.03
1274(d)(2)	304.03
1274(e)	304.03
1274A	304
1274A(a)	304.03[A]
1274A(b)	304.03[A]
1274A(c)	304.02[A]
1275	304
1295(a)	1104.01[A]
1361	206.01
1361(c)(2)(B)(v)	206.01
1362(a)	206.01
1362(b)	206.01
1362(d)(1)	206.01
1362(d)(2)	206.01
1362(d)(3)	206.01
1366	206; 206.02
1366(d)	206.02[B]
1374	206.02[A]
1374(d)	206.02[A]
1374(d)(7)	206.02[A]
1375	206.01
1378(a)	701.01[A]
1378(b)	701.01[A]
1381–1383	209.05; 1903.04[B]
1384–1388	1903.04[B]
1397B	1305.01
1397B(a)	1305.01

Code Sec.	Par. (¶)
1397B(b)(1)	1305.01
1397B(b)(1)(B)	1305.01
1397B(b)(4)	1305.01
1397B(b)(5)	1305.01
1397C	1305.03
1400B	1305.03
1400C	1706
1400F	1305.01; 1305.02
1400F(c)(2)	1305.02
1400I	806.01; 1105.05[C]
1400I(a)	806.01
1400I(b)	806.01
1400I(c)	806.01
1400I(d)	806.01
1400I(f)	806.01
1400L	806.02
1400L(b)	806.02
1400Z-2(a)	1304.02
1400Z-1(b)	1304
1400Z-2(b)(1)	1304.02[B]
1400Z-2(b)(2)(B)(i)	1304.02[B]
1400Z-2(b)(2)(B)(ii)	1304.02[B]
1400Z-2(b)(2)(B)(iii)	1304.02[B]
1400Z-2(b)(2)(B)(iv)	1304.02[B]
1400Z-2(c)	1304.02[B]
1400Z-2(d)(1)	1304.01; 1304.01[B]
1400Z-2(d)(2)(A)	1304.01[A]
1400Z-2(d)(2)(B)	1304.01[A]
1400Z-2(d)(2)(C)	1304.01[A]
1400Z-2(d)(2)(D)	1304.01[A]
1400Z-2(d)(3)	1304.01[A]
1400Z-2(e)(1)	1304.02[A]
1400Z-2(e)(2)	1304.02
1400Z-1(f)	1304; 1304.01[B]
1400Z-2	1304
1445	102.04
1563(a)	401.04[C]; 1301.01[C]
2032	101.01[F]
2032A	101.01[F]
4981	2201.03
6045(a)	1303.02
6045(b)	1303.02
6045(e)	1303.01[A]
6045(e)(1)	1303
6045(e)(5)	1303
6221–6241	203.02[G]
6240–6255	203.02[F]
6621	805.05[C]
6662(d)(1)(C)	809.01
6721	1303.03
6722	1303.03
6723	1303.03
7203	1303.03
7519	701.01[B]
7701	205.01
7701(a)(2)	203.02
7701(a)(3)	205.01
7701(l)	404.01
7704	1105
7704(c)	1105.01
7704(g)	1105.02; 2103.03
7872	303.03; 303.03[A]; 303.03[B]; 303.03[D]
7872(a)	303.03[B]
7872(b)	303.03[B]
7872(c)	303.03
7872(c)(2)	303.03[A]
7872(c)(3)	303.03[B]
7872(d)(1)	303.03[A]
7872(f)(2)	303.03

Regulations

Reg. §	Par. (¶)
1.15A.453-1(d)(2)(ii)(A)	1401.01[C]
1.42-5	805.01
1.42-5(c)(1)	805.01
1.48-1(c)	102.02[C]
1.48-1(e)(1)	801.01
1.48-1(e)(2)	102.02[C]; 801.01
1.48-4	603.02[A]
1.48-4(c)(3)	603.02[B]
1.48-4(c)(4)	603.02[B]
1.48-4(e)	603.02[B]
1.48-12(b)(2)	804.01[A]
1.48-12(b)(2)(v)	804.01[A]
1.48-12(b)(2)(x)	804.01[A]
1.48-12(b)(3)(ii)	804.01[C]
1.48-12(b)(3)(iii)	804.01[C]
1.48-12(b)(3)(iv)	804.01[C]
1.48-12(c)(3)(ii)	804.01[B]
1.48-12(c)(5)	804.01
1.48-12(c)(10)(i)	804.01[D]
1.48-12(c)(10)(ii)	804.01[D]
1.48-12(f)(3)	804.03
1.50-1	603.02[A]
1.50-1(b)(2)	603.02[A]
1.50-1(b)(3)	603.02[A]
1.50-1(c)	603.02[A]
1.50-1(c)(3)	603.02[A]
1.50-1(d)	603.02[A]
1.61-2(b)	1701.03[D]
1.61-6(a)	1001.01; 1001.01[A]
1.61-7	303.01
1.61-8(a)	401; 403
1.61-8(b)	403.01; 703.01; 502.01[B]
1.61-8(c)	401.02; 602.01; 602.02
1.61-12(b)(1)	1201.01[B]
1.108-2(f)	1201.01[A]
1.108-6	1201.01[C]
1.109-1(a)	602.02[B]
1.109-1(b)	602.02[B]
1.121-1(c)	2004.01[A]
1.121-4(a)	2004.02
1.121-4(b)	2004.02[A]
1.121-4(c)	2004.02[B]
1.121-a(1)	2004.01
1.162-1(a)	703.05; 703.06; 703.07
1.162-3	703.03
1.162-3(a)	703.03
1.162-3(a)(3)	703.03
1.162-3(c)(1)	703.03
1.162-3(c)(2)	703.03
1.162-3(d)	703.03
1.162-3(e)(2)	703.03
1.162-4	703.01; 703.01[F]; 801.03[A]
1.162-7(a)	703.04
1.162-7(b)(1)	703.04
1.162-7(b)(2)	703.04
1.162-7(b)(3)	703.04
1.162-11(a)	401.02; 402.01; 501
1.163-1(b)	303.02
1.163-1(d)	1701.03[D]
1.163-11	1701.01
1.164-3(b)	704.01; 1702
1.164-4(a)	704.02
1.164-4(b)(1)	704.02
1.164-6(b)	102.03
1.164-6(d)(1)	102.03
1.164-6(d)(2)	102.03
1.164-6(d)(3)	102.03
1.164-6(d)(5)	102.03
1.164-6(d)(6)	102.03
1.165-1(d)(2)	1501.02[C]

Reg. §	Par. (¶)
1.165-2(a)	801.05; 1504.02
1.165-7	801.03
1.165-7(a)(2)(i)	1501.02[A]
1.165-7(a)(2)(ii)	1501.02[A]
1.165-7(b)(1)	1501.02[A]
1.165-7(b)(2)(i)	1501.02[A]; 1703.02[B]
1.165-7(b)(2)(ii)	1703.02[A]
1.165-7(b)(4)(i)	1703.01[A]
1.165-7(b)(4)(ii)	1703.01[A]
1.165-7(b)(4)(iii)	1703.01[A]
1.165-7(b)(4)(iv)	1703.03
1.165-9(b)	2001.01
1.165-11(e)	1501.03[A]; 1501.03[B]
1.166-2(a)	1201.02[B]
1.166-2(b)	1201.02[B]
1.166-2(c)	1201.02[B]
1.166-5(b)	1201.02[C]
1.166-6(a)(1)	1202.02[B]; 1202.02[C]
1.166-6(a)(2)	1202.02[B]
1.166-6(b)(1)	1202.02[C]
1.166-6(b)(2)	1202.02[C]
1.166-6(c)	1202.02[C]
1.167-7(b)(2)(i)	801.03[A]
1.167(a)-2	900
1.167(a)-4	501.03; 601.02
1.167(a)-5	102.02[A]
1.167(a)-8(a)(4)	1504.02
1.167(g)-1	1804
1.168(i)-8	1301.01[E]
1.168(i)-8(d)(2)	1301.01[E]
1.169-2(a)(2)	802.01
1.169-2(a)(4)	802.01
1.169-4	802.01[A]
1.170A-1	1702
1.170A-4	1602.02
1.170A-4(b)(1)	1601.03[A]
1.170A-6	1601.04; 1601.04[B]
1.170A-7(a)(1)	1601.04
1.170A-7(b)(1)(i)	1601.04[A]
1.170A-7(b)(3)	1601.04[B]
1.170A-7(c)	1601.04
1.170A-7(e)(4)	1601.04[B]
1.170A-12	1601.04
1.170A-13(c)(2)	1601.01[B]
1.170A-13(c)(3)	1601.01[B]
1.170A-13(c)(3)(ii)	1601.01[B]
1.170A-13(c)(3)(iv)(B)	1601.01[B]
1.170A-13(c)(5)	1601.01[B]
1.170A-13(c)(5)(ii)	1601.01[B]
1.170A-13(c)(5)(iv)	1601.01[B]
1.170A-13(c)(6)	1601.01[B]
1.170A-14(b)	1601.04[C]
1.170A-14(c)	1601.04[C]
1.170A-14(d)(3)	1601.04[C]
1.170A-14(d)(4)	1601.04[C]
1.170A-14(d)(5)	1601.04[C]
1.170A-14(e)	1601.04[C]
1.170A-14(g)	1601.04[C]
1.170A-14(g)(2)	1601.04[C]
1.170A-14(g)(4)	1601.04[C]
1.175-2(b)	802.03
1.178-1(b)(5)	501.02
1.178-1(b)(5)(i)	501.02
1.190-2	703.02
1.190-3	703.02
1.194-1(b)	802.02
1.194-1(c)	802.02
1.194-2(b)(5)(ii)	802.02
1.194-2(b)(6)	802.02
1.194-3(a)	802.02
1.194-3(c)	802.02
1.194-4	802.02
1.212-1(b)	703; 2001.02
1.212-1(k)	703.08
1.216-1(a)	1901.02[A]
1.216-1(b)	1901.02[A]
1.216-1(d)(1)	1901.01[A]

Reg. §	Par. (¶)
1.216-1(d)(2)	1901.01[B]; 1901.02[A]
1.216-1(d)(4)	1901.01[D]
1.216-2(b)(1)	1901.02[B]
1.216-2(d)	1901.02[B]
1.217-2(a)(3)	1705.02
1.262-1(b)(4)	2001
1.263(a)-1	102.01
1.263(a)-1(a)	703.01[A]
1.263(a)-1(f)	102.01[B]; 703.01[B]
1.263(a)-1(f)(3)	103.01
1.263(a)-1(f)(4)	102.01[B]; 703.01[B]
1.263(a)-1(h)	102.01[A]; 703.01; 801
1.263(a)-2	102.01[A]; 502.02; 703.05; 801.03[A]
1.263(a)-2(d)	402.01
1.263(a)-2(d)(1)	102.01[A]; 103
1.263(a)-2(f)	102.01[A]; 1301.01[B]
1.263(a)-2(f)(4)	102.01[A]
1.263(a)-3	703.01; 703.01[A]; 801; 801.03[A]; 1301.02[E]
1.263(a)-3(d)	703.01[A]; 801
1.263(a)-3(e)	801.01
1.263(a)-3(e)(2)	801.01
1.263(a)-3(e)(2)(iii)	801.01[B]
1.263(a)-3(e)(2)(iv)	801.01[B]
1.263(a)-3(e)(2)(v)	801.01[A]
1.263(a)-3(e)(3)(i)	801.01[C]
1.263(a)-3(e)(3)(ii)	801.01[C]
1.263(a)-3(e)(3)(iii)	801.01[C]
1.263(a)-3(e)(4)	801.01[D]
1.263(a)-3(e)(5)(i)	801.01[E]
1.263(a)-3(e)(5)(ii)	801.01[E]
1.263(a)-3(e)(6)	801.01[D]; 801.01[E]
1.263(a)-3(f)(2)	601; 602
1.263(a)-3(h)	703.01[C]
1.263(a)-3(h)(4)	703.01[C]
1.263(a)-3(h)(5)	703.01[C]
1.263(a)-3(h)(8)	703.01[C]
1.263(a)-3(i)	703.01[D]
1.263(a)-3(j)	801.02
1.263(a)-3(j)(2)(ii)	801.02[B]
1.263(a)-3(j)(2)(iii)	801.02[A]
1.263(a)-3(j)(2)(iv)	801.02
1.263(a)-3(j)(2)(iv)(B)	801.02
1.263(a)-3(j)(2)(iv)(C)	801.02
1.263(a)-3(j)(3)	801.02[B]
1.263(a)-3(k)	801.03
1.263(a)-3(k)(3)	801.03
1.263(a)-3(k)(4)	801.03[A]
1.263(a)-3(k)(5)	801.03
1.263(a)-3(k)(6)(i)	801.03[B]
1.263(a)-3(k)(6)(ii)	801.03[B]
1.263(a)-3(k)(7)	801.03[B]
1.263(a)-3(l)	801.04
1.263(a)-3(l)(2)	801.04
1.263(a)-3(l)(3)	801.04
1.263(a)-3(n)	703.01; 703.01[E]
1.263(a)-4(f)(5)(ii)	703.01[C]
1.263A-0	103.01
1.263A-1(e)(2)	103.01[B]
1.263A-1(e)(3)	103.01[B]
1.263A-1(g)	103.01[B]
1.263A-8-1.263A-15	103.03
1.263A-8(b)	103.03
1.263A-9(a)	103.01[C]
1.263A-10(b)(1)	103.01[C]
1.263A-11(c)	103.01[C]
1.263A-11(d)	103.01[C]
1.263A-12(c)(2)	103.01[C]
1.263A-12(d)(1)	103.01[C]
1.263A-12(e)(2)	103.01[C]

Reg. §	Par. (¶)
1.263A-12(f)	103.01[C]
1.266-1(a)(2)	103.03
1.266-1(b)	103.03
1.266-1(c)(3)	103.03
1.266-1(e)	103.03
1.267(d)-1(b)	1301.01[C]
1.301.7701-1	205.01
1.301.7701-2	205.01
1.337(d)-7	2201.02
1.337(d)-7(d)(1)	2201.02
1.337(d)-7(d)(2)	2201.02
1.337(d)-7(d)(3)	2201.02
1.338-6	102.02[D]
1.441-1(c)	701.01
1.441-2	701.01
1.441-3	701.01[A]
1.441-3(c)	701.01[A]; 1101.01[B]
1.446-1(c)	303.02; 701.02[A]
1.446-1(e)(2)	903.01
1.446-1(e)(2)(ii)	903.01
1.446-1(e)(2)(iii)	903.01
1.448-1T(e)(4)	209.02[A]
1.453-9	1204.02[D]
1.453B-1(c)	1402.01[A]
1.461-1(a)	402.01; 703.05
1.461-1(a)(2)	701.02[B]
1.461-1(c)(3)	701.02[B]
1.467-1(c)(2)(iii)	404.02[A]
1.467-3(b)	404.02
1.467-3(c)	404.02
1.467-3(c)(3)	404.02[A]
1.469-1(e)(3)(vi)(D)	1103.01[A]
1.469-1(e)(4)(iv)	1101.02[B]
1.469-1(f)(2)	1102.03
1.469-1(f)(4)	1102.03
1.469-1(f)(4)(i)	1104.03[C]; 1104.04[B]
1.469-2(c)(2)(iii)(A)	1104.01[A]
1.469-2(c)(2)(iii)(C)	1104.01[A]
1.469-2(c)(2)(v)	1104.01[A]
1.469-2(d)(2)	1104.01[B]
1.469-2(e)(2)(ii)	1104.01[C]
1.469-2(e)(2)(iii)(A)	1104.01[C]
1.469-2(e)(2)(iii)(B)	1104.01[C]
1.469-2(f)(5)	1103.03
1.469-2(f)(5)(ii)	1103.03
1.469-2(f)(5)(iii)	1103.03
1.469-2(f)(6)	1103.02
1.469-4	1102
1.469-4(b)(1)	1102.01
1.469-4(b)(2)	1102.01
1.469-4(c)(1)	1102.01
1.469-4(c)(2)	1102.01
1.469-4(d)(1)	1102.01
1.469-4(d)(2)	1102.02
1.469-4(d)(3)	1102.02
1.469-4(d)(5)	1102.02
1.469-4(e)	1102.03
1.469-4(f)	1102.03
1.469-4(g)	1102.03
1.469-5(f)(1)	1101.03[A]
1.469-9(e)(2)	1103.06
1.469-9(e)(3)(i)	1103.06[A]
1.469-9(e)(3)(ii)	1103.06[A]
1.469-9(f)(1)	1103.06[B]
1.469-9(f)(2)	1103.06[B]
1.469-9(j)	1103.06[C]
1.483-3(b)(2)	304.01[B]
1.483-3(b)(2)(i)	304.01[B]
1.483-3(b)(2)(iii)	304.01[B]
1.483-4(b)(3)	304.01[B]
1.528-1(b)	1902
1.528-3(a)	1903.01[A]
1.528-3(b)	1903.01[A]
1.528-3(c)	1903.01[A]
1.528-4(b)	1903.01[B]
1.528-4(c)	1903.01[B]
1.528-4(d)	1903.01[B]
1.528-6(a)	1903.01[D]
1.528-6(b)	1903.01[D]
1.528-6(c)	1903.01[D]

Reg. §	Par. (¶)
1.528-7	1903.01[E]
1.528-8	1903.03
1.528-9(a)	1903.01[C]
1.528-9(b)	1903.01[C]
1.528-9(c)	1903.01[C]
1.528-9(d)	1903.01[C]
1.528-10(c)(1)	1903.02
1.528-10(c)(2)	1903.02
1.602-1–1.602-10	802.01[A]
1.612-4(a)	1101.02[B]
1.704-1	203.02[C]
1.706-1(b)(3)	701.01[A]
1.706-1(b)(3)(iv)	701.01[A]
1.706-1(b)(8)(ii)	701.01[A]
1.707-1(c)	703.04[E]
1.722-1	203.02[A]
1.742-1	203.02[A]
1.856-6(b)(1)	2201.01[A]
1.856-10	2203. 02
1.857-2(a)(3)(ii)	2201.01[A]
1.860-1–1.860-5	2203.04
1.1001-1(b)(1)	102.03
1.1001-1(b)(2)	102.03
1.1001-2	1301.01[B]
1.1001-2(a)(1)	1203.01[A]; 1602
1.1001-2(a)(2)	1203.01[A]
1.1001-2(a)(3)	1203.01[A]
1.1001-2(a)(4)(i)	1203.01[A]
1.1001-2(a)(4)(ii)	1203.01[A]
1.1001-2(a)(4)(iii)	1203.01[A]; 1602
1.1002-1(d)	1302.01
1.1011-1	1301.01[A]
1.1011-2(b)	1602.02
1.1017-1	1201.01[B]
1.1031(a)-1(a)	1302.01
1.1031(a)-1(b)	1302.01[A]
1.1031(a)-1(c)	305.01[B]; 1302.01[A]; 1302.02
1.1031(b)-1(a)	1302.02[A]
1.1031(b)-1(b)	1302.02[A]
1.1031(b)-1(c)	1302.02[B]
1.1031(d)-1(a)	1302.01[B]
1.1031(d)-1(b)	1302.01[B]; 1302.02[C]
1.1031(d)-1(c)	1302.02[C]
1.1031(d)-1(e)	1302.02[C]
1.1031(d)-2	1302.02[C]
1.1031(k)-1(g)	1302.01[A]
1.1033(a)-2(a)	1502.01
1.1033(a)-2(b)	1503
1.1033(a)-2(c)(2)	1503.01[B]
1.1033(a)-2(c)(3)	1503.01[C]
1.1033(a)-2(c)(7)	1503.01
1.1033(a)-2(c)(9)	1503.02[A]
1.1033(a)-2(c)(10)	1502.03; 1502.03[B]
1.1033(a)-2(c)(11)	1502.03
1.1034-1(a)	2003.02
1.1034-1(b)(6)	2003.02[A]
1.1034-1(c)(2)	2003.02[B]
1.1034-1(c)(3)(ii)	2003.03
1.1034-1(f)	2003.02[C]
1.1034-4	2003.02[B]
1.1038-1(a)(1)	1204.01
1.1038-1(a)(2)	1204.01
1.1038-1(a)(3)	1204.01
1.1038-1(a)(4)	1204.01
1.1038-1(b)(1)(ii)	1204.02
1.1038-1(b)(2)(i)	1204.02
1.1038-1(b)(2)(ii)	1204.02
1.1038-1(b)(2)(iii)	1204.02
1.1038-1(c)(4)(ii)	1204.02[C]
1.1038-1(d)	1204.02[D]
1.1038-1(f)(2)	1204.01[A]
1.1038-1(g)(1)	1204.01[C]
1.1038-1(g)(3)	1204.01[B]
1.1055-1(b)	1701.03[A]
1.1060-1(b)	102.02[D]
1.1060-1(c)	1202.02[D]
1.1060-1(d)	1302.01[D]
1.1060-1(e)	102.02[E]

Reg. §	Par. (¶)
1.1223-1(a)	1301.02[C]
1.1223-1(b)	1301.02[C]
1.1223-1(j)	1301.02[C]
1.1231-1(f)	1301.02[B]
1.1237-1(a)(2)	1003
1.1237-1(a)(3)	1003
1.1237-1(a)(4)	1003.01
1.1237-1(b)(3)	1003.01[A]
1.1237-1(c)(2)	1003.01[B]
1.1237-1(c)(2)(i)(a)	1003.01[A]
1.1237-1(c)(3)	1003.01[B]
1.1237-1(c)(3)(ii)	1003.01[B]
1.1237-1(c)(3)(iii)	1003.01[B]
1.1237-1(c)(4)	1003.01[B]
1.1237-1(c)(5)	1003.01[C]
1.1237-1(e)(2)	1003.02[A]
1.1237-1(e)(2)(i)	1003.02[A]
1.1237-1(e)(2)(ii)	1003.02[A]
1.1237-1(e)(2)(iii)	1003.02[A]
1.1237-1(g)(1)	1003.02[B]
1.1237-1(g)(2)	1003.02[B]
1.1241-1(a)	502.02[B]
1.1241-1(b)	502.02[B]
1.1245-3	1301.03[A]
1.1245-3(b)	1301.03[A]
1.1245-3(c)	1301.03[A]
1.1273-1(e)(3)	304.03[B]
1.1274-2(b)(3)	304.03[E]
1.1274-2(c)	304.03[D]
1.1274-2(f)(1)	304.03[C]
1.1274-2(f)(1)(ii)	304.03[C]
1.1274-2(g)	304.03[D]
1.1274-2(h)	304.03[C]
1.1274-3	101.02[C]
1.1274-3(a)(2)(iv)	304.03[E]
1.1274-3(b)(3)	304.03[E]
1.1274-4(a)(1)	304.03
1.1274-4(c)(1)	304.03[B]
1.1274A-1(c)(1)	304.02[A]
1.1274A-1(c)(2)	304.02[A]
1.1274A-1(c)(3)	304.02[B]
1.1275-4(c)(3)	304.03[D]

Reg. §	Par. (¶)
1.1275-4(c)(4)(ii)	304.03[D]
1.1275-4(c)(4)(ii)(B)	304.03[D]
1.1275-4(c)(7)	304.03[D]
1.6045-4	1303
1.6045-4(b)(1)	1303.01
1.6045-4(b)(2)	1303.01
1.6045-4(c)	1303.01
1.6045-4(e)(1)	1303.01[A]
1.6045-4(e)(3)	1303.01[A]
1.6045-4(e)(4)	1303.01[A]
1.6045-4(e)(5)(i)	1303.01[A]
1.6045-4(e)(5)(ii)	1303.01[A]
1.6045-4(f)	1303.01[B]
1.6045-4(h)(1)	1303.02[A]
1.6045-4(h)(2)(i)	1303.02[A]
1.6045-4(h)(2)(ii)	1303.02[A]
1.6045-4(i)	1303.02[A]
1.6045-4(i)(5)	1303.01[B]
1.6045-4(k)	1303.02[A]
1.6045-4(l)	1303.02[A]
1.6045-4(m)	1303.02[B]
1.6045-4(m)(1)	1303.02[B]
1.6045-4(m)(2)	1303.02[B]
15A.453-1(a)	1401.02
15A.453-1(b)	1401.01
15A.453-1(b)(2)(i)	1401.02[A]
15A.453-1(b)(2)(ii)	1401.02[A]
15A.453-1(b)(2)(iii)	1401.02[A]
15A.453-1(b)(2)(iv)	1401.02[B]
15A.453-1(b)(2)(v)	1401.02[A]
15A.453-1(b)(3)(i)	1401.02[B]
15A.453-1(b)(3)(ii)	1401.02[B]
15A.453-1(b)(3)(iii)	1401.02[B]
15A.453-1(c)(1)	1401.02[E]
15A.453-1(c)(2)(i)	1401.02[E]
15A.453-1(c)(2)(i)(B)	1401.02[E]
15A.453-1(c)(3)(i)	1401.02[E]
15A.453-1(c)(3)(ii)	1401.02[E]
15A.453-1(c)(4)	1401.02[E]
15A.453-1(c)(6)	1401.02[E]
15A.453-1(d)(2)(i)	1401.01[C]
15A.453-1(d)(2)(iii)	1401.01[C]

Reg. §	Par. (¶)
15A.453-1(d)(3)(i)	1401.01[C]
15A.453-1(d)(3)(ii)	1401.01[C]
15A.453-1(d)(4)	1401.01[C]
15A.453-1(e)(1)(i)	1401.02[B]
15A.453-1(e)(2)	1401.02[B]
15A.453-1(e)(4)	1401.02[B]
15A.453-1(e)(4)(v)	1401.02[B]
31.3401(a)(15)-1	1705.03[A]
301.6221-1(a)	203.02[G]
301.6241-1(a)(6)	203.02[G]
301.7701-1(a)	202.02
301.7701-3	205.01

Proposed Regulations

Reg. §	Par. (¶)
1.163(j)-1	303.02[D]
1.163(j)-2	303.02[D]
1.163(j)-3	303.02[D]
1.163(j)-4	303.02[D]
1.163(j)-5	303.02[D]
1.163(j)-6	303.02[D]
1.163(j)-7	303.02[D]
1.163(j)-8	303.02[D]
1.163(j)-9	303.02[D]
1.163(j)-9(g)	303.02[D]
1.163(j)-10	303.02[D]
1.163(j)-11	303.02[D]
1.167(j)-9(h)	303.02[D]
1.168-2(c)(4)(ii)(A)	904.01[B]
1.168-2(e)(3)	901.02[B]
1.168-2(e)(5)	901.02[B]
1.199A-2(b)(2)(iv)(C)	209.04
1.199A-7	209.05
1.199A-8	209.05
1.199A-9	209.05
1.199A-10	209.05
1.199A-11	209.05
1.199A-12	209.05
1.216-1(e)(2)	1901.01[B]
1.280A-1(c)(1)	1803.01
1.280A-1(c)(2)	1803.01
1.280A-1(e)(1)(iii)	1803.01[B]
1.280A-1(e)(1)(iv)	1803.01[B]
1.280A-1(e)(3)(ii)	1803.01[B]
1.280A-1(e)(3)(iv)	1803.01[B]
1.280A-1(e)(4)(i)	1803.01[B]
1.280A-1(e)(4)(ii)	1803.01[B]
1.280A-1(e)(6)	1803.01[B]
1.280A-1(e)(7)	1803.01[B]
1.280A-2(b)(3)	1801.02[B]
1.280A-2(c)	1801.02[C]
1.280A-2(d)	1801.02[D]
1.280A-2(e)	1801.02[A]
1.280A-2(g)(2)	1801.02
1.280A-2(i)(2)	1801.04[A]
1.280A-2(i)(2)(ii)	1801.04[A]
1.280A-2(i)(2)(iii)	1801.04[A]
1.280A-2(i)(3)	1801.03; 1801.03[B]
1.280A-2(i)(4)	1801.05[B]
1.280A-2(i)(5)	1801.04[B]
1.280A-3(c)(2)	1803.02[B]
1.280A-3(d)(2)	1803.02[B]
1.280A-3(d)(3)	1803.02[B]
1.280A-3(d)(4)	1803.02[B]
1.280A-3(e)	1803.01
1.465-2(a)	302.02
1.465-2(b)	302.02
1.465-4(a)	302.03[B]
1.465-5	302.03[B]
1.465-6(d)	302.03[A]
1.465-11	302.02
1.465-27	302.04
1.465-38	302.02[A]
1.465-41	302.03[C]
1.1400Z-2(a)-1(b)(1)	1304.02
1.1400Z-2(a)-1(b)(2)	1304.02[A]
1.1400Z-2(a)-1(c)(1)	1304.02[A]
1.1400Z-2(a)-1(c)(2)	1304.02[A]
1.1400Z-2(a)-1(c)(3)	1304.02[A]
1.1400Z-2(b)-1(b)	1304.02[B]

Reg. §	Par. (¶)
1.1400Z-2(b)-1(c)	1304.02[B]
1.1400Z-2(c)-1(a)	1304.02[B]
1.1400Z-2(c)-1(b)	1304.02[B]
1.1400Z-2(d)-1(a)	1304.01
1.1400Z-2(d)-1(a)(1)	1304.01[B]
1.1400Z-2(d)-1(a)(2)	1304.01[B]
1.1400Z-2(d)-1(b)	1304.01[B]
1.1400Z-2(d)-1(e)	1304.01
1.1400Z-2(e)-1(a)(1)	1304.02[A]; 1304.02[B]
1.7872-2(a)(2)(ii)	303.03
1.7872-4(c)	303.03
1.7872-4(d)	303.03
1.7872-4(e)	303.03
1.7872-10(a)(5)	303.03[B]
1.7872-11(g)	303.03[D]
1.7872-11(g)(3)	303.03[D]
1.7872-13	303.03

Temporary Regulations

Reg. §	Par. (¶)
1.469-5T(f)(4)	1103.06
1.163-8T	303.02[C]; 1701.01[B]
1.163-8T(a)(3)	303.02[C]
1.163-8T(c)(1)	303.02[C]
1.163-8T(c)(2)(C)	303.02[C]
1.163-8T(c)(3)	303.02[C]
1.163-8T(c)(4)(i)	303.02[C]
1.163-8T(c)(4)(ii)	303.02[C]
1.163-8T(c)(4)(iii)(B)	303.02[C]
1.163-8T(c)(4)(v)	303.02[C]
1.163-8T(c)(5)(i)	303.02[C]
1.163-8T(c)(5)(ii)	303.02[C]
1.163-8T(d)(1)	303.02[C]
1.163-8T(d)(3)	303.02[C]
1.163-8T(e)(1)	303.02[C]
1.163-8T(j)(1)	303.02[C]
1.163-8T(j)(2)	303.02[C]
1.163-10T(p)(1)	1701.01[A]
1.163-10T(p)(3)(ii)	1701.01[A]
1.163-10T(p)(5)	1701.01[A]
1.167(a)-4T	601.02
1.167(a)-5T	102.02[D]
1.263(a)-2T	502.02
1.280H-1T	701.01[B]
1.337(d)-7T	2201.02
1.444-1T(a)(5)	701.01[B]
1.444-1T(b)(4)(ii)(B)	701.01[B]
1.444-2T	701.01[B]
1.444-2T(c)(2)	701.01[B]
1.444-2T(c)(3)	701.01[B]
1.446-1T(e)(2)	903.01
1.448-1T(b)	701.02[A]
1.448-1T(e)	701.02[A]
1.469-1T(e)(3)	1103.01
1.469-1T(e)(3)(iv)	1103.01
1.469-1T(e)(3)(v)	1103.01
1.469-1T(e)(3)(vi)	1103.01[A]
1.469-1T(e)(3)(vi)(B)	1102.01
1.469-1T(e)(3)(vii)	1103.01[B]
1.469-1T(e)(3)(viii)	1103.01
1.469-1T(e)(4)(v)(A)	1101.02[B]
1.469-1T(e)(4)(v)(B)	1101.02[B]
1.469-1T(f)(2)(i)(A)	1104.03[A]
1.469-1T(f)(2)(i)(C)	1104.03[A]
1.469-1T(f)(2)(ii)	1104.02[B]
1.469-1T(f)(2)(ii)(B)	1104.03[B]
1.469-1T(f)(3)(i)	1104.04[B]
1.469-1T(f)(3)(iii)	1104.04[B]
1.469-1T(f)(4)(ii)(A)	1104.03[C]
1.469-1T(g)(2)	1101.01[B]
1.469-1T(g)(3)(i)	1101.03[B]
1.469-1T(g)(3)(ii)	1101.03[B]
1.469-1T(g)(3)(iii)	1101.03[B]
1.469-1T(g)(4)(i)	1104.02
1.469-1T(g)(4)(ii)	1104.02
1.469-1T(g)(5)	1104.04[A]
1.469-1T(g)(5)(ii)	1104.04[A]

Reg. §	Par. (¶)
1.469-1T(h)	1104.04[A]
1.469-2T(b)(1)	1104.01
1.469-2T(c)(1)	1104.01[A]
1.469-2T(c)(2)	1103.03
1.469-2T(c)(2)(i)(A)	1104.01[A]
1.469-2T(c)(2)(i)(C)	1104.01[A]
1.469-2T(c)(2)(ii)	1104.01[A]
1.469-2T(c)(2)(v)(A)(*1*)(*ii*)	1104.01[A]
1.469-2T(c)(3)(i)	1104.01[A]
1.469-2T(c)(3)(ii)	1104.01[A]
1.469-2T(c)(3)(iii)(B)	1104.01[A]
1.469-2T(c)(4)	1104.01[A]
1.469-2T(c)(5)	1104.01[A]
1.469-2T(d)(1)	1104.01[B]
1.469-2T(d)(2)	1104.01[B]
1.469-2T(d)(4)	1104.01[B]
1.469-2T(d)(5)	1104.01[B]
1.469-2T(d)(7)	1104.01[B]
1.469-2T(e)(1)	1104.01[C]
1.469-2T(e)(2)	1103.01[B]; 1104.01[C]
1.469-2T(e)(2)(i)	1104.01[C]
1.469-2T(e)(3)(ii)(A)	1104.01[C]
1.469-2T(e)(3)(ii)(D)(*1*)	1104.01[C]
1.469-2T(e)(3)(vii)	1104.01[C]
1.469-2T(f)(3)	1103.04
1.469-3T(d)	1104.04
1.469-5T(a)	1101.03[A]
1.469-5T(b)(2)(ii)	1101.03[A]
1.469-5T(b)(2)(iii)	1101.03[A]
1.469-5T(e)(1)	1101.02[A]
1.469-5T(e)(2)	1101.02[A]
1.469-5T(f)(2)(i)	1101.03[A]
1.469-5T(f)(2)(ii)	1101.03[A]
1.469-5T(f)(3)	1101.03[A]
1.1031(d)-1T	1302.01[D]
1.7519-2T(a)(4)(ii)	701.01[B]
1.7519-2T(b)	701.01[B]
1.7872-5T(c)	303.03[B]
301.9100-7T	902.01[A]

Revenue Rulings

Rev. Rul.	Par. (¶)
54-607	1301.02[C]
55-79	1401.02[C]
55-89	601.03
55-540	305.02[B]; 405.02
55-749	1302.01[A]
56-225	1901.01[C]
56-531	502.02[B]
56-543	1503.01[C]
57-198	301.03[A]; 1701.03[E]
57-244	1302.03
57-400	301.01[B]
57-488	1001.02
57-537	403.02; 503
57-565	1002.01[B]
58-1	401.04[B]
58-402	1301.01[B]
59-91	1002.01[B]
59-173	1502.03[A]
59-229	1302.02[B]; 1302.02[C]
60-3	1001.02
60-43	305.01[B]
60-122	402.02[A]
60-180	602.02[A]
60-327	704.02
60-329	1501.01
61-217	501.03
62-8	601.01
62-177	1901.02[A]
62-178	1901.02[A]
63-127	1503.01[B]
63-221	1502.01
64-31	1902.01
64-183	1502.03[A]

Rev. Rul.	Par. (¶)
64-205	1601.04[C]
64-237	1503.02[A]
65-79	102.02[C]
65-95	303.01
65-141	403.01
65-155	1302.02[A]; 1401.02[D]
65-265	102.02[B]; 901.02[A]
66-7	1301.02[C]
66-209	403.02; 1302.01[A]
66-215	102.02[C]
66-373	703.06
67-123	602.01
67-188	1202.01[B]
67-297	1701.02[A]; 1701.03[E]
67-337	704.02
67-349	102.02[C]
67-417	102.02[C]
68-13	1401.02[C]
68-19	502.01[B]
68-36	1302.01[C]
68-37	1502.03[A]
68-50	102.02[C]
68-193	102.02[B]; 901.02[A]
68-260	501.01[B]
68-331	1302.01[A]
68-387	1901.01[D]
68-431	201
68-478	1001.02
68-528	102.02[A]
68-530	102.02[A]
68-643	303.02; 303.02[A]
68-650	1701.02
69-43	1201.02[A]
69-76	1901.02[A]
69-89	201
69-169	102.02[C]
69-188	1701.02[A]
69-456	704.03
69-511	502.01[A]
69-582	1701.02[A]
70-103	102.02[C]
70-146	601.02; 602.01
70-160	102.02[C]
70-164	1501.01
70-254	703.06
70-360	301.01[A]
70-376	1503.01
70-399	1503.02[A]
70-408	501.01[A]
70-413	703.06
70-540	303.01
70-604	1903.04[C]
70-647	303.02
71-41	1503.02[A]; 1503.02[C]
71-49	704.01[C]
71-160	1501.02[C]
71-243	603.02[A]
71-268	704.01[A]
71-283	502.02[A]
71-475	103.03
71-476	703.08
71-590	704.03
72-85	503; 1301.02[B]
72-238	1202.02[C]
72-372	1503.01
72-404	1901.01[A]
72-424	1503.02[C]
72-433	1503.02[C]
72-456	1302.02[D]
72-519	406.02
72-549	1503.02[C]
72-601	1302.01[A]
73-18	1503.03
73-35	1502.03[A]
73-36	1202.01[A]

Rev. Rul.	Par. (¶)
73-72	1503.01
73-176	502.04
73-276	401.03
73-393	703.04[B]
73-451	1401.01[B]
74-2	102.02[C]
74-8	1502.01
74-17	1903.04[A]
74-52	704.01; 704.02
74-99	1903.04[A]
74-104	102.01
74-187	1701.03[E]
74-265	102.02[B]; 901.02[A]
74-324	905.01[B]
74-391	102.02[C]
74-392	102.02[C]
74-532	1502.01
75-99	303.02[A]
75-178	102.02[C]
75-194	1602.02
75-226	401.03
75-271	1701.03[D]
75-281	303.02
75-291	1302.01[A]
75-292	1302.01[A]
75-346	704.01
75-370	1903.04[C]
75-371	1903.04[B]; 1903.04[C]
75-455	704.02
75-494	1903.04[A]
75-524	1301.02[C]
76-45	704.02
76-110	1401.02[C]
76-134	1501.01
76-185	1601
76-301	1302.01[A]
76-319	1503.02[A]
76-495	704.01; 1702
76-521	1501.01

Rev. Rul.	Par. (¶)
77-29	704.01
77-188	102.01
77-192	1503.02[A]
77-270	703.01[F]
77-294	1401.01[B]
77-337	1302.01[A]
77-362	102.02[C]
77-422	1503.02[F]
77-490	1501.01
78-4	1302.01[A]
78-103	704.01; 1702
78-164	1202.01
78-303	1601.04[B]
79-91	1401.01[B]
79-137	1901.01[D]
79-174	1501.01
79-201	704.02
79-261	1503.02[A]
79-276	1001.01
79-402	1503.03
80-56	1202.02[C]
80-58	1204
80-72	302.03
80-93	703.01[F]
80-121	1301.01[B]
80-172	2004.01[A]
80-175	1503.01
80-184	1502.03[A]; 1503.02[C]
80-216	1003
80-235	101.02[A]
80-299	1901.01[B]
81-83	1001.02
81-152	1902.01
81-160	703.05
81-163	1602.02
81-181	1502.01
81-240	102.02[C]
81-300	703.04[E]
81-301	703.04[E]
82-74	1501.02[B]

Rev. Rul.	Par. (¶)
82-202	301.03[B]; 1201.01[A]
82-225	302.03[B]
83-49	1503.02[C]
83-51	1701.03[B]
83-70	1503.02[C]
83-74	1903.03
83-105	102.01
84-52	205.02
84-102	203.02[B]
84-111	204.02[A]
84-121	1302.01[A]
85-113	302.03
86-15	102.02[C]
86-67	301.01[A]
86-101	205.02
86-120	1204.01
87-22	303.02[A]; 1701.02[B]
87-41	703.04[C]
87-56	901.02[A]
87-57	701.01[A]
87-59	1501.01
87-130	1901.01[A]
88-38	401.04[B]
88-103	1503.01
90-34	1302.03[A]
90-38	903.01
90-61	1501.01
91-31	301.03[B]; 1201.01[A]
92-53	1201.01[A]
95-37	205.02
97-64	2202.01
2002-9	704.04
2002-83	1302.01[A]
2003-77	805.03[B]
2004-39	2202.01
2005-74	2002.01[D]
2006-27	1701.03[D]
2010-25	1701.01[C]
2016-29	805.01

Revenue Procedures

Rev. Proc.	Par. (¶)
75-21	305.02[B]
75-25	1001.02[B]
75-28	305.02[B]
76-30	305.02[B]
78-25	1001.02[B]
79-48	305.02[B]
86-14	904.01[B]
87-15	1701.02[B]
87-56	102.02[B]; 603.02[B]; 901.01[A]; 901.02[A]
87-57	901.01[B]; 901.01[C]; 901.01[D]; 902.01[B]
89-15	901.01[C]
92-29	1001.02[B]
2000-35	102.04
2000-37	1302.01[A]
2001-28	305.02[B]; 405.02
2002-12	703.03
2002-22	202.02
2002-28	703.03
2003-82	805.05[A]
2004-34	403.01; 701.02[B]
2004-38	805.01
2004-51	1302.01[A]
2005-14	2002.02
2006-45	701.01[A]
2006-46	701.01[A]
2007-12	1303
2010-13	1002.04
2011-41	101.01[F]
2013-13	1801.01

Rev. Proc.	Par. (¶)
2013-16	1201.01[D]
2014-12	804
2014-20	1201.01[C]
2015-56	801.02[C]
2018-59	303.02[D]
2019-8	901.03[A]; 902.01[B]; 902.02
2019-11	209.04
2019-12	704
2019-33	901.03[B]

IRS Letter Rulings

LTR	Par. (¶)
7820003	303.01
8229120	301.02
8421018	1601.02
8429004	1503.01
8547001	1201.02[A]
8614002	301.03[A]
8648005	102.02[C]
8749009	302.03[A]
8810034	1302.01[A]
200404044	1302.01[A]
200518016	804.01[D]
200652041	2002.01
200720016	704.01[C]
200725018	2002.01
200730012	704.01[C]

Notices

Notice	Par. (¶)
81-16	904.01[B]
84-16	904.01[B]
88-74	1701.01[B]
95-53	404.01
2006-27	1001.03
2006-28	1001.03
2006 52	803
2008-35	1001.03
2009-53	1708.01
2013-70	1708.01
2017-32	1701.03[D]
2017-40	1701.03[D]
2017-45	2202
2018-18	805.01
2018-28	303.02[D]
2018-34	1701.03[D]
2018-35	403.01; 701.02[B]
2018-48	1304
2018-63	1701.03[D]
2019-7	209.02[B]
2019-27	209.05
2019-42	1304

Treasury Decisions

Treasury Decision	Par. (¶)
8176	1602.02
8517	304
8820	402.02[A]
8859	805.01
9307	903.01
9564	102.01[A]; 703.01; 801
9636	102.01[A]; 703.01
9753	805.01
9847[fill colspan="2" character="period"]}	209
9848	805.01
9872[fill colspan="2" character="period"]}	804

Announcements

Announcement	Par. (¶)
86-5	904.01[B]
2006-88	1001.03

Field Service Advice

Field Service Advice	Par. (¶)
200033002	102.02[C]
200110001	102.02[C]
200127001	1503.02[C]

General Counsel's Memoranda

General Counsel's Memoranda	Par. (¶)
11933	601.01
19573	1202.02[A]
38975	1503.02[C]

Index

References are to paragraph (¶) numbers.

A

Abandonment losses . . . 1203, 1203.02, 1504
. for improvements . . . 801.05, 1504.02[B]
. for land . . . 1504.02, 1504.02[A]

Accelerated Cost Recovery System (ACRS)
. adopted in Tax Reform Act of 1986 . . . 900
. computation of deductions . . . 904.01
. election to use straight-line depreciation for . . . 904.01[A]
. for pre-1987 property . . . 904
. property excluded from using . . . 905.02[A]
. for property under construction . . . 901.02[B]
. recovery of cost of real estate under . . . 901, 904.01
. recovery period for . . . 904.01, 904.01[A]
. schedules used for . . . 904.01[B]
. tax-free transfers of recovery property under . . . 905.02[C]

Accelerated depreciation . . . 905.01, 1301.03[B], 1301.04[D]

Accounting method. *See also individual methods*
. decreased income as result of change in . . . 1104.01[B]
. increased income as result of change in . . . 1104.01[A]
. operating expenses and taxes . . . 701.02[B]
. other than accrual or cash, allowance of . . . 701.02

Accounting period, fiscal or calendar . . . 701.01. *See also* Tax year

Accrual method
. accrual of real property tax under . . . 701.02[B]
. advance rents under . . . 402.01
. apportionment of property tax under . . . 102.03
. bonuses under . . . 701.03[A]
. for contingent payment obligation realized for year of property sale . . . 1401.01[C]

Accrual method—continued
. deduction of interest paid under . . . 303.02, 303.02[A]
. deferral for advance payments . . . 701.02[B]
. economic performance requirement under . . . 701.02[B], 701.03[A]
. inclusion based on financial accounting treatment . . . 701.02[B]
. reporting income in year it is earned under . . . 701.02[B]
. sale on contract for deed under . . . 1301.01[B]
. strategies for timing income and expenses under . . . 701.03-701.03[B]
. taxpayer types required to use . . . 701.02[A]

Accumulated earnings tax . . . 204.02[B]

Acquisition of corporate control to replace involuntarily converted property . . . 1503.02[F]

Acquisition indebtedness
. home equity debt . . . 1701.01[C]
. maximum for deduction of . . . 1701.01
. for pre-1987 indebtedness . . . 1701.01, 1701.01[D]
. for qualified residence . . . 1701.01, 1701.01[B]

Acquisition transaction . . . 100-105
. basis, importance of . . . 101-101.02[C]
. buying expenses in . . . 102.01-102.02[E]
. construction of real property . . . 103-103.03
. energy efficient home tax credit . . . 105
. financing. *See* Real estate financing
. low-income housing tax credit . . . 104
. overview of . . . 100, 200
. by partnership . . . 203.02[A]
. real property purchase . . . 102-102.04
. reporting requirements for . . . 102.02[E]
. structure affecting tax consequences of . . . 100
. taxes imposed in . . . 704
. writeoff of expenses in . . . 702.01-702.01[C]

Active trade or business, writeoff of expenses for . . . 702.01-702.01[C], 702.02

Adaptation of property . . . 801.04

Additions and improvements to property . . . 800-806.02
. adjustments to basis for . . . 101.01, 800
. as capital expenditures . . . 801
. depreciation of . . . 602.02, 901.02-901.02[C], 904.02-904.02[B]
. for pre-1987 ACRS property . . . 904.02-904.02[B]
. substantial improvements as, rules for . . . 904.02[A], 904.02[B]

Advance payments, deferral for . . . 701.02[B]

Advance rent . . . 401.03, 402.01
. assignment of lease treated as . . . 403.02
. reporting . . . 403.01, 502.02[A]
. treatment by lessor of . . . 403.01, 406.02

Advertising expenses as deductible business expenses, reasonable . . . 703.07

Agency relationship
. among partners in general partnerships . . . 203.01[A]
. as requirement fir straw corporation ownership of real estate . . . 201.02

Agent in four-way exchange . . . 1302.03[B]

Agricultural cooperatives, qualified business income . . . 209.05

Air control facilities . . . 802.01[C]

Alcohol fuels credit as subject to passive activity loss rules . . . 1104.04

All events test satisfied upon occurrence of economic performance . . . 701.02[B]

Allocation of costs, asset acquisition . . . 102.02-102.02[E]

Allocation of expenses for use of home as day-care facility . . . 1801.05-1801.05[B]

Allocation of interest for construction of property . . . 103.01[C]

Allocation of partnership income for property or services provided . . . 203.02[C]

Allocation of partnership service costs . . . 203.02[C]

Allocation of real estate purchase costs . . . 102.02-102.02[E]
. for buildings and personal property . . . 102.02[C]
. for determining relative values . . . 102.02[A]
. for land and buildings . . . 102.02[A]

Allocation of real estate purchase costs—continued
. for land improvements and personal property . . . 102.02[B]
. real estate as part of a going business . . . 102.02[D]
. reporting requirements . . . 102.02[E]

Alternative cost limitation for common improvements . . . 1001.02[B]

Alternative depreciation, calculating . . . 902.01-902.01[B]

Alternative depreciation system
. for alternative minimum taxable income before 1999 . . . 902, 902.02[C], 1301.04[C]
. for corporate distributions . . . 902
. election to apply . . . 902, 902.01[A]
. for pollution control facilities . . . 1301.04[C]
. for real property used outside of United States . . . 902, 902.02
. types of property requiring use of . . . 902, 902.02-902.02[C]
. use of optional tables to compute . . . 902.01[B]

Alternative minimum tax
. adjustments to taxable income . . . 1301.04[C]
. basic computation of . . . 1301.04[A]
. effects on ownership, operation, and sale of real estate of . . . 1301.04
. optional ten-year writeoff of costs to avoid adjustments for . . . 1301.04[E]
. small business exception to . . . 1301.04[B]
. tax credits allowed to offset . . . 1301.04[A], 1301.04[F]
. tax preferences . . . 1301.04[D]

Alternative minimum tax credit against regular tax . . . 1301.04[F]

Alternative minimum taxable income
. adjustments to regular taxable income to determine . . . 1301.04[C]
. before 1999 . . . 902, 902.02[C], 1301.04[C]
. tax preferences in determining . . . 1301.04[D]

Amelioration of pre-existing conditions . . . 801.02[E]

American Taxpayer Relief Act of 2012 . . . 101.01[F]

Amortization provisions for property improvement costs
. for pollution control facilities . . . 802-802.01[C]
. for reforestation expenses . . . 802, 802.02

Anti-churning rules for depreciation . . . 905.02
. property excluded from being recovery property under ACRS for . . . 905.02[A]
. related party transfers bringing property to be subject to . . . 905.02[B]
. tax-free transfers . . . 905.02[C]

Applicable federal rate (AFR)
. for installment sales of timeshares and residential lots . . . 1401.01[A]
. for loan interest . . . 303.03
. for Section 467 rental agreements . . . 404.01

Appraisals, real estate
. to determine fair market value . . . 1601.01
. fee for . . . 1601.01[B]
. by qualified appraiser . . . 1601.01[B]
. types of . . . 1601.01[A]

Appreciated property
. basis of . . . 101.01[F]
. gain on distribution of . . . 206.02[A]
. gifts of . . . 701.03[A], 1601.03-1601.03[C]
. sale of . . . 204.02[C]
. tax consequences of distributions of corporation's . . . 208.01

Architect's fees . . . 801.05

Architectural barriers, deduction for removal of . . . 703.02

Arm's-length transactions, loans as . . . 303.03

Assessment of tax deficiency attributable to second disposition by related purchaser . . . 1401.03[B]

Assessments, nondeductible . . . 704.02

At-risk rules
. activities subject to . . . 302, 302.01
. avoiding . . . 302.03[B]
. computing at-risk amount for . . . 302.03[C]
. deduction under, allowance of . . . 302.02-302.02[B]
. determining amounts at risk for . . . 302.03, 302.03[A]
. qualified nonrecourse financing . . . 302.04–302.04[B]

At-risk rules—continued
. for real estate limited partnerships . . . 2102.01[A]
. taxpayers subject to . . . 302.01

Attorney fees for lease services . . . 501.01[A]

Audit rules, post-2017 partnership . . . 203.02[G]

B

Bad debt deduction
. determining worthless debt for . . . 1201.02[B]
. distinction between Code Sec. 165 loss and . . . 1201.02[A]
. in foreclosures . . . 1202, 1202.02[B], 1202.02[C]
. income recognition from prior . . . 1204.01[A]
. low bids to maximize . . . 1202.02[C]
. nonbusiness bad debts ineligible for . . . 1201.02[C]

Bankruptcy Act (repealed) . . . 1201.01[B]

Bankruptcy as proof of worthlessness of debt . . . 1201.02[B]

Bankruptcy Tax Act of 1980 . . . 1201.01[B]

Bargain sale to charity . . . 1602.02

Basis of partnership interest . . . 203.02[A], 203.02[B]

Basis of property
. acquired by gift . . . 101.01[E]
. acquired by inheritance . . . 101.01[F]
. acquired from spouse or former spouse . . . 101.01[G]
. acquired in exchange . . . 101.01[C]
. acquired on exercise of an option . . . 101.01[D]
. addition and improvement costs added to . . . 101.01, 800
. adjusted . . . 101, 302, 902.01[B], 1301.01[A], 1301.03, 1301.03[A], 1503.01[A]
. allocation among multiple properties of . . . 1302.01[C], 1503.03
. alternative cost method for inclusion of . . . 1001.02[B]
. apportionment of . . . 1000, 1001.01-1001.01[B]
. artificially inflated purchase price . . . 101.02[C]

Basis of property—continued
. borrowing against previously owned property . . . 101.02[B]
. calculating . . . 101.01-101.01[H]
. contingent obligations . . . 101.02[A]
. deposits for extensions of public utilities to subdivided real estate included in . . . 1001.02
. for determining low-income housing credit . . . 805.03[B]
. distribution in excess of . . . 203.02[D]
. election of insolvent or bankrupt debtor to reduce . . . 1201.01[B]
. following lessee improvements . . . 602.02[B]
. gifts of property . . . 101.01[E], 1603
. importance of . . . 101-101.02[C]
. inclusion of development costs in . . . 1001.02-1001.02[B]
. installment sales . . . 1402.01
. in involuntary conversion . . . 1503.01[A], 1503.03, 1503.03[B]
. lease cancellation payments affecting . . . 502.02[A]
. mortgage . . . 101.02
. original . . . 101.01, 101.02, 203.02[A], 301, 1301.01[A]
. owner-constructed . . . 101.01[B]
. in partially tax-free exchanges . . . 1302.02[C]
. purchased . . . 101.01[A]
. reacquired by repossession . . . 1204.01[C], 1204.02[A], 1204.02[B]
. recovery in contingent sales of . . . 1401.02[E]
. reduced by commercial revitalization deduction . . . 806.01
. reduced by rehabilitation credit . . . 804.01[E], 804.03
. speculative obligations . . . 101.02[A]
. stepped-up . . . 101.01[F]
. substituted . . . 1302.01[B]

Below-market rate loans . . . 303.03-303.03[D]

Benefits and burdens of ownership . . . 201

Betterments to property . . . 801.02
. amelioration of pre-existing conditions . . . 801.02[E]
. application to buildings . . . 801.02[B]
. building refresh . . . 801.02[C]
. building remodel . . . 801.02[D]

Betterments to property—continued
. increase in efficiency, capacity, etc. . . . 801.02[G]
. regulatory requirements . . . 801.02[F]
. replacements . . . 801.02[A]

Bipartisan Budget Act of 2015 . . . 203.02[G]

Bonus depreciation . . . 901.03[B]

Bonuses under accrual and cash accounting methods . . . 701.03[A]

Boot received in like-kind property exchanges . . . 1302.02, 1302.02[C]

Borrowed amounts not included in at-risk amounts . . . 302.03[A]

Broker or intermediary in three-way exchange . . . 1302.03[A]

Broker, real estate, reporting requirements of . . . 1303.01[A], 1303.02

Build-to-suit like-kind exchanges . . . 1302.01[A]

Building construction
. allocation of interest for . . . 103.01[C]
. capital expenditures for . . . 103

Building demolition, land valued for . . . 102.02[A]. *See also* Demolition costs

Building envelope components, tax credit for energy efficient . . . 1708.01

Building improvements
. as betterments . . . 801.02[B]
. as capital expenses . . . 703.01[F]

Building refresh . . . 801.02[C]

Building rehabilitation tax credits . . . 804-804.03

Building remodel . . . 801.02[D]

Building residual method for determining capitalization rate . . . 1601.01[A]

Buildings, allocation of costs . . . 102.02[C]

Built-in gains tax . . . 2201.02

Business expenses, deductible . . . 702-702.02, 703-703.09

Business income (passthrough deduction) . . . 209–209.05

Business interest . . . 303.02[D]
. carryforward of disallowed business interest . . . 303.02[D]

Business interest—continued
. election out of real property business . . . 303.02[D]
. election out of farming business . . . 303.02[D]
. election procedure . . . 303.02[D]
. partnerships and S corporations . . . 303.02[D]
. proposed regulations . . . 303.02[D]
. safe harbor for REITs . . . 303.02[D]
. small business exception . . . 303.02[D]

Business property, casualty losses on property used partially as . . . 1703.03

Business use of home . . . 1801
. business expenses unrelated to . . . 1801.04[A]
. as day-care facility . . . 1801.05-1801.05[B]
. determining gross income from . . . 1801.04[A]
. direct expenses for . . . 1801.03, 1801.03[A]
. exclusively and regularly . . . 1801.02-1801.02[D]
. indirect expenses for . . . 1801.03, 1801.03[B]
. for inventory storage . . . 1801.02[A]
. limitation on deductions . . . 1801.04–1801.04[B]
. order of deductions for . . . 1801.04[B]
. as place to meet patients, clients, or customers . . . 1801.02[C]
. as principal place of business . . . 1801.02[B]
. safe harbor deduction for . . . 1801.01
. sale of residence having . . . 2001.01
. separate structures next to home accepted as . . . 1801.02[D]
. tax exclusion for home . . . 2002.01[C]
. tests for deducting expenses of . . . 1801.02-1801.02[D]

Buy downs . . . 301.02

Buying expenses for real estate . . . 102.01-102.01[B]

C

C corporations
. accounting method for . . . 701.02[A]
. attributes comparison . . . 208.03
. closely held. *See* Closely held corporations
. grouping activities of . . . 1102.02

C corporations—continued
. related parties rule for S corporations and . . . 701.04[C]

Cancellation of lease
. by acquisition of fee interest by lessee before term ends . . . 502.01[A]
. amount received by lessor for, as gross income . . . 502.01[B], 502.02[B]
. deductible expense of payments by lessee for . . . 502-502.01[A]
. lessor's recovery of costs for . . . 502.02[A]
. payments by lessor treated as acquisition payments for property rights in . . . 502.02
. payments to sublessee for . . . 502.02[A]
. unamortized costs on . . . 502.03

Capital assets
. combining gains and losses for selling . . . 1301.02[B]
. holding period for . . . 1301.02[C]
. list of property not considered to be . . . 1301.02[A]

Capital expenditures. *See also individual expenditures*
. for constructing or improving buildings . . . 103, 703.01-703.01[F], 801-801.05
. types of legal fees considered to be . . . 703.08
. types of nondeductible . . . 801

Capital gain property
. gifts of . . . 1601.03[B]
. REIT . . . 2201.01[C]
. REIT shareholders . . . 2202.01

Capital gain tax rate . . . 1301.03[B]
. in D.C. Enterprise Zone . . . 1305.03
. in renewal community . . . 1305.02

Capital gains and losses on sale of property . . . 1301.02[A]

Capitalization of costs
. under Code Sec. 266 . . . 103.03
. of developing property parcels . . . 1001
. of impact fees . . . 704.04
. maintenance and repairs . . . 703.01[E]

Capitalization of income to value donated property . . . 1601.01[A]

Capitalization of rentals method for cost allocation . . . 102.02[A]

Carrying charges, capitalization of . . . 103.03

Cash method of accounting
. advance rents under . . . 402.01
. application of OID rules for . . . 304.02[A]
. bonuses under . . . 701.03[A]
. for contingent payment obligation realized for year of property sale . . . 1401.01[C]
. deduction of interest paid under . . . 303.02, 303.02[A]
. deduction of rent paid under . . . 402
. deduction of taxes paid under . . . 704.01
. deferring deductions under . . . 701.03[B]
. deferring income under . . . 701.03[A]
. limitations on taxpayers eligible to use . . . 701.02[A]
. real property taxes for seller and purchaser under . . . 102.03
. reporting income when actually or constructively received under . . . 701.02[A]
. sale on contract for deed under . . . 1301.01[B]
. timing of income and expenses under . . . 701.02[A], 701.03

Casualty, business . . . 1501–1501.03[B]

Casualty basis rules . . . 101.01[H]

Casualty defined . . . 1501.01

Casualty, gains produced by . . . 1500
. postponing recognition of . . . 1501.02[B]
. from reimbursements exceeding basis of property in casualty . . . 1501.02, 1501.02[B], 1501.02[C]

Casualty, restoration of damage from . . . 801.03[A]

Casualty loss deduction
. basis of property reduced by . . . 1501.02[D]
. limitations for 2018 through 2025 . . . 1703

Casualty losses
. in absence of insurance . . . 1501.02
. adjusted gross income limitation . . . 1703.01[B]
. deductible . . . 1301.02[A], 1501.02[A], 1703-1703.03
. deductible for . . . 1703.01[A]
. disaster area losses . . . 1501.03-1501.03[B]
. as indirect or direct expenses . . . 1801.03[B]
. involuntary conversions due to . . . 1500
. limitation for nonbusiness . . . 1703.01-1703.01[B]

Casualty losses—continued
. measuring decline in fair market value for . . . 1501.02[A]
. personal residence . . . 1703.02[B], 1703.02[C]
. reduction in qualified basis due to . . . 805.05[D]
. reimbursement of . . . 1501.02
. separate components of . . . 1501.02[A]

Certified historic structure
. conservation purpose for preservation of . . . 1601.04[C]
. defined . . . 804.02[A]
. demolition of . . . 1504.01
. rehabilitation tax credit . . . 804

Certified historic structures, tax credit for rehabilitation of . . . 804.02
. certification requirements for . . . 804.02[A]
. nonqualified buildings for . . . 804.02[B]
. recapture of . . . 804.03

Certified pollution controlled equipment, amortization of cost of . . . 802.01
. amortizable basis for . . . 802.01[B]
. amortization period of . . . 802.01[A], 802.01[B]
. for coal-fired electric generation plant . . . 802.01[C]
. requirements for electing . . . 802.01[A]

Charitable contributions, deductions for
. of appreciated property . . . 1601.03-1601.03[C]
. as business expense . . . 1601.02
. controlling . . . 701.03[A]
. disallowed . . . 1601, 1601.02
. for real estate donations . . . 1601
. for real property interests for conservation purposes . . . 1601.04[C]
. valuing gifts for . . . 1601.01

Charitable gifts . . . 1601-1601.04[C], 1602.02

Children of owner employed in real estate business . . . 703.04[B]

Circulation expenditures of periodicals, amortization of . . . 1301.04[C]

Closely held corporations
. material participation in . . . 1101.03[B]
. net active income of . . . 1104.02
. stock transfers for . . . 208.01
. subject to passive activity loss rules . . . 1101.01, 1101.01[A], 1104.02

Commercial buildings, rehabilitation of older . . . 804.01-804.01[E]
. basis reduction by credit amount . . . 804.01[E]
. energy-efficient expenditure deduction . . . 803
. expenditures incurred by predecessor . . . 804.01[B]
. nonqualifying expenditures . . . 804.01[D]
. recapture of credit for . . . 804.03, 1301.03[B]
. substantial rehabilitation test . . . 804.01[A], 804.01[B]
. wall test . . . 804.01[C]

Commercial revitalization deduction . . . 806.01, 1103.05[C]

Commissions and fees
. added to basis to determine gross profit . . . 1401.02[A]
. as deductible business expenses versus amortizable . . . 703.05
. kickbacks in nature of . . . 703.05[B]
. like-kind exchanges . . . 1302.02[D]
. real estate commissions . . . 703.05[A]

Commissions for finding tenant as lessor cost . . . 501.01[A]

Commitment fees . . . 703.05

Common ownerships . . . 202.02

Community property states
. list of . . . 202.04
. real estate ownership in . . . 202.04

Comparable sales, appraisals using
. appraisals using . . . 1601.01[A]
. interest-free or below-market loans . . . 303.03, 303.03[B]

Compensation as ordinary and necessary business expense . . . 703.04-703.04[E]

Compensation of partners . . . 703.04[E]

Components as separate units . . . 801.01[E]

Computer software, advance payments on lease or license of . . . 403.01

Condemnation award
. determining . . . 1502.03, 1502.03[A]
. special assessments deducted from . . . 1502.03[B]
. treatment of severance damages the same as . . . 1503.02[C]

Condemnation of property
. basis rules . . . 101.01[H]

Condemnation of property—continued
. defined . . . 1502.01
. gain or loss from . . . 1502.02
. postponing recognition of gain from . . . 1502, 1502.02, 1503.02[C]
. severance damages in . . . 1502.03[A], 1502.03[B], 1503.02[C]
. special assessments against remaining property from partial . . . 1502.03[B]
. special rule for replacement property in . . . 1503.02[C]
. threat or imminence of . . . 1502.01, 1503.01[C]

Condemnation processings, legal expenses incurred in . . . 703.08

Conditional sales contract . . . 305.04

Condominium management associations . . . 1900

Condominiums
. assessments or dues on . . . 1900
. defined . . . 1902
. dues, fees, or assessments on . . . 1903.01[C]
. equitable apportionment rule for sale of . . . 1001.01
. homeowners associations for . . . 704.01, 1903-1903.04[C]
. improvements to . . . 801.01[B]
. overview . . . 1900
. tax treatment of condominium association . . . 1902.02
. tax treatment of unit owners of . . . 1902.01
. use as residence of substantially all units of . . . 1903.01[B]

Conservation purpose for contribution of real property interest . . . 1601.04[C]

Construction costs
. capital expenditures for . . . 103
. capitalization of . . . 103.01-103.01[C]
. direct versus indirect . . . 103.01[B]
. interest paid for, capitalization of . . . 103.01[C]
. noncapitalized . . . 103.01[B]
. small taxpayer exception to uniform capitalization rules . . . 103.01[A]

Constructive ownership rules
. in applying indirect ownership interests . . . 1401.03[A]
. in applying loss disallowance rule . . . 1301.01[C]

Constructive receipt of income
. in deferred exchanges . . . 1302.01[A]
. doctrine of . . . 701.02[A]

Contingent payment obligation, fair market value of . . . 1401.01[C]

Contingent interest . . . 304.03[D]

Contingent sale defined . . . 1401.02[E]

Contingent sale price agreement, fixed maximum period for . . . 1401.02[E]

Controlled corporations
. leases between shareholders and . . . 401.04[B]
. matching lessee's rental deduction to lessor's income for . . . 401.04[C]

Controlled entity defined . . . 1301.02[A], 1401.03[A]

Controlled group
. loss disallowance rule for . . . 1301.01[C]
. members of, as related persons for installment sales . . . 1401.03[A], 1401.03[B]

Conversion of property to commercial use . . . 801.04

Cooperative housing corporations . . . 1901
. depreciation of . . . 1901.02[B]
. distributions by . . . 1901.01, 1901.01[C]
. exclusion of gain in . . . 2002.01[C]
. gross income of, derivation of . . . 1901.01, 1901.01[D]
. improvements . . . 801.01[B]
. interest and taxes on . . . 1901.02[A]
. one class of stock required for . . . 1901.01, 1901.01[A]
. overview . . . 1900
. qualification as . . . 1901.01
. right of occupancy for . . . 1901.01, 1901.01[B]
. shares of stock owned by taxpayers for . . . 1900
. tax benefits for . . . 1901
. tenant-stockholders of . . . 1901.01, 1901.02-1901.02[B]

Co-ownership, liability under . . . 202.02

Corporate capital gains and losses . . . 1301.02[A]

Corporate contribution basis rules . . . 101.01[H]

Corporate ownership, choice of . . . 208

Corporate veil, liability protection of . . . 208.01

Corporation, real estate. *See also* C corporations
. acquisition of trade or business assets of acquired corporation by . . . 702.01[A]
. alternative minimum tax . . . 1301.04
. at-risk rules applicable to . . . 302.01
. distribution of property by . . . 204.02[C]
. extraordinary amounts paid in guise of compensation to officers of . . . 703.04[A]
. legal characteristics of . . . 204.01
. material participation by . . . 1101.03[B]
. minimum tax credit refundable . . . 1301.04[F]
. officer compensation . . . 703.04[A]
. operation of . . . 204.02[B]
. organization of . . . 204.02[A]
. ownership by . . . 202, 202.02, 204-204.02[C], 208-208.03
. taxation of . . . 204.02
. taxation of, accumulated earnings . . . 208.01
. taxation of, in excess of partner's partnership basis . . . 203.02[D]

Corporation-shareholder loans . . . 303.03, 303.03[C]
. loss disallowance rule for . . . 1301.01[C]

Cost allocations for real estate purchases. *See* Allocation of real estate purchase costs

Cost-recovery method of reporting open transactions . . . 1401.02[E]

Cost segregation (allocation) studies for building costs
. to calculate depreciation for components . . . 903
. for recharacterizing existing property . . . 903.01

Court awards for damage or theft loss as casualty reimbursement . . . 1501.02[C]

D

Day-care facilities, use of home as . . . 1801.05-1801.05[B]

D.C. Enterprise Zone, zero percent capital gain tax rate from assets in . . . 1305.03

Dealer property
. characterization of . . . 1002.01-1002.01[B]

Dealer property—continued
. defined . . . 1002
. election to reduce basis of . . . 1201.01[B]
. gain or loss on sale of . . . 1002
. installment sales for . . . 1002.02[A], 1401.01[A]
. investment property versus . . . 1002.01[A]
. subdivided realty as . . . 1002.01[B]
. tax effects of classification as . . . 1002.02-1002.02[B]
. tests applied to classify . . . 1002.01[A]
. timeshares and residential lots as . . . 1002.02[B]
. used in nondealer activity . . . 1104.01[A]

Debt instrument
. contingent interest on . . . 304.03[D]
. fair market value of issue price of . . . 304.03[E]
. limiting imputed principal amount of . . . 304.03[E]
. OID rules applied to existing . . . 304.02[B]

Debt proceeds, tracing . . . 303.02[C]

Debt reallocation . . . 303.02[C]

Debt refinancing . . . 303.02[C]

Debt repayments, hierarchy of . . . 303.02[C]

Debt settled at discount . . . 1201
. alternative options for . . . 1203
. loss on . . . 1201.02[A]
. for qualified principal residence debt . . . 1201.01[D]
. for qualified real property business debt . . . 1201.01[C]
. tax treatment of credit for . . . 1201.02-1201.02[C]
. tax treatment of debtor for . . . 1201.01-1201.01[E]

Debtor, tax treatment of . . . 1201.01-1201.01[E]
. insolvent or bankrupt . . . 1201.01[B]
. reduction of tax attributes in . . . 1201.01[B]
. solvent . . . 1201.01[A]

Declining-balance method of depreciation defined . . . 905.01[A]

Deductions
. of abandoned improvement plans . . . 801.05

Deductions—continued
. of abandoned improvements . . . 1504.02[B]
. of abandoned land . . . 1504.02, 1504.02[A]
. accelerating . . . 701.03[A]
. advertising . . . 703.07
. amortization . . . 301.01[A]
. at-risk rules . . . 302, 302.02-302.02[B]
. of business expenses . . . 701.03[B], 1601.02
. for business use of home . . . 1801-1801.04[B]
. cash accounting method . . . 701.02[A]
. of casualty losses . . . 1301.02[A], 1501.02[D], 1703-1703.03
. of charitable donations . . . 1601-1601.04[C], 1602.02
. commercial revitalization . . . 806.01, 1103.05[C]
. of commissions and fees . . . 703.05-703.05[B]
. compensation . . . 703.04-703.04[E]
. deferring . . . 701.03[B]
. depreciation. *See* Depreciation deduction
. disallowed for rent in leases with purchase option . . . 405
. dividends paid . . . 2201.01
. for energy efficient commercial buildings . . . 803
. of expenses and interest mismatched between cash and accrual method related parties . . . 701.04[B]
. of farmers' land condition items . . . 802.03
. for home equity debt . . . 1701.01, 1701.01[C]
. for homeowners . . . 1700-1708.02
. of insurance premiums . . . 703.06
. of interest paid . . . 703.09
. of legal expenses . . . 703.08
. of lender's costs for mortgage loans . . . 301.01[B]
. for materials and supplies . . . 703.03
. for miscellaneous itemized expenses . . . 1301.04[C]
. for mortgage interest . . . 1701-1701.03[E]
. of moving expenses . . . 1705-1705.03[B]
. of operating expenses and taxes . . . 701.03-705.02
. order of . . . 302.02[A]
. of partnership losses . . . 206.02[B]
. of points (loan origination fees) . . . 1701.02-1701.02[B]

References are to paragraph (¶) numbers.

Deductions—continued
. of pre-1987 indebtedness . . . 1701.01, 1701.01[D]
. prior property tax . . . 102.03
. of property taxes . . . 704-704.04, 1702
. qualified business income (passthrough deduction) . . . 209–209.05
. recapture of prior deductions . . . 302.02[B]
. for removal of architectural barriers . . . 703.02
. for rent on leased property having lease cancellation payments . . . 701.03[A]
. of rent on vacation or other residence . . . 1803-1803.03
. of rent owed matched to lessor's income . . . 401.04[C]
. of rent paid in property or services . . . 402
. of school site donations . . . 1601.02
. of soil and water conservation expenditures . . . 802, 802.03
. for "tax losses" . . . 302
. by tenant-stockholders of cooperative housing corporations . . . 1901.01, 1901.02-1901.02[B]
. of transfer taxes . . . 704.03

Deep-rent skewing . . . 805.05[A]

Demand loans . . . 303.03[B]

Demand obligations not treated as installment sales . . . 1401.02[B]

***De Minimis* safe harbor** . . . 703.01[B]

Demolition costs . . . 102.02[A], 1504, 1504.01

Depletion as AMT tax preference . . . 1301.04[D]

Deposit of loan proceeds in bank account . . . 303.02[C]

Depreciation . . . 900-905.02[C]. *See also* Alternative depreciation system; *individual depreciation methods*
. accelerated . . . 905.01, 1301.03[B], 1301.04[D]
. additions and improvements, . . . 901.02
. alternative depreciation system . . . 303.02[D], 902–902.02[C]
. basis of . . . 602.02
. calculating . . . 102.02[B], 601.02, 900, 905
. changing methods for . . . 905.01[B]
. cooperative housing corporation . . . 1901.02[B]
. defined . . . 900
. excess . . . 1301.03[B]

Depreciation—continued
. overview of . . . 900
. of pre-1981 property . . . 905-905.02[C]
. of pre-1987 property . . . 904-904.02[B]
. of pre-1999 property . . . 1301.04[C]
. sale of depreciable property . . . 1401.03[A]
. tables . . . 901.01[D]
. taxable income adjustments . . . 1301.04[C]

Depreciation deduction
. additional first-year . . . 806.02, 901.03[B]
. adjusted basis of property reduced by claiming . . . 1301.03
. for business use of home . . . 1801.01, 1801.03[B]
. calculating . . . 101, 901.01-901.01[G]
. for costs of additions or improvements over recovery period . . . 602.02, 901.02-901.02[B]
. expensing election . . . 901.03[A]
. first-year bonus depreciation . . . 901.01[F], 901.03[B]
. of improvement costs . . . 501.03, 601
. improvement property after 2017 . . . 901.01[F]
. increasing . . . 102.02[B], 102.02[C]
. land improvements . . . 901.02[A]
. leasehold improvements . . . 901.01[E]
. by lessee shared with lessor . . . 601
. for lessee-constructed improvements and additions . . . 601.03-602.02[B]
. for lessee-replaced furniture and fixtures . . . 601.01
. by lessor, conditions allowing . . . 601, 601.01
. MACRS . . . 901
. mid-month convention . . . 901.01[C]
. motorsports entertainment complexes . . . 901.01[G]
. property under construction . . . 901.02[B]
. recovery periods . . . 901.01[A]
. reduction in basis for investment credit treated as . . . 1301.03[B]
. for rehabilitation of low-income housing . . . 1301.03[B]
. restaurant property . . . 901.01[E]
. retail improvements . . . 901.01[E]
. right to claim . . . 201
. straight-line method . . . 901.01[B]
. of tenant-stockholder of cooperative housing corporation . . . 1901.02[B]
. by trusts . . . 207.02

Depreciation recapture
. defined . . . 1301.03
. for property sold on installment basis . . . 1401.02[A]
. reporting gain in excess of, installment method for . . . 1401, 1402.02
. on Section 1245 personal property . . . 1301.03, 1301.03[A]
. on Section 1250 realty property . . . 1301.03, 1301.03[B]

Depreciation rules, pre-1987 . . . 602.02[A]

Depreciation tables . . . 901.01[D]
. for alternative depreciation system . . . 902.01[B]

Designation agreement for real estate transaction reporting, eligible persons for . . . 1303.01[A]

Development costs
. deductible versus capitalized . . . 1001
. inclusion in basis of . . . 1001.02-1001.02[B]

Direct costs of constructing real property, capitalization of . . . 103.01[B]

Disabled access credit as subject to passive activity loss rules . . . 1104.04

Disaster area losses . . . 1501.03-1501.03[B]

Disaster Relief Act . . . 1501.02[C]

Disaster relief exclusion from income . . . 1704

Discounted loans, amount at risk for . . . 302.03[A]

Disguised sales rule under Code Sec. 707(a)(2) . . . 203.02[B]

Disposition of appreciated property, gain on . . . 1104.01[A]

Disposition of installment obligations . . . 1402-1402.03

Disposition of interest in passthrough entity . . . 1104.01[C]

Distributions
. after-tax year . . . 2202.02
. corporations . . . 204.02[C]
. partnerships . . . 203.02[D]

District of Columbia first-time homebuyer tax credit . . . 1706

Dividends
. deficiency . . . 2203.04

Dividends—continued
. designation of qualified . . . 2201.01[B]
. dividends-paid deduction . . . 2201.01

Divorce, transfer of property incident to . . . 101.01[G]

Domestic corporation, U.S. real property interest in . . . 102.04

Donee's death affecting basis of gifted property . . . 101.01[F]

Down payment assistance . . . 1701.03[D]

Dwelling unit classification . . . 1803.01

E

Easement, sale of . . . 1301.01[B]

Economic performance rules . . . 701.02[B]

Economic Recovery Tax Act of 1981 . . . 904

Electric vehicle credit as subject to passive activity loss rules . . . 1104.04

Employee compensation . . . 703.04[C]

Employee relocation loans . . . 303.03[B]

Empowerment zone asset, rollover of capital gain from . . . 1305.01

Energy credits . . . 1708-1708.02
. nonbusiness property credit . . . 1708.01, 1708.01[A]
. residential energy efficient property . . . 1708.02

Energy efficient commercial buildings, deduction for expenditures for . . . 803

Energy efficient home tax credit . . . 105, 1001.03

Energy Policy Act of 2005 . . . 1708

Entity, business. *See also individual types*
. choice of . . . 208
. choice of fiscal versus calendar year for . . . 701.01
. comparison chart for choice of . . . 208.03
. real estate tax issues affected by choice of . . . 201.01
. with tiered structure, tax year of . . . 701.01[B]
. types of ownership of . . . 200

Equitable apportionment rule for sale of portions of property . . . 1001.01
. manner of apportionment of basis for . . . 1001.01[A]

Equitable apportionment rule for sale of portions of property—continued
. methods of apportionment of basis for . . . 1001.01[B]

Escrow accounts for installment payments . . . 1401.01[B]

Estate beneficiary as seller in installment sale . . . 1401.03[B]

Estate executor and beneficiary
. loss disallowance rule for . . . 1301.01[C]
. as related parties for sale of real estate . . . 1301.02[A], 1401.03[A]
. related party rules for . . . 701.04[C]

Estate tax
. effect of lifetime gifts on . . . 1600
. repeal of . . . 101.01[F]

Estates subject to passive activity loss rules . . . 1101.01

Evaluation of localities, expenses for . . . 102.01

Evidence of indebtedness of buyer as not constituting payment . . . 1401.02[B]

Excess business losses . . . 705
. excess loss defined . . . 705.01
. partnerships and S corporations . . . 705.02

Excessive compensation
. of family members as employees . . . 703.04[B]
. of real estate corporation officers . . . 703.04[A]
. of shareholder-employees of corporation . . . 703.04

Exchange
. basis of property acquired in . . . 101.01[C]
. delayed . . . 1302.01[A]

Exercise of option, basis of property acquired through . . . 101.01[D]

Expenses, controlling timing of . . . 701.03

Expenses, rental, match to lessor's rental income . . . 401.04[C]

Expensing, safe harbor . . . 102.01[B]

Expensing election . . . 901.03[A]

Extraordinary services tests . . . 1103.01

F

Fair market value
. determined for buyer's obligation . . . 1401.01[C]
. of like-kind property . . . 1401.02[D]
. measuring decline in, for casualty losses . . . 1501.02[A]

Family members
. as employees, compensation of . . . 703.04[B]
. gifts of mortgaged property to . . . 1602, 1602.01

Farm passive losses
. agricultural cooperatives, qualified business income . . . 209.05
. alternative minimum tax . . . 1301.04[C]

Farm property
. charitable deduction for donation of irrevocable interest in . . . 1601.04[B]
. installment reporting allowed for disposition of . . . 1401.01[A]
. land conditioning items for . . . 802.03
. sales by individuals of . . . 304.01
. subdivided realty as dealer property . . . 1002.01[B]
. valuing real estate as . . . 101.01[F]

Farming business interest deduction . . . 303.02[D]

Federal disaster area, presidentially declared
. deductible losses in, making election for . . . 1501.03
. for preceding year . . . 1501.03[A]
. revoking election for . . . 1501.03[B]
. special rules for replacement property in . . . 1503.02, 1503.02[D]

Federal disaster loan as reimbursement for casualty . . . 1501.02[C]

Financial Institutions Reform, Recovery and Enforcement Act of 1989 (FIRREA) . . . 805.01

First disposition of property in installment sale . . . 1401.03[B]

First-time homebuyer credit . . . 1707
. recapture . . . 1707.01

Foreclosure on real estate . . . 101.01[H]
. bad debt for mortgagee in . . . 1202
. deduction of loss on . . . 201, 1202
. expenses of . . . 1202.02[A]
. gain or loss on, calculating . . . 1202.01[A]

Foreclosure on real estate—continued
. gain or loss on, characterizing . . . 1202.01[B]
. as involuntary conversion . . . 1202.01
. mortgagee as creditor and purchaser of property in purchased . . . 1202.02[C]
. proceeds as less than debt amount in . . . 1202.02[B], 1202.02[C]
. REIT . . . 2201.01[A]
. under real estate loan (mortgage) . . . 300
. tax treatment of creditor in . . . 1202.02-1202.02[C]
. tax treatment of debtor in . . . 1202.01-1202.01[B]

Foreign Account Tax Compliance Act . . . 203.02[G]

Foreign person, real property interest acquired from . . . 102.04

Foreign tax credit, AMT . . . 1301.04[A]

Form 10-K . . . 102.01[B], 703.01[B]

Form 720, required payments of partnerships and S corporations paid using . . . 701.01[B]

Form 982, discharge of indebtedness income . . . 1201.01[D]

Form 1065, partnerships . . . 701.01[B], 1102.04

Form 1099, information return for real estate transaction using . . . 1303.02[A], 1303.02[B]

Form 1099-C, discharge of indebtedness . . . 1201.01[D]

Form 1120S, S corporations . . . 701.01[B], 1102.04

Form 8594, asset acquisition statements . . . 102.02[E]

Form 8609, Low-Income Housing Credit Allocation, certification of projects using . . . 805.02[B]

Form 8716, tax year election . . . 701.01[B]

Form 8823, Low-Income Housing Credit Agencies Report of Noncompliance . . . 805.01

Form 8283, appraisal summary . . . 1601.01[B]

Form 8877, Request for Waiver of Annual Recertification Requirement

Form 8877, Request for Waiver of Annual Recertification Requirement for the Low-Income Housing Credit—continued
for the Low-Income Housing Credit . . . 805.01

Form W-2, qualified business income (passthrough deduction) . . . 209.01, 209.02[A], 209.04, 209.05

Fuel cell power plant, tax credit for . . . 1708, 1708.02

G

Gain or loss, built-in . . . 203.02[B], 2201.02

Gain or loss, casualty . . . 1500, 1501.02-1501.02[B]

Gain or loss from condemnation of property . . . 1502.02

Gain or loss on foreclosure sale . . . 1202.01[B]

Gain or loss on repossession of seller-financing property . . . 1204, 1204.01

Gain or loss on sale of real estate
. adjusted basis in . . . 1301.01[A]
. amount realized in . . . 1301.01[B]
. character of . . . 1301, 1301.02-1301.02[C]
. computing . . . 1301.01-1301.01[E]
. disallowed . . . 1301.01[C]
. nonrecognition transactions . . . 1402.01[A]
. partial dispositions . . . 1301.01[E]
. of personal residence . . . 2000-2004.02[B]
. of spouses or former spouses . . . 1301.01[D]
. tax treatment of . . . 1301.02[A]

Gain or loss on tax-free exchange of property . . . 1302

Gain on sale or disposition of property interest . . . 1104.01[A]

General business credit . . . 1104.04, 1301.04[A]
. carryover of . . . 1201.01[B]
. tax credit components of . . . 804

General partnerships . . . 203.01[A]
. acquisition of interest in . . . 702.01[A]

Gift taxes
. adjustment of basis of property for . . . 101.01[E]
. on lifetime gifts . . . 1600

Gift taxes—continued
. treatment of loans for . . . 303.03[A]

Gifts, debt forgiveness of . . . 1201.01[A]

Gifts, loans as . . . 303.03
. gift and income tax treatment of . . . 303.03[A]

Gifts of easements . . . 701.03[A]

Gifts of property . . . 1600-1603
. appreciated property . . . 1601.03-1601.03[C]
. basis of property following . . . 101.01[E], 1603
. capital gain . . . 1601.03[B]
. charitable . . . 1601-1601.04[C], 1602.02
. for conservation purposes . . . 1601.04[C]
. to family . . . 1602.01
. of loss property . . . 1603
. mixed motives for . . . 1601.02
. mixed property . . . 1601.03[C]
. with mortgage . . . 301, 1602, 1602.01
. ordinary income . . . 1601.03[A], 1601.03[C]
. overview of . . . 1600
. partial interests in . . . 1601.04-1601.04[C]
. post-1920 and pre-1958 . . . 101.01[E]
. post-1958 and pre-1977 . . . 101.01[E]
. pre-1921 . . . 101.01[E]
. remainder interest in . . . 1601.04[B]
. in sale-leaseback among related parties . . . 305.03[B]
. to spouse or former spouse . . . 101.01[G]
. undivided portion of . . . 1601.04[A]
. valuation . . . 1601.01-1601.01[B]

Going business, real estate as part of . . . 102.02[D]

Grading of land, costs of . . . 102.02[B]

Graduated rents . . . 402.02
. decreasing . . . 402.02[A], 404
. increasing . . . 402.02[B], 404

Grantor of trust . . . 207
. taxation on trust income of . . . 207.03

Grantor trusts . . . 207.03

Gross profit defined . . . 1401.02[A]

Gross profit ratio for installment payments . . . 1401.02[A]
. applied to payments received . . . 1401.02[B]
. refigured following reduction in selling price . . . 1401.02[A]

Gross rent for tenant in low-income housing unit . . . 805.02[B]

Ground rent, payments on . . . 303.02

Guaranteed loans as not increasing at-risk amount . . . 302.03[A]

Guaranteed payments to partners . . . 203.02[E]
. characterized as payments for services or interest . . . 1104.01[C]
. services classifiable as payments to outsiders versus . . . 703.04[E]

H

Hardest Hit Fund . . . 1701.03[D]
. Form 1098, Mortgage Interest Statement . . . 1701.03[D]
. safe harbor . . . 1701.03[D]

Historic structures. *See also* Certified historic structures, tax credit for rehabilitation of
. demolition of . . . 1504.01
. depreciation recapture of costs of rehabilitating . . . 1301.03[B]
. straight-line depreciation for rehabilitation costs for . . . 1301.03[B]

Holding period
. for capital assets . . . 1301.02[C]
. reaquired property . . . 1204.01[B]
. for replacement asset for empowerment zone . . . 1305.01
. subdivision by investor . . . 1003.01[A]

Home affordable modification program (HAMP) . . . 1201.01[D]

Home construction contracts . . . 701.02[C]
. long-term construction contracts . . . 701.02[C]

Home equity debt . . . 1701.01, 1701.01[C]

Home mortgage interest, deduction . . . 1701.01

Home office. *See* Business use of home

Homeowners' association of condominiums
. assessments as income to . . . 1903.04[C]
. assessments by . . . 704.01
. association property held by . . . 1903.01[A]
. election for tax-exempt status of . . . 1903, 1903.03

Homeowners' association of condominiums—continued
. income and expenditures of, exempt function . . . 1903.01[C], 1903.01[D], 1903.04[B]
. inurement of . . . 1903.01[E]
. nonexempt . . . 1903.04-1903.04[C]
. overview . . . 1900
. qualification for tax-exempt status of . . . 1903.01
. taxation of . . . 1903.02
. use of residences . . . 1903.01[B]

Homeowners, deductions available to . . . 1700-1708.02

Horticultural cooperatives, qualified business income . . . 209.05

Housing allowance for ministers and military personnel, deduction of home mortgage interest despite . . . 1701.03[D]

Housing credit . . . 805.01

Hybrid accounting methods . . . 701.02

I

Impact fees as deductible business expenses versus capital expenditures . . . 704.04

Improvement plans, abandonment of . . . 801.05, 1504.02[B]

Improvements and additions to leased property. *See* Depreciation deduction; Leasehold improvements and additions

Improvements to land and buildings
. as capital expenditures . . . 801-801.05
. sold as subdivided lots . . . 1003.01[B]

Improvements to real estate developments
. alternative cost limitation for . . . 1001.02[B]
. estimated future costs . . . 1001.02[B]
. holding period following . . . 1301.02[C]
. as separate interest . . . 1001.02[A]

Imputed interest . . . 101.02
. conditions for applying . . . 304.01[B]
. on deferred payment sales . . . 304
. real estate sales subject to . . . 304.01-304.01[B]

Imputed interest rules . . . 304, 304.01
. interest rates under . . . 304.03, 304.03[A]

Incidental expenses of real estate purchases . . . 102-103.03. *See also individual expenses*

Income acceleration under accrual method . . . 701.03[B]

Income deferral under accrual method . . . 701.03[A]

Income forecast method for property sold in contingent payment sale . . . 1401.02[E]

Income reporting for real estate . . . 201

Income tax of lessor paid as additional rent . . . 401.02

Incorporation, taxable . . . 204.02[A]

Independent contractors
. licensed real estate agents receiving certain payments treated as . . . 703.04[D]
. tax and administrative burden reduced by using . . . 703.04[C]

Indian coal production credit as subject to passive activity loss rules . . . 1104.04

Indirect costs of constructing real property, capitalization of . . . 103.01[B]

Individual ownership of real estate . . . 202-202.04
. choice of . . . 208
. sole . . . 202.01

Inheritance
. basis of property acquired by . . . 101.01[F]
. of property on which lessee made improvements . . . 601.03

Installment accounting method . . . 701.02, 1401
. general rules for reporting payments under . . . 1401.02[A]
. interest on deferred tax under . . . 1401.04
. like-kind exchanges including obligation of buyer reportable using . . . 1401.02[D]
. personal property sold at gain reported using . . . 1401.02[C]
. reacquisitions . . . 1204.02[D]
. reporting sale using . . . 1401.02, 1401.03[A]

Installment obligations
. basis of . . . 1402.01
. cancellation of . . . 1402.01[B]
. deferred tax on . . . 1401.04

Installment obligations—continued
. disposition of . . . 1402-1402.03
. exceptions to recognition of gain or loss on . . . 1402.01[A]
. forms of . . . 1401.01
. interest rates applied to . . . 304.03[B]
. nonrecognition transactions . . . 1402.01[A]
. as part of liquidation of subsidiary . . . 1402.01[A]
. pledging . . . 701.03[B], 1401.04, 1402.02
. repossession of property . . . 1402.03
. satisfaction for amount other than face value of . . . 1402.01
. sold to accelerate receipt of income . . . 701.03[B]
. transfer at death of . . . 1402.01[A]
. transfer between spouses of . . . 1402.01[A]

Installment payments
. components of . . . 1401.02
. gross profit ratio applied to received . . . 1401.02[B]

Installment reporting
. of contingent sales . . . 1401.02[E]
. disallowed for dealer sales . . . 1401.01[A]
. disallowed for sales of depreciable property to related persons . . . 1401.03[A]
. for disposition of farm property . . . 1401.01[A]
. election not to use . . . 1401.01[C], 1401.02
. of gain using installment method from like-kind exchange . . . 1302.02[A]
. of gain using installment method from seller-financed sale . . . 1401
. general rules . . . 1401.02[A]
. not used for sale of property resulting in loss . . . 1401.01
. payments received for purposes of . . . 1401.02[B]
. requirements for . . . 1401.01

Installment sale
. application of imputed interest rules for . . . 304.01
. of dealer property . . . 1002.02[A]
. dealer sales . . . 1401.01[A]
. defined . . . 1401.01
. escrow arrangements for . . . 1401.01[B]
. multiple assets sold in single . . . 1401.02[C]
. of passive activity interest . . . 1104.03[D]

Installment sale—continued
. reacquisition of property sold in . . . 1204.02[A], 1204.02[B], 1204.02[D]
. reduction of selling price following . . . 1401.02[A]
. of related parties . . . 1401.03-1401.03[B]
. resale of property by related purchaser following . . . 1401.03[B]
. sale qualifying as . . . 1401.01
. seller-financed . . . 1400-1402.03
. unstated interest in . . . 1401.02[F]

Insurance
. business use of the home . . . 1801.03[B]
. mortgage . . . 1701.01
. National Flood Insurance Act . . . 1503, 1704
. premiums as currently deductible versus capitalized . . . 703.06
. reimbursement for casualty losses . . . 1501.02, 1501.02[B], 1501.02[C]

Intangible drilling costs
. as AMT tax preference . . . 1301.04[D]
. optional 10-year writeoff of . . . 1301.04[E]

Intellectual property, advance payments on lease or license of . . . 403.01

Interest
. business . . . 303.02[D]
. contingent . . . 304.03[D]
. on deferred tax . . . 1401.04
. defined . . . 303
. excessive . . . 304.03[E]
. investment . . . 303.02[B]
. prepaid . . . 303.02[A]
. reporting requirements . . . 303.03[D]
. tax-exempt . . . 1301.04
. unstated, in contingent installment sale . . . 1401.02[E]

Interest-free loans . . . 303.03-303.03[D]

Interest income
. on loans and investments made in ordinary course of trade or business . . . 1104.01[A]
. reporting . . . 303.01

Interest paid
. allocation . . . 103.01[C]
. construction period . . . 103.01[C]
. cooperative housing corporation . . . 1901.02[A]
. deduction of . . . 303.02, 303.02[A], 703.09, 1701
. investment . . . 303.02[B]
. pre-1987 construction . . . 103.02

Interest paid—continued
. for property construction, allocation of . . . 103.01[C]

Interest rate
. commercially reasonable . . . 302.04[A]
. for imputed interest and OID rules . . . 304.03
. maximum . . . 304.03[A], 304.03[E]
. variable . . . 304.03[C]

Internal Revenue Service (IRS)
. allocation formula for dwelling units of . . . 1803.02[B]
. deficiency assessments for gain on involuntary conversions made by . . . 1503.01[C]
. joint administration of low-income housing credit program by state agencies and . . . 805.01
. power to reallocate income of . . . 401.04[B]
. sale-leaseback guidelines of . . . 305.02[B]
. view of lease with option to purchase by . . . 305.04

Intra-family leases . . . 401.04[A], 401.04[B]

Inventory assets, sale of . . . 1401.02[C]

Investigatory expenses for creation or acquisition of active trade or business . . . 702.01, 702.01[A]

Investment Advisors Act of 1940 . . . Part VI Intro.

Investment credit for leasehold improvements and additions . . . 600

Investment credit for rehabilitation expenses . . . 804-804.02[B]
. basis reduced by . . . 804.01[E]
. credit split on short-term lease property . . . 603.02[B]
. election to pass credit to lessee . . . 603.02[A]
. expansion in 1978 of . . . 804
. for expenditures incurred by predecessor . . . 804.01[B]
. for historic structures . . . 800, 804.02
. leasehold improvements . . . 603-603.02[B]
. nonqualifying expenditures . . . 804.01[D]
. of older commercial buildings . . . 804.01
. passive activity loss rules . . . 1104.04

Investment credit for rehabilitation expenses—continued
. qualified rehabilitations by lessee . . . 603.01
. qualified rehabilitations by lessor . . . 603.02
. substantial rehabilitation test for . . . 804.01[A], 804.01[B]
. wall test for qualified rehabilitated building claiming . . . 804.01[C]

Investment income defined . . . 303.02[B]

Investment interest . . . 303.02[B]

Investment property
. acquisition of corporate . . . 1503.02[F]
. capital gains and losses on . . . 1301.02[A]
. residence converted to . . . 1804

Involuntary conversion of property ownership . . . 101.01[H]
. from casualty . . . 1500, 1503
. control in . . . 1503.02[F]
. deficiency assessments by IRS for gain on . . . 1503.01[C]
. in disaster. *See* Federal disaster area, presidentially declared
. of outdoor advertising displays . . . 1503.02[E]
. postponing recognition of gain from . . . 1502, 1503, 1503.01[C]
. replacement period for . . . 1503.01[C]
. for residences . . . 2002.01[C]
. resulting in gain . . . 1503, 1503.01[A]
. statement supporting . . . 1503.01[B]
. from threat or imminence of condemnation . . . 1502.01, 1503

J

Joint ownership of real estate . . . 202, 202.02
. in community property states . . . 202.04
. for replacement residence . . . 2003.02[C]
. by spouses . . . 202.03, 202.04

Joint ventures
. defined . . . 203.01[C]
. as partnerships for tax purposes . . . 203.01[C]
. property provided to . . . 1103.01[B]

K

Kickbacks as deductible as ordinary and necessary expenses, legal . . . 703.05[B]

References are to paragraph (¶) numbers.

L

Land
. abandonment of . . . 1504.02, 1504.02[A]
. allocation of costs . . . 102.02[A]
. interest on vacant land . . . 303.02[B]
. sales between family members . . . 304.01[B]

Land improvements
. in allocation of asset costs . . . 102.02[B]
. capitalization of . . . 703.01[F], 801-801.05
. depreciation of . . . 901.02, 901.02[A]
. for lots sold . . . 1003.01[B]
. made necessary after ten years . . . 1003.01[C]

Landlord, payments between tenant and . . . 400-406.02

Landscaping costs as land improvements . . . 102.02[B]

Lease acquisition . . . 500-501.03
. overview of . . . 500

Lease acquisition costs . . . 501
. amortization of . . . 501, 501.03
. apportionment of . . . 501.02
. classification of payments as . . . 501.01-501.01[C]
. lessee's . . . 501.01[B]
. lessor's . . . 501.01[A], 502.03

Lease as sales contract . . . 405.01

Lease cancellation payments . . . 502.01-502.01[B]
. to accelerate rent deductions . . . 701.03[A]

Lease disposition . . . 502-503
. by cancellation . . . 502-502.04
. by modification . . . 502.04
. by sale . . . 503
. by termination . . . 602.02[B]

Lease, disqualified . . . 902.02[A]

Lease distinguished from sale . . . 405.02

Lease financing . . . 305-305.04. *See also* Sale-leaseback transaction
. renewal options for . . . 402.02[A], 501.02, 602.02[A]

Lease with option to purchase
. IRS treatment of . . . 305.04
. as part payment of purchase price . . . 402, 405

Leaseback or long-term agreement, recapture in . . . 404.02[B]

Leased property
. buildings . . . 801.01[A]-801.01[C]
. condominiums and cooperatives . . . 801.01[B]
. network assets . . . 801.01[C]
. plant property . . . 801.01[C]
. real or personal property . . . 801.01[C]
. replacement of condemned . . . 1503.02[C]

Leasehold improvements and additions . . . 600-603.02[B]
. amortization of . . . 602.02[A]
. to benefit particular lessee . . . 601.02
. as capital investments . . . 602.02-602.02[B]
. depreciation of . . . 901.01[E]
. at lease termination . . . 602.02[B]
. by lessee . . . 602-602.02[B]
. by lessor . . . 601, 602
. not intended as rent . . . 602.02
. overview of . . . 600
. purchase of property following lessee's . . . 601.03
. as rent . . . 602.01
. restoration or maintenance by lessee as . . . 601.01
. Section 1231 assets used in trade or business . . . 1302.01[A], 1302.01[D]

Leasehold interests as capital assets . . . 503, 1301.02[B]

Leaseholds
. exchange of . . . 1302.01[A]
. replacement of . . . 1503.02[C]

Legal expenses as deductions versus capital expenditures . . . 703.08

Lessor's expenses paid by lessee as indirect rent . . . 401, 401.02

Liability issues
. of co-ownerships . . . 202.02
. of corporation versus partnership . . . 208.01
. of individual ownership . . . 202.01
. of partners . . . 203.01[A]

Liability protection of corporate veil . . . 208.01

Licensed real estate agents as independent contractors versus employees . . . 703.04[D]

Life insurance premiums . . . 703.06

Like-kind exchange
. basis rule for . . . 1302.01[B]

Like-kind exchange—continued
. boot received in . . . 1302.02
. commissions and expenses in . . . 1302.02[D]
. gain attributable to money or other property received as part of . . . 1401.02[D]
. identifying property for . . . 1302.01, 1302.01[A]
. multi-party . . . 1302.03-1302.03[B]
. property held for investment . . . 1302.01[A]
. property subject to liabilities in . . . 1302.02[C]
. real property . . . 101.01[C]
. requirements for tax-free . . . 1302.01
. sale-leaseback treated as . . . 305.01[B]
. taxable receipt of other property or money in . . . 1302.02[A]

Like-kind real estate defined . . . 1302.01[A]

Limited liability companies (LLCs)
. as entity classification . . . 205.01
. formation of . . . 205
. limited liability for members of . . . 205
. partnerships converting to . . . 205.02
. tax advantages of partnerships for members of . . . 205

Limited partnership interests . . . 1101.02[A], 2102.02

Limited partnerships . . . 203.01[B]. *See also* Real estate limited partnerships
. development of . . . 2101-2101.03
. exceptions to passive activity rules for . . . 1101.02[A], 1105.03
. master . . . 2100, 2103-2103.04
. material participation rules for . . . 1103.06[B]
. as tax shelters . . . 2101.01

Liquidation
. corporation property . . . 204.02[C]
. in kind of lease rentals . . . 602.02[B]
. of subsidiary . . . 1402.01[A]

Loan agreement for mortgage . . . 301.01[A]

Loan proceeds, disbursement of . . . 303.02[C]

Local benefit, taxes for . . . 704.02

Lodging, depreciation for . . . 901.02[A]

Long-term contracts
. for construction, percentage-of-completion accounting method for . . . 701.02[C]
. redetermined for minimum tax purposes . . . 1301.04[C]

Loss on installment sale reported in full for year of sale . . . 1401.01

Loss on sale or disposition of property interest treated as deduction from passive activity . . . 1104.01[B]

Loss property, gifts of . . . 1603

Low-income housing
. recovery periods for . . . 904.01[B]
. as Section 1250 property . . . 1301.03[B]
. tax credit . . . 805.01, 805.02[B]
. types of property considered to be . . . 1301.03[B]

Low-income housing, tax credit for . . . 100, 805-805.05[D]
. accelerated portion of . . . 805.05[C]
. acquisition transactions . . . 104
. annual recertification of tenant income for . . . 805.01
. applicable credit rates for . . . 805.03[A]
. application for . . . 805.01
. apportionment of . . . 805.01
. average income test . . . 805.02[B]
. basis of . . . 805.01
. calculation of credit . . . 805.03
. casualty losses . . . 805.05[D]
. ceiling on . . . 805.01
. certification . . . 805.02[B]
. costs eligible for . . . 805
. history of . . . 805
increased tenant income affecting . . . 805.05[A]
. investor incentive . . . 805.01
. joint IRS and state agency administration of . . . 805.01
. large partnerships . . . 805.05[B]
. minimum set-aside . . . 805.02[B]
. monitoring compliance of allocating . . . 805.01
. passive activity loss attributable to . . . 1103.05[C]
. of publicly traded partnership . . . 1105.03
. qualification for . . . 805.01, 805.02
. qualified basis for determining . . . 805.03[B]
. qualified low-income building . . . 805.02[A]
. rent restrictions for . . . 805.02[B]

Low-income housing, tax credit for— continued
. recapture of . . . 805.05-805.05[D]
. for rehabilitation expenditures . . . 805, 805.04
. state agencies award tax credits . . . 805.01
. state credit authority . . . 805.02[B]
. types of . . . 805.01

M

Maintenance cost capitalization . . . 703.01[E]

Maintenance provision for lessee . . . 601.01

Maintenance safe harbor . . . 703.01[D]

Master limited partnerships
. defined . . . 2103
. development of . . . 2100
. evolution and growth of MLP concept . . . 2103.02
. origins of . . . 2103.01
. real estate MLPs . . . 2103.04
. tax legislation . . . 2103.03

Matching of rental deductions and lessor's rental income . . . 401.04[C]

Material participation in activity . . . 1101.03
. by corporation . . . 1101.03[B]
. by individual . . . 1101.03[A]
. investing not counted as . . . 1101.03[A]
. by limited partnership . . . 1103.06[B]
. rental activities not requiring . . . 1101.03
. self-rented property for . . . 1103.02
. for separate activities . . . 1102-1102.04
. tests of . . . 1101.03[A]

Materials and supplies, repair regs . . . 703.03

Mid-month convention for real estate depreciation . . . 901.01[C]

Military allowance, deduction of mortgage interest despite . . . 1701.03[D]

Mine development expenses, optional 10-year writeoff of . . . 1301.04[E]

Mine exploration expenses, optional 10-year writeoff of . . . 1301.04[E]

Mineral rights as interests in real property . . . 1302.01[A]

Minimum tax credits of qualifying corporations, unused . . . 1301.04[B]

Mining exploration and development costs . . . 1301.04[C]

Minister allowance, deduction of mortgage interest despite . . . 1701.03[D]

Miscellaneous itemized deductions . . . 1301.04[C]

Mixed-use residences . . . 1800-1804. *See also* Business use of home
. exclusion of gain on sale or exchange of . . . 2002.02
. overview of . . . 1800
. sale transaction for . . . 2003.03

Modification of lease . . . 502.04

Modified accelerated cost recovery system (MACRS)
. additions and improvements . . . 901.02–901.02[C]
. computation of the deduction . . . 901.01–901.01[G]
. defined . . . 901
. depreciation for property under construction using . . . 901.02[B]
. expensing and bonus depreciation . . . 901.03–901.03[B]

Mortgage acquisition costs . . . 301.01[A]

Mortgage appraisals . . . 102.02[A]

Mortgage costs . . . 301.01-301.01[B]
. assumed by partners . . . 203.02[B]
. borrower's . . . 303.01[A]
. in business use of home . . . 1801.03[B]
. lender's . . . 301.01[B]
. points as . . . 1701.02-1701.02[B]

Mortgage, deduction of interest paid on . . . 303.02

Mortgage discount points charged to seller, income from . . . 303.01

Mortgage financing . . . 301, 1400
. artificially inflated . . . 101.02[C]
. buy downs . . . 301.02
. line-of-credit . . . 1701.01[D]
. not considered to be payment . . . 1401.02[B]
. payoff of . . . 301.03-301.03[B]
. prepayment of . . . 301.01[A], 301.03, 301.03[A]
. purchase-money . . . 1201.01[E], 1201.02

Mortgage financing—continued
. redeemable grounds rents treated as . . . 1701.03[A]
. as security for real estate loan . . . 300
. shared appreciation . . . 1701.03[B]
. tax ramifications of . . . 301
. troubled . . . 1200-1204.02[D]

Mortgage included in original cost basis . . . 101.02-101.02[C]

Mortgage insurance . . . 1701.01

Mortgage interest deduction . . . 1701

Mortgage interest tax credit . . . 1701.03[C]

Mortgage prepayment . . . 301.01[A], 301.03, 301.03[A]

Mortgaged property
. abandonment of . . . 801.05, 1203, 1203.02
. contribution to corporation of . . . 204.02[A]
. conveyance to mortgagee of . . . 1203.01-1203.01[B]
. foreclosure on . . . 101.01[H], 201, 300, 1202-1202.02[C]
. gifts of . . . 301, 1602, 1602.01
. like-kind exchange of . . . 1302.02[B]
. partnership contributions . . . 203.02[B]
. sale of . . . 301, 1203.01[A], 1203.02, 1301.01[B]

Motorsports entertainment complexes . . . 901.01[G]

Moving expenses . . . 1705-1705.03[B]
. costs deductible as . . . 1705.03
. deduction suspended . . . 1705.01
. distance requirement for deducting . . . 1705.02[A]
. for employees or self-employed person . . . 1705
. length of employment requirement for deducting . . . 1705.02[B]
. qualifications for deducting . . . 1705.02-1705.02[B]
. reimbursements of . . . 1705.03[A]
. for work outside of United States . . . 1705.03[B]

N

Natural business year . . . 701.01[A]

National Flood Insurance Act . . . 1503, 1704

National Housing Act . . . 1301.03[B]

Net fair market value of asset . . . 1401.02[C]

Net leases . . . 401.02

Net operating loss (NOL)
. of insolvent or bankrupt debtor, "expiring" . . . 1201.01[B]
. redetermined for AMT . . . 1301.04[C]

New York Liberty Zone, tax benefits for . . . 806, 806.02

Network asset improvements . . . 801.01[C]

Nominee corporations for real estate ownership . . . 201.01

Nonbusiness bad debts . . . 1201.02[C]

Noncapital assets, types of . . . 1301.02[A]

Nondepreciable property, portfolio income from rental of . . . 1103.04

Nonrental activities, rentals incidental to . . . 1103.01[A]

Nonresidential real property, depreciation of
. alternative depreciation system for . . . 902.01, 902.01[A]
. first year . . . 901.01[C]
. use of optional depreciation tables for . . . 901.01[D]

Nontaxable exchanges of property, holding period following . . . 1301.02[C]

Normal commercial practice concept for at-risk rules . . . 302.03[B]

O

Oil and gas property, working interests in . . . 1101.02[B], 1101.03

Omnibus Budget Reconciliation Act of 1987, repeal of installment method for dealers in property in . . . 1401.01[A]

Omnibus Budget Reconciliation Act of 1993, transitional depreciation system under . . . 901

Operating expenses of real estate . . . 703-703.09

Operating income of closely hold C corporations
. offset by passive losses . . . 1101.01[A]
. offset by tax credits . . . 1104.04[A]

Option on property, basis of property following exercise of . . . 101.01[D]

Ordinary and necessary expenses
. deduction of operating . . . 703
. development costs as capitalized or deductible . . . 1001
. legal kickbacks as . . . 703.05[B]
. repairs and maintenance of trade or business as . . . 703.01-703.01[F]
. salaries and other compensation as . . . 703.04

Ordinary income
. gain offsetting deduction from . . . 1202.02[C]
. insurance proceeds as . . . 1501.02[B]
. recapture provisions converting capital gain into . . . 1301, 1301.03[B]
. Section 1250 recapture by corporations treated as . . . 1301.03[B]

Ordinary income property, gifts of . . . 1601.03[A], 1601.03[C]

Organization costs
. of corporation . . . 204.02[A]
. of partnership . . . 203.02[C]

Original issue discount (OID) on deferred payment sales . . . 304

Original issue discount (OID) rules . . . 101.02, 304, 304.01, 304.02-304.02[B]

Outdoor advertising display, tax-free replacement of . . . 1503.02[E]

Ownership, form of entity . . . 200-209.05. *See also individual forms*
. non-tax functions by corporation for . . . 201.01
. overview of . . . 200
. for tax purposes . . . 201-201.02

Ownership in trust . . . 207-207.03

P

Parking transactions for replacement property . . . 1302.01[A]

Partner
. active participation by . . . 302.01
. admission of new . . . 203.02[B]
. C corporation as . . . 701.02[A]
. disguised payments as share of partnership income . . . 703.04[E]
. disposition of entity interest by . . . 1104.01[C]
. gain or loss recognized by . . . 203.02[B], 206.02[B]
. guaranteed payments . . . 703.04[E]

Partner—continued
. loss disallowance rule for . . . 701.04[B], 1301.01[C]
. passive activity loss rules applied to payments to . . . 1104.01[C]
. as related person in installment sales . . . 1401.03[B]
. required payments to . . . 701.01[B]
. retiring, gain or loss of . . . 1104.01[C]
. services rendered by, compensation for . . . 703.04[E]
. success to deceased, gain or loss of . . . 1104.01[C]

Partnership agreement
. items of income or loss given to partners under . . . 203.02[C]
. transfer following death of partner described in . . . 208.01

Partnership income, disguising payments to partners for services as shares of . . . 703.04[E]

Partnership interest
. basis of . . . 101.01[H], 203.02[A], 206.02[B]
. contribution of services in exchange for . . . 203.02[B]
. liquidation of . . . 203.02[A]

Partnerships
. attributes comparison . . . 208.03
. business interest deduction . . . 303.02[D]
. excess business losses . . . 705.02
. grandfather rules for publicly traded . . . 1105.02
. installment sale between corporations and . . . 1401.03[B]
. matching lessee's rental deduction to lessor's rental income for . . . 401.04[C]
. passive activity deductions for . . . 1101.01, 1104.01[C]
. post-2017 audit rules . . . 203.02[G]
. property provided to . . . 1103.01[B]
. publicly traded, passive activity loss rules applied to . . . 1101.02[A], 1105-1105.03
. as related persons for sales of depreciable property . . . 1401.03[A]

Partnerships, real estate. *See also individual types*
. accounting method of . . . 701.02[A]
. benefits of . . . 203, 208.01
. contribution of money or property to . . . 203.02[B]
. conversion to LLCs of . . . 205.02

References are to paragraph (¶) numbers.

Partnerships, real estate.—continued
. deferral period of current tax year of . . . 701.01[B]
. defined . . . 203.01
. distinctions between S corporations and . . . 206
. distribution of refinancing proceeds of . . . 206.02[B]
. general partnerships . . . 203.01[A]
. incorporation of . . . 204.02[A]
. joint venture treated as, for tax purposes . . . 203.01[C]
. large, rules for . . . 203.02[F]
. legal characteristics of . . . 203.01-203.01[D]
. limited partnerships . . . 203.01[B]
. loss disallowance rule for . . . 701.04[B]
. operation of . . . 203.02[C]
. organization and syndication costs of . . . 203.02[C]
. ownership by . . . 208.01
. recapture of low-income housing credit for large . . . 805.05[B]
. syndicate organized as . . . 203.01[D]
. tax year for . . . 701.01[A]
. taxation of . . . 203.02-203.02[G], 208.02

Passive activities
. classification of . . . 1101.02, 1103
. defined . . . 2102.01[B]
. disposition of interests in . . . 1104.03[D]
. installment sale of interest in . . . 1104.03[D]
. offset of losses and credits for . . . 1104
. transfer at death of . . . 1104.03[D]

Passive activity credits . . . 1104.04
. carryover of suspended . . . 1104.04[B]
. of closely held corporation . . . 1104.04[A]

Passive activity deductions . . . 1104.01[B]
. carryover of disallowed . . . 1104.03[C]
. computing . . . 1104.02
. in computing tax liability . . . 1104.04
. disallowed . . . 1104.03-1104.03[D]
. for partners and S corporation shareholders . . . 1104.01[C]

Passive activity gross income . . . 1104.01[A]
. computing . . . 1104.02
. in computing tax liability . . . 1104.04
. income items not considered, list of . . . 1104.01[A]
. for partners and S corporation shareholders . . . 1104.01[C]

Passive activity gross income—continued
. passive activity deductions against . . . 1104.01[B]

Passive activity loss rules . . . 1100-1105.03
. activities subject to . . . 1101, 1101.02-1103.06[C], 2102.01[B]
. determining activity for applying . . . 1102, 1102.01
. in determining alternative minimum taxable income . . . 1301.04[C]
. disallowed credits under . . . 1104.04[B]
. disallowed deductions under . . . 1104.03-1104.03[D]
. exceptions to . . . 1101.01[A], 1101.02-1101.02[B], 1101.03, 1103.05-1103.05[C], 1103.06, 1103.06[C], 1105.01
. general provisions of . . . 1101-1101.03[B]
. grouping activities for applying . . . 1102.01-1102.04, 1103.06[A]
. material participation . . . 1101.03–1101.03[B]
. overview of . . . 1100
. preventing current recognition of cash as well as paper losses . . . 1100
. reporting . . . 1102.04
. tax credits subject to . . . 1104.04-1104.04[B]
. taxpayers subject to . . . 1101, 1101.01-1101.01[B]

Passive losses
. of closely held corporations . . . 1104.02
. computing deductible . . . 1104.01
. disallowed . . . 1104.03-1104.03[D]
. farming activities . . . 1301.04[C]
. to offset operating income . . . 1101.01[A], 1104.04[A]
. suspended . . . 1104.03[D]
. tax treatment of . . . 1104-1104.04[B]

Passthrough deduction (qualified business income) . . . 209–209.05

Patron, gross income of . . . 1104.01[A]

Payments in lieu of taxes (PILOT), deduction of . . . 704.01[C]

Payments to landlord . . . 400-406.02
. overview of . . . 400

Payoff of mortgage . . . 301.03
. payment discounts for . . . 301.03[B]
. prepayment penalties for . . . 301.03, 301.03[A], 1701.03[E]

Payroll taxes for family members employed in real estate business . . . 703.04[B]

Penalties
. prepayment . . . 301.03, 301.03[A], 1701.03[E]
. for sales and exchanges of real estate . . . 1303.03

Percentage lease agreements . . . 401.01

Percentage-of-completion method of accounting for long-term construction contracts . . . 701.02[C]

Personal holding company tax . . . 204.02[B], 208.01

Personal property
. in allocation of asset costs . . . 102.02[B], 102.02[C]
. charitable deduction for irrevocable remainder interest in . . . 1601.04[B]
. defined . . . 1601.04[B]
. improvements . . . 801.01[C]

Personal residence
. business use . . . 1801-1801.05[B]
. calculating casualty losses for . . . 1703.02[B], 1703.02[C]
. as charitable gift . . . 1601.04[B]
. converted to investment property . . . 1804
. gain from sale of . . . 1301.02[A]
. held for gain . . . 2001.02
. postponement of tax requirements on sale of . . . 2003.01
. qualification for exclusion of gain on sale of. *See* Sale of principal residence
. rental of . . . 1802-1802.02
. rental use of, sale following . . . 2001.01
. replacement period for . . . 2003.01[A]
. tax basis of rehabilitated . . . 1704
. tax-free rollover of gain from sale of . . . 2003-2003.03

Personal service corporations
. accounting method of . . . 701.02[A]
. material participation in . . . 1101.03[B]
. minimum distributions to owner-employees of . . . 701.01[B]
. subject to passive activity loss rules . . . 1101.01, 1101.01[B]
. tax year of . . . 701.01[A]

Personal service income not included in passive activity gross income . . . 1104.01[A]

Plant property improvements . . . 801.01[C]

Pledge of installment obligations . . . 701.03[B], 1401.04, 1402.02

Points for mortgage loan . . . 1701.02-1701.02[B]

Pollution control facilities, alternative depreciation system for minimum tax on . . . 1301.04[C]

Pollution control facilities, special amortization provisions for . . . 802, 1301.04[D]
. for coal-fired electric generation plant . . . 802.01[C]
. limitations for longer-lived facilities . . . 802.01[B]
. requirements for using . . . 802.01[A]

Portfolio income not included in passive activity income . . . 1104.01[A]

Pre-existing condition amelioration . . . 801.02[E]

Pre-opening expenses . . . 702.01[C]

Prepaid interest, deduction of . . . 303.02[A]

Prepayment penalty for retiring mortgage debt . . . 301.03, 301.03[A], 1701.03[E]

Previously owned property, property basis in loan against . . . 101.02[B]

Principal residence. *See also* Personal residence
. basis of new . . . 2003.02[B]
. basis on sale of . . . 101.01[H]
. first-time homebuyer credit . . . 1707, 1707.01
. fixing up expenses for sale of . . . 2003.02[A]
. nonqualified use . . . 2002.01[B]
. purchase of new . . . 2004.01[B]
. qualified principal residence indebtedness for . . . 1201.01[D]
. tax exclusion for . . . 2002-2002.02
. tax treatment for sale and purchase of . . . 2003.02-2003.02[C]

Property adaptation . . . 801.04

Property additions and improvements . . . 800-806.02

Property contributed to partnerships . . . 1103.01[B]
. gain or loss on . . . 203.02[B]

Property restoration . . . 801.03-801.03[C]

Property taxes. *See also* Real estate tax
. accrual of . . . 701.02[B]
. apportionment of . . . 102.03
. cooperative housing corporation . . . 1901.02[A]
. deduction of . . . 704-704.01[B], 1702 1801.03[B]
. individual deduction . . . 704
. payments in lieu of . . . 704.01[C]
. prior deduction of taxes . . . 102.03
. reimbursement for . . . 102.03

Property treated as rental payments . . . 401.03

Public utilities, deposits for extension to subdivided real estate of . . . 1001.02

Purchase-money mortgage
. financing . . . 1201.01[E], 1201.02
. mortgage reacquisition of property sold subject to . . . 1203.01[B], 1204.02[C]
. reduction of . . . 1201.01[E]

Purchase-money obligation. *See* Mortgage financing

Purchase price
. allocation to land and improvements of . . . 602.02[A]
. basis artificially inflated by value of . . . 101.02[C]
. buying expenses . . . 102.01
. negotiation over . . . 1201.01[E]
. under residual method . . . 102.02[D]

Q

Qualified appraisal of donated real estate by qualified appraiser . . . 1601.01[B]

Qualified basis for low-income housing credit . . . 805.03[B]
. reduction for casualty losses for . . . 805.05[D]
. reduction in . . . 805.05

Qualified business income (passthrough deduction) . . . 209
. agricultural or horticultural cooperatives . . . 209.05
. calculating deduction . . . 209.04
. eligible trades and businesses . . . 209.02
. overview . . . 209.01
. qualified business income . . . 209.03
. rental real estate, safe harbor for . . . 209.02[B]
. specified trades and businesses . . . 209.02[A]

Qualified conservation contribution . . . 1601.04[C]

Qualified disaster relief payments . . . 1704

Qualified dividend income . . . 2202
. after tax-year distributions . . . 2202.02
. capital gain dividend . . . 2202.01

Qualified empowerment zone asset . . . 1305.01

Qualified homeowners associations . . . 1903

Qualified improvement property depreciation . . . 901.02[B]

Qualified intermediary, property transfers to . . . 1302.01[A]

Qualified low-income housing project . . . 805.02-805.02[B]
. recapture of credit for owner of . . . 805.05-805.05[D]

Qualified nonrecourse financing for real estate . . . 302.03
. deductions for . . . 302
. from related person . . . 302.04[A]
. requirements for, four . . . 302.04
. for subsequently acquired property . . . 302.04[B]

Qualified opportunity zones . . . 1304
. business . . . 1304.01[A]
. eligible gains . . . 1304.02[A]
. gain recognition . . . 1304.02[B]
. mixed investments . . . 1304.02[A]
. 90 percent test . . . 1304.01[B]
. partnership . . . 1304.01[A]
. pass-through entities . . . 1304.02[A]
. qualified opportunity fund . . . 1304.01
. stock . . . 1304.01[A]
. tax deferral . . . 1304.02
. tax-free appreciation . . . 1304.02[B]
. tax incentives . . . 1304

Qualified principal residence debt, exclusion reducing basis in . . . 1201.01[D]

Qualified real property . . . 901.03[A]
. definition . . . 901.03[A]
. section 179 deduction . . . 901.02[A], 901.03[A]

Qualified real property business debt, discharge of . . . 1201.01[C]

Qualified rehabilitation expenditures
. credit for . . . 603

Qualified rehabilitation expenditures— continued
. by lessee . . . 603.01
. by lessor . . . 603.02-603.02[B]
. nonqualifying expenditures for . . . 804.01[D]

Qualified rehabilitated building, wall test for . . . 804.01[C]

Qualified residence defined . . . 1701.01[A]

Qualified residence interest . . . 1701, 1701.01

Qualified small business stock as replacement asset . . . 1305.01

Qualifying indebtedness for installment sales . . . 1401.02[B]

Qualifying as a REIT . . . 2203
. asset requirements . . . 2203.03
. income requirements . . . 2203.02
. ownership and organization requirements . . . 2203.01

R

Raw land held for investment . . . 703

Readily tradable obligations not treated as installment sales . . . 1401.02[B]

Real estate
. acquired for resale . . . 103.01[B]
. carrying charges on . . . 103.03
. casualty losses on, determining . . . 1703.02[A], 1703.02[C], 1703.03
. construction of . . . 103-103.03
. held primarily for sale to customers, sale of . . . 1002.01[B], 1003-1003.02[B]
. improvements . . . 801.01[C]
. leveraged . . . 208.02
. as part of going business . . . 102.02[D]
. sales and exchanges of . . . 1300-1305.03
. securitized . . . 200
. seller-financed sales of . . . 1400-1402.03
. small taxpayer exception to uniform capitalization rules . . . 103.01[A]
. tax accounting for . . . 701-701.04[C]
. troubled financings of . . . 1200-1204.02[D]

Real estate acquisition
. allocation of costs . . . 102.02
. buying expenses . . . 102.01-102.01[B]
. incidental expenses of . . . 102-103.03
. from foreign person . . . 102.04
. by purchase . . . 102-102.04

Real estate commissions, deduction versus offset of purchase price of . . . 703.05[A]

Real estate developments, improvements made to whole of . . . 1101.02[A]

Real estate financing . . . 300-305.04
. overview of . . . 300

Real estate investment trusts (REITs) . . . 2200-2203.04
. additional taxes . . . 2201.03
. after-tax year distributions . . . 2202.02
. built-in gains tax . . . 2201.02
. capital gains . . . 2201.01[C], 2202.01
. dividends-paid deduction . . . 2201.01
. income from foreclosure property . . . 2201.01[A]
. overview of . . . 2200
. qualified dividends . . . 2201.01[B]
. qualified subsidiary . . . 2201.04
. qualifying as a REIT . . . 2203–2203.04
. tax treatment of . . . 2201–2201.04
. tax treatment of shareholders . . . 2202
. taxable subsidiary . . . 2201.04

Real estate limited partnerships . . . 2100-2103.04
. development of . . . 2101-2101.03
. Master Limited Partnership . . . 2100, 2103-2103.04
. overview of . . . 2100
. return from . . . 2101.03
. tax treatment of . . . 2102-2102.02

Real estate master limited partnerships . . . 2103-2103.04

Real estate mortgage investment conduits (REMICs) . . . 2300-2302.02[B]
. distributions from . . . 2302.02[A]
. income and basis in . . . 2302.02[B]
. investor interests in . . . 2301
. overview of . . . 2300
. regular interests in . . . 2302.01
. residual interests in . . . 2302.02-2302.02[B]
. tax treatment of . . . 2302

Real estate operating expenses . . . 703-703.09
. advertising . . . 703.07
. before the repair regulations . . . 703.01[F]
. commissions and fees . . . 703.05
. compensation . . . 703.04
. corporation officer compensation . . . 703.04[A]

Real estate operating expenses— continued
. *de minimis* safe harbor . . . 703.01[B]
. election to capitalize maintenance and repairs . . . 703.01[E]
. employee compensation . . . 703.04[C]
. family members as employees, compensation of . . . 703.04[B]
. independent contractor compensation . . . 703.04[C]
. insurance . . . 703.06
. interest . . . 703.09
. kickbacks . . . 703.05[B]
. legal expenses . . . 703.08
. licensed real estate agent compensation . . . 703.04[D]
. materials and supplies . . . 703.03
. partner compensation . . . 703.04[E]
. real estate commissions . . . 703.05[A]
. removal of architectural barriers . . . 703.02
. repair or improvement . . . 703.01[A]
. repairs . . . 703.01-703.01[F]
. routine building maintenance safe harbor . . . 703.01[D]
. small taxpayer safe harbor . . . 703.01[C]

Real estate tax. *See also* Property taxes
. accrual . . . 701.02[B]
. back . . . 704.01[B]
. deductibility of . . . 704-704.01[B]
. impact fees . . . 704.04
. local benefit taxes . . . 704.02
. payments in lieu of taxes . . . 704.01[C]
. prepaying . . . 701.03[A]
. real property taxes . . . 704.01
. safe harbors . . . 704
. special assessment . . . 704.02
. transfer taxes . . . 704.03

Real property. *See* Real estate

Reallocation of rental income and deductions . . . 401.04[B]

Recapture income as currently taxable . . . 1401

Recovery periods for depreciation . . . 901.01, 901.01[A]
. for ACRS . . . 904.01-904.01[B]
. for property under construction . . . 901.02[B]

Redeemable ground rents . . . 1701.03[A]

Refinancing residence debt
. acquisition indebtedness . . . 1701.01[B]
. points for . . . 1701.02[B]

Refined coal production credit as subject to passive activity loss rules . . . 1104.04

Reforestation expenses, deduction or amortization of . . . 802, 802.02

Refreshing a building . . . 801.02[C]

Registered historic district
. defined . . . 804.02[A]
. nonqualified buildings for credit in . . . 804.02[B]

Regrouping activities to apply passive activity loss rules . . . 1102.03

Regulations. *See* Repair regulations

Rehabilitation of building. *See also* Certified historic structures, tax credit for rehabilitation of; Commercial buildings, rehabilitation of older
. low-income housing credit for . . . 805-805.05[D]
. low-income housing depreciation deduction for . . . 1301.03[B]
. substantial rehabilitation test for . . . 804.01[A], 804.01[B], 805.01
. tax credits for . . . 804-804.03, 805.01, 1103.05[C], 1105.03
. wall test for . . . 804.01[C]

Reimbursement of casualty losses . . . 1501.02, 1501.02[C]

Related parties
. acquisition of debt by . . . 1201.01[A]
. anti-churning rules . . . 905.02[B]
. blocked from creating tax losses through property sales and deductions for expenses and interest . . . 701.04
. deductions for expenses and interest between . . . 701.04[B]
. defined . . . 701.04[C]
. gain on sale by . . . 1301.02[A]
. installments sales to . . . 1401.03-1401.03[B]
. lease of property between . . . 401.04
. like-kind exchanges between . . . 1302.01[A]
. losses on sales and exchanges between . . . 701.04[A]
. resale rule for . . . 1401.03[B]
. sale-leasebacks among . . . 305.03[B]

Related persons
. defined . . . 1401.03[B]
. qualified nonrecourse financing from . . . 302.04[A]

Related persons—continued
. for rule denying installment reporting of sales of depreciable property . . . 1401.03[A]
. second dispositions by . . . 1401.03[B]

Related purchaser, resale following installment sale by . . . 1401.03[B]

Relative values of land and buildings . . . 102.02[A]

Relief agency repairs or restorations as reimbursement for casualties . . . 1501.02[C]

Relocation assistance by employer . . . 2002.01[D]

Remainder interests
. exchange of . . . 1302.01[A]
. gifts of . . . 1601.04[B]

Remodeling a building . . . 801.02[D]

Renewal communities
. capital gain from sale of asset in . . . 1305.02
. commercial revitalization expenditures on . . . 806.01

Renewal community employment credit as subject to passive activity loss rules . . . 1104.04

Renovations as capital expenditures versus repairs . . . 703.01[F]

Rent
. allocation of . . . 404.01
. cost of improvements treated as . . . 602.01
. as deductible for business use of home . . . 1801.03[B]
. defined . . . 401
. excess . . . 401.04[A]
. forms for . . . 401
. graduated . . . 402.02-402.02[B]
. in gross income of landlord . . . 403
. indirect payment of . . . 401, 401.02
. for lessor-shareholders . . . 401.04[B]
. owed for repaying lessor for cost of improvements . . . 601.02
. paid in property or services . . . 401, 402
. of part of home . . . 1802-1802.02
. percentage . . . 401.01, 401.03, 401.04[B]
. resale of improved property to lessor as . . . 401.03
. unreasonably high, in lease with option to purchase . . . 305.04

Rent—continued
. vacation or other residence . . . 1803-1803.03

Rent, additional . . . 401.02
. substantial cost of improvements treated as . . . 602.01, 602.02

Rent restrictions in low-income unit to qualify for tax credit . . . 805.02[B]

Rental activities
. activities not considered . . . 1103.01[A], 1103.01[B]
. defined . . . 1103.01
. exceptions to passive activity loss rules for . . . 1103.06
. grouping . . . 1102.02
. incidental to holding property for investment . . . 1102.01, 1103.01[A]
. material participation not required . . . 1101.03
. as passive activities . . . 1101.02
. tests of . . . 1103.01

Rental agreement rules, exemptions from . . . 404.02[A]

Rental agreements
. deferred or stepped . . . 404, 404.01
. Section 467 . . . 404-404.02[B]

Rental deduction
. of lessee matched to lessor's rental income . . . 401.04[C]
. for part of home . . . 1802-1802.02
. tenant's . . . 402

Rental incident to development of property . . . 1103.03
. of nondepreciable property . . . 1103.04

Rental losses, limitations on . . . 1803.02-1803.03

Rental real estate
. active business requirement for . . . 702.02, 703
. active participation . . . 1103.05–1103.05[C]
. for 15 days or more . . . 1803.02[B]
. income and deductions for . . . 1803.02
. interest paid on debt for . . . 303.02[B]
. for less than 15 days per year . . . 1803.02[A]
. residential. *See* Residential rental property
. safe harbor for . . . 209.02[B]

References are to paragraph (¶) numbers.

Rental real estate activities of business
. active participation for . . . 1103.05-1103.06[C]
. exception to passive activity loss rules for business . . . 1103.06
. grouping of . . . 1103.06[A]
. tax credits from . . . 1104.04[B]

Repairing damaged property, cost of . . . 1501.02[A]
. by lessee as reimbursement to lessor . . . 1501.02[C]

Repair regulations
. before the regulations . . . 703.01[F]
. building systems . . . 801.02[F]
. materials and supplies . . . 703.03
. safe harbor . . . 703.01[D]
. transaction costs . . . 102.01[A]

Repairs deductible as ordinary and necessary business expenses
. before the repair regulations . . . 703.01[F]
. business use of the home . . . 1801.03[B]
. classification of expenditures for . . . 703.01[F], 801
. Code Secs. governing . . . 703.01
. election to capitalize . . . 703.01[E]
. forced . . . 703.01[F]
. kept separate from general renovations and replacements . . . 703.01[F]
. new buildings or permanent improvements not allowed as . . . 703.01[A]
. routine building maintenance safe harbor . . . 703.01[D]
. size of expenditure for . . . 703.01[F]

Replacement cost method of real estate valuation . . . 1601.01[A]

Replacement cost to value land and buildings . . . 102.02[A]

Replacement parts . . . 801.02[A], 801.03[A]

Replacement period following sale of principal residence . . . 2003.01[A]

Replacement period for involuntary conversion of property . . . 1503.01[C]

Replacement property for involuntarily converted property . . . 1503
. acquisition required during replacement period for . . . 1503.01[C]
. basis of . . . 1503.01[A], 1503.03, 1503.03[B]

Replacement property for involuntarily converted property—continued
. in condemnation . . . 1503.02[C]
. corporate stock as . . . 1503.03[A]
. corporation formed to obtain . . . 1503.02[F]
. direct conversion to . . . 1503.03[B]
. federally declared disasters . . . 1501.03-1501.03[B], 1503.02[D]
. like-kind test of . . . 1503.02[C]
. method of election . . . 1503.01[B]
. nonrecognition election by grantors and grantor trusts for . . . 1503.01
. outdoor advertising displays . . . 1503.02[E]
. from unrelated person . . . 1503.02[B]
. similar property . . . 1503.02[A]
. used in business or investment, special rules for . . . 1503.02, 1503.02[A], 1503.02[C]

Replacements to arrest deterioration and prolong property life as capital expenditures . . . 703.01[F], 801

Reporting person for real estate transactions . . . 1303.01[A]
. information return for each transferor made by . . . 1303.01[B]

Reporting requirements
. grouping . . . 1102.04
. real property purchase . . . 102.02[E]
. sales and exchanges . . . 1303-1303.03

Repossession of property . . . 101.01[H]
. seller-financed . . . 1204-1204.02[D], 1402.03

Research and experimental expenditures, amortization of . . . 1301.04[C], 1301.04[E]

Research credit as subject to passive activity loss rules . . . 1104.04

Residential construction contracts . . . 701.02[C]

Residential energy efficient property, tax credit for purchasing . . . 1708, 1708.02

Residential lots
. dealer sales of . . . 1002.02[B]
. installment reporting for sales of . . . 1401.01[A]

Residential real property as Section 1250 property . . . 1301.03[B]

Residential rental property, depreciation of
. alternative depreciation system for . . . 902.01, 902.01[A]
. first-year . . . 901.01[C]
. use of optional depreciation tables for . . . 901.01[D], 902.01[B]

Residual method, purchase price under . . . 102.02[D], 1302.01[D]

Restaurant property . . . 901.01[E]

Restoration or property
. damage from casualty . . . 801.03[A]
. previous case law . . . 801.03[C]
. qualifications . . . 801.03
. replacement of a major component or a substantial structural part . . . 801.03[B]

Retail improvements . . . 901.01[E]

Revenue Act of 1978 . . . 102.02[C]

Revenue Reconciliation Act of 1989 . . . 1302.01[A]

Revised Uniform Limited Partnership Act . . . 203.01

Robert T. Stafford Disaster Relief and Emergency Assistance Act . . . 1503, 1704

Routine building maintenance safe harbor . . . 703.01[D]

Royalties, licensing . . . 1104.01[A]

S

S corporations
. advantages of, as real estate ownership entities . . . 208.02
. apportionment of losses of . . . 206.02[B]
. attributes comparison . . . 208.03
. basis rules for . . . 206.02[B]
. built-in gain on assets of . . . 206.02[A], 208.02
. business interest deduction . . . 303.02[D]
. election for status as . . . 206.01
. excess business losses . . . 705.02
. grouping activities of . . . 1102.02
. income and loss . . . 206.02
. installment sales between related parties of . . . 1401.03[B]
. loss disallowance rule for . . . 1301.01[C]
. matching lessee's rental deduction to lessor's rental income for . . . 401.04[C]
. maximum of 100 shareholders for . . . 208.02

S corporations—continued
. property provided to . . . 1103.01[B]
. qualification as . . . 206.01
. related party rules for . . . 701.04[B], 701.04[C], 1401.03[A]
. requirements for qualification as . . . 206.01
. tax treatment of . . . 206, 206.02-206.02[B], 208.02
. tax year election . . . 701.01[B]
. tax year for . . . 701.01[A]
. termination of . . . 206.01

Safe harbor
. rental real estate . . . 209.02[B]

Safe harbor expensing
. business use of the home . . . 1801.01
. purchase of real property . . . 102.01[B]
. real estate operating expense . . . 703.01[B], 703.01[C], 703.01[D]

Sale-leaseback transaction
. AFR applied to . . . 304.01[A]
. drawbacks of . . . 305.01, 305.03[C]
. equity participation . . . 305.03[C]
. IRS guidelines for . . . 305.02[B]
. lease with option as conditional sales contract . . . 305.04
. as like-kind exchange . . . 305.01[B]
. process of typical . . . 305
. recognition for tax purposes of . . . 305.02-305.02[B]
. related party . . . 305.03[B]
. split financing . . . 305.03[A]
. straight . . . 305.01
. as substitute for mortgage financing . . . 305.01
. Supreme Court guidelines for . . . 305.02[A], 305.03[B]
. tax benefits of . . . 305.01[A]
. tax-exempt entities as seller-lessees in . . . 305.03[D]
. variations on . . . 305.03-305.03[D]

Sale of easement . . . 1301.01[B]

Sale of land between family members . . . 304.01, 304.01[B]

Sale of principal residence . . . 2000-2004.02[B]
. before May 7, 1997 . . . 101.01[H]
. for business or rental property in home . . . 2001.01
. exclusion of gain for taxpayers over 55 . . . 2004-2004.02[B]

Sale of principal residence—continued
. first-time homebuyer credit recapture . . . 1707.01
. gain or loss on . . . 2001-2001.02
. overview of . . . 2000
. qualifications for excluding gain on . . . 2002.01-2002.02, 2004.01
. reporting requirements for . . . 1303
. as subject to imputed interest rules . . . 304.01
. tax exclusion . . . 2002-2002.02
. tax-free rollover of gain . . . 2003-2003.03

Sale of property at loss, deduction gained by accelerating . . . 701.03[A]

Sale or exchange treatment on sale of lease . . . 503

Sales and exchanges of real estate . . . 1300-1305.03. *See also* Installment sale; Mortgaged property; Tax-free exchange of property
. amount realized on . . . 1301.01[B]
. eligible gain . . . 1304.02[A]
. empowerment zone investment, rollover of . . . 1305.02
. gain or loss on. *See* Gain or loss on sale of real estate
. gain recognition . . . 1304.02[B]
. information return for . . . 1303.02-1303.02[B]
. 90 percent test . . . 1304.01[B]
. opportunity fund . . . 1304.01
. opportunity zone property . . . 1304.01[A]
. overview of . . . 1300
. partial dispositions . . . 1301.01[E]
. penalties for . . . 1303.03
. qualified opportunity zones . . . 1304
. recapture provisions applied to . . . 1301
. related parties in . . . 701.04[A]
. reporting requirements for . . . 1303-1303.03
. selling expenses in . . . 1301.01[A]
. of spouses or former spouses . . . 1301.01[D]
. tax deferral . . . s02
. taxes on . . . 1301.01[B]

Schedule K-1 . . . 203.02[G]

Second disposition of property in installment sale . . . 1401.03[B]

Section 467 rental agreements . . . 404.01

Section 1231 assets used in trade or business
. capital gain on . . . 1301.02[A], 1301.02[B]

Section 1231 assets used in trade or business—continued
. capital loss on . . . 1301.02[A], 1301.02[B]
. defined . . . 1301.02[B]
. holding period for . . . 1301.02[C]
. like-kind exchanges of . . . 1302.01[D]
. nonrecognition on like-kind exchange of . . . 1302.01[A]
. ordinary gain on . . . 1301.02[A], 1301.02[B]
. ordinary loss on . . . 1301.02[A], 1301.02[B]
. recapture rule for . . . 1301.02[B]
. types of assets considered to be . . . 1301.02[B]

Securities Act of 1933 . . . Part VI Intro.

Securities Exchange Act of 1934 . . . Part VI Intro.

Security deposits
. advance payments for . . . 403.02, 404.01
. lessee's deduction of . . . 406.01
. return with interest of . . . 502.02[B]
. used versus held in trust . . . 406, 406.02

Self-rented property . . . 1103.02

Seller-financed property, repossession of . . . 1204–1204.02[D]
. basis of reacquired property in . . . 1204.01[C]
. exception for receipt of money or property in . . . 1402.03
. following installment sale . . . 1204.02[A]
. general rule for . . . 1402.03
. holding period for reacquired property following . . . 1204.01[B]
. income recognition upon . . . 1204.01[A]
. nonrecognition of gain or loss on . . . 1204, 1204.01
. prior bad debt deductions . . . 1204.01[A]
. recognition of gain . . . 1204.02-1204.02[D]

Seller-financed sales of real estate . . . 1400-1402.03

Selling expenses for real estate . . . 1301.01[B]
. added to basis to determine gross profit . . . 1401.02[A]

Services contributed to partnership in exchange for partnership interest . . . 203.02[B]

Services enhancing value of property, types of . . . 1103.03

Severance damages for condemned property . . . 1502.03[A]
. gain from . . . 1503.02[C]

Shared appreciation mortgage (SAM) . . . 1701.03[B]

Shareholders
. corporate, loans to . . . 303.03
. leases of property between controlled corporations and . . . 401.04[B]
. tax treatment of REIT . . . 2202–2202.02

Shareholders, S corporation
. deferral of income to . . . 701.01[A]
. disposition of entity interest by . . . 1104.01[C]
. loss disallowance rule for . . . 701.04[B]
. passive activity deductions for . . . 1101.01, 1104.01[C]
. required payments to . . . 701.01[B]
. as subject to at-risk rules . . . 302.01

Short-term lease property, investment tax credit split on . . . 603.02[B]

Significant services tests . . . 1103.01

Small businesses
. business interest deduction election . . . 303.02[D]
. sales by . . . 304.01
. stock gain excluded from income . . . 1301.04[D]
. uniform capitalization rule exception . . . 103.01[A]

Small Business Job Protection Act of 1996 . . . 601.02

Small business stock, AMT tax preference of gain on sale of . . . 1301.04[D]

Small construction contracts . . . 701.02[C]

Small taxpayer safe harbor . . . 703.01[C]

Soil and water conservation expenditures, deduction of . . . 802, 802.03

Solar water heating property, tax credit for . . . 1708, 1708.02

Sole individual ownership . . . 202.01

Sole proprietor, operator equity interest of . . . 702.01[A]

Special assessments as nondeductible . . . 704.02

Split financing for subordinated land lease . . . 305.03[A]

Spouses
. gain on sale of residence by . . . 2002.01[A]-2002.01[C]
. joint ownership by . . . 202.03, 202.04
. of owner employed in real estate businesses . . . 703.04[B]
. property acquired from . . . 101.01[G]
. separate returns filed by . . . 202.04
. transfer of installment obligation between . . . 1402.01[A]

Start-up expenses of businesses
. election to deduct . . . 702
. investigatory expenses . . . 702.01[A]
. pre-opening expenses . . . 702.01[C]
. types of . . . 702.01[B]
. writeoff of . . . 702.01, 702.01[B]

State allocating agencies for low-income housing credit . . . 805.01
. authorization for credit by . . . 805.02[B]

State and local taxes on sales of real estate . . . 1301.01[B]

Statutory recovery periods . . . 404.02

Stock acquisitions . . . 702.01[A]

Stock as replacement property . . . 1503.03[A]

Straight-line depreciation method . . . 900, 901.01[B]
. defined . . . 905.01[A]
. over ACRS recovery period . . . 904.01[A], 904.01[B]
. for rehabilitation costs for commercial and historic buildings . . . 1301.03[B]
. of Section 1250 property . . . 1301.03[B]

Straw corporations for property ownership . . . 201.01, 201.02

Stripping transactions . . . 404.01

Subdivided property
. calculation of amount and character of gain realized on sale of . . . 1003.02-1003.02[B]
. character of income from sale of . . . 1000
. as dealer property . . . 1002.01[B]
. five-percent rule . . . 1003.02[A]
. five-year rule for . . . 1003.02[B]
. inclusion of development costs in basis of . . . 1001.02
. by investor . . . 1003
. qualification for special tax treatment of . . . 1003.01-1003.01[C]

Subdivided property—continued
. selling price in case of exchange for . . . 1003.02[A]
Subdivision of real estate tract . . . 101.01[H]
Sublease treatment for transfer of less than entire interest . . . 503
Subleases of property on which lessor passed investment credit . . . 503
Subsidiaries, REIT . . . 2201.04
Sum-of-the-years digits method of depreciation . . . 905.01[A]
Syndicates
. costs of partnerships . . . 203.02[C]
. organization as partnerships of . . . 203.01[D]

T

Tax accounting for real estate . . . 701
Tax avoidance or evasion
. constant rental accrual in . . . 404.02
. lease between related parties used for . . . 401.04
. loans for . . . 303.03
. nonrecognition treatment of related party property exchanges not having as principal purpose . . . 1302.01[A]
. rules for Section 467 rental agreements to prevent . . . 404, 404.02[A]
. straw corporation for . . . 201.02
. using artificially inflated real estate purchase price . . . 101.02[C]
Tax credit
. adoption . . . 1301.04[A]
. alcohol fuels . . . 1104.04
. allowed for AMT . . . 1301.04[A]
. alternative minimum tax credit . . . 1301.04[F]
. building rehabilitations . . . 804-804.03
. child . . . 1301.04[A]
. disabled access . . . 1104.04
. District of Columbia first-time homebuyer . . . 1706
. electric vehicle . . . 1104.04
. energy credits . . . 1708-1708.02
. energy efficient home . . . 105, 1001.03
. energy efficient property . . . 1708.02
. first-time homebuyer . . . 1707, 1707.01
. foreign, as allowed for AMT . . . 1301.04[A]
Tax credit—continued
. general business . . . 804, 1104.04, 1201.01[B], 1301.04[A]
. for homebuilders . . . 1000
. Indian coal production . . . 1104.04
. investment . . . 603-603.02[B], 800, 804, 1104.04
. low-income housing . . . 100, 104, 805-805.05[D]
. mortgage interest . . . 1701.03[C]
. nonbusiness energy property . . . 1708, 1708.01, 1708.01[A]
. nonrefundable personal . . . 1301.04[A]
. for older commercial buildlings . . . 804.01-804.01[E]
. passed to lessee . . . 603.02[A]
. for passive activities . . . 1104.04-1104.04[B]
. to promote socially desirable goals . . . 800
. qualified rehabilitation expenditure investment . . . 603-603.02[B], 804-804.01[E]
. refined coal production . . . 1104.04
. for rehabilitation of certified historic structures . . . 804.02-804.03
. renewal community employment . . . 1104.04
. research . . . 1104.04
. residential energy efficient property . . . 1708, 1708.02
. for savers . . . 1301.04[A]
. split between lessor and lessee . . . 603.02[B]
. work opportunity, as allowed for AMT . . . 1301.04[A]
Tax credit projects, syndicators as source of equity financing for . . . 805.01
Tax Cuts and Jobs Act
. depreciation . . . 901.01[F]
. qualified business income (passthrough deduction) . . . 209, 209.01
. recovery period for qualified improvement property . . . 901.01[F]
. rehabilitation tax credit . . . 804
. uniform capitalization rule exception for small taxpayers . . . 103.01[A]
Tax effect loans . . . 303.03
Tax-exempt bond-financed property, alternative depreciation system used for . . . 902, 902.02, 902.02[B]

Tax-exempt entities as seller-lessees in sale-leasebacks . . . 305.03[D]

Tax-exempt interest as AMT tax preference . . . 1301.04[D]

Tax-exempt use property, alternative depreciation system used for . . . 902, 902.02, 902.02[A]

Tax-free exchange of property . . . 1302-1302.03[B]
. four-way . . . 1302.03[B]
. multiparty . . . 1302.03-1302.03[B]
. partially . . . 1302.02-1302.02[D]
. reporting requirements for . . . 1303.01-1303.03
. three-way . . . 1302.03[A]

Tax-free replacement of property . . . 1503-1503.03[B]

Tax-free transfers of recovery property under ACRS . . . 905.02[C]

Tax losses
. from leveraged real estate . . . 208.02
. partnership-generated . . . 2102.01

Tax planning . . . 701.03
. to accelerate income and defer deductions . . . 701.03[B]
. to defer income and accelerate deductions . . . 701.03[A]

Tax Reform Act of 1976, at-risk rules enacted in . . . 302

Tax Reform Act of 1984
. gift tax treatment . . . 303.03[A]
. OID rules expanded by . . . 304
. depreciation recapture under . . . 1401.02[A]
. pre-opening expenses added to definition of business expenses by . . . 702.01[C]
. recovery period for real estate extended by . . . 904.01

Tax Reform Act of 1986
. ACRS depreciation system adopted in . . . 900
. at-risk rules extended in . . . 302
. credit for qualified rehabilitation expenditures under . . . 603
. interest in master limited partnerships following passage of . . . 2100
. investment credit repealed under . . . 603
. lease improvements . . . 601.01
. lease termination . . . 602.02[B]
. low-income housing project gross income . . . 1104.01[A]

Tax Reform Act of 1986—continued
. nonrecourse financing . . . 302.04[A]
. passive activity loss rules . . . 1100
. passive loss rule . . . 2102.01[B]
. real estate transaction reporting mandated by . . . 1303
. REMICs . . . 2300
. repeal of tax incentives in . . . 104, 1201.01[A]
. retention of improvements by lessee under . . . 602.02[B]
. transfer tax treatment under . . . 704.03
. write-offs of cost of improvements to benefit particular lessee discontinued by . . . 601.02

Tax Relief Act of 2010 . . . 101.01[F]

Tax shelters
. abusive . . . 101.02[C]
. accounting method of . . . 701.02[A]
. defined . . . 101.02[C], 701.02[A]
. limited partnerships as . . . 2101.01
. proliferation of . . . 302
. real estate . . . 2101.02

Tax treatment of REITs . . . 2201–2201.04
. additional taxes . . . 2201.03
. built-in gains tax . . . 2201.02
. capital gains . . . 2201.01[C]
. dividends-paid deduction . . . 2201.01
. foreclosure property . . . 2201.01[A]
. qualified dividends . . . 2201.01[B]
. shareholders . . . 2202–2202.02
. subsidiaries . . . 2201.04

Tax year. *See also* Accounting period, fiscal or calendar
. changing . . . 701.01[A]
. required . . . 701.01[A], 701.01[B]
. special rules applied to entities selecting . . . 701.01, 701.01[A]
. election for other than required . . . 701.01[B]

Taxes for real estate . . . 700-702.02
. capitalized under former Code Sec. 189 . . . 103.02
. deduction of . . . 201
. overview of . . . 700

Taxpayer Relief Act of 1997
. business use of the home . . . 1801.02[B]
. exclusion for principal residence under . . . 2002, 2004
. leasehold improvements . . . 602
. tax reporting for large partnerships under . . . 203.02[F]

Telephone service as home business expense . . . 1801.03[B]

Tenants
. abatement agreement for work performed by . . . 602.01
. improvements to benefit particular . . . 601.02
. payments between landlords and . . . 400-406.02
. payments for cancellation of lease by lessor to . . . 502.02[A]
. of qualified low-income housing projects . . . 805.02[B], 805.05[A]
. rent deductions of . . . 402

Tenants in common, ownership by . . . 202.02, 208. *See also* Joint ownership of real estate

Tentative minimum tax in AMT computation . . . 1301.04[A]

Term loans . . . 303.03[B]

Third-party mortgages . . . 1204.02[C]

Tiered structures, required tax year of entities having . . . 701.01[B]

Timeshare ownership interest, installment reporting for sales of . . . 1401.01[A]

Timeshares, dealer sales of . . . 1002.02[A], 1002.02[B]

Total contract price in gross profit ratio defined . . . 1401.02[A]

Trade or business property
. group of assets constituting . . . 102.02[D]
. as noncapital asset . . . 1301.02[A]
. Section 1231 assets . . . 1301.02[B]
. start-up expenses . . . 702.02
. valuing property for estate tax purposes as . . . 101.01[F]

Transfer taxes, state and local, deductibility issues for . . . 704, 704.03

Troubled financings . . . 1200-1204.02[D]

Trusts. *See also individual types*
. allocation of depreciation deduction for . . . 207.02
. defined . . . 207
. grantor trusts . . . 207.03
. installment sale in which seller is beneficiary of . . . 1401.03[B]
. loss disallowance rule for . . . 1301.01[C]
. matching lessee's rental deduction to lessor's rental income for . . . 401.04[C]

Trusts.—continued
. related parties for real estate sales by . . . 1301.02[A], 1401.03[A]
. subject to passive activity loss rules . . . 1101.01
. tax treatment of . . . 207.01
. use for real estate operation or investment of . . . 207

U

Uniform capitalization rules
. application of . . . 103.01[C], 103.02
. enactment of . . . 103.01-103.01[C]
. expenses other than interest . . . 103.01[B]
. gross receipts test . . . 103.01 [A], 303.02[D]
. interest capitalized under . . . 103.01[C]
. small taxpayer exception . . . 103.01 [A]

Uniform Limited Partnership Act . . . 203.01

Uniform Partnership Act . . . 203.01

Uniform Settlement Statement . . . 1303.02[B]

Unit of property . . . 801.01-801.01[C]

United States Housing Act of 1937 . . . 1301.03[B]

Unstated interest in contract of sale . . . 304.01[A], 1401.02[F]

Unsuccessful attempt to obtain business lease . . . 501.01[C]

Utility costs for business use of home . . . 1801.03[B]

V

Vacant land, interest paid on . . . 303.02[B]

Vacation home
. gain on sale of . . . 1301.02[A]
. maintenance and repairs of . . . 1803.01[B]
. for personal purposes . . . 1803.01[A], 1803.01[B]
. rental of . . . 1803-1803.03

Valuation date for disposition of interest in passthrough entity . . . 1104.01[C]

Valuation of real estate gifts . . . 1601.01-1601.01[B]

References are to paragraph (¶) numbers.

Variable interest rate obligations, interest rate for . . . 304.03[C]

W

Wall test
. not applied to certified historic structures . . . 804.02
. for retention of existing external walls in rehabilitations . . . 804.01[C]

Water and soil conservation expenditures, deduction of . . . 802, 802.03

Welfare benefit fund, related parties for . . . 1301.02[A]

Whiteco factors for tangible personal property . . . 102.02[C]

Wind farms . . . 102.02[D]

Withholding exemption for acquisition or personal residence . . . 102.04

Withholding requirements
. for children employed in business of parent . . . 703.04[B]
. Code Sec. 1445 . . . 102.04
. for employees . . . 703.04[B], 703.04[C]
. not applicable to independent contractors . . . 703.04[C]

Work opportunity tax credit . . . 1301.04[A]

Wraparound mortgages for installment sales . . . 1401.02[B]

Writeoff of deductible or amortizable expenses . . . 702.01, 702.02
. incurred for additions or improvements to business property for pollution control . . . 800
. incurred in investigating creation or acquisition of active trade or business . . . 702.01[A], 702.02
. for low-income housing . . . 1301.03[B]
. of pre-opening expenditures . . . 702.01, 702.01[C]
. of start-up costs . . . 702.01, 702.01[B]

Y

Year, tax accounting. *See* Accounting period, fiscal or calendar; Tax year

Z

Zoning change for land, cost of obtaining . . . 901.02[C]